How Not To Say What You Mean
A Dictionary of Euphemisms

Reviews of previous editions

'A most valuable and splendidly presented collection; at once scholarly, tasteful, and witty.' *Lord Quirk*

'Euphemists are a lively, inventive, self-regarding and bumptious bunch. Holder goes among them with an etymological glint in his eye.' *Iain Finlayson, Financial Times*

'this fascinating book . . . don't put this dictionary in the loo – there's another euphemism for you – or else guests will never come out. It's unputdownable once you open it.' *Peter Mullen, Yorkshire Post*

'Concise, well-organized entries' *Library Journal* (USA)

'I am astonished at its depth and wit' Sam Allen (American lawyer and philologist)

'This bran tub of linguistic gems . . . A delight for browsers who love the vivid oddities of language . . . a valuable collection.' *City Limits*

'A very funny collection' *Financial Times*

'Many printable gems' *Daily Telegraph*

'Good bedside reading' *Sunday Telegraph*

'It will surely take its place . . . as a browser's delight and it will entertain book lovers for many hours, whilst at the same time providing useful background information, as well as instruction and clarification to many.' *Reference Review*

'An informative, amusing collection' *The Observer*

'Hugely enjoyable and cherishable' *Times Educational Supplement*

'Lovers of word play will have a field day' *Herald Express, Torquay*

'Excellent, informative, entertaining.' *Wilson Literary Bulletin* (USA)

'Great fun, but not for the maiden aunt.' *Sunday Telegraph*

How Not To Say What You Mean
A Dictionary of Euphemisms

R. W. HOLDER

OXFORD
UNIVERSITY PRESS

OXFORD

UNIVERSITY PRESS

Great Clarendon Street, Oxford OX2 6DP

Oxford University Press is a department of the University of Oxford.
It furthers the University's objective of excellence in research, scholarship,
and education by publishing worldwide in

Oxford New York

Auckland Bangkok Buenos Aires Cape Town Chennai
Dar es Salaam Delhi Hong Kong Istanbul Karachi Kolkata
Kuala Lumpur Madrid Melbourne Mexico City Mumbai Nairobi
São Paulo Shanghai Singapore Taipei Tokyo Toronto

Oxford is a registered trade mark of Oxford University Press
in the UK and in certain other countries

Published in the United States
by Oxford University Press Inc., New York

Database right Oxford University Press (maker)

First published as *A Dictionary of American and British Euphemisms* by Bath University Press 1987

Revised edition published by Faber and Faber Limited 1989

Second edition first published as *A Dictionary of Euphemisms* by Oxford University Press 1995,
and in paperback 1996

This third edition first published as *How Not to Say What You Mean:
A Dictionary of Euphemisms* in 2002

British Library Cataloguing in Publication Data
Data available

Library of Congress Cataloging-in-Publication Data

Holder, R. W.
How not to say what you mean: a dictionary of euphemisms / R. W. Holder.
p. cm.
Includes bibliographical references (p.) and index.
ISBN 0-19-860402-5
1. English language–Euphemism–Dictionaries. 2. English language–Synonyms and antonyms.
3. English language–Terms and Phrases. 4. Vocabulary. I. Title.

PE1449 .H548 2002
423'.1–dc21

2002074261

ISBN 0-19-860402-5

3

Typeset in 7.5/8.5pt OUP Swift Light by Kolam Information Services Pvt. Ltd, Pondicherry, India
Printed in Great Britain by Clays Ltd, St Ives plc

Contents

An Explanation

When I started gathering euphemisms in 1977 with a dictionary in mind, nothing similar had been published. I was free to choose the form the collection should take, to speculate on the etymology, and to lay down the criteria for entry or rejection. It was not, I felt, a subject to be taken too seriously, considering the ridiculous nature of many of the euphemisms we use in everyday speech.

I accepted Fowler's definition: 'Euphemism means the use of a mild or vague or periphrastic expression as a substitute for blunt precision or disagreeable use' (*Modern English Usage*, 1957). A second test soon emerged: that the euphemistic word or phrase once meant, or prima facie still means, something else. Because many euphemisms have become such a part of standard English that we think only of the current usage, I sometimes remind the reader of what the word means literally, or used to mean.

In speech and writing, we use euphemism when dealing with taboo or sensitive subjects. It is therefore also the language of evasion, of hypocrisy, of prudery, and of deceit. Fewer than one in a hundred of the entries in the Dictionary cannot be classified under a specific heading shown in the Thematic Index. Some of the entries may be judged by the reader to be dysphemisms, or neither euphemism or dysphemism. The selection is of necessity subjective, and there may also be cases where one woman's euphemism is another man's dysphemism. With regard to inclusive language, for the sake of brevity I stay with the old, politically incorrect rule that the use of the masculine pronoun may, where appropriate, also include the feminine.

I have left out anything which does not feature in literary or common use, unless it adds to our understanding of how language evolves. I also omit anything which I have only found in another dictionary. Inevitably, living in England and having worked during the past quarter century mainly there and in Ireland, the selection reflects the speech on this side of the Atlantic, despite my frequent visits on business to Canada and the United States. Happily English literature is universal, with Indian, South African, and Australian writers as available as those from North America and the British Isles.

The subjects about which we tend to use euphemisms change along with our social attitudes, although euphemisms associated with sexual behaviour and defecation have shown remarkable staying powers. We are more open than the Victorians about mental illness, brothels, and prostitution, less prudish about courtship and childbirth, less terrified about bankruptcy. In turn we can be less direct than they were when referring to charity, education, commercial practice, and race, among other things. In the last twenty-five years there has been a shift in our attitude to such matters as female employment, sexual variety, marriage, illegitimacy, the ingestion of illegal drugs, abortion, job security, and sexual pursuit. Even in the seven years which have elapsed between the previous collection and this one, out of some 1,200 new entries, the heaviest concentration is in these subjects, while euphemisms relating to alcohol or to death, for example, have remained relatively unchanged.

The derivation of many euphemisms through association is obvious, such as death with resting or sleeping, or urination with washing. Another source is from a foreign language, and I include examples from Latin, German, French, Italian, Spanish, Arabic, Turkish, Persian, Hindi, Japanese, and Tagalog, many of which were brought home by servicemen. Rhyming slang is also used euphemistically. Some other usages take more puzzling out. For example, to understand why a mentally ill person might be described as being *East Ham* demands knowledge of the London railway network, in which the East Ham station is one stop short of Barking. I try not to bore the reader by pointing out obvious imagery, but the etymology of euphemism, so much of which passes into standard English, does not seem to have been the subject of published academic research.

It seemed a denial of what I was trying to achieve if I had to define one euphemism by the use of another. However, with certain words this is unavoidable. In the case of *lavatory*, for example, there is no synonym which is not, like lavatory itself, a euphemism. We have no specific word for a woman who copulates and cohabits with a man outside wedlock, and I use *mistress* without any qualifying prefix. I also use *promiscuous* and *promiscuity* as definitions in a sexual, rather than a general sense. Because *fuck* and *shit* are ugly words which jar with constant repetition, I use the euphemistic *copulation* and *defecation* in their stead. Then there are words which have undesirable connotations which make them better avoided as definitions, such as *cripple, bastard, whore*, and *spinster*. No area of definition has given me as much pause as that concerned with mental illness, where the use of *mad* and *lunatic* can be misleading as well as offensive. To confuse matters, we use the word *mad* to describe conditions of the mind ranging from mild annoyance or folly to acute dementia, and many of the euphemisms we use about mental illness cover the same wide spectrum. The definitions selected in each case, and there are many, are what seem to me the commonest usages, but I remain aware of their inadequacy.

The illustrative quotations have been often chosen because they interest me, rather than being the first published example of the usage. Many of those from obscure 19th-century authors have been taken from Joseph Wright's magisterial *English Dialect Dictionary*. Where I have lifted a quotation from another compiler, I say so. For the rest, the quotations come from my own reading, the scope of which has naturally been limited. Even though the majority of my readers have hitherto been in North America, I have stayed with British spelling except where the usage itself is confined to America, when *defence* becomes *defense* and *centre* becomes *center*.

Labels such as *American* or *Scottish* indicate that the usage is restricted to the regional English specified; and in this case, *American* refers mainly to the United States. My use of *narcotics* as a definition is made in the knowledge that many drugs illegally ingested have other effects than narcosis. There is not however space enough in the text to enlarge on specific scientific differences and remain within the constraints suggested by my publisher. Because we have a Thematic Index, cross-references have been kept to a minimum in the text. The use of small capitals indicates where they can be found.

Professional and scholarly authors owe a debt to their editors but not to the same extent that I do. My interest in language is a hobby which has given me great pleasure, but my occupation has been not as an academic but as a manufacturer, which provided ample opportunity for reading while travelling as well as frequent contact with people in Europe and America, but not much time for writing. Dr Michael Allen of Bath University published the original edition in 1987 when it seemed unlikely to find a sponsor. The second edition benefited greatly from the advice and other assistance given me by Julia Elliott, Sara Tulloch, and Patrick Hanks at the Oxford University Press. The changes in style which have improved the presentation and range of this edition were suggested by Alysoun Owen and I owe much to Elizabeth Knowles, the most understanding of editors, and to Andrew Delahunty, who made many helpful suggestions. I must also thank the many readers who have written to me on specific points. None appear more enthusiastic than those in Australia, although I regret that I cannot use any of the material they have sent me, despite its linguistic ingenuity. There are limits to what may be placed on a family bookshelf.

My task is not dissimilar to that facing Sisyphus. The language continues to evolve and it is a poor week in which I do not note two or three new euphemisms, or decide that one previously noted has proved ephemeral. As I complete this explanation, the stone is near the top of the hill but already, with the acceptance of new entries closed, it has started to roll downwards once again.

R. W. Holder

West Monkton
2002

Bibliography

Quotations have been included in the text to show how words and phrases were or are used, and when. The date given for each title refers to the first publication or to the edition which I have used. Where an author has deliberately used archaic language, I mention this in the text.

The following dictionaries and reference books are referred to by abbreviations:

BDPF	*The Dictionary of Phrase and Fable* (Brewer, 1978)
DAS	*Dictionary of American Slang* (Wentworth and Flexner, 1975)
DRS	*A Dictionary of Rhyming Slang* (Franklin, 1961)
DSUE	*A Dictionary of Slang and Unconventional English* (Partridge, 1970)
EDD	*The English Dialect Dictionary* (Wright, 1898–1905)
Grose	*Dictionary of the Vulgar Tongue* (Grose, 1811)
Johnson	*A Dictionary of the English Language* (Johnson, 1775)
N&Q	*Notes & Queries*
ODEP	*The Oxford Dictionary of English Proverbs* (Smith and Wilson, 1970)
OED	*The Oxford English Dictionary* (1989)
SOED	*The Shorter Oxford English Dictionary* (1993)
WNCD	*Webster's New Collegiate Dictionary* (1977)

Adams, J. (1985) *Good Intentions*
Agnus, Orme (1900) *Jan Oxber*
'Agrikler' (1872) *Rhymes in West of England Dialect*
Ainslie, Hew (1892) *A Pilgrimage to the Land of Burns*
Aldiss, Brian (1988) *Forgotten Life*
Alexander, William (1875–82 edition) *Sketches of Life among my Ain Folk*
Allan, Keith, and Burridge, Kate (1991) *Euphemism and Dysphemism*
Allbeury, Ted (1975) *Palomino Blonde*
  (1976) *The Only Good German*
  (1976) *Moscow Quadrille*
  (1977) *The Special Connection*
  (1978) *The Lantern Network*
  (1979) *The Consequence of Fear*
  (1980) *The Twentieth Day of January*
  (1980) *The Reaper*
  (1981) *The Secret Whispers*
  (1982) *All Our Tomorrows*
  (1983) *Pay Any Price*
Allen, Charles (1975) *Plain Tales from the Raj*
  (1979) *Tales from the Dark Continent*
Allen, Paula Gunn (1992) *The Sacred Hoop*
Allen, Richard (1971) *Swedehead*
Alter (1960) *The Exile*
Amis, Kingsley (1978) *Jake's Thing*
  (1980) *Russian Hide-and-Seek*
  (1986) *The Old Devils*
  (1988) *Difficulties with Girls*
  (1990) *The Folks that Live on the Hill*
Anderson, David (1826) *Poems Chiefly in the Scottish Dialect*

Anderson, R. (1805–8 edition) *Ballads in the Cumberland Dialect*
Anderson, William (1867) *Rhymes, Reveries and Reminiscences*
Andrews, William (1899) *Bygone Church Life in Scotland*
Anonymous (1996) *Primary Colors*
Antrobus, C. L. (1901) *Wildersmoor*
Archer, Jeffrey (1979) *Kane and Abel*
Armstrong, Andrew (1890) *Ingleside Musings and Tales*
Armstrong, Louis (1955) *Satchmo*
Ashton, Rosemary (1991) *G. H. Lewes*
Atkinson, J. C. (1891) *Forty Years in a Moorland Parish*
Atwood, Margaret (1988) *Cat's Eye*
  (1996) *Alias Grace*
Aubrey, John (1696) *Collected Works*
Axon, W. E. A. (1870) *The Black Knight of Ashton*
Ayto, John (1993) *Euphemisms*

Bacon, Francis (1627) *Essays*
Bagley, Desmond (1977) *The Enemy*
  (1982) *Windfall*
Bagnall, Jos (1852) *Songs of the Tyne*
Balchin, Nigel (1964) *Fatal Fascination*
Baldwin, William (1993) *The Hard to Catch Mercy*
Ballantine, James (1869) *The Miller of Deanhaugh*
Banim, John (1825) *O'Hara Tales*
Barber, Lyn (1991) *Mostly Men*
Barber, Noel (1981) *Taramara*
Barham R. H. (1840) *Ingoldsby Legends*
Barlow, Jane (1892) *Bogland Studies*

Barnard, Howard, and Lauwerys, Joseph (1963) *A Handbook of British Educational Terms*

Barnes, Julian (1989) *A History of the World in 10 $\frac{1}{2}$ Chapters*

(1991) *Talking it Over*

Baron, Alexander (1948) *From the City, From the Plough*

Barr, John (1861) *Poems and Songs*

Bartram, George (1897) *The People of Clapton*

(1898) *The White-Headed Boy*

Bathurst, Bella (1999) *The Lighthouse Stevensons*

Beard, Henry, and Cerf, Christopher (1992) *The Official Politically Correct Dictionary and Handbook*

Beattie, Ann (1989) *Picturing Will*

Beattie, William (1801) *Fruits of Time Parings*

Beatty, W. (1897) *The Secretar*

Beevor, Antony (1998) *Stalingrad*

Behr, Edward (1978) *Anyone Here Been Raped and Speaks English?*

(1989) *Hirohito: Beyond the Myth*

Bence-Jones, Mark (1987) *Twilight of the Ascendancy*

Benet, Stephen (1943) *A Judgment in the Mountains*

Benn, A. W. (1995) *The Benn Diaries* (edited by Ruth Winston)

Besant, Walter and Rice, James (1872) *Ready Money Mortiboy*

Binchy, Maeve (1985) *Echoes*

Binding, Hilary (1999) *Somerset Privies*

Binns, Aethelbert (1889) *Yorkshire Dialect Words*

Blacker, Terence (1992) *The Fame Hotel*

Blackhall, Alex (1849) *Lays of the North*

Blackmore, R. D. (1869) *Lorna Doone*

Blair, Emma (1990) *Maggie Jordan*

Blanch, Leslie (1954) *The Wilder Shores of Love*

Blessed, Brian (1991) *The Turquoise Mountain*

Block, Thomas (1979) *Mayday*

Blythe, Ronald (1969) *Akenfield*

Bogarde, Dirk (1972) *A Postillion Struck by Lightning*

(1978) *Snakes and Ladders*

(1981) *Voices in the Garden*

(1983) *An Orderly Man*

Boldrewood, Rolf (1890) *A Colonial Reformer*

Bolger, Dermot (1990) *The Journey Home*

Book of Common Prayer (1662)

Boswell, Alexander (1803) *Songs*

(1871 edition) *Poetical Works*

Boswell, James (1785) *The Journal of a Tour to the Hebrides with Samuel Johnson*

(1791) *The Life of Samuel Johnson*

(1792–3) *London Journal*

Boyd, William (1981) *A Good Man in Africa*

(1982) *An Ice-Cream War*

(1983) *Stars and Bars*

(1987) *The New Confessions*

(1993) *The Blue Afternoon*

(1998) *Armadillo*

Boyle, Andrew (1979) *The Climate of Treason*

Bradbury, Malcolm (1959) *Eating People is Wrong*

(1965) *Stepping Westward*

(1975) *The History Man*

(1976) *Who Do You Think You Are?*

(1983) *Rates of Exchange*

Bradley, Edward (1853) *The Adventures of Mr Verdant Green*

Brand, John (1789) *The History and Antiquities of Newcastle-upon-Tyne*

Brewer, E. Cobham (1978 edition) *The Dictionary of Phrase and Fable*

Brierley, Benjamin (1854) *Treadlepin Fold and Other Tales*

(1865) *Irkdale*

(1886) *The Cotters of Mossburn*

Brown, Harry (1944) *A Walk in the Sun*

Brown, Ivor (1958) *Words in our Time*

Browning, D. C. (1962) *Everyman's Dictionary of Literary Biography*

Bryce, J. B. (1888) *The American Constitution*

Bryson, Bill (1989) *The Lost Continent*

(1991) *Neither Here Nor There*

(1994) *Made in America*

(1995) *Notes from a Small Island*

(1997) *A Walk in the Woods*

(1999) *Down Under*

Buchan, John (1898) *John Burnet of Barns*

Buckman, S. S. (1870) *John Darke's Sojourn in the Cotswolds*

Bullock, Alan, and Stallybrass, Oliver (1977) *The Fontana Dictionary of Modern Thought*

Bunyan, John (1678–84) *The Pilgrim's Progress*

Burgess, Anthony (1959) *Beds in the East*

(1980) *Earthly Powers*

Burleigh, Michael (2000) *The Third Reich*

Burmester, F. G. (1902) *John Lot's Alice*

Burnet, Gilbert (1714) *History of the Reformation of the Church of England*

Burnley, James (1880) *Poems and Sketches*

Burns, Robert (1786) *Poems in the Scottish Dialect*

Burroughs, William (1959) *The Naked Lunch*

(1984) *The Place of Dead Roads*

Burton, Anthony (1989) *The Great Days of the Canals*

Burton, Robert (1621) *The Anatomy of Melancholy*

Bush, Robin (1997) *Somerset Bedside Book*

Butcher, Harry C. (1946) *Three Years with Eisenhower*

Butler, Samuel (1903) *The Way of All Flesh*

Byrnes, J. H. (1974) *Mrs Byrnes's Dictionary of Unusual, Obscure and Preposterous Words*

Byron, G. G. N. (1809–24) *Works*

Bywater, Abel (1839) *The Sheffield Dialect*

(1853) *The Shevvild Chap's Annual*

Cahill, Thomas (1995) *How the Irish Saved Civilization*

Caine, T. H. H. (1885) *The Shadow of a Crime*

Cameron, Peter (1997) *Andorra*

Carleton, William (1836) *Fardorougha, the Miser*

Carrick, J. D. (1835) *The Laird of Logan*

Carter, Angela (1984) *Nights at the Circus*

Carter, V. Bonham (1965) *Winston Churchill as I Knew Him*

Caufield, Catherine (1990) *Multiple Exposures*

Cawthorne, Nigel (1996) *Sex Lives of the Popes*

Chambers, Robert (1870) *Popular Rhymes of Scotland*

Chamier, E., quoted in *Oxford Dictionary of English Proverbs*
Chandler, Raymond (1934) *Finger Man*
  (1939) *Trouble Is My Business*
  (1940) *Farewell My Lovely*
  (1943) *The High Window*
  (1944) *The Lady in the Lake*
  (1950) *The Big Sleep*
  (1951) *The Little Sister*
  (1953) *The Long Goodbye*
  (1958) *Playback*
Chapman, Kit (1999) *An Innkeeper's Diary*
Charlton, Jack (1996) *The Autobiography*
Chase, C. David (1987) *Mugged on Wall Street*
Cheng, Nien (1984) *Life and Death in Shanghai*
Christie, Agatha (1939) *Evil Under the Sun*
  (1940) *Ten Little Niggers*
Clancy, Tom (1986) *Red Storm Rising*
  (1987) *Patriot Games*
  (1988) *The Cardinal in the Kremlin*
  (1989) *Clear and Present Danger*
  (1991) *The Sum of All Our Fears*
Clare, John (1827) *The Shepherd's Calendar*
Clark, Alan (1993) *Diaries*
  (1995) *Barbarossa*
  (2000) *Diaries Into Politics*
Clark, Charles (1839) *John Noakes and Mary Styles*
Clark, Colin (1995) *The Prince, the Showgirl and Me*
Clark, Miles (1991) *High Endeavours*
Clay, John (1998) *Tales from the Bridge Table*
Cleland, John (1749) *Memoirs of a Woman of Pleasure* (Fanny Hill)
Cobbett, William (1830) *Rural Rides*
Coghill, James (1890) *Poems, Songs and Sonnets*
Cole, John (1995) *As it Seemed to Me*
Collins English Dictionary (1979 edition)
Collins, Jackie (1981) *Chances*
Collins, Wilkie (1860) *The Woman in White*
  (1868) *The Moonstone*
Colodny, Lee, and Gettlin, Robert (1991) *Silent Coup*
Colvil, Samuel (1796) *The Whig's Supplication*
Colville, John (1967) *The Fringes of Power*
  (1976) *Footprints in Time*
Commager, Henry (1972) *The Defeat of America*
Condon, Richard (1966) *Any God Will Do*
Congreve, William (1695) *Love for Love*
Cookson, Catherine (1967) *Slinky Jane*
  (1969) *Our Kate*
Coren, Michael (1995) *Conan Doyle*
Cork, Kenneth (1988) *Cork on Cork*
Corley, T. A. B. (1961) *Democratic Despot*
Cornwell, Bernard (1993) *Rebel*
  (1997) *Sharpe's Tiger*
Cornwell, Patricia (2000) *The Last Precinct*
Cosgrave, Patrick (1989) *The Lives of Enoch Powell*
Coyle, Harold (1987) *Team Yankee*
Crews, Harry (1990) *Body: A Tragicomedy*
Crisp N. J. (1982) *The Brink*
Crockett, S. R. (1894) *The Raiders*
  (1896) *The Grey Man*
Croker, T. C. (1862) *Fairy Legends and Traditions of South Ireland*

Cromwell, Oliver (1643) *Letter*
Cross, William (1844) *The Disruption*
Crossman, Richard (1981) *Backbench Diaries*
Cussler, Clive (1984) *Deep Six*
  (1994) *Inca Gold*

Dalrymple, William (1989) *In Xanadu*
  (1993) *City of Djinns*
  (1997) *From the Holy Mountain*
  (1998) *The Age of Kali*
Davidson, Lionel (1978) *The Chelsea Murders*
de Bernières, Louis (1994) *Captain Corelli's Mandolin*
de Guingand, Francis (1947) *Operation Victory*
de la Billière, Peter (1992) *Storm Command*
de Mille, Nelson (1988) *Charm School*
Deedes, W. F. (1997) *Dear Bill*
Defoe, Daniel (1721) *Moll Flanders*
Deighton, Len (1972) *Close-up*
  (1978) *SS-GB*
  (1981) *XPD*
  (1982) *Goodbye Mickey Mouse*
  (1985) *London Match*
  (1987) *Winter*
  (1988) *Sky Hook*
  (1989) *Spy Line*
  (1990) *Spy Sinker*
  (1991) *City of Gold*
  (1993/1) *Blood, Tears and Folly*
  (1993/2) *Violent Ward*
  (1994) *Faith*
Desai, Boman (1988) *The Memory of Elephants*
Dickens, Charles (1840) *The Old Curiosity Shop*
  (1843) *The Life and Adventures of Martin Chuzzlewit*
  (1853) *Bleak House*
  (1861) *Great Expectations*
Dickens, Monica (1939) *One Pair of Hands*
Dickinson, William (1866) *Scallow Beck Boggle*
Dickson, Paul (1978) *The Official Rules*
Dictionary of Cautionary Words and Phrases (1989)
Dictionary of National Biography (1978 edition)
Diehl, William (1978) *Sharky's Machine*
Dills, Lattie (1976) *The 'Official' CB Slanguage Language Dictionary*
Dixon, D. D. (1895) *Whittingham Vale*
Dixon J. H. (1846) *Ancient Poems, Ballads and Songs of the Peasantry of England*
Dodds, Michael (1991) *Last Man to Die*
Doherty, Austen (1884) *Nathan Barlow*
Donaldson, Frances (1990) *Yours Plum: The Letters of P. G. Wodehouse*
Douglas, George (1901) *The House with Green Shutters*
Doyle, Arthur Conan (1895) *The Napoleonic Stories*
  (1917) *His Last Bow*
Doyle, Ezra (1855) *Polly's Game*
Doyle, Roddy (1987) *The Commitments*
  (1990) *The Snapper*
  (1991) *The Van*
  (1993) *Paddy Clarke Ha Ha Ha*
  (1996) *The Woman who Walked into Doors*
  (1999) *A Star Called Henry*

Dryden, John (1668–98) *Poetical Works*
du Maurier, Daphne (1938) *Rebecca*
Dunning, Robert (1993) *Somerset One Hundred Years Ago*

Egerton, J. C. (1884) *Sussex Folks and Sussex Ways*
Eliot, George (1871–2) *Middlemarch*
Ellis, William (1750) *The Modern Husbandman*
Ellman, Lucy (1988) *Sweet Desserts*
Emblen, D. L. (1970) *Peter Mark Roget: The Word and the Man*
Emerson, P. H. (1890) *Wild Life on a Tidal Water*
(1892) *A Son of the Fens*
Enright, D. J. (editor) (1985) *Fair of Speech*
Erdman, Paul (1974) *The Silent Bears*
(1981) *The Last Days of America*
(1986) *The Panic of '89*
(1987) *The Palace*
(1993) *Zero Coupon*
Etherege, George (1676) *The Man of Mode*
Evans, Bergen (1962) *Comfortable Words*
Evans, Nicholas (1995) *The Horse Whisperer*
(1998) *The Loop*
Evans-Pritchard, Ambrose (1997) *The Secret Life of Bill Clinton*
Evelyn, John (published in 1818 posthumously) *Diary*

Faderman, Lilian (1991) *Old Girls and Twilight Lovers*
Faith, Nicholas (1990) *The World the Railways Made*
Farmer, J. S. and Henley, W. J. (1890–4) *Slang and its Analogues*
Farran, Roy (1948) *Winged Dagger*
Farrell, J. G. (1973) *The Siege of Krishnapur*
Faulks, Sebastian (1993) *Birdsong*
(1996) *The Fatal Englishman*
(1998) *Charlotte Gray*
Fergusson, Bernard (1945) *Beyond the Chindwin*
Fergusson, Robert (1773) *Poems on Various Subjects*
Fielding, Helen (1996) *Bridget Jones's Diary*
(1999) *The Edge of Reason*
Fielding, Henry (1729) *The Author's Face*
(1742) *The History and Adventures of Joseph Andrews*
Fiennes, Ranulph (1996) *The Sett*
Fine, Anne (1989) *Goggle-Eyes*
Fingall, Elizabeth (Countess of) (1977) *Seventy Years Young*
Flanagan, Thomas (1979) *The Year of the French*
(1988) *The Tenants of Time*
(1995) *The End of the Game*
Fleming, Lionel (1965) *Head or Harp*
Fletcher, John (1618) *Valentinian*
Follett, Ken (1978) *The Eye of the Needle*
(1979) *Triple*
(1991) *Night over Water*
(1992) *By Stealth*
(1996) *The Hammer of Eden*
Forbes, Brian (1972) *The Distant Laughter*
(1983) *The Rewrite Man*
(1986) *The Endless Game*
(1989) *A Song at Twilight*

Forbes, Colin (1983) *The Leader and the Damned*
(1985) *Cover Story*
(1987) *The Janus Man*
(1992) *By Stealth*
Ford, Robert (1891) *Thistledown*
Foreman, Amanda (1998) *Georgiana, Duchess of Devonshire*
Forsey, Eugene (1990) *A Life on the Fringe*
Forster, Margaret (1997) *Rich Desserts and Captain's Thin*
Forsyth, Frederick (1984) *The Fourth Protocol*
(1994) *The Fist of God*
(1996) *Icon*
Foster, Brian (1968) *The Changing English Language*
Foster, R. F. (1988) *Modern Ireland 1600–1972*
(1993) *Paddy and Mr Punch*
Fowler, H. W. (1957) *Modern English Usage*
Fowles, John (1977) *The Magus* (revised)
(1985) *A Maggot*
Fox, James (1982) *White Mischief*
Francis, Dick (1962) *Dead Cert*
(1973) *The Gift*
(1978) *Trial Run*
(1981) *Twice Shy*
(1982) *Banker*
(1985) *Break In*
(1987) *Hot Money*
(1988) *The Edge*
(1994) *Wild Horses*
(1996) *To the Hilt*
(1998) *Field of 13*
Francis, M. E. (1901) *Pastorals of Dorset*
Franklin, Benjamin (1757) *The Way to Wealth*
Franklyn, Julian (1960) *A Dictionary of Rhyming Slang*
Fraser, George MacDonald (1969) *Flashman*
(1970) *Royal Flash*
(1971) *Flash for Freedom*
(1973) *Flashman at the Charge*
(1975) *Flashman in the Great Game*
(1977) *Flashman's Lady*
(1982) *Flashman and the Redskins*
(1983) *The Pyrates*
(1985) *Flashman and the Dragon*
(1992) *Quartered Safe Out Here*
(1994) *Flashman and the Angel of the Lord*
(1997) *Black Ajax*
Frazier, Charles (1997) *Cold Mountain*
Freemantle, Brian (1977) *Charlie Muffin*
French, Patrick (1995) *Younghusband*
(1997) *Liberty or Death*
Fry, Stephen (1991) *The Liar*
(1994) *The Hippopotamus*
Funk, Charles E. (the elder) (1955) *Heavens to Betsy and Other Curious Sayings*
Furst, Alan (1988) *Night Soldiers*
(1995) *The Polish Officer*

Gaarder, Josten (1996) *The Solitaire Mystery* (translated by S. J. Hails)
Gabriel, Marius (1992) *The Original Sin*
Galloway, George (1810) *Poems*
Galsworthy, John (1924) *The White Monkey*

Galt, John (1821) *The Ayrshire Legatees*
  (1823) *The Entail*
  (1826) *The Last of the Lairds*
Gardner, James F. (1983) *Elephants in the Attic*
Garland, Alex (1996) *The Beach*
Garmondsway, George and Simpson, Jacqueline
  (1969) *The Penguin English Dictionary*
Garner, James F. (1994) *Politically Correct Bedtime Stories*
Gascoigne, George (1576; 1907–10 edition) *Works*
Gaskell, E. C. (1863) *Sylvia's Lovers*
Genet, Jean (1969) *Funeral Rites* (in translation)
Gentles, Ian (1992) *The New Model Army in England, Ireland and Scotland, 1645–1653*
Ginsberg, Allen (1984)
Gissing, Algernon (1890) *A Village Hampden*
Goebbels, Josef (1945) *Diaries* (translated by Richard Barry)
Golden, Arthur (1997) *Memoirs of a Geisha*
Goldman, William (1984) *The Colour of Light*
  (1986) *Brothers*
Gorbachev, Mikhail (1995) *Memoirs* (translated by Georges Peronansky and Tatjana Varsavsky)
Gordon, Alexander (1984) *Northward Ho!*
Gordon, Frank (1885) *Pyotshaw*
Gordon, J. F. S. (1880) *The Book of Chronicles of Keith . . .*
Gordon, Lyndall (1994) *Charlotte Brontë*
Gores, Joseph N. (1975) *Hammett*
Gosling, John and Warner, Douglas (1960) *The Shame of a City*
Graham, Dougal (1883) *The Collected Writings*
Graham, Harry (1930) *More Ruthless Rhymes for Heartless Homes*
Grant, David (1884) *Lays and Legends of the North*
Graves, Robert (1940) *Sergeant Lamb of the Ninth*
  (1941) *Proceed Sergeant Lamb*
Grayson, H. (1975) *The Last Alderman*
Greeley, Andrew M. (1986) *God Games*
Green, Jonathon (1991) *Neologisms: New Words since 1960*
  (1996) *Chasing the Sun*
Green, Shirley (1979) *Rachman*
Greene, G. A. (1599) *Works*
Greene, Graham (1932) *Stamboul Train*
  (1934) *It's a Battlefield*
  (1967) *May We Borrow Your Husband?*
  (1978) *The Human Factor*
Grinnell-Milne, Duncan (1933) *Wind in the Wires*
Grisham, John (1992) *The Pelican Brief*
  (1994) *The Chamber*
  (1998) *The Street Lawyer*
  (1999) *The Testament*
  (2001) *A Painted House*
Grose, Francis (1811 edition) *Dictionary of the Vulgar Tongue*
Guinness, Alec (1985) *Blessings in Disguise*

Hackett, John (1978) *The Third World War*
Haggard, H. Rider (1885) *King Solomon's Mines*
Hailey, Arthur (1973) *Wheels*
  (1975) *The Money-Changers*
  (1979) *Overlord*

  (1984) *Strong Medicine*
  (1990) *The Evening News*
Hall, Adam (1969) *The Ninth Directive*
  (1979) *The Scorpion Signal*
  (1988) *Quiller's Run*
Hallam, Reuben (1866) *Wadsley Jack*
Hamilton, Ernest (1897) *The Outlaws of the Marshes*
  (1898) *The Mawkin of the Flow*
Hardy, Thomas (1874) *Far From the Madding Crowd*
  (1888) *Wessex Tales*
Harland, John and Wilkinson, T. T. (1867) *Folk Lore*
Harris, Frank (1925) *My Life and Loves*
Harris, Robert (1992) *Fatherland*
  (1995) *Enigma*
  (1998) *Archangel*
Harris, Thomas (1988) *The Silence of the Lambs*
Hartley, John (1870) *Heart Broken*
Harvey, William (1628) *Anatomica de Motu Cardis* etc.
Hastings, Max (1987) *The Korean War*
Hastings, Selina (1994) *Evelyn Waugh*
Hattersley, Roy (1995) *Who Goes Home*
Hawks, Tony (1998) *Round Ireland with a Fridge*
Hayden, Eleanor (1902) *From a Thatched Cottage*
Heath, Robert (1650) *Clarastella together with poems occasional* etc.
Hector, William (1876) *Selections from the Judicial Records of Renfrewshire*
Heffer, Simon (1998) *Like the Roman: The Life of Enoch Powell*
Hemingway, Ernest (1941) *For Whom the Bell Tolls*
Henderson, George (1856) *The Popular Rhymes, Sayings and Proverbs of the County of Berwick*
Henderson, William (1879) *Notes on the Folk Lore of the Northern Counties* etc.
Herd, David (1771) *Ancient and Modern Scottish Songs*
Herr, Michael (1977) *Dispatches*
Herriot, James (1981) *The Good Lord Made Them All*
Hetrick, Robert (1826) *Poems and Songs*
Hewett, Sarah (1892) *The Peasant Speech of Devon*
Heywood, John (1546) *Works*
Hibbert, Samuel (1822) *A Description of the Shetland Islands*
Higgins, Jack (1976) *Storm Warning*
Hogg, James (1822) *Perils of Man*
  (1866) *Tales and Sketches*
Holder, R. W. (1992) *Thinking about Management*
  (2000) *Taunton Cider and Langdons*
Holmes, Richard (1961) *Dr Johnson and Mr Savage*
Holt, Alfred (1961) *Phrase and Word Origins*
Hood, Thomas (c.1830) *Poems*
Horne, Alastair (1969) *To Lose a Battle*
  (with D. Montgomery) (1994) *The Lonely Leader: Montgomery 1944–1945*
Horrocks, Brian (1960) *A Full Life*
Horsley, J. W. (1887) *Jottings from Jail*
Housman A. E. (1896) *A Shropshire Lad*
Howard, Anthony (1977) *New Words for Old*
  (1978) *Weasel Words*
  (1993) *Lives Remembered*

Howat, Gerald (1979) *Who Did What*
Hudson, Bob, and Pickering, Larry (1986) *First Australian Dictionary of Vulgarities and Obscenities*
Hudson, Kenneth (1977) *The Dictionary of Diseased English*
(1978) *The Jargon of the Professions*
Hughes, Robert (1987) *The Fatal Shore*
Hughes, Thomas (1856) *Tom Brown's Schooldays*
Hunt, Holman (1854) *Letter*
Hunt, Robert (1865–96 edition) *Popular Romances of the West of England*
Hutchinson, Lucy (c.1850) *Letter*
Hynd (1949)

Iacocca, Lee (1984) *Iacocca*
Ingelo (1830) *Reminiscences*
Inglis, James (1895) *Our Ain Folk*
Innes, Hammond (1982) *The Black Tide*
(1991) *Isvik*
Irvine, Lucy (1986) *Runaway*

James, Haddy (Surgeon) (1816) *Journal*
James, P. D. (1962) *Cover Her Face*
(1972) *An Unsuitable Job for a Woman*
(1975) *The Black Tower*
(1980) *Innocent Blood*
(1986) *A Taste for Death*
(1994) *Original Sin*
(2001) *Death in Holy Orders*
Jane, Fred (1897) *The Lordship, the Passen and We*
Jefferies, Richard (1880) *Hodge and his Masters*
Jennings, Gary (1965) *Personalities of Language*
Johnson, Samuel (1755) *A Dictionary of the English Language*
Johnston, Henry (1891) *Kilmallie*
Joliffe, Gray, and Mayle, Peter (1984) *Man's Best Friend*
Jolly, Rick (1988) *Jackspeak: The Pusser's Rum Guide*
Jones, R. V. (1978) *Most Secret War*
Jonson, Ben (1598–1633) *Works* (edited by Herford and Simpson, 1925–52)
Joyce, James (1922) *Ulysses*

Katzenbach, John (1995) *The Shadow Man*
Kay, Valerie, and Stevens, Peter (1974) *Beyond the Dictionary in English*
Kee, Robert (1984) *The World We Left Behind*
(1993) *The Laurel and the Ivy*
Keegan, John (1989) *The Second World War*
(1991) *Churchill's Generals*
(1998) *The First World War*
Keith, Leslie (1896) *The Indian Uncle*
(1897) *My Bonnie Lady*
Kelly, James (1721) *A Complete Collection of Scottish Proverbs*
Keneally, Thomas (1979) *Confederates*
(1982) *Schindler's Ark*
(1985) *A Family Madness*
(1987) *The Playmaster*
Kennedy, James (1998) *Silent City*
Kennedy, Patrick (1867) *The Banks of the Boro*
Kersh, Gerald (1936) *Night and the City*
King, Stephen (1990) *I Shall Bear Witness*

(1996) *The Green Mile*
Kinloch, George R. (1827) *The Ballad Book*
Kirkton, James (1817) *The Secret and True History of the Church of Scotland* etc.
Klemperer, Victor (1998) *I Shall Bear Witness* (translated by Martin Chalmers)
(1999) *To the Bitter End* (translated by Martin Chalmers)
Koontz, Dean (1997) *Sole Survivor*
Kramarae, Cheris, and Treichler, Panla (1985) *A Feminist Dictionary*
Kyle, Duncan (1975) *The Semenov Impulse*
(1983) *The King's Commander*
(1988) *The Honey Ant*

Lacey, Robert (1986) *Ford*
Lauderdale, John (1796) *A Collection of Poems*
Lavine, Emanuel (1930) *The Third Degree*
Lawless, Emily (1892) *Grania*
Lawrence, Karen (1990) *Springs of Living Water*
le Carré, John (1962) *A Murder of Quality*
(1980) *Smiley's People*
(1983) *The Little Drummer Girl*
(1986) *A Perfect Spy*
(1989) *The Russia House*
(1991) *The Secret Pilgrim*
(1993) *The Night Manager*
(1995) *Our Game*
(1996) *The Tailor of Panama*
(1999) *Single and Single*
Lee, Christopher (1999) *This Sceptred Isle*
Lee, John Alexander (1937) *Civilian into Soldier*
Lee, Joseph J. (1989) *Ireland 1912–1985*
Lewis, Matthew (1795) *The Monk*
Lewis, Nigel (1989) *Channel Firing*
Liddle, William (1821) *Poems on Different Occasions*
Lingemann, Richard (1969) *Drugs from A to Z*
Linklaker, Eric (1964) *Fatal Fascination*
Linton, E. Lynn (1866) *Lizzie Lorton of Greyrigg*
Lockhead, Liz (1985) *Time Confessions and New Clichés*
Lodge, David (1962) *Ginger You're Barmy*
(1975) *Changing Places*
(1980) *How Far Can You Go?*
(1988) *Nice Work*
(1995) *Therapy*
Lomax, Eric (1995) *The Railway Man*
Londres, Albert (1928) *The Road to Buenos Ayres* (translated by Eric Sutton)
Longstreet, Stephen (1956) *The Real Jazz Old and New*
Lowson, Alexander (1890) *John Guidfellow*
Ludlum, Robert (1979) *The Matarese Circle*
(1984) *The Aquitaine Progression*
Lumsden, James (1892) *Sheep-Head and Trotters*
Lyall, Gavin (1965) *Midnight Plus One*
(1969) *Venus with Pistol*
(1972) *Blame the Dead*
(1975) *Judas Country*
(1980) *The Secret Servant*
(1982) *The Conduct of Major Maxim*
(1985) *The Crocus List*
Lyly, John (1579) *Euphues, the Anatomy of Wit*

Lynd, Robert (1946) *Dr Johnson and Company*
Lynn, Jonathan and Jay, Antony (1981) *Yes Minister*
(1986) *Yes Prime Minister*
(1989) *The Complete Yes Prime Minister*
Lyons, Mary (ed.) (1996) *The Memoirs of Mrs Leeson*

Maas, Peter (1986) *Man Hunt*
McBain, Ed (1981) *Heat*
(1994) *There Was a Little Girl*
McCarthy, Mary (1963) *The Group*
(1967) *Vietnam*
McCarthy, Pete (2000) *McCarthy's Bar*
McCourt, Frank (1997) *Angela's Ashes*
(1999) *'Tis*
McCrum, Robert (1991) *Mainland*
McCrum, Robert, Cran, William, and McNeil, Robert (1986) *The Story of English*
MacDonagh, Michael (1898) *Irish Life and Character*
Macdonald, Ross (1952) *The Ivory Grin*
(1971) *The Doomsters*
(1976) *The Blue Hammer*
McInerney, Jay (1992) *Brightness Falls*
Mackenzie, George Stewart of Coul, quoted in Prebble (1963)
Mackie, Marlene (1983) *Gender Relations in Canada*
Maclaren, Ian (1895) *Beside the Bonnie Briar Bush*
Maclean, Rory (1998) *Under the Dragon*
MacManus, Seumas (1898) *The Bend of the Road*
(1899) *In Chimney Corners*
McNab, Andy (1993) *Bravo Two Zero*
(1997) *Remote Control*
McNair, Tom (1973) *A Guide to Hip Language and Culture*
MacTaggart, John (1824) *Scottish Gallovidian Encylopaedia*
Maggs, Colin (2001) *The GWR Bristol to Bath Line*
'Maidment, James (1844–5) *Spottiswoode Miscellany*
(1868) *A Book of Scotch Pasquils, 1568–1715*
Mailer, Norman (1965) *An American Dream*
Major, Clarence (1970) *Black Slang: A Dictionary of Afro-American Slang*
Major, John (1999) *The Autobiography*
Manchester, William (1968) *The Arms of Krupp*
Mandela, Nelson (1994) *Long Walk to Freedom*
Mann, Mary (1902) *The Fields of Dulditch*
Manning, Olivia (1960) *The Great Fortune*
(1962) *The Spoilt City*
(1965) *Friends and Heroes*
(1977) *The Danger Tree*
(1978) *The Battle Lost and Won*
Mantle, Jonathan (1988) *In for a Penny*
'Mark VII' (1927) *A Subaltern on the Somme*
Marmur, Jacland (1955) *The Kid in Command*
Marsh, Ngaio (1941) *Surfeit of Lampreys*
Marshall, William H. (1811, 1817, 1818) *Review and Abstract of the County Reports to the Board of Agriculture* etc.
Marvell, Andrew (*c.*1670) *Poems*
Mason, A. E. W. (1927) *No Other Tiger*
Mason, David (1993) *Shadow over Babylon*

Mason, William S. (1815) *A Statistical Account or Parochial Survey of Ireland*
Massie, Allan (1986) *Augustus*
Massie, Robert (1992) *Dreadnought*
Masters, John (1976) *The Himalayan Concerto*
Mather, Joseph (1862) *Songs*
Matthew, Christopher (1978) *The Diary of a Somebody*
(1983) *How to Survive Middle Age*
Mayberry, Tom (1998) *The Vale of Taunton Past*
Mayhew, Henry (1851) *London Labour and the London Poor*
(1861) *Mayhew's London*
(1862) *London's Underground*
Mayle, Peter (1993) *Hotel Pastis*
Mazower, Mark (1993) *Inside Hitler's Greece*
Mencken, Henry L. (1940–8) *The American Language*
Milligan, Spike (1971) *Adolf Hitler: My Part in his Downfall*
Milton, Giles (1999) *Nathaniel's Nutmeg*
Mitchell, David (1982) *The Spanish Civil War*
Mitford, Jessica (1963) *The American Way of Death*
Mitford, Nancy (1945) *The Pursuit of Love*
(1949) *Love in a Cold Climate*
(1956) *Noblesse Oblige*
(1960) *Don't Tell Alfred*
Mockler, Anthony (1984) *Haile Selassie's War*
Moir, David (1828) *The Life of Mansie Wauch*
Moncrieff, William (1821) *Tom and Jerry, or Life in London*
Monkhouse, Bob (1993) *Crying with Laughter*
Monsarrat, Nicholas (1978) *The Master Mariner*
Moore, L. W. (1893) *His Own Story*
Morison, David (1790) *Poems*
Morley, Robert (1976) *Pass the Port*
Mort, Simon (1986) *Original Selection of New Words*
Mortimer, Geoffrey (1895) *Tales from the Western Moors*
Moss, Robert (1985) *Moscow Rules*
(1987) *Carnival of Space*
Moss, W. S. (1950) *Ill Met by Moonlight*
Moyes, P. (1980) *Angel Death*
Moynahan, Brian (1983) *Airport International*
(1994) *The Russian Century*
Mucklebackit, Samuel (1885) *Rhymes*
Muggeridge, Malcolm (1972) *Chronicles of Wasted Time*
Muir, Frank (1990) *The Oxford Book of Humorous Prose*
(1997) *A Kentish Lad*
Muir, George (1816) *The Clydesdale Minstrelsy*
Murdoch, Alexander (1873) *Lilts on the Doric Lyre*
(1895) *Scotch Readings*
Murdoch, Iris (1974) *The Sacred and Profane Love Machine*
(1977) *Henry and Cato*
(1978) *The Sea, the Sea*
(1980) *Nuns and Soldiers*
(1983) *The Philosopher's Pupil*
(1985) *The Good Apprentice*
Murray, C. S. (1989) *Crosstown Traffic*
Murray, D. Christie (1886) *Rainbow Gold*
(1890) *John Vale's Guardian*

Murray, Elisabeth (1977) *Caught in the Web of Words*

Nabokov, Vladimir (1968) *King, Queen, Knave*
Naipaul, V. S. (1964) *An Area of Darkness*
(1990) *India: A Million Mutinies Now*
Nares, Robert (1820) *A Glossary or Collection of Words* etc.
Neaman, Judith N., and Silver, Carol S. (1983) *Kind Words: A Theasaurus of Euphemisms*
New Larousse Encyclopaedia of Mythology (1968)
Nicholson, William (1814) *Poetical Works*
Nicholson, John, and Burn (1777) *The History and Antiquities of the Counties of Westmoreland and Cumberland*
Ninh, Bao (1991) *The Sorrow of War* (translated by Frank Palmos)
Norfolk, Lawrence (1991) *Lemprière's Dictionary*

O'Callaghan, Sean (1998) *The Informer*
O'Connor, Joseph (1991) *Cowboys and Indians*
O'Donoghue, Maureen (1988) *Winner*
O'Hanlon, Redmond (1984) *Into the Heart of Borneo*
(1996) *Congo Journey*
O'Reilly, R. (1880) *Sussex Stories*
O'Rourke, P. J. (1991) *Parliament of Whores*
Oakley, Ann (1984) *Taking it like a Woman*
Ogg, James (1873) *Willie Waly; and other Poems*
Olivier, Laurence (1982) *Confessions of an Actor*
Ollard, Richard (1974) *Pepys*
Ollivant, Alfred (1898) *Owd Bob, the Grey Dog of Kenmuir*
Onions, C. T. (1975) *The Oxford Dictionary of English Etymology*
Ousby, Ian (1997) *Occupation: The Ordeal of France 1940–1944*
Oxford English Dictionary (1989 edition)

Pae, David (1884) *Eustace the Outcast*
Parker, Dorothy (1944) *The Portable Dorothy Parker*
Parris, Matthew (1995) *Great Parliamentary Scandals*
Partridge, Eric (1947) *Shakespeare's Bawdy*
(1959) *Origins*
(1969) *A Dictionary of Slang and Unconventional English*
(1972) *A Dictionary of Clichés*
(1972) *A Dictionary of Historical Slang* (with Jacqueline Simpson)
(1973) *Usage and Abusage*
(1977) *A Dictionary of Catch Phrases*
Paterson, R. C. (1998) *A Land Afflicted*
Patten, Chris (1998) *East and West*
Patterson, A. (1895) *Man and Nature on the Broads*
Patterson, James (1999) *Pop Goes the Weasel*
(2000) *Roses are Red*
Patterson, Richard North (1992) *Degree of Guilt*
(1994) *Eyes of a Child*
(1996) *The Final Judgement*
(1996) *Silent Witness*
Paxman, Jeremy (1998) *The English*

Payn, James (1878) *By Proxy*
Peacock, Edward (1870) *Ralf Skirlaugh, the Lancashire Farmer*
Peacock, F. M. (1890) *A Soldier and a Maid*
Pearsall, Ronald (1969) *The Worm in the Bud*
Pease, Howard (1894) *The Mark o' the Deil*
Peck, M. Scott (1987) *The Different Drum: Community-Making and Peace*
(1990) *A Bed by the Window: A Novel of Mystery and Redemption*
Pegge, Samuel (1803) *Anecdotes of the English Language*
Pei, Mario (1969) *Words in Sheep's Clothing*
(1978) *Weasel Words*
Pennecuik, Alexander (1715) *Description of Tweeddale and Poems*
Pepys, Samuel (1660–9) *Diary*
Pereira, M. (1972) *Singing Millionaire*
Perelman, S. J. (1937) *Strictly from Hunger*
Pérez-Réverté, Arturo (1994) *The Flanders Panel* (translated by Costa Margaret Jull)
Peshall (1773) *Ancient and Present State of the City of Oxford*
Phillips, Julia (1991) *You'll Never Eat Lunch in This Town Again*
Picken, Ebenezer (1813) *Miscellaneous Poems and Songs*
Pilcher, Rosamund (1988) *The Shell Seekers*
Pincher, Chapman (1987) *The Spycatcher Affair*
'Pindar, Peter' (1816) *Works*
Pinnock, John (1895) *Tom Brown's Black Country Annual*
Playboy's Book of Limericks (1972) (edited by Clifford Crist)
Pope, Alexander (1735) *Poetical Works*
Pope-Hennessy, James (1967) *The Sins of the Fathers*
Powetski, Grace (1992) *Guardian Angel*
Poyer, Joe (1978) *The Contract*
Praed, Campbell (1890) *Romance Station*
Prebble, John (1963) *The Highland Clearances*
Price, Anthony (1970) *The Labyrinth Makers*
(1971) *The Alamut Ambush*
(1972) *Captain Butler's Wolf*
(1974) *Other Paths to Glory*
(1975) *Our Man in Camelot*
(1978) *The '44 Vintage*
(1979) *War Games*
(1982) *The Old Vengeful*
(1985) *Here Be Monsters*
(1987) *A New Kind of War*
Proudlock, Lewis (1896) *The Borderland Muse*
Proulx, E. Annie (1993) *The Shipping News*
Pynchon, Thomas (1997) *Mason and Dixon*
Pythiam, B. A. (1979) *A Concise Dictionary of Current English*

Quiller-Couch, Arthur (1890) *I Saw Three Ships*
(1891) *Noughts and Crosses*
(1893) *The Delectable Duchy*

Rabelais, Francois (1532) *Pantagruel* (in translation)
(1534) *Gargantua* (in translation)

Radford, Edwin, and Smith, Alan (1973) *To Coin a Phrase*

Rae, John (1993) *Delusions of Grandeur*

Ramsay, Allan (1737) *Collection of Scots Proverbs* (1800 edition) *Poems*

Ramsay, E. B. (1858–61) *Reminiscences of Scottish Life and Character*

Ranfurly, Hermione (Countess of) (1994) *To War with Whitaker*

Rawson, Hugh (1981) *A Dictionary of Euphemisms and Other Doubletalk*

Ray, John (1678) *A Collection of English Proverbs*

Read, Piers Paul (1979) *A Married Man* (1986) *The Free Frenchman* (1995) *A Patriot in Berlin*

Reeman, Douglas (1994) *Sunset*

Rees, Nigel (1980) *Graffiti*

Rendell, Ruth (1991) *Kissing the Gunner's Daughter*

Richards, David Adams (1988) *Nights Below Station Street*

Richards, Frank (1933) *Old Soldiers Never Die* (1936) *Old Soldier Sahib*

Ritchie, A. I. (1883) *The Churches of St Baldred*

Robbins, Harold (1981) *Goodbye Janette*

Roberts, Michael (1951) *The Estate of Man*

Roberts, Monty (1996) *The Man Who Listens to Horses*

Rock, William F. (1867) *Jim an' Nell*

Rodger, Alexander (1838) *Poems and Songs*

Roethke, Theodore (1941) *Open House*

Roget's Thesaurus (1966 edition)

Ross, Alan (1956) *Noblesse Oblige*

Royle, Trevor (1989) *The Last Days of the Raj*

Runyon, Damon (1990 but written in 1930s) *On Broadway*

Rushdie, Salman (1995) *The Moor's Last Sigh*

Russell, S. C. (c.1900) *A Strange Voyage*

Ryan, Andy (1998) *Tenth Man Down*

Ryan, Chris (1999) *The Kremlin Device*

St Pierre, Paul (1983) *Smith and Other Events: Tales of Chilcotin*

Salinger, J. D. (1951) *The Catcher in the Rye*

Sale, Charles (1930) *The Specialist*

Sanders, Laurence (1970) *The Anderson Tapes* (1973) *The First Deadly Sin* (1977) *The Second Deadly Sin* (1977) *The Tangent Objective* (1979) *The Sixth Commandment* (1980) *The Tenth Commandment* (1980) *Caper* (1981) *The Third Deadly Sin* (1982) *The Case of Lucy Bending* (1983) *The Seduction of Peter S.* (1984) *The Passion of Molly T.* (1985) *The Fourth Deadly Sin* (1986) *The Eighth Commandment* (1987) *The Timothy Files* (1990) *Sullivan's Sting* (1992) *McNally's Luck* (1994) *McNally's Caper*

Sassoon, Siegfried (1928) *Memoirs of a Fox-Hunting Man*

'Saxon' (1878) *Galloway Gossip Sixty Years Ago*

Sayers, Dorothy (1937) *Busman's Honeymoon*

Scott, Andrew (1805) *Poems*

Scott, Paul (1968) *The Day of the Scorpion* (1971) *The Towers of Silence* (1973) *The Jewel in the Crown* (1975) *A Division of the Spoils* (1977) *Staying On*

Scott, Walter (1803) *Minstrelsy of the Scottish Border* (1814) *Waverley* (1815) *Guy Mannering* (1816) *The Antiquary* (1817) *Rob Roy* (1818) *The Heart of Midlothian* (1819) *The Battle of Lammermoor* (1820) *The Abbot* (1822) *Nigel* (1824) *Redgauntlet*

Seitz, Raymond (1998) *Over Here*

Service, John (1887) *The Life and Recollections of Dr Duguid of Kilwinning* (1890) *The Notandums*

Seth, Vikram (1993) *A Suitable Boy*

Seymour, Gerald (1977) *Kingfisher* (1980) *The Contract* (1982) *Archangel* (1984) *In Honour Bound* (1989) *Home Run* (1992) *The Journeyman Tailor* (1995) *The Heart of Danger* (1997) *Killing Ground* (1998) *The Waiting Time* (1999) *A Line in the Sand*

Shakespeare, William *Plays and Sonnets* (as noted)

Sharpe, Tom (1974) *Porterhouse Blue* (1975) *Blot on the Landscape* (1976) *Wilt* (1977) *The Great Pursuit* (1978) *The Throwback* (1979) *The Wilt Alternative* (1982) *Vintage Stuff*

Shaw, Irwin (1946) *Short Stories: Five Decades*

Sheldon, Sidney (1998) *Tell me your Dreams*

Sheppard, Harvey (1970) *A Dictionary of Railway Slang*

Shipley, Joseph (1945) *A Dictionary of Word Origins*

Shirer, William (1984) *The Nightmare Years 1930–1940* (1999) *This is Berlin*

Shorter Oxford English Dictionary (1993 edition)

Sidney, Philip (1586) *Works*

Simon, Ted (1979) *Jupiter's Travels*

Simpson, John (1991) *From the House of War* (1998) *Strange Places, Questionable People*

Sinclair, Keith (1991) *A History of New Zealand*

Skelton, John (1533) *Magnyfycence*

Slang Dictionary (The) (1874)

Slick, Samuel (1836) *Clockmaker*

Smith, Martin Cruz (1981) *Gorky Park*

Smith, Michael (1999) *Foley: The Spy who Saved 10,000 Jews*

Smith, Murray (1993) *The Devil's Juggler*

Smith, Tony (1986) *Family Doctor, Home Adviser*
Smith, W. H. C. (1991) *Second Empire and Commune*
Smith, Wilbur (1979) *Wild Justice*
Smith, Sir William (1923) *Latin–English Dictionary*
Smith, William G., and Wilson, F. P. (1970) *The Oxford Dictionary of English Proverbs*
Smollett, Tobias (1748) *Roderick Random*
  (1751) *Peregrine Pickle*
  (1771) *Humphrey Clinker*
Sobel, Dava (1996) *Longitude*
Sohmer, Steve (1988) *Favourite Son*
Solzhenitsyn, Alexander (1974) *The Gulag Archipelago* (translated by Thomas Whitney)
Somerville, A. E., and Ross, Martin (1894) *The Real Charlotte*
  (1897) *Some Experiences of an Irish RM*
  (1908) *Further Experiences of an Irish RM*
Spears, Richard (1981) *Slang and Euphemism*
Spence, Charles (1898) *From the Braes of the Carse*
Stamp, Terence (1994) *The Night*
Stegner, Wallace (1940) *The Women on the Wall*
Steinbeck, John (1961) *The Winter of our Discontent*
Stevens, Gordon (1996) *Kara's Game*
Stevenson, Robert Louis (1884) *The Resurrection Man*
Stewart, George E. (1892) *Shetland Fireside Tales*
Stewart, Graham (1999) *Burying Caesar*
Stoker, Bram (1895) *The Watter's Mou'*
Strachey, Lytton (1918) *Eminent Victorians*
Strain, E. H. (1900) *Elmslie's Drag-Net*
Strong, Terence (1994) *The Tick Tock Man*
  (1997) *Rogue Element*
  (1998) *Deadwater Deep*
Styron, William (1976) *Sophie's Choice*
Sullivan, Frank (1953) *The Night the Old Nostalgia Burned Down*
Sutcliffe, Halliwell (1899) *By Moor and Fell*
  (1900) *Shameless Wayne*
  (1901) *Mistress Barbara Cunliffe*
Sutherland, James (1975) *The Oxford Book of Literary Anecdotes*
Sutherland, William (1821) *Poems and Songs*
Swift, Jonathan (1723–38) *Works*

Taraporevala, Soomi (2000) *Pursis*
Tarras, William (1804) *Poems*
Taylor, Mary (1890) *Miss Miles*
Taylor, William (1787) *Scots Poems*
Teisser du Croix, Janet (1962) *Divided Loyalties*
Tennyson, Alfred (1859) *The Idylls of the King*
  (1885) *The Spinster's Sweet Arts*
Tester, William (1865) *Poems*
Thackeray, William (1837–55) *Works*
Theroux, Paul (1971) *Jungle Lovers*
  (1973) *Saint Jack*
  (1974) *The Black House*
  (1975) *The Great Railway Bazaar*
  (1976) *The Family Arsenal*
  (1977) *The Consul's File*
  (1978) *Picture Palace*
  (1979) *The Old Patagonian Express*
  (1980) *World's End and Other Stories*
  (1981) *The Mosquito Coast*
  (1982) *The London Embassy*
  (1983) *The Kingdom by the Sea*
  (1988) *Riding the Red Rooster*
  (1989) *My Secret History*
  (1990) *Chicago Loop*
  (1992) *The Happy Isles of Oceania*
  (1993) *Millroy the Magician*
  (1995) *The Pillars of Hercules*
Thom, Robert (1878) *The Courtship and Wedding of Jack o' the Knowe*
Thomas, Clive (1993) *Playing with Cobras*
Thomas, Hugh (1961) *The Spanish Civil War*
  (1986) *Armed Truce*
  (1993) *The Conquest of Mexico*
Thomas, Leslie (1977) *Bare Nell*
  (1978) *Ormerod's Landing*
  (1979) *That Old Gang of Mine*
  (1981) *The Magic Army*
  (1986) *The Adventures of Goodnight and Loving*
  (1989) *Orders for New York*
  (1994) *Running Away*
  (1996) *Kensington Heights*
  (1997) *Chloe's Song*
Thomas, Michael (1980) *Green Monday*
  (1982) *Someone Else's Money*
  (1985) *Hard Money*
  (1987) *The Ropespinner Conspiracy*
Thompson, Rupert (1996) *The Insult*
Thompson, David (1881) *Musings among the Heather*
Thwaite, Anthony (1992) *Selected Letters of Philip Larkin 1940–1985*
Tomalin, Claire (1997) *Jane Austen*
Torriano, Giovanni (1642) *A Common Place of Italian Proverbs and Proverbial Phrases*
Townsend, Sue (1982) *The Secret Diary of Adrian Mole Aged 13¾*
  (1984) *The Growing Pains of Adrian Mole*
Train, John (1983) *Preserving Capital and Making it Grow*
'Treddlehoyle' (Rogers, Charles) (1838–75) (ed. Isaac Binns, 1876–83, and reprinted in *Leeds Mercury*, 1892–3) *The Bairnsla Foak's Annual an Pogmoor Olmenack*
Tremain, Rose (1999) *Music and Silence*
'Trevanian', (1972) *The Eiger Sanction*
  (1973) *The Loo Sanction*
Trevor-Roper, Hugh (1977) *Introduction to Goebbels' Diaries*
Trollope, Anthony (1885) *The Land-Leaguers*
Trollope, Joanna (1992) *The Man and the Girls*
Tulloch, Sara (1991) *The Oxford Dictionary of New Words*
Turner, E. S. (1952) *The Shocking History of Advertising*
Turner, Graeme (1968) *Our Secret Economy*
Turner, Graham, and Pearson, John (1965) *The Persuasion Industry*
Turow, Scott (1987) *Presumed Innocent*
  (1990) *The Burden of Proof*
  (1993) *Pleading Guilty*
  (1996) *The Laws of our Fathers*
  (1999) *Personal Injuries*

Twain, Mark (1884) *The Adventures of Huckleberry Finn*
Tweeddale, John (1896) *Maff*
Tyrrell, Syd (1973) *A Countryman's Tale*

Upfield, A. (1932) *Royal Abduction*
Ustinov, Peter (1966) *The Frontiers of the Sea* (1971) *Krumnagel*

Vachell, Horace (1934) *The Disappearance of Martha Penny*
van Druten, J. (1954) *I am a Camera*
van Lustbaden, Eric (1983) *Black Heart*
Vanderhaeghe, Guy (1997) *The Englishman's Boy*
Vedder, David (1832) *Orcadian Sketches*
Verney (Lady) (1870) *Lettice Lisle*

Wainwright, J. (1979) *Duty Elsewhere*
Wallace, James (1693) *A Description of the Isles of Orkney*
Wambaugh, Joseph (1972) *The Blue Knight*
(1975) *The Choirboys*
(1981) *The Glitter Dome*
(1983) *The Delta Star*
Ward, Geoffrey C. (1990) *The Civil War*
Ward, Mary (Mrs Humphrey) (1895) *The Story of Bessie Costrell*
Ward, T. (1708) *Some Queries to the Protestants* etc.
Wardrop, Alex (1881) *Johnnie Mathison's Courtship and Marriage*
Waugh, Auberon (from *Private Eye* and *Daily Telegraph* diaries as noted)
Waugh, Evelyn (1930) *Labels*
(1932) *Remote People*
(1933) *Scoop*
(1955) *Officers and Gentlemen*
(1956) *Noblesse Oblige*
Webster, John (1623) *The Duchess of Malfi*
Webster, Noah (1977 Merriam edition) *New Collegiate Dictionary*

Wentworth, Harold, and Flexner, Stuart R. *Dictionary of American Slang* (1975 edition)
West, Morris (1979) *Proteus*
West, Nigel (1982) *MI5, 1945–72*
Westall, William (1885) *The Old Factory*
Weverka, Robert (1973) *The Sting*
Wheeler, Ann (1790) *The Westmoreland Dialect*
Whicker, Alan (1982) *Within Whicker's World*
Whitehead, Anthony (1896) *Legends of Penrith*
Whitehead, S. R. (1876) *Daft Davie*
Willock, A. Dewar (1886) *Rosetty Ends*
Wilson, Harry L. (1915) *Ruggles of Red Gap*
Wilson, John (1603) *The Bachelor's Banquet*
Wilson, John Mackay (1836) *Tales*
Wilson, Thomas (1843) *The Pitman's Pay*
Winchester, Simon (1998) *The Surgeon of Crowthorne*
Winton, Tim (1994) *The Riders*
Wodehouse, P. G. (1922) *Girl on Boat*
(1930) *Very Good, Jeeves!*
(1930) *Letter in Donaldson, 1990*
(1934) *Right Ho, Jeeves!*
Wodrow, Robert (1721) *The History of the Sufferings of the Church of Scotland* etc.
Wolfe, Tom (1987) *The Bonfire of the Vanities*
Wood, Frederick (1962) *Current English Usage*
(1979) *Dictionary of English Colloquial Idioms* (with Robert Hill)
Woodward, Rob (1987) *Veil*
Wouk, Herman (1951) *The Caine Mutiny*
Wright, Elizabeth Mary (1932) *The Life of Joseph Wright*
Wright, Joseph (1897) *Scenes of Scottish Life*
(1898–1905) *The English Dialect Dictionary*
Wright, Ronald (1989) *Time among the Maya*

Young, Edward (1721) *The Revenge*
Yule, Henry and Burnell, A. C. (1886) *Hobson–Jobson*
'Zack' (Keats, Gwendoline) (1901) *Tales of Dunstable Weir*

A

A1 amphetamine ingested illegally
An evasion among many in the argot of those who illegally ingest narcotics:
> Goodman had learnt the alternative names for amphetamines. These included: A1, beans, bombido, bumblebees, cartwheels, chicken powder, co-pilots, crank, cross-roads, diet pills, eye-openers, footballs, French blues, greenies, hearts, lightning, line, macka, miniberries, roses, speed, splash, sulph, thrusters, toffee whizz, truck drivers, turnabouts, wakeamine and zoom. (Fiennes, 1996)

AC/DC indulging in both heterosexual and homosexual practices
The reference is to the incompatible direct and alternating current in electricity supply. Also spelt phonetically as *acey-deecy*:
> Young attractive housewife, AC/DC, would like to meet married AC/DC people to join well-endowed husband for threesomes or moresomes. (*Daily Telegraph*, May 1980)
> So, he was acey-deecy... Lots of old altar boys play hide-the-weenie when they shouldn't. (Sohmer, 1988)

à trois in a sexual relationship involving three people
From *ménage à trois*, describing a couple married or living together and the outside sexual partner of one of them:
> I've been living *à trois* with a married couple. Do I shock you? (I. Murdoch, 1977)

abandoned *obsolete* working as a prostitute
Literally, forsaken, but not, it would seem, by her clients:
> The foolish idea... that once abandoned she must always be profligate. (Mayhew, 1862)
The punning *abandoned habits* were the flashy clothes prostitutes wore when riding in London's Hyde Park.

abbess *obsolete* a female bawd
Partly humorous and partly based on the suppositiond that nunneries were not solely occupied by chaste females:
> ... who should come in but the venerable mother Abbess herself. (Cleland, 1749, writing of a brothel)

abdominal protector a shield for the male genitalia

The *abdomen* is the lower cavity of the trunk, which the shield, commonly called a box, does not cover. If you hear a commentator suggest a player writhing in agony on the ground has been hit 'in the lower abdomen', it means he has had a disabling blow in his genitalia. See also WINDED.

aberration a sexual act or preference which is not heterosexual
Literally, a deviation from the norm:
> There's a great deal of tolerance for, well, aberrations. (Burgess, 1980)

ableism insensitivity towards lame or injured people
Used by those who may describe the fit as *temporarily abled*, presumably on the basis that their turn will come:
> Likewise 'ableism' or 'oppression of the differently abled ('disabled' is discriminatory) by the temporarily abled', is firmly proscribed. (*Daily Telegraph*, 23 January 1991, quoting from a publication put out by Smith College, Mass.)

ablutions a lavatory
Originally, the religious rite of washing, whence washing the body on any occasion, and then the place in which you washed. An army usage:
> We were told to choose a bed site... shown where the Ablutions were. (Bogarde, 1978, describing being drafted into the army)

abnormal *obsolete* homosexual
In the days when heterosexuality was the only accepted norm:
> ... lived an institutional life with other men in uniform without ever seriously arousing the suspicion that he was what is called abnormal. (P. Scott, 1975)
Whence *abnormality*, homosexuality:
> The fact that he revealed a hatred of 'abnormality' was only to be expected. 'What a filthy Lesbian trick.' (M. McCarthy, 1963)

abode of love a brothel
Where *love* imports copulation:
> These abodes of love seen from the other side are strangely transfigured. All is order, cleanliness and respectability. (Londres, 1928, in translation)

above ground see REMAIN ABOVE GROUND

above your ceiling promoted to a level beyond your abilities
Not merely rummaging about in the attic:
> L. M. is a very nice chap... but he is definitely above his ceiling. (Horne, 1994— Montgomery was speaking of

Leigh-Mallory, the senior allied airman
during the 1944 invasion of Europe)

absent parent a parent who does not live
with his or her infant child or children
Usually, the father, who is not just away on a
business trip:
> We must be careful that we do not empty
> our surgeries of angry absent parents only
> to fill them with angry lone parents
> instead. (*Daily Telegraph*, 5 July 1994,
> quoting the British Social Security
> Secretary)

See also LONE PARENT and SINGLE PARENT.

absorption a military conquest
Literally, the chemical or physical process of
assimilation:
> These measures, together with the
> 'absorption' of the Baltic states in the
> north, advanced the western frontiers of
> the Soviet Union by hundreds of miles.
> (A. Clark, 1995, writing about the
> Russian seizure of eastern Poland in
> 1939)

abuse the use of a person or object for a
taboo or illegal purpose
Literally, any kind of maltreatment or misuse.
Descriptive as both noun and verb of sexual
activity, especially by adults with children:
> If Mayhew's figures for the abuse of
> children are suspect, so are his figures for
> rape. (Pearsall, 1969)
> ... the cases for 'carnally abusing' girls
> between the ages of ten and twelve were a
> mere fifty-six. (ibid.)

To *abuse yourself* is to masturbate, of either sex,
and see SELF-ABUSE.
Abuse is also descriptive of the illegal ingestion
of narcotics or the excessive consumption of
alcohol:
> ... both now dead ... Anthony from
> drink and 'abuse' in Dublin. (A. Clark,
> 1993)

abuse a bed *obsolete* to cuckold
Not just to leap about on it:
> See the hell of having a false woman. My
> bed shall be abused. (Shakespeare, *The
> Merry Wives of Windsor*)

academic dismissal expulsion from college
Not the end of classes for the day:
> No student ever gets expelled any more,
> though he may suffer 'academic dismissal'.
> (Jennings, 1965)

academically subnormal of very low ability or intelligence
Logic tells us that half of any class will be
above the mean, and half below it:

The BBC had been offered the series and
had turned it down because one of the
pupils was 'academically subnormal'.
(F. Muir, 1997, writing about of the
television programme *Please Sir*)

academy *obsolete* a brothel
Literally, a school, from the original garden
where Plato taught:
> ... the show of a shop was shut, the
> academy open'd; the mark of mock-
> modesty was completely taken off.
> (Cleland, 1749)

Continuing the joke, if such it was, the
prostitutes were termed *academicians*.

accident[1] involuntary urination or defecation
Literally, anything which happens, whence,
in common use, anything undesirable:
> I've never punished him, the way our
> mothers and nurses did, when he has an
> 'accident'. (M. McCarthy, 1963)

accident[2] an unplanned pregnancy
To treat impregnation as though it were an
unforeseeable happening may seem unduly
innocent or cavalier:
> I have the means to prevent
> any ... accident. I promise I'll be very
> careful. (Styron, 1976)

A child born under these circumstances may
also be called an *accident*.

accommodate yourself to urinate
At some distance from the Latin meaning, to
make fit:
> ... our guide stopped on the path and
> accommodated himself in a way that
> made me think his reverence for the
> [holy] spot was far from fanatical.
> (E. Waugh, 1932)

accommodation house *obsolete* a brothel
A place where male lust was *accommodated*:
> ... took him along to one of the
> accommodation houses in Haymarket and
> got him paired off with a whore. (Fraser,
> 1973, writing in 19th-century style)

See also *house of accommodation* under
HOUSE 1.

accost to approach a stranger with a
taboo request or suggestion
Originally, *accost* meant to lie alongside,
which may be what a prostitute has in mind:
> Gladstone refers to being 'accosted', i. e.
> the initiative was the prostitute's, not, as in
> the past, his. (Parris, 1995—the Liberal
> Prime Minister habitually sought out
> prostitutes in the streets, to reform them,
> so he averred)

Also of begging in a public place.

accouchement the period of childbirth
What was a euphemism in French becomes
doubly so in standard English use:
    Queen Victoria had taken a personal
    interest in the Empress's accouchement
    and has sent...one of her ladies-in-waiting
    to be present at the birth. (W. H. C. Smith,
    1991)

account for to kill
Used of animals by humans and of humans by
soldiers. The usage might imply a reckoning
of the number slain but it may equally refer to
a single victim:
    A more suitable way of describing such
    an event, the Foxhunters' Society
    suggested delicately, might be a casual
    'the animal was accounted for'. (Whicker,
    1982)

accumulate (of securities) do not sell
Jargon of the financial analyst whose job is to
promote activity among investors rather than
pass them bad news:
    Merrill Lynch described a trading
    statement for Pilkington as 'encouraging'
    but downgraded its rating of stock to
    'accumulate' from 'buy'. (*Daily Telegraph*,
    21 March 2001—the share price duly
    fell)

ace *American* to kill
From taking a trick at cards:
    The gaunt man, his hands enclosed in
    blood-covered surgeon's plastic gloves,
    looked up at him. 'Someone's aced the
    lady.' (Diehl, 1978)

acid lysergic acid diethylamide
Better known as LSD. To *drop acid* is to ingest
it illegally:
    ...he was dropping acid and bombed out of
    his gourd. (Sanders, 1977)
An *acid-head* or *acid freak* is someone addicted
to LSD:
    ...mantras on the lips of fashion-conscious
    acid-heads across Europe and the United
    States. (Dalrymple, 1998)

acorn academy *American* an institution
for the mentally ill
Where you consign a NUT 1:
    'Your Honor, were these the acts of a sane
    man?'—and Dan would be hidden away in
    an acorn academy for a period of years.
    (Sanders, 1973)

acorns *American* the testicles
A variant of NUTS:
    ...shrieked as the spray hit him in the
    acorns. (Wambaugh, 1975)

acquire to steal

Literally, to gain possession of, as by purchase.
Whence *acquisition*, obtaining by stealing or
subterfuge:
    Lafarge was 'at present furthering
    arrangements for the acquisition of one
    hundred Slingshots'. (Hall, 1988—he was
    trying to steal them)

act (the) copulation
Sometimes *tout court* but more often as the *act
of shame* (if outside marriage); *of generation, of
intercourse, of love*; or *the sexual act*:
    My prepuce contracted so that the act
    would have been difficult. (F. Harris,
    1925)
    ...she with Cassio hath the act of shame
    A thousand times committed.
    (Shakespeare, *Othello*)
    The embrace of the sexes in the act of
    generation. (*EDD*)
    An act of intercourse took place, in the
    course of which both partners achieved
    climax. (Amis, 1978)
    It was the time after the act of love.
    (M. West, 1979)
    The sexual act is fully covered, but not in
    these pages. (Longstreet, 1956)
However, *a sexual act* may imply no more than
a pinched bottom.

act like a husband to have a sexual relationship with a female to whom you are
not married
But not of an encounter with a prostitute:
    Jessie confessed that her sister accused
    her of letting me 'act like a husband'.
    She must have seen the stain on my
    chemise. (F. Harris, 1925)

Actaeon *literary* one who cuckolds another
In the legend Actaeon was no more than a
casual observer of Artemis's nakedness, and
she had no husband to take offence. Nevertheless she turned him into a stag and set his
own pack on him:
    Divulge Page himself for a secure and
    wilful Actaeon. (Shakespeare, *The Merry
    Wives of Windsor*)

action¹ vice or illegal activity, or its proceeds
Usually illegal gambling, narcotics, or prostitution:
    ...one waits while the Federal authorities,
    mayors and the Mafia decide...how
    much of the action they want. (Allbeury,
    1976)
A *slice of the action* is a share in the activity or
proceeds. See also PIECE OF THE ACTION.

action² the brutal harassment of supposed opponents

The *Aktion* of the Nazis, normally directed at Jewish citizens:

> Schindler had not dared believe that this red child had survived the Aktion process. (Keneally, 1982)

action³(the) a chance of casual copulation

The ambience or venue where like-minded individuals may be met:

> Then he stared around to check the action. (Sanders, 1982—he had gone to a bar in search of a woman for casual sex)

active not physically impaired by age or illness

Descriptive of geriatrics who have retained mobility:

> Active Adult Golf Community.
> (advertisement in Gainesville, Florida, November 1987, for houses adjacent to a golf course)

or of those who continue to engage in sexual activity:

> They say Willie Maugham had [youth pills], too, and he was still active, if you know what I mean, the day he died. (B. Forbes, 1972)

activist a political zealot

No longer merely a supporter of the philosophy of activism. Describing those supporting an autocracy:

> On the few occasions when Chinese people supposedly demonstrated outside foreign embassies, activists had always been there to direct everything. (Cheng, 1984)

but more often, in the West, an *activist* is a person willing to break the law in pursuit of his beliefs.

actress *obsolete* a prostitute

Until a liberating decree of Charles II female roles on stage were played by males. Thereafter, for some three centuries, acting was not considered a respectable profession for a woman:

> The actress and the singer were considered nothing much more than prostitutes with a sideline. (Longstreet, 1956)

acute environmental reaction *American* an inability to continue fighting

Vietnam jargon, for a condition where it is hard to tell mental illness from self-preservation or cowardice:

> Most Americans would rather be told that their son is undergoing acute environmental reaction than to hear he is suffering from shell shock. (Herr, 1977)

Adam's arsenal the male genitalia

The source from which the human race was first engendered, so we are led to believe:

> It wasn't just that she was unusually partial to Adam's arsenal…(Fraser, 1971, of a lusty female)

Of the same tendency is, or was, *Eve's custom-house*, where Adam was supposed to have 'made his first entry'. (Grose)

adapt to dye

Of human hair:

> She 'mutates' or 'adapts' or 'colour-corrects' her hair. (Jennings, 1965)

additional means illegal drugs taken for body-building purposes

A method used by the Communist regime in East Germany (and cheats elsewhere) to achieve athletic success:

> What is certain that a large number of GDR sportsmen used 'additional means'. (*Sunday Telegraph*, 27 January 1994)

adjust your dress to do up the fasteners on your trousers

Once fly-buttons, now zips. Still sometimes seen in the admonition in public lavatories for males: 'Please adjust your dress before leaving.'

adjustment¹ an adverse price movement

If you are buying, a *price adjustment* means you will pay more:

> Price adjustment adds £5m to Carsington bill. (*Waterbulletin*, August 1983)

However, if you own shares, an *adjustment* means the prices have gone down:

> Last week's yo-yo swings imply that significant financial risks remain internationally. We are now in a period of adjustment. (*Sunday Telegraph*, 2 November 1997—share prices had fallen heavily)

See also CURRENCY ADJUSTMENT.

adjustment² the concealment of an illegality

In particular, the perversion of justice through bribery or influence:

> They caught him molesting a child in a public school in Queens. The desk sergeant had enough sense not to book him. The final adjustment cost about eighteen thousand dollars. (Condon, 1966)

adjustment³ the cure of the mentally ill

Correcting a deviation from the norm:

> Lucy is a very disturbed child, and a long way from adjustment. (Sanders, 1982)

adjustment⁴ the subjective alteration of published accounts

With publicly owned corporations, usually showing increased profits or assets, and with those privately owned, attempting to reduce profit and so avoid paying tax:

> The purpose of the 'adjustments' was to put the bank in the best possible light when the year-end figures ultimately appeared in the annual report. (Erdman, 1986)

administrative leave *American* suspension from duty for alleged malpractice
Not appearing to prejudge the issue:

> Administrative leave is the same thing as being suspended...the first step to being fired. (P. Cornwell, 2000)

admirer a woman's regular sexual partner outside marriage
In Jane Austen's day and writing, an *admirer* indulged in formal courtship. Half a century later the euphemistic use had developed:

> ...met her admirer at a house in Bolton Row that she was in the habit of frequenting. (Mayhew, 1862)

Still occasionally used humorously.

adult[1] pornographic
Used in connection with literature, films, stage shows, and erotica deemed unsuitable for children but, by implication, in accord with the tastes of fully grown people:

> ...nothing but taverns, junkyards, and adult book stores. (Sanders, 1980)

However the American *adult trailer park* merely bars residents with children.

adult[2] adulterous
The way grown-ups supposedly behave:

> The Duchess had never made any secret of her adult relationships in the years before she married. She had affairs with...(*Daily Telegraph*, 14 January 1994)

advantaged neither poor nor feckless
Political jargon of those who believe that individual prosperity may result more from injustice and greed than from thrift and application. Thus the poor may be described as the *least advantageous section of the community*:

> By constantly devoting attention and resources to the least advantageous section of the community, deprivation will be eliminated altogether. (Hattersley, 1995—but see *John*, 12: 8)

adventure[1] a war
Originally, a chance happening. Normally a description of a conflict in which the aggressor expects easy gains:

> Stalin will [not] allow himself to be dragged into the Pacific adventure. (Goebbels, 1945, in translation)

adventure[2] a sexual relationship with other than your regular partner
Again from the original meaning, a chance or exciting event:

> I cannot have an adventure with Martin. He would boast of me. (Theroux, 1980)

adventuress a promiscuous female
Not just a female who travels the world or does exciting things:

> ...she was also an adventurer, in the precise sense of the word—one who has adventures, as opposed to an adventuress—one who has lovers. (Blanch, 1954)

adventurous (of a woman) promiscuous
Addicted to many an ADVENTURE 2:

> It was hardly news that Nora was adventurous. Soon after I met her on date number two, it was Nora Goggins who gave me my first blow job. (Turow, 1993)

adverse event (an) a death
Medical jargon but not of losing your wallet:

> Although the possibility of an adverse event occurring might be negligible (less than one in a million) this does not mean that it might not occur to someone. (*Daily Telegraph*, 5 December 1996, reporting on sudden death among young people through disease)

adviser the representative of an imperial power in a client state
Doing much more than merely *giving advice*:

> The Spanish Communist leaders moved out in the wake of their Russian 'advisers'. (Boyle, 1979)

aerated drunk
Literally, describing a liquid charged with gas, rather than a body charged with liquid:

> Now they know Master Frank; they know he's apt to get a bit aerated (or merry as other people might say). (Tyrrell, 1973)

Aerated, of a person, may also mean angry or agitated.

aesthete a male homosexual
Literally, one who affects a higher appreciation of beauty than others:

> ...aesthetes—you know—those awful effeminate creatures—pansies. (N. Mitford, 1949)

Whence *aestheticism*, male homosexuality:

> He had been at the House, but remarked with a shade of regret that he had not found any aestheticism in his day. (E. Waugh, 1930—the *House* is a college at Oxford, not a legislature in Washington or Westminster)

aesthetic procedure (an) cosmetic surgery

Intended to make the patient more beautiful:
> They were concerned that my teeth never showed, even when I smiled, but they said the cure was simple. They had what they called an aesthetic procedure. (Iacocca, 1984)

See also PROCEDURE.

affair(e) a sexual relationship with someone other than your regular partner

The English version is now more common:
> ...having a vigorous and even dangerous wife, and an affair problem. (Bradbury, 1975)

In French it might include the person involved as well as the relationship:
> He comes to see the singer Floriana. He's her latest *affaire*. (Manning, 1960)

Also of homosexual relationships:
> His affairs with men had been few. (P. Scott, 1971)

A *man of affairs* is merely a businessman.

affair of honour *obsolete* a duel

From the days when insults were taken seriously:
> 'There is a small open space behind the horse lines,' said he. 'We have held a few affairs of honour there.' (A. C. Doyle, 1895)

affirmative action preferential treatment for particular classes of people when making appointments

Originally, in America, denoting attempts to promote black people. Now used of similar preference given to those who are not dominant white, fit, heterosexual males:
> And of course, there's Affirmative Action. Apparently there aren't too many black or Hispanic Masterwomen. (M. Thomas, 1982)

afflicted subject to physical or mental abnormality

Not just labouring under the effects of a temporary disability. An *affliction of the loins* was a venereal disease:
> I do not understand what kind of an affliction of the loins you can have to render mercury beneficial. (Dalrymple, 1993, quoting from a letter dated *c.*1817—it was probably syphilis)

affordable cheap

Used of household equipment and of small and often skimpy houses built for the poor:
> The associations took over from the councils as the main providers of social housing in 1988, with the intention of providing 'affordable' accommodation for people unable to meet the full cost of buying or renting in the open market. (*Daily Telegraph*, 23 October 1995)

African American black

Another twist in the tortuous path of evasion where skin pigmentation is concerned:
> Black people may be black, but many now prefer 'African American'. (*Daily Telegraph*, 23 February 1991)

African-descended *American* black

A euphemism not used of Egyptians, Moroccans, Boers, and many others of African descent:
> Jackson...a long, loose-joined African-descended male...(Turow, 1996)

afterlife death

Used especially by Quakers, spiritualists, and others who have confidence that death is not the end:
> 'It is the smell of afterlife.' 'It smells more like that of afterdeath,' said Jessica. (Sharpe, 1978)

afternoon man a debauchee

He is supposed not to be an early-riser:
> They are a company of giddy-heads, afternoon men. (R. Burton, *c.*1621)

Probably obsolete despite its use by Anthony Powell in the title of his 1933 novel.

after-shave a perfume used by males

The original justification for its use, in the days when men did not use perfume, was the alleviation of smarting after using a razor blade. The continuing choice of macho names for these products indicates that the taboo against male use of cosmetics is not quite dead:
> His sweet-whisky fragrance of after-shave lotion stung my eyes. (Theroux, 1982).

afterthought a child born in wedlock following an unplanned conception

Among the processes connected with the event, premeditation is not prominent:
> Being the youngest in the family—what is commonly called an 'afterthought'—she was also a little spoilt. (Read, 1986)

ageful *American* old or geriatric

Coined by the POLITICALLY CORRECT, among whom any mention that people grow old, and therefore often infirm, is taboo. In British legal jargon, to be *of full age* is to be eighteen years or older.

agent a participant in a taboo employment

In espionage, a spy, and specifically a *secret agent*. In male homosexual penetrative activity, the donor—the recipient is the *patient*. In warfare, a poison, such as the notorious *Agent Orange* used by the Americans in Vietnam for defoliation.

We also use *agent* in job descriptions to enhance our status. Thus the British *estate agent* (the American *realtor* or *real estate agent*) is at law the agent of neither the buyer nor the seller. There is an infinite variety of American *agents*, often no more than junior employees with no delegated responsibilities.

aid a gift from a rich to a poor country
Or, as Lord Bauer pointed out, a gift from the poor in a rich country to the rich in a poor country:
> MPs are to launch an enquiry into allegations that British aid was used to buy a fleet of 35 Mercedes limousines for the government of Malawi. (*Sunday Telegraph*, 29 October 2000)

Tied aid means that the donor is arranging credits or spending cash to assist its exporters.

air (the) peremptory dismissal from employment or courtship
Referring to the figurative or actual ejection from the premises in which the work or courting took place:
> If Victoria wants to give Jamie the air, it's no business of ours. (Deighton, 1982)

air support an attack from aircraft
Military jargon for raids to help soldiers on the ground. The usage is so common that we forget the logical meaning of the phrase, including the phenomenon whereby a laminar flow of air supports an aircraft in flight.

airhead a person of limited intelligence or ability
With supposedly no brain in the cranium:
> The downfall of the mighty always tickles the police, who generally see themselves as unappreciated vassals keeping the world safe for the airheads on top. (Turow, 1996)

airport novel a book written for a person who does not read regularly
For the captive traveller market and considered by the literati to be unworthy of their attention:
> I've even redone some of the airport novels which made Mr Follett so rich. (*Daily Telegraph*, 3 July 2000)

Ajax see JAKES

alcohol an intoxicant
The standard English is a shortened form of *alcohol of wine*, from the meaning, a condensed spirit. This in turn was derived from *kohl*, 'a fine powder produced by grinding or esp. by

sublimation' (*SOED*).

Alderman Lushington see LUSH

alienate to pilfer or steal
Either from the meaning to make less close, or from the legal jargon, to transfer ownership:
> You can 'alienate' as much pineboard as that? (Keneally, 1982—he was stealing from a pile of lumber)

all night man *obsolete British* a dealer in corpses
He took newly buried corpses for sale to teaching hospitals, especially in Scotland. There was no property, or ownership, in a corpse and a paucity of donors who were fearful of a piecemeal return to earth of themselves or their relatives at the expected Resurrection of the Dead.
See also RESURRECTION MAN.

all-nighter a contract with a prostitute to stay with her all night
Prostitutes' jargon:
> The price of a short-time with massage stayed the same, and an all-nighter cost only an extra three-fifty. (Theroux, 1973)

all over with death for
From the meaning, finished, but showing little faith in the hereafter:
> Then with a groan, his head jerked back, and it was all over with him. (A. C. Doyle, 1895)

all-rounder a person of both heterosexual and homosexual tastes
In a sport it describes someone with ability in various aspects of a game:
> She was a bit of an all-rounder. Both sexes, general fun and games. (Davidson, 1978)
See also BATTING AND BOWLING.

all the way (of sexual activity) with full penetration
As different from intermediate stages of caressing:
> 'Have you had sex together?' He blushed. 'Well, ah, not exactly. I mean, we've done...things. But not, you know, all the way. (Sanders, 1981)

all up with about to die
A variant of ALL OVER WITH:
> It's all up with him, poor lad...His bowels is mortified. (Fraser, 1971)

allergic to lead see LEAD

alley cat a prostitute
Both are reputed to frequent narrow lanes:

These alley cats pluck at your sleeve as you
pick your way along the steep cobbled
footpath. (Theroux, 1975)

As a verb, of a male, it means to be
promiscuous:

> ... couldn't stand the thought of the guy
> alley-catting around. (Sanders, 1977)

alternative different from existing social
arrangement, practicality, or convention

The use implies that the methods or tastes
proposed or chosen are preferable to or more
efficacious than those generally adopted,
whether it be *alternative medicine*, *gardening*,
nutrition, *religion*, *education*, *defence* (pacifism),
lifestyle, *sexuality* (homosexuality), or whatever:

> Eva Wilt's ... Alternative Medicine
> alternated with Alternative Gardening and
> Alternative Nutrition and even various
> Alternative Religions. (Sharpe, 1979)
>
> I'm into Marxist aesthetics. I'm interested
> in alternative education. (Bradbury, 1976)
>
> ... an 'alternative defence workshop' led by
> Mrs Joan Ruddock, CND Chairman. (*Daily
> Telegraph*, November 1983)
>
> Should we admire marriage or 'alternative
> lifestyles'? (*Daily Telegraph*, 14 December
> 1998, quoting Tony Blair)
>
> Homosexuality, with the inevitable
> personal disorientation it generates, was
> shrugged off as 'alternative sexuality'.
> (*Daily Telegraph*, November 1979)
>
> His relations with the women he
> photographed appear to have remained
> professional and friendly and—even
> though he never married—scandal
> never fastened on an alternative
> proclivity. (*Daily Telegraph*, obituary of
> August 1990)

amateur a promiscuous woman

Literally, a person who loves doing something, whence a performer who does it without payment:

> ... stark except for her riding boots. That
> took me aback, for it ain't usual among
> amateurs. (Fraser, 1971)

In the 19th century, an *amateur* was a
prostitute who also had other employment:

> ... working at some trade or other before
> losing their virtue ... called the 'amateurs'
> to contra-distinguish them from the
> professionals. (Mayhew, 1862)

amatory rites acts of copulation

Not the marriage service:

> ... my two friends soon translated both
> their sleeping arrangements and their
> deafening amatory rites to the bed in
> Nathan's quarters. (Styron, 1976)

amber fluid/liquid/nectar lager

From television advertising on behalf of an
Australian brand also brewed in Britain.

ambidextrous having both heterosexual
and homosexual tastes

Of men and women, from the ability to use
either hand with equal skill.

ambiguous homosexual or bisexual

Literally, having more than one meaning or
being hard to classify:

> By associating herself with the free love
> movement, by marrying a man with
> ambiguous sexual interests ... (Pearsall,
> 1969)

ambivalent having both heterosexual
and homosexual tastes

Literally, entertaining two opposite emotions
at the same time:

> Sexually I'd say some of the company was
> on the ambivalent side. (P. Scott, 1975)

ambrosia an intoxicant

Originally, the food, and less often the drink,
of the gods:

> Bring your own ambrosia or take pot luck.
> (Sharpe, 1976)

ambulance-chaser someone who greed-
ily touts for business

Referring to the practice, supposedly originated by American lawyers, of following an
ambulance to hospital in the hope of being
briefed by the victim to sue someone:

> Mader was a shyster in the Quorn
> Building. An ambulance-chaser, a small
> time fixer, an alibi builder-upper.
> (Chandler, 1939)

Now used as a verb and also of other seekers
after custom:

> During the summer months we were
> constantly being associated with potential
> bidders but we are quite clear that we want
> to remain independent. We want all
> ambulance-chasing merchant banks to
> understand that. (*Daily Telegraph*, 17
> November 1997)

America First isolationism

It was the name of an organization campaign-
ing for neutrality in the Second World War.
This stance was supported by 67% of a sample
in a poll conducted in 1939. Of the same
sample, 12% wanted aid sent to those fighting
Nazism and 2% were prepared to agree to
providing military assistance. (Deighton,
1993)

> Sloan did not care if Hitler gobbled up the
> whole of Europe—he was for America First.
> (M. McCarthy, 1963)

ammunition lavatory paper

Of the same tendency as the jocular BUM FODDER.

amorous favours copulation
Usually granted by a female rather than a male, but not always:

> It had become embarrassingly and sickeningly plain that the fickle Kim was bestowing amorous favours simultaneously on Melinda. (Boyle, 1979—Kim was the traitor Philby and Melinda the wife of his fellow traitor, Maclean)

For *amorous sport*, see SPORT (THE).
He who displays *amorous propensities* has lewd thoughts:

> I'll come no more behind your scenes, David; for the silk stockings and white bosoms of your actresses excite my amorous propensities. (J. Boswell, 1791—Dr Johnson was speaking to Garrick)

An *amorous tie* is a sexual commitment to another person:

> I have few friends and no 'amorous ties'. I am alone and free. (I. Murdoch, 1978)

amour[1] a sexual partner to whom you are not married
Literally, love or affection, but now standard English.

amour(s)[2] an act (or acts) of copulation outside marriage
The *act of love*:

> ... the jolly athletic amour so obviously and exquisitely enjoyed. (Styron, 1976)
> Those women who live in apartments, and maintain themselves by the product of their vagrant amours. (Mayhew, 1862—but not with hobos)

ample fat
Literally, wide and commodious, but only in this sense of a woman:

> ... a generous figure. 'Ample', she used to call it, or, an a kinder manner, 'my Edwardian body'. (Bogarde, 1978)

amply endowed having large genitalia or breasts
A synonym of WELL ENDOWED. If describing a female, she is unlikely also to have a dowry, her *endowment*, albeit large, being only physical:

> Exceptionally good-looking, personable, muscular athlete is available. Hot bottom plus large endowment equals a good time. (*Sunday Telegraph*, September 1989, quoting an advertisement by a prostitute to which Representative Frank responded: the advertiser cannot have been puffing because he later appointed her as his personal aide in Congress)

amusement with prizes gambling
Amusing, we may assume, for the owner of the automatic machines programmed to take a percentage off those who put money into them:

> AWP (Amusement with prizes) machines are a feature of all Rank's gaming business. (*Annual Report* of The Rank Organization plc, March 1996)

amusing (of art) pornographic
Jargon from a milieu where overt vulgarity is deplored:

> Pictures medium only, but some amusing. ('amusing' means 'erotic', doesn't it, in an auctioneer's catalogue description). (A. Clark, 1993)

angel dust an illegal narcotic or hallucinogenic drug
A heavenly feeling is sometimes induced:

> And that shooting ... wasn't just some kind of angel dust. (Deighton, 1981)

Angel foam was at one time a name for champagne.

angel of the night a prostitute
With no halo:

> The men appeared to be mostly elderly, the women all young. 'Angels of the night,' whispered the lieutenant. (Dodds, 1991)

angle with a silver hook *obsolete* to pretend to have caught a fish which you have bought
Not the behaviour of a sportsman or a gentleman. There followed some figurative use, to indicate willingness to accept a bribe.

Anglo-Saxon (of language) crude or vulgar
The supposition is that many obscenities in English have that ancestry:

> She was wildly aroused when Robbie employed certain Anglo-Saxon words. (Turow, 1999)

animal rights the attribution to selected animals of human characteristics
The fanaticism of some in a cause which has overtones of anthropomorphism can be distasteful to many who also abhor cruelty to animals:

> A gaunt, fearless woman with piercing eyes, now aged 50, and an animal-rights vegan to boot. (Evans-Pritchard, 1997)

annex to conquer and occupy
Literally, to attach:

> Nobo had been severely injured in a bombing outside Seoul in 1910, at the time

Korea was being annexed to Japan. (Golden, 1997)

anoint a palm see PALM 1

anointed *Irish* expected to die soon
It refers to the practice of so treating the bodies of mortally ill Roman Catholics:
 ... sure there isn't a winter since her daughter went to America that she wasn't anointed a couple of times. I'm thinkin' the people th' other side o' death will be throuncin' her for keepin' them waitin' on her this way. (Somerville and Ross, 1894)

anorak an enthusiast for an unintellectual pastime
Thought boring by those who use the word and may think themselves superior and avant-garde. The usage comes from the article of clothing favoured by those who take their pleasures in the open:
 For years people have been going round doing the wally voice for anoraks or trainspotters—and when a politician comes along with a similar voice we elect him prime minister. (*Guardian*, 1 October 1994—writing about John Major)

another state (in a) dead
Not on a day trip to France:
 They are in another, and a higher, state of existence. (J. Boswell, 1785)
See also BETTER COUNTRY.

Anschluss a military conquest
Literally, the German word means connection. This was how Germany described its occupation of Austria in 1938, becoming a euphemism in both German and English:
 After justifying the Anschluss of Austria ... he denied that he had broken the Munich agreement by occupying Prague. (Kee, 1984, reporting Hitler's speech of 28 April 1939)

answer the call¹ to die
Usually of those killed in war, called to arms and then, it might be hoped, to life eternal.

answer the call² to urinate
In this case, answering a CALL OF NATURE:
 ... was answering an urgent call behind bushes when they stopped close by. (Cookson, 1967)

anti- avoiding a statement of your allegiance
When the cause being promoted is likely to have few adherents, you declare yourself to be against something which sensible, well-meaning, or gullible persons are likely to abhor. Thus in the 5th century, Athanasius set

himself up as *anti-Arian*, and millions since have repeated his doctrinal niceties each Sunday. Many of us are *anti-fascist* but not Communists:
 The anti-fascist protection barrier is particularly deep and formidable where the railway crosses the Alexander Ufer. (Deighton, 1988—most of us called it the 'Berlin Wall')

anti-freeze a spirituous intoxicant
Some humorous use, because it may warm you in cold weather.

anti-personnel designed to kill or maim
It could mean no more than opposed to people:
 'Anti-personnel weapon' is a sophisticated euphemism for 'killer weapon'. (Pei, 1969)

antisocial criminal or offensive
Literally, reclusive or self-centred:
 ... he was 'jointed' for his 'anti-social behaviour', the IRA's euphemism for petty crime. (*Sunday Telegraph*, January 1990—jointed means shot in the knees or ankles)
Also used to describe those opposed to autocracy, who are criminal in the eyes of the autocrat:
 'Anti-social elements are there,' said the IG, patting his carbine again. (Dalrymple, 1998—an 'IG' is an Inspector-General of Police)
An *anti-social noise* is a fart:
 'And he accused me of making anti-social noises.' ... Then, as though to demonstrate, he emitted a precise fart. (L. Thomas, 1994)

anticipating *American* pregnant
Another way of saying EXPECTANT.

antlers an indication of cuckoldry
Formerly given as a pair, to be worn by the cuckold:
 Oh, there is many a fine lady of the *ton* as gives 'er wedded lord a pair of hantlers. (Fraser, 1997, using cockney speech)

antrum (amoris) the anus
Homosexual use and usage. An *antrum* is a cave or grotto:
 ... or perhaps it would be the other way round, the mature man busy with the young man's *antrum*. (Pérez-Réverté, 1994, in translation)
 ... the golden sceptre, erect and ready to be tempered in the *antrum amoris* of his mature companion. (ibid.)

apartheid the suppression of black people by white

Literally, separate development, but practised in South Africa a century after the United States declared that its black citizens should be separate but equal, which also meant separate but unequal.

ape *mainly American* mad
Usually of a temporary condition, from the supposed simian behaviour:
> Victor had something Jake will never have. It drove him ape. (Sanders, 1977)

appendage the penis
Literally, something attached or hung on:
> ... her mean little hand ready to perform its spiritless operation on my equally jaded appendage. (Styron, 1976—it can't have been that jaded)

appetites an obsession with sex
In the singular, an *appetite* is a craving for anything, normally for food:
> ... consigned to an early grave by his wife's various appetites. (Sharpe, 1974)

apple-polish *American* to seek favour or advancement by flattery
You rub the skins to make them look more palatable:
> Why try to apple-polish the dinge downstairs? (Chandler, 1939—*dinge* was an offensive term for a black person)
Whence an *apple-polisher*, who so behaves:
> ... he thought Cutter was a shallow, self-serving apple-polisher with delusions of grandeur. (Clancy, 1989)

apples *obsolete* the testicles
Victorian humour or exaggeration:
> By this piece of boldness, with its French phrase and its sexual innuendo about apples (Victorian slang for testicles), Vivian springs to life. (Ashton, 1991, quoting an article written by G. H. Lewes on 13 April 1850)

appliance an item of medical equipment worn on the body
Literally, anything which is applied for a specific purpose. A shortening of *surgical appliance*, which might describe a scalpel. An *appliance* may be a truss, a hearing aid, a wooden leg, or anything else you don't want to be precise about—but not spectacles.

apportion to allocate components of a purchase price in a single transaction so as to evade tax
There is a narrow and ill-defined line between tax evasion (which is illegal) and tax avoidance (which isn't):
> If ... he officially paid a lower price which was beneath the higher rate threshold, and

made up the difference by appearing to buy 'fixtures and fittings' for cash, then he would have been guilty of 'apportioning'. (*Daily Telegraph*, 17 August 1999, reporting on the British minister Peter Mandelson's dealings in real estate)

appropriate¹ to steal
Originally, it meant to take for your own use, without any taint of impropriety:
> All old *mali* had actually done, though, was appropriate his half share of what he had hoed and sweated to grow. (P. Scott, 1977—the *mali*, or gardener, had been dismissed for theft)

appropriate² in line with your dogmatic prejudices
Appropriate and *appropriately* are described (by R. Harris, 1992) as 'the favourite words in the bureaucrat's lexicon, the grease for sliding round unpleasantness, the funk-hole for avoiding specifics'. They are also beloved by the POLITICALLY CORRECT:
> Freedom of speech is still guaranteed by the Constitution, but it can be exercised only so long as it is 'appropriate'.
> (A. Waugh in *Daily Telegraph*, 13 August 1994, commenting on the refusal of an American publisher to publish writings by the Pope because they were considered anti-feminine)
and also beloved by tyrants:
> In the House of Assembly, Harare's Commons, [Ushekowokunza, Home Affairs Minister] called it 'appropriate technology', a euphemism for electric shock treatment that drew appreciative nods from his colleagues. (*Daily Telegraph*, September 1983, reporting on the torture of white officers in the Zimbabwe air force)

approved school *British* a penal institution for children
The *approval* was by the Home Office as being suitable for the incarceration of young criminals. You would be wrong to assume that educational establishments not so described lacked the blessing of society.

apron-string-hold *obsolete* the occupation by a man of his wife's property
The use satirized English and Welsh land tenure—freehold, leasehold, or copyhold. It also indicates what people thought of a man who lived off the estate of his wife, whose property by law vested in him on marriage, either beneficially or during her lifetime:
> A man being possessed of a house and large orchard by apron-string-hold, felled almost

all his fruit trees, because he expected the death of his sick wife. (Ellis, 1750)

ardent spirits spirituous intoxicants
Referring to the burning of the throat, not from the DUTCH COURAGE which may follow:
> He had committed the sin of lust, he had drunk ardent spirits. (B. Cornwell, 1993)

Arkansas toothpick *obsolete* a dagger
This is a sample entry, many weapons being given geographical attributions, either mocking the uncouthness of the local inhabitants or applauding their manliness:
> ...the Kentucky abolitionist Cassius Marcellus Clay, wearing 'three pistols and an Arkansas tooth pick'. (G. C. Ward, 1990, quoting an 1862 source)

See also GLASGOW KISS.

arm candy a good-looking female companion
Escorted by a man in public:
> Hurley, then seen merely as Grant's arm-candy, became famous when she wore a dress by Gianni Versace. (*Daily Telegraph*, 24 May 2000)

armed struggle (the) terrorism
The language of Irish dissidents, among others:
> ...you go saying I'm in the Armed Struggle, then you've got real trouble. (Seymour, 1992—the speaker was a terrorist)

armour *obsolete* a contraceptive sheath
As worn, or not, by Boswell:
> I took out my armour, but she begged that I might not put it on, as the sport was much pleasanter without it. (J. Boswell, c.1792)

army form blank *British* lavatory paper
The only bits of paper in the army without an identifying number.

around the Horn see RUN (A)ROUND THE HORN 1, 2

arouse to cause sexual excitement in another
Literally, to awaken from sleep. It is used of either sex, heterosexually or homosexually:
> ...he aroused her in a way that her husband had never done. (Allbeury, 1976—and not by a new alarm clock)

Whence *arousal*, such sexual excitement:
> ...the muted talk of women made him excited and he had to roll onto his stomach to conceal his arousal. (Boyd, 1982)

arrange to do something underhand or taboo
Used to describe preparing accounts or reports in a misleading manner; bribing or coercing officials; obtaining an unfair preference; or castrating domestic cats:
> You always ought to have tom cats arranged, you know—it makes 'em more companionable. (Noel Coward—reported speech)

To *arrange yourself* is to put your clothing back to normal after a taboo activity, such as urination or extramarital copulation:
> She was...arranging herself. She seemed a bit dazed. She whacked her shoulder on the bedroom door, trying to squeeze by him. (Anonymous, 1996)

An *arrangement* is what ensues, including a pot for urine in a bedroom, a bribe, a settlement with your creditors (or *Deed of Arrangement*), regular extramarital sexual activity, etc.:
> The majority of diplomats and businessmen away from home for long periods made 'arrangements' for themselves. (Faulks, 1993)

arranged by circumstances *Irish* (of a marriage) necessitated by the pregnancy of the bride
Not the *arranged marriage* of the Indian subcontinent:
> We had our share...of marriages arranged by circumstances. (Flanagan, 1988)

arse a person viewed sexually
Literally, the buttocks but, because they were the subject of taboo while a donkey wasn't, it was changed to *ass*, which quickly acquired similar connotations and persists in America. Thus in obsolete British use, a jackass became a *Johnny Bum*, *Jack* and *ass* being vulgar, while *bum* was still respectable. The commonest use, of male or female, is when they are described as a *bit* or *piece of arse* or *ass*:
> Am I to believe you would risk something like this for a piece of arse? (Diehl, 1978)
> The stewardesses all agreed he was a piece of ass. (Follett, 1978)

An *arse* or *ass man* is a promiscuous person:
> ...sexy as he smiled at the girl who was one of Engineering's assistants. He was the house ass-man. (M. Thomas, 1982)

An *arse-bandit*, sometimes shortened to *bandit*, is a male homosexual:
> He's a Moonie or somethin', isn't he? he said as he stuck on the Sports Channel—And an arse bandit. (R. Doyle, 1990)

An *arse peddler* is a prostitute, heterosexual or homosexual.

art pornographic
A survival from the days when pornographers were liable to prosecution, and a favoured

defence was that the matter in question was artistic rather than titillating:

> She finally makes it in 'art' (that is French soft-porn) movies before tragedy strikes. (*Sunday Telegraph*, 3 May 1998)

article an object which is the subject of taboo

Such as a chamber pot for urine, or *article of furniture*, as it was once called:

> Article (meaning 'chamber pot') is non U. (Ross, 1956)

artillery¹ *American* a hypodermic needle

From loading the charge and the explosive effect:

> ...a piece of community artillery passed from junkie to junkie. (Wambaugh, 1975)

artillery² armed supporters of a gangster

The weapons used are pistols, not howitzers or field guns:

> 'DJs', so called, to mix the stuff, and 'scramblers', who get paid in drugs to make the connections, 'mules' to carry it and move it two times every day from garages and apartments where it's stored, and his 'artillery', Honcho, Gorgo, and them motherfuckers so nobody think they can move up on [him]. (Turow, 1996)

Aryan without Jewish ancestry

Originally, 'a native or inhabitant of Ariana, the eastern part of ancient Iran' or 'a member of any of the peoples who spoke the parent language of the Indo-European (or esp. Indo-Iranian) family' (*SOED*). This was a Nazi classification in their anti-Jewish obsession:

> *Coffee* Eva's Aryan 60 grammes a constant source of envy on the part of Frau Voss. We give her 5 grams as a present. Bliss. We invite the Reichenbachs for genuine Aryan coffee. (Klemperer, 1998, in translation— diary entry 26 November 1940: Klemperer's wife, Eva, was not Jewish)

aryanize to steal from Jews

Originally, for the Nazis, it meant to remove any Jewish link or involvement, and then to take over without paying any compensation:

> Reka, the most reputable, the best department store in Dresden, was aryanised last year. (Klemperer, 1998, in translation—diary entry of 9 October 1937)

as Allah made him naked

The way he was born:

> Recognizedly not wearing anything... as Allah made him. (Davidson, 1978)

In the same sense others attribute the manufacture to God.

asbestos drawers an imagined concomitant of female lust

Designed to contain the HOT PANTS affected by the person so described:

> Needs asbestos drawers, I hear. Another little number from the sticks with a rich husband and hot pants. (M. Thomas, 1982)

Asian levy *British* a bribe

This was paid by ship-owners to the National Union of Seamen at £30 a head annually for each lowly paid Asian crew member employed on a British-registered ship in return for the union raising no objection:

> The old NUS had a history of controversial financial deals including the now notorious 'Asian levy'. (*Daily Telegraph*, 28 September 1999)

ask for your papers to resign from employment

Usually from an official position in a huff, the *papers* being the supposed commission which you were handed on appointment:

> ...his plumbing is done and he has asked for his papers. (Sayers, 1937—he was a diplomat, not an artisan)

asleep see FALL ASLEEP

ass see ARSE

assault to attack sexually

Literally, to use any force against another:

> If I'd been assaulted by men of my own race I would have been an object of pity. (P. Scott, 1973—a white woman had been raped by Indians)

And as a noun:

> ...the main proceedings, which happened to be a rape trial (in the papers of the *Intelligencer* the crime would be referred to as 'assault on a woman'). (King, 1996)

or with adjectival embellishment, as an *indecent assault*—see INDECENCY.

assembly area *American* an internment camp

Second World War term for the place of long-term incarceration of Americans of Japanese descent.

asset a spy

Literally, anything useful or valuable. Common espionage jargon, according to the spy novelists:

> No, [from] an asset we have in place in Norway. (Clancy, 1986, giving a source of information)

A *unilaterally controlled Latino asset*, or UCLA, was a spy or saboteur working for the US Central Intelligence Agency in Latin America:

...the CIA had played a direct role in placing underwater mines in three Nicaraguan harbors. This...had all been done by 'unilaterally controlled Latino assets' the UCLA's. (Woodward, 1987)

assignation a meeting for extramarital copulation
Literally, the allotment of something, whence a tryst:
> I have never really seriously thought of marriage...What suits me best is the drama of separation, of looking forward to assignations and rendezvous. (I. Murdoch, 1978)

Also of the act itself:
> Palmerston died there on the billiard table, reputedly after an assignation with one of the maids. (*Daily Telegraph*, 11 February 1995, referring to Brocket Hall)

assist the police (with their inquiries) see HELP THE POLICE (WITH THEIR INQUIRIES)

assistance a regular payment to the poor from public funds
Literally, help of any kind. To be *on assistance* is to be receiving such payments. See also PUBLIC ASSISTANCE.

assistant see PERSONAL ASSISTANT

associate with to meet in an illegal or taboo capacity
It describes those with criminal connections or copulating outside marriage:
> As in Hispaniola, many native women became associated intimately with the conquerors. (H. Thomas, 1993)

association a cartel
Literally, the act of combining for any purpose. However, some *trade associations* move into illegal price-fixing rather than sticking to legal topics of mutual interest.

astride copulating with
Equine imagery and normally used of the male:
> Harry—you are sure you have not been astride Mrs Lade? (Fraser, 1977)

asylum an institution for the mentally ill
Originally, a place where pillage was sacrilegious, which is why there was so much fuss about Henry II's murder of Becket. Then it became a safe place or benevolent institution. Now a shortened form of *lunatic asylum*:
> 'You don't think I ought to be in the Asylum, do you?' she said. (W. Collins, 1860)

at government expense in prison

The expression is not used for the provision for politicians, public employees, soldiers, and others maintained from the public purse:
> ...because a black guy built like the Bonaventure Hotel is likely to have done his long stint of muscle-building at government expense. (Deighton, 1993/2—describing an ex-convict)

at half mast with trouser zip undone
Referring to a flag incorrectly hoisted, except in mourning. The phrase is used as a coded message from one male to another in mixed company.

at Her Majesty's pleasure *British* indefinitely
The wording is used when a judge chooses not to place any term on the confinement of the prisoner due to madness or other factors.

at it engaged in some taboo activity
In appropriate circumstances, the phrase can apply to anything from picking your nose to bestiality. In the East End of London, it usually refers to being a villain; elsewhere is may indicate sexual activity:
> At least one of his uncles is 'at it', as they say, and drives around in a silver-grey Mercedes. (Read, 1979, of a habitual thief) Shit, for all he knew they could have been at it in Paris right from the beginning. (Winton, 1994, of homosexuality)

at liberty involuntarily unemployed
Actor's jargon in a profession where it does not do to say you are out of work:
> 'Laurence Olivier' (very careful checking every time for correct spelling) 'at liberty'. (Olivier, 1982, recounting when he was advertising for work)

See also BETWEEN SHOWS.

at rest dead
A tombstone favourite which might seem to suggest a torpid AFTERLIFE, although playing a harp and singing hymns could be quite restful, I suppose. Also as *at peace*.

at the last day when you are dead
The *last day* is, for devout Christians, the Day of Judgment, although the numbers of those in the dock might seem to merit a longer sitting:
> The subject of the sermon preached to us...was the certainty that at the last day we must give an account of the deeds done in the body. (J. Boswell, 1791)

at your last about to die
Not just of cobblers. See also LAST CALL.

at yourself masturbating

AT IT in a personal manner:
> Do you know what he's doing in there?
> At himself... Every time a new
> American magazine comes in with the
> women's underwear he goes in.
> (McCourt, 1997)

athlete a male profligate
Copulation is thought to provide the male
with good exercise:
> Errol was the greatest 'athlete' in
> Kenya... and was undoubtedly the love of
> Diana's life. (Fox, 1982)

athletic supporter a brief tight under-
garment worn by males to hold the genitalia
Not a football fan:
> The speaker stumbled sleepily past
> him... towards the Silex, dressed in
> nothing but an athletic supporter. (Wouk,
> 1951)

athwart your hawse copulating with you
A *hawse* is a rigid cable, and in this naval use,
the female is astride it:
> I was near crazy, with that naked alabaster
> beauty squirming athwart my hawse, as
> the sailors say. (Fraser, 1973)

attendance centre British a place to
which young criminals are required to
report for disciplinary training
Taken literally, the term might equally
apply, for example, to a theatre or a skating
rink.

attention deficit disorder idleness or stupidity
A medical condition which can also be used to
avoid condemning a child as being stupid,
idle, or naughty:
> They said I had a learning disorder. ADD.
> Attention Deficit Disorder. (Theroux, 1993)

attentions sexual activities with someone other than a regular partner
What in the singular may be no more than a
mark of respect, interest, or good manners
assumes sexual overtones in the plural:
> Jack Profumo... had become involved with
> a young lady who was also enjoying the
> attentions of the Soviet Military Attaché.
> (A. Clark, 1993—the community of interest
> would have been less noteworthy if
> Profumo had not also been Minister of
> Defence)

au naturel naked
Borrowed from the French by the Americans
more than by the British, who have fewer
taboos about nakedness.

auction of kit British one of the consequences of death
Naval usage. Shipmates pay inflated prices in
the knowledge that the proceeds will go to
the dependants of the dead person. The
practice was formerly referred to as the
punning *sale before the mast.*

auld kirk (the) Scottish whisky
The ecclesiastical derivation is unclear, except
perhaps for those of us who have sat through
a sermon in an unheated Scottish church in
winter:
> Whisky for me—a dram o' guid Auld Kirk.
> (Coghill, 1890)

aunt[1] a promiscuous woman or prostitute
The modern American use for an elderly
prostitute was anticipated by Shakespeare:
> ... summer songs for me and my aunts,
> While we lie tumbling in the hay.
> (*Shakespeare, The Winter's Tale*)

aunt[2] a lavatory
To whom many women say they are paying a
visit. In Victorian days it was their *Aunt Jones.*

aunt[3] an elderly male homosexual
Those so described are generally a generation
older than those whose company they seek.
Less often as *auntie:*
> Some mincing auntie in a cell with
> flowered curtains... (Ustinov, 1971)

Aunt Flo menstruation
The lady who comes regularly to visit you, and
a pretty awful pun.

auto-da-fé killing by burning
Literally (translated from the Portuguese)
the *act of faith* of the Inquisition, itself in
its own eyes no more than an inquiry. The
Spanish *auto de fé* was no less palatable.
However, before the Anglo-Saxons start
preening themselves, they should recall that
the English contemporary foul-mouthed Lord
Chancellor, Thomas More, reintroduced and
rejoiced in the burning of Protestants. On 5
November 2000 Pope John Paul II in Rome
proclaimed him to be the patron saint of
politicians.

auto-erotic practices masturbation
By either sex, and not just thinking evil
thoughts or watching pornographic videos:
> When the first menstruation coincided
> with the discovery of sex and possibly
> auto-erotic practices, this alarm
> combined with guilt feelings often created
> a climate for all kinds of neuroses. (Pearsall,
> 1969)
Also as *auto-erotic habits.*

avail yourself of to copulate with casually
Usually of a male:
> ...any man who availed himself of the 'tree rats' or 'grass bidis' was properly dealt with. (C. Allen, 1975)

available[1] willing to start a sexual relationship
Mainly of females and outside a regular partnership, with or without payment:
> Aileen was the only girl who had ever turned him down. The rest were always available—however nice—however respectable. (J. Collins, 1981)

available[2] involuntarily unemployed
Used by those who still are ashamed of not having a job:
> 'I'm, as they say, "between jobs".'
> 'Available.' 'That too.' (N. Evans, 1998)

available casual indigenous female companion *American* a prostitute
Circumlocution combined with euphemism:
> Even now the US State Department cannot bring itself to use the word *prostitute*. Instead it refers to 'available casual indigenous female companions'. (Bryson, 1994)
Elsewhere, as an *available lady*:
> The added appeal for the various available ladies...was that the people next door were all rich and lonely foreigners. (Whicker, 1982, writing of a café in Warsaw)

away[1] *obsolete* dead
With an implication of a temporary parting, perhaps:
> Rachel mournynge for hir children and wolde not be comforted, because they were awaye. (Coverdale Bible, *Jeremiah*, 31: 15—

the Authorized Version says 'because they were not')

away[2] in prison
The use was more common when the stigma of incarceration was greater:
> Apart from six months spent 'on the gallop', mostly in Eire, he's been away for eighteen years. (Stamp, 1994—he was an Irish terrorist)

awful experiment (the) the prohibition of sale and consumption of intoxicants in the USA from 1920 to 1933
Awful for those denied intoxicants or faced with illegality to obtain them: much more *awful* for the impetus it gave to organized crime:
> A generation or so has come between us and the Awful Experiment. (Longstreet, 1956)

axe[1] to kill after judicial process
Originally by beheading, then by any other form of killing:
> They were brought to Berlin and axed. (Shirer, 1984, referring to two German Socialist leaders handed over to the Nazis by Pétain's Vichy government in 1940)
Some figurative use:
> You were out to ax me. (Turow, 1987—an attorney had tried to discredit a hostile witness)

axe[2] to dismiss summarily from employment
Invaluable to sub-editors short of space. Occasionally too of a broken courtship.

Aztec two-step (the) diarrhoea
An affliction of visitors to Mexico—you have to keep dancing to the lavatory. Also as the *Aztec hop*; and see MONTEZUMA'S REVENGE.

B

B anything taboo beginning with the letter B

Specifically for *bloody* as in the expression *B fool*; for *bugger* in the expression *B off*; for *bitch* in the insulting *silly B*, of a woman; for *benzedrine* in the expression *B-pill*; etc.

BO the smell of stale sweat

The initial letters of the advertising slogan of the makers of Lifebuoy Soap, which claimed to correct the condition which they termed *body odour*:

> Not the BO that surges down the airline cabin when British businessmen take their suit jackets off; not offensive, like that. (P. McCarthy, 2000)

babysitting undisclosed telephone monitoring

The watchful third party in the home:

> Thomasson reports that Buzhardt made reference to 'baby-sitting people', a reference the reporter did not understand. (Colodny and Gettlin, 1991)

baby-snatcher a person with a much younger regular sexual partner

Usually heterosexual, with the woman older than the man:

> He had been living with an older woman...baby-snatching as everybody called it. (I. Murdoch, 1978)

Rarely the older person is referred to as a *baby-farmer*. See also CRADLE-SNATCHER.

bacchanalian drunken

Literally, anything to do with Bacchus, or Dionysus, who was the god of wine and debauchery:

> Burgess fell from grace at the Foreign Office as a result of another bacchanalian holiday trip. (Boyle, 1979—the authorities were less vigilant about Burgess's treachery)

A *devotee, son*, or *priest of Bacchus* is a drunkard. *Bacchanals*, a carouse, lives on in the English pub sign *Bag o' Nails*.

back door¹ the anus

Mainly homosexual use. However, a *back-door man* was also a married woman's extramarital sexual partner. If he did the *back-door trot*, it was not because the husband had come home unexpectedly, but to the lavatory with diarrhoea. See also FRONT DOOR.

back-door² to pass information improperly

Open communications are supposedly made through the front door:

> Don't backdoor me. I'll hear it from the DA in court. (Turow, 1996—a policeman was trying to pass information to a judge outside the courtroom)

backdoor³ involving bribery or impropriety

Again from the concealment:

> *Hoo-men* or 'backdoor business' was what oiled the heels of the new entrepreneurial China. (Strong, 1998)

back-gate parole *American* the natural death of a prisoner

The portal through which the coffin is carried.

back passage the anus

Medical jargon.

back teeth floating having drunk too much beer and wishing to urinate

You claim to have raised the level of liquid in your body that far:

> I've got to go to the john. My back teeth are floating. (Sanders, 1973)

Also as having your *back teeth afloat*.

back-up in retail inventories holding excess stock

Literally, an accumulation due to a jam:

> Chairman and chief executive Paul Fireman said the softer demand for athletic apparel and footwear had resulted in a 'back-up in retail inventories'. (*Daily Telegraph*, 12 December 1997—the sub-editor was not deceived: his headline was 'Sales of Reeboks have run out of puff')

backhander a bribe

Literally, a blow with the back of the hand. The giver of the bribe figuratively rotates his palm to conceal the passing of the money:

> Last year, a special adviser alleged in a video recording that Mr Chirac had sanctioned and witnessed a £500,000 backhander to a colleague. (*Sunday Telegraph*, 15 July 2001—M. Chirac was the president of France)

backside the buttocks

This standard English use ignores the other parts of the body similarly situated, from the back of the head to the heels. Some figurative use:

> But then it was just my...backside was at risk. (Price, 1978)

backward¹ very stupid

Educational jargon which indicates more than doing poorly in a class of normal children. Lay people use *backward* of adults who are slow-witted or illiterate.

backward² poor or uncivilized

It is used of sovereign states. The first of a series of patronizing post-colonial euphemisms:

> ...countries which have progressively and with increasing euphemism been termed backward, underdeveloped, less-developed, and developing. (Bullock and Stallybrass, 1977)

See also SOUTH 1 and THIRD WORLD.

backward³ through the anus

Describing sexual activity, from the Great Diarist onwards:

> ...and so to Mrs Martin and then did what je voudrai avec her, both devante and backward, which is also muy bon plazer. (Pepys, 1660–69)

bad working as a prostitute

A judgement on morals rather than job proficiency:

> ...lost her place for staying out one night with the man who seduced her; he afterwards deserted her and then she became bad. (Mayhew, 1862)

bad fire (the) hell

An evasion from the days when the devil, his place, and all his works must not be directly mentioned:

> People who say such things go to the bad fire! (Fraser, 1994, writing in 19th-century style)

bad man the devil

Otherwise known as the *good man*:

> The gite has a drop o' the bad man's bluid on it. (Johnston, 1891—a *gite* is a dress)

And, especially in Scotland, as the *bad lad*.

bad-mouth to denigrate

It applies to personal comment or commercial skulduggery:

> She knew Stafi disliked Russians in general, and Sorotkin in particular, but that was no reason to badmouth him in her presence. (Read, 1995)
> This legendary trio were busy bad-mouthing the Segal/Fitzwalter management. (*Private Eye*, May 1981)

bad powder a fart

Like the slow and smelly combustion of a faulty charge in a firearm, which is why men, who use this phrase, say it has been *burnt* or *let off*.

badge *American* a policeman

Of the same provenance as BLUE 1 and BUTTON 2:

> You gonna go walkin around Center City with a stiff, better have a badge along. (Turow, 1990)

A *badge bandit* is a highway patrolman who may or may not pocket the fine he imposes on you.

badger a prostitute

Formerly, a licensed huckster who had to wear a badge, from which the standard English meaning, to importune excessively, and so to the prostitute who accosts men in the street. The usage survives in the *badger game*, in which the victim is led by a prostitute into a sexually compromising situation, and then blackmailed:

> Any man who accompanies a night-club or dance-hall hostess to her apartment...runs a risk of being robbed or subjected to the well-known badger game. (Lavine, 1930)

bag¹ to steal

The method of concealing and taking away the loot:

> The idea of being had up to the Doctor for bagging fowls, quite unmans him. (T. Hughes, 1856)

Still common use among schoolchildren. An American *bag job* is the unauthorized taking of documents by a government agency.

bag² (the) dismissal from employment or courtship

A synonym of SACK.

bag³ to kill by hunting

Standard English, referring to the birds and small mammals which are put into the hunter's *bag*. You can only speak figuratively if you claim to have *bagged* a rhinoceros or lion. A *bag* of partridges etc. indicates how many were killed by the hunter in a day. Some allusive military use of killing humans:

> We've bagged quite a few snipers. (J. Major, 1999—explaining that British soldiers in Bosnia were not fired on because they shot those who targeted them)

bag⁴ to act as an intermediary in bribery

The container in which the bribe is carried:

> ...he'd been bagging for various judges for decades. (Turow, 1999)

See also BAGMAN.

bag⁵ see IN THE BAG 1 and 2

baggage *obsolete* a prostitute

Formerly in standard English, a worthless person, male or female. Shakespeare uses the

euphemism in one of his more complex
sexual puns:

No barricado for a belly know't;
It will let in and out the enemy,
With bag and baggage. (*The Winter's Tale*)

bagged *American* drunk
From BAG 3? You certainly may feel like death
later:

Al Mackey. He was more than half bagged.
(Wambaugh, 1981)

bagman someone employed in a taboo
activity
Originally a tramp, with his bag of belongings
over his shoulder. Now a passer of bribes, a
person who distributes narcotics illegally,
etc.:

'Shri Adam Zogoiby', who had allegedly
been the 'bagman' in the affair, carrying
suitcases containing huge sums of used,
out-of-sequence banknotes to the private
residences of several of the nation's most
prominent men, and then, as he subtly
put it in his evidence, 'accidentally
forgetting' them there. (Rushdie, 1995—in
Indira Gandhi's India, not all those bribed
were men)

bags trousers
An abbreviation of *leg-bags* and a survival from
the 19th-century taboo on trousers:

The shapeless flannels which he called his
bags. (Manning, 1965)

bait and switch obtaining investment
funds by deceit
Financial jargon:

The phenomenon has been described by
some market participants as 'bait and
switch' where banks win mandates
offering certain terms which are
subsequently changed because they are
unachievable. (*Daily Telegraph*, 6 July 2001—
but normally not after just one month, as
in the case reported)

bake to kill
The culinary imagery seems inappropriate:

All he had left to hope for was the
governor, who as a rule didn't issue
clemency to folks who had baked half a
dozen of his constituents. (King, 1996)

baker flying *American* menstruating
The red quartermaster (or baker) flag is flown
when a ship is loading fuel or ammunition,
warning other craft to stand clear.

balance of mind disturbed *British* a temporary insanity
Legal jargon, especially of suicides where
people want to bury the corpse in consecrated

ground, or merely to reject the probability
that someone had been driven to suicide as a
rational choice:

The verdict of the coroner was that he took
his life while the balance of his mind was
disturbed. I know little of my son's mind
but I reject the comfortable euphemism.
(P. D. James, 1972)

baldy fellow the erect penis
A male vulgarism:

I'd show her the money an' tell her I'll give
her some of it if she'll say hello to the baldy
fella. (R. Doyle, 1991)

bale out (of a male) to urinate
Like the removal of water from small boats.

ball to copulate with
Of either sex, probably punning on the slang
meaning, an orgy:

Sure I balled Victor. I wish he had bathed
more often, but sometimes that can be fun.
(Sanders, 1977)

ball-bearing a term of male abuse
Perhaps another way of saying *pillock*, which is
noted under PILL 1:

Terrible as that little ball-bearing is, he is
less dangerous for us than Herbert
Morrison. (Crossman, 1981)

ball money *obsolete English* money ex-
torted from the bridegroom at a wedding
Ostensibly for the provision of a *ball* for the
onlookers to play with but in effect a levy on
the groom.

balls the testicles
Common male usage. Also used of courage, of
either sex:

I got to admire him for that: the balls.
(Sanders, 1980)
Maybe Mama even hustles him right
here: she's got the balls for it. (Sanders,
1977)

bamboo curtain the censorship and
other restrictions in China to limit
knowledge of and contacts with foreigners
The Russian *Iron Curtain* in eastern form:

I had always understood that Western films
were kept well away from the People's
Republic to make sure no one ever got a
hint of the life enjoyed on the affluent
side of the bamboo curtain. (Dalrymple,
1989, after watching *Dr No* with
Tibetan, Chinese, and Ulgar subtitles in
Kashgar)

bamboozled *American* drunk

Literally, hoaxed, and perhaps suggesting that you have been deceived in liquor.

banana a penis

Which a male may be said to have *peeled* when he copulates:

> Lookin' for somewhere to stick his banana, wha', said Yvonne. (R. Doyle, 1990)

banana republic a poor and possibly corrupt country

A derogatory expression to describe those whose economies may appear to depend on the fruit as a main crop:

> ...meet once a month to hear a lecture on current affairs by a congressman, political science professor, repentant Communist, or the deposed dictator of a banana republic. (Sanders, 1992)

banana skin a potentially embarrassing or dangerous situation

Alluding to the supposed tendency of pedestrians to fall over after slipping on those discarded in the street. Journalistic jargon, mainly used of politicians but sometimes of other threatened species:

> Townsend, the Irish captain, is aware of the potential banana skin that awaits his side. (*Daily Telegraph*, 24 June 1994—it had to be a large specimen to threaten the entire soccer team, which did indeed slip, losing its match against the Mexicans)

bananas mentally disturbed

Probably because the fruit is favoured by monkeys. The phrase is often used to refer to mild hysteria:

> ...there's a poor cop called Captain Salvatore going bananas. (L. Thomas, 1979)

bandwagon a cause or chance for profit which attracts opportunists

Literally, a vehicle carrying musicians in a circus parade:

> I'm on the bandwagon with him. (N. Mitford, 1960—someone had joined a scheme in which easy profits were made)

A *band-wagoner* is an opportunist:

> ...sufficiently politically confused to rank either as a bandwagoner or a half-baked pain in the neck. (P. Scott, 1973, writing of Ghandi in 1943)

bang¹ (of a male) to copulate with

The common violent imagery:

> It'd be amusing to bang her under all those ducal Gainsboroughs. (M. Thomas, 1980)

As a noun, it denotes a single act of copulation:

> Did you ever give the maid a bang? (Mailer, 1965)

A *bang-tail* was a prostitute. See also GANG-BANG.

bang² a taboo activity or condition

It refers to the use of illicit narcotics, from the concept of *hitting*, and see HIT 4. Also used of syphilis, from the punning rhyming slang *bang and biff*.

bang up to imprison

From the slamming of the door:

> Bang me up again, he thinks. Prison's the place where you go when you don't want to make decisions. (le Carré, 1996)

bank *obsolete* to fail in business

The *bank* was the bench on which Lombard money-lenders conducted their business. It was turned over—*rupted*—if they failed to meet their commitments. In the late 19th-century banks were failing regularly and the phrase was still in use:

> Dunnot ye know at Turner's is banked. (M. Taylor, 1890)

A *banker* was a bankrupt, which seems odd to us today when it is the bankers who do most of the bankrupting of others.

bar a place for the sale and consumption of alcohol

A plank was used both as a counter and a barrier, giving the world perhaps its most multinational word. A *bar-fly* is a drunkard. However, *bar steward* is a term of personal abuse, for *bastard*:

> He has nobody, poor old bar steward, to lerve him. (Burgess, 1980)

bar girl *American* a prostitute

She seeks custom in bars. The shortened form, *B girl*, may allude to the fact that she may not merit an 'A' rating in her profession:

> He's got a finger in the B-girl rackets. (Theroux, 1973)

Barclays *British* an act of masturbation by a male

Rhyming slang on *Barclays Bank*, WANK 1. Noteworthy, among many similar vulgarisms, because it was used by the comedian Kenneth Williams in his diaries.

bareback copulating without a contraceptive

The common equestrian imagery, but this time without a saddle:

> I always ride bareback myself. (Wambaugh, 1981, of copulation)

Men or women can be *bareback riders*:

> ...no females except the local bareback riders. (Fraser, 1971—the implication is that they had venereal disease)

barker *American* a handgun
Neither a fairground tout nor a dog, but from
the noise:
> You knew you'd have to carry a barker on
> this job? (Sanders, 1970)

barking mad
From canine behaviour:
> Anyone who thinks this must be barking.
> (*Daily Telegraph*, 19 October 2000—the
> British Rail operator was asked by
> government simultaneously to increase
> traffic density, to eliminate delays, and to
> operate a zero defect safety policy)

A cockney may in similar fashion describe
another as *East Ham*, which is *one stop before
Barking* on the London tube railway network.

barley-fever *obsolete* drunkenness after
drinking whisky
Referring to the grain used in the manufacture of Scotch whisky:
> This was the first time he had ever fallen a
> victim to the barley-fever. (Moir, 1828)

A *barley-cap* was a drunkard who habitually
drank whisky. *John Barleycorn*, sometimes
knighted, is still whisky:
> I turn myself over to a higher power, LNU,
> who'll keep me safe from John Barleycorn,
> the devil. (Turow, 1993—*LNU* is an
> imaginary person, from *Last Name Unknown*
> in police jargon)

barrack-room lawyer an opinionated
but well-informed know-all
Usually an old soldier who combines knowledge of army regulations with experience and
bloody-mindedness. In America also as *barracks lawyer* and in the navy as *ship's lawyer* or
sea-lawyer:
> 'Who says that now?' cries this barrack-
> room lawyer. (Fraser, 1982)
> 'That was in church!' retorts Jemima,
> who has the makings of a fine sea-lawyer.
> (ibid.)

barrel-house *American* a brothel
Originally, a cheap saloon, where the intoxicants were served from *barrels*:
> The cribs, saloons, dancing-schools, the
> barrel-houses…(Longstreet, 1956)

base born *obsolete* illegitimate
Nor merely of humble parentage in the days
when primogeniture was paramount:
> One Sarah Gore came to me this morning
> and brought me an Instrument from the
> Court of Wells to perform publick penance
> next Sunday at C. Cary Church for having a
> base born child, which I am to administer
> to her publickly next Sunday after divine
> Service. (Bush, 1997, quoting James
> Woodforde, 3 January 1768: had the

practice continued, modern churchgoers
would sit down late to luncheon of a
Sunday)

base-head a person addicted to cocaine
A combination of HEAD 3 and a *base*, or pure
form of, drug:
> Dirty, skinny, disordered base-heads yelling
> at each other. (O'Rourke, 1991)

basement *American* a lavatory
It is frequently located there in shopping
malls, public rooms, etc. Usually in the query
'Where's the basement?', which may be made
in a building manifestly devoid of a lower
level.

baser needs the desire to copulate
The dated assumption was that regular sexual
activity is good for a man's health but is
morally reprehensible:
> What you need is a sensible wife to take
> care of your baser needs. (Sharpe, 1982)

bash to work as a prostitute
The slang *bash* means to walk, as in the army
square-bashing, parade-ground drill:
> Lettin' a woman bash on the bloody streets.
> (Kersh, 1936)

On the bash is so working:
> Anybody would think that I was asking you
> to go on the bash. (ibid.)

bash the bishop (of a male) to masturbate
From the likeness of the flaccid penis to the
chessman. Also as *flog the bishop*. See also
SHAKE HANDS WITH THE BISHOP.

basket[1] a term of vulgar abuse
It sounds like the taboo *bastard*. Used only
between males figuratively and often jocu-
larly. In obsolete British use, the punning
basket-making was extramarital copulation by a
male.

basket[2] the male genitalia seen through
tight trousers:
Homosexual jargon:
> The movement arched his entire body and
> made his basket bulge under the cloth of
> his trousers. (Genet, 1969, in translation)

basket case a destitute person or society
incapable of self-reliance
This is the container in which food might
be distributed as an act of charity. It is used
of a person, or of a nation, and also figuratively:
> The other part of him couldn't understand
> why a nurse in a nursing home should be
> so grief-stricken over the death…of an
> obvious basket case. (Peck, 1990—the arms

and legs of the person who died had been amputated)
Poland, which is economically a basket case... (*Daily Telegraph*, February 1982)
You cock teasers have turned millions... into a generation of sexual basket cases. (Styron, 1976)

basted *American* drunk
Literally, being roasted and periodically covered with molten fat. The common culinary imagery.

bat a drunken carouse
A *bat* was a drunkard some time before we though of him as a player of cricket or baseball. The use survives in the phrases *on the bat*, on a carouse, and *over the bat*, drunk.

bath-house a chamber for mass killing
The Nazis stripped their victims and herded them into gas chambers on the pretence that they were going to be washed in the process of decontamination:
Of four thousand in the next four trainloads, two and a half thousand went at once to the 'bath-houses'. (Keneally, 1982, writing of Auschwitz)

bathroom *American* a lavatory
In the long line of euphemisms which associate washing with urination and defecation:
... asked where the bathroom was. The restroom was filthy. (Diehl, 1978—and what was the lavatory like?)
Whence *bathroom paper* or *tissue*:
Mummy they have a lovely house, *but their bathroom paper hurts*. (E. S. Turner, 1952, quoting from an advertisement)

bats in the belfry mental abnormality
The phrase covers anything from absent-mindedness through eccentricity to madness, when the wild ideas may circle in your head like the mammals in the church tower at twilight:
Dear man, you've got bats in the belfry. (A. E. W. Mason, 1927)
Bats and *batty* are used as adjectives:
Told him he was bats. (C. Forbes, 1992)
If two batty old people are soaked in old hatred... what can you do? (L. Thomas, 1997)
For a native of the Caribbean, a *battyboy* is a homosexual male:
However, he kept well clear of West Indian men, whose traditional reaction to 'battyboys', their name for gays, is violent assault. (Fiennes, 1996)

battered *American* drunk

Covered with *batter* before being fried, or feeling roughly handled? Probably a bit of both, with the culinary imagery uppermost.

batting and bowling *British* having both heterosexual and homosexual tastes
The imagery is from the game of cricket, in which most players tend to specialize in one or the other. See also ALL-ROUNDER.

battle fatigue the inability to continue fighting
Not just tiredness from missed sleep or over-exertion:
... wondering suddenly how much guilty truth and how much honest battle fatigue there had been. (Price, 1979—an officer had admitted being a coward)
In wartime it is difficult to distinguish between psychological illness, idleness, and cowardice.

battle of the bulge a desire to slim
The *bulge* is the evidence of obesity around the waist and hips:
The 'battle of the bulge' became a corsetier's problem. (E. S. Turner, 1952)
The original battle was Eisenhower's, when the Germans broke through in the Ardennes in December, 1944. The modern campaigns seldom achieve comparable losses.

battyboy see BATS IN THE BELFRY

bawd the keeper of a brothel
Standard English, from the original meaning, dirt:
... like sanctified and pious bawds The better to beguile. (Shakespeare, *Hamlet*)
Bawdy has many of the meanings of DIRTY 1. A *bawdy house* is a brothel:
I would not wreck it, turn it into a bawdy house, or receive any members of the press here. (Bogarde, 1978, reporting the conditions of his lease)

bay window a fat person's stomach
Literally, the architectural feature of a house which protrudes from the lower floor only:
The big man folds his arms protectively over a bay window girded in a filthy apron. (Vanderhaeghe, 1997)

be excused to go to the lavatory
No more than politely to obtain release from the company of others. Perhaps the first thing we learned when we started school.

be nice to to copulate with
Prostitutes' jargon and see NICE TIME:
Wouldn't you like to be nice to Dasha? (Amis, 1980—Dasha was not what we would call a *nice girl*)

be with to copulate with
Of either sex, usually extramaritally and in the past tense. Also, of males, as *be into*:
> The girl talked. We know you've been with her. (Mailer, 1965)
> He had never been into a girl either. (Bradbury, 1975)

Been there is a claim by a male to have copulated with a specified female.

bean counter an accountant
Hardly a euphemism but more a term of disparagement of those in a profession which, like the law, is regarded by others with a mixture of fear, envy, and derision:
> Our firm had an account with the restaurant...and somewhere along the way our bean counters in the basement would find a way to bill the client for the cost of the food as well. (Grisham, 1998)

bear[1] to be pregnant or to give birth
The standard English use makes us forget that anyone who lifts up a baby *bears* a child and is of *child-bearing* age:
> Asses are made to bear, and so are you. (Shakespeare, *The Taming of the Shrew*, punning cleanly for once)

bear[2] *American* a policeman
Threat and violence are characteristics which the quadruped and the officer of the law are thought to have in common. Among the many derivatives, we may note the following: *bear bait*, a speeding motorist; *bear cage*, a police station; *bear in the air*, a police helicopter, especially one on traffic duty; *bear bite*, a ticket for speeding; *bear trap*, a police radar operation (in which illogically the *bears* do the trapping); *lady bear*, a policewoman.

beard a person acting as a decoy
The derivation is from the false *beard* worn as a disguise, despite which the use is of both sexes:
> 'He's the beard.' That's what they call the other man who pretends to be the lover. (Sanders, 1981)
> She was a beard for Mark, to keep Robbie unsuspecting about who was really informing on him. (Turow, 1999)

beast to copulate with
With the male adopting the approach of a quadruped:
> She switched on a German porn video which depicted four Teutonic blondes being beasted from behind by a like number of musclebound types. (Fiennes, 1996)

beast with two backs (the) copulation
From the facing position of the parties. The *beast* can be *made* or *played*:
> Your daughter and the Moor are now making the beast with two backs. (Shakespeare, *Othello*)
> She had the goods on me and in an idle moment I played the beast with two backs with her. (M. McCarthy, 1963)

Whence also the *two-backed beast* and the *two-backed game*:
> I...know what it had been like with Deborah and him, what a burning two-backed beast. (Mailer, 1965)
> She had a hearty appetite for the two-backed game. (Fraser, 1977)

beastliness male sexual activity
In the 19th century it meant copulation, when it was not thought proper for women to relish the activity:
> While you were at your beastliness ...(Fraser, 1971, writing in archaic style)

Now it means masturbation, which is hardly fair, as most animals don't masturbate:
> ...the detrimental effects on sportsmen of masturbation, referred to in the sermon as beastliness. (Sharpe, 1982)

beat on see RAISE A BEAT

beat the gong *American* to smoke opium
From the oriental association of ideas. A *beat pad* is where communal smoking takes place, now usually of marijuana.

beat the gun to copulate with a proposed spouse before marriage
The *gun* is the starter's pistol. Used specifically of conception before marriage even if only evident afterwards. Also as *beat the starter*; and see CHEAT THE STARTER.

beat your meat (of a male) to masturbate
And as *beat your dummy* or *beat off*:
> 'To see that you don't beat your meat,' said the constable coarsely. (Sharpe, 1976, explaining why a prisoner was kept under observation)
> Twenty minutes, he'll beat off and save the money. (Diehl, 1978—a man was waiting impatiently for a prostitute)

beau a woman's male sexual partner
Not necessarily beautiful, but paying court to her and, especially if she is married to another, implying that she has a sexual relationship with him:
> 'You don't do it famously.'...'I haven't heard a word of complaint from any new beau.' (Mailer, 1965)

beaver the female genitals viewed sexually

From the slang meaning, a beard, whence the pubic hair:

> Frank, who was seventeen at the time, remarked...he liked beaver too. His father told him to wash his mouth out and sent him to bed. (N. Evans, 1995)

bed¹ childbirth

The *bed* is the symbol of birth, marriage, and copulation. To be *brought to bed* is standard English for the delivery of a child:

> At the height of the gale a soldier's wife was brought to bed. (Graves, 1940)

bed² to copulate with

Formerly, where the marriage was made binding through consummation:

> Woo her, wed her and bed her.
> (Shakespeare, *Taming of the Shrew*)

In modern use, it applies to copulation by either sex, although men tend to *bed* women and women to *bed with* men:

> She had bedded with most of the criminal fraternity, including Roger Clinton, in a decade-long career of vertiginous debauchery. (Evans-Pritchard, 1997)

Bedtime business is copulation:

> I don't care about your bedtime business. Let them bounce on you like a squashy mattress! (Rushdie, 1995)

Bed-hopping is promiscuity:

> Given more privacy, some bed-hopping might have developed. (Hailey, 1979)

bed and breakfast a single act of overnight extramarital copulation

Punning on what a guest house offers:

> No mention of any bed-and-breakfast work, setting up ex-military members of parliament for possible blackmail. (Lyall, 1980)

beddable (of a female) sexually attractive

In proper use, capable of marriage and of bearing children:

> I'm wary of strong, clever women, however beddable they may be. (Fraser, 1973)

bedewed (of a female) sweating

A lady is not supposed to sweat in public or, in some circles, at all:

> ...a lady might get 'bedewed', but she didn't sweat. (Jennings, 1965)

bedfellow a person with whom you copulate extramaritally

Literally, a person with whom you share a bed, whence also, in standard use, someone with a shared interest:

> I've had better bedfellows, mistresses more given to the art of love. (F. Harris, 1925)

bedpan SEE PAN

bedroom eyes (with) (of a woman) appearing to offer a sexual invitation

The imagery is from BED 2:

> A redheaded number with bedroom eyes...(Chandler, 1939)

bedwetting involuntarily urinating in a bed

This standard English makes us forget that there are many other ways of making a bed damp.

bedwork copulation

Literally, in slang, a job so undemanding that you could do it in bed.

beef a person or the genitalia of a male viewed sexually

Beef has most of the sexual meanings of MEAT 1 and 2. Thus it may mean a prostitute, the penis, or copulation:

> ...feeding him beef like a shogun in a geisha house. (Wambaugh, 1975)

beefcake a male seen as a sexual object

The derivation is from the former meaning, a picture of a male for erotic female gratification, the converse of CHEESECAKE. Both heterosexual and homosexual use:

> ...the bellboys were choice beefcake—dressed as native bearers, bare-chested, in loincloths and sandals. (Anonymous, 1996)

been having urinated

Polite usage and effectively the past tense of GO 3:

> Hari's realization that I hadn't 'been' rather cast a blight on the evening.
> (P. Scott, 1973)

Occasionally also of defecation.

beg a child of *obsolete* to seek to impregnate (a woman)

From a wish by a male to generate an heir:

> I think he means to beg a child of her.
> (Shakespeare, *I Henry VI*)

behind the buttocks

It could be any part of you, from your head to your heels:

> ...reference to a female's buttocks as her 'behind'. (Jennings, 1965)

Occasionally used for the anus, in a non-sexual sense or homosexually:

> It was a serious insult, because that was the hand they used to wipe their behinds. (Simon, 1979)

This bee-hind is for sale, boy. (Mailer,
1965)

behind the eight ball *American* in serious difficulty
From a potentially losing position in the game
of pool:
> Verdi would get the message that he could
> find himself behind the eight ball.
> (Deighton, 1994)

behind the wire in prison
Especially of prisoners of war who were
confined in camp encircled with barbed or
electrified wire.

bell money *obsolete Scottish* a levy on a
bridegroom at a wedding
Not a corruption of BALL MONEY but a
payment ostensibly demanded by the ringers:
> At a wedding, the boys and girls of the
> neighbourhood assemble in front of the
> house, calling out 'Bell money, bell money
> shabby waddin, canna spare a bawbee'.
> Money is then given to them. (*N&Q*, 1865,
> quoted in *EDD*—such rudeness hardly
> deserved rewarding)
It will be noted that weddings were an
occasion for extortion long before the days
of the outside caterer and the professional
photographer.

belly plea a claim that the accused is
pregnant
A pregnant woman could not be hanged and
therefore so advised the judge if she were
convicted on a capital charge:
> My mother pleaded her belly, and
> being found quick with child...(Defoe,
> 1721)
To *slink a (great) belly away* was to have an
induced abortion:
> Lady Castelmayne, who he believes hath
> lately slunk a great belly away...(Pepys,
> 1664—at least it saved Charles II lumbering
> the British with another dukedom)

belly up bankrupt
The phrase is used of companies, with piscine
imagery:
> ...no government on earth in the mid-
> 1960s let a company like MDC go belly up.
> (Erdman, 1981)

bellyful of lead see LEAD

below medium height of unusually
short stature
Tallness short of gigantism is seen to be an
attribute of manliness, and shortness the
reverse:
> He was below medium height...(obituary
> in *Daily Telegraph*, December 1989)

below stairs[1] *British* employed as a domestic servant
The construction of town houses afforded day
accommodation for the servants in cellars or
semi-basements and sleeping space in the
attics, communication taking place through
the *back stairs* of gossip fame:
> To have one affair might be manageable:
> but to bed so many, and to stoop below the
> stairs, and then get caught, was a bed too
> far. (Parris, 1995, writing of the Victorian
> literary figure Charles Dilke)

below stairs[2] the genitalia
A variant of DOWN BELOW:
> The wretched bitch was halfway down my
> throat and rummaging below stairs with an
> expert hand. (Fraser, 1994)

below the salt socially inferior
The salt, being then a scarce commodity
needed by all, was put in the middle of the
dining table in medieval times. The diners
were seated in descending social order from
the head of the table:
> ...in comparison with other professions—
> the Church, Education, the Law, the higher
> levels of journalism, and the BBC—I am
> afraid it must be admitted that advertising
> sits rather below the salt. (E. S. Turner,
> 1952)
The saline distinction usually only works
against you but:
> ...it's a big dinner and you'll be well
> above the salt. (N. Mitford, 1960)

belt a taboo article or activity
From the slang meaning a blow. It is used of
copulation, illegal narcotics, and other taboos.
A *belt* is also a drink of spirits:
> Dundee and Spencer had a couple of belts
> on the drive into Manhattan. (Sanders,
> 1984)
The (Washington) Beltway, or ring road, is used
for 'government' in Washington DC, as
Westminster and *Whitehall* are for Britain.
However, it does not mean that those within
it habitually take illegal narcotics, become
alcoholics, and are sexually promiscuous:
> It continued for another two and a half
> years, the longest sustained leak in the
> history of the Washington Beltway.
> (Evans-Pritchard, 1997)
To *belt* is to engage in such taboo activities and
a *belter* was a prostitute.

bench to cause to withdraw from active
participation
He is relegated to the substitutes' *bench* while
others continue to play:
> ...if I say you're benched, you're benched.
> (Deighton, 1982—a commander grounding
> a flier)

A *bench-warmer* is a less competent performer: Chelsea's foreign formation, for a start, can be all but ignored, unless Hoddle should want Dennis Wise, currently a bench-warmer. (*Daily Telegraph*, 10 October 1998—Wise was one of the few indigenous players at Chelsea soccer club)

bend *obsolete* to drink intoxicants to excess
Probably a shortened form of *bend the elbow*, from the locomotion of the drinking vessel:
Bend well to the Madeira at dinner. (E. B. Ramsay, 1859)
See also ELBOW-BENDING. *Bent* still means drunk.

bend sinister an imputation of illegitimacy
The heraldic *bend sinister* runs from the upper right to the lower left corner of a coat of arms. To suggest that someone, whether or not entitled to a coat of arms, has a *bend sinister*, is to imply that he is actually or figuratively a bastard.

bend the rules to act illegally
The implication is that the law has not really been broken:
...if he sometimes 'bent the rules'...he believed that the end justified the means. (P. Scott, 1973)

bender a drunken carouse
A modern survival of the obsolete BEND:
He went on terrible benders and...would turn up unconscious in some Kamathipura gutter. (Rushdie, 1995)

benders *obsolete* the legs
From one of the 19th-century taboos, especially in New England, where even tables had *benders*.

bends (the) menstruation
Literally, decompression sickness and its painful symptoms:
She was having her monthly period, she said, a real bastard, cramps, the bends, you name it. (le Carré, 1986)

benefit state aid paid to the needy
Literally, an advantage. *Benefit* was formerly the specific advantage of being a member of a fund from which you could draw if you were ill. If the illness lasted too long, or you failed to keep up your subscriptions to the fund, you went *out of benefit*. The modern use is of regular or ad hoc payments:
Jobless CSE candidates 'should be given £13 benefit'. (*Daily Telegraph*, December 1980)

benevolence *obsolete* an arbitrary tax
Literally, generosity. English monarchs extracted such taxation from their rich subjects under the guise of loans which were described as *benevolences* but never repaid. The 1689 Bill of Rights brought this method of taxation to an end, until revived in the Second World War with a tax called the *Post-War Credit*, which would eventually repaid in a depreciated currency without interest.

bent¹ dishonest
Not straight, as in the punning *bent copper*. It may also refer to something stolen:
Having sold a stolen or *bent* car to a complainant...(Lavine, 1930)

bent² (of a male) homosexual
As different from *straight*, heterosexual:
...he's bent as a tin spoon. (Bogarde, 1981)

Best Brian a devoted, industrious, and uncritical servant
Doing the donkey-work for his master:
Branson regarded his finance director as Best Brian, a reliable acolyte. (*Sunday Telegraph*, 24 September 2000—his name was in fact Trevor)

bestiality copulation of a human with an animal
Literally, appertaining to a beast. Legal jargon for such a relationship with a mammal quadruped of either sex. In the case of *Rex v. Brown*, where the accused's amorous attentions were directed towards a duck, he was convicted of an attempt at bestiality only, despite achieving his desires, and left to reflect on the axiom that hard cases make bad law.

bestow your enthusiasm on (of a female) to copulate with promiscuously
So acting without payment:
Swiftly, concealed from the puritan gaze of 'Master', several of them acquired girlfriends there, eager to bestow their enthusiasm on the liberating British. (Horne, 1994, writing of staff officers in Belgium in 1945—*Master* was Montgomery)

bestride to copulate with
Usually of the male, with common equine imagery:
The tools of the fools who bestrode her. (*Playboy's Book of Limericks*)

bestseller a book of which the first impression is not remaindered
Publishers' puff—there could only be one *best* in any given period. An *international bestseller* is a novel set with American spelling. *Instant*

bestseller indicates an expensive pre-release advertising campaign.

betray to copulate with a third party while married

Literally, to prove false:

> He swiftly confessed, saying that he 'betrayed the covenants of marriage'. (*Daily Telegraph*, 29 September 1998—the adultery of a pastor who was a spiritual adviser to Clinton had been publicized)

In modern use, one spouse *betrays* the other. Formerly a male might *betray* a single woman by copulating with her with her consent:

> ...servant girls ceased to be seduced and began to be betrayed. (Mencken, 1940)

better country (a) life after death

The belief or hope of those who profess certain religions. Also as a *better state* (which here is not synonymous with *country*) or a *better world*:

> ...strive to take it with faith and patience, looking to a 'better country'. (Sir James Murray in a 1915 letter)

> I wish...that God may grant you every blessing, that you may be happy in this world for its short continuance, and eternally happy in a better state. (Lynd, 1946—quoting Dr Johnson's letter to Mrs Thrale on her marriage to Piozzi)

> To the memory of Ray Mock, my uncle, who long ago moved to a better world. (Koontz, 1997)

between shows involuntarily unemployed

Theatrical jargon, not used of those rehearsing for a new part. Also as *between jobs*, especially for those who do not tread the boards:

> 'I worked on lots of pictures a his over the years.' 'Did he know you were between shows?' (Wambaugh, 1981—the first speaker was an out-of-work dancer)

> 'What do you do?'...'I'm between jobs.' 'Are you an actor?'...'No.' (Hall, 1988)

between the legs on or around the genitalia

The term may be used to denote the location of anything from prickly heat to amorous fondling:

> ...her left hand around my neck stroking the back of my hair, her right hand still stroking me between the legs. (N. Barber, 1981)

between the sheets copulating

From the bedlinen:

> We still suited very well between the sheets. (Fraser, 1970)

Shakespeare used *twixt the sheets*:

> ...twixt my sheets,
> Has done my office. (*Othello*)

between the thighs of (of a male) copulating with

Used of extramarital sexual activity:

> A man can learn more between the thighs of a good woman than he ever needs to know. (Sharpe, 1974—academically and anatomically incorrect for all its vivid imagery)

beverage an intoxicant

Originally, any kind of drink, and then standard American English for any alcoholic drink served in a bar or *beverage room* by a waiter or *beverage host* (or *hostess*). In Britain, shortened to *bevvy* (with *bevvied* meaning well supplied with intoxicants) or *bevy*:

> Friday evening, no work tomorrow, arseholed by midnight, rollocked, well bevvied. (Boyd, 1998—*arse-holed* in this context means drunk)

> He has been showered with the kind of hospitality normally saved for a national hero, and he's sunk a bevy or two along the way. (Hawks, 1998)

beyond help dead

Not just out of reach:

> I was with him in moments, but he was beyond all help. He had suffered a massive coronary. (J. Major, 1999—a member died while speaking in the House of Commons)

beyond the blanket outside marriage

Referring to the date of conception:

> You're a bastard...That's what they call people who aren't born inside the nine months of marriage, people conceived beyond the blanket. (McCourt, 1997—he must have meant 'are born' etc.)

bibi a prostitute

In Hindi it means lady, whence the 19th-century British Indian use, denoting a white woman married to a white man:

> The *bibi*, or white wife, was a great rarity; but the *bubu*, or native wife, was an accepted institution. (Blanch, 1954)

Later a *bibi* in British Indian army use became an Indian prostitute:

> Sahib, you want nice Bibi, me drive you to bungalow of nice half-caste, plenty clean, plenty cheap. (F. Richards, 1936)

Also as *grass bibi* or *bidi*.

bicycle a promiscuous woman

Also known as the TOWN BIKE, because so many RIDE 1 her:

She was a convenient bicycle for men for a few hours. (Seymour, 1999)

biddy a sexually complaisant woman

In 19th-century England *biddy* meant a young prostitute, in Ireland a chicken, and everywhere, including America, it was a short form of the Irish name *Bridget*, at a time when many maidservants were Irish:

> ...for a pound of sausages you could find a biddy who would actually chuck her old man out of bed and send him to sit downstairs till you'd finished. (Seymour, 1980, writing of Germany immediately after the Second World War)

big pregnant

A shortened form of *big with child*, but also used before the swelling is visible. A *big belly* indicated pregnancy:

> They said shoo's big, but doctor said 'twas nought at all but cowld. (E. Doyle, 1855)
> ...the consequences of which was a big belly, and the loss of place. (Cleland, 1749—a servant who became pregnant might expect summary dismissal)

big animal *obsolete American* a bull

The word *bull* was taboo, from its sexual overtones. The fastidious had a plentiful choice of synonyms for *big animal*, including BRUTE, COW BRUTE, GENTLEMAN COW, HE-COW, MALE BEAST, *male cow*, MAN COW, *seed-ox*, and STOCK BEAST.

big-boned fat

The phrase is used of children and adults, seeking to suggest that their frame needs the extra padding:

> ...in his beefy adolescence his mother had tactfully described him as 'big-boned', though 'burly' was how he now liked to see himself. (Boyd, 1981)

big C (the) *American* cancer

The dread affliction which may lead to the BIG D:

> ...ailments are apt to be called by their own names or by superstitious shortened forms: arthritis, emphysema, cancer (or the Big C). (Johnson and Murray in Enright, 1985)

big D (the) death

Also as the *big jump*, or, for military men, the *big stand-easy*:

> He said there was a kid of five, son of a guy he knew. Seemed the boy was for the big jump. (Forsyth, 1996—the child was mortally ill)

big house *American* a prison

Usually, as with *big pasture* or *big school*, for male convicts:

> She has other worries besides trying to keep her ex-lover out of the Big House. (Lavine, 1930)

The *little school* is usually for women or children prisoners.

big jobs defecation

Nursery usage, sometimes shortened to *bigs* or *biggies*:

> ...done our bigs and wiped our bottoms. (Amis, 1978)
> ...the town's New Age mongrels who continue to use the Green as their favourite spot for dropping biggies. (Chapman, 1999)

LITTLE JOBS is urination.

big prize (the) copulation

A male may hope to win it after lesser awards during courtship:

> ...allowing moist liberties but with steel-trap relentlessness withholding the big prize. (Styron, 1976)

bijou inconveniently small

Estate agents' jargon which seeks to persuade you that a minute dwelling is a jewel:

> Now she lived in a tiny house off the King's Road...the sort of house agents called 'bijou'. (Deighton, 1988)

bikini wax the removal of women's pubic hair

It is the skin which is waxed, not the *bikini* costume:

> Her fag hairdresser gives a great bikini wax. (Sanders, 1982)

See also WAX 1.

bill a policeman

Derived perhaps from the weapon once carried by constables, but there is probably a simpler etymology:

> 'Eyes front,' said Murf. 'It's Bill.' A policeman in a helmet and gleaming rain-cape was coming towards them. (Theroux, 1976)

Also as *old Bill*, which may refer to an individual or to the force generally:

> He was in Borstal for robbery, involved in many fights, acquitted of a stabbing murder in '79 and of knifing Ol' Bill in '83. (Fiennes, 1996)

Billingsgate foul language

The language was once used by the women sellers of fish, rather than by the male porters, in the London market which was closed in 1982. According to Dryden , 'Parnassus spoke the cant of Billingsgate', and in modern use:

...his ears had surely overflowed with such billingsgate. (Styron, 1976)

bimbo a sexually complaisant female
From the Italian, meaning little (male) child. She is not a prostitute but may be prepared to exploit her youth and good looks:
> But why should a bimbo file cause such alarm? (Evans-Pritchard, 1997—the list was of women supposed to have caught the eye of Governor Clinton)

bin an institution for the insane
Literally, a container, and a shortened form of *loony bin*:
> We shall be found stark staring mad with horror and live sixty more years in an expensive bin. (N. Mitford, 1949)

bind to cause to suffer from constipation
Literally, to tie fast:
> Up and took phisique...only to loose me, for I am bound. (Pepys, 1662)
> Then the water will be madly binding. (N. Mitford, 1945)

binge to go on a drunken carouse
Literally, to soak:
> A man goes to the ale-house to binge himself. (*EDD*)
In modern use, mainly as a noun, which can cover overeating as well as drunken excess.

bint a prostitute
The British army picked up the Arabic word for young woman and carried it across the world:
> The women put it down to the rations we got, and the men down to the bint, as they called it. (Bogarde, 1978)

biographic leverage blackmail
The jargon of espionage and American politics:
> Jonathan smiled at the cryptic jargon...'biographic leverage' meant blackmail. (Davidson, 1978)

bird¹ a young female companion
The word, when referring to a young woman, has also meant a mistress, as in Holman Hunt's *Bird in a Gilded Cage* of 1854, and, in America, a prostitute who might operate from a *bird-cage*, or brothel:
> He stared at Amy as he shook Barry's hand, a calculated taunt which seemed to say, 'I like your bird, mate.' (Fiennes, 1996)

bird² imprisonment
Derived from the caging. Usually in the phrase to *do bird*, to be imprisoned:
> If it was anywhere else in the system I was doing bird they wouldn't have left you alone with me. (Rendell, 1991)

bird³ the vagina
A vulgar male use, and, in such circles, the *bird's nest* is pubic hair:
> This bitch wears these short shorts...when I'm down on my knees...I kneel there and look right at her bird. (Wambaugh, 1975)

bird circuit *American* a vicinity with saloons frequented by male homosexuals
Here the game is the cock rather than the hen.

bird dog¹ *American* a small gambler who follows the betting pattern of heavy gamblers
Literally, the animal that retrieves the quarry brought down by its master. In this instance, the master is likely to be party to criminal interference with the runners.

bird dog² *American* an unsuspected accomplice to a criminal
Again from collecting the carcass on another's behalf:
> Your bird dog, the State Senator. (Chandler, 1939, describing such a relationship)
To *bird-dog* is so to act:
> So he would be bird-dogging occasionally and bring you things? (Colodny and Gettlin, 1991—a naval Yeoman stole secret documents and passed them to his superior)

bird dog³ *American* a police detective
Hoping to find the quarry and bring it in:
> The man can't draw his gun without losing a few toes, but he's one hell of a bird-dog. (Clancy, 1991)

birth control the prevention of conception
Standard English, although the phrase would better describe stratagems by midwives to prevent the arrival of babies at weekends or other times inconvenient to themselves.

birthday suit (your) nakedness
What you were born in. Also as *birthday attire*, *gear*, or the obsolete *finery*:
> I went in the morning to a private place, along with the housemaid, and we bathed in our birthday soot. (Smollett, 1771—I am sure they had one each)
> ...the figure I made outshone all other *birthday* finery. (Cleland, 1749, of a naked woman)

bisexual having both homosexual and heterosexual tastes
In biology, it means having both sexes in the same plant or animal. Often shortened to *bi*.

bit¹ a woman viewed sexually by a male
A synonym of PIECE 1 but not used of a spouse. Seldom of a prostitute:
> 'Opal,' said Cicero, 'Whose bit is that?' (Londres, 1928, in translation)

Normally in a phrase such as *a bit of all right* (or *alright* for the less literate), *arse, ass, crumpet, fluff, goods, hot stuff, how's your father, jam, meat, muslin, skirt, stuff, you-know-what*, etc., most of which are elaborated under those headings:
> One of them...was his own bit of goods. She was a married woman whose husband was away working. (F. Richards, 1936)

A *bit on the side* is a regular sexual partner other than your spouse, adverting to the *side*, or additional, plate served with a formal meal:
> She had been used, had been just the fun you can't get when you're married, a bit on the side. (Bradbury, 1976)

bit² (a) copulation
By either sex:
> ...taking a little bit now and then from her husband's valet. (Condon, 1966)

A *bit of the other* is not a homosexual encounter but refers to copulation with *other than* a regular partner:
> ...off they go to this girlie restaurant ...Duffy's not averse to a bit of the other. (le Carré, 1991)

bit missing (a) of low intelligence
Not an absent girlfriend:
> A bit missing by the way she asked. Someone took advantage of her, I suppose. (P. D. James, 1962)

bitch *American* a male homosexual
The word is used in homosexual jargon of someone thought to be as spiteful or vindictive as a woman so offensively described. In obsolete use, a *bitch* was a prostitute and to *bitch* was to visit brothels.

bite the bullet to take a difficult or costly decision
A soldier being flogged was given a bullet to bite to prevent his crying out in pain. Today only metaphorical *bullets* are bitten:
> I suppose he thought it would be best to bite the bullet and pay out one large sum of money rather than be bled to death over the years penny by penny. (Atwood, 1996)

bite the dust to die
A synonym of LICK THE DUST, and usually of violent death, although not necessarily after falling from your horse in a Western movie. Rare figurative use:
> ...Jerry will unleash some devil's device and another brilliant novelist will bite the dust. (Thwaite, 1992, quoting a letter from Philip Larkin written in 1944)

black-and-white *American* a police car
The vehicles have distinctive paintwork:
> ...didn't even notice the cops gliding up in the black-and-white. (Wambaugh, 1981)

black bag (associated with) an illicit enquiry
Usually relating to telephone tapping or the robbery of documents, from the holdall in which tools are carried:
> I'd like you to authorize a black-bag job on Rathbone's town house. (Sanders, 1990)

black dog (the) melancholia
Black for the negative aspect, but the canine seems to be unfairly impugned:
> But what will you do to keep away the *black dog* that worries you at home? (J. Boswell, 1791, quoting from a letter by Dr Johnson dated 1779)

black economy the sum of goods and services provided without tax or official cognizance
Depressingly *black* for the tax collector, perhaps, but not normally so for those who pay for governmental voracity and profligacy:
> All public-spirited citizens will want to help the Inland Revenue in its battle against this 'black economy' of untaxed income and benefits. (A. Waugh in *Private Eye*, March 1981—the satirist was writing ironically)

black fish commercially caught fish sold illegally
In attempts to conserve fishing stocks, limits are set on the size, quantity, and species of fish which may be sold. Unfortunately a trawl cannot be programmed to be selective, and excess or forbidden catches have either to be thrown back in the sea or landed illegally:
> ...the fishing boats are preoccupied with quota restrictions and netting regulations, and the only criminals left are scraping a living from quota-jumping 'black fish'. (Bathurst, 1999)

black hole *obsolete* a prison
So called because it was insanitary, unlit, and below ground. Sometimes shortened to *hole*:
> Nothing but law and vengeance, blackhole and fining. (Cross, 1844)
> They'l other foin us, or else send us to't oil. (Bywater, 1839)

Most British towns had their *black hole*, although, when British schoolchildren used to be taught British history, the only one they were told about was the Calcutta version of 1756.

black job a funeral

Mourning clothes are that colour:

> One of Lord Portsmouth's eccentricities
> was that he took an obsessive interest in
> funerals ('black jobs') and slaughterhouses.
> (Tomalin, 1997)

black lad the devil

The Prince of Darkness entered a house by the
chimney in the days of coal fires and soot.
Also as the *black gentleman, man, prince, Sam,
spy*, etc.:

> The auld black lad may have my saul, if I
> ken but o' ae MacNab. (Ford, 1891)
> The Black Man would gi'e her power . . . to
> kep the butter frae gatherin' in the kirn.
> (Service, 1890—a *kirn* is a churn)

black market illegal dealing in goods in
short supply

Here the colour denotes illegality:

> A black market is beginning to appear, in
> sharp contrast to the orderly arrangements
> of the food markets. (Goebbels, 1945, in
> translation)

black meat a black woman viewed sexually by a white man

Usually a prostitute:

> I see right away he was crazy for black
> meat. (Fraser, 1994)

See also WHITE MEAT 2.

black money cash gained or used illegally

The proceeds of any vice, from bribery to
prostitution and illegal gambling; also undeclared gains or profits on which tax has not
been paid. Also as *black cash, pounds, francs,
dollars, marks*, etc.:

> Hasn't the wily oriental got black money
> tucked away? (Davidson, 1978)
> Their ancient—and fabulously rich—
> private syndicate operations around the Far
> East had been persuaded to provide black
> cash. (Strong, 1998)
> . . . to do with black dollars . . . after returns
> from the orient. (ibid.)

black smoke opium

Also as *black pills* or *stuff*:

> Imagine a clergyman peddling the black
> smoke. (Fraser, 1985)

black stuff (the) *Irish* stout

Usually Guinness, but people also relish
porter produced by Messrs Murphy and
Beamish:

> Just as Geraldine delivered me a pint of the
> black stuff, a young guy called Brian called
> into the pub. (Hawks, 1998)

black up (of a white actor) to take the role
of a non-white character by applying
dark make-up

Unacceptable today on several counts, especially as being seen to mitigate against the
employment of black actors:

> This means that actors should be cast
> because of their talent. But this policy has
> been refined. We do not believe that white
> actors should black up. (*Daily Telegraph*, 12
> August 1996, quoting Martin Brown, a
> union official. Mr Brown did not take
> exception to the fact that a black actor had
> played Macbeth the previous year)

black velvet a dark-skinned prostitute

Originally used by white British soldiers in
India, but the pun became more widely
accepted:

> In sophisticated circles Black Velvet is a
> mix of champagne and Guinness. But in
> the outback the phrase has a different
> meaning derived from an obscure Ugandan
> dialect. (*Private Eye*, January 1982—see
> UGANDA for the obscure in-joke)

blackbird *obsolete* a black African slave
conveyed to America

The jargon of the whites engaged in the
TRIANGULAR TRADE:

> Things were making life more difficult in
> the blackbird trade. (Fraser, 1971)

To *blackbird* was to be a slave trader. A
blackbirder was either a ship carrying slaves
or someone who transported or dealt in them:

> When the stinking ships of the
> blackbirders crossed the bars below the
> delta . . . (Longstreet, 1956)

Also as *black cattle, hides, pigs*, or *sheep*.

blackmail extortion by threats

Mail was a tribute or tax, becoming *black* when
paid by a Lowland Scot to a Highlander:

> And what is black-mail? A sort of
> protection money that Low-country
> gentlemen . . . pay to some Highland chief
> that he may neither do them harm nor
> suffer it to be done to them by others.
> (W. Scott, 1814)

Standard English. A century ago Dr Wright in
EDD was so rash or naïf as to say the use was
obsolete.

blank¹ a mild oath

A blank space may be left in print for the
taboo word:

> A nice hope I've got with that blank
> sketchy jumper. (Sassoon, 1928, describing
> a horse, not a sweater)

Also adjectivally as *blanking*.

blank² *American* to kill

The victim is sent into a void:

> . . . none of whom seemed particularly
> distressed by the sudden blanking of Victor
> Maitland. (Sanders, 1977)

blast¹ a mild oath
Perhaps from the obsolete meaning, lightning, with a use similar to the German *Blitz*. Partridge in *DSUE* says 'Among the lower classes a euphemism for bloody'.

blast² *American* to kill by shooting
Referring to the discharge:
> We just got a message for the guy. We don't blast him. Not today. (Chandler, 1939)

blast³ to ingest narcotics illegally
From the feeling experienced:
> I'm higher than a giraffe's toupee. I started blasting when I was 13. (Longstreet, 1956)

blast⁴ an intoxicant
Again from the feeling of elevation induced:
> ...get me another blast, will you? Easy on the ice. (Sanders, 1982)

blasted drunk
The sufferer may feel as if he has been blown up:
> Takes a real sailorman to know how to get blasted. (Clancy, 1986)
Also of illegal narcosis.

blazes hell
The eternal fires burn sinners, without consuming the body or making it insensible to pain:
> You can count on J. B. to blazes and beyond. (Fraser, 1977)

bleed to extort money from on a regular basis
Like a 19th-century surgeon, but not for the good of the victim. The obsolete British *bleed the monkey* was to steal rum from the *monkey*, or mess tub.

bleeding a mild oath
For the once taboo *bloody*.

bleeding heart a person who ostentatiously expresses concern about or seeks to relieve the suffering of others
The dividing line between a *bleeding heart* and a DO-GOODER is not wide or distinctly marked.

bleep an obscenity or a taboo word or expression
An electronic note is introduced by broadcasters etc. to replace obscene or offensive matter in a recording.

blighty a serious but not fatal wound
Blighty, from the Hindi *bilayati* meaning foreign, became their home country for British servicemen abroad, and not just those serving in India:
> Thought we'd see a bit of the place before we go back to Blighty. (R. Wright, 1989, quoting a British soldier based in Belize)
In the First World War a wound which caused repatriation was thought by some to be preferable to remaining to be killed in the trenches:
> What we used to call 'a nice blighty one'; sent me back to England. (Price, 1974)

blind a drunken carouse
The use seems to pre-date the cliché *blind drunk* or its Scottish form *blind-fou*.

blind copy a document of which a copy is given to a third party without the person to whom it is addressed being informed
Good manners suggest that the addressee should be told of other recipients. Less often as *silent copy*.

blind pig *American* an unlicensed place for the consumption of intoxicants
Hidden from the *pigs*, or police, perhaps?
> Howitson had raided it as long ago as February, 1966, and had discovered that it was, in fact, the front for a blind pig. (Lacey, 1986)

blindside *American* to rob or cheat
Not merely approaching out of peripheral vision. The jargon of basketball:
> Geraldine Forsyth had been blindsided by an unscrupulous polo player. (Sanders, 1994, but not on the polo field)

blip off *American* to kill
Blips indicate that an oscilloscope or other monitoring equipment is working. They vanish if the instrument malfunctions or is switched off.

blitzed drunk
The victim is devastated, as was England during the German Blitz:
> Miller has no health or weight problems and furthermore plans to get blitzed on February 1. (*Daily Telegraph*, 10 January 1995—he had foresworn alcohol during January)
Despite escaping the attentions of the Luftwaffe, more Americans than British use the expression.

block (of a male) to copulate with
With obvious imagery:
> There was a young lady of Thun,
> Who was blocked by the man on the moon.
> (*Playboy's Book of Limericks*)

block out to kill

The imagery is from the word-processor or computer, where matter can be made instantly to disappear from the screen or file, sometimes inadvertently:

> I'm aware of his CV...That's why I wanted him blocked out. (Strong, 1997)

blockbuster¹ *American* a real-estate dealer who induces whites to sell their homes through threat of other racial groups moving into the area

The use puns on the Second World War bomb. In this case, the *block* of real estate occupied mainly by white families may be more valuable if redeveloped.

blockbuster² a novel which is expected to sell well

Publishers' jargon. See also BEST-SELLER.

blocking detachment a unit positioned to stop retreat or desertion

A characteristic of the Red Army between 1942 and 1945 and of the Wehrmacht in the closing stages of the Second World War:

> Some of the best-fed and best-equipped battalions to be found in the Soviet Union were not sent to face the Germans...Assigned to follow the fighting forces, their job was to shoot men who tried to retreat and provide 'blocking detachments' which sent soldiers at gunpoint over minefields and into enemy gunfire. (Deighton, 1993/1)

blood menstruation

Or the first onset:

> My blood, for instance, it came late, as if worried it might upset things.
> (R. Thompson, 1996, of a tomboy)

Bloody may mean menstruating, either *tout court* and in various phrases such as *the bloody flag is up*.

blood disease *obsolete* syphilis

The condition was doubly taboo as being incurable and contracted in a shameful manner. Less often as *blood poison*:

> *Syphilis* became transformed into *blood-poison*, *specific blood poison* and *secret disease*. (Mencken, 1940)

blood money extortion

In standard usage, a reward for bringing about another's death or compensation paid to surviving relatives in respect of a killing:

> ...collecting 'blood money', that is, shaking down prostitutes, poor peddlers, &c. (Lavine, 1930)

blooming a mild oath

Used for the taboo *bloody*.

blot (out) to kill

Literally, to eradicate:

> The Emperor left here for Ethiopia today, flying to the frontier, and then in by ground. I hope he doesn't get blotted. (Mockler, 1984—in January 1941 Haile Selassie was as much at risk from his subjects as from the Italians who were being defeated)
> You can even blot me out suddenly so that I don't know about it. (Fraser, 1977)

blow¹ *obsolete* (of a male) to copulate

Usually in a phrase such as *blow the groundsels*, which meant that the parties were on the floor at the time. To *blow off* is to ejaculate semen:

> Blew off all over the booth. (*Playboy's Book of Limericks*)

blow² *American* a prostitute

A shortened form of the obsolete *blowen*, perhaps.

blow³ orally to excite the genitals of another

Homosexually or heterosexually:

> He was cruising down the interstate and his daughter's husband is blowing him. (Diehl, 1978)

A *blow job* is such activity:

> 'You want me to give you a blow job?' She got off the bed and came towards him. (Sharpe, 1976)

blow⁴ (off) to fart

A common vulgarism. See also BLOW A RASPBERRY.

blow⁵ to boast

Seldom in modern use *tout court* but usually in a phrase such as *blow smoke*, *blow your own horn*, or *blow your own trumpet*:

> You think I'm blowing smoke? (Sanders, 1994)
> Some staff member or some consultant can blow his horn and look oh, so smart and oh, so good to some journalist. (*Daily Telegraph*, 11 January 1997, quoting President Clinton)

blow⁶ a mild oath

Of the same tendency as BLAST 1.

blow⁷ to betray to authority

Probably a shortened form of *blow away* or *blow up*, to lose or destroy:

> Did you tell the man to blow me? (Hall, 1979—the speaker is a betrayed spy)

The British *blow the gaff* means to betray or give away confidential information, *gaff* being gossip. See also BLOW THE WHISTLE ON.

blow⁸ an illegal narcotic
The common imagery of *hitting*:
> And did Hardcore tell you that the idea was
> to make it look like this white man had
> been killed in a drive-in while he was
> buying blow? (Turow, 1996)

Also, as a verb, to smoke such a narcotic, in
phrases such as *blow a stick, Charlie, horse, snow*,
etc.

blow a gasket to become mentally deranged
Usually describing a temporary condition,
capable of simple repair:
> 'Christ!' said Larry, scratching a roundel of
> mosquito-bite scabs on his right cheek. 'So
> you *have* blown a gasket.' (O'Hanlon, 1996)

blow a raspberry to make a noise like a
fart with your lips
See RASPBERRY 1 for the origin in rhyming
slang:
> The bank man blew the Marseilles
> equivalent of a raspberry and went home.
> (L. Thomas, 1977)

Much figurative use, often by those without
an appreciation of the etymology.

blow away *American* to kill
Usually by gunfire at short range, although
the corpse is left for disposal by others:
> He got blown away. I went to his funeral.
> (Sanders, 1977)

blow-in *Irish* a foreigner who meddles in
domestic affairs
Used in the South rather than the North:
> [Cosgrave] fumed against 'blow-ins'—a jibe
> apparently aimed at Bruce Arnold, the
> English-born reporter of the Irish
> Independent. (J. J. Lee, 1989—it was
> through lying about the tapping of
> Arnold's telephone that Charles Haughey
> eventually fell from power)

blow job see BLOW 3

blow me one *American* give me a
draught beer
The summary request is to the bartender,
who then scoops, or occasionally blows, off
the froth which has resulted from pouring the
liquid under pressure into a glass.

blow the whistle on to make public a
taboo or questionable activity of another
The action of the referee who thus stops play
after a foul:
> He was a number one hitman for the
> Cosa Nostra and he blew the whistle on
> them. (Diehl, 1978)

See also WHISTLEBLOWER.

blue¹ *American* a policeman or prison
warder
From the normal colour of the uniform. Also
as a *bluebottle, bluebird, blue-belly, blue jeans, blue
suit,* or *blue-and-white*:
> Okay, [the elevator] was on the sixth floor
> when the first blues got to the Kipper
> townhouse. (Sanders, 1980)
> We blue suits liked the mouse. (King,
> 1996—they were prison warders)

In Britain a *man in blue* or a *bluecoat* is a
policeman, working perhaps out of a *blue
lamp*, a police station, named after the
standard exterior lit sign.
For the Nazis, the *blue police* were to enforce
their rule in occupied territories:
> ...speak to the SS men, to the Ukrainian
> auxiliary, to the Blue Police and to the OD
> details. (Keneally, 1982, writing of Nazi-
> occupied Poland; German control rested
> with the army and these four organizations
> in descending order of importance, the OD
> being Jews placed in authority over other
> Jews)

blue² erotic
Probably from the French *bibliothèque bleue*, a
collection of seamy works of literature, rather
from the colour of the brimstone which awaits
evil-doers:
> She starred in dozens of blue movies
> before coming above ground. (Deighton,
> 1972)

blue hair an old woman
Referring to the dye, or *blue rinse*:
> This joint is where you find busloads a
> blue-hairs when they get off the freaking
> cruise ships. (Wambaugh, 1981)
> ...the idea of spending the rest of my days
> in God's waiting room...some Florida
> condo surrounded by blue-rinse matrons.
> (Strong, 1998)

blue-on-blue shelling or bombing your
own troops
The derivation is from the colour marked on
military chinagraph maps to indicate your
own positions:
> I could see all the more clearly the
> potential for blue-on-blue (accidental
> attacks on friendly forces) particularly from
> the air. (de la Billière, 1992)

Blue Peter *British* (of education) undisciplined or ineffective
The derivation is from a television programme for children in which, among other
activities, they were shown how to construct
models out of waste materials. The use is
derogatory of primary education where formal instruction in the 'three Rs' may be
neglected in favour of letting the children

express their personalities through unstructured activities:

> ...marginalised and often trivialised into the so-called *Blue Peter* technology and cardboard engineering. (*Daily Telegraph*, 7 September 1995)

blue ribbon teetotal

It was the favour worn by those who had foresworn the demon drink:

> One minor victory was won by the 'blue ribbon' brigade; in 1917 all bars closed nightly at 6 o'clock. (Sinclair, 1991—when America entered the First World War the brothels were also shut down)

blue room a lavatory on an aircraft

Crew jargon, perhaps from the subdued lighting:

> ...a passenger deliberately burnt himself to death in the right aft 'blue room' or toilet. (Moynahan, 1983)

blue ruin *obsolete* gin

From the colour and the effect on addicts in the 19th century.

> My ole man and me want some blue ruin to keep our spirits up. (Mayhew, 1862)

Also known as MOTHER'S RUIN.

Blue stone was whisky, and in modern addict slang *blue* is a prefix for a variety of illegal narcotics from the colour of the pills, including *blue devils, flags, heaven, joy,* and *velvet.*

board (of a male) to copulate with

Usually outside marriage, and using naval imagery:

> I am sure he is in the fleet. I would he had boarded me. (Shakespeare, *Much Ado About Nothing*)

and in later use:

> I tried to board her at Kiva, but the caravanserai was too crowded. (Fraser, 1975)

To *board a train* is to copulate with a woman in immediate succession to other men:

> I just can't board a train like horny old Spencer. (Wambaugh, 1975)

board lodger *obsolete* a prostitute

The definition covered two categories: those who obtained their finery in addition to their accommodation from a pimp, thus staying under his control; and those who worked on their own, paying commission to the bawd of the brothel to which they took men:

> Board lodgers are those who give a portion of what they receive to the mistress of the brothel in return for their board and lodging. (Mayhew, 1862)

boat people refugees from Vietnam fleeing by sea

The fugitives were political and economic victims of the Communist victory. In obsolete British use, to *boat* was to send convicts to penal settlements in the West Indies or Australia, whence to imprison anywhere.

bobby a policeman

The derivation is from the pet form of the Christian name of Sir Robert Peel, who reorganized first the Dublin police and subsequently, in 1828, those in London:

> The bobbies over there came across it as a matter of routine. (Bagley, 1977)

bobtail[1] a prostitute

I suppose from her pelvic motion. In obsolete use it might also mean a eunuch, whose *tail* had been *bobbed,* or cropped.

bobtail[2] *American* a dishonourable discharge from the army.

The bit about 'honorable and faithful service' was clipped off the bottom of the printed certificate of discharge.

bodice-ripper a novel containing pornographic scenes

Usually written by women, and featuring an aggressive male attitude to casual copulation:

> Anthony Looch's guide to bodice rippers. (*Daily Telegraph*, 17 December 1994, featured in a section normally devoted to literature)

bodily functions urination and defecation

The equally important breathing, sweating, digesting, etc. do not count:

> You slept there, bathed, performed your bodily functions...(Sanders, 1973)

bodily wastes urine and faeces

Discharged in the BODILY FUNCTIONS. Occasional figurative use:

> ...the fan is full of bodily wastes. (M. Thomas, 1987—an allusion to the cliché *the shit hit the fan*)

body a corpse

Short for *dead body*:

> At Worcester must his body be interr'd. (Shakespeare, *King John*)

body bag *American* a container for the transfer of a corpse, especially that of a serviceman

Unlike the British, who traditionally bury their soldiers 'in some corner of a foreign field', the bodies of Americans killed abroad are returned to the United States for disposal:

> The KIAs were provided with HRPs which earlier had been called body bags, the new public relations title translated as 'human

remains pouches'. (Simpson, 1991—a *KIA* was 'killed in action')

Whence the *body-bag syndrome*, a reluctance by American commanders to involve soldiers in any action which might lead to casualties:

British officers speak of 'body-bag syndrome' as the major brake on NATO operations. (*Daily Telegraph*, 21 March 2001)

body image physical beauty

Not a portrait, photograph, X-ray, or scan but the jargon of the beauty parlour or cosmetic surgeon which avoids saying that the person paying them is ugly or ageing:

Britons began to follow Americans in their search for a better 'body image'. (Whicker, 1982)

body odour see BO

body rub (a) masturbation by a prostitute

One of the services which may be offered, usually to males, in a MASSAGE PARLOUR by a *body worker*.

body shaper a corset

An invention of advertisers to persuade the buyer that she (normally) is neither fat nor buying a corset. Also as *body briefer*, *hugger*, and *outline*.

boff[1] (of a male) to copulate with

The common violent imagery, from the slang meaning to hit, rather than a corruption of *buff*, to rub:

He boffs her or he doesn't boff her. She leaves. (Sanders, 1977)

boff[2] to fart

Common usage. The etymology is obscure.

bog a lavatory

A shortened form of *bog-house*, from the marshy ground which might surround it in the days before modern drainage, the septic tank, or the cesspit:

At the court held in October 1753...Edward Clanvill was charged with a 'public nuisance in emptying a bogg house (privy) in the street'. (Tyrrell, 1973)

And in modern use:

...been in the bog a long while...What do you suppose he's doing there? (Theroux, 1979—what indeed?)

bogy[1] *obsolete British* a policeman

Literally, a devil, from the apparition with the power of causing you alarm from the nursery upwards and likely to make your horse rear, or *boggle*, by suddenly appearing in its path:

Well, the bloody bogies are cleaning the streets up. There won't be a girl about.

(Kersh, 1936—the police were clearing prostitutes from the London streets prior to a coronation)

bog(e)y[2] a military foe

Another sort of devil:

...the target identification aircraft, which could vector the fighter bombers on to any bogey approaching on their radar screens. (de la Billière, 1992)

boiled *American* drunk

The common culinary imagery:

A crowd that can get boiled without having to lie up with Dr Verringer. (Chandler, 1953)

boiler room an operation for the unscrupulous selling of securities

Punning on the intense heat applied. Also as *boiler house* or *shop*:

...an ex-con called Sidney Coe who had time for a boiler room operation in Kansas City. (Sanders, 1990—Sidney did not have 'time' to run the operation, among his other duties, but instead had served a term in prison)

The Dutch authorities are finally acting to close down the 'boiler-shop' share-pushing operations based in Amsterdam. (*Daily Telegraph*, August 1986)

See also BUCKET SHOP.

boilerplate comprehensive disclaimers and provisions in an agreement

As used in warships, providing excessive protection of lawyers, accountants, brokers, and merchant bankers rather than of the client who pays them all:

...so that the attorneys for the underwriters could satisfy themselves on matter of title and other boilerplate. (M. Thomas, 1982)

bollocks the testicles

The old variant *ballocks* suggest derivation from BALLS, of which it is a synonym both anatomically and figuratively, as a vulgar denial or riposte.

bollocky *American* naked

Used of men only, it might seem:

I'm going bollocky. I don't even care. (Theroux, 1989—he was going swimming)

bolt suddenly to leave home, to desert a spouse, or to bilk your creditors

Like the unmanageable horse. In marriage, usually of a woman leaving her husband:

He mightn't want to send you off, but he'll be jolly pleased now you've bolted. (I. Murdoch, 1978)

And of a debtor:

Matthews was on the point of fleeing his creditors in the usual fashion, by bolting to France. (Ashton, 1991)

bolt the moon see MOONLIGHT FLIT

bombed out under the influence of narcotics or alcohol
Either or both:
    ... he was dropping acid and bombed out of his gourd most of the time on pills and booze. (Sanders, 1977)
A *bomb*, *bomber*, or *bombita* is usually a marijuana cigarette or a dose of cocaine.

bona roba *obsolete* a prostitute
From the fine clothes she wore to attract custom:
    She was then a bona roba. (Shakespeare, *2 Henry IV*, of Jane Nightwork)

bondage sexual activity involving physical restraints or abasement
Literally, a condition of slavery or of being tied up.

bonds of life being gradually dissolved dying slowly
Bath Abbey, from which this example comes, offers many delightful morbid evasions in its epitaphs:
    The Bonds of Life being gradually dissolved She Winged her Flight from this World in expectation of a better, the 15th January, 1810.

bone[1] *obsolete* to steal
Bone may mean a finger, which has overtones of stealing, as in FINGER-BLIGHT, or there could be an allusion to the ossivorous habits of canines:
    From her grave in Mary-bone
    They've come and boned poor Mary. (Hood, c.1830—he worked hard on his puns, of which this is by no means the feeblest)
The modern American *boning*, enrichment through sharp practice, may owe something to improving the edible weight of meat by removing the bone before sale.

bone[2] associated with human death
What is eventually left after burial, along with the teeth, if any. Many obsolete uses such as *bone-house*, a coffin; *bone hugging*, carrying a corpse to a grave; *bone-orchard* or *bone-yard*, a burial ground; etc.:
    ... we usually plant one or two in the bone-orchard before we start for home. (N. Mitford, 1960, writing of a party of elderly tourists)
See also MAKE YOUR BONES.

bone-ache *obsolete* syphilis

Punning perhaps on the symptoms and the *bone*, the penis in old vulgar use.

boner an erection of the penis
From the rigidity:
    She was coming on to me outside the men's room. I've got a boner like Babe Ruth's bat. (Bryson, 1991)

bonk to copulate
The usual violent imagery. Also as a noun:
    Anyway it was worth trying and worth the occasional bonk from the bomb-maker with the bad breath. (Fiennes, 1996)

booby a mentally ill person
Literally, a fool. Usually in a phrase such as *booby hatch* or *hutch*, an institution for the insane:
    A year later the bride was in the booby hatch. (Sohmer, 1988)
    Check the booby hutches ... for escapees. (Sanders, 1981)

booby-trap *American* a garment to contain women's breasts
A possibly ephemeral pun on the slang *boobies*, a woman's breasts, often shortened to *boobs*.

book *American* a sentence in prison
Normally for a year. The derivation might be from a criminal *record*, which is entered for future reference. If the judge *threw the book at you*, you would expect a longer period of confinement than twelve months.

bookmaker a person who accepts bets for a living
Not an author but from a shortened form of the 19th-century *betting-book maker*. Now standard English.

boom-boom[1] *American* defecation
Nursery usage, from the firing of ordnance.

boom-boom[2] copulation
Again from the firing of a gun? That would imply only male activity, but it is used of either sex:
    'No more boom-boom for that mamma-san,' the Marine said, that same tired remark you heard every time the dead turned out to be women. (Herr, 1977)

boom-passenger *obsolete British* a convict sentenced to transportation
Not a libidinous passenger on a cruise but a prisoner chained to the boom on deck while being taken to a penal colony.

boondock *American* to court sexually
Supposedly from the Tagalog *bundok*, a mountain, whence the isolated place where a car

might be parked, and carried home by servicemen serving in the Philippines. *Boondagger*, a female homosexual taking the male role, may be a punning corruption of *boondocker*.

boost¹ *American* to steal

Literally, to give a lift to:

> You were in Fulton Superior Court apologizin' for boosting car radios. (Diehl, 1978)

Whence *booster*, a casual thief:

> I'm usually better at it than the average TV booster. (J. Patterson, 1999)

The articles stolen are concealed in a *booster bag* or *bloomers*.

boost² *American* to make a fraudulent bid at an auction

Again, from giving a lift to something.

boost³ to importune excessively in selling

Pushing too hard:

> Africans living by their wits in Olbia, Chinese seamen boosting lighters in Oristano. (Theroux, 1995)

boot (the) summary dismissal from employment

From the kick to speed the departing servant, which today would land you in court if not in hospital:

> You know they can't sack teachers.
> You've got to do something really drastic before they give you the boot. (Sharpe, 1976)

The British *Order of the Boot* is such dismissal.

boot money a wrongful payment to an amateur in sport

A relic from the days when talented people played sport for fun rather than money and the respective status of amateurs and professionals was strictly regulated. Supposedly the money was left in the player's *boot*, with a suggestion that it was to help pay for his sporting footwear:

> But by the early Eighties under-the-counter payments—such as 'boot money' from kit manufacturers and inflated expenses—became increasingly prevalent. (*Daily Telegraph*, 28 August 1995)

bootleg smuggled or stolen

Originally it referred to intoxicants, supposedly from the bottles concealed on the legs when transporting supplies illegally to American Indians. Standard English of smuggled intoxicants during Prohibition:

> ...had got his hands on some bootleg liquor and was giving a party. (Theroux, 1978)

Now of anything stolen. Also as a verb:

> Do you think...that he might come back and bootleg a copy and give it to you? (Colodny and Gettlin, 1991, reporting the cross-examination of Admiral Welander in 1971)

A *bootlegger* is a smuggler or thief and a *bootlegger turn* is a rapid manoeuvre rotating a car through 180 degrees using the handbrake, to avoid a pursuing vehicle:

> The principal wasn't trained to drive, wouldn't have known how to perform the bootlegger turn. (Seymour, 1999)

boracic *British* indigent

Rhyming slang, *boracic lint*, skint. Usually denoting a temporary embarrassment, when the sufferer may describe himself as *brassic*.

born in... an impolite way of indicating that someone is subject to an imperfection associated with the supposed natal place. Thus *born in a barn* may greet the failure to close a door:

> Henno called him back to ask him to close the door; he asked him if he had been born in a barn. (R. Doyle, 1993)

Born in a mill indicates that the person so designated is not listening or paying attention, rather than that he is deaf. In obsolete use, *born in the vestry* denoted that you were illegitimate, because your parents had not been married in the body of the church.

Borough English *obsolete* a form of disinheriting the eldest son

The subject came up in a discussion on 16 October 1773, concerning *Marcheta Mulierum*, a custom whereby the Lord of the Manor was entitled to *jus primae noctis*:

> Dr Johnson said, the belief that such a custom having existed was also held in England, where there is a tenure called *Borough English*, by which the eldest child does not inherit, from a doubt of his being the son of the tenant. (J. Boswell, 1773—Blackstone in his *Commentaries* disagreed with the omniscient Doctor)

borrow to steal, take, or plagiarize

The loan may be involuntary and the object will be consumed or not returned.

> In the Army it is always considered more excusable to 'win' or 'borrow' things belonging to men from other companies. (F. Richards, 1936)
> Mr B....has made his name in the art world by 'borrowing' from the paintings and sculptures of others. (*Daily Telegraph*, 24 November 2000)

both oars in the water *American* mentally normal
Euphemistic in the negative, from the uneven progress of a boat propelled with one lateral oar:
> They're not exactly demented, but neither Isaac Kane nor Sylvia Mac has both oars in the water. (Sanders, 1985)

both-way having both heterosexual and homosexual inclinations
When you *swing both ways*—see SWING 2:
> Maybe he wasn't a fag. One of those both-way people you were always reading about. (Goldman, 1986)

bother to make unwelcome approaches to
Usually sexual, by a male:
> ...grandma whispering hoarsely, 'Leave me alone, will you?' ...I only knew he was bothering her. (Cookson, 1969—as a child she shared her grandparents' bedroom)

bottle¹ (the) an addiction to intoxicants
Bottles and intemperance have long gone together, especially if the preference is for wines and spirits:
> The bottle was enjoyed by both as a launching pad for the missile of social grace. (Ustinov, 1971)

To *take to the bottle* or *bother the bottle* is to be an alcoholic:
> Mitzi had taken to the bottle, since reality was too bleak for her. (Ustinov, 1966)
> It's not madness to drink in all this, though he bothers the bottle mightily. (Winton, 1994)

The regimen of the baby invites many puns, of which *on the bottle* is most common:
> I doubt whether Mama is particularly fond of sloppy philosophers who are always on the bottle. (Gaarder, 1996, in translation)

To *circulate the bottle* is to invite successive people to drink wine, and to do so *freely* implies drunkenness among them:
> I had dined at the Duke of Montrose's, with a very agreeable party, and his Grace, according to his usual custom, had circulated the bottle freely. (J. Boswell, 1791)

Bottled means drunk:
> We none of us were ever quiet when we was bottled. (Cookson, 1967)

bottle² an act of urination
A shaped glass container is used by a recumbent male in a sickbed:
> You don't want the bottle, or anything like that? You're ready to see your visitor? (Price, 1979, of a hospital patient)

bottle³ to sodomize
Rhyming slang on *bottle and glass*, arse:
> I want to bottle you, mate, Tom says. Kim has never heard the expression but he immediately understands it. (Burroughs, 1984)

bottle⁴ courage
Only euphemistic when you lose it, but not only of DUTCH COURAGE:
> He couldn't face up to the fact that his bottle had gone. (Strong, 1997—he was an adult who had lost his nerve, not a baby crying in a cot)

bottle⁵ *British* to injure with a broken glass bottle used as a weapon
The jargon of aggressive youths who habituate bars and nightclubs:
> People are 'bottled' or 'glassed' for catching a stranger's eye. (*Sunday Telegraph*, 23 January 2000)

bottle blond(e) a woman with hair dyed yellow
The dye or bleach comes in a glass container:
> Wiry bottle blonde with heavy features...(*Daily Telegraph*, 16 June 1995)

bottle club an unlicensed establishment selling alcohol to customers
In theory the diners and others brought their own *bottles* of wine etc.:
> Incidentally, dozens of new bottle clubs—a sort of combination of nightclub and speakeasy—have opened in London in the last two months. (Shirer, 1999, quoting an Ed Murrow broadcast of 18 January 1940)

bottle shop a liquor store
Not selling ketchup or soft drinks;
> Nor were there [in Soweto] any shops, apart from occasional bottle shops and small groceries. (Simpson, 1998)

bottom the buttocks
Literally or physically, the soles of your feet:
> God gave them bottoms to be smacked on. (Bradbury, 1976)

An American *bottom woman* is a pimp's favourite prostitute, which seems illogical until you consider why he should be attracted to her.

bottom line the sticking point in terms of policy or price
The cliché, meaning the end result, comes from the arrangement of a profit and loss account, where the profit, or loss, is the lowest figure. It might appear tautological to state that the *bottom line* is something below which you cannot go, but:

The trouble was that, because Britain's bottom line was so often abandoned, the Chinese assumed it would always be abandoned. (Patten, 1998)

bought and sold *obsolete* bankrupt
The derivation is from the disposal of the debtor's possessions:
> For Dickon thy master is bought and sold. (Shakespeare, *Richard III*)

bounce¹ to copulate
From the motion, especially on a sprung mattress:
> We all bounced about in bed together from time to time and enjoyed it. (Fraser, 1970)
A *bounce*, or *bouncy-bouncy*, is an act of copulation:
> One bounce with that female Russian shotput and you'd bust your truss. (Sharpe, 1977)

bounce² to be dishonoured by non-payment
Referring to cheques, returned to the person who drew them, like a rubber ball dropped to the ground and caught again.

bounce³ to dismiss peremptorily from employment or courtship
From the notional rebounding after hitting another surface, such as the sidewalk:
> If the case is cleared, or I get bounced, the two of you go back to your regular duties. (Sanders, 1985)
A *bouncer* performs the same function at a public gathering, forcibly excluding the unwanted or unruly.

bounce⁴ to persuade by violence
Criminal and police jargon, of extortion, forcibly extracting a confession, etc.:
> You push the victim on the floor. When he comes out this time, we're going to grab him and bounce him a little. Nothing heavy. (Sanders, 1977)

bounce⁵ to induce another hastily to accept an engagement or liability
Without violence, but through persuasion that a quick decision is needed:
> Soviet support for the heavy Cuban involvement in Angola...was achieved...through 'bouncing' the Russians. (*Sunday Telegraph*, November 1983)

bouncers the breasts of an adult woman
A male vulgarism, not of rubber balls, but from the pendulous tendency of breasts when unsupported:
> 'Look at the bouncers on that one.'
> Hosbach smacked his lips, eyeing the new girl. (R. Moss, 1987)

bout an act of copulation
The imagery is from wrestling:
> I was sorry to hear that Sir W. Penn's maid Betty was gone away yesterday, for I was in hope to have had a bout with her before she had gone, she being very pretty. (Pepys, 1662, who added 'I have also a mind to my own wench, but I dare not, for fear she prove honest and refuse and then tell my wife')

bowel movement (a) defecation
Medical jargon:
> Most constipation is 'imagined'. A daily bowel movement can be a needless fetish. (Hailey, 1979)
See also MOVEMENT 1.

bowler hat the discharge, especially prematurely, of an officer from the armed services
What was once the standard business headgear replaces the uniform cap:
> Command in the desert was regarded as an almost certain prelude to a bowler hat. (Horrocks, 1960, writing of the British 8th Army in North Africa)
Now also of civilian premature discharge, and as a verb:
> If Frank had been bowler-hatted and replaced by Bret...(Deighton, 1988)
Those who receive a *golden bowler* are paid well for being retired or leaving early.

box¹ a coffin
Formerly, as a verb also, to place a corpse in a coffin prior to interment:
> Ol Joe Sharman died. Donald made the coffin and they'd boxed him. (Emerson, 1892)

box² a shield for the male genitalia
Mainly sporting use but now also of riot protection gear:
> The cricket boxes issued to constables as items of their 'new protective equipment range' are made of nasty plastic with very little room for accommodation. (*Police*, July, 1981)

box³ *American* the vagina
Viewed sexually by a male, presumably as a temporary container:
> Her box is so big she wouldn't even feel your hand unless you wore a wristwatch. (Wambaugh, 1975)

boy an adult male
Used by and of those seeking to perpetuate an illusion of youthfulness:
> Boy. He must be forty-four. (J. Collins, 1981)

and in a derogatory sense, by white people of
adult black servants:
> My most frequent disguise was as a
> chauffeur, chef or a 'garden-boy'. (Mandela,
> 1994, telling of his period at liberty in 1961
> when evading arrest)

boy scouts *American* state police
They wear clothes reminiscent of a
Baden-Powell scoutmaster and are seen as
enjoying a lower status than other officers of
the law.

boyfriend a male sexual partner
Of almost any age over puberty. Heterosexual
or homosexual:
> ... occasional liaisons which she alluded to
> by saying ... 'He's an old boyfriend of
> mine.' (Theroux, 1976)
> It is not known whether he will take his
> South African boy friend, [a] ballet
> dancer ... with him. (*Private Eye*, March
> 1981)

See also GIRLFRIEND.

boys'¹ (room) a lavatory for exclusive
male use:
Not just for juveniles:
> I went into 'Boys' and looked around.
> (Theroux, 1979)
> You should know we never lock the boys'
> room. (Sharpe, 1977)

boys² any group of men engaged in a ne-
farious or dangerous enterprise
It may be a criminal gang, or those in their
pursuit. Servicemen:
> The boys are busy tonight. (Horne, 1994—a
> bomb had been dropped nearby)

or insurgents, such as the Rhodesian *boys in the
bush*:
> There are still going to be some boys in the
> bush dreaming of marching into Salisbury.
> (*Sunday Telegraph*, December 1970—as
> indeed they did)

or politicians, especially in America, usually
in phrases such as the *boys in the backroom*,
who pull the strings behind the scene and
must not be confused with the *backroom boys*,
who innovate on behalf of their employer; or
as the *boys upstairs*, from the location of many
managerial offices:
> Snyder had appealed to Christiansen for a
> reduction of his weekly quota. Christiansen
> said he'd talk to the boys upstairs.
> (Weverka, 1973)

brace *American* to kill
Literally, to fasten tightly or strengthen.
There is also a slang meaning, to waylay, none
of which gives us a satisfactory etymology:
> You and your friend go up to brace him.
> (Sanders, 1973—they were to kill)

bracer a spirituous intoxicant
Something to strengthen you, you hope.

Brahms *British* drunk
Rhyming slang on *Brahms and Liszt*, pissed. See
also MOZART, which is rarer.

branch water *American* water which is
offered from a bottle
It is supposed to come from an unpolluted
tributary, or *branch*, of a stream, and therefore
not to spoil the taste of your whisky with the
taint of chlorine. Many bartenders depend on
a closer, less costly source.

brass-rags in enmity
Literally, clothes used by sailors for cleaning
on board ship:
> Seems there has been a bit of a tiff between
> the young people before they parted brass-
> rags. (Sayers, 1937)

brasser a prostitute
From the obsolete *brass* (*nail*), rhyming slang
for TAIL 1, which lives on in the cliché *as bold
as brass*:
> [Sex] was in the air ... brassers and
> sailors holding up every corner. (R. Doyle,
> 1999)

brassière a garment to contain women's
breasts
Originally in French a sleeved garment, thus
becoming euphemistic there before the English accepted it to cover the taboo *breasts*
with a double evasion. Now standard English, often shortened to *bra*, pronounced
as the French *bras*, thus completing the
circle.

break a commandment to copulate outside marriage
Yes, the one proscribing adultery:
> Look, there is a pretty man. I could be
> contracted to break a commandment with
> him. (Pepys, 1666—the speaker was the
> 'bonny lass' Lady Robinson)

break luck *American* as a prostitute to
obtain the first customer of the day
Owing nothing to the slang *break a lance*, to
copulate, but probably because her *bad luck*
has ended with the arrival of a customer.

break the news *American* to obtain a confession or other information through
violence
The victim is made aware of the extent of his
predicament:
> 'Breaking the news' ... and numerous other
> phrases are employed by the police ... as
> euphemisms to express how they compel

reluctant prisoners to refresh their
memories. (Lavine, 1930)

break the pale *obsolete* to be promiscuous

The *pale*, as in *paling*, was a piece of wood,
then a fence, then a fenced-in curtilage, and
finally a district under the control of a centre
with hostile natives prowling outside. If you
broke the pale, you were somewhere where you
should not have been:

... he breaks the pale,
And feeds from home. (Shakespeare, *The
Comedy of Errors*)

break the sound barrier *American* to
belch or fart

A pretty tasteless pun.

break wind to belch or fart

Standard English of belching. The taboo about
polite use of the word *fart* is, as these things
go, fairly recent:

A man may break a word with you, sir, and
words are but wind,
Ay, and break it to your face, or he break it
not behind. (Shakespeare, *The Comedy of
Errors*)

In modern use:

I'll kill the first son of a bitch who even
breaks wind. (M. West, 1979)

break your elbow *obsolete* to give birth to
a child outside marriage

The fracture was sometimes caused by a
figurative bed:

And so she broke her elboe against the bed.
(Heath, 1650, of a single woman who had a
child)

If a woman *broke her elbow in the church*, she
was judged not immoral but a bad housekeeper after marriage. A woman who copulated outside marriage was said to *break her
knee*, in a direct translation from a French
euphemism. If she *broke her leg above the knee*,
referring to a ruined horse and the position of
her genitals, she gave birth while unmarried,
the putative father also being said to have
broken his leg:

If her foot slip and down fall she,
And break her leg above the knee.
(Fletcher, 1618)

break your neck to have an urgent desire
to urinate

Normally of a male, without suicidal tendencies. It indicates that *break-neck* speed is
required.

**break your shins against Covent Garden
rails** see COVENT GARDEN

breathe your last to die

Circumlocution and evasion rather than euphemism, as you cannot expect to live
more than two or three minutes after the
event:

... the quicker that one breathed his last,
the better, and I hurried up with my
lance ... and drove it into his throat.
(Fraser, 1969)

For the Nazis, a *breathing problem* was a routine
cause of death given to the family of a
murdered person:

He received notification ... of her death in
Brandenburg from 'breathing problems'.
(Burleigh, 2000—an epileptic woman was
killed as a matter of policy, along with
others who had chronic illnesses, in 1940)

brew¹ *British* to burn

Referring to an armoured vehicle in wartime,
from the brewing of tea by soldiers over an
open fire, often raised by pouring petrol into
sand:

You'll have seen a tank being brewed.
(Seymour, 1980)

A *brew-up* was the infusion of the tea or,
in sardonic humour, the combustion of a
tank:

You would hear the fire order given by the
tank commander as the enemy came into
view. Then—'well done—good shooting—
another brew up.' (de Guingand, 1947)

brew² beer

It is indeed *brewed*, along with many other
substances:

They sat in wicker rockers on the porch,
and opened another round of brew.
(Grisham, 1994)

brewer's goitre frontal obesity in a male

The thyroid gland, from the swelling of which
you may find yourself with a *goitre*, is situated
in the neck, not around the waist:

— the crenellated face, the brewer's
goitre slung under his belt ... (Keneally,
1985—in practice, the belt is usually
slung ineffectively under the pro-
tuberance)

brick short of a load (a) of low intelligence

Of the same tendency as many similar
expressions denoting a shortage from the
norm.

Bridewell *obsolete British* a police station

The original in London was a holy well with
supposed medicinal properties, then a hospital for the poor, then a prison:

Crowley went to the 'nearest Bridewell'
and told the officer of his wife's accusation.
(Pearsall, 1969—his wife had accused him
of raping his daughter)

Bridport dagger *obsolete* a hangman's rope
The Dorset town, with a climate suited to growing flax, was noted for its ropewalks. An inn at Tyburn was so called:
> He was soon chatting up Hangmen and their 'Prentices, while standing them pints at their Local, the Bridport Dagger. (Pynchon, 1997)

If you were *stabbed by a Bridport dagger*, you were hanged.

brief to disclose information which is misleading or incomplete
Literally, to inform another of the relevant facts:
> Washington and London share the same problem between 'briefing' and 'leaking'; the rule of thumb is that a 'leak' is when someone else does it. (Seitz, 1998)

brig a prison
Shortened form of *brigantine*, a ship often used as a naval prison:
> I'm not sure he'll end up in the brig, but he'll lose all rank. (Higgins, 1976)

Civilian as well as military use.

Brighton pier *British* homosexual
Rhyming slang for QUEER 3. There are in fact two such maritime features in the Sussex town.

bring down to kill by shooting
Military and sporting jargon:
> Since 1998. 15,638 partridges and 20,233 pheasants have been brought down. (*Sunday Telegraph*, 9 June 2001)

bring off¹ to cause to achieve a sexual orgasm
Of either sex, by whatever means:
> He remained in her for what seemed like ages...bringing her off again and again. (M. Thomas, 1980)

bring off² to cause the abortion of a foetus
It is physically removed from the mother:
> I was left in the club...like any tiresome little skivvy, but unlike her we were able to arrange to have it brought off. (P. Scott, 1975)

bring your heart to its final pause to die
One of many tiresome Victorian circumlocutions:
> ...and bring his heart to its final pause. (Eliot, 1871)

bristols the breasts of an adult female
Rhyming slang on *Bristol City*, titty, after the soccer team rather than the conurbation:
> Laidback, funloving author, 44, is anxious to meet respectable bit of stuff with big bristols and own teeth. (advertisement in *Private Eye*, November 1988)

broad a sexually complaisant female
The 15th-century adjectival meaning, vulgar, survives only when we speak of humour or the accents of country folk. As a shortened form of *broad woman*, it refers to moral laxity rather than girth:
> Give me some pictures where the good guys get the dough and the broads once in a while. (Deighton, 1972)

broads *obsolete* playing cards
In the days when they were still the Devil's pictures:
> Will you have a...touch of the broads with me? (Mayhew, 1851—it was an invitation to play cards)

broken home a family with young children whose parents have parted
Not a building struck by some natural disaster:
> Lucy was raised in what used to be called a 'broken home'. (Turow, 1996)

bromide job a superficial excuse or explanation
Bromide, either as *sodium bromide* or *potassium bromide*, is given medicinally as a sedative and, by popular myth, to soldiers in their tea to reduce their libido:
> It's only a bromide job, of course; it's not sharp-end work. (Seymour, 1995)

Bronx cheer a fart
Simulated orally or generated anally.

bronze eye the anus
A male homosexual use:
> ...he didn't mind sodomizing a client, but his own bronze eye was closed to all comers. (Fry, 1991)

Also as *second eye*, and not just of the Cyclops.

broomstick match see JUMP THE BROOMSTICK

brother¹ was used in phrases to describe those in less reputable employment or the subject of taboo. Thus a *brother of the bung* was a brewer; a *brother of the gusset* was a pimp; a *brother starling* was someone with whom you shared your mistress; etc.

brother² *American* a black man who may resent a society dominated by whites

Used in the black community:
> ...dude called Washington Lee was a brother, not the house nigger on some editorial board. (McInerney, 1992)

A *blue-eyed brother* is a white man who espouses black militant causes:
> That settled them down. Suddenly I was a blue-eyed brother. (Grisham, 1999—he was a white lawyer working among poor blacks)

See also SISTER 2.

brown¹ the anus

Usually in the derisive phrase *in your brown*:
> Yeh do in your brown, said Anto.—He asked yeh do yeh drink in the Hikers, not do yeh sit on the wall outside. (R. Doyle, 1991)

brown² to sodomize

The imagery needs no elaboration:
> Did he brown yeh, Jimmy? Outspan asked.—No He just ran his fingers through me curly fellas. (R. Doyle, 1987)

brown envelope a bribe

The cover in which it is handed over is unidentifiable:
> He should provide introductions to those who might be slipped a brown envelope. (Seymour, 1998)

brown-hatter a male homosexual

With an implication of buggery:
> A lot of brown-hatters and word merchants...(Sharpe, 1974)

Less often as a verb:
> Harrison's lot are a lot of wankers and Slymne's go in for brown-hatting. (Sharpe, 1982)

See also DICK'S HATBAND.

brown-nose to flatter

Not from exposure to the sun but from the figurative proximity of your proboscis to the anal area of the object of your sycophancy:
> Hungerford—you missed the beginning but this is a course you can't fail so there is no need for brown-nosing. (Goldman, 1984—a pupil had been flattering his teacher)

A *brown-noser* or *brown-nose* so acts:
> What a little brown-noser. What do you want from Daddy? (J. Patterson, 1999)
> Unit Two, a cadre of teacher's pets captained by the infamous brownnose Iovescu, sat firmly atop the heap. (Furst, 1988)

A toady may figuratively replace his *nose* with his *tongue*:
> Also his tongue was busy and almost perfectly brown. (de Bernières, 1994, describing an obsequious officer)

brown stuff (the) faeces

Normally only figurative use:
> If anyone realizes I'm helping you, the brown stuff could fall on me from a great height. (Strong, 1997)

brown sugar heroin

A variant of SUGAR 3, from the colour:
> 'What are you using these days, Bones?' 'A little brown sugar now and again, you know, keep my head straight.' (Follett, 1996)

brownie a spirituous intoxicant

Whisky or brandy, not vodka or gin, from the colour, and owing nothing to the nocturnal elf:
> I had to toddle off to the sherbert cupboard and administer a stiff brownie and water. (*Private Eye*, July 1981)

In America a *brownie* may be no more than a roast potato:
> He ate two brownies, clearing the plate. (Grisham, 1999)

brownie points the supposed rewards of currying favour with your superiors

Baden-Powell's *Brownies*, whose name puns on the colour of the uniform and the benevolence of the creatures who perform good deeds around the home by night, win promotion, to the exalted position of sixer or beyond, through the award of points for good works or achievement:
> Then you'll find out who slid the blade into Sidney Leonides. And you'll get brownie points for clearing a homicide. (Sanders, 1987)

browse to steal and consume food within a store

The thief adopts the feeding habits of a ruminant, carrying his booty past the checkout desk in his stomach.

brushfire war a conflict in which a major power is not directly involved

It involves figuratively the undergrowth rather than the standing timber:
> The language of the mad foments violence...'Brushfire wars', 'limited actions', 'clean atom bombs'. (M. West, 1979)

brute *obsolete American* a bull

A shortened form of COW BRUTE, from the days of prudery about bulls. See also BIG ANIMAL for further evasions.

bubble to inform against

Rhyming slang for *sneak*, from *bubble and squeak*, the fried dish of cabbage and potato:

Someone will bubble. Someone always does. (le Carré, 1993)

bucket¹ a place for defecation
A male usage, especially where a smaller receptacle is provided for urination inside communal living quarters. Some figurative usage:
> Get off the bucket. I'm serious. (Theroux, 1978)

bucket² *British* a prison
Rhyming slang on *bucket and pail*, jail.

bucket³ to kill by drowning
A way of disposing of an excess of kittens:
> Hadn't someone better bucket them at once? (N. Mitford, 1960—they were newly-born kittens)

bucket shop an insubstantial vendor of overvalued securities or cut-price services
Not an ironmonger, but selling bombed-out shares or empty airline seats.

budget cheap
Advertising jargon. The implication is that the cost will not exceed the amount which you have allocated for the purpose.

buff¹ the bare skin
A shortened form of (flenched) *buffalo*, used of in phrases such as *to the buff* and *in the buff* to describe human nakedness, especially when that condition is taboo:
> I went home directly, stripped to the buff, and fell into bed. (Sanders, 1992)
> Nudity was nothing special in our circle; over the years many of the painters and their friends posed for one another in the buff. (Rushdie, 1995)

To *buff* was to strip:
> I didn't 'buff it'; that is, I didn't take my shirt off. (Mayhew, 1851)

buff² *obsolete* to copulate with
The common imagery of rubbing:
> I wor fit for booath cooartin' and buffin'. (Mather, 1862)

bug¹ to conceal an apparatus for eavesdropping
From the size, colour, and shape of the device:
> He was ready to give me permission to bug his church pew. (Diehl, 1978)

bug² *American* a mark indicating the use of union labour in manufacture
Mainly in the printing trade, but also once found on Canadian beer cans.

bug-eyed drunk

Referring to the protrusion of the eyeballs:
> Victor did not deny his condition. 'Banjaxed, bombed, bug-eyed, and bingoed,' he said without slurring his words. (Deighton, 1993/2)

bug out *American* to retreat
From the slang meaning, to quit rapidly. *Bug-out fever*, in the Korean War, was cowardice:
> 'Bug-out fever', the urge to withdraw precipitately in the face of the slightest threat from the flank... (M. Hastings, 1987)

Buggins' turn *British* promotion on the grounds of seniority rather than merit
The mythical *Buggins* is an incompetent or unambitious employee who stays a long while in the same job:
> ...the attempt [in 1937] to break up the prevailing system of Buggins' turn and bring forward dynamic, progressive, unorthodox leaders. (Keegan, 1991, writing about the British army)

bughouse mentally unbalanced
Perhaps from the insects figuratively buzzing round in the head:
> It's enough to make a man bughouse when he has to play a part from morning to night. (A. C. Doyle, 1917)

The noun in America denotes an institution for the mentally ill:
> You're bigger bloody fools than anybody outside a bughouse. (Marsh, 1941)

bugle an erection of the penis
Presumably because it is rigid and can be played upon:
> He could've given himself a bugle now, out here in the hall, just remembering what she was like and her smile. (R. Doyle, 1991)

bulge an indication of sexual arousal in a male
Seen through an outer garment, but not a pot belly:
> She thought she saw the bulge of him, and she believed she had control of him. (Seymour, 1997)

bull¹ (of a male) to copulate with
The function for which uncastrated animals are preserved:
> He would guarantee all the female slaves had been bulled by his crew. (Fraser, 1971)

bull² a promiscuous male
From his bovine habits:
> He is the village bull. The women dare not refuse him. (Manning, 1960—he was also a priest)

bull³ egocentric boasting

A shortened form of *bullshit*, with the same meaning, or, in America, *bull-rinky*:

> You're full of bull this morning. (Steinbeck, 1961)
> I come to ask you why my boy died, and you trot out that same bull-rinky about communists you always trot out at election time. (Anonymous, 1996)

A *bullshitter* is someone who boasts or acts officiously.

The letters *BS* are used for *bullshit* and *bullshitter*, in all senses as noun or verb:

> He was a great romancer and wrote the biggest BS of them all. (F. Richards, 1933)
> ...sitting around, BS-ing, talking about how law school was coming. (Goldman, 1986)

The 19th-century *bull-scutter* was 'anything worthless or nasty' (*EDD*).

bull⁴ *American* a policeman

Originally a detective, probably from his aggressive behaviour:

> Only on rare occasion will the cop...offer any information to the 'bull' or 'dick'. (Lavine, 1930)

The word is now applied to any armed protector of property.

bull⁵ a female homosexual taking the male role

A shortened form of *bull-dyke*:

> So you gave that old bull a key. (Theroux, 1976, writing about a female homosexual)
> I know the model. Bull dyke. (Sanders, 1977)

bull pen *American* a prison

Where the BULL 4 puts his victims:

> ...ordered them thrown into the bull pen. (Lavine, 1930—some men had been arrested)

It is also any common dormitory for males.

bullet (the) peremptory discharge from employment

What happens when they FIRE you. Only in spy fiction is the gun loaded:

> ...never knowing whether they're getting a medal or a bullet. (le Carré, 1980)

bum *American* a vagrant or beggar is not a euphemism, being a shortened form of *bummer*, from the German *bummeln*, to stroll or idle, whence to tramp, and not from *bum*, the buttocks. The obsolete Scottish *bum*, a coarse woman, predates that etymology. *Bum* is also slang for worthless, whence perhaps its use of a cheap prostitute. *Bum-fighting*, copulation, probably comes from the mean-

ing buttocks, as does *bum-bandit*, a male homosexual. A *bum-boy* does not work on a *bum-boat* but is a catamite:

> He was also a bum-boy and sold himself. (Dodds, 1991)

bum-fodder lavatory paper

The jocular term has given rise to a shortened form, *bumf* or *bumph*, an excess of paperwork or documentation:

> Astounding how the bumph accumulated even after a short absence. (Grayson, 1975)

bump¹ (the) peremptory dismissal from employment

The displacement is sudden:

> They got bumped off the staff of the hospital. (Chandler, 1939)

bump² *American* to induce an employee to leave employment

In a situation where the employer would pay heavily for the dismissal of an employee, the technique is to *bump* him within the organization from one job to another, each more unpleasant or demeaning than the last, until he leaves of his own accord.

bump³ (the) pregnancy

Literally, any swelling of the body, usually caused by a blow. A *bumper* is not the putative father but a stripper in a stage show.

bump⁴ to copulate

From the pushing of the bodies against each other:

> One could imagine brother and sister bumping like frogs in broad daylight. (Theroux, 1978—they committed incest)

Occasionally also as *bump bones*.

bump⁵ (off) to kill

The blow is fatal:

> I don't go around bumping everyone I meet, you know. (Keneally, 1985)
> 'He had to take risks.' 'Like bumping chaps off?' (le Carré, 1980)

A *bump* is such a killing, possibly by a *bumpman*, a professional assassin:

> Normal routine in the case of a bump is to stay clear. (Hall, 1969, referring to a murder)

bump⁶ to cause a pre-booked passenger to travel by a later aircraft

Airlines routinely overbook seats if they can, to allow for the frequent NO-SHOW. If too many passengers turn up, the last arrivals or the most docile are left off the flight:

> 17 passengers were 'bumped' in all: although after the desk closed he heard the girl being told to allow for six to eight extra

Sudan Airways personnel on the flight.
(*Private Eye*, December 1981)

bun¹ a prostitute

The still current mariner's fetish about mentioning the word *rabbit* before a voyage to
ward off ill luck dates from the time when
fraudulent chandlers supplied cheap rabbit
meat, which doesn't keep when salted, for
pork, which does. The superstitious had,
before a trip, to touch the tail of a hare or, if
none were to hand, the pubic hair of a
woman, including one who might for a fee
allow hers to be touched. Thus the *bun*, a
shortened form of *bunny* (the diminutive for
the rabbit), came to mean the hair and the
prostitute.

See also BUTTERED BUN.

bun² a lump of faeces

From the shape in the highway:
> ...the crunchy snow which is spread
> here and there with cinders from
> people's furnaces and dotted here and
> there with frozen horse buns. (Atwood,
> 1988)

bun in the oven (a) pregnancy

Punning on the rising of cake mixture and the
growth of the foetus:
> I rather fancied she had a bun in the oven.
> (Theroux, 1971—she was not a cook)

bun on (get/have/tie a) to be or become
drunk

Perhaps a shortened form of *bundle*, a quantity
of anything:
> We'll celebrate tonight, if you do. And if
> you don't, well, then we'll tie a bun on
> anyway, just to forget it all. (van Druten,
> 1954)

bun-puncher *British* a person who never
drinks intoxicants

Army usage, in a society where abstention
from intoxicants can be as taboo as drunkenness in civilian life:
> If a teetotaller he was known as a 'char-
> wallah', 'bun-puncher' or 'wad-shifter'.
> (F. Richards, 1933)

bunch of fives a fist used as a weapon

Less often it means an open hand used for
chastisement:
> Wright did not hesitate to call his pupils'
> attention to his 'bunch of fives', a term he
> was specially fond of using to denote his
> powerful hand, which might now and
> again come into palpable contact with a
> pupil's cheek. (E. M. Wright, 1934, writing
> about her husband, Joseph, who edited the
> *EDD*)

bundle *obsolete American* to copulate with
your sweetheart before marriage

Similar customs to that described below
prevailed in Scotland and elsewhere, in
country districts and with parental consent:
> The New England custom of 'bundling',
> namely the supposedly chaste lying in
> bed together of young, affectionate,
> unmarried persons of opposite sexes for
> the sake of company and the saving of
> fuel...(Graves, 1941, writing of the 18th
> century)

And in English North Country use:
> My God! do you expect me to bundle with
> that 'un? (Cookson, 1967)

bung¹ *obsolete* a drunkard

Literally, a stopper for a cask:
> Away...you filthy bung. (Shakespeare, *2
> Henry IV*)

A drunkard might be said to have been to
Bungay Fair, punning on the Suffolk market
town.

bung² a bribe

The notes are literally or figuratively *bunged*
into a pocket. *Bung* is used specifically in
Britain for illegal cash payments made when a
footballer transfers to a new club:
> Arsenal sack Graham over cash 'bung' for
> transfer. (*Daily Telegraph*, 22 February
> 1995—Graham was Arsenal's manager)

bung up and bilge free *British* copulating

Naval usage, from the recommended way of
storing a cask of rum aboard ship, whence
anything in good order. The *bung* puns on the
orifice rather than on a method of contraception:
> I used to be bung but now I'm pill.
> (Bradbury, 1976—referring to contracep-
> tion)

bunk flying *American* boasting

Air force usage. The daring exploits which you
relate are dreamed or otherwise invented in
bed.

bunny¹ an unmarried sexual companion

Homosexual or heterosexual, in the former
case taking the female role. The use comes
from the pet name given to someone who
may share the timid character of the rabbit.
Also descriptive of females, in many
phrases denoting the venue, such as *beach*,
jazz, *ski*, or *surf bunny*.

bunny² a towel worn during menstruation

From its shape and feel. Whence the
Australian *buns on*, menstruating.

bunny hugger a person obsessed with the welfare of a selective choice of non-human mammals

Foxes, rabbits, and badgers score more highly than rats and mice. A dysphemism, especially among the practitioners of COUNTRY SPORTS:

Judging from letters sent to the Press, many bunny-huggers believe that the average mink lives the life of a fur-clad Buddhist monk. (Robin Page in *Daily Telegraph*, 6 September 1998—those describing themselves as animal lovers had released some 6,000 mink from captivity in the unfulfilled hope or expectation that the predators would live a vegetarian life of self-denial and peaceful coexistence among the native fauna)

Burke *obsolete* to murder

The celebrated Irishman killed people to replenish his stock of corpses which he sold for medical research until he was hanged in Edinburgh in 1829. The modern usage as a mild insult, usually spelt *berk*, comes via rhyming slang from the *Berkshire* or *Berkeley Hunt*, viewed figuratively and not anatomically.

burn¹ *obsolete* to infect with venereal disease

The sensation of one of the symptoms felt by the male, especially when urinating:

Light wenches will burn. Come not near her. (Shakespeare, *The Comedy of Errors*)

A man who *burned his poker* was so infected and a *burner* was the infection.

burn² *American* to kill

Originally, by electrocution, from the singeing of the contact points on the corpse. Latterly, of any death, especially by shooting:

Do you really think Knox burned Kipper and Stonehouse? (Sanders, 1980)

burn³ to extort from or to cheat

Probably a shortened form of *put the burn on*, to compel, through figurative application of HEAT 1 or by physically contra-rotating the skin at the wrist:

I thought he was the one who burned me. (Theroux, 1976, writing of a cheat)

In narcotic jargon, it may mean to take money for illicit supplies and fail to deliver, or to give information to the authorities about another's addiction.

burn with a (low) blue flame *American* to be very drunk

The imagery is from a dying fire, about to go out.

burra peg see CHOTA PEG

burst to have an urgent need to urinate

With a full bladder; a shortened form of the phrase *bursting for a pee*. Occasionally as *bust*.

bury to inter (a corpse)

So long standard English that we assume the thing buried is a dead body, unless we elaborate by saying *buried alive*. So too with *burial*, with its assumption of prior death.

bury a Quaker *obsolete* to defecate

A *Quaker* for the Irish was a turd, perhaps from their brown clothing. A *Quaker's burial ground* was a lavatory, and a tasteless pun.

bush the pubic hair

Of male or female, with obvious imagery:

The small, trimmed bush, soft as down...(Sanders, 1982, describing a naked female)

bush-house *obsolete British* a house selling intoxicants

Often opening on fair or market days, it signalled its availability by hanging a bush outside:

Starting from the 'Bush-house' where he had been supping too freely on the fair-ale. (*EDD*, quoting a source from 1886)

Whence the proverb *Good wine needs no bush*.

bush marriage a marriage performed without due ceremony

In a remote place where the trappings of the traditional ceremony are unavailable:

...most of them were bush marriages performed by some joker wearing a coconut mask and a feathered jock-strap. (Sanders, 1977)

bush patrol *American* an al fresco sexual encounter

Punning on the pubic hair, the remote location, and the military exercise.

bushwhack to ambush

Literally, to hack a path through woods or to propel a craft by pulling on overhanging foliage:

...had bush-whacked a Russian baggage train and were busy looting it. (Fraser, 1973)

business any taboo or criminal act

It may refer to defecation or, less often, urination, by humans or animals; to sexual activity; to killing; to illegal drug use; etc.

Frensic finished his business in the lavatory. (Sharpe, 1977—Frensic was not a plumber)

Clem, a pedigree Labrador, evidently feeling at home, did his business. (Sharpe, 1976)

A 5.9 dropped in his trench, while he was
absent on a business essential to health.
(Mark VII, 1927, writing of the First World
War)
This was the first time they'd done the
business in a good while; two months
nearly. Made love. (R. Doyle, 1991)
Mine was a large lady, already in the
business for some time. (Londres, 1928, in
translation)
...you'd tried to give the Führer the
business. (Price, 1978—someone had tried
to kill Hitler)
In the jargon of prostitution, a *business woman*
is a prostitute.

bust¹ financially ruined
Literally, broken. Standard English.

bust² to arrest during a police raid
Again from the concept of breaking:
    Professor Philip Swallow...was among
    sixteen people arrested on Saturday...'I've
    never been busted before,' he said. (Lodge,
    1975)
A *bust* is such a raid:
    In the busts, the FBI captured a shoulder-
    fired rocket launcher, Semtex explosives,
    hand-grenade canisters, eleven pipe
    bombs, and an arsenal of M-14 rifles.
    (Evans-Pritchard, 1997)

bust³ a drunken carouse
Either broke or broken after it.

bust a cap to ingest illegal narcotics
From the breaking of the seal on the
container.

bust a string to become mentally unbalanced
Probably alluding to tennis rather than playing a fiddle:
    I thought that owl had bust a string. I
    thought its body-clock was out of sync. But
    there you go. Owls are smarter than
    squirrels. (O'Hanlon, 1996)

bust bodice a garment for holding women's breasts
A *bodice* is a garment which covers the upper
parts of the body. Barely euphemistic, except
when shortened to *BB*:
    Others have compared them to Madonna's
    bust bodice. (A. Waugh in *Daily Telegraph*,
    14 December 1994—they were two brick
    cones containing a theatre)
    Start-rite shoes for Wills and Rory,
    summer vest for Aunt Dolly, esoteric
    haberdashery for the Duchy...BBs for
    Clary and Polly. (Howard, 1993, giving
    a shopping list from the Second World
    War)

The usage lapsed rather when Brigitte Bardot
appeared on the scene.

busy *British* a policeman
Probably a shortened form of *busybody*, a nosy
or interfering person:
    ...don't hang around. The bloody street's
    alive with busies. (Kersh, 1936)
    His mother was head of the local civic
    association, a busybody who had led a
    campaign to stop construction of a
    synagogue in their leafy, affluent, very
    Catholic neighbourhood. (Evans-Pritchard,
    1997)

butch (of a female) masculine
A shortened form of *butcher* and not from an
old Manx word meaning witch. A woman so
described may also be a homosexual playing
the male role. Rarely of homosexual men:
    He marked them down as two very butch
    guys. (B. Forbes, 1986)

butler's perks opened but unfinished
bottles of wine
Not always decanted and kept for future use
by the master:
    From time to time Kenneally was liable to
    over indulge in "butler's perks", as half-
    empty bottles of wine are sometimes
    referred to in country houses. (*Daily
    Telegraph*, 30 October 1999)

buttered bun a woman who has copulated successively with more than one
man
Usually a prostitute, owing nothing to the
American *butt*, the buttocks, but a lot to BUN 1.

butterfly a male homosexual
From the light and pretty appearance of the
diurnal insect:
    ...if it ever comes out that Dunce's top
    aide is a butterfly, it's not going to do
    his candidacy any good. (Sanders, 1984)

buttock *obsolete* to copulate
Perhaps with a *buttock and twang*, a prostitute;
not, you hoped, with a *buttock and file*, because
she would rob you. A *buttock ball* was copulation (Grose). You had to pay *buttock-mail* if you
committed adultery:
    Yer buttock-mail and yer stool of
    repentance. (W. Scott, 1814)

button¹ **(man)** *American* a professional
killer
Presumably you press him for action:
    Know what a button is, DeLoroza? A
    shooter. (Diehl, 1978)
    His head was alive and jumping with
    notions of button men. (M. Thomas, 1980)

button² *American* a policeman
He wears them on his uniform:
> The buttons won't have any time to
> worry about what's going on down on
> East 55th Street. (Sanders, 1980)

buy to secure the services of a prostitute
The precise nature of the accord and satisfaction is not stipulated:
> A geisha of the first or second tier cannot
> be bought for a single night. (Golden, 1997)
See also BUY LOVE.

buy a brewery to become an alcoholic
Or as much of its produce as you can drink:
> Then the jackaroo married the station and
> bought a brewery. (Kyle, 1988—he married
> the owner and became a drunkard)

buy it to be killed or wounded in action
A military usage, from acquiring the missile
which hits you:
> They bought it—all except me. I'd gone for
> a walk... you know, with a spade.
> (Manning, 1978, writing of soldiers killed
> in the Western Desert)
The American *buy the farm* is to be killed, from
the dream occupation on retirement:
> Who knows when M.M. will buy the farm?
> (Deighton, 1982—M.M. was a fighter pilot)

buy love to copulate with a prostitute
Normally of heterosexual encounters:
> 'I don't buy love,' I warned her, 'but how
> much do you generally get?' 'From one
> dollar to five.' (F. Harris, 1925)

buyer a person addicted to illegal narcotics
Addict jargon—he also probably buys food
and clothing from time to time:
> The label is drugs—Converse was a heavy
> buyer. (Ludlum, 1984)

buzz on (a) drunk or under the influence
of narcotics
From the ringing in the ears or general air of
excitement:
> ... we'd drink, get a little buzz on, and then
> go into the ocean to swim and sober up.
> (Theroux, 1973)
Whence *buzzed*, drunk:
> He seemed a trifle buzzed when he
> arrived, blew the ceremony several
> times, most noticeably when he
> forgot the business with the
> ring. (Goldman, 1984—the priest was
> drunk)

by(e) *obsolete* an indication of illegitimacy
Literally, ancillary. A *by(e)-blow*, *-chap-*, *-scape*,
etc. indicated illegitimate birth of one who
was *by(e)-come*, *-begot*, etc.:
> I really was a niece of a one-time
> Governor and not some by-blow of
> Lili Chatterjee's family. (P. Scott, 1973)
By(e)-courting, by a male, was done deceitfully
without any intention of marriage:
> Bitterly did I regret I had done my
> by courtings so near home. (Crockett,
> 1896)
In Scotland a *by(e)-shot* was an elderly unmarried woman, not always as a result of Cupid's
bad marksmanship:
> If she cannot restrain her loquacity, she is
> in danger of hearing the reproach of a by-
> shot. (Tarras, 1804)

by yourself mad
In a world of your own, perhaps:
> But monie a day he was by
> himself, He was so sairly frighted.
> (Burns, 1785)
We retain the usage in the expression *by* (or
beside) *himself with rage*.

C

C anything taboo beginning with the letter C

It is used for cancer, which is also referred to as the BIG C, or for cocaine or CRACK 3. US army laxatives in the Second World War were called CC pills, the equivalent of the British NUMBER NINE.

cabbage to steal

Cabbages were odd snippets or spare lengths of cloth which were traditionally the perquisite of tailors, who sometimes consigned good material into that category. The term than passed into, and has stayed in, general use, mainly of pilfering:

If I cabbage that ring tonight, I shall be all the richer tomorrow. (*N&Q*, 1882)

cadge *obsolete* to steal

The linguistic progression appears to have been from selling as an itinerant vendor to stealing, then to our modern meaning, to sponge or beg:

A thieving set of magpies—cadgin' 'ere and cadgin' there. (M. Ward, 1895)

cage a prison

Dangerous convicts in the 19th century wore yellow clothes, at a time when a canary was a popular pet. The imagery also comes, as with CHOKEY and other slang words for prison, from reference to a confined space.

California widow *obsolete American* a deserted wife

Her husband might literally or metaphorically have left her to strike gold elsewhere. *California blankets* in the Great Depression were newspapers used to pad clothing for warmth, as they are still used by those sleeping rough.

call (the) death

Your God needs you elsewhere:

I preached... in the evening to a still more serious congregation at Stoke (? Chew Stoke); where Mr Griffin is calmly waiting for the call that summons him to Abraham's bosom. (John Wesley, 1780, quoted in Bush, 1997)

The past participle of the verb, *called*, is usually amplified by the addition of a sporting destination, such as *home* or *away*:

He had been ca'ed away atween the contract an' the marriage. (J. M. Wilson, 1836—the *contract* was the betrothal)

Called to higher service embodies in one phrase an avoidance of a direct reference to death, an implication that the dead person was specifically summoned by a deity, the hint of meritorious deeds of a religious nature on earth, and the acknowledgement that heaven is the destination where the good work will continue:

In March, 1875, Mr Empson was stricken down with paralysis, and was called to higher service on June 28th the next year. (Tyrrell, 1973)

call a soul *obsolete* to announce a death

The *calling* was done from a flat tombstone in the churchyard after matins:

Last Sunday fwornuin, after service...
the clerk caw'd his seale. (R. Anderson, 1805)

call down *obsolete* to announce publicly that you will not pay your wife's debts

A relic from the days when the wife's possessions passed to her husband on marriage and all she retained was the right to pledge his credit for food and clothing for the home. The *calling down* was done by the town crier and from then on, in theory at least, the husband had no responsibility for paying further debts contracted by his wife. Failing the town crier, a notice might be inserted to the same effect in a local newspaper, as sometimes happened in Britain within living memory.

call girl a prostitute

Originally operating from a CALL HOUSE, but the name became more applicable to those summoned by telephone:

A low church missionary who was discovered as being the business manager of a ring of syphilitic call-girls. (Ustinov, 1971)

A *call-boy*, who once did no more than make sure actors did not miss their cues, is a male prostitute:

He made an additional two hundred as a call-boy for discriminating gay customers. (Wambaugh, 1981)

Call-button girl is obsolete:

Prostitutes, 'call-button girls' as they call themselves, roam from airport to airport. (Moynahan, 1983)

call house *American* a brothel

Where you originally found the CALL GIRL:

... it's no worse than playing the piano in a call house. (Perelman, 1937)

call of nature the need to urinate or defecate

The visit demanded by your bodily functions:

I was probably off the road, behind the bush, answering a call of nature. (Follett, 1978)

'When nature calls, heh, heh, heh,' he'd
said...and made his way out into the trees.
(M. Thomas, 1980)

call off all bets to die
When, under certain conditions, a horse
is withdrawn from a race, all wagers are
invalid.

call out to challenge to a duel
The contest took place in the open air, and
those who pick a quarrel still invite their
opponent to 'come outside':
> If you were not my brother I'd call you out
> for saying that. (Deighton, 1987—a son had
> spoken disparagingly of their father)

call the tricks to solicit as a prostitute
A TRICK is the customer:
> They weren't allowed to call the tricks
> like the girls in Storeyville. (L. Armstrong,
> 1955)

caller (a) menstruation
A usage which uses the same imagery of
interruption as the more common VISITOR.

callisthenics in bed copulation
Callisthenics is training in graceful movement:
> ...other than callisthenics in bed, and
> from some rumours I hear, you're getting
> plenty of that. (Hailey, 1979, describing a
> libertine)

calorie counter a fat person
Advertising jargon, suggesting that the physical condition is not due to gluttony, the lack
of exercise, and so on:
> ...don't risk offending them by calling
> them fat. Their ads are addressed to
> 'weight watchers' and 'calorie counters'.
> (Jennings, 1965)

camel a smuggler of illegal narcotics
It describes those operating from Africa,
where you are unlikely to find a MULE, into
Europe:
> Algeciras is known as 'the marijuana
> gateway to Europe', being the unloading
> point from Tangier and the Ceuta
> enclave for most 'camels'; the jeep and
> truck drivers of hash loads from the Rif.
> (Fiennes, 1996)

camp homosexual
Originally it described male homosexuality,
but now refers to either sex. The origin is
obscure, which gives free rein to speculation
among etymologists. Ware suggests that it is
'probably from the French' who are naturally
blamed for things of which we may disapprove. Partridge urged us to consult the *EDD*,
but which of Dr Wright's definitions caught

his fancy is hard to decide: 'gyrating in the
air', 'gossiping', 'a heap of potatoes or turnips
earthed up in order to be kept throughout the
winter': we can only guess. The progression
from using exaggerated gestures to male
homosexuality is well documented in the
OED:
> The red shadow is at large. Did you ever see
> anything quite so camp? (P. Scott, 1975—
> the dialogue about a male homosexual in
> 1946 was probably anachronistic,
> especially when placed in India)

To *camp it up* in Britain means no more than to
accentuate or display male homosexual characteristics; in America it may imply participation in group male homosexual activity. To
camp about can mean no more than to act
jokingly:
> ...just words, they weren't meant
> seriously. I was just camping about.
> (Bogarde, 1981)

camp down with to live with as a sexual
partner
Permanence is implied in the arrangement
without any suggestion that it is under canvas
or homosexual:
> Race left Linda with a weeks old baby
> and camped down with his House of
> Commons harpie/secretary. (*Private Eye*,
> July 1981)

camp follower a prostitute
Those who provided goods and services for an
army marched with it:
> ...to prevent their men from contracting
> certain indelicate social infections
> from...hem hem—female camp-followers
> of a certain sort. (Fraser, 1975, writing in
> 19th-century style)

can¹ *American* a lavatory
Originally, a bucket. Now used of any kind of
plumbing sophistication:
> Snyder had paced the small office and
> gone to the can a couple of times.
> (Weverka, 1978)

can² *American* to dismiss from place or
employment
Figuratively, being put in the *ash-can* rather
than flushed down the CAN 1:
> He worked for maybe a month and then he
> was canned. (Sanders, 1980)

Also used of dismissal from academia for
misconduct or underachievement.

can³ *American* a prison
Literally, a container. Usually of a short-stay
lock-up or a confined cell:
> You wanna sit in the can for twenty years?
> (Weverka, 1973, seeking to emphasize the
> rigours of close confinement)

can on (a) drunkenness
The phrase antedates the practice of drinking beer out of cans, and refers to intoxication from any cause. See also CANNED.

canary[1] *obsolete* a convict
Some were obliged to wear yellow clothes and lived in figurative cages. A canary was also a female accomplice to a crime in 19th-century London:
> Sometimes a woman, called a 'canary', carries the tool and waits outside. (Mayhew, 1862)

canary[2] a sexually available female
The common avian imagery, although she might also be a singer:
> Canary... for woman is just used in smart fiction about jazz. (Longstreet, 1956)

canary[3] an informer to the police
From the cliché *sing like a canary*, and see SING:
> And they were as pretty a pair of canaries as you could ever hope to meet. You could hear them singing to the KGB before you were out of the room. (R. Harris, 1998)

canary trap a stratagem used to detect those who abstract, copy, and circulate confidential documents
A way to catch a CANARY 3 who informs political associates or journalists rather than the authorities:
> What about internal security... the project documents?... You mean canary traps?... You use the machine to make subtle alterations in each copy of important papers. (Clancy, 1988)

candy illegal narcotics
At one time *candy* was cocaine, and then embraced marijuana or LSD on a sugar lump. *Nose candy* is a narcotic in powdered form:
> C'mon t'daddy little girl. C'mon an' get your nose candy. (J. Collins, 1981)
The punning *candy man* or *candy store* is a dealer in illegal drugs:
> 'Well,' said the kid with the buzz cut, 'if you ain't a candy store, there's a couple guys watching sure think you are.' (Koontz, 1997)

canhouse *American* a brothel
The derivation may be from the slang *can*, the buttocks:
> The little girls, looking so sweet and demure, knew all the words for canhouses... and seemed ready to illustrate them with anyone. (Longstreet, 1956)
The use of *can* to mean a prostitute may be a back derivation from *canhouse*, or vice versa.

canned drunk
The usual culinary imagery, also owing something to having a CAN ON. *Half-canned* means the same thing.

canned goods *American* a virgin
Describing an adult female, untainted (or free of disease) and unopened (with maidenhead intact). Occasionally of a male.

cannon a pickpocket
We are faced with two tributaries to this etymological stream. Some maintain that the derivation comes from the thief bumping into his victim, causing him to stumble, which enables the thief to take the wallet or watch in the confusion, with imagery from the billiards or pool table. The older general meaning, a thief, comes from the Yiddish *gonif*, whence the shortened *gon*, whence *gun*, whence *cannon*.

canoe *American* to copulate with
If a young man took a woman for a trip in such a craft, there was no room for a chaperone, which gave them unwonted seclusion when they went ashore:
> Her Old Man... had been hearing about me and Daisy canoeing from the first night we'd got together. (L. Armstrong, 1955—they were not into aquatic sports)
Canoodle, to fondle sexually, dates from the mid-19th century, which means it is not a compound of *canoe* and *cuddle*:
> Helen had fallen from a balcony while... canoodling with a Dutch sea captain. (*Private Eye*, May 1981)

canteen medal an exposed trouser fly button
Originally, a wine cellar, a *canteen* acquired its general use as a public place of refreshment, and especially for British servicemen who expressed disdain for any medal awarded other than for an act of bravery.

capital involving killing
Literally, of the head but now seldom referring to beheading. A *capital crime* is one which involves a killing, leading to a *capital charge* before the court and, upon conviction in some parts of the world, to *capital punishment*, death, which in some American states will take place in a *capital sentences unit*.

capon *American* a male homosexual
Literally, a castrated cock. In obsolete use it meant a eunuch.

captain is at home (the) I am menstruating
A red coat was once worn by British officers.

card¹ *obsolete Irish* to punish by laceration

A 19th-century toothed tool for combing wool was a weapon used to harm those who assisted unpopular or absentee landlords:

> The widows...who...had paid their rents in full were visited a party of women with blackened faces and were 'carded'—had sheep's combs drawn through their flesh. (Kee, 1993)

card² an argument supported by prejudice or favouritism

The *card*, with a suitable prefix such as *race* or *Welsh*, is *played* to win a trick unfairly:

> When Peter Walker played the 'Welsh' card yet again, I dictated him a note and Carys translated it into Welsh before we dispatched it. (J. Major, 1999—Walker, the Secretary of State for Wales, could not speak Welsh)

card short of a full deck (a) stupid

A variant of FIFTY CARDS IN THE PACK:

> Lewis has occasionally been dismissed as a card or two short of a full deck. (*Daily Telegraph*, 10 June 1997—an optimistic and genial television journalist with the BBC was subject to criticism by his more abrasive and confrontational peers)

cardiac incident a malfunction of the heart

Medical jargon, but every heartbeat might be so described. With a *cardiac arrest*, the heart stops beating.

cardigan *American* a contraceptive sheath

The use is at two removes from the Crimea, where the pugnacious earl gave his name to an article of clothing.

cardinal is at home (the) I am menstruating

Princes of the Church wear a red biretta and robes of office.

cards (your) *British* dismissal from employment

At one time, revenue stamps were affixed weekly to cards, originally to provide basic insurance and pension rights but latterly as a tax on employment paid by both the employer and the employee. It was necessary to show a properly stamped card either to a new employer or to the authorities when claiming money while unemployed:

> Get your cards! You take a week's pay and you get out of my place. (Deighton, 1972)

An employee wishing to leave employment might *ask for his cards*.

care *British* the guardianship of children by a local authority

Often the children subject to this procedure, described as being *in care*, may be unruly or criminal or have no parent fit or able to look after them, and are confined to an institution:

> 'And I won't be put in care?'...'That kid goes into care over my dead body.' (P. D. James, 1994)

It should not be assumed that children living normally at home with their parents are uncared for.

career change dismissal from employment

True as far as it goes, but unlikely to be the whole story:

> The company's claim that its trading director had suddenly decided it is time for a career change after 23 years with Sainsbury's was a surprise to the rest of us...but a £270,000 pay-off rather gives the game away. (*Daily Telegraph*, 29 October 1998—it transpired that the recipient had not arranged another career to change into)

If you dismiss a lot of people, you may set up a *career transition center*, as a clearing house:

> Workers headed home...with their redundancy pink slips and an invitation to drop in on what Boeing euphemistically calls its Career Transition Center to begin the search for new work. (*Sunday Telegraph*, 6 December 1998)

careful stingy

From the concept that thrift is praiseworthy but avarice is a deadly sin:

> [Harold Wilson] is careful. In the narrow financial sense he always seemed to enjoy receiving hospitality. (Bevins, 1963)

caress yourself (of a female) to masturbate

From the literal meaning, to touch gently:

> She admitted having caressed herself ever since she was ten. (F. Harris, 1925)

caring the ostentatious display of social conscience

Originally used in this derogatory sense by those critical of hypocrisy or self-advertisement in others:

> They will probably become nuns or prison wardresses or join the caring professions. (A. Waugh, *Private Eye*, July 1980)

Now standard English of nurses, home helps, and the like, or *carers* in the jargon, a pun perhaps on their being concerned for, and their looking after, other people. *Uncaring* means cruel, selfish or insensitive, often in a double negative:

Ulyatt, who was not a cruel man, or an
uncaring one, simply shut his eyes. (Kyle,
1975)

carnal pertaining to copulation
Literally, of the flesh. Legal jargon and
standard English in several phrases such as
carnal act, knowledge, necessities, or *relations:*
...the only time I've completed the carnal
act with my nose full of water was in
Ranava Ilona's bath. (Fraser, 1977)
'Know you this woman?' 'Carnally, she
says.' (Shakespeare, *Measure for Measure*)
Maitland had carnal relations with
several other women during this period.
(Condon, 1966)
I have been afflicted for ninety years by
the carnal necessities of women.
(Sharpe, 1978—the venerable speaker
was a libertine excusing a dissolute life)

carpet¹ to reprimand
Unlike the workshop or servants' quarters,
the master's room had a floor covering on
which the defaulter had to stand:
Do I carpet the head of the risk department
or what? (McCrum, 1991)
Beware the French *sur le tapis,* which means
only up for consideration.

carpet² a wig
A variant of the RUG worn by an American
male:
...snowy-white hair. If it wasn't a carpet, it
had enjoyed the attention of an artful
coiffeur. (Sanders, 1979)

carpetbagger a seeker of short-term gain
Originally, an absconding American banker,
who so carried away the bank's reserves when
he left. Then widely used of Northerners who
sought easy pickings in the South after the
Civil War. In modern use it refers to a tout
who seeks to put together a deal without any
personal investment or risk, as by seeking a
buyer for a property which does not belong to
him. The verb is rare:
Only *then* he is not on the take, he is not
carpetbagging his country's inheritance. (le
Carré, 1996)
The term is also used in Britain of those who
place small deposits with mutual building
societies, in the hope of profit if the societies
abandon their mutual status; and of politicians seeking a safer constituency.

carry¹ to be pregnant (with)
Of the same tendency as BEAR 1 but some-
times without stating the burden:
She was in the seventh month of
pregnancy and carrying big.
(J. Collins, 1981)
To *carry a child* is specific:

Mrs Thrale is big, and fancies that she
carries a boy. (Johnson)

carry² to have an illegal narcotic on you
A shortened form of *carry drugs.* Because of
the risk of detection in a body search, a rule
among drug users says *Never carry when you can
stash.*

carry³ *American* to be in possession of a
handgun
Again a shortened form, and used of both
legal and illegal sidearms:
'Ahhh, I'm carrying,' Boone said. 'Someone
will spot the heat.' (Sanders, 1977—Boone
was a policeman)

carry⁴ to drink too much intoxicant without appearing drunk
Such a gift was supposed to be an indication
of good breeding:
...as gentlemen should, carried their
two bottles of an evening. (Strachey,
1918
To *carry* a *(heavy) load* means to be drunk,
usually on beer.

carry a card to be a member of the Communist party
The use was developed in the 1920s when
such membership was not flaunted in
polite circles because it might lead to ostra-
cism:
Maurice Dubb who was probably the first
academic to carry a card...(Boyle, 1979)

carry a torch for to desire sexually
The imagery is from a religious processional
light. Usually of unrequited love:
Maggie Young-Hunt came in today. Out of
coffee, so she said. I think she's carrying a
torch for me. (Steinbeck, 1961—the visit
took place in daylight)

carry off to cause the death of
It is used of dying from an epidemic or sudden
illness:
...if one of the characters did happen to
be carried off in the course of nature...
(N. Mitford, 1949)

carry on with to have an extramarital
sexual relationship with
The 19th-century use implied no more than
companionship or courtship:
I carry on with him now and he likes me
very much. (Mayhew, 1862)
In modern use, of either sex, the relationship
is explicit and often censurable:
...administered a public wigging to
Princess Margaret when she was carrying
on with that nancy-boy pop singer. (*Private
Eye,* April 1981)

carry the banner *American* to be destitute
Perhaps from the activities of the Salvation Army, who provide food and shelter for the homeless, among their many good works. Other phrases used of and by hobos are *carry the balloon*, from the rolled bedroll, and *carry the stick*, as used in walking.

carry the can to receive undeserved punishment while the culprit goes free
Some authorities suggest that the can contained beer. Common use in the First World War suggests that it was more likely to have carried food prepared behind the lines for those in the trenches. The full version *carry the can back* may have referred rather to the unpleasant and dangerous duty of taking the CAN 1, with its malodorous cargo of urine and faeces, back to the rear from the trenches; and see REARS. The phrase is also used of a guilty person singled out or available for punishment among several miscreants:
　　...whoever inflicted that fatal wound has
　　not been brought to justice...you alone
　　stand to carry the can. (*Daily Telegraph*,
　　1 November 1995)
See also as TAKE THE CAN BACK.

carsey a lavatory
From the Italian *casa*, a house, and defined by Dr Johnson as 'A building unfurnished':
　　'Mens resting Room' which he assumed
　　was the carsey. (Follett, 1991)
Also as *carsy, karsey, karzey*, and *karzy*.

carwash (a) *American* copulation under a shower
The imagery seems rather remote:
　　Home to Pittsburgh! Chris. The kindest,
　　sharpest, sexiest girl in the United States
　　of America. A carwash or two.
　　(O'Hanlon, 1996)

case¹ *obsolete* a brothel
As with *carsey*, from the Italian (or Spanish) *casa*, a house, and occasionally so spelt. And as *casa* or *casita*:
　　Four casas, four women, often four
　　Frenchwoman, to the square hectare.
　　(Londres, 1928, in translation, writing
　　of the density of prostitutes in Buenos
　　Aires)
　　Some people used to call her Caso Maggie.
　　(Kersh, 1936)
　　...the representative of the law hurries to
　　the Casita and the woman pays at once.
　　(Londres, 1928, in translation)
A *casino* is where we can gamble in public.

case² anything which is the subject of taboo
It may be someone displaying a degree of eccentricity in conduct. In medical use, a patient, especially where it might be a breach of confidence to divulge the identity. In funeral jargon, the corpse:
　　We cremate quite a few cases. (J. Mitford,
　　1963)
A recidivist is a *hard case*.

cash flow problem an insolvency
Cash flow, the money we receive against what we have to pay, is always a problem, needing constant attention. This usage is of corporate trading while insolvent:
　　Once *that* word gets out we are going
　　to have what is euphemistically
　　called a cash flow problem. (Sharpe, 1977)
Also used of temporary personal indigence.

cash in your checks to die
Equally common as *cash* (or *pass*) *in your chips*, from turning your counters into money when you quit the gambling table.

cast¹ to give birth prematurely
Standard English of quadrupeds, from the meaning to cause to fall:
　　Just a pair still-born at the hinner een'
　　Puir dwarfed last anes,
　　Wee, deid, cast anes. (Lumsden, 1892,
　　writing about lambs: *hinner een'* means
　　latter end)
Whence two obsolete punning phrases of bipeds, both meaning 'to give birth while unmarried'. To cast a girth used equestrian imagery, and to *cast a laggin* (or *leglin*) *girth* came from the spilling of the staves of a tub when the hoop round them is displaced:
　　...slipping a foot, casting a leglin-girth or
　　the like. (W. Scott, 1822)

cast² *obsolete* to use magical powers of divination
If you were *cast for death*, you had not been selected to play Julius Caesar but were terminally ill:
　　He's cassen her planets, and he's sure she'll
　　dee. (E. Peacock, 1870)

cast your pellet to defecate
Literally, to *cast* is to let fall:
　　...the squatting early morning figures of
　　male labourers casting their pellets upon
　　the earth. (P. Scott, 1973)

casting couch (the) sexual activity between a female seeking a favour and a male in a position to grant it
Originally used of aspiring actresses:
　　...married a veteran Hollywood stunt
　　man...saved her from being just another

hooker working the casting couches.
(J. Collins, 1981)
This particular piece of furniture is found less often outside the theatrical profession:

Young lady, I do not need a casting couch. I can have any woman I want. (*Private Eye*, May 1981, quoting a journalist)

casual (the) an institution which housed the destitute

A shortened form of the British *casual ward*, accommodation available for tramps arriving on foot without reservation at uncertain intervals. Those who tramped the road and slept in such places were known as *casuals*, a word which now applies to people in temporary employment:

The 'casuals'... may be more properly described as men whose employment is accidental, chanceful, or uncertain. (Mayhew, 1851).

cat[1] a prostitute

Usually of females but occasionally of a male:

If you want to bugger a male cat, that means you're a queer. (Theroux, 1973, and not of bestiality)

Cat-house, a brothel, is more widely used:

'What are those places?' Asked Treece. 'Warehouses,' said Jenkins. Treece thought he said whore-houses... They didn't look like his idea of a cathouse. (Bradbury, 1959)

A male human *cat* was not necessarily associated with TOMCATTING, being sometimes no more than a smartly dressed man:

I had on a brand new Stetson... fine black suit and new patent leather shoes... I was a sharp cat. (L. Armstrong, 1955)

cat[2] the vagina

PUSSY 1, using the same imagery, is much more common:

The rest of them were putting cigarettes in their cats and puffing on them. (Theroux, 1975)

cat about *American* (of a male) to be sexually promiscuous

Not necessarily with a CAT 1:

Alf... had a persistent lurid curiosity concerning Robbie's catting about. (Turow, 1999)

catch a rich marriageable adult

The imagery comes from angling. In former times a (*good*) *catch* might be either male or female so long as he or she was rich:

Gabriel had been quite a 'catch'. (Boyd, 1982)

catch a cold[1] *British* to contract gonorrhoea

Army use, punning on the meaning, to get yourself into trouble. Shakespeare may have had the same thing in mind when he wrote:

A maid, and stuff'd. There's goodly catching of cold. (*Much Ado About Nothing*)

catch a cold[2] to have a trouser zip undone

An oblique warning from one male to another, received by me on the quay at Destin, Florida, on a mild day in November 1987.

catch a cold[3] to suffer a loss

Normally as a speculator or gambler:

The 1960s speculative bubble burst and while the rest of the world caught a cold, Japan got pneumonia. (*Daily Telegraph*, 5 December 1994)

catch a packet[1] to be killed or severely wounded

Usually after being struck by something solid, like shrapnel. The common use from the First World War changed to mean getting into trouble until the Second World War, when the phrase reverted to its former meaning, and also came to embrace the ordeal of a town which was severely bombed or of a unit which was subjected to a heavy attack:

The same thing's happening to the 2nd Northants, they've caught a packet too. (Price, 1978, of a badly mauled regiment)

catch a packet[2] to contract venereal disease

A common use among servicemen in the Second World War.

catch fish with a silver hook *obsolete* to pretend to have caught fish which you have bought

An expression among anglers, where such behaviour is opprobrious, as was that of the man who liked to SHOOT WITH A SILVER GUN. See also ANGLE WITH A SILVER HOOK, which was an even less gentlemanly activity.

catch the boat up *British* to have contracted venereal disease

Naval usage. Jolly (1988) suggests a derivation from the days of pressing, when seamen were not allowed ashore for fear that they would desert. A *sick boat* would circulate among the fleet and take patients, with or without venereal disease, to a naval hospital ashore. On discharge from hospital, the sailor would be required to rejoin his ship wherever it was.

category killer a cut-price store in a shopping precinct

Articles are sold at prices which deter competition, until there is no competition for those specific products, when the prices may rise:

> ...unenclosed developments, usually built in a U-shape around a central parking lot and containing at least one *category killer* store—a place like Toys 'R' Us or Circuit City selling a particular type of product in such volume and at such prices as to deter any nearby competition. (Bryson, 1994)

cattle¹ a category of despised persons
More dysphemism than euphemism. Evelyn used the word of prostitutes:

> Nelly...concubines and cattell of that sort.

A similar derogatory use was of slaves in the Southern States:

> Could be payin' [a right nice price] for the right kind of cattle. (Fraser, 1971, writing in 19th-century style about a slave owner)

cattle² an act of copulation
Rhyming slang on *cattle truck*, and used figuratively, if at all:

> I don't give a flying cattle if you give me fifteen thousand pounds a week. (Kersh, 1936)

caught¹ pregnant
Mainly female use of unwanted pregnancy, with obvious imagery:

> If the girl gets caught and pregnancy results...(F. Harris, 1925)

caught² infected with venereal disease
Medical practitioners report that this is the commonest way in which their diseased and embarrassed young patients introduce the subject of their visit.

caught short having an urgent desire in an inconvenient place to urinate or defecate
Of both sexes, from the days when coaches or trains stopped at regular intervals but offered no lavatory accommodation between one stage or station and the next:

> Well, this virus carried a gun, I nearly got caught short. (Steinbeck, 1961)

cavalry prostitutes who solicit from motor vehicles
The usage, if not the practice, is peculiar to the Far East, leaving the INFANTRY, as usual, to slog it out on foot.

cease to be to die
Hardly euphemistic for an atheist. Of more interest perhaps is the biblical use for the menopause:

> It ceased to be with Sarah after the manner of women. (*Genesis*, 18: 11)

ceasefire a continuation of fighting

A usage when the opponents are operating under different rules, and especially if politicians wish to give the impression that hostilities are coming to an end:

> Lord Carrington will negotiate no more ceasefires in Bosnia until the warlords there have reached stalemate or exhaustion, he announced yesterday. (*Daily Telegraph*, 24 July 1992)

Cecil the penis
One of the many male forenames by which the appendage is known. To *dip Cecil in the hot grease* is to copulate:

> I know all he wants is to dip Cecil in the hot grease. (Sanders, 1981)

celebrate to drink intoxicants to excess
Literally, to mark a happy or festive occasion, when intoxicants may be drunk. When a drunken person is said to have been *celebrating*, there is no suggestion of prior festivities:

> No, I haven't been celebrating. I can drive. (Seymour, 1998)

celebrity a person employed as an entertainer
Literally, deserving fame. Jargon of the entertainment industry:

> On the fringe of the famous...constantly invaded by idle chatter and envious gossip which inevitably, it seems, surrounds what is euphemistically called today a celebrity. (Bogarde, 1978)

cement to prevent defecation
Used of medicine taken after an attack of diarrhoea, although concrete might seem more appropriate:

> I'd already got the trots. They're supposed to cement you up. (P. Scott, 1975, describing pills)

And in various compound uses, such as:

> The water came from a communal tap down by the road, so it was cement-sandwich country as far as I was concerned. (Lyall, 1972)

cement shoes weights attached to a corpse
For those murdered, especially in Chicago, and dumped in deep water:

> There were more bodies down there at the bottom of the lake with cement shoes than there was garbage. (Weverka, 1973)

certain age (a) old
The precise figure is often uncertain, although none of us is not of a certain age, unless we cannot trace a certificate of birth:

> They were a certain age, they had bumps and braces and wooden legs. (Theroux, 1979)

certain condition (a) see CONDITION 2

certifiable mentally unstable but still at liberty
Medical experts and a magistrate had at one time to certify that a mentally ill person could be involuntarily incarcerated:
> I won't put him in an asylum. He really and truly isn't certifiable. (M. McCarthy, 1963)
See also SECTION.

chair¹ (the) judicial death by electrocution
From the furniture to which the victim is strapped:
> We get a lock on the case, you could face the chair. (Mailer, 1965)

chair² *American* a senior manager
It is POLITICALLY CORRECT, being sexually neutral, but not euphemistic, for those who conduct a meeting to be so described:
> In the view of Professor Steiner, who is the 'chair' of the English Department at the University of Pennsylvania...
> (*Sunday Telegraph*, 21 January 1996)

chair-days *obsolete* old age
Before the advent of hip replacements:
> ... in thy reverence and thy chair-days, thus
> To die in ruffian battle. (Shakespeare, *2 Henry VI*)

Chalfonts *British* haemorrhoids
Rhyming slang for piles, from the town Chalfont St Giles. See also FARMER GILES.

chalk-board a blackboard
A usage originally in the classroom, to avoid offence to black people:
> The cook put her tatting aside and stood next to the chalk-board. (Proulx, 1993)

challenged differing from the norm in a taboo fashion
Not faced with a duel, but of those thought to be facing life at a disadvantage. The use extends to the bald, who are *follicularly challenged*; to the deaf, who are *aurally challenged*; to the blind, who are *visually challenged* (and not by 'Halt! Who goes there?'); to the mentally ill, who are *cerebrally challenged*; to those of low intelligence who are *developmentally* or *intellectually challenged*; to a dwarf, who is *vertically challenged*; to a lame person, who is *physically challenged*; to a crook, who is *ethically challenged* (a phrase used on 18 June 1996 by the chairman of the committee investigating inter alia Hillary Clinton's deals in Arkansas); and so on.

> Here are Barry Pearson (right) and Tim Lyle, the follically-challenged duo who run the corporate management boutique. (*Daily Telegraph*, 1 November 1997)
> There was also the matter of the not inconsiderable number of intellectually challenged members of the Nazi party. (Burleigh, 2000, writing of compulsory sterilization programmes)

There are also figurative uses. Thus to be *parentally challenged* is to be a nasty person, or bastard:
> They are mostly feckless, ill-informed and otherwise unemployable people. One or two are parentally challenged. (*Daily Telegraph*, 19 November 1993, quoting Howard Davies, who, as the Director of the Confederation of British Industry, was castigating journalists)

etc.

challenging unprofitable
One of the code words used by company chairmen when things are going badly, disregarding the fact that the firm is *challenged* by its competition every day:
> Trading conditions in Continental Europe, however, remain challenging. (Pilkington plc Chairman's Report, June 1994, heralding a period of decline in its fortunes)

chamber a receptacle for urine
A shortened form of *chamber-pot*, which was formerly kept for nocturnal urination under the bed or in a small cupboard in the bedroom. The urine, or *chamber-lye*, might be collected, fermented, and put to various good uses, like the washing of clothes or the dressing of wheat:
> We leak in the chimney, and your chamber-lye breeds fleas like a loach. (Shakespeare, *1 Henry IV*—a *loach* was a small fish)

chambering copulation
The activity normally takes place in an upstairs room:
> Harriet heard more than she wanted of the chambering next door. (Manning, 1978)

chance illegitimate
From the unplanned nature of such impregnations in many standard English and dialect phrases such as *chance bairn*, *begot*, *born*, *child*, and *come*:
> 'Chance children', as they are called... are rare among the young women of the costermongers. (Mayhew, 1851)
A *chanceling* was an illegitimate child, both literally and as an insult:
> Offspring of a pair a conncelins. (Bywater, 1853)

change¹ (the) the menopause
A shortened form of the standard English *change of life*:

Too young for the change, I suppose.
(J. Trollope, 1992)

change² *obsolete* to grow into a difficult or stupid child
Babies born wise and beautiful grew up stupid, ugly, and mischievous if the fairies did a switch in the cradle:

My granny never liked her, said she was 'changed'. (Service, 1887)

Thus a *changeling*, such a child, resulting from the malevolence of the fairies and not from incest and other inbreeding which was endemic in rural areas before the Railway Age.

change³ to replace by a clean one a soiled napkin on a baby
The baby in fact remains unchanged, albeit cleaner and sweeter-smelling for a while:

The baby now began to scream. 'I expect he wants changing,' said David. (N. Mitford, 1960)

change someone's voice to injure (a male)
Literally or figuratively by a blow to the testicles. The vocal adjustment is seldom permanent:

Damn, if anyone talked that way about Cathy I'd have changed his voice for him. (Clancy, 1987)

change your bulbs to become subject to mental abnormality
Presumably from the difference in light emitted when those of different wattage are selected:

It's Grandpa's dying that's changed her bulbs. (de Bernières, 1994—she had seen what she thought was a ghost)

change your jacket to desert an old allegiance
A modern variant of TURN YOUR COAT:

This was made possible because there were those in the new Socialist Order who had 'changed their jackets' following Franco's death. (letter in *Daily Telegraph*, 17 December 1998)

change your luck *American* (of a white male) to copulate with a black woman
The *changing* comes from switching from red to black in roulette after a losing streak.

chant *obsolete* falsely to describe a horse for sale
Literally, singing, but singing the nag's praises dishonestly. A *chanter* or *horse-chanter* was the equine equivalent of a second-hand car salesman, except that for age, temper, hooves, soundness, teeth, coat, etc. you must read mileage, roadworthiness, tyres, compression, fuel consumption, bodywork, etc.

chap *obsolete* a male suitor
Originally, a buyer, then in colloquial use any man, and in the 19th century specifically a suitor:

On the suspicion of an offence, the 'gals' are sure to be beaten cruelly and savagely by their 'chaps'. (Mayhew, 1851)

Chapping was courtship for a female, but not with the *old chap*, the devil:

Speak truth, then ye needna fear
Tae meet the auld chap face to face.
(Thomson, 1881)

chapel of ease¹ a mortuary
Originally, a place of worship for the convenience of parishioners residing a long way from their parish church. Also as *chapel of rest*:

From 'undertaker' tout court to 'funeral parlor' to 'funeral home' to 'chapel' has been the linguistic progression. (J. Mitford, 1963)

'James' had already mercifully been removed to the 'Chapel of rest'. (I. Murdoch, 1978)

chapel of ease² a lavatory
A punning British use, of the place where you might *ease yourself*, and especially of an ornate public urinal for men, such as used to grace the streets of London.

Chapter Eleven see GO 2

character saleable
Literally distinctive, the derivation coming from the Greek instrument for marking and engraving. This is real-estate jargon for any property about which the selling agent cannot think of anything better to say.

charge¹ *American* an erection of the penis
DAS suggests derivation from 'activation from an electric charge and/or the sensation of electric shock', an etymology with which most males would find themselves uncomfortable. Likening the phenomenon to the loading (or charging) of a piece of ordnance in preparation for a discharge is more acceptable.

charge² an illegal injection of narcotics
The imagery is again from loading, or revitalizing, as in the cliché *a shot in the arm*, the use of which does not imply wrongdoing or

illegality. (You may read a report that a troop of Brownies received a shot in the arm after some gift or other good fortune, as though the small girls and Brown Owl—or Tawny—were about to behave in an animated fashion after being injected with heroin.)

charity girl *obsolete American* a sexually complaisant young female

A Second World War usage: patriotism was an excuse for promiscuity with servicemen. A *charity dame* was her mother, acting with the same abandon.

charity money protection money paid to an extortioner

A development of post-Communist Russia:
> As damp snow settled on Leninsky
> Prospekt, a black Zil, an old-regime car,
> drew up outside a rouble casino. 'They've
> come for charity money,' said the owner as
> he handed over a thick wad of roubles
> wrapped in a napkin to the steel-toothed
> driver. (Moynahan, 1994)

Charlie a substitute word for a taboo subject

It may mean a homosexual male, the police, an enemy (especially the Viet Cong), a prostitute, the male or female genitalia, menstruation (in the phrase *Charlie's come*), a stupid person (or *right Charlie*), cocaine or crack drugs (or *Charlie girl*), etc.
> 'By goles, Jon, we'll see murder done, so we
> will!' 'I'll run for the charlies.' (Fraser, 1997,
> writing of the Regency period)
> They could sure as shit believe that Charley
> was shooting at them. (Herr, 1977)
> Charlie girl, coke, cocaine. He's big.
> Cannabis too. (Fiennes, 1996—of a
> dealer)

If you are told *Charley's dead*, your trouser zip may be undone, or, in the days when they were worn, your petticoat was showing under your skirt.

Charlies, a woman's breasts, is obsolete.

Charlie Ronce a pimp

A brother to JOE 1 in rhyming slang, for *ponce*.

Charlie uncle a stupid man

Using the first two phonetic letters of a taboo FOUR-LETTER WORD.

charm *obsolete* to effect a magical cure

A *charm* was originally the singing of a song, whence an incantation, and the medical virtuosity of a *charmer*, or white witch:
> Soom folk says it's hall bosh about
> charmin' yer cock...Mah feyther took a
> feather o' his cock to t'old witch an' she
> charmed un. (*Good Words*, 1869, quoted in
> *EDD*—an avian remedy was supplied, not
> an aphrodisiac)

Thus to be *charming* was to be in good health:
> An' how's Coden Rachel?—She's charmin',
> thankee. (Quiller-Couch, 1890)

charms the sexual attractiveness of a female

The arts or attributes which work such magic on men:
> I had a full view of all her charms. (Cleland,
> 1749)

If, as a woman, you decide to SHOW YOUR CHARMS, you do more than display an amulet.

charwallah *British* a teetotaller

Originally, the *wallah* or man who brought round the *char*, or tea, for troops serving in India. See also BUN-PUNCHER.

chase to seek to copulate with extramaritally

Usually of a male, from following in a predatory way, but women do it also. The object of the pursuit is normally given, like *hump, skirt*, or *tail*:
> ...known to tipple a bit and chase hump.
> (Mailer, 1965)

chase the dragon to smoke a narcotic

Formerly of opium, with the traditional Chinese association, but now of heroin:
> This turned out to be a euphemism for
> smoking heroin—'chasing the dragon'—
> and Tosh took to the practice with
> abandon. (Fiennes, 1996)

chaser an intoxicant of a different kind from that just taken

It follows the previous libation down the throat. Usually of beer after spirits or vice versa. Less often of a further portion of what you have been drinking.

chat *British* an interview in which the police may seek to make a suspect incriminate himself

Literally, an informal or light-hearted conversation. The British police use the word when they want to obtain evidence without the inconvenience of a caution or a defence lawyer in attendance:
> This time there had been no caution, no
> suggestion that this was anything but an
> informal preliminary chat. (P. D. James,
> 1994)

cheat to copulate with someone other than your regular sexual partner

Of either party, within or outside marriage, from the deception usually involved:
> Eight months married and cheating on me
> with a piece of merchandise like that.
> (Chandler, 1943)

cheat the starter to conceive a child before marriage
Sporting imagery, from starting a race before the signal to go. As with BEAT THE GUN, the phrase was also formerly used of premarital copulation without impregnation between an engaged couple.

cheaters *American* cosmetic padding
The attempt is to deceive by enhancing the size of thighs, buttocks, and breasts. See also FALSIES.

check out *American* to die
The imagery is said to have come from the medical examination on demobilization, but leaving a hotel or cashing in when you quit gambling are just as likely:
    If you get found, you check out. See you in the morgue. (Chandler, 1953)

cheese eater *American* a cheat
A figurative use. *DAS* says 'Euphem. for rat'.

cheesecake an erotic picture of a female
The word puns on the sweet confection and the smile-inducing cheese demanded by photographers. Mainly Second World War use:
    [I] had literally thousands of cheesecake pictures taken of me. (*Daily Telegraph*, 10 May 2001, in the obituary of an actress)
See also BEEFCAKE.

chemical involving the use of illegal drugs
Many of the agents ingested are indeed produced through chemistry, although the term is also applied to those of biological origin:
    We wouldn't make nasty accusations about affairs of chemical addictions. (Grisham, 1998)
To be *chemically inconvenienced* or *affected* means that you are incapacitated by illegal drugs or, less often, by alcohol.

chère amie a sexual mistress
The French euphemism is carried into English:
    Phryne, the chère amie of a well-known officer in the Guards... (Mayhew, 1862)
Occasionally translated as *dear friend*; and see FRIEND.

cherry a woman's virginity
In vulgar use, the hymen:
    ...asking me to look after you was the most risky thing she could do if you wanted to hang on to that cherry of yours. (P. Scott, 1968)
A *cherry-picker* is a libertine.

cherry-pick fraudulently to select bargains
You select only the best of the fruit. Financial jargon of trades done in the morning on discretionary accounts where the gains or losses can be allocated fraudulently when the paperwork is completed later or at the close of business:
    Since rules for designating customer accounts are lax, the broker can do blank trades in the morning, then 'cherry-pick' the profitable ones at lunchtime, and allocate them to the intended beneficiary. (*Sunday Telegraph*, 27 March 1994—suggesting that an American politician had so enjoyed good fortune in the market)

chestnuts the testicles
A variant of the NUTS theme:
    Listen, I'm gonna stand down here freezing my chestnuts and pressing on this buzzer and shouting your name. (Turow, 1993—he was being refused entry to an apartment)

chew to practise fellatio
A variant of EAT 1:
    'He wanted you to gobble ze goo?' she asked. 'What?' 'Chew on his schlong,' Maggie said impatiently. (Sanders, 1981)
To *chew the fat* means merely to gossip, among males.

chew a gun to kill yourself
You put the barrel in your mouth and aim upwards:
    Doing good deeds apparently keeps people from chewing on guns. (Wambaugh, 1981)

chi-chi of mixed white and Indian ancestry
A derogatory use. It means dirty in Hindi:
    'The late Mr Elphinstone,' she said, her voice unsteady, 'had a weakness for chhi-chhi women.' (Rushdie, 1995)

chic sale *American* a primitive outdoor lavatory
The American humorist Chic (Charles) Sale had a stage act on the construction of privies, and wrote *The Specialist* in order to establish his copyright in the material.

Chicago typewriter a sub-machine gun
A combination of the staccato noise of the machine and the city's reputation for lawlessness:
    There it was, now they had it all. Chicago typewriters...Did Bottles Capone, Al's brother, or Jake 'Greasy Thumb' Guzik have anything they didn't? (Furst, 1988)

chick a prostitute
The common avian imagery of any young
female. Also as *chickie*:
> What was the name of the chick with the
> big behind who sat on my knee in the car?
> (Bradbury, 1959)
> Mayhew got himself a little number
> down at China Beach, little chickie
> workin' the skivvie houses down there.
> (Herr, 1977)

A *chickie house* is a brothel.

chicken¹ a youth attractive to homosexuals
A variant of CHICK. A *chickenhawk* is a homosexual adult who seeks out boys for sexual
purposes, punning on *sparrowhawk*:
> Chicken worried him, though. There were
> these children of eleven, twelve and
> thirteen. (Fry, 1991)
> I just happen to like boys...but I don't do
> chickenhawks. (M. Thomas, 1980)

If however someone describes you as NO
(SPRING) CHICKEN, it means you are showing
your age.

chicken² cowardly
From the supposed nature of the domestic
fowl. To *chicken out* is to behave in a craven
way:
> I'm not chicken. I'm just being realistic.
> (Ryan, 1999)
> Panditji, Congress-tho, is always
> chickening out in the face of radical acts.
> (Rushdie, 1995)

An American *chicken colonel* is not being
accused of cowardice but is wearing the
ordained badge of rank on his shoulders.

child of God a member of the untouch-
able class in Hindu society
Dirty work, including the collection of human
excreta, is reserved for them. A member of
another caste touching them is defiled:
> She decided he was a Harijan, a child of
> God, an untouchable. (P. Scott, 1971)

child of sin *obsolete* an illegitimate child
The *sin* was its conception, at least so far as
the mother was concerned. Also as *child or
grief* or LOVE CHILD:
> I have fallen! I am a mother, and my
> poor dear boy is the child of sin.
> (Mayhew, 1862)
> She's never been the same since she lost
> that child of grief. (Macdonald, 1971)

child of Venus a prostitute
Supposedly mothered by the goddess of love.
The term is also used of a woman who
relishes sexual activity:
> ...a merry little grig and born child of
> Venus. (F. Harris, 1925—a *grig* was

originally a dwarf before becoming a
cheerful person)

child-bed (in) giving birth
Not a cot but standard English for parturition:
> Two months later I heard she had married
> this same Count de Beton, and she died in
> child-bed a year or two later. (A. C. Doyle,
> 1895)

chill to kill
The common cooling imagery:
> A hundred guys could have chilled this
> little wart. (Chandler, 1939)

China white heroin
From the colour, the origin, and the porcelain, perhaps:
> Offered me a whole piece of unstepped-on
> China white. (Wambaugh, 1981)

Chinese is used in phrases to indicate dishonesty, wiliness, duplicity, or muddle,
some of which follow.

Chinese bookkeeping false accounting
> She...was aware how many actors were
> ripped off by their company's Chinese
> bookkeeping. (Whicker, 1982)

Chinese copy a production model stolen
from another's design
Used as a noun or verb:
> ...some big-time outfit'll Chinese copy
> his equipment and take his market
> away by underpricing him. (M. Thomas,
> 1982)

Chinese fire-drill (a) pandemonium
> It's the usual Chinese fire-drill...But we're
> keeping on top. (Strong, 1998)

Chinese paper a security of doubtful
value
> When something happened to break the
> flow, it came tumbling down on
> leverage until it...was buried under the
> Chinese paper. (Train, 1983, describing
> a buyout financed by subordinated
> debentures)

Chinese parliament a disorganized discussion group
It would seem the converse of what happens
in Beijing, where mute and subservient
nominees appear only to be harangued at
length by their masters:
> We call this stage of planning and
> preparation 'walk through, talk
> through', and operate a Chinese
> parliament while we're doing it.
> (McNab, 1993)

Chinese (three-point) landing a crash
on the runway
Punning on the mythical Oriental Wun Wing
Lo. Tricycle undercarriages came later.

Chinese tobacco opium

Chinese wall the pretence that price-sensitive information will not be used by an
adviser or his associates to their own
advantage
Said to have been first used in this context by
F. D. Roosevelt in 1927. The paper-thin nature
of such a wall may prevent sight but is
unlikely to affect hearing:
> The next hurdle for the Swiss is the
> 'inquiry'—the exchange uses the word
> investigation—by the Securities and
> Futures Authority, which is trying to
> decide whether the bank's Chinese walls
> were breached by its dealings. (*Daily
> Telegraph*, 19 January 1995—the
> bank's market-makers had accumulated
> shares in electricity companies while
> other bank employees were advising a
> predator on a takeover within the same
> sector)

Chinese whisper an unsubstantiated ru-
mour
> Too often these Chinese whispers make the
> end product unrecognisable. (J. Major,
> 1999)

chippy[1] *American* a prostitute
Usually at the lower end of the profession,
from *chip*, a BIT or PIECE 1:
> He pays some chippie fifty to gobble his
> pork. (Diehl, 1978)
A *chippie-joint* is a brothel.

chippy[2] *American* to ingest illegal narcotics on an irregular basis
Where using illegal drugs is the norm, non-
addiction may be taboo (as in FISH 1 for
homosexual females). In such a culture a non-
addict may wish to avoid being thought stuffy
by not entirely eschewing narcotics, as it were
merely *chipping* at a mass. This may be
inferred from *chippy-user*, 'one who uses
narcotics infrequently' (Lingemann, 1969).
To confuse matters, a *chippy* in black slang is
a regular taker of strong narcotics, although
in Britain he is merely a carpenter.

chirp *American* to be an informer to the
police
Underworld slang using the common *singing*
imagery (Chandler, 1950). Whence *chirper*, an
informer:
> I am by no means a chirper. (Runyon, 1990,
> from 1939)

chisel to steal or cheat
The imagery is from the removal of slivers
from wood with a sharp instrument. The
thefts so described may be minor and repeti-
tious, and the cheating mean:
> Gotham liked to chisel whatever 'float' it
> could over the weekend. (M. Thomas, 1980,
> describing the banking practice of stealing
> the interest on customers' money by
> being dilatory about transfers on Fridays)
On the chisel is so to behave:
> He'd be pretty sore if I was on the chisel.
> Not that I don't like money. (Chandler,
> 1953)
A *chiseller* so behaves or, in America, saves
expense by avoiding compliance with a law or
regulation of which he disapproves.

choke your chicken (of a male) to masturbate
The derivation is from the likeness of the
penis to a chicken's plucked neck:
> I went to Chi Town to clean up, but I
> ended up choking my chicken.
> (Dills, 1976—he had unsuccessfully
> sought to pick up a woman for sex in
> Chicago)
Whence *chicken-choker*, a masturbator, which
is also said to be 'a friendly term truckers use
for each other' (ibid.).
I have what may be a rogue example of the
meaning to urinate:
> Whenever Walker was about to go and
> answer a call of nature, he would
> announce 'Well, I'm gonna choke my
> chicken'. (de la Billière, 1992—we must
> assume the gallant general was not
> mistaken in his assumption of his
> colleague's intentions)

chokey a prison
The Hindi *chauki*, originally meaning four-
sided, became a space surrounded by walls,
whence a police station or customs house and
then a prison:
> I've got to cart Voluptia off the chokey.
> She's been interfering down in the
> circumcision booths. (Bradbury, 1976)

chop[1] to kill
Originally standard English, meaning to kill
an animal by a blow from the hand. When
killing humans, the blow is with a sharp
instrument:
> Unless he chopped us both (which seemed
> far-fetched, pirate and Old Etonian though
> he was)...(Fraser, 1977)
To *get the chop* was to be killed in battle. The
newspaper jargon *chop shot* is a picture of the
corpse of someone who has been killed:
> You don't get many chop shots these days.
> (M. Thomas, 1980, referring to a public
> execution)

chop² (the) sudden dismissal from employment
The metaphorical blow with a sharp instrument, of individual rather than multiple dismissals. The employer does the *chopping*:
> Joint editor Allan Segal was chopped last month. (*Private Eye*, May 1981)

For the chop describes the status of a candidate for dismissal:
> Tusker had been for the chop the moment Solly Felbergerstein set eyes on him. (P. Scott, 1977)

chopper¹ a sub-machine gun
Underworld jargon referring to its ability to chop down its targets:
> The man with the chopper... (Chandler, 1950, describing someone so armed)

chopper² the penis
Perhaps from its divisive sexual function and common slang. Of the same tendency as the obsolete *cleave*. My daughter, whose job included editing crossword puzzles, erred by allowing 'a butcher's chopper' as a clue for 'cleaver', which calls to mind Dr Wright's definition:
> Broach—a butcher's prick. (*EDD*)

chota peg a spirituous intoxicant
Chota is small in Hindi, although the measure may not be:
> Better a few too many chota pegs than the possible alternative. (P. Scott, 1968)

A *burra peg* is an even larger measure of spirits. These British Indian phrases are now passing out of use as those who lived or served in India die off. See also PEG.

chubby fat
Literally, like the thick, coarse-fleshed fish, whence agreeably plump, especially of babies. You meet the adjective in advertisements calculated to avoid upsetting mothers who have to select capacious clothes for an obese child.

chuck (the) peremptory dismissal from employment
You would be wrong to infer that the parting was forcible. Also, as a verb, of the ending of a courtship:
> Anyway he wouldn't have killed himself because I chucked him. (P. D. James, 1994)

chuck horrors *American* acute withdrawal symptoms
Used of drug addicts denied access to a supply to which the body has become accustomed. The phrase is used of those under medical supervision, and of those displaying the same symptoms in prison, being similarly deprived of narcotics. Whence perhaps the further meaning, a claustrophobic fear of being imprisoned.

chuck seven to die
Probably obsolete, as people do not play with single dice so much these days. Those who do will recall that the cube has no seven.

chuck up to vomit
Not playing catch with a ball. Usually associated with drunkenness.

chucked drunk
It compares the rotation of a lathe to the giddiness of intoxication.

church triumphant the dead
A Christian use, especially of those who are considered to have well served the *church militant here on earth*, while the less devoted or martial among us are doomed to languish among the vanquished.

churn to deal unnecessarily in a client's securities in order to generate commission
The imagery is from constantly turning the milk to obtain butter or cream. In this case, the investor is milked and the advisers get the cream:
> Your account can be 'churned' even though you haven't signed for discretionary trading. (Chase, 1987)

circular error probability the extent to which ordnance will miss the target
A Gulf War usage, from the illustration by concentric rings on a chart:
> There was something called circular error probability, which simply meant the area where a bomb or missile was likely to fall. (Simpson, 1991)

circular file *American* a waste-paper basket
Most of them are round; and see FILE THIRTEEN.

circular protector *obsolete* a contraceptive sheath
This was what they used to be called in advertisements, although the description could have meant anything from sheep fencing to an envelope for junk mail.

cissy a male homosexual
Literally, an effeminate man, probably a corruption of *sister* via *sissy* or *sis*:
> You know how cissies hate pregnant ladies. (N. Mitford, 1949)

Civil Co-operation Bureau *South African* an extralegal governmental agency
This organization was established by the white South African government to harass and generally discomfort its critics and opponents:

> After telling the enquiry about the plans of the Civil Co-operation Bureau to hang the dead foetus of a monkey outside Archbishop Desmond Tutu's house, General Rudolph 'Witkop' Badenhorst, Chief of Military Intelligence, complained that he was receiving anonymous calls at home. (*Sunday Telegraph*, March 1990—I hope that the practice of designating a classification 2.2 in a university examination as a 'Desmond' after the courageous cleric will remain a constant reminder of his achievements)

civilian impacting the inadvertent killing or wounding of non-combatants
A Gulf War neologism:

> Some of the military spoke of 'civilian impacting'. (Simpson, 1991)

claim responsibility for to admit to
A usage of terrorists, especially in Northern Ireland, who saw murder and arson as creditworthy:

> He turned on the radio...is just coming in of a bomb explosion...no one has yet claimed responsibility. (McCrum, 1991)

claimant a poor person supported in part or whole by the state
They *claim* money to which they are entitled from public agencies etc.:

> Reductions for Students, OAPs and Claimants. (Theatre Wales poster, October, 1981—despite the standard English use of *claimant* as anyone who makes a claim, no self-sufficient person would be so unwise as to ask if he might pay a lesser price for his ticket)

There is also an organization called the *Claimants' Union* which seeks to maximize the receipts of its members from public funds.

Clapham an allusion to gonorrhoea
In the 19th century to *come home by Clapham* was to have been infected with clap, or gonorrhoea, Clapham Common being a haunt of prostitutes. Today male homosexuals use the Common for the same purpose, which may explain the embarrassment and immediate resignation of a government minister who went wandering there on his own and suffered what he later described as 'a moment of madness'. Pope's prognosis was invalid when he wrote: 'Time, that at last matures a clap to pox.'

claret blood
Boxing jargon, of blood from the nose. To *tap the claret* was to make your opponent's nose bleed:

> Blacked his eye, an' he tapped m'claret. (Fraser, 1997, writing of a pugilist)

classic proportions (of) fat
Originally, *classic* meant belonging to the literature of Greek or Latin antiquity when that was considered the only stuff worth reading, less taxing literature being written in the vernacular, or Romance, whence our modern romantic novels. The female models chosen by Rubens and other old masters, or *classic* painters, were nearly always on the plump side.

clean¹ free from unpleasantness, danger, or illegality.
The opposite in many uses of DIRTY. It may denote that a sexual partner has no venereal disease, that the enemy is not in a location, that someone is not carrying drugs or a handgun, etc.:

> I was a lucky devil to drop on such a lovely clean skirt. (F. Richards, 1936—the woman was free of disease)
> ...this village is clean and this village is all Charlie. (Theroux, 1975, writing of Vietnam)
> 'What's the point if he's clean?' 'If he's carrying something.' (Kyle, 1975—someone was suspected of having a pistol)

A *clean* atom bomb has less radioactive fallout than a *dirty* one:

> The language of the mad...'Clean atom bombs'. (M. West, 1979)

To have *clean hands* is not to have accepted a bribe or acted dishonestly.

clean² to kill or evict indigenous inhabitants of a different race or religion to your own
The practice is age-old but the language more recent:

> The displacement of the Arab majority had been achieved only by a process which Yigal Allon, the commander of the Jewish military forces in Galilee (and later Deputy Prime Minister of Israel), himself described as a 'cleansing'. 'We saw a need to clean the Inner Galilee', he wrote in his memoirs, 'and to create a Jewish territorial succession in the entire region of Upper Galilee. We therefore looked for means to cause tens of thousands of sulky Arabs who remained in Galilee to flee...Wide areas were cleaned.' (Dalrymple, 1997)

The world paid more attention to the *ethnic cleansing* in Bosnia and Croatia, perhaps because there were more television channels than half a century earlier, and no networks

controlled by Serbian or Croat sympathizers.

clean house to remove incriminating evidence

By destroying either documents or witnesses
or both:

> Once he muttered darkly that Bill Clinton's
> people were 'cleaning house', and he was
> 'next on the list'. (Evans-Pritchard, 1997—
> he was murdered soon after and his file on
> Clinton was stolen)

clean up[1] to bring the proceeds of vice
into open circulation

A variant of LAUNDER:

> The money from this stuff needed cleaning
> up. (Davidson, 1978)

Or the money may be *sent to the cleaners* for the
same purpose:

> Black money tucked away ready to go to
> the cleaners. (ibid.)

clean up[2] to copulate

The derivation is from the slang, meaning
to win:

> I went to Chi Town to clean up. (Dills, 1976)

cleanliness training *American* teaching
young children controlled urination
and defecation

Not just learning to wash your neck and keep
nits out of your hair. The British talk of *potty
training*, which is explicit (see POT 3).

cleanse[1] to free from enemy occupation
or sympathizers

The traditional job of the infantry:

> ...paramilitary elements trained and
> drilled in a special school and sent to
> 'cleanse' (US word) pacified hamlets.
> (M. McCarthy, 1967)

See also CLEAN 2.

cleanse[2] to remove the placenta from domestic cattle

Veterinary jargon:

> I was 'cleansing' a cow (removing the
> afterbirth). (Herriot, 1981)

clear not menstruating

Some ancient taboos relating to menstruating
women still persist in India and elsewhere:

> I could only visit them on my 'clear' days.
> (Taraporevala, 2000, referring to her Parsee
> relatives)

clear up *American* to desist from the
regular use of illegal narcotics

Literally, to tidy up or redress any situation.
Drug abusers' jargon.

clear your desk to be summarily dismissed from employment

The instruction is given to prevent an employee compiling and stealing a dossier of
useful documents or otherwise causing disruption:

> Last February Derek Linton and a fellow
> director were given the fabled five minutes
> to clear their desks at the advertising
> agency they themselves had founded 18
> years earlier. (*Telegraph Magazine*, 1 June
> 1995)

cleavage the visible division between a
clothed woman's breasts

Literally, the action of splitting apart:

> Donna's cleavage was opening like a barn
> door. (le Carré, 1996)

click[1] *obsolete* to steal

Literally, to snatch or seize hold of

> ...wanting to click the cunzle (that is hook
> the siller). (W. Scott, 1814)

A *clicker* was a thief, a body-snatcher, or
a pestering touting shopkeeper. (Body-
snatchers were not thieves as there was no
property in a corpse.) Stolen goods might be
taken from *Clickem Inn* to be sold at *Clickem Fair*
(the forerunner of the car-boot sale).

click[2] to conceive a child

The commonplace sound of a successful
connection having been made:

> I let him into the secret. Irene's hoping
> we've clicked. (N. Barber, 1981)

click with to form a romantic attachment
with

Literally, to reach an accord with:

> Look, righ', you could've tried to click with
> her yourself. But you didn't. An' Joey did.
> So fair fucks to him. (R. Doyle, 1987—*fair
> fucks* in this context means no more than
> good luck)

clicket to copulate

From the French *cliqueter*, to make a clicking
noise and using the same imagery as CLICK 2.
It is used properly of foxes, less often of deer
and hares, and almost never of humans.

climax a sexual orgasm

Literally, the culmination of anything:

> A climax was never reached by either of
> them, but that did not spoil their pleasure.
> (P. Scott, 1968)

climb (of a male) to copulate with

Referring to the action of getting on top of the
female. Also as *climb in with, climb into bed
(with), or climb aboard*:

> You mean you're going to climb some
> gorgeous chorus girl. (Condon, 1966)
> I'd just as soon go to bed with a giant clam
> as climb in with Eva Wilt. (Sharpe, 1979)

... sufficient affection and desire for her still to want to climb into bed if I got half a chance. (Fowles, 1977)

I suspicioned from Nance's smirks, that Tom was finding occasion to climb aboard now and then. (Fraser, 1997)

climb the ladder *obsolete* to be hanged
Either from the ascent to the scaffold or because the *ladder* itself was used for the drop:

When he was upon the ladder he prayed that God would inflict some visible judgment upon his Uncle. (Wallace, 1693)

However a woman who is said to *climb the ladder on her back* does no more than seek to turn male advances to advantage and advancement.

For *climb the wooden hill*, see WOODEN HILL.

clink a prison
Originally the jail in Southwark, but then used generally, helped no doubt by the onomatopoeic attractions of keys in locks and heavy doors shutting:

... the more troublesome firebrands... were popped neatly into clink. (P. Scott, 1971)

clink off *obsolete* to die
From a Scottish meaning, to depart:

In God's gude providence she just clinkit off hersell. (E. B. Ramsay, 1859)

clip[1] to swindle or rob
The association is with the shearing or the venerable practice of cutting the edges off silver coins. Now often it is used of picking pockets. A *clip artist* is a swindler and a *clip joint* a night club or similar establishment where customers are overcharged and otherwise cheated:

I took Celia and Victor Farris to dinner at one lush clipjoint and raised my voice in outrage at the miserable food and service. (Whicker, 1982)

clip[2] to hit with a bullet
Literally, to cut or shear, whence to mark as by removing cardboard from a ticket, which is what a *clippie* used to do on a bus. In America the person *clipped* is usually killed, but in British use he would only be slightly wounded, without being incapacitated.

clip his wick to kill
Like putting out a candle by cutting the wick below where it was burning:

Maitland found out. So they clipped his wick. (Sanders, 1977, writing of killing, not circumcising)

cloakroom a lavatory
Coats are often stored in or near lavatories:

To a small boy looking urgently for the cloakroom... (Jaeger, in Morley, 1976)

The shortened British form *cloaks* normally refers only to the place where outer garments are stored in a public place.

clobbered *American* drunk
The common beating imagery. It was used by Thurber in the *New Yorker* in 1951, but may now be obsolete.

clock fraudulently to alter the reading of a milometer
A motor trade device to increase the apparent value of a second-hand car. Some figurative use of falsely changing other statistics:

'The revenue and cost trends... are still not meeting our expectations,' he declared, which was a polite way of saying load was clocked. (*Daily Telegraph*, 3 May 2001)

cloot the devil
Literally, one of the divisions of a cloven hoof, a physical characteristic shared by Satan and cattle. Also as *clootie*:

I hate ye as I hate auld Cloot. (Barr, 1861)

Auld Hornie, Satan, Nick, or Clootie. (ibid.)

Clootie's croft was land set aside by a farmer and left untilled so that the devil would be content to leave the rest of the farm in peace:

The moss is soft on Clootie's craft. (G. Henderson, 1856—with its 'set aside' programmes, the bureaucracy in Brussels now performs the same function)

close[1] stingy
A shortened form of close-fisted, whence also NEAR 1.

close[2] having an extramarital sexual relationship with
From the requisite proximity:

Mr——and Mrs——a widow... have been close for two years. (*Daily Telegraph*, 28 March 1994—he was leaving his wife and said he intended to 'continue his relationship' with Mrs——)

A *close relationship* with a *close companion* or *friend* may be heterosexual or homosexual:

Among them was Paul——... and his close companion Jeremy——. (Chapman, 1999)

Di was having a close relationship with the muscular Tommy Yeardye. (Monkhouse, 1993—of the actress Diana Dors)

For *close friend* see FRIEND.

close an account to kill
With imagery from banking or story-telling? We were all hoping you would close his account. (Sohmer, 1988—an FBI agent had been told where a murderer was hiding)

close its doors to fail

Used of a bank, although it will prudently close its doors every day at the close of business, in the hope of reopening them on the morrow:

> ... if the run persisted, cash reserves would be exhausted and FMA obliged to close its doors. (Hailey, 1975—FMA was a bank)

close stool a portable lavatory
Originally for use in the CLOSET 1, but now usually found in the sickroom, if at all:

> Your lion, that holds his poll-axe sitting on a close-stool, will be given to Ajax. (Shakespeare, *Love's Labour's Lost*—see JAKES for the punning *Ajax*)

close the bedroom door to refuse to copulate with your spouse
The female usually does the *closing*, metaphorically if the spouses continue to occupy the same room:

> From the moment he had been a gubernatorial candidate she had closed the bedroom door. (Allbeury, 1980)

The phrase is not used of a husband banished to the spare room for snoring.

close your eyes to die
Or explicitly, *close your eyes for the last time*. If you close another's eyes, that person is already dead:

> I trust that I shall be able to close your eyes in peace. (R. Hughes, 1987, quoting a letter from a 19th-century convict in Australia to his parents in England)

closet¹ a lavatory
Literally, a small or private room. The word usually comes with the descriptive prefixes *earth* or *water*, whence the initials EC and WC, and the charming French noun *le water*.

closet² concealing in public your homosexuality
Again from the small or private room where you act according to your inclinations. Usually of a male, as in the phrases *closet queen* or *closet queer*, but occasionally of a female:

> I often wondered if she was a closet lez. (Sanders, 1977)

Whence *in the closet* for a homosexual who so acts:

> To me it figured that Bert was in the closet. (Turow, 1993—Bert was found to be subscribing to a periodical for homosexuals)

To *come out of the closet* or COME OUT is to cease to hide your homosexuality from the public.
In occasional and convoluted use, a *closet homosexual* may be a heterosexual male who affects homosexuality, as for example to avert the suspicions of a cuckolded husband:

> Dexter Dempster, New York's leading closet homosexual...(M. Thomas, 1980—Dexter was cuckolding someone)

clout *American* to steal
Probably from the meaning, to hit, whence perhaps by transference from the American HIT 3, to rob, and often referring to thefts from cars.

club¹ see IN THE CLUB

club² an agency promoting the sale of a specific product
Customers, styled as members, usually have a continuing obligation to buy despite not forming an association of like-minded people:

> Now, alas, the eel and pie shop was a video rental 'club'. (Deighton, 1988)

club³ a business which contrives to evade regulations
Especially those regulations which control the sale of alcohol or the dissemination of pornography. Thus those enrolled as members may be entitled to buy and consume alcohol in unlicensed premises, or to watch pornographic films which it would illegal to show to the general public.

clunk a corpse
Literally, the sound of a blow or a dull person, neither of which explains the etymology:

> He'll be a clunk before he hits the floor. (Sanders, 1973)

cluster the male genitalia
They are certainly proximate, and even more so in tight trousers:

> 'The cluster', he replied, 'is prominent these days.' (Matthew, 1983—a shop assistant was trying to sell tightly cut trousers)

co-belligerent a former enemy helping a conqueror in continuing war
By 1943, when Italy tried to change sides, COLLABORATOR 1 had become pejorative, and so

> ... the word 'co-belligerent' was invented to proclaim the new status. (Jennings, 1965)

The wise Italians had shown little belligerence between 1940 and 1943, and had no reason to show any more thereafter.

cooperate to assist another through fear or duress
Literally, to work with. Used of traitors, or the mass of a defeated population, in wartime:

> ... people in his area have begun to 'cooperate' with the Americans—the word 'collaborate' is avoided. (M. McCarthy, 1967)

The police suggest criminals should *cooperate* when seeking to extract information from them. The Soviet empire economically controlled and exploited its subject states through its *Economic Cooperation Council*, or Comecon.

co-respondent a male accused at law of having cuckolded another

Legal jargon for the man who has to *respond* jointly with the wife to a husband's petition on the grounds of adultery:

Merrick was, in his romantic way, a sort of professional co-respondent. (Bradbury, 1959)

Whence articles of clothing, such as *co-respondent's shoes*, of suede or two-toned leather, thought to be affected by philanderers.

In America a woman may also be a *correspondent*, being in Britain no more than a *party cited*:

...doubled as a paid correspondent in divorce cases—'the Woman Taken in Adultery'. (M. McCarthy, 1963)

cobbler a forger

Criminal and espionage jargon, of someone who forges credit cards, passports or other documents. To 'cobble' was literally to repair in a slipshod manner, although we expect more of our shoemakers.

cobblers the testicles

Rhyming slang on *cobblers' awls*, balls, which may or may not be a shortened form of balderdash. Mainly figurative use, with a *load of old cobblers*, meaning nonsense.

cobs the testicles

Literally, small stones, and either a shortened form of COBBLERS or a variant of the American NUTS, a variety being the hazel or *cob* nut

cock *obsolete* (of a male) to copulate with

Cock, the penis, is a venerable use:

Pistol's cock is up. (Shakespeare, 2 *Henry IV*—another of his lewd puns)

In modern speech we might say that we *cock a leg across*, *athwart*, or *over* a female:

...all the more difficult for me to cock a leg athwart Miss Fanny. (Fraser, 1971)

A *cocksman* is a philanderer:

He didn't think of himself as a cocksman but every now and then...something would get loose in his system. (M. Thomas, 1982)

To confuse matters, in black American slang, a *cock* may be a vagina. The *cockpit*, meaning the vagina viewed sexually, puns on the site of avian contest:

...the rose-lipt overture presenting the cockpit so fair. (Cleland, 1749)

See also ROOSTER.

cock-eyed drunk

Literally, askew.

cock the leg to urinate

Normally of a dog, but not of a bitch:

The poodle...shivered and cocked its leg nervously against the front door. (Bogarde, 1978)

Sometimes used humorously by and of men.

cock the little finger to be addicted to alcohol

From the manner in which some hold a cup:

Some say she cocks her wee finger...In short that she's gien to the drink. (Barr, 1861)

cockchafer¹ a treadmill

The flesh was rubbed raw by the coarse cloth used in prison garments. Punning on the Maybug, or *Melolontha vulgaris*:

He 'expiated', as it is called, this offence by three months' exercise on the 'cockchafer' (treadmill). (Mayhew, 1851)

cockchafer² a prostitute

Again punning on the beetle, from the soreness which might result after an encounter with her.

cocked drunk

Like a firearm prior to discharge rather than from any association with COCK-EYED. As usual in drunken terms, the half equals the whole:

Half cock'd and canty, hyem we got. (T. Wilson, 1843—*canty* means cheerful)

cocktail¹ *obsolete* a prostitute

Possibly a pun, also referring to *cockatrice*, a prostitute, from the fabulous serpent which killed by its glare:

Such a coxcomb as that, such a cocktail. (Thackeray)

cocktail² a mixture of alcohol or illegal narcotics

We have a choice of derivations, some more far-fetched than others. We can rule out the 'six-oared boat used by Kentish smugglers' and derivation from the Krio *koktel*, meaning a scorpion. In Yorkshire it once meant a flaming tankard of ale, which is getting closer. The obvious candidate is the French *coquetel*, from the feather used to stir the drink, but I still stay with the Aztec *xoc-tl*, named from the maiden Hochitl who introduced to the king a concoction devised by her father, thereby winning his heart and immortality. Commoner in America than in Britain, where it tends to be refer specifically to a drink based on a spirit without a generic meaning of intoxicants:

They had been having cocktails every night. (M. McCarthy, 1963)
Whence *cocktail bars, hours, lounges,* and the like.

coco mad
A Second World War usage, sometimes as cocoa:
> I mean for a moment he sounded perfectly normal, or is he really cocoa? (Fraser, 1992)

Probably taken from *off your (cocoa)nut*—see OFF 2—rather than anything to do with the famous clown.

coffee grinder *American* a prostitute
She may also be a belly dancer or stripper, and the three professions are not mutually exclusive.

coffee-housing cheating at cards
Referring to the behaviour of whist players in 18th-century London coffee houses:
> Coffee-housing...can range from the lifting of an eyebrow to the deliberate banging down of a card on the table. (Clay, 1998)

The 1874 *Slang Dictionary* gives *coffee-shop* as a 'watercloset, or house of office', presumably because, as today, passers-by used their lavatories.

cohabit to have a regular sexual relationship with
Literally, merely to live in the same abode, as do parents and children:
> My staff are all highly trained in the Swedish technique and strictly forbidden to cohabit with the customers. (B. Forbes, 1986—a bawd only allowed the women to copulate in the brothel)

coition copulation
It started by meaning mutual attraction, as of planets:
> While Titian was mixing rose madder
> His model sat poised on a ladder.
> Her position, to Titian, suggested coition
> So he nipped up the ladder and had her. (old limerick)

cojones *American* the testicles
A borrowing from the Spanish:
> But Burton spoke fluent Arabic, and he would have learned Maghrebi Arabic for such a venture, and his *cojones* were of legendary size. (Theroux 1995, of Burton's visit to Mecca, although what the testicular idiosyncrasy had to do with that exploit is unclear)

Cojones is also 'often used to indicate machismo. Offensive.' (*Dictionary of Cautionary Words and Phrases*, 1989—however any document prepared for a 'Multicultural Management Program' is likely to take offence easily)

coke cocaine used illegally
No more than a shortened form, without reference to the beverage. A *cokie* habitually uses the drug illegally:
> Out of the apartment houses came cokies and coke peddlers who look like nothing in particular. (Chandler, 1943)

A *coke-hound* is not a sniffer dog:
> He's a coke-hound and he talks in his sleep. (Chandler, 1939)

Coked is being under the influence of the narcotic:
> ...'coked' or 'bopped up' by gunmen. (Lavine, 1930)

cold¹ dead
Usually but not exclusively used of hot-blooded creatures, although *knocked out cold* refers to unconsciousness only. Whence several morbidly humorous 19th-century phrases, of which the most common was *cold meat*, a corpse:
> If you bother with us, I will make meat of you—cold meat. (F. Harris, 1925)

A *cold-meat party* was a funeral; a *cold-box* a coffin; a *cold cart* a hearse; a *cold cook* an undertaker; and *cold storage* the grave.

cold² not easily susceptible to sexual excitement
The opposite of HOT 1 but also of someone who fails to be sexually excited on a specific occasion:
> I have often been asked why on my African travels I was cold in regard to the native women. (F. Harris, 1925—what strange interlocutors he must have met)

Despite Mr Harris's unwonted abstinence, more of women than of men, as in Shakespeare's *cold chastity.*

cold³ an excuse for an ailment which is taboo or concealed
Servicemen in the Second World War who contracted gonorrhoea might say that they *had a cold.* Now used by politicians who wish to conceal infirmity:
> Andropov spent half his 15 months in power seriously ill, supposedly suffering from a 'cold' but in fact lying in a Kremlin hospital hitched up to a dialysis machine with kidney failure and diabetes. (*Sunday Telegraph,* 27 March 1994) See also CATCH A COLD 1 and 2 and DIPLOMATIC COLD.

cold deck a pack of cards which has been arranged for use by a cheat
Literally, one which has not been played with:
> It was even suggested he might at times ring in a cold deck (a previously 'prepared'

fresh deck of cards) on his own hand. (Clay, 1998)

cold feet cowardice or fear
There is a physical justification for this standard English use. We do experience the symptoms of coldness when we are frightened:
> I think I must have the merest touch of claustrophobia—or cold feet as they would call it in the mess. (Price, 1978, of a tank commander)

cold turkey the effect of sudden and sustained deprivation of narcotics
The sufferer resembles a bird which has been plucked. Usually of withdrawal from drug-taking, drinking alcohol, or smoking tobacco:
> You can't suddenly sign the pledge, go cold turkey. (B. Forbes, 1986)
> I'm giving up [smoking] again. Two days of cold turkey. (Strong, 1997)
To help a person shake off an addiction is to *cool a turkey*:
> If you're still wanting my help, I'll be at your disposal to help cool your turkeys. (Fiennes, 1996—he was working in a place which treated addicts)
In America other fowls may replace the turkey.

cold-water man *Scottish* a person who drinks no intoxicants
The use is perhaps obsolete, in a society where, for some, abstinence is taboo:
> 'Dae ye drink?' He's a cauld-water man. (J. F. S. Gordon, 1880)

collaborator¹ a traitor
He works disloyally for the conqueror, not loyally for another like-minded person:
> The English so often have these unknown French friends... Collaborators one and all. (N. Mitford, 1960)
Collaborationist is specific:
> I told him I was not a collaborationist, that I was a doctor. (Fowles, 1977, writing of a Greek in the Second World War)
To *collaborate* is so to act:
> ...the French government was required to order the administration to 'collaborate' with the German miliary authorities in the Occupied Zone. (Ousby, 1997)

collaborator² a ghost writer
The labour is mostly done by the ghost:
> Crawford Sloane's book, *The Camera and the Truth* had been published several months earlier. Written with a collaborator, it was his third. (Hailey, 1990)

collapsible container *American* a contraceptive sheath

Police jargon which transfers the male post-coital collapsing to the contraceptive:
> In any police report when you refer to a collapsible container, it's a rubber. (Wambaugh, 1981)

collar¹ to steal
Either from putting a collar on a dog in the days when they were taken for ransom (although in English Common Law they could not be the subject of theft) or, more probably, from securing possession of anything.

collar² an arrest
The act of grabbing a suspect by his collar so as to lead him away:
> But the evidence is of such a nature that it doesn't justify a collar—an arrest. (Sanders, 1973)
The miscreant may *get his collar felt*, as mentioned on BBC television on 25 February, 1997. An *accommodation collar* is an arrest by an American policeman to fill a quota and prove he is doing his job.

collar³ *American* a policeman
Whose task it is to make a COLLAR 2.

collateral damage killing or wounding civilians by mistake
Literally, damage running alongside:
> What an odd term, he thought. *Collateral damage.* What an off-hand way of condemning people whom fate had selected to be in the wrong place. (Clancy, 1989)

collect *American* to accept a bribe
Usually it refers to taking bribes on a regular basis:
> Woe to the cop who collects anything... and doesn't 'see the sergeant'. (Lavine, 1930)
Of the same tendency was the British *collector*, the highwayman who ordered you to stand and deliver.

collect a bullet to be shot
The *collection* is involuntary:
> Gen had collected a bullet. (Ryan, 1999—Gen died soon after)

Colombian gold high-quality marijuana
From the source, the colour, and the profits:
> Pot-smokers the world over recognize the taste of its product, known as Colombian Gold. (Theroux, 1979)

colonial *American* old
Real estate jargon of buildings which were not always there before the 1780s. *Antebellum*, referring to the Civil War, is more likely to be authentic, but don't count on it.

colony a distant territory ruled by ex-patriates
Literally, a place to which people emigrate in order to live but most British, French, German, and Italian *colonies* retained their majority of indigenous inhabitants. Immediately before the British Crown Colony of Hong Kong was returned to China, 98% of its population were people of Chinese extraction.

colour relating to racial descent
Literally, the universal human characteristic of skin pigmentation. A *colour problem* is tension between different racial groups:

It was now accepted that some form of control was unavoidable if we were not to have a colour problem in [Britain] on a similar scale to that in the USA. (Heffer, 1998, quoting Rab Butler in 1961)

To be *colour-blind* is to be unprejudiced concerning the skin pigmentation of others:

[Nat Bergman] seemed completely colour-blind and became my first white friend. (Mandela, 1994)

colour-tinted dyed
Describing hair, where it is more than circumlocution because the process is more drastic than the variation of a shade. Also, as a verb, to *colour correct*:

For dry, bleached or colour-tinted hair (instruction on bottle, 1980)

She 'mutates' or 'colour-corrects' her hair. (Jennings, 1965)

coloured[1] not exclusively of white Caucasian ancestry
Oscar Wilde correctly described himself on entering the United States as pink;

There are already white tables so why not have a table for the coloured fellers. (Theroux, 1973—they were not foresters)

In South Africa *coloured* or *Cape coloured* was used of those of mixed ancestry:

The pass system, for example, barely affected Indians or Coloureds. (Mandela, 1994)

A year ago the Cape Coloured teenager, who is due to make his Test debut against England at Port Elizabeth on Boxing Day, would have been content just to be in the crowd. (*Sunday Telegraph*, 24 December 1995)

An America you may also meet a *person of the coloured persuasion* or a *person of colour*:

I am not a black. I am a person of the colored persuasion. (Sanders, 1977)

The Reverend then spent a very long time blasting everyone who wasn't of colour and had money. (Grisham, 1998)

coloured[2] dyed

Hair is never colourless:

He could see the spark of rouge on her cheeks, the perfect part in her colored hair. (Turow, 1990—*part* is American for parting)

colourful amoral or defying convention
As different from grey, or boring:

In Fleet Street, a usefully libel-resistant catch-all term to imply (variously) a louche, pleasure-seeking or startling quality is 'colourful'. (Parris, 1995)

colt[1] *obsolete* to impregnate a woman
Punning perhaps on an old meaning, to cheat, because it was used of extramarital impregnation:

She hath been colted by him. (Shakespeare, *Cymbeline*)

colt[2] *obsolete English* a fine extracted from a recruit by other employees
The money was spent on intoxicants as part of a ritual called *shoeing the colt*, which tells us the etymology. This was one of many similar expressions relating to initiation ceremonies for apprentices.

comb out to massacre
How the Germans described their treatment of Soviet citizens:

... anti-partisan operations resulted in the deaths of a quarter of a million Russian civilians as a given area was encircled and then 'combed out', a euphemism for lining up the inhabitants of villages and shooting them. (Burleigh, 2000)

combat fatigue an unwillingness or inability to continue fighting
Not just weariness from broken nights, poor shelter, irregular food, unchanged clothing, lice, ulcers, and the other discomforts of active service but a reaction to prolonged exposure to danger and seeing the death and mutilation of comrades:

He is suffering from what you call combat fatigue, and is subject to fits of depression and hallucination. (Shaw, 1946)

As with BATTLE FATIGUE, it was difficult for those undergoing the same dangers and privations to distinguish between psychological disturbance and cowardice.

combat ineffective dead, seriously ill, or badly wounded
Not describing a gun which doesn't shoot straight but how a commander assesses his troops:

If he became combat ineffective, a subtle way of saying wounded or killed... (Coyle, 1987)

come to achieve a sexual orgasm

Of both sexes:
> 'I don't know why I let you come this
> evening,' says Flora. 'You haven't let me
> come,' says Howard. (Bradbury, 1975)

Come off is less common and seems to be used
of the male rather than the female experience. *Come* is used also to describe the fluid
secreted by the male and by the female during
copulation:
> 'It's Bernard Shaw's semen.'...'You mean
> it's come?' 'Yes.' (Bradbury, 1976)

come across¹ to do something unwill-
ingly under coercion
It refers to extortion, bribery, or making a
confession:
> ...ask why he had to pay when the other
> bird didn't come across. (Lavine, 1930)

come across² to have a casual sexual relationship with
Again acceding to a suggestion, usually from a
man, but without any coercion:
> I can see you now, selling pencils outside
> the high school, 'cause Alison Taylor won't
> come across. (R. N. Patterson, 1996/2)

come across³ to defect
Espionage jargon, from the actual or figurative passage of a frontier or line of battle:
> He's defected. He came across and that's
> that. (Seymour, 1980)

come again to resume your living physical state after death
An eagerly awaited expectation by some
devout people despite the manifest problems
such a happening might pose:
> He shall come again in His glory, to judge
> both the quick and the dead. (*Book of
> Common Prayer*, 1662)

Come back in the same sense is obsolete.

come aloft to have an erection of the
penis
Punning perhaps on the duties of deck-hands
on sailing ships:
> I cannot come aloft to an old woman.
> (Dryden, 1668)

come around to menstruate
Regularity is hoped for, except for those
wishing to become pregnant.

come down to cease to be under the influence of illegal narcotics
After a feeling of levitation and implying the
unpleasantness and ill-temper of one so
affected:
> Floating. When she came down it was
> pretty grim. (Bogarde, 1981)

come home by Clapham see CLAPHAM

come home feet first to be killed
Corpses are usually carried that way, although
the opposite happens with coffins:
> Whoever came home feet first, it wasn't
> going to be him. (Fraser, 1977)

come in at the window *obsolete* to be
illegitimate
The newcomer was figuratively introduced
into the household by any aperture other
than the front door. Following the window
in popularity were the side door, the back
door, the wicket, and the hatch. Also as *come o'
will*:
> In at the window or else o'er the hatch
> ...I am I howe'er I was begot.
> (Shakespeare, *King John*)
> Little curlie Geoffrey—that's the eldest, the
> come o' will. (W. Scott, 1815)

come into the public domain to cease
being a secret
It refers to embarrassing or scandalous information which politicians or public employees wish to conceal:
> Naturally we are, all of us, in the Service
> concerned that advice one has given
> could be misunderstood if it were to
> come into the public domain. (Lynn and
> Jay, 1986)

come off see COME

come on¹ to menstruate
Obvious derivation and wide female use:
> Have you come on badly or something?
> (P. Scott, 1968—an enquiry from one
> woman to another)

come on² an invitation to another to
make a sexual approach
Either sex may so encourage the other,
although it is more commonly done by the
female:
> 'Did she touch the young guy?...Stroke his
> hair. Put her hand on his arm. Anything
> like that?' 'You mean was she coming on?'
> (Sanders, 1981)

come-on³ a deceptive inducement to
enter into a long-term commitment
Advertising jargon for the offer intended to
tempt or trap the unwary:
> The electricity bill, a come-on for *Time/Life*
> books...(Allbeury, 1980, listing the
> contents of mail)

come out to announce your availability
as a sexual partner
Until the 1950s this was social jargon for the
parade of marriageable girls of wealthy
parents, in London especially, before supposedly eligible bachelors; see also OUT 1:

Girls had to come out, I knew. (N. Mitford, 1949)

The phrase is now used specifically of homosexuals who make public their sexual preference for the first time, being a shortened form of *come out of the closet*:

Lord Mountbatten was definitely gay himself though he never had to courage to come out of the closet. (*Private Eye*, May 1981)

The Bishops' group also says that a homosexual who has 'come out' should offer his resignation to his bishop. (*Daily Telegraph*, October 1979—note the quotation marks in an early use)

come through to act under duress
From the meaning, to achieve a desired result. It is used of the payment of a bribe or of giving information under duress:

They'll snatch your wife or take you out in the woods and give you the works. And you'll have to come through. (Chandler, 1939)

come to to copulate with
Particularly in a marriage where the spouses occupy separate beds:

I have come very seldom to you in the last few years. (Bogarde, 1981—a husband was speaking to his wife)

come to a sticky end to fail disastrously but deservedly
The fate of a fly on flypaper. It may describe an untimely death of a dissolute or criminal person, the incarceration of a rogue, an unwanted pregnancy of a flighty girl, or any other unpleasant upshot which allows third parties the satisfaction of saying 'I told you so'.

come to see to court
Literally, to visit, but a man who *comes to see your sister* is unlikely to content himself merely with a visual inspection. See also SEE 1.

come to the attention of the police to be a habitual criminal
The constabulary do not so refer to their benefactors:

More important, many of them, as the superintendent puts it, 'come to our attention'. (*Daily Telegraph*, 9 April 1996, of young unemployed adults living at the public expense in seaside hotels)

come to your resting place to die
Not reaching your overnight hotel but the common imagery of likening death to resting while you await resurrection or whatever may be in store. Also as *come to the end of the road*:

He drove me direct to this bungalow and then to the resting place which she had come to just the day before. (P. Scott, 1973)

She came to the end of the road only five years after we had laid father to rest. (Tyrrell, 1973)

I like the Shetland *come to yourself*, with its Buddhist overtones:

I faer dis ane 'ill come to himsel'. (*Shetland News*, 1890, quoted in *EDD*)

come together to copulate
Without necessarily reaching simultaneous orgasms:

When his mother Mary was espoused to Joseph, before they came together, she was found with child by the Holy Ghost. (*Matthew*, 1: 18)

come up with the rations *British* to be awarded as a matter of routine
An army use where campaign medals were not valued highly and those for bravery appeared to be awarded at random:

'Bit of decoration. Congratulations.' 'Came up with the rations.' He took the ribbon. But if he joked he was pleased in his soul. (J. A. Lee, 1937)

Now used of routine awards to British functionaries and time-servers.

come your mutton (of a male) to masturbate
The common MEAT 2 imagery. See also MUTTON.

comfort[1] copulation
The female so provides solace for the male:

Gossip declared that Bothwell sought comfort with his divorced wife Jean, with whom he spent several days a week. (Linklater, 1964—Mary Queen of Scots was not reputed to enjoy sexual activity)

comfort[2] urination
As in the *comfort break* at meetings:

But it was in one of those comfort breaks from the negotiations with the NUJ…that I realised my arguments had outstayed their welcome. (Cole, 1995)

An American *comfort station* is a public lavatory:

Art habitually terminated the beach section of his run by the comfort station coyly labelled 'Boys' and 'Girls'. (L. Thomas, (1979)

comfort women prostitutes working under duress
The lot of many Korean, Chinese, and Dutch females in territories captured by the Japanese:

...the forced recruitment of 'comfort women' by the Japanese army in the Second World War. (*Daily Telegraph*, 7 March 1994)

comfortable¹ *American* drunk
A feeling of wellbeing is induced at some stage.

comfortable² not in mortal danger
Hospital jargon, although a patient so described would seldom admit to being 'free from pain and trouble' (*OED*) unless deeply sedated. Thus we can sympathize with 'Mr Steve Wickwar, 27' who:
    sustained severe cuts after being attacked by a two-year-old male leopard...His condition at Northampton general hospital was said to be comfortable. (*Daily Telegraph*, April 1982—but why not 'a leopard, 2'?)

comic a document calculated to deceive
Literally, a publication containing colourful stories and pictures for children. It is used of expense claims by employees, records by commercial drivers, etc.:
    Shit, damn near every trucker he knew kept a phoney log, they called them comic books. (N. Evans, 1995)

coming of peace a military defeat
The words used by Hirohito in his broadcast of 15 August 1945, when he announced Japan's capitulation in such evasive and formal language that some of the military misunderstood his message and carried on fighting. He also asserted, with considerable understatement, that the war 'had turned out not necessarily to Japan's advantage'. (Keegan, 1989)

commerce copulation
Literally, exchange or dealings between people, but long used of copulation, especially if it is outside marriage. *Sexual commerce* is explicit. *Sinful commerce* is not thieving or receiving stolen goods but copulating with a prostitute:
    Jenny the tavern-girl was not alone in this world of sinful commerce. (Monsarrat, 1978, writing in archaic style)

commercial sex worker a prostitute
Neither a salaried nurse running a VD clinic nor even someone employed to categorize day-old chicks:
    A St John Ambulance worker...tells me that she is only allowed to describe (prostitutes) as CSWs—short for Commercial Sex Workers. (*Daily Telegraph*, 5 January 1994)

commission a bribe

Not the warrant to do something for another but from the reward in percentage terms for doing it. Commercial usage where a gloss of legality is used to conceal bribery:
    As for bribes...this is a capitalist society, General. We prefer to talk of commissions and introducer's fees. (W. Smith, 1979)

commission agent a person who accepted bets for a living
Neither an agent of those who place the bets nor rewarded by commission. In former times, some opprobrium used to attach to gambling and those who facilitated it.

commit to consign to an institution for the insane
Literally, to give in charge, and clearly the shorter form of a longer phrase:
    Polly, you ought to commit your father. (M. McCarthy, 1963—father was mentally ill but at liberty)
And see SECTION.

commit a nuisance to urinate in public
Usually of a male, where *commit* meant perform and *nuisance* is legal jargon for an offensive act:
    These are the same naughty young men who 'Commit a Nuisance'...Or it could be some old rustic twelve-pinter who is past caring. (Blythe, 1969—a 'twelve-pinter' is someone who has drunk at a sitting twelve pints of beer)
You may still see some of the old signs enjoining us to 'Commit no nuisance'—don't urinate here.

commit misconduct to indulge in extra-marital sexual activity
Used of either sex, and also as *commit infamy*. To *commit adultery* is standard English and not euphemistic, being the first use of the phrase:
    ...moments of passion reduced to 'committing misconduct'. (Pearsall, 1969)
    [He] would in time betray his wife...and might in his lifetime commit infamy with more than a thousand women and boys. (Tremain, 1999)

commit suicide to be murdered
One of the Nazi evasions when explaining the death of a prisoner:
    The Hamburg Gestapo chief Bruno Streckenbach came to a local arrangement in 1934 with the courts, whereby those who 'committed suicide' after he had smashed their kidneys with a knuckleduster were cremated to prevent autopsy. (Burleigh, 2000)

committed dogmatic as to political or social views

Literally, devoted, although people who use the phrase are not likely to elaborate on the cause which is the object of their devotion:

> Committed to what? Abortion, Marxism or promiscuity? It's bound to be one of the three. (Sharpe, 1976)

Whence, *commitment*, such dogmatism:

> He believed the best journalism was not the balanced, objective kind... but the 'journalism of commitment'. (Simpson, 1998)

Committee (the) an instrument of state repression

A common abbreviation in totalitarian states like the former Soviet Union. Thus the *Komitet Gosudarstvennoi Bezopasnosti*, or KGB, became the *Komitet*, or Committee:

> 'The Committee's involved,' Suchko went on, using the standard euphemism for the KGB. (R. Moss, 1985)

In Cuba you may still find the *Committee for the Protection of the Revolution*, which involves neighbours spying on each other in the manner of the Nazi *Blockwachter* organization.

commode a portable lavatory

Originally, a woman's tall headdress, whence a tall chest of drawers, and then any wooden bedroom cupboard, which many of these lavatories, disguised as furniture, came to resemble:

> An ice-box built in a Marie-Antoinette commode. (Ustinov, 1971)

commodious too large

Literally, convenient, but in real estate jargon, where we might have expected elegant spaciousness, all we find is a place too big to heat or keep in repair.

common customer *obsolete* a prostitute

Supplier might have seemed more appropriate:

> I think thee now some common customer. (Shakespeare, *All's Well that Ends Well*)

Also as *common jack*, *maid*, *sewer*, and (in modern use) *tart*. *Commoner o' th' camp* can also be found in the Bard's works.

common house[1] *obsolete* a brothel

From the sharing no doubt and not to be confused with Westminster's *House of Commons*:

> Do nothing but use their abuses in common houses. (Shakespeare, *Measure for Measure*)

See also HOUSE 1.

common house[2] *obsolete* a lavatory

Again from the sharing, and a feature of much 19th-century urban development. See also HOUSE 2.

communicable disease a venereal disease

For medical practitioners the phrase has two meanings. It can be either a disease like meningitis, which must be reported (communicated) immediately to the authorities, or a disease which can be transferred by contact from one sufferer to another. Lay use is normally only in the second sense.

community alienation lawlessness

Social-service jargon which seeks to avoid blaming thugs for anti-social behaviour. It does not mean the place has been taken over by foreigners:

> The village now exhibits the signs of this community alienation with its smashed telephone kiosks, litter and graffiti painted on its mellow walls. (*Thatch*, March 1982)

community of wives polyandry

Nothing so tame as the Women's Institute, Mothers' Union, or Ladies' Circle:

> In the 1650s people listened with delicious horror to reports of Ranter meetings, where, it was said, adherents drank freely, smoked, swore, took off their clothes and practised 'community of wives'—meaning group sex. (Gentles, 1992—the 'Ranters' were one of the many religious sects which emerged during the English Civil War, proving less enduring if more lively than, for example, the Quakers)

community relations social tension between those of a different racial background

The use seeks to avoid reference to COLOUR and can be found in various phrases relating to problems which may occur through the distrust, ignorance, jealousy, fear, or other factors which may be present when those of different racial backgrounds move into territory formerly occupied mainly by another ethnic grouping. Thus a *community affairs officer* is concerned to prevent, and a *community relations correspondent* to report on, discord between such groups, not to arrange or write about church fêtes and the like.

community treatment center *American* a prison

Not a doctor's surgery, hospital, or operating theatre.

companion a person with whom you have a regular extramarital sexual relationship

Originally in this sense, an employee who lived with and attended to another person. Of either sex, and heterosexual or homosexual:

> I'm thinking of getting a new companion. There's a little actress on the train who

would suit me. (G. Greene, 1932—the speaker a female homosexual)
Princess Stephanie of Monaco and her companion, Daniel Ducruet, her former bodyguard, pose with their second child Pauline. (*Daily Telegraph*, 7 June 1994)

A *constant companion* is journalese to describe such a relationship where one of the parties might sue for defamation:

Miss Kristina Olsen, his close friend and constant companion. (Allbeury, 1976)

company¹ a person with whom you have an extramarital sexual relationship
Literally, companionship and often of a transient relationship:

And your wife on the outside, looking around for company. (Sanders, 1977)

See also KEEP COMPANY WITH and STEADY COMPANY.

company²(the) the main US organization for espionage and foreign subversion
A pun on the initial letters of *Central Intelligence Agency* and the Spanish *Cia*, an abbreviation for *compañia*, company:

Your outrageous statement that we intend to commit bodily harm tarnishes our friends in the Company. (Ludlum, 1979)

compensated dating prostitution
As practised by some schoolgirls in Japan where copulation with females over the age of 13 is legal:

Few parents want to think that their daughters are involved in 'compensated dating'. (*Daily Telegraph*, 29 August 1996)

completion a sexual orgasm
Usually of the female, whether final or not:

In thanks, he summoned up a patient rigidity which brought her to six vast, grunting completions before she subsided into deep sleep. (M. Thomas, 1980)

complications the swelling of an adult's testicles during mumps
This symptom, additional in some cases to swollen glands in the neck, is very painful and may lead to infertility:

Measles without complications at nine and mumps when he was too young for complications at ten. (Price, 1972)

complimentary included in the price
The usage often seeks to mask an inferior or unwanted substitution for a discontinued service, such as a paper strip with which to clean your shoes in place of a night porter. However, there are exceptions:

We will shortly take your beverage order. The wine in your basket is complimentary.

(Republic Airlines Flight RC 207 Greenville—New York, May 1981)

compound with *obsolete* to copulate with
Literally, to mingle with:

My father compounded with my mother under the dragon's tail. (Shakespeare, *King Lear*)

comprehension the ability to read
Literally, understanding. Educational jargon, along with *literacy* and *numeracy*, to avoid having to mention the three r's, which used to be the foundation of every child's education in the days when teachers were not obliged to attend teacher training colleges:

MID-GLAMORGAN ADULT LITERACY/ NUMERACY SERVICE for help with: READING SPELLING ARITHMETIC. (Advertisement in *Rhymney Valley Express*, noted in *Private Eye*, October 1981, addressed to those who had failed to acquire these skills at school)

A British *comprehensive* school is one financed by the state which offers non-selective entry and is not necessarily characterized by comprehension:

46 per cent of children now leaving Mrs. Williams' 'comprehensive' secondary school system [are] unable to read or write. (A. Waugh in *Private Eye*, July 1981)

compromise to expose to embarrassment or danger
Literally, to accept a lowering of standards. It describes involving in or revealing adultery, homosexuality, murder, etc.:

He began to fiddle with his clothes... is he going to do it here, in public, to compromise me? (Bradbury, 1959)
Lord Randolph [Churchill]... in order to cover for his brother who had compromised Lady Aylesford... appeared prepared to expose the Prince of Wales's adultery with her. (Graham Stewart, 1999)
He was killed—and he was killed—because whatever that woman told him was so conclusive he had to be compromised hours later. (Ludlum, 1984)
I'd learned from an unidentified source that Flight 306 to Bangkok was compromised. (Hall, 1988—it was about to be blown up in mid-air)

con to trick
Not relating to the path of a ship or 'set in a notebook, learned, and conned by rote' but a shortened form of *confidence*, which was first used in this sense in 1866 of the advisers of the Confederate President Davis:

Many of the people you meet will be out to con you. (Sanders, 1980)

Whence the *confidence trick, or fraud*, practised by the *con man* (are there no 'con women'?) or *con artist*:

> Don't pull that con artist crap with me, pal. I've seen you working this street for three days. (Weverka, 1973)

concentration camp a place for arbitrary imprisonment of political and other opponents

They were originally the areas in which civilians were concentrated by the Spanish in Cuba and the British in South Africa to prevent the feeding and hiding of men engaged in fighting against them. The Nazis adopted the tactic and the terminology—*Konzentrationslager*. Their prisons, which started as places for extortion, ransom, and humiliation, became depots for slave labour and genocide:

> There are not only prisons now, there are concentration camps. (Manning, 1962, writing of the Second World War)

Sometimes abbreviated to *camp*:

> ... three-fifths of [Polish Jews] had disappeared into camps that used the new scientific methods... They had an official name... Vernitchtungslager, extermination camp. (Keneally, 1982)

concentration problem (a) idleness or inattention

Educational jargon in a world where there are no lazy or stupid children:

> You clearly have a concentration problem, 'are an idle bitch', and I was wondering... (Amis, 1978)

See also PROBLEM.

concern political dogmatism

Literally, care or interest:

> The Claimants' Union, a focus of responsibility and concern... (Bradbury, 1975, and see CLAIMANT)

In the same context, *concerned* means dogmatic:

> The kind of *decent*, modest radicalism... was a perpetuation of the concerned student politics... (Bradbury, 1965)

concerned *obsolete* drunk

Probably a shortened form of *concerned in liquor*, or something of the sort:

> He never called me worse than sweetheart, drunk or sober. Not that I knew his Reverence was ever concerned. (Swift, 1723)

concert party the concerted buying of shares in a company using different names

Stock Exchange jargon for an attempt to build up a key or large holding without putting on notice the board of the company or the Stock Exchange. There is also a more innocent use, where individuals have banded together to acquire a large holding which remains separately owned:

> The shares were suspended in June at $4\frac{1}{2}$p and resumed at $1\frac{1}{2}$p, closing unchanged. A concert party, including Victor Kiam, now owns 60—85%. (*Daily Telegraph*, 22 September 1998)

concession a reduction in an inflated demand

The jargon and practice of politics:

> The bids... are invariably padded so that the minister can be seen to make 'concessions' in head-to-head negotiations with the Treasury. (J. Major, 1999)

concessional free or subsidized

The use seeks to mask the granting of charity or privilege to individuals who receive *concessional fares* on public transport and to countries which receive *concessional loans* or *financing*:

> Most big companies that work in the regions where concessional financing is used believe that the countries other than their own twist and bend and creatively interpret these rules. (Patten, 1998)

concoct to falsify

Originally, to form from different ingredients, whence to invent:

> I never knew anybody—anybody—concoct his expenses like you. (L. Thomas, 1989)

concrete shoes (in) murdered and hidden

A more accurate description of CEMENT SHOES, and also as *concrete boots* or *overcoat*:

> ... it's tough to play golf in concrete shoes. *Comprende?* (M. Thomas, 1980)
> Aiden... has a three-day plan; repay two grand he owes his pornographer boss or else find himself trying on a concrete overcoat. (*Empire*, August, 1993)

condition¹ an illness

Literally, any prevailing circumstance, but in matters of health any *condition* is bad, be it of the heart, liver, bladder, or whatever:

> Throughout the aircraft, the old, then those with pre-existing medical conditions, began to die. (Block, 1979)

condition² a pregnancy

This usage is not reserved for unwanted or difficult pregnancies and merely avoids direct reference to the taboo surrounding pregnancy:

Naturally, Melinda did not mention her condition. (Boyle, 1979—Melinda Merling was pregnant by the spy Donald McLean before their marriage)

The *condition* may be adjectivally enhanced, as by *delicate*, *interesting*, or *certain*:

He said that a young woman who was obviously in 'a certain condition', but not having a ring...(Lodge, 1975)

conditioner a mild acid liquid
Sold to neutralize the alkaline effect of soap after washing hair. In former times people used vinegar to this end. A product which says it combines shampoo and conditioner is one which has been formulated with a pH of 7 and costs more.

confederation a pressure group
Literally, an alliance or union of states for joint action. Thus the *British Confederation for the Advancement of State Education* sought not so much to improve the quality of teaching in state schools as to close down those which achieved higher standards through the selection of pupils.

conference (in) unwilling to see or talk to callers
A standard excuse, which sounds grander than TIED UP:

Ahm afraid Miss Brimley is in conference. Can someone else answer your query? (le Carré, 1962)

The 'formal meeting for consultation and discussion' (*SOED*) is where we go when we are *at a conference*, unless were are in medical or academic employment, when a *conference* may be a paid holiday to be enjoyed with our peers and a chosen companion in a congenial place at the expense of a third party.

confident pricing charging more for the same product
The circumstances are that you expect the buyers not to make a fuss about it or stop buying:

This splendidly open-handed promise [to improve profits by £100m. a year] was to be achieved by...and 'a more confident pricing policy'. (*Daily Telegraph*, 5 April 1996)

confinement the period of childbirth
Literally, no more than be cooped up, as in prison. Standard English:

The women continue working down to the day of their confinement. (Mayhew, 1851)

Thus the use of *confined*, which might be taken as being unable to leave a sickroom, is to be giving birth, this usage having superseded the 19th-century meaning, constipated.

confirmed bachelor a homosexual
Mainly obituary use but:

Although he had been himself referred to in such phrases as a 'confirmed bachelor', even his personal life has largely been left alone. (*New Yorker*, July, 2000)

conflict a war
Literally, a strong disagreement or a single battle. It sounded better than war, especially when the Korean *conflict* burst upon us so soon after the Second World War.

confrontation a war
Literally, a meeting face-to-face. Indonesia's 1963 *confrontation* with the fledgling state of Malaysia included subversion and armed incursions, the latter being repulsed with the help of the British (a debt now forgotten). The word is also used by terrorists of indiscriminate violence against society:

Well for one thing we haven't ruled out the possibility of confrontation. (Theroux, 1976—terrorists were discussing tactics)

confused drunk
It certainly can take you that way.:

I gather our son was very confused that night; which is a mother's way of saying he was plastered. (Ludlum, 1979)

congress copulation
Literally, a coming together, as in the *Indian Congress Party*, which restricts its activities in the main to politics. Also as *sexual congress*:

I had heard precisely how that acrobatic quartet achieved congress. (Fowles, 1977—four people were copulating)

Eight days later in the little summer-house sexual congress took place. (Boyd, 1987)

conjugal rights copulation with your spouse
Legal jargon, from the parties being yoked together, and indeed in some societies a symbolic yoke formed part of the marriage ceremony. A woman is unlikely to seek these rights from her husband except in satire:

Wilt had enough trouble with his own virility without having Eva demand that her conjugal rights be supplemented oralwise. (Sharpe, 1976)

If a wife goes to court for the *restoration of conjugal rights*, she seeks pecuniary rather than sexual gratification.

conk (out) to die
From the unplanned stoppage of an engine and the consequent immobility:

Jassy and Victoria will scream with laughter when I do finally conk out. (N. Mitford, 1949)

...the paintings would automatically increase in value once Maitland had conked. (Sanders, 1977—Maitland was an artist)

connect¹ to copulate
The imagery is from joining or fastening together:
> ...two beautifully engraved figures of man and woman who were connecting at every tick of the clock. (F. Richards, 1936)

Connection in this sense normally means extramarital copulation, although usually in the singular:
> Privates in the Blues...often formed very reprehensible connections with women of property, tradesmen's wives, and even ladies. (Mayhew, 1862—'the Blues' is a British regiment)

and sometimes bestiality:
> ...others were homosexual, others who sought connection with animals (an ill-documented area in sexology). (Pearsall, 1969)

connect² a source of illegal narcotics
The *connection*, in the jargon of drug usage, runs from the manufacturer to the retailer:
> [She] had got too much in the bank to be shagging every creep with a connect because she's too scared to go out and cop on her own. (Turow, 1999)

connections people liable to favour or assist you unfairly
Literally, those to whom you are related or whom you know well, but also used of those susceptible to bribery:
> ...the redoubtable lady was able first to defraud the public and then evade the consequences because she had 'connections'. (Shirer, 1984—she used bribery)

connubial pleasures copulation
Although *connubial* means to do with marriage, the *pleasures* to which the phrase alludes can be taken within or without that institution:
> She never married, but it didn't prevent her from enjoying connubial pleasures. (Ludlum, 1979)

conquer a bed *obsolete* to copulate with a female
See also BED 2:
> When you have conquer'd my yet maiden bed. (Shakespeare, *All's Well that Ends Well*)

consensual relationship a regular extra-marital sexual relationship
Consensual indicates a legal as well as a sensual accord:

This suggests that Britain is moving rapidly towards Scandinavian-style 'consensual relationships', said the Office of Population, Census and Surveys. (*Daily Telegraph*, 14 June 1995)

consenting adults male homosexuals over the age of 18 who engage in sexual acts with each other
British law concerns itself less with female homosexuality:
> Two consenting adults had been ejected from the gents. (Sharpe, 1975—they were not consenting to their ejection)

console to copulate with
Literally, to alleviate sorrow. It is used of either sex, especially when a regular sexual partner is absent:
> Another girl of similar type, who had briefly consoled him in France. (Boyle, 1979—of the spy Philby)

Consolation is such copulation:
> Most whose wives were out of harm's way were quick to find consolation. (Manning, 1977)

consort with to have an extramarital sexual relationship with
A *consort* is someone who keeps you company:
> Some of them consorted with—with the worst type of native woman. (Fraser, 1975)

constructed *American* conquered or re-captured
The language of Vietnam:
> A 'constructed' hamlet meant not a newly built one but a former Viet Cong hamlet that had been worked over politically. (M. McCarthy, 1967)

If it was taken by the Vietcong and re-captured, it became, in the jargon, *reconstructed*.

consultant¹ a senior employee who has been dismissed
A usage by and of those who seek to conceal the loss of face arising from dismissal.

consultant² a salesperson
The suggestion is that they give the customer impartial advice:
> Virgin Associates Direct has a network of 6000 consultants demonstrating products in people's homes. (*Daily Telegraph*, 5 April 2000)

consummate (a relationship) to copulate
Originally, to accomplish to the full:
> I have had to learn self-control. She has refused to consummate our relationship. (Townsend, 1982)

Consummation is one of the essential ingredients of Christian marriage, in default of which a British or Vatican court, among others, may grant an annulment. To *consummate your desires* implies copulation, usually of men but:
> ...there is a house in Regent Street, I am told, where ladies, both married and unmarried, go in order to...consummate their libidinous desires. (Mayhew, 1862)

consumption pulmonary tuberculosis
Prior to penicillin, this was the dread disease which wasted away, or consumed, the sufferer:
> The girl had died since them. Consumption devoured her. (Keneally, 1979, writing of the 19th century)

Also known as *the white plague*, both phrases were replaced latterly by *TB*, for *tubercule bacillus*.

contact with sexual activity with
From the touching. In heterosexual encounters, it appears to apply only to the male, despite the mutuality of the transaction:
> ...he would need...to augment his size and permanence by food, booze, contact with a woman. (Keneally, 1982)

Contact sex involves more than kissing, voyeurism, and the like:
> Reynolds denied ever having had 'contact sex' with Miss Heard. He said the taped telephone conversations were simply manifestations of an embarrassing craving for 'phone sex'. (*Daily Telegraph*, 24 August 1995—even more embarrassing was the fact that Reynolds was a US Congressman and Miss Heard was a 16-year-old girl)

contagious and disgraceful disease a venereal disease
Legal jargon in the English law of defamation. If you wrongly imputed it when speaking about a woman, the plaintiff had no need to prove special damage. The Slander of Women Act 1891 also made an imputation of unchastity in a woman actionable without proof of special damage.

content¹ kept involuntarily under heavy sedation
Medical jargon:
> ...the few violent cases we have are kept pretty, uh, content. (Sanders, 1979, of an institution for the insane)

content² (your desire) to copulate
Normally referring to casual arrangements by either sex:
> It was the doctor who undertook to content her desire. (F. Harris, 1925)

continent see INCONTINENT 1 2

continuations *obsolete* trousers
They continued a Victorian male's upper garments in a direction too delicate to mention. See also UNMENTIONABLES 1 for more of these quaint usages.

contour a fat shape
Literally, the outline of any figure, but promising to *reduce your contour* is how advertisers try to sell you health foods, exercise equipment, and the like.

contract a promise of payment to murder (someone)
Underworld jargon for a murder treated as a commercial transaction with payment or a reward to the killer:
> There's a contract out on Billison and he's still alive. (Bagley, 1977—the implication was that he should already have been killed)

The *contract* may also be the proposed victim:
> I want you to know you could become a contract. (Deighton, 1981)

contribution a quantity of urine
Medical coyness when asking a patient to provide urine for analysis:
> 'The usual contribution, please,' she said motioning towards the lavatory door. (Sanders, 1981)

control unit *American* a cell for solitary confinement
There is no inference that the other prisoners are out of control.

controlled substance a narcotic
So called because its legal manufacture and distribution are regulated and supervised:
> ...there was no evidence that he was dealing in what the government laughingly calls a 'controlled substance'. (Sanders, 1987)

controversial¹ politically damaging
Bureaucratic jargon of a policy which may offend populist susceptibilities:
> 'Controversial' only means 'this will lose you votes'. 'Courageous' means 'this will lose you the election.' (Lynn and Jay, 1981)

controversial² disreputable and untrustworthy
Journalistic jargon, especially of businessmen:
> ...[the] moving spirit of the now defunct stockbroker——is working on a diamond company float on the Moscow stock exchange [and is] now sharing a Knightsbridge office with the controversial financier——' (*Sunday Telegraph*, 17 December 1994)

convalescent home an institution for geriatrics
Deposited by their descendants, the inmates go there to die rather than get better.

convalescing exiled
A Chinese Communist evasion:
...if a high official is said to have a cold he's likely to be fired, if he's 'convalescing' he has been exiled. (Theroux, 1988)

convenience a lavatory for public use
Literally, anything which accommodates. Often specifically described as *public*, *men's*, or *ladies'*, or merely in the plural:
...another tin outhouse with a sign saying Conveniences. (Theroux, 1983—it was a lavatory on a camp site)

convenient¹ *obsolete* a prostitute
She restricted her clientele to one regular customer:
Dorimant's Convenient, Madam Loveit. (Etherege, 1676)

convenient² tiny
Real-estate jargon, describing a garden which is manifestly inconvenient for drying washing, privacy, lighting bonfires, growing produce, and all the other uses to which a garden should be put.

conventional not involving nuclear or germ warfare
There is something bizarre in the notion that any weapons for killing or maiming are sanctioned by general agreement or established by social custom.

conversation *obsolete* copulation
The usage must have led to widespread embarrassment and misunderstanding:
His conversation with Shaw's wife. (Shakespeare, *Richard III*)
See also CRIMINAL CONVERSATION.

convey *obsolete* to steal
The article taken is carried off. A *conveyor* was a thief:
...conveyors are you all,
That rise thus nimbly by a true king's fall. (Shakespeare, *Richard II*)
Conveyance was theft and *conveyancing* swindling, the usage pre-dating, and not alluding to, the fees charged by lawyers for transferring title to real estate.

convince to compel by force
Criminal slang:
He knew exactly what methods Willi Kleiber would use to 'convince' Colonel Pitman to open the safe. (Deighton, 1981)

convivial habitually drunken
A journalistic evasion:
...obituaries are simply eulogies of the great and the good, any of whose peccadillos (unusual sexual tastes, drunkenness and so on) are tactfully powdered over with euphemism ('flamboyant', 'convivial' etc.) (Lewis Jones in *Daily Telegraph*, 1 December 1994)
Whence *conviviality*, drunkenness:
Randolph, easily diverted by conviviality, had not been a spectacular success as a correspondent. (Whicker, 1982—Randolph Churchill was an alcoholic and an unreliable journalist)

convoy concept an educational theory whereby the rate of instruction is lowered to the rate of the most stupid or least able to learn
A theory once espoused by teacher training institutions and practised by their products, thereby threatening to condemn some able children to a lifetime of menial work or unemployment:
The 'convoy concept' requiring all to travel at the pace of the slowest, the linguistically handicapped, was damaging. (Deedes, 1997, writing of classes containing immigrant children with a poor command of English)

cook¹ to kill
Perhaps not from the usual culinary imagery, despite the attractions of derivation from *cook your goose*, to cause to fail. Possibly from execution by electricity:
Those fucking sketches could cook him if we found the girl. (Sanders, 1977)
Also of stock in a dry country:
A drought...would cook half the stock in the country. (Boldrewood, 1890)

cook² fraudulently to alter
As in the common *cook the books*, to prepare accounts falsely, from the culinary art of rearranging ingredients to make a more acceptable dish. Sometimes also of records of events:
It is better not to use the word 'cook' in connection with either books or minutes. (Lynn and Jay, 1989)
The phrase was first used of the 'Railway King', George Hudson, who, after overreaching himself, falsified accounts so as to pay dividends out of capital. Among other achievements, he devised the now universal 'clearing' system for shared public services.

cook³ an addict who ingests heated illegal narcotics
Formerly of opium only, when heated over a flame.

Cook County see FIND COOK COUNTY

cookie a promiscuous female
Supposedly warm, sweet and fresh:
> ...you might come clean about that blonde
> cookie you've parked on big-hearted Mrs
> Swallow. Rumour has it that she's
> pregnant. (Lodge, 1975)

A *new cookie* is a younger female consorting
with a man who has abandoned his wife.

cookie pusher a male employee who
curries favour with his boss
From the act of handing round the cakes or
biscuits at a function largely attended by
women:
> ...do you see that furry-headed little
> cookie-pusher Brittan is having the
> fountains in Trafalgar Square drained for
> New Year's Eve? (*Private Eye*, December
> 1983—Brittan was the British Home
> Secretary) Also used generally of male
> homosexuals and owing nothing to the
> obsolete cookie, cocaine.

cool¹ dead
It alludes to the loss of body heat:
> ...if the old lady hadn't been cool for a
> month even the will certainly wouldn't
> have been proven. (Lyall, 1969)

In rare American use, to *cool* is to kill. A *cool
one* is a corpse:
> Mr Yow would not have brought me here if
> he'd known there was a cool one in the car.
> (T. Harris, 1988)

cool² not carrying illegal narcotics
The reverse of HOT 2 and perhaps owing something to the meaning poised and
unruffled. *Cool* is also a widely used adjective of the young, implying social acceptability.

cooler¹ a prison
Common imagery of the place where miscreants are sent to cool down:
> We could be put in the cooler for these.
> (Theroux, 1973)

cooler² an intoxicant which is diluted
and served in a large glass
Normally with ice, to cool you down.

coop *American* a prison
In this case for humans, not for hens and
rabbits:
> 'No convictions, but prints on file.' 'Been in
> the coop.' (Chandler, 1958)

cop¹ to steal
Literally, to catch or seize:
> I was taken by two pals to an orchard to
> cop some fruit. (Horsley, 1887)

cop² a policeman
Usually thought to be a shortened form of
COPPER but also because he *cops* or seizes you:
> The fuzz—that's what they call them now,
> not cops any more. (Ustinov, 1971)

A *cop shop* or *house* is a police station:
> I have to go to the cop house just about
> now. (Chandler, 1958)

Cop, prison, is obsolete.

cop³ *American* to obtain illegal narcotics
Through buying, stealing, or howsoever:
> ...she's too scared to go out and cop on her
> own. (Turow, 1999)

cop⁴ to experience sexually
As in *cop a feel*, to fondle a female sexually, or
cop a cherry, to copulate. Less often of
homosexual activity:
> He has shown the world what happened
> when a scrawny little Frenchman tried to
> cop his joint. (King, 1996; and see JOINT 2)

cop a packet to be killed or severely
wounded
A variant of CATCH A PACKET in all its
meanings, including contracting a venereal
disease. Sometimes also as *cop it*:
> I was really lucky. A lot of my mates
> copped it. (Manning, 1977)

Cop out, in this sense, is rare.

cop an elephant's to become intoxicated
Rhyming slang on *elephant's trunk*, drunk.
Occasionally a drunkard may be described as
elephant's. See also JUMBO.

cop out *American* to plead guilty to a
minor offence in return for the prosecution dropping a more serious charge
A part of the process of plea-bargaining.

cop the drop *American* to accept a bribe
The money is passed into an upturned
palm.

copper a policeman
Probably from the metal buttons on their
19th-century uniforms, but COP 2 offers an
alternative etymology:
> An' up comes a bleedin' rozzer an' lumbers
> me. Wot a life! Coppers. (Kersh, 1936)

copulate to fuck
Originally, to link together, whence to become joined together. As it is explicit in
standard English and less jarring than *fuck*, I
use the word, along with *copulation*, throughout this dictionary.

cordial¹ *obsolete* an intoxicant
Originally, any food or drink which comforted
the person who ingested it:

...make invitation the one to the other for pipes of foreign cordials. (Blackmore, 1869)
In modern use a drink so described, for example lime juice, is likely to please but not to intoxicate.

cordial² cold and unfriendly
Diplomatic jargon which indicates the opposite of the correct meaning, warm and friendly.

corked *American* drunk
Of people: the converse of wine, which should not be drunk when it is corked. The imagery is unclear.

corn¹ low-grade whisky
From the raw material, and often home-made. Also in many compounds, such as *corn juice*, *corn mule* (with a special 'kick'), and the obsolete *corn waters*:
Various sorts of distilled spirits, particularly one named Cornwaters. (Hibbert, 1822)

corn² copulation with a woman
A less common version of OATS, from the food a horse likes best and often. The obsolete *cornification*, lust, comes from the Latin *cornus*, a horn.

corn-fed *American* (of a female) plump
Especially referring to one below middle age, from the fattening of livestock on an augmented diet:
The Sunset Barn is what the drugstore counter was later to become for the corn-fed beauties of the Midwest. (Vanderhaeghe, 1997)

corned drunk
In America, from drinking too much CORN 1. In Scotland and England, where the usage has recurred at various times since the 18th century, it probably came from the old meaning PICKLED.

corner¹ to establish a monopoly in an essential product
Probably from driving cattle into the corner of a yard rather than from storing goods in a hidden place. To *corner* is British criminal jargon for selling shoddy goods at more than their worth by persuading greedy buyers that they are in short supply or have been stolen.

corner² a urinal
Male use, from the facility of urinating in an open space so long as the penis is concealed:
Oh, I'm so sorry, I was looking for a corner. (Olivier, 1982, quoting Winston Churchill who entered a theatre dressing room in 1951)

corner³ the penis
In the phrase *get your corner in*:
...if he did get his corner into a nice mine wife...(Keneally, 1979)

cornhole to sodomize
The derivation is from a vulgarism, meaning the anus:
...you think I'm gonna want the whole world watching him cornhole me. (Goldman, 1986)
I have a single citation referring to incest:
Ran from home because her old man was cornholing her every night. (Turow, 1993—her *old man* was her father, not her husband)

coronary inefficiency a weak heart
Medical jargon which verges on circumlocution or pomposity:
A coronary inefficiency had made it necessary for Robert Winthrop to use a wheelchair. (Ludlum, 1979)
If someone is said to have suffered a *coronary*, it means he has had a heart attack.

corporate entertainment bribery
When customers are given treats at the firm's expense. Also as *corporate hospitality*:
The boxes [at Covent Garden opera house] are largely used for corporate entertainment, that is to say buttering up clients. (H. Porter, *Daily Telegraph*, 22 October 1994—he also noted *business entertainment, freebie, conference*, JOLLY 2, *jaunt, concessionary fare, facility trip, sale preview*, and HOSPITALITY as being indicative of bribery)
He met the senior tutor of his old Oxford college in Newmarket, when both were enjoying the corporate hospitality of a merchant bank. (Rae, 1993— and also enjoying the horse racing)

corporate recovery the management or winding-up of insolvent companies
Accountants' jargon which seeks to draw attention to the often slim hope of revival rather than the probability of demise:
This compares with the 75 p.c. growth in the insolvency side—which the firm delicately calls 'corporate recovery'. (*Daily Telegraph*, 24 November 1990—the firm was the accountants Peat, Marwick, McClintock)

corpse (of a performer) to be unable to continue to act
Forgetting your lines or through uncontrollable laughter:
[Max Bygraves'] original act was so brash and feeble that he could scarcely

get through it without corpsing. (F. Muir, 1997)

correct ¹ in line with received opinion or enforced dogma
As in POLITICALLY CORRECT and not referring to a general adherence to high moral standards. What is *correct* depends on who is writing the rule-book, including the Nazis or the Russian Communist party:
> ...to ensure that political affairs would be handled correctly in an emergency. (Goebbels, 1945, in translation)
> From the correct point of view, there are no contradictions [in Soviet Russian policy]. (M. C. Smith, 1981)

correct² not behaving badly
A Nazi description of how they treated conquered people:
> Events inside France exploded the hope that the Germans would prove 'correct' in their Occupation. (Ousby, 1997)

correction a serious fall (in value)
Stock exchange jargon for a collapse after heavy selling, which seeks to imply that prices had previously risen too high:
> ...there were sufficient signs on the horizon to indicate that some major correction—for which read 'collapse'—is called for. (M. Thomas, 1982)

correctional of or pertaining to prison
The theory is that convicts are there to be taught better ways:
> Correctional—that's a good word. The inmates were corrected all right. Killed with a lethal injection. (P. D. James, 1994)
An American *correctional facility* is a prison and a *correctional officer* is a jailer. For the Soviet communists, *correctional training* included political imprisonment in *corrective training camps*:
> Those who said that...underwent corrective training that proved fatal in most cases. (Amis, 1980, writing about Russian dissidents)
See also HOUSE OF CORRECTION.

corrupt to copulate with outside marriage
Literally, to spoil or lead astray. It is the male who usually did this kind of spoiling:
> Angelo had never the purpose to corrupt her. (Shakespeare, *Measure for Measure*)

costume wedding the marriage of a pregnant bride
Her physical indications rather than her remorse at her premarital behaviour may inhibit the wearing of the traditional white dress.

cottaging seeking a male homosexual partner in a public urinal
Cottage is a slang name for urinal:
> The Tea Room Trade they call it in America; in England, Cottaging. (Fry, 1991)

couch potato a person who habitually spends leisure time watching television
Not a vegetable related to the pernicious couch-grass, or *triticum repens*, but a person vegetating on a sofa:
> Greg wound up the interview good-naturedly and expertly handed on the couch potatoes to the paddock commentator for profiles of the next race's runners. (D. Francis, 1994)

cough¹ (of a criminal) to give information to the police
A common variant of the singing theme, which can include confessing to your own guilt:
> I could go up Grosvenor Street and cough it all. (Theroux, 1976—he was threatening to give information)

cough² to die
The terminally ill suffer from laboured breathing and catarrh:
> All a matter of luck, whether one man stands his ground and wants to take people with him when he coughs. (Seymour, 1977)

cough medicine a spirituous intoxicant
Usually whisky, from the colour and from the pretence of medicinal value, in humorous speech. *Cough syrup* may mean the same thing, but can also, in criminal circles, be a bribe to prevent a possible informer talking.

counsellor one who seeks to advise those suffering misfortune
Literally, anyone giving advice and, specifically in America, a lawyer, but not always:
> 'I wish you'd take my advice and see a Counsellor.' 'Everyone wants me to see a shrink,' she burst out. (Sanders, 1981)
Counselling, as an occupation, fell into a certain disrepute in the 1990s, despite the worthiness of many practitioners:
> There are only three recession professions. One is garden design. The others are counselling and consultancy...two of these activities involve people who are not sure what they ought to be doing telling other people who are not sure what they ought to be doing what they ought to be doing. (Victoria Glendenning in *Daily Telegraph*, 27 January 1994)

count (the) death
Boxing imagery. The *long count*, though rarer, shows greater knowledge of the sport. To *put*

out for the count, again from boxing, is to make unconscious rather than to kill. To *count the daisies* is to be dead, the sums being done from the roots upwards, it would seem. See also POPPING UP THE DAISIES, PUSH UP THE DAISIES, and UNDER THE DAISIES.

counter-attack an unprovoked aggression
There is no requirement for a prior attack to counter:
> Thus did the Nazi dictator and his cohorts in Berlin see the German 'counterattack' on Poland become a European war. (Shirer, 1984, describing the invasion of Poland in 1939)

counter-insurgency waging war in another country
The insurgents are usually the native inhabitants who seek to establish their own administration in place of that imposed by those who use this expression, such as the French in Algeria, the British in various places, and the Americans in Vietnam:
> Kennedy men revealed the need for brand-new names; counter-insurgency, special warfare. (M. McCarthy, 1967)

counter-revolution any internal opposition to a totalitarian regime
The only permitted *revolution* is the one which brought the government to power.

country *American* not reconstituted
The language of the coffee shop(pe):
> Your choice of three crisp slices of bacon ... served with one large country egg. (Holiday Inn menu, May 1981—in the event, the chef chose the slices for me)

country blood *obsolete British* in part black ancestry
It described those of whom an ancestor served in the far-flung empire and had children by a locally born woman who was not white:
> In Miss Vezzis he drew a suitably comic portrait of the result, a half-caste woman in her 'cotton print gowns and bulgey shoes', and a rotter like Bronckhorst was supposed to have 'country blood'. (Royle, 1989)

country-club girls *American* prostitutes operating out of town
When the law closed New Orleans brothels in 1917 to remove temptation from servicemen, many of the prostitutes moved into the countryside:
> The country-club girls are ruining my business. (Longstreet, 1956—an operator left in the city was complaining)

country in transition a poor and backward country
The phrase fails to specify in which direction it is moving:
> ... those thrilling economies known to the IMF as Less Developed Countries or (a new euphemism) countries in transition. (*Daily Telegraph*, 15 September 1994)

country pay *obsolete American* payment in kind
In 18th-century New England specie was scarce and banks were mistrusted:
> My pay would be 'country pay', that is, payment in kind. (Graves, 1941, writing of that period: George Washington, wise man that he was, kept his savings in the Bank of England in London right through the War of Independence)

country sports killing wild animals for pleasure
The trio hunting, shooting, and fishing. Also as *country pursuits*, which do not seem to include hiking, gardening, or simply watching the grass grow.

county farm *American* an institution where people are detained involuntarily
Either through mental illness or as convicts:
> They met a gang of wandering hobos or a band of niggers escaped from the county farm. (King, 1996)

couple¹ (with) to copulate with
The standard meanings are to marry of humans and to copulate of animals:
> Thou hast coupled this Hindoo slut. (Fraser, 1975, writing in archaic style)
> Only ten minutes ago she had been coupling with me on the bed. (Fraser, 1969)
A *coupling house* used to be a brothel.

couple² an unmarried man and woman who have an exclusive sexual friendship with each other
Usually of those not actually cohabiting:
> 'We were a couple,' she murmured, 'and then we weren't. Because of her.' (R. N. Patterson, 1996)

couple³ *American* a woman's breasts
Usually viewed sexually by a male but:
> Reminded her of a girl at prep school who was voted best couple in the yearbook. (McInerney, 1992)

courses *obsolete* menstruation
From the meaning, a period of time:
> I had my courses, my flowers. (Fowles, 1985, writing in archaic style of a woman denying that she had been pregnant)

courtesan a prostitute
In the 15th century, it referred to someone at court. The derivation is more likely to be from the Italian *cortigiana*, despite the morals of Tudor courtiers:
> He regularly visited a famous courtesan in the Srinegar bazaar and enjoyed other favours too. (Masters, 1976)

courtesy included in the price
From the meaning, given freely; but the *courtesy coach* takes you to an inaccessible hotel which you would not have patronized without it. See also COMPLIMENTARY.

cousin Cis a drunken carouse
Rhyming slang for piss which, in the expression *piss-up*, has the same meaning. *DAS* says *sis*.

Covent Garden *obsolete English* engaged in or ancillary to prostitution
The London district, with the neighbouring Drury Lane, was a 17th-century haunt of prostitutes (see also DRURY LANE AGUE). As *Covent* is a corruption of *convent*, there were many ecclesiastical puns and witticisms. Thus a *Covent Garden Abbess* kept a brothel, or *garden house*, which contained *Covent Garden goddesses*. They often infected their customers with *Covent Garden gout*, or *garden gout*, venereal disease, the customers then being said *to have broken their shins against Covent Garden rails*.

cover[1] to copulate with
Standard English of stallions, from the mounting of the mare:
> [The stallion] started covering mares in 1983, and for the first half of the season he bred without any problems. (Monty Roberts, 1996)

Also of other mammals, but rarely used of humans:
> He'll ask you why you did it. 'Because your overseer's covering 'em, you'll say, using a lady-like term.' (Fraser, 1971—the overseer was copulating with slaves)

cover[2] to dye
A 1983 advertisement for dyes said it was for 'covering men's hair'.

cover your boots to urinate
A literal translation from the Hebrew in the Coverdale and the Geneva Bibles.

covert act any illegal behaviour
Not just hidden or secret in the literal sense:
> 'Do you mean acts of sabotage?' 'Er . . . could I just say covert acts?' (Lyall, 1985)

cow brute *obsolete American* a bull

A usage from the days when a bull was too overtly sexual to talk about. For a list of similar euphemisms, see BIG ANIMAL.

crack[1] to rob
By forcible entry of a building or specifically by *cracking* a safe, an art in which a *cracksman* specializes.

crack[2] to hit or kill
Not necessarily with a blow that damages the skull:
> I figure you cracked him in anger. (Turow, 1987, referring to a murder)

crack[3] an illegal compound narcotic
The compound is notorious for the immediate onset of addiction after use:
> Breathing short and shallow, just excited, afraid and juiced all at once, didn't even have time to think about the bag of crack you'd been able to buy. (Katzenbach, 1995)

A *crackhead* is one so addicted:
> Did you get a friend to drive you? Another crackhead looking for an easy score? (ibid.)

crack[4] to arrest
From *cracking a case*, it would seem:
> The first time where she got cracked, we sort of caught them in the act. (Turow, 1996—a policeman was speaking of a habitual criminal)

crack a bottle to drink wine
Perhaps the more impatient among us might break a neck to get at the contents more quickly, but the phrase is also used when the cork is withdrawn by conventional means.

crack a Jane to copulate extramaritally with a female virgin
From CRACK 1 or from *cracking a problem?* To *crack a doll* or *crack a Judy* means the same thing. The obsolete British phrases for the same achievement, to *crack a pitcher* or *a pipkin*, showed more imagination: both these pieces of pottery remain serviceable after the *cracking*, but not as desirable as those without blemish.

crack your whip (of a male) to copulate
Punning on the mastery of an animal trainer and the slang *whip*, or penis:
> She was crazy for me to get her that guy who wrote about cracking his whip all the time. (Sharpe, 1977)

cracked mentally unstable
The article is usable but flawed. There are various similar words using the same imagery. A *crackpot* may be no more than eccentric:

There is no percentage in her remaining engaged to a crack-pot. (Runyon, 1990, written in the 1930s)

although the adjectival use may imply greater mental instability:

Now the necessary removal of Bayldon was threatened by a hijack organised by some crackpot group. (B. Forbes, 1989)

Crack-brained means slightly dotty. *Crackers* can mean anything from mildly eccentric to raving mad:

His nephew by marriage...had gone crackers and killed a man. (King, 1996)

crackling a woman viewed sexually by a man

Literally, the crisp and tasty outside of roast pork. She is usually described as a *bit* or *piece of crackling*.

cradle-snatcher an older person marrying one much younger

In everyday English, someone who steals a baby, not its bed. Usually of a man and sometimes as a verb. Also as *cradle robber*:

They implied ungraciously that is the cradle-snatching Londoner and his fancy-girl wanted to use the church. (le Carré, 1995)

She was fifteen...Whoa. He'd shake a finger at himself. Fifteen. Cradle robber. Jailbait. (Turow, 1996)

See also ROB THE CRADLE.

crank an erect penis

Literally, an actuating lever which projects:

...locks [my diary] up at night to make sure your wife does not...riffle the pages looking for another passage about my hand on my crank. (Turow, 1993)

crap associated with hanging people

The meaning to defecate is venerable and not euphemistic; nor is *crapper*, a lavatory or a person who defecates. Death by hanging, with the muscular relaxation and the fear, caused a loss of urine and faeces:

The hangman was Jack Ketch...the crap merchant, the crapping cull, the switcher, the cramper, the sheriff's journeyman, the gaggler, the topping-cove, the roper or scragger. (R. Hughes, 1987, describing 19th-century criminal argot)

crash to return to normality after taking an illegal narcotic

To descend from a HIGH:

Brodie had said...'I'm crashing.' And she had gone to the mantelshelf...and taken out a vial of powder. (Theroux, 1976)

cream to ejaculate semen

A male vulgarism:

At the sight of his bride
When he got her inside,
He creamed all over the bedding.
(*Playboy's Book of Limericks*)

To *cream your jeans* is to experience premature ejaculation or extreme sexual excitement in a male.

cream for (of a female) to desire sexually

From the increased vaginal discharge:

'Honey,' he said, 'You're still creaming for me.' (Mailer, 1965)

Whence *creamer*, a promiscuous young woman:

Plenty of young creamers ready to spread their pussies. (Sanders, 1982)

crease to kill by violence

Mainly in America, from the collapse of the victim. In British use it means to hit with a bullet without severely wounding.

creative disputatious or dishonest

Thus for churchmen *creative conflict* is a bitter doctrinal argument. For a businessman *creative accounting* is false bookkeeping:

They give you a lot of crap about 'creative freedom' but all they're really talking about is 'creative bookkeeping'. (B. Forbes, 1989)

Creative tension means violent disagreement:

He denied that...relations were strained between Lord King and Sir Colin but conceded there had been 'creative tension' between two able executives. (*Daily Telegraph*, 14 January, 1993—their company, British Airways, had been accused of unethical behaviour towards a competitor)

Creative freedom for artists and academics can mean anything they want it to, other than something conventional.

creature (the) spirituous intoxicant

Literally, something created, and perhaps only a shortened form of *creature comfort*:

When he chanced to have taken an overdose of the creature. (W. Scott, 1815)

The use, which survives in Ireland, often spelt *cratur*, *crathur*, or *crater*, was common in 19th-century England too:

Never a drop of the crater passed down Chancy Emm's lips. (Mayhew, 1862)

creature of sale *obsolete* a prostitute

For sale might have been nearer the mark:

The house you dwell in proclaims you to be a creature of sale. (Shakespeare, *Pericles*)

credibility gap the extent to which you are thought to be lying

Or, which is more honourable, reluctant to come to terms with unpalatable truth. The phrase comes from US strategic analysis in the 1950s and was used in this sense by Gerald Ford in 1966 when questioning President Johnson's statements about the extent of American involvement in Vietnam:

> We do not recognise them helmeted, in a bomber aiming cans of napalm at a thatched village. We have a credibility gap. (M. McCarthy, 1967, referring to American pilots in Vietnam)

A *serious credibility gap* means that everyone thinks that you are a liar.

creep around to commit adultery
From the surreptitious manner in which it is usually done:

> She put up with six years of her husband beating her, but she wouldn't put up with his creeping around for a single day. (King, 1996)

creep-joint *American* a brothel
Originally, an illegal gambling operation without a liquor licence which moved from place to place to avoid detection by, or paying off, the police:

> Wieland says you were in Sampaloc. In a creep-joint. (Boyd, 1993)

Cressida a prostitute
She was the lady who gave Troilus a bad time and Chaucer, Shakespeare, and others a plot:

> The girl was a born Cressida, a daughter of the game. (Manning, 1960)

crib *American* a brothel
Literally, a poor sort of house:

> Miserable naked girls in the twenty-five and fifty cent cribs. (Longstreet, 1956—and who wouldn't be miserable on that money?)

A *crib girl* is a low-grade prostitute:

> The crib girls were the cheapest jump, but they didn't allow you to take your boots off. (Vanderhaeghe, 1997—there is no further explanation for such fastidiousness on their part)

A *crib man* is not a male prostitute but a thief who robs from private houses.

crime against nature (a) *American* sodomy or bestiality
As proscribed in the laws of many states:

> Most states have laws against fornication and even masturbation lying somewhere on their books... One of the most popular phrases is 'crime against nature'... but almost never do they specify what a *crime against nature* is. (Bryson, 1994—as he concludes, it could be anything from walking on grass to chopping down trees)

criminal assault the rape of a female
Any force offered against another intentionally (other than *in loco parentis*) is a crime, whether or not sexually inspired:

> ... leading a criminal assault by several Indians on an English girl. (P. Scott, 1975, describing a rape)

The woman may be said to have been *criminally used*:

> She was dragged from her bicycle into the derelict site... where she was criminally used. (P. Scott, 1971, writing of the same event)

criminal connection *obsolete* extramarital copulation
The *connection* is as in CONNECT 1, although adultery was never a crime in the British Isles if the other party were above a prescribed age and consented:

> These [prostitutes] seldom or never allow drunken men to have criminal connection with them. (Mayhew, 1862)

criminal conversation *obsolete* adultery
Usually committed by the woman, in whom it was thought more reprehensible, and abbreviated to *crim con* in legal jargon:

> In 1837, Mrs Charlotte Travanion née Brereton, of Cornwall, was accused of having criminal conversation with a man. (Pearsall, 1969)

criminal operation an illegal abortion
Not a planned robbery or cutting a hostage's finger off.

crinkly old or an old person
As wrinkled as a WRINKLY:

> ... there was no sign of the yachting-capped assholes or bejewelled crinkly women. (Bryson, 1991, describing shops on Capri out of season)

critical power excursion a nuclear meltdown
Jargon of the nuclear power industry which hoped it would never happen, until Chernobyl.

croak[1] to die
A dying person unable to clear mucus in the throat makes such a sound:

> They go mouching along as if they were croaking. (Mayhew, 1851)

Less often *croak* means to kill:

> ... the guy who had guts enough to croak 'Tough Tony'. (Lavine, 1930)

To *croak yourself* means to commit suicide.
A *croaker* was a doctor, perhaps from his attendances at the deathbed or his supposed professional shortcomings.

croak² *obsolete* to whinge
A common usage from the 17th century to the Second World War, from the tone of voice usually adopted:

> ... they were civilians and, like all civilians, spent their time in pettifogging or 'croaking'. (Farrell, 1973)

crocked drunk
From drinking out of too many crocks, or from being injured by the excesses:

> In New York they prefer to arrive crocked ... sorry, smashed ... and sober up during the interview. (B. Forbes, 1972)

Rarely, a *crock* is a drunkard.

crook the elbow *Scottish* to be a drunkard
A variant of *bend the elbow* (see BEND), which may imply no more than having a drink.

cross (of a male) to copulate with
From the attitude adopted on the female:

> They found on the grass
> The marks of her ass
> And the knees of the men who had crossed her. (*Playboy's Book of Limericks*)

A *cross girl* at one time was a cheating prostitute, who *crossed* or *double-crossed* her customers.

cross-bar hotel *American* a prison
Prisons are described as hotels in various underworld euphemisms. In this punning usage, the bar secures the gate. A *cross-bar* apartment is a cell:

> Preparing to move into a crossbar apartment on the Green Mile did not, as a rule, put even the most deviant of prisoners in a sexy mood. (King, 1996)

cross-dress to be a transvestite
Usually of male homosexuals playing the female role:

> She had never accepted his desire to cross-dress, regarding him as 'perverted' and 'disgusting'. (*Listener*, 12 July 1984)

cross-firing a commercial fraud to secure increased borrowings
The imagery is from what happens on the battlefield:

> It appears that the alleged fraudulent activity at Versailles could have involved a system called cross-firing. This involves setting up a fictitious company as a trading client, then approaching a bank for finance to support the deal with the phantom company. (*Daily Telegraph*, 4 March 2000)

cross the floor *British* to change political allegiance

The seating arrangements in Westminster have the opponents facing each other across the floor of the House. If you change parties, you sit on the other side:

> After he crossed the floor he became, in addition, a rat, a turncoat, an *arriviste* and, worst crime of all, one who had certainly arrived. (V. B. Carter, 1965, of Winston Churchill's defection from the Conservatives to the Liberals in 1904)

Sir Hartley Shawcross, thought to be increasingly disenchanted with the Labour Party of which he was a member, acquired the nickname 'Sir Shortly Floorcross'.

cross the Styx to die
In classical mythology, you were ferried to the other side of the Styx by Charon, so long as your relatives had remembered to put the fare in your mouth when they buried you. A dead Christian might figuratively *cross the River Jordan*, which is toll-free.

cross your palm to bribe
The derivation is probably from the request of a gypsy to have her palm *crossed with silver*, after which she will tell you your fortune. Divination falls within the sphere of influence of the devil, whose powers can be negated only by the use of the Christian cross. The gypsy keeps the silver.
See also PALM 1.

crower *obsolete American* a cock
Another evasion from the days when it was thought indelicate to talk about cocks, bulls, stallions, and asses.

crown jewels see JEWELS

crud human excreta
Originally, curdled milk. Mainly American army use, as in the expression *Cairo crud* for diarrhoea induced by Egyptian culinary experience. Civilians tend to prefer the adjectival form used figuratively:

> This Reape was a cruddy character. (Sanders, 1980)

cruise¹ to seek a sexual partner at random
Usually of a male, seeking someone of either sex according to his predilection, on foot or in a car, on the street, in a bar, or at a party:

> I don't want to cruise any more. I'm afraid I won't be able to get it up. (Sanders, 1982)

A *cruise* is such a foray:

> ... a spell behind bars for a sexual misdemeanour and recent cruises around New York's gay clubs. (*Private Eye*, May 1981)

In Victorian London and elsewhere a *cruiser* was a prostitute who solicited custom from a hansom cab:

A cruiser, bigod, of all the luck!—though what custom she expected in this deserted backwater I couldn't imagine. (Fraser, 1994, writing in archaic style)

cruise² to be under the influence of illegal drugs

The imagery is from flying or freewheeling: Directors didn't seem to drink much. A little champagne or white wine. Although at least six of them were cruising at five thousand feet on something else. (Wambaugh, 1981)

crumbling edge an inexorable slow downward movement

Jargon of the stock market, when dealers are uncertain when the sea of troubles will no longer erode the cliff:
But we could be in for a 'crumbling edge' with violent movements up and down, albeit on a downward trend. (*Sunday Telegraph*, 23 August 1998—the imagery fits ill with movements 'up')

crumbly an old person

Presumably about to disintegrate. The expression is used only by the young:
I'm drinking sherry with a lot of crumblies. (L. Thomas, 1996)

crumpet a person or persons of the opposite sex viewed sexually

Literally, a cake made of flower and yeast, and usually of females:
Never short of crumpet. That's one thing about this job. (Deighton, 1972—he was not a cook)
Usually in the phases a *bit* or *piece of crumpet*.

crush a sexual attraction towards another person

Is it from the wish to embrace the object of your affection? American *crushes* are heterosexual for the most part while British schoolgirls in single-sex schools have them homosexually, usually on an older female:
These are schoolgirl dreams. And why pick on me for your 'crush'? (I. Murdoch, 1977)

crystal cocaine

In concentrated form:
She was into crystal like it was gonna be banned tomorrow. (Murray Smith, 1993—the lady was not a collector of glass)

Cuban heels thick soles and heels to enhance height

As worn in the Caribbean and by the vain:
The prosecution had alleged that the bantam-weight Basham, who stands only a fraction above five feet three (without his

Cuban heels) had committed assault. (*Daily Telegraph*, 11 March 1995)

cuckoo¹ a male profligate

Despite the derivation from the bird which makes use of nests built by other birds, he does not necessarily cuckold anyone:
The cuckoo then on every tree
Mocks married men. (Shakespeare, *Love's Labour's Lost*)
To *cuckold the parson* was to copulate not with his wife but with your betrothed before the wedding.

cuckoo² mentally unbalanced

The cuckoo has the reputation of being a silly bird:
Old defectors, old spies, they get a bit cuckoo. (le Carré, 1980)

cuff¹ to arrest

The handcuffs are placed on the victim rather than hitting him about the ear:
I figure if you move fast, you should be able to cuff him tomorrow. (Sanders, 1977—of a criminal)

cuff² *American* to obtain on credit

If you were eating *on the cuff*, a waiter might note the debt on his starched shirt cuff:
Even at college he knew places where he could have eaten on the cuff or drink booze without showing ID. (Deighton, 1993/2)
The use is sometimes where there is an intention to defraud:
'You're not going to cuff the Grill, are you?' She grinned wolfishly. 'Maureen has an account there.' (ibid.)

cull to kill

Originally, to select for rejection, as deer, seals, etc. The standard English use is never of killing humans.

cult appealing only to a minority

From esoteric religions, we move to *cult* movies, books, art, or even radio or television shows:
Braden was a brilliant broadcaster and the show achieved a kind of cult status. (F. Muir, 1997)

cultural having characteristics differing from the norm

Originally, relating to good taste, manners, etc. but:
'Cultural'...is the sociologists' jargon for saying as Lewis Carroll once put it 'the word means what I choose it to mean'. (Shankland, 1980)
Cultural deprivation may be what an immigrant to a land with a different tradition to his homeland may be said to suffer and for which

the natives of the host country are sometimes castigated as being blameworthy. A *cultural bias* is anything which may be thought to favour one section of the community over another:

> Eventually the pen-and-paper tests were dropped altogether because they were 'culturally biased'. (*Sunday Telegraph*, 20 November 1994—the New York Police department found that black candidates performed less well in written tests than white)

Mao's *Cultural Revolution* was correctly named, creating anarchy to preserve the autocracy of the unbalanced tyrant.

cumshaw a bribe
The derivation is from the Mandarin used by beggars, although a normally reliable authority thought otherwise:

> The expression was originally 'come ashore money', a sailor's tip to the launch's boatman. (Jennings, 1965)

I am indebted to Mr John Black, who tells me that his father, when Accountant-General of Hong Kong, was a prime target for *cumshaws*, which he refused or passed on to worthy recipients as the case might be. The word still means a windfall or something for nothing in British naval slang.

cunning man *obsolete* a wizard
Cunning meant knowing and, as most wizards were in league with the devil, you had to talk nicely about them:

> A 'cunning man' was long resident in Bodmin, to whom the people went from all parts to be relieved of spells. (R. Hunt, 1865)

cup too many see IN YOUR CUPS

cupcake a homosexual
Why the inoffensive confection was chosen for this use is unclear. For an American, it may also mean an ineffective male:

> 'Odd? Queer? Gay?' Audley raised an eyebrow. 'A cupcake?' (Price, 1982)
> When guys in camouflage pants and hunting hats sat around in the Four Aces Diner talking about fearsome things done out of doors, I would no longer feel such a cupcake. (Bryson, 1997)

Cupid's arbour *obsolete* the vagina
As the God of Love, he provided the Victorians with many similar phrases—*Cupid's cave, cloister, corner, cupboard,* and so through the alphabet. In his Greek name, *Eros,* he also gave us *eroticism.*

Cupid's measles *obsolete* syphilis
The symptoms are similar at one stage:

> ... it was on this leave that he contracted his umpteenth case of Cupid's measles. (Fraser, 1992)

In America also as *Cupid's itch.*

curio a piece of loot
Literally, a collector's item:

> He was periodically concerned to acquire what he euphemistically called 'curios', more straightforwardly 'loot'. (Keegan, 1991, writing of Field Marshal Sir John Dill as a young officer in the Boer War)

curious homosexual
Literally, unusual:

> He was my tutor. Surely you don't imagine I go to curious parties with Pinkrose. (Manning, 1965)

currency adjustment a devaluation
Political use, to disguise the failure of the policies which led to its necessity. See also ADJUSTMENT 1.

currency girl a prostitute who accepts only foreigners as customers
Roubles won't do:

> A *valutnaya,* a currency girl, [earns] more in a half-hour trick than a navy captain in a year. (Moynahan, 1994, writing of post-Communist Russia)

curse (the) menstruation
A shortened form of *the curse of Eve,* who thus burdened all females:

> You've probably got the curse or something. (Bogarde, 1978)

curtains death
The derivation is from the end of a play, the darkening of a room, or, improbably, the screening of an execution. Also some figurative use:

> To have given Nixon knowledge of even the smallest part of that particular Haig connection would have meant curtains for Haig as Nixon's Chief of Staff. (Colodny and Gettlin, 1991)

custody suite *British* a prison cell
Usually in a police station:

> The police claimed that they had been instructed to refer to custody suites [instead of cells]. (*Daily Telegraph*, April 1986)

cut¹ to render (a male) sexually impotent
Of humans by vasectomy, of domestic animals by castration:

> The bull calves are cut. (Marshall, 1818)

cut² to dilute in order to cheat customers

Mainly of intoxicants and drugs sold illegally, from the practice of dividing before adulteration:

> The real thing. Pharmaceutical coke. Not the cut street stuff. (Robbins, 1981)

cut³ drunk
Literally, in dialect, tacking or weaving. Often as *half-cut*:

> On many a night we left the canteen half-cut. (F. Richards, 1936)

cut⁴ an illegal or concealed commission payment
Common criminal and commercial use, again from the dividing. Whence as a verb, to take such a payment:

> Crap games were played in the corridor with the keeper 'cutting' the game. (Lavine, 1930, writing of prisoners in a police station)

cut⁵ a reduction in the size of the increase desired or expected by the recipient
Normally of spending in the public sector:

> So, too, has [grown] the number of welfare lobbyists raised in that public-sector culture who protest that every reform is a 'cut' while spending continues to climb. (*Daily Telegraph*, 5 December 1995)

cut⁶ *American* to kill
Not necessarily with a knife:

> You Americans—you are so strange. You 'put a man down', or you 'cut him', or you 'burn him', or you 'put him away' or 'take him for a ride'. But you will never say you killed him. (Sanders, 1970)

cut a cheese to fart
The smell may be rich and unpleasant. In Somerset you may say that you have *cut a leg* in the same sense. The more general use is merely to *cut one*:

> ... none of them would say anything if he cut one. (McInerney, 1992)

Grose (1811) gives 'Cheeser. A strong smelling fart.'

cut-and-paste job a report sloppily prepared from various sources
The script might be thus edited prior to word processors, which have however retained the terminology:

> Mr Baker claims the articles have used 'selective quotations' from telephone conversations. 'The authors of the articles have carried out a "cut and paste" job of taking different bits of different conversations and

amalgamating,' he said. (*Daily Telegraph*, 22 September 1996)

The same term is disparagingly used of a non-fiction book where a hurried author has undertaken little original research.

cut down on to kill
Not necessarily with a blow from above:

> They want me to cut down on him... I am to burn this man. (Sanders, 1970—the speaker was an assassin, not a worker in a crematorium)

cut numbers to make employees redundant
It is thought safer to be imprecise about the commodity being counted:

> If you say they are not cutting numbers, I do not know how they are going to do it. (*Daily Telegraph*, 4 February 1999—it was being suggested that a takeover would save the combined company $100 million)

cut off dead
Always of premature or untimely death, with imagery from the gathering of a flower in bloom:

> ... whose headstones record an early death, a cutting-off before the prime. (P. Scott, 1968)

cut out to deprive (someone) of something valuable
Said formerly by sailors, from singling out a ship in the opposing fleet for concerted attack and capture. The term is also used about displacing a female's partner, especially on the dance floor.

cut the mustard (of a male) to be able to copulate
Cut means share in, but why *mustard*, unless from Wisconsin German/American English, borrowing *senf* which means pizazz in slang:

> You can't cut the mustard but how about watching? (Theroux, 1973)

There is some figurative use:

> None of this bailing out firms that can't cut the competitive mustard. (M. Thomas, 1982)

Also shortened to *cut it*:

> 'Are you married?' 'Divorced.' 'Ha! Couldn't cut it.' (J. Collins, 1981)

cut the painter to die
Like a boat cast loose on the water and used of old seafarers. *Cut adrift*, of the same tendency, is probably obsolete. *Cut your cable* should logically imply suicide but it is used of natural death, usually in old age.

Cyprian *literary* a prostitute
Aphrodite, the Greek Venus and goddess of
love, was associated with Cyprus:

> The Burlington Arcade, which is a well-
> known resort of Cyprians of the better sort.
> (Mayhew, 1862)

Cythera *literary* associated with copula-
tion
Again from Aphrodite, this time with her
Cretan connections:

> ... nor indeed were we long before we
> finished our trip to Cythera. (Cleland, 1749)

D

D anything taboo beginning with the letter D

Usually *damn*, *damned*, *damnable*, and the like which used to be less socially acceptable in polite speech than they are today:

And at last he flung out in his violent way, and said, with a D, 'Then do as you like.' (C. Dickens, 1861)

The *big D* is death:

The systematic encroachment of the big D. (le Carré, 1980)

D and C the abortion of a foetus

The medical abbreviation of *dilation and curettage*, a common operation for older women but, in the young adult, perhaps involving the removal of a foetus:

... a pro-choice ad that sold the Crackers on the notion that the founding fathers fought and died for the right to a D & C. (Anonymous, 1996)

DCM a notice of dismissal from employment

The initial letters of 'Don't come Monday' punning on the Distinguished Conduct Medal. Mainly American use: among British railway employees it denoted suspension for one day only.

dairies *obsolete* a woman's breasts

A vulgarism of obvious derivation:

Janey was one of your real fancy doxies, painted and feathered like a Mohawk and twice as noisy, clinging on Tom's arm with her dairies in his face. (Fraser, 1997—Janey was an actress and also, by this account, a contortionist)

daisy chain *American* a body of investors concertedly inflating the price of a quoted security

Not necessarily with an intention to defraud but one of many terms for the action of professional investors who collaborate to move prices and make short-term gains.

dally to copulate with extramaritally

Originally, to talk idly, but in this usage men do it more than women:

On the night of the divorce he was out with Australian harpie——with whom he dallied for a year or two. (*Private Eye*, April 1981)

Dalliance is such behaviour:

What time the gifted lady took
Away from pencil, pen and book,
She spent in amorous dalliance.
(They do these things so well in France.)
(Parker, 1944, on George Sand)

damaged¹ drunk

Mainly American use, from the temporary incapacitation.

damaged² having copulated before marriage

Such a woman, under former convention, would have become less desirable as a bride, and hence was described as *damaged goods*:

That's the girl that was pure, not damaged goods, and the girl you'd want to be mother of your children. (McCourt, 1999)

damaged³ of criminal habits

Those who used the adjective in this sense see villains acting because of the harm society is thought to have done to them rather than because of the harm they do to society:

No one can be bad, only 'damaged'. (*Daily Telegraph*, 3 October 1995, reporting on the treatment of young criminals)

dance¹ *obsolete* to be killed by hanging

Alluding to the kicking of the victim and the gyration of the corpse:

Spring's passage out was going to be at the end of a rope, and unless I shifted I'd be dancing alongside him. (Fraser, 1982)

You might also be said to *dance on air, at the end of a rope, off, the Tyburn jig, upon nothing,* etc.:

Matthew would be dancing on air by next sun-down. (Monsarrat, 1978)

The *dance-hall* was the condemned cell and the *dancing master* the hangman. To *dance a two-step to another world* is to be killed, but not necessarily by hanging

... no good keeping souvenirs of that sort when any moment we may be dancing a two-step to another world. (F. Richards, 1933, writing of First World War trench life)

dance² to be involuntarily under another's control

You have to move when another tells you to, and not necessarily because a gunman is shooting at your feet. Much figurative use.

dance a Haymarket hornpipe *obsolete* to copulate with a prostitute

The Haymarket in London was a haunt of prostitutes (and their clients) and the expression involves two vulgar puns:

Perhaps we'll dance another Haymarket hornpipe before long. (Fraser, 1975, writing in 19th-century style)

dance at *obsolete* to court

Not like the activities of Salome. Possibly referring to the courtship of birds:

I should have no opinion of you, Biddy, if
he danced at you with your consent.
(C. Dickens, 1861)

dance barefoot *obsolete* to remain unmarried when a younger sister marries
Probably from the effect on her dowry:
> I must dance barefoot on her wedding day.
> (Shakespeare, *The Taming of the Shrew*)

If in Yorkshire you remained a bachelor when
your younger brother married, you might be
said to *dance in the half-peck*. A peck was a liquid
measure of two gallons, of beer or cider normally, but occasionally of spirits, and a *peck-
man* was a distributor of smuggled spirits,
presumably because that was about all the
load he could carry. We can assume that
the elder brother was consoling himself at the
wedding feast. The economic pressures on
unwed females who were not allowed to work
to keep themselves, and on brothers who
were expected to provide labour for the farm
through having children, made it socially
desirable that brothers and sisters respectively should marry in descending age order.

danger signal is up (the) I am menstruating
Red is the colour indicating danger and a
warning to stay clear. See also BAKER FLYING.

dangerous to women adept at seduction
The expression does not necessarily imply
rape:
> 'Is Morny dangerous to women?' 'Don't be
> Victorian, old top. Women don't call it
> danger.' (Chandler, 1943)

Lady Caroline Lamb implied as much of Lord
Byron when she confided to her journal that
he was 'Mad, bad, and dangerous to know'.

Darby and Joan¹ an elderly married
couple living together
They were the characters in Woodfall's 18th-
century ballad, who grew old together. Rarely
seen as a verb:
> Darby and Joaning it into the sunset.
> (Bogarde, 1981)

Darby and Joan² *obsolete British* a pair
of male homosexuals
Army use in the days when a posting to India
lasted for five or seven years:
> The attitude of other soldiers towards the
> 'Darby and Joans' of the regiment was
> generally good-natured. (C. Allen, 1975)

dark¹ closed
Theatrical jargon, from the absence of footlights etc., when a play has flopped or a
theatre management has failed:
> The theatre is now 'dark'—only the
> bars and a buffet are open to earn

money. (*Sunday Telegraph*, November,
1981)

dark² (of people) having non-white ancestry
A usage by white people and not necessarily
offensive. Also as *dark-skinned* or *dark-complected*:
> I tried to tell him a dark-complected man is
> nothing in this country without an
> education to stand on. (Macdonald, 1952)

The noun *darky* to describe a non-white is
objectionable:
> Was it something about not taking
> on the darkies as conductors? (le Carré,
> 1983)

dark man the devil
The colour came from his evil night-time
deeds and the soot which adhered to him as
he made his way down the chimney:
> A drunk of really a noble class that brought
> you no nearer to the dark man. (Hardy,
> 1874)

dark meat¹ the flesh of poultry other
than the breast
A survival from the days when prudery
forbade the mention of breasts and legs,
which also became BENDERS or *lower limbs*.
See also WHITE MEAT 1.

dark meat² *American* a black woman
viewed sexually by a white male
The usual MEAT 1 imagery:
> Bill, you better try some dark meat and
> change your luck. (Sanders, 1982—Bill was
> not averse to the breast of poultry but
> unable to copulate with his white wife)

dark moon *obsolete* a wife's secret savings
A 19th-century expression, from the days
when a married woman was not allowed
independent assets and had to hide any
savings away without telling her husband, to
provide against future disaster:
> The farmer was delighted at the discovery
> of his wife's dark moon. (*N&Q*, 1867)

darn a mild oath
A shortened form of the obsolete *tarnation*,
which was a blend of 'damnation' and by
the 'tarnal' (Jennings, 1965—'tarnal' meant
eternal). Still widely used for *damn*, which
itself is now mild when less people believe in
Hell.

dash¹ to adulterate a drink
Literally, to mix or dilute, as in a culinary
recipe:
> This beer's dashed an' 'er aulus do dash it.
> (*EDD*)

dash² a mild oath
A literary convention replacing a taboo word like *damn* with a dash.

dasher *obsolete* a prostitute
Not because she sprinted but, because she *cut a dash*, was smartly turned out.

date a heterosexual companion
You specified the time of meeting:
> ...theories as to the girl's possible date. (Davidson, 1978—they were speculating about her companion, not her age)

On a *blind date* you take pot luck. In America a *date* may describe a prostitute:
> ...pictures and other materials about the women...were given to Bailey's DNC contact, so that prospective clients could choose among possible dates. (Colodny and Gettlin, 1991, describing facilities for obtaining prostitutes for Democratic visitors to Washington)

To *date* is to take out such a companion:
> If the Smiths hadn't been there I would have dated her myself. (Theroux, 1978)

dateless *obsolete* senile
Not leading a celibate life but unable to recall the passage of time:
> We were like to be turned out on t' wide world, and poor mother dateless. (Gaskell, 1863)

daughter of joy a prostitute
Whatever her mother's actual maiden name:
> Charles VI of France writes of going to 'hear the supplication which has been made to us on the part of the daughters-of-joy of the brothel of Toulouse called the Great Abbey'. (Cawthorne, 1996)

daughter of the game a prostitute
See GAME 2:
> The girl was a born Cressida, a 'daughter of the game'. (Manning, 1960)
And see CRESSIDA.

Davy Jones's locker a grave at sea
Grose says 'David Jones. The devil, the spirit of the sea'. The first literary use was by Smollett in 1751. Derivation from the biblical Jonah is sometimes suggested. The *locker* was the seaman's chest:
> All hands are snug enough in Davy Jones' locker. (Chamier, 1837—they had died at sea)

Davy Jones's natural children *obsolete* pirates
Another way of saying 'maritime bastards'.

dawn raid the unannounced and rapid accumulation of a large block of shares
City jargon, from the surprise military attack. The manoeuvre is used to avoid having to disclose a gradual accumulation or pay the price increase which would follow sustained demand.

day of action a politically motivated strike
For many, a day of inaction:
> In 1982, we ran into a new sort of dispute over the Health Service workers' strike. The print unions demanded that we print statements in support of the strike. The TUC staged a 'Day of Action' which printers were required to support. (Deedes, 1997)
See also INDUSTRIAL ACTION.

daylight associated with killing by shooting
What is improbably supposed to be seen through the body after the passage of a bullet:
> You'll want to be discreet...they'd as soon make daylight shine through you as anyone else. (Furst, 1988)

de-accession to dismiss from employment
Denying people access to the former place of work:
> Not much help here from Morgan, which is currently de-accessioning 1,500 staff. (*Daily Telegraph*, 12 June 2001)

dead cat bounce a temporary increase in the value of a security or currency of which the price has been falling but which remains overvalued
Like a rebound of a corpse dropped on a hard surface:
> Dealers in the Russian market, however, still think a deterioration is possible. 'It was just a dead-cat bounce,' one said. (*Daily Telegraph*, 15 August 1998)

dead meat a human corpse
Criminal jargon beloved of writers of detective stories. To *make dead meat of* is to kill a human being.

dead soldier an empty bottle of wine or spirits
The imagery is from the military appearance of a line of bottles:
> I'd take [a bottle of brandy] to him if he had a dead soldier. (Sanders, 1980)

dead to recklessly ignoring
A Victorian survival, which used to refer mainly to sexual behaviour, when a person might be *dead to honour* or *propriety*:

I cannot suppose that he is altogether Dead
to Propriety, though how long such
Restraint will continue I cannot say.
(Fraser, 1977—writing in archaic style of
how a kidnapper might behave towards his
female victim)

Dead to the world means asleep.

deadhead *American* a successful scrounger or non-payer
You can't include his cash when you count
the takings. Of a non-paying spectator at a ball
game, a fare-evader on a train, etc. The word
is also used of a cadger in a bar who doesn't
stand his round.

deal to sell illegal narcotics
The language of commerce is used to conceal
criminality:
    'A little grass now and then. Not from her.'
    'But she deals?' (Sanders, 1977)
Whence a *dealer*, who so behaves:
    Now the WCF had to cope with the
    dealers and the wildness on the fringe of
    Ladbrook Grove. (French, 1995—the office
    of World Congress of Faiths had been
    relocated in a seedy district of London)

deal from the bottom of the deck to lie
or cheat
The imagery is from card-sharping:
    For all we knew, he could be dealing from
    the bottom of the deck, just to make more
    money. (Forsyth, 1994)

dear friend an extramarital sexual partner
Male or female, but in the latter case less
explicit than CHÈRE AMIE.

dear John the ending by a woman of an
engagement or marriage
In the Second World War, the missive of
dismissal received by so many men serving
abroad started formally rather than by using
warmer appellations:
    The colonel concedes that he should have
    got out on receipt of his first 'Dear John'
    letter, particularly as this coincided with
    the break-up of the regiment. (*Daily
    Telegraph*, January 1984)
The phrase is now used of such a decision
communicated by any medium.

debauch to copulate with extramaritally
Literally, to corrupt:
    Men so disorder'd, so debauch'd and bold,
    That this our court, infected with their
    manners,
    Shows like a riotous inn. (Shakespeare,
    King Lear)
Boswell, who expressed the view that 'a man
may debauch his friend's wife genteely'

(J. Boswell, 1791), was clearly less moral than
his hero:
    Take care of me; don't let me into your
    houses without suspicion. I once
    debauched a friend's daughter: I may
    debauch yours. (ibid., quoting Dr Johnson
    who was speaking hypothetically—*take care*
    means beware)
Debauch, a drunken revel, is standard English.

debt of honour unpaid money lost at
gambling
Under English law gambling debts are not
recoverable, but a defaulter would lose his
good name, especially if the wager was with a
social equal.

decadent not conforming to accepted
tastes
Literally, in a state of decline from past
standards. Much used by autocrats about
anything of which they disapprove, from
homosexuality to artistic style:
    Shetland had accepted eight 'decadent'
    surrealist paintings that Goring had
    confiscated. (Deighton, 1978)

decant to urinate
Literally, to pour liquid from one container
into another:
    Just going to decant (and the awful phrases
    they come up with). (Barnes, 1991)

**deceive (your regular sexual part-
ner)** to copulate with another
Literally, to mislead as to the truth in any
respect, and of either sex:
    Harper nodded and made a private vow
    that he would not deceive his wife.
    (Theroux, 1980)

decent wearing clothes which hide any
suggestion of nakedness
You do not have to be fully clothed to be
adjudged *decent*, but your attire must not
suggest immodesty:
    . . . since I could see she was clothed—
    'decent', as girls used to say. (Styron,
    1976—and they still do)

deck *American* a packet of illicit narcotics
Usually heroin, from being wrapped in paper
like a pack of cards. To *deck up* is to pack
heroin for retail sale.

decks awash *American* drunk
Applied not only to sailors and owing much to
HALF-SEAS OVER.

decline an irreversible physical or mental
condition
Literally, a downward slope, but in this use, of
pulmonary tuberculosis in the 19th century

or mental health in the 20th, there is no prospect of the condition being improved and the slope turning upwards.

décolletage the breasts of an adult female

Literally in French, the cutting out of the neckline of a dress whence, in English, what may be revealed by excessive cutting out:

When Sara came and stooped down to pour the coffee, however, the display of her very ample decolletage turned Willy's thoughts in another direction. (Erdman, 1993)

decontaminate[1] *American* to embalm

The majority of corpses are no more *contaminated* than a leg of mutton, a side of bacon, or a flitch of beef:

The incentive to select quality merchandise would be materially lessened if the body of the deceased were not decontaminated and made presentable. (J. Mitford, 1963—the survivors will spend more if the corpse is spruced up)

decontaminate[2] to destroy evidence

You wipe a disk or destroy a file ahead of an investigation.

deed (the) copulation

Usually extramarital and always so if it is dirty or vile:

...one that will do the deed
Though Argus were her eunuch.
(Shakespeare, *Love's Labour's Lost*)

deep freeze *American* a prison

The common imagery of the COOLER 1:

If the cops didn't grab him and chuck him in the deep freeze...(Chandler, 1958)

deep six to kill or destroy

The original meaning was merely to dispose of, not from the traditional depth in feet of a grave but from the lowest mark on a naval heaving line in fathoms, below which all vanished. Used of destruction, death, or figuratively:

How do you propose we deep-six that Stratton? (Block, 1979—they were trying to make an airliner crash)
Barney would have expected his friend to deep-six it out of the window. (M. Thomas, 1980,
You can deepsix that crap. Eighty years old and still fucking. That I don't need. (Sharpe, 1977)

defecate to shit

The original meaning was to purify or cleanse. Thus William Harvey could write in the 17th century:

The blood is not sufficiently defecated or clarified, but remains cloudy. (Harvey, 1628)

Now *defecate* and *defecation* are used in medical and polite standard English.

defence aggression

As in a government department concerned with waging war which calls itself a *Ministry of Defence*:

The war cabinet, which will be called the Ministerial Council for the Defense of the Reich, was given sweeping powers by Herr Hitler (Shirer, 1999, writing of 31 August 1939, when Germany attacked Poland)

The British *D Notice*, short for *Defence Notice*, is an instruction to the media to suppress news, ostensibly on the grounds of state security.

defend your virtue to refuse to have a sexual relationship

Usually of a female and indeed:

A male defending his virtue is always a farcical figure. (M. McCarthy, 1963)

The phrase may also be used for the rejection of homosexual approaches.

defensive victory the postponement of defeat

Used to mask the reality of military disaster:

On the Cowland front, a complete defensive victory was secured yesterday. (Goebbels, 1945, in translation: the diaries of Klemperer show how such language persuaded many Germans to keep fighting in the spring of 1945 for a hopeless cause)

defile to copulate with extramaritally

Literally, to make filthy. The *defilement* is usually done by men in the face of female reluctance, passivity, or resistance:

Children who only hours ago had been virgins, defiled by men they had never seen before. (Ludlum, 1979)
[Irish] Law prohibits the defilement of girls under the age of 15. (*Daily Telegraph*, 3 June 1994)

To *defile yourself* is to engage in such activity:

Intercourse is not a necessity...I won't have my men defiling themselves. (French, 1995, quoting Younghusband)

To *defile a bed* does not imply involuntary urination:

My bed he hath defiled. (Shakespeare, *All's Well That Ends Well*)

and he who so copulates is a *defiler*:

...thou bright defiler
Of Hymen's purest bed. (Shakespeare, *Timon of Athens*)

deflower to copulate with (a female virgin)

OED gives a 14th-century quotation from Wyclif in this sense and Shakespeare speaks of 'A deflower'd maid' (*Measure for Measure*). The imagery of plucking a bloom can refer to the loss of the maidenhead other than by copulation:

> His female admirers had a model made of it in pure gold and organized a ceremony in which several virgins deflowered themselves on this object. (Manning, 1977)

Defloration is such copulation:

> ... the usual sanguinary symptoms of defloration. (Cleland, 1749)

degenerate a homosexual
To *degenerate* means to cease to be able to function as before, and as the function of sex is the propagation of the species, there might be some logic in so describing those who do not breed. However, the imagery comes from the meaning degraded or corrupt:

> They send their husky young recruits in there to entrap men like me ... And once they've established you're a degenerate ... (Cameron, 1997)

degrade to damage or render of less value
Literally, to reduce a substance in strength or purity. Military jargon:

> ... an air assault to 'degrade' by 50 per cent the strength of the Iraqi forces arranged north of the border. (Forsyth, 1994)

A *degraded* woman used to be one who had been detected in extramarital copulation, and *degradation* is prostitution:

> 'Do you suppose she has been ... degraded?' says he, in a hushed voice. (Fraser, 1971)
> ... the hiring of stage-struck girls by foreign impresarios who took them abroad and sold them into degradation. (Paxman, 1998)

dehire *American* to dismiss from employment
Barely euphemistic in a country when to *hire* has become synonymous with to employ.

delayering dismissing employees
Literally, dispensing with a layer of management in a hierarchical organization:

> These seismic changes effect everyone, but the most vulnerable are older people, ambushed in mid-career by strategies that mask their true intent under such euphemisms as 'right-sizing' and 'delayering'. (*Telegraph Magazine*, 1 July 1995)

Delhi belly diarrhoea
An alliterative use not confined to India or its capital:

> Kind of a bowel thing. Up all night. Cramps. Delhi belly. Food goes right through you. (Theroux, 1975)

delicate *obsolete* suffering from pulmonary tuberculosis
One of the 19th-century euphemisms for the common disease:

> The brother died young. He was delicate. (Flanagan, 1988, writing in 19th-century style)

Today a *delicate condition* indicates pregnancy.

deliver to drop (an explosive) on an enemy
Military jargon of bombs or ordnance. thus a *delivery vehicle* is not a milk float but a missile which carries a bomb.

demands of nature urination and defecation
You might think gravity came first, followed by breathing:

> ... walking with the sense of purpose proper to a man about to attend to the demands of nature. (Masters, 1976)

demanning the dismissal of employees
Not an operation to change masculinity:

> It is imperative the process of demanning continues. (*Daily Telegraph*, 8 March 1994—a chairman was announcing the dismissal of 2,000 employees)

demi-mondaine a prostitute
Married people who 'went to the world' in the French Second Empire were the *monde* and women on the fringes of that society unaccompanied by men were the *demi-monde*. The obsolete English *demi-rep*, a shortened form of *demi-reputation*, meant the same thing.

democrat/democracy have always meant different things to different people and seldom, outside the Parish meeting, 'rule by the people'. An example was the *German Democratic Republic*, Soviet Russia's totalitarian satellite. We are wise to look for a flaw in any concept or political argument claimed to be based on the principles of *democracy*:

> 'Vietnam's Democratic One-man Rule'—the Procrustean subject was Diem.
> A democratic 'dictator' or a 'democratic' dictator? (M. McCarthy, 1967)

demographic strain too many people
Demography is the study of population statistics, but this phrase does not mean that your eyes ache from reading too many censuses. It is taboo, as well as being simplistic and offensive, to suggest that poor countries face starvation because ignorant people breed too

fast and medical science allows too many to survive.

demographically correct containing a proportionate ratio of blacks, whites, Hispanics, etc.
Not merely counting or classifying them without error:
> ... sitting on a school desk in a dark suit, a demographically-correct display of acne-free teenagers in front of him.
> (Anonymous, 1996—a politician was doing a commercial in an election campaign)

demonstration a mass assembly to protest about a specific isssue
Literally, a showing, illustration, or proof:
> He never took part in demonstrations or marched on May Day parades.
> (M. McCarthy, 1963)

The shortened form *demo* has no non-euphemistic use.

demonstrator a car subjected to personal use by a motor trader
Motor-trade jargon seeking to imply that the vehicle has only been used for display to customers prior to sale rather than used by the trader, his employees, and their families as a cost-effective personal car.

demote maximally to kill one of your associates
Espionage jargon. The career as a spy of the victim certainly can fall no lower:
> Jonathan smiled at the cryptic jargon ... in which 'demote maximally' meant purge by killing. (Trevanian, 1972)

A *maximum demote* is such a killing:
> The assassinations are called 'sanctions' if the target is someone outside the CIA, and 'maximum demotes' if the target is one of their own men. (Trevanian, 1973)

deniably (of a lie or secret action) in a manner hard to expose
Usually of a statement made off the record or an act taken by a third party on behalf of another:
> ... the small country could inflict wounds itself, or even more safely, sponsor others to do so—'deniably'. (Clancy, 1987)

Whence the adjective *deniable* and the noun *deniability*:
> ... nothing more than an exercise in keeping its own nose clean—not being seen to be involved. Deniability was the polite word for it. (D. Mason, 1993)

deny yourself to to refuse to copulate with
Usually within marriage:

> Livia denied herself to me. I knew she had so determined by the way she refused to look at me. (A. Massie, 1986)

A spouse may also, if so minded, *deny a bed*:
> Otherwise I shall deny you my bed. (ibid.—Livia was again being difficult)

depart this life to die
The implication is that you will arrive in another state of being:
> Things went on smoothly for a dozen years when the old Frenchman departed this life. (Mayhew, 1851)

The *departed* are the dead:
> Mary said it was a memorial quilt, done by Mrs Alderman Parkinson in the memory of a dear departed friend. (Atwood, 1996)

A *departure* is death:
> This unsound mode of transport would have been her only criticism of William's orchestration of her departure. (Archer, 1979, writing about a funeral)

dependency[1] a subject territory
British imperial use for those distant parts of the globe ruled from London which were not dominions, colonies, or protectorates.

dependency[2] an addiction to narcotics or alcohol
The victim *depends* on regular ingestion:
> It is estimated that at least two million women have dependencies—addiction would be a better word—on prescriptive drugs. (Sanders, 1981)
> He was a Corkman, an alcoholic who, several months before, had spent some time in a treatment clinic for people with dependency problems. (O'Callaghan, 1998)

depleted *American* poor
Literally, emptied or reduced in quantity:
> Clara twice a week drove her Seville to the city's depleted neighbourhoods for the morning. (Turow, 1990—she went slumming)

deposit a turd
Usually in the phrase *make a deposit*, to defecate:
> Never read when you eat, guys, but always read when you make a deposit. (Theroux, 1993—not of visiting a bank)

deprived poor
Literally, having lost something, which is not so for most paupers:
> Deprived Families on Increase (headline in *Daily Telegraph*, 4 October 1983, meaning that there were more poor families rather than the other constructions which might be put upon the four words)

Whence *deprivation*, poverty:

By constantly devoting attention and resources to the least advantageous section of the community, deprivation can be eliminated altogether. (Hattersley, 1995)

derailed mad
The common transport imagery:
Was her father derailed, off his trolley, losing hold? (Turow, 1990)

derrière the buttocks
The French too have behinds and use the same euphemism, although without our salacious overtones:
...there were mischievous triple-rilled derrières. (E. S. Turner, 1952, writing of advertising of tight skirts)

deselect to dismiss (a political incumbent)
The action is taken by a caucus rather than the electorate.

designer stubble male unshaven facial hair
Something between a neat beard and being clean-shaven:
He sported dark glasses, his usual 'designer stubble' and wore a single-breasted pinstripe suit. (*Daily Telegraph*, 22 June—he was a wealthy pop musician)

designs on (have) to wish to seduce
Not just wearing a patterned dress or carrying plans:
...they contain no mention of his having had designs on the local girls. (Bence-Jones, 1987, writing about the dissolute Earl of Leitrim who was murdered in Donegal in 1878)

destroy to kill (a domestic animal)
The meaning to kill has long been standard English but there is a jargon use referring to sick, old, or unwanted poets:
If he makes another mess...I'll have him destroyed. (N. Mitford, 1945—he was a dog)

destruction *obsolete* the seduction (of a female)
Especially if there was no prospect of subsequent marriage:
I gather from [a remark] that you are one of those who go through life seeking the destruction of servants. (Bence-Jones, 1987—a young member of the Kildare Street Club in pre-1914 Dublin had drawn the attention of an older member to a pretty girl cleaning the windows of a house across the street)

detain to imprison for political purposes

Each of us is detained when our train is held up at a signal:
...they were stoned and scourged and imprisoned—or 'detained', as the authorities called it. (Seymour, 1977)

developing poor and relatively unindustrialized
The direction of the *development* is not specified:
...countries which have successively and with increasing euphemism been termed backward, under-developed, less-developed and developing. (Bullock and Stallybrass, 1977)

developmental associated with ignorance, idleness, or the lack of ability
Educational jargon, as in the *developmental class* for the unruly or stupid, and the *developmental course*, which used to be called cramming.

device any object which is the subject of a taboo
Literally, a mechanical contrivance. It is used specifically of armaments where, for a while, *nuclear device* was thought to sound more acceptable than *atom bomb*, and of contraception:
The pharmaceuticals don't agree with me. I had to go to the doctor and get a device. (Keneally, 1985)

devil's mark (the) *obsolete British* congenital idiocy
Mainly in rural use:
That's where your village idiots come from. They call it the Devil's Mark. I call it incest. (le Carré, 1962)
God, Satan, and the fairies seem to have been equally to blame for the results of inbreeding—see GOD'S CHILD and CHANGE 2.

devoted to the table gluttonous
Not merely fond of a piece of furniture:
Heavily overweight, [Joffre] was devoted to the table and allowed nothing, even at the height of the crisis in 1914, to interrupt lunch. (Keegan, 1998)

dick¹ the penis
Probably rhyming slang from PRICK, but the penis has many common male names—see, for example JOHN THOMAS, JOCK, TOMMY, and WILLY:
What she had said about things like his dick. (Amis, 1978)
Whence, as a verb, to sodomize:
...six bad [years] in San Quentin gettin' dicked by the residents. (J. Collins, 1981)

dick² *American* a policeman
Usually a detective:
> One of the more ambitious would go to the
> Detective Bureau and become a dick.
> (Lavine, 1930)

A policewoman may be described as a *Dickless Tracy*, punning on the cartoon character and her femininity, but not, I suggest, in her presence.

dick around (of a male) to be promiscuous
The derivation is from DICK 1. Figuratively, it means to mess around:
> Dicking around was his style and he was
> not alone in that. (Fiennes, 1996—the act
> does indeed need a partner)
> ... dicking around with his cows and
> windmills. (M. Thomas, 1982, writing about
> a painter)

Dick's hatband *obsolete* an indication of male homosexuality
Punning on the crown which the effete Richard Cromwell was unfit to wear in succession to his mighty father, Oliver, and the discoloration:
> Hello, thinks I, he ain't one of the
> Dick's hatband brigade, surely.
> (Fraser, 1977, writing in 19th-century
> style)

To *wear Dick's hatband* was to be known as a male homosexual.

dicked in the nob *obsolete* mentally unbalanced
In this use, the *nob* is the head:
> But, bless you, every good pug is dicked in
> the nob, or he'd not be a pug in the first
> place. (Fraser, 1997—a *pug* was a
> prizefighter, or pugilist)

dickens the devil
The origin is unclear, despite the notorious marital behaviour of the novelist:
> They had more chains on him than Scrooge
> saw on Marley's ghost, but he could have
> kicked up dickens if he'd wanted. That's a
> pun. (King, 1996)

dicky unwell
Rhyming slang on *Uncle Dick*, sick. Widely used to refer to our own indispositions; in others, it signifies a chronic state of ill-health:
> ... sent me home. Said I had a dicky heart.
> (Theroux, 1974)

diddle¹ to urinate
Literally, to jerk from side to side, which a male may do with his penis after urination to eliminate drips. *Dicky Diddle* was also rhyming slang for piddle.

diddle² to masturbate
Of both sexes, again from the jerking movement:
> ... she caught Leslie, then three, diddling
> herself and forced her to wear hand-splints.
> (Styron, 1976)

diddle³ *American* to copulate
Literally, in this sense, to CHEAT:
> I play golf with the insurance industry, a
> sin apparently even more troublesome to
> Americans than diddling a hairdresser.
> (Anonymous, 1996—a presidential
> candidate had been accused of copulating
> with his wife's hairdresser)

die to achieve a sexual orgasm
Of male or female:
> I will live in thy heart, die in thy lap, and be
> buried in thy eyes. (Shakespeare, *Much Ado
> About Nothing*)
> These lovers cry—Oh! Oh! they die.
> (Shakespeare, *Troilus and Cressida*)

die queer *obsolete Kent* to kill yourself
A use which might be misunderstood today.

die with your knees bent *American* to be killed in an electric chair
Sitting down at the time:
> ... the awful tide of dismay in their eyes as
> they realized they were going to die with
> their knees bent. (King, 1996)

To *die in a horse's nightcap* or *die in your shoes* meant to be killed by hanging.

diet of worms a corpse
Modern scientists tell us that the process of corporal dissolution is fungal, with worms obtaining little sustenance. Happily in 1670 or thereabouts Marvell knew better:
> ... then worms shall try
> That long preserved virginity,
> And your quaint honour turn to dust,
> And into ashes all my lust.

The *Diet*, or assembly, was held in the Rhineland city of Worms in 1521 and is remembered by generations of schoolchildren for the pun in English rather than for Luther's courage in attending.

dietary difficulties the barring of Jews from the German Imperial navy
German anti-Semitism was not a Nazi invention:
> Jews unwilling to give up their faith and be
> baptized were barred from the Imperial
> Navy, the official excuse being 'dietary
> difficulties'. (R. Massie, 1992)

differently affected by a taboo condition
In a series of phrases such as *differently abled*, crippled or of low intelligence;

differently advantaged, poor; *differently weighted*, obese:

> It can only be a matter of time before the differently-weighted push for job quotas in the fire departments and the police. (*Sunday Telegraph*, 6 March 1994)

difficult particularly objectionable
You may say this about other peoples' children, but it is wise to keep out of earshot of their parents if you do so.

dime out *American* to cheat, betray, or short-change
A shortened form, perhaps, of NICKEL AND DIME:

> That's the play, right, George? They want me to dime somebody out. (Turow, 1999)

diminished responsibility a suggestion of temporary insanity
A defence seized on by lawyers when the accused has no other:

> P——, 23, of Newcastle upon Tyne, denied murder but pleaded guilty to manslaughter on the grounds of diminished responsibilty. (*Daily Telegraph*, 22 May, 2001—a woman had thrown a baby of 10 months out of a third floor window)

ding-a-ling a penis
Referring to the pendent position of a bell clapper:

> The quads have been reporting progress on papa's ding-a-ling daily. (Sharpe, 1979—papa had snagged his penis on rose thorns)

Some figurative use as an insult:

> I spoke to a couple of ding-a-lings. (J. Patterson, 1999—they had been unhelpful)

dine well to be a drunkard and a glutton
The goodness lies in the excess of food and wine:

> Birkenhead...who, in the language of the day, 'dined well'. (Graham Stewart, 1999)

dip¹ to steal
Literally, to put into liquid, which involves a downward movement, and so a *dip* or *dipper* is a pickpocket:

> Dipping, lifting money out of a mug's pocket. (Kersh, 1936)
> Twenty years of muggers and dips, safe men and junkies. (Mailer, 1965—but don't place reliance on the *safe man* unless you wish him to open a safe for you)

The *dip squad* consists of police charged with apprehending pickpockets:

> He was not happy about being taken off the dip squad. (*Daily Telegraph*, 27 April 1996—a policeman returning to normal duty, after the investigation of an allegation of

dishonesty, sported a pigtail: when given new duties less to his liking he claimed to be a victim of sexual discrimination)

dip² a drunkard
A shortened form of *dipsomaniac*. To *dip your beak* or *your bill* means to drink intoxicants to excess.

dip your wick to copulate
Common male punning use—see WICK—on its immersion in an oil lamp:

> Worms, who had had an exhausting time dipping his wick, as he called it, all over Wimbledon. (Bogarde, 1978)

diplomatic cold a bogus excuse for non-attendance
First contracted by Mr Gladstone, as being more polite than a direct refusal. Those who wish to keep out of the public eye for a while may contract a *diplomatic illness*:

> This was interpreted by some as a 'diplomatic' illness, allowing him to dissociate himself from the campaign if it went disastrously wrong. (*Daily Telegraph*, 1994, reporting on Yeltsin's absence during a Russian attack on Chechnya)

direct action unlawful violence or trespass
Usually in support of a minority group opposed to legal activities taken by others, such as hunting or growing genetically modified crops:

> 'I mean direct action,' said Araba, ignoring Brodie. 'In a word, Susannah—violence.' (Theroux, 1976)

direct mail unsolicited enquiries sent by post
The communication seeks an order, a subscription, a donation, political support, etc. but the delivery is not more or less direct than the rest of your mail, most of which you actually want to read. *Junk mail* is accurate but not euphemistic.

directional selling promoting the product of an associated company without disclosing the financial link
Either the subsidiary of a supplier is trading under another name or a supposedly independent adviser is recommending a purchase in respect of which he will obtain an undisclosed commission or other benefit:

> While directional selling has long been suspected within the industry, this degree of openness is unheard of. (*Sunday Telegraph*, 16 August 1998—Thompson Travel had introduced a commission structure encouraging its subsidiary travel agent firm Lunn Poly to recommend

Thompson holidays rather than those of its competitors)

dirt information which may be damaging to another

It may be issued to embarrass or blackmail them, often in the phrase *have the dirt on* someone.

dirty¹ pertaining to anything harmful or damaging which may be the subject of a taboo

A *dirty* (atomic) *bomb* is going to go on killing more life for a longer period in a nastier way than a *clean* one. A *dirty joke* usually involves copulation or homosexuality. A *dirty book* may be itself clean but contains pornographic or salacious material. The *dirty deed* is extramarital copulation by a male:

... my mind leaped to the conclusion that he had taken her from me, and done the dirty deed on her. (Fraser, 1977)

A *dirty old man* seeks a sexual arrangement with a much younger person. A *dirty weekend* may be fine and sunny but is passed in overnight clandestine copulation:

They've simply gone for a dirty weekend at the Spread Eagle. (Matthew, 1978)

See also CLEAN 1.

dirty² to urinate or defecate (while wearing clothing or recumbent)

In phrases like *dirty yourself*, *your pants*, or *your trousers*. They are not used of splashing with mud.

... patients could only be kept lying on sand or sawdust, because they perpetually dirtied themselves. (Burleigh, 2000)

disability a limiting mental or physical condition

Literally, the fact of being rendered incapable, or *disabled*, but the two words have for so long been standard English that we forget there is normally no suggestion that the condition has been wilfully brought about:

The passage of the Americans with Disabilities Act in 1990 extended the same legal protections... to an estimated 43 million disabled Americans. (*Chicago Tribune*, 20 May, 1991)

Since the term 'disability' can include a former addiction to cocaine, marijuana etc., this means that an employer cannot enquire into past use of drugs, even for jobs such as airline pilots. (*Sunday Telegraph*, 6 March 1994)

disabled see DISABILITY

disadvantaged poor

Sociological jargon which has passed into standard English, suggesting that those so described have lost an advantage which they once enjoyed, such as having rich parents or good schooling:

I do want to help him—because he's black and probably grew up disadvantaged. (Theroux, 1982)

A 1965 Jules Feiffer cartoon tracks the progression from 'poor' to 'needy' to 'deprived' to 'disadvantaged'.

disappear¹ to be murdered

The implication is that the body is unlikely to be found:

...then he, Danny Lehman, might disappear for a period of thirty years, or he might disappear, period. (Erdman, 1987—the alternatives were imprisonment or death)

Also, rarely, incorrectly, as to murder:

Similar vehicles, devoid of ornaments and license plates, prowl the streets at night, looking for *subversivos* to 'disappear'. (A Guetemalan I know claims that *disappear* was first used as a transitive verb in his country.) (R. Wright, 1989)

disappear² to urinate

Mainly female use. Women do not in fact vanish after telling you that they are going to *disappear*, but they pay a fleeting visit to a lavatory.

discharge to ejaculate semen

As from Pistol's gun:

I will discharge upon her, Sir John, with two bullets. (Shakespeare, *2 Henry IV*—the 'bullets' were his testicles)

Discharge, meaning to dismiss from employment, comes from the literal meaning to free or to rid; but see FIRE.

disciple of a person addicted to participating in the activities of someone associated with something taboo

Thus a *disciple of Bacchus* is a drunkard, a *disciple of Oscar Wilde* is a male homosexual, etc.:

When I asked if you were a disciple of Oscar Wilde I meant it only in the sense of literature. (Burgess, 1980)

discipline see DOMINANCE

discomfort agony

The supposing comforting language of dentistry. When your dentist suggest you may *feel a little discomfort*, it is time to grip the arms of the chair.

discrimination selective and unfair treatment of others

Literally, the exercise of any choice or taste, but standard English is this use for over a century:

The prospect of having the fundamental choice of treatment taken away on the basis of age is quite simply age discrimination. (*Daily Telegraph*, 10 July 2001—women over 70 were being refused surgery for breast cancer)

disease of love a venereal infection
Where *love* indicates no more than copulation:
... advertisements of doctors who cured 'all the diseases of love'. (Manning, 1977)

disengage to retreat
The language of defeat:
But they cannot impose a decisive battle on us before our lines are on the terrain we have chosen; we are disengaging with great skill. (Klemperer, 1999, in translation)
A *disengagement* is such a retreat:
'Disengagement proceeds according to plan.' 'According to plan' has been much in favour recently. (ibid.—diary entry of 24 September 1943)

disgrace to impregnate a woman outside marriage
Literally, to bring into disrepute. A *disgrace* is the outcome, at least for the woman, but only if the news gets about, I suppose:
So don't talk about *making little* of people, or of him *disgracing* me. (Binchy, 1985)
I could not account to myself for the circumstances of the clerk's guilty wife living out all her after-existence on the scene of her disgrace. (W. Collins, 1860)

dish a sexually attractive woman
A male use, with common culinary imagery.
While one young dish was being lined up for a 'bunnymoon' (his word for a weekend away... (Faulks, 1996)

dishonoured *obsolete* (of a female) copulated with outside marriage
She has thus lost her HONOUR:
... he could think of a number of ways for a dishonoured woman to spend the rest of her life. (Farrell, 1973)

disinfection mass killing
The Nazi pretence was that Jews, Gypsies, and others killed by gassing were being put into a confined place for the purpose of eliminating lice etc.:
The underground chambers were named 'disinfection cellars', the above-ground chambers 'bath-houses'. (Keneally, 1982, writing of Auschwitz)

disinvestment the disposal of shares etc. as a political gesture
Not just a normal sale for economic reasons but because of opposition to an activity in which the corporation participates. The rare alternative, *divestiture*, literally means dispossession and has clerical overtones, because that is what can happen to naughty parsons.

dismal trade the arranging of funerals for payment
Literally, *dismal* means dreary:
There was no reason to believe the big-volume concerns will demonstrate a more tender regard for the pocket-books of their customers than has traditionally been the case in the Dismal Trade. (J. Mitford, 1963)
A *dismal trader* is not necessarily gloomy about business, and *dismals* were once mourning clothes.

disorderly house a brothel
Originally 19th-century legal jargon and still in use, even of the most tidy and well-conducted brothel:
If the neighbours chose to complain before a magistrate about a disorderly house... (Mayhew, 1862)

disparate impact *American* a difference in intelligence, education, or ability
Sociological jargon to explain away the result of any examination or test where one group consistently achieves better results than another:
Wherever there is 'disparate impact'—one race getting more marks than another—the Government assumes bias in the methodology of testing. (*Sunday Telegraph*, 20 November 1994—for ten years the NYPD had failed to evolve tests which resulted in whites and blacks achieving equal results)

dispatch to kill
Literally, to send. It has long been used for the killing of humans and other animals:
... we are peremptory to dispatch
This viperous traitor. (Shakespeare, *Coriolanus*)
Also as a noun, it still implies efficient and unspectacular killing:
If custody was out of the question, employ all feasible measures for dispatch. (Ludlum, 1979, writing of people not of mail)

dispense with (someone's) assistance to dismiss (someone) from employment
Usually peremptorily and with dishonour, of a senior official etc.:
The Fuhrer will dispense with his assistance (Goebbels, 1945, in translation)

disport amorously to copulate
Literally, no more than frolicking with sexual overtones:

Same old rut. A Richmond resident tells me
that it is once again that time of the year
when the deer in Richmond Park are
disporting themselves amorously. Notices
in the park are models of tact. They read
demurely: 'Warning, Excessive Deer
Activity'. (*Daily Telegraph*, October 1987)

disposal a killing other than by process of
law
Espionage and criminal jargon, from the need
to get rid of the body:
  Disposals are not in our line of country.
  (Allbeury, 1981, referring to such a killing)

dispossessed indigent
Those so described are unlikely to have
owned valuable possessions in the first place:
  There the spit-and-polish troops are
  immigration police; the hordes, the
  Mexicans, Haitians, and other dispossessed
  people seeking illegal entry. (Cahill, 1995)

dispute a strike
Shortened form of *industrial dispute*. Used
twice in three minutes by BBC Radio 4 on 15
June, 1983:
  A dispute among Southern Region guards
  has led to the cancelling of trains. (They
  were not arguing with each other, as might
  have been supposed.)
  A dispute among camera and technical
  staff has prevented the televising of
  sporting events. (Again, the difference of
  opinion was with the employer, not with
  the fellow workers.)

dissolution¹ death
Literally, the splitting up into constituent
parts, as the corpse into bones, or the body
from the soul:
  A fetch...come to assure...a happy
  longevity or immediate dissolution.
  (Banim, 1825—a *fetch* was a ghostly figure)

dissolution² a persistent course of licentious behaviour
The word is used of casual copulation, homosexuality publicly flaunted, heavy gambling,
drunkenness, the use of illegal narcotics, etc.
In each case normal constraint is *dissolved* and
he who so acts is *dissolute*.

distracted by having a sexual relationship with
Literally, having your attention drawn away
from something, in this case your spouse:
  The couple had a wobbly time last year and
  even separated for a while briefly when
  Brian became momentarily distracted by
  his (married) secretary. (*Sunday Telegraph*,
  27 February 2000)

distressed mentally ill
Medical and sociological jargon. Literally, it
means sorely troubled but today you call such
people distraught.

distribution the payment of a bribe
Usually where there are several recipients, or
where the organizer of a corrupt deal hands
on bribes to others, which may then be called
a *secondary distribution*:
  I also want acknowledgement from every
  recipient in the 'secondary distribution', as
  you so nicely put it. (Erdman, 1981)

disturbed¹ naughty or ill-disciplined
Sociological jargon which does not imply that
the miscreants have been interrupted in their
activities:
  Boys and girls who steal or vandalize, or
  wet the bed, or are found by their teachers
  or doctors disturbed...(Bradbury, 1976)

disturbed² mentally abnormal
Medical jargon, with an implication that the
condition is akin to unease:
  He had stopped looking for the
  hospital...'Are you disturbed?' went on
  the lunatic. (Amis, 1978—the lunatic was
  using the jargon used by others of himself)

ditch to land an aircraft in water
Not of seaplanes. A *ditch* is a drain dug to
receive water, whence the standard English
meaning, to discard in such a drain, or
elsewhere, any unwanted object. Originally a
Second World War punning use but now of
any aircraft making a forced landing, especially in the sea.

dive¹ *obsolete* to steal by picking pockets
From the movement of the hand:
  In using your nimbles, in diving in pockets.
  (Ben Jonson)
Grose notes *diver* as a pickpocket.

dive² *American* a place for the sale and
drinking of intoxicants
Often low-class, from the use of cellars, where
the rent is less. In the same sense Grose gives
diver as 'one who lives in a cellar'.

dive³ a pretence of having been knocked
down
Made by a boxer who, of his own volition,
goes to the canvas, a soccer player who seeks
to win an undeserved free kick, or a pedestrian seeking compensation from a motorist:
  Some gamblers tried to scare him into a
  dive. (Chandler, 1939—they wanted a
  boxer to throw a fight)
  ...there must be a fair chance the crafty
  old bugger took a dive hoping to get a big
  payday in court. (P. McCarthy, 2000,

commenting on a press headline, 'PRIEST
SUES CORPORATION OVER KNEE')

diver a male who indulges in cunnilingus
As with a *muff-diver*:
> ...the tufts of facial hair known as *bugger's
> grips* can also be described as muff-diver's
> depth marks. (Jolly, 1988)

divergence homosexuality
Moving away from the norm:
> Miles's divergence had been one of his
> most valuable assets. (Trevanian, 1972—
> Miles was a homosexual)

diversity¹ the presence of both black and
white employees
Literally, the condition of being different or
varied:
> The company selected the black candidate
> because only two of its 82 managers were
> from ethnic minorities and the board was
> feeling the pressure of federal rules
> demanding 'diversity' in the workplace.
> (*Daily Telegraph*, 9 April 1995—the
> unsuccessful white candidate was awarded
> $425,000 damages against the company, a
> judgment which was confirmed by the
> Supreme Court)

diversity² *American* giving preferential
status to a minority group
Or showing exceptional tolerance towards the
interests of a minority:
> At a posh suburban high school in
> Brookline, Massachusetts, the standard
> course of European history was
> discontinued for having failed to meet the
> requisite 'diversity' standard, while an
> entire menu of new courses, in black
> studies, women's studies, Asian studies,
> etc. supplanted it. (*Sunday Telegraph*, 21
> January 1996)

Such fortunate students would in due course
include in their résumés an account of their
diversity training qualifications and experience:
> At Cornell University, a student-
> employment 'diversity' training session
> included the showing of X-rated gay
> porno movies to show if applicants
> showed any signs of discomfort or
> distaste. (ibid.)

divert to steal
Usually of embezzlement, where the funds
are directed into the wrong channel, but
sometimes of goods:
> ...a large proportion of the profits had
> been, shall we say, diverted. (Erdman,
> 1987)
> Like the wharfingers, the lock-keepers had
> ample opportunity to 'divert' a certain
> amount of cargo. (A. Burton, 1989)

do¹ to copulate with
Mainly male usage, from his supposed initiative:
> Doing a filthy pleasure is, and short. (Ben
> Jonson)
> 'Where you might meet anyone and do
> anything.' 'Or meet anything and do
> anyone.' (Bradbury, 1975)

Both sexes *do it*:
> Always wanted to do it outside, you know,
> ever since I read *Sons and Lovers*. (ibid.)

do² to kill or injure
Also as *do for, do down, do in, do over*, etc.:
> Some of our chaps say that they had done
> their prisoners in whilst taking them back.
> (F. Richards, 1933)
> ...the thug swaggered off down the
> pavement, doubtless eager to tell his
> friends that he'd 'done' one of the visiting
> fans. (Paxman, 1998)

To *do yourself in* is to commit suicide:
> He has written a letter to my parents.
> I might as well do myself in. (Townsend,
> 1982)

do³ (over) to cheat or rob
Also as *do the dirty* or *do down*:
> Sometimes I'd go with a friend to France
> for the weekend, expeditions that were
> financed by him doing over his aunty's gas
> meter. (McNab, 1993)

do⁴ a battle
In standard usage, a party or function. Usually
of a less successful and bloody encounter,
such as the British *Arnhem do*.

do⁵ to charge with an offence
Police jargon:
> She's been done twice for drunk in charge.
> (Allbeury, 1976)

A person charged, especially with a motoring
offence, will refer to having been *done*.

do a bunk to urinate
Literally, to depart quickly. There are numerous slang and dialect phrases meaning to
urinate or to defecate which employ the verb
to do. I have listed many, SLASH for example,
under the noun, because slashes etc. are had,
done, or gone for, and the noun imparts the
sense. Phrases not noted elsewhere include
do a rural, to defecate out of doors; *do a shift*, to
urinate; and *do a dike*, to urinate or defecate.

do a line to ingest narcotics illegally
through the nose
From the sprinkling of power in a line:
> The only people present were Patty-Anne,
> Lasater, and Bill Clinton. 'He was doing a
> line. It was just there on the table.' (Evans-
> Pritchard, 1997)

do a number (of a criminal) to give information to the police
A variant of SING:
> Look, if Keiser's doing a number, I've arranged for you to get fifty to knock him off. (Maas, 1986—Keiser was talking to the police)

do a runner to leave without prior notice
Escaping, you hope, from your spouse, creditors, jailers, or anyone else who might have an interest in your peremptory departure:
> She's done a runner, yes. She's taken the kiddies, yes. (Seymour, 1995)

do away with to kill
So long standard English that it is hard to recall that the words mean something different:
> As the *Volkischer Beobachter* puts it, these enemies of the state will henceforth receive no mercy. They will be ruthlessly done away with. (Shirer, 1999, reporting on 8 November 1939, after a failed attempt on Hitler's life)

do business with to cease to be confrontational with
Mrs Thatcher's often-quoted (and copied) assessment of Gorbachev.

do-gooder a self-righteous person who forces his concerns on others
Nearly always used derogatorily:
> ... hated to ... make the other policeman think he was a do-gooder. (Wambaugh, 1975)

Do-gooding, as different from doing good, is so acting:
> What were her do-gooding parents but pious cheats? (Theroux, 1976)

do-lally-tap mad
The derivation is from the transit camp at Deolali near Bombay where time-expired British soldiers were sent to await repatriation. The heat and boredom were accentuated by the vagaries of intercontinental transport in the days of sail. If you arrived at the camp in the wrong season, you could be stuck there for six months, which would be additional to your contracted service:
> In India he had a touch of the sun, which we old soldiers called 'Deolalic Tap'. (F. Richards, 1933)

The 'old soldier' also uses another spelling:
> Oh, he's got the do-lally tap. (F. Richards, 1936)

In the Second World War sometimes shortened to *tap*:
> I was sure by now that this was your natural wild man, and not permanently tap. (Fraser, 1992)

do the business to copulate with
Often within marriage or a permanent relationship, and not to be confused with DO BUSINESS WITH:
> This was the first time they had done the business in a good while; two months nearly. Made love. He'd never called it that; sounded thick. Riding your wife was more than just riding. (R. Doyle, 1991)

do the right thing to marry a woman you have impregnated
After you had been seen to DO WRONG:
> He Did The Right Thing, by a girl who had only six months to live. (Lyall, 1982)

do what comes naturally to copulate
Of either sex:
> The pimps would come round and collect, do what comes naturally, and cut out. (L. Armstrong, 1955)

do wrong (to someone) to copulate with other than your regular sexual partner
Arguably such behaviour wrongs the transient as well as the permanent sexual partner:
> Then every two or three months he would do her wrong. Some girl would take an interest and Hobie would disappear in her dorm room often for days. (Turow, 1996)

do your duty by to impregnate (your wife) or to have a son by your husband
Much store was formerly set by both parties on a wife not copulating with other than her husband before they had jointly produced a son and heir:
> I regard it as my duty to have an heir. If my husband refuses to do his duty by me I shall find someone else who will. (Sharpe, 1975)

do yourself to masturbate yourself
Usually of females, and as *do it with yourself*:
> The thought of him inside her, made her squirm; for an instant she considered doing herself. (M. Thomas, 1980)
> 'Have you ever done it with yourself?' Dottie shook her head violently. (M. McCarthy, 1963)

dock to copulate with a female
The expression was at one time confined to copulation with a virgin, using the imagery of pruning.
This is a convenient place to note that etymologists do not always agree with each other. Farmer and Henley trace this meaning of *dock* to the Romany *dukker*. Partridge, in *DSUE*, looks to the standard English meaning, to curtail, which, in his judgment, 'is obviously operative'. Grose makes no suggestion as to the etymology but reports 'Docked smack smooth; one who has suffered an

amputation of his penis for a venereal complaint'. *EDD* correctly reports that *dock* means to undress, as in 'mun dock this gound off'. *OED* reminds us that the *dock* in which a prisoner stands comes from the Dutch word for a rabbit hutch. The *New Oxford Dictionary of English* adds further to our understanding with the definition 'to attach (a piece of equipment) to another', which is one way of describing the copulatory process. My contribution to the debate is to draw attention to a marine *dock*, a long, narrow, moist space into which a ship moves and may fit snugly. I am sorry that we shall never know what Alfred Holt, the erudite author of *Phrase and Word Origins*, thought.

doctor to change through deception
By adulterating intoxicants, administering drugs to racehorses, falsely adjusting accounts, castrating tomcats, etc.:
> One doctors a cat or a company's accounts. (Howard, 1978)
> They've doctored the tapes. (Colodny and Gettlin, 1991, of Watergate)

dodgy indicating some characteristic that is taboo or of doubtful legality
Thus for a sailor a *dodgy deacon* is a homosexual priest and a *dodgy car* is one which has been stolen:
> I might be able to sell a dodgy car now and again but that's never going to make us rich. (L. Thomas, 1977)
For a transport driver a *dodgy night* is one spent at home but entered on his time sheet as being passed with his vehicle:
> If you check your overtime sheets,
> or the appropriate lay-bys, you will
> find out…what the drivers'
> jargon 'dodgy nights' means. (Holder, 1992)

doe *obsolete* a prostitute
The progression from this 17th-century use was to a woman student at Oxford University and, in modern America, to a woman who goes to a party unaccompanied, but not a *stag party*.

dog and pony show *American* a bogus exhibition or insincere conduct calculated to deceive
Where you may put on a *dog and pony act*:
> I was here one time for a 'dog and pony show' put on by our government for your State Department. (Hailey, 1990, writing of a place in the Amazon basin where illegal coca crops were grown and, on that occasion, destroyed)

Well, my darling wife and I are having this sort of terrible argument, but I suppose we can do the dog and pony act. (Proulx, 1993—they could pretend to be on good terms)

dole a payment by the state to the involuntarily unemployed
Originally, a portion, whence a gift made regularly to the poor, as *dole-bread* or *dole-money*, and at funerals *dole-meats*:
> She's on the dole, so hopefully we'll trace her soon enough when next time she claims benefit. (Strong, 1997)
Now largely replaced by new euphemisms—see RELIEF 1.

doll[1] a sexually attractive female
Dr Johnson reminds us that *Doll* was a contraction of *Dorothy* as well as being 'A little girl's puppet or baby'. A female so described may be beautiful though slow-witted, but a *real doll* implies beauty and brains.

doll[2] a narcotic in pill form
Formerly a barbiturate or amphetamine. The punning title of Jacqueline Susann's novel *Valley of the Dolls* started or sanctified this usage.

dollar shop a store which will not sell in the local currency
A feature of Communist regimes where luxuries, and even some necessities, were reserved for foreign tourists and party officials. The currency did not have to be the American dollar so long as it was not from any Communist country.

dolly a mistress
Certainly from DOLL 1 but also perhaps owing something to her smart dress—*dolled up*:
> It seemed rather steep of my father to keep his dolly at home with my wife there. (Fraser, 1969, writing in 19th-century style)
A Victorian *dolly-common* or *dolly-mop* was a prostitute:
> Maid-servants, all of whom are amateurs, as opposed to professionals, more commonly known as 'Dolly-mops'. (Mayhew, 1862)

domestic a servant in the home
A shortened form of *domestic servant* or *domestic help*:
> We used to call them servants. Now we call them domestic help. (Chandler, 1953—and now we call them *domestics*, but not to their face)

domestic afflictions menstruation
It could mean myriad other things which cause unhappiness in the home.

dominance a sexual perversion in which a woman inflicts pain on a man
Literally, authority or control over another. Also known as *discipline*, with whips, thongs, handcuffs, and similar props.

Don Juan a male philanderer
The successful practitioner in seduction inspired the music of Mozart and the words of Molière, Byron, and Shaw, to name but a few. Whence *donjuanism*, such behaviour:
  Etlin has great courage and charm, yet his Donjuanism somehow detracts from his authority. (Read, 1986)

don the turban to become a Muslim
Certain Europeans, for reasons of conscience or expediency, changed religion while resident in a Muslim society:
  British travellers of the period regularly brought back tales of their compatriots who had 'donned the turban' and were now prospering in the Islamic world. (William Dalrymple in *Sunday Telegraph*, 20 February 2000)

done for subjected to a major misfortune
Killed, seriously wounded, defeated in a fight, or bankrupted:
  'They're both done for'... George lay spread-eagled at my feet. (Fraser, 1971)

dong a penis
Probably from DING-A-LING through *ding* and *ding-dong*, all making a comparison with a bell clapper:
  His dong was never as all-fired important to Wally as yours is to you. (Hailey, 1979)

don't name-'ems *obsolete* trousers
A 19th-century example of the great trouser taboo—see also UNMENTIONABLES 1.

doodoo excrement
From babytalk:
  The horse did a doodoo on the street and there was a smell. (McCourt, 1997)

doorstep[1] to abandon a baby
In the days when there was a stigma attached to unmarried woman having babies and little help for them if they did, the baby might be left on the doorstep of a prosperous house, the mother ringing a bell and then leaving. Some figurative use of the behaviour of parents towards unwanted children:
  When it became obvious...from the hour of my conception, that my parents intended to doorstep me...(N. Mitford, 1945)

doorstep[2] aggressively to interview an unwilling person

To catch a victim reluctant to be interviewed, a journalist may thrust a microphone at him, possibly with a camera also recording the scene, as he attempts to enter or leave his home.

dope a narcotic
Originally, a thick liquid, from the Dutch *doop*, sauce, as used once on the canvas fuselages of aircraft. Whence prepared opium, which has the same appearance:
  A younger sister whom she loved...had taken to dope. (F. Harris, 1925)
Now it may refer to any illegal narcotics. To *dope* is to give such narcotics to horses, athletes, or greyhounds, whence the *dope*, inside information or, in this case, which runner has been drugged? *Dope*, a simple person, comes from the drugged mien and behaviour.

dose a venereal infection
Literally, an amount of medicine, and the usage, normally of gonorrhoea, comes from the remedy formerly prescribed:
  And if I give that man a dose, that's my pleasure and he just gettin' what he's payin' for. (Simon, 1979—a prostitute was talking, not a medical practitioner)

dose of P45 medicine *British* the summary dismissal of employees
The tax form handed to those leaving employment is numbered P45:
  I also suspect the AA is wildly overmanned and Gardner will administer a large dose of P45 medicine. (*Sunday Telegraph*, 27 June 1999—the Automobile Association had just changed ownership)

dotty eccentric or mentally ill
Originally, of unsteady gait, whence feeble and then feeble-minded:
  There might be a basis of truth, but I felt she was pretty dotty. (Manning, 1965)

double dipper a person in receipt of bribery or a second source of income
Not taking a classic sauna, passing from the hot chamber to the cold:
  Keegan was an academy graduate who had put in his thirty and retired to become a double-dipper. (Clancy 1986—he had both his pension and a new job)

double entry dishonest
The development in Lombardy of *double-entry bookkeeping*, a self-balancing method of keeping accounts, was an important factor in making that region pre-eminent in European banking. The euphemistic use alludes to the keeping of two sets of books in parallel, one of which is intended to deceive:

A double-entry man. Hong Kong's full of
them. Twisters. (Theroux, 1982)

double-gaited having both homosexual
and heterosexual tastes
The imagery comes from equestrian sport:
> '...homosexuality isn't the handle it once
> was'...'Pascoe's wife didn't know he was
> double-gaited.' (Bagley, 1982)

double-header sexual activity by a male
with two females in each other's presence
Prostitutes' jargon, from the use of two
locomotives to pull a train and punning on
GIVE HEAD:
> ...she wasn't interested in the hundred-
> dollar bag of bones who Juicy Lucy said was
> coming back at eight o'clock for a
> doubleheader. (Wambaugh, 1981—'Juicy
> Lucy' is a name commonly given to a
> prostitute)

double in stud to copulate with two
people in each other's presence
Of either sex, despite being derived from the
maleness of STUD:
> ...maybe there were some who doubled in
> stud. (Longstreet, 1956)

double time copulation outside marriage
There is increased payment for overtime
working, and see TWO-TIME:
> Your wife is standing right beside
> you and you are practically accusing
> her of a little double time. (Chandler,
> 1953)

doubtful sexuality homosexuality
The choice is not really in doubt:
> L——was to be compared with A——in
> doubtful sexuality. (Mitchell, 1982)

douceur a bribe
Literally, a gratuity, in French and English:
> I bet he's had some little douceur slipped
> into his hand. (Manning, 1965)
I prefer the 19th-century spelling:
> Nobody is allowed to take dowzers. (EDD
> from 1885)

dove an appeaser or pacifist
The allusion is to the symbol of peace and the
opposite of HAWK. The use is not necessarily
pejorative and became hackneyed during the
Cold War.

down to prison
The place where the judge sends you after
sentencing, the cells often being situated in
the cellar of the courthouse:
> In all her nineteen years she had
> never once been permitted to visit

her father, who had been sent down
three months before she was born.
(Strong, 1994)
In the same sense, the tipstaff may be
instructed to 'take the prisoner down',
although the descent may be no greater than
from the dock to the floor of the room.
Prisoners of war were sent *down the line*.

down among the dead men drunk
The *dead men* are the skittles which have been
knocked over in ninepins. Whence also the
rarer *in the down-pins*.

down below the genitalia
Of either sex, despite that part of the body
being located above the legs. Also as *down
there*:
> We take it in turns to stroke and
> massage each other anywhere but
> what you used to call down below.
> (Amis, 1978)
> The first time she touched him 'down
> there' she thought she would die of
> mortification. (Forsyth, 1994)

down boy control your lust
The canine injunction is adopted to a manifestation of male sexual excitement:
> 'We'll have a nightcap at my place,' she
> said. 'Sounds good,' I said. 'Let's go.' 'Down
> boy, down!' she said. (Deighton, 1993/2)

down for the count to be convicted of a
offence
The imagery is from boxing:
> He's definitely going down for the count.
> What are your thoughts on his mental
> state? (J. Patterson, 1999)

down on providing oral sexual stimula-
tion of another's genitalia
Homosexual and heterosexual use, from the
posture adopted:
> 'When I'm up, Barbara's down,' says
> Howard...'When you're up who, Barbara's
> down on whom?' asks Flora. (Bradbury,
> 1975)

down population a compulsory dismissal of staff
Not the result of genocide or the inhabitants
of an Irish county:
> The consultants used to talk about 'down
> population'. (*Daily Telegraph*, 24 November
> 2000—a former employee of Express
> Newspapers was speaking about life under
> a new owner)

Down's syndrome a congenital disorder
due to a chromosome deficiency
This is an example of a phrase incorporating
syndrome being used to avoid a taboo word—in

this case what was formerly known as Mongolism. Here the stigma and the possible racial sneer are circumvented by naming the affliction after the English physician John Langdon Down (1828–1896):

> People they spoke to about mongolism— Down's syndrome as Angela insisted on referring to it. (Lodge, 1980)

In the same way we may prefer not to talk about schizophrenia:

> ... to rid the ailment of unpleasant associations, there are now moves to have it called Kraepelin's syndrome. (Winchester, 1998)

downer a depressant narcotic
Addict jargon:

> He hoped there might be some downers left ... where his girlfriend left a small cache. (Wambaugh, 1975)

downs depressant narcotics
Always in the plural and taken to have the opposite effect of UPS:

> ... took his pills by the fistful, downs from the left pocket of his tiger suit and ups from his right. (Herr, 1977)

downsize to dismiss employees
The volume you wish to reduce is the size of the payroll:

> It was an unhappy time. We had to downsize the company substantially and we had quite a serious divergence of opinion between the management and the workforce. (*Sunday Express*, 12 February, 1995—the *divergence* was not surprising as the workforce was suffering the job losses, not the managers)

downstairs[1] *obsolete* the house servants
Their normal location was in a semi-basement of a town house. Whence the British television series *Upstairs, Downstairs*.

downstairs[2] the genitalia
A genteel use by and of male and female without the possible sexual implication of DOWN BELOW.

downward adjustment a devaluation or an economic depression
The phrase attempts to lull fears by implying that events are still under control:

> ... the worst America has to endure is a 'downward adjustment of the economy'. (Jennings, 1965, noting the euphemism)

doxy *obsolete* a prostitute
Originally, a sweetheart, from the Dutch *dock*, a doll:

> A party taken on a cruise by wealthy degenerates, who had sold their doxies at

various places in the Caribbean. (Fraser, 1971, writing in 19th-century style)

drag the clothing of the other sex worn by a homosexual
Originally theatrical use, referring to a male actor (not necessarily a homosexual) in female clothes, the long train being *dragged* on the floor. A homosexual so attired is said to be *in drag*:

> A cop tried to intervene and was promptly felled by someone in drag. (Sharpe, 1977)

A *drag* is also an American homosexual party for males.

dragon (the) habitual illegal use of narcotics
The association is of opium with China, dragons, and so on:

> You're standing between me and the big, bad dragon. (Gabriel, 1992—he was stopping an addict getting heroin, not intervening between man and wife)

In many phrases such as *chase the dragon*, to be addicted to narcotics.

drain off to urinate
Usually of a male, with obvious imagery:

> Weak bladders, old men ... Might as well drain off himself. (Grayson, 1975)

dram a drink of spirituous intoxicant
You used to buy spirits from apothecaries, who used their own measurements, in this case one eighth of a fluid ounce which was originally the weight of a drachma, corrupted to *dram*:

> 'Come over for a dram,' he urged them. (Boyle, 1979)

draw a bead on to shoot at or kill
The *bead* is the foresight of an old-style rifle, rather than the bullet:

> I am going to draw a bead on this gentleman. I am preparing an operation to liquidate him. (Goebbels, 1945, in translation—he was particularly upset by the way in which the inhabitants of his home town had welcomed the Anglo-American invaders)

draw a blank *American* to be very drunk
Punning on the loss of awareness and an unsuccessful attempt in a lottery:

> For after the funeral I drew a near blank, as they said in those days about drunkenness in its most amnesiac mode. (Styron, 1976)

draw the enemy into a trap to retreat involuntarily
Military use when you want to disguise your predicament in order to keep up morale:

Of course the officers knew, but they were telling us we were drawing the enemy into a trap. (F. Richards, 1933, describing a retreat in the First World War)

draw the king's picture to counterfeit bank notes
Or the queen's, or the president's, as the case may be, from forging the likeness.

draw the long bow to boast or exaggerate
The longer the bow, the further the potential range. Also as *pull the long bow*:
  ...draw the long bow better now than ever. (Byron, 1824, of boasting)
  You will say, 'Ah, here's Flashy pulling the long bow,' but I'm not. (Fraser, 1973, writing in 19th-century style)
See also SHOOT A LINE.

draw water to have power or influence
Naval jargon, from the size of the ship:
  I'm not a friendless nobody nowadays...You think you draw water? Well, you ain't the only one. (Fraser, 1994)
The official or officer who *draws too much water* is not to be gainsaid.

dream associated with illegal narcotics
Especially heroin as in *dream dust*, although a *dream stick* was opium.

dress for sale *American* a prostitute
In this CB use, the *dress* is not what's on offer and the transaction contemplated is one of hire or licence. In 19th-century London a *dress lodger* was a prostitute clothed in suitable style by a pimp, working from a brothel called a *dress-house*:
  The dress-lodger probably lives some distance from the immoral house by whose owner she is employed. (Mayhew, 1862)
Today an American pimp who decks out a prostitute is said to provide her with *bonds* or *threads*.

dress on/to the left to be a male homosexual
The enquiry of a bespoke tailor of his customer as to which side his penis normally rests in clothing:
  And in the matter of how a gentleman should arrange himself within his undergarments, all leading authorities have concluded that he must dress to the left. (Rushdie, 1995)
  I wondered if the senator was attempting to discover whether I was 'dressing on the left'. (Behr, 1978—was he homosexual?)
See also LEFT-HANDED 2 for the sinister association.

drill[1] to kill by shooting
The imagery is of boring holes:
  I could drill you and get away with it. (Chandler, 1958—the speaker was not an army sergeant)

drill[2] to organize and train civilians in an illegal militia
Drilling instils the first rudiments of military discipline:
  ...the Ulster Volunteer force went on drilling...and not with dummy weapons. (R. F. Foster, 1988)

drink[1] an intoxicant or to drink intoxicants
The commonest euphemism for anything to do with intoxicants. Thus if a friend offers you a *drink*, you do not expect him to serve water. To *like a drink* is to have a perhaps modest alcoholic addiction. *Drink taken* or *in drink* mean intoxicated, as did the obsolete *given to the drink*:
  Some say she cocks her wee finger. In short that she's gien to the drink. (Barr, 1861)
To *have a drinking problem* or *drink too much* is to be an alcoholic:
  ...her father had had a drinking problem. (Theroux, 1982—he was not suffering from some restriction of the throat)
  He sometimes drank too much. (F. Harris, 1925)
A *non-drinker* drinks only non-alcoholic drinks. And see DRUNK.

drink[2] a bribe or tip
Given as such to save any embarrassment when handing over cash, but less explicit than the French *pour-boire*:
  'Has any money changed hands?' 'I dare say Jimmy was offered a 'drink' of some sort.' (Read, 1979)

drink[3] the sea
Used by airmen when forced to put down on water, or *in the drink*.

drink at Freeman's Quay to cadge intoxicants from others
Freeman's was also the mythical brand of cigarettes cadged by servicemen in the Second World War.

drink milk *Indian* (of a baby) to drown
The Parsees set a higher value on male children and drowned unwanted females in milk:
  ...if it were a daughter, Bapaiji swore she would make it drink milk; all good women, so she contended, hated their sex. (Desai, 1988)

drive a ball through to kill by shooting
Using the same imagery as DRILL 1:
> Supposing, he asked, landlords refused to
> give any reduction of rent: what were they
> to do? 'Drive a ball through them.' (Kee,
> 1993—the advice was tendered by a man in
> the crowd attending one of Parnell's
> meetings in Ireland)

drive-away the theft of fuel by absconding without paying
Those of us who pay also expect to drive away:
> I'd already checked the garage surveillance
> cameras...they were focused on the
> forecourt to catch drive-aways. (McNab,
> 1997)

droit de seigneur copulation by a male employer with a female employee
Literally, a right of the lord of the Manor, which was said to include, fictitiously in most cases, copulating with each virgin in his domain. In modern times such a privilege was claimed by other dominant males, especially in the entertainment industry:
> The droit de seigneur died with the
> Hollywood czars. (Deighton, 1972)

The feudal system functioned primarily on the lord's ability to demand unpaid labour from tenants or villeins, in return for protection. This practice coined euphemisms such as *bederipe* (reaping by request) and *boonwork* (granting a favour):
> William did additional ploughing as
> 'boonwork', and in the great communal
> effort of the summer and autumn helped
> to gather in the lord's harvest. (Mayberry,
> 1998—William de Mora was a 13th-century
> tenant farmer)

Another word for this forced labour, *love-boonwork*, can only have been used ironically.

drop¹ to kill
By shooting, after which the victim falls:
> But [the Iraqi soldiers] got so close
> that there was no way they were going
> to avoid us, so we dropped them.
> (McNab, 1993)

In Chicago, to *drop down the chute* meant to murder, as with the disposal of garbage in an apartment block:
> If he's alive, put him on ice until tonight.
> Then drop him down the chute. (Weverka,
> 1973)

drop² a quantity of intoxicant
Usually of spirits and seeking to imply a moderate consumption:
> The rum came up with the rations and was
> handed over by the Company-Sergeant-
> Major. If he liked his little drop, he took his
> little drop. (F. Richards, 1933)

Occasionally as a *drop of blood*:
> 'Give me a drop of blood, will you?' The
> bourbon tasted like linseed oil. (Mailer,
> 1965)

A *drop on* or *drop taken* indicates intoxication:
> Two of our chaps with a drop on shot all
> the bottles and glasses in a cafe.
> (F. Richards, 1933)
> My father was always giving out about it
> when he had a drop taken. (Flanagan, 1979)

drop³ to die
Usually suddenly, of natural causes. From the falling and a shortened form of *drop dead*:
> Louie's out mowing the lawn and he
> drops...Like that. The ticker. (Sanders,
> 1977)

The (*long*) or (*last*) *drop* was death by hanging:
> Unlike the festive hangings of earlier
> times, the drop was performed in church
> stillness. (Keneally, 1982)

drop⁴ to give birth to
Usually of quadrupeds but, of women, to *drop a bundle* meant to have an induced abortion:
> Ask the girls who dropped their
> bundles...(W. Smith, 1979, writing of such
> abortions)

drop⁵ a bribe
Literally, a place where stolen goods are left for collection by a third party:
> Over the years Robbie had made 'drops' to
> many judges. (Turow, 1999)

drop acid illegally to ingest LSD
The *dropping* may be onto a cube of sugar.

drop anchor fraudulently to cause a horse to run slowly in a race
The imagery is naval and the practice associated with crooked gambling.

drop beads *American* to identify yourself esoterically to another homosexual
By speech or body language. The wearing of beads by a male may imply effeminacy. If the string breaks, the beads spread themselves over a wide area.

drop car a vehicle used in an illegal enterprise
And abandoned during the getaway:
> He described how he bought a 'drop
> car' under a false name. (Evans-Pritchard,
> 1997)

drop-dead list a list of names of people to be dismissed from employment
The offensive expression *drop dead* expresses rejection.

drop in your tracks to die suddenly

The imagery is from racing and the death may or may not be from natural causes:
> ... if Kramer had not been so inconsiderate as to drop in his tracks. There was nothing like death for spawning myths. (D. Francis, 1978)

drop off to die
It is used of dying from natural causes. The derivation is from the colloquial meaning, to sleep, and from the fate of a dead bird:
> The soo took the fever, the kye droppit off. (A. Armstrong, 1890)
> It's the dropping off the perches ... Soon we shall all have gone. (N. Mitford, 1949)

drop the boom on to discriminate against
Literally, to activate a defensive obstruction to navigation. Of the withdrawal of credit facilities, exclusion from confidence, or dismissal from employment:
> [He] still worried that Harold would drop the boom on him. (McInerney, 1992—he was afraid of losing his job)

drop the crotte to defecate
From the French word for dung, *crotte*, rather than from the obsolete English *crottels*, horse dung. Also as *drop a log* or *wax*. Some figurative use:
> Buller splayed out and dropped his crotte on the edge of the path (G. Greene, 1978)
> Willie said, 'I almost dropped a log.' (Theroux, 1993—Willie had been taken by surprise)

drop the hook on *American* to arrest
The imagery is from fishing:
> The buttons in the prowl car were about ready to drop the hook on him. (Chandler, 1953)

drop your arse to have diarrhoea
Not merely to lower yourself into a chair:
> A guard appeared each time and dragged me down to the toilet, then stood over me while I dropped my arse. (McNab, 1993)

drop your drawers *American* (of a female) to copulate promiscuously
A British female would, if so inclined, *drop her pants*, the equivalent of the American *underpants*:
> ... those pressed, permanented country-club types ... would drop their drawers for a New York Jew. (M. Thomas, 1980—*permanented* means having their hair permanently waved)

drop your flag to surrender
Which a warship might do, by lowering it to denote submission.

droppings the excreta of animals
Standard English since at least the 16th century:
> There were steaming piles of elephant droppings in the middle of the road. (C. Allen, 1975)

drown the miller to be made bankrupt
According to the Scottish proverb, 'o'er much water drowned the miller', from the days when most flour mills were powered by a leat and a flood might destroy the mill. Whence the derivative use, meaning to add too much water to a glass of whisky.

drown your sorrows to drink intoxicants to excess
Supposed solace is brought about through intoxication:
> If I didn't know you better I'd have said you'd been drowning your sorrows. (Amis, 1978)

drumstick the thigh of a cooked bird
Another way of avoiding mention of the taboo leg. And see DARK MEAT 1.

drunk intoxicated
Standard English, from having had a DRINK 1 too many. A *drunk* may mean an alcoholic or, less often, a carouse:
> He also had some glorious drunks with the men he had met. (F. Richards, 1933)

Drury Lane ague *obsolete* venereal disease
The affliction might be caught from a *Drury Lane vestal*, a prostitute. Drury Lane, adjoining Covent Garden, was a notorious brothel area in pre-20th century London.

dry¹ prohibiting or not offering the sale of intoxicants
It does not mean that, in a *dry canteen*, no potable fluid is available. See also WET 2.

dry² wanting an alcoholic drink
Usually of a person wanting beer, with a pretence of dehydration:
> You dry, lad? S'm I, begod! mouth like an ash pit. (Cookson, 1967)

dry³ to forget your lines
Theatrical jargon, a shortened form of *dry up*, something which should not happen to a professional actor:
> I delivered the previous lines right on cue. But after the Yorick speech I let them think I'd dried. (Deighton, 1972)

dry bob copulation without ejaculation
A vulgarism which puns on the term for an English schoolboy who eschewed rowing in

favour of cricket. A *dry run* indicates copulation during which the male wears a contraceptive sheath, being a triple pun on the absence of a free seminal discharge, on the sensation, and on the meaning, a practice or rehearsal.

dry clean to check or evade for reasons of security

The removal of extraneous matter:

> On the way back to his offices at American Contract Services in Little Rock he would double back or take strange routes to 'dry clean' the cars that he thought were following him. (Evans-Pritchard, 1997)

dry out to desist from drinking alcohol after a period of excess

Not what you do in front of a fire after a walk in the rain:

> I have been at a health farm in the depths of Suffolk, slimming and drying out before the summer holiday. (A. Waugh, *Daily Telegraph*, 13 August 1994)

dry pox (the) *obsolete* syphilis

More usual as the *pox*, *tout court*:

> The disease communicated by the Malays, Lascars, and the Orientals generally...goes by the name of the Dry——. (Mayhew, 1862—he isn't always so squeamish)

duck *American* a urine bottle for males

Hospital jargon, from its shape.

duff¹ see FLUFF YOUR DUFF

duff² *American* the buttocks

Referring to the suety pudding or pastry and probably not associated with the slang expression *duff up*, to belabour, or the slang *duff*, a male homosexual.

dull to kill

With imagery from making dark rather than from stupidity:

> He dulled them, turned, left the room. (Goldman, 1986, writing about a double murder)

dumb down to make simpler

The phrase refers to public examinations, which retain the former names and grades but are set or marked so that a greater proportion of examinees appears to pass or do well; or to broadcasting, where effort is being made to attract a less cerebral audience:

> Under New Labour, this dumbing down will not affect children's ability to go on to higher education. (*Daily Telegraph*, 16 February 1998)

dummy¹ a stupid person

Literally, a representation of the human form, from the meaning, a dumb person. It may denote someone who is momentarily unthinking or distracted, or it may refer to the mentally ill:

> So don't get the idea all of Ellerbee's patients are dummies. (Sanders, 1990—Ellerbee was a psychiatrist)

dummy² the penis

The shape may be likened to the baby's comforter. Usually in the phrase, *flog the dummy*, to masturbate.

dump to defecate

An obvious and rather distasteful male usage as a verb or a noun:

> Everything hinged on that first dump of the day. (Theroux, 1971)

And some figurative use:

> But maybe you also recall how your Service dumped all over us on that one? (Lyall, 1985)

It is to be hoped that the prevalent roadside sign 'No Dumping' indicates the absence of such euphemistic use in Ireland.

dunny a lavatory

Not just an Australian usage. Probably a corruption of *dung*:

> He stuck out like a dunny in a desert. (Winton, 1994)

The *dunnie* van in rural Somerset collected the NIGHT SOIL for manure:

> In only one or two places, including Glastonbury, do people recall the 'dunnie van' going round. (Binding, 1999)

duration the time occupied by the Second World War

Shortened form of *duration of the war*. Common British usage, especially at the time when the outcome was uncertain and there was a taboo about predicting the future:

> ...you'd never get back to England. You'd be stuck there for the duration. (N. Barber, 1981)

dust¹ illicit narcotics in powdered form

There is a visual similarity:

> He pays off with the dust, and it's party time every Saturday night. (Sanders, 1950—he was not using gold dust)

See also DREAM and ANGEL DUST.

dust² to kill

Probably from wiping off or out, with blackboard imagery:

> The question is...did she hate him enough to dust him. (Sanders, 1985)

Dustman, a corpse, and *dustbin*, a grave, punned on the eventual state of an unembalmed corpse.

Dutch appears in many offensive and often euphemistic expressions dating from the 17th-century antagonism between England and the Low Countries. Thus anything qualified as being *Dutch* is considered bogus or inferior, from being IN DUTCH, in trouble, to speaking *double-dutch*, incomprehensibly. An exception is the contraceptive device called a *Dutch cap*, from its shape not its efficacy, or lack of it

Dutch (do the) to kill yourself
> You're not going to do the dutch,
> are you?...Commit suicide?(Sanders, 1980)

Whence the *Dutch act*, suicide.

Dutch auction an auction in which the auctioneer drops the price until a buyer makes a bid, being the reverse of a normal auction in which bidders raise the price until only one remains in the auction

Dutch bargain an unfair or unprofitable deal

Dutch cheer a drink of spirits—the Dutch are supposed to be gloomy when sober.

Dutch comfort an assumption that things cannot get worse

Dutch concert a cacophony
> Music played out of tune, drunken singing, or any other discordant noise:
> In the evening, as we were walking the ramparts, we were serenaded by a Dutch concert. (Emblen, 1970, quoting Roget—the noise came from frogs, ducks, crows, grasshoppers, peacocks, and asses)

Dutch consolation an assurance that, although things are bad, they could have been worse

Dutch courage bravery induced by intoxicants, implying a Dutchman is a coward when he is sober:
> A lot would depend on what time of the evening I would do it.
> A bit of Dutch courage would help.
> (*Sunday Telegraph*, 12 November 1995—describing the removal from a bar of a model galleon with a curse on whoever might touch it)

Dutch feast an occasion where the host becomes drunk while his guests are still sober

Dutch fuck lighting one cigarette from another, perhaps because the action is soon over, costs nothing, and may leave you with a burning sensation:
> ...then lit his cigarette from mine...
> That's a Dutch fuck, old chum. (Barnes, 1991)

Dutch headache a hangover—for such a drink-sodden people there could be no other medical cause

Dutch reckoning an inflated bill without details
> DUTCH RECKONING, or ALLE-MAL. A verbal of lump account, without particulars, as brought in spunging or bawdy houses. (Grose)

Dutch roll combined yaw and roll in an aircraft which behaves with the gait of a drunken sailor
> This usage, first noted by Moynahan in 1983 as modern airline pilots' jargon, shows that, with English speakers, old prejudices die hard.

Dutch treat an entertainment or a meal to which you are invited but where you have to pay for yourself
> She and Caliban enjoyed the better restaurants in town, and never ate at the same place twice. It was always a Dutch treat. (Grisham, 1992)

Where such costs are shared by agreement, it is called *going Dutch*:
> 'Here,' Ardis Peacock said half-heartedly, 'let's go Dutch.' 'No way...I asked you to lunch.' (Sanders, 1980)

Dutch uncle someone who reproves you sharply or gives you solemn advice, unlike the supposed geniality of real uncles
> I talked to him like a Dutch uncle. It doesn't seem to have done him any good. (Baron, 1948)

Dutch widow a prostitute

Dutch wife a bolster, once the sole bed-mate of many white bachelors serving in the Far East:
> ...he clutched tightly the bolster—sweat-absorbing bedfellow of sleepers in the East—known as a Dutch wife. (Burgess, 1959)

Dutchman a stupid person
> You so describe yourself rather than others when you express surprise or disbelief in the

phrase *I'm a Dutchman* which is sometimes
shortened to *I'm a Dutchy*:

> If those are not tables once used to
> wash the 'stuff', I'm a Dutchman.
> (Haggard, 1885)
> If they're snitches, then I'm a bleeding
> Dutchy. (Fiennes, 1996)

duty defecation
Probably from the requirement placed daily
on children:

> Many any unwary person has been
> knocked off his toes by a charging porker
> before the completion of his duties.
> (Simon, 1979, writing of defecation in the
> open air in India)

duty not paid smuggled

Especially of tobacco and alcoholic drinks
into countries with higher taxes than their
neighbours:

> The 1993 paper tells us that BAT's Brazilian
> subsidiary, Souza Cruz, [was] increasing
> its market share as a result of DNP,
> Duty Not Paid—the official term for
> smuggling. (*Daily Telegraph*, 16 February
> 2000)

duvet day an unjustified absence from
work tolerated by an employer
You stay in bed a while longer:

> The idea of mental health days (dubbed
> 'duvet days' in many companies) originated
> in Scandinavia. (*Daily Telegraph*, 6 October
> 1998)

E

EC see EARTH CLOSET

ear a microphone used in secret surveillance
The jargon of espionage and spy fiction:
> If they think you've got something to hide, they'll plant another ear. (D. Francis, 1978)

early bath dismissal from a game for foul play
Usually *taken* by the offending player. American offenders may find themselves *sent to the showers*.

early release dismissal from employment
Those *released* are less likely to receive favourable severance terms than those who take EARLY RETIREMENT:
> *Early Release Schemes*: The group expects to reduce the number of employees by about 15,000 during each of the next two financial years. (British Telecom report, 1993)

early retirement dismissal from employment
Not going to bed before ten o'clock or voluntarily deciding to take your pension before due time:
> Paul Bergmosen, in charge or purchasing, who was given 'early retirement' in 1977...(Lacey, 1986)

early treatment room a station to which a soldier might go after promiscuous copulation
As different, in the Second World War, from the medical establishments such as Casualty Clearing Stations, to which the wounded would be directed or taken:
> Laying down the necessity for Early Treatment Rooms, Monty—with perfect reason—observed that the man who has a woman in a beetroot field near his company billet will not walk a mile to the battalion E.T. room. (Horne, 1994—the choice of crop seems irrelevant)

earn to steal
Military usage, seeking to show entitlement perhaps. See also LIBERATE 2 and REQUISITION.

earn a passport to be rewarded as an assassin
Another duty, it would seem, of the women in the harem, who might be lent by the sultan to a minister with orders to kill him:
> Her task accomplished, she was reintegrated into the Royal household and rewarded for her services. In the argot of the Seraglio, this was known as 'earning a passport'. (Blanch, 1954)

earnest *obsolete* homosexual
Victorian slang and possibly what inspired Wilde's choice of title for *The Importance of Being Earnest*.

earpiece an informant keeping a watching brief
Neither a muff nor a deaf aid:
> He's there as [former Chairman] Sir David Alliance's earpiece. (*Daily Telegraph*, 8 March 2001, explaining a board appointment)

earth *obsolete* to inter (a corpse)
Mainly Scottish and Yorkshire dialect:
> There was a multitude fit for a city procession saw her earthed. (O'Donoghue, 1988)
The burial space was the *earth-dole*:
> A rich man at last, like a poor man, nobbut gets his yeth-dooal. (*EDD*)

earth closet a non-flush lavatory
Soil is used to cover the faeces:
> Hugh Flatt near the entrance of the earth closet which he still uses in the summer. The waste is mixed with sawdust and household waste to form a wonderful black, friable compost. (picture caption in Binding, 1999—Hugh is seen displaying a pan of, it is hoped, such compost)
Commonly abbreviated to EC.

earth moved for you (the) you had a sexual orgasm
Especially of females, but also used of male sexual activity:
> But she plays to the camera, eyebrows raised and euphemisms to the fore: 'So, Clurr, what everyone at 'ome wants to know is, did the earth move for you?' (*Daily Telegraph*, 1996, commenting on Cilla Black's performance as television presenter of *Blind Date*)

earthy vulgar
A venerable usage:
> Certainly we know that [Abraham Lincoln] enjoyed an earthy story. (Bryson, 1994)

ease nature *obsolete* to urinate or defecate
The allusion is to the subsequent relief. Also as *ease yourself, ease your bladder* (of

urination), and *ease your bowels* (of defecation):

> Desecration seems to have horrified royalist commentators more than iconoclasm: soldiers stabling horses in the nave of St Paul's Cathedral, and other places, setting hounds to hunt cats in the aisles of Lichfield, resorting to other churches to 'ease nature', using stone altars as chopping blocks for meat, dressing up in priests' or bishops' vestments, and brazenly smoking, drinking and swearing inside the sacred space of churches. (Gentles, 1992—it happened during a civil war, not a soccer tournament)

> One man I knew used to swear that he only eased his [bladder] once a month. (F. Richards, 1936)

> I had dismounted to... try to ease my wind-gripped bowels. (Fraser, 1973)

A CHAPEL OF EASE 2 or HOUSE 2 *of ease* was a lavatory.

ease springs (of a male) to urinate
Punning on the military order in which the rifle bolt is moved rapidly up and down the breech, which has a tenuous similarity to the stroking of the penis to prevent a drip of urine. Jolly (1988) suggests that a sailor who excuses himself from company in order to urinate may pretend to be seeing to the *springs*, or mooring lines, of a ship, which may need easing according to current or tide.

easement self-masturbation
Not a right of way, turbary, venery, piscary, or cow pasture but the supposed *easing* of your desires or tensions:

> Sometime long after midnight she took the easement of maiden, spinster, widow. (Frazier, 1997)

East (go or be sent) to be killed
It was the direction in which Jews and others were sent to the places of extermination by the Nazis:

> 'Where has Herr Hirschmann gone?' I was able to ask. 'The Germans sent him east.' (Keneally, 1985—in fact this particular victim may have gone West, from Belorussia)

East African activities extramarital copulation
A *Private Eye* refinement of the in-joke, based on UGANDA:

> I was distressed to see the old French word 'romance' used as a code name for East African activities. (A. Waugh in *Private Eye*, December 1980)

East Village *American* a less fashionable area of New York

Used by realtors and others to exploit the cachet of *The Village*:

> Property speculators tried to call the East Side of (10th Street) 'the East Village' but there were not many takers. (Deighton, 1981)

London has its SOUTH CHELSEA.

Eastern substances illegal narcotics
The association is between China, opium, and the geographical source of much cocaine etc.:

> The smell of exotic Eastern substances grown on the premises that wafts gently across the square. (*Private Eye*, May 1981, of cannabis)

easy terms hire purchase
The use is so widespread that we no longer address our minds to the reality that everything involved in such a transaction is more expensive and difficult, except the size of the initial payment.

easy way out (the) suicide
The use implies a lack of courage:

> ...they've told me it's cancer and I'm taking the easy way out. (P. D. James, 1972, quoting a suicide note)

easy woman a female with no reservations about casual copulation
Not necessary a prostitute:

> Whether we worked in a Massage Parlour or were rich... we were still the same to you. Easy women. (Bogarde, 1978)

Such a person may also be said to have *easy affections*:

> It appears that on the previous evening they rode into a neighbouring town where they spent the night with women of easy affections. (Mark VII, 1927)

See also *lady of easy virtue* under LADY.

eat to indulge in fellatio or cunnilingus
Usually specifying what is being figuratively consumed, such as MEAT 2, PORK 2, PUSSY 1, and other slang terms for the penis or vagina:

> Wouldn't you like to eat my pussy? (Robbins, 1981—the woman was not suggesting sacrificing her pet for the pot)

Occasionally as *eat out*:

> She used to give hand jobs. She let Moochie eat her out. (Theroux, 1989)

eat a gun to commit suicide with a firearm
By shooting yourself upwards through the mouth:

> ...his back against the filthy tiled wall, and he was trying to eat his gun. (Sanders, 1977)

eat flesh to copulate with a woman

A venerable pun:
> Suffering flesh to be eaten in thy
> house... contrary to the law. (Shakespeare,
> 2 Henry IV)

eat for two to be pregnant
The theory, unjustified in affluent families, is
that a woman needs double rations during
pregnancy:
> 'Do you ever remember me on a diet, Edie?'
> 'No, I can eat for two.' 'You don't mean...?'
> (Deighton, 1972)

eat-in kitchen American there is no separate dining-room
Real estate jargon for a small house or
apartment:
> Eat-in kitchen, lovely porch overlooks
> private yard. (Chicago Tribune, 30 July 1991)

eat porridge British to be in prison
A staple of the prison diet:
> The best offer you're going to get, mate is
> to eat your porridge here for a respectable
> time. (C. Thomas, 1993)
See also PORRIDGE.

eat stale dog American to take a deserved reprimand
I think this is analogous to *eat dirt*, with *dog*
being a shortened form of *dog shit*:
> I can eat stale dog and get by. (Chandler,
> 1939—he had been detected in wrong-
> doing)

eat the Bible American to perjure yourself
You lie after swearing on the Bible in court to
tell the truth:
> ...told the lieutenant not to count on me
> to eat the Bible. (Lavine, 1930)

eating disorder (an) anorexia nervosa or
bulimia
Not spilling egg down your shirt:
> The Princess of Wales also suffered from an
> eating disorder, which is thought to have
> added to the strain of her marriage. (Daily
> Telegraph, 22 April 1995)

eccentric severely ill mentally
Literally, not moving on a centrally placed
axis, whence, of human behaviour, whimsical
or unusual:
> The poor man is crazy, the rich man is
> eccentric. (old saw quoted in Sanders,
> 1977)

economical with the truth lying
Famously said by the Secretary of the British
Cabinet, Sir Robert Armstrong, in a legal
action ill-advisedly brought by Mrs Thatcher
in Australia to try to prevent the publication
of confidential, inaccurate, and largely inconsequential allegations about the secret service, as a result of which she enriched the
author, his lawyer, and the language. Also as
economical with the actualité:
> Mr Clark admitted he had been economical
> with the *actualité* (Sunday Telegraph, 20
> March 1994—a British minister had
> become involved in another ill-advised
> court case)

economically disadvantaged poor
The usage covers poverty arising from inadequacy, fecklessness, low intelligence, bad
education, idleness, misfortune, or ill-health:
> We happen to house people who are
> economically disadvantaged. (Daily
> Telegraph, 21 September 1995—the
> individual so classified was unemployed
> and had eight children)
Also as *economically abused, exploited*, or *marginalized*.

economically inactive unemployed
The actions of each of us impinge on the
economy, whether or not we create wealth:
> Both men claimed there had been an
> unlawful interference with their rights as
> EU citizens when they became
> 'economically inactive'. (Daily Telegraph,
> 21 March 1995—an Italian and a
> Portuguese with three dependants had
> migrated to England where they had
> been kept at public expense without
> working. When it was suggested that
> they should return to their country
> of origin, they issued proceedings for
> damages)

economy cheap
Literally, the avoidance of waste. That does
not mean necessarily that a traveller in other
than an *economy* seat in an aircraft is feckless.
In supermarket jargon *economy* may mean
large.

écouteur a person who obtains aural
gratification from the sexual activity of
others
Literally, the French word means a person
who listens, but has a specific meaning in
English:
> The shrieking bed springs were no
> accident. The manager's wife was an
> écouteuse. (Condon, 1966)

ecstasy an illegal stimulant
Easier to pronounce than *methylene dioxy-
methamphetamine*:
> He had introduced her to Ecstasy, the tense
> atmosphere of pubs with the big boys
> spoiling for fights, the private discos.
> (Fiennes, 1996)

edged slightly drunk

The obsolete Suffolk use was probably not the direct parent of the modern American, but both must have come from being *on the edge of drunkenness*, or some such phrase:

> When he was nicely edged he was a pretty good sort. (Chandler, 1934)

Edie *obsolete British* a prostitute

From the woman's name, denoting a cheaper type:

> The Edies of the East End, Piccadilly and the railway stations...(Gosling and Warner, 1960)

educable *American* dim-witted

Yet still capable of learning something at school.

education welfare manager a truancy officer

There was a time when those who played truant were called naughty and punished:

> The case was adjourned while the disease was investigated, despite objections from the local education manager, as truancy officials are now called. (*Daily Telegraph*, 25 May 1994—the 'disease' making it impossible for the child to attend school was the newly identified School Phobia Syndrome)

eel a penis

Possibly no more than a translation of a Japanese euphemism, using the common SERPENT imagery:

> Hatsumomo had found a clever way of putting into Dr Crab's mind the idea that my 'cave' had already been explored by someone else's 'eel'. (Golden, 1997)

effeminate (of a male) homosexual

Literally, having the characteristics of a woman:

> She wondered for a moment if he might be what people called effeminate. (Follett, 1978)

efficiency *American* a single-roomed apartment

An *efficient* use of space, I suppose:

> It was an efficiency—one large room, kitchenette, bath. (J. Patterson, 1999)

effing an oath

For *fucking*, used figuratively:

> It wasn't a case of where's my effing breakfast. (C. Allen, 1975)

And see F.

effluent a noxious discharge

Literally, anything which flows out but now understood to refer to sewage or untreated industrial waste. *Sewage* itself started life in this sense as a euphemism, from its original meaning, a draining of water.

effusion *obsolete* an ejaculation of semen

Literally, a spouting forth:

> The mere effusion of thy proper loins. (Shakespeare, *Measure for Measure*)

elastic subject to unprincipled retraction, disregard of law, or withdrawal under pressure

It may refer to a politician's principles, to a judge's attitude to inconvenient laws, or to a battle front during a retreat:

> Since Stalingrad the line in the east has been *elastic*, and the enemy never achieves a *breakthrough*. (Klemperer, 1999, in translation)

Whence *elasticity*, such conduct:

> There was a similar emphasis on judicial 'elasticity', for which read 'revolutionary consciousness'. (Burleigh, 2000, of the courts in Nazi Germany)

elbow-bending drinking intoxicants

Usually to excess, from the movement of the glass to the lips:

> Afrazi was a major leaguer at elbow-bending. (M. Thomas, 1980)

An *elbow-bender* is a drunkard. See also BEND.

electric methods torture

A refinement of Nazism:

> Bienecke used the 'electric methods' pioneered by the SD in France—not the sort of scientific advance to crow about. (Keneally, 1985, describing German behaviour in occupied Russian territory)

electronic underwear the use of a clandestine recording device

The microphone is hidden beneath outer clothing:

> That's the mob. They...tell each other they're tough and worry over which one of them's wearing electronic underwear, FBI issue. (Turow, 1993)

Electronic counter-measures or *penetration* mean spying through such clandestine means.

elephant and castle *British* the anus

Rhyming slang on arsehole, from the area named after a public house which stood at the start of the old road from London to Brighton.

elephant's drunk

Rhyming slang, for elephant's trunk. See also COP AN ELEPHANT'S.

elevated drunk

From the feeling induced at a certain stage of drunkenness:

JOHNSON. (who, from drinking only water, supposed every body who drank wine to be elevated.) I won't argue any more with you, Sir. You are too far gone. (J. Boswell, 1791—Sir Joshua Reynolds not unnaturally took offence at this sally)

If, in Britain, you are *elevated to the peerage*, it does not necessarily mean you are drunk as a lord.

There is also a rare use of *elevation* for drunkenness.

elevator does not go to the top floor (the) *American* there is mental deficiency

A use not replicated in the British *lift*:

> ... the man should really be committed. It's obvious his elevator doesn't go to the top floor. (Sanders, 1992)

eliminate to kill

Usually of political or espionage killings:

> We will just have to eliminate him. No time. No publicity. (G. Greene, 1978)

Whence *elimination*, such killing:

> Elimination is rather a new line for us. More in the KGB line or the CIA's. (ibid.)

embalmed very drunk

Based on the lifeless condition of the subject and the intake of fluid which led to it. *Embalming fluid* is cheap whisky.

embraces copulation

Literally, clasping in the arms with familial or sexual affection:

> ... solicited the gratification of their taste for variety in my embraces. (Cleland, 1749)

The singular is rare:

> When a girl's lips grow hot, her sex is hot first and she is ready to give herself and ripe for the embrace. (F. Harris, 1925)

Illicit embraces means adultery:

> Harold and Noreen must have been surprised again in their illicit embraces. (M. McCarthy, 1963)

embroidery exaggeration or lying

Literally, fancy needlework:

> Albert's tongue ... may have led him into the odd spot of embroidery. (J. Major, 1999—the Irish prime minister was reputed to have 'never walked past an open microphone in his life')

emergency[1] a war

Used by those who think the opposition is unworthy of them, such as the British in the civil war in Malaya against the Chinese Communists, or by those who do not want to acknowledge that there is a war going on, such as de Valera in Ireland during the British fight against Nazi Germany:

> Not only must the war be referred to as 'the emergency' but nothing could be printed which could conceivably offend either side. (Fleming, 1965 describing the Irish wartime press censorship)

emergency[2] a political suspension of civil rights

Usually declared by a ruler to retain or impose absolute power:

> Mrs Gandhi locked up the opposition, suspended the Constitution and declared an Emergency. (Dalrymple, 1998, writing of events in India in 1975)

emergent poor and uncivilized

The use is mainly of former colonial territories in Africa, some of which appear to be retreating into greater poverty and tribal division rather than achieving greater freedom and prosperity. Also as *emerging*:

> To avoid embarrassing its trading partners in emergent Africa, South African officials and trade organizations will not disclose the destination of its £800m. annual food exports. (*Daily Telegraph*, October 1981)
>
> Except for King Paul of Greece ... they came from the emerging nations. (Manchester, 1968, including Mali, Yemen, Nigeria, etc.)

emigrated killed

How the Nazis explained the absence of those sent to extermination camps:

> I replied to her on the 25th and the card came back today. Blue stamp on it 'returned', note in pencil 'emigrated' ... 'Emigrated' for *been* emigrated. Innocuous word for 'robbery', 'expulsion', 'sent to one's death'. Now, of all times, one can no longer assume that any Jews will return from Poland alive. (Klemperer, 1999, in translation: diary entry 27 February 1943)

Emmas *British* haemorrhoids

Possibly only a shortened form but also heard as *Emma Freuds*, from a British public figure.

emotional drunk

Excitable and sentimental behaviour is sometimes displayed:

> Tired and emotional after a long flight from Australia ... (*Private Eye*, September 1981)

employ *obsolete* (of a male) to copulate with

Master and mistress:

> Your tale must be, how he employ'd my mother. (Shakespeare, *King Lear*)

employment unemployment

This is one of those evasive opposites, such DEFENCE and HEALTH. Thus a government Department of Employment is concerned with finding jobs or providing for the unemployed.

empty nesters a childless couple
Either because the children have grown up and left home or because the woman is continuing to take full-time paid employment during years of possible childbearing, thereby hoping to attain a higher standard of living:

> Yesterday the euphemistic jargon ranged from 'open strategic stock' to 'lifestyle market segments'. The latter term translates as the observation that Bournemouth has more 'empty nesters' and fewer 'couples pre-children' than Kensington. (*Daily Telegraph*, 16 April 1997)

empty out to urinate
It could be no more than cold tea from a pot:

> I stepped out onto the back porch to empty out. (King, 1996)

Empty your bladder is an explicit circumlocution:

> Go to the bathroom, empty your bladder. (M. McCarthy, 1963)

Empty yourself is to defecate:

> It was the period when some men ate, or read, or wrote home, or dozed, or just went to the lavatory and emptied themselves. (Forsyth, 1994)

emunctory associated with farting
Literally, no more than relating to a bodily duct or orifice having an excretory use, including sweat glands:

> Perhaps I do have a tendency to emunctory moments, but so do many elderly men. (L. Thomas, 1994—he farted a lot)

enceinte pregnant
It means surrounded and is also euphemistic in French. When we use the word, we are doubly evasive or prudish:

> The idea that Kate might be enceinte had stolen more than once through her quiet thoughts. (M. McCarthy, 1963)

encourage to compel
The language of totalitarianism:

> At Christmas [1940, French schoolchildren] were 'encouraged'—a euphemism for 'required'—to send cards, messages and drawings to their leader. (Ousby, 1997—the leader was Pétain)

end to kill
The common scepticism about reincarnation:

> The sword hath ended him. (Shakespeare, 1 Henry IV)

The end is death:

> I could see his fear of the end growing inside him like a poison flower. (King, 1996)

The *end of the road* may describe any situation after which there will be no further developments, including death:

> Cheeky servants and cunning poachers ceased to annoy the Rev. Francis in 1811, for that year he came to the end of the road. (Tyrrell, 1973)

end of desire a sexual conquest
The termination is usually short-lived:

> He has somehow vaguely imagined that, the end of his desire attained, soul and sense would lie down together. (Sayers, 1937)

end up with Her Majesty to be imprisoned
Not the destiny of Prince Philip:

> We need to keep the drugs and the money in two separate transactions or someone's going to end up with Her Majesty in no time. (Fiennes, 1996)

endowed see WELL ENDOWED

energetic using violence
Literally, being very active:

> But the threat of being caught by Spain's sometimes energetic police force and being extradited has done little to deter British criminals from decamping to Spain. (*Daily Telegraph*, 9 January 2001)

energy release *American* an accidental release of radioactive material
An atomic power station should only release energy which is converted into electricity. Much nuclear jargon seeks to play down risks to health, real and imagined.

enforcer a criminal who terrorizes under orders
Usually working for an unpaid bookmaker, gang leader, etc.:

> She was a freelance enforcer, renowned for her skill in getting any job done quickly. (J. Collins, 1981)

Avoid confusion with the British *enforcement officer*, who performs much the same function, enforcing myriad regulations for a local authority but without violence or illegality.

engine the penis
Viewed sexually, and a variant of TOOL or the obsolete *machine*:

> . . . too much desirability can freeze a man's engine. (Keneally, 1985)

English *American* denoting or pertaining to sexual deviation

As in the coded advertisements for *English arts,
discipline, guidance, treatment*, etc., none of
which have anything to do with elocution or
any other kind of instruction in the most
versatile of languages.

English disease (the)[1] male homosexuality

A usage not often heard in England:
> We call this thing a disease and sometimes
> the English disease. (Burgess, 1980—a
> New Yorker was talking about male
> homosexuality)

English disease (the)[2] a propensity to go
on strike

This time the phrase was used both at home
and abroad. See also FRENCH LEAVE and
SPANISH PRACTICES.

English vice (the) the obtaining of sexual
gratification through pain

Not a piece of mechanical equipment secured
to a bench but a predilection supposed to
have developed from the experience of boys
and their masters in 19th-century single-sex
boarding schools:
> The popularity of flagellation—known as
> the 'English vice'—created a large corpus
> of literature. (Pearsall, 1969)

enhance to alter or increase in a surreptitious way

Thus dye may *enhance* a real or imagined blondeness of hair; an *enhanced radiation weapon* is a
neutron bomb, not a sun lamp; *enhanced
contouring* is cosmetic padding of clothing:
> ...her bra comes with 'built-in emphasis'
> or 'enhanced contouring'. (Jennings,
> 1965)

A public body which *enhances revenue* puts up
taxes.

enjoy to copulate with

Usually of the male, from the days when the
pleasure was supposed to be his alone:
> You shall, if you will, enjoy Ford's wife.
> (Shakespeare, *The Merry Wives of Windsor*)

A man may also, if so inclined, *enjoy favours* or
hospitality:
> He regularly visited a famous courtesan in
> the Srinagar bazaar and enjoyed other
> favours too. (Masters, 1976)
> The scandal mags said Kennedy, quote,
> Enjoyed her hospitality, unquote. (Sanders,
> 1977)

Enjoyment of her person is obsolete:
> ...prostituted for some time to old men,
> who paid a high price for the enjoyment of
> her person. (Mayhew, 1862)

An *enjoyed* female is one who is no longer a
virgin, whether or not her partner found it
pleasurable:

> After Mrs Mayhew, when I was
> seventeen, no mature woman who had
> been enjoyed attracted me physically.
> (F. Harris, 1925)

enjoy a drink to be a drunkard

You may also be said to *enjoy a cup, drop, glass,
nip, the bottle*, etc.

enjoy Her Majesty's hospitality to be in
prison

In jail you do not have to pay for your keep.
The phrase has to be adjusted for kings,
governors, and presidents.

enjoy yourself to masturbate yourself

A night alone rather than a night out:
> I was not the only European officer in the
> jungle who enjoyed himself secretly on
> occasion. (N. Barber, 1981)

enlightenment deception

In Nazi Germany and elsewhere, where effort
is made to manage news, especially if something labelled NEW is on offer from politicians:
> Shortly after Hitler came to power in 1933,
> Goebbels and his new Ministry for Public
> Enlightenment and Propaganda built a
> bureaucracy that controlled every aspect of
> broadcasting. (Shirer, 1999)

enlist the aid of science to undergo cosmetic surgery

The *scientist* removes wrinkles, causes superfluous hair to vanish, implants it where it is
scarce, etc.:
> A few years ago when my hair began to
> recede I enlisted the aid of science.
> (I. Murdoch, 1978)

entanglement an embarrassing or clandestine association

Literally, an ensnaring or enmeshing. It may
refer to extramarital sexual relationships and
other ill-advised adventures:
> Mr Hurd sought to extricate Lady Thatcher
> and other ministers from responsibility for
> the 'temporary and incorrect
> entanglement' of arms and aid in a
> protocol signed by Lord Younger. (*Daily
> Telegraph*, 3, March 1994—the British
> government was funding an engineering
> project in Malaya in exchange for a
> purchase of arms)

enter (of a male) to penetrate sexually

Barely euphemistic despite the limited area of
invasion:
> She let out a breath in a long
> quavering moan as he entered her.
> (Masters, 1976)

enter the next world to die

In various phrases, indicating devout belief or scepticism, including the *great perhaps* and the Bard's *undiscovered country*:

> It was better to enter the next world with a full belly. (F. Richards, 1933)
> ... within a month or so I shall have entered the great 'Perhaps', as Danton I think called 'the undiscovered country'. (F. Harris, 1925)

entertain¹ to copulate with

Another way of keeping a visitor occupied or amused, I suppose:

> She had 'entertained' him before and each time he had nearly ripped her in half. (J. Collins, 1981)

An *entertainment lady* is a prostitute:

> Many [Chinese] local councils are attempting to cash in and have begun charging the 'entertainment ladies', as they call them, for the right to work. (*Sunday Telegraph*, 6 December 1998)

entertain² to bribe

Commercial use, relating to excessive prodigality to a customer in return for business. *Entertainment* is such bribery.

entitlement state payment to the poor

A preferred usage, including by many who are not POLITICALLY CORRECT:

> I knew [Clinton] was a bounder, of course, but my hope was that he'd turn out to be the Carlos Menem of North America and slash entitlement spending. (Evans-Pritchard, 1997)

equipment a man's genitalia

Using the same imagery as TACKLE:

> When we find a potato that looks like a set of men's equipment we pass it round and laugh at it. (de Bernières, 1994)

equity equivalent contingent participation *American* a loan illegally tied to future profitability

One of the evasions describing methods which allow banks to participate in speculative ventures:

> Our interest wouldn't be in stock, of course. Glass-Steagall rules that out. It'd be what they call 'an equity equivalent contingent participation'. (M. Thomas, 1987)

erase to kill

Another way of saying RUB OUT:

> I'd have hired a drunken lorry driver and had her erased on a zebra crossing. (Sharpe, 1977)

erection an enlargement of the penis due to sexual excitement

Literally, the condition of being upright. Standard English of both buildings and penises:

> ... his toilet closet full of Japanese erection lozenges and love elixirs. (Ustinov, 1971)

Whence *erect*, having such an enlargement:

> He had woken erect himself. (P. Scott, 1975— he had not been sleeping standing up)

err to copulate outside marriage

Literally, to stray or wander, whence to sin generally and then specifically of copulation. In the 19th century an *erring sister* was a prostitute:

> No one knows whether the fierce moralist and respected lay preacher actually had sex with those he called his 'erring sisters'. (Parris, 1995, of Gladstone, whose practice it was to seek the company of London prostitutes at night)

Errant describes such behaviour and gave us the perfect crossword clue, 'Where to find errant pairs (5)'. (For those who don't try to solve cryptic crosswords, *errant* is an indication of an anagram of pairs—*Paris*.)

escort a paid heterosexual partner

Originally, a body of armed men, whence a person accompanying another. Usually in this sense a female who, on payment of a further fee, reveals herself as a prostitute:

> One was a persistent 'escort' of Arabs. (*Private Eye*, July 1981)

An *escort agency* provides the services of such people:

> But escort agency meant hookers for hire. (Theroux, 1982)

essence semen

Literally, an essential being and what is left after distillation:

> I want to drink your essence and I will. (F. Harris, 1925)

essential purposes urination or defecation

Not, in this instance, access to food, clothing, shelter, water, or air:

> The train rumbled up the west coast, with occasional stops for what we coyly termed 'essential purposes'. (Lomax, 1995)

essentials the male reproductive organs

The brain, heart, or liver assume less importance:

> ... once your essentials are properly trapped in the mangle there's nothing to do but holler. (Fraser, 1985)

eternal life death

It is what the devout, or the survivors, look for.

eternity (in) dead
Without necessarily any aspiration to reincarnation, celestial hymn-singing, or other
sought-after benefits:
> Silence, all of you! Another sound and we'll
> put you all in eternity! (Fraser, 1994)

ethical investment a policy of buying
only stocks in companies which do not
overtly offend the prejudices of dogma-
tists
The *ethics* are supposedly of those who invest
their cash, which is not to suggest that those
investing in other companies operating
within the law are unethical:
> The latest craze to be imported from
> America is for 'ethical investment'. Almost
> every week there seems to be a new unit
> trust launched which promises to invest
> your money only in 'socially screened'
> firms. (*Daily Telegraph*, 25 September 1987)

ethnic not exclusively of white ancestry
Literally, 'pertaining to nations not Christian
or Jewish' (*OED*), from which anyone who is
not a Christian or a Jew. As the practice of
those religions was largely confined to Europe
or those of European descent, the word came
to refer to those of other than white skin
pigmentation:
> The car had been stolen the previous night
> from outside a block of high-rise
> apartments in Brixton chosen because of
> its ethnic inhabitants. (B. Forbes, 1986—
> Brixton is an area of London with a
> majority of non-white people)
An ethnic minority in America may include
Hispanics as well as blacks, native Indians, or
other non-white inhabitants. In Britain what
was in the 1980s an acceptable euphemism is
now less so:
> Senior officers questioned by the enquiry
> used terms, including 'coloureds' and
> 'ethnics', that were offensive to black and
> Asian people. (*Sunday Telegraph*, 6 June
> 1999)

ethnic cleansing see CLEAN 2

ethnic loading making appointments for
reasons other than those of suitability or
qualification
A way of achieving a quota, although not to be
encouraged when choosing brain surgeons,
airline pilots, sprinters, or those in similar
occupations which call for special training or
physical attributes:
> America's problem is that its 'intellectual
> elite' is now chosen by a system of
> positive discrimination and ethnic
> loading. (A. Waugh in *Daily Telegraph*, 10
> April 1995)

Eumenides the Furies
The Greek word means kindly ones, and they
were liable to get angry with you if you failed
to flatter them, as would the GOOD FOLK with
our recent ancestors. Similarly, the Greeks
called the stormy and fearsome Black Sea the
Euxine, the hospitable. Some Christian prayers
to an all-powerful and avenging God make
strange reading too.

evacuation[1] defecation
Medical jargon and a shortened form of
evacuation of the bowel:
> ... supported the dysentery cases as they
> trembled and shuddered during their
> burning evacuations. (Boyd, 1982)

evacuation[2] see EVACUEE

evacuee a German citizen killed by the
Nazis
Mainly Jews, who were forcibly driven from
their homes:
> People have long been saying that many of
> the evacuees don't even arrive in Poland
> alive. They are being gassed in cattle trucks
> during the journey. (Klemperer, 1999, in
> translation—diary entry 27 February 1943)
The *evacuation* was to extermination camps:
> She was successfully retained by her
> company, at the last moment, from an
> evacuation group. (ibid.—those who think
> all Germans were equally guilty of such
> atrocity should read Klemperer: correction,
> everyone should read Klemperer)
> So deportation [from France] was labelled
> *Evakuierung* (evacuation)... (Ousby, 1997)

evasion a lie
More than merely an avoidance of the truth:
> I should say she indulged in certain
> evasions. (Styron, 1976)

Eve a female
Especially viewed sexually outside marriage:
> ... a local 'Eve-teasing' problem. The sexual
> harassment of women in public places,
> sometimes quite open, was a problem all
> over India. (Naipaul, 1990)
You may also see *Eve* as an indication of sex
on a lavatory door, with the correspond-
ing *Adam*. For *Eve's custom-house* see ADAM'S
ARSENAL.

even numbers or odd *American* heterosexual or homosexual
A question varying the ODD theme:
> 'What do you like better? Even numbers or
> odd?' ... I could see she recognized it as a
> bar line. (Turow, 1999)

evening of your days old age
Not the period after work each day:

...his mother came to reside with him for the evening of her days. (Tyrrell, 1973)

eventide home an institution for geriatrics

Where, if your family won't or can't care for you, you may spend the EVENING OF YOUR DAYS.

everlasting life death

The hope or expectation of the devout and a monumental variation of ETERNAL LIFE.

everlasting staircase *obsolete* a treadmill

The degree of arduousness was regulated by a jailor through a screw; and see SCREW 2:

The convicts' names for the treadmill were expressive: the everlasting staircase, or, because the stiff prison clothes scraped their groin raw after a few hours on it, the cockchafer. (R. Hughes, 1987)

excess[1] *American* to dismiss from employment

When the employer wants to cut costs by getting rid of *excess* labour:

Workers are never laid off; they're 'redundant', 'excessed', 'transitioned', or offered 'voluntary severance'. (*Wall Street Journal*, 13 April 1990, quoted in *English Today*, April 1991)

excess[2] to make a charge additional to the published tariff

As for an overweight package on an airline.

exchange flesh *obsolete* to copulate

This may be no more than the Bard's fertile imagery at work:

She would not exchange flesh with one that loved her. (Shakespeare, *The Winter's Tale*)

exchange of views a disagreement between dogmatically opposed parties

Mainly the language of diplomacy. Adjectival qualifications such as *cordial* or *helpful* do not indicate greater amity, nor is an *exchange of ideas* more propitious.

exchange this life for a better to die

Another monumental aspiration:

After a long illness which she bore without a murmur exchanged this life for a better on the 23rd day of March, 1815. (Monument in Bath Abbey)

excited by wine having drunk alcohol

Not just being a wine buff:

Addison and Thomson were equally dull until excited by wine. (J. Boswell, 1791)

excitement (the) copulation

Perhaps a usage of the male rather than the female:

I'll wear a shirt and tie...have the excitement with my wife, go to sleep...(McCourt, 1999)

excluded (the) poor people

Society denies them some of the advantages which come from being richer:

They will not be told it is their social duty to serve drink to the excluded. (*Daily Telegraph*, 9 July 2001—bankers were being urged by Government to allow uncreditworthy people to open bank accounts)

exclusive expensive

The places of business so described do not exclude people with the ability to pay:

A year or so later I found myself in the Crystal Room at London's exclusive Grosvenor House Hotel. (F. Muir, 1997)

excrete to defecate

Literally, to discharge from a body. It could therefore (but does not) refer to blood, sweat, tears, snot, urine, etc.:

Soldiers lucky enough to find a soup kitchen discovered that boiling soup froze solid before they could finish it, while those who dropped their trousers to excrete in the open, died as their bowels froze solid. (Deighton, 1993/1, writing about Germans on the Russian front)

execute to murder

Literally, to carry out any task, whence to effect the sentence of a court, especially a death sentence. It became standard English for beheading. Today terrorists have adopted the word to try to cloak their killings with legality:

'The execution of the hostages will begin then.' 'Execution.' She was using the jargon of legality. (W. Smith, 1979, of a terrorist)

executive measure a political murder

Another Nazi evasion of the Second World War:

'Lohse, I recommend that your office initiate an executive action aimed at Oberfuhrer Willi Ganz'...

Executivmassnahme, a classic 'soft word' whose intent can be convincingly denied long after the corpses are counted. (Keneally, 1985)

The CIA was said to describe an authorized assassination by one of its operatives as an *executive action*.

exemplary punishment death by hanging

Not being made an example by having to
stand in the corner for a few minutes:

> Few people want to take direct
> responsibility for hanging; understandably
> they prefer abstractions—'course of
> justice', 'debt to society', 'exemplary
> punishment'—to the concrete fact of a
> terrified stranger choking and pissing at
> the end of a rope. (R. Hughes, 1987)

exercise copulation

Usually taken in a HORIZONTAL position:

> The looks he gave me when he was talking
> about faith and the Blessed Virgin. It isn't
> only the bishops who like to get their
> exercise. (R. Doyle, 1996—a woman had a
> conversation with a priest shortly after
> revelations about the fatherhood of the
> Bishop of Galway)

For *exercise your marital rights* see MARITAL
RIGHTS.

exhibit yourself to show your penis to a
stranger in a public place

A form of male gratification, it would seem,
the display being mainly to women or
children:

> ...a wealthy old man charged...with
> exhibiting himself to toddlers. (Sanders,
> 1973)

To *make an exhibition of yourself* is merely to
behave stupidly.

expectant pregnant

A shortened form of *expectant mother*, who is
said to be *expecting*:

> Polish women workers (forced labour) were
> reputedly sent home if they were
> expecting. (Klemperer, 1999, in translation)

We take for granted that a person so
described is 'expecting' the birth of a baby
to herself, and not a birthday present or an
increase in salary.

expedient demise an unlawful killing by
a government agency

A *demise* is literally a failing or ending, whence
a death. The pretence is that a death so
described was natural but timely:

> You had to give orders for the expedient
> demise of two men. (Deighton, 1981—he
> called the book *XPD*)

expended killed

Mainly military use, treating soldiers as
merely another resource like ammunition:

> 'And what do you mean about me being
> expended'...'He has wanted to kill you.'
> (L. Thomas, 1978—this is a rare non-
> military example)

Expendable is the number of soldiers you can
afford to have killed or wounded in a battle,
or someone whose life may be sacrificed:

> 'You're what they call "expendable".' Clark
> nodded with sad honesty. (ibid.)

expenses an additional tax-free income

In standard usage, payments incurred by an
employee in the course of his duties and
reimbursed by the employer. There are few
who spend less freely on personal comforts
when the employer is paying the cost and
often the disbursement may not have
been made as claimed. Thus *expense-account*
living is synonymous with extravagance and
excess:

> ...colleagues who scrabble around in
> boardrooms and come in late (if at all) for
> Questions, with expense-account fumes on
> their breath. (A. Clark 2000, commenting
> on his fellow Members of Parliament)

experienced[1] having copulated

Of either sex:

> Stephanie was 'experienced'. Whatever
> had it been like with all those men?
> (I. Murdoch, 1977)

Whereas, in most disciplines, to gain experience you must practise often and become
adept, in this activity a single essay may be
enough.

experienced[2] *American* second-hand

Used about a motor car.

expert a person who makes a living by
professing knowledge

Others often find a claim of omniscience
spurious:

> The directorate of ARCOS was topheavy
> with so-called 'experts'. (Boyle, 1979)

And see TALKING HEAD.

expire[1] to die

To breathe out, but for the last time:

> As to other euphemisms—of words
> which connote death...'expire' for 'die'.
> (J. Mitford, 1963)

expire[2] *obsolete* to achieve an orgasm

A double euphemism on DIE:

> When both press on, both murmur, both
> expire. (Dryden)

expletive deleted an obscenity

Part of our linguistic debt to Richard Nixon,
and perhaps also to Rose Mary Woods, who
transcribed the tapes:

> Suddenly hearing that his words were
> being overheard by newsmen, Thompson
> ended with a grin and the words 'expletive
> deleted'. (Hackett, 1978)

The Nixon transcriptions (tape 13 February
1973) also used *adjective deleted* and *characterization deleted*, neither of which has passed
into the language.

expose to leave in the open to die
Infanticide was once common, especially of
female babies:
> Like many unwanted female infants of
> Rome, she had been 'exposed'—that is, left
> out in the open to die. (Cawthorne, 1996)
See also DRINK MILK.

expose yourself to show your penis to a
stranger in a public place
More common (etymologically) in Britain
than in America:
> He . . . had rung the doorbell and introduced
> himself to Stacie, then had exposed
> himself. (Condon, 1966)
And see *indecent exposure* under INDECENCY.

exterminating engineer *American* a controller of pests or vermin
This example illustrates the popular pastime
of upgrading our job descriptions to gratify
our self-esteem, and that of our spouses.
Logically, this particular *engineer* might be in
the process of personal dissolution, and even
if we accept that he is *exterminating* something, the choice is large. The British *rodent
operator* is no less pretentious and illogical—
might he not provide performing shrews for a
circus?

extinguish to kill
This possibly obsolete use seemed to be used
more of kings than commoners. It is also used
of genocide.

extra-curricular referring to taboo extramarital activity
Literally, anything at school, college, etc.
which is done in addition to the prescribed
course of study:
> Though industry pundits reckon Halpern—
> better known for his exuberant extra-
> curricular activities—itches to get back in
> the high street. (*Sunday Telegraph*, 5 June
> 2001—he had, when chairman of a
> multiple retailer, seen the details of his oft-
> repeated sexual activity with a young
> woman become public knowledge)

extramarital excursion a sexual relationship outside marriage
It might be, but is not, a skittles tour with the
lads or a day at the seaside with the Mothers'
Union:
> . . . similar situations—in reverse—when he
> returned from extra-marital excursions.
> (Hailey, 1979)

extramural referring to taboo extramarital activity
No different from EXTRA-CURRICULAR. The

verbal use is rare:
> Besides she's always liked to extra-mural a
> bit. (Bradbury, 1983, writing of a
> promiscuous wife)

extras bought sexual gratification
The service provided is usually masturbation
or copulation in a brothel which calls itself a
MASSAGE PARLOUR:
> Mr Bircher admitted giving the service
> with 'extras' on request, consisting of acts
> of masturbation by him and his wife. Basic
> massage was £15. Exotic massage cost £20.
> (*Daily Telegraph*, January 1984)

extremely ill under sentence of death
The coded public language of the rulers of
Communist China:
> . . . if a high official is said to have a cold
> he's likely to be fired, if he's 'convalescing'
> he has been exiled and if he is 'extremely
> ill' he is about to be murdered. (Theroux,
> 1988)

extremely sensitive source an illegal
interception of messages
The usage does not refer to the quality of the
equipment used:
> . . . being careful not to mention the phrase
> wiretapping, but using instead the
> standard cover language, 'extremely
> sensitive source'. (Colodny and Gettlin,
> 1991, writing about Watergate)

eye the anus
Male homosexual use, either *tout court* or in a
compound, as BRONZE EYE or SECOND EYE. An
eyeball palace is an American male homosexual
bar.

eye-candy *American* a nubile young
woman
Good-looking and by implication sexually
promiscuous:
> I have this gorgeous stick of eye-candy
> (LA-speak for glamourpuss) that absolutely
> *nobody* knows about. You want her
> number? (*Daily Telegraph*, 6 December 1994)

eye-opener an intoxicant or stimulant
taken on waking
Punning on the meaning, a surprise:
> A morning eye-opener (brandy, Scotch or
> whatever) would be also provided.
> (Sanders, 1980)
The usage seems to have originated with
British troops in France during the First World
War, especially, albeit surprisingly, among
airmen. Now generally used by people addicted to alcohol or drugs who need topping
up before they can face another day.

F

F fuck
Nearly always for the verb as an expletive.
Also as the *F word*:
> I thought Johnny Rotten of the Sex Pistols
> was going to butt my head: I said 'Lovely to
> see you, Mr Rotten.' He said 'F——off, f——
> face.' (newspaper report, 2000)
> The 'f' word was broadcast on Radio 4
> yesterday. (*Daily Telegraph*, 12 January 1995)
And see EFFING.

face your maker to be mortally ill
A prospect hoped for or feared by the devout:
> Often a poor soul facing his maker chooses
> to come and spend those final few hours
> with us. (Deighton, 1993/2—the speaker
> ran a refuge for the destitute)
It may also mean to die.

facile sexually compliant
Used only of women and in one of its senses a
synonym of *easy*, as in EASY WOMAN:
> . . . he soon made the acquaintance of Mme
> de Warens, a woman of facile morals.
> (Boyd, 1987)

facilitator an arranger of embarrassing,
illegal, or dubious business
It now supplants the FIXER, who has become
discredited:
> Single's are facilitators, Oliver . . .
> maximisers, creators. (le Carré,
> 1999)

facility¹ a lavatory
Literally, anything which makes a performance easier:
> A small outdoor facility and the forest.
> (Poyer, 1978, describing a chalet on the
> edge of a village)
Often seen in the plural, despite there being
only one:
> . . . containing a washbasin, a folding table
> and two seats, one of which contained
> what the timetable coyly called 'facilities'.
> (D. Francis, 1988, describing a
> compartment in a railway carriage)

facility² an agreement to lend money by
a bank
Banking jargon for the limit to which you
may borrow. It makes life easier for the
borrower, for a while.

fact-finding mission a holiday with expenses paid

The *missionaries*, often politicians, tend to seek
out the *facts* in distant and agreeable places:
> But it was hard to suppress the thought
> that the final touch was provided by a be-
> suited Commons Select Committee junket
> (sorry: fact-finding mission) to France. (*Daily
> Telegraph*, 18 April 1995)

fact-finding observer a neutral clandestinely assisting a belligerent
F. D. Roosevelt knew the *facts*, despite the anti-
British reports of his London ambassador,
Joseph Kennedy, long before he sent his
teams over to Britain prior to Pearl Harbor:
> At first the Atlantic campaign against the
> U-boats was the prime concern, but more
> and more US army, and army air-force,
> 'fact-finding observers' were to be seen in
> London. (Deighton, 1993/1)

fact sheet a selection of truths and untruths calculated to deceive
Literally, a summary of information issued to
confirm ephemeral publication, such as a
radio broadcast:
> Confidence in the claims of special interest
> groups was further undermined when the
> Commission of Racial Equality withdrew a
> 'fact sheet' on employment which wrongly
> said 'only one per cent of solicitors in
> England' were from ethnic minorities.
> (*Sunday Telegraph*, 27 August 1995—the
> correct figure was over 3%)

facts (of life) the human process of reproduction
Thus breathing, eating, and growing old are
not the *facts of life*, while conception, pregnancy, menstruation, birth, etc. are:
> I sometimes think your children are right
> and you don't know the facts of life.
> (N. Mitford, 1949)
Sometimes shortened to *the facts*:
> Linda's presentation of the facts had been
> so gruesome that . . . their future chances of
> a sane and happy sex life [were] much
> reduced. (N. Mitford, 1945)
A *fact of life* is an unpalatable truth.

fade to kill
Underworld slang from the many senses of
the word importing diminution:
> 'You fade him?' 'Not me. I just found him
> as he was.' (Lyall, 1965—he was a corpse)

fade away to die
Especially of former soldiers:
> Frank wrote to me regularly until he faded
> away in 1961. (Robert Graves in an
> introduction to a reprint of F. Richards,
> 1933)

fag a male homosexual

Probably from the fact that male cigarette, or *fag*, smokers were thought effeminate by pipe or cigar smokers:

> An eager young fag, very pert in urchin cut and ear-rings, had accosted him. (Davidson, 1978)

faggot a male homosexual

In obsolete British use, *faggot*, as a verb, meant to copulate, and, as a noun, a prostitute. I suspect the modern use comes from FAG, as pouftah comes from POUFF:

> You made me out to be a drunk and a faggot. (Giles Brandreth in *Sunday Telegraph*, 8 July 2001—reporting a conversation with Lord Snowdon)

fail to display the symptoms of old age

Literally, not to succeed, or to discontinue. The condition so described may long antecede death, when a vital organ may really cease to function, as with *heart failure*:

> 'People fail,' I said. 'Father is failing.' 'Your father is fine,' Christopher said. (Flanagan, 1995)

fail to win to lose

Not even to draw. This was the excuse of the pusillanimous Unionist General McClellan in the American Civil War:

> McClellan insisted that he had not lost; he had merely 'failed to win' only because overpowered by superior numbers. (G. C. Ward, 1990—in fact the numbers opposing him were inferior, but better led)

fair¹ poor

A classification denoting scholastic performance or the quality of goods and services which is just above the lowest rating or outright rejection. It should mean favourable, or at least halfway between good and bad.

fair² unfair

One of the opposites so loved by politicians. Thus the British term for a rent controlled below the open market or economic rent was a *fair rent*:

> Their regulated rent (euphemistically called a 'fair rent' by law) would buy dinner for one at a local restaurant. (*Private Eye*, July 1981)

See also DEFENCE, HEALTH, and LIFE 2.

fair-haired boy someone unfairly favoured

He may be dark-haired, or bald, but he is being helped to political office or promotion beyond his deserts:

> Alexandrov's too old to go after the post himself... Gerasimov's his fair-haired boy. (Clancy, 1988)

A *fair-haired girl* is a blonde.

fair trader *obsolete* a smuggler

Facing no excise duty, he charges his customer less:

> I am what is called a fair trader—in other words a smuggler. (Pae, 1884)

fairness at work *British* penalties and burdens imposed by government on employers beyond those agreed between employer and employee and their representatives

Unfair on the employer and, in the long term, damaging also to those employed because the majority pay the cost of the litigious minority through reduced earnings, lower investment, and a reluctance to recruit:

> The CBI remains convinced that without its hard work and lobbying the Government's Fairness at Work proposals would have been a lot more aggressive (from a boss's point of view) and much more pro-union than they are. (*Sunday Telegraph*, 1 November 1988)

fairy a homosexual

Usually denoting a male taking the female role, but also used collectively:

> A mob of howling fairies, frenzied because the best part went to younger stars who didn't lisp. (Theroux, 1976)

faithful not having a sexual relationship with anyone other than your regular sexual partner

Literally, true to your word or belief, but in this sense limited to one of the marriage vows:

> He loved his beautiful wife and, so far as I know, was faithful to her. (I. Murdoch, 1978)

fall¹ to commit adultery

The imagery is from *falling from grace*:

> It is their husband's faults,
> If wives do fall. (Shakespeare, *Othello*)

Less often as a noun, and of any promiscuity:

> The Queen was convinced that what she called 'Bertie's fall' was at least in part responsible for Prince Albert's death. (R. Massie, 1992—Bertie (later King Edward VII) had fallen in, with, on, and for Nellie Clifton, who had been introduced to his bed and embraces by fellow officers in camp in Ireland)

fall² to become pregnant

A common modern use, which does not imply illegitimacy. Also as *fall in the family way* or *fall pregnant*:

> Annabel Birley has fallen again and delivered another (legitimate) Goldsmith into the world. (A. Waugh in *Private Eye*, 1980)

The girl fell in the family way and was sent out of the house. (Mayhew, 1862)
... one of the Emalia girls fell pregnant, pregnancy being, of course, an immediate ticket to Auschwitz. (Keneally, 1982)

To *fall for a child* or *fall wrong to* are obsolete:
There was a lass... who fell wrong to a farmer's son where she had been serving, and he wouldn't marry her. (Saxon, 1878)

fall³ to die

On military service, from being hit by a bullet etc., although the death may not necessarily occur in battle:
John Cornford had fallen the day after his coming of age. (Boyle, 1979)

In Hitler's case, the word was used to cover his suicide:
Adolf Hitler fell in his command post in the Reich Chancellery (official announcement of Hitler's death, 1 May 1945, in translation)

And see FALLEN (THE).

fall⁴ to be sentenced to prison

The descent caused by the disgrace and the reversal of fortune:
I want you to follow my instructions when the case is tried, and if I fall I will find no fault with you. (Moore, 1893)

fall⁵ American an arrest

Against which possibility you may keep handy some *fall money*, to pay for a lawyer, put up bail, bribe the police, etc.

fall⁶ to be born

Of a quadruped which gives birth standing:
The calf is lately fell. (Ellis, 1750)

fall⁷ (of an aircraft) to crash

It also falls frequently as it manoeuvres, meets air pockets, and makes a controlled landing:
When the 747-400 fell, the Dalmanns lost their eighteen-year-old daughter. (Koontz, 1997)

fall among friends to be drunk

A variant of the biblical reference *fall among thieves*, which may be used to seek to explain to your wife what you imply is untypical and blameless behaviour (usually without success):
... 'the Fleetsh all lit up' commentary by Cdr Tommy Woodfruffe, who had lately fallen among friends. (*Daily Telegraph*, June 1990, in the obituary of the officer who had arranged the lighting for the Spithead Coronation Review of 1937, which is now remembered, if at all, for his drunken radio commentary)

fall asleep to die

The common sleeping imagery:
... fell asleep in Jesus... of enteric fever in Mesopotamia. (memorial in West Monkton church, Somerset)

fall off the back of a lorry to be stolen

In reality the days of insecure loads are long past:
You wouldn't believe what I paid for them. Fell off the back of a lorry. (Theroux, 1976—he had received stolen goods)

Stolen goods similarly *fall off the back* of other goods vehicles such as vans and trucks.

fall off the perch to die

With avian imagery:
If the excitement of sharing a bedroom with a shapely lass should cause Fred to fall off the perch... (*Sunday Express*, March 1980)

In similar fashion you may, in due time, *fall off the hooks*.

fall off the roof American to start menstruating

My correspondents have failed to suggest a plausible etymology. Usually shortened in the past tense to 'I fell off'.

fall off the wire to be in severe difficulty

Like a tightrope walker who dispenses with a safety net:
It struck Caroline that if Brooks fell off the wire in *this* case, Salinas might go with him. (R. N. Patterson, 1994—Brooks was a district attorney, not a trapeze artist, and Salinas was his deputy)

fall on your back to consent to copulation

Of a woman:
She won't be the first to fall on her back for your pleasure. (McCourt, 1999)

fall on your sword to resign after failure

The fate of defeated Roman generals:
Sources close to the company said that he had elected to 'fall on his sword' following a warning two weeks ago which forecast a loss of £2m. (*Daily Telegraph*, 7 May 1997, of a Chief Executive)

fall out American to die

The military imagery implies that you are no longer on parade.

fall out of bed American to fail commercially

An unplanned and usually painful experience:
But if Seaco fell out of bed, or the bond market cracked... (M. Thomas, 1982, referring to a failing corporation)

fallen (the) those killed in war
Those who FALL 3 in battle:
> Since Monday the *Dresdener Zeitung* is only printing mass graves, so to speak . . . and not much more remains than the earlier lists of the fallen. (Klemperer, 1999, in translation, writing of the last weeks of the Second World War)

fallen woman a promiscuous female
Normally, but not necessarily, a prostitute:
> Let's face it dear, we are nothing but two fallen women. (N. Mitford, 1949)
At one time you had to watch your words when a lady tripped over her skis or her shoelaces.

falling sickness (the) epilepsy
Falling over is one of the symptoms:
> To cure the falling illness wi' pills o' pouthered puddocks. (Service, 1887— *puddock* does not here have its normal meaning, a kite or buzzard, but is a corruption of *paddock*, a frog or toad)
Also as the *falling evil*.

fallout radioactive matter introduced into the atmosphere by human agency
Now standard English and no longer used of less noxious substances such as volcanic ash.

false committing adultery
The opposite of TRUE for either sex:
> False to his bed. (Shakespeare, *Cymbeline*)

falsies pads concealed under clothing for females
Mainly of devices to make breasts or thighs look more alluring. The padding of men's jackets at the shoulders, equally calculated to deceive, is not the subject of euphemism or derogatory comment.

familiar with having a sexual relationship with
The adjective *familiar* originally meant relating to your family, whence it was used of someone with whom you associated freely:
> The intimation is that you have been indecorously familiar with his sister. (Jennings, 1965)
It may apply to either sex.
A *familiarity of marriage* is not having breakfast together but copulation:
> She had neither aptitude nor liking for the familiarities of marriage. (Linklater, 1964, writing of Mary Queen of Scots)

family¹ not pornographic
Not as modern as we might think; Bowdler called his emasculation of the Bard *The Family Shakespeare*. Thus a *family show* is one in which the vulgarity is muted.

family² the Mafia
A society which had as its watchwords *Morte Alla Francia Italia Anela*:
> It ain't gonna be easy now, keeping the Feds and the Family from tumblin' on me. (Diehl, 1978)
(Theroux, 1995, points out that Mafia 'is identical to the obsolete Arabic word *mafya*, meaning "place of shade", shade in this case indicating refuge, and is almost certainly derived from it.' Although no longer dogmatic about derivations, I would be reluctant to let the 'death to the French in Italy' line of enquiry disappear.)
Nothing is new—in 18th-century England a *family* was an association of thieves.

family jewels see JEWELS

family planning contraception
This standard English use denotes the reversal of planning a family for most people most of the time. In many compounds, such as *family planning requisites*, contraceptives.

family way see IN THE FAMILY WAY

fan club people who clandestinely copy the actions of another
Stock-market jargon, where the one followed may be a successful manager or investor, especially if there is a suspicion that either enjoys inside knowledge:
> While there is a distinction between a legal 'fan club' and an illegal support operation, the black and white turns to grey when the 'fans' were selling Guinness short. (*Private Eye*, August 1989— they were not selling less stout than a full glass but shares in the company which brewed it)

fancy¹ to desire sexually
Either sex may *fancy* the other:
> You can't do it to an ordinary woman just because you fancied her at school. (I. Murdoch, 1978)

fancy² *obsolete* a girl's suitor
It would seem that the suit of those so described was encouraged:
> Crokey and lawn tennis for't young misses and their fancies. (*Weekly Telegraph*, 1894, quoted in *EDD*)

fancy³ *obsolete American* an attractive young female slave
Usually a black person with some white blood who might be the mistress of an owner or overseer, or placed in a brothel:
> These yellow wenches . . . being graceful delicate creatures of the kind they called 'fancy pieces' for use as domestic slaves.

(Fraser, 1971, writing of the early 19th century)

fancy man someone with whom a woman has a regular sexual relationship

Usually the woman is married and the parties are not cohabiting:

I can only remember two of them that had regular fancy-men. (F. Richards, 1936, writing of soldiers' wives)

A *fancy woman*, *bit*, or *piece* is a mistress:

They supposed that Donald must be keeping 'a fancy woman' in New York. (Boyle, 1979—in fact Maclean was keeping rendezvous with his Russian spymaster)

fanny the buttocks *American* or vagina *British*

Of the buttocks, it may refer to the male or female, as in the expression *sitting on your fanny*. Of the vagina, it is used both literally and figuratively:

She'd have your fanny for a dishcloth. (Sharpe, 1977)

Great fanny, the wife of the KGB Captain. (Seymour, 1982)

Although derivation from a shortened form of fantail has its advocates, it probably comes from Cleland's *Memoirs of a Woman of Pleasure*, which relates the adventures of Frances (Fanny) Hill as a prostitute in 18th-century London. He would rejoice to know that the Sybil Brand Institute, a woman's prison on rising ground in Los Angeles, is popularly known as *Fanny Hill*.

Fanny Adams nothing

Sharing the initial letters of *fuck all*. She was murdered in 1810, her memory being kept alive in naval slang for tinned meat. Also as *sweet Fanny Adams*, *sweet FA*, or *FA*:

'So what can the Inguish hope for?' I asked. 'Absolutely Sweet Fanny Adams,' Simon Dinsdale replied. (le Carré, 1995)

far from staunch cowardly

An example of the euphemistic use of understatement:

I would inevitably learn later, that some Americans had been far from staunch. (M. Hastings, 1987, quoting the British General Mansergh on the Korean War)

far gone drunk

Despite physically remaining in the same place:

I won't argue with you, Sir. You are too far gone. (J. Boswell, 1791)

Farmer Giles haemorrhoids

Rhyming slang for piles.

fast ready to copulate casually

Mainly of women, from the meaning highliving:

Anglo-Indians (regarded as 'fast') swinging their bums. (Theroux, 1973)

fast buck (a) money obtained unscrupulously

The dollars come quickly and easily, although not necessarily dishonestly. Perhaps punning on the stag, which is fleet of foot, but perhaps not. The expression is also used where the unit of currency is other than the dollar.

fat cat a person who exploits a senior appointment for personal gain

Usually of politicians and company directors, who display greed and self-satisfaction, although they do not actually purr:

There's a fat cat called Rippon who used to be in very big with Heath and who now floats round the City. (*Private Eye*, November 1980)

fate worse than death unsought extramarital copulation by a woman

A pre-Second World War use, acknowledging the convention that women should be virgins when they married:

So being rattled stupid by Solomon would be no fate worse than death for her. (Fraser, 1977)

Still used humorously.

father of lies the devil

Dysphemism rather than euphemism, from Satan's being credited with the invention of lying:

Terry Reeves believed this fantastical personage to be the Father of Lies himself. (Graves, 1941, writing in 18th-century style)

fatigue mental illness

In medical jargon *mental fatigue* is synonymous with nervous breakdown. See also BATTLE FATIGUE.

favour to copulate with

A form of Dr Johnson's *regarding with kindness*, I suppose, without some of the overtones of FAVOURS:

He thanks our transport lady whom Mr Muspole claims to have favoured in the snooker room. (le Carré, 1986—he did not give her an easy break)

A man may also in the same sense do a *favour* to a woman:

The victim's girlfriend's a nice bit of stuff, he'd tell his colleagues when he went down the canteen for a beer. I wouldn't mind doing her the odd favour. (Pérez-Réverté, 1994, in translation)

favours an extramarital sexual relationship

Granted by either sex to the other:
> The small luxuries of life that plenty of women were prepared to exchange their favours for. (G. Greene, 1978, and not of political allegiance)
> A fondness amounting to sexual mania for the favours of young men. (Sharpe, 1977)

To *force favours from* is to rape:
> But even as he forced his favours from her...(Keneally, 1987—or should it have been 'her favours'?)

Favours may also be *shared*:
> And who does she pick to share her favours with? (Bogarde, 1981)

feather-bed to grant excessive indulgence towards

The derivation possibly comes from the Rock Island Railroad whose train crews complained of hard bunks and were thereupon asked if they wanted feather beds (Holt, 1961). A *feather-bed soldier* in obsolete British use was one who went whoring a lot.

feather your nest to provide for yourself at the expense of others

Now standard English, with avian imagery. You can either do it by dishonesty:
> Mr Badman had feathered his nest with other men's goods and money. (Bunyan, 1680)

or through unprincipled self-enrichment:
> [The English] have planned Germany's subjugation with an eye to feathering their own nest. (Goebbels, 1945, in translation)

or, in former times, by marrying a rich widow.

fee note a request for payment

A precious usage of lawyers who wish to imply that their relationship with their customer (client) is not that of seller and buyer:
> My firm's Cost department has mentioned to me that it would be appropriate for fee notes to be submitted in connection with the winding up of your late father's estate. (letter dated 29 January 1998 to Mr Anthony Peter from his lawyers)

feed to suckle

You avoid mentioning the taboo *breasts*:
> Louisa was feeding her second baby in Scotland. (N. Mitford, 1945)

Not to feed a baby does not mean that you starve it.

feed a slug to kill by shooting

The SLUG 1 is a bullet. Also as *feed a pill*:
> ...rubbing his greasy hair, and then feeding him a slug while he was still purring. (Chandler, 1943)
> I want to make certain that both you and your friend feed Danny Boy the pills. (Sanders, 1973—two people were to be implicated not in medical care but in a shooting)

feed from home to be promiscuous

Perhaps just another Shakespearean image:
> ...he breaks the pale,
> And feeds from home. (*The Comedy of Errors*)

feed the bears *American* to receive a ticket for a traffic offence

The BEAR 2, or policeman, may or may not pass the fine on to the local municipality.

feed the ducks to cut off a penis

The perpetrator, a wronged Thai wife, throws the excision from the elevated living quarters on to the ground below where the ducks browse:
> The gruesome practice of penis disposal is referred to as feeding the ducks. (*Sunday Telegraph*, 30 November 1997)

feed the fishes to be seasick

Old humorous use, but never funny to the victim. You do not actually have to vomit over the rail.

feed the meter illegally to extend a period of parking

To prevent hogging parking space, you should move on after the parking period for which you have paid has expired.

feed your nose to inhale illicit narcotics through the nose

Usually ingesting cocaine or heroin:
> A woman like that...has got to be on. I'd be willing to bet she's feeding her nose. (Sanders, 1977)

feel to excite sexually with the fingers

Either sex may feel the other, the same sex, or themselves:
> Blank reached into his coat pocket to feel himself. (Sanders, 1981)
> To obliterate such thoughts, she slid her hands between her legs and felt herself. (N. Evans, 1995)

Males *feel up* females:
> He had probably been in the kitchen feeling Ella up. (Follett, 1979)

and a *feel-up* is what he does, has, or possibly enjoys:
> How is this genital whatname different from a feelup? (Amis, 1978)

A man who persuades a woman to permit this activity is said to *cop a feel*:

I...with my beloved Maria did not even try
to cop a feel. (Styron, 1976)

feel a collar to arrest
The wearer has his clothing felt as he is
apprehended:
New life, no Customs and Excise feeling his
collar, new identity. (Seymour, 1999)

feel a draft *American* to sense prejudice
The *draft* (or British draught) is the invisible
but uncomfortable sensation felt by some
blacks in the presence of some whites, with
imagery from the household phenomenon.

feel no pain to be drunk
From the numbing effect of the intoxicant
rather than unconsciousness:
'But they wasn't drunk.' 'Feeling no pain?'
'Not even that.' (Sanders, 1981, suggesting
mild inebriation)

feet first dead
This is the way corpses tend to be carried:
Cut up rough and you'll go out feet first.
(Deighton, 1981)

fell design a male attempt at seduction
Fell means cruel or clever, this derivation
being from the former. Now only humorous
use:
'Are you a virgin?' he said suddenly,
stopping right in the middle of his fell
design. (M. McCarthy, 1963)

fellow commoner *British* an empty bottle
Originally, an 18th-century student at Cambridge or Oxford University who was wealthy
and thus supposedly empty-headed as he did
not need to work or become a parson. Still
heard in some academic circles.

fellow-traveller a Communist sympa-
thizer or apologist
Trotsky's *poputchnik* and Lenin's USEFUL FOOL
who may be described as *fellow-travelling*:
I knew you had some Communist
friends...They thought you were a
sentimental fellow-traveller, just as we did.
(G. Greene, 1978)
If such zealous organizations...were not
disturbed by Churchill's new friends on the
left, then he was probably pretty safe from
charges of fellow-travelling. (Graham
Stewart, 1999)

female-Americans adult women living
in the United States
The language of those who think that all
women are the subject of unfair discrimination, or worse. The phrase does not encom-
pass, for example, Mexican girls:

My, my, Kravitz & Bane, that great bastion
of civil justice and liberal political action,
does, in fact, discriminate against
African-Americans and Female-Americans.
(Grisham, 1994—less than 10% of the
partners in a law firm were women: the
percentage of black women partners—
African-American-Female-Americans—was
not specified)

female domination a male fetish involving obtaining sexual gratification from
being assaulted or tied up by a female
who is usually a prostitute:
Not describing the reality of many happy
marriages:
'Big item in the FD market.' 'The what?'
George asked. 'Female domination. Whips
and bonds.' (Lyall, 1982)

female oriented *American* homosexual
The phrase is not used of a LADIES' MAN.
Female identified means the same thing.

female physiology menstruation
Physiology is literally the functioning of the
body:
I held her lightly, protectively, then
murmured in her ear, 'Beastly female
physiology.' (Fowles, 1977—she was
menstruating)

female pills medication to abort a foetus
In 1950 a British Code of Standards was
introduced to ban misleading or dishonest
medical advertising and:
...the use in any advertisements for
medicines or treatments of any phrases
implying that the product could be
effective in inducing miscarriage—
for instance 'Female Pills', 'Not to be
used in cases of pregnancy', and
'Never known to fail.' (E. S. Turner,
1952)

feminine complaint an illness which
affects only adult females
Not just that her husband has been out late
drinking again:
'Probably a feminine complaint,' Scaduto's
wife said. When I squinted she said,
'Plumbing.' (Theroux, 1982)

feminine gender the vagina
Oddly, in languages where it is declined, it is
usually male, as for example *con* or *cunnus*:
She went in to adjust her suspender.
It got caught up in her feminine gender.
(old vulgar song)

feminine hygiene associated with menstruation

Usually of the paraphernalia, such as towels, tampons, and the like. See also PERSONAL HYGIENE.

femme fatale a woman considered by men to be irresistibly attractive
She only kills figuratively:
> I suppose such corny little manifestations of endearment were what she thought appropriate to her role as a femme fatale. (Deighton, 1985)

fence knowingly to deal in stolen property
Thus providing a screen between the thief and the eventual buyer:
> He used to take things home and 'fence' them. (Mayhew, 1862)

A *fence* is someone who so acts.

fertilizer the excreta of cattle
It should mean anything which adds fertility to the soil, including compost and seaweed:
> Today's 'fertilizer' was 'manure' yesterday and 'meadow dressing' the day before. (Jennings, 1965)

fetch[1] *obsolete* a ghost
Its appearance presaged imminent death—*fetching you away*—or long life. If the viewer did not die of fright, the alternative outcome was necessary, to avoid discrediting the phantom.

fetch[2] to abduct
What was once used of animal predators was also appropriate to the Gestapo:
> The fox fetched the last duck I had. (*EDD*)
> As long as they don't come to 'fetch' me, as long as I have halfway enough to eat. (Klemperer, 1999, in translation—diary entry of 2 July 1942)

fiddle to steal by cheating
Literally, to play a stringed instrument, as certain untrustworthy itinerants once did, whence embezzling cash or manipulating accounts. A *fiddle* is any device, even within the law, whereby someone may be cheated or overcharged. With the same etymology, an obsolete Scottish *fiddle* was a child abandoned by gypsies.

fidelity copulation only with a regular sexual partner
It means faithfulness, in all its senses:
> ... expecting complete fidelity from Christine. (S. Green, 1979, writing about the slum landlord Rachman and his mistress Keeler)

field associate *American* a police officer charged with detecting police corruption
An unpopular and taboo task for which the name changes from time to time.

fifth column traitors within your ranks
General Mola, investing Madrid in 1936 with four columns of soldiers, foolishly boasted that he already had a fifth column in the city, meaning covert supporters of the insurgents, of whom many fewer remained when Madrid eventually fell some three years later. The modern use usually implies treachery:
> Their supporters would know about it, and would be making preparations to join in, as a fifth column. (Masters, 1976)

fifty cards in the pack of low intelligence
You need fifty-two cards, except for tarot.

fifty up (of a male) masturbation
Counting the strokes:
> ... hence the old tombola call: *Five-oh, under the blanket—fifty*. (Jolly, 1988)

fight in armour *obsolete* to copulate in a contraceptive sheath
Boswell used both the pun and the appliance, and had cause for regret when he omitted to do so. (J. Boswell, *c.*1792)

file Chapter Eleven see GO 2

file thirteen a wastepaper basket
Where you dispose of unwanted or superfluous correspondence or printed matter:
> They won't give them time off, or they'll put the application in 'File 13'—the wastepaper basket. (McNab, 1993)

In America, also known as *file seventeen*.

fill full of holes to kill by shooting
You may also, if so unfortunate, be *filled with lead* or *with daylight*.

fill in to maim or torture
The origin appears to be from British naval slang, meaning to beat:
> Then I realized that though the people sounded more in control, if they filled me in they'd do it more professionally. (McNab, 1993, writing about his imprisonment by Iraqis)

filler[1] a trivial item included in a serious newspaper
Filling the empty space among the advertisements and features in the absence of hard news:
> We used to produce fillers, which is what the papers use to cement the real news to the adverts: 'Sacked stripper organizes strike.' You know the sort of thing. (Deighton, 1972)

filler² a cheaper substitute surreptitiously introduced to increase apparent weight or volume
Either during manufacture, as china clay into cream chocolates, or during packaging, as coal dust into sacks of house coal.

fillet to steal
Literally, to remove the flesh from the bone:
  We did think some spare parts might be filleted, but luckily nothing's gone. (*Sunday Telegraph*, October 1981)

filly a young woman viewed sexually by a male
Literally, a female horse less than four years old:
  We pre-war soldiers always made enquiries as to what sort of a place it was for booze and fillies. (F. Richards, 1933)

filth *obsolete* a prostitute
Although, with poor personal cleanliness among rich and poor alike in those days, probably no filthier than anyone else:
  Wisdom and goodness to the vile seem vile: Filths savour but themselves. (Shakespeare, *King Lear*)

filthy relating to any taboo act
It may be masturbation, unwanted sexual approaches, lewd talk, and the like:
  ... the sailor tried to be filthy. (L. Thomas, 1977—he had attempted rape)
Filth is used to describe swearing and obscenity.

final solution (the) the killing of all Jews
The Nazi *Endlösung*:
  Comprehension was not aided by the Nazis' deliberate carrying over of the same terms—Final Solution, evacuation, resettlement—as euphemisms for mass murder. (Burleigh, 2000)

financial assistance *American* state aid for the poor
True as far as it goes, but it could as well be a loan, gift, or subsidy to the rich:
  'You're on welfare?' 'Financial assistance,' she said haughtily. (Sanders, 1985)

financial engineering accounting practices tending to distort or mislead
Not controlling a metal-working shop through the use of figures:
  ... as we have seen elsewhere, financial engineering cannot conceal the truth indefinitely. (*Daily Telegraph*, 16 November 1990)
A *financial engineer* so behaves:
  Famed for once being a cost-cutter and financial engineer, this year's performance

has won W——recognition as a professional manager of business. (*Sunday Telegraph*, 19 November 1995)

financial products forms of borrowing, moneylending, or selling insurance
The use of PRODUCT seeks to cloak the transaction with respectability:
  ... proliferation of new instruments and 'financial products'. Reshapings of lending and borrowing packaged to the advantage of a now totally institutionalized market. (M. Thomas, 1987)

financial services moneylending
The language of those especially who offer costly credit to the relatively poor. It should mean no more than accounting or banking.

financially constrained poor
We all have financial constraints, which is why few of us possess that second Ferrari:
  Yesterday was Thorn's chance to have a ball, telling everyone how wonderful it is renting out television, videos, fridges and even furniture to the 'financially constrained', as chief executive Mike Metcalf tactfully calls them. (*Daily Telegraph*, 19 November 1996)

financially excluded unable to open a bank account
Not unable to pay the entrance fee but uncreditworthy:
  It hopes that by offering bank accounts via Post Office branches it can ... help the 'financially excluded'. (*Daily Telegraph*, 22 February 2001)
See also EXCLUDED.

find¹ to steal
The pretence is as old as stealing, as in the obsolete Scottish phrase *find a thing where the Highlander found the tongs*, 'Spoken when boys have pick'd something and pretend they found it'. (Kelly, 1721—to Lowlanders the Highlander was an inveterate thief).
A 19th-century *finder* was a thief:
  The 'finders' and 'stealers' of dogs were the most especial subject of a parliamentary enquiry. (Mayhew, 1851)

find² to fabricate (evidence)
The language of the Nixon White House:
  There was no prior evidence of such a relationship between Rutherford and Anderson, and Stewart refused to try to 'find' one. (Colodny and Gettlin, 1991—Nixon was convinced that there was a homosexual relationship between the journalist and the naval Yeoman)

find a tree to urinate

It may be said about humans as well as dogs: The traffic was snarled on the George Washington Parkway...so Patrick pulled into Fort Marcy Park to find a tree. (Evans-Pritchard, 1997)

find Cook County to engage in electoral fraud

Cook County's votes were produced miraculously by the Democratic machine in Illinois to secure Kennedy's win over Nixon in 1960: 'They found Cook County,' was the jaundiced comment. (J. Major, 1999—writing of Mitterrand's decision in 1992 that the French had voted in a referendum in favour of the exchange rate mechanism)

finger¹ to inform on or point out in a criminal context

The pointing is usually figurative only: Snyder had hoped to pick up a few hundred bucks by fingering Hooker to Amon Lorrimer. (Weverka, 1973)

To *put the finger on* is also to betray. The betrayer is a *finger-man*.

finger² to point out an opportunity for a crime

This time the pointing out is to another criminal:

I figure he knew them, and they knew him. Maybe he fingered the job. (Sanders, 1977)

Again the agent is a *finger-man* or *finger guy*: The finger guy must know the party he fingers has plenty of scratch to begin with. (Runyon, 1990, written in 1930s).

finger³ to excite (another) sexually with a finger

Usually of a female by a male:

There was a young fellow of Bude
Who fingered his girl while they
queued...(vulgar limerick)

To *finger (yourself)* is to masturbate, of male or female:

...her other hand fingering, all five fingers fingering like a team of maggots at her open heat. (Mailer, 1965)

Bouts of screaming followed and then, as though in a trance, she had begun to finger herself. (Fiennes, 1996)

finger-blight the reduction of a crop due to stealing

An occurrence once common in apple orchards, *blight* being a natural phenomenon, while scrumping by children is not.

finger-man¹ ² see FINGER 1 2

finger-man³ a killer

He pulls the trigger:

...the finger-man loiters ahead undetected till the target blunders into him. (le Carré, 1980)

fingers get close to the thumb *obsolete* favouritism is shown to relatives or friends

The imagery is from the clenched fist:

Yes, sir, the fingers have got pretty close to the thumb. (Egerton, 1884, writing about a case of nepotism)

finish¹ to kill

It is used of humans or animals. If they have been previously wounded or are sick, you *finish them off*. *Finished* may mean dead.

finish² to achieve a sexual orgasm

Very common use of either sex.

finish yourself off wipe your genitalia dry

An injunction after washing for children, invalids, or geriatrics which avoids mentioning the taboo parts of the body.

fire to dismiss peremptorily from employment

Punning on *discharge*, which is standard English, meaning, to dismiss from employment, and on the rapidity with which the deed is usually done:

'Working?' 'Nope, I got fired.' (Theroux, 1976)

fire a shot *American* to ejaculate semen

Or more shots than one. The use of *ejaculate* and *ejaculation* in a sexual sense is now so pervasive that it can convey an unfortunate image to the reader of older literature:

The vicar ejaculated from time to time and looked increasingly bewildered. (Sayers, 1937)

fireman¹ a motorist exceeding the speed limit

From the corny question asked by a traffic policeman, 'Where's the fire?'

fireman² a person to whom unpleasant duties are delegated

With obvious imagery:

Since starting at the Pentagon, Buhardt had been a fireman helping...stave off or limit the fallout from a variety of scandalous episodes. (Colodny and Gettlin, 1991)

The Nazis called the Jews whom they used in death camps to enforce discipline over other prisoners, predominantly Jewish, *firemen*.

See also VISITING FIREMAN 2.

firewater whisky

As well as burning your throat and your guts, it is flammable:

> Would I be consultant in exchange for a generous consignment of firewater? (*Private Eye*, September 1981)

firm (the) a clandestine, illegal, or bogus organization

A 19th-century usage of the Fenians in Ireland and much loved by espionage writers:

> Ever since he joined the firm as a young recruit... (G. Greene, 1978, of a spy)

Also used by the Windsor family:

> ... masses of photographs of 'The Firm', as they somewhat affectedly style themselves. (A. Clark, 1993, reporting on the contents of British royal palaces)

first people *Canadian* the descendants of the indigenous population

Not Adam and Eve but the aboriginal population of the country:

> The constitution is filled with modish catchphrases of the late 20th century, affirmative action, first people (natives), collective human rights, and the equality of male and female persons. (*Daily Telegraph*, 23 October 1992, reporting a statutory innovation which the Canadian electorate rejected)

first strike unannounced aggression

A use referring to an attack before war has been declared; otherwise it would not be euphemistic. A *first-strike capability* is an ability to attack another with nuclear weapons without prior warning.

See also SECOND STRIKE.

first world rich

The language of those for whom talk of poverty and backwardness is offensive:

> And then 50,000 First World Citizens—Brits, Americans, French, German, Spanish, Swedish, Danish—name it. (Forsyth, 1994)

The *Second World* was inhabited by Soviet Russia and its satellites. See also THIRD WORLD.

fish¹ *American* a heterosexual woman

One caught by a male, as seen by female homosexuals among whom heterosexuality in females is taboo. A *fishwife* in the same argot is the wife of a male homosexual.

fish² a prostitute's customer

To be caught and gutted:

> You may sit and drink if you like. I shall tell the girls that you are not a fish. (Trevanian, 1973—he was in a brothel)

fish³ a torpedo

Second World War jargon, seeking to make light of danger:

> We had a fish coming at our ship at about 265 degrees. (N. Lewis, 1989—it had been fired by a German E-boat)

fish story a lie or exaggeration

Anglers have a habit of romancing about the size of their catch or the one that got away:

> It was an obvious fish story and nobody in the room bought it. (Cussler, 1994)

fishing expedition an attempt to obtain gratuitous information

Not knowing what you may catch, as cross-examining counsel, detective, journalist, or spy. Also as *fishing trip*:

> ... things that an investigative fishing expedition into the break-in could uncover and exploit politically. (Colodny and Gettlin, 1991, quoting a Nixon tape of June 1973)

> It's a fishing trip rather than a specific enquiry. (P. D. James, 2001)

fishing fleet *British* marriageable girls send abroad to find husbands

Single British girls were sent to Malta or India where single men on extended tours might be less discriminating in their choice of bride:

> ... girls who had come out from England... as members of the 'fishing fleet' to find a husband. (Farrell, 1973)

fishmonger's daughter *obsolete* a prostitute

As with *fish market*, a brothel, the allusion is olfactory:

> Excellent well, you are a fishmonger. (Shakespeare, *Hamlet*—Hamlet speaking to Polonius, implying that the latter's daughter, Ophelia, was a prostitute. Polonius misses the point, only to take another behind the arras in the third act)

fishy (of a male) homosexual

Punning on QUEER 3 and the meaning irregular:

> ... her only husband had been as fishy as Dick's hatband. (Fraser, 1975)

fistful a prison sentence of five years

Prison slang, a variant of FIVE FINGERS and HANDFUL 1.

fit up to incriminate falsely

Another way to FRAME 1:

> ... some of the criminals changed their stories and admitted PC Cooley had been 'fitted up'. (*Daily Telegraph*, March 1990)

five-fingered discount *American* a reduction in price due to theft

It refers to stolen goods sold below their market price. See also FINGER-BLIGHT.

five-fingered widow (the) *British* male masturbation
Army use among those long absent from the company of white women:
> The red light districts... were strictly out of bounds... Many turned, as a last resort, to the 'five-fingered widow'. (C. Allen, 1975, writing of service in India)

five fingers a prison sentence of five years
A variant of FISTFUL and HANDFUL 1.

five or seven *obsolete British* drunk
This pre-Second World War London use came from the standard court sentence for being drunk and disorderly or drunk and incapable—five shillings fine or seven days in jail.

fix¹ to make an illegal arrangement
In standard usage, to mend or adjust. Fix as a verb or noun may involve bribery, damaging a rival, a gambling coup, etc.:
> To a Metropolitan policeman fix could only mean nothing other than a bribe. (Deighton, 1978)
> ... named in several of the White House tapes whom Nixon planned to 'fix' after he had been reelected. (Colodny and Gettlin, 1991)
> There's eight or nine races on the card... and the fix can be in any time somebody says so. (Chandler, 1953)

fix² *American* to castrate
The treatment of domestic animals, which might, I suppose, consider it an illegal arrangement, or FIX 1.

fix³ an injection of illegal narcotics
Usually heroin:
> Frank, had you had a fix? (Davidson, 1978, asking about narcotic use, not navigational verification)

fix⁴ to kill
Not an illegal arrangement if done in battle:
> One such desperado appeared in a ditch, ten yards from the house in which we were sitting. We fixed him. (Horne, 1994—the 'desperado' was a German soldier with a bazooka)

fix up *American* to hire a prostitute for another's use
Literally, to arrange something. Business jargon in a society where overt bribery or giving preferential prices is illegal.

fixer an arranger of embarrassing, dubious, or illegal business

He is the agent who may convert a COMMISSION into a bribe, divert unpleasant publicity, or do any act relevant to FIX 1:
> He's a fixer, a smoother-out. (Price, 1970)
See also FACILITATOR.

fizzer *British* an accusation of a military offence
An army pun on *charge*:
> 'I'll put you on a fizzer!' Vince shouted as he went and took over from Stan on the Minimi. (McNab, 1993—a *Minimi* is a gun)

flag is up (the) I am menstruating
Punning on the redness of the danger flag and the blood. Also as *flag of defiance*, *fly the (red) flag*, and BAKER FLYING.

flake¹ *American* an eccentric or strange person
Of uncertain derivation, although there are plenty of theories to choose from. Dr Johnson gives 'Any thing that appears loosely held together', and the imagery of disintegration is common in terms for mental illness:
> 'What a character she is,' he said. 'A real flake.' (Sanders, 1986)

flake² *American* cocaine
Probably from chipping it from a mass, and see CHIPPY 2.

flamboyant homosexual
Literally, colourful or showy, which is how some male homosexuals are thought to comport themselves:
> ... obituaries are simply eulogies of the great and the good, any of whose peccadillos (unusual sexual tastes, drunkenness and so on) are tactfully powdered over with euphemism ('flamboyant', 'convivial' etc.) (Leslie Jones in *Daily Telegraph*, 1 December 1994)

flapper *obsolete* a young woman who flouts convention
In northern English dialect, a young prostitute; in western England, a petticoat; in *OED* a 'young wild duck or partridge'; and in the 1920s a participant in the *flapper era*:
> I was sure I would have enjoyed being a rich Canton flapper with a peacock called Bluey too. (Irvine, 1986)

flash to display your genitalia in public to a stranger
Usually an erect penis by a male to a female; less often by a female:
> Sweet, shy and doe-eyed at home, she would rush up to complete strangers in the streets, grapple with her skirts and shout '... Give me money or else I'll flash'. (Dalrymple, 1993)

A *flasher* so behaves:
> These men were rapists or Peeping Toms or flashers or child molesters. (Sanders, 1973)

flash-ken *obsolete* a brothel
Also as *flash-house* or *-panney*, where you would find a *flash-tail*, *-girl* or *-woman*, if that was your ambition:
> ...at last struck home at a likely flash-ken where they were keeping it up to some tune. (Fraser, 1997—supposedly they were 'keeping up' no more than wine and song)
> ...keeping a cold eye on the more obvious thieves and flash- tails. (Fraser, 1977, writing again in 19th-century style)

flash your tin *American* to reveal that you are a police officer
The metal shield is the badge of office:
> Chief, should Jason Two flash his tin or work undercover? (Sanders, 1977)

flat on your back (of a woman) copulating
Her probable posture:
> ...if I can't charm this one flat on her back, I've lost my way with women. (Fraser, 1971)

The American *flat-backer* in black speech is a prostitute.

flawed drunk
Perhaps a pun on *floored*, from the tendency to fall over, and the common DAMAGED 1 imagery.

fleece to defraud
By robbery or overcharging, from the shearing of sheep:
> ...all the petty cutthroat ways and means with which she used to fleece us. (Cleland, 1749—she was a cheating bawd)

And (for non-lawyers) see *knight of the Golden Fleece* under KNIGHT.

flesh your will *obsolete* (of a male) to copulate
It is hard to say whether Shakespeare invented the imagery and exactly what vulgar pun he had in mind:
> The night he fleshes his will in the spoil of her honour. (*All's Well That Ends Well*)

fleshpot a brothel
Originally a vessel in which meat was cooked, whence a source of luxury and debauchery offering a variety of vicious attractions:
> ...found the 'fleshpots' of Nairobi to be 'insidious and most likely to corrupt'. (C. Allen, 1979)

fleshy part of the thigh the buttocks

It was here that a military bulletin said Lord Methuen had been wounded in the Boer War. Apart from late 19th-century modesty, to be wounded in the buttocks might imply that you had not been facing the enemy.

flexible¹ unprincipled
Principally of politicians:
> Pym is preparing...a swift twitch of the rug from under the few remaining loyalist sheepshaggers. This is called being *flexible*. (*Private Eye*, May 1982—the British Foreign Secretary opposed Mrs Thatcher's policy after the invasion of the Falkland Islands)

Such behaviour is called *flexibility*:
> Conservative MPs, impatient for the pre-election bribery to start, call for 'flexibility'. (*Financial Times*, December 1981)

flexible² condoning adultery
Literally, adaptable:
> Friends say their marriage falls short of being completely open sexually. But they have a flexible arrangement. (*Sunday Telegraph*, 25 February 2001)

fling (a) an extramarital sexual relationship
From the meaning, indulgence in any unaccustomed excess:
> I had my fling with the Tanglin wife. (Theroux, 1973)

flip your lid to lose your senses
The *lid* is slang for the head:
> ...you suddenly decide to answer questions today? And from the press? You must have flipped your lid. (Lynn and Jay, 1989)

It describes temporary rather than permanent derangement.

flirty fishing proselytization through the promiscuity of young women
Females belonging to a cult established by David Berg, an American evangelist, were encouraged to recruit men through sexual seduction. The use of condoms was forbidden, resulting in numerous pregnancies:
> Those children that were the result of Flirty Fishing are known as Jesus Babes. (*Daily Telegraph*, 25 November 1995)

flit¹ to die
Literally, to remove to another place:
> She canna flit in peace until she sees you. (W. Scott, 1816)

flit² (do a) to leave accommodation without paying rent due
A shortened form of MOONLIGHT FLIT:
> The family on the corner, two years in arrears on the rent, were doing another flit,

all their furniture...stacked up on creaking barrows. (Bradbury, 1976)

flit³ a male homosexual who usually plays the female role
He affects female mannerisms by *flitting about*:
  He assured me that he had a luscious ass...Flits have always been attracted to me. (M. McCarthy, 1963)

float paper to issue cheques or other securities unsecured by bank deposits or assets
Before the computer, banks took several days to clear cheques, an interval which could be used for taking unauthorized credit:
  He could probably stall [bankers] for the necessary twenty-four hours. It wouldn't be the first time Lorimer had floated paper for a day or two. (Weverka, 1973)

floater¹ *American* an undesirable
A hobo with no fixed abode.

floater² *American* the corpse of a person who has been drowned
Morticians' jargon:
  Floaters...are another matter; a person who has been in the Bay for a week or more...(J. Mitford, 1963)

floating *American* drunk or under the influence of narcotics
Referring to the feeling of levitation and mental detachment.

flog off (of a male) to masturbate yourself
The common beating imagery. Also as *flog your beef, mutton, donkey, dummy*, etc.:
  ...dragged off to jail every time he...flogged his dummy on the porch. (Wambaugh, 1975)

flop (of a woman) to be promiscuous
She is thought readily to drop to a prone position:
  Lois flops at the drop of a hat. (Chandler, 1943—he was not suggesting that she tired easily)

floral tribute a wreath presented at a funeral
Tribute, protection money or rent paid on a regular basis, has evolved in standard English to mean a gesture of respect or praise on a single occasion. Brides prefer to carry bouquets.

flourish your genitals (of a male) to copulate
You do more than when you FLASH:
  I do not understand what kind of a affliction of the loins you can have to render mercury beneficial. You have, I dare say, been flourishing your genitals over and above that which nature requires. (Dalrymple, 1993, quoting from a letter c.1817)

flower¹ *obsolete* the virginity of a woman
What you lose if a man chances to DEFLOWER you:
  Threw my affections in his charmed power,
  Reserved the stalk and gave him all my flower. (Shakespeare, 'A Lover's Complaint')

flower² *American* a male homosexual
More widely dispersed than the PANSY, it might seem.

flowers *obsolete* the menstrual flow
Normally expanded to *monthly flowers*, from the flowing rather than the flowering:
  I had my courses, my flowers. (Fowles, 1985—she was denying that she was pregnant)

flowery¹ a prison cell
Rhyming slang on *flowery dell* and sometimes used to refer to the prison itself.

flowery² blasphemous or vulgar
Descriptive of language, although the concept of blasphemy now seems to be out of date except in Muslim communities.

fluff your duff (of a male) to masturbate
Probably likening the penis to a suety dish, with the same imagery as PULL THE PUD(DING):
  What are you doing here in the dark—fluffing your duff? (Sanders, 1982)

flush down the drain to dismiss peremptorily from employment
The imagery is obvious:
  If I bounce him and ask Thorsen to get me another man, he'll flush Boone down the drain. (Sanders, 1977)

flute an erect penis
As with BUGLE, a firm instrument which may be played:
  But it's his fault as much as Sharon's. Whoever he is.—It was his flute tha'—
  (R. Doyle, 1987—they were discussing the cause of Sharon's pregnancy)
A *fluter* in America is a male homosexual.

flutter a wager
A 17th-century use which is still current, from the excitement of gambling and often seeking to minimise the extent of an addiction.

flutter a skirt *obsolete* to be a prostitute

Attracting a possible client's attention. Today a *flutter* may be a short-term extramarital sexual relationship.

flutterer a machine to assist in lie detection

It records variations in the subject's pulse, temperature, sweat, etc.:

> What we used to call a lie detector, sir. A polygraph, known in the business as a flutterer. (le Carré, 1989)

flux¹ menstruation

Literally, the condition of flowing or, as with solder, causing to flow:

> Even her body's flux, which she could feel in a gentle, almost controlled flow, wasn't the inconvenient and disagreeable monthly discharge...
> (P. D. James, 1980)

flux² diarrhoea

Again from the flowing:

> Our bodies weakened with fluxes, our strength wasted with watchings, want of drink, wet and cold being our constant companions. (Gentles, 1992, quoting a soldier in the New Model Army before the Battle of Dunbar)

fly¹ *American* in plain clothes

It is used of a policeman assigned away from his normal precinct or uniformed duty, from the meaning knowing, but perhaps also referring to a *fly cab*, one plying for hire without a licence.

fly² to be under the influence of illegal narcotics

Usually the sense of levitation from smoking marijuana:

> This is top-grade grass. We'll fly. (Sanders, 1982)

fly a flag to have a trouser zip inadvertently undone

Whether or not a part of the shirt-tail is protruding. You may also, in this situation, be said to be *flying low*.

fly a kite¹ to tender a worthless negotiable instrument

Only the wind supports it. See also KITE.

fly a kite² *obsolete* to write a begging letter

A considerable industry and art in 19th-century England made possible by the advent of the penny post.

fly-by-night¹ an absconding debtor

Not from a witch, on or off her broomstick, or from the ominous bird, also known as the whistler or gobbleratch, whose nocturnal flight presaged imminent death, nor even the tourist on a package holiday on the cheapest ticket, but the tenant with unpaid rent who took his goods with him to prevent distraint by the landlord. Now standard English for anyone who is financially unreliable. See also MOONLIGHT FLIT.

fly-by-night² drunk

Rhyming slang for TIGHT 1, with perhaps a sideswipe at the unreliability of drunkards.

fly one wing low to be drunk

RAF slang from the Second World War referring to a damaged plane:

> ...half the officers in the club house were flying one wing low. (Deighton, 1982)

fly the blue pigeon¹ to steal lead

Usually from the roof of a church, where the birds might congregate, and from the colour of the metal, shortened in slang to *bluey*:

> And there's the bluey...the lead from the pipes and the roofs like of churches.
> (L. Thomas, 1981)

fly the blue pigeon² *British* to be a malingerer

A naval pun on SWING THE LEAD.

fly the yellow flag to have contagious fever aboard

The crew would not be allowed ashore. Now only figurative use:

> A ship that flies the yellow flag and cannot find a port. (Seymour, 1977)

flyblow an illegitimate child

Punning on the deposit of eggs left in meat by flies, and the taint:

> She is still a bairn. And the flyblow of the system. (Cookson, 1969—her autobiography was largely about her own illegitimacy)

flying handicap diarrhoea

The phrase puns on the celerity needed, the disability, and a typical name for a horse race.

flying low see FLY A FLAG

flying picket *British* a crowd from afar trying to stop others working

They travelled by road rather than by air. Perhaps obsolete since such intimidatory action has been made illegal.

flying squad a police detachment organized for rapid deployment

There have been earthbound *flying squadrons* from the 17th century. The London version formed in the 1920s is also known in rhyming slang as *The Sweeney*, from the demon barber, Sweeney Todd.

fog away *American* to kill
By shooting, perhaps also alluding to the smoke from the gun. Sometimes simply as *fog*.

fogbound of low intelligence
Unable to see things clearly:
    I also found myself giggling at the thought that maybe his lunch companions were so fogbound they wouldn't notice if he made everyone's lunch disappear. (Anonymous, 1996)

foggy drunk
Your eyes may be and your memory becomes. Also as *fogged*.

foin *obsolete* (of a male) to copulate
Literally, to make a thrust with a sharp weapon:
    When wilt thou leave fighting o' days and foining o' nights. (Shakespeare, *2 Henry IV*)

fold to fail in business
Either personally or corporately, from the collapsing:
    Second, they must let some of the banks fold to allow the financial sector to reconstruct. (*Daily Telegraph*, 15 January 1997, of the Japanese economy)
In America it may also mean to die.

fold your hand to concede defeat
By resigning or abandoning an enterprise, as in poker, when a player drops out of the bidding:
    I was waiting, and dreading, the first sign that Richard had folded his hand. (Anonymous, 1996)

follow to die after another named person
To be reunited elsewhere, it may be hoped:
    A gift from his dear widow, Mr Osnard, shortly before she followed him. (le Carré, 1996)

follow your passions to copulate promiscuously
Or one passion in particular:
    A geisha determined to follow her passions might take this risk. (Golden, 1997)

follower *obsolete* a male who is courting a female
Specifically a man who courted a domestic servant girl:
    No, sir, missus don't permit no followers. (Mayhew, 1862)
Then in upper-class use—those who had servants—of courting any girl:

    If she had no followers they would say she's a Lesbian. (N. Mitford, 1960)
To *follow* meant to court:
    He followed his wife ten year afore they were wed. (*Leeds Mercury*, 1893, quoted in *EDD*)

fond of excessively addicted to
More than just being favourably disposed towards. Thus a man who is *fond of the women* is a profligate, and he who *is fond of a glass* drinks too much alcohol, or, if *fond of food*, is a glutton:
    Burke was vice-commandant of the Dublin Brigade, and a bit too fond of the glass for a man holding that rank. (Flanagan, 1995)
    Marshall's size (he was fond of food) gave him an awesome presence at meetings. (*Daily Telegraph*, 23 February 1996)

fondle to caress sexually
Literally, to handle something or someone fondly:
    ... she had learned to slide her hand into his slitted pocket and fondle him. (Sanders, 1973)

food for worms dead
Unless cremated. Also as *worm-food*:
    But it was William who became food for worms. (Macdonald, 1976)
    You have to be faster, or you are worm-food. (Seymour, 1977)
See also DIET OF WORMS.

fool (about) with yourself to masturbate
Like the inconsequential action so described:
    Honey ... you don't care if I fool with myself a little. (M. Thomas, 1982)

fool around with to have a sexual relationship with
Either sex can do it, with no intention of pair-bonding or the like:
    He's looking for a girl to fool around with tonight. (Evans-Pritchard, 1997)
    Only fooled around with him a little. I wasn't Frenching him. (Wambaugh, 1975)

foot *obsolete British* to take money from new employees to buy intoxicants
An initiation ceremony, perhaps a shortened form of *foot the bill*:
    When he wor lowse on his prentis-ship his shopmates footed him. (Treddlehoyle, 1875)
A *footing* was such a levy:
    I paid five shillin' for footin when I started. (Pinnock, 1895)
This is a sample entry: there were many euphemisms for the practice of older workers extorting money from new apprentices.

footless drunk
Neither better nor worse than LEGLESS:
Jesus, the things I knew for a fact when I
was footless. (R. Doyle, 1996)

footpad see HIGHWAYMAN

for the birds mentally unbalanced
With your head in the metaphorical clouds:
I was for the birds when I was like that; I
didn't know who or where I was. (R. Doyle,
1996)

for the high jump in deep trouble
It originally meant to be sentenced to death
by hanging, whence to be killed by any
means:
Satchthorpe and Frimston are for the high
jump ... the Chief Constable's ... practically
said as much. (Grayson, 1975)

for your convenience provided ostensibly as a special service
The pretence of giving you something extra
when it is already in the price is mildly
irritating:
The notice said they were sanitized under
infra-red and ultra-violet light for
Koolman's protection and convenience,
but I suppose anybody would get the same
kind of towel. (Deighton, 1972)
However, all is forgiven when you meet an
unconscious pun:
For your convenience—Sanitor tissue seat
covers. (lavatory in Fall River,
Massachusetts, May, 1981)

forage to steal
Originally as a noun, food for cattle. Such food
was traditionally stolen for their horses by
armies on the march, whence, as a soldier, to
look for anything else to steal:
'Where the devil did you come by this?'
'Foraged, sir.' (Fraser, 1969)

force-protection *American* the avoidance
of combat by soldiers
The effectiveness of the US Army is not
increased by having to steer clear of danger:
... what the Americans see as a 'force-
protection issue'; the US military comes
under intense political pressure not to
suffer casualties. (*Daily Telegraph*, 21 March
2001)

force-put job *Devon* the marriage of a
pregnant woman
In dialect, *force-put* means a matter of necessity.

force yourself on to copulate with
The male usually does the *forcing*. Also as *force
your ardour* or *force your attentions on*:

You are not the sort of man to force
yourself on me against my will. (A. Massie,
1986)
This was the evening when the
conquerors of the Afrika Korps were to
force their pent-up ardour on the
ladies of Alexandria. (Manning, 1977—
she meant 'the conquerors in the Afrika
Korps')
Willie tried to force his attentions on her.
(Kee, 1993—Willie O'Shea wanted to
copulate with his wife, Katie, at a time
when she was bearing children by C. S.
Parnell)
To *force favours from* may indicate a greater
degree of female reluctance.

forehead challenged balding
Another variant of the CHALLENGED theme:
'Seth, am I supposed to feel sorry for you
because you're bald?' 'Going,' he says.
'Going bald. Forehead-challenged.' (Turow,
1996)

forget yourself to be guilty of a solecism
Not total amnesia but swearing when it is out
of place, making a sexual approach to a
woman who has not signalled that she would
welcome it, and the like.

fork (of a male) to copulate with
Punning on the pronging and the place where
the legs join the trunk. Referring to the latter,
Shakespeare used *the place between her forks* for
a woman's frontal crotch:
Behold yond simpering dame,
Whose face between her forks presages
snow. (*King Lear*—her pubic hair was
turning white)

forked plague (the) *obsolete* cuckoldry
Referring to the proverbial horns worn by the
cuckold, and see HORN 2:
This forked plague is fated to us.
(Shakespeare, *Othello*)

form a criminal record
Police jargon, probably from horse-racing,
punning on the special *form* on which these
details are recorded:
With regard to a police record, Artie
Johnson is the only one with any form.
(Davidson, 1978)

former person a perceived opponent of
the Communist state
Such people had already lost such rights as
were accorded to Soviet citizens:
They consolidated their positions with
trenches dug by forced labour gangs made
up of train-loads of 'former persons' sent to
the front. (Moynahan, 1994, writing of the
Russian civil war in 1919)

forty-four *American* a prostitute
An unusual example of non-British rhyming slang, for *whore*.

forum shopping choosing a jurisdiction to minimize alimony
For those who have the choice:
> ... it was little wonder that 'forum shopping'—looking for the best country to start proceedings—has become such a popular sport among rich husbands in the international scene. (*Daily Telegraph*, 15 May 2001)

forward *obsolete British* drunk
A use which may have referred to the truculence associated with drunkenness:
> Twer querish tack—beer and reubub weind an' bacca juice a-mixed, but I knowed we could get fururd on't. (Buckman, 1870—a mixture of tobacco juice, beer, and rhubarb wine was queerish tack indeed)

forward at the knees elderly
From the way some old people walk.

foul[1] to defecate in an unacceptable place
Usually of dogs on carpets or pavements, but occasionally of humans:
> Who had fouled his home? (Boyd, 1982—troops had defecated everywhere in a house)

To *foul yourself* is to defecate or vomit in your clothing:
> They fouled themselves where they lay. (Fraser, 1971)

foul[2] *obsolete Scottish* the devil
A shortened form of *foul ane* or *foul thief*, still heard in expressions such as *foul skelp ye*, the devil take you; and *foul may care*, devil-may-care:
> Our deacon wadna ca' a chair
> The foul ane durst him na-say.
> (R. Fergusson, 1773)
> Seek the foul thief onie place. (Burns, 1786)

foul desire a wish to copulate
Where *foul* means disgusting it seems that linguistically only males are thus taken:
> If foul desire has not conducted you. (Shakespeare, *Titus Andronicus*)

A man may also have *foul designs* on a woman who is not his normal sexual partner. If he *has his foul way with her*, he will copulate with her, not necessarily against her inclination. Still used humorously.

foul play *British* murder
Police jargon, and not of the way professional footballers behave on the pitch:
> He was shot.' 'Foul play—isn't that what you British call it?' (Deighton, 1978)

foundation of a lower academic standard
Educational jargon, for those whose *foundations* were not properly laid during years of schooling:
> The market is not flooded with students clamouring for foundation degree places. (*Daily Telegraph*, 3 February 2001)

foundation garment a corset
The imagery comes from building, although the word *buttress* comes more readily to mind:
> ... she may be half-perishing in the clutch of her 'foundation garment'. (Jennings, 1965)

four-letter man an unpleasant person
The letters are S, H, I, and T.

four-letter word an obscenity
Jennings (1965) demonstrated that there were then only eight among the catalogue of obscenities which contained four letters. However the most hackneyed among them do tend to have four letters.

four sheets in the wind see SHEET IN THE WIND

fourth a lavatory
The use seems to have originated at Cambridge University, probably from the lowest category of degree awarded on graduation, rather than from the three Estates of the Realm—the peers, the bishops, and the commons. The literati in the 19th century delighted in inventing candidates for the *fourth estate*. Carlyle says Burke first suggested the press, although Macaulay has a better claim. The joke, if such it be, still lingers on:
> Just to make sure the food and drink were equally up to the expectations of the fourth estate. (Deighton, 1982, meaning journalists)

foxed drunk
Literally, deceived, and so a variant of the obsolete deceived in liquor, which seeks to imply it was not your fault:
> ... poured drink into himself until he was completely foxed. (Fraser, 1970)

As usual, the half is the same as the whole:
> Here I was, half-foxed and croaking to myself in a draughty shack. (Fraser, 1971)

Both uses are now dated.

foxy *American* feeling promiscuous
I am unhappy with the coy SOED definition, 'feeling attractive':
> Over forty and feeling foxy. (on a woman's apron, JFK Airport, 1979)

fractured *American* drunk
The broken imagery again.

frag *American* to kill
A shortened form of *fragmentation device*, which is a long-winded way of saying hand grenade. The use originated in Vietnam where the grenade was used to kill over-keen or unpopular officers, often white, by conscript GIs, often black. (Some rich white boys evaded conscription, which did not prove to be a bar to at least one, who obtained the appointment of Commander-in-Chief of the US forces. Most blacks had to serve.) Some general use of killing by any means:
> Molly Turner was important to me and you fragged her. (Sanders, 1984—Molly was murdered)

fragile suffering from sub-acute alcoholic poisoning
Usually an admission of a HANGOVER by the sufferer himself.

frail suffering from sub-acute alcoholic poisoning
A variant of FRAGILE.

frail sister a prostitute
Her weakness is moral rather than physical:
> He couldn't stomach sweeping out no more saloons, nor sloshing out no more cuspidors, nor being at the beck and call of bar-keeps, piano players with two left hands, frail sisters and soiled doves. (Vanderhaeghe, 1997)

A *frail* was once any member of the weaker sex:
> In persuading frails to divulge what they know...(Lavine, 1930)

frailty (of a woman) copulation outside marriage
Literally, weakness of any kind:
> Was this common, too common, story of a man's treachery and a woman's frailty the key to the secret? (W. Collins, 1860)

frame[1] to incriminate falsely
Like mounting a picture, so that you can see it better:
> I take it you don't want your daughter-in-law framed. (Chandler, 1943—the speaker was not a photographer)

The result is a *frame-up*:
> It's a frame-up as sure as ever I saw one. (Deighton, 1981)

frame[2] a male who is attractive sexually to homosexuals
Probably from the slang *frame*, a body. Not necessarily a homosexual himself, although dress and posture may send a signal to other homosexuals, in which case the *frame* takes the female role.

frank[1] *obsolete* copulating promiscuously
Dr Johnson gives 'licentious', from the early meaning, liberal or generous:
> Chaste to her Husband, frank to all beside
> A teaming mistress but a barren bride.
> (Pope, 1735)

frank[2] unfriendly and without consensus
It is used of political talks between fundamentally opposed parties:
> Mr Mugabe had agreed on the need for urgent and 'frank' talks. (*Daily Telegraph*, December 1980—note the inverted commas)

Full and frank in a communiqué tells you that the parties failed to agree on anything:
> These [talks] lasted an hour and a half and were described as having been full and frank. (Kee, 1984—Chamberlain and Mussolini met on 11 June 1939; Great Britain and Italy were shortly to be at war)

fraternal assistance an invasion
Those on the left politically are wont to address each other, and perhaps even think of each other, as brothers:
> But the decision to say 'counter-revolution' instead of 'uprising', 'people' instead of 'party', 'fraternal assistance' instead of 'invasion' are choices of the highest solemnity. For Communism exists by casting spells—change the language and the world itself will change. (*Sunday Telegraph*, March 1989)
> Here was a man whose whole life had been devoted to Marxism-Leninism, who had helped plan the fraternal assistance to Czechoslovakia and Afghanistan. (R. Harris, 1998)

fraternization copulation with enemy civilians in military occupied territories
Strictly, friendship with or treating as brothers, but to an occupying soldier the *frater* was of less interest than his sister(s):
> Relics of the Great Fraternization Period, you know. (Bogarde, 1981, referring to German children fathered by occupying soldiers after the Second World War)

Non-fraternization, not mingling with the natives, was the official policy of the winning side:
> Here, as Odgers recalls, 'the troops had lectures on non- fraternization'. (Horne, 1994)

fratricide inflicting casualties by mistake on your own troops
Inadvertently or carelessly killing your brothers-in-arms:
> ... it is very difficult to avoid blue-on-blue, or fratricide, as the Americans call it. (de la Billière, 1992)

See also FRIENDLY FIRE.

freak¹ a male homosexual
Literally, an irrational event or a monster:
> They wanted to go down to Greenwich Village to see the freaks (Sanders, 1981)

freak² a devotee of any taboo or unconventional activity
Usually in a compound noun, such as *acid-freak*, someone who uses LSD habitually; *surf-freak*, one who spends excessive time in, under, or around rollers. In prostitutes' jargon, a *freak trick* is a customer who demands from her abnormal sexual activity.

freak³ to ingest an illegal hallucinogen
As a result of which you may *freak out*.

free included in the price
An advertising gimmick seeking to persuade a buyer that more is being handed over than has been paid for. A prospective purchaser may also be offered a separate article which is described as being free as an inducement to buy what the seller is peddling. See also COME-ON 3.

free from infection not suffering from venereal disease
In the army, a soldier can have measles, and a heavy cold, but be so described. Usually abbreviated to *FFI*.

free love unrestricted copulation outside marriage
The use implies an absence of concealment and disregard of convention. It is used for either sex:
> Dismal free love at a summer camp. (G. Greene, 1932)

free of Fumbler's Hall *obsolete* (of a male) sexually impotent
The inference was that the husband so described might toy sexually with his wife without being able to do more.

free relationship licence within a heterosexual partnership to copulate with third parties
There is an implication perhaps that a normal union in which the parties copulate only with each other involves sexual servility:

> Our marriage had broken up over my jealousy. Esther wanted a free relationship. (M. McCarthy, 1963)

free samples copulation permitted by a woman prior to marriage
The imagery is from a taster or trial quantity offered by a trader. The euphemism was much used of betrothed couples.

free trade *obsolete* smuggling
It was (and still is) a way of evading excise duty:
> My father let me have a horse from the stable and a ling-tow over my shoulder to go out on the free trade among the Manxman. (Crockett, 1894)

Today *free trade* in standard English describes commerce between states without tariff barriers, although international trade is seldom truly free because of non-tariff barriers, nationalism, and other factors.

free world those countries not under Communist control
A different kind of tyranny might be included under this heading, despite the imperfections of its political arrangements:
> The Western countries call themselves collectively the 'Free World'. (Jennings, 1965)

freed from earthly limitations dead
It is a kind of liberty to which few of us look forward with enthusiasm:
> That bright spirit was but freed from its earthly limitations. (E. M. Wright, 1932— her young daughter had just died)

freedom fighters terrorists
Even when opposing an autocratic regime, they normally seek to replace it with autocracy:
> We are not murderers...we are freedom fighters against international imperialism. (Sharpe, 1979)

freelance (of a woman) to be promiscuous
A complex pun on LANCE, to copulate (though normally of the male), being *free* from involvement with a pimp, or not demanding payment, and the *freelance* who works without being tied to a single employer. Also used as a noun to describe one who so behaves.

freeloader¹ a thief
He who helps himself:
> Though gas meters were considered more difficult to tamper with, this had not deterred some ambitious free-loaders. (Hailey, 1979)

freeloader² a systematic cadger
In this use, the greed is covered by a gloss of
legality:
>   Only 400 of the most abject freeloaders
>   bothered to turn up. (*Private Eye*, March
>   1980, describing a reception)
An event which attracts such people is known
as a *freebie*.

freeman of Bucks *obsolete British* a cuckold
Punning on the distinction, the English
county, and the horns of the stag.

Freemans cadged cigarettes
Army usage, referring to a fictional brand
smoked by habitual cadgers. See also DRINK
AT FREEMANS QUAY.

freeze¹ an attempt to contain public expenditure by reducing wages or recruitment
In an inflationary economy, absence of an
increase effectively reduces pay, and non-
recruitment saves costs:
>   There aren't any music-teaching jobs, said
>   Michael, they've all been cut back in the
>   freeze. (Lodge, 1980)

freeze² the refusal by a female to copulate with her regular sexual partner
First noted (etymologically) in Australia but
now a widespread usage.

freeze off to kill
The common imagery of CHILL:
>   Frisky Lavon got froze off tonight.
>   (Chandler, 1953)

freeze on to to steal
Alluding to the adhesive quality of ice. It
refers to minor peculation and stealing by
finding.

freeze out to eliminate minority shareholders unfairly
Commercial jargon, from the meaning to
exclude arbitrarily. Minority shareholders in
a British unquoted company have scant legal
protection if their total interest amounts to
less than 25 per cent of the equity.

freezer *American* a prison
The imagery of the ICE BOX 1:
>   You didn't spend three days in the freezer
>   just because you're a sweetheart.
>   (Chandler, 1953)

French is used by the English of anything
which they consider bogus, over-rated,
illegal, immoral, or otherwise undesirable, reflecting the mutual distrust be-

tween the countries which was not
lessened by the events between 1940
and 1945. The following examples give
a general flavour:

French¹ to indulge in oral sex
Using what the English call the FRENCH way:
>   I wasn't Frenching him. (Wambaugh, 1975)

French² an excuse for swearing
You pretend that the taboo word is foreign:
>   ...not when some poor fucker...you'll
>   excuse my French, Mr Carter...(Seymour,
>   1980)

French ache (the) syphilis
Shakespeare refers to the baldness caused by
this supposed import:
>   Some of your French crowns have no hair
>   at all. (*A Midsummer Night's Dream*)
In former times you might be be unfortunate
enough to contract *French disease*, *fever*, *gout*,
measles, or *pox*, or receive a *French compliment*,
each of which would cause you to become
frenchified, or syphilitic.

French article smuggled brandy
The euphemism passed into some general use
to include imports which had suffered excise
duty. Also, in smuggling argot, as *French cream*,
elixir, or *lace*. A *Frenchman* was a single bottle of
brandy. I'm not sure why in Ireland *French
cream* was whiskey:
>   Might he have the pleasure of helping
>   her to a little more of that delicious
>   French cream. (P. Kennedy, 1867, of
>   whiskey)

French drive a miscued shot at cricket

French kiss a kiss during which the
tongue is inserted into another's mouth
Such depravity has to be un-English:
>   'Yes, but not without tongues down each
>   other's throats, like they do now.' 'We used
>   to,' I said. 'It was called French kissing.'
>   (Lodge, 1995)
An *Aussie kiss* is a *French kiss* performed *down
under*.

French leave unauthorized absence
Originally of a soldier, implying a propensity
in French soldiers for desertion. Some civilian
and figurative use:
>   We could still, if we wished, take 'French
>   leave' of Vietnam. (M. McCarthy, 1967)

French letter a contraceptive sheath
worn by a male
The term may come from their being packed
in small envelopes, coupled with the supposed Gallic penchant for frequent copulation. I think any derivation from *letting*, or

preventing, as in the phrase *let or hindrance*, is unlikely:

> ...keep in their bags not even small change, only a powder-puff, a lipstick, a mirror, perhaps some French letters. (G. Greene, 1932)

Also as *FL*, *Frenchie*, or *French tickler*:

> Preyed on his mind, all those FLs did. (Sharpe, 1974)
> You can't feel a thing with a Frenchie. (Sharpe, 1976)
> ...you were screwing matron with a French tickler. (Sharpe, 1982)

French pigeon a pheasant shot out of season

The action of a bounder.

French renovating pills substances to induce abortion of a healthy foetus

Freely advertised in the 19th century, with a warning that pregnant women should not take them—in fact revealing their purpose.

French vice (the) cunnilingus or fellatio

And as the *French* way

> ...sodomy, buggery, or the fashionable 'French' vice clinically called *cunnilictio* and its corresponding variation, *fellatio*. (Pearsall, 1969)

fresh¹ *obsolete* not having taken alcohol

The word was used about an habitual drunkard:

> There is our great Udaller is weel enough when he is fresh. (W. Scott, 1822)

This is an example of a word or term having two opposite euphemistic meanings.

fresh² mildly drunk

Perhaps a shortened form of *fresh in drink* and from the meaning, lively:

> He wa' to say drunk—on'y fresh a bit. (Pinnock, 1895)

In the days of restricted opening hours, English inns used to stay open all day only on market days and farmers used to return home *market-fresh*:

> ...was already 'market-fresh' when we started back. (*Cornhill Magazine*, 1896, quoted in *EDD*, of a drunken farmer)

fresh³ making unwelcome sexual approaches to another

Another form of liveliness:

> I know I look a lot younger than I am...so maybe I shouldn't have been surprised that Andy got fresh. (Rendell, 1991)

freshen a drink to serve more alcohol

Formerly, the addition of more soda water to a partly drained glass, to make it sparkle again:

> 'Let me freshen your drink,' Delaney said. He went over to the liquor cabinet, came back with new drinks for both of them. (Sanders, 1973)

freshen up *American* to urinate

The standard invitation to an arriving traveller:

> Why don't you just freshen up and then stroll on down the path, first right, to my lodge? (M. Thomas, 1980)

fricasseed *American* drunk

The common cooking imagery. We may also marvel at the American-English conjugation of a French verb.

fried *American* drunk

More culinary imagery.

friend an extramarital sexual partner

Heterosexual or homosexual:

> You got a friend that don't work and a husband that works, you're all set. (Chandler, 1943)
> I have a very nice friend. It's against the law of course. (G. Greene, 1932—but not these days)

See also LADY FRIEND, WOMAN FRIEND, and MAN 1. *Friends*, *close friends*, or JUST GOOD FRIENDS may be enjoying such a relationship:

> She managed to let me know...that Dylan Thomas had once been a 'close friend'. (Fowles, 1977)

friend has come (my) I am menstruating

Punning on the arrival for a limited period and the relief at not being pregnant. Also as *my little friend*.

friendly lacking accord or sympathy

The language of diplomacy to describe discussions between mutually suspicious or antagonistic parties. This is one grade up the scale from FRANK 2.

friendly fire being bombed or shelled by your own side

The use seeks to play down one of the hazards of battle:

> ...strafed and bombed by American planes. (Afterwards the ghastly error was described in military double-talk as 'friendly fire'.) (Hailey, 1979)

frig¹ to copulate with

From *frig*, to rub, despite the etymological attractions of the old Cornish *frig*, a married woman, and of *Frigga*, Odin's wife, the aptly named Norse goddess of married love whom we commemorate weekly in the word *Friday*:

> I kept on frigging her with my man-root. (F. Harris, 1925)

You may still hear *frigging* as an expletive for *fucking*.

frig² (of a male) to masturbate
Again from the rubbing:
    ...under a haystack in the country we gave ourselves to a bout of frigging. (F. Harris, 1925)

frightener a person paid to intimidate illegally
Usually for the collection of usurious debt or to prevent the giving of evidence:
    'Why are you bothering?' he asked. 'I don't like frighteners.' (D. Francis, 1988—the speaker was being so threatened)

fringe unconventional, insubstantial, or fraudulent
Close to the edge of propriety or convention in the arts, as in the *fringe theatre*, or of honesty in commerce:
    The Bank of England's least favourite 'fringe' banker. (*Private Eye*, March 1981)

frippet a sexually available young woman
Usually unmarried. A *frip* was a scrap of cloth, whence something worthless. *Frippery* was clothing and the imagery is the same as SKIRT:
    I'll take my Bible oath you've got your little bit of frippet tucked away nice and convenient. (Amis, 1990)

froggie *British* a contraceptive sheath
From the *French* in FRENCH LETTER and a derogatory name for a nation noted for the culinary delicacy, frogs' legs. Naval use.

front¹ an organization hiding its real objective so as to appeal to the gullible and well-meaning
The method was first described by Munzenberg, the Communist propagandist, and remains useful after the collapse of Communism:
    The World Committee for the relief of Victims of German Fascism set the pattern for all future camouflaged 'front' organizations. (Boyle, 1979)

front² a seemingly honest person or business shielding a covert or illegal operation
Espionage and criminal use:
    ...invested in a wide range of new enterprises one of which was a 'front' for the Gehlen organization. (Allbeury, 1976)

front door (the) the vagina
As different from the BACK DOOR 1:
    You'll be able to hand out radical

deliverance to both of them now. One at the front door, and one at the back. (Bradbury, 1975—he would be able to copulate and to bugger)
Also as the *front parlour*.

front-running dealing illegally as an insider
You get your order in before that of your client:
    The alleged offences include 'front-running' in which dealers hurriedly execute orders for themselves, knowing prices will move in their favour by client orders they have just received. (*Daily Telegraph*, August 1989, reporting on Chicago commodity dealers)

frontier guards troops used for invasion without a declaration of war
The Chinese Communists so described their armies which invaded India in 1960s and Vietnam in the 1970s:
    Then a reference to 'Chinese Frontier Guards' alerted me. (Naipaul, 1964—he had though he was listening to an Indian broadcast until the use of the euphemism told him the source was Chinese)
    ...Chinese soldiers fighting in Vietnam but marked as 'Frontier Guards in South China'. (Theroux, 1988)

frottage sexual bodily contact between two people wearing clothing
Literally, touching or rubbing together:
    By the 1930s there was so much frottage going on in the public parks that a visiting French schoolmistress was horrified. (Paxman, 1998)

fruit¹ a male homosexual
Which came first, the RAISIN or the *fruit*? Probably the *raisin*, from the French meaning, lipstick:
    Pastor was screwing that Mexican fruit. (Deighton, 1972)

fruit² an irrational or unpredictable person
An abbreviation of FRUITCAKE.

fruit bowl the genitalia of a male
Not punning on FRUIT 1 but referring to the visual appearance:
    'We'll hide and jump out on him.' 'And all kick him in the fruit bowl.' (L. Thomas, 1997)

fruit machine a mechanical gambling device
The symbols on the rotating discs in the early versions are fruits:

An army-surplus dealer, a scrap-metal
merchant, a fruit-machine operator—or a
property man. (S. Green, 1979)
The alternative name, *one-armed bandit*, from
the actuating lever, is more fitting.

fruit salad a mixture of illegal narcotics
Either of indiscriminate ingestion of whatever
is to hand, or of the pooling of supplies by
those who meet to ingest narcotics together.

fruitcake a mentally abnormal or eccentric person
A shortened form of the cliché *as nutty as a
fruitcake*:
God knows they've got their share of
armed fruitcakes. (Lyall, 1985)

fry¹ to kill or be killed
It refers to judicial and other killing:
Frying some druggie-pirate-rapist-
murderers would surely appeal to the
citizens of the sovereign state of Alabama.
(Clancy, 1989)
If I don't get off on them, they'll fry.
(Marmur, 1955—soldiers were waiting to
be lifted from a beach under enemy fire)

fry² the testicles of lambs
It is how they are often cooked.

fuddled drunk
Literally, confused. We tend to use the term of
others rather than ourselves.

fudge to attempt to deceive by making
wrong entries
Especially of the falsification of accounts,
being a corruption of the standard English
fuddle, to confuse:
Perhaps he had been fudging his tax
returns. (Chandler, 1958)

fulfilment copulation
Literally, the accomplishment of anything:
In the corners couples embraced and
fondled, stopping just short of actual
fulfilment. (Bradbury, 1959)

full drunk
It survives in the Scottish *fou*:
The cup that cheers, but makesna fou.
(Tester, 1865—he was referring to tea)
Now also heard in various clichés such as *full
as a tick* or the less common *full as a boat*.

full figure (a) obesity
Having a *full figure* does not imply merely that
you have all normal anatomical appendages.
The expression is used of women more than
men:
Miss Lewinsky's already full figure
appeared to have gained several more

pounds in recent weeks. (*Daily Telegraph*, 20
August 1998)
A *fuller figure* means much the same:
Arabs and Turks are said to appreciate the
fuller figure in a woman. (A. Waugh in
Daily Telegraph, 11 July 1994)
Full-bodied is used more of wine than of
women.

full in the belly pregnant
Not merely having eaten a hearty meal. In
various forms:
He had run away with a girl with a full
belly and a father with a loaded musket.
(Monsarrat, 1978)

full treatment (the) copulation
The language of brothels which operate under
the style of MASSAGE PARLOUR, and the like:
Is it just your neck that's giving you trouble
or do you require the full treatment?
(Matthew, 1978)

fumble a manual sexual approach to another
Literally, to use your hands awkwardly,
whence to caress:
I must have carried twenty females to the
barges (and none of them worth even a
quick fumble). (Fraser, 1975)
To *fumble* means to caress a person sexually:
The dish you was trying to fumble up the
hall. (Chandler, 1958, and not describing a
waiter)
...a priest could still fumble beneath an
altar boy's cassock without the fear of
being pictured in the local paper.
(P. McCarthy, 2000)
Conversely, in the 18th century a *fumbler* was
a sexually impotent man and see FREE OF
FUMBLER'S HALL.

fumble for a check *American* to seek to
avoid payment for a shared meal etc.
You let the other person pick it up first.

fun sexual gratification from another
Originally *fun* meant a hoax or trick, whence
amusement. Now of either sex, especially in
personal sexual advertisements:
Country gentleman, 45, wealthy, tall,
educated, is looking for an attractive young
mistress. For fun. (advertisement in *Private
Eye*, April 1980)

fun and games sexual promiscuity
Literally, unconventional conduct:
She was a bit of an all-rounder. Both
sexes. General fun and games. (Davidson,
1978)

fun house *American* a brothel
One of the rarer appellations, from FUN:

I'm exaggerating, but it was splendidly furnished, with more mirrors than a fun house. (Sanders, 1986)

fun-loving hedonistic
A man who prefers wine and women to song:
The *Washington Post* had described him as 'fun-loving', which was journalese for a hearty preference for alcohol or sex. (M. Thomas, 1980)

funny¹ unwell
Literally, strange or unusual. Thus when we *feel funny* we are unlikely to be in a humorous mood. A *funny tummy* may well be the result of drinking too much alcohol.

funny² (of a male) homosexual
Literally, odd:
And you said last night he was 'that kind'... funny, kinky. (Bogarde, 1981)

funny³ mad
Again from the oddness, and usually in the euphemisms of institutions for the insane such as *funny farm*, *home*, or *place*:
Wasn't that the first picture of Pound to appear after he was let out of the funny farm? (Theroux, 1978)
... if Harold were really worried about joining his mother in the funny place, he should see a psychiatrist. (Wambaugh, 1975)

funny money cash which cannot be spent openly
Counterfeit notes or the proceeds of vice or crime:
As quick as he finds out that's funny money he'll put the finger on you. (Weverka, 1973)

furlough *American* involuntary dismissal from employment
Literally, paid leave of absence, whence suspension from duty without pay, and then dismissal. Airline pilots and cabin staff who were dismissed in the 1980s after striking were so etymologically described.

furry thing *British* a rabbit
Seamen must not mention rabbits before putting to sea under an old taboo based on the substitution by fraudulent chandlers of rabbit meat, which does not keep, for salt pork, which does.

fuzz the police
Perhaps a shortened form of *fuzzy bear*, which is noted under BEAR 2:
The fuzz—that's what they call them now, not cops any more. (Ustinov, 1971)
A *fuzz-buster* is a motor-borne radar detector:
In New York fuzz-busters were only illegal for trucks over eighteen thousand pounds. (N. Evans, 1995)

G

G anything taboo beginning with the letter G

A mild expletive, usually spelt *gee*, a shortened form of *jeez*, from *Jesus*; in America, the leader of a *gang* of convicts, or a *gallon* of whisky. A *G-man* is a federal agent, working for the US *government*. A *G-nose* sniffs narcotics, and not necessarily glue:

Behind his back, guys call him G-nose or Snowman, and it's not because he likes bad weather. (Turow, 1993)

gaffe the embarrassing statement of an unpalatable truth

Literally, a tactless remark, via the French word for a boathook:

Indeed [the remarks by the Countess of Wessex] neatly bear out our favoured definition of a 'gaffe' as a statement of the obvious by a prominent person. (*Daily Telegraph*, 9 April 2001—the Countess had been trapped into speaking openly on political matters)

gage *American* to be addicted to cheap and unpalatable whisky, chewing tobacco, or marijuana

The container so called holds a quart, which does not tell us the other derivations. Whence *gaged*, drunk, but not necessarily of whisky.

The people who don't smoke or gage, get razored in barrel-houses . . . (Longstreet, 1956)

gain to steal

Literally, to acquire something desirable. In the 15th century, *gain* meant booty.

gallant *obsolete* a woman's extramarital sexual partner

Literally, as an adjective, chivalrous:

Elspeth would be back in the saddle with one of her gallants by now. (Fraser, 1971, writing in archaic style of a profligate wife)

To *be gallant to a woman* was to copulate with one who was not your wife:

Is it the case you had been gallant to her before marriage? (Galt, 1826)

Gallantry was sexually licentious behaviour by either sex:

She was not without a charge of gallantry. (Hutchinson, *c*.1650)

See also OVER-GALLANT.

gallop (of a male) to copulate with

Using the common equine imagery:

. . . beaky, sharp-eyed old harridan, whom I wouldn't have galloped for a pension. (Fraser, 1971)

A *gallop* is a an act of copulation, or the female partner, always given a laudatory adjective:

She was a fine, rousing gallop, all sleek hard flesh. (ibid., and not of a mare)

game¹ wild animals killed primarily for human amusement

Standard English for animals hunted in the wild, birds conserved so that they can be shot, and certain large fish. *Big game* describes large mammals in Asia and Africa, in areas where they have not been hunted to extinction.

game² (the) female prostitution

The same imagery as SPORT but, for those involved, business rather than pleasure. A prostitute may be described as being *at*, *in*, or *on the game*:

I'm old at the game. (F. Harris, 1925)

They don't take only women who are in the game already. They get hold of innocent women. (Londres, 1928, in translation)

Every girl in Bayswater bangs to him if she wants to stay on the game. (G. Turner, 1968)

For Boswell it was the *noble game*. If however you were detected in adultery in Scotland, the kirk demanded a *game fee*:

Niest ye maun pay the game fee,
An' nae muir we sal trouble thee. (Liddle, 1821)

gamester¹ *obsolete* a prostitute

One who played the GAME 2:

She's impudent, my lord, and was a common gamester to the camp. (Shakespeare, *All's Well That Ends Well*)

gamester² a gambler

Gaming has meant gambling since the 16th century because most wagers turn on the outcome of *games*:

The credit of a race-horse, a gamester, and a whore, lasteth but a short time. (Torriano, 1642)

And in the ABC used by myself and my children:

G was a gamester who had but ill luck. (In those innocent days, we saw no impropriety in 'U was an usher who loved little boys'.)

gander-mooner *obsolete English* a husband copulating outside marriage

The month after the birth of a child was known as the *gander month* or *gander moon*, from 'the month during which the goose is sitting when the gander looks lost and wanders vacantly about' (*EDD*). During this period a husband was supposedly given licence to copulate with other than his wife.

gang *mainly Scottish* is used in many euphemistic phrases as an alternative to GO.

gang-bang successively to assault someone sexually
Heterosexually or homosexually:
  Mickie was gangbanged by bad convicts. (le Carré, 1996)
See also BANG 1.

garb of Eden (the) nakedness
Without even a fig leaf:
  ...usually clothed in her 'garb of Eden'— starkers. (Theroux, 1992)

garden *British* to sow mines in water from the air
Second World War usage which, by describing the operation horticulturally, avoided explicit lethal terms and adverted to the comparative safety of the operation:
  'Gardening' was arranging for the RAF to lay mines in a particular naval grid square outside a German harbour. An hour later, you could guarantee the harbour master...would send a message using that day's Enigma settings, warning ships to beware mines in naval square such-and-such. (R. Harris, 1995—this was helpful to the code-breakers at Bletchley Park)

garden gout/house see COVENT GARDEN

garden of remembrance the curtilage of a crematorium
Usually a few seats, some roses, a path, some slabs, and a lawn, all of which are soon forgotten:
  There is something comfortlessly empty about a 'garden of remembrance' after the loquacious populated feeling of a graveyard. (I. Murdoch, 1978)
An American *garden of honor* is that part of a cemetery where you can put up a plate naming a dead serviceman and a *garden crypt* a drawer for corpses facing outward:
  Crypts facing outside...are now called 'garden crypts'...'It's all part of the trend towards outdoor living,' explained the counsellor. (J. Mitford, 1963)

gardening leave suspension from office on full pay
Usually when a senior employee is instructed to stay away from his place of business, whether or not his hobbies include horticulture:

  ...given £228,000 in redundancy payments after just nine weeks on an American posting and eight months 'gardening leave'. (*Daily Telegraph*, 5 February 1994)
Less often when an employer wants to frustrate for a while an employee leaving to join a competitor:
  Kingfisher's chief executive insisted on lengthy 'gardening' leave which meant that Mr Holmes only joined M&S at the beginning of January. (*Daily Telegraph*, 8 March 2001)

gargle an alcoholic drink
Literally, a liquid suspended in the throat for medicinal purposes:
  Every night at about nine o'clock—when he heard the news music—he started getting itchy...but it wasn't the gargle he was dying for: it was this...the crack, the laughing. (R. Doyle, 1991)
The verb is perhaps obsolete:
  'Let's...gargle.' He poured drinks. (Chandler, 1939)

gas deliberately to kill or injure by poison gas
A usage about soldiers in the First World War; the chronically unfit, the gypsies, and the Jews in Nazi Germany; civilians in modern Iraq; and convicted murderers in some American states, where they may also *get the gas pipe*:
  He's not around any more to be asked. They gassed him. (Chandler, 1953)
  You may go down the toilet there, Victor, but I get the gas pipe. (Diehl, 1978— Victor would be incarcerated not incinerated)

gas-house *American* a bar selling mainly beer
For British devotees of real ale, an unusually frank description of the main quality of the product on offer. *Gassed* means drunk.

gash a woman viewed lecherously
Literally, in slang, an object obtained for nothing or something surplus to requirements:
  Maybe there's some of that Swedish gash hanging around. (Sanders, 1977)

gate¹ to confine to college as a punishment
Originally used with reference to those colleges in Cambridge and Oxford which had formidable barriers to prevent unobserved access and formidable porters in the gatehouse. An American *gated community* is an area with high security to keep intruders out rather than inhabitants in:

John Ridgway and his family lived in
one such fortress city, the 'gated
community' of the old Bradbury district.
(Fiennes, 1996)

gate² *(the) mainly American* peremptory
dismissal from employment
The way out for the last time, *given* or *shown*:
Amtrak board facing the gate. (*New York
Post*, September, 1981—they were
threatened with dismissal en bloc, not
about to board a train)

gathered to God dead
The dead person may also be *gathered to his
ancestors, his fathers* (but not *his mothers*), *Jesus,
Mohammed*, etc.:
Jane's father Patrick had been gathered to
God some six summers . . . (Fry, 1994)

gauge to kill
Literally, to measure, or a token of defiance,
which does not help us very much:
Nile and me, we fixin to gauge his daddy.
(Turow, 1996—daddy was going to be
murdered)

gay enjoying or doing something which
is the subject of a taboo
Literally, happy or cheerful. In the 19th
century a prostitute might be called a *gay girl*
or *lady*, leading the *gay life*:
I went through all the changes of a gay
lady's life. (Mayhew, 1862, quoting an old
prostitute)
Until the 1960s, *gay* was synonymous with
merry as an indication of intoxication:
It wasn't a very serious crime—getting
three amorous Kanaka girls gay on . . . gin.
(Alter, 1960)
Now standard English for homosexual:
Investigations were proceeding with a gay
club. (Davidson, 1978)

gazelles are in the garden (the) something is not quite as it should be
Said in company when someone wishes to tell
you that your nose is dripping, your trouser
zip is undone, a shoulder strap is showing, or
as the case may be.

gear anything which is the subject of
secrecy or taboo
Literally, equipment. In obsolete Scottish use
it meant smuggled spirits:
There were . . . two kinds of lads who
brought over the dutiless gear from
Holland. (Crockett, 1894)
In modern use, the male or female genitalia,
apparatus used to ingest narcotics, house-
breaking tools, etc. In America *geared up*
means drunk.

gears have slipped mind is deranged
Motoring imagery—you may move but ineffectively. The same *gears* may also *fail to
mesh*:
His gears have slipped. Not a lot, but some.
(Sanders, 1982)
It was just that the things she said and did
were highly askew. Her gears weren't quite
meshing. (Sanders, 1986)

gender-bending the deliberate adoption
of the characteristics of the opposite sex
No longer a pupil's struggles with Latin
grammar. Usually of unconventional dress or
behaviour by someone who is homosexual or
bisexual.

gender norming accepting different standards for women
A phenomenon of public-sector employment,
where favouring women over men is thought
to bring political advantage:
. . . uncongenial to most ordinary soldiers,
whose prospects of promotion are already
limited by 'gender norming'—the
deliberate skewing of test results to make
sure that more women pass. (*Sunday
Telegraph*, 11 April 1993)

general discharge *American* dishonourable dismissal from the forces
Other people get *honorable discharge*.

gentle *obsolete Irish* bewitched
Unlike the Christmas pantomime variety,
fairies were nasty creatures whom you called
the *gentle people* because it was wise to speak
kindly of them. Hawthorns were called *gentle
bushes* or *thorns*, despite their pricks, because
the fairies put spells on them. Land left
uncultivated for occupation by the fairies
was known as the *gentle place*:
All the land was excellent quality except
half an acre of rocky ground, which was
'allowed' to be a very 'gentle place'. (*Cornhill
Magazine*, February 1877)

gentleman someone in a situation or occupation the subject of vilification or
taboo
In obsolete British use, he might be poor and
involuntarily unemployed, a grim joke on the
wealthy who did not need to work:
He is a gentleman now, without seeking
the shelter of the workhouse. (O'Reilly,
1880)
The *gentlemen* were smugglers:
If the gentlemen come along don't you
look out o' window. (Egerton, 1884)
And in many phrases such as *gentleman of
fortune*, a pirate; *gentleman of the cloth*, a tailor,
punning on the clergy; *gentleman of the road*,

formerly a highway thief but in modern use, a tramp.

gentleman cow *American* a bull
19th-century prudery. Also as *gentleman ox*. For further examples see BIG ANIMAL.

gentleman friend a woman's sexual partner to whom she is not married
He does not have to be of gentle birth or indeed behave chivalrously towards her.

gentleman of color *American* a black man
Not (yet) considered offensive despite its inaccuracy in suggesting that other human skin pigmentation lacks colour:
  I used to introduce her to Mr Simon Pettibone, an elderly gentleman of color, who is the Club's manager and bartender. (Sanders, 1994)

gentlemen a lavatory exclusively for male use
Less often in a compound by the addition of *convenience* etc. than is the case with LADIES, and often shortened to *gents*:
  I always thought wearing a kilt was a pretty daft idea, but they do save time in the Gents. (*Private Eye*, August 1980)

gentry *obsolete Irish* the fairies
These malevolent creatures had to be flattered although the appellation may have been less of a compliment than they imagined, given Catholic Irish opinion of much of the Anglo-Irish Protestant *gentry*:
  Biddy was known, too, to have the power of seeing the 'gentry', beings who creep out from every mousehole and from behind every rafter the minute a family has gone to sleep. (Lawless, 1892)

geography the location of a lavatory
In genteel use, explained to a visitor, to avoid the need for exploration:
  Let me show you the GEOGRAPHY of the house. (Ross, 1956)

Georgian *British* old
Estate agents' jargon for a house usually in poor repair. The implication is that the structure was built between 1714 and 1830, when the first four Georges reigned, rather in the days of Kings George V and VI, from 1910 to 1952.

German distorted to fit Nazi dogma
In defence of their bizarre genetic theories, the Nazis were obliged to create new disciplines of *German chemistry, mathematics, science*, etc., especially where they felt a necessity to contradict the work of Jewish scientists.

Germanization was the process of adapting anything foreign to their own use, including taking fair-haired children from conquered countries for adoption and rearing in Germany:
  It is believed they were the rejected ones from the Germanization program. (Styron, 1976, of the killing of non-German children)

German Democratic Republic the totalitarian Soviet satellite state in eastern Germany
See DEMOCRAT/DEMOCRACY. It is sad to recall that Victor Klemperer, whose *Lingua Tertii Imperii* studied the abuse of language by the Nazis, should have ended his life condoning a regime as ruthless, unprincipled, and linguistically cynical as its predecessor.

get is used in many phrases, most of them vulgarisms, associated with copulation. Among those referring to male copulation are *get a leg over*: *get it, get it in, on, off, off with*, or *up*: *get in* or *into her bloomers, girdle, knickers*, or *pants*; *get lucky, round, there, or through*; *get your end in, hook into, muttons, nuts off, rocks off, way with, will(s) of*:
  No chance of 'getting off with' anyone else. (A. Clark, 2000)
  He was too drunk to get it up even with the help of a crane. (Archer, 1979)
  . . . those motel units where you're planning to get into my bloomers. (Sanders, 1982)
  Buck and Martin . . . were both trying to get in the girdles of the same sorority girls. (Turow, 1993, but presumably not simultaneously)
  He'd tell a woman *anything* to get in her pants. (Sanders, 1977)
  One of them was also boasting of having got lucky last night with a local girl. (P. McCarthy, 2000)
  Never seen her before tonight. Bet I get there, though. (Bradbury, 1959)
  We could both get our end in there. (Keneally, 1985)
  'I'd like to get my hook into her,' Davis said. (G. Greene, 1967)
  They couple like stoats, by the way, but only with men of proved bravery . . . you have to be blood-thirsty to get your muttons. (Fraser, 1977)
  Thanks for coming over, we got our rocks off. (M. Thomas, 1980)
  When he had got his wills o' her . . . (Kinloch, 1827)
Other phrases may refer to mutual copulation or by either partner, such as *get busy with, get into bed with, get it together, get laid, get your greens*, and *get your share*:

'Have you ever gotten busy with someone because Hardcore said so?' She does not like this subject, sex, at all. (Turow, 1996—she was a member of a gang of which Hardcore was the boss)
... to get voluntarily into bed with a wanted murderess. (Sharpe, 1979)
You and me'll be like the fat couples with the big bellies. We ain't never going to get it together. (Vanderhaeghe, 1997)
A place where even the most diffident foreigner can get laid. (Theroux, 1975)
She's not getting what I believe is vulgarly called her greens. (G. Greene, 1967)
'Everyone talks about what a stud he was.'... 'He was getting more than his share even then.' (M. Thomas, 1980)

Sometimes the same phrases are used of sodomy or bestiality:

I know a pillar of the community who gets it off with alligators. (Sanders, 1982—and more than once?)
... an amusing set of photographs of one man getting it off with a couple of sailors. (M. Thomas, 1980)

As a less disagreeable footnote, we may note that, in 1696, Aubrey wrote of Sir Walter Ralegh's 'getting up one of the mayds of honour'; and that, in obsolete use, to *get laid* meant no more than to get off to sleep:

I couldn't get myself laid for the noise he mead. (*EDD*)

get a marked tray *?obsolete American* to have contracted venereal disease
To avoid infection, the crockery was not used by other patients.

get a result *British* not to lose
The jargon of less literate soccer managers and players, who have problems in differentiating a draw or loss from an abandoned match:

Nobody fancied playing Leeds—it was difficult to get a result against us. (Charlton, 1996)

(Soccerspeak has its own grammar, in which the past participle replaces the past tense and an adjective becomes an adverb. Thus *The boy done good* does not imply that the player is or has been a philanthropist, as becomes apparent when even better play elicits the comment *The boy done excellent*.)

get along to grow old
A shortened from of *get along in years* or some such phrase:

He is getting' along, and we can't expect him to be nimble. (Hayden, 1902)

get away *obsolete Scottish* to die
The soul escapes from this Vale of Tears:

The Laird, puir body, has gotten awa. (Thom, 1878)

get fitted (of a female) to wear a contraceptive device
Usually on the first occasion:

... asking them if they would like to come in and, as he puts it, get fitted. (Bradbury, 1976, writing about young women in a clinic)

get it to be killed
Usually of violence in war:

Richards got it in Danang. (Theroux, 1973, writing about a soldier's death in Vietnam)

Also of wounding:

Then I realised he had got it. He doubled up. I grabbed his right arm but he screamed, 'That's where I'm hit.' (Ranfurly, 1994—diary entry of 18 March 1943)

get off[1] to achieve an orgasm
It applies to either sex:

At my age, just getting off takes my breath away. (M. Thomas, 1980)

get off[2] to see married
Usually of a woman, and a shortened form of *get off our hands* or some more charitable phrase:

You'd think she'd want to get her off all the quicker. (N. Mitford, 1949—*she* was the putative bride's mother)

get off[3] to ingest narcotics illegally
A feeling of floating is sometimes experienced. To *get on* is to become so addicted.

get off with to start a sexual relationship with
By either sex, or homosexually:

It became a sort of joke between us. To see if we could all get off with him. (R. Doyle, 1987)

get on to grow old
Standard English, being a shortened form of *get on in years*:

... there was only one of him and he was getting on. (N. Mitford, 1949)

get on your bike *obsolete* to be dismissed from employment
A reminder of the days when the majority of employees cycled to and from work:

They'll still keep him on. There's no talk at all of telling him to get on his bike. (*Private Eye*, July 1980)

get the needle *American* to be judicially killed
By lethal injection rather than electrocution:

And when have they last imposed [the death penalty]?...No one gets the needle in Manhattan. (P. Cornwell, 2000)

get the shaft *American* to receive harsh or unfair treatment
With many variations as to the offensive weapon figuratively used:
> The executives continue to take their pay and their perks while the workers get the shaft. (*New York Times*, 17 March 1992)

get the shorts to be insolvent
Or temporarily without any money:
> Suddenly he's got the shorts...he can't come up with the scratch and he's hurting. (Sanders, 1977)

get the upshoot *obsolete* to receive vaginally the male ejaculation
Another of Shakespeare's lewd puns:
> 'Then will she get the upshoot by cleaving the pin.' 'Come, come, you talk lewdly; your lips grow foul.' (*Love's Labour's Lost*)

get with child to impregnate a female
Within or outside marriage, and not merely acquiring a stepchild as part of a new marital package:
> At that time he got his wife with child. (Shakespeare, *All's Well That Ends Well*)

get your collar felt see COLLAR 2

get your feet under the table to achieve a comfortable or desired situation
The phrase was in common use of servicemen stationed far from home in the Second World War when some local family offered them frequent hospitality, often resulting from courtship with a daughter. Now also of someone wishing to get married:
> I don't think much of the girlfriend, do you? Elaine thinks she's desperate to get her feet under the table. (Helen Fielding, 1996)

ghost¹ a fictitious employee
Either an invented name on the payroll or that of someone who exists but does not work for the organization:
> As for the ghosts, some African governments have them on their payrolls. The Congo has just paid off 6,000 of them—fictitious employees...created to allow people to obtain five or ten salaries each month. (*Daily Telegraph*, 26 March 1994)

ghost² a writer whose work is published under another's name
Used by a public figure without literary expertise, and a shortened form of *ghost-writer*:

Ghost! Good God! The greatest political story in the century and they're looking for a 'ghost'. (A. Clark, 1993, referring to Mrs Thatcher's memoirs)
An American ghost-writer is said to have been hired to help with his second book. (*Daily Telegraph*, 1 December 2000)

ghost does not walk (the) *?obsolete* the cast will not be paid
Theatrical jargon, the *ghost* being the cashier. The reference is to the days when actors were less protected by a union and the only threat of striking was by Marcellus, with his partisan.

gift of your body (the) *obsolete* extramarital copulation by a female
Loan or *licence* might better describe the nature of the transaction:
> He would not, but by gift of my chaste body
> To his concupiscible lust. (Shakespeare, *Measure for Measure*)

gild to tell a lie about
Literally, to cover thinly with gold, and perhaps alluding to that misquoted cliché *gild the lily*—Shakespeare actually wrote 'to gild refined gold, to paint the lily' (*King John*). In phrases such as *gild the facts*, *proposition*, *truth*, etc.:
> 'He lied to me about the security clearance.' 'It's a bad word to use in law. I'd agree he gilded the proposition.' (M. West, 1979)

ginger homosexual
Rhyming slang on *ginger beer*, QUEER 3. Sometimes written in full:
> I can usually detect anything that's ginger beer. (B. Forbes, 1989, writing about the homosexual spy Donald Maclean)

Ginza cowboy *American* an ineffectual soldier
Ginza from the shopping centre in Tokyo and *cowboy* meaning unprofessional and slipshod:
> Most of the first American troops hopelessly attempting to stem the invasion [of South Korea] were 'Ginza cowboys'—young GIs from the occupation force in Japan, with little training and less discipline, unhappy and unready to fight. (Whicker, 1982)

gippy tummy diarrhoea
A corruption of *Egyptian tummy*, suffered by foreign visitors rather than the local inhabitants who have greater immunity to germs and bacteria in food and drink. Also as *gyppy tummy* and contracted elsewhere than in Egypt:

She knew she was in for a further attack of 'Gyppy tummy'. (Manning, 1977)

girl¹ a prostitute

Literally, a female child or servant, whence a sweetheart. Often in more explicit phrases, such as *girl of the streets*:

They turn the young Jewesses . . . into what are generically known as girls. (Londres, 1928, in translation)

The veritable girl of the streets is too 'vicious'. (ibid.)

Girlie often indicates that the women involved are being exploited for, or engaged in, prostitution, as in *girlie houses*, *parlors*, etc., which are brothels, and *girlie bars*, where prostitutes solicit custom; or in pornography, where *girlie flicks*, *magazines*, or *videos* aim to titillate men:

. . . a front for the girlie house Billie ran upstairs. (Weverka, 1973)

. . . direct traffic up to Billie's girlie parlor. (ibid.)

girl² any female less than 50 years old

The usage, often in the form of hyperbole, seeks to imply that the ageing process has been retarded or reversed:

. . . she was only a slip of a girl—what was she now—twenty-seven or eight. (J. Collins, 1981)

I first met Winston Churchill in the early summer of 1906 at a dinner party to which I went as a very young girl. (V. B. Carter, 1965—she was not in swaddling clothes but a woman of 19)

See also BOY.

girl³ *American* cocaine

Addict usage, the etymology being explained in the quotation:

Nobody called cocaine *white lady* any more, either. But the word *girl* had come to mean cocaine through a sort of perverse evolution. (McBain, 1994)

girler a male profligate

He who seeks sexual relationships with a GIRL 1 or 2:

I hear this Frank Sinatra's a fearful girler. (Theroux, 1978—fearful or fearless?)

girlfriend a female extramarital sexual partner

Not just a *friend* who is a *girl*, but of a relationship which is generally exclusive, from courtship to cohabitation, heterosexual or homosexual:

What was he so worried about? Maybe he'd got himself a girlfriend. (Kyle, 1975)

See also BOYFRIEND.

girls (room) a lavatory for exclusively female use

Usually adjacent to its male counterpart.

giro day *British* the day of the week in which the state makes payment to those without work and others thought deserving

With dependency, wholly or in part, on fiscal redistribution by government affecting some 40% of the population, it is not the day to choose to buy a stamp from any post office through which the majority of giro cash payments are made:

It's not Giro day. They're all up and about on Giro day. That's tomorrow. In the winter some of them only move once a week. (L. Thomas, 1996)

give is used occasionally *tout court*, but usually in a phrase, meaning copulation, such as *give a little*, *access to your body*, *in to*, *it*, *it to*, *out*, *the ferret a run*, *the time to*, *(up) your treasure*, *way*, *your body*, *your all*, *your body*, and *yourself*. In most cases, the female is credited with the generosity;

Maybe Bill gives at the office. (Sanders, 1982—Bill did not offer charitable donations but did not copulate with his wife)

She still give you a little? (Wambaugh, 1975, of an ex-wife: she was not paying alimony)

She decided to . . . give all soldiers who wished to take advantage of her free access to her body. (F. Richards, 1936)

I wouldn't pretend a geisha never gives in to a man she finds attractive. (Golden, 1997)

You been giving it to her, have you? (Allbeury, 1976)

A guy buys gifts for his wife because he knows she won't give out if he don't. (Sanders, 1970)

I was personally acquainted with at least two girls he gave the time to. (Salinger, 1951)

The summer solstice, when maids had given up their treasure to fructify the crops. (M. McCarthy, 1963)

Magill wasn't the first time I've given my Little All for my job. (Lyall, 1985)

I loved a man, gave him my heart and, God help me, gave him my body. (Higgins, 1976)

In small families the servants gave themselves to the sons. (Mayhew, 1862)

Occasional homosexual use:

. . . despite his decision to give himself to me, he was postponing the moment of going to bed. (Genet, 1969, in translation)

give a line to lie
As different from what you do when you
SHOOT A LINE:
> An experienced officer, sometimes I think I
> know pretty well when someone's giving
> me a line. (Turow, 1996)

give a P45 *British* to dismiss peremptorily from employment
Referring to the number of the tax form given
to the departing employee, including those
who retire or leave of their own volition:
> When nasty British journalists were
> suggesting he should be given his P45 he
> consoled himself with the knowledge that
> life...was nowhere near as bad as it was in
> the White House for his college friend Bill
> Clinton. (*Sunday Telegraph*, 8 August 1999)

give head *mainly American* to practise fellatio or cunnilingus
Neither etymological source, from the posture of the participant or the glans penis, is
attractive:
> The old bastard had his son-in-law giving
> him head in the back seat. (Diehl, 1978)

give (someone) the air to dismiss from
employment
The employee may also, if so unfortunate, be
given the BAG 2, the BOOT, the BULLET, the
breeze, the SACK, NOTICE, WARNING, the WIND
2, *his running shoes*, etc. Also, apart from *the
bag*, *the sack*, *notice*, or *warning*, the phrases
may be used of the unilateral ending of
courtship.

give the eye to look at a stranger in a
manner denoting a sexual interest
Unless it is the *evil eye*, which may cast an
unpleasant spell on the victim:
> They had been giving each other the eye on
> and off since he first saw her. (Fiennes,
> 1996)

give the finger to to make an obscene
gesture towards
The practice, of southern European origin,
seems to be encroaching on the venerable
Anglo-Saxon TWO-FINGERED message:
> 'Goodbye, you ninny!' she called, giving
> him the finger. (L. Thomas, 1994—a wife
> was deserting the husband to whom she
> had previously given her hand)

give the good news to kill
Whatever can the bad news be?
> As the boy shouted, Mark gave him the
> good news. His body disintegrated in front
> of my eyes. (McNab, 1993)

give (someone) the works to maim or
kill (a victim)

Literally, in slang, to act thoroughly:
> After a while we gave him the works,
> leaving him...up a dark street. (Mitchell,
> 1982)

give time to other commitments to be
peremptorily dismissed from employment
As with similar evasions, such as *give time to his
other interests*, a face-saving form of words for
senior employees:
> He is 'giving time to his other
> commitments' according to the board.
> (*Daily Telegraph*, 8 October 1993—he was
> dismissed after 'disappointing figures' and
> less than seven months in office)

give to God *Irish* to commit (a child) to a
priestly or monastic life
The donors are the parents and family:
> Every good Catholic family, he says, gives
> someone to God. (Burgess, 1980)

give up the ghost to die
The *ghost* is the spirit which you surrender to
heaven, or as the case may be, when it leaves
the body:
> Man dieth, and wasteth away; yea, man
> giveth up the ghost. (*Job* 14:10)
There are many obsolete dialect phrases
indicating that the dead will make no further
demand on terrestrial resources, such as the
Lancashire *give up the spoon*—you will sup no
more:
> Johnny gan up his spoon one day
> beawt havin' any mooar warnin' nor
> other folk. (Brierley, 1865, of a sudden
> death)

give your life to be killed in action
Whether or not you were conscripted:
> Some exceptional servicemen give their
> lives in remarkable operations. (J. Major,
> 1999)

given new responsibilities demoted
The *new responsibilities* are invariably less
demanding or rewarding than those relin-
quished:
> ...the two existing top managers...have
> been given new responsibilities. (*Daily
> Telegraph*, 2 September 1994, under the
> headline 'Simpson shakes up Lucas')

given rig *obsolete Scottish* a plot of land left
uncultivated to placate the devil
An example of the common practice of
seeking to mollify the devil and discourage
him from harming the rest of the farm:
> 'The Gi'en Rig', which was set apart or
> given to the Diel, to obtain his good will.
> (J. F. S. Gordon, 1880: however, our
> modern *set-aside* of agricultural land as

dictated by Brussels seems to attach no comparable benefits for the rest of the holding)

given to the drink see DRINK 1

glands *American* taboo parts of the body
Especially the breasts of a female or the testicles of a male.

Glasgow kiss *Scotland* a head-butt
Parts of the conurbation have an unenviable reputation for violence:
This is a Glasgow kiss, I said, and butted him in the face. (Barnes, 1991)

glass¹ an intoxicant
Usually wine or spirits:
The Duke ... laid the first stone out with no ceremony but three cheers and a glass. (Bathurst, 1999, of Skerryvore Lighthouse on 7 July 1841)
He, too, was happy to drink a glass. (Kyle, 1988—in fact he drank its contents)
A *glass too much* means drunkenness, and a *social glass* is alcohol taken in the company of others:
We only regretted that he could not be prevailed with to partake of the social glass. (J. Boswell, 1773—Dr Johnson had temporarily eschewed alcohol)

glass² *British* to wound (someone) in the face with a broken glass
An unfortunate example of the antisocial behaviour of some young males whose income exceeds their manners, education, intelligence, or sobriety:
People are 'bottled' and 'glassed' for catching a stranger's eye too long. (*Sunday Telegraph*, 23 January 2000)

glass ceiling a level above which certain categories of people are unlikely to be promoted
It is there but cannot be seen. Mainly used by women in a hierarchical structure:
'Don't whinge about glass ceilings,' is Prue Leith's advice to budding business women. (*Daily Telegraph*, 3 April 1995)

glass house *British* an army prison
The derivation is from the glass roof of the one at Aldershot, and perhaps advertising to the figurative heat applied to the inmates.

glean to steal
Literally, to pick up ears of corn left by the reapers. Usually of pilfering small articles.

globes *obsolete* the breasts of an adult female

Of obvious derivation and doubtful taste:
The Graceful peak where beauty sits,
The swelling globes, the pouting teats.
(Pearsall, 1969, quoting a verse from 1860)

glove money *obsolete* a bribe
By ancient custom, you gave gloves to anyone who had done you a favour or might be persuaded to do so, concealing the bribe inside. Sir Thomas More, when Lord Chancellor of England, kept the gloves which Mrs Croaker gave him but returned the hidden £40. We should not then be surprised that, despite the uncouthness of his language, he was later beatified.

glow *obsolete* to sweat
A usage of women and horses, from the visual effect on the skin. Sweat remains the subject of taboo because of the odour secreted from the armpits and the crotch.

glow on a state of mild drunkenness
The result of the associated sweating and perhaps alluding to the feeling of exhilaration:
I didn't feel like getting a glow on. Either I would get really stiff or stay sober. (Chandler, 1953)

glue *American* to pilfer
The object sticks to the hands of the thief.

go¹ to die
And its northern British alternative, *gang*, alone or in many phrases:
... he said 'I think I'm going, Peter.' He didn't speak again. (Manning, 1977)
Thus a sailor may *go aloft*, punning on the ascent of the rigging; a Scot might *go corbie*, from the crow, the messenger which brought bad tidings or did not return; cattle might *go down the nick*, to a slaughterhouse; an Egyptologist might *go forth in his cerements* (the waxed wrappings alluded to by Stringer to in Powell's *Dance to the Music of Time*); and all of us will ultimately *go away, for a Burton, forward, home, into the ground, off, off the hooks, on, out, over, round land, the wrong way, to a better place* (often specified in detail according to the delectations or aspirations of the deceased), *to grass, to heaven, to our rest, to our reward, to ourselves, to the wall, under, west*, etc.:
Not since my wife, Miriam ... went away. (Diehl, 1978—Miriam had died, not gone on holiday)
Hadna Pyotshaw grippit ma airm he was a gone corbie. (F. Gordon, 1885)
Looks like they's all goin' to go down t'nick. (Herriot, 1981, of a herd of cattle)
Comrades-in-arms who long ago went for a Burton beer ... (Maclean, 1998)

... leaving me to tell the story of his 'life's work' alone, while he went forward to receive the crown of righteousness laid up for him in another world. (E. M. Wright, 1932—the *life's work* was Joseph Wright's *English Dialect Dictionary*)

... he is not sick, that he doesn't have to go into the ground with her. (T. Harris, 1988)

I was assured yesterday that Lady Duncannon was gone off, surely it cannot be true, do write me word that I may contradict it. (Foreman, 1998, quoting a letter written in January, 1785—her ladyship had died but not, so far as we know, putrefied)

He went round land at las', an' was found dead in his bed. (Quiller-Couch, 1893)

... a chronic state of diarrhoea under which the animal wastes away and dies. That is what is perfectly understood as going the wrong way. (*EDD*, from western England)

He wanted to know who'd be paying Mr Torrance's bill now he's gone to his final reward. (McBain, 1994)

I expect he's gone to his rest long since, poor man. (P. D. James, 1972)

Now Sam's gone to the great massage parlor in the sky. (Sanders, 1977)

But it's a glory to know he has gone to his reward. (Sanders, 1980)

He had once said to Victoria that [Prince Albert] did not cling to life (as she did) and that, if he had a severe illness, he would go under. (Pearsall, 1969—Prince Albert died of typhoid caught at Windsor Castle, although Victoria preferred to think it was from mortification at the sexual behaviour of their son Bertie, of which more under FALL 1)

In obsolete use to *go right* was to die and go to heaven:

I knowed 'e went right, for a says t'I, a says, 'I 'a sin a angel'. (*EDD*)

go² to become bankrupt

Alone, or in phrases, some of which are shared with death. *Go at staves* was what happened to a barrel when the hoops were removed; *go for a Burton* did not mean you had slipped out for a pint; the individual or firm might also *go crash, smash, to the wall, under, west*, etc.:

If s shopkeeper conducted his affairs upon such a principle he would go smash. (Flanagan, 1988)

The American Bankruptcy Reform Act of 1978 specifies in successive chapters procedures for the protection of creditors or businesses, of which Chapter 11, which permits continued trading under court protection during insolvency, is perhaps the most common. A corporation claiming such relief is said to go or *file Chapter Eleven* (or as the case may be), indicating that it is insolvent:

The Lelands had first approached him in the summer of 1921, six months before they were driven to file Chapter Eleven. (Lacey, 1986—using the phrase anachronistically)

go³ to urinate or defecate

A shortened form of *go to the lavatory* or *bathroom* etc., with irregular conjugation in the perfect tense—I go, I went, I have been. As with GO 1 and 2, *tout court*, or in numerous phrases, such as *go about your business, for a walk (with a spade* etc.), *on the coal* (for a blacksmith, to ammoniate it), *over the heap* (for a collier), *places, round the corner, to ground* (in the open), *to the toilet* (or whatever term is used for a lavatory), *upstairs*, etc.:

... especially Lally who was longing to 'go' as much as we were. (Bogarde, 1978)

They should go about their private business one hundred yards from the ordinary encampment. (F. Harris, 1925)

I'd gone for a walk... You know, with a spade. (Manning, 1978)

What am I do to? I can't follow them when they go places. (Manning, 1977)

'Going to ground' is a phrase well known to the surgeons in the Birmingham hospitals. (*EDD*—meaning defecation)

... he went to the toilet down a bit of hosepipe through Miss Kilmartin's car window. (R. Doyle, 1993—referring to a child urinating)

'Do you want to go upstairs, Emma?' she asked... 'I'll come too,' said Louis... 'You can't go where she's going. (Bradbury, 1959)

The obsolete *going* was human excrement:

No man shall bury and dung or goung within the liberties of this city. (Stowe, 1633, referring to London)

go abroad *obsolete British* to accept a challenge to a duel

In the 19th century duelling was illegal in Britain but not in France. Not to accept a challenge made in Britain by fighting in France was considered cowardly by some:

I have called frequently today and I find that you are not going abroad. (Kee, 1993, quoting a letter dated 13 July 1881 from O'Shea to Parnell, whom he had challenged to a duel in Lille. Parnell wisely ignored him)

go again *obsolete* to reappear after death

But not perhaps in the form we might choose, if consulted:

... but Vauther went agen, in the shape of a gurt voul theng. (*Exmoor Courtship*, 1746, quoted in *EDD*)

go all the way to copulate after a series of sexual familiarities
Teenage usage.

go (any) further to proceed to more intimate sexual activity
Usually in the negative by a female who seeks to prevent copulation:
> ... though I wouldn't 'let him go any further' as we used to say, I did like the kiss more than I've liked anything for years. (Read, 1979)

go-around an aborted aircraft landing
A pilot only aborts a landing when he is uncertain that he can land safely, the decision being often reached on the final approach due to obstruction on the runway, bad weather, or some other danger:
> An average of 10 go-arounds are necessary at Heathrow every week. (*Daily Telegraph*, 16 October 1998)

go at yourself to masturbate
Not self-criticism:
> It's a sin when you're wide awake and going at yourself. (McCourt, 1997)

go beyond friendship to copulate with
The implication is that sexual partners cannot be friends:
> This was no more than a strong friendship but unfortunately, on one occasion, it went beyond friendship. (*Daily Telegraph*, 10 December 1999)

go bush *obsolete* to become mentally unbalanced
A result of loneliness and unfamiliar conditions:
> Like many British colonials in isolated outposts, he found his mind wandering up eccentric avenues: one of the signs of a man about to 'go bush'. (French, 1995)
See also GO NATIVE.

go case to work as a prostitute
From CASE 1, although the woman need not work in a brothel:
> I was green. It took me a week to realize that I was the only girl in the club not 'going case'. (Irvine, 1986—she was in a night club, not pregnant)

go down¹ to be killed
Formerly, by hanging, when you had to GO UP 1 first:
> The lasses and lads stood on the walls, crying 'Hughie the Graeme, thou'se ne're gae down.' (W. Scott, 1803)

Now of being shot:
> All we're looking to do is pull the remains of the [SAS] team out before anyone else goes down. (Ryan, 1999)

go down² to go to prison
See DOWN. The usage may also refer to the descent to the cells from the dock:
> I often heard talk about criminals ... If they got you, then you went down. (Simon, 1979)

go down³ to crash
Not just ceasing to be airborne:
> A plastic card in the seat pocket in front of me read: *In case of an Emergency* ... 'Forget that, muffin. If we go down, we're history.' (Theroux, 1993)
A plant crashing in the sea may be said to *go in*.

go down on see DOWN ON

go down the tube(s) to fail
Not a reference to a visit to the lamentable London subway system but from the mechanism through which carcasses were conveyed in the meat business, especially in Chicago:
> Does she know the rice farm's going down the tube? (le Carré, 1996)

go Dutch see DUTCH TREAT

go for your tea *Irish* to be murdered
A usage and practice of the IRA, of which the etymology is unclear:
> 'If they've got names it'll be a leak from over the water. Some loose-mouthed bastard will be going for his tea.' She knew the euphemism for execution. (Strong, 1994)

go into (of a male) to copulate with
When Baroness Burdett-Coutts, a friend of Queen Victoria, married a man 40 years her junior, the *Pink 'Un* published the following announcement:
> AN ARITHMETICAL PROBLEM: How many times does twenty-seven go into sixty-eight and what is there over? (quoted by F. Harris, 1925)

go into the streets to become a prostitute
From the open soliciting:
> While my boy lived, I couldn't go into the streets to save my life or his own. (Mayhew, 1862)

go native to adopt the prevalent attitudes of an institution
Falling in line with the lifestyle of the indigenous peoples. The phrase is used of politicians whose enthusiasm and fresh ideas are thwarted by bureaucrats:

When a Minister is so house-trained that he automatically sees everything from the Civil Service point-of-view, this is known in Westminster as the Minister having 'gone native'. (Lynn and Jay, 1981)

More generally of anyone surrendering to a prevailing dogmatism:

[Bishop] Wienken went native to the extent of being sharply disowned by Cardinal Michael Faulhauber. (Burleigh, 2000—the Bishop had appeared to approve Nazi euthanasia in 1940 and was later to become involved in negotiations with Eichmann)

go off¹ to achieve a sexual orgasm

Of both sexes:

There was an old whore of Montrose Who'd go off any time that she chose. (*Playboy's Book of Limericks*)

go off² to lose quality or putrefy

Standard English of food etc. and other figurative uses:

But no shell had hit near Sergeant Porter. He had just gone off for no reason. (H. Brown, 1944—the sergeant had not deserted but had lost his nerve)

go on the box *obsolete British* to be absent from work through illness

Long before television, this *box* was a sick club, from the container into which the weekly subscriptions were placed. Also as *go on the club*, being a shortened form of *sick club*.

go out with to have an exclusive sexual friendship or relationship with

Standard English, even though the parties may remain indoors. The phrase is also used by children pre-puberty of playground preferences among the opposite sex.

go over to defect

The term describes anyone changing one allegiance for another, whether in religion, espionage, or politics:

Evangelical of course. No, I was glad that Wilfred didn't go over. (P. D. James, 1975—Wilfred was a clergyman)

go over the hill to escape or desert

Also as *go over the side* for mariners, and *go over the wall*:

I guess he figured you'd gone over the hill. (Deighton, 1982, referring to an army absentee)

[Philby] didn't go over the wall until he had to. (Allbeury, 1981—Philby was a traitor)

go slow *British* a deliberate failure to complete the work allocated

A bargaining tactic which may in the short term cause an employer loss without corre-

sponding hardship to his employees. See also SLOWDOWN 1.

go south to lose value or fail

From the direction of the line on a graph. Financial jargon and some general use:

They had bought it from an actor whose career had gone south. (Grisham, 1999)

go state *American* as a criminal to give evidence against an accomplice

It would never do to turn QUEEN'S EVIDENCE in a republic:

Told me he gone state and all how he been goin on. (Turow, 1996—a witness was explaining why she had changed her story)

go steady to court to the exclusion of others

A pleasant, if dated, usage:

Either this was a popular spot for lovers or some people had been going steady for a very long time. (Bryson, 1995)

go the other way to become or act as a homosexual

Other than heterosexual:

'Well, you think I'd ever go the other way?' 'No … Not you, the old Davenport cocksman.' (Sohmer, 1988)

See also the OTHER WAY.

go the whole way to copulate

After preliminary fondling:

If it had gone the whole way and the man had aroused her senses, the poor child was in a fix. (M. McCarthy, 1963)

go through¹ to copulate with

Literally, to experience, use up, or transfix, from which etymologists can take their pick:

… nudging each other in the ribs and saying 'I wouldn't mind going through that on a Saturday night.' (Lodge, 1988—men were ogling a young woman)

go through² to kill

Literally, in slang, to use up:

[He] went through two of my people to get here. (J. Patterson, 1999—he killed them)

go to bed with to copulate with

Of either sex, and of homosexuality, although not necessarily in or on a bed:

Years ago she had gone to bed with him for a few weeks. (Amis, 1978—you might suppose they were a pair of invalids)

'The idea of going to bed with Donald,' he spluttered. (Boyle, 1979—the splutterer was Guy Burgess)

go to heaven in a string *obsolete* to be hanged

The fate of 16th-century English Roman Catholics when dynastic changes prevented their continued burning of Protestants:

> Then may he boldly take his swing,
> and go to Heaven in a string. (T. Ward, 1708, quoted in *ODEP*)

go to it *obsolete* to copulate
Literally, to set about a task (as in its use as a slogan in 1940 urging the British populace to work harder):

> The fitchew nor the soiled horse goes to't
> With a more riotous appetite.
> (Shakespeare, *King Lear*)

go to Paul's for a wife *obsolete* to seek a prostitute
Prostitutes used to frequent the fashionable walks around London's St Paul's cathedral, as Falstaff was aware:

> I bought him in Paul's ... an I could get me but a wife in the stews. (Shakespeare, *2 Henry IV*)

go to the Bay *obsolete British* to be transported to Australia as a prisoner
The destination was Botany Bay in New South Wales:

> 35 per cent are known to have been charged with as many as four earlier offences before they 'napped a winder' or 'went to the Bay'. (R. Hughes, 1987, rebutting the myth that other than hardened offenders were hanged or transported)

go to the fat farm *American* to be obese
Not visiting a piggery:

> .... an insecure girl, unfondly remembered by schoolmates as having 'gone to the fat farm'. (*Daily Telegraph*, 27 January 1998)

go to the wall to fail or be destroyed
It may apply to corporate bankruptcy, to death, and to any enterprise which does not succeed:

> The progeny of those who made the grade flourished; those found wanting went swiftly to the wall. (N. Evans, 1998)

go up[1] *obsolete* to be killed by hanging
Especially in 19th-century America. Occasionally also of natural death:

> You'd better give it up if you don't want to go up. (Cookson, 1969—the thing to be given up was working with lead paint)

go up[2] to be under the influence of illegal narcotics
When you be come UP 2, but may GO DOWN 2 if you are caught.

go up the river *American* to be sentenced to jail
Referring to the location of the penal institutions with relation to New York City, New Orleans, and elsewhere:

> The long-term prisoners waiting to go up the river ... (L. Armstrong, 1955)

go with to copulate with outside a permanent relationship
More often used of women than men despite the reciprocity:

> [Keeler] hurt [Rachman] terribly when she went with other men. (S. Green, 1979)

go wrong *obsolete* (of a woman) to copulate outside marriage
Doubly blameworthy if she were also impregnated:

> 'When I was sixteen,' she said, 'I went wrong.' (Mayhew, 1862)

goat-house *obsolete* a brothel
A *goat* was a promiscuous male, from the Grecian god Pan and the general reputation of billy goats:

> [Baldwin defaced] pictures of the Welshman in his photograph collection, ensuring his devilish resemblance to 'the Goat' nickname. (Graham Stewart, 1999—the Welshman was the promiscuous David Lloyd George)

To *play the goat* was to act lasciviously, although to *play the giddy goat* is merely to behave stupidly.

gobble to practise fellatio on
Usually in phrases using MEAT 2 imagery or in explicit slang:

> If he pays some chippie to gobble his pork ... (Diehl, 1978)
> I had her gobbling my pecker behind the lifeboats. (M. Thomas, 1980)

Also as a noun:

> ... the search for a half-decent English gobble has been my Holy Grail. (Blacker, 1992)

God's child *obsolete* an idiot
The defect was often attributed to divine agency rather than the consanguinity of the parents:

> Such as him were called 'God's children'. (O'Reilly, 1880)

God's own medicine a narcotic or hallucinogen
Opium was so named in the 19th century, when it was freely available both for infants and for adult use. Now mainly referring to morphine when used illegally, and abbreviated to *gom*.

God's waiting room a retirement institution for geriatrics
Making a charitable assumption about posthumous selection:

> In a private nursing home—one of those
> places they call God's waiting room.
> (B. Forbes, 1986)

Parts of Florida also share the appellation.

goer a sexually promiscuous woman
A male usage, perhaps adverting to an old car,
or *banger*, which is still roadworthy and starts
when needed:

> Babes were divided into those termed 'a
> goer'—a woman who looked as if she'd
> be sexually available and willing—and
> those known to be sexually active.
> (*Daily Telegraph*, 21 December 1995—a
> *babe* is a young female working in a
> male environment: there appeared
> to be no third category, chaste virgins)

A *party-goer*, whether male or female, is a
gregarious hedonist.

gold-brick *American* a shirker
A common 19th-century trick was known as
the *gold brick swindle*, whereby prospectors
sought to sell base metal to the unwary by its
colour. Whence trickery of any kind, and then
specifically those who feigned illness in the
army to avoid duty:

> The gold brick swindle is an old one but
> crops up constantly. (*National Police Gazette*,
> 1881)
> Tarrant was the greatest goldbrick on the
> base. (Deighton, 1982)

gold-digger¹ *obsolete* a person employed
to remove human excrement
Sardonic humour, as with HONEY. Also known
as a *gold-finder*; in America a *goldbrick* was a
turd.

gold-digger² a woman who consorts
with a man because he is rich
Working a single, but often exhausted, vein, a
large difference in age being a usual feature:

> If she was a gold-digger, a common
> accusation in these cases, picking a man
> with eight children…was not an obvious
> choice. (Forster, 1997—the master of the
> house was 46 and the servant he married
> was 24)
> This [case] was never about a gold
> digger seeking money. (*Daily Telegraph*,
> 29 September 2000—as the former
> stripper was 26 years old and the
> man owning a fortune of
> $1.6 billion was 89, it was clearly
> love at last sight)

gold-plating excessive bureaucratic regulation and enforcement

Literally, no more than adding an attractive
gloss to something. Under English common
law, everything is legal unless express pro-
hibited by law, when the law must be obeyed
and enforced. The imposed European system
operates on the converse principle whereby,
under a process known as *tolérance*, unnecessary or intrusive regulations are suitably
modified or ignored:

> What they did object to was 'gold
> plating'—Britain adding so much to
> European Directives and enforcing them
> with such zeal that British companies are
> at a disadvantage to competitors with less
> rigorous enforcement. (*Daily Telegraph*, 11
> March 1996)

golden large or excessive
In the financial jargon phrases *golden goodbye*
or *handshake*, a payment made in lieu of
damages when an employee is dismissed
before his contract expires; a *golden hallo*, to
induce someone to join a firm or match his
benefits accrued in the post he is leaving;
golden handcuffs, to prevent his leaving to join a
competitor; a *golden parachute*, which ensures
a soft landing if he is dismissed; and, less
often but with more wit, a *golden retriever* to
induce a former employee to return:

> I would not be looking for a golden
> goodbye—why should I deserve that?
> (*Sunday Telegraph*, 28 January 2001, quoting
> the chief executive of Marks & Spencer)
> They have something called a 'Golden
> Handshake'. If they want to get rid of a
> foreigner they offer him a chunk of money
> as compensation for the loss of his career.
> (Theroux, 1977)
> It gives employees an equity-type stake in
> the bank as well as acting as a form of
> 'golden handcuffs'. (*Daily Telegraph*, 18
> March 1994)
> Research director Peter Jensen got
> £252,000 including a £186,000 golden hello
> when he arrived in January. (*Daily Telegraph*,
> 27 August 1998—this did not prevent the
> shares in his employer falling from 177 to
> 35 pence within a year)
> But when a person fell from a position of
> influence, there was no safety net, no
> golden parachute. (Sohmer, 1988)

For *golden bowler* see BOWLER HAT.

golden ager *American* a geriatric
Not someone living in a mythical *golden age*,
but an elderly person supposedly enjoying the
GOLDEN YEARS.

golden boy someone unfairly favoured
or marked for undue promotion
Also as *blue-eyed boy* or FAIR-HAIRED BOY:

> Horton graduated from golden boy
> tipped for the top, to the man the old

guard loved to hate. (*Sunday Telegraph*, 7 January 1996)

golden years (the) old age
Referring not to the cost of increasing medical treatment but rather to ripened corn:
> They are addressed as 'senior citizens' and congratulated on their attainment of the 'golden years'. (Jennings, 1965)

golly a mild oath
Perhaps the commonest corruption of *God*, a usage anticipating by some 40 years Florence Upton's *Golliwog* books, in which the black hero came to the rescue of the Dutch Dolls. Other such corruptions included *goles*, *golles*, *gollin*, *golls*, *gom*, *gommy*, *goms*, *gomz*, *goom*, *gull*, and *gum*, of which *by gum* is a lone survivor.

gone¹ pregnant
Usually indicating the period since conception:
> 'What's he going to do about our Doreen who is six months gone? (Tidy, in *Private Eye*, March 1981)

gone² drunk or under the influence of narcotics
Rational behaviour and comprehension have departed:
> She was so 'gone' by the time I finished clearing up...(Bogarde, 1981—she had taken drugs)

gone about besotted with
From the symptoms of infatuation. Still common as *gone on* but *gone over* is obsolete:
> Mr Hawkins was *fearfully* gone about Francis Fitzpatrick—oh, the tender looks he cast at her. (Somerville and Ross, 1894)

gone walkabout been stolen
The practice of Australian aborigines. The phrase may be used of anything from minor thefts to complex frauds, where funds may have been moved through various accounts:
> ...the whole of the money put in for the development of the DeLorean Car had disappeared—or 'gone walkabout'. (Cork, 1988)

goner a person about to die or who has just died
Also spelt phonetically:
> I thought she was a goner, I'm afraid. You've never seen anyone so pale. (Fry, 1994)
> Better say your prayers. If we crash, you're a gonner. (Manning, 1962)

good folk *obsolete* the fairies
These malevolent creatures had to be flattered, especially in Ireland and Scotland where they were also called the *good neighbours* or *people*:
> The guidfolk are not the best of archers, since the triangular flints with which the shafts of their arrows are barbed do not always take effect. (Hibbert, 1822)
> If ye ca's guid neighbours, guid neighbours we will be;
> But if you ca's fairies, we'll fare you o'er the sea. (Ayrshire ballad, 1847)
> ...so young that you were in girl's skirts lest you be carried away by the good people. (Flanagan, 1988—until the 19th century Irish fairies, in search of baby boys, were thus duped)

good friend(s) having an ongoing extra-marital sexual relationship
A journalistic evasion when reporting such a condition might be considered defamatory:
> ...he mustn't say *good friends*, that was always taken as a euphemism for extreme intimacy. (Price, 1974)
See also FRIEND.

good lunch (a) a meal at which a large amount of alcohol is drunk
The quantity or quality of the food in less important:
> At Prime Minister's questions, the Speaker selected to ask a Supplementary Question a Tory backbencher, 'returning from a good lunch' (as it was put to me). (Cole, 1995)
See also DINE WELL.

good time a sexual experience with a stranger
A conventional suggestion by a soliciting prostitute, or *good-time girl*:
> I'll try to give you a good time. (F. Harris, 1925)
Less often the approach is by a male:
> The man was offering her a drink and a good time in Spanish. (Theroux, 1979)

good voyage *obsolete British* the use of a warship for commercial freight
Until the beginning of the 20th century, naval Captains accepted civilian cargo in their ships, especially to remote destinations or where there was a risk of piracy, pocketing the cash:
> The practice known as freight or 'good voyages' was to Mr Pepys's eyes the most pernicious of all. (Ollard, 1974)

goodbye peremptory dismissal from employment
It is the employer who initiates the farewell:
> ...since released, not surprisingly, to pursue 'other business interests', the

banking euphemism for goodbye. (*Private Eye*, April 1988)

goods (the) something illicit or harmful in your possession

Physically, of stolen property or illegal narcotics; figuratively of any information of a damaging or shameful nature, which can be used in extortion or coercion:

> But what if a twist exactly like her was a suspect, and you had to get the goods on her? (Sanders, 1980)

goof *American* a habitual user of illegal narcotics

Literally, a stupid person, whence many uses to do with unsophistication and incompetence. A *goofball* is the addict or the narcotic and *goofed* means under narcotic influence:

> Clearest of all was that solitary *hoo* of the goofball in the crowd. (Theroux, 1978)
> Goofballs are one of the barbiturates laced with benzedrine. (Chandler, 1953)

goolies the testicles

If Eric Partridge had served in India rather than on the Western Front, he might have known that the derivation both of the game of marbles, *gully*, and of this euphemistic use came from the Hindi *goli*, a ball:

> Then when he's off guard you give it to him in the goolies. (Sharpe, 1974)

To discourage Iraqis from castrating their prisoners in the 1930s, the Royal Air Force issued *goolie chits*:

> Aircrew carried special 'goolie chits' offering rewards for the sparing of their private parts in the event of capture. (*Daily Telegraph*, 7 March 2001)

goon squad members of a police or military unit capable of acting violently or ruthlessly

A *goon* was, in dialect, a simpleton, whence a German guard in a prisoner-of-war camp:

> Either Jericho has been taken and has told the goon squad everything, or he's up to something. (Forsyth, 1994—Jericho was an informant in Iraq)

goose¹ *obsolete* a prostitute

The common avian imagery. If she were a *Winchester goose*, she had syphilis, from the insalubrious church-owned property in south London where the meaner prostitutes lived:

> ...but that my fear is this
> Some galled goose of Winchester would hiss. (Shakespeare, *Troilus and Cressida*)

goose² to pinch the buttocks of

A male, or less often female, sexual approach, as delicate as a nip from the bird's beak, or as indelicate:

> Leroy goosed the girl from behind, causing an alarmed but happy squeak to emerge from her lips. (J. Collins, 1981)
> They chivvied each other and laughed a lot. Once she goosed him. (Sanders, 1982)

gooseberry the devil

Not obsolete because the use survives in the expression *play gooseberry*, to play the devil with a courting couple by keeping them company when they would rather be left alone:

> Th'match ther wur betwixt a tailor and owd gooseberry. (Axon, 1870)

gooseberry bush SEE PARSLEY BED

gooseberry lay *American* a crime easily carried out

A *gooseberry* was a washing line, from which clothes might be stolen as easily as taking berries off a bush, whence to *gooseberry*, to pilfer clothing, and then any similar theft.

Gordon Bennet(t) a mild oath

For *God*, from the American press proprietor who sponsored H. M. Stanley in his African travels and balloon races, not the London stipendiary magistrate who came to prominence some decades later.

governess *obsolete* a female bawd

The 19th-century brothel she ran brought back memories of the schoolroom:

> The most prominent of the 'governesses' who ran brothels for flagellants was Mrs. Theresa Berkley of 28 Charlotte Street. (Pearsall, 1969)

governmental relations *American* bribery or coercion

Not just voting, paying your taxes, and being told what to do by officials:

> Governmental relations (lobbying) was repulsive but paid so well every D.C. firm had entire wings of lawyers greasing the skids. (Grisham, 1998)

grab¹ *obsolete Irish* to accept a tenancy after another's eviction

During the agrarian disturbances of the 19th century, to accept a tenancy of a farm after the eviction of a previous occupier was considered by nationalists as treacherous:

> But Mick Tobin, now...he was prepared to grab. (Flanagan, 1988—Mick was later killed by his ejected predecessor)

grab² to steal

The common imagery which links seizing with theft:

> 'How are you going to get the money?' I asked. 'Grab it. Steal it,' he said. (L. Thomas, 1977)

Grace of Wapping (the) *obsolete London*
the killing of a pirate
Wapping lies on the north bank of the
Thames where a port used to be:
> ...the tide lapping Wapping Old Stairs,
> where pirates were taken and tied to the
> piles at low water until three tides—the
> Grace of Wapping—had flowed over them.
> (P. D. James, 1994—they were probably
> killed before they were tied up)

graft¹ *obsolete* to cuckold
The imagery is of figuratively *grafting*, or
implanting, the horns of cuckoldry on the
victim's head.

graft² bribery
Literally, hard work, from the original meaning, digging a grave. Now standard English.

grandstand *American* to accentuate a difficulty in order to win praise
Where the spectators whom you wish to
impress are located, but the expression is
not confined to sport:
> I relied on you to grandstand enough to let
> her get wise to you. (Chandler, 1958)
A *grandstand play*, is such behaviour:
> ...kept details to yourself. A real
> grandstand play. (Diehl, 1978—a
> policeman had tried to solve a case on his
> own)

granny farming a form of vote rigging
Registering votes by proxy on behalf of
muddled and deceived geriatrics:
> In a process known as 'granny farming',
> they persuaded elderly and house-bound
> voters to sign a proxy form, without telling
> them that they would be used for the Social
> Democrats. (*Daily Telegraph*, 11 March, 2001)

grape (the) wine
Standard English since the 17th century. The
obsolete punning *grape-shot* meant drunk but
a *whiff of grapeshot* was something more
debilitating—see WHIFF OF.

grass¹ to inform against
Rhyming slang on *grass in the park*, coppers'
nark:
> 'Favours. Grassing.' Blamires said. 'I've
> nobody to grass on.' (Kyle, 1975)
A *grass* is an informer:
> There's a copper in that boy, you mark my
> words. He's a natural grass. (le Carré, 1986)

grass² marijuana
Shortened form of *grass-weed* in common use
and occasionally as *green grass*:
> Frank was restive about the marijuana.
> 'You surely wouldn't make trouble about a
> scrap of grass.' (Davidson, 1978)

> We are smoking too, man, you know?
> Grass. Green grass. You know what I mean?
> (Simon, 1979)

grass widow a woman of marriageable
age separated for an extended period
from her husband
The derivation is from the *grass* of the hill
stations to which wives were sent during the
Indian hot season, or a corruption of *grace
widow*? Originally it might mean a mistress or
an unmarried woman who had had a child:
> Grass widows and their fatlings to lie in
> and nurse here. (R. Hunt, 1896)
If the husband was away for long periods,
there might be an inference that the *grass
widow* was promiscuous:
> ...here husband having run off on her, so
> that now she was no more than a grass
> widow. (Atwood, 1996—for which loss she
> found nightly consolation in the arms of
> her lodger)
Some humorous use of husbands who regularly absent themselves to play sport:
> When [Denis Thatcher] played cricket for
> the old boys, Margaret washed up the tea
> things in the clubhouse like any other grass
> widow of the period. (*Sunday Telegraph*, 7
> May 1995)

gratify *obsolete Scottish* to bribe
Literally, to please or indulge:
> People were still obliged to gratify the
> keepers for any access they had to visit or
> minister to their friends. (Wodrow, 1721)

gratify your passion(s) to copulate
A venerable but perhaps obsolete usage, and
as *gratify his* or *your (amorous) desires* or *works*:
> He cannot afford to employ professional
> women to gratify his passions. (Mayhew,
> 1862)
> She did gratify his amorous works.
> (Shakespeare, *Othello*)
To *gratify yourself* is to masturbate:
> ...he never let his sexual feelings for his
> fellow passenger get the better of him, nor
> ever 'gratified himself in an unnatural
> way'. (Winchester, 1998)
Whence *gratification*, copulation:
> ...since the Roman Church regarded such
> errors as venal... I had much gratification
> at little expense. (Graves, 1940)

grave (the) death
Standard English figurative use:
> There will be sleeping enough in the grave.
> (Franklin, 1757)
In obsolete Scottish use, the *gravestone gentry*
were the dead:
> My bed is owre amang yon gravestane
> gentry. (A. Murdoch, 1873)

gravy *American* an intoxicant
SAUCE 1 is much more common.

gravy train (the) supplemental benefits received gratuitously
There is a continuing excess of the pleasant but unnecessary complement to the main dish for those who *ride* this vehicle:

> The gravy train has not stopped entirely for Grub Street hacks. (*Private Eye*, July 1981)

graze to steal and eat food in a supermarket
Like cattle in a pasture, you eat what you pick up between the rows and pass the checkout desk with empty hands and a full stomach. In obsolete use, to *graze on the plain* or *common* was to be dismissed from employment as a house servant:

> He turnde hir out at durs, to grase on the playne. (Heywood, 1546)

grease¹ to bribe
The usage predates OIL, of which it is a euphemistic synonym. Either *tout court*, as a verb or noun, or in phrases such as *grease hands, palms, paws, the skids, the system*, etc.:

> With gold and grotes they grease my hands,
> In stede of ryght that wrong may stand. (Skelton, 1533—a *groat* was a silver coin worth four pence)
> Every D.C. firm had entire wings of lawyers greasing the skids. (Grisham, 1998)
> He lacked the financial resources with which Oskar greased the system. (Keneally, 1982)

grease² *American* to kill
The allusion is perhaps to converting the body into a fatty substance, or a corruption of CREASE:

> If... he makes any threatening movement—anything at all—grease him. (Sanders, 1973)

greased *American* drunk
Things may indeed seem to run more smoothly for a time:

> You come over early and we can get greased before the mob arrives. (Sanders, 1982—they were hosting a party, not sun-bathing)

great *obsolete* pregnant
A shortened form of *great with child*:

> O silly lassie, what wilt thou do,
> If thou grow great they'll heez thee high. (Herd, 1771—society would reward her not with a home of her own and a weekly stipend, but with death by hanging)

Also as *great-bellied*:

> 'Tis strange to hear how long they will dance, and in what manner, over stools, forms, tables; even great-bellied women sometimes (and yet never hurt their children) will dance so long that they can stir neither hand nor foot. (R. Burton, 1621, writing about St Vitus' Dance)

great and the good (the) *British* people comprising or approved by the political establishment
An often derogatory use by those who aspire to, but do not achieve, entry to the charmed circle:

> Maynard, astute businessman... Maynard, supporter of charity... Maynard, the great and the good. (D. Francis, 1985, describing a rogue conspiring to be knighted)

great certainty (the) death
Also as the *great change, leveller, out, perhaps* or, for the dying Charles II, *secret*, before or after expressing concern about 'poor Nellie's' future:

> 'The Great Certainty looms,' said Mr Flawse. (Sharpe, 1978)
> Here was a beloved relative and perishing fellow-creature, on the eve of the great change... (W. Collins, 1868)
> I thought this is the end, China, and you're going to find the Great Perhaps. (Fraser, 1992)

Great Game the 19th-century rivalry between Britain and Russia for empire and influence in Asia
In retrospect, the players were more amateur than professional:

> ... William Moorcroft, the self-appointed British spy who penetrated Central Asia to play some of the opening moves in the Great Game. (Dalrymple, 1993)

great majority the dead
A shortened form of the *great majority of souls*, who are presumed to be in heaven, limbo, or elsewhere:

> Life is the desert, life the solitude. Death joins us to the great majority. (Young, 1721)

Greek Calends (the) never
The Romans were meant to settle their taxes and other accounts on the Calends, or first day, of each month, but the Greek calendar had no Calends:

> The emergence of chaos in Germany ... would put off the pacification of Europe to the Greek Kalends. (Goebbels, 1945, in translation)

Greek gift a present with dire consequences

A throwback to the Trojan Horse and Virgil's *timeo Danaos et dona ferentes*:

> The control France was granted [by Hitler] over her navy also proved a Greek gift. (Ousby, 1997—on 2 and 6 July 1940 Churchill convinced the world that Britain would not surrender by ordering the destruction of major elements of the French fleet at Mers-el-Kébir after it had refused to continue the fight against Germany or take refuge in a neutral port)

Greek way (the) pederasty

The supposed sexual tastes of the ancient Greeks:

> Hooking, that's mostly for oddball stuff now, golden showers, Greek, not straight sex. (Turow, 1993—*golden showers* involves urinating on the sexual partner)

green goods *American* counterfeit bank notes

GOODS for the stolen element and *green* for the colour of the notes. A *green-goods man* is a forger:

> He was just in here looking for a green-goods man. (Weverka, 1973)

green gown *obsolete* an indication of unchastity in an unmarried woman

On the eve of May Day, convention allowed the lads and lasses to spend all night in the woods, supposedly gathering flowers. During the night, many dresses were stained by the grass of the meadows:

> Then some greene gowns are by the lassies worne
> In chastest plaies. (Sidney, 1586)
> ... she had the salutation 'with a greene gowne'... as if the priest had been at our backs, to have married us. (G. A. Greeene, 1599, quoted in *ODEP*)

The *green sickness* was:

> The disease of maids occasioned by celibacy (Grose).

To *give green stockings* was to commit the solecism of getting married before your elder sister.

green needle (the) *American* a lethal injection of cyanide

Used in judicial killings.

greenmailer *American* a corporate raider who seeks to get paid to go away

The *green* of the US dollar replaces the *black* of BLACKMAIL:

> ... the first place to which takeover artists and greenmailers and LBO peddlers come for cash and complicity. (M. Thomas, 1987—an LBO is a leveraged buy-out)

grey¹ (of merchandise) branded and authentic but sold at below the manufacturers' stated price

Especially of luxury goods and clothing where the manufacturer seeks to maintain higher prices in an affluent country than can be charged elsewhere. Thus the product is known as *grey goods*, the trade known as the *grey market*, and those involved are called *grey marketeers*:

> Tesco was reported to have sold grey goods worth £30 million last year. (*Daily Telegraph*, 17 July 1998)
> It... offered cheap Calvin Klein clothing to its ABC Cardholders after obtaining stock on the grey market. (*Sunday Telegraph*, 22 February 1998—*cheap* in this context means less costly than normal)
> By buying goods without the manufacturer's consent, grey marketeers... operate in an area so named because it is neither illegal nor accepted business practice. (*Daily Telegraph*, 17 July 1998)

grey² (of people) lacking personality or initiative

The adjective is used about subservient politicians and functionaries, who may also be described as *grey suits*, from their attire:

> The grey men in the home team were each speaking in turn about peace and unity. (Simpson, 1998, writing about politicians in Belgrade)
> He had been appointed four years earlier to the post of premier by the late President Cherkassov as a skilled administrator, a grey suit with a background in the petroleum industry. (Forsyth, 1996)

greymail *American* a threat to tell state secrets if prosecuted

A type of BLACKMAIL, the shade variation indicating less criminality:

> He would also use a 'CIA defense'—so called greymail tactics that had been successfully practised by other defendants involving national security. (Maas, 1986)

Grim Reaper (the) death

Grim for the death's head or skeleton in northern English dialect, and *Reaper* from the scythe he carries:

> The goal was to outmanoeuvre the Grim Reaper. (J. Mitford, 1963)

grind to copulate with

Probably from the rotary pelvic motion:

> ... a young person of Harwich,
> Tried to grind his betrothed in a carriage.
> (*Playboy's Book of Limericks*)

A *grind* is the act, or the female participant, who is always referred to in flattering terms—

where do all the *bad grinds* go? An American
grind-mill was a brothel:
> It was a business in the grind-
> mills...(Longstreet, 1956, and not of
> flour-making in New Orleans)

grind the wind *obsolete British* to be punished on a treadmill
Introducing rotary power with no end product:
> The prisoners style the occupation
> 'grinding the wind'. (Mayhew, 1862)

groceries sundries *obsolete* intoxicants
So described on the bill by the grocer so that
the servants, and perhaps the husband, might
not know the extent of the purchases of
alcohol by the lady of the house.

groggy *obsolete* drunk
The celebrated British Admiral Vernon, who
died in 1757, was known as *Grog*, because he
wore a grogram cloak. He introduced to the
navy a drink consisting of rum and water,
which was called after his nickname. If you had
grog on board or became *groggy*, you were drunk,
and, if habitually so, a *grog-hound*. As drunkenness induces an unsteady gait, today you may
say you are feeling *groggy* without having
consumed any alcohol or incurring any opprobrium, merely feeling dizzy or unwell.

groin the genitalia
Literally, the place where the abdomen meets
the thigh. Sports commentators talk of an
injury to the *groin* when the player has
suffered a more telling and painful blow.
Non-sporting use is less common:
> He was grabbed by a sensitive portion of
> his lower groin. (Lavine, 1930)
> They should get to know one another
> better by rubbing groins together. (*Sun*,
> March 1981)

grope to fondle another person sexually
Literally, to use the hands for feeling anything. Usually of a male whose activity may be
inexpert or unwanted:
> You mean fornicating in the sauna or in a
> mop closet or underwater groping is okay?
> (Sanders, 1973)
Whence a *groper*, an unattractive male suitor,
replacing two more logical obsolete meanings, a blind person or a midwife.

gross height excursion a dangerous and
unplanned loss of aircraft height
Civil aviation jargon in an environment
where nothing must be acknowledged as
dangerous or unplanned:
> ...a nose dive is never called a nose dive. It
> is a 'gross height excursion'. (Moynahan,
> 1983)

gross indecency bestiality or sodomy
Legal jargon when buggery was not consid-
ered a lawful activity:
> ...he was arrested by members of the
> Metropolitan vice squad for an act of gross
> indecency in Hyde Park. (B. Forbes, 1986)
See also INDECENCY.

ground associated with death
From the days when most corpses were
buried rather than burned. *Ground-sweat* was
the dampness arising from the soil, whence
burial and the adage 'A ground sweat cures all
disorders'. A *ground-lair* was a family burial
plot and *ground-mail* the fee paid to the church
for interment:
> Measuring off the different allotments
> under liberal principles, both as to the
> extent of ground and the rate for ground
> lair. (*Aberdeen Chronicle*, 10 July 1819)
> 'Reasonable charges!' said the sexton; 'ou,
> there's grund-maill—and bell-siller—and
> the kist—and my day's wark.' (W. Scott,
> 1819—a *kist* is a coffin)

group sex a sexual orgy
It could mean no more than a meeting of the
Mothers' Union, all being female so long as
the vicar stays away:
> If God had meant us to have group sex, I
> guess he'd have given us all more organs.
> (Bradbury, 1976)

growth a carcinoma
Literally, something which has grown and,
even of human tissue, not necessarily malig-
nant. A common usage to avoid reference to
the dread cancer.

grunt *American* to defecate
The association is with the straining noise.

grunter a pig
Used among fisherman to avoid saying the
word *pig*, there being a taboo arising from
sickness on board caused by rotten pork:
> When Kate referred to a pig, she said
> grunter. (Cookson, 1969—Kate was
> married to a mariner)
See also FURRY THING.

guardhouse lawyer *American* an opinionated know-all and troublemaker
Also known as a BARRACK-ROOM LAWYER.
Guard duty involves much tedium, providing
fertile ground for bores and agitators. General
as well as military use.

guardian an occupying conqueror
Literally, one who protects or manages the
affairs of another:
> ...the indigenous Ughur inhabitants had
> shared a mutual hatred of the Chinese

'guardians' on and off for over a thousand years. (Strong, 1998)

guest¹ a prisoner
Seldom *tout court*; more often as *guest of Uncle Sam* or *of Her Majesty*:
> ... to book a prisoner—I beg your pardon, 'guest'. (Lavine, 1930)

The obsolete Scottish *guest* was a ghost, an unwelcome visitor or a linguistic corruption:
> Brownies, fays and fairies,
> And witches, guests. (Liddle, 1821)

guest² a customer
Literally, a recipient of free entertainment or hospitality, but not in the hotel or theme park business:
> In Euphemismland crowds are audiences, customers Guests ... (Whicker, 1982, writing about Disneyland)

See also PAYING GUEST.

guest worker an alien employed without the right of permanent residence
Those so employed are paid, like the German *Gastarbeiter*, usually for menial work shunned by the indigenous population:
> A new development [in Israel] was that their dislike and fear of Palestinians had reached such a pitch that their answer now to Palestinian demands was the hiring of immigrant laborers and field hands from Thailand, the Philippines and Poland— desperate so-called 'guest workers'. (Theroux, 1995)

guidance to the market a profit warning
Financial jargon, from a world where it is important not to be detected in giving price-sensitive information to favoured individuals and an unambiguous profit warning will lead to a sharp fall in the share price:
> When is a profit warning not a profit warning? When it's just 'specific steady guidance to the market'. (*Daily Telegraph*, 9 February 2001)

guiding light *British* an unachievable aspiration to prevent pay rises
Also known as *guidelines*, one of the euphemisms used by government seeking in a market economy to discourage wage increases through exhortation:
> ... the Government expected that a 2.5 per cent 'guiding light' would be observed. (Crossman, 1981, referring to

a White Paper issued in February 1962: time would have been better spent on studying the experiences of King Canute)

See also PAUSE 2 and RESTRAINT 1.

guinea-hen *obsolete* a prostitute
A pun on her fee and the common avian imagery:
> Ere I would say, I would drown myself for the love of a guinea-hen, I would change my humanity with a baboon. (Shakespeare, *Othello*)

gumshoe *American* an investigator in plain clothes
He has an ability to walk quietly on rubber soles. He may be a policeman or a private detective:
> Don't you call me 'sister' you cheap gumshoe. (Chandler, 1958, insulting a policeman)
> The president's private eye ... had become for all intents and purposes the exclusive gumshoe of White House counsel John Dean. (Colodny and Gettlin, 1991)

gun a criminal who carries a handgun
Criminal jargon:
> Especially if they're killers—guns for hire. (Bagley, 1977)

However, in America he can also be an unarmed thief, from the Yiddish *gonif*.

gunner's daughter *obsolete* a flogging
Literally, the barrel of the gun over which the victim was strapped, thus *kissing* or *marrying* her:
> I was made to kiss the wench that never speaks but when she scolds, and that's the gunner's daughter. (W. Scott, 1824)

A *son of a gun* was an illegitimate child, conceived on a long voyage and of doubtful paternity, although these connotations are forgotten in modern use.

gypsy's warning (a) *American* no warning at all
Showing a surprising lack of confidence in Romany second sight. In Britain and Ireland, if her palm were crossed with silver to negate the influence of the devil, in whose sphere necromancy falls, a *gypsy's warning* foretold misfortune. In Ireland also it meant gin, which often led to other misfortunes.

H

H anything taboo beginning with the letter H
Usually *hell*, in the expression *What the H?* In addict use, *heroin*:
> Daddy is fillin' the gun full of beautiful H. Soon you will be ridin' a wave. (J. Collins, 1981)

habit an addiction to narcotics
Not used of the equally addictive alcohol or tobacco. Your preference may be indicated by a modifier as, for example, *nose habit*, and the degree of addiction in a phrase assessing the cost:
> ... $50 a day habit. (Lingemann, 1969)

To *kick the habit* is not to treat your monastic attire roughly but to stop taking illegal narcotics.

had it dead or beyond repair
Of man, beast, or worn-out machinery:
> You've had it. You're snuffed. You're wiped out. (Theroux, 1976)

Hail Columbia *American* an expression of annoyance
Hail from hell and *Columbia* from America:
> I got Hail Columbia from father for that escapade. (Sullivan, 1953)

To *raise Hail Columbia* is to cause a fuss.

hair of the dog a morning drink of an intoxicant
Usually after too many the previous evening, the effects of which it is supposed to alleviate. A shortened form of *hair of the dog that bit you*. In America a *horn of the ox (that gored you)* means the same thing:
> Do you feel like swilling the hair of the dog with me? (D. Francis, 1978)
> ...three guys bellying up to the bar in an adjoining room, starting their day with a horn of the ox that gored them. (Sanders, 1979)

hair trigger trouble a tendency to premature ejaculation
Like a pistol where the *trigger* is set for too light a pull:
> The King, they said, suffered from a condition for which the medical name is 'hair trigger trouble'. (A. Waugh in *Daily Telegraph*, 29 April 1996)

haircut a severe financial loss
The locks are shorn. This kind of *haircut* is *taken*, rather than *got*, as in a barber's shop:

> The total of the Golden Grove haircut was less than $200 million in capital and reserves. (M. Thomas, 1982)
> The rouble collapsed. Russia defaulted on $33 billion of bonds. And bank stocks finally 'took a haircut'. (*Daily Telegraph*, 29 August 1998)

hairpiece a wig
Literally, no more than a piece of hair, on or off the scalp:
> He patted his hairpiece lovingly. (R. Moss, 1987)

half¹ a quantity of beer
Shortened form of *half a pint*:
> Pints were for men...only boys drank halves. (Sharpe, 1975)

In obsolete use, to *half-pint* was to drink beer:
> Two miners were 'half-pinting' in the public house. (R. Hunt, 1865)

In America as *half a can*:
> 'Bring me half a can.' A half-can meant a nickel's worth of beer. A whole can meant a dime's worth. (Longstreet, 1956—those were the days!)

Half and half is mild and bitter beer in the same glass:
> He would not play except for a pint of half and half. (Mayhew, 1862)

half² wholly
Used of drunkenness in many phrases where the *half* is not a partial condition but usually equals the whole, as in *half and half, half canned, cooked, corned, cut, foxed, gone, in the bag, on*, etc. Although incapacity through ingesting alcohol or narcotics is often described by the same euphemism, only with alcohol is the condition often divided by two:
> 'Were you drunk at the time?' 'Well, I'll tell you what it is, gentlemen. I was half-and-half.' (*Evesham Journal*, 1879, quoted in *EDD*)

half-and-half oral followed by vaginal sex
Prostitutes' jargon:
> Would the gentleman, she wanted to know, care for a half-and-half? (First, 1995—the question was posed by a prostitute)

half-deck a mentally disturbed person
The partly open craft is less seaworthy than one fully decked:
> But all those people on Dr Diana's list sound like half-decks. (Sanders, 1985—Diana was a psychiatrist)

half-inch to steal
Rhyming slang for PINCH 1, mainly of petty pilfering:

You used to 'arf inch suckers orf the barrers. (Kersh, 1936—a *sucker* was an orange)

half-seas over drunk

All the other states of drunkenness preceded by *half* indicate a condition of intoxication no less than the whole. In this case there is no *seas-over* to be halved. It is used either of total drunkenness:

I'm half-seas o'er to death. (Dryden, 1668–98)

or of a milder case:

It was no longer the custom to get drunk, but to get half-seas over was still fairly usual. (F. Harris, 1925)

And as *half-sea*:

Hoarse elder John sat at his knee, In proper trim—more than half sea. (Spence, 1898)

halve the footprint to implement multiple closures

Financial jargon for what usually happens after a takeover or merger, where duplicated functions are identified, branches closed, and people dismissed:

Bank of Scotland said it planned to 'halve the footprint' of the 1,700 NatWest branches. (*Daily Telegraph*, 25 September 1999—the bank failed in its attempted takeover, being itself absorbed into another larger bank in 2001)

hammer¹ to declare a defaulter

London Stock Exchange jargon, from the hammering to gain silence in which to make the announcement on the once noisy and crowded trading floor.

hammer² a philanderer

The common male violent imagery:

I used to be a great hammer, you know...Not any more. (Amis, 1988)

Whence to *hammer away*, to copulate:

It is also in this room that our producer hammers away...grunting like a wild pig. (Dalrymple, 1998—the producer was not a carpenter)

Do not confuse these usages with Thomas Cromwell, the *malleus monachorum*, or hammer of the monks, who proved more adept at dissolving monasteries than picking a wife for his sovereign.

hampton the penis

Rhyming slang on *Hampton Wick*, a district to the west of London, for PRICK:

No worse off physically than for a couple of sharp tweaks of the hampton. (Amis, 1978)

Unusually, both words in the phrase are commonly used as rhyming slang, but whereas *hampton* is only met literally, WICK is also used figuratively.

hand an employee

Mainly American use, playing down any suggestion of servitude. Compound job descriptions are common, such as *cowhand*, *deckhand*, *farmhand*, etc. However an *old China hand* (and they are always 'old', however young) does not work in a crockery store but is credited after residence in the Far East with understanding the intricacies of the geographical area mentioned:

...the hours he spent with old Asia hands, drinking brandy and hearing tall stories about wars and coups. (McCrum, 1991)

See also HELP 1 and OBLIGE.

hand-fasting obsolete Scottish trial marriage

What seems innovative in social behaviour is not always so:

It was not until more than twenty years after the Reformation that the custom of 'hand-fasting', which had come down from Celtic times, fell into disrepute, and consequent disuse. By this term was understood cohabitation for a year, the couple being then free to separate, unless they agreed to make the union permanent. (Andrews, 1899)

hand in your dinner pail to die

The common imagery of making no more demand on terrestrial resources:

Uncle Wilberforce having at last handed in his dinner pail...[he] had come into possession of a large income. (Wodehouse, 1930—he was the heir)

hand job the masturbation of a male by someone else, especially a prostitute

The *hand* or *hand relief* usually indicates self-masturbation:

He declined her offer of a compensating handjob. (M. Thomas, 1980)

I'm as well off with my hand and my imagination. (R. Doyle, 1996)

hand trouble mainly American unwelcome male attempts to fondle a woman sexually

She, not he, has trouble with his hands:

Bonnie had encountered men with hand trouble. (Hynd, 1949)

handful¹ a prison sentence of five years

Criminal jargon of the same tendency as FISTFUL and FIVE FINGERS.

handful² a badly behaved person

Literally, what you can hold in your hand. It may describe a precocious or naughty child or a wayward spouse.

handicap a mental or physical defect
Literally, a disadvantage imposed on a competitor to make an equal contest:

> We fight shy of abbreviations and
> euphemisms. [The Americans] rejoice in
> them. The blind and maimed are called
> 'handicapped', the destitute
> 'underprivileged'. (E. Waugh, 1956—
> comment on how things have changed in
> half a century is superfluous)

Now those with mental conditions are *mentally handicapped*, lame people are *physically
handicapped*, those with poor sight or blind are
visually handicapped, the deaf are *aurally handicapped*, etc. Nor does their condition prevent
them being CHALLENGED.

handle¹ to embrace a woman sexually
Literally, to hold with the hands:

> A did in some sort indeed handle women.
> (Shakespeare, *Henry V*, and not of a pimp)

The obsolete English dialect use was not
euphemistic:

> In love making, where the swain may not
> have the flow of language, he may
> sometimes attempt to put his arm
> around the girl's waist; this is
> called 'handlin' on her' (*EDD*—as
> ever, Dr Wright uses *love making* for
> courtship)

handle² the power over another to coerce
or extort
From the leverage:

> In this permissive age homosexuality isn't
> the handle it once was. (Bagley, 1982)

handout¹ *American* a bribe
Originally, food and clothing given to the
poor, whence money regularly paid to alleviate poverty by the state and any payment
for which there appears to be no consideration:

> Six weeks' suspension and six weeks at
> reduced pay for taking a handout. (Diehl,
> 1978)

handout² a written or printed statement
issued publicly containing tendentious
information
In standard usage, a summary intended to
record or amplify verbal information:

> The question which has not been raised
> in the Press here, force-fed as it is
> on NASA hand-outs... (*Private Eye*, July
> 1983)

handshake a supplementary payment on
leaving a job
Not necessarily GOLDEN and paid on summary
dismissal or early retirement:

> Had he agreed to suppress his feelings for
> five months—thereby collecting a full

pension and a brigadier's handshake over
£8,000...(M. Clark, 1991)

handyman special *American* a derelict
building
Real-estate jargon for a dilapidated house:

> * HANDYMAN SPECIAL * Huge house w/lots of
> potential. (*Chicago Tribune*, 30 July 1991—
> and lots of cockroaches, damp, dry rot,
> woodworm, etc.)

hang to kill by breaking the neck through
suspension
Formerly, it meant death by crucifixion, but it
is now standard English in the present sense,
the past sense being *hanged* not *hung*:

> 'No, Grace, we don't hang them any more.'
> 'Not even murderers?' 'Specially not them.'
> (N. Mitford, 1960)

A *hang-fair* was an execution by hanging in
public and a *hanging judge* was one who readily
sentenced people to death:

> The innkeeper supposed her some harum-
> skarum young woman who had come to
> attend the 'hang-fair' next day. (Hardy,
> 1888)
> He's got one or two unlikely convictions
> out of them. A hanging judge, some people
> said. (Christie, 1939)

hang a few on to drink intoxicants
Mainly American and usually to excess:

> He had only hung a few on and was, for
> him, slightly sober. (Longstreet, 1956)

Also as *hang one on*, which is never limited to a
single drink.

hang a red light on *American* to drive out
of business
The imagery is from a closed road—for once
the RED LAMP does not advertise a brothel:

> I have enough influence around this town
> to hang a red light on you. (Chandler, 1958)

hang in the bell-ropes *obsolete* to be
jilted
Especially after the banns had been called.
From denying the campanologists their reward:

> ...the 'deserted one' is said to be hung
> in the bell-ropes. (*N&Q*, 1867, quoted
> in *EDD*)

hang on the bough *obsolete Scottish* (of a
female) to remain unmarried
The imagery is from unplucked and wasted
fruit, although for a woman forbidden to earn
her living, remaining unmarried was once
less attractive than it is now:

> Ye impident woman! It's easy to see why ye
> were left hangin' on the bough. (Keith,
> 1896)

hang out the besom *obsolete* to live riotously during your wife's absence
A *besom* is a broom, once the preferred mode of transportation of witches, the aged menial who wielded it, and, in the 19th century, a prostitute because 'A girl described as "a besom" without a qualifying adj. would imply unchastity'. (*EDD*)
Inn signs were often poles with tufts on them, which looked like *besoms*. One way and another, a man *hanging out the besom* was consorting with unchaste women, or frequenting the pub, or both. However, a woman who was said to *hang out the broomstick* was no more than scheming to get herself a husband, the sign telling people that she was open for business.

hang out to dry *American* to be exposed publicly to protect others
Left on the washing line:
    Mitchell and Dean gave him assurances that he wouldn't be left to hang out to dry. (Colodny and Gettlin, 1991)
Whence a *hang-out*, such a stratagem:
    Is it too late to go the hang-out road? (ibid.—Nixon was asking if his accusers might be bought off by sacrificing one White House witness)

hang paper *American* to issue cheques or other securities fraudulently
Punning on house decoration:
    Jimmy gave me some good skinny on how to hang paper with minimum risk. (Sanders, 1990—*skinny* was originally 'a course or class in chemistry' (*DAS*) whence slang for any instruction)
See also PAPER-HANGER 2.

hang up your boots to cease to participate in a sporting activity
Not confined to ball games:
    I'd always thought of thirty-five as approximately hanging-up-the-boots time. (D. Francis, 1985, of steeplechasing)

hang up your hat[1] *obsolete* to marry a wealthy woman
Especially if she provides the matrimonial home and he retires from gainful employment:
    Snelling 'hung his hat up'—that is the local phrase—at the abode of Ephraim Shorthouse, whose daughter Cecilia had grown to marriageable age. (D. Murray, 1890)
Less often as *hang up his ladle*.

hang up your hat[2] *obsolete* to die
A reminder of the days when all adults wore headgear out of doors. Various other objects might also in similar fashion he *hung up* by those who would need them no more, such as a *dinner-pail*, *mug*, or *spoon*.

hangover symptoms of prior sub-acute alcoholic poisoning
Now standard English, from the *hanging over* of the ill effects until the next day:
    'How's the hangover?' From the sound of it, on the mend. The hair of the dog had bitten. (D. Francis, 1978)

hanky-panky extramarital sexual familiarity
Originally, trickery. It is what mothers used to tell their daughters to watch out for if spending an evening alone with a male.

Hanoi Hilton *American* a North Vietnamese prisoner-of-war camp
Of the same tendency as POTSDAM:
    ...two other general officers had been excused a stay in the Hanoi Hilton because of him. (Clancy, 1989—he had rescued downed fliers)

happen to to cause to die
Things *happen* to us every moment of our lives, but this particular *happening* old people especially prefer not to spell out, preferring the phrase *if anything happens to me*...

happy dust *American* cocaine
An addict usage:
    ...that happy dust gonna take you a real great snow ride. (J. Collins, 1981)

happy event the birth of a child
Although:
    ...an unhappy condition followed by a happy event, although the event is by no means always happy. (Atwood, 1996)

happy hour a period when a bar sells alcohol more cheaply
A period, not necessarily of sixty minutes, when people stopping work are encouraged in theory to drop in, relax, and relieve the tensions of the day, but in reality to drink too much and arrive home drunk, broke, and late:
    I bought two more [beers]: it was, after all, happy hour. (Theroux, 1979)

happy release the death of a terminally ill patient
We use it of others in pain, although they may feel otherwise. Less often as *happy dispatch*, a translation of the Japanese *hara-kiri* but without implying suicide. The *happy hunting grounds* are said to be the post-mortem destination of American Indians, while Dr Johnson professed to believe that, when dead, he might sit in a *happier seat*:

...although when in a celestial frame...he has supposed death to be 'kind Nature's signal for retreat', from this state of being to 'a happier seat', his thoughts upon this awful change were in general full of dismal apprehension. (J. Boswell, 1791—the Doctor was human after all)

hard denoting an extreme version of anything taboo or shameful

Thus *hard core* is explicit pornography: a *hard case* is a confirmed criminal; *hard drugs* are the more dangerous and addictive narcotics and hallucinogens; *hard drink*, the *hard*, or the *hard stuff* is spirits, and to *harden a drink* is to add more alcohol to it:

Playboy Enterprises acknowledged yesterday that it pays to be wicked by spending $80m. (£57m) on three hard-porn television networks. (*Daily Telegraph*, 4 July 2001)

If I don't have a drop of the hard I'm for it. (Cookson, 1967)

Would you have available a drop of the hard stuff? (L. Thomas, 1997)

I carried [a drink] to the kitchen and hardened it up from the bottle. (Chandler, 1943)

hard of hearing deaf

Not describing a noise which is indistinct. Deafness, when so described, is not, like blindness, understood to be an absolute condition, except where described as *stone deaf*:

'I'm hard of hearing, you know,' she said. 'Practically deaf.' (Sanders, 1980)

hard-on an erection of the penis

Of obvious derivation. Used both literally and, as an insult, figuratively, for PRICK:

...getting a hard-on listening to a beautiful woman screwing another guy. (Diehl, 1978) 'Jesus,' she said, groaning, 'what a hard-on you are.' (Sanders, 1977—the groan was out of frustration, not desire)

To *have a hard-on for* is to lust after:

And this Piper guy had a hard-on for old women. (Sharpe, 1977)

hard room a prison cell

It certainly has no feather bed and soft furnishings:

...defacing the walls of some of the subterranean 'hard-rooms'—a polite departmental euphemism for prison cells. (Deighton, 1985)

hard up poor

Usually of a temporary shortage of funds and perhaps a shortened form of the slang phrase *hard up against it*.

hardware[1] *obsolete American* whisky

This 19th-century use was resurrected during the Prohibition years as an evasion for the nature of the goods.

hardware[2] any modern armaments

Military jargon for things made of metal such as tanks, bombs, planes, guns, and missiles:

'You're talking about hardware.'...'We don't buy machine guns at the local ironmongers.' (Theroux, 1976)

harmful elements those citizens opposed to an a totalitarian regime

The jargon of Communism and Nazism which still persists in repressive societies:

Stuhlecker commissioned him to form a unit to 'cleanse the country from harmful elements'. (Burleigh, 2000, writing of the Nazis in Latvia in 1942)

harpic *British* mentally unbalanced

The brand name of a lavatory cleaner which claimed to clean the bowl 'right round the bend':

God, he must be harpic. (Fraser, 1992, using Second World War slang)

Harry the devil

Usually as *old Harry*, the *Lord Harry*, or the *living Harry*:

By the livin' Harry, if I could win over tae them. (Wardrop, 1881)

We still *play old Harry* when something upsets us:

[I must] not let the first law of nature, or any other individual consideration, play old Harry by setting up a dualism which destroys the dream in the misery of the business. (Mark VII, 1927, writing of trench life in the First World War)

harvest *American* to kill for personal gratification

Fresh euphemisms are needed from time to time to describe or attempt to justify the activities of those who kill animals other than for self-protection or food:

Trophy-hunters, or harvesters, as some prefer to be called, track and kill their prey...Mr O'Neill was glad that he had 'harvested' his bear without unleashing the Inuit hunter's dogs on his prey. (*Daily Telegraph*, 29 April 1998—Mr O'Neill had paid for a licence to kill a single male polar bear; the intrepid hunter and two of his companions in error killed females)

hash marijuana

Not from the dish of diced meat and vegetables but a shortened form of *hashish*. A *hash-head* is an addict.

hatch the birth of a child
Emergence from an egg is less taboo than the method of mammalian delivery:
> The female mind...takes an interest in the 'Hatch, Match and Despatch' of its fellow creatures. (Payn, 1878)

hatchet (man) someone entrusted with a job requiring ruthlessness or destructive criticism
The association is with the cutting tool, of anyone from a killer to those entrusted with introducing unpopular policies:
> If he's dead, he's worth five grand to you and five to the hatchet. (D. Francis, 1988)
> 1981 is not exactly turning out to be a vintage year for..., Sir James Goldsmith's hatchet man. (*Private Eye*, April 1981)

A *hatchet job* is such activity, especially applied to a piece of reportage:
> This series is going to be very sympathetic to the police...I'm not out to do a hatchet job. (Sanders, 1973)

haul your ashes *American* (of a male) to copulate
The imagery is from the extraction of matter from a furnace which is red and glowing, perhaps owing something to a meaning of *haul*, to harm another physically, with the common violent imagery:
> I pop in a red, get a little shot, you get your ashes hauled. Same dif. (Diehl, 1978, or, in translation, 'I like self-induced narcosis, you prefer sexual promiscuity—it's a matter of taste')

haute cuisine small portions of expensive food
Literally, high-quality cooking:
> When I'm away I live in hotels, where I get junk tricked out as haute cuisine. (Follett, 1979, and get charged accordingly)

Havana rider *obsolete American* an aircraft hijacker
The preferred destination of many such when the practice first emerged:
> Research in America has come up with a picture of the 'Havana riders', as airline staff call them. (Moynahan, 1983)

have to copulate with
Of either sex, meaning to possess, albeit temporarily:
> I was so impatient I had her without getting out of my chair. (Fraser, 1969)
> You must have had lots of men...Have you enjoyed it? (Amis, 1978)

Most of the sexual phrases commencing with *have* are so common that we forget their intrinsic stupidity. Only hermaphrodites do not *have sex* and we *have something to do with* everyone we meet. The common usages are *have a bit, a man/woman, at, it, it off, (sexual) relations (with), sex, something to do with, your end away, your (wicked) way with,* and *your will of:*
> I woke up and had at her again. (Fraser, 1970)
> The true test is when you can watch your wife having it off with someone else and still love her. (Sharpe, 1976)
> You perhaps ought to have relations once to make sure of a happy adjustment. (M. McCarthy, 1963)
> The euphemistic modern to have (something) to do with a woman. (Partridge, 1947)
> He has been having his end away. (P. Scott, 1977)
> Piper prowled the dark streets in search of innocent victims and had his way with them. (Sharpe, 1977)
> ...rollicking Regency days when the squire laid-about-him with his crop and had his wicked way with simple village maidens. (Whicker, 1982)
> ...sweeping her off at his saddlebow and having his wicked will of her. (Fraser, 1982)

There are countless vulgarisms, many with vivid imagery, of which a single sample may suffice:
> He had her right there, bent over the pit of the well...I had my nose in the butter many a time, he said. (Frazier, 1997)

Also of homosexual activity:
> Khaliq will insist on having it off with the other ranks. (M. Thomas, 1980)

have the painters in to be menstruating
Common female usage, with reference to the staining and colour, the protective sheeting, the temporary indisposition, and the inconvenience.

have your ticket punched *American* to do something or assume a position whereby you will attract favourable notice
Your presence on the bus has been recorded:
> He had come to Washington to have his ticket punched, that is, to hold down a Pentagon desk assignment, a pre-requisite in the modern Navy for being awarded the rank of admiral. (Colodny and Gettlin, 1991)

hawk *mainly American* a person who advocates aggression as a way of defence
The idea comes from Calhoun's War Hawks a political party of 1812, and was revived during the Cold War. See also DOVE.

hawk your mutton to be a prostitute

Literally, to offer meat for general sale. Also as *hawk your meat* or *your pearly*:

> I told her to hawk her pearly somewhere else. (Sharpe, 1976—a *pearly* is an oyster, to which bivalve the vagina is coarsely likened)

In obsolete use, to *hawk your meat* might mean no more than to display an immodest amount of bosom.

he-cow *obsolete American* a bull
19th-century prudery. Also as *he-thing*, which must have taken some working out. See BIG ANIMAL for more examples.

A *he-biddy* was a cock, better known as a ROOSTER.

head¹ *obsolete* to kill by beheading
As in the modern use, where we *head* gooseberries etc. by taking the top off:

> Has not heading and publickly affixing the head been thought sufficient for the most atrocious state crimes? (Maidment, 1868)

A *heading* was such an execution, carried out by a *heading-man* on a *heading-hill*, for the convenience of onlookers.

head(s)² a lavatory on a ship
Originally, in a warship, but now general:

> There was a small head off the little cabin. (Sanders, 1977)
> He heard the liquid pour in the bowl of the heads. (W. Smith, 1979)

head³ a narcotics addict
Alluding to the effect on the mind. Usually in combination as, for example, *snow-head*, a person addicted to cocaine.

head case an idiot
It may describe anything from inattention through eccentricity to madness:

> His teachers in the school didnae think he was very bright. They though he was a head case. (Theroux, 1983)

head count reduction the dismissal of numbers of employees
Not a diminution in the frequency of counting them. Commercial jargon where a decision is made to reduce numbers either peremptorily or over a period:

> He said 891 staff had left in the first quarter, bringing the total headcount reductions to 2,041. (*Daily Telegraph*, 10 February 1999, writing about BOC)

head for the hills to distance yourself from any threat in a craven manner
The *hills* are the traditional refuge of the escapee, whence much figurative use:

> Some business leaders headed for the hills, anxious to avoid the shellfire; others moved in quickly behind China's line.

(Patten, 1998—the *shellfire* was Chinese bluster and bullying prior to the British handover of Hong Kong to China. Patten notes elsewhere that those Hong Kong Chinese most subservient to the Chinese policy appeared also the keenest to secure foreign passports for themselves and their families)

head job (a) fellatio
Not an appointment to manage a school or even what the barber does for you:

> . . . receiving a listless headjob from an aging black prostitute. (Wambaugh, 1975)

A *head chick* is a prostitute who offers such a service. See also GIVE HEAD.

headshrinker a psychiatrist
An evasion is needed because consulting a psychiatrist, though a status symbol for some, is a shameful matter for others. The usage puns on the practices of primitive tribes apropos their enemies, and is shortened to *shrink*, while *headshrinking* describes the process:

> One day I may need some headshrinking work done. (Ustinov, 1971)
> . . . ending up on some shrink's couch twice a week. (Hailey, 1979)

headache¹ *obsolete England/Ireland* a corn poppy used for narcotic purposes
The *papaver rhoeas* may not have had the potency of its oriental cousins, but it was what was available. There was a fetish against unmarried girls touching the flowers, because the drowsiness and feeling of goodwill induced by closer acquaintance might make them easier to seduce:

> Corn-poppies, that in crimson dwell,
> Call'd head-aches from their sickly smell.
> (Clare, 1827)

The narcotic made from the poppies was called *headache-wine*.

headache² a female excuse for not participating in a sexual activity
Whether it be going out with a male for the evening or copulation:

> You were glad you found out about the headache before investing too much time and money and hope in her. (Chandler, 1953)

headbanger an irrational or confused person
From the supposed habit of the mentally ill of beating the head against the wall, whence the need for padded cells. Also as *head case*:

> I was now alone with 'Dennis Skinner and the headbangers'. (Benn, 1995—he and Skinner were on the left fringe of the British Labour party)

She looks at me as if I'm a headcase when I ask for chopsticks. (P. McCarthy, 2000)

headhunter¹ *American* a police internal disciplinary inspector

His quarry is any dishonest policeman:
Headhunters made rank consistently better than other investigators. (Wambaugh, 1975)

headhunter² a recruiting agent

Again punning on the practices of primitive tribes, and now standard English. It is considered chic for someone changing a managerial job to indicate his importance (and vanity) by saying he had been *headhunted*:
'You came here in 1995 by invitation.' 'You could say I was head-hunted.' (P. D. James, 2001)

headlights the breasts of an adult female

Viewed sexually by a male, especially in the days when the lamps were not recessed into the bodywork of the car:
... built like the brick shithouse you've always heard about, five foot ten in her stocking feet and female every inch of it, a phenomenal set of headlights ... (Turow, 1993)

health illness

As with DEFENCE and LIFE 2, the taboo subject is avoided by talking about the converse. Thus the pharmaceutical industry sells *health care products* to the sick; the British *National Health Service* provides, as best it can, for the ill and dying; and we refer to such things as *health clinics* or *farms*, *health insurance*, etc.

healthy in accordance with approved policy

One of the favoured evasions of the Nazis:
They were to grasp the essence of a case, approaching it with a 'healthy prejudice' and in line with the main principles of the Führer's government. (Burleigh, 2001, writing of instructions to German judges)

heart condition a malfunction of the heart

Medical jargon, in which all *conditions* are bad:
He had suffered from a heart condition for several years. (*Daily Telegraph*, November 1980)
Sometimes shortened to a *heart*, as in the phrase *having a heart*, but who doesn't?

heart's desire copulation

When the expression refers to some other aspiration, the object is usually named:
... the naked rector, blindfolded by one of the milkmaids and thinking he was about to have his heart's desire ... (B. Cornwell, 1997—it is

strange that milkmaids acquired a reputation for sexual impropriety; the chances of dalliance in the cowshed would seem to have been remote)

hearts (of oak) *British* penurious

Rhyming slang on *broke*, from a national savings and benefit society of the same name:
It left me 'earts of oak. (Kersh, 1936)

hearth rival *obsolete* a mistress

Not to mention the rivalry in bed:
She must have been Njal's mistress at some time or what the Norsemen charmingly have called Bergthora's 'hearth rival'. (Balchin, 1964)

heat¹ an action which causes alarm or anxiety

The body temperature rises when we are in danger. The usage covers things like police activity against specific criminals, military attacks, enquiry into scandal, illegal coercion, etc.:
It's life or death, nothing in between. This is immediate heat. (Murray Smith, 1993, writing about a blackmail threat)

heat² a handgun

The derivation is from the warmth of the barrel and perhaps punning on HEAT 1 and on firing. Also as *heater*:
'Ahh, I'm carrying,' Boon said. 'Someone will spot the heat.' (Sanders, 1977)
'All right, Dad. Shed the heater.' ... He put his enormous Frontier Colt on the floor. (Chandler, 1939)

heave (the) summary dismissal from employment

Literally, causing a heavy object to move:
When the cuts came I fancy half the staff would have written in suggesting he was top target for the heave. (Seymour, 1998)

heaven associated with the ingestion of illegal narcotics

In various jargon uses by addicts, such as *heaven dust* for cocaine and *heavenly blue* for pills of that colour.

heavily built obese

Mainly of teenage children:
Both girls are white, 5ft 2in and heavily built. (*Daily Telegraph*, 22 February 1997)

heavy involving significant sexual activity

Heavy here means important. In various phrases such as a *heavy date* which may involve *heavy necking* and result in a *heavy involvement*, which may lead to marriage:

Thought you had a heavy date tonight, Molly? (Deighton, 1981)

heavy landing an aircraft crash on the runway
All *landings* of a machine heavier than air are of necessity *heavy*. Aviation jargon for an accident which is not calamitous:
> ...DC 10 of the big American carrier careered off the runway at Istanbul after a heavy landing. (Moynahan, 1983)

heavy of foot *obsolete* in a late stage of pregnancy
How sad it is that many of these useful phrases are no longer used:
> James cam to me ae morning when she was heavy o' fit. (Service, 1887)

heel-tap a small volume of alcohol left in a glass
A *tap* was the sole or heel of a shoe, whence the liquid at the bottom of the glass:
> Seize the bottle and push it about. Don't fill on a heel-tap, it is not decorous. (A. Boswell, 1803)

The expression survives in *no heel-taps*—everyone must drain his glass.

heeled carrying a gun
Literally, armed and equipped:
> I noticed Collins's hand stray under his jacket and wished I'd thought to come heeled myself. (Fraser, 1982)

Well heeled does not mean it is a good gun, but that the person so described is wealthy.

heels foremost dead
You will almost certainly be carried that way as a patient on a stretcher on the way to hospital, but if so described, you are a corpse.

heightened interrogation torture
As authorized by the Nazis and other authoritarian regimes:
> Down in the cellar the Gestapo was licensed to practise what the Ministry of Justice called 'heightened interrogation'. (R. Harris, 1992)

heinie *American* the anus
The progression from the familiar form of the German name *Heinz* to any German, and then to this anatomical vulgarism, is unclear:
> There was always a certain tone Edgar took on. Like he'd gotten some icy fluorocarbon up the heinie. (Turow, 1996)

heist *mainly American* a theft
A variant of HOIST 1, referring to taking a truckload of goods or to an armed robbery:
> 'This is a heist!' Frisky yelled. 'Out of there and line up.' (Chandler, 1939)

helmet a police officer in uniform
The derogatory jargon used by those who are permitted to wear plain clothes:
> They had a taste for lapel pins...All things which said 'I am not a helmet'. (*Daily Telegraph Magazine*, August 1990)

help¹ *mainly American* a domestic servant
In standard use, any employee and a shortened form of *hired help*. In the home it implies voluntary assistance rather than servitude:
> I don't want my help to know or guess. (F. Harris, 1925—about her promiscuity)

help² the services of a ghost writer
Publishing jargon, which ignores the invaluable assistance given to all authors by their editors (especially mine):
> The odd thing about this kind of collaboration is that the celebrity...in seeking 'help' with a novel, inevitably appears dimmer than if she had never done a book at all. (*Daily Telegraph*, 9 September 1994)

help the police (with their inquiries) *British* to be in custody and presumed guilty of an offence with which you have not been charged
The purpose of the wording is not to prejudge guilt and so avoid the possibility of a subsequent conviction being quashed or an action for defamation:
> When someone is helping the police with their inquiries it may not be proven that he is a murderer but the suggestion is there. (Sharpe, 1976)

To *assist the police* means the same thing, although to *help the police* in some parts of the globe can mean something quite different:
> 'He is helping us with our inquiries.' 'What a pompous name for torture.' (Theroux, 1977)

help yourself to steal
Literally, not to await service by another. Usually of pilfering, especially where the goods are unguarded.

hemp¹ pertaining to death by hanging
The material of the rope. The *hemp-string* was a noose; the *hemp quinsy* or *hempen fever*, death by hanging; and a *hempen widow* someone whose husband, a *Hampshire gentleman*, had been hanged:
> In a' probability he wad form a bonnie tossil at the end of a hemp string. (Willock, 1886—a *tossil* was a tangle)

> The hemp quinsy, as the lags call hanging. (Keneally, 1987, writing in 19th-century style)

hemp² marijuana
A shortened form of *Indian hemp*:
> Reefers, grefa, the hemp...(Longstreet, 1956, listing illegal narcotics)

hen associated with a bride
The usage, which survives in *hen party*, a meeting between the bride and her female friends immediately prior to a wedding, and in *hen night*, a social gathering limited to females, once occurred in northern English phrases more to do with extortion than with celebration. *Hen brass* or *hen silver* was demanded by onlookers for *hen-drinking*, ostensibly to toast the bride, and in a refined form firearms were used:
> Formerly a gun was fired over the house of a newly married couple, to secure a plentiful issue of the marriage (probably to dispel the evil spirits that bring bad luck). The firing party had a present given them...and this was termed hen-silver. (*Penrith Observer*, September 1896)

The male equivalent is not *cock* but STAG.

hereafter (the) death
Religious use, anticipating some sort of continuing existence:
> The contents of that box were all that held off the Hereafter. (D. Francis, 1978)

hermaphrodite *obsolete* a homosexual
Literally, a creature combining the features of both sexes, from the machinations of the nymph Salmacis whose body was fused with that of Hermaphroditus when he refused her sexual advances

hic jacet *obsolete* a tombstone
Punning perhaps on the coat of an unsophisticated person and the Latin, 'here lies':
> By the cold Hic Jacets of the dead. (Tennyson, 1859)

hick *?obsolete American* a corpse
In standard usage, an unsophisticated country dweller, who might be killed for anatomical dissection if he wandered alone into town in the days when concern about preserving a whole cadaver for resurrection made corpses for medical teaching scarce in both America and Britain.

high drunk or under the influence of narcotics
Referring to the feeling of elevation or elation, but not describing those who have lapsed into torpidity or unconsciousness:
> We'd had some people in for cocktails, and we all got quite high. (M. McCarthy, 1963) The user smokes them in big puffs getting high. (Longstreet, 1956)

high-fly (the) *obsolete England* sending out begging letters
The career was made economically viable by the introduction of the penny post. Today we have a more descriptive title in *junk mail*, which also includes general advertising matter.

high forehead (a) baldness
Hair on the scalp is a sensitive subject for most men:
> 'And the receding hairline?' 'Receding what?'...'High forehead,' he said. (Lynn and Jay, 1986)

highball *American* to ingest a taboo substance
For railroad engineers, a *highball* was a clear track; for drinkers, an alcoholic mixture in a tall glass; for drug addicts, an amalgam of narcotics:
> She had been 'highballing' a mixture of cocaine and crystal and was totally 'strung out'. (Evans-Pritchard, 1997)

higher state (of existence) (a) death
Not drunker or more under the influence of drugs, nor even in the realm guarded by St Peter above the clouds. The comparison with earthly existence is spiritual:
> ...unite in the praise and prayer to our heavenly Father, from whom we daily receive so much good, and may hope for more in a higher state of existence. (J. Boswell, 1773)

See also *called to higher service* under CALL.

highgrade *American* to steal
The derivation is from the meaning, to take the easiest pickings, of timber from a forest, ore from a mine, etc. A *highgrader* is a discriminating thief who goes for items of the highest value.

highwayman a thief on the highway
Not just any wayfarer. He was usually on horseback, when he was a *high pad*, as distinct from the *footpad*, who robbed on the *pad*, or path, on foot. His robbery was known as the *high law* and he was the *high lawyer*.

hijack to take illegal possession of (a vehicle)
Standard English and doubtfully euphemistic, despite its interesting etymology. Originally, American Prohibition use, when it became easier to steal liquor from smugglers than to smuggle on your own account, and the command to raise the hands from the *hi-jacker* was a laconic 'High, Jack':
> Hijackers stopped cargoes at interurban boulevards. (Longstreet, 1956, describing the days of Prohibition)

Now used of the theft of all types of motor vehicles, of aircraft piracy, and also figuratively:

> A man armed with grenades hijacked a Russian jetliner yesterday and took the plane on a three-country odyssey. (*Sun-Ledger*, 21 February 1993)
> But the environmentalists are the main group to have figured out that science can be hijacked for ideological purposes. (*American Spectator*, February 1994)

hike¹ (off) *obsolete* to dismiss peremptorily from employment

The WALK 2 imagery:

> Another minute an' he'll hyke me aff. (Proudlock, 1896)

See also TAKE A HIKE 1.

hike² an unwarranted increase in selling price:

Literally, a raise, of anything, but more pejorative than the neutral increase:

> I ... expect that allowing for the effect of the oil price hike the inflation figures will begin to improve well before Christmas. (*Guardian*, 25 September 1990)

hillside men *obsolete Irish* outlaws

A 19th-century use when most of the population wished to be freed from English control but abhorred violence:

> He was no bog-trotter ... but ranged on the side of the moonlighters and the hillside men. (Flanagan, 1988—a *bog-trotter* was either an outlaw or a dispossessed tenant; for *moonlighter* see MOONLIGHT 2)

hindside the buttocks

BACKSIDE is more common. Perhaps obsolete but for some figurative use:

> Although Richard had a tendency to look after his bureaucratic hindside, Barcella knew him and trusted him. (Maas, 1986)

historic old

A usage of estate agents which sometimes traps them in tautology:

> Historic Saxon barn. (*Sunday Telegraph*, May 1981, implying construction before 1066)

hit¹ a drunken carouse

From the effect of the alcohol and rhyming slang on *hit and miss*, PISS, which is occasionally given in full:

> Sorry about my breath—I've been out on the hit and miss. (*Daily Telegraph Magazine*, August 1990)

hit² to kill

Usually describing an assassination by a bullet, known as a *hit* and carried out by a *hitman*:

> This is some kind of Mafia hit? (Diehl, 1978)
> You've narrowed the field down to a couple thousand hitmen. (ibid.)

hit³ to steal from

Criminal slang, indicating the place from which the robbery was made. In America to *hit* may also mean to beg on the street with menaces.

hit⁴ an ingestion of illegal narcotics

From the immediate physical effect:

> I want another hit before you bring him in. I want to be really up for what I have to do. (Robbins, 1981).

To *hit the pipe* is to smoke opium or marijuana.

hit-and-run a single promiscuous encounter

Punning in Britain on the version of cricket and in America on baseball:

> I don't go for hit-and-run. If someone wants to make love with me, I want him to stay with me. (R. N. Patterson, 1996)

Hit in this sexual sense has a venerable ancestry:

> She'll find a white that shall her blackness hit. (Shakespeare, *Othello*)

hit on to attempt or achieve a sexual relationship with a female

Either trying to *make a hit with*, make a good impression on, her, or the usual violent imagery:

> ... people start sending drinks over to me, like fifty at a time. Then they're all hitting on me. (Theroux, 1990)
> Did you hit Sonny because he was a Russian or because he was hitting on me? (de Mille, 1988—she and Sonny had been copulating with each other)

hit the bottle to drink intoxicants to excess

Of a single debauch or sustained drunkenness. Also as *hit the hooch* or *hit it*:

> I just wondered ... whether he'd planned to use the rest of the day to hit the bottle. (Gaarder, 1996)
> ... hitting the hooch like you birds been. (Chandler, 1943)
> ... poor old Carlisle, who between you and me had been hitting it a bit of late. (*Private Eye*, September 1981)

hit the bricks¹ *American* to go on strike

From walking out on to the sidewalk in the days before employees drove to work.

hit the bricks² *American* to escape or desert

Again from the sidewalk. *Hit the hump* is a synonym for the hill over which the fugitive disappears.

hit the sack with to copulate with
To *hit the sack* or *hay* means no more than to go to bed on your own:
> ...blame a Colonel for hitting the sack with a hooker. (Ustinov, 1971)

hit the silk see SILK

hit the wall *American* to become a fugitive
Climb over the wall would seem more appropriate:
> Cuz hit the wall man. Ain no tellin where that mother gone. (Turow, 1996—Cuz was not a cousin but a fellow gangster: nor was he a *mother* who had borne children)

hobby-horse *obsolete* a prostitute
Literally, an article in Morris dancing which became a children's toy. Shakespeare gives us another vulgar pun on *hobby*, a wanton, and on the usual equine imagery:
> My wife's a hobby-horse. (*The Winter's Tale*)

hochle *obsolete Scottish* to flaunt promiscuity
Literally, to sprawl about. Dr Wright gives as definition 'To tumble lewdly with women in open day.' (*EDD*—do not be misled into thinking that there was an 'open day' for tumbling lewdly with women).

hoist[1] to steal
In 19th-century Britain it implied shoplifting. In modern America, it is used as a noun of robbery from the person by a pickpocket:
> Blisters Schultz had scraped together just enough to pay his motel bill, but self-esteem depended on better luck with the hoists. (D. Francis, 1973)

hoist[2] to drink intoxicants
From lifting the glass, with some imprecision about the quantity:
> The pub was full of hollering men...Murf said 'I think I should split.' 'Forget it. Let's hoist a few.' (Theroux, 1976)

hoist your skirt (of a female) to copulate casually
With obvious imagery:
> Every girl in the reseau would hoist her skirt for you. (Allbeury, 1978)

hold to possess narcotics illegally
For your own use or resale:
> 'You holding anything?' the kid asked again, still staring at the ocean. 'Looking to

make a score or move some merchandise?' (Koontz, 1997)

hold-door trade (the) *obsolete* prostitution
From the practice of leaning while waiting against a partly opened door:
> Brethren and sisters of the hold-door trade. (Shakespeare, *Troilus and Cressida*)

hold paper on *American* to have a warrant for the arrest of
Criminal and police jargon:
> 'You holding paper on him?' I still wanted to know what it was for, what Kam, whoever he was, was supposed to have done. (Turow, 1993)

hold the bag *American* to accept the blame or the consequences
Rather like the game of pass the parcel, with the loser being the person holding it when the music stops:
> She'll be left holding the bag for a long time. *I* get over it. (R. N. Patterson, 1994)

hold-up a robbery
Literally, a delay of any kind, and I suppose a considerate thief may still *hold up* his hand to stop you before taking your valuables. Formerly, of stopping stagecoaches and robbing the occupants, but now of any robbery, especially where violence is threatened:
> You'll hold me up now, I suppose! (Chandler, 1939)

hold your liquor to drink a lot of alcohol without appearing drunk
Intermediate urination does not disqualify you but vomiting does:
> He can't drive, he can't cook, he can't hold his liquor. (Theroux, 1978)

hole[1] *obsolete* to kill
The derivation is from the entry of the bullet or the excavation of the grave:
> Keep yourself from being holed as they holed Mr Bingham the other day. (A. Trollope, 1885)

The modern cliché a *hole in the head* is not your mouth but death from a bullet.

hole[2] copulation with a female
From a male vulgarism for the vagina:
> He says I should be nice to Dolores, you never know, and he winks again, I think I'll be gettin' me hole tonight, he says. (McCourt, 1999)
> When a girl gets hot, her hole gets bigger. (Theroux, 1989)

holiday a term in prison
It is one way of explaining the absence:

Not since I took that little state-financed holiday. (Lyall, 1969)

holiday ownership a compounded annual rent paid in advance
When victims became aware of the scams and other disadvantages of *time-sharing*, another phrase had to be coined to ensure that the gullible would continue to part with their money:

So you must agree that buying a holiday ownership apartment at the Lanzarote Beach Club will actually SAVE YOU £20,000. (*Daily Telegraph*, August 1989—see SAVE for this kind of frugality)

hollow legs the ability to drink a lot of beer, wine, or spirits
The volume has to be stored somewhere, it seems. Sometimes in the singular:

Born with hollow legs! I watched with fascination while the gold liquid disappeared like beer. (D. Francis, 1978)
A thirtynine-year-old woman with a hollow leg. (R. Doyle, 1996—she was a drunkard)
The cliché is also applied to gluttony.

holy of holies[1] the vagina
The kind of tasteless pun which a libertine like Frank Harris would relish:

I want to see the Holy of Holies, the shrine of my idolatry. (F. Harris, 1925)

holy of holies[2] a lavatory
Again a tasteless double pun on what should be a quiet and secret place. The Latin version, *sanctum sanctorum*, loses all in the translation.

holy wars the expansion into the Middle East in the Middle Ages by western adventurers
We know them better as the Crusades. Although the pretext, and motive for some, was religious, a major cause for the aggression and attempted conquest was the pressure on resources caused by the rising population in western Europe prior to the fortuitous onset of the Black Death. After humanity had been culled for a century, the problem was starting to recur when the Age of Discovery revealed softer victims in the Americas, Africa, and the East. As what goes round comes round, parts of the world now experience a *jihad*.

holy week the period of menstruation
You can take your pick from a variety of tasteless puns and allusions.

home[1] a residential institution
Literally, the individual house in which you live with your family. A *nursing home*, for example, can be a hospital or a place which accommodates geriatrics.

home[2] a newly built house for sale
It is occupation by the buyer which makes the transformation:

Down here, the real estate agents sold homes, not houses. (McBain, 1994)

home economics cooking and housekeeping
The tuition needs a name which avoids sexual stereotyping:

In Home Economics, which really means cooking and sewing, I've learned how to install a zipper and make a flat-fell seam. (Atwood, 1988)

home equity loan a second mortgage
The security being deferred to the first mortgagee, the terms are onerous and only accepted by those in dire financial straits:

'Home equity loan' sounded ever so much more palatable than 'second mortgage'. (M. Thomas, 1987)

homelands *South African* areas into which black people were forcibly resettled
Nominally independent regions which were established as part of the policy of APARTHEID:

South Africa's ethnic homelands are crumbling from internal corruption and bankruptcy and outside pressures by President F. W. de Klerk and the African National Congress. (*Sunday Telegraph*, March 1990)

homely *American* plain-looking (used of women)
Literally, unaffectedly natural:

It was the homeliest members of your class who became teachers. (M. McCarthy, 1963)

homo a homosexual
A shortened form of homosexual. In Latin, a man, but the derivation is from the Greek word meaning same:

I'll never understand women. Sometimes I think these goddamned homos have got something. (Deighton, 1982—implying that all homosexuals are male)

honest chaste
Not necessarily truthful or trustworthy in other respects:

I do not think but Desdemona's honest. (Shakespeare, *Othello*)
A man may still *make an honest woman* of someone by marrying her after impregnating, or openly cohabiting, with, her.

honey *American* associated with human excrement
Referring to the colour and texture rather than the smell or sweetness. A *honey bucket* is a

portable lavatory for the army; a *honey-barge* carries away lavatory waste for the navy; a *honey cart* does the same function for airlines; and a *honey-dipper* is not a bee but a person who empties lavatories:

> 'I emptied the honeybucket!' shouted an American voice. (L. Thomas, 1981)
> ... the sanitary servicing vehicle ('honey cart' to the crews)... (Moynahan, 1983)
> The V.C. got work inside all camps as shoeshine boys and laundresses and honey-dippers. (Herr, 1977)

honey trap an attempt to seduce for subsequent blackmail or exposure

The sweet experience ensnares the victim, who is usually male. Both as a noun and as a verb:

> He was later awarded £20,000 damages in a French court which heard allegations that he had walked into a honey trap designed to disgrace him. (*Daily Telegraph*, 24 February 2001—the seductress was named as *Miss Bare Breasts of Belgium*)
> ... the arrest of a Marine Embassy official who had been 'honey-trapped' by a woman working for the KGB. (Pincher, 1987)

honk *American* to feel the genitals of a male

Like squeezing an old-style bulb horn, although probably more painful. Prostitutes' and police jargon, indicating a sexual approach:

> Sabrina... gave his genitals a squeeze... He knew he had been 'honked' as the vice cops called it. (Wambaugh, 1975)

honour chastity in a woman

Literally, maintaining moral standards:

> You sitting there with your legs crossed and a hole in the head and me trying to explain how I shot you to defend my honour. (Chandler, 1958)

honourable age (of) geriatric

It was dangerous under Communism to suggest that the sick and senile old men who clung to office until death, or even a few days after, were unfit to govern:

> We had in recent years a true gerontocracy, with the average age of the members of the leadership over seventy. Even though many new faces had joined the Central Committee since I had taken over, people of an 'honourable age' still predominated. (Gorbachev, 1995, in translation)

honour(s) *British* a system whereby politicians reward supporters and discourage dissidents

Although nominally under royal patronage, those chosen for inclusion are selected by government on populist or political grounds, an *honour* being the reward or bribe:

> ... allegations that he had received financial benefits from... a London solicitor whom he subsequently recommended for an honour. (*Sunday Telegraph*, 10 June 2001)
> They certainly wouldn't bother to ingratiate themselves with royalty if they knew how the Honours system actually operates. (A. Clark, 1993—fawning businessmen were at a meeting attended by the Prince of Wales)

For acts of bravery, some *honour* is still attached to an award:

> Before I had time to congratulate him on his Honour he hurried away. (Ranfurly, 1994, diary entry of 2 January 1942—David Stirling had been awarded a medal for bravery)

hook[1] to steal

The imagery is from angling. In East Africa it still applies to the technique of introducing a pole with a *hook* on the end through the shutters of your bedroom, with razor blades let into the shaft to stop you grabbing it:

> I guessed he had hooked it from the Miskito Indian on the Rio Sico, after his showerbath. (Theroux, 1981, of pilfered soap)

In obsolete British use a *hooker* was such a thief.

hook[2] a threat used to influence conduct

Again the imagery is from angling, with a fish on the line:

> He had a hook of some sort into her. (Chandler, 1958)

hook[3] an enticement leading to trickery

Baited for the dupe:

> 'Let's hear what the guy has to say.' The hook was in. (Weverka, 1973)

hooked under a compulsive addiction

Standard English. The addiction may be for a sport, a pastime such as a watching a specific television programme, or something taboo, especially narcotics:

> The kid never did get hooked on the hard stuff. (Sanders, 1977)

hooker a prostitute

From catching, *hooking*, a customer rather than General Hooker's exploits in Washington brothels or prostitutes in the *Corlears Hook* or *Caesar's Hook* districts of New York:

> Even the hookers had done no more than cast an eye. (Mailer, 1965)

A *hook-shop* was a brothel where prostitutes took those they had *hooked*:
> Some nights we go about and don't hook a soul. (Mayhew, 1862—they were prostitutes, not Salvationists)

hooky *American* human excrement
Perhaps from the shape. It is used for *shit* in the literal, allusive, figurative, and expletive senses of that overworked word. To *play hook(e)y* is to play truant.

hoosegow a prison
From the Spanish *juzgado*, a court, and from being judged in court and sent to jail:
> In that case, stew in a French hoosegow for the rest of your natural. (Sharpe, 1982)

hoovering the abortion of a foetus
Specifically by vacuum aspiration under medical supervision:
> I already had two hooverings when I wasn't sure. (McInerney, 1992)

hop a narcotic
Originally, opium, from the twisting vine rather than a corruption of some Chinese word. A *hophead* is an addict, who may resort to a *hop-joint* where he may become *hopped*, or under illegal narcosis:
> They take him over to the hospital ward and shoot him full of hop. (Chandler, 1943)
> Frank wasn't just a deviant and not just a hop-head. (Davidson, 1978)
> 'Coked' or 'hopped up' gunmen...(Lavine, 1930)

hop into bed to copulate casually
Usually on a first or single occasion and not propelling yourself on one leg only:
> 'How about hopping into bed?' 'At half-past four on a Sunday afternoon?' (D. Francis, 1978)

The American *whore-hopping* is not brothel leapfrog but copulation with two or more prostitutes in succession:
> Red-necks who had come down for the beer-drinking and the whore-hopping. (Theroux, 1979)

hop off to die
Avian imagery. Formerly as *hop the living* and also, in modern use, as *hop the twig*:
> And so the Captain has 'hopped the living'? I thought he was going to live forever, and I half suspect someone has been soaping the stairs. (Ashton, 1991, quoting a 19th-century letter)
> It's not often multi-millionaires hop their twig. (Bagley, 1982—and even they do it only once)

hop-pole marriage *obsolete Kent* a marriage not consecrated in church
Either the parties lived together unwed or they decided to do so after the conception of a child, their resolve being shown by jumping over a stick or *hop-pole*.
See also JUMP THE BROOMSTICK.

hopper *American* a lavatory
Literally, an inverted cone through which solids are discharged into a container:
> Mom was on the hopper with her knees pressed together. (Theroux, 1973)

hopping-Giles *obsolete British* a lame person
St Giles was the patron saint of cripples in the days when they were accepted as a common and unremarkable feature of society, and before the word *cripple* was considered derogatory and it became taboo to allude in direct terms to any physical abnormality. A crippled person would also respond to the name *Hopkins*.

horizontal pertaining to copulation
From the normal posture of the parties. In many phrases such as *horizontal aerobics*, in which both participants take exercise; *horizontal collaboration*, or how some Frenchwomen greeted the German invader, earning the sobriquet *collabos horizontales*; *horizontal conquest*, where the victor takes the spoils; the *horizontal life*, or prostitution; *horizontal jogging*, the *horizontal position*, or copulation; etc. A *grande horizontale* is a well-known prostitute or unchaste woman:
> When their horizontal aerobics are concluded, they lie awhile, insensate and numb. (Sanders, 1987)
> ...'horizontal collaboration' between 'respectable' women and Germans...was excoriated. (Burleigh, 2000—nonetheless the German troops fathered some 50,000 children by Frenchwomen during the occupation)
> Women who associated with German troops would come to be known as *collabos horizontales*. (Ousby, 1997)
> ...diamonds and rubies...and other battle honours of her horizontal conquests. (Ustinov, 1966)
> ...women didn't seem to go in for all this casual, take-it-or-leave-it horizontal jogging that seems to lie at the very root of our society. (Matthew, 1983)
> Propinquity—that's what leads to the horizontal position. (N. Barber, 1981)
> Some will have been dismayed by her failure to shine in the various roles she has adopted to date—as a journalist on *Paris Match*, as a television personality, grande

horizontale, film star. (A. Waugh in *Daily Telegraph*, 16 November 1996 writing about a royal duchess)

horn¹ the erect penis

Common enough in the 16th century for Shakespeare's punning vulgarism:

I can find no rhyme to 'lady' but 'baby'—an innocent rhyme; for 'scorn', 'horn', a hard rhyme. (*Much Ado About Nothing*)

For one author at least a *horn-emporium* was a bookshop which sells erotic literature for males:

Scrutinising the neighbourhood for a new, more convenient horn-emporium, was a pressing need. (Amis, 1988)

horn² to cuckold

Antlers, the traditional emblem of cuckoldry, were figuratively placed on the head of the deceived husband:

... by those that do their neighbours horn. (Colvil, 1796)

... evidence of Julie and Ronnie putting horns on the head of [her husband]. (Sanders, 1979)

To *wind the horn* was to acknowledge that you had been *horned* by a *horn-maker*:

Our horn'd master (waes for him)
Believes that sly boots does adore him. (Morison, 1790—but not sly enough to take in the servants)

Virtue is no horn-maker. (Shakespeare, *As You Like It*)

horn of fidelity *obsolete* a magic drinking cup

Morgan le Fay sent it to King Arthur to enable him to test the chastity of the ladies of his court. Legend records that only four out of the hundred managed to *drink cleane*, thus preserving the liquid and their honour.

horn of plenty the penis

Punning on HORN 1 and the cornucopia which, before brimming over with good things, was no more than the capital adornment of the goat which suckled Zeus:

She left her bikini top on, but she removed the bottom and then wrestled off my trunks. She held our suits in one hand and with the other grabbed hold of the horn of plenty. (Turow, 1993)

horn of the ox see HAIR OF THE DOG

horny¹ the devil

He has *horns* on his head. Usually *old horny*, *hornie*, *horney*, or *hoorny*:

Should Hornie, as in ancient days,
'Mang sons o' God present him. (Burns, 1786)

In 19th-century Ireland, it was also an abusive word for a policeman.

horny² excited sexually

Despite, or perhaps because of, the maleness of HORN 1, used of both sexes:

Even if they did put bromide in his tea he still felt horny every morning and woke up with an erection like a tent pole. (Bogarde, 1978)

The stewardesses were plain and presumably horny. (M. Thomas, 1980)

horse¹ *American* a corrupt prison warder

He carries contraband into, and messages out of, a prison.

horse² heroin

Probably a corruption of *heroin*, despite the attractions, etymologically speaking, of *riding* under its influence. Whence Deighton's punning title for a novel, *Horse under Water*.

horse apples *?obsolete American* the turds dropped by a horse

Especially in a street, where they might pile up like apples on a fruiterer's shelf:

... 'horse apples', 'cowpats', 'prairie chips', 'muck', 'dung', etc. (Jennings, 1965, listing common euphemistic synonyms)

horse collar *American* an expression of disgust

The accoutrement is chosen in favour of the more robust *horse shit*.

hose¹ to cheat

From the spraying with water or bullets, rather than the stocking on the leg:

I know about Marcus Wheatley... who hosed someone on a dope deal. (Turow, 1987)

hose² *American* to seek to confuse

Spraying another with excessive or irrelevant detail:

'He's hosing him,' Sennett said with anguish behind me. (Turow, 1999)

It may also mean to flatter.

hospice an institution for the incurable or dying

Originally, a resting place for travellers, especially pilgrims, and often run by members of a religious order. The current use first emerged in Dublin at the end of the 19th century.

hospital¹ an institution for the insane

The usage glosses over the taboo nature of the affliction:

American lunatic asylums are now simple hospitals. (Mencken, 1940)

hospital² a place of illegal confinement
Jargon of totalitarian regimes and the American Central Intelligence Agency.

hospital job a contract which can be loaded with excessive charges
In normal manufacturing use, it is a contract to which you can divert resources when business is slack, delivery not being urgent because the patient is unable to walk away while awaiting treatment. The dishonesty starts when such a contract is loaded with waiting time and scrap because the customer, usually a public body spending other people's money, is too inefficient or indifferent to detect malpractice.

hospitality free intoxicants
In standard usage, the provision of a welcome and entertainment to a visitor. In broadcasting, a *hospitality room* is the place where the tongues of amateur broadcasters are loosened prior to going on air and to which the staff repair for free drinks:
> The landlord...was happy to stay open as long as Seddon Arms wanted a drink. Maxim was beginning to guess at the scale of the 'hospitality' which the arms business could afford. (Lyall, 1980)
> In the hospitality room George Foster stood with his clip-board in one hand. (Allbeury, 1982—and a free drink in the other, no doubt)

hostess a prostitute
She entertains guests in a bar or club where the provision of food and drink may be a secondary function:
> Once a hostess, always a hostess. You always were a bit of a whore. (Kersh, 1936)
What were once called *air hostesses* now prefer to be known as *cabin flight attendants*.

hot¹ sexually aroused
From the increased bodily temperature and flushing caused by excitement, and also used of other emotions, such as anger, which give rise to the same symptoms. Being *hot* or having *the hots* is feeling lust for someone:
> I have never in my life seen so many ladies so hot in such a small place. (S. Green, 1979, and not describing a Turkish bath)
> Now he's got the hots for this young chick. (Sanders, 1973)

hot² obtained or held illegally
Used of stolen goods to be disposed of on the *hot market*, or the proceeds of vice—*hot money*. Both of these commodities are likely figuratively to burn you if you touch them:

Boudreau sold cheap liquor and handled fixes downtown and sometimes sold hot goods. (Weverka, 1973)
Not rich enough for the hot market. (Price, 1979, of stolen property)

hot³ infected with venereal disease
Normally of a male, from the burning sensation when urinating if infected with gonorrhoea, and also perhaps from the risk of infecting another.

hot⁴ radioactive
Nuclear jargon, perhaps taken from a *hot spot* on a bearing, where heat indicates potential malfunction and possible danger.

hot back (a) *obsolete* lust
HOT 1 certainly, but not usually confined to the BACK:
> When gods have hot backs, what shall poor men do? (Shakespeare, *The Merry Wives of Windsor*)

hot-house *obsolete* a brothel
Punning on a horticultural structure which may have relied more on the *hot-bed* principle, whereby the burial of rotting vegetable matter produced heat, than on glass:
> She professes a hot-house, which, I think, is a very ill house too. (Shakespeare, *Measure for Measure*)

hot pants an indication of sexual arousal
In Britain, where men wear *trousers*, only used about a female, but in America it may apply to both sexes:
> If she ever got hot pants, it wasn't for her husband. (Chandler, 1953)
> I've still got hot pants for her, if you want to call that love. (M. McCarthy, 1963)

hot-pillow *American* associated with promiscuous copulation
The bedding, whether *pillow* or *sheet*, has no time to cool down between customers in a *hot-pillow* or *hot-sheet hotel, motel*, or *joint*:
> That notorious hot-pillow hotel on the far side of San Jorge. God knows, Stone had never been fastidious about where he'd take his girls for a quickie. (Deighton, 1972)
> It looked like a hot-pillow joint to me. (Sanders, 1994)
> The hotel was noted for its hot-sheet business. (M. Thomas, 1980)

hot place (the) hell
Where the fires for ever burn. Now rare, even among evangelical Christians.

hot seat an electric chair used for execution

...the killers who end up in the
gas chambers or the hot seat. (Chandler,
1953)

Much figurative use of an uncomfortable
position of authority where something has
gone wrong and there is nobody else whom
you can blame.

hot seating employing shift workers
Analogous to HOT-PILLOW, although in this
case it is the chairs and things such as
computers which are passed in quick succession from one occupant to another. Also as
hot-desking.

hot shot *American* a fatal dose of illegal
narcotics
Punning perhaps on the meaning, a lively
person. The impurities of illegal narcotics,
often adulterated in the distribution
chain, constitute an additional risk to addicts.

hot stuff a highly sexed person
One who is likely to give a partner a *hot time*,
in or out of bed.

hot-tailing sexual promiscuity
A potent compound of HOT 1 and TAIL 1:
She's going to be hot-tailing it with
every...(Price, 1982—a man with a broken
spine was speaking of his wife)

hot-wire to steal a vehicle by bypassing
the ignition switch
A mixture of HOT 2 and modification of the
electrical circuitry:

hourly hotel *American* an establishment
which lets rooms for casual copulation
Day and night, with or without a prostitute:
...bustin' the massage parlours, movie
pits, hourly hotels. (Diehl, 1978)

house[1] a brothel
Literally, a dwelling or any other building
given over to a special purpose, such as a
theatre or debating chamber. The use for a
brothel *tout court* is obsolete, along with *house
of accommodation* or *assignation* (which let
rooms for casual copulation); *house in the
suburbs, of civil reception, of profession, of resort,
of sale, of sin, of tolerance*, etc.:
Some of the girls about here live in houses.
(Mayhew, 1862—but not chastely with
their families)
They enter houses of accommodation,
which they prefer to going with them to
their lodgings. (ibid., writing about
prostitutes)
...keepers of houses of assignation, where
[ladies of intrigue] might carry on their
amours with secrecy. (ibid.)

I was as well acquainted here as I was in
our house of profession. (Shakespeare,
Measure for Measure)
Shall all our houses of resort in the suburbs
be pull'd down? (ibid.)
I saw him enter such a house of sale—
Videlicet, a brothel. (Shakespeare, *Hamlet*)
Common house, ill-famed house, scalding house
(where you were likely to contract disease),
and *introducing house* are also obsolete:
Lord Euston was said to have gone to an ill-
famed house. (F. Harris, 1925)
His eager beaver interest in an 'introducing
house' in St George's Road, near Lupus
Street, was particularly resented by his
colleagues as it catered almost exclusively
to Members of Parliament. (Pearsall,
1969—I'm surprised it was not called a
house of commons. The busybody was
Gladstone, whose obsession with female
prostitution and casual contacts on the
streets with prostitutes would cause
greater comment today than they did then)
Current euphemisms include *house of evil* or *ill
repute, house of pleasure*, and *house of ill fame*:
I had to live in a house which was little
better than a house of ill fame. (Foreman,
1998, quoting a letter written in 1795)
A girl who had been forced into a house of
ill-repute... (Lavine, 1930)
In Bangkok we saw some blue movies in a
palatial house of pleasure. (Whicker,
1982—it was not a cinema. His companion
was Randolph Churchill)

house[2] *obsolete* a lavatory
Again, the building given over to a particular
purpose. Although Dr Johnson defines lavatories as *houses*, he does not so define a *house*.
In varying compounds such as *house of
commons, of ease, of lords*, and *of office*:
I had like to have shit in a skimmer
that day over the house of office.
(Pepys, 1660)

house[3] *obsolete* an institution for the
homeless
A shortened form of the dread *workhouse*,
which was also known as a *house of industry*:
Many old people...have to enter the
'house', as it is nick-named, like humble
suppliants. (F. Gordon, 1885)
The House of Industry for the reception of
the poor of eleven of our fourteen parishes.
(Peshall, 1773)

house[4] intended to avert criticism for
prejudice
The usage implies tameness where a person is
appointed in an attempt to be POLITICALLY
CORRECT:
...dude called Washington Lee
was a brother, not the house

nigger on some editorial board.
(McInerney, 1992)
See also OBLIGATORY, STATUTORY, and TOKEN.

housecleaning *American* the elimination of undesirable or embarrassing items
The imagery comes from the annual major assault that used to be made in the spring on carpets, curtains, etc. It refers to an investigation and subsequent reorganization in an institution when inefficiency or corruption have reached levels which threaten the security of those in charge; and to the destruction of records which might embarrass them:
> In the afternoon hours of August 8, Ford staff members heard of frantic housecleaning under way at the White House. (Colodny and Gettlin, 1991, describing the aftermath to Watergate)

house man *American* a security guard
Police jargon, and not the *man of the house*:
> I'm the house man here. Spill it. (Chandler, 1939)

house of correction a prison
So named in the hope that there will be no recidivism. The American *house of detention* is specific:
> Lyburn...is unlike any other house of correction in the world. (Ustinov, 1971)
> Incarceration in the House of Detention means loss of wages and a job. (Lavine, 1930)

house-proud obsessed with domestic cleanliness and tidiness
This tedious affliction may have little to do with pride in the family residence itself.

house-trained no longer given to involuntary urination or defecation
Usually of domestic pets, but sometimes of young children. Figurative use of a subservient male in the home, and of anyone who is induced to comply with the practices and abuses of those over whom he is nominally in charge:
> The Civil Service phrase for making a new Minister see things their way is 'house-training'. (Lynn and Jay, 1981)

housekeeper a resident mistress
Most women who follow the occupation of keeping house for a bachelor or widower lead sexual lives of impeccable propriety, although there are some who retain the title after changing the nature of the relationship along with their testamentary expectations:
> Several housekeepers...chosen for their willingness to endure the

bed and board of old Mr Flawse. (Sharpe, 1978)

housemate *American* a regular sexual partner with whom you cohabit
Not just a fellow lodger or member of the family:
> For the more flip, Americans offer LIL, for live-in lover, or housemate. (Whicker, 1982—he was discussing how to introduce to strangers a woman with whom he shared such a relationship)
Flatmate does not carry the same sexual inference.

how's your father casual copulation or its outcome
A male usage, perhaps from an opening conversational gambit. Where copulation is meant, usually in the phrase, *a bit of how's your father*. Less often of unplanned pregnancy:
> The girl was in the club, knocked up, a bun in the oven—'ow's yer father. (Lyall, 1982)

hulk *obsolete* a floating prison
Originally a ship, and then the hull of a ship no longer seaworthy but deemed good enough for the confinement of convicts. Often in the plural:
> From his 'unhappy position' in York Castle, awaiting transfer to the hulks...(R. Hughes, 1987)

human difference a facility below the norm
Not referring to the infinite variety among specimens of *homo sapiens*, nor even to those with acute eyesight or hearing:
> ...many people in the deaf community define their deafness not as a disability, but merely as a 'human difference'. (*Chicago Tribune*, 20 May 1991)

human intelligence the use of spies
Espionage jargon for the acquisition of *intelligence*, or information, by *human* agency rather than the interception of radio signals, satellite photography, etc.

human relations sexual activity
Literally, members of our family or everyone with whom we come in contact:
> She had no idea of elementary human relations. (Fraser, 1969—she was unaware of the process through which babies are conceived)

human resources personnel
Pretension rather than euphemism, perhaps, although it could mean virtually anything from your bank balance to an oilwell:

He's something big in personnel now, but they call it Human Resources. (P. McCarthy, 2000)

Often shortened to *HR*.

human rights individual licence beyond that permitted by existing institutions
The phrase comes from the 1948 United Nations' Universal Declaration of Human Rights, a concept to which no exception can be taken by those who consider mankind to be paramount on earth. In practice, *human rights* sometimes provides a slogan for those who wish to overturn an established form of social living acceptable to or tolerated by a majority, using violence if necessary.

human sacrifice the dismissal of employees
Punning on ancient rites to propitiate the gods:
    Sometimes human sacrifice is appropriate, but we have not quite reached that point yet. (*Daily Telegraph*, 20 November 1998—shares in a company had hit a fourteen-year low)

human waste sewage
Not discarded packaging or cans, amputated limbs or corpses, the unemployed or those without fulfilling lives. Jargon of civil engineers, to distinguish it from surface water and other effluent.

hump to copulate with
Venerable enough for Grose to note 'once a fashionable word for copulation'. The imagery is from porterage rather than from the BEAST WITH TWO BACKS. Also as *hump the mutton*:
    His trouble was seducin'. Story is he humped the faculty wives in alphabetical order. (Bradbury, 1965)
    She completed her undressing while we were positively humping the mutton all the way to the couch. (Fraser, 1977)

hung suffering from sub-acute alcoholic poisoning
Not an illiterate usage of *hanged* but a shortened version of *hungover*:
    'Sweating out your booze?' 'You look hung yourself.' (Mailer, 1965)
    He put down the receiver with all the gentleness of the badly hungover. (D. Francis, 1978)

hung like (of a male) claiming the fabled sexual prowess of
In various clichés. *Hung like a bull, horse*, or *stallion* implies large genitalia:
    I hear he's hung like a horse. (Sanders, 1986)

Hung like a rabbit suggests a penchant for frequent copulation.

hunt to go looking for a homosexual partner
Often in public urinals:
    Gilbert's given up 'hunting', he says all he ever wanted was love and he's got mine. (I. Murdoch, 1978)

hunt the brass rail *?obsolete American* to frequent bars
There used to be a brass rail in many saloons on which you might rest a foot:
    Virgins, reporters, house-wives, kept-wenches, customer's men hunt the brass rail. (Longstreet, 1956)

hunt the fox down the red lane *?obsolete British* to become drunk
Having too many CHASERS, no doubt. The *red lane* is the throat:
    I am sorry, kind sir, that your glass is no fuller...
    So merrily hunt the fox down the red lane. (J. H. Dixon, 1846)

hurt to assault sexually
It may indicate psychological as well as physical injury:
    'At least I know,' she said to Carlos, 'that you didn't hurt Elena.' (R. N. Patterson, 1994—Carlos had been wrongly accused of paedophilia)

husband[1] a pimp
Referring to his relationship with the senior of the women in his stable:
    ... to denounce a woman to her 'husband' if the creature makes advances to you. (Londres, 1928, in translation)

husband[2] a homosexual who takes the male role
Male or female, cohabiting sexually with another homosexual:
    The 'husband' he tripped with a heel behind her ankle. (Sanders, 1982, describing a fight with two women)

hush money a bribe to ensure silence
Hush for the ensuing quiet. Less often as *hush payments*:
    People objected to the bald language, the discussions of hush payments and stonewalling. (Colodny and Gettlin, 1991, describing the tapes of Nixon's conversations in the White House)

hustle[1] *American* to steal from or cheat
Literally, to push or crowd, whence to sell at inflated prices by skilful banter or to seek to

obtain cash by any means for the purchase of illegal drugs:

> Duty-free baubles were interminably hustled by stewardesses. (Deighton, 1988)

hustle² to engage in prostitution

From vigorous importuning in public by a *hustler*, or prostitute:

> I hustled at a dead run until the streets were empty and the bars closed. (Theroux, 1973)

> I don't think she's an out-and-out hustler. (Allbeury, 1976)

hygiene facilities a lavatory

Hygeia was a the Greek goddess of health, which seems quite a step from lavatories and sanitary towels (see PERSONAL HYGIENE):

> ... such was the Menezes's monopoly of hygiene facilities that Carmen's people were reduced to performing their natural functions in the open air. (Rushdie, 1995)

hygienic free from venereal disease

Not necessary clean or healthy in other respects:

> But there were a few men in formal evening dress with stiff collars, looking for company that was certified as hygienic. (R. Moss, 1987)

hygienic treatment *American* the temporary preservation of a corpse

Funeral jargon, which ignores the fact that newly dead meat is aseptic. We are conditioned to the sight of sides of meat or dead birds hanging in the butcher's shop, but we regard with alarm the untreated corpses of those formerly near and dear to us:

> Although some funeral directors boldly speak of 'embalming', the majority consider it preferable to describe the treatment by some other term as ... 'Hygienic Treatment'. (J. Mitford, 1963)

I

I hear what you say I do not agree with you

A convenient form of words because it avoids the need to enter into discussion or argument.

I must have notice of that question I do not intend to answer you

This response is best used in an interview broadcast live when you wish to hide known facts as well as ignorance. Radio and television are too ephemeral for there to be a risk of your bluff being called.

ice¹ to kill

The derivation is from lowering the body temperature rather than the ice formerly used in morgues. Also as *put on ice*:

I heard what the rat did to you for icing High Ball Mary. (Diehl, 1978)

Somebody put this Domino on ice about four hours ago—it wasn't no amateur hit. (ibid.)

ice² an illegal narcotic

Formerly only cocaine, from the numbing sensation:

I'll just be snorting some ice around the USA. (Murray Smith, 1993)

Also as *ice cream*.

ice box¹ *American* a prison

Originally a cell used for solitary confinement, where you were sent to cool down. Also as *ice-house*:

A prisoner went to the 'ice-box' or solitary...(Lavine, 1930)

...three days in the icehouse...(Chandler, 1953)

ice box² *American* a mortuary

This usage has survived the refrigeration of mortuaries:

He's got seven stiffs down there in the ice box. (Diehl, 1978)

ice queen a reserved and chaste young woman

Male use, from her supposed frigidity, but not a champion skater:

Her nervousness gave her the reputation of an ice queen and she was not often asked out. (Follett, 1991)

ideal for modernization dilapidated

In this real estate agents' newspeak, *ideal* means only fit for:

Stone-built detached cottage. Ideal for modernization. (*Western Daily Press*, May 1981)

identification proof of the ability to pay

A passport or driving licence will not suffice. The desk staff in a hotel who ask for *identification* will want to take an imprint of your credit card before handing you the room key.

ideological supervision censorship

In political circles, *supervision* always carries menacing overtones:

Dubcek cracked; he agreed censorship ('ideological supervision') could be restored and accepted the 'temporary stationing' of the invasion forces. (Moynahan, 1994, writing of events in Czechoslovakia in April 1968)

idiosyncrasy homosexuality

Literally, any tendency or unusual preference:

[The Queen] seemed quite comfortable in the company of Anthony Blunt, even after his 'idiosyncrasy' was known. (*Daily Telegraph*, 24 March 1995—Blunt was the Surveyor of the Queen's Pictures, having for years been a Communist spy)

ill¹ menstrual

Common female usage:

'When were you ill last?' 'About a fortnight ago,' she replied. (F. Harris, 1925)

Mrs Pepys was *ill of those*:

Thence home and my wife ill of those upon the maid's bed. (Pepys, 1669)

ill² suffering from a taboo disease

Either a venereal disease or AIDS:

The poor girl may not even have known she was ill. (F. Harris, 1925—a prostitute had syphilis)

'How can you be sure that Étienne knew Eric was ill?' '...you do love euphemisms, don't you?' (P. D. James, 1994—Eric was infected with the AIDS virus)

ill³ drunk

The symptoms of drunkenness can be identical with those of various illnesses:

'Roddy felt ill.' 'Ill,' said Jerry. 'Drunk, you mean.' (Deighton, 1988)

ill⁴ mentally unwell

Now probably obsolete, with our better understanding of mental sickness. Also as *ill-adjusted*:

She had some art treasures which she heaped upon me when she was what we will politely call 'ill', but claimed back again the moment she was well. (Coren,

1995, quoting Dr Conan Doyle writing
about a patient)
We aren't here to provide a haven for the
ill-adjusted. (Bradbury, 1959)

ill-wished *obsolete* bewitched
The malady might be cured by a visit to the
conjuror, or white witch:
   ...the child had been ill-wished...and
   would never be better until 'the spell was
   taken off her'. (R. Hunt, 1865)

illegal operation an induced abortion
In the days before such procedures became
legal:
   What about you, doctor—and your little
   professional mistake? Illegal operation, was
   it? (Christie, 1939)

illegal substance see SUBSTANCE

illegitimate born outside wedlock
This is a dog Latin word coined in an
age when people worried a lot about paternity:
   A yearly average of 1,141 illegitimate
   children thrown back on their wretched
   mothers. (Mayhew, 1862)
The meaning unlawful developed later.

illicit pertaining to extramarital copulation
Literally unlawful, although English common
law saw no criminality in adultery, leaving
jurisdiction to the Church. Usually in phrases
such as *illicit embraces*, *connection*, *commerce*,
intercourse, etc.:
   He...agreed that much more misery than
   happiness, upon the whole, is produced
   by illicit commerce between the sexes.
   (J. Boswell, 1791)

illuminated drunk
A rare version of LIT or *lit up*.

imaginative journalism sensationalist
fabrication
It is unwise to call a journalist a liar because
the press has more chances of hurting you
than you have in return:
   ...a piece of imaginative journalism was
   being perpetrated by one of its own
   journalists. (*Private Eye*, June 1981)

imbibe to drink intoxicants
Literally, to drink any liquid. Anyone who is
said to *imbibe* is being accused of being an
alcoholic.

immaculate in fair decorative order
No used residence is ever 'spotlessly clean
or neat, perfectly tidy, in perfect condition'
(SOED). This is the puffing of estate agents

for a house which looks fit to move into
without immediate attention.

immigrant *British* a non-white citizen of
the United Kingdom
White people who have moved to Britain are
not included in this category in popular
speech, despite the fact that:
   Most 'immigrants' have been here for
   many years, and two of every five of them
   were born in the United Kingdom.
   (Howard, 1977)

immoral associated with prostitution
Literally, contrary to virtue, but confined to
sexual misbehaviour in various legal jargon
phrases. Thus *immoral earnings*, which it is a
crime for a pimp to *live on*, are what a
prostitute gets paid:
   It would mean my arrest on a charge of
   living on immoral earnings. (Theroux,
   1973)
Immoral girls are prostitutes:
   Though they'd twice given him the boat
   fare home he had spent it on drink and
   probably on immoral girls. (Bradbury,
   1976)
An *immoral house* was a brothel:
   The dress-lodger probably lives some
   distance from the immoral house.
   (Mayhew, 1862)
A building used for *immoral purposes* is either a
brothel or another place where a prostitute
takes her customers:
   ...full of brothels, almost every house
   being used for an immoral purpose. (ibid.)
The American Mann Act, known as the
Immorality Act, makes it unlawful to transport a female across a state line with intent to
'induce, entice or compel her to give herself
up to the practice of prostitution, or to give
herself up to debauchery or any other
immoral purpose'.

impaired hearing deafness
In standard usage, to *impair* means to damage
or weaken, and while this description is
correct of those who served in the artillery
without the protection of earmuffs, it is
normally not so for the rest of the population
who are so afflicted:
   ...the deaf shall be called 'people with
   impaired hearing'. (*Daily Telegraph*,
   1 October 1990, quoting a memorandum
   issued by Derbyshire County Council's
   Equal Opportunities and Race Relations
   Department)

impale (of a male) to copulate with
Originally, it meant to surround with a fence
(or paling), whence to thrust a stake into
something, and so to the common connection
between thrusting and copulation:

Before she could turn round I had impaled
her and was subsiding into a chair with her
on my lap. (Fraser, 1971)

importune to offer sexual services for
money
Literally, to beseech. Legal jargon of prostitutes who solicit customers in public places.

impotent sexually infertile
Literally, powerless in any respect, but used in
this sense of either sex:
    ...advertisements for doctors who cured
    'all the diseases of love' and promised the
    impotent 'horse-like vigour'. (Manning,
    1977)

improper involving promiscuity
Literally, lacking propriety in any respect. The
obsolete *improper house* was a brothel:
    Neither are the magistracy or the police
    allowed to enter improper or disorderly
    houses, unless to suppress disturbances.
    (Mayhew, 1862—other than in their private
    capacity as customers, we might suppose)
An *improper connection* was adultery:
    I asked him if there was any improper
    connection between them—'No, sir,
    no more than between two statues.'
    (J. Boswell, 1773)
An *improper suggestion* is an invitation to a
stranger to indulge in a sexual act:
    ...one of the tarts plucked at Kavanagh's
    sleeve and made an improper suggestion.
    (Fraser, 1975)

improvement[1] *obsolete Scottish*   forcible
depopulation
The Scottish Highland Clearances replaced
people by sheep in the glens to increase
income for the lairds and chiefs:
    The necessity for reducing the population
    in order to introduce valuable
    improvements. (Prebble, 1963, quoting Sir
    George Stewart Mackenzie of Coul)
Many of those evicted emigrated to the
American colonies, where they stayed loyal
to the crown in the War of Independence and
subsequently removed themselves to New
Scotland, or Nova Scotia, rather than stay
among the successful rebels.

improvement[2] a reduction in quality or
service
Any statement that a change introduced by a
manufacturer or provider of services will
result in *improvement* for customers should
be viewed with suspicion. The only thing it is
normally intended to improve is the profitability of the operation:
    Improvement means deterioration.
    (Hutber's Law, propounded by the former
    City Editor of the *Sunday Telegraph*)

improving knife (the) cosmetic surgery
Some may think that the scalpel might be put
to better use in aid of life-threatening ail-
ments:
    The world craze for the improving knife
    was just starting and Japanese secretaries
    would go to a small private hospital off
    the Ginza during lunch-hour. (Whicker,
    1982—they wanted to look more like
    Caucasians)

in[1] imprisoned
Criminal jargon; a shortened form of *in prison*
or INSIDE.

in[2] (of a male) copulating with
A common vulgarism:
    Climbing into bed with...Lady Fleur, when
    that noble lord was not only in it but in
    her. (Sharpe, 1978)

in a pig's ear no, or that is nonsense
The *pig's ear* was the receptacle kept on the
bridge of a naval vessel into which the
watchman and others might urinate without
having to leave their post. Non-naval use is
always figurative:
    'Looking forward to our association, as they
    say.' In a pig's ear, Lorimer thought, as he
    trudged the deserted streets looking for a
    taxi. (Boyd, 1998)

in Abraham's bosom dead
Where Dives reputedly saw Lazarus, although
it seems poor recompense for a lifetime of
penury and abuse:
    The sons of Edward sleep in Abraham's
    bosom. (Shakespeare, *Richard III*)

in bits suffering from a hangover
Coming apart:
    — That's good. I was in bits meself this
    mornin'.—Were yeh?
    — Yeah. The oul' rum an' blacks, yeh
    know. (R. Doyle, 1990)

in calf pregnant
Literally of cows, vulgarly of women. Also as
in foal, *pig*, *pod*, and *pup*:
    [Queen Victoria] had just discovered that
    she was in foal for the ninth time. (Fraser,
    1975)
    'I'm in pig, what d'you think of that?'
    'A most hideous expression, Linda dear.'
    (N. Mitford, 1945)
    I've 'ad seven girls i'pod and wor going wi'
    a married woman. (Bradbury, 1976)

in care see CARE

in Carey Street *British* bankrupt
From the location of the London Bankruptcy
Court.

in circulation (of a woman) available for copulation

Normally of a prostitute:
> ... cannot conceive that a grown-up girl can earn her living in any other way. At twelve she is in secret circulation. (Londres, 1925, in translation)

in conference see CONFERENCE

in drink see DRINK 1

in Dutch in trouble

A survival from the maritime antagonism between the English and the men of the Low Counties:
> Got me in proper Dutch, you did. (B. Forbes, 1986—he had been exposed to criticism by another's action)

See also DUTCH.

in flagrante delicto in the act of extra-marital copulation

Legal jargon, often shortened to *in flagrante*. The French form, *en flagrant délit*, is rare:
> An SA man... had once caught a Jewish cattle dealer and a younger 'Aryan' girl *in flagrante delicto* behind a locked door of a room in an inn. (Burleigh, 2000)
> In the old days you at least knew this death *en flagrant délit* meant hell-fire for ever. (Read, 1979)

The phrase is also used to describe other kinds of wrongdoing where the offender is caught in the act.

in for it pregnant

A common use, especially of pregnancy outside marriage.
> Both James's Anna and Edward's Elizabeth were... in the less delicate language of Lord Portsmouth's brother Coulson '*in for it*'. (Tomalin, 1997, quoting from a letter of Jane Austen dated 5 January 1801)

in full fling *obsolete* enjoying an exclusive sexual relationship

A *fling* is a temporary bout of uncharacteristic hedonism:
> It seems she's in full fling with Valhubert. (N. Mitford, 1960)

in heaven dead

Religious use, and by monumental masons:
> I am indebted to my dear parents (both now in heaven) for having had habits of order and regularity instilled into me from an early age. (W. Collins, 1868)

There are many other phrases of the same tendency, such as *in the arms of Jesus*.

in left field *American* eccentric or mentally unstable

A baseball term, with perhaps a hint of the normal *sinister* connection:
> Sometimes they make sense and sometimes they're way out in left field. (Sanders, 1985)

in liquor drunk

In fact the LIQUOR is in you.

in name only without copulation

Used of a marriage, especially where the parties have continued to live with each other:
> My husband was... in name only. (Ludlum, 1979)

in purdah menstruating

But not living apart, as in some Hindu and Muslim societies:
> Do we know how long she's going to stay in purdah? (B. Forbes, 1983—a menstruating actress was holding up a production)

in relation with copulating with

There is no suggestion of consanguinity:
> ... she must have been in relation with both [O'Shea and Parnell]. (Kee, 1993—she was married to one and having children by the other)

in rut copulating

Literally, the state of excitement of a stag during the mating season:
> I could hear Deborah in rut, burning rubber and a wild boar. (Mailer, 1965)

in season able to conceive

Standard English of mammals other than humans, when the use becomes a vulgarism:
> The point of [women] being in season all the time with only brief interruptions...' (Amis, 1978)

in the altogether naked

The derivation is from the biblical passage, or is a shortened form of *altogether without clothes*:
> Thou wast altogether born in sins. (*John* 9: 14)

in the arms of Morpheus asleep

A euphemism only when used of someone who should have kept awake:
> At this hour when it is very hot he is usually to be found 'in the arms of Morpheus' which means, I understand, that he is sleeping. (Farrell, 1973)

Morpheus, the god of dreams, was the son of Hypnos, the god of sleep. Those unversed in Greek mythology are likely euphemistically to confuse the two deities.

in the bag[1] taken as a prisoner of war

Sporting imagery, referring to what the hunter shoots and carries away:

> Tell him if he tries to stick it out, he'll only end in the bag. (Manning, 1977, writing about the Second World War)

in the bag² *American* drunk

Like a hunted animal which has no hope of escape:

> He had a shotgun next to the chair, and he was half in the bag from booze. (Clancy, 1989)

in the barrel *American* about to be dismissed from employment

Or *fired*, which makes it twice removed from the standard English *discharged*.

in the box *American* (of a male) copulating

See BOX 3. For the Victorians a *good man in the box* was not an experienced philanderer but a rousing preacher, that *box* being a pulpit.

in the cart in serious difficulty

An adult male, who was not ill or wounded, would only find himself riding *in the cart* on his way to the scaffold. Apart from degrading the victim (only women and children rode in carts), it was common for the noose to be fixed around his neck and then for the cart to be driven off, leaving him hanging.

in the churchyard dead

And buried:

> My wife's in the churchyard there, and my children are all married. (W. Collins, 1860)

in the closet see CLOSET 2

in the club pregnant

A shortened form of *in the plum(p) pudding club*:

> Chaps having it off get taken aback when young women are put in the club. (Davidson, 1978)

Whence to *join the club*, to become pregnant.

in the departure lounge about to be dismissed from employment

The take-off in this case is involuntary:

> Any suggestion that [Stuart Proffitt] was in the departure lounge for reasons of moral or intellectual integrity was simply window-dressing. (*Sunday Telegraph*, 1 March 1998—Proffitt was an editor who had refused to accept a compromise intended to protect his employer's commercial interests in China)

in the family way pregnant

Probably an alteration of *in the way of having a family*, although the phrase is only used of the mother, with a suggestion usually that the pregnancy was unplanned. Also formerly as *in the increasing way* or *in that way*:

> But she's not so fucking happy when she's in the family way. (Manning, 1977)

> Both James's Anna and Edward's Elizabeth were already 'in the increasing way' as Eliza put it. (Tomalin, 1997, quoting from a letter of Jane Austen dated 5 January 1801)

> Mrs Clement too is in that way again. I am quite tired of so many children. (ibid.—letter dated 13 March 1817)

in the glue in personal difficulty

Unable to move freely:

> What about you? Are you in the glue? (T. Harris, 1988)

There are many other figurative expressions meaning the same thing, some vulgarisms, of which *in the nightsoil* is one of the less offensive.

in the hay copulating

Literally, in bed, from the days when your palliasse was filled with hay or straw:

> Tell me friend, what's she like in the hay? (Fraser, 1971)

in the mood ready to copulate

Female usage, especially in the negative when she wishes to avoid copulation with her regular partner:

> 'I'm not in the mood tonight,' Saroya told Robin. (*Daily Mirror*, February 1980)

in the rats suffering from delirium tremens

Army usage. Pink elephants, snakes, and rats are the reputed visitors in the delusions of those so afflicted:

> Seeing the pool of scared snakes... sent him 'in the rats'. (F. Richards, 1936)

in the raw naked

Literally, informal or untreated:

> I know what you were doing in the middle of the hay in the raw. (Sharpe, 1977)

in the red owing or losing money

A survival from the days when bankers and others used red ink for debit balances and black for credits. *In the black* is still used to indicate solvency or profitability.

in the ring engaged professionally in cheating at auction

Now used of fraudulent dealers who abstain from bidding against each other at a public auction and hold a private auction later among themselves. The use was formerly of those in a cartel of manufacturers, agreeing minimum prices. In the 19th century the term was used for stealing:

These parties are connected with the thieves, and are what is termed 'in the ring', that is, in the ring of thieves. (Mayhew, 1862)
See also RING 2.

in the sack copulating
Literally, in a bed, and usually extramaritally:
A medical examiner took a smear. The German girl has been in the sack tonight. (Mailer, 1965)
Into the sack means getting into bed for sexual activity:
'Would you get into the sack with a phallic symbol?' 'I go to bed with you, don't I?' she said lightly. (Theroux, 1976)

in the saddle copulating
Of either sex, using the common equine imagery:
Elspeth would be back in the saddle with one of her gallants by now. (Fraser, 1971)

in the skin naked
Particularly of nudity in public and breach of convention:
She must sunbathe in the skin. (L. Thomas, 1979, noting the absence of strap marks)
The more common *in the buff* comes from a shortened form of *buffalo*, whence the hide, whence the skin.

in the soil dead
Usually of those interred:
'And my father?' Benny falls back into despair. 'In the soil, son,' he says, wiping away fresh tears. (le Carré, 1996)

in the tank *American* drunk
The *drink tank*, or cell, is where inebriates are placed to sober up:
Spermwhale was almost in the tank, a fifth or bourbon or scotch in the huge red hand. (Wambaugh, 1975)

in the trade earning a living by prostitution
The phrase covered anyone in the business, from prostitute to bawd or pimp. The British *in trade* was a derogatory reference by landed gentry or professional people to those who manufactured or distributed goods, whom they thought to be their social inferiors.

in trouble¹ pregnant
A common use where the pregnancy is unintended and the female is unmarried.

in trouble² detected by the police in criminal activity
A shortened form of *in trouble with the police* or *with the courts*. Usually only describing the period between detection and sentencing.

in your cups drunk
You need only one cup, if it is large enough, or refilled sufficiently often:
...in his cups could do an admirable soft-shoe clog. (Sanders, 1973)
If you have taken a *cup too many* it means you are drunk.

in your nip naked
None of the 30 dialect meanings of *nip* given in the *EDD* helps us as to the etymology:
— Yeh'd be better off goin' around in your nip, said Jimmy Sr. They laughed at that...— I'd need shoes, though, says Bimbo.—An' somewhere to put your cigarettes, wha'. (R. Doyle, 1991)

inamorata a mistress
From the Italian *innamorata*, literally no more than a female with whom someone is in love:
As a member of the Souls and for twenty years the *inamorata* of the painter, Edmund Burne-Jones...(S. Hastings, 1994)
Inamorato is the male equivalent, although rarer.

incapable *British* very drunk
The legal offence *drunk and incapable* applies to a drunkard who has lost physical control:
She was so drunk, incapable—isn't that the word they use...? (Theroux, 1976)
The law accused a rowdy or violent drunkard of being *drunk and disorderly*.

incentive travel free trips for employees and their families
Either arranged as a bribe, often by a drug company, which may hold a conference in an exotic location, or given as a reward for travelling expensively on business with your employer paying:
But the Inland Revenue is taking a close interest in perks—especially 'incentive travel' which is corporate speak for staff junkets. (*Daily Telegraph*, 22 May 1997)

incident a war
Literally, a single occurrence, as a *border incident*, where opponents may loose off a few shots at each other. Many *incidents* have no fixed duration:
...the China 'incident', the cruel war which now had been raging for four years against the Kuomintang government. (Keegan, 1989)

inclusive language changing the former literary convention that the use of the male gender may also imply the female
The purist may find the constant repetition of 'he or she', 'him or her', and 'his or hers' more intrusive than inclusive:

It is a matter of 'gender', or 'inclusive language' as the feminists call it. (*Sunday Telegraph*, 9 May 1993)

income protection arranging your affairs to avoid tax

Although legal, the practice is looked upon with disfavour by those not in a position to do it themselves:

Tax avoidance, or as Mr Treyer preferred to call it, Income Protection. (Sharpe, 1978)

income support *British* money paid by the state to poorer people

One of a sequence of phrases meant to mask any suggestion of charity in such payments:

...she was only £10 a week better off than when she was on income support (as national assistance is now called).
(A. Waugh in *Daily Telegraph*, 8 October 1994)

inconstancy promiscuity

Used of those with regular sexual partners:

Inconstancy was so much the rule among the British residents in Cairo, the place, she thought, was a bureau of sexual exchange. (Manning, 1978)

incontinent[1] promiscuous

Literally, lacking self-restraint, and the opposite of *continent*, copulating only with your regular partner:

He had rekindled her...she had never been particularly continent. (le Carré, 1980)

Obedience to the marriage vows is *continence* or *continency*:

In her chamber, making a sermon of continency to her. (Shakespeare, *The Taming of the Shrew*)

incontinent[2] urinating or defecating involuntarily

From the literal meaning, without interval, and again the opposite of *continent*:

The geriatric ward where...he found himself surrounded by the senile and incontinent. (G. Greene, 1978)

Incontinency is the state of being so affected:
...embarrassed by the incontinency which had overtaken him. (M. Thomas, 1980)

incontinent ordnance mis-hits

Figuratively, hitting at the wrong time in the wrong place:

Bombs dropped outside the target area are 'incontinent ordnance'. (Commager, 1972)

inconvenienced *mainly American* with permanently impaired faculties

As in *The National Inconvenienced Sportsmen's League* (quoted in Rawson, 1981). The deaf

may be described as *aurally inconvenienced*, the blind as *visually inconvenienced*, and so on.

increase in head measurement greater conceit

When the head becomes figuratively swollen:

...after Alamein, a change in [General Montgomery's] character was detected by those near to him—an increase in the head measurement. (Horne, 1994)

incurable bone-ache *obsolete* syphilis

Not rheumatism or arthritis. Until Fleming's discovery of penicillin, the condition might be arrested but not cured, and mental institutions had many patients suffering from neurosyphilis, or general paralysis of the insane:

Now the rotten diseases of the south...incurable bone-ache.
(Shakespeare, *Troilus and Cressida*)

incursion an unprovoked attack

Literally, a running into, but long used in the military sense:

The White House describing the invasion (or, as it preferred, 'incursion') of Granada...(McCrum et al., 1986)

indecency an illegal sexual act

Nearly always by a male, but also used when an older woman copulates with a boy under the age of sixteen. Literally, it means unseemliness of any kind. In former use, it might refer to any extramarital sexual behaviour:

Numbers lie on the kitchen floor, all huddled together, men and women (when indecencies are common enough). (Mayhew, 1851)

An *indecent offence* is sexual:

Accused by fellow officers of an indecent offence with a local youth...(*Private Eye*, July 1980)

An *indecent assault* is nearly always by a man against a woman, covering anything from pinching her bottom to attempted rape. *Indecent exposure* is the display of the penis to strangers in public.

See also GROSS INDECENCY.

indescribables *obsolete* trousers

From the vintage years of 19th-century prudery. See also UNMENTIONABLES 1.

Indian hemp cannabis

A lot of hemp comes out of India other than *cannabis sativa indica*, the source of marijuana.

indigenous having remote ancestors from the territory where you live

Literally, native, a word which has unacceptable colonial connotations:

Americans should celebrate 'Columbus Day' as *Indigenous People's Day*. (Seitz, 1998)

indiscretion *obsolete* a child born out of wedlock
It was the mother who was supposed to have been indiscreet rather than the father.

indiscretions repeated acts of adultery
Literally, acts taken without caring about the embarrassment or distress they may cause:
> The Princess of Wales, who normally overlooked her husband's indiscretions...(R. Massie, 1992, writing of Alexandra, not Diana)

indisposed[1] menstruating
Literally, unwell:
> *Flag 3*. A sanitary pad or towel. Hence the flag (*or danger signal*) *is up*: she is 'indisposed'. (*DSUE*)

indisposed[2] having a hangover
Again from feeling unwell:
> When a rich man gets drunk, he is indisposed. (Sanders, 1977)

individual behavior adjustment unit *American* a cell for solitary confinement
Circumlocution combined with evasion. It could refer to anything from a dose of medicine to a turnstile.

indulge to drink intoxicants
Literally, to humour or gratify, and used normally of those who say they won't or don't:
> 'Drinks, Chester,' she said. 'The usual for the Reverend and me. Mr Rigg isn't indulging.' (Sanders, 1980)
Those who *overindulge* get drunk.

industrial action *British* a strike
Now standard English for industrial inaction. The plural is not used even when there is more than one strike:
> Khadiq's flight was delayed, successively by industrial actions involving luggage handlers at Heathrow and air controllers in France. (M. Thomas, 1980—the American author was misusing British English with 'actions' as well as writing 'luggage' for 'baggage')

industrializing country a poor and relatively undeveloped state
A coinage based on aspiration rather than reality:
> The term 'developing nations' was to be superseded by 'industrialising country'. (*Daily Telegraph*, 12 May 1993, quoting a directive issued by Leeds Metropolitan University)

inexpressibles *obsolete* trousers
See UNMENTIONABLES 1 for similar prudery:
> The navigator...wears inexpressibles of corduroy retained in their position by a leather strap round the waist. (*Bath Chronicle*, 21 November 1839, quoted in Maggs, 2001)

infamy *obsolete* prostitution
Literally, notoriety:
> Girls sold to infamy. London as centre of hideous traffic. (*News of the World* headline, quoted in Paxman, 1998)

infantry low-grade prostitutes
Soliciting on foot, unlike the more fortunate CAVALRY:
> When Theodora grew up, she too became a full-time courtesan, working with the so-called 'infantry', the lower end of the market. (Cawthorne, 1996)

infidelity adultery
Literally, an absence of faith, whence any dishonest act:
> In conducting these amours they perpetuate infidelity with impunity. (Mayhew, 1862)
Infidelities imply a consistent pattern of such conduct with different partners:
> Mavis had seized the opportunity to catalogue his latest infidelities. (Sharpe, 1979)

inflame to induce lustful feelings in (another)
The firing is figurative:
> She was the sort of woman 'who might be trusted not by one single word or sign, by glance of the eye or touch of the hand or tone of the voice, to inflame him unworthily'. (French, 1995)

informal acting illegally or without required permission
Literally, casual or easy-going, which is not one of the properties of a receiver of stolen property, or *informal dealer*:
> No action would be taken against 'informal' dealers who came forward, and nor would the money be confiscated. (Davidson, 1978)
A British *informal market* is a gathering which is allowed to function in a street or elsewhere despite the lack of an official licence.

information lies and a selection or suppression of the truth
As in the British *Ministry of Information* during the Second World War, which suppressed, distorted, edited, and invented 'news'. Today

the function is performed if required by the Foreign Office:

> Indeed he chose Sir John Rennie, a career diplomat and one-time head of the Foreign Office's Information Research Unit, responsible for what had once been called psychological warfare. (N. West, 1982)

Disinformation is the publication of rumours and lies intended to confuse or mislead.

informer a private individual who reports the activity of another surreptitiously to authority

Dr Johnson gives 'One who discovers offenders to the magistrate', but the word is now used mainly of police spies:

> I was aware of the likelihood that he was an informer, planted by those who wished me ill. (Cheng, 1984)

initiation the first act of copulation

In standard usage, becoming a member of a club etc., usually with due ceremony. It may be used of either sex. *Initiation into womanhood* is specific:

> She thought vaguely about the morning and 'her initiation into womanhood'. (Boyd, 1982—she was on her honeymoon)

initiative a concerted official reaction to a crisis

Almost invariably belated and ineffective, as were the successive British governmental *wage initiatives* which were intended to suspend the law of supply and demand in the hiring and remuneration of employees:

> ... there was a top-level conspiracy—no, wrong word ... *initiative* ... a top-level initiative among the Joint Chiefs. (Block, 1979)

inner city slum

Used to describe the derelict housing, abandoned shops, etc. which remain when those who can afford to have escaped to the suburbs to avoid noise, smells, and mugging.

inoperative untrue

Literally, invalid or not functioning:

> ... the press office that had been damaged by being forced many times to retract earlier statements about Watergate as 'inoperative'. (Colodny and Gettlin, 1991)

Inquiry and Control Section the agency for persecuting Jews

Perhaps the most despicable organization of Vichy France:

> Inside were long trestle tables manned by gendarmes under the supervision of the Inquiry and Control Section, formerly the Police for Jewish Affairs. (Faulks, 1998)

inquisition torture

It would be tempting providence to say that the usage is obsolete. When the 16th-century Spaniards captured heretics, the activity of the men of God went far beyond questioning:

> ... the priests who worked for the Inquisition three hundred years ago, and who could prove from the Bible that God wanted people racked and tortured. (Keneally, 1979)

insatiable having a wish for frequent copulation

Literally, not capable of satisfaction in any particular respect. Used of either sex, within or outside marriage:

> Her mother had warned her that men were insatiable, especially in heating climates. (P. Scott, 1977)

inseparable forming an exclusive sexual relationship with

Not Siamese twins nor even cohabiting:

> It had long been noticed that Lizzy and Furnivall had been, as Benzie discreetly puts it, 'inseparable' long before they were married. (J. Green, 1996—Furnivall was a 19th-century libertine and philologist without whom the *OED* might not have been produced)

inside in prison

Mainly criminal use:

> ... an unfortunate habit to be inside, those who treat H.M.'s prisons as hotels. (Ustinov, 1971)

inside track an unfair or illegal advantage

19th-century oval racetracks were operated without staggered starts, giving the animal on the inside less far to run than the competition. Now used of unfair promotion, the giving of advance information, and the like.

insider a person using confidential information for private advantage

In standard usage, any person with such knowledge or information, usually of a financial deal, whether or not the confidentiality is abused:

> As an insider, I'd get my arse in a sling if I wheel and deal. (Sanders, 1977)

Whence the criminal offence of *insider dealing*.

institutionalize to confine (a person) involuntarily

Especially the mentally ill:

> Nathan is insane, Sophie! He's got to be ... *institutionalized*. (Styron, 1976)

instrument the penis

Viewed sexually and with common imagery:

I can make my instrument stand whenever I please. (F. Harris, 1925, quoting Maupassant)

insult (of a foreigner) to associate sexually with a Chinese woman
A Communist tactic to keep non-Chinese at a distance from nationals:
'Then you know it is an offence to insult Chinese women.' Dancer was well aware of the xenophobic Beijing idiom for having casual relations. (Strong, 1998)

intact still a virgin
Literally, untouched or unimpaired. This specific use may come from the legal jargon for a female virgin, *virgo intacta*:
'He undressed you and looked at you in a mirror. But he didn't enjoy himself with you. He didn't touch you or lie on top of you, did he?' 'The girl is intact,' he said. (Golden, 1997)

integrated casting giving black actors roles traditionally taken by white actors
The object is to provide greater opportunities for non-white actors to perform regardless of historical authenticity:
Referring to cases where blacks have undertaken major Shakespearean roles hitherto regarded as white ... Mr Brown said 'This is a victory for integrated casting'. (*Daily Telegraph*, 12 August 1996)

intelligence spying
The ability to comprehend has been thus debased since the 16th century.

intemperance regular drunkenness
The converse of *temperance*, moderation, although in an establishment which styles itself a *Temperance Hotel*, alcohol is unavailable:
... had, through intemperance, been reduced to utter want. (Mayhew, 1851)

intentions whether marriage is proposed
In the olden days, when husbands were expected to keep their wives in the manner to which they were accustomed and the rituals of courtship were meant to be observed, a girl's father might, if so minded, ask her suitor what his *intentions* were. To the modern parent, they are usually self-evident.

intercourse copulation
Literally, any verbal or other exchange between people, which is why we should think no ill of Sir Thomas More, nor question his canonization:
For justifying himself he wrote a full account of the intercourse he had with the Nun and her complices. (Burnet, 1714)

By the late 18th century *sensual intercourse* meant copulation:
The conversation today, I know not how, turned ... upon sensual intercourse between the sexes, the delight of which [Dr Johnson] ascribed chiefly to the imagination. (J. Boswell, 1791)
and *irregular intercourse* was not the spasmodic coupling of spouses but extramarital copulation:
So then Sir, you would allow of no irregular intercourse whatever between the sexes? (ibid.—Dr Johnson had been condemning the 'licensed stews of Rome')
Now standard English as a shortened form of *sexual intercourse*:
Have you ever had intercourse, Dorothy? (M. McCarthy, 1963)

interesting condition see CONDITION 2

interfere with to assault sexually
Journalistic and forensic jargon for illegal male sexual acts against boys and females:
They are quite alive and nobody has interfered with them, not yet. (N. Mitford, 1960, writing about boys who had absconded from boarding school)

interim not given security of employment
Literally, temporary:
Interim managers may be seen by many as glorified temps, but in an increasingly cost-conscious business environment they are here to stay. (*Independent*, 20 March 1998)

intermediate *obsolete* not heterosexual
A Victorian usage which seems to have embraced homosexuality:
Membership of the intermediate sex was an excellent excuse for contracting out of society and any sexual embroilment. (Pearsall, 1969)

intermission a period of television advertisements
Literally, a temporary cessation which, on some channels, seems more like constant interruption.

internal affairs *American* the investigation by policemen of allegations against the police
Most police forces are reluctant to wash their dirty linen in public, or at all, and complaints against them, sometimes malicious, are the subject of taboo:
In Internal Affairs in his sneakers and sweatshirts, investigating complaints against his fellow officers. (Diehl, 1978)

The Soviet Russian *Ministry for Internal Affairs* controlled the fearsome MVD, or SECRET (STATE) POLICE.

internal security the repression of dissidents

Its function in a tyranny is to protect the rulers against the ruled.

interrogation with prejudice torture

The Communist KGB used *with prejudice* in the same way as the CIA—see TERMINATE:

'Interrogation with prejudice' left Vikov crippled. (M. C. Smith, 1981)

intervention¹ a military invasion

Literally, placing yourself between two other parties. The Russian invasion of Afghanistan aroused only muted protests from western left-wingers, the BBC's news editors choosing to describe it in all its bulletins as an *intervention*.

intervention² a surgical operation

Medical jargon for another kind of invasion.

intimacy copulation

Literally, close familiarity. Used more of extramarital copulation than of that within marriage:

A social escort who... would amateurishly offer 'intimacy', as they called it. (Theroux, 1973)

An *intimate* is a mistress:

Edward VII had introduced the resort to golf; a local intimate of his, a dressmaker, had only recently died. (Whicker, 1982—the resort was Carlsbad)

So too as an adjective:

You also need a bath and a change. Especially if you propose to be intimate with anyone other than myself. (Bradbury, 1975)

intimate part the genitalia of either sex or the breasts of a woman

A less frequent version of PRIVATE PARTS:

... glimpsing an occasional movement of white skin which... might, for all one could tell, belong to an intimate part. (Farrell, 1973)

intimate person the penis

A refinement of the PERSON theme:

The idea that any of them had... decorated his intimate person with a doughnut was absurd. (Blacker, 1992)

intrigue (an) a clandestine sexual relationship

In this sense, an *intrigue* is a plot, whence something done surreptitiously. Usually in the plural:

... only stipulating for the preservation of secrecy in their intrigues. (Mayhew, 1862)

introduce yourself to a bed to copulate with (someone)

On a single occasion perhaps:

Jupiter, who was enamoured of her, introduced himself to her bed by changing himself into a shower of gold. (Norfolk, 1991—gold still seems to facilitate this kind of introduction)

introducer's fee a bribe

Literally, a sum paid to a third party who brings the principals together:

As for bribes... this is a capitalist society, General. We prefer to talk about commissions and introducer's fees. (W. Smith, 1979)

introducing house *obsolete* a brothel

Prostitutes frequented it by day:

Introducing houses, where the women do not reside, but merely use the house as a place of resort in the daytime. (Mayhew, 1862)

See also HOUSE 1.

intruder an armed invader

More sinister than merely turning up without an invitation:

... so many intruders from across the Pakistan border were killed. (Naipaul, 1990)

invade (of a male) to copulate with

Partridge says 'A literary euphemism' (*DSUE*) and the *OED* agrees with him but only in the sense 'to make an attack upon a person, etc.'.

invalid coach *American* a hearse

An invalid description.

inventory adjustment a loss caused from prior overvaluation of goods

Usually arising from a failure to write down slow-moving, damaged, or unsaleable stocks and not providing for pilferage. Also as *inventory correction*:

Company officials blame the losses on share investments and 'inventory adjustments'. (*Daily Telegraph*, 19 February 1993)

The market has clearly written off 2001 as a year of brutal inventory correction. (*Financial Times*, 14 June 2001)

inventory leakage stealing

Not an imperfectly corked bottle in the stores. Trade jargon for routine pilfering by staff and customers.

invert a male homosexual

Figuratively, turned upside down, as seen from a heterosexual's point of view:

> 'We don't call anyone a queer, homo, pouf, nancy or faggot.' 'What in hell do you call them?'... 'Inverts.' (Bogarde, 1978)

Whence *inverted*, homosexual and *inversion*, homosexuality:

> Said I was that way. 'Inverted'? Isn't that the word? (Turow, 1999)

investigate to create, exaggerate, exploit, or distort (the account of an event)
The perpetrator calls it an enquiry:

> 'What d'you mean—smear?' 'Have it your way—investigate, if you prefer. Just so you keep on digging until something starts to smell. Choose your own euphemisms.' (Price, 1979)

Whence *investigative journalism*, *reporting*, etc.:

> 'I do investigative reporting when I think it's needed.' 'Yeah, investigative, meaning one-eyed, slanted.' (Hailey, 1979)

investor a gambler
A usage by promoters of football pools and other lotteries to delude subscribers into believing that they are not wasting their money.

invigorating cold
Describing water for swimming, weather for walking, etc. Those who say your participation in the activity to which they are themselves committed would be *invigorating* want you to suffer with them.

involuntary conversion *American* an aircraft crash
You *convert* an operational aircraft to scrap. True as far as it goes, which is not far enough.

involved actively and uncritically committed to an extreme policy
Literally, complex, although those so described are often simple and unthinking:

> Charming girl, very committed, very involved. You must have read about her campaign... (Theroux, 1976)

Involvement is such devotion to extremism:

> You don't understand the first *thing* about involvement. (le Carré, 1995)

involved with enjoying a sexual relationship with
Usually not of a transitory nature but:

> Khan cites the case of one off-duty flight attendant who became 'involved' with two passengers and a crewman on a single flight. (*Daily Telegraph*, 18 April 1995—she had copulated with all three)

Irish illogical or defective

The prefix appears in many offensive and sometimes euphemistic expressions dating from the time when Irish people were deemed to be backward in both Old and New England.

Irish evidence a perjurer
Either because Irish Catholics, forced to swear on a Protestant bible, felt no compunction to tell the truth, or from the denigration of all things Irish by the English:

> The publick shall be acquainted with this, to judge whether you are not fitter to be an Irish Evidence, than to be an Irish peer. (J. Boswell, 1791, quoting a letter from Richard Savage to Lord Tyrconnel)

Irish fever (the) typhus
The disease was endemic in 19th-century Dublin slums, many of which, prior to the forced Union in 1801 with England, Scotland, and Wales, had been town houses of an elegant capital:

> Irish slums were graphically illustrated in the *Builder*; typhus was known as the 'Irish fever'. (R. F. Foster, 1988)

Irish hoist *American* a kick in the pants
The way New Englanders treated an Irishman who ignored the warning NINA (the indication on situations vacant notices that No Irish Need Apply).

Irish horse *British* an inedible gobbet of meat
The navy called beef *salt horse*, reserving Irishness for the fat and gristle.

Irish hurricane *British* a calm sea
Another naval usage.

Irish pennant *American* a loose end
In both the literal and the figurative senses:

> Always loose ends. You know what they call them in the Navy? Irish pennants. (Sanders, 1985)

Irish promotion a reduction in wages
For doing the same or a similar job.

Irish thing (the) alcoholism
An offensive usage except perhaps when used by an Irish writer:

> Ya father? Well, ya know, he's got the problem, the Irish thing. (McCourt, 1997—father was an habitual drunkard)

Irish toothache¹ being pregnant
Adverting to the supposed confusion of the Irish in English eyes, and the dental troubles of undernourished pregnant women.

Irish toothache² an erection of the penis

Although this condition is not unconnected with pregnancy, the connection appears tenuous.

Irish vacation *American* a term in prison
Alluding to the supposed lawlessness of 19th-century Irish immigrants into America, or to a tendency of the authorities to pick on them, or to the preponderance of Irishmen among the jailers:
> The author knitted police court news...rude winks about rough lads who might be going away for 'an Irish vacation'. (Proulx, 1993)

Irishman's rise a decrease in pay
For doing the same job.

iron¹ a handgun
The metal is inexactly specified:
> He punched Malvern with the muzzle of the gun...'Keep your iron next to your own belly.' (Chandler, 1939)

A steel was always a sword or bayonet.

iron² a male homosexual
Rhyming slang on *iron hoof*, a POUFF.

iron out to kill
Not from IRON 1 but from the flattening of the victim. Occasionally as *iron off*.

irregular not acting in a conventional or usual way
It may refer to copulation, where the use is specific of a relationship between a Roman Catholic priest and his mistress. Sometimes as *irregular conduct* or *an irregular situation*:
> Johnson...was very careful not to give encouragement to irregular conduct. (J. Boswell, 1791)
> No, no, I mean it's you who've had time and the irregular situation. (I. Murdoch, 1974—a man was talking to his mistress)

Irregularity can refer to dishonesty or fraud, or to constipation, or to the menstrual cycle:
> These 'irregularities' had allegedly taken the form of loans she had not repaid (sic). (*Private Eye*, April 1981)
> Irregularity was one of my problems these days, so I was unusually prepared. (P. Scott, 1975, describing menstruation)

it¹ the sexual attractiveness of females as perceived by males

A survival from the 1930s prudery about sex:
> 'It is not beauty that makes every head (except one) turn on the beach to look at her.' 'It's IT, my boy,' said the Major. (Christie, 1940)

it² copulation
A usage without any prior reference to the subject matter:
> I would have asked you anyway...you see, I like it with you. (Bradbury, 1976)

it³ the male or female genitals
Again, the subject has not been previously introduced:
> Whereas in Jake's youth he had gawped at a girl with upper clothing disarranged to reveal a, to him, rare glimpse of 'them', he is now horrified to find himself staring much lower down at a sharply focussed full-colour close-up of 'it'. (F. Muir, 1990, writing of K. Amis's *Jake's Thing*)

itch to feel lustful
Usually of a woman, from the supposed aphrodisiac properties of cantharides which, by exciting vaginal itch, is said to stimulate sexual desire:
> A tailor might scratch her where'er she did itch. (Shakespeare, *The Tempest*, with another of his obscure sexual puns)

Less often of men in the same sense:
> I was beginning to itch for her considerably. (Fraser, 1969)

Itchy feet is the propensity to leave a regular sexual partner for another, as with the SEVEN-YEAR ITCH.

item (an) a continuing sexual partnership between two people outside marriage
Perhaps merely from an *item* of news or gossip:
> The *Daily Telegraph*...revealed a few years ago that she and Chairman of the Ramblers' Association at the time, were 'an item'. (*Daily Telegraph*, 15 April 1995)

itinerant *Irish* a gypsy
Even when parked up:
> Turned out it was a local fella and there's me thinking it must be, y'know, itinerants. (P. McCarthy, 2000)

J

J. Arthur *British* masturbation
Rhyming slang on the film mogul (and lay
preacher) J. Arthur Rank:
> ...having to slip into the bog at the office
> and give yourself a quick J. Arthur into this
> little bottle. (Matthew, 1983)

jab a vein to inject an illegal narcotic
Addict jargon:
> ...smoke marijuana or opium, or sniff
> snow, or jab a vein. (Longstreet, 1956)
Occasionally as *jab off*.

jack¹ the penis
One of the male names often used. Whence
Jack in the orchard, copulation, and *jack off*, to
masturbate:
> The schmuck hasn't done anything but
> indict homos and jack-off artists for two
> years. (Diehl, 1978)

jack² *American* a policeman
The JOHN 4 in familiar speech—many *Johns*
are *Jack* for short:
> ...a uniformed cop was using a
> small walkie-talkie...Another jack was
> sitting and writing in a notebook.
> (Lyall, 1972)

jack it in to die
Literally, to give up an attempt or enterprise.

jack of both sides *obsolete* a male homosexual
Literally, someone who is willing to give his
support to either of two opposing sides.

jack off see JACK 1.

jacket *American* a criminal record
The cover in which the papers are kept:
> ...you don't think people like that
> have jackets, do you? (Sanders,
> 1985, referring to people in the learned
> professions)

jag house *American* a brothel
A *jag* was a load, and used to denote
drunkenness just as LOAD 1 does today, and
to have a *jag on* was to be drunk. From being
an inn, the *jag house* became a brothel and is
now used of one which caters for male
homosexuals.

jagged *American* drunk
From the roughness rather than the *jag*, or
load.

jail bait *American* a sexually mature
female below the legal age of copulation
Bait is used of any young person who may
attract an older one sexually, and especially of
boys attractive to homosexual men. Illegal
copulation with a young girl carries a risk of
imprisonment:
> Two chickies, delicious little morsels of jail
> bait. (J. Collins, 1981)

jakes a lavatory
Just as you visit the JOHN 1 in modern
America, so in the past you visited *Jake's place*.
Dr Johnson's examples from Shakespeare,
Swift, and Dryden are all lavatorial, although
he defines the word as 'a house of office',
using another euphemism:
> I will...daub the walls of a jakes with him.
> (Shakespeare, *King Lear*)
Wits in the 18th and 19th centuries used *Ajax*,
punning on the King of Salamis. In modern
Irish English, it has been corrupted to *jacks*:
> He'd gone to the jacks. It was the only
> thing that ever made him hurry. (R. Doyle,
> 1996)

jam to copulate
Alluding to the pressing tightly together:
> 'He had a good grip on her and she closed
> her eyes and they did it.' 'Did what?' he
> said hoarsely. 'Jammed.' (Theroux, 1978)

jam rag an absorbent worn during menstruation
From the staining:
> She'll go to the shops and get my jam-rags
> for me. (R. Doyle, 1996)

jane¹ *obsolete* a prostitute
Rhyming slang for *Jane Shore*, a whore, the
mistress of King Edward IV:
> Louis Quatorze kept about him, in scores,
> What the Noblesse, in courtesy, term'd his
> Jane Shores. (Barham, 1840)

jane² a lavatory
A feminine, or feminist, JOHN 1, although it is
not noted in *A Feminist Dictionary* (1985).

Japanese insincere
Etiquette in Japan decrees that you should
never indicate dissatisfaction to a stranger:
> Unhappy, indeed, Japanese, laughter all
> round. (A. Clark, 2000)

jar a drink of an intoxicant
Usually beer, from the container in which it
may come:
> 'Have you been drinking?' 'A jar or two,' I
> admitted. (Lyall, 1975)
If you are said to *enjoy a jar*, the implication is
that you are a drunkard.

jasper *American* a female homosexual
A variant of JOHN 3 with possible punning on the meaning segregated.

jawbone *American* credit
You talk the seller into parting with the goods without paying for them. Usually in the phrase *on jawbone*:
> Many ranchers did all their William Lake business on jawbone, paying once a year when they sold their crops of beef.
> (St Pierre, 1983)

jerk¹ *American* to fail a pupil
Tugging them out of the class:
> Not a single student was put up for elimination by the instructors in our school in the first class. The army had to step in and jerk them. (Deighton, 1993, writing about civilian training for air force pilots in 1939)

jerk² a stupid or ineffective person
A common insult as a shortened form of JERK OFF 1 and, less often, a *jerk-off*:
> Look, you think this is some penny-ante organization I'm running, you stupid jerk. (Poyer, 1978)
> It is impossible, even for a flinty-hearted jerk-off such as your narrator, not to be won over. (Bryson, 1989)

jerk off¹ (of a male) to masturbate
From the movement of the hand:
> He's jerking off thirty times a day, that fuckin' guy, and they're all set to give him a medical. (Herr, 1977)

jerk off² illegally to inject heroin slowly
The addict allows the narcotic to mingle with blood in the phial so that a mixture can be injected.

jerry a pot for urine
Dr Wright says it is a shortened form of 'Jeremiah, a chamber utensil' (*EDD*). There may have been some allusion to the *Jericho*, a lavatory, which was one of the unlikely places to which people said they were going. The German soldier, or *Jerry*, wore a helmet of much the same shape but that is probably only a shortened form of *German*.

jet lag a hangover
In standard use, disruption of the biological clock through time change. On long flights some people drink too much alcohol, but are reluctant to admit that as the cause of their later being off-colour:
> I am still under the weather due to jet lag et al. (*Private Eye*, March 1981)

jewels the male genitalia

American rather than British use, from their pendulous proclivity:
> If I'd given him a bright 'Good Morning, Sam!' he'd have kicked me in the jewels. (Sanders, 1979)
Also as *crown jewels* or *family jewels*:
> ...drew up the knees to protect the family jewels. (ibid.)

Jewish question (the) the killing of all Jews
Mass murder was the answer to the *question* which the Nazis formulated in those parts of Europe under their control, especially in the later stages of the Second World War:
> Wisliceny had barely returned to Bratislava from Salonika when on 20 September he and three other SD 'specialists in the Jewish question' were transferred to Athens to set up a department for Jewish affairs under Blume. (Mazower, 1993—the Italians, who had controlled the Athens area until September 1943, had refused to implement anti-Jewish policies there)

Jezebel a prostitute
She was the flighty wife of Ahab in the Old Testament:
> 'But that's...' She was about to say 'a mortal sin' but desisted. 'It makes me a Jezebel, doesn't it?' (Read, 1986)
Until quite recent times, a young woman might be termed a *Jezebel* if she wore make-up on the streets. The epithet was also favoured by the vituperative preacher, John Knox.

jig-a-jig copulation
From the movement involved. In many similar expressions such as *jig-jig* or *jiggy-jig*:
> 'Dated her,' I said. 'You mean a little boom-boom.' 'Jig-jig,' he said. 'But it comes to the same thing. (Theroux, 1978)
> ...the familiar cry of 'jiggy-jig, Sahib'. Very small boys did the soliciting for these native girls. (F. Richards, 1936)
Then come *jig*, *jiggle*, *zig-zig*, and so on. Mainly Far Eastern use.

jiggle (of a male) to masturbate
Literally, to move back and forth:
> 'Nothing of the sort, he lay there jiggling like.' (I guessed what she meant...frigging himself.) (F. Harris, 1925, writing of Carlyle's behaviour on his wedding night. Evidently Mrs Carlyle had more to put up with than the celebrated cup of tea thrown at her by her husband, or less)

Jim Crow *American* the unfair treatment of black people by whites
In early usage, any poor man, from the character in a song in the Negro minstrel show written by Tom Price (1808—60):

It was my first experience with Jim Crow. I was just five, and I had never ridden in a street car before. (L. Armstrong, 1955, writing about segregation on public transport in New Orleans)

Jimmy an act of urination
Rhyming slang on *Jimmy Riddle*, which is also used for urine:
Cdr 'Biffy' Dunderdale and Charles Fraser-Smith...devised maps printed on silk in invisible ink which 'you could develop with your own Jimmy Riddle'. (After the war the silk was sold as scarves to unsuspecting debutantes.) (*Daily Telegraph*, 9 November 1996, listing aids to those who might be captured in wartime)

Jimmy Brits diarrhoea
Again rhyming slang and not shortened to *Jimmy*. Occasionally as *Edgar Brits*.

job an act that is the subject of taboo
In nursery use, used of defecating, and also as BIG JOBS; referring to copulation, a participant is said to be ON THE JOB; of robbery, as in the film title *The Italian Job*; etc.

job action *American* striking or failing to perform an allotted task
The job inaction is the equivalent of the equally deceptive British INDUSTRIAL ACTION:
The pilots' job action in February cost American $225 million and affected hundreds of thousands of travelers. (*New York Herald Tribune*, 10 August 1999)

job turning *American* reducing the responsibility and pay associated with an appointment
The procedure is adopted by an organization when, to fill a QUOTA or to avoid being sued for DISCRIMINATION, it is obliged to appoint to a situation someone whom it thinks to be of inferior qualifications, ability, or experience.

jock the penis
A vulgarism on its own:
He washed his jock in public and he's shy. (Sanders, 1977)
but standard English in *jock-strap*, the genital support garment:
...some joker wearing a coconut mask and a feathered jock-strap. (ibid.)

jocker a male extramarital sexual partner
Heterosexual or homosexual, in which latter case he plays the male role:
So I'm her jocker. So what? This is a lady, a person. (Turow, 1999)
Roxie hustles the guys who want a queen, and the kid goes for the ones who want a jocker. (Wambaugh, 1972)

joe[1] a ponce
Rhyming slang on *Joe Ronce*, whose origins and achievements do not seem to have been recorded for posterity.

joe[2] a spy
Espionage jargon, for one of your own spies:
A joe in the parlance is a living source, and a live source in plain English is a spy. (le Carré, 1989)

john[1] a lavatory
The *cousin John* people said they had to visit as they absented themselves from company:
Running back and forth, practically living in the john. (Theroux, 1975)
(I once worked for a manufacturer of casements in Cardiff called 'Jonwindows'. Happily our range was more extensive than the title might have suggested.)

john[2] *American* a woman's extramarital sexual partner
Sometimes, but not necessarily, he is married to a third party.

john[3] a male homosexual playing the male role
A homosexual pair were once called *John and Joan*, although this may not be the origin of this usage, as the name John appears to be some kind of catch-all so far as taboo activities are concerned.

john[4] *American* a policeman
A shortened form of *John Law*:
So the Johns came for him. (Chandler, 1939)
I'd have no trouble with John Law. (Sanders, 1982)

john[5] *American* a potential customer for a prostitute
Prostitutes' jargon:
Our hustlers sat on their steps and called to the 'johns' as they passed by. (L. Armstrong, 1955)
A *cheap john* is a brothel.

John Barleycorn whisky
The allusion is to its raw material:
Leeze on thee, John Barleycorn,
Thou King o' grain. (Burns, 1786)

John Thomas the penis
The common use of a masculine name or names and without sexual implications. Also as *John Peter* or *John Willie*:
John Thomas doesn't even have a chance to lift his head. (G. Greene, 1978)
What I call your penis and what you prefer to regard as your John Willie. (Sharpe, 1978)

John Thomas and *John Peter* may be shortened to *JT* and *JP*, the latter not necessarily on a Justice of the Peace:

> She had old JP out there, touch, kiss, prod, and consume, aided by some quick dancing work with the fingertips. (Turow, 1993)

Johnnie's out of jail *American* your trouser zip is undone

The prisoner has not in fact escaped.

johnny a contraceptive sheath

From FRENCH LETTER via *frenchie* and *Johnny Frenchman*:

> Millroy was unrolling a small tight ring of rubber... 'A rubber Johnny,' Millroy said. (Theroux, 1993)

Also as *Johnnie*.

Johnson a penis

A diminutive version of JOHN THOMAS, perhaps:

> Though I s'pect he's got himself a microscopic Johnson, his wife runnin' off like that. (Anonymous, 1996)

We cannot claim any link with St Johnstone, whose ribbon or tippet was a hangman's noose.

join¹ *obsolete* to copulate

Of the same tendency as the common COUPLE 1:

> Lovers passed the virulent lice to each other when they joined fast and secret in some hidden corner. (Keneally, 1982)

join² to be as dead as

The imagery is of a coming together again in some physical or spiritual existence rather than in the grave. Thus you may join your deceased spouse or a variety of others:

> He was about to join his ancestors. (Sharpe, 1978)

If you *join the (great) majority*, you are not just voting for a plausible politician:

> ... he was really doing no more than joining that majority. (Price, 1985—he was dying)

join the club see IN THE CLUB

joiner a person who seeks popularity or business by attaching himself to associations etc. in which he has no special interest

Literally, a skilled carpenter. Pejorative use:

> He appeared to be a genial greeter and joiner, an intellectual lightweight. (Sanders, 1977)

joint¹ a marijuana cigarette

The derivation is from what was formerly the equipment of an opium user rather than the place in which the smoking may be done:

> Two or three people can get high on one joint (marijuana cigarette). (Longstreet, 1956—the words in brackets would be superfluous today)

joint² *American* the penis

With the common MEAT 2 imagery:

> ... drawings of a man's joint, a woman's cooze. (Sanders, 1982)

See also UNLIMBER YOUR JOINT.

joint³ *Irish* to incapacitate by shooting

Another type of butchery:

> According to Belfast's grisly argot, he was 'jointed'—shot through both elbows, both knees, and both ankles. (*Sunday Telegraph*, January 1990, reporting on a victim of the IRA)

jolly¹ drunk

An old variant of MERRY:

> They're not up all night at balls and parties, and they don't get jolly in the small hours. (Pearsall, 1969, quoting 19th-century music-hall patter)

jolly² an unnecessary treat paid for by a third party

A business use by those attending and by those not asked to attend, but seldom by those who organize and pay for it.

jolly³ extramarital sexual activity

Heterosexual or homosexual, from the enjoyment:

> ... found the names of Thomas J. Kealy and Constance Underwood, and what they had been paying for their jollies. (Sanders, 1984—the names were in a prostitute's notebook)

jolt (a) anything taboo which gives you a shock or impetus

For illegal narcotics users, an injection of heroin; for criminals, a time in prison; for drinkers, any intoxicant, but usually whisky:

> I think maybe I'll get a jolt too. (Sanders, 1982)
>
> I went out to the kitchenette and poured a stiff jolt of whisky. (Chandler, 1939)

Jordan *obsolete* a pot for urine

Dr Johnson thought it might have come from the Greek while Onions (1975) favoured a river source:

> They will allow us ne'er a jordan and then we leak in the chimney. (Shakespeare, 1 Henry IV)

Certainly, if in Edinburgh you heard from above the cry *jordeloo*, you were well advised to avoid the area into which the malodorous liquids were being thrown. *Gardeloo, gardez l'eau*, was unpleasant enough, by all accounts.

joy¹ copulation
For male or female, as in *mutual joy(s)*:
> ...the woman seeking mutual joys courts him to run the race of love. (Lucretius, in translation)

Whence the punning *joy ride*, a single act of copulation; *joy-girl* or *joy-boy*, a prostitute; and *joy-house*, a brothel:
> I had no fatigue, indeed, I felt better for our joy ride. (F. Harris, 1925)
> The gambling casino on the lake, and the fifty-dollar joy girls. (Chandler, 1953)
> I ain't been in a joy house in twenty years. (Chandler, 1940)

joy² heroin
The sensation illegal users seek:
> The Family doesn't sell crack or joy. That's on principle. (Fiennes, 1996)

Joy is also used attributively in many compounds, such as *joy popper*, an occasional user; *joy powder*, morphine; *joy flakes*, cocaine; *joy ride*, being under narcotic influence; *joy rider*, a person taking drugs; *joy smoke*, marijuana; *joy stick*, an opium.

joy ride¹ ² see JOY 1 2

joyride³ to take and drive away a motor vehicle without consent
Under the English Larceny Act, codifying the common law, the offender committed no crime, apart from a possible theft of fuel, because there was no intention 'permanently to deprive the owner thereof'. *Joyriding* is now an offence in its own right.

Judy a prostitute
The derivation is either from the common girls' name which became a name for common girls or, more probably, from *Judith*, the beautiful Jewess who is said to have tricked Nebuchadnezzar's general Holofernes in order to save the town of Bethulia. The general lost his head to her and to the axe:
> When monks like Negga were shooting down their officers or bribing potential Judiths to seduce their Holofernes... (Mockler, 1984)

Then a *Judy* became a mistress:
> He went tul his wife at Wortley, an his judy went to Rotherham. (*Dewsbury Olm*, 1866, quoted in *EDD*)

And now, in Ireland at least, she is an attractive young woman:
> Some great lookin' judies. (R. Doyle, 1987—the advantages of a public house were being discussed)

jug¹ a prison
From the Scottish *joug*, a pillory rather than the ewer. To *jug* is to imprison:
> He is arrested. He is jugged. (Manning, 1960)

jug² an intoxicant
Referring to the container:
> I had a way of puttin' in my time with a private jug, on the sly. (Twain, 1884)

juggle *obsolete* to copulate
If Shakespeare was running true to form, punning on the play with balls:
> She and the Dauphin have been juggling. (*1 Henry VI*)

jugs a woman's breasts
Probably from their shape and the purpose of producing and holding milk:
> Blue eyes. Peaches-and-cream complexion. Big jugs. (Sanders, 1970)

Grose tells us that a *double jug* was a man's backside.

juice¹(the) intoxicants
The common modern use probably came from the literal meaning, liquid of fruit, rather than from the Scottish *juice of the bear*, whisky. *Juniper juice* was gin but the *juice* can be any spirits:
> The cops will probably want you to stay off the juice. (Deighton, 1972)

And as a verb:
> ...would gather after a long day in the IO shop to juice a little. (Herr, 1977—in fact they gathered in the IO shop after a long day elsewhere)

Whence *juiced*, drunk, *juice head*, a drunkard, and *juice joint*, a bar.

juice² *American* a payment made or demanded illegally
What comes in if you SQUEEZE 1:
> The bookie was a big operator and sent his juice money directly to City Hall. (Weverka, 1973—I suspect he sent it direct to City Hall, without an intermediary, but not necessarily promptly)

Whence the *juice dealer*, or loan shark, who uses for collection a hoodlum called a *juice man*.

juice³ semen
Not blood, sweat, or tears:
> There was a moment just before the juice from him was in my mouth, when I already had the taste of it. (R. Thompson, 1996)

juiced up (of a female) lustful
From the increased sexual secretion:
> ...he knew how to get a girl juiced up better than anyone she'd ever known. (M. Thomas, 1982)

Whence, *juicy*, experiencing such arousal:
> They will claim that only the other day they saw a man whose bottom reminded them a little of Mel Gibson and that they

got really quite juicy thinking about it. (Fry, 1994)

jump¹ to rob
From the pouncing. An English 19th-century use since revived in America:

Instead of 'jumping' those stores for an average of forty dollars...(Lavine, 1930)

jump² a single act of copulation
Normally a male usage, but he does not literally have to leap on his partner:

You've never had a quick jump in the hay in your life. (Steinbeck, 1961)

To *jump* is to copulate and a *junior jumper* is a youthful rapist.

jump³ to leave in a forbidden or illegal way
Thus to *jump ship* is to stay ashore wrongly, of a sailor, although it may be used of other desertion:

Moscow Centre officers who were thinking of jumping ship...(le Carré, 1980)

A prisoner not on remand may, if he absconds, *jump bail*; and if you leave somewhere such as a restaurant without paying your bill in America you may be said to *jump a check*.

jump the broomstick to live together as a couple without marrying
This symbolic leap replaced the wedding ceremony:

Besides I ain't married proper. No more than if I jumped a broomstick. (B. Cornwell, 1993, writing in archaic style)

Whence the *broomstick match*, or common-law marriage:

I never had a wife but I had two or three broomstick matches. (Mayhew, 1851)

You might also have been said to *jump the besom*.

jump the last hurdle to die
With steeplechasing in mind.

junk illegal narcotics
Originally old rope, whence hemp, whence narcotics generally:

Now every nerve became an open mouth that screamed for junk. (Gabriel, 1992)

A *junkie* is an addict:

A cheap junkie's arms and legs are covered with unhealed scabs. (Longstreet, 1956)

A *junker* in this world is not a Prussian aristocrat but a pedlar in narcotics, as is a *junkman*:

I just retired a junkman. (Diehl, 1978—he had killed one)

Junked up is the state of being under the influence of narcotics:

Will you go out now, before he gets junked up for the evening? (Chandler, 1939)

junket an unnecessary treat provided free by another
Literally, a dessert of flavoured milk curdled by rennet. Now describing an occasion where the provider seeks to obtain a business advantage without overt bribery:

...lurking in the background of every junket there is likely to be a provenance or motive that is not especially palatable. (H. Porter in *Daily Telegraph*, 8 October 1994)

just good friends see FRIEND

justify *obsolete* *Scottish* to kill by order of a court
It meant to bring to justice, whence either to convict or acquit, which must have been the source of some confusion:

Our great grand-uncle that was justified at Dumbarton. (W. Scott, 1817—we can only learn great grand-uncle's fate by reading on)

K

kangaroo court an ad hoc investigation
A method of disciplining supposed offenders
who fail to comply with unenforceable rules,
instructions, or customs. The practice is found
in closed societies such as prisons, the forces,
terrorist organizations, or trade unions. The
offender is made figuratively to jump to it,
like the marsupial. A prison *kangaroo club* is a
clique of long-serving inmates:
> He was president of the Kangaroo Club and
> would hold court to instruct them in their
> duties. (Lavine, 1930, describing the
> initiation of new prisoners)

kayo to kill
From the boxing *KO*, to knock out:
> ...this stiff got kayoed at the end of
> October. (Diehl, 1978)

keel over to die
The capsizing of a boat, or the figurative fall
of a bird from its perch:
> He told me he might keel over at any time.
> (A. Waugh, *Private Eye*, August 1980)

keelhauled *obsolete* drunk
It was Dutch practice to drag defaulters under
the keel of a boat for punishment, and we still
use *keelhauling* of a verbal reprimand. If you
were very drunk, you might look and feel like
the victim of a real *keelhauling*:
> They wad fuddle an' drink till they were
> keel-haul'd. (W. Anderson, 1867)

keep to maintain a mistress
The usage implies both provision for her
upkeep and keeping her sexual activities for
your sole use:
> One officer offered to keep me if I would
> come and live with him. (Mayhew, 1862)
The man was the *keeper* and the woman a *kept
mistress*, *wench*, or *woman*:
> ...amongst the kept mistresses... I hardly
> knew one that did not perfectly detest her
> keeper. (Cleland, 1749)
> Virgins, reporters, housewives, kept
> wenches. (Longstreet, 1956—which was
> the oddity in that class?)
> Most kept women have several lovers.
> (Mayhew, 1862)
The relationship commences when the woman is *taken into keeping*:
> In France, as soon as a man of fashion
> marries, he takes an opera girl into
> keeping. (J. Boswell, 1791—there must
> have been few *men of fashion* or a plethora of
> artistes)

keep company with to have a sexual rela-
tionship with
Literally, to accompany whence, in standard
English, to court:
> Their sweethearts or husbands have been
> keepin' company with someone else.
> (Emerson, 1890)
See also COMPANY 1.

keep sheep by moonlight *obsolete* to be
killed by hanging
You watch them from the gallows, as did
those
> ...that shepherded the moonlit sheep a
> hundred years ago. (Housman, 1896)

keep up with the Joneses to live beyond
your means or extravagantly
The *Joneses* are your mythical neighbours who
always seem able to afford the new curtains
you have coveted or the garden tractor you
have been collecting brochures about, and
with whom you seek to compete.

keep your legs crossed (of a female) not
to be promiscuous
The imagery is obvious. Also as *keep your legs
together*:
> I don't think she keeps her legs crossed all
> the time. (Price, 1972)
> [She] had kept her legs tightly together.
> (Price, 1975)

keep your pants on (of a male) not to be
promiscuous
Also as *keep your pants zipped*:
> 'Have you found someone else?' he asked.
> 'Nope, I've kept my pants on.' (Grisham,
> 1998)
> But playing around like that... Can't keep
> his pants zipped. (Clancy, 1991)

kerb-crawling looking for a prostitute
Done by a man who drives slowly in an area
known to be frequented by prostitutes:
> [George Wigg] was now fulfilling that
> function in the Lords, where his self-
> righteous pomposity would continue until
> pricked by his arrest for kerb-crawling.
> (Heffer, 1998—the 'function' was toadying
> to the then Prime Minister, Harold Wilson)
Whence also to *crawl a kerb*:
> Sailor spotted Tosh's red beacon hair and
> explosive silhouette and for the first time
> in his life he crawled a kerb. (Fiennes, 1996)

Khyber the anus
Rhyming slang for *Khyber Pass*. Sometimes also
in the vulgar riposte *up your Khyber*. Less often
in full:
> Does he listen? Does he, my Khyber Pass.
> (le Carré, 1993)

kick¹ to die
Probably from the involuntary spasm of a slaughtered animal. Usually as *kick in, it, off* or *up*:

> Thou's no kick up, till thou's right aul.
> (Picken, 1813—you won't die till you're old)

The common *kick the bucket* is supposed by some to come from the *bucket*, or beam, to which a Norfolk pig was tied to facilitate the slitting of its throat and which it kicked in its death throes. It may as well have come from the practice of the victim or suicide standing on a bucket after being strung up to a beam, the bucket then being kicked away:

> It all went. So he kicked the bucket, literally. (Sanders, 1977—he committed suicide)

To *kick the wind* or the punning *kick your heels* was to be killed by hanging:

> In a few moments most of them would be kicking their heels in a different world from this one. (F. Richards, 1933)

kick² (the) peremptory dismissal from employment
Usually affecting a single employee. The assault is figurative.

kick over the traces to behave in an immoral or an unruly fashion
Like an unschooled horse:

> What about his missus? Does she ever kick over the traces? (Sanders, 1992—an enquiry was being made about her adultery)

kick the habit to cease ingesting unprescribed drugs
See also HABIT.

kick the tyres to examine superficially
Business jargon, from the actions of inexpert buyers of used cars:

> ...a simplistic agrarian vision which the war-weary nation had bought without kicking the tires. (M. Thomas, 1980)

kickback a clandestine illegal payment
The derivation is from the vicious habits of starting handles in the days before motors had electric starters. Used of hidden commissions, bribery, and commissions on the proceeds of illegal activities:

> It's the job if I get a kickback. (Chandler, 1939)

kid an adult
A child since the 16th century, before which it was only the young of a goat. Untypically missed by Dr Johnson and his team. As with MIDDLE-AGED, the usage seeks to minimize age:

> He was still a kid, no more than thirty, thirty-two. (M. Thomas, 1980)

In obsolete English to *kid* meant to impregnate or to give birth, of both women and goats.

kill a snake *Australian* to urinate
Not the usual penis-as-serpent image, but from going into the bush.

kind (of a female) prepared to be promiscuous
Literally, friendly or considerate. Of a male, it may mean exercising tenderness or restraint in sexual activity:

> 'Your Highness,' he said at last, 'will you be kind to our treasure...It's a polite way of suggesting you don't make too much of a beast of yourself on the honeymoon. (Fraser, 1970)

kindness *obsolete* bribery
Another form of consideration:

> ...what hath passed between us of kindness to hold his tongue. (Pepys, 1668—he was worried that the person who had bribed him would talk about it)

King Lear *British* a male homosexual
Rhyming slang for QUEER 3, with perhaps an allusion to the monarch's madness.

king over the water *obsolete British* a Stuart pretender in exile
Possibly used of Charles II and James II during their 17th-century absences from the throne, and certainly much in vogue after the Hanoverian kings took over after Queen Anne died in 1714:

> He so far compromised his loyalty, as to announce merely 'The King', as his first toast...Our guest...added, 'Over the water'. (W. Scott, 1824)

Stuart supporters would normally pass their glass over a glass of water without venturing verbal amplification. Loyalty to the Stuarts, especially after 1715, also implied adherence to Roman Catholicism, which in turn involved civil disabilities if not prosecution.

kingdom come death
Despite society's unsatisfactory experience with theocracies, we do not demur at the plea *Thy kingdom come* in the Lord's Prayer:

> ...Piper being blown to Kingdom Come in the company of Mrs Hutchmeyer. (Sharpe, 1977)

kinky displaying bizarre sexual tastes
A kink is a bend, as in a hosepipe. *Kinky* implies a number of perverted deviations when formerly it was applied only to male homosexuality:

And you said last night that he was 'that kind'...funny, kinky. (Bogarde, 1981)

kiss *obsolete* to copulate with
This dates to the era when kisses were only exchanged within the family. If you got that far with a third party, you might expect to proceed much further. Whence the euphemistic definition by Dr Wright:
> Obs. To lie with a woman. (*EDD*)

kiss-and-tell involving the sale of personal memoirs of promiscuity
Usually done by women, telling the tabloid press about sexual relationships with older men who are public figures, in return for what is called *kiss-money*.

kiss off¹ *American* to die
The gesture of parting.

kiss-off² *American* summary dismissal from employment or another's presence
Again from the parting:
> 'Yes. Sure. Fine,' Delaney said heavily, feeling this was just a polite kiss-off. (Sanders, 1973)

Those dismissed on the west coast may call it a *New York kiss-off*. In New England it becomes a *California kiss-off*. This again demonstrates the common practice of attributing bad manners or behaviour to our rivals.

kiss St Giles' cup *obsolete* to be killed by hanging
A victim was traditionally offered a cup of water at St Giles-in-the-Fields on his last journey from Newgate to Tyburn.

kiss the ground *obsolete* to die
Referring to the involuntary falling and not in any way associated with the practice of kissing the tarmac to express your pleasure at arrival:
> I will not yield
> To kiss the ground before young Malcolm's feet. (Shakespeare, *Macbeth*, although here it might have meant no more than to pay homage)

kissed by the maiden *obsolete Scottish* judicially killed
The *maiden* was a guillotine:
> [The Duke of Argyll] was taken to Edinburgh to be kissed by the *Maiden*. (Paterson, 1998—it happened in June 1685)

Kit has come *British* I am menstruating
Kit can be a shortened form of Charles, and see CHARLIE.

kitchen-sinking making excessive provision

From the cliché *everything bar the kitchen sink*. It is the practice of those taking control of a business which has been doing badly to ensure that none of the previous losses or managerial errors can be attributed to them:
> There will be an element of 'kitchen sinking' in these numbers. (*Sunday Telegraph*, 4 April 1993—excessive reserves had been provided)

kite to issue (a negotiable instrument that is not covered by the drawer)
A shortened form of *fly a kite*, an operation which involves launching an object without visible support:
> 'Just don't start kiting checks,' Delaney warned. (Sanders, 1985)

A *kiteman* may still try to issue such paper, but with less success since electronic banking and computerization.

kitty¹ the vagina
A variant of PUSSY 1.

kitty² *obsolete* a prison
Common in the northern counties of England in the 19th century:
> The blacksmith—hauling off the breakers of the peace to the 'Kitty'. (D. D. Dixon, 1895)

Note the modern use when, in some communal activity involving expense, we each put something *in the kitty*.

knackers the testicles
A *knack* was a toy or small object, made by a *knacker*, whence a saddler, who bought old or dead beasts for their hides, whence his modern counterpart who disposes of dead cattle. The use may come from the meaning small objects but Dr Wright is persuasive when he gives:
> Two flat pieces of wood or bone...Of unequal length. (*EDD*)

Partridge suggests 'Prob. ex dial knacker, a castanet or other "striker"' (*DSUE*) and the imagery from the small Spanish chestnut is attractive, although unconvincing.

Those who, in their exhaustion, claim to be *knackered* are likely to consider themselves candidates for the *knacker's yard* rather than winded by a blow to the testicles.

knee-trembler a person who copulates while standing up
From the required movement:
> That knee-trembler put Angela in an interesting condition. (McCourt, 1997)

kneecap *Irish* to maim by shooting in the knees
A form of punishment used by the IRA in Northern Ireland.

knees up (of a female) copulating
The position sometimes adopted:
    ... he's had more hot dinners in my house
    that I've had nights with my knees up.
    (Lyall, 1972)
A *knees-up* is no more than a party or informal
dance.

knight *British* a person associated with
any illegal, taboo, or despised occupation
A source of much former wit. A *knight of
Hornsey* was a cuckold, punning on the
London borough and the horn of cuckoldry;
a *knight of the road* was a mounted thief; and a
knight of the Golden Fleece was a lawyer,
although here I fear the preterite may be
the wrong tense.

knight starvation *British* excessive and
ostentatious zeal in pursuit of a knight-
hood
An ailment aggravated by the HONOUR(S)
system. The usage puns on an advertising
slogan coined by Horlicks to sell a malted
milk product as a nightcap:
    Some might say he deserves the money for
    taking on such a thankless task, and only
    the ungracious will mutter about knight
    starvation. (*Daily Telegraph*, 4 February
    1998—a businessman had been appointed
    Chairman of the Arts Council)

knob the penis
A male vulgarism using the same imagery as
KNOCKER. As the word is also used for the
head, there can be occasions where misunderstanding occurs.

knobs a woman's breasts
A less common vulgarism than KNOCKERS, but
again using the same imagery:
    ... and who do I see in a tight sweater, with
    knobs like this? (Theroux, 1989)

knock *obsolete* to copulate
The activity might take place in a KNOCKING-
SHOP. A single act of copulation can also be
called a *knock*:
    Throw her away and she'll always come
    back for another weekend of cheap knock.
    (Fowles, 1977)

knock around habitually to beat
By husbands of wives and parents of children:
    I gather he likes to knock her around a bit.
    (le Carré, 1989)

knock down to kill
You *knock down* animals by shooting them:
    She knocked down squirrels with exquisite
    faces. (Mailer, 1965)

knock it back to drink intoxicants to
excess
On a single occasion or regularly, from the
angling of the glass as you drink:
    ... he'd begun to knock it back at half past
    ten in the morning. (P. Scott, 1977)

knock off[1] to kill
As a bird from a branch, but in American use
it may also apply to humans:
    So you wouldn't knock him off ... but you
    might throw a scare into him. (Chandler,
    1939)
To *knock on the head* is also to kill, of humans
and other animals.

knock off[2] (of a male) to copulate with
Usually in a casual relationship, perhaps with
imagery from stealing.

knock off[3] to steal
It refers to minor thefts, from the concept of
dislodging them from a counter or barrow.

knock off[4] to drink (an intoxicant)
Usually beer, and specifying in pints the
amount consumed. See also KNOCK IT BACK.

knock off (someone's) rudder to cause
mental imbalance to (someone)
Like the boat which can no longer be steered:
    There's been a tragedy in this fellow's life
    and it has knocked off his rudder. (Mark
    VII, 1927)

knock-out a fraudulent auction
Auctioneers' jargon which puns on *knock
down*, to register a sale by the fall of the
hammer, and the boxing term *knock out*, to
end a contest by rendering your opponent
unconscious. The phrase is used of cases
where there is a conspiracy between the
auctioneer and one or more of the bidders
to cheat the seller.

knock over to kill
By shooting, using the language of hunting:
    I heard ... he had been knocked over in the
    last months of the war ... The rumour
    proved false ... He is alive and kicking.
    (F. Richards, 1933)

knock up to impregnate a female
Usually when it is an unwanted pregnancy:
    ... they told me that seven of the girls were
    knocked up—well, pregnant. (N. Mitford,
    1960)
In the days before alarm clocks, when people
lost their jobs if they were late for work,
factory workers would be *knocked up* by
someone paid to knock on their doors or
windows to wake them.

knocker the penis
From the shape of a door knocker and punning on its sexual function:
Susie was a perfect fool for any chap with a big knocker. (Fraser, 1982)

knockers a woman's breasts
Again from the shape of a door knocker and its movement in a vertical plane when activated:
I could see a roomful of libidinous Japanese with their mouths open, transfixed by a wobbling pair of Russian knockers. (Theroux, 1988)

knocking-shop a brothel
Derived from the obsolete KNOCK but still a common usage:
At the fifth knocking-shop, I struck pure gold. (Fraser, 1971: the gold was figurative—he had found a bawd to hide him)
Formerly also as *knocking-house*, *knocking-joint* or *knocker's shop*:
...in twenty minutes they had organized a taxi to a 'knocker's shop'. (M. Clark, 1991—they were 'taking a look at the tarts')

knot *obsolete* to copulate
From the meaning, to unite or bring together:
...a cistern for foul toads
To knot and gender in. (Shakespeare, *Othello*)
I am not sure about:
...young people knotting together, and crying out 'Porridge'. (Pepys, 1662)

know to copulate with

It was a euphemism in Hebrew, Greek, and Latin, which explains why the translators for King James I (of England) found it so useful:
And he knew her not till she had brought forth her first-born son. (*Matthew* 1: 25, of Joseph and Mary)

know the score see SCORE 1

known to the police having a criminal record or having been suspected of a crime
The usage ignores the fact that the police know many people who are not criminals, not excluding lawyers and politicians:
Hamilton was a frightening man, known to the police. (Monkhouse, 1993—Hamilton had been arrested three times in connection with crimes of violence but never convicted)

knuckle sandwich *American* a punch in the face
An equivalent of BUNCH OF FIVES which uses the same imagery:
First the velvet glove, then the knuckle sandwich. (Sanders, 1977)

konk off to die
Presumably what happens if you *konk* (or *conk*) *out*, like a motor:
I know why you've come to see me. You think I'm going to konk off. (Blessed, 1991—he was visiting a nonagenarian)

L

labour¹ childbirth
Literally, physical toil, but so long standard
English that we do not think about it as a
euphemism.

labour² unemployment
A *Labour Exchange* was an office where those
without work went to seek a job and claim
money, whence being *on the labour* meant
being unemployed and in receipt of state cash
rather than *labouring*:
> Being on the labour wouldn't have been
> that bad if you could've come up here
> every night. (R. Doyle, 1991—*here* was the
> pub)

labour education arbitrary imprisonment
Usually for political dissenters in China, like
the Chinese woman who, in 1981, wished to
marry a French diplomat and was sentenced
to two years *re-education through labour* for the
offence of 'illegally living together with a
foreigner'. (*Daily Telegraph*, November 1981)

lack of moral fibre *British* cowardice
Mainly Second World War military use, often
as *LMF*:
> ...stamped on the record of failed officers.
> *Lack of moral fibre*. If Second-Lieutenant
> Audley suffered from LMF...(Price, 1978)
Under conditions of active service, it is not
easy for comrades to distinguish between psychological illness, prudence, and cowardice.

lack of visibility concealment or obfusca-
tion
Financial jargon for opaque or worrying
published accounts:
> 'Lack of visibility' is usually code for not
> liking the view. At Granada, the picture is
> indeed foggy. (*Financial Times*, 14 June 2001)

lad an exclusive male premarital sexual
partner
Literally, a boy or young man, especially in
Scotland and the north of England. Elsewhere
specifically one who looks after horses:
> But when I was nineteen he sought me out
> and he became my lad. (Cookson, 1969)
So too with *LASS*.

laddish mildly pornographic
To be *one of the lads* is to act in a gregarious if
immature way in male company:
> Copies of British tabloid newspapers,
> 'laddish' men's magazines, a satellite

television magazine and a pair of reading
glasses lay strewn across a Moorish-style
coffee table. (*Daily Telegraph*, 31 August
1998, describing the residence in Spain of a
British fugitive)

ladies a lavatory exclusively for female
use
Usually adjacent to GENTLEMEN. Also as *ladies'
convenience, room* etc.:
> I tapped a kidney in the ladies room.
> (Theroux, 1978)

ladies' man a man who delights in the
company of women
A slightly derogatory use by other males who
may not share his dress sense or his ability to
show interest in every topic of female conversation. He may also be a profligate:
> Blamey was a big 57-year-old who liked to
> wear a broad-brimmed bush hat and
> seemed to enjoy his reputation as a
> ladies' man. (Deighton, 1993—General
> Blamey commanded the Australian
> forces in the Middle East between 1940
> and 1942)

lady a prostitute
As in the oldest joke:
> 'Who was that lady I saw you with last
> night?' 'That was no lady. That was my
> wife.'
A *lady's college* was a brothel where you might
contract *lady's fever*, syphilis. Also as *lady-
boarder, lady of a certain description, easy virtue,
no virtue, pleasure* (who might also be a
mistress), *the night, the sisterhood, the stage, the
streets*, or just plain *ladybird* (who might also
be a sweetheart):
> ...played for the lady-boarders and their
> friends. (Longstreet, 1956—the women
> worked in a brothel)
> There are two kinds of person who supply
> the police with all the information they
> want; one, that of unmarried ladies of a
> certain description...(H. James, 1816)
> Talking of London, [Dr Johnson]
> observed...a man of pleasure [thinks of it
> as] the great emporium for ladies of easy
> virtue. (J. Boswell, 1791)
> So when he visited ladies of no virtue, it
> might be for purposes of fornication.
> (Masters, 1976)
> Here was my Lord Bouncker's lady of
> pleasure. (Pepys, 1665)
> The lady of the night studied Abel
> carefully. (Archer, 1979)
> I was looked up to as a kind of pattern to
> the ladies of the sisterhood. (Lyons, 1996—
> the boast was made by a celebrated 18th-
> century Dublin prostitute)
> We call them ladies of the stage. They
> prefer that. Most of them have been in

front of the footlights at one time or
another. (Innes, 1991)
What, lamb! What, ladybird! God forbid.
(Shakespeare, *Romeo and Juliet*)

lady bear *American* a policewoman
A version of BEAR 2.

lady dog a bitch
The very fastidious or prudish use the phrase
to avoid confusing the inoffensive quadruped
with the spiteful and domineering biped so
offensively described.

lady friend a female extramarital sexual
partner
She does not have to be a woman of breeding
or distinction, but the use implies slightly
more acceptability than WOMAN FRIEND:
    It's my lady friend. I've reason to
    suspect that she's getting a bit on the
    side. (P. D. James, 1972)

lady-in-waiting[1] a concubine in the Japanese court
Literally, a female who attends to female
royalty:
    A dozen concubines, euphemistically
    termed ladies-in-waiting, nightly awaited
    the drop of the imperial handkerchief at
    their feet to follow him into his quarters.
    (Behr, 1989, writing about the Emperor
    Meiji, Hirohito's dissolute father)

lady-in-waiting[2] a pregnant woman
Mainly humorous use, punning on the court
official. The obsolete English *lady in the straw*
was a woman in the process of being
delivered of a baby.

lady-killer a male profligate
But without murderous intent.

lady of intrigue *obsolete* a promiscuous
woman
Not Mata Hari but:
    By ladies of intrigue we must understand
    married women who have connection with
    other men than their husbands and
    unmarried women who gratify their
    passions secretly. (Mayhew, 1862)

laid out drunk
Either like a boxer who has been floored by
his opponent (in this case alcohol) or like a
cadaver. See LAY OUT.

laid to rest dead
A monumental favourite, as in AT REST:
    She came to the end of the road only
    five months after we had laid Father to
    rest, so they were not parted long.
    (Tyrrell, 1973)

Anyone dying at sea might be *laid in the lockers*,
for subsequent burial on land, but if you
died beyond the Thames estuary town of
Gravesend, your corpse would be disposed of
at sea.

lame duck[1] the holder of an office to
which he has not been re-elected
His successor will soon hold the reins of
power, perhaps with a different policy. The
term is often used of an outgoing president
of the United States who becomes ineffectual during his last months of office, if not
before.

lame duck[2] a failing enterprise
Peter Pindar described Pitt as 'A duck con-
founded lame' which may have been no more
than political abuse. In the 19th century, the
phrase was used of personal failure in business:
    [A lame duck is] a stockjobber who
    speculates beyond his capital, and cannot
    pay his losses. (*The Slang Dictionary*, 1874)
In 1971 John Davies, a British minister in the
Heath government, used the phrase to describe manufacturing companies seeking
state cash to compensate for losses caused
by their own ineptitude. Giving such assistance was said to be contrary to government
policy, and the cash was then paid over. See
also U-TURN.

lance (of a male) to copulate with
Literally, to pierce, with the common thrusting imagery:
    She would fall in a faint,
    And only revive when lanced freely.
    (*Playboy's Book of Limericks*)

land of forgetfulness (the) death
Some of us sinners on this ball of clay can
hope this is true:
    I was told of a vast number of my
    acquaintance who were all gone over to the
    land of forgetfulness. (J. Boswell, 1791)

land of Nod (the) sleep
A pun on Cain's travels when he 'dwelt in the
land of Nod' (*Genesis* 4: 16):
    There's queer things chanced since ye hae
    been in the land of Nod. (W. Scott, 1818)
Mainly nursery use for coaxing children into
the frightening dark.

landscaped tidied up
Estate agents' and builders' puff for the
garden of a new house from which most of
the rubble has been removed or covered with
a thin coating of soil.

language swear words
A shortened form of *bad language*:

I'll have no man usin' language i' my house. (D. Murray, 1886—he was not a Trappist abbot)

In America *language arts* is educational and sociological jargon for the ability to speak coherently.

lard the books dishonestly to increase a claim for repayment

You enrich the mix by adding too much fat:

The housekeeper at Twin Beeches regularly larded her books with non-existent bills. (Deighton, 1972)

large¹ pregnant

Occasional female use:

It was when I was large with our Lizbeth. (*EDD*)

large² small

Or smaller than *jumbo* or *family* in hypermarket hype:

The smallest tube of toothpaste you can buy is the 'large size'. (Jennings, 1965)

larger obese

Jargon of the clothing industry, without stating the norm against which the measurement has been made. It may also refer to females who are taller than the norm:

...a brand aimed at 'larger' women. (*Daily Telegraph*, 15 September 1994)

lass an exclusive extra-marital female sexual partner

A usage not confined to the Scots. See also LAD.

last call (the) death

In various other combinations also, sometimes referring to the dead person's occupation or interests. Thus the *last call* tends to be taken by actors or actresses, who make their *last bow*, although never their last curtsey. Cowboys head for the *last round-up* but those of us who pay the *last debt* may in fact die insolvent. The *last trump* is not for card players only but for those who hear the call to the seat of judgment. The *last end* and the *last resting place* are specific, at least until the resurrection, as is the *last voyage* or the *last journey*:

Just before the armistice George made his last journey to Banbury; a month later everyone in the village knew he was near the last journey of all. (Tyrrell, 1973)

See also AT YOUR LAST.

last favour (the) copulation

Granted after other familiarities. Also as *last intimacies*:

A man...has a secret horror of an innocent young woman allowing the last intimacies

to a man whom she does not passionately love. (Pearsall, 1969, quoting Patmore, *c.*1890)

For the diarist, the *last thing*:

I had my full liberty of towsing her and doing what I would but the last thing. (Pepys, 1663—to *towse* was to pull or shake about, whence *towser*, a dog used in bear-baiting, and then any mastiff)

last shame (the) *obsolete British* a term of imprisonment

A usage at a time when more stigma attached to criminality.

last waltz *American* the walk to death by execution

A waltz traditionally ends the ball.

latchkey (of a child) arriving home to an empty house because neither parent is then available and specifically the mother is absent at work

With implications of parental neglect:

'In a world of latchkey children,' he said, 'children whose only companion is the television set...' (M. Thomas, 1985)

late¹ dead

Usually in connection with someone recently deceased. Venerable enough to have been used by Caxton in 1490 but still sometimes confused with unpunctuality.

late² failing to menstruate when expected

With fears of unplanned pregnancy:

He thought of her telling him she was late, had never been late before, and was he going to walk out on her. (Seymour, 1980)

late booking fraudulently reserving profitable deals for favoured clients

A practice of commodity or money dealers who prefer to defer nominating the beneficiaries of their better deals until the end of the day, when they can allot the less successful trades to passive investors:

Regulators said that Mr Armstrong, who joined Jardine, Fleming in 1982 from Scottish Equitable, was in the practice of executing deals known as 'late booking'. (*Daily Telegraph*, 30 August 1996—Armstrong was banned for life by the Hong Kong regulators, his employers were fined £12 million, and over £200,000 was repaid to those who had been cheated)

late developer a poor scholar

Used by parents who have hope rather than by teachers who have experience:

late disturbances | **lay down your life**

She was a late developer and a bit of a slow-coach. (I. Murdoch, 1977)

late disturbances a recent war
Late means former:
> The year of 1688 brought to England the worst turmoil since the 'late disturbances', as Mr Pepys had once described a brutal civil war and a royal beheading.
> (Monsarrat, 1978)

Also as *late unpleasantness*, describing the American Civil War and the First World War. Another version after the Second World War was *late nastiness*:
> ...it was a great mercy we couldn't fight tanks in the dark in the late nastiness.
> (Price, 1987—by *fight* he meant *fight with* rather than *fight against*, night sights not having then been invented)

latrine a lavatory
As with LAVATORY itself, the derivation is from the Latin *lavare*, to wash. Usually denoting primitive and communal structures, as in the army:
> Latrines...often consisted of no more than a small mud hut with an open door.
> (C. Allen, 1975)

latter end¹ the buttocks
Of the same tendency as BOTTOM. Also in the form *latter part*.

latter end² death
It should mean no more than our closing years before death:
> I spoke severely, being naturally indignant (at my time of life) to hear a young woman of five-and-twenty talking about her latter end! (W. Collins, 1868—she was not referring to her anatomy)

laughing academy an institution for the insane
Not a school for comedians. Inappropriate laughter is a symptom of insanity:
> The way you're going in to bat to get the old man back in the laughing academy...(Wambaugh, 1975)

launder to bring funds dishonestly obtained into apparently legal circulation or account
Used of money which has been stolen or which is the proceeds of vice, especially drug dealing; and of public funds secretly diverted from the purpose for which they were voted:
> ...accused of 'laundering' some of the marked banknotes used to pay the Schild ransom. (*Daily Telegraph*, July 1980)
> Cash from various Ministries is 'laundered' and diverted to the secret service. (*Daily Mirror*, February 1980)

A bank permitting such transactions or a seemingly legal trading company through which the funds pass is known as a *laundry*.

lavabo a lavatory
'I will wash', from the Latin Vulgate version of *Psalms* 26: 6—*Lavabo inter innocentes manus meas*—and still used interchangeably with LAVATORY, but not very often:
> They follow me even to the lavabo. (Theroux, 1975)

lavatory a room set aside for urination and defecation
Originally, a place for washing in, and then the place where you went to wash:
> Remember that our 'lavatory' is a euphemism. (E. Waugh, 1956—and I use it to define others)

lavender *American* related to male homosexuality
The perfume made from the plant is considered effeminate. A *lavender convention* is a meeting of male homosexuals, or *lavender boys*.

lay¹ to copulate with
The male usually *lays* the female, from his superior attitude or from assisting her to a prone position:
> Laying me's part of your terms of service? (Bradbury, 1975)

Shakespeare used *lay down*:
> The sly whoresons
> Have got a speeding trick to lay down ladies. (*Henry VIII*)

A woman who has copulated is said to have been *laid*.

lay² a promiscuous woman
As seen by a man:
> He smiled to himself, watching her thinking about the high cost of a free lay. (Weverka, 1973)

It is remarkable that, in malespeak, there are only *good lays* in this context.

lay a child *obsolete British* to apply a cure for rickets
It was necessary to take the child to a smithy where three smiths of the same name worked and there subject it to procedures which are detailed in the *EDD*, none of which we would view with confidence today.

lay a leg on (of a male) to copulate with
Or, more commonly, *lay a leg over* or *across*:
> Where was a' his noble equals when he bute to lay a leg un my poor lassie? (D. Graham, 1883)

lay down your life to be killed in wartime

There are overtones of voluntary sacrifice:

> David Haden-Guest...also laid down his
> life. (Boyle, 1979)

A civilian may *lay down his burden or his knife
and fork*. A Scotsman might also have been
said to *lay down his clay*, the *clay* being the
human body:

> I'll soon lay down the clay, yet ere I go
> away I'd like to see the brig across to Torry.
> (Ogg, 1873)

lay hands on to beat

Someone who expresses a wish to *lay his hands
on you* is seldom a faith healer or a bishop
wishing to confirm you. Occasionally it means
to kill, especially in the phrase, *lay hands on
yourself*, to commit suicide.

lay off to dismiss from employment

Formerly for a short period only, until business picked up, but now of permanent
dismissal:

> I didn't know my old man had been laid
> off. (Theroux, 1977)

lay out to prepare (a corpse) for burial

You straighten the limbs before the onset of
rigor mortis might make it hard to accommodate the body in the coffin.

lay paper to pass worthless financial instruments

The *paper* is bouncing cheques, forged bank
notes, or bogus securities. The imagery is
from the 'paper-chase', in which participants
followed a trail of torn-up paper dropped by
their quarry.

lay pipes *American* to seek votes through
bribery

From the political commissioning of unnecessary public works to give employment to
potential voters. *To lay some pipe* is a male
vulgarism for copulating.

lay to rest to inter a corpse

The common sleeping imagery:

> But that did not lessen the sadness I
> felt at not being able to make her life
> more comfortable, or the pain of
> not being able to lay her to rest.
> (Mandela, 1994—he was not allowed
> to leave prison to attend his mother's
> funeral)

See also AT REST.

lead associated with shooting

From the composition of the bullet. The victim
might have a *bellyful of lead*, be *filled with lead*, be
loaded with *lead ballast*, *eat lead pills*, wear *lead
buttons*, or suffer from *lead poisoning*;

> You won't float long if I put lead into you.
> (Fraser, 1970)

Talk to me like that...and you are liable
to be wearing lead buttons on your vest.
(Chandler, 1943)
Hey, reb! Here's a lead pill for your
sickness. (B. Cornwell, 1993)
...one of the fastest guns I'd ever seen and
he's been itching to give me lead poisoning
for months. (Fraser, 1994)

Soviet soldiers fought fanatically partly because:

> There seemed little difference between the
> enemy bullet and that fixed ration from
> the Soviet state, the NKVD's 'nine ounces
> of lead'. (Beevor, 1998, of the Second World
> War)

To be *allergic to lead* is to be a coward:

> Sir Gerald was, to put a fine point on it,
> allergic to lead. He was very deeply anxious
> not to get killed—injured even. (Whicker,
> 1982—after securing a safe billet far
> behind the lines at Bari, Gerald was killed
> when an ammunition ship blew up in the
> harbour)

lead apes in hell *obsolete* (of a woman) to
die without having copulated

Alluding to simian sexual vigour:

> I must not dance barefoot on her wedding
> day
> And for your love for her, lead apes in
> hell. (Shakespeare, *The Taming of the Shrew*—
> see DANCE BAREFOOT)

lead in your pencil (of a male) sexual potency

Likening the ejaculation to the core of
graphite (not lead) in the punning PENCIL 1,
which shareas a Latin stem with *penis*:

> Wally shook some dregs of Angostura into
> the gin. 'That'll put lead in your pencil,' I
> said. (Theroux, 1973)

leak¹ an act of urination

Of obvious derivation. *Leaks* may be had, done,
gone for, needed, sprung, taken, etc. by either
sex in mildly vulgar use:

> ...shuffling through the house in carpet
> slippers to take a leak. (Theroux, 1978)

To *leak* is occasionally used meaning to
urinate:

> ...we were allowed out for twenty minutes
> drinking and leaking. (Lyall, 1972)

leak² to release (information) furtively

Done by a politician who wishes to sound out
public opinion about future policy or release
information which cannot be attributed to
him; or by an employee who improperly
passes on confidential information for private gain or political advantage; or by a
traitor:

> Until fingered by his ex-wife in 1984,
> former Navy Officer John Walker leaked

secrets to the Soviets for nearly 20 years. (*Life*, Autumn 1989)

A *leak* is an instance of this phenomenon, and an administration or organization which is a constant source of such information is called *leaky*:

The Master in College...acting on a hint from a leaky chaplain, made enquiries and managed to get hold of Wolfenden's letter. (Faulks, 1996)

leakage the persistent unauthorized release of confidential information
What happens when there is a LEAK 2:

We discussed leakages. Lady S. said that the surest way of making people repeat things was to say 'Don't quote me'. (Colville, 1967)

leaky menstruating
Of obvious derivation:

As leaky as an unstaunch'd wench. (Shakespeare, *The Tempest*)

Also used of a person prone to involuntary urination.

lean on to put pressure on (a person) so as to extract a benefit
The benefit may be silence of a witness, money from a victim, etc. and is used of actual or threatened violence:

I know his victims. I know who he leaned on. (Theroux, 1976)

leaner a cheat at cards
Attempting surreptitiously to see another's hand:

Although he considered a few players 'leaners'...he said he had seen relatively few deliberate attempts to see opponents' cards. (Clay, 1998)

leap in the dark (a) death by hanging
A sack or blindfold covered the victim's eyes. Hobbes is reported to have so described his own imminent (natural) death.

leap on (of a male) to copulate with
The common imagery of violent movement:

You can't take a vow of celibacy...You'll be leaping on someone and then feeling guilty. (I. Murdoch, 1985)

Shakespeare used *leap into* of marriage:

I should quickly leap into a wife. (*Henry V*)

Leap into bed is specific of both sexes. Male animals may be said to *leap at* females:

His bulls leap at a cow. (Marshall, 1811—the stud fee was five shillings)

leap the broomstick *obsolete* to live together as a couple without marrying
A variant of JUMP THE BROOMSTICK and also as *leap the besom*. It applied to couples who were by choice cohabiting without

being married, or to those without access to a priest:

Leaping a broomstick was the deep country way of marriage. (B. Cornwell, 1993)

leaping house *obsolete* a brothel
Where a customer might LEAP ON a prostitute. Also as *leaping academy*:

Dials the signs of leaping houses. (Shakespeare, *1 Henry IV*)

...teaching 'em Latin in the environs of a leaping-academy. (Fraser, 1982, writing in 19th-century style)

learn on the pillow to acquire proficiency in a foreign language from a (sexual) mistress who is a native speaker
The expression is used to draw attention to the sexual impropriety rather than the linguistic achievement.

learning difficulties (with) unable to keep up with your peers in class
One so described may suffer from a mental condition beyond a difficulty in memorizing or concentrating. The phrase was first adopted in the British Warnock Report of 1979:

...the mentally handicapped shall be defined as 'people with learning difficulties'. (*Daily Telegraph*, 1 October 1990)

learning disabled having chronic difficulty with schoolwork
An extension into education of the DISABLED imagery:

His own term was 'cryptophobic'...but I think in today's lingo we'd say 'learning disabled'. (Turow, 1993)

Whence *learning disability*, such difficulty:

If someone in your family has a learning disability ('mental handicap'), he or she needs security. (advertisement for the Royal Society for Mentally Handicapped Children, *Sunday Telegraph*, 30 January 2000)

leather¹ to thrash (someone)
The material of the belt used:

Father leathered me though. (Boyd, 1982)

leather² *American* a male homosexual
Referring to the style of dress adopted. Also as *leather-queen*.

leave¹ to desert (a spouse)
When we use the word, we ignore the fact that married companies part company daily, to come together again in the evening:

He shocked Victorian society even more by leaving her. (Howard, 1978)

leave² (someone) to die
An involuntary desertion:
'I think,' the maid replied, 'Mr Ford will be
leaving us.' (Lacey, 1986—Henry Ford was
dying)

leave alone not to be associated with
Normally relating to illegal narcotics or sexual
activity:
You remember old Philip Haskell, master
of foxhounds one year, and the next thing
you know—...At least father has been
leaving young boys alone. (Flanagan,
1995—Philip chased youths as well as
foxes)

leave before the gospel to withdraw
from the vagina before ejaculation
Attending church but forgoing the Mass.
Especially Roman Catholic use and practice
when mechanical and chemical forms of
contraception are eschewed.

leave of absence suspension from employment during investigation of a supposed offence
Literally, no more than a vacation, but used by
the employer to avoid defamation before an
offence is proved:
'But not canned; just put leave of absence.'
'Without pay,' I said bitterly. (Sanders,
1986—an employee had been accused of
theft)

leave shoes under a bed to copulate casually
Normally of a male, and not of staying in a
hotel on business:
Haven't been leaving your shoes under a
strange bed...(Sanders, 1979)

leave the building to die
The *building* is your body where your soul
resides while you are living:
I could quietly die—or as Papa said, 'leave
the building'. (Theroux, 1978)
If you affect clichés, especially those with
biblical antecedents, you are more likely to
leave the land of the living:
Let us cut him off from the land of the
living, that his name be no more
remembered. (*Jeremiah*)
Americans may also be said to *leave town*.

leave the room to go to the lavatory
The request which echoed throughout our
schooldays, with the variant *May I leave the
class*?

leave your can *obsolete* to desist from
drinking alcohol
Euphemistic in the negative, when used of a
drunkard:

His countenance had the ruddiness which
betokens one who is in no haste to 'leave
his can'. (J. Boswell, 1791)

leave your pillow unpressed *obsolete* (of
a male) not to copulate with your wife
Not using the marital bed:
Have I my pillow left unprest in Rome,
Forborne the getting of a lawful race?
(Shakespeare, *Antony and Cleopatra*)

led astray having voluntarily done something for which you later express regret
or shame
Men use this as an excuse when they come
home drunk, women if they eat fattening
food, and both sexes if they commit adultery:
She had been led astray before I met
her...and she was a common prostitute.
(Mayhew, 1862)

left field *American* crazy or unconventional
The imagery is from baseball, referring to the
area less favoured by right-handed hitters:
...a touch fundamentalist, but not too
left-field to scare away sensible money.
(Barnes, 1989)

left-footer a person not conforming to
the practices or beliefs of the majority
Someone so described may not play football
and, if he does, he may well prefer his right
boot. It may refer to a homosexual:
I can pass myself off as a left-footer. (Fraser,
1983—he could ape homosexuality)
In the British navy the term was also applied
to Roman Catholics.

left-handed¹ *obsolete* indicating illegitimacy
From the bar sinister on a coat of arms, which
is a sign of bastardy.

left-handed² homosexual
Using the same imagery as LEFT-FOOTER:
'You don't think Andy's a bit left handed,
do you?' he asked Paddy over a nightcap.
'You never hear of him going with girls.' (le
Carré, 1996)
A homosexual may also be said to have *two left
hands*:
He couldn't stomach...being at the beck
and call of bar-keeps, piano players with
two left hands, frail sisters, and soiled
doves. (Vanderhaeghe, 1997)

left-handed wife a woman living with a
man to whom she is not married
He takes her left hand, and not her right,
in a *left-handed alliance*. (My wife, along
with many other virtuous ladies, could be

so described, literally but not euphemistically.)

leg-over an act of copulation
Usually by a male outside marriage, from the position adopted:
> He is on the terrace *tout nu*. She cannot resist him. *Voilà*. It is a leg-over. (Mayle, 1993)

leg-sliding promiscuity
By either sex, from the movement involved:
> Everyone's allowed a bit of leg-sliding these days. (le Carré, 1980)

legal resident a spy accredited as a diplomat
As different from the *illegal resident* who spies in the host country under cover:
> ... he should never have been appointed to the vital position of legal resident in the USA. (Deighton, 1981—he was a Russian spy)

legless very drunk
From your inability to walk steadily, or at all:
> Bagley getting legless on Southern Comfort. (*Private Eye*, June 1981)

lend to lose ownership of
As in the old proverb 'He who lends, gives'. If you *lend* someone a match, or a cigarette, you are unwise to expect repayment. In 1941 the British had exhausted their ability to pay for more supplies from neutral America, which nevertheless wanted the British Empire to be able to continue fighting Germany and Italy on its behalf, all other opponents having been defeated or withdrawn. The US Congress agreed to lease arms to Britain under the fiction that the cost would be repaid after the war, using *lease-lend* to describe the arrangement. It was abruptly and wisely brought to an end by Harry Truman in 1945.

length a term of imprisonment
A rare version of the common STRETCH 1.

lesbian a female homosexual
The poetess Sappho lived on the island:
> It was commonly rumoured that Tanya was a Lesbian. (Bradbury, 1959)

Lesbianism is female homosexuality:
> I practised Lesbianism, which was certainly sterile. (F. Harris, 1925)

and the adjectival form is *lesbic*:
> ... the perverse intertwining of two figures in lesbic passion. (ibid.)

You may sometimes hear the corruptions *lez*, *lezzer*, or *lizzie*:
> She would not screw. I wondered if she was a closet lez. (Sanders, 1977)

> —Ah, she's nice though. She says I have the right kind o' nipples.—Lezzer. (R. Doyle, 1990)

To get into Mortimer's outfit you have to be a lizzie or a drunk or an Irishwoman. (Manning, 1978—the *outfit* was the First Aid Nursing Yeomanry, or FANY, whose members were commonly referred to as *fannies*)

less lacking a quality in a way which is the subject of a taboo
Thus *less academic* children are stupid or unteachable; a *less attractive* person is ugly or repulsive in other ways (it will not be long before we learn, for example, that Cinderella had two *less attractive* sisters); *less edited* is pornographic; *less enjoyable* is boring, of books, plays, and art; *less gifted* is of inferior ability or intelligence; *less* or *lesser developed* is poor and backward, of a country; *less prepared* is of inferior attainment; etc.:
> She said the move showed 'the dramatic increase in the acceptance of a wide range of adult programming. This kind of less-edited programming is here to stay'. (*Daily Telegraph*, 4 July 2001, reporting on pornographic television programmes)
> ... loans to lesser developed countries such as Zaire and Jamaica. (M. Thomas, 1960)
> ... the selection of the best qualified black applicants ... in preference to less gifted or less prepared blacks. (Pei, 1969)

let go to dismiss from employment
The usage seeks to imply that the worker is being done a favour:
> It wore the sheriff down after a while and he let George go. (Chandler, 1943—George was a deputy, not a criminal)

let in (of a female) to permit copulation
The derivation is obvious:
> I still thought it good policy not to let him in yet a while. I answered then only to his importunities in sighs and groans. (Cleland, 1749)

let off to fart
A shortened form of *let off wind* rather than from the firing of a gun:
> 'He keeps letting off,' she repeated in a whisper ... 'I think it's because he's scared.' (L. Thomas, 1986)

To *let fly* implies a more violent, noisier, release.

let out *American* to dismiss from employment
A version of LET GO, but with no implication that an employer can ever detain workers against their will:

Jay Allen, the most brilliant among us
younger men, would soon be let out.
(Shirer, 1984—a journalist was about to be
dismissed)

lethal control killing
Control by killing rather than of killing:
'I mean lethal control.' 'Shoot them.'
'Yeah.' (N. Evans, 1998)

letterhead appointed other than on
merit
It is used of an attempt to bolster the image or
credibility of an organization through its
association with an eminent person or one
who comes from a MINORITY:
Some years ago, Sackville recounted, he
flew to Houston, Texas for a meeting
where he was to represent a British
Corporation on whose board he served as a
letterhead lord. (Seitz, 1998)
See also STATUTORY and TOKEN.

leveraged involving excessive borrowing
Especially where a predator takes over a
corporation incurring debt which he hopes
to service or repay out of the victim's assets:
Anyway, this investment banker
specializes in 'leveraged buyouts'; it's
the new thing in Wall Street fashion.
(M. Thomas, 1987)

liaison an extramarital sexual relationship
Originally, the culinary thickening of a sauce,
whence a close relationship:
... striking up an occasional liaison which
she alluded to by saying... 'He's an old
boyfriend of mine.' (Theroux, 1976)
Less often the person with whom the relationship is enjoyed, or as the case may be, is so
described:
... how she had taken her mother's Visa,
forged the signature, and bought the
current 'liaison' from the council houses a
500-cc Yamaha. (Seymour, 1995)

libation a drink of an intoxicant
Literally, the ceremonial offering of a drink:
'... this may be a good time for a drink. Do
you concur, Senator?' 'A small libation
would not be inappropriate,' he said in a
wry manner. (Sanders, 1984)

liberal *obsolete* (of a female) promiscuous
She carried freedom a little too far:
It's sign she hath been liberal and free.
(Shakespeare, *1 Henry VI*)

liberate¹ to conquer
Literally, to free:
'Nehru turned them out in the liberation of
Goa.' 'Liberation... did you say *liberation*?'

(Dalrymple, 1998—Goa was a Portuguese
enclave in the subcontinent which India
invaded and annexed)

liberate² to steal
Originally, a use by soldiers in the Second
World War, when freeing occupied territories
and looting property whose owner had van-
ished tended to go hand in hand:
It's a gold watch... a *liberated* gold watch.
(Price, 1978)
Now in general use of thieving:
'Are you going to be warm enough in that
jacket?' 'I'm all right. I liberated it from a
second-hand shop.' (Theroux, 1976)

liberate³ to permit or encourage to flout
social convention
Again the concept of setting free:
The custom of keen gardeners who once
shopped for bedding plants and potting
compost was replaced by that of cross-
dressing businessmen and 'liberated
people' who indulged in group sex in the
swimming pool. (*Daily Telegraph*, 28
November 1998—the proprietor of what
had formerly been a garden centre said
after his conviction for living off immoral
earnings—'I did not have sex parties. I had
liberated parties')
Whence *liberation*, as in WOMEN'S LIBERATION.

liberate⁴ peremptorily to dismiss from
employment
The victim is thereby freed from performing
the arduous duties of office or employment:
... a papal decree was issued by which Dr
Errington was 'liberated' from the
Co-adjutorship of Westminster, together
with the right of succession to the See.
(Strachey, 1918—Manning, lately an
archdeacon in the Anglican Church, thus
cleared the way for his own succession to
Wiseman as Roman Catholic Archbishop of
Westminster)

lick of the tarbrush see TARBRUSH

lick the dust to die
Usually today after being killed in a Western,
from where a corpse lies in dry country, but
with a biblical lineage:
His enemies shall lick the dust. (*Psalms* 72: 9)
See also BITE THE DUST.

lid an ounce of marijuana
The quantity which fitted into the lid of a
tobacco tin and made about 40 hand-rolled
cigarettes:
Tommy smoked a couple of lids a week.
(Wambaugh, 1981)

lie in to await the imminent birth of a child

Greek, Latin, and Teutonic roots of *lie* all mean bed where, in the language of euphemism, you only give birth or copulate:

> Within ten days she'll be lying in. (Graves, 1940)

A *lying-in wife* was a midwife:

> As well as can be expected. That's the answer of a lying-in wife. (J. M. Wilson, 1836)

Formerly to *lay in* was synonymous:

> When the gal is in the family way, the lads mostly sends them to the workhouse to lay in. (Mayhew, 1851)

lie with¹ to copulate with

It has long been assumed that the adult male and female cannot *lie* in each other's company without copulating, within or outside marriage:

> To tell thee plain, I aim to lie with thee. (Shakespeare, *3 Henry VI*)

Lie on might be more accurate of the male, but is less used:

> Lie with her! lie on her! (Shakespeare, *Othello*)

Lie together implies extramarital copulation:

> Foreign students were positively encouraged to lie together, he said sardonically, so that they didn't go out and pursue the natives. (D. Francis, 1978, writing about Moscow University)

lie with² to be buried beside

Of husband and wife or parent and child:

> I'd like my husband to lie with his son. (Stevens, 1996)

life¹ (the) any taboo way of earning your keep or existing

Prostitutes' jargon for prostitution, thieves' for stealing, and also used by drug addicts, especially when they alternate between scheming to get money to buy illegal narcotics and being under their influence.

life² death

As in *life assurance* sold through *life cover* in a *life policy* by a *life office* to a *life*, or person whose death will lead to payment.

life everlasting see EVERLASTING LIFE

life of infamy prostitution

How the righteous profess to see it:

> ...she may have been a servant out of a place...and betaken herself here to a life of infamy. (Mayhew, 1862—*here* was a brothel)

We still may hear talk of a prostitute leading a *life of shame*.

life preserver a cosh

It is not intended to preserve that of the victim:

> Macarthur was hit with a life preserver...on the back of the head. (Christie, 1939—it killed him)

lifestyle sexual orientation

An evasion used especially when questioning potential blood donors so as to screen out any likely to be HIV-positive without making further tests:

> This lifestyle, choice—whatever it was called—remained beyond him. Not the acts, but the very philosophy. (Turow, 1990)

lift¹ to steal

Usually of pilfering, from the casual removal:

> Billy can lift your jock strap, and you wouldn't feel a thing. (Weverka, 1973—Billy was an adept pickpocket)

Specifically of plagiarism in the 20th century, of picking pockets in the 19th century, and of disinterring corpses for sale in 18th-century Scotland:

> Resurrectionists...who were as ready to lay their murdering hands on the living, as to lift the dead. (S. R. Whitehead, 1876)

A *lifter* is a thief, usually by picking pockets. *Shoplifter*, a thief from a store, has been in use since the 17th century and the verb, to *shoplift*, since the 19th:

> I know it's bad for them, but thousands of people shoplift. (D. Francis, 1981)

lift² the feeling after an ingestion of illegal narcotics

Literally, a feeling of wellbeing or encouragement:

> 'Want a lift?' 'I can use something,' Janette said. She took a small vial from the bag. (Robbins, 1981)

lift³ an arrest

Mainly police jargon, from removing a suspect from circulation:

> The lift and then the interrogation, the interrogation and then the imprisonment. (Seymour, 1982)

Also as a verb in the same sense.

lift⁴ a thick sole and heel to enhance height

Only the subject of evasion when worn by a male:

> Beware Greeks wearing lifts. (*Financial Times*, 1988, quoting a quip about the presidential candidate Dukakis who was so shod, the motto being after—long after—Virgil's *timeo danaos et dona ferentes*, 'I fear the Greeks even when they are bearing gifts')

lift a gam *Irish* to fart
A *gam* was a leg in slang. It was also a school of
whales but their propensity for blowing does
not contribute to the etymology.

lift a hand to to strike (a person)
And not by way of greeting:
> Wud ye lift yer han' to a woman? (*EDD*)

lift a leg[1] (of a male) to copulate
Getting himself into a convenient attitude:
> I'll ne'er lift a lawless leg
> Again upon her. (Burns, 1786)
And see LEG-OVER.

lift a leg[2] to urinate
In standard usage it applies to a dog, which
does it literally:
> She opened the front door, and watched
> [the dog] go over to the hedge where he
> lifted his leg. (Ustinov, 1966)

lift the books *obsolete* to withdraw from
regular service at a church
A major decision in the days when church
attendance was a social necessity, apart from
any spiritual benefit:
> He saved a public scandal by lifting his
> books—resigning his membership.
> (Johnston, 1891)
If you were to *lift your lines*, you would receive
a disjunction certificate on changing from one
congregation to another:
> 'What has Jeemes Simpson done?' 'He's
> lifted his lines.' (*Longman's Magazine*, May
> 1891)

lift your little finger to drink intoxicants
On a single occasion, from the conveyance of
the glass to the mouth, or more often of a
drunkard:
> Liquors a bit, don't you know; lifts his little
> finger. (F. M. Peacock, 1890)
In the same sense you may *lift* other parts of
your anatomy, including your *arm*, your *elbow*,
or your *wrist*.

lift your hair to kill (someone)
And retain the scalp as a trophy:
> That's what Indians is known for. Slipping
> behind you and lifting your hair when you
> least expect it. (Vanderhaeghe, 1997)

light[1] promiscuous
Of no moral weight but *light ladies*, *wenches*, or
women were not successful dieters or those
emulating Florence Nightingale but prostitutes:
> I wouldn't have thought that many of the
> light ladies of Calcutta had the opportunity
> to bestow their favours in the Japanese.
> (Fraser, 1992, and not differentiating them
> from the dark ladies)

> Light wenches will burn. Come not near
> her. (Shakespeare, *The Comedy of Errors*—
> they were not condemned to the stake
> but would give you venereal disease)
Commentators charged that throughout
his papacy [Pope John XI] continued
committing 'infinite abominations
among light women'. (Cawthorne,
1996—he occupied the throne of St Peter
from 931 to 936)

light[2] **(a)** (in a request to light a cigarette)
a male recognition signal
Such a request was once a universal homosexual password:
> ... it was not granted to me to live a
> moment of happiness, because a sailor's
> face in front of me went blank when I
> asked him for a light. (Genet, in 1969
> translation)

light[3] *American* not obviously black
The language of segregation or prejudice:
> I couldn't go in there with her. Even if
> I was light enough to pass, like her.
> (Macdonald, 1952)

light-fingered thieving
It indicates a propensity to lift small objects:
> ... Rose and Crown public house, resorted
> to by all classes of light-fingered gentry.
> (Mayhew, 1862)
An old superstition has passed into oblivion:
> The baby's nails must not be cut till he is
> a year old, for fear he should grow up a
> thief, or ... 'light-fingered'. (W. Henderson,
> 1879)

light-footed[1] (of a female) promiscuous
She might also have been *light-heeled* and a
light-skirts was a prostitute.

light-footed[2] (of a male) homosexual
Being LIGHT ON HIS TOES.

light-housekeeping *American* living as
man and wife without marriage
A pun on LIGHT 1 and the avocation of the
coastguard.

light in the head of low intelligence
Not a turnip on Hallowe'en:
> The kid's a little light in the head. His
> brother takes care of him. (Sanders, 1970)
Perversely, one such might also be described
as THICK.

light on his toes homosexual
Some affect a mincing walk or appear to walk
on tiptoe:
> Your assistant in the theatre, sir, your
> dresser, he's a bit light on his toes as well,
> isn't he? (Monkhouse, 1993)

light the lamp (of a prostitute) to accept customers
The brothel's sign is a red lamp:
> She confided in me that she had lit the lamp four hundred times, in one week, in her Casita. (Londres, 1928, in translation)

lightning low-quality spirits
Alluding to the effect when it strikes you. Usually denoting whisky in America and gin in Britain.

like a drink to be addicted to alcohol
The term is used of others, but not of ourselves. To *like a pipe* is not to use one for smoking tobacco but to be addicted ingesting illegal narcotics:
> 'He a junkie?' 'Man likes a pipe, I'm told.' (Katzenbach, 1995)

like that homosexual
Usually of a male.

like the ladies to be a philanderer
Not merely the opposite of being a misogynist:
> Getty liked the ladies, and if he had not known much success with them it was not for want of trying. (Whicker, 1982)

lily *American* a male homosexual
The derivation is from the woman's name and the pale colouring, despite the flower being the emblem of chastity and innocence.

limb *obsolete* a leg
A classic example of 19th-century prudery, when in America not just humans but dining tables had *limbs*. See also LINEN.

limb of the law a policeman
Alluding perhaps to the cliché, *the long arm of the law*:
> Be't priest, or laird, or limb o'law. (Nicholson, 1814)

Rarely shortened to *limb*. A *limbo* was a prison, from the place where unbaptized infants dwell along with those who predeceased Christ and various other unfortunates:
> I have some of them in limbo patrum. (Shakespeare, *Henry VIII*)

limited idle, stupid, or incompetent
Educational jargon of children, to avoid precision or offence. Used of an adult, it means lacking in ability or intelligence. This is one of the sillier euphemisms, as we are all confined within limits, of memory, knowledge, experience, common sense, and physical power.

limited action a war

The stronger participant so describes it, especially if his domestic population is not at risk:
> ...the language of the mad foments [violence]...'Bushfire wars', 'limited actions'. (M. West, 1979)

An American *limited covert war* is one aided by the CIA without Congress being informed:
> Para-military action of any type, Tyler argued, was war, and he had gingerly coined the euphemism 'limited covert warfare'. (Woodward, 1987)

limp-wrist a male homosexual
From the action of masturbating:
> He looked like a peroxided limpwrist. (Wambaugh, 1983)

Whence adjectivally as *limp-wristed*:
> His limp-wristed nancy-boy of a son...(*Private Eye*, January 1980)

line¹ to copulate with
Literally, of a dog or wolf, but obsolete of humans:
> Winter garments must be lined,
> So must slender Rosalind. (Shakespeare, *As You Like It*)

line² a nasal ingestion of narcotics
From the way it is sprinkled for sniffing:
> Hey, baby, come back to my place, we'll do a couple lines. (Turow, 1999)

line your pocket wrongfully to enrich yourself
The money provides the *lining*:
> ...adept in the field of corruption and lining his own pocket. (Goebbels, 1945, in translation)

In America, as *line your vest*:
> I think he's been lining his vest. (R. Moss, 1987—he was not a tailor but an official suspected of peculation)

An obsolete form was *line your coat*, although Shakespeare's observation of human behaviour is, as ever, timeless:
> And throwing but shows of service on their lords,
> Do well thrive by them, and when they have lin'd their coats,
> Do themselves homage. (*Othello*)

lined *obsolete* pregnant
Punning on LINE 1 and the insertion of additional material in a garment:
> ...she got lined by a big black buck. (Graves, 1941)

linen *obsolete* a shirt
From the days when legs were BENDERS and cocks became ROOSTERS:
> If such standard English words as 'leg' and 'shirt' were found beyond the

pale...(James Gordon Bennett caused a
certain frisson when his *New York Herald*
refused to print the former as 'limb'
and the latter as 'linen')...(J. Green,
1996)

lingua tertii imperii the evasive abuse of
lanugage by the Nazis
Literally, the language of the Third Reich:
Camouflage also shaped the distinctive
vocabulary of the Reich which the
philologist Victor Klemperer has ironically
called LTI: *Lingua Tertii Imperii*. (Ousby,
1997)

link prices to arrange an illegal cartel
Manufacturers or distributors either divide
markets on a geographical basis or agree to
quote the same prices as each other.

linked with having a sexual relationship
with
A favoured journalistic evasion:
Since the break-down of her marriage,
the Duchess has been linked with a
Texan oil executive...and...her
financial adviser. (*Daily Telegraph*, 14
December 1994)

liquid consisting of, serving, or containing alcohol
Literally, anything from water to sulphuric
acid. Usually in compounds. A *liquid refreshment* is an intoxicant. A *liquid restaurant* serves
intoxicants as well as food. A *liquid lunch*,
dinner, or *supper* is not one with a soup course
but where excessive alcohol is drunk with
little or no food:
...indebted...to the owner of a 'liquid'
restaurant. (Lavine, 1930, writing during
the Prohibition years)
Following our liquid lunch, he agreed to
totter round the greens with me. (*Private
Eye*, August 1981)
Barley and his friends had enjoyed a liquid
supper under plastic muskets. (le Carré,
1989—the muskets were part of the bogus
décor of a London pub)

liquidate to kill other than by process of
law
Originally, to clear away, whence the implication for ruthless efficiency:
The silent liquidation of many friends in
the Soviet Union without a single bleat of
protest from the freedom-loving
west...(Boyle, 1979)
In legal jargon and the commercial world, a
liquidator kills off failed companies.

liquidity the ability to pay your debts as
they fall due
Only euphemistic when you lack it:

Sir Jeremy came to me saying that he
lacked liquidity...that's the delicate way
these European aristocrats say in deep shit.
(Deighton, 1993/2)
A *liquidity crisis* for a company means that it is
insolvent and for a person that he is bankrupt, in each case still staving off the threat or
reality.

liquor a spirituous intoxicant
Originally, any liquid, in many spellings:
Lecker made her drunk as David's sow.
(*Gentleman's Magazine*, 1742, quoted in *EDD*)
Liquored means partly drunk and *full of liquor* or
in liquor mean drunk:
He was in liquor when he made his first
appearance. (Monsarrat, 1978)

lit drunk or under the influence of narcotics
From the generally exhilarated state rather
than the redness of the nose:
An old con like me don't make good
prints—not even when he's lit. (Chandler,
1939)
Also as *lit up*.

little bit a young sexually attractive
woman
She may be a prostitute:
There's always a little bit at that truck 'em
up stop. (Dills, 1976—and not referring to
the cuisine)
See also BIT 1.

little boys' room a lavatory for exclusive
male use
Fairly common male adult use, despite the
cloying imagery. *Little girls' room* providing
similar facilities for females is equally nause-
ous but less common:
She slid out of the chair. 'Just goin' to the
little girls room, hon.' (J. Collins, 1981)

little friend see LITTLE VISITOR

little gentleman in black velvet *obsolete* a mole
King William III, who was hated by the
Jacobites (and still is by many of the Irish),
was riding a horse which stumbled on a
molehill. He fell off, broke his collar bone,
and died from complications which ensued. It
was treasonable to impugn what Catholics and
others saw as the usurping Hanoverian monarchs. If you wished to venerate the mole, you
were better to refer to him obliquely:
The little gentleman in black velvet
who did such service in 1702. (W. Scott,
1816)
See also KING OVER THE WATER.

little house a lavatory

It was often a small detached shed in the yard or garden:

> Frequently younger children would wait for their older brothers and sisters and go together to the little house. (Binding, 1999)

Also as *petty house*.

little jobs urination
As different from BIG JOBS, defecation, in nursery use.

little local difficulty a major crisis
The term used by the British prime minister Macmillan after losing his three senior Treasury ministers in January 1958 when they were unable to accept his lack of political principle or his pragmatism. Now used ironically:

> 'I'm afraid we have a little local difficulty, sir.' Stephen considered him with nonchalance, enjoying the panic in his eyes. (McCrum, 1991)

little Mary the stomach
This is perhaps the sole survivor in modern speech of the 19th-century evasions about any part of the body which might conceivably have some connection with sex, urination, defecation, or childbirth.

little people the fairies
The fairies were malevolent, unlike their namesakes in Christmas pantomimes, and you had to speak nicely about them. Also as *little folk*.

little something an intoxicant
Usually in an enquiry to a guest.

little stranger an unborn child
Nursery usage, to avoid telling the truth about pregnancy and to prepare a toddler for the arrival of a sibling.

little visitor (a) menstruation
But no less in terms of duration or discomfort than a VISITOR. Common female use, and as *little friend*, which implies a welcome as indicating the woman is not pregnant. *Little sister* is rare.

little woman a mistress
Literally, in ponderous male humour, a wife:

> I think we can take it there's a 'little woman' in the case. (P. D. James, 1962)

live as man and wife to live as a married couple without being married
It is of course what nearly all married couples do:

> Irene and I lived together as man and wife. (L. Armstrong, 1955—she was his mistress)

Of a married couple, *not to live as man and wife* means that they have ceased to copulate with each other:

> They shared their farmhouse at Bittadon, near Ilfracombe, Devon, but were not living as man and wife. (*Daily Telegraph*, 24 October 1997)

live by trade to be a prostitute
Those of us who earn a living in commerce may hope that this usage is obsolete. Also as *live by trading*:

> Oh, there's no doubt they live by trading. (*EDD*)

live-in girlfriend a mistress
She resides with a man who is single, or separated or divorced from his wife:

> ... attending Hollywood high society affairs as his live-in girlfriend rather than as his wife. (*Daily Telegraph*, September 1981)

See also GIRLFRIEND.

live in (mortal) sin (of a couple) to live together without being married
They commit the *mortal sin* of adultery or of fornication:

> For the first year we lived in sin. (Sanders, 1973)
> But then aren't you living in mortal sin? (N. Mitford, 1945)

live on to make a living from sexual services
Descriptive of either a mistress or a pimp. *Live off* means the same thing:

> In this life [of prostitution] I have known, loved, lived for, lived on, lived off ... many men. (L. Thomas, 1977)

live tally *obsolete* to live as a couple without being married
A *tally* is a corresponding piece which exactly fits another, like an indenture:

> Aw'd advise thi t'live tally if theaw con mak it reet wi some owd damsel. (Brierley, 1854—most men would prefer a young damsel, I suspect)

live together to live as a couple without marriage
It usually implies cohabitation:

> If parties is married, they ought to bend to each other; and won't, for sartain, if they're only living together. (Mayhew, 1851)

The term is correctly used of homosexual couples.

live with to copulate with
Perhaps the commonest usage:

> You lived with women. You lived with that old actress. (I. Murdoch, 1978)

Also of homosexual relationships.

lived-in untidy
You so describe another's house, usually with an implication of untidiness and dirt. A *lived-in face* denotes debauchery on the part of its wearer.

livener an intoxicant taken early in the morning
Either by someone who was drunk the previous evening or by a habitual drunkard:
    Your Lordship has heard of people having 'liveners' in the morning. (*Birmingham Daily Post*, 1897, quoted in *EDD*)

living space conquered territory
The Nazi German *Lebensraum* to be annexed from Poland, Russia, and others—'to obtain by the German sword sod for the German plough':
    Lebensraum which should have meant 'living-room' but actually signified the occupation of Europe and as much of Russia as Hitler had been able to lay his hands on. (Sharpe, 1979)
Even more sinister was the Nazi policy of *Lebensborn*, under which fair Polish or Czech children were taken from home and placed with German families to be raised as Germans and thus augment the Teutonic stock.

lizzie see LESBIAN

load[1] the quantity of intoxicants which has made someone drunk
The drunkard *carries a load* or *has a load on*:
    Sure I seen him drunk. Lots of times. He's have a load on. (Sanders, 1977)

load[2] *American* the genitalia of a male
Homosexual use:
    The long-haired youth entered, came close to Firenza's side, pressed his nylon-sheathed load against the doctor's arm. (Sanders, 1977)

loaded[1] drunk
Carrying a LOAD 1:
    I'm not loaded, as they haven't told me when the bars around here open up. (Ustinov, 1971)
Sometimes used of being under the influence of illegal narcotics.

loaded[2] fraudulently increased
The demand for payment is made heavier by the inclusion of fictitious or inflated entries.

loaded[3] laced with intoxicants
A non-alcoholic drink may be so treated, with or without the knowledge of the drinker:
    We sipped our loaded coffee. (Chandler, 1939)

loaded[4] wealthy
Used in a disparaging or envious way:
    There might be someone; she wouldn't tell me; not if he wasn't loaded. (Rendell, 1991)

load-shedding a failure of the electricity grid through inability to generate sufficient power
In Britain this was one of the features of the electricity industry when it was owned and operated by the state, whose employees used evasive language to explain inefficiency:
    ...'load shedding'—the bureaucratic word for power cuts—took place three hours every day. (*Daily Telegraph*, 13 August 1999)

local *British* an inn
Shortened form for *local pub* etc. A man does not use the word to describe his village post office or other common amenity in the vicinity.

local bear *American* a policeman attached to a small force
As different from a state trooper. See also BEAR 2. Sometimes also as *local boy* or *yokel*.

lock out (of an employer) to refuse to make work available for employees
Not referring to thieves and other would-be trespassers who are *locked out* of the premises each evening, or as the case may be. The jargon of industrial disputes:
    We have been given two days...to carry on production or we should be locked out. (Allbeury, 1982)

locked drunk
As in an arm-lock or a prison cell? Probably neither:
    —I was fuckin' locked, said Declan Cuffe. Rum an' blacks, yeh know. (R. Doyle, 1987—*blacks* is stout)

log-rolling *American* giving selfish or insincere support
Neighbours used to help each other manhandle heavy wood for winter burning, whence figuratively mutual political back-scratching:
    The members [of Congress]...make a compact by which each aids the other. This is called log-rolling. (Bryce, 1888)
In modern use, it covers insincere commendation, and any reward for sycophancy:
    If either were appointed...it would be a piece of disgraceful log-rolling. (Manning, 1965)

loins the male genitals in their reproductive role
Literally, the region of your body between your ribs and your hips:

A tongueless man may pass through his
loins his unsung music. (Kersh, 1936)
A *surge in the loins* is the ejaculation of semen:
In no time at all I felt the surge in my loins,
and it was as I wrenched with the supreme
moment that I awoke. (de Bernières, 1994)

lone love self-masturbation
As different from narcissism:
As a girl she had spent her thirteenth year
troubled by the belief that she alone had
discovered such an act...So it had been a
considerable relief when her cousin Lucy,
older by some months, had set her straight
on the matter of lone love. (Frazier, 1997)

lone parent a parent living alone with
dependent offspring
Usually an unmarried mother or a parent
whose spouse lives apart through divorce or
other separation, without any suggestion that
the child has other than two progenitors:
The main reason given by divorced lone-
parents for marital breakdown was
infidelity. (*Bath Report*, June 1991)
See also ONE-PARENT FAMILY and SINGLE
PARENT.

long acre *Irish* the roadside verge
Where itinerants set up camp and graze their
horses.

long-arm inspection *American* a medical
inspection of the penis
DAS says the inspection is of the erect penis.
See also SHORT-ARM INSPECTION.

long home (your) death
More accurately, perhaps, the grave:
Horn sent her off to her long home to lie.
(Burns, 1786)
Those who die may also go on their *long
journey*:
I expect this is our last time around, Dick,
but I hope to take a few of them on the
long journey with us. (F. Richards, 1933,
writing of going back into the First World
War trenches after leave)
The *long day* is the Christian Day of Judgment,
when a considerable catalogue of offences
will come up for simultaneous hearing, requiring a lengthy sitting; whence the admonition:
Between you and the lang day be it. (Pegge,
1803)

long illness (a) *American* cancer
The language of the obituary notice. A *short
illness* may indicate suicide.

long in the tooth old
Horses are aged by the recession of their
gums:

...he wanted to link up with some nice
little bit less long in the tooth. (Christie,
1939)

long pig human flesh
The flesh of the human and the pig have a
similar taste:
The Fijian's chief table luxury was human
flesh, euphemistically called by him 'long
pig'. (Theroux, 1992)

long-term buy a poor investment
The jargon of the analyst:
They are required to analyze corporate
clients but these pieces of research
never say anything negative. The
worst phrase you might read is 'neutral'
or 'long-term buy'. (*Sunday Telegraph*,
8 August 1999)

long-term friend a permanent sexual
partner
Or as permanent as these relationships ever
are. Either heterosexual:
...a house in Aylesbury where he lives with
a long-term woman friend. (*Daily Telegraph*,
April 1990)
or homosexual, when it may be a pointer
or evasion used in an obituary of a single
man.

long-term relationship an exclusive extramarital sexual arrangement
What you hope to have with a LONG-TERM
FRIEND:
Any wealthy man who might have been
interested in an expensive, long-term
relationship would certainly think less of
her and even change his mind if he knew
she was carrying on with the chef of a
noodle restaurant. (Golden, 1997)

long walk off a short pier (a) death by
drowning
Usually murder:
...such topics as hanging, cyanide, and a
long walk off a short pier. (Sanders, 1979)

longer-living *American* geriatric
From the moment we are born each of us is
longer-living than those younger than ourselves.

loo a lavatory
Probably a corruption of *l'eau*, although this
theory does not find favour everywhere:
She sat in the loo on the pink tufted
candlewick of the seat cover. (Bradbury,
1976)

look after (your) other interests to be
peremptorily dismissed from employment

If the *other interests* are said to be *expanding*, the departure is even more precipitate. The *interests* may also be *pursued*:

> He suddenly needs more time to pursue that old favourite 'my other expanding interests'. (*Private Eye*, April 1987)

look at the garden to urinate out of doors
Males say they are going to do it. They may also specify which part of the curtilage they intend to examine, such as the *compost heap*, the *roses*, or the *lawn*.

look in a cup to foretell the future
For some, the tea leaves reveal all:

> I'm just broucht a si o' tea wi' me, an' I wis just wantin' you to luik in a cup for me. (G. E. Strewart, 1892)

Divination has always been the subject a taboo.

look on the wine when it was red to be drunk
Or white, perhaps:

> Let it not for one moment be imagined that I had looked on the wine of the Royal Hotel when it was red. (Somerville and Ross, 1897)

looking glass *obsolete Irish* a pot for urine
I draw your attention to the obvious joke involving the traveller who wished to adjust his tie, and the waitress, in *EDD* vol. iii, p. 635.

loop *obsolete* to kill by hanging
The association is with the noose:

> Like moussie thrappl't in a la',
> Or loon that's loopit by the law. (Ainslie, 1892—the mouse was throttled and a loon was a person of low rank)

looped *American* drunk
From *looping the loop*, acting like a fool (or *LOOPY*), or the inability to walk in a straight line? We can only guess:

> And stop drinking too much Lenny. You sound half looped every time I talk to you. (Erdman, 1993)

loopy mentally abnormal
The imagery might come from railway shunting practice—see UP THE LOOP. The condition may be anything from severe to eccentric:

> 'Ah,' said the Bishop, 'and suppose one of your children were sick in some way?' 'Loopy?' 'If you like.' (Fry, 1994)

> The reason is typically Muriel Spark, both down-to-earth practical and mildly loopy at the same time. (L. Barber, 1991)

loose¹ promiscuous

Used of women rather than men, from the relaxation of tighter standards. A *loose woman* is a prostitute:

> There were 8,600 prostitutes known to the police, but this was far from...the number of loose women in the metropolis. (Mayhew, 1862)

The obsolete *loose in the hilts* punned on a dagger unfit for use:

> A sister damned: she's loose i' the hilts. (Webster, 1623, quoted in *ODEP*)

And see ON THE LOOSE.

loose² suffering from diarrhoea
Originally diarrhoea was the *loose disease*, and the opposite of constipated, which (from the Latin) meant compressed (and, as *constipado*, means no more than having a cold in Spanish). The word is used about humans and other animals.

loose cannon a person whose unpredictable conduct may cause difficulties or embarrassment
The imagery is from the gun on a naval vessel which, if not properly secured, fired in another direction than the aimed broadside and caused mayhem on a rolling deck:

> Mr Clinton's policy team...view Mr Carter as a loose cannon. (*Daily Telegraph*, 19 September 1994)

loose house a brothel
Where you might expect to find LOOSE 1 women:

> You'd think she had started a loose house in the dead centre of the village. (Cookson, 1967)

loose in the attic mentally unstable
Attic is a slang word for head:

> He's a goddam loony. He's just uh...a little loose in the attic. (Diehl, 1978)

You may also hear *loose in the head*, or any of the other slang words for head.

loosen your bowels to cause to defecate
Although not necessarily become LOOSE 2:

> It was fit to loosen the bowels of a bronze statue. (Fraser, 1975)

Lord of the Flies the devil
Beelzebub, *fly-lord* in Hebrew, was Prince of the Flies in Syrian mythology.

Lord sends for you (the) you are dead
A Christian use, in expectation of joining Jesus in heaven:

> A woman like me doesn't part with pearls and diamonds until the good Lord sends for her. (Sharpe, 1977)

If the *Lord has you*, you are dead.

lose¹ fraudulently to destroy
What may happen to embarrassing or incriminating files, documents, and tapes:
> It was decided to temporarily lose particularly incriminating correspondence between Derby and the Deputy-Under-Secretary of the India Office. (Graham Stewart, 1999)

lose² to dismiss from employment
The essence of this *loss* is that it is involuntary on the part of those dismissed:
> That'll be fewer breakdowns, less overtime to make up for breakdowns, and of course, I'll be able to lose several men. (Lodge, 1988—an employer was explaining the benefits of the installation of automated machinery)

lose³ to be bereaved of
An evasion, especially when speaking of the death of a relative:
> Hendrix, like...Lennon, lost his mother at an early age. (C. S. Murray, 1989)

lose hold to become mentally unbalanced
Also as *lose it*, *lose the plot*, or *lose your grip*:
> Was her father derailed, off his trolley, losing hold? (Turow, 1990)
> 'Were you really mental?' She tapped her forehead. 'Had you lost it?' (L. Thomas, 1996)
> Rather lost the plot after his wife died. (R. Harris, 1995)

lose the vital signs to die
Medical jargon which does not mean getting lost on a journey. A dead soldier may *lose the number of the mess* and a sailor may in similar punning fashion *lose the wind*.

lose your (good) character to be discovered in any impropriety
Normally, after being convicted of a crime. In a single woman, the phrase is used to refer to copulation before marriage:
> I might not lose, with my character, the prospect of getting a good husband. (Cleland, 1749)

lose your cherry (of a woman) to copulate for the first time
The *cherry* is the maidenhead:
> In thirty years you can get born, grow up, go to college, lose your cherry, have a couple of kids. (Diehl, 1978)
The obsolete Scottish *lose your snood* meant the same thing, the silken snood being worn as a symbol of virginity:
> A 'body kens it's lang syne you tynd your snood. (Hamilton, 1897—*tyne* means lose)

lose your lunch to vomit
Usually when drunk or through seasickness. You may also *lose* other meals in this sense.

lose your reputation *obsolete* (of a woman) to be known as promiscuous
She may also, in the same way, *lose her virtue*:
> We cannot go there. The night watchman will see us. You will lose your reputation. (Bradbury, 1976)
> Every woman who yields to her passions and loses her virtue is a prostitute. (Mayhew, 1862)

lose your shirt to be ruined or suffer an excessive financial loss
Figuratively, having nothing left to wear. An American may in the same sense *lose his vest* or *his pants*.

loss a bereavement
What happens when you LOSE 3 somebody:
> But she told her other gentlemen she could feel he had had a loss. (le Carré, 1980)

loss of innocence copulation before marriage
Usually of women, in the days when extra-marital sex for them was taboo:
> That motive was unquestionably not to be traced to the loss of her innocence and her character. (W. Collins, 1860)

loss of separation flying dangerously close to another aircraft
Air traffic jargon:
> ...the Tristar then flew within a few miles of an Aer Lingus Boeing 747 heading for Shannon and had 'loss of separation' (flew closer than the legal safety limit) with two other planes. (*Daily Telegraph*, 21 August 1991)

lost¹ engaged in prostitution
Although still aware of their whereabouts:
> They weren't by any means all lost women when they came. (Londres, 1928, in translation)

lost² killed
Usually through violence:
> My...my wife and son, sir...lost in the uprising...murdered. (Fraser, 1975)
> *Lost at sea* is specific of drowning.

lot a battle in which there were many casualties
A First World War usage which sought to play down the horror of the carnage:
> I was in the last lot, sir. In Flanders. (Kyle, 1988)

Lothario a male who constantly makes sexual proposals to women

He was a character in a play of 1703, *The Fair Penitent*, by Rowe:

> He pointed out the office lothario and the office seductress. (Sanders, 1981)

lotion an intoxicating drink

Originally, the action of washing, whence any liquid applied externally to the body:

> I suggested to our noble friend that a lotion might not come amiss. (*Private Eye*, March 1980)

love see ABODE OF LOVE, BUY LOVE, LOVE AFFAIR, LOVE CHILD, LOVE MUSCLE, LOVE NEST, LOVE-MAKING, and MAKE LOVE TO.

love affair a short-term sexual relationship

A debasement of the original meaning, a courtship between two unmarried persons. Now used even for a single act of extramarital copulation:

> Do you want me to drop in for a short love affair? (I. Murdoch, 1978)

love child an illegitimate child

The use should not suggest that children born within wedlock are unloved:

> ... little to dispute save the paternity of 'love children'. (Bartram, 1897)

In the days when illegitimacy mattered, also as *love-bairn*, *love bird*, *love begotten*, *lover child*, etc.

love muscle the penis

No longer the heart, as depicted on cards for St Valentine's Day:

> ... a prisoner in the Rutland penitentiary who somehow got a bunch of guys he'd found through the personals to pay him fifty bucks apiece with a letter promising he was 'going to put a liplock on your love-muscle' as soon as he was released. (Turow, 1993)

love nest a place in which a mistress is housed

Where you keep your BIRD 1:

> As a love-nest, the place had its points. (Chandler, 1943)

love that durst not speak its name (the) male homosexuality

A 19th-century use reminding us of Oscar Wilde, but still seen occasionally:

> ... stiff collar and tie, always formal, even when declaring the love that durst not speak its name. (Burgess, 1980)

loved one the corpse

The phrase is today widely used of both the living and the dead without enquiry as to its appropriateness:

> As for the Loved One, poor fellow, he wanders like a sad ghost through the funeral men's pronouncements. (J. Mitford, 1963)

Evelyn Waugh entitled his 1948 novel about the Californian funeral industry *The Loved One*. It is in other respects free from euphemism, like most of his writing. The dedication turned out to be to the wrong Mitford sister, Nancy, and not Jessica, whose 1963 *The American Way of Death* was to make a stir and her reputation.

lovemaking copulation

Originally it implied no more than courtship:

> Christopher, in lovemaking, as in most things, would pursue methods unknown to her. (Somerville and Ross, 1894— Christopher was someone who would not have read, let alone put into practice, lessons from the Kama Sutra)

Now it refers only to copulation:

> Rachman's love-making was clinical and joyless. (S. Green, 1979)

lover an extramarital sexual partner

Usually of a man on a regular basis, for which it is standard English:

> In a marriage, if the lover begins to be bored with the complaisant husband, he can always provoke a scandal. (G. Greene, 1978)

The plural, *lovers*, indicates the two persons involved such an arrangement, usually male and female:

> Soon, however, everybody knew that they were lovers. (F. Harris, 1925, writing of Parnell and Mrs O'Shea)

and today sometimes of the same sex:

> 'Are you and she lovers?' asked Treece. 'No, she's never done anything to me,' said Viola. (Bradbury, 1959)

low-budget cheap

The word *budget* is used to avoid the association of cheapness and nastiness, especially in the production of films and television programmes. *Low-cost*, with the same inferences, is more generally used.

low flying speeding in a motor vehicle

As distinct from *flying low* (see FLY A FLAG). The two are not used interchangeably.

low girls prostitutes

Of the meaner sort:

> The most of the low girls in this locality do not go out till late in the evening, and chiefly devote their attention to drunken men. (Mayhew, 1862)

low profile with an avoidance of publicity
The imagery is from tank warfare, where you try to keep behind cover to reduce the target. A usage of politicians and other public figures when they do what ought not to be done and leave undone what ought to be done.

lower abdomen (of a male) the genitalia
A useful evasion for sports commentators when a player has suffered a disabling blow.

lower ground floor a cellar or basement
To be found in restaurants and shops which seek to maximize their space but wish to avoid any implication of sending customers BELOW STAIRS 1.

lower part anything to do with sexual activity
The location of the genitalia, what some see as the less attractive side of marriage, or a bit of both:
    I believe we shall have a happier union if all that 'perfectly natural but lower' part is eliminated from it. (French, 1995—being so instructed by his fiancée, it is not surprising that Francis Younghusband's later sexual conduct was a trifle bizarre)

lower stomach the genitalia
Of male or female:
    ...caressed the hair of her lower stomach affectionately. (Bradbury, 1976)

lower the boom¹(on) to arrest
The assumption from the nautical imagery is that the victim is already in harbour and will not be allowed out:
    We lowered the boom on Ross Minchen. He's behind bars right now, with his lawyer fighting to get him out. (Sanders, 1986)

lower the boom² to refuse to grant further credit to
The *boom* prevents the delivery of further goods or services until the account is settled.

lubricate to bribe or facilitate through bribery
Another form of GREASE 1 and OIL:
    [Rich] lubricated his claim for a pardon with more than $130 million of charitable donations. (*Daily Telegraph*, 30 January 2001—pardoning him was one of Clinton's last acts as President, an action which led to unfavourable comment from his political opponents and others)

lubricate your tonsils *American* to drink intoxicants
Despite alcohol being water-based:
    Can I bring something to lubricate your tonsils? (Sanders, 1992)
Lubricated means drunk.

Lucy in the sky with diamonds lysergic acid diethylamide
Or *LSD* and the title of a Lennon/McCartney song of 1967.

lumber *obsolete British* to copulate
Probably rhyming slang on HUMP from *lumber and lump*:
    Zoe lumbers for a fiver. (Kersh, 1936)

lump *American* a corpse
Criminal and police jargon, a shortened form of *lump of meat*:
    The lump is on the way down now. The big problem...is whether to do a cut 'em-up before lunch or after. (Sanders, 1973, writing about a medical post-mortem examination)

lunch box the male genitalia
Probably alluding to the shape through tight clothing. Mainly homosexual use.

lunchtime engineering bribery
Describing excessive hospitality, where a vendor plies the customer's purchasing agent, clerk, or manager with intoxicants etc.

lungs a woman's breasts
Viewed sexually, but without much anatomical accuracy, by a male:
    '...it's not a bad piece.' 'Good lungs,' Eddie admitted. (Sanders, 1982—the woman so described was not a singer)

lush a drunkard
Literally, succulent:
    He was a lush. He got the sack. (Theroux, 1983—he was dismissed for drunkenness, not given some dry white wine)
Formerly a *lush* was an intoxicant:
    We gets in some lush, and 'as some frens, and goes in for a regular blow-hout. (Mayhew, 1862)
Lushy and *lushed* mean drunk:
    And when Tom kicked up shines...or would get himself lushy three days at a time, or gallivant with whores and mollishers...(Fraser, 1997—*mollishers* were women)
    ...on a bench by a railing of the boat, lushed to the gills. (L. Armstrong, 1955)
All these drunken images were once recalled by reference to a London lawyer, Alderman Lushington.

Lydford law arbitrary punishment

This is a sample entry of many British local geographical euphemisms. The tin-mining districts of Devonshire and Cornwall, known as the Stannary, made and policed their own laws. On one occasion a judge in the Devon border town of Lydford caused a tin-miner to be hanged in the morning before sitting in judgment on him the same afternoon.

M anything taboo beginning with the letter M

Especially marijuana in addict use.

madam the female keeper of a brothel

The lady of the HOUSE 1 from the days of Shakespeare's *Madam Mitigation* (*Measure for Measure*) onwards:

'What can I do for you, Madam?' 'Miss,' she said. 'In my country a lady doesn't like being mistaken for a madam.' (Deighton, 1978)

made at one heat *obsolete Somerset* stolen

When farm tools and household utensils were made in the local smithy, each article was formed by successive reheating and quenching. Only a thief avoided this laborious progression.

Magdalene a prostitute

Christ's disciple, Mary, was supposed to have been one before she changed her ways:

After that our Magdalenes were left alone. (Fraser, 1982, writing in 19th-century style about prostitutes)

magic word (the) please

Not *abracadabra*, but a reminder to children who may forget their manners.

mail a letter see POST A LETTER

main thing (the) copulation

For Pepys and other males subsequently in their encounters with females:

... here finding Mrs Lane, took her over to Lambeth where we were lately, and there did what I would with her but only the main thing, which she would not consent to. (Pepys, 1663, with *but* meaning except)

mainline illegally to inject a narcotic intravenously

With railroad imagery and immediate effect:

He made himself a fix ... and he mainlined it. (Pereira, 1972)

The *main line* is the vein in the arm:

A high-wire performer who hit the main line in his own office. (Chandler, 1953)

mainstreaming seeking to favour chosen categories of person

The intention is to give preference to the interests of those other than white males unfairly, especially in employment and pro-

motion (according to critics), or to give others their rightful opportunity in a society dominated by white males:

Ms Harman's policy of 'mainstreaming', whereby every new government policy was examined for its impact on women, will be diluted. (*Sunday Telegraph*, 4 October 1988)

make¹ to copulate with

Normally the male *makes* the female:

The team made eight hits And a girl in the bleachers called Alice. (*Playboy's Book of Limericks*)

Either side can *make it* with the other:

Georges Simenon, who says he made it with ten thousand different women. (Hailey, 1979)

This old meat made it with Bernard Shaw. (Bradbury, 1976)

A *make* can be an act of copulation, or a promiscuous woman, usually described as an *easy make*.

make² a theft

Criminal jargon:

'It's not a make,' I said. 'You're in trouble.' (Chandler, 1939—he was not just being accused of stealing)

In the British army, to *make* an object was to loot or steal it.

make a call to urinate

The CALL OF NATURE, punning on the social visit:

'I just want to make a call,' said Willoughby, and he disappeared into the toilet. (Bradbury, 1959)

make a decent woman of to marry a woman you have impregnated

A less common version of MAKE AN HONEST WOMAN OF:

You ought to hear Hope when she gets scared he'll never come back and make a decent woman of her. (Stegner, 1940—the putative father was in the navy)

make a hole in the water to kill yourself by drowning

Plunging from a height, but not of diving:

Why I don't go and make a hole in the water I don't know. (C. Dickens, 1853)

make a mess to urinate or defecate involuntarily or in an inappropriate place

Nursery and geriatric use when involuntary by humans, indoors by domestic pets:

If he makes another mess ... I'll have him destroyed. (N. Mitford, 1945, of a dog)

make a play for *American* (of a male) to seek to engage heterosexually

One of the moves in football and see PLAY:

'Don't make a play for me, Peter.' 'I wasn't planning to.' (Sanders, 1983)

make a purse for yourself *obsolete* to steal or embezzle

You filled it without having to earn the contents:

> The wife of one of his acquaintance had fraudulently made a purse for herself out of her husband's fortune. (J. Boswell, 1791—the wife died without telling her husband where the money was. He told Dr Johnson he was more hurt by her lack of confidence in him than by losing the money. The wife's sin was, in the eyes of men and the law, heinous, she not being entitled to own property in her own right)

make a (an improper) suggestion to propose casual copulation

Men do it to women and prostitutes do it to men:

> ...if anyone had made a suggestion to her then, she would have slapped his face...But look at her: she'd sleep with any Tom, Dick or Harry for two or three pounds. (Kersh, 1936)

make an honest woman of to marry a woman you have impregnated

There was a time when HONEST was a word of some worth and this phrase was used seriously:

> It was your son made her sae, and he can make her an honest woman again. (W. Scott, 1822, writing about a pregnant woman)

Now only used humorously:

> But if you're really so old-fashioned...it's called 'making an honest woman of me'. (Price, 1970)

make away with[1] to kill

The victims are usually domestic animals. Of humans, usually reflexive and referring to suicide:

> ...ready to make away with themselves. (R. Burton, 1621)

make away with[2] to steal

The act of physical removal.

make babies together to copulate with each other

Usually within marriage and not anticipating a multiple birth or using IVF. To *make a child*, which is marginally less cloying and not euphemistic, means to become a parent:

> Aren't you ever sad...that we haven't made a child? (G. Greene, 1932)

make it to survive (an operation etc.)

Euphemistic in the negative:

> ...the doctor came out to tell them her father hadn't made it. (Turow, 1999)

make little of *Irish* to copulate with outside marriage

Usually with the woman as the object, after which she is made large by impregnation:

> You let *David Power*, the doctor's son, make little of you, and get you into trouble? (Binchy, 1985)

make love to to copulate with

In gentler times, it meant no more than to court:

> ...generally they had made love to her, and, if they did not, she presumed they did not care about her, and gave them no further attention. (Somerville and Ross, 1894, describing a flirt)

Now standard English:

> He should make love to her, or, in the parlance, screw her. (Masters, 1976)

Also relating to homosexual activity:

> The allegation that (Burgess) had ever made love to Maclean...(Boyle, 1979)

To *make love to yourself* is to masturbate:

> She sometimes made love to herself on the bath mat. (M. McCarthy, 1963)

make nice-nice to copulate

Nice, it might seem, for both parties:

> Sylvia Forsyth was making nice-nice with Timothy Cussack, her sister-in-law's former lover. (Sanders, 1994)

make off with to steal

Standard English. It is never your own property, or wife, that you take with you.

make old bones to live long

Euphemistic in the negative, in which the phrase is normally used:

> I feel I shall never make old bones. (N. Mitford, 1945)

make out with to have a sexual relationship with

Make in with might appear more logical:

> I know you were making out with that German maid. (Mailer, 1965)

make room for tea to urinate

A jocular and almost genteel usage, although based on flawed physiology. You may also claim to be *making room for it*, *another beer*, etc.:

> 'Knock that back and have another.' 'I'll make room for it first if you don't mind.' (Amis, 1986)

make sheep's eyes at to show sexual interest in (another)

Like the unintelligent staring of the wide-eyed beast. In former times you might *cast sheep's eyes at* the object of your desire:

> I have often seen him cast a sheep's eye out of a calf's head at you. (Swift, 1738—*calf* also implies youthful longing, as in *calf love*)

make sweat with to copulate with
There are many other communal activities which increase the body temperature of the joint participants, such as a singles at tennis on a hot day:

> He thought his body would still smell from the sweat he made with the woman from Trapani in the back of the car the night before. (Seymour, 1997)

make the beast with two backs see BEAST WITH TWO BACKS (THE)

make the (bed) springs creak to copulate
The usual BED 2 imagery. The *springs* may also *squeak* under the same provocation:

> We've been married a long time and made the springs creak times without number. (Fraser, 1971)
> 'It would improve everyone present if the bedsprings squeaked a bit more often.'
> 'Let's leave sex until after tea,' said Treece. (Bradbury, 1976)

make the chick scene (of a male) to copulate
Not usually with a CHICK, or prostitute:

> ...that roaring faggot...He makes the chick scene from time to time. (Mailer, 1965)

make the supreme sacrifice to be killed on war service
Not necessarily in action:

> Fellow members who had made the supreme sacrifice...(Boyle, 1979, writing of those who had died or been killed in the forces)

make time with *American* (of a male) to seek to engage sexually
The imagery is unclear:

> It doesn't help when they go into the bar and find a couple of guys trying to make time with them. (Sanders, 1983—the bar was in a club for women)

make tracks to escape or leave in a hurry
Most of those about whom this phrase is used are anxious not to *make tracks* which others might follow:

> I shouldn't be surprised if he's made tracks. (Sayers, 1937)

make up to to attempt to court
Either sex can *make up to* the other:

> ...me mother would have a fit if she thought I was making up to you. (Cookson, 1967)

make use of to do something taboo in connection with
Thus to *make use of prostitutes* is not to find them chaste employment but to copulate regularly with them: to *make use of drugs* is not to control your hypertension under medical supervision but to ingest narcotics illegally; so too with firearms, where to *make use of a weapon* is to maim or kill:

> I saw a Jewess climb on to the fence of the ghetto, stick her head through the fence and attempt to steal turnips from a passing cart. I made use of my fire-arm. The Jewess received two fatal shots. (Deighton, 1993/1, quoting from Schoenberner's *Der Gelbe Stern*, translated by Susan Sweet in 1969)

make water to urinate
Discharge would be more accurate. Standard English:

> Heave up my leg, and make water against a lady's farthingale? (Shakespeare, *The Two Gentlemen of Verona*)

See also WATER.

make way with to have a sexual relationship with
Maritime imagery, perhaps, although to *make way* normally means to allow to pass:

> [He] tried to make way with Oretta, who had him by about thirty years. (Turow, 1999)

make whoopee *obsolete* to copulate
Literally, to celebrate or carouse:

> I heard two people in the next room making whoopee—the old man's archaic term for fornication. (Styron, 1976)

make your bones to kill (someone)
Committing a murder was said to be a prerequisite of full membership of the Mafia. Some figurative use, indicating worthiness for a position of authority or experience:

> The men behind him were old-time spooks who had made their bones on the Berlin Wall when the concrete was not even dry. (Forsyth, 1994)

make yourself available to indicate promiscuity
Not a politician modestly suggesting he be chosen as a candidate but a woman signalling sexual desire to a man:

> He...would have toyed with her and cast her aside...if she had been callow enough

to make herself immediately available to him. (W. Smith, 1979)

maladjustment severe mental illness
Literally, faulty adjustment of anything:
> I was good at diverting myself, and others, from the deeper causes of my 'maladjustment'. (Irvine, 1986—she was in an institution for the insane)

In educational jargon, *maladjusted*, of children, means that they are naughty or ill-disciplined.

malady of France *obsolete* syphilis
Also known as the FRENCH ACHE:
> My Moll is dead i' th' spital
> Of malady of France. (Shakespeare, *Henry V*—an anachronism as the disease had not been imported from the Americas in 1420)

See also FRENCH.

male homosexual
As in *male videos* or *movies*, for the delectation of those who are *male identified* or *oriented*. But not *tout court* on a lavatory door.

male beast *obsolete American* a bull
From the high days of Victorian prudery. And as *male cow*. See also BIG ANIMAL.

male parts the genitalia
Not the beard, manly breast, or other physical indications of masculinity:
> His hair and beard hung in untidy yellowish ropes over his bronzed body, almost as far as his male parts. (Farrell, 1973)

See also PRIVATE PARTS.

man¹ a woman's male sexual partner
Sometimes her husband; sometimes as different from her husband:
> He is not my man, he is my husband. (*Evesham Journal*, 1899, quoted in *EDD*)

Man friend is explicit in this sense of someone other than her husband.

man² *American* a policeman or warder
Mainly criminal jargon. *The Man* is a prison governor:
> If he went to The Man to complain about it, you got him alone some place, more places to ambush a man in prison....(McBain, 1981)

man about town a philanderer
Literally, a person often seen in society:
> In his youth, Marcus Sieff had the reputation of being something of a man about town, and he married four times. (*Daily Telegraph*, 24 February 2001)

man cow *obsolete American* a bull
See also MALE BEAST and BIG ANIMAL.

man friend see MAN 1

man of pleasure a profligate
Not just enjoying being alive but also seeking the company of a *lady of pleasure* (see LADY):
> Talking of London [Dr Johnson] observed...a man of pleasure [thinks of it] as an assemblage of taverns, and the great emporium for ladies of easy virtue. (J. Boswell, 1791)

man-root the erect penis
The source of procreation:
> ...moving her pussy the while up and down harshly against my man-root. (F. Harris, 1925)

See also ROOT 1.

management privileges promiscuous copulation with a female employee
A feature, it is said, of the entertainment industry. Also as *managerial privileges*:
> On the bed upstairs, Julie had let him enjoy what are known in show business as 'management privileges'. (Allbeury, 1981)
> Tammy gave what we call 'managerial privileges' to agents, impresarios and the rest of the gang. (Allbeury, 1980)

manhood the male genitalia
Literally, the state of being an adult male:
> ...tying a handkerchief round the remains of his once proud manhood. (Sharpe, 1979—he had snagged his penis on a rosebush)

To *eliminate manhood* is to castrate:
> I know what you mean about eliminating manhood—even in animals. (Hailey, 1979)

The *needs of manhood* are copulation:
> The boy who...would probably never sleep with a woman not bought and paid for once he was grown to manhood's times and needs. (King, 1996)

manure the rotted matter incorporating the excreta of cattle, has so long been standard English that we may forget its origin as a euphemistic corruption of *main d'œuvre*. The linguistic progression went from holding land, to farming it, to fertilizing it.

many pounds heavier much fatter
Perhaps written more of women, who can be more sensitive on the subject of weight than men:
> From time to time, she returned to the screen many pounds heavier. (*Daily Telegraph*, 19 March 2001, in an obituary of the actress Ann Sothern)

marbles the testicles
The association is with the glass spheres, or alleys, which used to be made of marble. However, it is not only men who, if mentally unstable, figuratively *lose their marbles*:
> ... now openly saying that Sir Ian has lost his marbles. (*Private Eye*, August 1981)

march to a different drummer to be mentally ill
And out of step:
> Money talks; even when it is being spent by someone who marches to a different drummer. (Simpson, 1998)

marching orders dismissal from employment
Not immediately into action but permanently out of it:
> Sir John Brown said the oil giant ... had given 12,000 employees their marching orders by the end of July with another 2,500 expected by the end of the year. (*Daily Telegraph*, 11 August 1999)

marginalized not belonging to a dominant racial or sexual group
Supposedly living on the edge of a society which does you no favours:
> ... the political drive for 'empowerment' of 'marginalised' groups such as blacks, women and gays. (Mary Kenny in *Sunday Telegraph*, 30 January 1994)

Maria Monk the male semen
Rhyming slang for SPUNK, from *The Awful Disclosures of Maria Monk*, a scurrilous anti-Catholic and pornographic book published in the 19th century and said to be still in print. My apologies to the poetess who died in 1715, and whom I once wrongly associated with this vulgarism.

marital aid an instrument to use in seeking sexual pleasure
Less likely to feature in any sexual exchange within wedlock than in solitary activity:
> ... in their bedroom drawers I would find what the dirty shops called 'marital aids'. (Theroux, 1983)

marital rights copulation by a man with his wife
In the days when this phrase was used seriously, the sexual meaning transcended the economic and other *rights* which a husband acquired over his wife and her possessions when they married. Both lay and ecclesiastical law held that it was a woman's duty to copulate with her husband on request, even at the risk of dangerous, debilitating, and unwanted pregnancies. Today the phrase

is used only by husbands with willing wives and a dated sense of humour.

mark[1] *obsolete Scottish* an invulnerable spot on the body of a wizard or witch
It played an important role when it came to unmasking them:
> ... through which mark, when a large brass pin was thrust till it was bowed, both men and women, neither felt a pain, nor did it bleed. (Ritchie, 1883)

mark[2] a swindler's victim
First watched, or *marked*, for his suitability. He who *walked penniless in Mark Lane* had been swindled, although not necessarily in that London street.

mark[3] *American* to injure in custody with bruising or contusions
Police jargon, where it was desirable that evidence of the maltreatment of a suspect in questioning should not be apparent to others:
> You told me not to mark him. (Macdonald, 1952—a jailer was talking of a prisoner who had been assaulted)

marriage joys copulation
But what of shared children, companionship, warmed slippers, and cooked meals? Also as the *marriage act*, which is not nuptials:
> The sweet silent hours of marriage joys. (Shakespeare, *Richard III*)
> Heterosexuality and 'the marriage act' were keenly promoted. (French, 1995—the promotion was by Younghusband in *Wedding*)

martyr to (a) suffering from
The death or persecution is only figurative. The *Daily Telegraph* on 7 September 1978 hesitated to call the Prime Minister a liar, a *martyr to selective amnesia* being a more telling and memorable indictment. He who describes himself as *a martyr to indigestion* is merely telling you he has occasional dyspepsia.

Mary marijuana
The abbreviation is used in pop songs for oblique reference to narcotics. Because some English speakers pronounce the J in *marijuana*, sometimes also as *Mary Jane* or *MJ*.

Mary Fivefingers male self-masturbation
The lady is either the same as, or closely related to, the FIVE-FINGERED WIDOW. Also as *Mary Palm*:
> I ... was at home conducting a perverse and private romance with Mary Fivefingers. (Turow, 1993)
> KGB men never go out with girls, they just live with Mary Palm. (de Mille, 1988)

masculinity the male genitalia
Or one of the component parts:
> ... lays out his masculinity on the tabletop,
> where Gasha Rani mistakes it for a Havana
> cigar. (Dalrymple, 1998)

massage[1] to bribe
Literally, to apply friction to muscles, to
loosen them up. Also as a noun.

massage[2] *American* to assault violently
Police jargon for the use of force to obtain
information:
> 'Shellacking', 'massaging',... and
> numerous other phrases are employed
> by the police... as euphemisms to
> express how they compel reluctant
> prisoners to refresh their memories.
> (Lavine, 1930)

massage[3] masturbation
One of the services obtainable in a MASSAGE
PARLOUR:
> 'You want a massage,' she says. I says forget
> it. They don't mean massage. (Theroux,
> 1975)

massage[4] to overstate or wrongly increase (figures)
It is done by brokers seeking to talk up a
stock, or accountants wishing to show profits
or assets higher than they really are:
> The massaging of profits came at a 'vital
> time' for the company, which was floated
> by Walker in 1985. (*Daily Telegraph*, 3 June
> 1994—some officers were accused of false
> accounting)

massage[5] to flatter
Another way figuratively to STROKE another:
> The D.A. was massaging him, Paget
> thought, as he would any defense lawyer
> with a guilty client in a mildly troublesome
> case. (R. N. Patterson, 1992)

massage parlour a brothel
The friction applied is not to tone up the
muscles:
> Whether we worked in a Massage Parlour
> or were rich... we were still the same to
> you. Easy women. (Bogarde, 1978)

masseuse a prostitute
Usually working in a MASSAGE PARLOUR. The
archetypal press baron, Lord Gnome seldom
ventured abroad unless...
> accompanied by my personal assistant-
> cum-masseuse Miss Rita Chevrolet. (*Private
> Eye*, February 1980)

mate to copulate
Literally, to pair, of animals and, less often,
humans:
> Mating pythons are a very rare and a very
> strange sight. (F. Richards, 1936)
> He'll never be able to mate with a woman
> again. (M. West, 1979—but what other
> partner may he have had in mind?)
A *mating* is an act of copulation:
> ... half a dozen mamas enjoyed
> unexpectedly vigorous matings that
> evening. (Erdman, 1974)

mattress (in compounds and phrases) relating to copulation
The common association of beds and copulating, in such phrases as *mattress drill* and *beating
the mattress*. *Mattress extortion* is sexual blackmail or persuasion:
> So you con him into moving to sunny
> Florida. Maybe a little mattress extortion
> there. (Sanders, 1982)

mature old
Literally, fully developed:
> ... the high payers at the front wind up
> with some of the more mature girls.
> (Moynahan, 1983—older stewardesses tend
> to work the first-class section in aircraft)
Matured, less common, is a synonym:
> Angela Neustatter's... career has been in
> journalism where, as on the screen,
> newness and freshness are especially
> esteemed and, in her words, 'to hell with
> us matured folk'. (*Daily Telegraph*, 28
> January 1996)
A *mature student* is not necessarily a wise and
well-rounded one, but an adult who has
rejoined academe as a pupil, usually on a
full-time basis.

maturer fatter
The language of those who seek to sell clothes
to older women, who generally have put on
weight and acquired a *maturer figure*.

maul to caress (a reluctant female)
Literally, to handle roughly, but to an unwilling partner, any male fondling is excessive:
> Because you give me the occasional
> meal... doesn't mean you have the right to
> maul me. (Archer, 1979)

mausoleum crypt *American* a drawer for
a corpse facing on to a corridor
The slots which are harder to sell, given the
absence of a view:
> The crypts facing the corridor are called
> 'Mausoleum Crypts'. (J. Mitford, 1963)
A far cry from the tomb Mausoleus' widow
built at Halicarnassus around 353 BC, with the
help of a few thousand slaves.

me-too (of goods and services) exactly
copying

Commercial use where a product is launched virtually identical with that of a competitor in an attempt to exploit a market he has developed:

> Everybody knows there are 'me-too' drugs...But they sometimes lead to new discoveries. (Hailey, 1984)

measure for the drop to dismiss from employment

It is one of the duties of the hangman, although weight was more important than height if the job were to be performed properly, and punning on *dropping*, or ceasing to select, a player in a team game:

> Time to move you on...Time to measure you for the drop. (le Carré, 1989)

meat¹ a person viewed sexually

Male or female, heterosexually:

> Away, you mouldy rogue, away. I am meat for your master. (Shakespeare, *2 Henry IV*)

or homosexually:

> Together, he and Jimmy had shared some of the choicest meat inside the prison. (McBain, 1981)

A *bit of meat* is a man's sexual partner:

> I don't want you coming round here after my little bit of meat. (F. Richards, 1933)

A young prostitute is *fresh meat* and an old one, *stale meat*:

> ...since to the accustomed rake the most prized flesh is the newest, some now counted her stale meat. (Fowles, 1985)

meat² (and two veg) the male penis or genitalia

Usually, as *meat* alone, in a phrase such as TUBE OF MEAT or *hot meat*:

> A lot of [young women] look like they need...a hot meat injection. (Styron, 1976)

Meat and two veg may be used without any sexual overtones:

> ...carrying a carving knife with which she planned, she shrieked, 'to cut off his meat and two veg'. (Monkhouse, 1993)

meat³ a human corpse

Although not for consumption:

> —told him to forget Stalin, that Stalin was history, Stalin was meat. (R. Harris, 1998)

A *meat wagon* is an ambulance, a hearse, or a police van:

> The have the meat wagon following him around to follow up on the business he finds. (Chandler, 1943, writing about Marlowe, his corpse-prone private eye)
> ...pictured in the local paper getting out of a meat wagon with a blanket over his head. (P. McCarthy, 2000—the fate of a priest who sexually assaulted boys)

meat rack *American* a meeting place for male homosexuals

Punning on MEAT 1 and the butcher's display:

> The meat racks, the quick sex, the beatings...(J. Collins, 1981, describing a male homosexual's life)

In obsolete British use, a *meat-house* was a brothel.

meathead a fool

Wise people also have *meat* of the same kind in their heads:

> Rev, in this town, with this Administration? Don't be a meathead. (M. Thomas, 1987)

medal showing a visible undone fly button on trousers

A pre-zip warning from one male to another. Also as an *Abyssinian medal*, from a campaign which lasted from 1893 to 1896 without reflecting much glory on the invaders.

medical correctness the avoidance in speech of direct reference to a taboo condition or illness

Not diagnosing patients accurately or treating them wisely:

> Medical Correctness is motivated by compassion, but seized by a dangerous illusion, that if you change words, you change reality. (M. Holman in *Financial Times*, October 1994)

See also POLITICALLY CORRECT.

medicine spirituous intoxicants

This substance is seldom ingested to treat disease:

> ...[drunkards] fond of taking their medicine. (Mayhew, 1851)

The pretence that we drink spirits for our health is not new, nor does it confound our critics.

medium small

Literally, between little and big, but not in the grocery business or at the coffee shop.

medium machine an atomic bomb

The Soviet Russian equivalent of similar American and British false names intended to deceive, from the *tank* onwards:

> ...Yepishev had been...Deputy People's Commissar for Medium Machine Building...'What's a medium machine?'...'Code-name for Soviet atomic bomb programme.' (R. Harris, 1998)

meet your Maker to die

This and similar expressions are used even by those with no confidence that the rendezvous will be kept. Similarly, a Muslim might, if so favoured, *meet the Prophet*:

He intended to meet the Prophet shod, smiling, and at peace. (M. Thomas, 1980)

meeting (at/in a) where you claim to be when you do not wish to speak to some-one

The standard rebuff by telephone or through an intermediary:

> Ray Nethercott, Allied's managing director, who made £1.2m. when the company floated, has such an exciting life that he is forever in meetings. (*Daily Telegraph*, 22 August 1998—a journalist was trying without success to talk to him about a problematic flotation of shares)

melanin-enriched (of people) black

Enrichment would imply an additive rather than the natural skin pigment:

> I understand the governor likes his ladies...melanin-enriched. (Anonymous 1996)

mellow drunk

Literally, ripe, and a euphemism since the 17th century:

> Two being 'half-drunk', and the third 'just comfortably mellow'. (Bartram, 1897)

melons *American* the breasts of an adult female

Either *tout court*, or as *watermelons*, perhaps for those with a larger bust.

member the penis

Literally, any limb of the body:

> Affection and the erect male member tend to go hand in hand, if you'll pardon the expression. (Amis, 1978)

The obsolete British *Member for Horncastle*, meaning a cuckold, was a complex vulgar pun on the Lincolnshire parliamentary con-stituency.

membrum virile the penis

Literally, in Latin, the male MEMBER:

> And not a bad label for his membrum virile either. (Sanders, 1980)

memorial *American* relating to death

Literally, maintaining a memory of anything. A *memorial society* is the equivalent of the old British *funeral club*:

> Memorial societies...constitute one of the greatest threats to the American idea of memorialization. (J. Mitford, 1963— *memorialization* is trade jargon for extracting as much money as possible from the bereaved in the form of fancy caskets etc.)

A *memorial counsellor* is a salesmen of funerals or their accessories:

> A cemetery salesman identified on his card

as a 'memorial counsellor'...(ibid.)

A *memorial house* is a building with room on the walls for tablets recording deaths, usually attached to a *memorial park*, or cemetery:

> ...[interred] not in a graveyard or cemetery, but rather in a 'memorial park'. (ibid.)

men in suits managers or those in a learned profession other than medicine

A derogatory use by those who produce wealth through skills or physical labour:

> It never mattered to him, an Anchorage boy, what the men in suits thought. (Seymour, 1995)

men of respect *American* members of the Mafia

What they call themselves. Others use less flattering appellations.

men's magazine a pornographic publica-tion for male readers

Now likely to be aimed at the homosexual market:

> He even had a little stash of men's magazines in an old hatbox at the back of his clothes. (Bryson, 1989)

men ('s room) a lavatory for male use only

Usually so described in a severe building where nobody is trying to sell you anything:

> I went into the men's room, just to look in the mirror. (Theroux, 1973)

The counterpart of *men* is WOMEN, but you are likely to seek in vain a *women's room*.

ménage à trois three people living to-gether in a sexual relationship

Literally, domestic arrangements for three and sometimes shortened to *à trois*. To *maintain a clandestine ménage* is to house a mistress:

> Although he was indeed married, he also maintained a clandestine ménage. (Jones, 1978)

menses menstruation

Literally, in Latin, month(s). Formerly stan-dard English in the singular but now always in the plural:

> He would say...'I'se glad to see ye after yer mense', before beginning the churching. (Linton, 1866—*churching* was the rite of supposedly cleansing women after childbirth)

> A woman does not get gout unless her menses are stopped. (Condon, 1966)

mental mad

Literally, pertaining to the mind:

> Non-U mental/U mad. (Ross, 1956)

To be *mentally challenged* is not to be solving a difficult crossword:

...the general-for-specific euphemism *sick* is frequently used to describe someone who is *mentally challenged*. (Allan and Burridge, 1991, just as *mentally challenged* is frequently used to describe the condition of or those suffering from mental illness or deficiency)

mental disease *obsolete* syphilis
A common usage in the days when those with third-degree syphilis, along with dipsomaniacs, formed the majority of those in lunatic asylums:
>...even in 1966 Winston's son Randolph referred to his grandfather as suffering from a 'severe mental disease'. (R. Massie, 1992—Lord Randolph Churchill had contracted syphilis either from a prostitute at Oxford or from a maid at Blenheim after his wife's confinement with Winston)

merchant banker a male term of abuse
Additional to any association with the disrespect in which some hold the calling. Rhyming slang for *wanker*:
>...a whisper directed to some inattentive figure: 'Show some respect, you merchant banker.' (*Daily Telegraph*, 16 November 1996)

mercy *obsolete Scottish* whisky
It brought—still brings—warmth and comfort:
>The Baillie requires neither precept nor example wi' his tumbler when the mercy's afore him. (Galt, 1826)

mercy death the murder of a patient thought to be terminally ill
And as *mercy killing*:
>Mercy death suspected in hospital. (headline in *Daily Telegraph*, 30 December 1994)

Also favoured by the Nazis:
>...the Gestapo is now systematically bumping off the mentally deficient people...the Nazis call them 'mercy deaths'. (Shirer, 1984)

merger accounting the false statement of subsequent profitability
Literally, the creation of provisions against the cost of assimilating an acquisition:
>By the alchemy of merger accounting, some of the 'cost' could be recycled into profits. (*Daily Telegraph*, 16 November 1990—it was suggested that some £60 million were thus shown as profit by Burton after its contested acquisition of the store group Debenhams)

merry drunk

Cheerful, but not offensive. A venerable usage but still current.

merry-begot *obsolete* illegitimate
Conceived in pleasure rather than in drink:
>That Joe Garth is a merry-begot. (Caine, 1885)

meshugga mentally unstable
From the Yiddish *shagig*, to go astray or wander (*OED*):
>'They say he's meshugga.' 'No sign of that today.' (Deighton, 1988)

mess¹ to commit adultery
Probably a shortened form of *mess about*, to act in a sloppy, unconventional, or disorganized way:
>I got a decent wife. I don't go messing any longer. I just don't have the energy. (Sharpe, 1977)

mess² faeces or urine in an unwanted place
Mainly of household pets, but also of other animals:
>...the goat which was for ever trotting in and making a mess in the fireplace. (W. S. Moss, 1950)

To *mess your pants* is to defecate into them involuntarily:
>I was so scared I messed my pants. (Hailey, 1990)

mess with yourself to masturbate
Again from the meaning, to *mess about*:
>I thought he was fuckin' gorgeous. I used to mess with myself thinking about him. (R. Doyle, 1993)

message *American* an advertisement
Television jargon.

Mexican brown *American* marijuana
Not the tan you look for in Cancun:
>That's what speed and Mexican brown does for you. A hardballer. (Wambaugh, 1983)

Also as *Mexican green* or *red*. A *Mexican mushroom* is the hallucinogenic *Psilocybe Mexicana*.

Mexican raise *American* a promotion with no increase in pay
Many Mexicans working in the United States without permits are subject to exploitation. A *Mexican promotion* means the same thing.

mickey *Irish* the penis
An example of the common practice of using a masculine name:
>Mister Quigley couldn't get his mickey to go hard. (R. Doyle, 1993)

In Australian slang a *mickey* is the vagina, but whether this comes from the Shakespearean

MOUSE or from seeing things upside down I cannot say.

Mickey (Finn) a drugged intoxicant
Named after a late 19th-century Chicago innkeeper of evil repute. The commonest additive is chlorine, reacting with alcohol with dire effects (which also explains why ex-servicemen who soldiered in remote parts of the globe where all drinking water was heavily chlorinated still tend to drink their spirits neat). Sometimes as *Mickey tout court* or as *MF*:
> I'll tell pop to slip a mickey in your margarita. (Sanders, 1992)
> Had I been slipped an MF? (Burgess, 1980)

Mickey Mouse fraudulent
From the cartoon character via the slang meaning, bogus or ineffective:
> It was the revenue who made the first breach of Fleet Street's Spanish practices by exposing the Mickey Mouse payments to printers. (*Daily Telegraph*, 11 August 1994)

middle age the decades prior to becoming a geriatric
Halfway to three score years and ten is 35 but no man under 45 or woman under 50 would admit to having reached *middle age*:
> ... in that advanced stage of life that we euphemistically call middle age (Deighton, 1982)
> Though himself only in early middle-age, the King reminded his listeners that: 'For the second time in the lives of most of us we are at war.' (Kee, 1984—George VI was 44 at the time)

middle-aged spread obesity
A normal function of ageing:
> Middle-aged spread is a genuine fact of life ... The flesh can resist the flow of gravity for so long. (Matthew, 1983)

midnight baby *American* an illegitimate child
The time would seem to have been chosen from the supposed moment of conception rather than that of the birth:
> I never knew who my daddy was. I was what they called a midnight baby. (Sanders, 1984)

midwives' mercy *obsolete* infanticide of an unwanted or deformed baby
A usage in the days of high infant mortality and no antenatal treatment:
> She's had a child previously, you know—which died, I presume of midwives' mercy. (Atwood, 1996)

migraine a condition blamed for avoiding an obligation or to excuse an indiscretion
Mainly called in aid by women who seek to excuse unwarranted absence from work, or refusal to copulate with their regular sexual partner; or to suggest that they are not drunkards:
> She had stayed at home with a hangover that she called a migraine. (Manning, 1978)
Men so afflicted tend to have bad backs.

migration forcible deportation as slave labour or for killing
One of the Nazi evasions used in France:
> So 'deportation' was labelled *Abwanderung* (migration), *Evakuierung* (evacuation), *Umseidlung* (resettlement) and, closer to reality but still not that close, *Verschickung zur Zwangarbeit* (sending away for forced labour). (Ousby, 1997)

military intelligence spying
It could mean no more than knowing how to fire a gun:
> Foreigners have spies; Britain has military intelligence. (Follett, 1978)

militia an armed body operating outside normal military regulations
Literally, a body supplementing, and under the control of, regular forces:
> He more than anyone else knew that the Militia existed in order to betray. (Genet, 1969, in translation)
The French *milice* in the Second World War facilitated the rule of the German occupier, including rounding up Jews for deportation and murder:
> ... the *Service de l'Ordre Légionnaire*—which is now the Milice—the scum of the scum. (Price, 1978)

milk regularly to defraud
Persistently taking small amounts from a till, inventory, etc.:
> But you lowered the boom on swindlers who were milking a phony charity last year. (Deighton, 1993/2)
Also of stealing by siphoning fuel from motor vehicles.

milk run a comparatively safe wartime flight
From the regular doorstop delivery common in Britain:
> We'll be over the sea most of the way ... Another lousy milk run. (Deighton, 1982)

mingle bodies to copulate
A purist might say that only a limited portion of each does the *mingling*:
> ... in the eight times their 'bodies had mingled' since that first evening. (Boyd, 1982)

minor function (the) urination
Defecation is not, however, designated the *major function*:
> ... going to the W.C. (Generally for the minor function). (Franklyn, 1960)

minor wife a mistress
A Far Eastern usage:
> I used to drink a lot ... I went to whores and kept a minor wife. (*Sunday Telegraph*, 30 November 1997—he became a monk after his wife had cut off his penis)

minority those of a different colour or religion from the majority of the population
Not those who choose to go hunting with dogs or lose an election:
> ... the minorities ran the risk of losing others' sympathy and support. (Jennings, 1965)

And in several evasive phrases:
> 'Minority ethnic'—meaning black, Asian or Chinese—was adopted [by the London Metropolitan Police] because 'ethnic minority' was deemed too vague because it includes Irish and Mediterranean peoples. (*Sunday Telegraph*, 6 June 1999)
> I used to be coloured, right? Then I was a negro. And then I turned into an Afro-American. After that I was just a member of a Minority Group. Now, I'm black. (Theroux, 1982)
> What's the deal here—you don't let minority-type people sit at your front booths? (McInerney, 1992, writing of seating in a restaurant)

minus indicating lack of common sense or eccentricity
In various phrases implying incompleteness, such as *minus buttons* or *screws*:
> ... he'd throw down his pen and admit the fellow was minus some buttons, crazier than a bed bug. (Burgess, 1980)

mirror operation a firm formed to continue a previous business while avoiding its liabilities
Not one manufacturing glasses or publishing a type of newspaper daily:
> Mr Chorlton claimed last night that Club Encounters was a mirror operation with the same client base, created to avoid expensive 'unreasonable'

litigation lodged against Close Encounters of the Best Kind by a former business associate. (*Daily Telegraph*, 30 October 1997)

misadventure the consequence of error or negligence
Medical jargon. Elsewhere in life *misadventures* tend to be caused by bad luck. A *therapeutic misadventure* means that the patient died after receiving incorrect treatment and a *surgical misadventure* tells us that the scalpel slipped.

misbehave to engage in sexual activity outside marriage
Either heterosexual or homosexual:
> Elspeth, I have reason to believe, misbehaved in a potting-shed at Windsor Castle with that randy little pig the Prince of Wales. (Fraser, 1994—the holder of that title was later crowned as Edward VII)
> *The Times* reported: 'They saw two men under a tree misbehaving.' (Parris, 1995—a young soldier and a government minister were masturbating each other in St James's Park, London)

misconduct see COMMIT MISCONDUCT

misfortune *obsolete* an illegitimate child
Literally, ill-luck, which it was at one time for the mother and child:
> ... had 'had a misfortune'—in the shape of a bouncing boy. (Bartram, 1897)

An illegitimate child might also be called a *misbegot* or a *mishap*. In its literal sense, an accident, a *mishap* was also the premature delivery of a foetus, in which case the animal or woman was said to *misgo*:
> 'Tis a thousand pities her should'a miswent. (*EDD*)

miss[1] *obsolete* a mistress
If a man *kept a miss*, he was not attending to the care and maintenance of his young female offspring:
> Priests, lawyers, keen physicians, kept misses. (Galloway, 1810)

miss[2] to fail to menstruate at due time
Shortened form of *miss a period* and often with overtones of unwanted pregnancy:
> 'Has 'er missed then?' 'No, but us've 'ad some worryin' times.' (conversation in South Devon between two males in 1948)

Mis(s) is a common abbreviation for miscarriage.

missionary position (the) copulation during which the male lies atop the female

Not the status of those who take the Gospel among the heathen but from the practice of missionaries among the Polynesians, who had favoured a quadripedal approach:

'The guy's on top and the girl's on the bottom and they're—well, you know, screwing?'...'Not the missionary position.' (Theroux, 1973—but it was)

misspeak to lie
Originally, to speak evil or to speak incorrectly. One of Richard Nixon's Watergate contributions to linguistics:

...do they bar him for his 'misspeakings', or do they just take over and appoint someone else as candidate? (*Private Eye*, October 1986)

mistake¹ a child unintentionally conceived
Usually within marriage but also of illegitimacy:

Told him he was rubbish, a mistake. (D. Francis, 1987)

mistake² urination or defecation other than in a prepared place
By young children or domestic pets:

That was enough to make her father overlook the chewed shoes and occasional mistakes with which the dog was littering the house. (Clancy, 1987)

mistress a man's regular extramarital sexual partner
Originally, the female head of the household, but now always used in this sense except when shortened to *Mrs* or as the title of a schoolteacher:

My mistress is my mistress. (Shakespeare, *Titus Andronicus*)

Kept mistress is explicit:

It's not fair to the girl, this life as a kept mistress. (F. Harris, 1925)

misuse to copulate with outside marriage
Literally, to treat wrongly:

Did you ever misuse my Sophie...did you ever have her? (Keneally, 1979)

See also USE 1.

mitotic disease cancer
Medical jargon avoiding the dread word, from *mitotis*, the process whereby a cell splits into two identical parts:

The label used by many Australian doctors in place of 'cancer' is mitotic disease. (Allan and Burridge, 1991)

mob an association of criminals
From the Latin *mobile vulgis*, the rabble:

Wasn't it enough to pay protection on his place to the mob? (J. Collins, 1981)

mobility impaired crippled
Literally, weakened in strength. Circumlocution which implies that the weakening was effected by some external agency.
See also IMPAIRED HEARING.

model a prostitute
Shortened form of *model girl*, a mannequin. I am sure that many women so described lead conventional sexual lives. However, prostitutes who advertise their availability through telephone booths and other media often profess to be so employed, as do high-class prostitutes who have no need to advertise:

Miss Keeler, 20, a freelance model, was visiting Miss Marilyn Rice-Davies, an actress. (*Daily Telegraph*, December, 1962)

modern (of weapons) nuclear
A perhaps obsolete military usage, to differentiate from old-fashioned ways of killing people:

...the power, range and prospective development of 'modern' weapons—a frequent euphemism—would favour a surprise attack against the United States. (H. Thomas, 1986, quoting US Chiefs of Staff paper of September 1945)

modern conveniences *British* a lavatory and bathroom indoors
Usually shortened in classified advertisements to *(all) mod cons*. The *all* suggests hot running water rather than a jacuzzi.

mole a conspirator or spy within an organization
Espionage and labour union jargon, from the habit of the mammal to work underground, and its blackness, but not its blindness:

There were no 'moles' at large in Washington. 'Indifference, not treachery, was at the root of America's attitude.' (Boyle, 1979)

molest to assault sexually
Originally, to inconvenience, but so pervasive is the euphemism that a female may be reported as having been brutally assaulted but not *molested*, unless the assailant's motives were sexual as well as predatory:

I revived her by threatening to carry her into the bushes and molest her. (Fraser, 1975)

A *child molester* is a paedophile.

moll *obsolete* a prostitute
Originally, a sweetheart, which survives in the gangster's *moll*. The derivation is from the common girl's name, and a *moll-shop* was a brothel. *Moll Thompson's mark* meant nothing

more than emptiness, of a bottle, punning on the initials *MT*.

Molotov cocktail a simple petrol bomb
Molotov was Stalin's Foreign Minister in the Second World War. His long and sinister career included making a pact with Hitler in 1939 and organizing the postwar occupation of Eastern European states. The weapon by which he is remembered was in fact invented by the Finns for use against their Russian invaders.

mom-and-pop staid and old fashioned
Like your aged parents and often of a small retail business:
> ...a small-time mom-and-pop dope store would be allowed to flourish unmolested. (McBain, 1981)
Some figurative use:
> Are you gonna be a mom-and-pop camcorder with Kuralt-ian notions of 'on the road', or are you up to heavyweight digital effects and dazzling graphics? (*Fly Rod and Reel*, March 1991)

momentary trick (the) *obsolete* copulation
The duration of a casual encounter:
> ...for the momentary trick
> Be perdurably fined. (Shakespeare, *Measure for Measure*)

Monday morning quarterback *American* a fantasist who judges by hindsight
The spectator who watches the weekend game may take his criticism to work with him on Monday:
> ...the Monday morning quarterback who could have won the ball game if he had been on the team. But he never is. He's high up in the stands with a flask on his hip. (Chandler, 1958)

monkey¹ (the) *American* addiction to illegal narcotics
Probably from *having a monkey on your back* which you cannot shake off:
> You think it's the monkey that's killing you. (Macdonald, 1971, writing of a heroin addict, not a zoo-keeper)

monkey² *obsolete British* a mortgage
Again something which it is hard to get free from:
> Oh yes, there's a monkey sitting on his chimney. (*EDD*—he had an onerous mortgage)

monkey's (a) an obscenity
Shortened form of *monkey's fuck*, a matter of trifling importance, and usually in the phrase *give a monkey's*:

> ...doesn't it worry you that ninety-nine point nine per cent of the population couldn't give a monkey's? (Lodge, 1988)

monkey business promiscuity
Literally, any mischief which a monkey might get up to. Used sometimes as a warning to a man to behave decorously towards a young woman:
> 'No monkey business,' he agreed. 'Shit, I won't touch her.' (Sanders, 1977—an artist was speaking to a young model's mother)

monosyllable *obsolete* the vagina
The taboo *cunt*:
> Perhaps a bawdy monosyllable such as boys write upon walls. (*DSUE*, quoting Lucas's *The Gamesters*, 1714)
Grose says 'A woman's commodity'.

Montezuma's revenge diarrhoea
Usually, but not necessarily, contracted in Mexico by visitors from the United States:
> You get Montezuma's revenge when you've been off on holiday somewhere. (BBC Television, 18 November 1996)
Montezuma II was the Aztec emperor when Cortes invaded Mexico, and was killed by his own people in 1520 after he had told them to submit to the invader.
Also as the AZTEC TWO-STEP, *Mexican toothache*, *Mexican two-step*, *Mexican foxtrot*, etc.

monthly period menstruation
Not how many days a month lasts. Standard English, sometimes shortened to *monthlies*:
> ...her monthly period. We call it menstruation. (Sharpe, 1978)
> Molly was easily excited, especially about the eighth day after her monthlies had ceased. (F. Harris, 1925)
Month's is obsolete:
> ...my wife...gone to bed not very well, she having her month's upon her. (Pepys, 1662)
Monthly courses is also obsolete but a woman my still suffer from *monthly blues*:
> 'You all right?' 'Yes.' 'Monthly blues?' (de Mille, 1988)

mooch *obsolete* to pilfer
Originally, to hang about, whence to beg, and then to steal:
> I don't mean to say that if I see anything laying about handy that I don't mooch it. (Mayhew, 1851)
This is an example of a word which has reverted from its euphemistic to its proper use in modern speech.

mood freshener an illicit drug
From the stimulus:

It was enough to send you racing to the bathroom for a discreet puke or a quick blast of mood freshener. (McInerney, 1992)

moon to expose the buttocks to others by lowering clothes in public
A *moon-like* expanse of flesh is so revealed:
... the Chinese soldiers provoking incidents by dropping their pants and presenting the bare bums northward, mooning the Soviet border. (Theroux, 1988, writing about the Manchurian border)

moon people lunatics
Not lowering their trousers in public or belonging to an eastern cult but from the venerable association of the Latin *luna* with *lunacy*:
She put me—can you imagine—into an *asylum for lunatics*. Moon people. (Anonymous, 1996)

moonlight[1] *obsolete British* associated with smuggling
The time when the stuff was shipped ashore and transported. Smuggled spirits were called *moonlight* and a habitual smuggler was said to have been *bred in the moonlight*:
Thirty 'crack' hands, who had been bred in the moonlight from boyhood. (Vedder, 1832)

moonlight[2] *obsolete Irish* to wound
Violence in 19th-century agrarian disturbances tended to take place at night, with warnings about arson and assault being signed *Captain Moonlight*:
He had deposed to his experience of being moonlighted in the thigh. (*Daily Telegraph*, November 1888)

moonlight[3] to work at a second job
The work is often done in the evening, without paying tax on the earnings:
A joiner who 'moonlights' at weekends for his mates... (Shankland, 1980)
The word is also used of those who continue draw unemployment monies from the state without revealing earnings from casual employment.

moonlight flit the clandestine departure of an absconding debtor
Formerly, a tenant in arrears with his rent, whose chattels could be distrained by the landlord so long as they remained in the rented premises, but not elsewhere:
He has e'en made a moonlight flitting. (W. Scott, 1822)
You might in similar fashion have made a *moonlight flight, march, touch,* or *walk,* or have been said to *bolt* or *shoot the moon*:

Nobody was allowed to shoot the moon. (Besant and Rice, 1872)
The term is also used of avoiding other creditors:
He was fain to make a moonlight flitting, leaving his wife for a time to manage his affairs. (Galt, 1821)
See also FLIT 2.

moonraker *obsolete* a smuggler
Contraband, especially spirits, was often concealed in a pool for later recovery by trawling in the moonlight and onward transmission:
Getting ready for the moonrakers at the great pool. (Verney, 1870)

moonshine whisky
From an illicit still, which is operated at night to avoid detection:
... made their living by odd ends of trade, from moonshine, from cutting lumber... (Keneally, 1979)

moose *American* a prostitute
Neither a corruption of MOUSE nor punning on the deer (or dear), but a Korean War usage from the Japanese *musume*, a girl (*DAS*).

mop up to kill or capture (surviving opponents)
Military jargon with imagery from cleaning spillage:
Franco ruled. It was all over bar the mopping up. (Boyle, 1979)

morally challenging evil
A variant on the CHALLENGED theme:
Arthur Niebe, the head of the SS Reich Criminal Police, a figure so morally challenging that he is virtually airbrushed out of many accounts of the resistance. (Burleigh, 2000)

more than a (good) friend a person with whom you have an extramarital sexual relationship
Another kind of FRIEND:
It would have taken no special investigation to establish that they were more than good friends. (Price, 1971)
And in similar phrases, such as *more than just friends*:
No mention had been made of that one time they had briefly become more than just friends. (N. Evans, 1998)

morning after (the) a hangover
Shortened form of *the morning after the night before*, when excessive or adulterated alcohol had been consumed.

most precious part the male genitalia

Valued in this usage, by the male at least, for copulation rather than urination:

> Corporal Browne was hit in the most precious part of his body. (Farran, 1948)

moth in your wallet (a) stinginess
The *Tineola bisselliella* doesn't normally go for leather, although it favours an undisturbed site for its eggs:

> Symington would pick up the tab...there were no moths in his wallet. (Sanders, 1983)

mother[1] *American* an elderly male homo-sexual
The obsolete British meaning was a bawd.

mother[2] *American* a term of vulgar abuse
Shortened form of *motherfucker*, but those who use it are unlikely to know that Oedipus was said to have sired four children by Jocasta in a complex saga which includes blinding and suicide as well as incest. Used as an insult, but an inanimate object may also be so casti-gated:

> I remember back in Quang Tri we had an A.P.C. was a real mother. Always throwing tracks, breaking down. (Boyd, 1983, writing about an armoured personnel carrier)

mother five fingers masturbation of a male
A relation no doubt of the FIVE-FINGERED WIDOW:

> Always looking for something better. Know what I mean? Then I end up with Mother Five-fingers. (Sanders, 1981)

mother's blessing *obsolete* a narcotic ad-ministered to a baby
The *blessing* was the peace which came from silencing a crying child:

> Give the babies a dose of 'Mother's Blessing' (that's laudanum, sir, or some sich stuff) to sleep 'em when they're squally. (Mayhew, 1862)

The usage and practice continued until after the Second World War.

mother's ruin gin
In the 19th century, cheapness led to wide female addiction and consequent demoraliz-ation. Now only humorous use:

> ...struggling to get his arms round a Europack of litre-sized Mother's Ruin. (*Private Eye*, April 1980)

Occasionally as the punning *mother's milk*.

motion (a) defecation
Medical jargon, not of sitting up in bed but from the movement of the bowels. *Motions* are faeces:

> She had dreams of cooking by perpetual motion, or rather by perpetual motions.

(Sharpe, 1976—Mrs Wilt's 'biological' lavatory was supposed to generate heat for domestic purposes)

motion discomfort airsickness
Airline jargon, in support of the pretence that any regular passenger actually enjoys flying:

> 'I am still suffering from motion discomfort.'... 'It means air sickness.' (N. Mitford, 1960)

The *motion discomfort bag* you may find on an American airliner is for you to vomit in.

mount to copulate with
Standard English of animals. Occasional use of humans puns on the action of mounting a horse:

> Like a full-acorn'd boar, a German one, Cried 'O' and mounted. (Shakespeare, *Cymbeline*)

The punning *mounting drill* was popular among cavalrymen:

> It occurred to me, as I put Mandeville through her final mounting drill, that she wasn't fit to fill my dear one's corset. (Fraser, 1994)

A male may describe his complaisant sexual partner as *a good mount* ; it remains a mystery where the *bad mounts* get to.

mount a corporal and four (of a male) to masturbate
It puns on the constitution of an army guard and the thumb and four fingers.

mountain chicken the hind legs of a giant toad
A Dominican specialty:

> We ate a big dish of 'mountain chicken', a rich white meat fried in batter. Each succulent serving was revealed, too late, to have been the hindlegs of a giant toad. (Whicker, 1982—and unfortunate for the toad also)

mountain dew whisky
From the process of distillation and the place where it is done:

> A 'greybeard' jar of the real Glengillodram mountain dew. (Alexander, 1882)

mouse *obsolete* a sexually attractive female
Perhaps a pet name, or perhaps not:

> ...tempt you again to bed; Pinch wanton on your cheek; call you his mouse. (Shakespeare, *Hamlet*)

mousehole the vagina
Not necessarily viewed sexually:

> Scissored her legs open—and pulled a length of magician's scarves, knotted end

to end, out of her mousehole. (Theroux, 1978)

mouth *obsolete* to kiss lecherously
Literally, to utter. Also as *mouth with*:
> He would mouth with a beggar, though she smelt brown bread and garlick. (Shakespeare, *Measure for Measure*)

move in on to form a sexual relationship with
As different from MOVE IN WITH:
> —You moved in on Joey, Nat'lie? he asked.—Yeah.—I did. The girls laughed again.—Yis're disgusted, aren't yis? said Imelda.—She likes him, yis stupid fuckin' saps. (R. Doyle, 1987)

move in with to cohabit and copulate with
Not of a married couple changing residences:
> As to his moving in with you, all I'll say is that some of the folks round here are a little old-fashioned. (N. Evans, 1998)

move on to die
While the corpse might seem incapable of movement, perhaps the spirit will remain mobile:
> I want to leave something which might be useful to other people after I move on. (W. F. Deedes in *Daily Telegraph*, 2 March 1998)

movement[1] an act of defecation
It is the bowels which *move*, not the participant:
> Observe the time of day he has his movement. (M. McCarthy, 1963)

Move your bowels, to defecate, is standard English:
> He lay in bed, reading nothing; he moved his bowels. (Bradbury, 1959—he was a hospital patient)

movement[2] an institution or collection of institutions
Usually characterized by deep-rooted conservatism to protect the status quo and reluctant to *move* in any direction, exemplified on occasion by the British Building Society or Trade Union *movements*.

Mozart drunk
Rhyming slang on *Mozart and Liszt*, pissed. See also BRAHMS.

Mr Plod see PLOD

Mr Priapus an erection of the penis
PRIAPUS, the Pan of Mysia, is depicted in that condition:
> ... as I write and describe them, cause Mr Priapus to swell in my breeches. (Pearsall, 1969, quoting 19th-century pornography)

Mrs Chant *British* a lavatory
Rhyming slang for AUNT 2 in female use.

Mrs Duckett a mild oath
Again rhyming slang.

mud in your trousers involuntary defecation
Usually through terror:
> By God, I nearly had mud in me trousers tonight. (Winton, 1994—he had had a shock)

muddy *obsolete* tipsy
Not at all clear in the head and not with clothing soiled from falling:
> He has an elderly woman ... who lives with him, and jogs his elbow when his glass has stood too long empty ... not that he gets drunk, for he is a very pious man, but he is always muddy. (J. Boswell, 1791)

mudlark *obsolete London* a scavenger or thief
It referred either to those who frequented the exposed banks of the River Thames at low tide to pick up anything of value, or those who picked up stolen goods which an accomplice had tossed over the rail of a ship:
> The mudlarks are generally known as thieves. (Mayhew, 1862)

muff the female pubic hair
This usage has survived the practice of using *muffs* to warm the hands when conveyances were unheated:
> I had a photograph of that sanctimonious prick Merriman with his nose in some call girl's muff. (M. Thomas, 1980)

A *muff-diver* indulges in cunnilingus.

mug to rob by violence in a public place
In obsolete British use to *mug* was to bribe with drink, from the container:
> Having ... mugged, as we say in England, our pilot. (Ingelo, 1830)

In 19th-century London it came to mean robbery by garroting, perhaps because the victim was considered a *mug*, or stupid person. Now all too common, and for us the *mugger* is no longer merely 'the broad-nosed crocodile from India' (*SOED*).

muggy drunk
Literally, moist, and usually of the weather:
> They're rayther muggy oft. (Charles Clark, 1839, writing of drunkards)

Muggy may also mean stupid.

mule a carrier of illegal narcotics in bulk
Like the beast of burden used especially on mountain tracks, and owing nothing to the American slang *mule*, whisky illegally distilled, with its fierce kick:
> Some smuggle for their own use, but most are 'mules', paid $1,500 or so a trip. (Moynahan, 1983)

multicultural embracing people of differing skin pigmentation
Multicoloured would be deemed offensive:
> All-black schools in multi-cultural Brent would be a form of apartheid. (*Daily Telegraph*, October 1983)

Whence *multiculturism*, the integration of non-white people into a mainly white population:
> ... 'multiculturism'... provides certain minorities with a way through the university, and little fiefdoms within the curriculum for those on the vocal left lucky enough to identify themselves with them. (*Daily Telegraph*, 23 January 1991— the standard of entry was alleged to be lower for applicants who were not white)

municipal farm *American* a prison
Where convicts are put to work:
> A striker caught with a slingshot was sentenced to the municipal farm. (Lacey, 1986)

Murphy game (the) *American* (of a prostitute) cheating a customer
Perhaps from the simplest of *Murphy's Laws*, that if something can go wrong, it will:
> ... there were rooms for hire above the bar and that Star's specialty was the Murphy game... rolling drunk customers. (Maas, 1986)

muscle to assault criminally
From the force used:
> You couldn't muscle anyone, Peter. You're a softy. (Sanders, 1983)

A *muscleman* or *muscle* does the assaulting:
> ... kind of muscleman for a big protection gang in Tokyo. (M. West, 1979)
> Not so much between the ears, but he was a good muscle. (Sanders, 1980)

To *muscle in on* something is to seek an undeserved benefit.

mush *obsolete British* to rob from houses
Shortened form of the slang *mushroom*, an umbrella. Itinerants, known as *umbrella* or *mushroom men*, went from house to house offering to mend umbrellas, which provided good cover for crooks and gave the trade a bad name. *Mush* is still a mode of male address, importing no ill-will or accusation of dishonesty.

musical *obsolete* (of a male) homosexual
Homosexuals considered themselves to be more artistic that heterosexuals:
> In Harry's estimation they were both homosexual—or 'musical', as the Noel Coward set would say. (Follett, 1991)

muster your bag *British* to be ill
Naval usage, from having to take your kit to the sick bay.

mutate to dye
Literally, to change genetically and permanently:
> She 'mutates' or 'colour-corrects' her hair. (Jennings, 1965)

mutilate to castrate
Originally, in this sense, to cut off a limb. Now mainly used of American tomcats.

mutt *British* deaf
From the rhyming slang *Mutt and Jeff*, better known as the First World War service and victory medals than for the comic cartoon characters, but for most people no longer remembered as either.

mutton a person viewed sexually by another
The common MEAT 1 imagery:
> The duke... would eat mutton on Fridays. He's now past it. (Shakespeare, *Measure for Measure*)

A *mutton* was a prostitute, and a *mutton-monger* was a profligate male, illogically it might seem, as he was a buyer, not a seller:
> Bit of a mutton-monger, I shouldn't wonder... You'll just have to prime him with raw eggs, stout and oysters, what? (Fraser, 1997)

See also COME YOUR MUTTON.

mutton dressed as lamb a woman affecting the dress or style of someone much younger
A derogatory expression:
> 'Youthful excess is one thing,' said the Dean, 'but mutton dressed as lamb is another.' (Sharpe, 1974)

muzzy tipsy
Literally, of the weather, dull and overcast. Quite common female use of themselves.

my word *British* faeces
Rhyming slang for *turd*. Mainly used of canine deposits on pavements etc.

N

N-word (the) the word *nigger*
The word *nigger* is strictly taboo unless used by a black person:
> One does not have to drive too far out of town to see a Confederate flag snapping in the wind or hear the odd mention of the 'N-word'. (*Daily Telegraph*, 18 April 1997)

nab to steal
Literally, to catch or arrest:
> They ha' nabb'd my gold. (C. Clark, 1839)
In obsolete use to *nab the snow* was to steal washing from a line, the usage clearly complimenting the laundress. To *nab the stoop* was to stand in the pillory.

naff off go away
OED says that *naff* is a 'a euphemistic substitution for fuck', which is more likely than Partridge's suggestion that it is back slang for *fan*, a shortened form of FANNY. The origin of the slang meaning, dated or unfashionable, is unclear.

nail¹ *American* (of a male) to copulate with
Perhaps from the slang *nail*, a penis, or from an analogy with SCREW 1. The rhyming slang *hammer and nail*, TAIL 1, opens yet another line of etymological enquiry:
> Until April [Congressman Gary Condit] was just another horny congressman, nailing—as with many, if not most, of his colleagues—one of the town's vast herd of obliging interns. (*Sunday Telegraph*, 15 July 2001)

nail² a cigarette
A shortened form of the perhaps obsolete *coffin nail*, from the adverse effect on health:
> Smoke if you want to...I thought you were desperate for one of those East German nails. (Deighton, 1994)

nameless crime (the) buggery
A common use when homosexual acts between males were illegal. The charge sheet of an accused would refer to 'the abominable crime of buggery'. Murder and rape earned no such descriptive embellishment.

nancy a male homosexual
The derivation is from the female name. Originally as *Miss Nancy* and also as *nancy boy*:
> He looked a bit of a nancy boy to me. (Matthew, 1978)

nanny-house *obsolete* a brothel
A *nanny* was a prostitute, from the female form of goat rather than her nursing skills:
> ...speech smacking of grogshop or nanny-house. (Graves, 1940, writing in archaic style)

Napoleon's revenge diarrhoea
As suffered by British tourists in France:
> A lady friend, travelling through France with her family, was stricken with a rather severe attack of 'Napoleon's revenge'. (*At Your Convenience*, 1988)

nappy an infant's towel to contain excreta
A shortened form of *napkin*, a small piece of cloth, and now standard English.

narrow *obsolete* miserly
Not widespread in generosity:
> Archibald, Duke of Argyle, was narrow in his ordinary expenses. (J. Boswell, 1773)
Narrowness was stinginess:
> Dr Johnson said, I ought to write down a collection of the instances of his narrowness, as they almost exceeded belief. (ibid.)

narrow bed a grave
Where we await our summons to the *narrow passageway to the unknown*, perhaps:
> The narrow passageway to the unknown which everyone must cross. (J. Mitford, 1963)

nasty¹ (the) a spirituous intoxicant
Unpleasant to the teetotaller. Now humorous use only and as the *nasty stuff*
> 'What you need is a wee bit of the old nasty.' I uncorked the Armagnac. (Sanders, 1982)
> How about a bit of the old nasty stuff before we turn in? (Sanders, 1977)

nasty² drunk
Not from taking too much of the NASTY 1 but from the way drunks feel and behave:
> I shared a car back to London with Peter and we sat in the back getting thoroughly nasty on a clutch of freebie bottles of Hine or Martell. (Fry, 1994)

nasty complaint (a) venereal disease
It might seem to suggest having a rotten cold, or telling the waiter there's a hair in your soup:
> After a business trip to the Middle East, Brown found he was suffering from a nasty complaint. (*Private Eye*, February 1989)

national assistance *British* monies paid by the state to the poor

Not bankrolling a poorer sovereign state. See also ASSISTANCE.

national emergency British the Second World War

It was indeed that, but much more besides before Russia and the United States were attacked and joined the fray:

> When I find this war, in the ninth month of its second phase, still referred to coyly as the 'national emergency' ... (Heffer, 1998, quoting Enoch Powell)

national indoor game (the) copulation

Certainly played by many, and not usually al fresco.

national savings lending to the government

There are many other ways in which citizens may save, contributing to a *national* accumulation of wealth:

> One form of lending to the government is called 'national savings'. This is one of those maddeningly misleading expressions which summon patriotism to the aid of deception. (Heffer, 1998, quoting Enoch Powell)

national security guard an instrument for civil repression

The *security* being *guarded* is that of an autocrat:

> The shark pool ... was established by Nassir's feared henchmen from the National Security Guard. (*Daily Telegraph*, August 1980)

See also SECURITY.

national service British compulsory conscription into the armed forces

The usage concealed the military nature of the engagement while conscription remained in force after 1945 (prior to which people had simply been *called up*). Others out of uniform may also have thought they were serving the state:

> ... advocating alliance with Russia, the imposition of national service and the creation of a cross-party coalition government. (Graham Stewart, 1999, reporting Churchill's policy in 1938)

nationalize to appropriate

Standard English for compulsorily taking an undertaking from private ownership, with or without compensation, into state control and ownership. See also PUBLIC OWNERSHIP and PUBLIC–PRIVATE PARTNERSHIP.

native black

Literally, as in Dr Johnson's definition, 'an original inhabitant', but extended in

the colonial era to all people who were not white:

> 'He admits to having abandoned twenty men to their deaths,' Vera said. 'They were only natives.' (Christie, 1939)

Native American a person with North American Indian ancestry

For the transatlantic observer, a harsh usage which appears to disparage the greater part of those who were born in the United States and look upon it as their native land, quite apart from what the indigenous inhabitants of other American territories may feel:

> 'An Indian,' I said ... 'I mean, a Native American.' (Theroux, 1993)

native elixir (the) Irish whiskey

Native certainly to Scotland as well as Ireland, although its properties as an *elixir*, prolonging life or acting as a panacea for all ills, are not universally accepted, especially by the wives of those who happen to appreciate its beneficial nature:

> 'Poor Griffith,' Childers said to me, 'a bit too fond of the native elixir, eh?' (Flanagan, 1995—Griffith was the half-English negotiator for Irish independence in 1922 and Erskine Childers was the English supporter of Irish Republicanism, whom they later killed)

natural[1] obsolete an idiot

Probably a shortened form of *natural (born) fool*, an expression which antedated this use by a century (*EDD*):

> We had our natural. He was known as daft Jamie. (Inglis, 1895)

natural[2] (of parentage) illegitimate

Originally, describing a child who was sired by the father of a family as distinct from an adopted child. From the late 16th century until recently, *natural* imputed illegitimacy:

> Edward VII, a most wide-ranging man in his attraction to ladies, was his natural father. (Condon, 1966)

Today it is again used, as long ago, to describe the biological parents of an adopted child.

natural break British the intrusion of advertisements in a television broadcast

The licensing authority stipulated that the interruptions for advertising should not spoil the continuity of a programme. Whence also the humorous *natural break* in a meeting, for urination.

natural functions (the) urination and defecation

Eating, sweating, and breathing are just as *natural*, to name but a few. In obsolete form as *natural necessities* or *purposes*:

...reaching peaks of embarrassment whenever he wished to fulfil one of his natural functions. (R. V. Jones, 1978)

...severall...under that relligiouse confynment, wer forced to give way to ther naturall necessities...bedewing the pavements of churches with other moysture than teares. (Paterson, 1998, quoting James Gordon on Scottish Covenanting enthusiasm for long sermons in 1638)

natural vigours (in a male) lust
Especially when it was thought lust came less *naturally* to females:
I have my natural vigours, like any man. (Fowles, 1985)

nature stop *American* a halt on a road journey for urination
Not at a viewpoint with a camera.

nature's garb nudity
Without even a fig leaf. A naked person was also said to be *in his naturals*.

nature's needs urination and defecation
A variant of NATURAL FUNCTIONS:
For another of nature's needs I also inserted a large rubber bag. (Theroux, 1975)

naturist a nudist
Not someone especially interested in the environment but one with a penchant for wearing NATURE'S GARB, either alone or in the company of like-minded people.

naughty promiscuous
Originally only of a female, as such conduct was not considered wicked in a male:
She had been naughty as a girl, she said, especially with one boy. (F. Harris, 1925)

naughty-house *obsolete* a brothel
From the sense, wicked:
This house, if it be not a bawd's house, it is pity of her life, for it is a naughty house. (Shakespeare, *Measure for Measure*)
Naughty lady, a prostitute, seems to have survived into modern times:
...to which, incidentally, came many of the naughty ladies of Paris to improve their complexions. (Fingall, 1937)

nautch girl a prostitute
Literally, a professional Indian dancing girl:
She kept a troupe of nautch-girls who were also prostitutes. (F. Richards, 1936)

Neapolitan bone-ache syphilis
The disease you caught from the Italians, if not the French or the Spanish:
Vengeance on the whole camp or, rather, the Neapolitan bone-ache for that,

methinks, is the curse...(Shakespeare, *Troilus and Cressida*)
Also as the *Neapolitan favour*.

near¹ stingy
A derivative of CLOSE 1:
Some were beginning to consider Oak a near man. (Hardy, 1874)

near² imitation
Mencken gave 'near-silk, near-antique, near-leather, near-mahogany, near-silver and near-porcelain' (1941). Consumer protection legislation has thinned the list. *Near-beer*, supposedly with low alcohol content, was sold in unlicensed premises in Britain until after the Second World War:
Near-beer costs two shillings a glass: call it just beer—forget the 'near'. (Kersh, 1936)

necessary (house) *obsolete* a lavatory
The Italian *necessario* or the French *nécessaire*:
...the unlucky medicine chest played the same part that Martie Antoinette's nécessaire did in the escape to Vincennes. (N. Mitford, 1945)
A contrivance for emptying every Necessary House in the City of London...(Monsarrat, 1978, writing in archaic style)
A *necessary woman* was not the TOKEN female committee member but the emptier of lavatories:
Trott the Necessary Woman, who stalked the house at all hours...to empty and then clean the several privies. (ibid.)

neck to kiss and caress amorously
From the placing of an arm round the other's neck at some stage:
...to copulate, or at least neck, in the relative comfort of a parked sedan. (Ustinov, 1971)

necklace *South African* to murder by igniting a rubber tyre placed on the shoulders of a victim
A method used by blacks on other blacks, for crime or for being of a different political persuasion:
...some stone throwing, petrol bombing, and necklacing of innocent people. (BBC News, 30 August 1989, reporting on rioting in South Africa)

necktie party a lynching
The *necktie* is the noose:
The solitary bent branch enough to tell any Western fan that it would eventually be used for a necktie party. (Deighton, 1972)
Also as a *necktie sociable*. The victim might be *measured for a necktie*:

...then he knew he was being measured for a necktie. (Price, 1985, and not by an outfitter)

The outcome was to *have his neck stretched*:
He shot the associate...and was taken off to have his neck stretched. (Bryson, 1995)

or wear a designated *necktie*. After a revolt in the Baltic provinces in 1906, the Russian Prime Minister Stolypin caused more than 2,000 rebels to be shot or hanged:
He followed on with such gusto that the noose became known as the 'Stolypin necktie'. (Moynahan, 1994—this did not stop the British Ambassador in St Petersburg naming him as 'the most notable figure in Europe')

need help to be incompetent or bankrupt
Each of us *needs* and receives *help* from others in every aspect of our daily lives:
It says the NEMC and its chief executive, Jennie Page, need help in the running of the project. (*Daily Telegraph*, 7 January 2000, writing about the New Millennium Experience Company, which was responsible for the ill-fated London Millennium Dome)

needle to strengthen (an intoxicant) by adulteration
Originally, by introducing an electric current through a rod shaped like a needle, whence any form of lacing:
The smell of needled beer...(Longstreet, 1956)

needlepusher a person addicted to illegal narcotics
Injected by a hypodermic needle:
Some needlepusher found the body. (J. Patterson, 1999)

negative or **negatively** are used in the same way as *less*, to avoid precision or as an evasion, in many phrasal euphemisms, of which a sample only appears below:

negative aspect(s) an unacceptable consequence
The usage resurfaced when the media tycoon Rupert Murdoch objected to the publication by HarperCollins, one of his subsidiaries, of a book which he judged might have damaged his business interests in China:
Bell, referring to the Patten book, scurried to reassure Disney that Murdoch 'has outlined to me the negative aspects of publication which I fully understand'.
'Outlining the negative aspects' is of course a recognized Murdochean euphemism for a threat of immediate execution. 'Fully understanding the negative aspects' is a euphemism for the execution itself. (Frank Johnson in *Daily Telegraph*, 28 February 1998—Disney was an American Murdoch employee and Bell the head of HarperCollins. The editor of the London *Times*, also owned by Murdoch, showed his awareness of the *negative aspects* of the story, which he ignored, choosing for his front page a piece about the late Duke of Windsor's handkerchief)

negative cash debt
Or a reduction in liquidity:
Over the past 10 years (the building industry) has generated £140m of negative cash. (Peter Long, quoted in *Daily Telegraph*, 23 January 2001)

negative containment a leak of radiation from a nuclear reactor
The phrase is used because:
To report there had been an 'escape' of radioactive matter would be alarmist. (*Daily Telegraph*, 9 March 1994)

negative contribution a sale at a loss
Commercial jargon. The *contribution* is that part of the price left after deducting the cost of labour and materials. A *positive contribution* indicates that some or all of the overhead and selling costs have been recovered. A *negative profit contribution* means that you have lost money after deducting all your costs.

negative employment unemployment
Not just in an American *negative employee situation*, where staff are dismissed:
It is impossible to calculate how many jobs would be destroyed by the seductive, compassion-seeming policy of setting a minimum wage, but even the TUC acknowledges there might be 'negative employment effects'. (*Daily Telegraph*, 24 August 1995—the TUC is the British Trades Union Congress)

negative equity owing more on an asset than it is worth
Particularly of mortgages on dwellings:
Their mortgage was £60,000...They were not quite 'negative equity' but damn near. (Seymour, 1995)

negative growth a decline
Politicians so speak of the national product, businessmen of turnover or profits:
With International Leisure somewhat becalmed at 112p having shown negative growth in two years...(*Private Eye*, September 1986)

negative incident an event which may cause harm or adverse publicity

A dread event in the world of public relations: 'Will they have a representative on the train?' 'To minimize negative incidents...I'm using their jargon, dammit.' (D. Francis, 1988)

negative (income) tax state payment to the poor

The proposition seems to have been first expounded by Milton Friedman under the title *negative tax*. An object would be to eliminate the present cumbersome methods of individual assessment and distribution of money to the poor and others.

negative patient care outcome death

Medical jargon. The phrase could be taken to mean that a test has proved the absence of infection.

negative propaganda the unfair denigration of opponents

Not much different from any other kind of *propaganda*, you might suppose, the word having come far since 1622, when Pope Gregory XV set up a body of cardinals under that title to *propagate* Roman Catholicism:

Denigration—or 'negative propaganda', if you are given to squeamish euphemism—is an essential part of any election, even an internal one. (Cole, 1995)

negative stock-holding orders which cannot be delivered

This is how your computer tells you about empty shelves in the warehouse when you have overdue orders and clamant customers. Normally computers deduct orders or sales from unallocated stocks to throw up reorder or manufacture schedules.

negatively impacted disappointing or loss-making

Bankers, whose existence depends on confidence, adopt linguistic contortions to avoid any word like *loss*:

Last week it revealed a slight downturn in third quarter figures and warned that fourth quarter results would be 'negatively impacted'. (*Daily Telegraph*, 28 September 1998—Goldman Sachs was explaining why its planned flotation had been postponed)

negatively privileged poor

Sociological jargon and a correct statement only of those who have elected to lead a life of monastic asceticism. See also PRIVILEGED and UNDERPRIVILEGED.

negotiable we do not expect to receive the asking price

Estate agents' jargon, often shortened to *neg.* in classified advertisements.

negotiate to yield or appease

The language of diplomacy, where bullies or appeasers are involved:

Halifax...had urged the Polish Foreign Minister, Beck, to negotiate (i.e. yield) upon Hitler's demand to annex Dantzig. (Crossman, 1981—Halifax was in 1939 the British Foreign Secretary)

negro *obsolete* a slave

Rawson (1981) tells us that *negro quarter* was recorded in 1734 and, as ever, gives an erudite exposition of the usage:

I'll be no man's negro I will be no man's slave. (Grose, 1811—his headword is *negroe*)

For nearly 300 years the word *negro*, a black person, has been in and out of fashion, sometimes being used as a euphemism for the taboo *nigger*. It is now definitely out.

nelly a homosexual

Either male or female, although a *nelly fag* is male A *nelly* is 'a weak-spirited or silly person' (*SOED*). The derivation might just owe something to the expression *not on your nelly* (rhyming slang on *Nelly Duff*, or *duffer*), whence an allusion to the *duff* in FLUFF YOUR DUFF.

Nelson's blood rum

The corpse of the Admiral was returned from Trafalgar via Gibralter in 1805 for burial in London. The preservative in which was immersed was probably brandy, not rum. Tradition has it that the spirit was depleted on the voyage because sailors siphoned it off and drank it.

neoplasm a cancer

Literally, a fresh growth. Mainly medical jargon.

nephew *obsolete* a son

An evasion when the church expected celibacy and clerical errors became cardinal sins:

He made six of his close relations, 'nephews' or illegitimate sons, cardinals. (Cawthorne, 1996, writing about Pope Sixtus IV, 1471–84)

nerve agent a noxious gas

Military jargon. It could mean anything which excites the senses and so stimulates a nerve, not excluding a woman's perfume.

nervous breakdown a severe mental illness

Not paralysis, where some of the *nerves* really do *break down*:

The man before him had similarly had a nervous breakdown and had had to be brought South by an Indian sub-assistant surgeon. (C. Allen, 1975)

Now standard English covering conditions varying from depression to madness.

nest *obsolete* the vagina
With visual imagery:
> ... in your daughter's womb I'll bury them:
> Where, in that nest of spicery, they shall
> breed. (Shakespeare, *Richard III*)

The usage persisted in 19th-century slang.

nether parts the genitalia
Literally, the lower parts, but not of the feet
or ankles:
> And when he approached me he was
> unclothed, and his hair concealed his
> nether parts. (Dalrymple, 1997)

Also as *nether regions*. Shakespeare uses *the
Netherlands*, punning vulgarly on the 'Low
Countries':
> The Netherlands?—O, sir, I did not look so
> low. (*The Comedy of Errors*)

networking using social contacts for political or financial purposes
From the jargon of information technology
rather than the British *old-boy network*, the
mutual support of former schoolfellows:
> I hate the word 'networking', but I love
> parties and clubs. (*Sunday Telegraph*, 24 July
> 1994—he may have hated the word but he
> seemed to enjoy the result)

neutral unfavourable
The coded language of the corporate analyst:
> They are required to analyze corporate
> clients, but these pieces of research never
> say anything negative. The worst phrase
> you might read is 'neutral' or 'long-term
> buy'. (*Sunday Telegraph*, 8 August 1999)

neutralize to kill
Much more than rendering *neutral*, or inert:
> It means they don't know he's
> been ... neutralized. (Follett, 1978)

never-never (the) a contract for hire purchase
From the former ethic that you should *never*
buy something for which you could not pay
cash, because you would *never* be out of debt.
Whence figurative adjectival use:
> Critics rebuked [the 1979 Irish budget] for
> raising expectations it could not satisfy,
> and for fostering a never never mentality
> among a public who now irritatedly
> refused to pay the price of profligacy.
> (J. J. Lee, 1989—the budget proposed a 2%
> levy on farmers who, as a class, paid only
> 1% of their gross income in tax)

new regressive
Political use, tending to conceal a reversion to
primitive, tyrannical, unsuccessful, or unpopular policies, of which Hitler's *New Order* was
the most infamous:
> There was no 'New Order' involving some

kind of remodelling of relations between
fascist sates; the term was a euphemism for
German imperial dominance. (Burleigh,
2000)
> The [German] courts and police assumed
> responsibility for enforcing a mood of
> Panglossian optimism, by punishing even
> the most inadvertent or innocent of
> remarks which impugned the 'new times'
> in the 'new state'. (ibid.)

Also as the *New Deal*, *New Labour*, etc.

new age travellers *British* vagrants
Itinerants who reject conventional attitudes
to employment and trespass:
> In addition [to gypsies] there are estimated
> to be 2,500 to 5,000 'New Age Travellers'.
> (*Daily Telegraph*, 19 August, 1992)

new Australian *Australian* an immigrant
Not a baby born there. After Australia decided
to accept immigrants who were neither
British nor white, it was necessary to adopt
a phrase which avoided any reference to their
skin pigmentation or country of origin.

New Commonwealth a group of countries in which the majority of people
are not white
After the Second World War *Empire*, even
without the prefix *British*, had too many overtones of conquest and white supremacy, and a
new name was needed for the agglomeration of
former colonies and dependencies which continued to consult with each other, along with
the English-speaking white *Dominions*:
> At the Commonwealth Prime Minister's
> Conference in September (1962) it was
> clear that neither the 'old Dominions' nor
> the 'New Commonwealth' were happy
> about the developments in the
> negotiations [to enter the European
> Community]. (Crossman, 1981)

new economic zones the barren places to
which opponents were exiled
They were too busy there trying to stay alive
to cause trouble, or they starved to death.
In this way the victorious Communist Vietnamese sought to eliminate potential dissidents who were unable to get hold of a
boat:
> Vietnam's 'New Economic Zones' (in fact
> areas of internal exile where many starve
> and perish) ... (*Daily Telegraph*, February
> 1980)

Newgate *obsolete British* a prison
It denoted other prisons than the notorious
one in London. There were many compounds
to do with jail, crime, or hanging such as
Newgate bird, a thief, and *Newgate solicitor*, a
corrupt lawyer.

news management *American* the suppression of information
For military or political purposes. The *management* embraces delay, obstruction, and manipulation rather than attempts to get lies published.

next door to having taboo features associated with
Usually of criminals or those with mental illness. Thus *next door to a padded cell* implies mental deficiency:
> Stevens was sane enough, but Taylor was next-door to a padded cell. (Fraser, 1994)

nibble¹ an act of casual copulation
Literally, a small bite:
> 'She makes a damn pretty widow'... 'Wouldn't mind a nibble myself.' (Lyall, 1972)

nibble² a theft
Usually taking only a part, in the hope that the depredation will pass unnoticed:
> Did I think the guys wouldn't take a nibble out of this? (Turow, 1993—two policemen had discovered a hoard of cash)

nice time a single act of copulation with a prostitute
Prostitute's jargon when soliciting:
> You've given me the ticket and I've given you a nice time. (G. Greene, 1932)

See also MAKE NICE-NICE.

Nick¹ the devil
Named after one of the Nordic evil spirits or monsters
> O thou! Whatever title suit thee,
> Auld Hornie, Satan, Nick, or Clootie.
> (Burns, 1785)

Today usually as *old Nick*; seldom as *Nickie* or *Nicker*.

nick² to steal
Literally, to cut an edge, from which the use was originally only of pilfering:
> We dinna steal. We only nick things whiles. (Crockett, 1896)

nick³ a police station or prison
From the slang meaning to catch, the inmate having been caught or *nicked*.

nick⁴ to castrate
The animal is cut in the process:
> Through mist or fog to nick a sturdy hog. (Dickinson, 1866)

nick⁵ a vasectomy
Again from the cutting.

nickel and dime *American* to short-change or cheat
Before the Second World War, stores such as Woolworth offered goods to the value of 5c and 10c, giving value but with a sacrifice of quality:
> The kind of guy who'll nickel-and-dime his own mother. (M. Thomas, 1987)

niece¹ *obsolete* a daughter
The mediaeval Popes tended to be poor genealogists. See also NEPHEW.

niece² a mistress
The older male seeks to justify the constant presence of his younger companion:
> The swashbuckling Patton was seldom without comfort—later veiled from the sight back home of the only woman he truly feared, his wife Beatrice, as a visiting 'niece'. (Horne. 1994—Jean Gordon, the *niece* who accompanied him on his campaign in Europe, killed herself two weeks after his death)

night (the) death
The common association with darkness and sleep
> Still there are works which, with God's permission, I would do before the night cometh. (Strachey, 1918, quoting Dr Arnold in 1842)

night bucket a receptacle for urine
Usually in communal male sleeping quarters, where its use can avoid the ingress of cold air through repeated opening of a door in winter. Less often as the punning *night jar*, which should not be confused with the *Caprimulgus europaeus*:
> I'm saying if I'm to help you here, it's with both of us knowing that everybody empties their own night jar. (Frazier, 1997)

night games copulation
And in America as *night baseball*, which is often played away from home:
> 'He was too old for games.' 'What kind of games?' 'Night games,' she said softly. (Theroux, 1992)

night girl a prostitute
The time, not the duration, of plying her trade:
> You see nothing in [fish and chip shops] but drunken soldiers and night girls. (McCourt, 1997—and fish and chips, we must assume)

night job a contract in which a prostitute devotes the entire night to a single customer
Also known as an ALL-NIGHTER:

They ran to wake up mama, who was sleeping after a night job. (L. Armstrong, 1955)

night loss the involuntary ejaculation of semen during sleep
Mainly female use, referring to the soiled bedlinen. Also as *night emission* or NOCTURNAL EMISSION.

night physic (of a male) copulation
The medicine once thought necessary to be taken regularly for his health.

night soil human faeces
Soil has meant excrement since the 16th century, and primitive lavatories were cleaned at night, sometimes by a *nightman* in an operation called, in London at least, a *wedding*:
> ...thrust our ragged clothes, with a stick deep into the night soil of the necessary house. (Graves, 1940, writing in archaic style)

Now mainly jocular figurative use, *in the nightsoil* being a synonym for *in the shit*. *Night water*, urine, is obsolete:
> You try to tell us that the might of this great army rests upon goddam night water? (Keneally, 1979—Confederate soldiers were forbidden to make any noise at night)

night stool a portable lavatory
Sickroom use. It looks like a square seat.

nightcap a drink of intoxicant
You don't place it on your head but drink it before retiring:
> A 'nightcap', which consisted of a stoup of mulled claret, well spiced and fortified with a glass of brandy. (Lowson, 1890)

Now also of any such drink in the evening:
> May I please offer you a nightcap? (M. Thomas, 1980—he was trying to pick up a stranger)

nightclub hostess a prostitute
A *nightclub*, in proper usage, is a place of refreshment and entertainment open to the public until late at night. Some are indeed properly conducted, but not all
> A night-club or dance-hall hostess...are the modern equivalents of the old-time disorderly house and the street walker. (Lavine, 1930)

nightingale¹ *obsolete* a police informer
From the *singing* properties of bird and man.

nightingale² *obsolete British* a soldier who cried out while being flogged.

To show more fortitude, the victim was given a bullet to bite, thus further enriching the language.

nightingale³ *obsolete* a prostitute
Usually operating in the hours of darkness:
> There he was abovestairs, in bed wi' three nightingales. (Fraser, 1997, writing in 19th-century style)

nightwork *obsolete* copulation
As it was in Shakespeare's days and plays:
> Ha, 'twas a merry night. And is Jane Nightwork alive?...She was then a bona-roba. (*2 Henry IV*)

nil by mouth allow to die
Normally, an instruction in hospital to starve a patient before an operation.

NINA *American* we do not employ Irish people
The initials in a classified advertisement to be seen frequently not that many decades ago:
> The Irish were never liked up there in New England, and there were signs everywhere saying No Irish Need Apply. (McCourt, 1999)

nineteenth (hole) the bar at a golf club
The first eighteen involve striking a ball and walking after it. Occasionally the *nineteenth* may where you drink other than in the clubhouse, or what you drink:
> We finished the eighteen holes and went back to the castle for the nineteenth. (D. Francis, 1996)

nip¹ to steal
Either by *pinching* or by giving short measure:
> Ye was set aff frae oon for nipping the pyes. (A. Ramsay, 1737)

nip² a drink of spirits
Originally, a *nipperkin*, an eighth part of a pint, the quantity normally served:
> Down to the bar to snatch a furtive 'nip'. (Doherty, 1884)

nip³ to castrate
From the action of the tool employed:
> It was to 'nip' some calves...or more correctly to emasculate them by means of the Burdizzo bloodless castrator. (Herriot, 1981)

no (like NOT) is used as a prefix in many phrases where the statement of the contrary is used as a euphemistic device. The following are some examples:

no active treatment allow to die

Hospital jargon in the case of a terminally ill patient. If your visitors see NAT on the notes at the foot of your bed, it is time to tell them where your will is kept.

no better than she should be promiscuous

Usually said of a younger woman by an older:
> ... dissolute young Guards officers dining and spending the night with women no better than they should be. (S. Hastings, 1994)

Also as *no better than she ought to be*.

no (spring) chicken (usually of a woman) old

A *chicken* is the young of a domestic fowl, whence a child.
> And Caroline is twenty-seven. No chicken. (Bogarde, 1981)
> She's old enough in the picture. 'I'm no spring chicken myself.' (Macdonald, 1976)

no Einstien/genius/scholar unacademic

no oil painting/beauty ugly

etc.

no comment I admit nothing

Political and business use in reply to journalists. It is a defence of those who know that, when scandal is in the air, to be quoted is to be misquoted, and selectively.

no i/v access allow to die

Hospital jargon indicating the end to intravenous feeding of a dying patient.

no longer with us dead

Especially of a former associate, but not describing one who has merely taken another job
> None of us could believe that the charming Deborah ... was no longer with us. (Mailer, 1965)

No longer in service comes from the jargon of espionage:
> Fensing is no longer in service ... officially we're calling it a suicide. (Hall, 1988)

no mayday *American* allow to die

Or do not try to resuscitate, from the international distress call, a corruption of *m'aider*.

no more dead

Not euphemistic for those who are dubious about the afterlife:
> Mrs de Moleyns, a loving wife, a tender mother, a good true friend to the poor in her village, is now no more. (Dunning, 1993)

no right to correspondence (have) to be dead

Russian Communist usage. The dead cannot read:
> 'No right to correspondence'—and that almost for certain means 'He's been shot'. (Solzhenitsyn, 1974, in translation)

no show the fraudulent use of a name on a pay sheet

Either the person fails to report for work but, with the connivance of another, continues illegally to collect his pay; or a name is entered on the pay sheet of someone who does not exist or is not employed there, the pay being drawn by a third party. For the airlines, however, a *no show* is a passenger who books a flight but fails to check in.

nobble[1] *obsolete* to steal

Literally, to tamper with a horse illegally, whence to do other evil deeds connected with dishonesty:
> Ah thowt ah'd tak a wauk an nobble a few specimens for me-sen. (Treddlehoyle, 1892)

nobble[2] to kill

Again from tampering with a horse:
> 'I saw a bloke nobbled here,' she said. 'I mean killed.' (Theroux, 1976)

noble game (the) prostitution

According to Boswell, having paid an actress to participate. See also GAME 2.

nocturnal emission an involuntary ejaculation of semen

Spitting, vomiting, sweating, sneezing, or ejaculation during copulation are not included:
> He got a good deal of pleasure from nocturnal emissions. (Sharpe, 1978)

nocturnal exercise copulation

Another form of NIGHT PHYSIC:
> ... if I'm not down to twelve stone by the time we reach Calcutta, it won't be for want of nocturnal exercise. (Fraser, 1975)

nocturne *obsolete* a prostitute

Literally, a night scene in a painting or a dreamy musical composition. Whence George Sand's apocryphal pun to Chopin: 'One nocturne deserves another.'

noddy *British* a policeman

By translation from PC Plod (see PLOD) whose exemplary behaviour graced the *Noddy* books:
> ... hardly worth the shoe leather of the luckless noddy taking statements. (Blacker, 1992)

noggin an intoxicating drink

Originally, an eighth of a pint of any liquid:

Only share of two noggins wid my brother.
(Carleton, 1836)
Now used of any type of beer or spirits, but
not of wine.

non-aligned vacillating in allegiance
The representatives of countries which so
described themselves met in Belgrade in 1961,
claiming with more or less sincerity that they
favoured neither Washington nor Moscow.
Jennings in 1965 described them as 'no more
than potential parasites', as though their
approval for either of the then Great Powers
might have been obtained by bribery or
support for an autocrat. Perish the thought!.

non-Aryan see ARYAN

non-heart beating donor a corpse
It sounds better to the recipient of a trans-
planted organ, or his relatives:
    [Transplant surgeons] proposed alternative
    for dead ... 'non-heart beating donor'. (*Daily
    Telegraph*, 12 May 1993, quoting the *British
    Medical Journal*)

non-industrial poor and relatively uncivilized
One of the long line of euphemisms adopted
to avoid offending post-colonial rulers:
    'Civilized' and 'primitive' were to be
    replaced by 'industrial' and 'non-
    industrial'. (*Daily Telegraph*, 12 May 1993,
    quoting a document issued by Leeds
    Metropolitan University)

non-performing asset a loan on which
interest is not being paid
Bankers' jargon. It is in fact the borrower who
is failing to *perform*.

non-person a person without civil rights
A Communist appellation of those, not being
supporters or advocates of Communism,
whose fame or achievements embarrassed
the current oligarchy:
    Kropsky was banished twenty years ago. He
    became a non-person. (Ludlum, 1979)

non-profit *American* avoiding taxation
Not any old loss-making enterprise, but one set
up in such a way that the eventual beneficiary
avoids tax through a tax-exempt charity:
    The profits that are now extracted by the
    promoters of 'non-profit' cemeteries are
    spectacular. (J. Mitford, 1963)

non-traditional (casting) using a black
actor in a role written for a white
Stage jargon:
    ... the term 'non-traditional' is inadequate.
    What we have is theatrical PC. (*Daily
    Telegraph*, 6 February 1993—a black actor

without make-up had been cast to play the
    part of a white New Englander)

non-white a person whose ancestry is not
entirely white
Particularly those with black ancestry:
    Non-whites are even more overwhelming
    in their desire for work. (Pei, 1969)
Howard (1977) described it as 'the latest silly
extremity into which we have been forced by
euphemism'.

nonsense sexual activity outside normal
courtship
Literally, an absurdity:
    He was a calm, down-to-earth creature who
    brooked no kind of 'nonsense'. (Bogarde,
    1981—he was the proprietor of an erotic
    photographic studio)

normalization the suppression of rebel-
lion or protest
The *normality* sought is the state desired by
those who do the suppression:
    The so-called policy of 'normalization'
    ... was just an abdication of responsibility
    that would be dearly paid for in blood.
    (McCrum, 1991)

North to prison
Not as fatal as being sent EAST by the Nazis,
but the direction of the some of the Gulags if
you lived in Moscow:
    When his five years were up he went back
    to Moscow and immediately telephoned
    Svetlana, was arrested again and sent
    'north' for another five years. (F. Muir,
    1997—say what you will, Stalin had style
    when it came to damping the ardour of
    what he considered an unsuitable
    prospective son-in-law)

North Britain Scotland
More common when Scots thought of themselves as British, despite Britain being in
foreign eyes synonymous with England:
    Near to this Marble are deposited the
    Remains of Hugh Campbell Esqre of
    Mayfield in the County of Ayr North
    Britain 5 Jan 1824. (Memorial in Bath
    Abbey)
Abbreviated to *NB*, especially in mail. Major
Hancock, the officer commanding the gar-
rison of Edinburgh Castle in 1947, received a
readdressed letter 'not SS Edinburgh Castle—
try Edinburgh NB'.
Whence *North British*, Scots or Scottish:
    The poet Burns wrote in the North British
    dialect. (Wodehouse, 1930—Jeeves was
    correcting Wooster's enunciation)
A *North Briton* was a Scot, although John
Wilkes, who used the nom de plume, was a
Londoner.

nose a cocaine addict
The allusion is to sniffing the powder:
> Higgins taught her everything there was to know about cocaine, turned her into the biggest nose in town. (McBain, 1994)

Having a *nose habit* is such addiction.

nose job (a) cosmetic surgery on the nose
Women tend to be less content with their nasal inheritance than men:
> Turn out that she always wanted a nose job. (Clancy, 1989)

nose open lustful
Bulls and stallions flare their nostrils when sexually excited. Of humans, the phrase is used figuratively:
> 'I seen her mooching around upstairs.' Murf licked his lips. 'She's got your nose open?' (Theroux, 1976)

not (like NO) is used in many phrases where understatement or contradiction is used as a euphemistic device. A sample follows.

not a great reader illiterate
Still heard among old country folk in southwest England, and probably elsewhere,

not all she should be sexually promiscuous
More common when chastity was more fashionable:
> To suggest those girls were naughty and Not All They Should Be, the 1970s artist showed them smoking cigars. (Whicker, 1962, writing about nymphs painted on the ceiling of a bar in Monte Carlo)

Also as *not all she ought to be*.

not all there stupid or confused
It describes a mental state, not that of an amputee:
> That poor creature who's not quite all there. (Christie, 1940)

Atypically, *all there* means keenly intelligent.

not as young as I was old
None of us is as young as we were, even as the eye crosses the page:
> You aren't as young as you once were yourself, you know. (Golden, 1997)

not in your first flush of youth old
But not yet geriatric.

not inconsolable promiscuous in the absence of a regular sexual partner
See CONSOLE:
> It is feared she waited for [Kim Philby] in vain. Not that the Lady Francis, a creature

of some resilience, proved inconsolable. (Boyle, 1979)

not interested in the opposite sex homosexual

not long for this world about to die
> Mrs Finucane...says she's not long for this world and the more Masses said for her soul the better she'll feel. (McCourt, 1997)

not rocket science simple
Usually of a technological theory or a mechanical problem

not sixteen annas to the rupee of low intelligence
This is one of many phrases indicating a shortage from a full complement. Under British Indian currency, there were four pice to the anna and sixteen annas to the rupee. Today the anna is not used. Despite decimalization, we may still hear *not sixteen ounces on the pound*.
See also TWELVE ANNAS TO THE RUPEE.

not very well very ill
Hospital and valetudinarian jargon, which ignores the presumption that *very well* implies perfect health. Also as *not at all well*, which may indicate a fatal condition.

etc.

not at home at home but unwilling to speak to a caller
The converse of *at home*, a specific invitation to visit at a set time:
> Want to see Mrs Morny.' 'She's not at home.' 'Didn't you know that when I gave you the card?'...'I only knew when she told me.' (Chandler, 1943)

not available (to comment) unwilling to be publicly compromised or shown up
The coded language of those who do not wish to be interviewed and of the journalists who wish to interview them.

not dead but gone before dead
Also as *not lost but gone before*, *before* meaning ahead, to await the arrival of a survivor, it would seem.

not in at home but unwilling to see or speak to a caller
A synonym for NOT AT HOME:
> Weren't you told she was not in? (Chandler, 1943—a caller was being rebuffed by the servant of the person he wished to speak to)

not invented here we reject and denigrate all other ideas than our own

A defensive mechanism of those who are
employed to think and innovate, whose
position is threatened if a third party achieves
what they are being paid to do:
> They didn't think of it, so they'll piss all
> over it. *Not invented here*! (M. Thomas, 1980)

Often abbreviated to NIH.

not seeing anybody not having a sexual
relationship with anybody
Despite enjoying 20/20 vision:
> She had recently split up with a partner
> and 'wasn't seeing anybody'. (Lodge, 1995)

notice dismissal from employment
Shortened form of *notice of dismissal*, which is
given or received. *Notice* as a verb is obsolete
> Notice me as much as ye like, I'll not clean
> them pigs out. (M. Francis, 1901)

nouvelle cuisine small portions of food
sold at high prices
The presentation on the plate may be attractive, the shortage of edible matter providing
ample space for the artistic pretentions of the
chef:
> She says both her cooking and its
> presentation are more voluptuous than
> nouvelle cuisine. (*Country Homes*, June,
> 1990)

See also HAUTE CUISINE.

nullification killing
One form of cancelling out:
> They are also reported being used to kill
> enemy divers, in the case of the US, as part
> of a 'swimmer nullification' programme.
> (*Sunday Telegraph*, 29 March 1992,
> writing about captive whales being
> trained by the CIA)

number is up (your) you are about to be
killed
First World War usage, from the game of
House, where each player has a numbered
card, and punning on a soldier's individual
army number. It indicates the fatalism of the
trenches, where death appeared to come on a
chance basis:
> It's all right, you laughing, but I know my
> number is up. (F. Richards, 1933)

number nine *British* a laxative
The standard army purgative. Some figurative
use when a sluggard might be told he needed
a dose of number nines.

number one(s)¹ urination
Mainly nursery usage.

number one² self-interest
Perhaps from the adage *Number one comes
first*:

...he believes trade policy should be
founded on protection. Look after Number
One. (A. Clark, 1993)

number two(s) defecation
Mainly of small children. Adult usage is rare:
> Stand over him and, as he put it 'do
> number two—oh lots of it—all over me'.
> (Theroux, 1973)

nunnery *obsolete* a brothel
The religious orders provided many allusive
words for sexual subjects before and for some
decades after the dissolution of the monasteries in the 1530s, partly out of envy at the
wealth of the Church and partly because of the
dissolution of many individuals in Holy Orders:
> Get thee to a nunnery. (Shakespeare,
> *Hamlet*—he is accusing Ophelia of being a
> prostitute)

A prostitute might be referred to as a *nun* and
see ABBESS.

nurse to suckle (a baby)
Perhaps from the *wet nurse*, who suckled
another's child, or from the cradling of the
child as it feeds:
> Priss...was nursing her baby...'I never
> expected a breast-fed grandson,' said Priss's
> mother. (M. McCarthy, 1963)

The obsolete *nurse-child* was illegitimate,
brought up away from its mother.

nursing home an institution for geriatrics
Literally, a hospital for any sick person:
> One very old man whittling away the end
> of his life in a Georgia nursing home. (King,
> 1996)

nut¹ a mentally ill person
Nut is slang for a human head and this is a
shortened form of *gone in the nut*, or some such
expression:
> It was the laugh of a nut. (Chandler, 1940)

A *nut college*, *farm*, *hutch*, or *house* is an
institution for the insane:
> ...round up of nut-houses, likely nutters
> on parole. (Davidson, 1978)

A *nut-coat* is a straitjacket:
> And if you think you're gonna put that nut-
> coat on me, you got another think coming.
> (King, 1996)

The FBI list of mad or unstable people likely to
attack a public figure is called the *nut-box*.
A *nutter* is anything from an irrational person
to a madman, described as *nutty*, *nuts*, or *off his
nut*.

nut² to headbutt another
Again from the meaning, a head:
> He spied her and decided on rape. She
> screamed, so he nutted her—that's the term

we use for headbutting—and carried on.
(Fiennes, 1996)

nuts the testicles
Also as, and perhaps a shortened form of,
nutmegs; and see COBS:
  ... the new government ... will cut our nuts
  off. (M. Thomas, 1980—the threat was
  figurative only)

nymph *obsolete* a prostitute
In standard usage, a mythical semi-divine
and beautiful maiden. More explicitly

as *nymph of darkness, of delight, of the pavement,*
etc.

NYR an airman lost in action
Second World War usage, as an abbreviation
of *not yet returned* from a mission over enemy
territory:
  'We've got a lot of NYRs, Lester.'
  'Not yet returned doesn't mean
  dead.' (Deighton, 1982—but it meant
  shot down or crashed, with death a
  probability)

O

O opium
Addict use, and not of oxygen:
> To me 'O' means opium, not physics.
> (Fiennes, 1996)

oats copulation
Usually by a male, within or outside marriage, with an implication of regular need, as in the daily nourishment of horses:
> I'll have to go out later, so you'll have to wait even longer before you get your oats. (R. Forbes, 1986—copulation, not porridge, was what was being suggested)

An *oat opera* is pornography:
> 'Whatever you think is best, Percy,' Harry said, turning the page of the oat opera he was reading. (King, 1996)

objective biased
How autocrats may describe independent critics:
> ...with the job of deciding which British journalists were 'objective' enough to be allowed to travel to South Africa. (Simpson, 1998—the regime would not admit possible critics)

obligatory appointed other than on merit
Describing membership of committees, boards, etc. where it may be thought expedient or politically necessary to have other than those chosen from a male dominant group:
> ...she's my recommendation...for our obligatory female. (Price, 1985)

See also STATUTORY and TOKEN.

oblige *British* to work as a domestic servant
The employee, always female and often elderly, is shown to be conferring a favour on her employer by undertaking a menial task for money:
> Mrs Benbow regretted that 'what with my husband's heart and the questions going on by the police' she would not be obliging me in future. (le Carré, 1995)

oblique homosexual
The common imagery of divergence from the *straight*, or heterosexual:
> ...whether she has unmasked his disguise, or because his tastes were oblique, or because she is a man who thinks she is a woman...(Bradbury, 1983)

obtain to acquire illegally
Usually of stealing but also of acquiring forbidden or other embargoed goods:
> '...many shall pleasures...not the least of which is obtaining Cuban cigars.'
> 'Obtaining' was the Director's favourite euphemism. (van Lustbaden, 1983)

occupied defeated and annexed
Not all conquerors depart:
> Let us hope the Administration will not be foxholed by Beijing, and will stand with Congress, which unanimously passed a resolution declaring Tibet an occupied country. (*New York Times*, 13 April 1993—and not *occupied* only by Tibetans)

occupy (of a male) to copulate with
From the physical entry rather than gaining her attention:
> These villains will make the word as odious as the word 'occupy', which was an excellent good word before it was ill sorted. (Shakespeare, *2 Henry IV*)

And in modern use:
> Karl was not ready, having been occupied with a Negro girl in his tent. (F. Harris, 1925)

OD yourself to commit suicide
Taking an *OD*, or overdose, of drugs, legally or illegally acquired:
> I'm gonna shoot it all up my arm in one blast. I'm gonna OD myself. (Gabriel, 1992)

ODC *Northern Ireland* a prisoner who is not a terrorist
Jailers' jargon:
> Maghaberry prison, which housed former terrorist prisoners and ODC's—ordinary decent criminals...(O'Callaghan, 1998)

odd homosexual
Literally, out of the ordinary:
> The successful challenges that have been made to the popular media images of lesbians as 'odd girls' and 'twilight lovers'...(Faderman, 1991)

odorously challenged smelly
An ingenious extension of those before whom that traditional symbol, the gauntlet, is thrown down—see CHALLENGED for other examples:
> The list of minority victim-groups with special rights [in the United States] is growing longer every year, and now includes Hispanics, Asian-Americans, women (all 51 per cent of the population), the obese, and finally the smelly (odorously challenged). (*Sunday Telegraph*, 20 November 1994)

of mature years old

The phrase does not refer to a girl of 19 or a youth of 21, indicating not full development but incipient decline:

A good many of my students were civil servants, some of them of mature years. (Forsey, 1990)

See also MATURE.

off [1] *American* to kill

Perhaps a shortened form of BUMP 5 (OFF):

Maybe he stiffed the waiter and the guy followed him down here and offed him. (Sanders, 1973)

To *off yourself* is to commit suicide:

I just don't want to off myself like so many cops do. (Wambaugh, 1975)

off [2] with its implications of departure and decay precedes many phrases indicating types of mental illness as follows:

Off at the side, of a mild condition, is obsolete:

Not 'all there'—'off at the side'. (Linton, 1866)

Off your head covers anything from a temporary forgetfulness to lunacy, with many slang variants for *head*, such as *chump, gourd, napper, nut, onion*, and *turnip*:

I must be going off my chump. (Wodehouse, 1930)

He feared she had gone off her gourd, and he was scared. (Sanders, 1982)

The fixture was scratched owing to events occurring which convinced the old boy I was off my napper. (Wodehouse, 1930)

When...she informed him one day that she was engaged...he went right off his onion. (Wodehouse, 1922)

Unless he had gone off his turnip, I suppose. (le Carré, 1980—the victim had not lost his appetite)

Another group of phrases comes from disabled transport, with the vehicle figuratively leaving the *rails*, its *tree* (or axle), or the *rocker* or *trolley* which picks up the overhead electric supply of a tram or trolley-bus:

...a very unstable personality placed in this environment would go off the rails. (*Macleans Magazine*, 9 November 1993)

Who the hell is she? She's off her tree. (le Carré, 1989)

I think he was really off his rocker for a bit. (Amis, 1988)

There are moments when I wonder if I'm tipping off my trolley. (Deighton, 1985)

The American *off the wall*, from the unpredictable bounce off the fence in baseball, can be used of mental illness or figuratively:

...it was a crazy cackle, and maybe she really was off the wall. (Sanders, 1982)

It's bizarre. Oil nuts? A processing plant? It's off the wall. (O'Hanlon, 1996)

off-colour [1] vulgar or offensive

The colour is not necessarily BLUE 2:

I don't want any of your off-colour stuff from the Drones' smoking-room. (Wodehouse, 1934)

off-colour [2] ill

It may describe a temporary affliction, which may make the victim paler than usual. Also used of menstruation.

off duty menstruating

A female use, inferring also that she is unavailable for copulation. Also as *off games*, punning on SPORT and a pupil's minor indisposition:

...errant husbands who have looked to her for corrective therapy during periods when their wives have been in the country/abroad/off games. (*Private Eye*, December 1983)

off-line *American* dead

From the meaning, no longer connected:

'She was off-line, Judge. Clearly.' Dead, in other words. The cops are always at their toughest when the subject is dying. They have a thousand euphemisms. (Turow, 1996)

Off-line is also a synonym for *out of line*, meaning behaving improperly or illegally.

off the chandelier bogus

It describes bids at an auction, where the auctioneer is trying to run up the bidding by pretending there is another active bidder in the hall:

...the bidding, which moved slowly from $4 to $6 million, proved to be all 'off the chandelier'. (*Daily Telegraph*, January 1990)

Depending on the décor, such bids may also come *off the ceiling, wall*, or whatever else catches the auctioneer's eye, other than a genuine bid.

off the payroll [1] dismissed from employment

Joining the rest of humanity which was never on that particular payroll in the first place:

So the old boy hadn't known I was 'off the payroll'. (Shirer, 1984—the newspaper proprietor had not known that a journalist on one of his newspapers had been dismissed)

off the payroll [2] employed by a competitor

Not paid by the same master:

If a transmission took place without these words, the ex-CIA man would know that whoever was out there...was off the payroll. (Forsyth, 1996)

off the peg inferior or ill-cut

In standard usage, this describes garments which are bought ready-made rather than individually tailored:

In an off-the-peg dress...she did not look her best. (Ellman, 1988)

off the rails¹ see OFF 2

off the rails² being detected in reprehensible conduct
Criminal or sexual, of someone hitherto considered above reproach, and implying a continued pattern of bad behaviour:
> Johnny Depp is a dream as the bad boy tempting a nice girl off the rails. (*TV Quick*, 9 December 1992)

off the reservation acting beyond your authority
Moving outside the RESERVATION where you are meant to live:
> B'ai B'rith raced to condemn the off-the-reservation rabbi. (Clancy, 1991—the rabbi had been expressing extremist views)

off the voting list dead
I am not sure if this usage is accurate in Northern Ireland, Cook County (see FIND COOK COUNTY), or Florida.

off the wagon habitually drinking alcohol after a period of abstinence
After having been ON THE WAGON:
> When a man like that goes off the wagon, he bites dust. (Kersh, 1936)

off-white wedding the marriage of a pregnant bride
She may or may not eschew the pleasure of wearing a virginal white dress:
> I married Pauline hastily—a quiet off-white wedding in the parish church. (Lodge, 1962)

offer yourself to ask a man to copulate with you
Usually promiscuously:
> She tracked me down to my rooms in Oxford and offered herself to me. (Amis, 1978)

The obsolete *offer kindness* was at the gift of either sex:
> Offerd her such Kindnes, as sticks by her ribs a good while after. (J. Wilson, 1603, quoted in *ODEP*)

oil to bribe
A synonym of GREASE 1. Often as the punning *palm-oil*.

oiled drunk
Things may for a time seem to run more smoothly:
> Phipps, described by Yakimov as 'a trifle oiled', had attacked the Major. (Manning, 1965)

The commonest cliché, whatever the state of inebriation, is *well oiled*:
> He was well oiled by the time the coffee waiter returned. (Deighton, 1988)

The obsolete British *oil the wig* was to become drunk, and in Scotland *oil of malt* was whisky.

okay no longer suffering from a taboo condition
Usually recovered from a mental illness:
> 'Is she out of hospital?' Lucille asked. Susan nodded. 'Is she, y'know, *okay* now?' (Anonymous, 1996)

old or **auld** is a prefix to numerous *nicknames,* or names for NICK 1, the devil, who was liable to appear if you spoke about him directly: whence our expression *talk of the devil,* if a person about whom we have been speaking in his absence comes into view. Instead of using the word *devil,* people spoke of (the) *old* or *auld bendy, blazes, bogey, boots, boy, chap, child, cloot, cloutie, dad, Davy, driver, gentleman, gooseberry, Harry, hornie, lad, mahoon, man, Nick, one, poger, poker, Roger, ruffin, Sandy, scratch, serpent, smoker, sooty, thief, toast,* etc. Some of these names are dealt with elsewhere, without the prefix. It was not uncommon for a farmer to leave a patch of ground untilled for the devil's use (today Brussels calls it setaside), in the hope that he might be induced to leave the rest of the farm alone:
> The old man's fold, where the druid sacrificed to the demon. (*EDD*)
and see *clootie's croft* under CLOOT.

old Adam (the) a man's lust
Referring to the unregenerate character of our common ancestor before life became complicated for him and he passed on to us, with St Paul's help, our sexual complexes:
> I felt the old Adam stir at the sight of her. (Fraser, 1973)

old bill see BILL

old faithful menstruation
By coming back regularly, it lifts anxiety about unwanted pregnancy.

old-fashioned derelict
Real-estate jargon:
> When applied to houses old-fashioned means a draughty ruin. When applied to clubs it means bad food and no women. (Theroux, 1982)

old maid an unmarried woman who is unlikely to marry

A *maid* was an unmarried girl and, after the 17th century, in the normal linguistic progression, an unmarried female of any age:

> There will the devil meet me, like an old cuckold, with horns on his head, and say, 'Get you to heaven, Beatrice, get you to heaven, here's no place for you maids.' So deliver I up my apes and away to St Peter. (Shakespeare, *Much Ado About Nothing*—see LEAD APES IN HELL for the simian allusion)

Now standard English:

> I'm able to keep myself, and to wait as long as I choose till I get married. I'm not afraid of being an old maid. (Somerville and Ross, 1894)

old man¹ see OLD

old man² the penis

Male usage, possibly adverting to OLD MAN 1, the devil, and the role of the penis in licentious behaviour, although the term is used when it is in a flaccid state:

> ...just as much as his old man needed to set it trying to haul itself up into his abdomen. (Amis, 1978)

old man's friend pneumonia

It is an illness which allows the elderly to die quickly and without much pain. Penicillin may now preserve them for more lingering, painful, and degrading deaths.

older woman (the) an elderly female

Advertising jargon which omits to state what her age is compared with. Similarly, the advertisers' 'larger woman' is not merely bigger than a midget, but unusually tall or fat.

oldest profession (the) prostitution

With its biblical references:

> It was maybe the oldest profession... but New Orleans was proud and ashamed of its cathouses. (Longstreet, 1956)

See also PROFESSION.

on¹ drunk

In a mild state:

> I shouldn't like to say how he was drunk... he was a little bit on like. (*EDD*)

This use is obsolete except in the expression *half on*, where, as usual with drunkenness, the half equals the whole.

on² pregnant

Today in a phrase, such as *four months on*. In former use, *tout court*:

> I doubt she's on again, poor lass. (*EDD*—*doubt* means suspect)

on³ habitually using illegal narcotics

A shortened form of *on drugs*:

> But a woman like that living a life like that, has got to be on. (Sanders, 1977)

on⁴ potentially promiscuous

On in the sense, happening or going ahead:

> Those legs at the corner table might be on, but they could just be here for conversation. (Blacker, 1992—the *legs* belonged to a female)

on a budget poor

A *budget* was a small purse, whence the amount you had to spend, from which grew the modern meaning, to estimate and plan your receipts and expenditure. *On a budget* was used in British television advertisements addressed at poor people in September, 1998, although the poor are probably the least in a position to undertake forward financial planning.

on a cloud under the influence of illegal narcotics

From the floating feeling. The *cloud* is sometimes numbered *nine*, after the cumulonimbus which may reach 30,000 to 40,000 feet.

on health grounds through incompetence

A formula used where a senior executive is summarily dismissed, inferring that his health is at risk rather than that of the company:

> Mary Allen, who took over in September after the resignation 'on health grounds' of Genista McIntosh, has disclosed that she found the company ungovernable. (*Daily Telegraph*, 10 November 1997—the company was the London Royal Opera House, which, despite large public subvention, faced insolvency)

on heat¹ able to conceive

Standard English of mammals other than humans, from the increased bodily temperature associated with the condition.

on heat² lustful

Of either sex:

> Are you on heat for her, Reverend? (B. Cornwell, 1993)
> Those bloody women! Like a lot of randy she-cats. And there's that bitch back again, on heat as usual. (Manning, 1962—she was a princess, not a dog)

In heat is less common:

> 'I'm no bitch in heat,' she said between tight teeth. 'Take your paws off me.' (Chandler, 1958)

In the heat means copulating:

> ...make love to her afterwards. Would you like to hear tapes [of] Mike Santos in the heat? (M. West, 1979—Mr Santos was not a sprinter)

on her way *obsolete* pregnant
The destination is unstated:
> She's two months on her way.
> (Shakespeare, *Love's Labour's Lost*)

on ice in prison
Stored like edible provisions:
> I learnt a bit in Brixton—I was 'on ice' there for two years. (Fiennes, 1996—Brixton is an English prison)

on the beach dismissed from employment
It is used of sailors, especially if they have been discharged in a foreign port:
> You hear that, you Port Mahon bumboatman, you? You ought to be on the beach! (Fraser, 1971)

on the black working without paying tax
Probably a development of BLACK MARKET:
> He brought the drinks back, shouldered his way through...the building site workers who were all on the 'black'. (Seymour, 1995)

on the bottle see BOTTLE 1

on the box *obsolete* *Scottish* ill and needy
The *box* was the Poor Box kept in church, in which donations for the poor were left:
> Fifteen got assistance from the Poor's Fund; or as it was generally expressed...fifteen ...were on the box. (Pennecuik, 1715)

on the chisel see CHISEL

on the club *British* ill and absent from work
From the days when employees might join a benefit society, paying weekly subscriptions against possible ill health.

on the couch engaged in casual copulation
This mythical article of furniture is put to the same use as the CASTING COUCH:
> My wife thinks I have endless lines of big-titted girls trying to get me on the couch. (Deighton, 1972)

on the cross engaged in robbery as a prostitute
It is the victim who is figuratively crucified, or *double-crossed*:
> The hostile gaze of the decent did not prevent men and women 'on the cross' from constructing pecking orders. (R. Hughes, 1987)
See also *cross girl* at CROSS.

on the dole see DOLE

on the gallop *Irish* (of a criminal) evading capture
A variant of the standard English ON THE RUN:
> Apart from six months spent 'on the gallop' in Eire, he's been away for eighteen years. (Stamp, 1994, writing about a terrorist bomb-maker who had spent much of his life in prison)

on the grind engaged in prostitution
Punning on the *grind* of honest daily toil and GRIND, to copulate.

on the job copulating
A common pun on being engaged in work:
> 'We told him you'd been on the job continuously'...He paused fractionally as the implications of that statement flashed through his mind. (Price, 1970)
The rarer *in mid-job* means the same thing:
> If he could snap his fingers and boof, there he was in mid-job, very pleasant. (Amis, 1978)

on the labour see LABOUR 2

on the left *American* operating illegally
The usual sinister connection, usually of operating without a licence:
> ...a small shop whose manager made more money selling drink 'on the left' than he did by dry-cleaning. (Clancy, 1988)
In Britain it means being able to enjoy reading editorials in the *Guardian*.

on the loose engaged in prostitution
As different from a LOOSE 1 female, who may have other employment, or none:
> When I lived with S. he allowed me £10 a week, but when I went on the loose I did not get so much. (Mayhew, 1862)

on the make seeking a sexual relationship
Literally, overly ambitious or greedy in an impatient way. Of either sex:
> Once in a while...a man and a woman talk without dragging bedrooms into it. This could be it, or she could just think I was on the make. (Chandler, 1953)

on the needle addicted to illegal narcotics taken by self-injection
The *needle* is the hypodermic syringe. Whence also the punning *needlework*, such addiction:
> Was this talcum powder loyalty, I wondered; did they go in for this type of needlework as well? (Rushdie, 1995—the sisters described were not seamstresses)

on the nest *American* pregnant
From the sedentary behaviour of a broody hen.

on the pad *American* in receipt of regular bribes

Police jargon, from the notebook in which the transactions may be recorded, albeit usually in coded form:

> Everybody's on the pad then ... The pimps, the barkeeps, they just put up the dough. (Turow, 1987)

on the panel[1] *British* ill and absent from work

Prior to the advent of medicine on demand, a *panel* of doctors was published, informing the poor where they could get advice and treatment on a charitable basis. Half a century later, the phrase is still in use.

on the panel[2] *obsolete Scottish* in court accused of a crime

The derivation is from the *panel* of magistrates or of the offenders—we cannot be sure:

> Mr James Mitchel was upon the panell at the criminal court for shutting at the Archbishop of St Andrew's. (Kirkton, 1817)

on the parish *obsolete British* destitute

Money needed for communal use was levied by means of a *parish* or *parochial rate* on property. Part of it went towards providing for the homeless and destitute. Also as *on the parochial*:

> This meant that one in every forty people in England and Wales was 'on the Parish'. (J. J. Lee, 1989, writing of 1904)
>
> They did their very best to get him gang on the 'parochial'. (*Aberdeen Weekly Free Press*, March 1901, quoted in *EDD*)

on the pill see PILL 2

on the piss engaged in a drunken carouse

Usually from drinking beer, where the volume requires frequent urination. The phrase does not mean that, like the former Indian premier, Desai, you drink your urine for medicinal purposes.

on the pull seeking an individual sexual partner

You seek individual company in the society of others, if nothing more:

> She wasn't on the pull that night and, even if she had been, any public profile was too low to grace her boudoir. (Blacker, 1992)

on the ribs *obsolete* indigent

Probably from the protrusion of the ribs of an undernourished person:

> 'How's life, Duke?' 'On the ribs.' 'You skint?' 'Dead skint.' (Kersh, 1936)

on the roof *American* engaged in a carouse

It may be shingled rather than tiled:

> I was on the roof last night and I've got a hangover. (Chandler, 1944)

on the run a fugitive from justice

Standard English, and not of taking part in a marathon:

> Alfred Sirven, the mysterious power behind the group, is now on the run in the Philippines. (*Daily Telegraph*, 30 January 2001—M. Sirven's activities when the Elf oil company was owned by the French government were exposed when a minister and his mistress fell out)

on the seat in the lavatory

Not in an armchair, and often as an explanation for a delayed response:

> Tell them I'm on the seat, my compliments. (Seymour, 1977)

on the shelf (of a female) unmarried and unlikely to marry

The imagery is from slow-moving inventory in retailing:

> Nearing thirty, she cheerfully admitted she was 'on the shelf—'it's a spinster's life for me.' (Rushdie, 1995)

A synonym, *on the peg*, is obsolete.

on the side (of a benefit or pleasure) enjoyed illegally or immorally

Things so described include a bribe, undeclared and therefore untaxed income, or extramarital copulation, where a *bit* or *thing on the side* may be occasional indulgence or a mistress. The imagery is from the additional food on a separate plate served with the main dish:

> Bendon'd had a thing on the side, his secretary Constanza. (Turow, 1999)

on the skids (of a commercial enterprise) failing

A *skid* is a piece of wood on which an object is placed to facilitate unstoppable movement, such as the launching of a ship:

> His current affairs flagship World in Action is on the skids. (*Private Eye*, May, 1981)

on the square living honestly

Criminal jargon in a society where it is reprehensible to be law-abiding:

> Going on the square is so dreadfully confining. (Mayhew, 1862)

The Freemasons so describe their participation in their secret society, not because they lead honest lives but from the set-square used in building.

on the street(s) see STREET (THE)

on the stroll engaged in prostitution

From the leisurely walk while seeking custom:

> Hello, Mayann. What in the world are you doing out on the stroll tonight?
> (L. Armstrong, 1955—Mayann did not bother to explain)

on the take accepting bribes
It may describe a pattern of conduct rather than a single payment:

> You're on the take from one of the mobs. (Deighton, 1978)

on the tiles engaged in a night-long carouse
In the nocturnal company of tomcats:

> I saw you sneaking up the stairs. Been having a night on the tiles, have you? (Sharpe, 1975)

See also ON THE ROOF.

on the town[1] engaged in a carouse
Literally, on a rare visit to a city's theatres etc. without much thought of expense, and used of both sexes without any implication of the debauchery imported by ON THE TILES.

on the town[2] *obsolete* working as a prostitute
Where she sought trade:

> She had been on the town for fifteen years. (Mayhew, 1862)

on the trot a fugitive from justice
A synonym of ON THE RUN:

> I'm looking for someone, and if he's here, he's probably told you he's on the trot. (Follett, 1978)

on the wagon refraining from drinking intoxicants
Taking potable fluids only from the *water wagon*. It may describe a single case of abstinence, as with someone about to drive a car, or a former alcoholic who is trying to cure himself of the addiction:

> On the wagon now, of course, and what he drunk was with a wink and shake of the head. (Longstreet, 1956)

on the wall *American* in prison
Within, rather than *on*, we might have thought:

> He a drug kingpin. He gone be on the wall for life. (Turow, 1996)

on top of (of a male) copulating with
The common posture rather than masculine dominance:

> Isn't there anything else to interest you, except twenty minutes on top of a girl? (Kersh, 1936)

on vacation in prison
The common black humour:

> He slammin. He on vacation. (Turow, 1996—in that case for not less than twenty years)

on your back (of a female) copulating
The posture commonly adopted:

> One way to travel. On my back.
> (L. Thomas, 1977—she had not booked a wagon-lit)

on your bones indigent
Starvation has consumed the flesh:

> Give us a chance, constable. I'm right on my bones. (Galsworthy, 1924)

on your shield dead
The shield doubled for a stretcher if you were killed in battle:

> ...the only way out was on your shield. (Keneally, 1982, writing about trying to resist the Nazi police)

on your way out dying
The common imagery of departure:

> ...a pretty little nurse to special him on his way out. (Price, 1979)

The phrase is also used of someone about to lose his job or his place in a team.

onanism masturbation
Onan spilled his seed on the ground, for which he was slain by the Lord (*Genesis* 38: 9, 10). The expression is used of males and, illogically, of females:

> One night I got thinking of E...and for the first time in months practised onanism. (F. Harris, 1925)

> Those poor girls, he went on, were dying by the thousand from consumption, but really from self-abuse or onanism, as it was often called. Masturbation would also arrest growth, distort the pelvis, and prevent the development of the breasts. (Pearsall, 1969, quoting MacFadden's *The Power and Beauty of Superb Womanhood*, 1901—and what about blindness?)

one-armed bandit see FRUIT MACHINE

one bubble left of level mentally unsound
Another way of indicating imbalance:

> The guy is one bubble left of level. (Turow, 1999)

one foot in the grave near death
Through old age or terminal disease.

one for the road an extra drink of intoxicant before leaving company

The warming, or stirrup, cup formerly taken before cold winter journeys on horseback or in an unheated coach.

one-night stand a single night of copulation with a chance partner
Punning on a travelling show, which plays a single performance before moving on:
> An opportunity for extracurricular sex occurred...Afterwards there had been still more opportunities—some the usual one-night stands. (Hailey, 1979)

A *one-nighter* means either the same thing, or the partner with whom the night is enjoyed (or as the case may be):
> This little lady is a born one-nighter. (D. Francis, 1982)

one o'clock at the waterworks *American* your trouser zip is undone
The hour at which an employee might leave his office and appear in public.

one of those a homosexual
Usually of a male:
> When you asked him if he knew any girls—the shadow of homosexuality, is he one of those? (le Carré, 1986)

In former use among sober and godly matrons, *one of those* might be a prostitute.

one of us a person with similar tastes and manners
Euphemistic only in the negative when implying that someone is not your social equal:
> ...he's not what Aunt Fenny calls one of us. (P. Scott, 1968, referring to a policeman commissioned into the army)

one off the wrist an act of masturbation
Not your stolen Rolex:
> I'm afraid Mother was enjoying a quick one off the wrist. (Fry, 1994—*Mother* was a man)

one over the eight an excessive intake of intoxicants on a single occasion
There are eight pints in the gallon, which was considered a sufficient amount of beer or cider for a regular drinker in an evening:
> 'Had one over the eight,' diagnosed Mr Blore accurately. (Christie, 1939)

one-parent family a parent living alone with dependent offspring
There are normally two parents still alive, of whom one is permanently absent from the home, or, in the case of many young females, was never there at all:
> The one-parent family is going to be the big social problem of the 1980s, with the present rate of divorce. (Price, 1979)

See also LONE PARENT and SINGLE PARENT.

one thing copulation
It is a commonly held belief among adult females that a man's interest in them is solely sexually based:
> I'd really—only—wanted—one—thing. She told me so this morning. (Amis, 1978)

one too many an intoxicant taken to excess
Whence *had one too many*, became drunk:
> ...had one too many in a bar somewhere. (M. McCarthy, 1963)

one-way ride an abduction where the victim is murdered
To *The undiscover'd country, from whose bourn No traveller returns*:
> Charlie Luciano—now nicknamed Lucky Luciano on account of the one way ride that he came back from...(J. Collins, 1981)

one-way street *American* a heterosexual person
Homosexual jargon.

open access needing no academic qualification
A device for enrolling those from a MINORITY group, or for boosting admissions:
> But both courses are 'open access'. (*Daily Telegraph*, October 1983, describing degree courses at two London polytechnics which also offered REMEDIAL lessons in the English language so that students could embark on their studies with an ability to read and write)

open housing *American* a policy which allows no restriction on new residents in a district
White Christians frequently opposed any Jews or blacks moving into their locality. With *open housing*, such restriction, based on snobbery and prejudice but also on economic grounds, is not permitted.

open legged (of a woman) promiscuous
The derivation is obvious:
> ...the risks to my health, in being so open legg'd and free...(Cleland, 1749—but she did in fact make a charge)

open marriage a marriage in which neither spouse hides extramarital copulation
The *openness* consists in not lying to the other about lying with others:
> A groovy couple with an open marriage...(Bradbury, 1976)

open palm see PALM 1

open relationship a non-exclusive sexual friendship
An OPEN MARRIAGE without the wedding bells:
> You and I have had an open relationship with no strings. (Lodge, 1988)

open your bowels to defecate
A *bowel* is literally an intestine, whence any internal organ, and was so used by Cromwell:
> The enemy in all probability will be in our bowels in ten days. (Letter, 1643)
Now medical jargon:
> 'Have you had your bowels open?' he asked. (Bradbury, 1959)

open your legs (of a woman) to copulate promiscuously
It will not happen if you KEEP YOUR LEGS CROSSED:
> I'll teach her not to open her legs for bloody Germans. (Allbeury, 1978, writing about a Frenchwoman in the Second World War)

opening medicine a laxative
Not the first dose in a series, but *opening* bowels:
> Any pukka old soldier would have much preferred a dose of opening medicine. (F. Richards, 1933—to compulsory church parade)

operation (an) surgery
Literally, a work, deed, or action. Standard English:
> One morning, just as Canon Gloy
> Was starting gaily for the station,
> The Doctor said: 'Your eldest boy
> Must have another operation!' (Graham, 1930—'What!' cried the Canon. 'Not again? That's *twice* he's made me miss my train!')
See also PROCEDURE.

operational difficulties the ostensible reason why your journey will be delayed
The excuse given by transport operators, especially of trains and aircraft, to cover up breakdowns or incompetence. Also as *operating difficulties*:
> The Aeroflot flight was eight minutes late. For 'operational reasons' the girl at information explained. (Seymour, 1982—for most airlines eight minutes late is early)
> 'Operating difficulties', I assume, which is BR-speak for some ASLEF slob, having drunk fourteen pints of beer the previous evening, now gone 'sick' and failed to turn up. (A. Clark, 1993—BR was the state-owned British railway network and ASLEF the main union to which engine drivers belonged)

operator a swindler

Literally, anyone who carries out an operation, but beware of so describing a surgeon in his hearing:
> 'What does that mean—operator?' 'Well, I've done a bit of villainy.' (L. Thomas, 1978)
The word is also used of politicians and businessmen who use unconventional or questionable tactics to achieve their ends, and of dealers in illicit drugs.

optically challenged having defective eyesight
The usage covers anything from poor eyesight to blindness. Also as *optically handicapped*, *inconvenienced*, or *marginalized*.

oral sex cunnilingus or fellatio
Passionate kissing is not so described:
> [Rachman] preferred oral sex, something that obviated the need for a bed. (S. Green, 1979)
In the same sense, *oral service* is not what your dentist provides.

orchestras the testicles
Rhyming slang on *orchestra stalls*, BALLS:
> ... catching one a direct bullseye in the orchestras, thus putting one completely *hors de combat* for at least a week. (Matthew, 1983)

order of the boot (the) *British* summary dismissal from employment
After the ancient *Orders* of chivalry. Also as the *order of the push*.

orderly market a situation where suppliers do not compete on price
Either through a cartel, a monopoly, or though collusion between competitors:
> Even better, other mergers left it with only a single, German, competitor, which should make for what industrialists like to call an 'orderly market'. (*Daily Telegraph*, 26 September 1995)

orderly progress the maintenance of a monopoly
A world where politicians and public servants keep their jobs and control the market without interference from competitors or outsiders:
> Last week he sang of 'orderly progress' as 'preferable to the dangers of unbridled competition'. (*Sunday Express*, May 1981—a politician, for whom any competition was by definition 'unbridled', was opposing the sale of a state monopoly)

ordure excreta
Literally, filth. Either faeces or vomit:
> Barbarians! The place is covered in ... human ordure. (Boyd, 1962—soldiers

had defecated in every room)
But it's hard enough...without havin' that
ordure there atop ye. (Keneally, 1979—
soldiers were vomiting)

organ the penis
Shortened form of *sexual organ* or *organ of sex*:
He displayed the organ, the secondary
function of which is the relief of the
bladder. (Manning, 1965)
Seldom of the vagina:
...that organ of bliss in me, dedicated to its
reception. (Cleland, 1749)
Organs means the penis and testicles:
You've got to have a healthy view of your
organs. (Bradbury, 1976—you do it with
mirrors?)

organization (the) a band of criminals
Literally, a body of people working in concert.
Underworld jargon:
It's the business of the organization, and I
don't know anything about that. (Seymour,
1992)

organize to induce to join a trade union
In the jargon, a company which is not obliged
to negotiate with a trade union is not
organized, however well its affairs may be
managed.

orientation homosexuality
We have moved a long way from the
Christian desire to site a building so that it
faces towards the east, or *Orient*. In this use, a
shortened form of *sexual orientation*:
Trent had made no secret of his
orientation, had gone public six years
before. (Clancy, 1988)

Oscar a male homosexual
Not an actor receiving a coveted award but
from the late Mr Wilde. The use is more
common in America and Australia than in his
native Ireland or Britain.

other (the) promiscuous copulation
Always in the phrase *a bit of the other*, which is
given at BIT 2.

other place (the) *British* a house of parliament
For reasons of pedantry, it is not done for a
member of one of the legislative bodies to refer
to the other directly in the course of debate.
Also as *another place*, which should mean
anywhere beyond the confines of the chamber.

other side (the) death
For spiritualists, across the barrier between
this world and the next. For some others, the
far bank of the Styx or Jordan, on the way to
the Elysian Fields or life eternal.

other side of the tracks (the) *American* the poor section of town
When the railroad arrived, it was often
located on the edge of town where property
was cheaper, and it could be placed down-
wind of houses to minimize smoke, noise,
and fire hazards. Eventually the town would
develop around the station, with the richer
inhabitants staying in the more salubrious
quarter and the poorer living *on the other side of
the tracks*. Now also some figurative use.

other way (the) homosexual
The phrase applies to either sex:
He wouldn't look at his servants. His
inclinations, if she knew it, are all the
other way. (G. Greene, 1932—female
servants sometimes caught the eye of the
master of the house)

other woman (the) a mistress
The usage overlooks the fact that all woman-
kind is *other* than the wife or permanent
partner:
If Polly were not the 'other woman', she
would advise Gus to go back to her.
(M. McCarthy, 1963)

others *Irish* menstruation
The etymology is unclear:
—I told him I thought I was pregnint.—
GOOD JAYSIS! Jimmy roared laughing.—
Yeh fuckin' didn't!—I did, Jimmy....Me
others were late. (R. Doyle, 1987)

out¹ available for marriage
A shortened form of *out in society*, when girls
approaching marriageable age had their
season in which they met bachelors, among
others. Despite the attraction of linking
matrimony with the chase, I fear that we
cannot call in aid the hunting jargon *out*,
engaged on horseback chasing fox or deer:
'Weren't you out last Saturday?' she
asked...'That's a nice cob you were on.'
(Sassoon, 1928)

out² overtly homosexual
Having COME out of the CLOSET 2. Whence the
verb, meaning publicly to expose another's
homosexuality:
Militant activists claim that they are now
'negotiating' with five other bishops (who,
it is said, are being urged to admit to
homosexuality or be 'outed'). (*Sunday
Telegraph*, 12 March 1995)
In this context an *outing* is not a Sunday
school treat but such involuntary exposure:
It is here that Outrage's tactics, particularly
in threatened 'outings' of individual
clergymen, are likely to cut sharpest.
(ibid.—Outrage is a homosexual pressure
group)

out³ *obsolete* involved in a duel
The venue was generally in the open air:
'And for the sake of practice you insulted
six fencing masters in a week before your
duel?' 'I had the privilege of being out
seven times in as many days, sire,' I said.
(A. C. Doyle, 1895)

out of circulation menstruating
Female usage, often to a male, with imagery
from the lending library.

out of context said inadvisedly
A use by politicians when they have forgotten
what exactly they may have said, wish they
had never said it, or were unaware
that anyone was recording it. As journalists
are known to be selective in their quotations, this defensive manoeuvre is often
effective.

out of the envelope acting eccentrically
or without authority
Pilots' jargon, the *envelope* being the param-
eters within which an aircraft is designed to
perform, as to rates of climb, stall, turn, etc.:
He's somewhat out of the envelope, to use
an old test pilot's phrase. (BBC Radio 5, 26
June, 1994)

out of town *American* in prison
Suggesting the convict may be away on
business. Some humorous use.

out of your skull mentally unwell
You may also be described as being *out of your
gourd*, *head*, *senses*, *tree*, etc.:
'You're fucked,' I said. 'You're out of your
gourd.' (Turow, 1996)
He's out of his skull...ready for certifying.
(Bogarde, 1981)
Lady Macbeth was...clearly out of her tree.
(N. Evans, 1995—and not after hiding in
Birnham Wood)

out to lunch *American* mentally unstable
The imagery is of a short absence from home,
whence indicating a mild and perhaps temporary affliction:
His wife died two years ago and he's been
somewhat out to lunch ever since. (Diehl,
1978)

outdoor plumbing *American* a primitive
lavatory
A humorous use of a shed with a seat, a hole,
but no water or drainage.

outfit a criminal gang
Another type of ORGANIZATION:
'You said you saw what they did to Archie.'
'Who are we talking about here? Outfit?'
(Turow, 1993—Archie had not been fitted

for a suit but garroted and dumped in a
refrigerator)

outhouse a lavatory
In a courtyard or down the garden, away from
the dwelling house. It was the place you
visited if you said you were going *out the back*:
[He made] a gentlemanly statement of his
wish to use the outhouse. (Keneally, 1979)

outplace to dismiss from employment
Not being sent to work away from the plant
or office:
...despite the fact that your company is
doing rather well, you have been sacked or,
rather, 're-engineered', 'downsized',
'unassigned', 'proactively outplaced' or
'put in the mobility pool'. (*Sunday Telegraph*,
27 October 1996)

outrage to copulate with a woman
against her will
Literally, to offend in any way:
She complained that...some British
soldiers had assaulted and outraged
her...She could have identified at least
forty men who had outraged her.
(F. Richards, 1933—she was a French
prostitute)

outsourcing *British* handing management over to or buying services from
the private sector
It is embarrassing for a socialist to concede
that state or municipal ownership is often not
compatible with economy or efficiency:
Estelle Morris, the schools minister,
announced that...some at least of
Leeds' functions would be privatised,
though she preferred to call it
'outsourcing'. (*Daily Telegraph*, 3
February 2000)

oval office *American* the vagina viewed
sexually
Punning on the personal office of the President of the United States, without any
implication that the holder of that position
would ever be guilty of sexual impropriety:
Ace, he was looking for a girl...'Gone
visit the oval office?' asked a man.
(McInerney, 1992)

overactive naughty
An excuse or delusion of parents whose lack
of discipline may have caused the problem:
'We do have a special course for the Over-
Active Underachiever,' continued the
headmaster. (Sharpe, 1982)

over-civilized decadent
Nazi dysphemism in a culture where to
appreciate beauty was to be effete:

They are nearer to France, Europe's most over-civilized country. (Goebbels, 1945, in translation, writing about his native Rhinelanders who did not resist the Anglo-American invaders)

over-familiar making an unwanted sexual approach to a female
Literally, being too affable. See also FAMILIAR.

over-gallant making an unwanted sexual approach to a female
Literally, in this sense, being too polished in behaviour:
Sammy was...How shall I put it? I think the kindest way would be 'over-gallant'. (Boyd, 1982)
See also GALLANT.

over-geared insolvent
Gearing is the relationship between assets and debt. Unless you are its banker, to imply that a company is insolvent is taboo as well as being actionable.

overindulge to drink intoxicants to excess
On a single occasion or habitually:
...the thought for a moment I might have been over-indulging. (Private Eye, July 1981)
See also INDULGE.

over-invoicing the payment of money additional to the agreed price in a place selected by the recipient
In markets where corruption is rife and taxation heavy, a customer may ask a foreign supplier to inflate the price of imports, with the difference being paid as a bribe or as a return of the excess in another country.
See also UNDER-INVOICING.

over-privileged rich
But no more privileged than PRIVILEGED.

over-refreshed drunk
Not much different from REFRESHED. Over-sedated still means, and over-excited used to mean, the same thing:
...post-prandial euphoria that Harry Woods euphemistically termed 'over-refreshed'. (Deighton, 1978)
Only...the recognition that she was a tad over-sedated prevented her from falling down. (le Carré, 1996)
I am very much afraid he is over-excited with wine. (W. Collins, 1860)

over the bat see BAT

over the broomstick obsolete cohabiting and copulating outside marriage

The outcome if you decided to JUMP THE BROOMSTICK:
...this woman in Garradstreet here, had been married very young, over the broomstick (as we say), to a tramping man. (C. Dickens, 1861)

over the Jordan dead
What happens when you reach the OTHER SIDE:
'All those soldiers that I killed at Alamein, and in Normandy', and about it not being long before he joined them 'over the Jordan'. (Horne, 1994, writing about the aged Montgomery)

over the top¹ obsolete attacking an enemy from a trench
First World War usage. The top was the parapet of the trench over which the attackers climbed: and to go over the top was to risk being killed or maimed:
Darling, you can't really imagine ONE going over the top? (N. Mitford, 1960—a man was explaining why he declined to participate in the Second World War)

over the top² achieving sexual orgasm
Usually of a female:
She made love to herself on the bath mat...She always felt awful afterwards...especially when she took herself...'Over the Top'. (M. McCarthy, 1963)

over the wall¹ escaping from prison
Of obvious imagery. The phrase is used whatever the means of egress.

over the wall² British in prison
Naval jargon, from the meaning of wall, the side of a ship, over which the prisoner passed on his way to jail ashore:
The Court Martial sentenced him to six months over the wall and he got dismissed from Service as well. (Jolly, 1988)

over there engaged in warfare on foreign soil
For the British, France in the First World War:
[Peter] was seventeen and a half; next year would see him fighting. He had learned much of what it was like over there from his brother. (S. Hastings, 1994, quoting from E. Waugh)
For the American military over there meant service in Europe in both World Wars.

overdo the Dionysian rites to become drunk
Dionysus discovered the art of wine-making. Being of catholic tastes, the god sought

pleasure also in sexual orgies, plays, human sacrifice, and flagellation.

overdose an attempt at suicide by self-poisoning with drugs
Medical jargon, whether the protagonist fails or succeeds, and often abbreviated to *OD*, which may refer either to the attempt or to the person who makes it:

> She's a person, not a *goddamned OD*!
> (Clancy, 1989—she had attempted to kill herself)

overdue [1] pregnant
Failing to menstruate at the expected time but not necessarily denoting an unwanted pregnancy.

overdue[2] in difficulty or crashed
Aviation jargon, of an aircraft which has failed to report routinely during flight, or has not landed as expected:

> Overdue connoted something quite different from late in airline parlance. (Block, 1979)

overflight a spying mission
Literally, crossing a country in the course of a commercial flight by a recognized and agreed path. The American government in May 1960 so described the mission of Gary Powers, who was shot down over Russia in a U2 aircraft. In 1962 the Russians exchanged Powers for their spy Rudolf Abel.

overfriendly involving sexual impropriety
The excess of amity is usually shown by a male:

> Verity makes no secret of having had an overfriendly involvement with a pupil's mother in Leeds, where he was headmaster of the grammar school for ten years. (*Daily Telegraph*, 18 August 1998)

overhaul indoctrination
The language of Nazi Germany in its early years of government:

> ...decrees...according to which all...are to get an annual four week 'national political overhaul' (overhaul, *again* the mechanistic terminology). (Klemperer, 1998, in translation—diary entry 13 June 1934)

overhaul of profit margins the peremptory dismissal of employees
As it is believed by many that industrial costs 'walk on two feet', the expectation is that paying less people will increase profit:

> ...520 jobs are to be chopped out of the company's portfolio of regional newspaper titles. The headline of the press release: 'overhaul of profit margins at Westminster press'. (*Daily Telegraph*, 1 July 1995)

overhear *American* a clandestine listening device
Evasions are necessary because of sensitivity about illegal eavesdropping:

> I asked if there was an 'overhear', the feds' delicate term for a bug. (Turow, 1999)

oversee *obsolete* to bewitch
Literally, to inspect or supervise, but one glance was enough for a true witch. Also as to *overlook* or *overshadow*:

> It have brought all kind of disaster along with it. It must have been overseen when I took it. (Gissing, 1890)
> Wha kens what ill it may bring to the bairn, if ye overlook it in that gate? (W. Scott, 1819)
> The last witness said deceased had been 'overshadowed' by someone. (*North Devon Herald*, 1896, quoted in *EDD*)

overtired drunk
Alcohol makes you sleepy, or TIRED 2:

> I had on occasion stepped in at the last moment when he was overtired-emotional to write and file some *Daily Telegraph* piece for him. (Whicker, 1982—he was Randolph Churchill, when working as a war correspondent in Korea)

Overtiredness is drunkenness:

> [George Brown] turned up to the first production meeting—in the morning—in an advanced state of over-tiredness. (*Private Eye*, 1980)

owned second-hand
A refinement of the PRE-OWNED theme. In 1999 prospective customers were being invited in advertisements to buy *owned Rolls-Royce* motor cars, as though there were also a store of abandoned vehicles from which to draw, if they so chose.

own goal an accusation or campaign which damages the originator
The result for a soccer player of inadvertently scoring against his own side:

> Occasionally there was an 'own goal'. Usually there was a warning. (McCrum, 1991, describing terrorists attempting to blow up others but killing themselves)

P

P urine
The initial letter of *piss*. Also, as a verb, to urinate and in the vulgar expression *p off*. See also PEE.

PC see POLITICALY CORRECT

PG see PAYING GUEST

pacify to conquer
Literally, to bring peace to:
> ...the unsettled areas where we are still engaged in pacifying the Taijacks, Uzbecks and Khokandians. (Fraser, 1973—the areas had long been settled by the nations named, but not by the Russian invaders)

Pacification is such conquest. Thus, for the British in Africa, their colonial rule was the *era of pacification* (C. Allen, 1970). For the Americans in Vietnam, it was an attempt to beat the Vietcong:
> Pacification...forced upon an already violated population. (Herr, 1977)

An American *pacification camp* or *center* was, in Vietnam, a political prison:
> ...concentration camps are 'pacification centers'. (Commager, 1972)

pack it in to die
Literally, to desist:
> That's where Jack's mate from Hong Kong packed it in. (Theroux, 1973)

package on (a) drunkenness
Carrying a LOAD 1 and owing nothing to the obsolete English *pack*, rum, named after the English general Pakenham who had the misfortune of being killed in the battle of New Orleans two months after the signing in Europe of the peace treaty between the combatants.

package store *American* a place which sells intoxicants
A survival from the days when buying liquor to drink at home was taboo:
> Their father had been an alcoholic who had worked occasionally and not well as an auto mechanic to provide money that he had transferred regularly and immediately to the nearest package store. (Clancy, 1991)

And see GROCERIES SUNDRIES.

packet¹ a serious wound or death
Literally, a small pack, hence an article sent by post, as in the *packet boat* which carried the mail. See also CATCH A PACKET 1.

packet² a venereal disease
Another unwelcome small pack for soldiers in the Second World War—see CATCH A PACKET 2. Today, if you *catch a packet*, it may mean no more than having a number of bills descend on you at once.

pad dishonestly to inflate
Used of claims and accounts, from *padding* clothing to cause an apparent increase in size:
> The surcharges, padding and fictitious costs that were an inevitable part of every account. (Deighton, 1972)

There is no etymological link with the obsolete *pad*, to rob, as in *foodpad* (see HIGHWAYMAN), which came from *pad*, a path.

Paddington *obsolete* relating to hanging
The geographical location in London of the gallows:
> Tyburn being in the parish of Paddington, execution day was known as Paddington Fair, the hood drawn over one's head was the Paddington spectacles, and in dying one danced the Paddington frisk. (R. Hughes, 1987)

paddy wagon *American* a police vehicle
There was a preponderance of those of Irish origin in New England police departments but not necessarily among those incarcerated:
> McCord and the other burglars being led out of the building and into a paddy wagon...(Colodny and Gettlin, 1991—the building was Watergate)

pagan *obsolete* a prostitute
Prostitution was no occupation for the upright:
> *Prince Henry* What pagan may that be?
> *Page* A proper gentlewoman. (Shakespeare, *1 Henry IV*)

paint a picture to attempt to deceive
Normally through lying:
> Someone's painting you a fucking picture! Can't you see that? (Wolfe, 1987)

paint the tape *American* fraudulently to record deals at fictitious prices
The reference is to the *ticker tape* by which market information was diffused:
> Some of the amazing prices you read of in auctions are created by the owner selling to himself—what is called 'painting the tape' on Wall Street. (Train, 1983)

paint the town red to carouse
Usually of a single session of celebratory drunken debauchery. It has been suggested, somewhat improbably, that the phrase originated in the American west, where a drunken spree might start in a brothel area and then

move uptown, although a reverse itinerary would have seemed more likely.

painted woman *obsolete* a prostitute
Not an artist's model but someone who used cosmetics before the practice became in succession permitted, normal, and then obligatory.

painters are in (the) I am menstruating
From the disruption and discoloration. Dated female use.

pair a woman's breasts
Viewed sexually by a male. A female said to have a good or magnificent *pair* is neither an identical twin nor being complimented on her eyes or ears.

palm¹ an indication of bribery
The hand of the recipient is upturned:
> You yourself
> Are much condemn'd to have an itching palm. (Shakespeare, *Julius Caesar*)

Whence to *anoint a palm*, to bribe, and many punning terms for bribery such as *palmistry*, *palm oil*, *soap*, or *grease*:
> It would be hard to dispute that a little such palm-grease must, on occasion, have found a compliant hand. (Monsarrat, 1978)

The recipient's *palm* may be *slippery*:
> ...birth and wedding certificates, confidential medical reports acquired by the usual greasing of slippery palms. (Rushdie, 1995)

On receipt of the bribe or tip, the *palm* may be *tickled*:
> At length, by tickling the palm of his hand, he promised to be ready for me by six the next morning. (Emblen, 1970)

An *open palm* indicates a desire to be bribed or excessively tipped:
> Its restaurants are opulent and noted for exorbitant prices and some of the world's worst food served with a condescending flourish and an open palm. (Whicker, 1982—the name *Palm Beach*, the resort about which he was writing, had been chosen with considerable foresight)

palm² to cheat by prestidigitation
The cards are concealed in the *palm* of the hand. Used figuratively of other forms of cheating and sharp practice, as in the phrase *palm off with*, to give (someone) something which is worthless or of less value than had been agreed.

pan a pedestal-type lavatory
Literally, any bowl. Whence the figurative *down the pan*, irretrievably lost. A *bedpan* is used for defecation and urination, not for eating from or washing in:

> One night I heard him fling the bedpan across the room. (L. Thomas, 1977)

panhandler a beggar
From the receptacle he thrusts at you and not necessarily a resident of western Florida:
> I saw some [refugees] the next day—panhandlers holding politely worded signs. (Theroux, 1995)

Many *panhandlers* are importunate and some so described are thieves.

pancake¹ the faeces of cows
The shape on the grass.

pancake² to land (an aircraft) with the undercarriage retracted
It flops down, the usage possibly owing something to PANCAKE 1.

panel¹ (the) *obsolete* *British* the list of doctors available to treat the poor
Those whom poor sick people consulted prior to the National Health Service. To be ON THE PANEL meant to be absent from work due to illness.

panel² *obsolete* a prostitute
There seems to be no link between this *panel* and the American *panel-house* or *panel-joint*, a brothel, where the rooms were divided into wooden cubicles:
> Panels march by two and three
> Saying, Sweetheart, come with me. (old ballad quoted in *EDD*)

pansy a male homosexual
Like the delicate flower, *viola tricolor*:
> You're just a filthy pansy! No wonder your marriage has failed. (Masters, 1976)

pant after to desire sexually
Usually a male *pants after* a female who is not his sexual partner, desire making him figuratively breathless:
> That boy was panting after you. I saved you from him. (Sheldon, 1998)

panther sweat *American* whisky
DAS suggests: May have originally been a euphemism for 'panther piss':
> 'Ran alky through her,' he said, 'in a beatup truck, white lightning, panther piss...whatever you want to call it.' (Sanders, 1980)

But where did *panther piss* come from, in the absence of panthers?

paper aeroplane a project to construct a new aircraft
Usually drawn in outline with a draft specification in the hope of securing backing for development costs from a potential customer

or government. The pun is less obvious with *paper helicopter*:

There is a heavy health warning about assuming that paper helicopters always fly. (*Daily Telegraph*, 2 March 1994, reporting on a document prepared by a manufacturer)

paper-hanger¹ *American* a policeman punishing a motorist for speeding

Referring to the *ticket* which may be handed out on such occasions. With similar punning humour, the officer may be described as *doing his paperwork*

paper-hanger² a person who passes false negotiable instruments

Usually of cheques which have been stolen or are not covered by deposits:

I've been stung too many times by the summer people. Paperhangers, I call them. (Theroux, 1974—an innkeeper was bemoaning his losses from cashing cheques for holidaymakers)

See also HANG PAPER.

paper out on having a commercial agreement to murder

Such a CONTRACT can rarely have been written down:

'It wasn't no amateur hit.' 'Are you tellin' me there was paper out on her?' (Diehl, 1978)

paper the house to fill a theatre by giving tickets away

Punning theatrical jargon, the *house* being the audience.

Paphian associated with prostitution

Paphos, or Cyprus, was sacred to Venus, the goddess of love:

Cyprians of the better sort ... well acquainted with its Paphian intricacies. (Mayhew, 1862)

parallel importing a measure of illegality or breach of contract

Describing political arrangements, where government is ineffective:

... most citizens welcomed the end of anarchist gang terrorism ... the system of 'parallel police' and 'parallel justice' was approved. (Mitchell, 1982, writing about the Spanish Civil War)

or trading, where goods are sold at prices below those stipulated in that market by the manufacturer:

By buying goods without the manufacturer's consent, grey marketeers—or parallel traders as they prefer to be known—operate in an area so named because it is neither illegal nor accepted business practice. (*Daily Telegraph*, 17 July 1998)

The practice of sourcing outside the usual channels—also called 'parallel importing'—triggered a controversial European Court ruling last month. (*Daily Telegraph*, 27 August 1998)

Parallel pricing is where two suppliers or bidders operate a cartel.

parallel parking *American* having a mistress

One vehicle legally at the kerb and another beside it in the street.

paralysed very drunk

And immobile:

Dead drunk, paralysed, spifflicated. (Chandler, 1953)

paralytic very drunk

Again immobile, but not from paralysis or palsy:

We had a marvellous wedding, Jerry and me. I was paralytic. (Theroux, 1983—but what did Jerry think about it?)

paramour a person with whom you have a regular extramarital sexual relationship

Originally a suitor, acting 'through love', and of both sexes, although latterly women have acquired more *paramours* than men:

Married women go there with their paramours, for they are sure of secrecy. (Mayhew, 1862)

parboiled drunk

Literally, thoroughly boiled, whence overheated. The common culinary imagery.

Paris Mean Time Greenwich Mean Time adapted to French chauvinism

It was an insult to French pride that the meridian was judged to have been centred on an observatory in England:

Even then [in 1911], they [the French] hesitated to refer directly to Greenwich mean time, preferring the locution 'Paris Mean Time, retarded by nine minutes and twenty-one seconds'. (Sobel, 1996)

parity the achievement of the best in any aspect of employment

Trade union jargon. The equality you seek is always better in terms of wages, hours of work, holidays, pensions, paternal leave, or whatever.

park¹ *American* to kiss and embrace in a parked car

In a secluded spot or one devoted to such activity:

He saw the grove of trees where he had parked with Alison. (R. N. Patterson, 1996/2)

park² to transfer (stocks) to an accomplice so as to conceal ownership
Using the same imagery as WAREHOUSE:
> Last year he also, on five occasions, arranged with Keith Place of Natwest, to 'park' stock with each other... with an understanding to repurchase. (*Daily Telegraph*, 25 June 1994)

park women *obsolete* prostitutes
As found in 19th-century London, where a plethora of open spaces offered convenient location:
> Park women, properly so called, are those degraded creatures, who wander about the paths most frequented after nightfall in the Parks, and consent to any species of humiliation for the sake of acquiring a few shillings. (Mayhew, 1862)

parliament¹ *obsolete British* a lavatory
An excruciating Victorian pun on sitting.

parliament² *obsolete* smuggled or illegally distilled spirits
Because no excise duty had been paid on it:
> It's as good parliament as ever gentleman tasted. (Croker, 1862)

parlor house *American* a brothel
The room in which you might be expected to meet a female visitor:
> The parlor houses, cribs, brothels and bagnios had disappeared... and a thousand prostitutes had been thrown out of work. (Gores, 1975)

parsley bed *obsolete* the place where new girl babies are found
EDD defines it as 'A euphemism for the uterus' but the ensuing quotation and dissertation do not support the definition (vol. iv, p. 427). Parsley seeds itself and, like the gooseberry bushes which provided similar antenatal accommodation for boys, thrives without weeding, resulting in unkempt areas in many Victorian gardens where the stork might discreetly drop its bundle:
> How do babies come? What is the parsley bed the nurses and doctors say they come out of? (Pearsall, 1969, quoting from 1879)

part to die
Usually of a spouse, in the hope of being united later, perhaps:
> She told me, that to part was the greatest pain she had ever felt, and that we would meet again in a better place. (J. Boswell, 1791)

part with patrick *obsolete Scottish* to abort a foetus prematurely

A version of the former standard English, *part with child*:
> Or he wan back she parted wi' patrick. (D. Graham, 1883)

partake to drink alcohol
Really no more than to share in, in this case sharing a drink:
> Harangued in good-humoured way by one who has clearly partaken... (Deedes, 1997)

partially sighted nearly blind
To refer directly to a HANDICAP is taboo.

partner a person having a regular unmarried sexual relationship with another
Usually they also cohabit. The word is used of homosexuals and heterosexuals:
> Maternity nurses at the Royal United Hospital in Bath have been told to call fathers of newborn babies 'partners' rather than 'husbands', so as not to upset single mothers. (*Sunday Telegraph*, 20 March 1994)

partner with Revlon to dye your hair
Revlon is a firm which manufactures dyestuffs:
> She's still a blonde, but I think she partners with Revlon. (McBain, 1994)

parts the human genitalia
A shortened form of PRIVATE PARTS:
> 'You find the model ugly?' 'Not at all. I mean her... parts.' (Amis, 1978)
The former meaning, virtues, might lead to misunderstanding today:
> I think highly of Campbell. In the first place, he has very good parts. (J. Boswell, 1773)

party a battle
A Second World War version of the First World War SHOW 2, understating the danger and the unpleasantness:
> Dutch civilians weeping... for the few returning guests departing from what someone on the staff had chosen to call a party. (Bogarde, 1978, writing about the battle of Arnhem)

party girl *American* a prostitute
Literally, a girl who attends parties, whence one who is invited to be available for male guests, or one who attends in the hope of meeting a customer:
> There were some snide references to what had befallen her, including a mention that she was known as a 'party girl'. (Sanders, 1986)

party member a Communist
The usage dates from the period prior to the Second World War when you kept quiet about being a Communist because many

would consider you to be a traitor with revolutionary tendencies:

> That's why people convert to Catholicism, or become party members. (Bradbury, 1959)

pash a homosexual desire

A shortened version of *passion*. Formerly much used to denote such feelings between schoolgirls for each other, or for a female teacher:

> Are you getting a pash for that little thing? (G. Greene, 1932—but people normally had *pashes on* not *pashes for*)

Less often of one-sided heterosexual feeling:

> Janet seems to be getting a pash for this Savory man. (ibid.)

pass¹ to die

The passage from this world to the next. Also as *pass away, beyond the veil, into the next world, off the earth* (or a synonym), *in your checks, into the next world, on,* or *over*:

> Things are mixed up since Mr Forsythe passed. (Sanders, 1994—Mr Forsythe was not a bridge or football player but had been murdered)
> Flora must have thought she was going to do, for just before she passed away...(L. Armstrong, 1955)
> His own mongrel, misinterpreting his teachings as commands to bite the tyres of passing military trucks, passed prematurely beyond the veil. (de Bernières, 1994)
> He was the first to pass into the next world. (F. Richards, 1933)
> ...some strong healthy men have been unlucky enough to pass off this Ball of Clay in double-quick time since we have been at this station [in India]. (F. Richards, 1936).
> She murmured something sensitive just before she passed on. (Bradbury, 1976)

It is mainly the devout who *pass over*, arriving on the banks of the Styx, the Jordan, the Great Divide, or wherever. You do not have to be gambler to *pass in your checks*. For all categories of *passers*, their *passing* is death:

> The Phelan grandchildren, like their parents, had attracted new pals and confidants since Troy's passing. (Grisham, 1999)

pass² an unsolicited sexual approach

Usually by a male to a female he does not know well, from the reconnaissance before attacking:

> Too many passes had been made at it and it had grown a little too smart in dodging them. (Chandler, 1943, describing a woman's face)

Occasionally of homosexuals:

> Burgess sought Rees out later earning a mild rebuff for 'making a tentative pass' at him. (Boyle, 1979)

Although normally *made*, it seems that *passes* can also be *thrown*, as in football:

> Threw a pass. Yes, as a matter of fact he did. (Amis, 1988)

pass air *American* to fart

You may also, if so minded, *pass gas* or *wind*.

pass water to urinate

The phrase is so common that we do not confuse it with driving by a river or handing someone a jug at table:

> The nurse took him into a little cubicle and asked him to pass water into a bottle. (Bradbury, 1959)

And see WATER.

passing see PASS 1

past its sell-by date outmoded or useless

A cliché from the dating of food sold by retail, which is intended to convince the customer of its freshness:

> They were considered past their sell-by date, middle-aged southerners who had no active record since the, fifties. (O'Callaghan, 1998, explaining how the Provisional IRA members, largely based in the North, viewed their IRA predecessors)

past (your) something shameful or secret about your past life

It usually refers to criminal activity or to adultery, the latter in the days when it was not socially accepted, especially in a woman:

> 'Part of your past, I presume?' 'No. At least, not as you mean it.' (Manning, 1965)

pasture (of a male) to copulate

Grazing as it were:

> Fielding thought of Hecht pasturing in that thick body. (le Carré, 1962)

patron *obsolete* a man who keeps a mistress

Originally, he who stands in the relationship of a father, whence the concept of protecting:

> An impotent or unkind man will produce a woman predisposed to fall in love instantly with her succeeding patron. (Chandler, 1944)

pause¹ the natural cessation of menstruation

Literally, a cessation of something which will be resumed but, in this usage, a shortened form of *menopause*.

pause² a statutory restriction on increases in pay

One of a series of terms used by politicians of attempts to hold down wages as a supposed cure for inflation brought about in part by their ill-conceived fiscal policies:

> In 1961...Selwyn Lloyd introduced what he euphemistically described as the Pause, to combat growing inflationary pressure. (S. Green, 1979—Lloyd was the British Chancellor of the Exchequer)

pavement girl *American* a prostitute
Standing on roadside at which her trucker customers pull up rather than in any old STREET:

> A little further down the road a famous 'pavement girl' wolf-whistles up to greet him and make fun of him. (Ninh, 1991)

Also as *pavement princess*.

pavement people homeless beggars
The place where they beg and sometimes also sleep:

> Jenny Hoyle, the Taunton Town Centre Manager, has not been heard to utter nasty words like 'vagrant'—she prefers the sublime phrase 'pavement people'. (Chapman, 1999)

paw to fondle sexually
Perhaps punning on *paw*, the hand, and on the vigour with which an impatient stallion strikes the ground with his hoof:

> When you ask any of the men here, they just paw you. (Chandler, 1953)

pay a visit to urinate
Shortened form of *pay a visit to the lavatory* and punning on making a social call. Very common of urination but seldom of defecation.

pay lip service insincerely to say you agree with or support
Talking not acting:

> New Labour, you say you are about social change. I ask you to stop paying lip service. (*Daily Telegraph*, 14 July 2001—an author was pressing for fewer restrictions on immigration into Britain)

pay nature's debt to die of natural causes
From the necessity of death in the natural order. Also as *pay nature's last debt*.

pay the supreme sacrifice to be killed in combat or judicially
More often *made* than *paid*. Also as *pay the supreme price*:

> Death in war is unfortunate but unavoidable. Every man who joined MK knew that he might be called on to pay the supreme sacrifice. (Mandela, 1994—MK, *Unkhonto we Sizwe*, was the military arm of the African National Congress)

His friends were convinced it was his political radicalism that explained why he was singled out to pay the supreme price for disobedience. (Gentles, 1992, describing Robert Lockyer who was executed after the Leveller mutiny of 1649)

pay with the roll of a drum *obsolete British* to avoid payment
It was illegal to seek to arrest a soldier for debt while he was on the march.

pay your debt to society to be killed judicially
Usually for murder.

paying guest a stranger lodging for payment in a private house
A standard usage which is thought to add gentility to a commercial transaction and often abbreviated to *PG*. Whence the *guest house*, where visitors pay for accommodation.

payoff a bribe or illegal reward
Not what you receive on leaving lawful employment:

> Ezra is still in the saddle, even after that payoff business in Malawi. (M. Thomas, 1980)

payroll adjustment the summary dismissal of staff
Not merely correcting an error in a previous computation:

> The American company Wal-Mart went one better with 'normal payroll adjustment'. (*Daily Telegraph*, 20 August 1996, quoting William Lutz)

peace a preparation for violence
First noted in Hitler's notorious *peace speech* of 17 May, 1933, which heralded his assaults upon his neighbours. The concept and language were adopted by Communists and other aggressors, with *peace councils, offensives,* and the like:

> Its official name was Operation Peace for Galilee, even though the siege of Beirut, far to the north of Galilee, had been going on for weeks. (Simpson, 1998, writing of the 1982 invasion of Lebanon by Israel)

Peace-keeping action is an invasion of another's territory, the units taking part being described as a *peace-keeping force*.

peace at last death
A tombstone and obituary favourite, referring to the dead person and not to the survivors.

pear-shaped unsuccessful
Probably from the form of an analyst's graph, the use having started as jargon in financial

circles. As with the fruit, the weight is at the lower end:

> Yesterday it all went pear-shaped for Michael...(*Daily Telegraph*, 20 June 1997—Michael's plans had come to naught)

pecker the penis
Literally, an instrument for making a hole by pecking:

> ...caution a feller about despairing of his poor engine and perhaps hitting his pecker with a hammer. (Theroux, 1973)

The British *pecker* was the nose, whence the expression *keep your pecker up, keep cheerful,* an exhortation which an American might find impracticable as well as impertinent.

peculiar homosexual
A variant of QUEER 3:

> The idea came to her that Dick was, well, *peculiar.* (M. McCarthy, 1963)

In obsolete British use a *peculiar* was a mistress, someone you kept for your own exclusive use.
For Webster in 1833 the *peculiar members* were the testicles.

peculiar institution (the) *obsolete American* slavery
19th-century usage, when slavery was thought to be an integral part of the economy of the South. It also continued in some Unionist states for much of the Civil War:

> ...it was unthinkable that the American flag should impose the South's 'peculiar institution' on new lands won by Americans from every part of the country. (G. C. Ward, 1990—dispossessing American Indians was all right, it seems)

peddle your arse to be a prostitute
From *peddle,* to offer for sale, and see also ARSE, with the alternative *ass:*

> I'm too old to peddle my ass. (Sanders, 1981)

Some homosexual use also.

pee to urinate
The first letter of *piss,* and the usual spelling of **P**:

> During the next few days I peed endlessly into containers which were duly transported to the laboratory and analysed. (Oakley, 1984)

A *pee* is an act of urination:

> The Brigadier, on his way back from a quick pee in the bushes...(Bogarde, 1978)

Pee-pee for urination is rare in English (although common in colloquial French).

peel a banana *American* (of a male) to copulate

Either from the movement of the prepuce or from the removal of clothing.

peeler a policeman
After the original BOBBY, Sir Robert Peel:

> If they'd been tipped every peeler in London would have been there in plain clothes waiting for us. (Clancy, 1987—the police would have been *tipped off,* not given gratuities)

Whence perhaps the American slang *peel,* to arrest.

peeper a private detective
They were at one time frequently involved in the observation of adultery:

> 'Merely an ex-cop trying to hustle a living.'
> 'That's tall talk for a peeper.' (Macdonald, 1952)

Peeping Tom a sexual voyeur
Leofric, the Anglo-Saxon Lord of Coventry, agreed to postpone an increase in taxes if his wife, Godiva, rode naked through the streets. The townspeople were forbidden to watch, and how anybody would have known if Tom hadn't peeped is a matter for conjecture:

> Luje tried to persuade himself that he wasn't *spying* . It wasn't like he was being a Peeping Tom or anything. (N. Evans, 1998)

peg¹ an intoxicating drink, usually of spirits
Anglo-Indian use and a shortened form of CHOTA PEG:

> We had our pegs on the verandah. (Fraser, 1977)

peg² *obsolete* to drink intoxicants to excess
Not from PEG 1 but from the communal drinking bowl in which each person's share was marked with a peg:

> What with rum and pepper—and pepper and rum—I should think his pegging must be nearly over. (C. Dickens, 1861—the drunkard also used to knock on the floor when he wanted fresh supplies)

peg out to die
Not necessarily of drink but from the scoring at cribbage, where the first to finish moves his peg to the end of a row of holes on a board and *pegs out.*

pencil¹ the penis
From the shape and construction rather than the shared Latin ancestry. Now only as LEAD IN YOUR PENCIL, although Partridge gave *pencil and tassel* as a child's penis and scrotum (*DSUE*).

pencil² not legally binding

Attributive use, from the ability to erase what is written in pencil:

> Book studio space and make it firm, no pencil deals. I want it in dry ink. (B. Forbes, 1972)

A busy or self-important person who *pencils* an appointment in a diary is likely to cancel it or fail to keep it.

penetrate¹ (of a male) to copulate with
Sharing the etymological stem with *penis*.

penetrate² to enter (a building) without consent
The language of espionage. Those involved may also figuratively *penetrate* an organization of which they disapprove or which they suspect of subversion.

penman a forger
Literally, a skilled writer with a pen. Criminal jargon:

> Then there are the 'blanks', the unfilled identity cards, on which the penman can work at will using the originals to produce forgeries of superb quality. (Forsyth, 1994)

penny short of a pound simple-minded
239 out of 240 in the old imperial coinage, using the common imagery as in NOT SIXTEEN ANNAS TO THE RUPEE and similar phrases which imply that someone is NOT ALL THERE:

> Slow-and-Lucky, who's a penny short of a pound and walks his Alsatian dog all day, the dog as daft as Lucky is. (le Carré, 1993)

people cuts the dismissal of employees
Not surgery or fencing:

> Mr Saltmarsh said much of the rest of the savings would be found in 'people cuts'. (*Daily Telegraph*, 20 May 1999)

people of/with those having a particular characteristic
POLITICALLY CORRECT language adopted by those so described. Thus *people of colour* are black:

> Black people may be black, but many now prefer 'African American' or 'people of colour'—though *never* 'coloured people'. (*Daily Telegraph*, 23 February 1991)

People with impaired hearing are deaf and *people with learning difficulties* are those who are unable to keep up with their peers in class:

> ... the deaf shall be described as 'people with impaired hearing' and the mentally handicapped as 'people with learning difficulties'. (*Daily Telegraph*, 1 October 1990)

People of size, which might be thought to include all of us and not just interior decorators fixing wallpaper, does not refer to stature but to girth:

> ... mainstream society should shed its prejudices against those known in the current politically correct jargon as 'people of size'. (*Sunday Telegraph*, 13 November 1994)

The usage was to be found before 1939:

> Among those not allowed to emigrate to Britain, Palestine or the colonies were the infirm, anyone with a criminal record, those who could not support themselves and 'people with unacceptable politics'—a euphemism for communists. (Michael Smith, 1999)

We can only rejoice with Mr B. F. Freeman, who won $50,000 in a 'Create a New Word' competition by suggesting *people with differing abilities* to describe those suffering from a physical disability (Beard and Cerf, 1990). Now we know at last why Arnold Palmer or Tiger Woods routinely turn in lower scores on the golf course than ourselves.

people's imposed by autocracy
The language of totalitarianism or contempt in various compounds, as follow:

people's army an army pledged to the support of a regime when the former non-political or professional army has been disbanded

people's car a device for financing Nazi re-armament
In 1938 any German who had paid 750 marks at a rate of not less than 5 marks a week received an order number, but none received a car. Today *Volkswagen* has long shaken off its dubious beginnings.

people's court a tribunal supporting the regime without trained judges or juries, and without justice or mercy
There is a certain irony in the fact that the three Communists acquitted by a properly constituted court in 1934 of involvement in the Reichstag fire should have been the first victims of the Nazi *Volksgerichtshof*.

people's democracy an autocracy
Usually Communist, and newspeak at its best, since its citizens are denied effective voting rights or access to a free press.

people's justice summary killing without trial
Without even the legalistic routine of a PEOPLE'S COURT to delay the process:

> Spare them after all? When they should be punished according to the people's justice. (Kyle, 1983, writing of the Czar and his family)

people's lottery a national lottery operated by a licensee

people's militia an armed force supporting those who have seized power
It may be institutionalized to keep a watch over and counterbalance what remains of a professional army.

people's palace a mansion for the exclusive use of an autocrat
As in Syria:
> And it was he who told me that his palace in Damascus, built at a cost of 120 million dollars—and of course no one but the Commander was allowed to enter it—was called Kasr el Sharb, the People's Palace. (Theroux, 1995—the 'Commander' (of the Nation) was the autocrat Assad)

people's republic an autocracy
Usually Communist and slightly less offensive than PEOPLE'S DEMOCRACY, although the *people* are unlikely to notice any difference:
> ... fatuous violation of language that in our day terms the grotesque dictatorship a 'People's republic'. (Theroux, 1979)

people's tribunal a political court on the lines of a PEOPLE'S COURT
> ... normally the only indication that the People's Tribunal had done its work was the appearance in the street outside of the common red placards announcing that the accused had been guillotined. (Kee, 1984, writing of Germany in 1939)

Percy a penis
A shortened form of PERSON, usually in the phrase POINT PERCY AT THE PORCELAIN.

perform¹ to defecate or urinate when required
A shortened form of *perform a natural function* or some such expression:
> Temple felt an urge to perform a natural function. (Boyd, 1987)

Common nursery usage to describe a child being trained to control urination or defecation:
> On the rare occasions when by pure chance—he 'performed', she moderated her pantomime of approval. (M. McCarthy, 1963)

Also used of domestic pets.

perform² to indulge in sexual activity
Normally heterosexual, of a male:
> You see ... he can perform, or he wants to, anyway he does. (Amis, 1978)

Whence the *performer*:
> ... the writer or artist ... is a better performer in love's lists than the navvy. (F. Harris, 1925)

Also of homosexuality and sexual deviation.

period¹ the time of menstruation
Shortened form of MONTHLY PERIOD of menstrual flow:
> 'Next Monday?' asks Howard. 'No good,' says Flora. 'That's my period.' (Bradbury, 1975)

period² old and dilapidated
Literally, a passage of time, but for this attributive use the estate agent is unlikely to go into historical detail, having given the impression that the property is venerable:
> Impressive stone-built period house (available for the first time in 50 years). Ideal for renovation. (*Western Daily Press*, May 1981)

periodic rest a term in prison
Usually of a habitual criminal. The phrase was used of the incarceration of Jimmy Hoffa, the former boss of the Teamsters' Union, who was jailed through the efforts of Robert Kennedy and released by Richard Nixon in 1971.

permissive less constrained by custom in personal conduct
Formerly meaning not obligatory, and then relaxed or lenient, as in the British *permissive society* resulting in part from reforms initiated by Roy Jenkins in the 1960s, which decriminalized acts of homosexual behaviour between consenting adults and generally led to a less censorious attitude to promiscuity.

person the male genitalia
A shortened form of *personal parts*, which also describes the vagina. Specifically of the penis, shortened to PERCY, punning on the male name.

person of/with someone having a particular characteristic
Used in much the same way as PEOPLE OF/WITH. Thus a *person of colour* is a black person, and a *person with AIDS* becomes a *PWA*, an abbreviation not usually accorded to the victims of other diseases. To avoid mentioning sex, the bedroom, or unmarried copulation we have to turn to an American circumlocutory bureaucrat:
> At the other end of the scale, the US Census Bureau came up with 'Person of the opposite sex sharing living quarters'. As an introduction it seemed a mite unromantic. (Whicker, 1982—he was pondering how to describe his mistress)

persona non grata someone caught spying
Literally, any unwelcome person, but used specifically of a diplomat accused of spying on a host nation. Sometimes abbreviated to *PNG*, and forming an unusual verb:

They're already PNG'd, and they're going
on the next Pan Am. (Clancy, 1988—two
spies with diplomatic status were leaving
the country)

personal assistant a secretary
The use once enhanced the status of the
employer and the salary of the employee.
Sometimes shortened to *assistant*:
> ...two remarkably pretty girls, dark-
> haired, upright of carriage, secretaries
> perhaps, assistants rather. (Amis, 1988)

personal correction flogging
As practised in 19th-century English boarding
schools by even so reputedly enlightened a
pedagogue as Thomas Arnold:
> [Dr Arnold] was particularly disgusted by
> the view that 'personal correction', as he
> phrased it, was an insult or degradation to
> the boy on whom it was inflicted.
> (Strachey, 1918)

personal hygiene the paraphernalia of
menstruation
Hygiene originally meant knowledge and practice that relates to the maintenance of health,
and menstruation is not an illness but a
natural process. Also, of containers in lavatories for the disposal of towels and tampons, as
feminine hygiene.

personal hygiene station a lavatory on a
spacecraft
Not just for menstruating women.

personal parts see PERSON

personal relations sexual activity with
another
In literal terms you have *personal relations* with
everyone you meet. Of copulation:
> Personal relations, as they used to say. But
> what's personal about relations?...Two
> victims sharing groins. (Bradbury, 1965)
And of homosexuality:
> Burgess had ample opportunity to indulge
> his fetish for 'personal relations' under
> cover of the rigidly enforced nightly
> blackout. (Boyle, 1979)

personal representatives those who administer the estate of a person who dies
intestate or without a living executor
The *person* whom they supposedly *represent* is
dead.

personal services extramarital sexual activity
The term is often used by prostitutes:
> Recruiting 'a lady of my acquaintance' for
> personal and espionage services...(Boyle,
> 1979)

personality a nonentity
Literally, the fact of being a person, with
individual characteristics. Jargon of the entertainment industry:
> He wouldn't allow the *TV Times* to
> describe him as a TV personality.
> That's just for jokeless comics wishing
> they could sing and dance. (Deighton,
> 1972)

persuade to compel through violence or
threats
Literally, to convince by argument:
> No less than 260 of our illustrious
> legislators are vulnerable to KGB
> 'persuasion'. (*Private Eye*, 1981, suggesting
> that British legislators are not immune to
> human frailties)

persuader a weapon
Criminal jargon:
> ...pistols, whips, blackjacks, lengths of
> rubber hose called persuaders...(Lacey,
> 1986)

pet¹ to caress physically during courtship
Probably from the stroking of the domestic
animal:
> ...held in his gentle brutal mitts for a
> petting session. (Ustinov, 1971)

pet² *American* a mistress
The imagery is of the domestic animal kept
for its owner's pleasure, or pleasuring:
> Cynical as a Park Avenue pet after her
> butter and egg man goes home. (Chandler,
> 1958)

peter *mainly American* the penis
One of the common male names for the penis
and not, as has been suggested, from petard, a
mine:
> 'Twas the peter of Paul the Apostle.
> (*Playboy's Book of Limericks*)

petit ami the partner of a male homosexual playing the female role
Less common linguistically than PETITE AMIE:
> Your *petit ami* was calling me a horrid baggy
> little man. (Sharpe, 1977)

petite very small
Not merely describing a young girl. Jargon of
the garment trade.

petite amie a mistress
The little female friend but not normally or
necessarily French. Also as *petite femme*, which
is not a comment on her size:
> Time the *petite femme* got herself into a
> *negligée*. (N. Mitford, 1945)

petrified *American* drunk

Showing no sign of movement, as if turned into stone. The imagery is the same as the common STONED.

petticoat dominated by a female

For the Victorians a *petticoat* was a female, without expressly sexual overtones:

I can safely say here there is not a *petticoat* in the whole history. (Haggard, 1885)

It is not necessary to dilate further to sufferers on what is meant by *petticoat government*:

Adair's idea of 'petticoat government' included the power of the Women's Council of the Cherokee. (P. G. Allen, 1992)

petting-stone *obsolete Northern England* a stone at the church gate at which a bride supposedly renounced her ill humours

Such were unfortunately to be found only in Northumberland and Durham. A bride, after leaving the marriage service, had to jump, stride, or be carried across the stone. If she failed to do so, the marriage was doomed. The ritual was later commuted for a cash payment before being abandoned:

There was a 'petting-stone' for the bride to jump over. (*Durham Tracts*, 1893, quoted in *EDD*)

petty house see LITTLE HOUSE

phantom *American* a person paid while not working or a nonexistent employee whose wage is drawn by another

The victim is usually a public-sector employer. Either the person named on the payroll exists but, as a friend of a politician or a supervisor, gets paid while not working; or the payroll numbers are inflated by the name of a person who has no connection with the enterprise or does not exist, with someone stealing the wages. See also TWIN-TRACKING.

pharmaceuticals illicit narcotics

Usually carried personally, as with aspirins or toothpaste:

... whom Caryn still saw, but only as a matter of form and pharmaceuticals. (M. Thomas, 1982—she obtained her supply from him)

pharmacy a private store of illegal narcotics

Literally, a place where drugs are dispensed:

... Barney convoying personal pharmacies through airports. (M. Thomas, 1980)

phoenix seeking to avoid the payment of liabilities

Usually in the phrase *phoenix company* which, like the fabulous bird, arises from the ashes of a receivership or liquidation with a different name but the same proprietor(s), the same assets, and a trail of unpaid suppliers:

James O'Donoghue of the Serious Fraud Office said: 'These firms are cropping up all over the place. A lot of them are phoenix companies: one gets closed down and two or three more open up.' (*Daily Telegraph*, 22 March 1997—the companies were engaged in conning the public into buying whisky in cask as a supposed investment)

physic a laxative

Literally, any medical treatment:

The physic will clean him out real good. (L. Armstrong, 1955)

See also NIGHT PHYSIC.

physical involvement a sexual relationship

Not just shaking hands, which is all the words might imply:

Her solicitors have been instructed to sue any hack who dares to suggest a physical involvement. (*Private Eye*, March, 1981)

pick¹ to steal

OED notes a use in 1300, which makes it one of the oldest euphemisms in the language, and in regular use since then:

A charge of picking and unlawfully intermitting with his neighbour's goods. (Hector, 1876)

To *pick a pocket* is explicit, and we are still plagued with *pickpockets* who steal articles from our clothing:

I told him my intentions, but he was not satisfied, and said, 'Do you know, I should as soon have thought of picking a pocket, as doing so'. (J. Boswell, 1773—Johnson had been vexed at his companion's riding ahead)

The obsolete forms of *pickle* and the Scottish *pike* also meant to steal:

Ye pykit your mother's pouch o' twalpennies. (W. Scott, 1818—a *twal-penny* was a shilling)

pick² *obsolete* to give premature birth

Of animals, from the dialect meaning, to throw:

... produces a calf prematurely ... in local phrase, 'picks her cau'f'. (Atkinson, 1891)

pick a daisy to urinate

A punning female use, perhaps from the bending down and the *daisy*, or chamber pot, so called from the common floral decorative motif of the rim. To *pick a pea* punned with less subtlety. To *pick a rose* brought to mind a nozzle producing a fine spray. These, and other flowers, might also be *gathered*, *plucked*, or *pulled* by a woman wishing to urinate.

pick-me-up a drink of an intoxicant
Literally, a medicine taken as a tonic, whence
jokingly used of spirits:
> If I had any more of these pick-me-ups I'd
> be under the table. (Theroux, 1979)

pick off to kill
Choosing whom you aim at:
> Go ahead. You can pick him off. (Genet,
> 1969, in translation, writing of a killing)

pick up to acquire a sexual partner casually
Of either sex, often at a first meeting:
> Rachman continued to pick up other girls.
> (S. Green, 1979)

The person thus met is a *pick-up*:
> You don't think they make me look like a
> tart?...I'll go up the Broadway looking for
> pick-ups. (Theroux, 1976)

A *pick-up joint* is where such meeting may take
place, and often a haunt of prostitutes:
> This is a pick-up joint, after all. Singles
> come here hoping to bed a staffer from
> Kennedy's or Glens. (J. Patterson, 1999)

pick up a knife *obsolete* to fall off a horse
An object of shame in the days when most
people could ride. The pretence was that the
loss of your seat was intentional. Much
humorous use.

pick up a nail to contract gonorrhea
The discomfort felt by the male when urinating or undergoing a pre-penicillin cure was
akin to the lameness of a horse.

pickled drunk
The common culinary imagery but this time
also alluding to the preservation of anatomical specimens in alcohol:
> ...you were a bit pickled at the time and so
> not to be blamed for what you did.
> (Wodehouse, 1930—the action was to have
> knocked down a pedestrian while drunk
> and driven on, considered less
> reprehensible then than now)

pie-eyed drunk
Unable to focus rather than with eyes like
pies:
> Brother Yank doesn't believe in getting his
> nose in the trough before 10 p.m., by
> which time one and all are absolutely pie-
> eyed. (*Private Eye*, April 1981)

piece¹ a female viewed sexually by a
male
Literally, a part of something and a synonym
of BIT 1:
> The greatest little piece in the business,
> and for half a page in your rag—she'll do it.
> (Deighton, 1972)

More often as a *piece of arse* or *ass, crackling,
crumpet, goods,* or *skirt. Piece of buttered bun,
muslin, on a fork,* or *of trade* (a prostitute) are
obsolete. A *piece of gash, spare,* or *rump* is a
woman considered readily available for promiscuous copulation:
> I was day after day closeted with this choice
> piece of rump, and not so much as
> touching her, let alone squeezing or
> grappling. (Fraser, 1975)

A *piece on the side* is a mistress. A *piece of work* is
a smart or clever woman with other than
sexual attributes in male eyes.

piece² a handgun
Used of both cannons and personal weapons
since the 16th century, and of crossbows
before that. It is a shortened form of *fowling-
piece* or *carrying piece*:
> 'You carry a piece?' he asked suddenly. 'Oh
> no,' I said, 'I don't believe in violence.'
> (Sanders, 1980)
> A carrying piece has got but one business.
> That business is killing. (Vanderhaeghe,
> 1997)

piece of the action a share in the proceeds or enjoyment of vice, illegality, or
any taboo activity
Usually prostitution, narcotics, or gambling.
Occasionally also of someone trying to benefit
from the enterprise or initiative of another:
> He has claimed a piece of the action in the
> video production of operas at Covent
> Garden. (*Private Eye*, May 1981)
See also ACTION 1.

piece off *American* to bribe
From the actual or figurative peeling of bills
from a bankroll, to buy silence or a favour,
and especially of bribing a foreman to give
you a job in return for part of your wage.

pig a police officer
An ancient form of abuse noted by Grose. *Pig-
feet* is less common but no less offensive:
> ...they'd tell the pig-feet if they came
> asking around. (Lyall, 1982)

pig's ear a receptacle for urine on the
bridge of a ship
Placed so that a sailor on watch had no need
to leave his post, and from the shape rather
than the obsolete Scottish *pig,* a pot for urine:
> Into my putrid channel
> At night each wifie tooms her pig. (Ogg,
> 1873—to *toom* is to empty)
Whence the expression *in a pig's ear,* meaning
certainly not:
> You're as pure as an angel you are, in a
> pig's ear as if you'd never seen the inside of
> a man's bedroom. (Atwood, 1996)

pigeon the dupe of a criminal

Venerable enough to be in Grose but still modern criminal use. The *pigeon-drop* is the trick where the victim pays money to thieves for a share in a bogus bankroll which they profess to have found. Whence, in America, to *pigeon* is to steal, as the voracious birds do. See also STOOL PIGEON.

piggyback to use another's reputation for your financial or social ends

Apart from the basic meaning, a *piggyback* is a ride given to a child on the back of an adult:
    You're doing me the very same way. You're piggybacking. (Theroux, 1978)

pigment black skin colour

Literally, a substance providing colour, without which we would all be albinos:
    And that's your fate too, Henry. He's makin' good use of your pigment. (Anonymous, 1996—the black Henry was supporting a white candidate)

pile into (of a male) to copulate with

Literally, to get actively involved. We see also the common violent and penetrating imagery:
    I'm 'bout worn out pilin' inter that li'l darlin'. (Fraser, 1971)

piled with French velvet *obsolete* infected with syphilis

A complex pun on the *pile* of shorn cloth and the FRENCH ACHE:
    Thou art piled, for a French velvet. (Shakespeare, *Measure for Measure*)
See also FRENCH.

pill¹ *obsolete* the penis

This Scottish/northern English use, from Norwegian dialect, survives in the word *pillock*, which is commonly used figuratively (and usually in ignorance) as a mild insult.

pill² (the) a contraceptive taken orally by females

Not just any medicament prepared for swallowing:
    In the pre-pill world of our youth
    . . . (Bradbury, 1976)
Whence *on the pill*, taking such contraceptive regularly and by implication able to copulate without impregnation.

pill³ *obsolete* to blackball from membership of a club

From the slang meaning, a ball:
    After someone he had put up for the Kildare Street Club had been pilled, he never entered the doors of the Club again. (Fingall, 1977—the Kildare Street Club in Dublin was habituated by the Protestant gentry, especially prior to 1914)

pillow partner a person with whom you copulate

Of either sex, but not a spouse:
    I can usually have the use of a native pillow partner. (Fraser, 1971)

pills the testicles

From *pill*, a ball, rather than from likeness to medical tablets, and see BALLS.

pin the penis

Of the same tendency as PRICK but much less common.

pin-up an erotic picture

Or its subject. In the Second World War titillating and sometimes crude pictures of women were displayed in barrack-rooms etc. using drawing-pins. The same description is now also given to representations of males similarly displayed in offices etc., and to those pictured.

pinch¹ to steal

Literally, to nip between the fingers:
    He had spent most of his life in clink for pinching anything from a roll of linoleum to a hurricane lamp. (Bogarde, 1972)

pinch² to arrest

From the grasping of the subject:
    He got acquitted for that there note after he had me 'pinched'. (Mayhew, 1851)
In American use a *pinch* is also an arrest:
    Maybe he knows something that could hang a pinch on her. (Chandler, 1958)

pine overcoat a coffin

Accorded, it would seem, to those who die of violence rather than naturally. See also WOODEN BOX.

ping-ponging passing a rich client from one specialist to another

A medical version of the long rallies in table tennis.

pink pound the purchasing power of homosexuals

A version of the coloured currencies which trade at a rate outside that dictated by the open market, of which the European agricultural *green pound*, reflecting the distortions and intricacies of the Common Agricultural Policy, is an example. The *pink* is from the traditional colour of the boudoir, and the usage reflects the higher spending power of those without families to support:
    The pink pound is going from strength to strength. (*Daily Telegraph*, 11 March 1995)

pink slip *American* a notice of dismissal

If that is the message, the paper on which it is figuratively written is *pink*, whatever the colour. Less often referring to retirement:

> I'm forty-seven hours and forty-five minutes from owning my own pink slip. (Wambaugh, 1983—he was about to retire)

To be *pink-slipped* is to be summarily dismissed:

> The first month, eleven of the twenty-three staffers were pink-slipped. (Sohmer, 1988)

pint (the) beer or stout
The traditional imperial measurement:
> Some have given up the pint entirely. (McCourt, 1999—and not referring to those who have adopted metrication)

pioneer¹ a soldier sent to intervene in a foreign war
Originally, one who clears the way for his own following troops, although in the Second World War the British *Pioneer Corps* usually handed that privilege to the infantry or Royal Engineers:
> China had sent several fresh brigades of 'volunteers' and 'pioneers' into the fray. (Ustinov, 1966)

pioneer² *Irish* a person who has forsworn intoxicants
Showing the way to others.

pipe an illegal narcotic
The instrument used for ingestion:
> 'He's a junkie?' 'Likes a pipe, I'm told.' (Katzenbach, 1995)

piran *Cornish* drunk
Cornwall was the county where tin was mined from Roman times until recently:
> St Piran is the patron saint of tinners, popularly supposed to have died drunk. (*EDD*)

piss (the) an intoxicant
Usually beer, because of the consequent urination:
> You should stay off the piss for a while. (Winton, 1994)

See also ON THE PISS.

piss pins and needles (of a male) to be infected with gonorrhea
It refers to the sensation while urinating. Also as *piss pure cream*. The obsolete *piss your tallow* was to ejaculate before vaginal entry:
> Send me a cool rut-time, Jove, or who can blame me to piss my tallow? (Shakespeare, *The Merry Wives of Windsor*)

pissed drunk
Referring to the need to dispose of beer drunk to excess, but also of being drunk on wine or spirits:

> I am not introspectively drunk. I am merely pissed. (Sharpe, 1977)

The American *pissed* can also, like the British *pissed off*, mean dejected:
> The thing I remember was that Ritchie was so pissed. (R. N. Patterson, 1996—the amorous Ritchie's disaffection was not caused by drink but by the unplanned absence of his wife)

Occasionally in America shortened to *P.O.*:
> I think the president was very angry...in fact royally P.O.'d might be a very good word for it. (*Washington Post*, March, 1987, quoting Maureen Regan)

pistol *obsolete* the penis
Of obvious imagery. Whence Shakespeare's punning character.

pit-stop an occasion for leaving company for a short taboo activity
Normally the need is for urination. With somewhat inverted logic, the derivation is from the replenishment and repair of a car during a race. Less often, but more logically, the desire is to ingest narcotics:
> The hiatus allowed the control-room crew to...make necessary pit-stops. (Clancy, 1989)
> She had obviously just made a pit stop in the Ladies, and a few tiny specks of white dust still clung to her upper lip. (Pérez-Réverté in translation, 1994)

place a lavatory
Only heard in the male enquiry *Where's the place?* in a restaurant or similar establishment.

place-man a spy
Originally, someone who holds a responsible *place* in government service. In this use punning on having been *placed* there by his masters:
> Soviet officials had access to a variety of French political and military secrets through experienced 'place men' such as Burgess's associate. (Boyle, 1979)

place of correction *obsolete* a prison
Named for an honest, but usually unfulfilled, aspiration:
> Your places of correction could be as quiet as Chelsea Hospital. (Ustinov, 1971)

place of ill fame a brothel
A less common variant of a HOUSE 2:
> The Red house was a place of ill-fame—a bawdy house to put it plain. (Norfolk, 1991)

place of safety an inhumane prison
Himmler's favoured term for his concentration camps.

planned unexpected and unwelcome
A common usage when we prefer not to
admit that we have been wrong or lacking in
foresight:

> Surprise and mobility, coupled with
> overwhelming air support, turned 'planned
> withdrawals' into creeping rout. (Boyle,
> 1979)

The appearance of *as planned* in any corporate
statement should always be greeted with
scepticism and invite further enquiry.

planned parenthood *American* the induced abortion of a foetus
The antithesis of *planning*, it might seem:

> A rash of violence and killings at abortion
> centres throughout the United States (or
> Planned Parenthood Clinics as they are
> delicately called). (A. Waugh in *Daily
> Telegraph*, 14 January 1995)

planned termination the induced abortion of a foetus
Performed under medical conditions. Less
often it may refer to a suicide.

planning the restriction of development
A reactive rather than proactive process
seeking to regulate the use of land and
buildings, carried out by *planning officials* or
planners.

plant[1] to bury a corpse
The imagery of horticulture, without the
crop:

> Y'wouldn't want to be planted without
> ceremony. Why not put Baptist? (Manning,
> 1962)

plant[2] falsely to place incriminating evidence
Again with horticultural imagery:

> With the evidence you'd arranged for him
> to find... Or to put it bluntly, planted.
> (Crisp, 1982)

plant[3] an item introduced editorially into
a periodical for promotional or political
purposes
Journalistic jargon. The story is not necessarily false or misleading.

plant the books *obsolete* to cheat at cards
The *books* were the playing cards and the
planting was arranging the deck before dealing.

plasma an intoxicant
Literally, the substance in the blood in which
other elements are suspended:

> And speaking of the old nasty—it's past
> noon and you could use some plasma.
> (Sanders, 1985)

plastered drunk
Literally, covered with a substance that sticks
to a surface, as does the smell of intoxicants,
but perhaps only referring to the immobility
of a limb in plaster:

> You could tell by his eyes that he was
> plastered to the hairline. (Chandler, 1953)

plastic chicken circuit (the) dinners organized by institutions
Usually on an annual basis with speeches and
obligatory attendance for some functionaries.
As Chamberlain's Second Law teaches us,
'Everything tastes more or less like chicken',
especially in the world of mass catering:

> He hit the plastic chicken circuit as
> president of the Confederation of British
> Industry. (*Daily Telegraph*, 2 March 2000)

plater a person who engages in fellatio on
another
Often a prostitute. From the concept of eating
MEAT, presumably ham, as fellatio is also
known in those circles as a *plate of ham*.

play to indulge in sexual activity
The imagery of SPORT:

> As well a woman with an eunuch play'd
> As with a woman. (Shakespeare, *Antony and
> Cleopatra*)

A *play house* was a brothel, not a theatre. See
also MAKE A PLAY FOR. There are many other
compounds and phrases referring to copulation, masturbation, or homosexual activity,
exemplified by the entries which follow.

play around to copulate casually
Usually with more than a single regular
partner:

> Not with the chauffeur... I don't have to
> dig down that far if I want to play around.
> (Chandler, 1939)

play at hot cockles (of a female) to masturbate
The *cockles* are the vulva.

play away to commit adultery
Punning on the team game played on the
opponents' ground:

> His work... gave him ample opportunity to
> play away from home. (N. Evans, 1998—
> and not of a professional footballer)

play games to be promiscuous
Usually of a woman, with a single extramarital partner:

> She was playing games with Vannier.
> (Chandler, 1943)

play hookie to commit adultery
Of either sex, with the imagery of playing
truant from school:

The safest racket in the world is to rob a married man or woman who is playing hookie. (Lavine, 1930)

play in the hay to copulate
But not necessarily al fresco; and see also IN THE HAY:
> If every girl who's ready to play in the hay was to get married, we'd have damned few spinsters. (Fraser, 1969)

play mothers and fathers to copulate
Usually outside marriage. Also as *play mummies and daddies* or *mums and dads*:
> And at a moment like this my wife has to play mothers and fathers with that bastard. (C. Forbes, 1985)
> He'll probably want to play mummies and daddies too. (Pérez-Réverté in translation, 1994—a man asked a woman to come to his apartment on the pretext of talking business)

play on your back (of a woman) to copulate
See ON YOUR BACK:
> Lulls him while she playeth on her back. (Shakespeare, *Titus Andronicus*)

play Onan to withdraw before ejaculation
A method of preventing impregnation; and see ONANISM;
> Very soon I played ONAN and like the biblical hero 'spilt my seed upon the ground'. (F. Harris, 1925)

play the ace against the jack to copulate
The *ace* is a vulgarism for the vagina and the JACK 1 is the penis, the whole punning on a game of cards.

play the beast with two backs to copulate
See BEAST WITH TWO BACKS.

play the field to be sexually promiscuous
Of either sex, from betting on several runners in the same race:
> You've had enough of playing the field so now you're looking for a young, beautiful and preferably well-born virgin. (P. D. James, 1994)

play the goat (of a male) to be promiscuous
But to *play the giddy goat* means merely to act stupidly.

play the organ to copulate or masturbate
Of either sex, punning on the musical instrument; and see ORGAN.

play the pink oboe to engage in sodomy or be a male homosexual
The *pink* is from the colour of the boudoir and the vulgar *oboe* is a penis. Also as *play the skin flute*:
> He looks like a guy who plays the skin flute. (Sanders, 1984)

play tricks to copulate with other than your regular sexual partner
Usually of a female, punning perhaps on the prostitute's jargon TRICK.

play with to excite sexually
Usually heterosexually. To *play with yourself* is to masturbate:
> At the time we were playing with ourselves, I kept thinking of Mary's hot slit. (F. Harris, 1925)
etc.

play a card to deploy an argument based on prejudice or emotion
See CARD 2. The suit is usually specified:
> To claim to speak for all the black individuals in this country is to patronize, stereotype and 'play the race card'. (*Daily Telegraph*, 24 April 1997)

play-fellow a sexual partner
Of either sex, but not your spouse:
> To seek her as bed-fellow,
> In marriage pleasures play-fellow. (Shakespeare, *Pericles*)
Also as *playmate*.

play with a full deck to be mentally alert
Euphemistic only in the negative:
> The writer of that piece of filth is obviously not playing with a full deck. (Sanders, 1992)
And see FIFTY CARDS IN THE PACK.

playboy *obsolete* the devil
Not the modern wealthy hedonist:
> The devil sitting cheek be jowl with him in his own chimbley corner...an' himself an' the playboy sloughed out o' the same pipe. (MacManus, 1898—to *slough* was to swallow)

player *American* a non-critical and unthinking supporter
A shortened form of TEAM PLAYER:
> Bill Clinton had appointed him to the Board of Arkansas Private Investigators. He was a player. He knew how to keep his mouth shut, too. (Evans-Pritchard, 1997)

please yourself on *obsolete* (of a male) to copulate with
In the days when females were not meant to take much pleasure in it:
> Perhaps they will please themselves upon her. (Shakespeare, *Pericles*)

pleasure to copulate with
Normally, of the male, who was presumably enjoying rather than conferring *pleasure*:
> Three doe-eyed, heavy hipped women pleasuring one man. (Masters, 1976)

Pleasures may be copulation:
> ...afternoon pleasures are exchanged for a few days' work. (B. Forbes, 1972—a producer was casting female roles in a film)

Pleasuring can be copulation or masturbation by either sex:
> Not the most joyous pleasuring I have taken part in... (Fraser, 1969)

A *pleasure house* is a brothel:
> It was a pleasure house, where those rich ofay (white) business men and planters would come. (L. Armstrong, 1955)

pledge (the) an undertaking never to drink intoxicants
Signed, taken, kept, or *broken* by those who have, usually as a member of a church, forsworn the 'demon drink':
> He felt the Band of Hope had been worthwhile when some of the old boys came to see him during a holiday in the village. It warmed his heart to be told 'I've kept the pledge'. (Tyrrell, 1973)

plink to shoot
Onomatopoeic, from a strip comic:
> The matter had started with a drive-by shooting—fundamentalists plinking at Alevis in a café. (Theroux, 1995)

plod a policeman
At second remove from the measured gait when one such might be seen patrolling on foot, perhaps via *Mr Plod*, Enid Blyton's character and Noddy's friend:
> Why hadn't it been given straight to us? Why are the... 'plods' involved? (Seymour, 1989—an investigator from the narcotics squad was denigrating the local police)
> I was as sure as can be that Mr Plod would 'pull' that McLaren F1 sooner or later, even though we were constantly being overtaken by common or garden Fords and Vauxhalls. (*Daily Telegraph*, 19 August 1995—the McLaren F1 is a very fast and sporty car)

plotcock *obsolete* the devil
To *plot* was to 'scald in boiling water' in northern English and Scottish dialect, as a chicken before plucking, and the *cock* was a symbol of the occult powers:
> Seven times does her prayers backwards pray,
> Till Plotcock comes with lumps of Lapland clay. (A. Ramsay, 1800—all genuine witches pray backwards, and Lapland was

their fabled homeland before being taken over by Father Christmas)

plough¹ (of a male) to copulate with
It puns on the entry of the share into the furrow and the chance of issue:
> He plough'd and she crop'd. (Shakespeare, *Antony and Cleopatra*)

plough² to fail a candidate in an examination
Of uncertain origin. Possibly the American *plowed*, drunk, comes from the inability of the subject to pass a test of sobriety.

plough under *American* needlessly to cause the death of
The way a farmer disposes of an unwanted crop. Wendell Willkie, opposing Roosevelt's third term as President, appealed to isolationists and pacifists in the electorate by accusing Roosevelt of being a warmonger, determined to 'plow under every fourth American boy'. Because Willkie lost, we forget how close he came to winning.

ploughman's(a) *British* bread and cheese
A shortened form of *ploughman's lunch*, from a campaign initiated on the part of cheesemakers to promote the consumption of cheese in pubs. Thereafter innkeepers were progressively able to charge more for what had previously been a cheap snack, especially if garnished by a lettuce leaf and a slice of tomato:
> ...the cricket pitch being watered, ploughman's lunches being served in the Barley Mow... (*Daily Telegraph*, 30 July 1994)

pluck (of a male) to copulate with
DAS says 'Rhyming euphem. for the taboo "fuck"'. However, to *pluck a rose* was to copulate with a female virgin, and the imagery may come from the gathering of a flower.

plucked *obsolete British* not awarded a degree at a graduation ceremony
In universities an unpaid tradesman had the right to pluck the gown of the chancellor awarding the degree if he were owed money by the candidate. The degree would not then be conferred until the debt had been paid.

plucked from us unexpectedly or prematurely dead
With floral imagery, the deity being credited with choosing the choicest blooms:
> The most heavenly girl in the whole world has been plucked from us. (Mailer, 1965)

plug¹ to kill by shooting

Literally, to stop a hole, which I suppose the bullet may do, after making it:

> I'd plug you as soon as I'd strike a match. (Chandler, 1943)

plug² to have penetrative sex with

Heterosexual or homosexual:

> That's why I plugged the girl, even after she puked. (Turow, 1996)
> There was a high private pleasure in plugging a Nazi...she was loose...as if this was finally her natural act. (Mailer, 1965—she was sodomized)

plug³ to give unwarranted publicity to

Disk jockeys thus advertise popular music on radio etc., sometimes in return for a bribe. Also as a noun.

Plum Book (the) *American* a list of the patronage at the disposal of an incoming president

An election campaign can only be financed if there is an expectation of supporters receiving a success fee, usually in the form of a *plum*, or desirable, even if quite unsuitable, post:

> Some 3,000 jobs are annotated in Washington's notorious Plum Book, a compilation of juicy positions ripe for picking. (Seitz, 1998)

plum(p) pudding club see IN THE CLUB

plumb (of a male) to copulate with

Literally, to sound a depth:

> There once was a plumber of Leigh
> Who was plumbing a girl by the sea.
> (vulgar limerick)

plumber *American* a presidential staff member acting improperly

His function, after the Ellsberg disclosures in 1971, was to trace or stop any LEAK 2:

> Young and Krogh were later dubbed the Plumbers, because they were assigned to stop news leaks. (Colodny and Gettlin, 1991, reporting on the cross-examination of Admiral Welander on 22 December 1976)

plumbing¹ a lavatory

Referring to the ancillary piping:

> Unless you've shifted the plumbing around here, I can find it. (M. McCarthy, 1963)

plumbing² the parts of the body concerned with urination and defecation

A genteel and rather coy use, likening the body to an aspect of domestic construction:

> Helena had known about sex from a very early age but treated it as a joke like what she called her plumbing. (M. McCarthy, 1963)

pocket to steal

Normally of trifles small enough to go into it, without premeditation but now also of embezzlement. See also POUCH.

pocket job (a) male masturbation

By himself or another. Also as *pocket pool* or, in Britain, *pocket billiards*, from the *pockets*, balls, and cue used in the game:

> ...reduced to performing pocket jobs. (Styron, 1976)
> You're playing with yourself. Lay off the pocket pool. (Theroux, 1978).

Pocket the red is a vulgarism meaning to copulate.

poetic truth lies

A translation of an expression used by Goebbels, who was appointed Minister of Advertising by Hitler in 1933:

> Convenient lies ('poetic truths') as he called them. (Trevor-Roper, 1977)

point Percy at the porcelain (of a male) to urinate

The *porcelain* is the material of the urinal; and see PERCY.

pointy head an intellectual

Derogatory use by those less favoured:

> ...all he did was prance around in white regalia, set fire to crosses, wind up the liberal pointy heads. (Evans-Pritchard, 1987—he was in the Ku Klux Klan)

poison a preferred intoxicant

A jocular reference to the possible harmful effects:

> 'What's your poison?' Dundridge said he'd have a gin and tonic. (Sharpe, 1975)

poison pill the deliberate assumption of corporate liabilities to deter or repel an unwanted predator

A tactic of the defended bid, with success perhaps leaving a sour taste in the mouth and failure a similar discomfort for the winner:

> 'Poison pill' meant that AbCom would issue a dilative new stock...and that would double or triple the cost of AbCom to an unfriendly enquirer. (M. Thomas, 1985)

poke¹ (the) *obsolete* summary dismissal from employment

Punning on the meaning to *push*, and a *poke* is also a sack, as in the phrase *buy a pig in a poke*, to be deceived or cheated:

> He's gi'en him t'poke. (*Leeds Mercury Supplement*, April 1896, quoted in *EDD*)

poke² (of a male) to copulate with

The common imagery:

Don't get to poke too many women too
often. (Bradbury, 1976)
A *poke* is either a single act of copulation:
Nice trouble-free way of victualling your
girl-friend between pokes. (Amis, 1978)
or the female participant, as seen by the male.
Some homosexual use; and the American
pogey bait, candy, was the 'inducement held
out by old sailors for the favours of fat-
cheeked smooth-bottomed young cabin boys'
(Styron, 1976).

poke³ a prison
Possibly from the meaning sack, and as *pokey*:
He just got out of poke three months ago.
(Sanders, 1970)
'Another night in the pokey,' forecast
Maddison gloomily. (L. Thomas, 1996—Mrs
Maddison had assaulted a policeman)

pole an erect penis
An obvious vulgarism. In archaic use, to *pole*
was to copulate with, of a male.

police action a war
First noted in September 1948, when the
fledgling Indian state conquered Hyderabad:
In a remarkably successful manoeuvre
against Hyderabad's state forces
(codenamed 'Operation Polo' and referred
to euphemistically as 'police action'),
Indian troops destroyed their rivals within
four days. (French, 1997)
The phrase became notorious in the Korean
War:
Truman agreed with a reporter who asked
'Would it be correct to call it a police action
under the United Nations?' This was a
phrase which would later haunt Truman.
(M. Hastings, 1987)

polish the mahogany to urinate
The allusion is to the wooden lavatory seat. I
thought this was obsolete until I heard it on
television in February 1994.

political and social order internal repression
The Brazilian version of familiar autocratic
language:
The Department of Political and Social
order, a bland title for the administration
of terror and thumbscrews. (Simon, 1979)

political change a humiliating defeat
Kissinger's contemporary description of the
conquest of South Vietnam by the North and
the final American withdrawal.

political (re-)education the arbitrary imprisonment of dissidents
A Communist phrase to describe and justify
internal repression.

political engineering *American* using government patronage to engender political support
Specifically, describing awarding defence pro-
curement projects to provide work in as many
congressional districts as possible, regardless
of expense or efficiency.

politically correct conforming in behaviour or language to dogmatic opinions
The subject is wittily and provocatively
examined in *The Official Politically Correct
Dictionary and Handbook* (Beard and Cerf,
1992). For those who espouse *political correctness*, every topic the subject of taboo must be
referred to by euphemism or circumlocution,
or ignored, while the conduct of its devotees
can rival fascism in its rigour:
Many men now consider themselves to be
the victims of political correctness and
pluralism that leaves them at a
disadvantage in competition for work.
(*Independent*, 21 July 1991)
Sometimes shortened to *PC*:
PC holds that Western civilization is the
product of racial and sexual hierarchies
which should be unseated. (*Sunday
Telegraph*, 21 July 1991)

pollute to affect in a taboo manner
Literally, to corrupt or make dirty. To *pollute
yourself* is to masturbate, while to *pollute* a
female was to copulate with her extramaritally. *Polluted* may describe being drunk or
under illegal narcotic influence.

polygraph a lie detector
Literally, a machine giving a number of
simultaneous read-outs:
What we used to call a lie detector, sir. A
polygraph. (le Carré, 1989)

pony an act of defecation
Rhyming slang on *pony and trap*, a crap. Some
figurative use:
The voice must have realized I was giving
him a lot of old pony. (McNab, 1993—he was
lying during interrogation by the Iraqis)

poodle a sycophant
Literally, a type of lapdog:
Last week Jacques Chirac nominated Jean-
Claude Trichet...who has a long line of
form as a trained poodle. (*Daily Telegraph*,
12 November 1997—the nomination was
as head of a European bank where, as a
good European, he could promote French
interests)

poontang *American* casual copulation
A corruption of the French *putain*, a prostitute, and formerly used in the Southern states

of copulation by a white male with a black female:

> A growin' Southern boy's got to have his poontang. (Styron, 1976)

Also, in the Second World War, as *poontan*:

> Weber from Company B says a carton [of cigarettes] will get you a whole load of poontan. (McCourt, 1999, writing about occupied Germany in the late 1940s)

poop¹ to defecate

A usage of the nursery and of domestic pets.

poop² to fart

Onomatopoeic and sometimes used figuratively as an insult:

> [King George VI's] equerries seem to be a collection of old poops. (Horne, 1994)

pooped drunk

Originally, flooded by the sea coming over the stern, but not only of sailors:

> ... seldom sober by seven and almost always pooped by eight. (Sharpe, 1979)

pooper-scooper a shovel for removing animal faeces from a public place

From POOP 1. The term is also a vulgarism associated with sodomy, and a *pooper-scooper* is an offensive name for a male homosexual.

poor-mouth to ignore or refer to in unfavourable terms

A more consistent practice than the occasional denigration implied when you BAD-MOUTH:

> Naturally the Chinese have always poormouthed the foreign-built railways' contribution to their economic well-being. (Faith, 1990)

poorly¹ very seriously ill

Hospital jargon, replacing the normal meaning, unwell, and seeking to comfort the family of the patient.

poorly² menstruating

Again unwell, and often in the phrase *my poorly time*.

pop¹ to ingest narcotics illegally

Either from *popping* them into your mouth as a pill or into vein by injection. Whence *popper*, such a pill or injection:

> The ammoniac aftersmell of poppers hung in the air. (M. Thomas, 1982)

pop² an act of copulation

Possibly from the sensation of orgasm, but more likely because *pop* can be a synonym of go, meaning a single occasion:

> Azalo figured she'd be lucky to get twenty bucks a pop. (Sanders, 1985—Azalo was a prostitute)

To *pop* is to copulate, of a male:

> Someone [the Candidate] popped at the 1984 convention. (Anonymous, 1996)

pop³ to pawn

Perhaps from *popping in* to effect the transaction with UNCLE:

> I had to pop the silver, you know what I mean. (Guinness, 1985)

And in the old song:

> Up and down the City Road,
> In and out the Eagle.
> That's the way the money goes.
> Pop goes the weasel.

The Eagle was a London public house of which a former landlord was the father of one of my aunts by marriage, a shameful connection of which other family members were long kept unaware. The *weasel* was the *weasel and stoat*, overcoat.

pop⁴ to kill

Causing another to POP OFF or from the sound of the gun?

> We don't pop people any more. We've learned from the Argentines. People just disappear. (Sanders, 1984)

pop off to die

Literally, in slang, to depart, rather than from a cork leaving a bottle, and usually of natural causes:

> Look here, Hugh, I'm afraid Percy has popped off. (Matthew, 1978—Percy the budgerigar had died)

pop the question to propose marriage

The question used to be asked by the male, and when *popped* related only to wedlock, in the days when there were still taboos about courtship and men were supposed to have honourable intentions:

> Just heard yesterday that my divorce comes on today so was elated and popped question to Dutch girl. (E. Waugh, July, 1936 in S. Hastings, 1994—he had in fact been divorced for some years but wished also to have a papal annulment)

pop your clogs to die

You would need your shoes no more:

> It's either join us or pop your clogs. (Fraser, 1983—he was to be killed if he refused to join the pirate crew)

popping up the daisies dead

The corpse is supposed to provide sustenance for the common churchyard wild flower. Some jocular use, even of those cremated.

popsy a woman available for casual copulation

Originally, and still used as, a term of endearment to a girl, whence an attractive young female. The euphemistic use is usually generic and not of prostitutes:

> ...enough popsy to satisfy an army. (Fraser, 1977)

population transfer forcible resettlement

Not the natural movements which take place on a surprising scale in a civilized country but the language used for the forcible uprooting of a racial group for political reasons, as practised by the Germans under Hitler, the Russians under Stalin, the South Africans under apartheid, etc.

porch climber¹ *American* a thief from houses

A convenient mode of access to an upstairs window:

> He was a two-bit porch climber with a few small terms on him. (Chandler, 1939)

porch-climber² an illegal narcotic

I suppose from the effect it has on those who ingest it:

> Even the ups give it a wide berth and pretend they do not know porch-climber is sold there. (Vanderhaeghe, 1997)

pork¹ *American* a Federal benefit diverted to local political purposes

From the richness of the meat:

> The prison library was in back of the building that was going to become the prison auto shop—at least that was the plan. More pork in someone's pocket was what I thought. (King, 1996)

The punning *pork chopper* receives a sinecure in return for past favours. And see PORK BARREL.

pork² the penis viewed sexually

The usual MEAT 2 imagery and as *pork sword*:

> I've known greater beauties, and a few that were just as partial to pork. (Fraser, 1982—the ladies were not gourmands)
> 'She isn't getting any.'...'Any what?' 'Cock. The old pork sword.' (B. Forbes, 1989)

pork³ (of a male) to copulate with

Putting the PORK 2 to work:

> Larren's porkin her and takin the money to keep her in style. (Turow, 1987)

pork-barrel diverting public funds for political advantage

The container in which the PORK 1 is delivered:

> It would be a pity if so many Conservative achievements...were to be lost to the pork-barrel demands of a single MP. (*Daily Telegraph*, 7 December 1996)

Also in America as a verb:

> America's production of space centres...symbolise[s] an ancient discipline which lies at the heart of politics here: pork-barrelling. (*Private Eye*, July, 1983)

pork pies lies

Rhyming slang. Also as *porkie pies* or *porkies*:

> 'You mean Susan's hairdresser?' Lucille asked. 'And Jack's porkpie.' (Anonymous, 1996—at issue was not Jack's hat but his veracity about his relationship with the hairdresser)
> There's nothing wrong with making people happy by telling a few porkies. (L. Thomas, 1996)

porridge *British* prison

Partridge suggests a pun on STIR but the dish is also a staple item of food in prisons.

porthole the anus

Male homosexual use:

> Pecker tracks in the porthole, didn't you say? (Turow, 1993, reporting scars from being sodomized)

positive militaristic and aggressive

How tyrants like to see and describe themselves:

> ...was in tune with Japan's increasingly aggressive or, to use the euphemistic Japanese term, 'positive' foreign policy. (Behr, 1989)

possess to copulate with

Historically the male *possessed* the female, despite the physical contradiction:

> I have bought the mansion of a love, But not possess'd it. (Shakespeare, *Romeo and Juliet*)

And explicitly:

> We find men who have violated the best principles of society, and ruined their fame and their fortune, that they might possess a woman of rank. (J. Boswell, 1791—Johnson had suggested that copulation with a duchess was more pleasurable than with a chambermaid)

post a letter to defecate

Punning on an excuse for absenting yourself from company and the process of defecation. In America as *mail a letter*.

postal *American* mentally unstable

The imagery escapes me:

> When someone goes berserk with a semi-automatic in a crowded diner, he is said to

have 'gone postal'. (*Sunday Telegraph*, 20 May 2000)

posterior(s) the buttocks
Originally, later in line, from which BEHIND: Her posterior, plump, smooth, and prominent. (Cleland, 1749)

posterior assault sodomy
An attack from the rear:
...putting upon view, for a fee, fictitious Sea-Creatures that others must bend down to see, becoming thereupon subject to posterior assault. (Pynchon, 1997, naming *unwise practices* which were to be found aboard a Sixth-rate vessel on a long voyage)

pot¹ to kill by shooting
Referring to hunting for the cooking *pot*, but now also used of attempts to kill or wound:
...wasn't anything much else to shoot at so I took to potting them. (Sharpe, 1978)
A *pot-shot* is one taken without premeditation.

pot² a habitual drunkard
The drinking vessel rather than the slang for a belly. Whence *pot valour*, drunken courage and, rarely, *potted*, drunk.
See also POT-WALLOPER.

pot³ a receptacle for urine
Literally, any container for liquids:
I had taught him to use a pot. (N. Mitford, 1960)
Also as the diminutive *po*:
Eeny-meeny, miney-mo,
Sit a........on a po.
When he's done, wipe his bum...(old rhyme)

pot⁴ marijuana
Either derived from the American Indian *potaguya* or from the container in which the leaves and stalks are cooked or brewed. The shortening of *pot liquor* to *pot* favours the latter:
...to graduate to student parties to smoke pot. (Bradbury, 1976)

pot hunter an egoist seeking public recognition
Not an archaeologist or drunkard but literally or figuratively after a *pot*, a cup or trophy given to a winner.

pot walloper *obsolete* a drunkard
To *wallop* was to boil hard as well as to beat, and the *pot* held the intoxicant. This was a pun on the granting of suffrage under the Reform Act of 1832 to any adult male householder who had *walloped his pot* (cooked food in his house) in a parish for a period of six months previously. Women may have

done the cooking but that did not entitle them to a vote.

potation an alcoholic drink
Literally, the act of drinking, whence anything drunk:
...returned next day only partially recovered from the potation that had celebrated the event. (Somerville and Ross, 1894)

potboiler a repetitive or facile work by an established artist or author
The hob on a fire was there to keep the *pot* on the *boil*, for use when required
Then, when I got in the swing of things and began turning out four potboilers a year...(Sanders, 1980)
To *keep the pot boiling* is to publish such work or republish what is already available in print:
I am glad that all these must have helped to keep the Graves pot boiling. (*Sunday Telegraph*, 5 November 1995, reviewing an edition of Robert Graves's *Collected Short Stories*)

Potomac fever *American* a desire to be elected to high Federal office
Not an ague caught from the river flowing through the nation's capital:
Baxter contracted a terminal case of Potomac Fever. He started to dream of the White House. (M. Thomas, 1980)

Potsdam *obsolete British* a prison for captured soldiers
Where the Kaiser had a palace. In the First World War capture was referred to as dining there with him:
...so this was 'Potsdam', this moist foul-smelling cell. (Grinnell-Milne, 1933)

potty¹ mad or eccentric
Perhaps from having *gone to pot* or using the same imagery as *crackpot*, meaning unwise or bizarre:
It was only a question of time before the goat-major would go stone potty. (F. Richards, 1936)

potty² a receptacle for urine
A nursery version of POT 3:
She's on the potty. (Goldman. 1984—a child was explaining why her mother could not come to the telephone)

pouch to steal
Originally Scottish but now widely used as a synonym of POCKET:
I had given Master Boy Scout a fair amount of money...doubtless he had merely pouched it. (B. Fergusson, 1945—he had paid a tribesman for help

behind the lines in Burma in the Second
World War)

pouff a male homosexual
Not from the English dialect meaning 'a big
stupid person' (*EDD*) but probably from the
exclamation, implying a lack of substance or
value. Also as *pooftah*:
> Don't tie the tapes under your chin... or
> they'll think you're a pouff. (D. Francis,
> 1978)
> If Prince Charles shows no interest, he *must*
> be a pooftah. (A. Waugh in *Private Eye*, July
> 1980)

As the novelist pointed out, the use of these
derogatory terms obliges us to use circumlocution when we describe a round footstool:
> ...sitting animatedly forward on what
> used to be called a pouf or pouffe but
> obviously couldn't be these days.
> (Amis, 1978)

pound (of a male) to copulate with
The common violent imagery:
> ...hoped the little bubblegummer had
> been well pounded by the piano-tuner so
> she could go...to the home for unwed
> mothers. (Wambaugh, 1975)

pound salt *American* go away and leave
me alone
A shortened form of *go pound salt up your ass*.
Less often as *pound sand*.

pourboire a bribe
Significantly more has to change hands than
would pay for a drink:
> And he'll need to make cash transfers to
> someplace...where government officials
> are not insulted by the offer of a small
> pourboire. (Sanders, 1977)

powder a narcotic taken illegally
In the form in which it is often marketed:
> Why would any fool use powder for
> pleasure when he can have a woman?
> (Clancy, 1989)

A *powdered lunch* is one where narcotics are
ingested illegally in addition to or instead of
food:
> 'Did you see him...wasted by lunch-time.'
> 'Liquid lunch.' 'Powdered lunch.' (Garland,
> 1996—see also WASTED)

You do not however have to be a drug addict if
you TAKE A POWDER.

powder room a lavatory for the exclusive
use of females
It used to be that part of a warship where the
gunpowder was stored. To minimize danger
from flashbacks, the size of the passage to the
gun deck was restricted and children were
used to pass the powder to the guns. Today

the *powder* is scented talc which women put
on their faces.

powder your nose[1] to go to the lavatory
A phrase normally used by females:
> Back in the Long Gallery some of the
> women went upstairs to 'powder their
> noses'. (N. Mitford, 1949)

powder your nose[2] to snort cocaine
Punning on POWDER and the visit to a
lavatory:
> 'I'm just going to powder my nose,' Potts
> said slyly. 'Coming?' (Boyd, 1998)

pox (the) syphilis
Literally, any disease that brings pustules on
the skin but, as Dr Johnson reminds us, 'This
is the sense when it has no epithet':
> I couldn't be sure she hadn't got the pox.
> (Archer, 1979)

prairie-dogging *American* unnecessarily
standing up to look over the partition of
a work station
The derivation is from the animal's behaviour
on emerging from its hole:
> There was lots of 'prairie-dogging' out of
> the cubes. (J. Patterson, 2000—the *cubes* are
> the workplaces in an open-plan office)

prairie oyster[1] the testicle of a calf
Eaten as a delicacy, especially in America:
> ...a Testicle Festival, which for a while
> enjoyed even greater popularity, except
> perhaps with the calves who supplied the
> food, euphemistically served as 'prairie-
> oysters'. (N. Evans, 1998)

prairie oyster[2] a pungent alcoholic drink
with a raw egg in it
Perhaps because the egg is swallowed whole,
as is an *oyster*. The American *prairie dew* is an
illegally distilled spirit.

pre-arrangement *American* the payment
for a funeral before death
Funeral jargon for selling burials and their
trappings to the living, especially those who
are morbid or lonely. Also as *pre-need*:
> The cemetery industry has found an
> answer to high cost through
> pre-arrangement. (J. Mitford, 1963)
> A 'pre-need memorial estate'; in other
> words, a grave for future occupancy. (ibid.)

pre-dawn vertical insertion an invasion
by parachutists
Neither inserting your card for clocking on on
early shift nor starting the day with copulation but how the American invaders of
Grenada on 27 October 1983 described their
mission.

pre-driven *American* (of a car) not new
Anything to avoid saying 'second-hand'. See
also PRE-OWNED, PREVIOUSLY OWNED, and
USED.

pre-emptive unprovoked and without
warning
Used of warfare or violence. *Pre-emption* is
buying first, whence denying the purchase to
others. In the phrases *pre-emptive strike* and *pre-emptive offensive*:

> It would be important...for the forces of
> the Pact to be fully prepared...for the
> more likely contingency of a pre-emptive
> offensive. (Hackett, 1978)

A *pre-emptive action* or *pre-emptive self-defence*
may be no more than killing one person:

> He had written a legal opinion
> asserting that pre-emptive action would
> be no more an assassination than
> would a case in which a policeman
> gets off the first shot at the man who is
> pointing a gun at him. 'Pre-emptive
> self-defense' he called it. (Woodward,
> 1987)

pre-owned (of a car) not new
The jargon of the motor trade, forgetting the
initial ownership of every new car by the
manufacturer and the dealer:

> (Pre-owned)—the modern euphemism for
> 'second hand'. (Pei, 1969)

See also OWNED, PRE-DRIVEN, and PREVIOUSLY
OWNED.

precautions contraception
Shortened form of *precautions against pregnancy*:

> She hoped she might be pregnant,
> since she had taken no precautions.
> (M. McCarthy, 1963)

precocious spoilt and ill-mannered
Originally, developing early. Used of children
other than your own, out of earshot of their
parents.

predilection homosexuality
Literally, a tendency or preference for anything:

> 'Predilection?' he said, giggling. 'What a
> sensitive way of putting it!' (Sanders, 1986)

preference (a) being homosexual
Shortened form of *sexual preference*, but not
used about heterosexuals:

> Names and addresses; sweethearts and
> wives; habits and preferences. Complete
> with photos and medical sheets. (Deighton,
> 1994)

pregnancy interruption an induced abortion

An *interruption* is a disturbance with an
assumption of resumption. This medical
jargon is sometimes enlarged to *voluntary
pregnancy interruption* or *VPI*.

preliterate uncivilized
Anthropological and social science jargon to
describe primitive societies which remain
illiterate, denoting concern on behalf of those
who cannot read what they would be concerned about.

premature *obsolete* conceived before marriage
How couples used to explain a birth before
they had been married the requisite nine
months.

premium costing more
An attributive use of a noun, which originally
meant an award or prize, whence something
worth more than its face value. Advertising
jargon.

preparation room *American* a morgue
Not merely the area in which the mortician
embalms the corpse:

> He suggests a rather thorough overhauling
> of the language...'preparation room not
> morgue'. (J. Mitford, 1963—listing advice
> on euphemisms for undertakers talking to
> customers)

prepare *American* to embalm
For viewing by the survivors rather than by St
Peter:

> So the worst racket of all was built up: the
> embalming or 'preparing' of the 'loved
> one'. (E. S. Turner, 1952)

prepared biography *American* a draft obituary of a living person
A delicate expression masking the inevitabil-
ity of death:

> In America, incidentally, an obituary held
> in reserve for future use is...described as a
> 'prepared biography'. (John Gross in
> Enright, 1985)

preparedness *American* the military help
given by the United States to Britain in
the Second World War before Pearl
Harbor
Isolationism was so widely supported that
Roosevelt and his supporters had to conceal
their actions in euphemism:

> [Henry Ford] had financed an expensive
> advertising campaign in the country's
> largest newspapers savagely attacking
> 'preparedness'. (Lacey, 1986—Ford's anti-
> Jewish paranoia attracted him to elements
> of Nazism)

present a bribe
The gift is a payment for a service which
should be provided free:
> I stood behind Nazir as he discussed the
> 'present' necessary to 'reopen' the border.
> (Dalrymple, 1989, writing about entering
> Pakistan—the border had been wrongly
> closed so that the guards could extract
> bribes from travellers)

present arms to have an erect penis
Punning on the military drill in which the
rifle is held vertically in front of the body:
> ... by the time she was done I would be
> ecstatically ruined, and certain sure I'd
> never be able to present arms again.
> (Fraser, 1971)

preserved *American* drunk
A variant of the more common PICKLED, with
alcohol the preservative agent.

press *obsolete* to kidnap for service in the
navy
By a *press gang*, which seized men in public
places:
> His negro servant, Francis Barber,
> having left him, and been some time at
> sea, not pressed as has been supposed,
> but with his own consent... (J. Boswell,
> 1791—Dr Johnson was seeking Barber's
> release)

press conjugal rights on to copulate with
(a reluctant wife)
See CONJUGAL RIGHTS:
> Some fear that he might have been
> pressing his 'conjugal rights' could have
> accounted for it. (Kee, 1993—Parnell was
> afraid that Katie O'Shea, with whom he
> lived as man and wife and by whom he had
> children, might also be having to copulate
> with her husband)

press your attentions on (of a male) to
copulate with
Usually extramaritally. It might literally mean
no more than, for example, the concentration
of a dentist filling a patient's tooth.

pressure torture
Exerted on someone in custody:
> '... he's trained to withstand pressure.'
> 'Interesting usage, pressure.' (Seymour,
> 1989—a prisoner was being tortured)

pressure of work an excuse for neglect,
inefficiency, or discourtesy
The phrase is seldom used by businesslike
people:
> I feel an awful worm, not having written to
> you for so long, but a genuine pressure of
> work stopped me. (P. G. Wodehouse in a

letter of 1930, in Donaldson 1990—note
the qualification *genuine*)

prestigious expensive
Originally it meant concerned only with
juggling, or prestidigitation, but now used as
conferring prestige:
> City of London's most prestigious fully-
> serviced apartment block. (*Times*, May 1981,
> but not referring to Buckingham Palace)

preventable diseases *American* syphilis
and gonorrhea
Army usage from the Second World War.
They were to prove insidious enemies.

preventative a contraceptive sheath
Preventing, it was hoped, disease and impreg-
nation but not necessarily worn by the former
British *preventative man*, a coastguard.

preventive detention arbitrary imprisonment
Literally, a long sentence for a dangerous or
hardened criminal. In a totalitarian state the
phrase describes the incarceration of critics,
without process of law.

previously owned (of a car) second-hand
One of a series of euphemisms to avoid the
reality that others have been driving the
vehicle:
> Buyers looking for a 'previously owned'
> motor car (to use the current trade
> euphemism) tend to be very selective. (*Daily
> Telegraph*, October 1987)
See also PRE-OWNED, OWNED, and USED.

prey to (a) suffering from
The victimization is in most cases figurative,
as with those who describe themselves as
being a *prey to dyspepsia*, for example. Not so
the obsolete British *prey to the bicorn*, a
cuckold. The *bicorn* was a mythical two-
horned beast which devoured men whose
wives dominated or deceived them. Its counterpart, the *chichevache*, which ate obedient
wives, was reputed to feed but rarely.

priapus an erect penis
Priapus was the Pan of Mysia, usually depicted
in such a condition:
> He threatened her with a priapus that had
> already once inflicted upon her an almost
> mortal wound. (Nabokov, 1968)
Rarely used as a mild male insult, as synonym
for DICK 1 or PRICK:
> 'Up yours as well, Priapus,' he said, and I
> hung up laughing. Outrageous man!
> (Sanders, 1994)
Whence *priapism*, such an erection, which
may be a natural phenomenon or a dangerous
medical condition:

Priapism, a condition caused by a sudden obstruction of the blood vessels so that blood cannot flow away from an erect penis. (T. Smith, 1986)
See also MR PRIAPUS.

price crowding a price increase not authorized by the proprietor
Mainly supermarket jargon, for a practice under which a manager seeks to create a reserve which can be used to make good losses for which he might be held responsible.

prick a penis
Once standard English but now a vulgarism:
    What did in for him
    Was a prick in the skin,
    When the prick should have been in Ophelia. (*Playboy's Book of Limericks*, referring to Hamlet's demise)
Also used figuratively as a term of mild abuse or rebuke among males.
See also CHOPPER 2.

pride an erect penis
Shortened form of *pride of the morning*, an erection of the penis upon waking, which comes from the proper meaning, a mist or shower heralding a fine day:
    Said a just-wed professor named Ted,
    To a redhead coed in his bed…
    Won't you swallow my pride dear instead?
    (*Playboy's Book of Limericks*)
Prides may mean the penis and testicles:
    I had nothing but my two hands to cover my prides with. (Frazier, 1997)

prima donna *obsolete* a prostitute
The term for a principal female singer or dancer in an opera or ballet has, outside the theatre, come to denote a temperamental and self-important person, from the reputed behaviour of some artistes. In 19th-century London she was neither of these things:
    By lorettes I mean those I have touched on before as prima donnas. (Mayhew, 1862—a *lorette* I assume to be a nun (see NUNNERY), from those who took their vows in one of the orders established under the auspices of *Our Lady of Loreto*, the Italian town in which the Virgin Mary reputedly made her home after being transported there by angels in 1295)

prime saleable
Literally, first, whence implying of first quality. Commonly used of perishable foodstuff, especially meat.

prime the pump deliberately to cause inflation by excessive government spending

The fiscal theory, now largely discredited, is that higher taxation or borrowing spent on more public works will lead to economic growth without inflation or depreciating the value of the currency:
    The new administration coming into power in just two weeks would have to 'prime the pump' through massively increased government expenditure. (Erdman, 1986)

primed *obsolete Scottish/English* drunk
Like a pump and perhaps also alluding to an explosive charge:
    When he was 'primed', was Nathan's wont to pass,
    No licensed house without another glass. (Doherty, 1884)

Prince of Darkness the devil
Not the eldest son of King Edward III, the *Black Prince*, but another evasive way of talking of the devil.

prince (the) *obsolete* menstruation
Presumably from the pleasure and relief at his appearance:
    Georgiana noted every variation in her menstrual cycle with obsessive diligence. 'The Prince is not yet come,' she wrote to her mother in October [1779]. (Foreman, 1998)

princess an expensive prostitute
From the meaning, a classy type of female or one who affects airs:
    Willy goggled at a couple of painted princesses swaying by in all their finery. 'Whores,' says I. (Fraser, 1973, writing in 19th-century style)
Also as *pavement princess*.

privacy an opportunity to urinate or defecate
Not just wanting to be alone:
    After he had eaten, Lawford went out into the bushes for privacy. (B. Cornwell, 1997)

private enterprise illegal trading by an employee
Literally, trade or industry not financed by or under the direct control of the state:
    But there was a great deal of what you might call private enterprise on that run. (Price, 1970, writing about smuggling by airline staff)

private office *obsolete* a lavatory
What was once also called a *house of office*. Today only rather grand or self-important people run *private offices*, with individual secretarial help and lots of potted plants.

private parts the human genitalia
Those not normally exposed to public gaze.
Also as *privates*:
> 'No more private selves, no more private
> corners in society, no more private
> properties, no more private acts.' 'No more
> private parts,' said Barbara. (Bradbury,
> 1975)

> He had not let Oliver in until his
> privates were covered with water.
> (Bradbury, 1976)

And of animals, where they are not covered
up:
> Buller was licking his private parts with the
> gusto of an alderman drinking soup.
> (G. Greene, 1978—Buller was a dog)

See also PARTS, PRIVITIES, and PRIVY PARTS.

private patient *British* a person paying
for specific medical care
Not waiting to be treated under the National
Health Service which, as a relic of command
economy theory, cannot plan to have immediate resources available free and on
demand for each of some sixty million people
whose needs are random. The usage ignores
the fact that each *patient* is *private*, whether
the bills are paid through taxes, insurance,
income, or savings.

privileged rich
Sociological jargon not really implying that
those so described have honourable distinc-
tions; in the eyes of those who use this
dysphemism, the opposite is true. See also
UNDERPRIVILEGED.

privileges sexual activity
Literally, special rights, like those of a
Member of Parliament to libel others in the
House of commons with impunity:
> He'll still continue to pay her hourly fee
> whenever he spends time with her...But
> he's also entitled to other 'privileges'.
> (Golden, 1997, of a geisha)

privities the human genitalia
The concept is of privacy:
> ...felt great pain in her privities, as if her
> swooning had not spared her and some
> rude forcing had taken place. (Fowles,
> 1985)

privy a lavatory
Again from the privacy:
> Hadjimoscos, sick in a privy, had spewed
> out his false teeth. (Manning, 1960)

A *privy-stool* was a lavatory seat and bucket:
> ...chairs and privy-stools necessary for a
> royal visit. (Monsarrat, 1978)

privy parts the human genitalia
An older version of PRIVATE PARTS:

> He moved their privy parts to the front.
> (Plato, in translation, reporting some
> genetic engineering by Zeus)

PRN *British* administer diamorphine
Perhaps from the Latin, *pro re nata*, 'for the
affair born', used by doctors to mean 'as
required', of any medication. It may be used
as a coded message in a hospital for euthena-
sia of a patient in pain and mortally afflicted.

pro a prostitute
A shortened form of PROFESSIONAL, or *prostitute*, or both:
> You the bloke that floated them pros out to
> the *Everett*? (Theroux, 1973—some
> prostitutes had been sent out to a ship)

A *pro-pack*, a contraceptive kit which was
issued to soldiers in the Second World War,
came from PROPHYLACTIC, despite being for
use (for the most part) with an AMATEUR.
Neither of these definitions should necessarily be applied to a *PRO* (public relations
officer) or to the *pack* of information with
which he is likely to encumber you.

pro-choice *American* in favour of abortion on demand
Not the selection of a prostitute, or even
suggesting that those not wishing to have
children might remain celibate:
> They ran an old tape on television last
> night, denouncing the pro-choice
> movement. (R. N. Patterson, 1992)

See also PRO-LIFE.

pro-life *American* opposed to abortion on
demand
A belief so strongly held by some as to justify
their murdering abortionists acting within
the law:
> I turned her down flat, but was at once
> beset with memories of Sister Floreas, who
> took the pro-life war into the most
> overpopulated regions of Bombay, and who
> had gone to a place in which unwanted
> pregnancies were presumably no longer a
> problem. (Rushdie, 1995—Sister Floreas
> was dead)

probe (of a male) to copulate with
But not with a blunt-ended exploratory
surgical instrument:
> Says Barbara frankly, 'I was probed.' 'That's
> true,' says Howard. 'At the purely external
> level you got screwed.' (Bradbury, 1975)

problem an unwanted and often irreversible condition
The word is used in many phrases to conceal
truth or inadequacy. Thus a *cash problem* in an
individual is a shortage of money, and not a
superfluity or a lack of pockets to put it in. In

a company a *cash flow problem* means that it is overtrading or insolvent. A *communication problem* means that nobody understands us or we don't understand them. A *crossword problem* means we cannot complete the crossword (a *problem problem?*) although a *problem crossword* is one we may expect to solve. A *drink problem* is alcoholic addiction by a *problem drinker*:

> ...the fact that she was a 'problem drinker'...(Styron, 1976)

However, a *drinks problem* at a party would indicate only that you might be running out of supplies. A *heart problem* is a malfunction of that organ, with other organs or bodily parts similarly identified according to your disability. The onset of menstruation may herald a woman's *problem days*, but if she suffers from a *women's problem* she may have a disorder of the womb or of some other part exclusive to her sex. Staying with health, the obese may have a *weight problem*:

> If you are destined to be fat, food makes you fat. But I have never had a weight problem. (I. Murdoch, 1978)

A society which includes many races may face a *colour problem*, while a black person may be said offensively to have a *pigmentation problem*:

> ...wants to send anyone with a pigmentation problem back to Islamabad. (Sharpe, 1979)

Politicians profess to face innumerable *problems*, not all of their own making. Thus Hitler was tested by a so-called *Austrian problem*, which he resolved by having Austria's chancellor murdered and then by invading the country.

procedure any taboo or unpleasant act
Literally, a method of behaving. In medical jargon, as a shortened form of *medical procedure*, it is something which may well cause a patient pain, then or later:

> Dr Carolyn Ryan shook her head. 'I have two procedures tomorrow.' (Clancy, 1991— as a surgeon, she was refusing a glass of wine)

For police and lawyers, a *procedure* is a civil or criminal legal action, a synonym of *proceedings*. For a pregnant woman it may be the abortion of a healthy foetus. For the Nazis, it meant mass murder:

> Schindler had heard rumours that 'procedures in the ghetto' were growing more intense. (Keneally, 1982, writing of Poland in the Second World War)

process the penis
Literally, anything which sticks out:

> ...washing my process and asking me if I've got the clap. (Theroux, 1973)

proclivities unconventional sexual preferences
Literally, any personal choice:

> Shaleen had never made any secret about her proclivities. She had a wild thing going for a make-up girl. (Turow, 1999)

procure to arrange (prostitution) on behalf of another
Literally, to obtain, of anything, but legal jargon in this sense:

> ...she had never heard of my sister, but she would undertake to procure her for me for seventy-five dollars. (Fraser, 1973)

Whence a *procurer*, a pimp, and *procuress*, a bawd:

> A middle-aged man doing the same thing was a dull dirty procurer. (Theroux, 1973)

product a service
Jargon of bankers and other financial institutions which seeks to suggests that their activities actually *produce* something:

> Beginning with the M&S Chargecard, followed by personal loans and a number of investment products. (*Daily Telegraph*, 3 March 1994)

product shrinkage the supply of a lesser quantity at the previous price
Not settlement in a package:

> The device known as 'product shrinkage' is using the confusion caused by metrication of weights and measures to reduce the content of thousands of brands of canned and packaged goods. (*Sunday Telegraph*, 11 February 2001)

production difficulties strikes
The universal code words used by British national newspapers prior to the taming of the print unions and the introduction of new technology which reduced their power to disrupt:

> On at least one day this week, our readers will be deprived of copies of this newspaper...The failure to deliver will be due, not in the language of our trade to 'production difficulties' but to the decisions of the TUC to stage a day of action ostensibly in support of hospital workers. (Deedes, 1997, writing about the 1970s)

profession (the) prostitution by females
Prostitutes' jargon:

> ...containing some bitter denunciations by an old member of the profession. (Londres, 1928, in translation)

See also OLDEST PROFESSION, PROFESSIONAL (WOMAN), and PRO.

professional unsporting

The behaviour of those paid for playing a sport and for whom winning is no longer a game:

> The feeling persists that he was being professional, which is often a euphemism for unsporting. (*Daily Telegraph*, 21 April 1997—a soccer player had ignored the convention that the ball should be returned to the opposition if deliberately put out of play after an injury to a player)

A *professional foul* is a cynical infringement of the rules to deny an advantage to an opponent.

professional car *American* a hearse
Funeral jargon. *Processional* would be more appropriate.

professional (woman) a prostitute
How those so employed prefer to describe themselves, likening their trade to the *learned professions*:

> He cannot afford to pay professional women to gratify his passions. (Mayhew, 1862)

progressive opposed to conventional methods or manners
Literally, moving towards improvement:

> And this was at a time when progressive educationalists in Britain were arguing that children should not be given homework because it put those from working-class homes at a disadvantage. (Rae, 1993—the former headmaster of Westminster, a leading London school, was reporting on the education in an Indian leper colony of poor children, who demanded homework)

Politically, *progressive* is being a Communist or holding left-wing views:

> Day Release Apprentices have their weekly hour of progressive opinions. (Sharpe, 1979)

proletarian Communist
The *proletariat*, from the Latin *proletarius*, 'the lowest class in the Servian arrangement' (Wm Smith, 1933) first described those in feudal service and then anyone who worked for a wage, among whom middle-class revolutionaries traditionally seek support. Whence a *proletarian democracy*, a Communist autocracy; *proletarian internationalism*, Soviet Russian imperialism; etc.

promised *obsolete* engaged to be married
From the days when a man (and very occasionally a woman) might be sued for *breach of promise* if an engagement were broken off and it was considered shameful for a woman to remain unmarried and so become an OLD MAID:

> Loud, of course, and facetious were the lamentations that Francie had not returned 'promised' to one or other of these heroes of romance. (Somerville and Ross, 1894)

promoted to Glory dead
A usage of the Salvation Army, whose members live as closely as any may get to the Christian ethic, and deserve any glory that may be going.

prong (of a male) to copulate with
The common FORK imagery:

> I hear she's some kind of guru to the old man...Think he's pronging her? (M. Thomas, 1985)

prophylactic a contraceptive sheath
Literally, associated with the prevention of any disease. Used in the Second World War to describe any process to reduce the incidence of venereal disease:

> ...his paybook, his handkerchief creased according to regulation, and one prophylactic. (A. Clark, 1995, listing the standard personal equipment of a member of the SS *Totenkopf* division)

proposition to suggest engaging in a sexual act
Made to other than a regular sexual partner, of both heterosexuals and homosexuals:

> He might feel like hitting the first [homosexual] who propositioned him. (Davidson, 1978)

A *proposition* is such a suggestion:

> I didn't take her up on a proposition she made to me...a bodily proposition. (Masters, 1976)

proposition selling the use of misleading hypotheses to confuse a buyer
The commercial use of leading questions:

> His technique is old-style American 'proposition selling'. The salesman puts forward a series of numbskull propositions with which you have *no choice but to agree*. (*Daily Telegraph*, August 1989, reporting on a time-sharing scam)

protect to reunite by force
The language of Hitlerism:

> He had warned that Germany would know how to 'protect' ten million Germans living on the border...Everyone knew what Hitler meant by 'protect'. (Shirer, 1984)

protect your interests aggressively to annex border states or territory
The language of autocrats:

> He nearly succeeded in persuading his superiors to annex portions of Sinkiang...and then occupying territory

to 'protect Russian interests'. (Dalrymple, 1989)

protected sex copulation or sodomy using a condom:

Not girls looked after by chaperones but seeking to *protect* against the transfer of disease:

> As she had recently come from abroad and despite the fact they had protected sex, he thought it prudent they should both attend hospital to be tested for the Aids virus.
> (*Daily Telegraph*, 2 December 1995—the case was of legal interest when the woman was convicted of the offence of causing grievous bodily harm to the male, because she had knowingly infected him with the AIDS virus)

protection extortion

The practice of selling immunity from your own depredations is well documented, from Anglo-Saxon payment of *Danegeld* in England to the Mafia in America and Italy:

> He was supplying Rachman's clubs with protection. (S. Green 1979)

Being *in* or *into protection* is engaging is such extortion:

> I'm going into protection... scare the shopkeepers silly. (I. Murdoch, 1977)

protective custody arbitrary imprisonment

The pretence is that the victims are incarcerated to prevent any harm befalling them:

> *Shutzhaft* (Protective Custody) a catch-all word whereby men, women and children disappeared and were never seen again. (Deighton, 1978)

protective reaction *American* bombing enemy territory

One of the Vietnam coinages (Commager, 1972).

protector[1] a man keeping a mistress

The 19th-century convention was that a woman living alone should have a man to look after her:

> They are dismissed... and set once more adrift. They do not remain long... without finding another protector. (Mayhew, 1862)

protector[2] a contraceptive sheath

As used in PROTECTED SEX.

protectorate a conquered and subject territory

Coined by the European colonizers of Africa, who seemed more anxious to *protect* themselves against a rival grab for the territory than to *protect* the indigenous population from any evil. Then used of a territory, such as Palestine, captured from an occupying power given to another nation, in this case the captor, to control without making it a colony. Hitler adopted the word for his de facto annexation of Bohemia and Moravia:

> With a war on, the Germans have organized their own winter games there, with skiers, skaters, and hockey teams from Italy, Hungary, Yugoslavia, Slovakia, the Protectorate and Germany. (Shirer, 1999—the games were held in January 1940)

provision an arbitrary adjustment in figures to be publicly reported

Literally, a reserve made against contingencies, to avoid a misleading statement of assets or profits. A *provision* is normally made on a subjective basis by managers, who may wish, by using a high figure, to reduce what appears as profit and therefore become subject to tax or, by understatement, to seek to show a stronger financial position than is the reality.

pruned *American* drunk

Probably from feeling like a tree or plant which has had its appendages or extremities removed rather than from *prune juice*, a spirituous intoxicant.

psycho a mentally ill person who is prone to violence

From the Greek, it means relating to the breath, whence of the soul or mind. *Psycho* is probably no more than a shortened form of *psychopath*::

> 'Keep that psycho away from me,' Wade yelled, showing fear for the first time. (Chandler, 1953)

psychological warfare the dissemination of lies and half-truths

From 1939 until the end of the Second World War, the phrase also included truthful broadcasting from Britain to Germany and to countries occupied by Germany:

> ... the Foreign Office's Information Research Unit, responsible for what had once been termed psychological warfare. (N. West, 1982)

psychologically disadvantaged under the influence of narcotics

An interesting variant of the DISADVANTAGED theme:

> Wilson, who won a lawsuit in 1992 claiming that his father, Murray Wilson, had bullied him into giving away the publishing rights to his songs while he was 'psychologically disadvantaged' (spaced out on drugs)... (*Daily Telegraph*, 7 October 1994—Wilson was one of the Beach Boys)

public assistance money paid regularly by the state to the needy
Not just helping an old lady to cross the road. See also ASSISTANCE.

public convenience see CONVENIENCE

public house an establishment where intoxicants may be sold and drunk
A *house* open at times to the *public*. Indeed, it used to be called a *public* but is now referred to, even in France, as a *pub*:
> Being also a public, it was two stories high (W. Scott, 1814)

public ownership control and management by politicians and bureaucrats
The use of the phrase is normally confined to commercial businesses, utilities, etc. No member of the public should be so rash as to try to assert ownership rights over them:
> Various failings, real or imaginary, in state-run undertakings created the need for fresh euphemism, and 'public ownership' was promptly produced. (S. Hoggart, in Enright, 1986)

public–private partnership *Britain* accepting private finance and management for a public service
Having long opposed privatization when out of office, Labour needed a new term for it when elected:
> A CDC 'public private partnership' (new speak for privatization) may take three years or more. (*Daily Telegraph*, 5 April 1998, writing about the Commonwealth Development Corporation)

public sector borrowing requirement government overspending
The *public sector* is that part of a mixed economy which is controlled, financed, and managed by government, the activities of its components not being subject to commercial pressures such as the need to generate cash or make profits, while losses can be met by further borrowing:
> A series of heavy expensive settlements has piled up that debt, euphemistically called the Public Sector Borrowing Requirement. (*Daily Telegraph*, December 1980)

public tranquillity internal repression
As in the *Department of Internal Tranquillity* in China.

puddle the result of involuntary urination
Literally, a shallow and temporary pool of rainwater. The usage is of small children and domestic pets:

> My foot landed in the middle of Telek's puddle. (Butcher, 1946—Telek was Eisenhower's dog)

pull¹ to cause a horse to lose a race
Racing jargon, from the jockey's handling of the reins. To *pull up* means, in racing circles as in motoring, to cause to come to a standstill.

pull² to seek to strike up an acquaintance with a member of the opposite sex
Commonly known as going ON THE PULL. The word is also used of casual copulation:
> If someone does recognize me, word will go back that the brigadier's pulling outside duty. (Ludlum, 1984—he was meeting a woman in a truck stop)

pull a daisy see PICK A DAISY

pull a train *American* to copulate in immediate succession with a number of males
The imagery is from coaches behind an engine:
> ...trying to persuade her to pull the train for a few of the choirboys. (Wambaugh, 1975—the *choirboys* were off-duty policemen)
See also *board a train* at BOARD.

pull his trigger to cause to ejaculate semen
The PISTOL imagery:
> I know how to pull his trigger. His wife doesn't. (Sanders, 1981)

pull in (for a chat) to arrest
Police jargon, the CHAT being an interrogation:
> What do you say to a man from SAVAK when he says...We'd like you to replace Barnheni as office manager, because we'll be pulling him in for a chat very soon. (M. West, 1979—SAVAK, an acronym in Persian translated as *National Security and Intelligence Organization*, was the Shah's version of the Gestapo)

pull off *American* to refrain improperly from investigating a crime or prosecuting a criminal
From the meaning, to draw back from:
> The detectives who were offered all kinds of inducements to pull off...(Lavine, 1930)

pull (yourself) off (of a male) to masturbate
See also the more common PULL THE PUD(DING).

pull out of a hat to produce irresponsibly
As the conjurer produces the rabbit:

The *Veterinary Journal* said he 'pulled figures out of a hat to fit his arguments'. (*Private Eye*, May 1981)

Pull out of the air has the same meaning.

pull rank to use seniority to secure an unfair advantage

It applies to those in hierarchical employment, such as sailors or public officials, and is euphemistic only when not used of normal commands and orders.

pull the long bow see DRAW THE LONG BOW

pull the pin *American* to retire from employment

The imagery is from uncoupling of rolling stock on a railroad, allowing the engine to run free, and not from activating the primer on a hand grenade:

... he wondered if he could afford to pull the pin when he got twenty-five years in. (Wambaugh, 1983)

The phrase is also used of a man deserting his wife, with the same imagery.

pull the plug on to kill by withdrawing mechanical life support

Punning on the electrical connection to life support machinery and the flushing of a lavatory. Whence also a meaning, to murder:

Hubby Luther pulled the plug on her. (Sanders, 1986)

pull the pud(ding) (of a male) to masturbate

The *pudding* is the penis:

... worry about the Republicans, who will soon know every time you pull your pud. (Anonymous, 1996)

pull the rug to render bankrupt

The imagery is from causing a person standing on a mat to fall when you jerk it. The use is of a banker who declines to give more credit or a creditor who obtains judgement for a debt. Whence figuratively of unilateral action by another precipitating a crisis:

He thinks the United Nations peacemongers could pull the rug. (Forsyth, 1994—some parties were in favour of leaving Iraq in possession of conquered Kuwait)

pump bilges (of a male) to urinate

The water is expelled over the side of a boat:

See if you can put a Martini together while I pump bilges. (Clancy, 1989)

Also as *pump ship*.

pump up (of a male) to copulate with

Presumably from the motion involved, likened to inflating a tyre:

If you work for a big corporation, the head of the firm is always pumping up the secretary. (*Sunday Telegraph*, 20 March 1994—to say *always* is to put rather a fine point on it)

pump your shaft (of a male) to masturbate

Again from the motion involved :

So there he stood, pumping his turgid shaft. (Sanders, 1973)

Also as *pump your pickle*, alluding to the shape of a gherkin.

punch *American* (of a male) to copulate with

With the common violent imagery:

Danny introduces Angel to this broad which Danny has been punchin' since high school. (Diehl, 1978)

punish the bottle to drink wine to excess

In former times, *jars* or *pots* could suffer similar abuse:

What with worry and waiting, he'd been punishing the pot, and was cut enough to be quarrelsome. (Fraser, 1997, writing in 19th-century style)

punk[1] *obsolete* a prostitute

The Worcestershire dialect meaning was 'Trash; an article of inferior quality' (*EDD*) It would be hard to draw any inferences from the alternative meaning, the scaly poloporous, better known perhaps as *polyporus squamosus*:

She may be a punk, for many of them are neither maid, widow, nor wife. (Shakespeare, *Measure for Measure*)

punk[2] *American* a male homosexual

From the meaning, rotten (of wood), whence worthless or of low quality. The word came into general use in connection with adolescent excess. Thus devotees of a loud tuneless noise with a strong beat (often accompanied by flashing coloured lights), who wore ritual decorated leather garments and impractical hairstyles, were known as *punks* and the noise was called *punk rock*.

punk[3] low-quality marijuana

Again from the meaning, of low quality. *Punk pills* may be any narcotic illegally taken orally.

punter *British* an inexperienced visitor who can be overcharged or robbed

Literally, someone who bets on horses or greyhounds, whence a habitual loser:

Many airport taxi-drivers object to driving their fellow-countrymen, motivated by the prospect of picking up a 'punter', someone who can safely be overcharged. (Moynahan, 1983)

pup to impregnate a woman
Canine imagery, without any suggestion of bitchiness:
    I want all these wenches pupped. (Fraser, 1971)
In coarse speech, to *pup* is also to be delivered of a child and *in pup* means pregnant, of a woman as, in standard English, of a dog.

puppy fat obesity in a child
Usually of a young female, with the implication that the plumpness will vanish as the child grows up, without any dietary change or regular exercise.

pure¹ *obsolete* a mistress
From her freedom from disease rather than her chastity or modesty.

pure² *obsolete* dog turds
This was one of the opposites, like DEFENCE and HEALTH, faeces being manifestly impure:
    ... the leather-workers used a substance for darkening skins that was known as 'pure' and that was gathered from the streets each night by the filthiest of local ingredients—'pure' being a Victorian term for dog turds. (Winchester, 1998)

purge¹ beer
Probably from its laxative effect:
    We had a drop of 'neck-oil', which like 'purge' was a nickname for beer. (F. Richards, 1936)

purge² to attack violently
Another form of cleaning out:
    The next day what the [Israelis] euphemistically call a 'purging operation' was effected. In this instance they 'purged' Fatah. (Price, 1971)

purge³ to cause diarrhoea
Literally, to rid of an impurity:
    The water causes violent and excessive purging...nigh ten times a day. (Dalrymple, 1989)
Now standard English.

purification of the race the systematic killing of gypsies, Jews, and mentally or physically subnormal Germans
How the Nazis sought to justify mass murder:
    The Nazis' refashioned warfare was a means of achieving the racial 'purification' of Europe, and involved both relocating entire populations and killing every Jewish man, woman and child that they could round up or capture. (Burleigh, 2000)

pursue to court
What a FOLLOWER used to do:
    Gaston Palewski, Nancy Mitford's great love, also pursued [Hermione, Countess of Ranfurly]. (*Daily Telegraph*, 13 February 2001, in an obituary of the Countess, whose fascinating diaries were published as *To War with Whitaker*)

pursue other interests see LOOK AFTER (YOUR) OTHER INTERESTS

push¹ (of a male) to copulate with
The usual thrusting imagery but also from the rhyming slang, a *push in the truck*:
    'You pushing her?'...'Every chance I get.' (Sanders, 1970—the lady was not confined to a wheelchair)
Whence, in West Africa and perhaps elsewhere, *push*, copulation:
    Sing, dance, cook, plenty push. (Sanders, 1977—a female servant was being extolled to a bachelor)

push² (the) peremptory dismissal from employment
Given by the employer. Seldom of an employee leaving of his own volition:
    It is conceivable that not all employees relished the chance of encouraging ambitious young men to give their firm 'the Push'. (E. S. Turner, 1952)

push³ a sustained attack in war
Jargon from the Second World war:
    The gen is that the jerries are preparing a push on Alam Haifa. (Manning, 1977)

push⁴ to distribute (narcotics) illegally
Literally, to sell energetically or fraudulently, as with a *share pusher* who sells securities at false values. A *pusher* is an illegal distributor of narcotics:
    He was on the weed. I pretended I was a pusher. (Chandler, 1958)

push (someone's) buttons to excite sexually
Like actuating a machine:
    He wondered if he would still push her buttons. (J. Patterson, 1999)

push the button on *American* to kill or cause to be killed
Again from actuating a machine, or perhaps from switching off a light:
    You never gonna get the guys who pushed the button on him. They too big for you. (Sohmer, 1988—his FBI partner had been murdered)

push up the daisies to be dead

Referring to the supposed nourishment of the common churchyard flower. Less often as *push up the weeds*:

> If I'd been born fifty years sooner I'd have been pushing up the daisies by now.
> (N. Mitford, 1960)
> And there are more, who are pushing the weeds up. (Seymour, 1977)

pushing academy *obsolete* a brothel

Where you could learn how to PUSH 1, and punning on the meaning, a fencing school. Also as a *pushing shop*:

> ... for the income of the whores of the so-called *pushing academies*. (Keneally, 1987)
> He spent an hour a day at the pushing shop down near the railway, rooting himself stupid. (Keneally, 1987)

pussy¹ the vagina

A commoner version of CAT 2:

> She could not even get her forefinger into her pussy. (F. Harris, 1925)

The punning *pussy-whipped* means besotted, of a male:

> An old man like that. Our father. Pussy-whipped. (Sanders, 1980)

In America, a *pussy lift* is an operation to tighten the vagina and so enhance sexual enjoyment:

> ... Piper with the happy illusion that pussy lifts were things cats went up and down in. (Sharpe, 1977)

pussy² a woman thought available for promiscuous copulation

Her PUSSY 1, in this context, is of more interest than her sweet nature:

> ... Brancusi
> Unafraid of black pussy,
> Walked under the ladder and had her.
> (*Playboy's Book of Limericks*—the sculptor was using a black model)

put to copulate

From the placement rather than any association with holing out at golf :

> ... you been put-putting with blondie here, my wife. (Mailer, 1965)

A *put*, a single act of copulation, may be *had* or *done* by a male. *Put and take* describes the mutual act of copulating.

To *put a man in a belly* puns on the male ingress and the conception:

> So you may put a man in your belly.
> (Shakespeare, *As You Like It*)

To *put it in* or *put it up* are explicit of male copulation:

> They thought it would save their kids or their daddies, letting me put it up them. (Allbeury, 1980—a German guard explained the basis of his relationship with women prisoners)

To *put it about* is to copulate promiscuously of a either sex:

> Certainly not some blonde tart who undoubtedly put it about if the mood took her. (C. Forbes, 1987)

To *put out* is normally only of female promiscuity:

> Any girl ... is caught in a sexual trap. If she won't put out the men will accuse her of being bourgeois. (Lodge, 1975)

Put to, from the meaning, to start work, is obsolete:

> As rank as any flax-wench that puts-to,
> Before her troth-plight. (Shakespeare, *The Winter's Tale*)

put a move on *American* to make a sexual approach to (a stranger)

Usually by the male:

> ... too sore and shaken to put a move on her. (Wambaugh, 1983)

Occasionally in the plural:

> He doesn't seem to understand the etiquette of putting the moves on a woman. (de Mille, 1988)

put (a person's) lights out to kill

Lights are eyes, but the phrase also puns on extinguishing a lamp:

> All men who were lucky at gambling very soon had their lights put out. (F. Richards, 1933, writing of First World War trench life)

put against a wall to kill

The classic form of execution by shooting in a prison yard:

> They will put anyone that answers back against a wall. (A. Clark, 1995, quoting Bormann's instructions to the Nazi Home Army in 1945)

put away¹ to kill

Especially of old, diseased, or unwanted pets:

> I have left instructions for Buller to be put away—as painlessly as possible. (G. Greene, 1978—Buller was a dog)

To *put yourself away* is to commit suicide.

put away² *obsolete* to bury

From the days when the poor were anxious that a proper burial in hallowed ground should give them as good a chance of resurrection as the better-off might anticipate:

> Some poor comrades undertook to see her put away. (Hartley, 1870)

put away³ to confine involuntarily to an institution

Referring to criminals and those with severe mental illness:

> He was a bit 'tropo' ... They put him away in the end. (Simon, 1979)

put (it) away⁴ to consume (intoxicants)
Not merely returning the bottle to its rack,
and usually to excess:
> ... it was really astounding to see [her] put
> away the booze. (Styron, 1976)
> ... the walking wounded of the day watch
> *really* put it away. (Wambaugh, 1983)

put daylight through to kill by shooting
Mainly First World War usage but with
common imagery:
> He wouldn't have given him that chance,
> but soon put some daylight through him.
> (F. Richards, 1933)

put down¹ to kill
Normally of old, diseased, or unwanted
domestic pets:
> ... an old smelly Border terrier which Uncle
> Matthew had put down. (N. Mitford, 1945)

Less often of murdering people:
> I am going to be forced to put down the
> first hostage. (W. Smith, 1979)

Formerly also of judicial execution:
> The most ... accomplished lady ... was
> suffered to be put down like a common
> criminal. (Hogg, 1822)

put down² to denigrate or oppress
Either by a dominant group or by an individual snub:
> The majority keeps putting down the
> minority. (*Daily Telegraph*, 1 March 1995—
> obese men complained that they were the
> butt of lewd jokes by women)

put in the mobility pool summarily dismissed from employment
The jargon of management consultants who
see employees as units of output, possessing
job *mobility* just as those in a *typing pool* might
sometimes have been competent stenograph-
ers:
> ... despite the fact that your company is
> doing well you have just been sacked or,
> rather ... 'put in the mobility pool'. (*Sunday
> Telegraph*, 27 October 1996)

put in your ticket to die
A ship's officer surrenders his *ticket* on
retirement.

put off *obsolete* to kill
It was used of animals:
> Ir ye gaun to pit aff da auld koo? (*Shetland
> News*, 1990, quoted in *EDD*)

put on to deceive or mislead
From the imposition on another's credulity:
> ... if he's putting us on I'm going to pull his
> arms off. (Forsyth, 1994)

put on file rejected for employment

An excuse by a prospective employer where
he fears there might be a claim for unlawful discrimination if the candidate were
rejected outright or given the true reason
for rejection:
> Photos are demanded—if you're ugly you
> are 'put on file'. (*Sunday Telegraph*, 14
> January 1996: the applicants wished to be
> employed as showgirls)

put on the spot to kill
From the slang meaning, to accuse or embarrass:
> Youthful killers on the East Side can he
> hired to 'knock off' or 'put a guy on the
> spot'. (Lavine, 1930)

put out see PUT

put out a contract on (someone) to pay
for a killing
As in CONTRACT.

put out of your troubles to kill
Or *put out of your misery*, as the case may be:
> Shore's you're born, he'll turn State's
> evidence ... I'm for putting him out of his
> troubles. (Twain, 1884)

put out to grass to cause to retire prematurely
The imagery is from the horse which escapes
the knacker:
> If you think you are going to be put out to
> grass, you are mistaken. (Price, 1979—a
> man was being moved from his normal job
> prior to retiring age)

put the arm on to extort money etc. from
(a person) by threats of violence
The imagery is from wrestling. Also as *put the
black on*, where *black* is a shortened form of
BLACKMAIL, and *put the burn on*, from BURN 3.
And as *put the bite on*, *put the muscle on*, or *put
the scissors on*:
> Other guys roll over and lie still the moment
> you put the arm on them. (le Carré, 1980).
> ... put the bite on you and you paid him a
> little now and then to avoid scandal.
> (Chandler, 1951)
> I was looking for a job, no question about
> it. But I wasn't trying to put the muscle on
> them. (Colodny and Gettlin, 1991—he was
> being accused of blackmail)
> ... if I don't get them in one pound notes,
> I'll put the scissors on you. (Kersh, 1936)

put the boot in to disrupt or upset
through offensive behaviour or the
threat of violence
Literally, what a ruffian may do when he has
knocked you down. Figuratively of any harmful or dishonest action:

Leseter's success with the horses was achieved by 'putting in the boot'—fixing the races. (Evans-Pritchard, 1997)

or of deliberately making a hurtful remark:

Mrs Lupey says living successfully in a family is largely a matter of timing, and, I must say, I picked exactly the right moment to put the boot in. (Fine, 1989)

put the clock back fraudulently to alter the reading of a mileometer

Motor trade jargon; and see CLOCK.

put the clog in deliberately to injure an opposing player

In the game of soccer, where the players wear boots rather than wooden footwear:

There were many who thought the Dutch had put the clog in on the Saudi striker. (*Daily Telegraph*, 22 June 1994)

To *clog* is to attempt to maim.

put the finger on see FINGER 1

put the juice to *American* to kill by electrocution

The *juice* is the electric current used in the CHAIR 1:

'Didn't ever think I'd be helping the cops put the juice to no one,' he said. 'But the dude was a killer.' (Katzenbach, 1995)

put the skids under wilfully to cause to fail

The imagery is from the way of launching a ship or getting tree trunks to a mill. Once on the skids, the motion cannot be voluntarily arrested.

put to to cause to mate with

Standard English of mares etc.:

We put her to Sandcastle yesterday morning. (D. Francis, 1982)

The stallion is said, while attending to such duty, to STAND 2. See also PUT.

put to rest dead

When the dead person is said to be AT REST:

...didn't expect things to change much until she was put to rest. (Sanders, 1986)

put to sleep to kill (of a domestic animal)

What you do with old, ill, or unwanted pets:

'I'll have it put to sleep,' he shouted...'Oh, darling,' she pleaded, 'he's only a puppy.' (Ustinov, 1966)

put to the question *obsolete* to torture

The language of the Inquisition, but also a common method of medieval criminal investigation elsewhere.

put to the sword to kill

Usually of a large number of helpless victims, by any form of violence:

...took Siakat by storm and put not only the Egyptian garrison, but every man, woman and child in the place to the sword. (F. Harris, 1925)

put under the sod dead

And presumably buried:

Charlie, who was put under the sod, poor chap, a year come Michaelmas...(Pease, 1894)

To *put underground* is to kill:

If you don't keep quiet for ten minutes, I'll put you underground too. (G. Greene, 1932)

put yourself about to be promiscuous

Mainly of males, from circulating freely:

By all accounts our friend put himself about a bit. (Blacker, 1992)

put yourself away see PUT AWAY 1

python the penis

The common serpentine imagery. Not viewed sexually and perhaps only used in the phrase SIPHON (or syphon) THE PYTHON, to urinate.

Q

quail *obsolete* a prostitute
Not from the Celtic *caile*, a young girl, but the common avian imagery, this time from the reputedly amorous game bird:
> Agamemnon, an honest fellow enough, and one that loves quails. (Shakespeare, *Troilus and Cressida*)

Quaker gun *American* a decoy cannon
A usage from the Civil War because, like the *Quakers*, it wouldn't fire in anger:
> After a while a whole battery of Quaker guns were discovered at Centreville. (G. C. Ward, 1990)

qualify accounts to throw doubt on published figures
Literally, to *qualify* means to modify in some respect, and there are some technical *qualifications* in auditors' reports which do not indicate that the directors are suspect and the company is headed for receivership, but not many.

quantitatively challenged fat
But not Sumo wrestlers:
> Without some such ordinance the fate of the quantitatively challenged teenager in the United states—and there are many of them—is sad to contemplate. (A. Waugh, *Daily Telegraph*, 4 October 1993)
And see CHALLENGED.

quarantine a military blockade
Originally, the period of forty (*quarante*) days in which a widow might stay in her deceased husband's house, whence any period of isolation against disease etc. J. F. Kennedy used the phrase of the 1962 blockade of Cuba.

queen¹ *obsolete* a prostitute
From the old meaning, any female animal, and especially a CAT 1:
> To call an honest woman slut or queen. (W. Scott, 1820)
A *queen-house* was a brothel.

queen² a male homosexual
Usually an older man playing the female role or affecting effeminate mannerisms or dress:
> He won't hold your hand or ask for your autograph like that old Harley Street queen you normally see. (Deighton, 1972)

Queen's evidence *British* betraying a fellow malefactor
Or *King's evidence*, depending on the occupant of the throne. The derivation is from the convention that the crown prosecutes in British criminal cases:
> But a suspect may, if he refuses to co-operate, perhaps by 'turning Queen's evidence' or becoming a 'supergrass' ...(David Pennick in Enright, 1985)

queer¹ drunk
Originally, not in your normal state of health, and still occasionally used of a drunkard, with a suggestion that his condition may have been caused by something else. The meaning to make drunk is obsolete:
> Queered in the drinking of a penny pot of malmsey. (W. Scott, 1822)

queer² of unsound mind
Perhaps a shortened form of *queer in the head*. In this usage, people may be *a bit queer*, implying a harmless and mild condition.

queer³ homosexual
Almost always of males. It is used adjectivally:
> I'm not, um, queer. Well, you know, I don't like boys. (Theroux, 1975)
and as a noun:
> Three or four queers talking together in queertalk. (from a poem of 1947, in Ginsburg, 1984—*queertalk* is different from gobbledegook)

queer⁴ (the) *American* forged banknotes
Criminal usage:
> He was all for printing the queer. (Sanders, 1990)

question¹ to arrest
Police jargon, much used when publicizing particulars of a suspect to avoid the legal implications of a direct assertion of guilt. If the police announce that they would like to *question* someone corresponding with your description, you should take an overnight bag to the interview.

question² a persistent problem to which there appears to be no answer
Common political usage:
> I have always expressed my belief that the present Parliament and Government would fail to settle the Irish land question. (Kee, 1993, quoting Parnell from 1881)
Such a *question*, in German and French as well as English, may also concern matters to which allusive reference may be thought preferable, especially during the Second World War:
> One of [Mitterrand's] friends...held a leading position in the Paris office of the *Commisariat-Général aux Questions Juives*, the Vichy agency charged with hunting down

Jews, listing them for deportation and, in due course, looting their property. (*Sunday Telegraph*, 2 October 1994)

questionable immoral or illegal
Literally, something which should be inquired into, but now almost always in a derogatory or euphemistic sense. A *questionable motive* is concealed or dishonest, a *questionable act* offends the law or propriety, a *questionable remark* or *joke* is one in bad taste, and a *questionable payment* is a bribe.

quick *obsolete* pregnant
From its first standard English meaning animate, and used of pregnancy after the foetus has started kicking:
    She's quick; the child brags in her belly. (Shakespeare, *Love's Labour's Lost*)

quick one a drink of intoxicant
Not necessarily drunk by an addict:
    His short sharp nose looked as if it had hung over a lot of quick ones in its time. (Chandler, 1943)

quick time a single act of copulation with a prostitute
The jargon of prostitutes who have a time-based tariff:
    Want a quick time, long time, companionship, black leather, bondage? (graffito quoted in Rees, 1980)

quickie[1] a drink of intoxicant
Another form of QUICK ONE:
    And maybe we'd better break open the bottle for a quickie. (Sanders, 1980)

quickie[2] a single act of copulation
Not necessarily with a prostitute:
    Stone had never been fastidious about where he'd take his girls for a quickie. (Deighton, 1972)

quietus death
Literally, a legal discharge from an obligation, whence removal from an office:
    When he himself might his quietus make With a bare bodkin. (Shakespeare, *Hamlet*)
and in modern use:
    It looks as if Armstrong has got his quietus. (Christie, 1939)

quit to die
From the departure and as *quit the scene*. To *quit cold* or *quit breathing* is to be killed:
    Quit cold—with a slug in his head. (Chandler, 1939)
    Tafoya asked if there was anybody 'that should quit breathing permanently'. (Maas, 1986)

quod prison
It was formerly spelt *quad*, a shortened form of *quadrangle*, the area in which students were confined for punishment:
    He has got two years now. I went to see him once in quod. (Mayhew, 1862)
To *quod*, to send to prison, is obsolete:
    ...been quodded no end of times. She knew every beak as sat on the cheer. (ibid.—the *beak*, or magistrate, sat on the chair)

quota appointed to meet an arbitrary target for types of employee rather than on suitability, aptitude, or qualification
Originally an American phenomenon where employers of more than fifteen people were required to reflect in their workforce the local mix of race to a minimum ratio of 80%:
    Quota employees have become a standard office joke. (*Sunday Telegraph*, 20 November 1994)

R

R-word (the) recession

Not to be said in financial circles:

> After a record nine-and-a-half years of
> consecutive growth, the nation's
> 'Goldilocks economy'—not too hot, not too
> cold but just right—is flagging and all the
> talk is of the dreaded R-word, recession.
> (*Daily Telegraph*, 3 February 2001)

rabbit an incompetent performer in sport

The allusion is to the timid creature *Oryctolagus cuniculus*, which was known as a *coney* for two centuries after its introduction to England by the Normans. As *coney* and *cunny* sound much the same, prudery required another appellation for the long-eared, fecund, burrowing animal.

RD see REFER TO DRAWER

race defilement sexual relations between a non-Jewish German and a Jew

An early manifestation of Nazi persecution:

> Gunter Powitzer had been arrested at
> the beginning of 1937 for 'race
> defilement', after getting his non-
> Jewish girlfriend Friedl pregnant.
> (M. Smith, 1999)

Late in the Second World War, even friendship between and Jew and a non-Jew became a Nazi crime:

> The secret intent [of a Jew] to buy
> [a table service] was a misdemeanour,
> the connection with an Aryan sales
> girl could be interpreted as race
> defilement. (Klemperer, 1999, in
> translation)

race-norming *American* setting different pass standards in examinations for blacks and whites

A method of achieving a QUOTA:

> Race-norming is an unfair practice. (*Chicago Sun-Times*, 14 May, 1991—unfair both to those discriminated against and to those patronized)

race relations the reality within a community of differing racial descent or nationality

Not international diplomacy but relating to any attempt in a community to combat prejudice against and conflict between people of different race, colour, or nationality. Whence the *race relations officer*, who monitors conduct and offers advice, particularly in mixed communities; *race relations laws*, which decree individual or institutional behaviour; the *race relations board*, which seeks out and sponsors litigation against alleged offenders; and the pejorative *race relations industry*, which, in the eyes of its critics, has an obsessive attitude to matters which they feel would be better left to individual choice.

racial displaying prejudice against or hostility towards an ethnic group

Originally, referring to humanity in its entirety, as when Dr Marie Stopes was president of the *Society for Constructive Birth Control and Racial Progress*. The Nazis adopted and fostered a nascent tendency to intolerance, with their doctrines of the Nordic German master race, their spurious *racial science*, and their *racial purity*, for which to qualify it was necessary to prove that there was no gypsy, Jew, or Slav among your ancestors since 1750. That led to *racial purification*, the killing of Gypsies and Jews especially, but also of other mentally ill and physically deformed Germans:

> [By 1940 the SS] had already done sterling work in matters of racial purification. (Keneally, 1982)

The 1941 German invasion of Russia was, for the Nazis, a *racial war*:

> The idea of *rassenkampf*, or 'race war', gave the Russian campaign its unprecedented character. (Beevor, 1998)

racism intolerance towards or ill-treatment of those of a different race or nationality

Literally, a belief that people from different races may have inherent qualities and differences, as that Armenians and Parsees tend to be very intelligent, and Kenyans better long-distance runners. Now much pejorative use of prejudice, discrimination, and conflict towards a MINORITY:

> ... the Catholic bishops, too, have excitedly discovered 'racism awareness courses'. (*Daily Telegraph*, 20 April, 1992)

Also as *racialism*.

racist an intolerant bigot in matters of race and nationality

Originally, one who perceived or studied differences between races but now only used in a pejorative sense. Also as *racialist*.

racked *American* drunk or under the influence of illegal narcotics

Not tortured on a *rack*, but otherwise laid out, it would seem.

racy prepared to copulate extramaritally

A variant of FAST, both meaning high-living or reckless in behaviour:

The Eden Hotel...where the racy girls
hung out, was entirely rubble. (Shirer,
1984)

radical accepting or advocating extreme
political policies
Literally, going back to the roots:
> Had we proceeded in a more radical
> fashion in our treatment of prisoners of
> war the numbers of German soldiers
> ...surrendering...would have been
> smaller. (Goebbels, 1945, in translation)

The word is now used pejoratively:
> ...avid, punitive, radical ladies...
> enlisting my support for experimental
> sex-play in the nursery schools. (Bradbury,
> 1976)

In obsolete English dialect a *radical* was an
impudent, idle, dissipated fellow; but do not
assume that there was any connection with
academia. In the 1930s the New York police
Radical Squad existed mainly to break up
Communist rallies.

rag (the) *British* a brothel
British Indian Army usage, perhaps from the
slang name of the London Army and Navy
Club:
> In this brothel, or Rag as it was called by
> the troops...(F. Richards, 1936)

rag water *obsolete* gin
So called because those who became addicted
to it ended up *in rags*.

rag(s) on menstruating
Usually *had* or *got*:
> That stupid little cunt...is refusing to
> work because she's got the rags on.
> (B. Forbes, 1989—she was an actress,
> not a prostitute)

Rag week, punning on the university fund-
raising occasion, and *ragtime*, punning on the
music, are the duration of menstruation.

ragged drunk
The way you may feel later.

railroad *American* to treat in a ruthless
and unfair way
The imagery is from the immutable track:
> ...railroaded to jail in an incredibly short
> time. (Lavine, 1930)

Now also used of summary dismissal from
employment:
> Her father, in real life, had been framed
> and railroaded out of his position.
> (M. McCarthy, 1963)

and of pressing for a precipitate or uncon-
sidered response to a proposal.

railroad bible *American* a pack of playing
cards

Gambling was prevalent on long train journeys:
> In the United States a pack of cards became
> known as a 'railroad bible'. Some 300 card
> sharks operated the Union Pacific. (Faith,
> 1990—for the sake of passenger safety,
> I hope he meant 'operated on the
> Union Pacific')

rainbow fascist an intolerant person obsessed with ecological matters
Dysphemism rather than euphemism, but
descriptive of those who ignore or break the
law in their pursuit of environmental or
animal issues.

raincoat[1] *American* a male contraceptive
sheath
Punning on the RUBBER and the avoidance of
getting wet.

raincoat[2] a private investigator
The clothing they wear in a job which exposes
them to the elements:
> It will be interesting to see if Lloyds is
> prepared to use the raincoats (private
> investigators). (*Daily Telegraph*, 6 August
> 1994—the insurance body was pressing
> defaulting members, or names, to cover
> their losses)

rainmaker a person valued in an organization primarily for his contacts
He attracts clients or voters as his African
namesake generates precipitation:
> You got the makings of a serious
> rainmaker, Henri—bring me all the black
> caucus business. (Anonymous, 1996—
> Henri was a black campaign assistant)

raise a beat to have an erection of the
penis
From the observable pulse. Also as *have a beat on*
or *raise a gallop*. Some figurative use, as when an
exhausted man may declare that he *could not
raise a beat*, without any suggestion that he
might be required to indulge in sexual activity.

raise a belly to impregnate a woman
Referring to the subsequent swelling:
> He raised so many bellies in the gay capital
> that the registrar of births had to increase
> his staff owing to the way he had exercised
> his. (Pearsall, 1969, quoting 19th-century
> pornography—the *gay capital* was London,
> not San Francisco)

raisin a male homosexual
I suspect from the French meaning, lipstick;
FRUIT 1 many have come later:
> [Maugham] had more wrinkles than
> Auden, that other amazing raisin.
> (Theroux, 1978)

rake-off a payment made under bribery or extortion

Usually on a regular basis, with imagery probably from the roulette table:

> I'll give you a third, as I gave Curtis. The 'rake-off' don't hurt anyone. (F. Harris, 1925—the inverted commas show the novelty of the usage)

ram[1] (of a male) to copulate with

The usual violent imagery and a rarer variant of PUSH 1, punning on RAM 2:

> Flirting and ramming with white women...(Fraser, 1975)

ram[2] a promiscuous male

Like the fecund animal:

> Must 'ave been quite a ram in 'is day. (Ustinov, 1971)

ram-riding (a) *obsolete* public humiliation

An adulterous wife or a henpecked husband might be compelled to mount a sheep in this venerable ceremony:

> They had seized the woman—and some were taking her along in a Ram Riding. (Quiller-Couch, 1891)

Also as a *riding*:

> I found the stairs full of people, there being a great Riding there today for a man, the constable of the town, whose wife beat him. (Pepys, 1667)

ramp to rob, cheat, or overcharge

Originally, to snatch. The overcharging use may owe something to the upward inclination. A *ramp* usually refers to cheating or overcharging, not robbery.

ramps (the) *obsolete British* a brothel

Army use, possibly because you paid dearly for your pleasure, then or later.

randy *British* eager for copulation

A *ran-dan* was a carouse:

> Is the laird on the ran-dan the night? (Tweeddale, 1896)

and *randy* is a corruption of it. In the late 19th century 'A randy sort o' a 'ooman' (*EDD*) was one who enjoyed a good party, but the association with intoxicants has now gone:

> I want you just as you are. Final. Got it? I'm randy now. (Bogarde, 1981)

This use makes the British look with misgiving on the American shortened form of the name *Randolph*.

Rangoon itch a fungal infection of the penis

Burmese prostitutes were notoriously disease-ridden:

> The houses you come away from with fungus on your pecker known as 'Rangoon itch'...(Theroux, 1973)

The *Rangoon runs* were not journeys to and from the city, but diarrhoea.

rank capable of being impregnated

Literally, fresh or strong-smelling:

> ...the ewes, being rank,
> In the end of autumn turned to the rams. (Shakespeare, *The Merchant of Venice*)

rap the accusation of a criminal offence

Literally, a rebuke or slap:

> I'd rather be under a murder rap, which I can beat. (Chandler, 1953)

A *rap sheet* is a list of previous convictions:

> As far as he knew, she might be a felon with a list of heinous crimes on her rap sheet. (Koontz, 1997)

rap club *American* a brothel

To *rap* is to talk or chatter, or to perform *rap music*:

> In the face of a crackdown on street prostitution many of the girls...are taking shelter in 'rap clubs'—which have replaced massage parlors in the sex-for-sale world. (*New York Post*, 22 June 1973)

Also as *rap parlor* or *studio*.

raspberry[1] a fart

Rhyming slang on *raspberry tart*. To *blow a raspberry* is to simulate the sound orally through pursed lips. Much figurative use indicating a mild admonition, refusal, or reproach:

> ...popped question to Dutch girl and got raspberry. So that is that, eh. Stiff upper lip and dropped cock. (E. Waugh, July 1936, quoted in S. Hastings, 1994)

raspberry[2] a lame person

Rhyming slang on *raspberry ripple*, a cripple.

rather exceedingly

Many expressions introduced by *rather* are on the borderline of understatement and euphemism. Thus a *rather naughty child* is almost certainly a spoilt and undisciplined brat, and a hospital patient who is described as being *rather poorly* is very ill.

rational agreeing with a prejudice

Literally, using logic or reason. The language of a bigot:

> A rational debate for their purposes is one which reached the approved conclusions. (*Daily Telegraph*, 26 June 2001)

rationalize arbitrarily to reduce

Literally, to think in a rational manner, whence to deal sensibly with a problem. To *rationalize* a workforce is summarily to dismiss employees. So too with other resources:

> Every time the Government...encouraged local authorities to 'rationalise' their recreational areas, school pitches have been lucratively sacrificed for houses and supermarkets as a way of keeping down the rates. (*Daily Telegraph*, 3 March 1994)

rattle¹ to copulate with
Of a male normally, from the shaking about which may be involved:

> All I'd done was rattle Mandeville's wife. (Fraser, 1973)

rattle² a promiscuous woman
From RATTLE 1:

> It was her thinking she was the thinking man's rattle. (Amis, 1978)

A *rattle* can also be a single act of copulation.

rattle³ *American* to urinate
Rhyming slang on *rattle and hiss*, perhaps with the usual serpentine imagery in mind.

rattled *mainly American* drunk
I suspect, from the antiquity, that the derivation is from the Scottish meaning, to beat, with the common violent imagery.

raunchy lustful or pornographic
It originally meant sloppy, whence, with an unusual rapidity of progression, poor, then cheap, then drunken:

> But then things got a little raunchy. They wanted to go down to Greenwich Village and see the freaks. (Sanders, 1981)

Now almost entirely used in its sexual sense:

> ...importuning me with words delectably raunchy and lewd. (Styron, 1976)

ravish to copulate with a woman against her will
Originally, to seize or carry off anything:

> The ravish'd Helen, Menelaus' wife,
> With wanton Paris sleeps. (Shakespeare, *Troilus and Cressida*)

and in more modern use:

> I don't know why, but that ravishing of Lily made her dear to me. (F. Harris, 1925)

The dated female expression of delight *How ravishing!* came from the meaning 'ecstatic' rather than from any Freudian fantasies.

raw naked
The undressed state:

> But screw the pyjamas. I sleep raw. (Sanders, 1983)

razor to maim or kill by cutting
Here the cut-throat open blade is not used for shaving:

> ...razored in barrelhouses and end up being shot in a saloon. (Longstreet, 1956)

re-educate to seek to change a political allegiance by imprisonment or violence
The Communists achieved more by brutality than the Americans in Vietnam through appeals and bribery:

> ...turn every deserter into a defector by 're-educating' him in a camp. (M. McCarthy, 1967)

Whence *re-education*:

> Then the Red Guard unit did a little re-education of their own, putting the boot in. (Strong, 1998)

re-emigration *obsolete* encouraging black immigrants to Britain to return to their place of birth
A usage after repatriation had become a dirty word:

> ...[Enoch Powell] repeating that repatriation (which he called 're-emigration') was also a vital part of Conservative policy. (Cosgrave, 1989)

reading Geneva print *obsolete* drunk
This is a sample entry of several literary puns on the city noted for its piety and its printing, and on *gin*, which was also then called *Geneva*, from the French *genièvre*, the juniper berry:

> You have been reading Geneva print this morning already. (W. Scott, 1816)

ready for capable of being impregnated
Of a mammal other than a human:

> Wild animals are taken by a female ready for a male. (J. Boswell, 1791—Dr Johnson was talking about elephants)

realign (of currency) to devalue
Realignments are always downwards:

> [Mrs Thatcher] privately began telling colleagues critical of entry [into the Exchange Rate Mechanism] that we could easily realign. (J. Major, 1999)

ream to sodomize
Literally, the engineering term for enlarging a hole by inserting a metal tool:

> ...maybe a night in the slammer where the boogies will ream you. (Sanders, 1985—a policeman was threatening a male homosexual)

reaper (the) death
Father Time carries a scythe as well as an hourglass. Usually as the GRIM REAPER.

rear to defecate
The etymology suggested elsewhere based on soldiers falling out *to the rear* seems

implausible. The derivation was more probably from REAR (END) and REARS.

rear end the buttocks
Not the heels or the shoulder blades. Both
homosexual and male heterosexual use:
   ... her sumptuous rear end. (Styron, 1976)

rears lavatories
Those in a communal block are usually
situated behind the dwellings whose occupants used them.

reasonable submissive to coercion or the
threat of force
The language of bullies and tyrants:
   My official did not see why it should not be
   a peaceful [settlement] if, as he said, the
   Poles were 'reasonable'. (Shirer, 1999,
   quoting a broadcast on 22 August 1939,
   nine days before Germany invaded
   Poland: as Klemperer reminds us, Hitler
   and Stalin had already agreed to divide
   Poland between themselves—diary entry
   7 June 1939)

rebased reduced
It refers to dividends, pay, and suchlike. The
base might have been set higher, but never is:
   The dividend has been 'rebased'—cut
   to you and me. (*Sunday Telegraph*,
   23 December 1996)

rebuilding costs reparations on a defeated foe
The language of Nazi Germany:
   Hitler ... preferred to call the financial
   burden the Reich imposed on defeated
   nations, not *Beatzungcosten* (occupation
   costs) but *Aufbaucosten* (rebuilding costs).
   (Ousby, 1997)

receding (of a male) nearly bald
A shortened form of *receding hairline*. Among
men, baldness is always a delicate subject,
except in others.

receive to be prepared to see an unexpected guest
A usage of those whose privacy is guarded by
servants:
   She is [in], but I gotta go through all that
   etiquette shit and see if she's receiving.
   (Sanders, 1992)

receiver a dealer in stolen property
From his willingness to 'receive anything
bought' (Mayhew, 1862). Now standard English, and not to be confused with the official
charged with winding up the affairs of a
bankrupt business.

receiver-general *obsolete* a prostitute

Punning on the officer appointed by the court
in a case of insolvency and her *reception* of
men *generally*.

recent unpleasantness a war
A version of *late unpleasantness* and its variant,
LATE DISTURBANCES, seeking to play down or
forget the horror.

recognition *British* the receipt of a hon-
orific title
Not just knowing a likeness but the use of
government patronage in awarding HONOURS:
   ... someone who hopes that it may result at
   some future date in their recognition.
   (A. Clark, 1993—he was as caustic about
   those who through flattery or bribery
   (political donations) seek such 'awards', as
   he was anxious to secure for himself the
   appointment as a Privy Counsellor)

record (a) the evidence of a criminal conviction
We all have *records* of a sort, although we
modestly prefer to use the French *résumé* or
the Latin *curriculum vitae* when we talk about
them:
   He had a record and I knew about that, but
   I picked him up. (L. Thomas, 1996)

recreational drug an illegal narcotic
As opposed to one taken for medical purposes:
   Sloth, gluttony, recreational drugs were
   out. (McInerney, 1992)

recreational sex promiscuous copulation
Re-creation might, incorrectly, seem to imply
a desire to achieve impregnation of the
female:
   We're both happily married. We just have
   a common interest in recreational sex.
   (Lodge, 1995)
See also REST AND RECREATION.

rectification of frontiers the annexation
of territory by force
The party which seeks the putting right, from
Hitler onwards, is never minded in turn to
divest itself of territory.

red cross morphine
Addict jargon. It can be stolen from a first aid
kit. A *red devil* is a barbiturate, from the colour
of the pill.

red eye *American* poor-quality potable
alcohol
Usually whisky, from one of its effects on the
drinker, and not to be confused with the *redeye (special)*, the overnight flight from the
Pacific to the East coast in which travellers
lose four hours and a good night's sleep:

I'm on the redeye back to the Big Apple. (M. Thomas, 1980)

red flag is up (the) I am menstruating
Punning on the discoloration and the danger signal.

red-haired visitor (a) menstruation
A VISITOR who also calls on brunettes and blondes.

red ink a loss
In the olden days, black ink on a bank statement indicated a credit balance and *red ink* a debit:
> As Telewest intended, this Bluewater stuff quite overwhelmed the red ink that washed through the company's results yesterday. (*Daily Telegraph*, 24 March 2000)

red lamp a brothel
The traditional sign displayed outside. Less often as *red light*:
> There was a Red Lamp at Bethune situated about five yards off the main street. (F. Richards, 1933)
> Why don't we put red lights outside the hostels too? (J. Major, 1999—he was ridiculing the idea that unmarried mothers should be housed in hostels)

A *red light precinct* or *district* is a brothel area where you would expect to find more than one *red-lighted number*:
> They paid for promotion or detail to the red-light precinct. (Lavine, 1930, writing about the New York police)
> ... also featured at the red-lighted number of the brothel area of a town. (Longstreet, 1956)

red rag (the) menstruation
Punning perhaps on RAG(s) ON and the cliché, a *red rag to a bull*.

Red Sea is in I am menstruating
Alluding to the adventures of Moses and others recorded in *Exodus*, and possibly punning on the *sea* which covered the channel of their escape.

red squad (the) *American* police concerned with subversion
When others than Senator Joseph McCarthy feared Communist influence in America:
> The New York Police Department has a Red Squad. They change the name every two years or so—Radical Bureau, Public Relations, Public Security. Right now they call it the Security Investigation. (M. C. Smith, 1981)

redistribution of property looting

Not penal taxation of the rich but Second World War use of soldiers in Europe:
> He didn't call it stealing though, 'redistribution of property' he called it. (Price, 1978)

redistribution of wealth punitive taxation
As Abe Lincoln observed, making the rich poor doesn't make the poor rich:
> ... wilful and cruel disruption of the economic fabric that was called the redistribution of wealth. (Allbeury, 1976)

redlining *American* refusing credit solely because of the place of residence of the applicant
The address is highlighted in a list, figuratively or in fact:
> ... entire areas of the city, poor areas, humble areas were beyond the credit ... the inhabitants of those districts were exiled from creditworthiness. That foul practice was called redlining. (M. Thomas, 1987)

redneck *American* a poorly educated and bigoted white man
Dysphemism rather than euphemism describing a person who works in the open, perhaps at an unskilled job, but not someone who used to be called a *Red Indian*:
> The Stanton campaign will be presented tonight by a hyperactive redneck. (Anonymous, 1996)

reds (the) menstruation
A common female use.

reduce the headcount to dismiss employees
It is the bodies, not the *headcount*, who suffer the *reduction*:
> Smith is determined to turn the business round and stripping out costs and reducing the headcount will undoubtedly help. (*Sunday Telegraph*, 8 August 1999)

A *headcount reduction* is what happens:
> He said 891 staff had left in the first quarter, bringing total headcount reduction to 2,041. (*Daily Telegraph*, 10 February 1999)

reduce your commitments involuntarily to leave employment
Not just paying off your debts or moving to a cheaper house:
> ... a former finance director of Mirror Group Newspapers facing charges of false accounting and conspiring with Robert and Kevin Maxwell, has reduced his commitments ... (*Daily Telegraph*, 2 March 1995)

reduction in force *American* the summary dismissal of an employee or employees
Whence the acronym *riff*, used as noun and verb:

> Ask any Federal Government employee what it means when he receives his Reduction in Force letter, and he will say 'I've been riffed'. (letter to *New York Times Magazine* quoted in Wentworth and Flexner, 1975)

redundant dismissed from employment
Originally meaning, in superabundance, which an individual *made redundant* can hardly be:

> 'And now they've turned you out?' he asked 'Who said they had?' 'I thought you said something about being made redundant.' (Sharpe, 1974)

reefer a marijuana cigarette
Possibly from the method of hand-rolling the cigarettes:

> A two-time loser making home from a reefer party. (Chandler, 1943)

reengineer summarily to dismiss employees
It is people who are thrown away, rather than parts of the product:

> In a reengineering, a number of people get reengineered out of a job. (*Sunday Telegraph*, 6 May 1995—quoting a lawyer in a London legal firm which had just 'released' eleven partners)

refer to drawer this cheque is unpaid through lack of funds
Banks use this evasion because it is dangerous to dishonour a cheque by mistake and thereby imply that the drawer has acted fraudulently. Commonly abbreviated to *RD*.

referred *British* failed
Originally, put back. University jargon.

refresh your memory[1] to give information through duress
Police usage and quite different from consulting an aide-mémoire:

> They compel reluctant prisoners to refresh their memories. (Lavine, 1930, describing violence by the New York police)

refresh your memory[2] to correct previous perjury
Where a witness is recalled to the stand after having given misleading or false evidence. He may also *refresh his recollection*:

> ... after the indictment they'll give her a chance to 'refresh her recollection'. (Turow, 1990)

refreshed drunk
After a REFRESHER 1 too many:

> Mickie, I think you're a touch refreshed. (le Carré, 1996)

refresher[1] a drink of an intoxicant
Referring to the supposed bracing effect:

> He marches out, with his hat on one side of his head, to take another 'refresher'. (Jefferies, 1880)

refresher[2] *British* a fee paid to a British lawyer for days in court after the first
The advocate's oratory, if not his throat, might dry if not so rewarded.

regroup to fail to advance
Through apprehension, inexperience, or cowardice:

> ... instead of thrusting with all speed inland, they had walked around the beachheads, preparing to be attacked by a ferocious enemy and 'regrouping'—that popular British army expression so often to be found masking fatal inactivity. (Horne, 1994, writing about the Normandy landings)

regular[1] in the habit of daily defecation
Laxative advertisements enshrined this use:

> I've always been regular as clockwork, and then, bingo. (Ustinov, 1971)

regular[2] menstruating at a predictable time
There is a danger of confusion with REGULAR 1:

> 'What are you talking about?' 'She was a regular girl.' (R. Harris, 1998—she was perhaps pregnant)

regular[3] small
In the jargon of packet sizes, this comes after ECONOMY, *jumbo*, *family*, MEDIUM, etc.

regularize to invade and conquer
The intended implication is that the political situation is being returned to normal. It took one Polish, one East German, and twelve Russian divisions to *regularize* the position in Czechoslovakia in 1968.

relate to copulate
Literally, to be connected in any way:

> 'Can't you just say 'fuck' once in a while?' But Piper wouldn't. 'Relating' was an approved term. (Sharpe, 1977)

relations see *have relations (with)* under HAVE, HUMAN RELATIONS, and *sexual relations* under SEXUAL INTERCOURSE

relations have come (my) I am menstruating

From the limited duration and inconvenience of the visitation, or, in some cases, the relief at seeing them. The kinship is sometimes identified as being with *country cousins*, from their ruddy complexion.

relationship an extramarital sexual involvement with another

In fact, we have a *relationship* with everyone we meet, as buyer or seller, friend or enemy:
> For just over three months Jeanie has had a relationship with a Russian. (Allbeury, 1982)

Often with adjectival embellishment such as *close*, *long-term*, *special*, or as the case may be.

release¹ to dismiss from employment

The employee has not hitherto been held against his will:
> ...since released (not surprisingly) to pursue 'other business interests' (the banking euphemism for goodbye). (*Private Eye*, April 1988)

Also as a noun:
> The pilot's release from the team is a result of administrative action. (*Daily Telegraph*, January 1987)

release² a death

The soul has left the body for more congenial climes. Much used after a painful terminal illness in the cliché HAPPY RELEASE.

release³ *obsolete* to kill

Again from the separation of the soul from the body, but in days when there was more general belief in life after death:
> Let these serve as a sacrifice for the Innocent spirits so cruelly released at Jhanoi. (Fraser, 1975, writing in archaic style)

release⁴ sexual activity

The theory is that unrelieved sexual tension is unhealthy, especially for an adult male:
> ...indulged in this pastime night after night as much to give him some 'release' (she actually used the odious word). (Styron, 1976, writing about masturbation)

relief¹ public aid given to the indigent

Originally, a feudal payment to an overlord on coming into an estate:
> The parish granted no relief and even if it had done so it is very doubtful whether the strikers or their wives would have accepted it. (F. Richards, 1936)

relief² urination

You usually *need* or *obtain* it:
> Archie had needed immediate relief in the bathroom. (Davidson, 1978)

Whence the American *relief-station*, a lavatory.

relief³ sexual activity

As with RELEASE 4, from a supposed relieving of sexual tension. It is used of copulation or masturbation:
> ...the Euphoric Spring had heated your blood to the extent that you're prepared to fly me six thousand miles to obtain relief. (Lodge, 1975)
> He played blue movies in his head featuring himself and Robyn Penrose, and crept guiltily to the *en suite* bathroom to seek a schoolboy's relief. (Lodge, 1988)

relieve *American* to dismiss from employment

The use suggests that the employer is doing the employee a kindness. The British *relieve of duties* is usually of an official for misbehaviour or dereliction of duty, pending a full enquiry and dismissal.

relieve of virginity to copulate with a female virgin

Perhaps no more than a circumlocution:
> Dottie had wanted to be 'relieved' of her virginity. (M. McCarthy, 1963)

relieve of your sufferings to be dead

Usually in the past tense:
> ...lingering a year until relieved of his sufferings in 1841. (Dalrymple, 1989, writing about James Prinsep, who translated Ashoka's edicts)

relieve yourself to urinate

Obtaining RELIEF 2 and as *relieve your bladder*:
> He felt a sudden urge to relieve himself. (Diehl, 1978—he was not on guard duty)
> Drinking excessive amounts of tea leads to a strong urge to relieve the bladder. (Golden, 1997)

To *relieve your bowels* is to defecate:
> They were in the dawn, brass lotah in hand, to relieve their bowels in the spaces between the houses. (Masters, 1976)

relinquish to leave (employment) after being dismissed

The usage implies wrongly that the giving up was voluntary:
> Mr Barker 'relinquished' these roles in May last year on the same day that Hartstone issued its second profit warning. (*Daily Telegraph*, 16 July 1994)

relocation sending people to a place for killing them

A Nazi use for the rounding up of Jews to send to the extermination camps:
> In Berlin, they wrote 'relocation', and believed themselves excused. (Keneally, 1982, citing a German wartime edict)

relocation camp *American* an institution for the imprisonment of enemy aliens
The language is the same as that of the Nazis, but the intention was merely to safeguard the Union against possible subversive action by Japanese Americans, of whom many lived in the Pacific states:
> ...most of them interned at the time in 'relocation camps'. (Jennings, 1965—in fact those interned remained staunchly loyal to their adopted country)

reluctant to depart suggesting that the verdict of dismissal was wrong
A cricket usage, where unwillingness immediately to accept the decision of the umpire is considered unsporting:
> He removed...Graham Gooch, who was reluctant to depart after nicking an inside edge. (*Daily Telegraph*, 27 April 1996—Gooch was a professional cricketer)

remain above ground not to die
I include this entry to illustrate the dangers and risks confronting those who use euphemisms:
> Mrs Van Butchell's marriage settlement stipulated that her husband should have control of her fortune 'as long as she remained above ground'. The embalming was a great success. (J. Mitford, 1963—Mr Van Butchell showed more enterprise than taste)

remainder¹ to kill
A rare usage, from the resultant corpse:
> He did not feel pity often, but he almost felt it for whoever was to be remaindered there. (Goldman, 1986—he was an assassin)

remainder² to dispose of (surplus stock of a book) by selling cheaply
The jargon of the publishing trade and the humiliation of an author:
> The book was a total failure—even, my literary agent told me gleefully, when remaindered. (*Sunday Telegraph*, 14 November 1998)

remains a corpse
Funeral jargon:
> Today though, 'body' is Out and 'remains' or 'Mr Jones' is In. (J. Mitford, 1963)

remedial applicable to the dull, the lazy, and the badly taught
Literally, helping to cure something, but not, in common educational jargon, used to describe special instruction to overcome a specific weakness in an otherwise normal child:
> ...the staff even have to lay on a remedial English course for students with a 'less than adequate mastery of the English language'. (*Daily Telegraph*, October 1983, reporting on a former polytechnic)

As with mental illness, the use of euphemism to mask levels of disability is no kindness for those who require long-term help.

remittance man *obsolete* an unsuccessful, embarrassing, or improvident member of a wealthy family sent to reside in a distant country
He received, rather than sent, the *remittance* so long as he stayed away:
> Remittance man—a form of Kenya settler said to depend on remittance from UK to stop him returning. (C. Allen, 1979)

removal¹ a murder
But not necessarily making off with the body. *DSUE* says: 'Ex a witness's euphemism in the Phoenix Park assassination case'. (On 6 May 1882 Burke and Cavendish, the Permanent Under-Secretary for Ireland and the Chief Secretary, were hacked to pieces with surgical knives in Phoenix Park, Dublin. Five of the murderers were hanged, but the killings led to a harsh Prevention of Crimes Act, the abolition of trial by jury, and a worsening of relations between England and Ireland.)

removal² dismissal from employment
Venerable enough to be noted by Dr Johnson in 1755.

removal³ a burial
Moving the corpse for the last time before the resurrection:
> Very few had attended Bridget Manning's removal...Halpin had photographs of the burial. (J. Kennedy, 1998)

removed *obsolete* dead
Not murdered. It was the soul which took flight, while the corpse remained:
> When a person has just expired, the Scotch people commonly say, he is removed. (*Monthly Magazine*, 1800, quoted in *EDD*)

rent boy a young male homosexual prostitute
Probably not from the obsolete meaning of *rent*, a payment in respect of an illegal transaction:
> Colombo was sucked into the sad and dangerous world of London rent boys. (Fiennes, 1996)

rent stabilization see STABILIZATION

renter a prostitute
Male or female, working on a part-time basis.

repose *American* to be dead and buried
The common imagery of the corpse being
asleep (see FALL ASLEEP):
> The companions will repose one above the
> other in a single grave space. (J. Mitford,
> 1963)

In funeral jargon, a *reposing room* is a morgue:
> Reposing room or slumber room, not
> laying-out room. (ibid.)

repositioning the summary dismissal of
staff
Used in this sense by Stanford University.
(*Daily Telegraph*, 20 August 1996). True as far as
it goes, but not the whole story.

reproductive freedom *American* the right
to abort a healthy foetus
Not the right to multiple parenthood, which
Chinese citizens do not enjoy. The phrase is
also used to denote the effect on a woman's
life of the availability of contraceptives.

requisition to steal
Literally, to take over on a temporary basis for
military or urgent purposes:
> Captain Martin... suggested we
> 'requisition' the...drum kit to prevent it
> falling into German hands. (Milligan,
> 1971—the drums were taken from the Old
> Town Church Hall of Bexhill-on-Sea in
> 1940)

reservation an area of land not taken
from American Indians by white settlers
The HOMELANDS of South Africa were not an
original idea:
> ...the vegetation—or lack of it—wasn't all
> that different from the reservation of his
> youth. (Clancy, 1991—an American Indian
> was in the Middle East)
See also OFF THE RESERVATION.

resettlement mass murder
Literally, voluntary or involuntary removal of
residence. However, the Nazi *Unsiedlung* took
Jews from the ghetto, or from the Jewish
House in which they were obliged to live, to
their death:
> ...the huge 'resettlements' from the
> Warsaw ghetto...were coincident
> with the establishment of
> ...Treblinka and its gas chambers.
> (Styron, 1976)

reshuffle to dismiss from employment
In the case of governments, the numbers of
cards in the pack remain the same, as in a
ministerial *reshuffle*, where the head of government dismisses ministers and appoints
others in their place. In an industrial *reshuffle*
many of the cards no longer remain in the
pack:

Ericsson spoke of negative momentum at
the end of 1995 and early 1996 as 12,000
Public Communications staff were re-
shuffled. The 1996 rise in orders can be
seen as evidence that the new slimmed-
down unit found its footing. (Goldman
Sachs Research paper, February 1997)

residential provision *British* a place in a
boarding institution
More than mere inelegance or circumlocution
because sociological jargon must avoid the
taboo *board school*, a prison for young criminals, and the equally abhorrent *boarding
school*, attended by fee-paying pupils outside
the state system. The *resident* may be a
homeless geriatric, a lunatic, a chronic invalid, or a prisoner.

resign to be dismissed from employment
The word is used by and of the employee to
save face:
> I worked as a personal secretary in London
> until I was fi...until I resigned. (Bradbury,
> 1976)

resign your spirit *obsolete* to die
The usage seems to discount the prospect of
reincarnation:
> Resigned her Spirit to Him who gave it on
> the 13th day of March 1818. (memorial in
> Bath Abbey)

resistance any dissent or divergence from
the standards of an autocracy
Those Germans who were not Nazis were
deemed to be against them and so characterized, without having to emulate the courage
of the Poles, Dutch, and other nationals living
under German occupation:
> People who are mad or had epileptic fits
> were shot for 'resistance'. (Burleigh, 2000,
> describing Buchenwald concentration
> camp in 1938)

resisting arrest while in custody
Police usage to explain the wrongful wound-
ing or killing of a prisoner:
> I like it better you get a slug in the guts
> resisting arrest. (Chandler, 1939)
See also SHOT WHILE TRYING TO ESCAPE.

resolved without trial *American* involving the acceptance of a guilty plea
Part of the process of plea bargaining, but not
implying that the accused was acquitted for
want of prosecution:
> ...it should be 'resolved without trial', an
> oblique reference to a guilty plea. (Turow,
> 1990)

resources control *American* the destruction of crops

The language of Vietnam. It should mean no more than farming or rationing:
... bombing, defoliation, crop-spraying, destruction of rice supplies, and what is known as 'Resources Control'.
(M. McCarthy, 1967)

rest and recreation sexual activity
Originally, a short period of leave during wartime. Often abbreviated to R & R:
The Russians had probably been a patrol team, and had chosen the farm for a little informal R & R.
(Clancy, 1986—they had raped a girl there)

rest home an institution for the aged or mentally ill
Not punning on the fact that its residents will spend the *rest of their lives* there. For geriatrics:
A ninety-two-year-old who died in a rest home. (J. Mitford, 1963)
and for those with mental illness:
This is a discreet private loony bin. A rest home, it's called. (Atwood, 1988)

rest room *American* a lavatory
Wide use by both sexes:
... asked where the bathroom was. The restroom was filthy. (Diehl, 1978—but in what state was the lavatory?)
An attempt by the funeral industry to use *restroom* for morgue not surprisingly found few takers.

resting unemployed
Theatrical jargon which seeks to imply that the idleness is voluntary:
... the demoralization of so many of my out-of-work companions. 'Resting' is one of the least restful period's of an actor's life. (I. Murdoch, 1978)

restorative a drink of intoxicant
Restoring calm or relaxation, I suppose. Not common.

restorative art *American* embalming
Funeral jargon:
... transferred from a common corpse into a Beautiful Memory Picture. The process is known in the trade as embalming and restorative art. (J. Mitford, 1963)

restore order to invade and conquer (a country)
The excuse of the Russians in Hungary and Czechoslovakia, and of others elsewhere:
This has involved moving in masses of arms and men of the ANC's 'armed wing', the 'MK' to step up the violence—thus creating an excuse for the South African Defence Force (SADF) to be sent in to

'restore order' and to topple Buthelezi.
(*Sunday Telegraph*, 27 March 1994)

restraint[1] an attempt to limit wage increases
One of a series of euphemisms used by governments which seek to curb the inflation generated in part by their own profligacy or incompetence, by limiting wages and salaries. See also FREEZE 1 and PAUSE 2.

restraint[2] a recession
A usage of politicians who wish to avoid the dread word 'recession' and to imply that the economic mess is caused other than through their own policies:
The country [under Harold Wilson] was going through a period of severe economic restraint. (Mantle, 1988)

restricted growth dwarfishness
Restricted comes from a Latin verb meaning to hold back deliberately, and the only true human *restricted growth* was among the hapless Chinese women whose feet had been bound to keep them small. A BBC programme broadcast on 15 January 1987 was devoted to *people of restricted growth*.

restructure to dismiss from employment
Not altogether misleading, as the new *structure* will be different from the old, with fewer folk to pay:
The men (and one woman) are unemployed, swept from their jobs by a deadly combination of recession and 'restructuring'. (*Telegraph Magazine*, 1 July 1995)

restructured presented in a dishonest or misleading way
It applies to financial reports and the like:
When the Saudis take a look at some of these 'restructured' balance sheets, they are going to need about ten seconds to figure out what pushing oil back to ten bucks a barrel would do to a twenty-to-one debt to equity ratio at Texaco. (M. Thomas, 1987—and did, as it turned out, although other factors also came into play)

result[1] *British* a victory
The jargon of soccer managers and others. If a team is matched against a stronger side, a draw may also qualify as a *result*, but a loss never is, even when it is. Some figurative use of any favourable outcome:
All-in-all, it sounds like a result, as they might say in the Mount Pleasant sorting office. (*Daily Telegraph*, 24 September 2000—Mount Pleasant is the principal postal sorting office in London and many employed there are soccer fans)

result² *British* a sexual conquest
The derivation and illogicality is as in RESULT 1,
but which came first I do not know:
> It wasn't Friday but most were still looking
> for a result. (McCrum, 1991, describing
> youths at a function)

resurrection man *obsolete Scottish* a steal-
er of corpses
When it was widely supposed that those who
died in Christian belief would in due course
undergo a *resurrection* of the body, few wished
to risk having their corpses dissected in
pursuit of medical knowledge for a fear of a
dismembered or partial return to earth. In the
19th century the pre-eminent medical school
was in Edinburgh, and the demand for bodies
led to suppliers raiding churchyards:
> The Resurrection Man—to use the by-name
> of the period—was not to be deterred by
> any of the sanctities of customary piety.
> (Stevenson, 1884)

This punning usage may first have been
applied to Burke and Hare, who carried the
business a stage further by murdering chance
victims when a paucity of natural deaths
caused fresh corpses to be in short supply.
Also as *resurrection cove* and *resurrectionist*.

retainer a series of payments made to an
extortioner
Literally, a sum paid to retain the services of a
lawyer etc.:
> I can afford a substantial retainer. That's
> what it's called, I've heard. A much nicer
> word than blackmail. (Chandler, 1958)

retard a simpleton
Literally, anything delayed or held back:
> How long is the old girl going to take? No
> one said she was a fucken ree-tard.
> (Theroux, 1978)

In educational jargon, *retarded* is used to
describe a person with a congenital inability
to learn.

retire¹ to kill
The victim certainly stops working:
> I just retired a junkman. (Diehl, 1978)

retire² to go to urinate
When the monarch *retires* on a public occasion, she does not abdicate. Whence a *retiring-
room*, a lavatory, which may be any old
lavatory in America but, if so described in
Britain, is reserved for royalty or honoured
guests.

retire³ to dismiss from employment
The victim does not cease to work in that post
voluntarily:
> George Owen was 'retired' from Mercury
> by Lord Young, C & W's well-rewarded

chairman. (*Daily Telegraph*, 6 December
1994)

retiring-room see RETIRE 2

retread a single woman who has previously lived with a man in a sexual relationship
The imagery is from a tyre, suggesting that
the previous owner has had the better use
when the article was pristine:
> The girls who don't marry are regarded
> with suspicion... and those who did, or
> who end long-term relationships, are now
> seen as 'retreads' to be avoided. (*Sunday
> Telegraph*, 3 September 1995)

retrenched dismissed from employment
Literally, reduced in the interests of economy,
but illogically used of those who have gone
rather than those who remain in the workforce:
> Factories closed. Retrenched workers
> committed suicide. (Naipaul, 1990)

return fire to attack without warning
Nazi Germany's internal justification of the
invasion of Poland, and later of Holland:
> According to the National Socialists, the
> war began today, on 3rd September 1939,
> as a result of groundless declaration of
> war by the English and the French.
> In 1st September 1939 we merely
> 'returned Polish fire'. (Klemperer,
> 1999, in translation—diary entry of
> 3 September 1944)

return to to die
The destination is normally specified, such as
to *ashes*, *dust*, etc.:
> Great travail is created for all men... from
> the day that they go out of their
> mother's womb, unto that day when
> they return to the mother of all things.
> (R. Burton, 1621)

returned to unit *British* failed
Army usage, often abbreviated to *RTU*, to
describe those who fail to complete a course
to qualify for an elite corps, to become an
officer, etc.:
> They would be conditionally accepted or
> RTU'd to their original units. (Allbeury,
> 1982)

revenue enhancement raising taxes
What is *enhancement* for the tax collector is the
opposite for his victims. Less often as *revenue
emolument*, an *emolument* being originally the
fee you paid to a miller for grinding your corn.

reverse discrimination a failure to appoint the more suitable candidate

Discrimination, tout court, might seem sufficient to have covered the concept:

> White men have scored two major victories in reverse discrimination rulings by the US Supreme Court, confirming that the mood in America is turning sharply against race-based 'affirmative action'. (*Daily Telegraph*, 19 April 1995)

reverse engineering unauthorized copying

Not the gear which propels backwards. You obtain your competitor's product, take it apart, and then incorporate the technical improvements in your own.

reviver a drink of an intoxicant

Referring to its supposed ability to liven up the drinker, but not used only, as you might suppose, of the first potation.

revolutionary Communist

You might have thought that things would stop revolving after the Communists had attained power, but you would have been wrong:

> Mikoyan concludes the revolutionaries should establish 'revolutionary organs of power' (a euphemism for Communist dictatorship). (*Daily Telegraph*, June 1980)

Such power, if threatened, has to be met with *revolutionary firmness:*

> Western governments wouldn't be capable of handling them with 'Revolutionary firmness'. Meaning eight armoured divisions and a couple of MVD brigades...And a thousand cattle trucks for the lucky survivors. (Price, 1972)

Revolutionary elections are those rigged by the Communists:

> ...the post-war evolution of, say, Tito's partisan movement into a one-party state should prevent excessive naivete about what EAM's organizers meant when they talked about 'revolutionary elections'. (Mazower, 1993—EAM, the Greek Communist party, held a ballot while still under German occupation. EAM chose all the candidates and made electors sign the ballot papers. No prizes were awarded for predicting the outcome)

revolving-door[1] unduly lenient and ineffective

It describes the treatment of criminals who, soon after capture, are released to continue their former activities, figuratively entering (and leaving) the police station, court, or jail through such an access:

> The people of California are sick of revolving-door justice. (*Daily Telegraph*, 4 March 1995)

revolving door[2] involving excessive change of management

Those appointed come and go, figuratively without having entered the building:

> Ian Townsend, chief executive, is quitting [Sheffield United] to become chief executive of Medical House...The revolving door at Sheffield adds to the wider concern over soccer club management. In March, Sheffield's previous chief executive, Charlie Green, was forced to stand down. (*Sunday Telegraph*, 16 August 1998—managers of other businesses are fortunate not to have their effectiveness assessed weekly on the basis of the random achievement of eleven employees)

rib joint *American* a brothel

Probably from the obsolete *rib*, a woman, after the manner of Eve's creation. *DAS* says 'from 'tenderloin' reinforced by 'crib joint', which might be right, although most sexual euphemisms have less complex ancestry.

rich friend a man with a much younger mistress

Not just someone of either sex who happens to be better off than we are. See also FRIEND.

Richard a turd

Rhyming slang on *Richard the Third*. This English king had a bad press from the Tudors and Shakespeare, which is why he is commonly considered more of a shit than Edward, William, Henry, or George, of whom there were also more than three.

ride[1] to copulate with

Usually of a man, with the common equine imagery:

> You ride like a kern of Ireland, your French hose off. (Shakespeare, *Henry V*)

but also of a woman, especially if above the man:

> Gabby groaned as she rode him at a little under a canter. He lay easing himself up to her. (L. Thomas, 1979)

A *ride* is either a female viewed by a male for copulation, or the act:

> Reckon you'll count it a pretty dear ride you had, friend. (Fraser, 1971)

and, at least in Dublin, it may mean a male so perceived by a female:

> Anita shouted after him.—Mandy said you're a ride, Darren! (R. Doyle, 1991: the demure Mandy denied this: 'I did not, Anita. Fuck off.')

To *ride St George* was to copulate with 'The woman uppermost in the amorous congress, that is, the dragon upon St George' (Grose). It was said to be the best way to beget a bishop.

ride² *obsolete Scottish* to be a thief or marauder
The language of the Borders, where *riding out* or *riding* and robbery were almost synonymous:
> Ride, Rowlie, hough's i' the pot. (Nicholson and Burn, 1777—*hough* was the last piece of beef, and it was time to rustle some more)

ride abroad with St George but at home with St Michael *obsolete* to be a henpecked braggart
The phrase had nothing to do with begetting bishops (see above), or shopping at Marks & Spencer.

ride backwards *obsolete* to be taken to your execution
The way in which the victim was obliged to sit in the cart. Men did not ride in carts unless they were seriously ill, wounded, or being taken to the gallows.

ride-by carried out from a moving motor vehicle
It is used of a crime, such as shooting someone from a car or snatching a handbag from the pillion of a scooter:
> In nine months, she has mastered all the terminology: 'ride-by' (shooting on the move); 'drive-up' (firing from a stop); 'drive-through' (the car is the weapon); 'chase-aways' (the enemy flees). (Turow, 1996)

ride the red horse to menstruate
In America the horse may be white, from the colour of the absorbent cloth. Also as *ride the rag*.

ride the wooden horse *obsolete* to be flogged
From the *horse*, or stool, to which the victim was strapped.

ride up Holborn Hill *obsolete* to be taken in London to your execution
Holborn Hill was on the road from Newgate prison to the Tyburn gallows:
> I shall live to see you ride up Holborn Hill. (Congreve, 1695)

riding master a woman's extramarital sexual partner
Punning on the teacher of equestrianism:
> I was the Queen's current favourite and riding-master. (Fraser, 1977, writing in 19th-century style)

riding time the season of impregnation of sheep
Vulgarly also of women:
> Warn him ay at ridin time
> To stay content wi' yowes at home. (Burns, 1786—*yowes* means ewes)

right-sizing the dismissal of employees
Right for the management or owners, perhaps:
> 'We enter 1995 with the bulk of our right-sizing behind us,' Lou Gerstner, chairman of IBM, on last year's 35,000 redundancies. (*Daily Telegraph*, 20 January 1995)
See also DOWNSIZE.

rights at work the legal imposition of additional costs and obligations on employers
Not just the entitlement to wages, holidays, overtime pay, safe working conditions, and other normal arrangements between employer and employee:
> 'Rights at work' is, of course, Labour code for reversing at least some of the Conservative trade union reforms, and bestowing new privileges on the unions. (*Daily Telegraph*, 3 October 1995—*of course* indicates the tendentious nature of the comment)

ring¹ the vagina or anus
Viewed sexually. Heterosexual use:
> ...I'll fear no other thing
> So sore as keeping safe Nerissa's ring. (Shakespeare, *The Merchant of Venice*)
and homosexual:
> Listen, Ted—he's you know, after yer ring! (Parris, 1995—a boy was warning another about his friendship with a homosexual British Member of Parliament)

ring² a cartel
The concept is of meeting in, and making complete, a circle:
> Wellington City Council, which recently protested strongly against the submission of equal tenders by a number of British firms, has now decided to accept the tender for electric cable which is ...below the 'ring price'. (*Times*, 13 May 1955)
Apart from commercial use, dealers at auctions are reputed to operate in *rings*.

ring eight bells to die
The watch is over. Jolly (1988) draws our attention to the punning Alastair Maclean novel title, *When Eight Bells Toll*.

ring the bell to impregnate a woman
Normally intentionally, from the fairground trial of strength which involves a blow with a sledgehammer to drive an object up a vertical column. If the object reaches the top, the bell placed there will ring.

ringer a racehorse etc. fraudulently substituted for another

In early 20th-century slang, a *ringer* was a person who closely resembled someone else. The cliché a *dead ringer* does not denote that the substitute is deceased, but that the likeness is perfect. It is just possible that the usage came from *ringing the changes* in campanology.

rinse a dye applied to the hair

Literally, a cleaning by water. Mainly female hairdressing jargon. Older women with white hair tend to favour *blue rinses*:

 ... married the Buick dealer on the adjacent lot, and got a blue rinse. (Bradbury, 1976)

Rio trade a desperate gamble

Made by a dealer or punter seeking to recover previous heavy losses:

 At first I thought it was a Rio trade, which is where someone makes a last-ditch attempt to recover losses by betting their bank or, if that fails, books a one-way ticket to Brazil. (*Daily Telegraph*, 19 November 1998—a trainee dealer had lost over ten million pounds by mistakenly entering a transaction to sell securities worth over eleven billion)

rip off to cheat or steal from

The imagery is from tearing paper off a pad or banknotes off a roll. Of cheating:

 We got ripped off for half a million, and we respond with free psychiatric treatment and maintenance for the villain's family. (M. West, 1979)

and, as a noun, of stealing:

 Such rip-offs of their material are strictly banned by the GTV hierarchy. (*Private Eye*, May 1981)

To *rip off a piece of arse* or *ass* is to copulate with a female, when you may CHEAT perhaps, but are not stealing:

 ... picks up a hooker and rips off a piece of ass. (Theroux, 1973)

ripe *American* drunk

And ready to fall.

ripped *American* drunk or under the influence of illegal narcotics

Feeling torn by alcohol or drugs:

 Last night you got ripped on tequila. (*Midnight Zoo*, 1991)
 Dave Gilbert ... told Min once he's been ripped on LSD and put the top of a hamburger bun on in place of a distributor cap. (Lawrence, 1990)

ripple (of a female) to experience a succession of orgasms

Like waves beating on a shore:

 A bird sang low; the moonlight sifted in;
 The water rippled, and she rippled on.
 (Roethke, 1941)

ripples on (have) *obsolete* to be mildly drunk

Ripples are the attachments to the side of a cart to enable it to carry more than its normal load:

 "E 'ad the ripples on'—drunk he was not, though he had exceeded his rightful allowance. (*EDD*)

rise an erection of the penis

In America you call an increase in pay a *raise*, to avoid misunderstanding.

riser a thick sole and heel to enhance the appearance of height

Worn by a man: women are not ashamed of wearing *high heels*:

 He was half the size of anyone else ... wore risers. (le Carré, 1993)

rivet (of a male) to copulate with

Literally, to pass a rigid metal fastener though a hole:

 When I was an undergraduate you got sent down if you were caught riveting a dolly. (Sharpe, 1974)

roach[1] the butt of a marijuana cigarette

I have no plausible etymology:

 The waitress took the roach, sniffed it, and said, 'Thank you, dear. Just what I need.' (Sanders, 1986)

roach[2] *American* a cockroach

In a prudish anxiety to avoid any mention of the word *cock*, *rooster-roach* was found unsatisfactory and the shortened form *roach* became a standard usage:

 'He spattered a cockroach with a trifle spoon.' 'That's lovely,' agreed Loretta. 'Except for the roach,' said Sol. (L. Thomas, 1994)

It is offensive to call an policeman a *roach*, and dangerous if he hears you.

road apples *American* horse turds in the street

From the way it piles up naturally, as a fruiterer may display his wares.

road is up for repair (the) I am menstruating

A pun on the red warning light, the restriction of the passage, and the temporary nature of the affliction.

rob the cradle to form a sexual attachment with a much younger person

The *robber* may be male or female:
> Hello, you must be Jerry's wife. I'd heard he'd robbed the cradle. (Evans-Pritchard, 1997—quoting flattery by President Clinton)
> I could eat him up! But that would be robbing the cradle. (Atwood, 1988—two older women were talking about a younger man)

rock an illegal narcotic
Because of its crystalline nature:
> Fucking punk kid got burned in a drug deal. Fuck, some drug deal. Fifty bucks worth of rock. (Katzenbach, 1995)

rock and roll *British* a regular payment by the state to the involuntarily un-employed
Rhyming slang for DOLE.

rock crusher *American* a convict
The activity in which prisoners were traditionally engaged.

rocks the testicles
Of no greater size, it would seem, than a man's STONES. Usually in the phrase *get your rocks off*, to copulate, not be castrated.

rocky¹ of unsound mind
Unstable, like an unbalanced chair:
> I guess you're a bit rocky. You haven't escaped from anywhere, have you? (G. Greene, 1932)

rocky² *American* drunk
Again from the lack of balance.

rod¹ a handgun
Literally, a straight piece of wood:
> I don't never let Frisky carry a loaded rod. (Chandler, 1939—Chandler was a craftsman who at least knew when he was writing bad English)

rod² the penis
Referring to its propensity to rigidity:
> The liveliest part of his body became spiritualized, and his rod itself. (Genet 1969, in translation)

rodded carrying a handgun
A ROD 1:
> The derby hat saw if I was rodded. He took the Luger. (Chandler, 1939)

roger (of a male) to copulate with
Commonly supposed to come from a name traditionally given to a bull. However it was also a name shepherds bestowed on a ram. A third source may have been the rare use meaning a penis, likening its behaviour to what goes on under the *Jolly Roger*, or pirate flag:
> ... find oneself rogered by one of his libidinous heroes. (Bradbury, 1976)

Also spelt *rodger*.

roll¹ to copulate with
Of either sex, from the movement:
> A beautiful blonde virgin from Boulder Swore no man on earth had yet rolled her. (*Playboy's Book of Limericks*)

A *roll* is copulation:
> ... our last meeting had been the monumental roll in her pavilion. (Fraser, 1975)

The cliché a *roll in the hay* does not necessarily imply copulation in an agrarian setting:
> A hotel room rented ... for a roll in the hay. (Chandler, 1953)

roll² *American* to rob with violence
Often applied to a drunkard who is knocked, or *rolled*, over before being robbed. Also in general use of street theft:
> ... rolled by a tough hackie and dumped out on a vacant lot. (Chandler, 1953)

roll³ to kill
After violent assault:
> ... both now dead. James 'rolled' by rough trade in Blackheath. (A. Clark, 1993)

roll over¹ (of a female) to agree to extra-marital copulation
Literally, to submit, like a domestic cat being scratched:
> He was good-looking, the girls rolled over for him in droves. (le Carré, 1995)

roll over² (of a criminal) to give information against other criminals
Another form of submission:
> The ATF likes to work with criminal defendants who have 'rolled over' to avoid prosecution. (Evans-Pritchard, 1998)

roller-coaster involving dramatic changes of fortune or reputation
It describes a career like a fairground ride, the downs being more memorable than the ups:
> The appointment of Mr Burnside, who has had a roller-coaster career, has raised more eyebrows in the sports community. (*Daily Telegraph*, 27 June 1998—Mr Burnside had previously been employed by British Airways as adviser to the Chairman during an acrimonious dispute with Virgin)

rollocked drunk
It is difficult to work out what the device for holding an oar on a rowing-boat has to do with inebriation:

Friday evening, no work tomorrow, arse-
holed by midnight, rollocked, well bevvied.
(Boyd, 1998)

Roman *American* sexually orgiastic
From the fabled orgies of the ancient Romans
rather than any depravities of the modern city
or its church. Now found in advertisements
offering access to sexual depravity, such as
Roman culture or the *Roman way.*

Roman candle a failure of a parachute
Failing to open fully, it resembles the firework:
> ... we were all well acquainted with details
> of a Roman candle. (Farran, 1948, writing
> about parachuting)

Roman spring (a) lust in the elderly
It attempts to do for geriatrics what an Indian
summer does for the climate.

romance copulation with one person outside marriage or a stable relationship
In standard usage, a courtship, from the
romance, or tale of chivalry, which was set
down in vernacular French rather than in
Latin:
> I am distressed to see the old French word
> 'romance' used as a code name for East
> African activities. (A. Waugh in *Private Eye*
> 1980—see EAST AFRICAN ACTIVITIES for
> another code name)

Also as a verb:
> Stanford Court, where he'd romanced
> another highly recognisable blonde star,
> Frances Day. (Monkhouse, 1993)

romantic entanglement a sexual relationship
Often more sordid than *romantic,* and as
romantic affair or *relationship*
> Half of fashionable London has its
> ... romantic entanglements. (Flanagan,
> 1988, writing of the 19th century)
> And naturally everyone understands that
> [Congressman Gary Condit] lied because he
> wanted 'to protect his family'. If he had a
> romantic relationship, that's his business.
> (*Sunday Telegraph*, 15 July 2001)

To be *romantically linked* can imply anything
from demure heterosexual courtship to
homosexual activity:
> His younger son, Lord Alfred Douglas, was,
> as they say, romantically linked to Oscar
> Wilde. (Parris, 1995)

See also ROMANCE.

romp to copulate
Literally, to frolic or play boisterously:
> What these Indians don't know about the
> refinements of romping isn't worth
> knowing. (Fraser, 1975)

A *romp* may be an act of extramarital copulation, or the person with whom it is undertaken:
> I'd rather think of her as the finest romp
> that ever pressed a pillow. (Fraser, 1970)

roof rabbit a cat
I include this entry as a reminder of the
terrible privations in those parts of Europe
still under German occupation in the winter
of 1944/45, and especially in Holland, where a
strike by railway workers was met with a Nazi
embargo on all food deliveries:
> Things were not so bad as in Holland,
> where the cats were served as 'roof rabbit',
> nor nearly so severe as on the mainland.
> (de Bernières, 1994, writing about
> starvation on a Greek island at that time)

room and board with Uncle Sam *American* imprisonment
In a federal penitentiary, from the shared
letters U and S:
> Using narcotics without a licence can get
> you room and board with Uncle Sam.
> (Chandler, 1993)

rooster a cock
A survival from 19th-century American prudery, when any mention of a *cock* was taboo:
> ... engine noises clinging to the trees, the
> rooster crowing. (Theroux, 1993)

root¹ a penis
The source of procreation or the shape of *root*
vegetables:
> ... a thicket of curling hair that spread
> from the root all around thighs and navel.
> (Cleland, 1749)

See also MAN-ROOT.

root² (about) to copulate
With porcine imagery, probably, rather than
from ROOT 1:
> ... he spent an hour a day at the pushing-
> shop ... rooting himself stupid. (Keneally,
> 1985)
> Where did you learn to root about like
> that? Didn't know such things went on
> outside a Mexican whorehouse. (Mailer,
> 1965)

A *root rat* is a male profligate:
> They're supposed to be so holy but some of
> them are unbelievable root rats. (Theroux,
> 1993, writing of male Mormon
> missionaries in Polynesia)

rootless Jewish
The language of Nazi Germany and Communist Russia, where Jews were seen as a threat
because of their intelligence, their independence, and their shared religion and
culture:

Nine Kremlin doctors were said to be
plotting to kill the leadership. Seven of
them were described as 'rootless
cosmopolitans', Sovspeak for Jews.
(Moynahan, 1994, writing about the
paranoid Stalin's 'Doctor's Plot' in
January, 1953)
And a couple of hundred rootless
internationalists—interruption: 'Jews'—
want to set nations of millions at one
another's throats. (Hitler speech reported
in Klemperer, 1998, in translation—diary
entry of 11 November 1933)

rope¹ (the) death by hanging
Noose and all:
> We're dealing with big violent organized
> gangs. Comes of scrapping the rope. (Kyle,
> 1975)

rope² *American* marijuana
From the association with HEMP 2.

roses (your) menstruation
The usual reference to the colour of blood:
> Such a bad headache. Had her roses
> probably. (Joyce, 1922)

rosy drunk
Referring to the facial glow. The meaning
wine may have been merely the anglicizing of
rosé:
> ...fetched the rosy, and applied
> himself to...another glassful.
> (C. Dickens, 1840)

rough trade an uncouth male in a sexual role
Aggressive and often badly dressed or un-
washed, he may be the consort, of a wealthy or
cultured woman:
> ...being admonished...for her public
> Ugandan activities with her 'rough trade'
> boyfriend. (*Private Eye*, April 1981)

Much homosexual use, both of an uncouth
person and of consorting with him:
> I don't do chickenhawks and I don't do
> rough trade and I don't work men's rooms.
> (M. Thomas, 1980)

round the bend mentally unbalanced
Going out of sight. Less often as *around the
bend* or *round the twist*:
> 'Keitel also is going round the bend,' Jodl
> observed. (C. Forbes, 1983)
> But I was around the bend. I was sort of like
> Lady Macbeth—obsessed by the blood.
> (Anonymous, 1996)
> 'At least you can smile at it.' Dennis, half-
> smiling himself. 'If I didn't, I'd go round
> the twist.' (Proulx, 1993)

See also HARPIC.

roundheels *American* a promiscuous woman
Like the unsuccessful boxer, the shape of
whose *heels* facilitates a quick descent to the
canvas:
> Little roundheels over there...she's a
> blonde. (Chandler, 1951)

routine (nursing) care only allow to die
Hospital jargon for the procedure where extra
medication or resuscitation would only pro-
long suffering.

rover a promiscuous person
Hunting for sexual partners:
> He is single, but he is no rover. (Turow,
> 1987)

roving eye a tendency towards promiscu-
ity
Usually, but not exclusively, an ocular affliction of males, and not referring to the
ceaseless vigilance of a mariner on watch:
> This was a predator, a huntress, Artemis for
> pants. Old Cap'n Hawley called it a 'roving
> eye'. (Steinbeck, 1961)

rub groins together to copulate with each other
As the GROIN is where the abdomen meets the
thigh, the *rubbing* may concern other organs
more immediately:
> ...they should get to know each other
> better...by rubbing their groins together.
> (*Sun*, March, 1981)

rub off to masturbate
Usually of a male. Also as *rub up*, or *rub yourself*:
> Lucy was standing between his legs and
> rubbing him up. (Sanders, 1982)
> ...he rubbed himself and the orgasm came.
> (F. Harris, 1925)
To *rub someone up the wrong way* does not mean
that you are infelicitous in your intimacy.

rub out to kill
The act of erasing:
> Somebody rubbed him out this
> afternoon with a twenty-two.
> (Chandler, 1939)

rub the bacon to copulate
One of the common MEAT 2 images. Also as
rub the pork:
> If [they] did have the hots for each other,
> maybe Scoggins walked in on them while
> they were rubbing the bacon. (Sanders,
> 1979)
> As long as you and I keep rubbing the
> pork...(Sanders, 1982—a man was talking
> to his mistress)

rubber *American* a contraceptive sheath

A usage for what in the British Isles used to be an inoffensive article of stationery:
> Inside my valise
> Are some rubbers and grease. (*Playboy's Book of Limericks*)

The synonym *rubber johnny* is common but *rubber cookie* is rare.

A merchant advertising *rubber goods* may sell sexual apparatus as well as contraceptives:
> A druggist with a *Rubber Goods* sign taped to the window. (Theroux, 1973)

rubber cheque a cheque which is dishonoured
It is liable to BOUNCE 2:
> Rubber checks make bankers break out in a rash. (Sanders, 1992)

rubber heel *American* a detective
From their habit of walking around quietly. See also GUMSHOE.

rubber tire see SPARE TYRE

ruddy a mild oath
Literally, glowing with a pink hue. Used in place of the once taboo bloody:
> You ask for the impossible. You ask for the ruddy impossible. (Hemingway, 1941)

rude noise a belch or fart
Which a child may say it has made, or be reprimanded for making.

rug a wig worn by a male
The covering of a bare area:
> Your hair is beautiful. Is it a rug? (Sanders, 1973)

Whence the figurative use of exasperation, to *pull your rug out in handfuls* etc.

ruin *obsolete* to copulate with (a female) outside marriage
The implication was that her marriageable worth had been lowered:
> I've often heard the boys boasting of having ruined girls. (Mayhew, 1851)

Such a female would have been said to have been *ruined in character*:
> ... seduced by shopmen, or gentlemen of the town, and after being ruined in character ... (Mayhew, 1862)

rum-johnny the Indian mistress of a white man
She didn't drink alcohol but was so called through a corruption of *ramjani*, a dancing girl in Hindi, or *rama-jani* in Sanskrit:
> ... relaxing with his friends in their *chummery* (bachelor quarters) or whoring with his *rum-johnny*. (Dalrymple, 1993)

Do not confuse this meaning with the similar corruption of *Ramazami* (a common Muslim name) to *rum-johnny*, which referred to Indian servants seeking work from new European arrivals in the port of Calcutta.

rumble to steal
Probably from the name of the improvised seat at the back of a carriage from which servants might pass purloined goods to an accomplice, or *running rumbler*, in the street:
> Methodically, the stewards first 'rumble' the dry stores. (Moynahan, 1983)

run¹ to smuggle
From one of the myriad meanings of *run*, in this instance a single voyage or excursion:
> You can lay aground by accident and run your goods. (Slick, 1836)

A *run* is a smuggling trip:
> A fine clear run ... all the goods snugly stowed away. (Ainslie, 1892)

There seem still to be plenty of *gunrunners* around:
> There were people in India and Pakistan who would have been prepared to run guns or to go to Hyderabad to fight us. (Royle, 1989—General Das was seeking to justify the Indian invasion of the princely state)

run² to flee in defeat from a battlefield
The motion is away from the enemy, not towards him, and the usage is by the winners:
> What? Do they run already? Then I die happy. (General Wolfe, 1759, as Montcalm's troops left the Plains of Abraham)

Whence also to escape:
> After another half hour she realized he'd probably run. (Turow, 1999—he had been under surveillance)

run³ an unexpected and sustained series of demands on a bank for repayment
The phenomenon occurs when depositors fear for their savings:
> ... if the run persisted, cash reserves would be exhausted and FMA obliged to close its doors. (Hailey, 1975)

run⁴ (the) peremptory dismissal from employment
A mordant wit may also give you your *running shoes*.

run⁵ deliberately to ignore
When we disobey traffic signals:
> She ran a red light and turned a corner. (Follett, 1996—the lady was not a bawd who repented of her ways)

run (a)round the Horn *American* repeatedly to mislead, frustrate, or deceive
The fluctuating winds of the Cape so hindered the progress of sailing ships:

'I won't run you round the Horn,'
Sendecker spoke quietly, 'but I can't tell
you more than I already have.' (Cussler,
1984)

There is a specific use when the police move a
suspect under arrest from one police station
to another to frustrate a lawyer trying to gain
access. Also as *waltz around the Horn*:

By the time his lawyer finds out, we've
moved him again. We waltz him 'around
the Horn.' It's an old routine. (Sanders,
1973)

run around with to have a sexual relationship with

In normal use, no more than to comport with
socially:

Gus had walked out on her because she had
been 'running around' with a Party
organizer. (M. McCarthy, 1963)

run away permanently to leave the matrimonial home

Usually describing a wife's action, but not
necessarily with or for another man:

The fact that she did not even take her
handbag with her is proof... that she was
not running away. (I. Murdoch, 1978)

run into a bullet to be killed

Often used when there is a pretence that the
killing was accidental:

If it develops that a rival ran into a spare
bullet while someone was practising target-
shooting, that's just too bad. (Lavine, 1930)

run off¹ permanently to leave the matrimonial home

Usually of a wife, for another man and less
often of a husband:

I wish to God she would run off with
somebody. (Foreman, 1998—he wanted to
be rid of his wife)
Rita's third husband had run off with a
male dancer. (I. Murdoch, 1978)

run off² an act of urination

Like emptying a tub.

run on (a) menstruation

Common female usage.

run out of steam (of a male) to be sexually
impotent

The imagery is of an engine which has
exhausted its fuel:

... normal except they've run out of steam
and can't make it with a woman any more.
(Hailey, 1979)

runner¹ *obsolete* a policeman

Today they all ride around in pairs and cars,
although the Victorian *runners* were not
renowned for their youth or celerity. (As with
RUN 1, there are many euphemistic meanings
for *runner*, including smuggler, fugitive, conveyor of illegal bets, etc.)

runner² an escape

From *running away*. Thus to *do a runner* is not
to repair a curtain or assault an athlete, but to
make yourself scarce:

Checheyev... high-tailed it to Bath to
advise Larry to do a runner. (le Carré,
1995)

runny nose an addiction to cocaine

From sniffing it and the consequent damage
to the nasal tissue:

'He had a problem. He owes me a little.'
'What kind of problem?' 'A runny nose.'
(Anonymous, 1996)

runny tummy (a) diarrhoea

Referring to the looseness of the stool rather
than *running* to a lavatory. Also as the *runs*:

... don't eat any of those gaddam
grapes... they'll give you the runs. (Price,
1978)

rush job the marriage of a pregnant bride

The hastily arranged wedding used to be to
the putative father.

rush the growler *American* to send for
beer to drink at home

A *growler* is a large pitcher. If you dallied on
the return journey, the beer might become
warm:

Meanwhile my jug is getting low. How
about rushing the growler for me?
(Sanders, 1980)

rusticate to banish

Standard English of dismissing British students from university for a while because of
idleness or misconduct, even if they continue
to reside in a town. The Chinese Communists
take things more literally:

His parents had been rusticated—sent
shovelling. (Theroux, 1988—they were city
dwellers banished to the countryside)

S

sack (the) dismissal from employment
In the days when workmen had to provide
their own tools, they were kept in a bag or
sack at the employer's workshop, or carried
in them to work. To be given it, or *sacked*, by
your master meant you were dismissed:
> ...sacked by a British bank for interfering
> with a woman in Fixed Deposits. (Theroux,
> 1973)

An unsatisfactory member of the Sultan of
Turkey's harem who *got the sack* received
more peremptory and drastic treatment: she
was stitched up in one and thrown into the
Bosporus.

saddle soap flattery
Its quality is to make the seat more comfortable by softening it:
> ...he pointed out he would save the saddle
> soap in future and come up with easier
> missions. (Coyle, 1987—a soldier had been
> getting the tough assignments despite
> flattering his commander)

See also SOFT SOAP.

saddle up with (of a male) to copulate
with
The common equine imagery. Also as *get in the
saddle*:
> He had been saddling up with all the
> wenches on his estate and breeding
> bastards like a buck rabbit. (Fraser, 1979)
> Just before they get in the saddle they say,
> 'Okay, put your clothes on—you're under
> arrest.' (Theroux, 1973)

safe *American* a contraceptive sheath
A rarer form of SAFETY:
> Cordelia knows it's called a safe. Perdie told
> her once, when she was little and mistook
> one for a balloon. (Atwood, 1988)

safe house a refuge
Not merely one which is unlikely to collapse:
> The Russian spy master had a 'safe house'
> for a time at 3 Rosary Gardens. (Boyle,
> 1979)

safe sex sexual activity with another in
which a protective sheath is used
No longer merely worrying about an unwanted pregnancy or a curable disease:
> She brushes back Gina's badly braided hair
> and tells her to get hip to safe sex. (*Oakland
> Tribune*, 1 March 1991)
Safer sex means the same thing.

safety *American* a contraceptive sheath
The use pre-dates SAFE SEX, coming from the
days when all men had to worry about were
paternity suits, cuckolded husbands, breach
of promise actions, and venereal disease.

St Colman's girdle has lost its virtue *obsolete* there has been extramarital copulation
The mythical but magical garment encircled
only those who were chaste. The euphemism
was used in 1890 when Parnell's adultery
with Katie O'Shea, which had been widely
known in political circles but not publicized,
was exposed in open court, thereby ruining
his career.

salami tactics the gradual elimination of
non-Communists from a coalition
The phrase described the slicing away by the
Communists in Hungary of their coalition
partners after the Second World War:
> Why should the Russians try to annex
> the whole of Europe...if they try anything
> it will be salami tactics. (Lynn and Jay,
> 1989)

salt to cheat by improper addition
Normally, to add salt to food, to improve or
disguise its taste. The common euphemistic
use is in mining, where valuable ores or
minerals are introduced into samples to
deceive assayers and investors:
> It now shows that there was no gold in the
> mine, that the claims were a fraud and
> the samples were salted. (*Daily Telegraph*,
> 10 May 1997)
Accounts may also be salted, with non-
existent deliveries being charged or excessive
prices claimed.

salt and pepper *American* a black and a
white person in a sexual relationship
In this offensive use, the male is usually black.

salute upon the lips a sexual kiss
From the days when heterosexual kissing
outside marriage was exceptional:
> ...he repeatedly subjected me to the *assault*
> of his *salutes* upon my lips. (Fraser, 1977,
> writing in 19th-century style)

salvage to steal
Mainly Second World War usage, when
advancing troops came across a lot of abandoned property.

Sam *American* a policeman
Especially if on counter-narcotic duties for
Uncle Sam.

same gender oriented *American* homosexual

SGO for short, and not just referring to those who prefer the social company of others of their own sex.

sample a quantity of urine
Medical jargon. If a nurse asks you to provide a *sample*, it might as well be of saliva or blood or just about anything, but it isn't.

sanction an assassination
Literally, no more than a penalty, except in this espionage jargon:
> ...he had performed a half-dozen counter-assassinations ('sanctions' in the crepuscular bureaucratese). (Trevanian, 1973)

sand rat *British* a cheap prostitute
Army use in the Far East, from the prevalent rodent in bashas, or sleeping huts:
> The few cases that were contracted were with the Burmese and Chinese sand-rats. (F. Richards, 1936, writing of venereal disease)

Sandy McNabs *British* crab-lice
Army rhyming slang on crabs, or *phthirus pubis*, the proper name indicating where the infection, usually sexually transmitted, is to be found:
> I had no idea what the crabs (or, as Smudge Smith said, 'Sandy McNabs') were. (Milligan, 1971)

sanitary man a cleaner of lavatories
Sanitary means pertaining to health:
> ...latrine buckets introduced which the sanitary men emptied every night. (F. Richards, 1933)

For the avoidance of doubt, the old-fashioned *sanitary inspector* in Britain now calls himself a *public health inspector*. The American *sanitation man* remains a *dustman* in the British Isles.

sanitary towel an absorbent padding worn during menstruation
Once again health and cleanliness are confused. Also as *ST* and, in America, as *sanitary napkin*:
> She sold sanitary towels to the younger women in the pension, passing them over wrapped in plain paper, with a secrecy that suggested a conspiracy. (Manning, 1977)
> Don't block the toilet with sanitary napkins. (Bradbury, 1959)

sanitized cleaned or rendered harmless
You read it on the irritating paper strips across lavatory bowls and toothmugs in certain types of hotel which need to convince you that they clean the rooms between customers.

Also of files etc. from which damaging evidence has been eliminated:
> Erlichman says he never received that material, and doesn't know whether he got all of what Welander had turned over to Haig, or if the batch was sanitized by either man. (Colodny and Gettlin, 1991)

sapphic a female homosexual
Sappho was the poetess who lived on Lesbos, thus doubly enriching the language:
> I never picked you for a sapphic...were you always that way? (M. McCarthy, 1963)
> One of the fillies started an affair with a lady passenger...I had to make up to an emigrant to tempt my Sappho back to me. (Londres, 1928, in translation)

Sapphism is female homosexuality:
> *Mrs Keppel and Her Daughter* is a 'must' for anyone interested in the remarkable sexual licence which Edwardian couples afforded themselves, or in the sapphism with which their daughters experimented. (*Daily Telegraph*, 18 May 1996)

sartorially challenged badly dressed
An extension of the CHALLENGED theme which has added a new dimension to the world of euphemism:
> The sartorially-challenged Sir John Harvey-Jones...(*Daily Telegraph*, 30 March 1994— Sir John was not considered a snappy dresser)

sauce¹ (the) intoxicants
Usually spirits and implying excess. Someone *on the sauce* is either an alcoholic or has been on a carouse:
> I had been on the sauce and behaving badly. (Theroux, 1978)

See also GRAVY.

sauce² (of a male) to copulate with
Perhaps from the meaning, to give cheek:
> Said as if the name was a reason for my never having sauced her. (Fry, 1994, of copulation)

sauna a brothel
Since antiquity public wash-houses have catered for other masculine needs than cleanliness:
> ...more magazines restrict advertisements for 'saunas' or 'escorts' to a few pages. (*Sunday Telegraph*, 28 August 1994, reporting on attempts to curtail advertising by prostitutes)

You are, however, more likely to be offered a sauna in a sauna parlour than a massage in a MASSAGE PARLOUR.

sausage the penis

Nursery use, without sexual connotations. In the same society it may also mean a turd. Now unfortunately also found in various vulgarisms, like *sausage jockey*, a promiscuous woman, and *sausage sandwich*, copulation.

save to spend
A commercial inducement to buy something you don't need because of a supposed reduction in price. The British *saver fare* on railways was a cheaper one offering less comfort and convenience:
> The price: somewhere between Saver and First. (*Daily Telegraph*, 12 November 1997, describing a new service offered by a railway company)

A single woman who *saved it*, refused to copulate before marriage:
> A wet tongue kiss, a few minutes in their arms...but...she was saving it for her husband. (Longstreet, 1956)

say a few words to make a speech
Would that they were only a few on most occasions.

say Kaddish for to mourn the death of
Kaddish is a Jewish prayer 'specially recited also by orphan mourners' (*OED*):
> He had said Kaddish for so many of his own generation. (Forsyth, 1994, referring to an octogenarian Jew)

scald *obsolete* to infect with a venereal disease
From the burning sensation, especially in the male, who might have been infected in a *scalding-house*, or brothel.

scalp to kill
Originally the scalp was the skull, as in the American *scalp dolly*, or wig, and thence the hair on the head. The verb form arose from the practice of the American Indians, in which the skin and hair were removed from their victims both to prove their success and to retain as a trophy.
To *scalp* is also used figuratively meaning to cheat, in a commercial transaction:
> ...her air of innocence made her seem like a tout; and yet she did not scalp me, but asked for the exact price that was printed on the ticket. (Theroux, 1995)

scandal sheet a form on which expenses are claimed
A newspaper so described is also likely to contain exaggerated or fictional episodes.

scarlet woman a prostitute
The woman 'arrayed in purple and scarlet colour... THE MOTHER OF HARLOTS' (*Revelations*, 17.4/5), whence any adulteress:

> The Colonel evidently objected to its presence in his house at the same time as his Scarlet Woman. (Sharpe, 1978)

Our Protestant ancestors found it a useful abusive epithet for the Church of Rome.
Whence the obsolete *scarlet fever*, or lust for soldiers, involving a treble pun—on the disease, on the colour of their uniform, and on the activities of the *scarlet woman*:
> Nursemaids are always ready to succumb to the 'scarlet fever'. A red coat is all powerful with this class, who prefer a soldier to a servant. (Mayhew, 1862)

scheduled classes those condemned by birth to menial employment
Indian society retains gradations which would provide endless occupation for those whose function it is to seize upon and punish any form of DISCRIMINATION:
> ...the Dulits (or scheduled classes or harijans or untouchables, to take the wounding nomenclature back through its earlier stages)...(Naipaul, 1990)

school *American* a prison
The *big school* is for men and the *little school* for women and children.

schtup (of a male) to copulate with
A version of TUP perhaps, although a Yiddish origin is more likely:
> Don, all I asked was that you should refrain from schtupping your secretary. (Follett, 1996)

scissor-and-paste job a book or article not based on original research
The author figuratively clips and inserts material from published sources:
> [It] is a competent scissor-and-paste job. It gathers together the essential information from earlier biographies. (*Sunday Telegraph*, 3 June 2001)

scoop an alcoholic drink
This was the method of taking potable liquid for sale from a large container in the days before environmental health officers invented and the public lost much of its gastric immunity to a measure of impurity in foodstuffs:
> They did this every Christmas, went to one of their houses and had a few scoops before the dinner. (R. Doyle, 1991)

scorched *American* drunk or under the influence of illegal narcotics
After you BURN WITH A (LOW) BLUE FLAME? A bit far-fetched, but the imagery is the same.

score[1] (of a male) to copulate

Usually of a single episode on a casual basis without payment:

> Brunton was all set to score with a Moral Philosophy student in his rooms—a female student. (Price, 1979—but clearly not that moral)

The punning *know the score* is to be sexually experienced, of both men and women.

score² to commit a successful crime

Mainly of crime committed to pay for illegal drugs:

> At first...we thought it was a junkie looking to score. (Sanders, 1985)

Whence to buy such narcotics:

> There were drive-up windows to garages to which people could come to score. (Turow, 1987)

or the purchase:

> Just enough jewelry and twenty dollar bills to hold out the promise of a quick and easy score. (Katzenbach, 1995)

score adjustment *American* giving higher marks to non-whites

A device to conceal lower scholastic achievement or to compensate for inadequate schooling etc.:

> The little-known practice is also referred to in certain government and employment circles as 'within-group norming' or 'score adjustment strategy'. (*Chicago Times*, 14 May 1991)

Scotch mist *British* drunk

Rhyming slang on PISSED, punning on the drizzle which blots out the landscape, and on the whisky.

scour to administer a laxative to

Literally, to clean thoroughly the inside of anything. A beast with *scour* has diarrhoea, which humans also caught from bad beer, or *scour-the-gate*:

> There's first guid ale,
> And second ale and some,
> Hink-dink and ploughman's drink,
> And scour-the-gate and trim. (Chambers, 1870)

The *scours* is diarrhoea:

> If I'd known I'd have the scours this bad I'd not have eat one mouthful of that venison. (Frazier, 1997)

scrag to kill

From the meaning, neck, whence death by throttling or garotting:

> So I guess there is nothing for me to do but scrag myself. (Runyon, 1990, written in the 1930s—he was disappointed in love at the time)

scratch¹ *obsolete* the devil

Because of his propensity to 'seize rapaciously' (*OED*). Usually as *old scratch*:

> Give over action to like Old Scratch. (Slick, 1836)

scratch² a wound

A brave soldier seeks to minimize the extent of his injury:

> She gave a little scream. 'You are wounded! Your arm!' 'It's a scratch, nothing more.' (Fraser, 1970)

scratch³ *American* to kill

Literally, to retire from a contest by eliminating your name from a list:

> I scratch the Colonel in Hong Kong, Corrigan shows up. I scratch Corrigan, there's the dame. (Diehl, 1978)

screw¹ (of a male) to copulate with

Referring to the entry into a reciprocal aperture:

> 'Well you, Howard,' says Flora,
> 'who did you screw last night?'
> (Bradbury, 1975)

Either sex may be said to *screw around*, to copulate indiscriminately:

> Blokes who screw girls who screw around a lot are usually blokes who screw around a lot. (Amis, 1978)

A *screw* is a female sexual partner, always with a laudatory adjective. As I note elsewhere, in male vanity or fantasy, there are no bad *screws*.

Also figurative use as an expletive:

> She was drowned out by a chorus of 'Screw the profiteers'. (Hailey, 1979)

screw² a prison warder

Not from turning the key in the lock so much as from tightening the screw on the apparatus on which a prisoner underwent forced exercise, or hard labour:

> ...known as a hard-boiled screw. (Lavine, 1930)

screw³ to cheat

A venerable standard English usage, from the accentuated application of force implicit in the screwing process. It is the victim who usually so refers to his plight in the passive sense:

> Your chance of being screwed by a Canadian factory owner then were as good as your chance of being screwed by an American factory owner. (*Sunday Night Toronto*, 12 February 1974)

screw loose (a) mental instability

The imagery is from falling apart:

> I don't mean mad as in zany or whacky. I mean mad as in screw loose or tonto. (L. Barber, 1991)

Whence *screwy*, having an abnormal mental condition or behaving in an eccentric manner:

> 'The girl is screwy,' I said. 'Leave her out of it.' (Chandler, 1958)

The American *screw factory* is an institution for the mentally ill:

> ...had to be taken to the screw factory. (Wambaugh, 1975)

To be *screwed up* is to be confused or upset, while to *screw up* is to handle a situation badly.

screwed drunk

Probably a pun on TIGHT 1:

> ...a glance sufficed to show even Philippa...that he was undeniably screwed. (Somerville and Ross, 1897)

To be *half-screwed* is to be no more sober.

screwed down dead

As the coffin is sealed after a last peep at the corpse:

> Then don't talk as if I'd been screwed down. (Cookson, 1967)

scrubber a prostitute

Of the meaner sort, perhaps from the status and posture of the floor cleaner:

> Not all of them were scrubbers. Jane Wentworth wasn't...Marilyn would have fitted into that line of likely pick-ups. (Price, 1979)

A London *Times* 1972 headline 'Heath's Whitehall Scrubbers' Party' was changed in the second edition to 'Celebrating a Whiter Whitehall', without giving the office cleaners time to consult their lawyers.

scuppered killed in battle

The derivation from the *scuppers* of a ship seems inappropriate, unless it is where a corpse might lie. Some figurative use:

> We're here to raise money for a very important charity, and we're not going to let that be scuppered. (*Daily Express*, 8 June 1992)

scuttered *Irish* drunk

The *EDD* gives thirteen definitions of dialect meanings for *scutter*, including to make short runs or have diarrhoea, which have some association with the symptoms of drunkenness:

> Having one of those beside the bed would have been very handy for when you come home scuttered at night. (R. Doyle, 1991, referring to a machine to help those with bad eyesight)

sea food *obsolete American* whisky

A Prohibition use 'to mislead the police or strangers' (*DAS*). Most bootleg liquor came by sea or over the Great Lakes.

sea-lawyer see BARRACK-ROOM LAWYER

season (the) the annual period in which upper-class marriageable girls were put on display

In the days when COME OUT meant no more than to appear in society:

> 'The Season' being a sort of ritual marriage market to which every parent then subscribed anxiously. (Blanch, 1954—not every parent, only the rich ones)

seat the buttocks

A transference from the thing you sit upon to the part of the body on which you sit. As with BOTTOM, a familiar coy evasion.

The American *seat cover* is a nubile female in a car:

> Lay an eyeball on that seat cover comin' up in that show-off lane. (Dills, 1976)

and to *check the seat covers* in Citizens' Band slang is to look for or at an attractive woman in a car.

secluded inconveniently isolated

Estate agent's jargon to describe a house with limited or no access to public transport, utilities, shops, etc. *Seclusion*, for a violent criminal or lunatic, is involuntary solitary confinement.

second eye see BRONZE EYE

second strike retaliation

Nuclear warfare jargon, and not a further blow from the party making the FIRST STRIKE. A *second-strike capability* is your ability to reply in kind to a nuclear attack, inflicting *second-strike destruction*:

> Both superpowers have to bear in mind the high probability of second-strike destruction. (Hackett, 1978)

secret parts the human genitalia

Those not generally revealed in company rather than the subject of ignorance:

> *Hamlet* Then you live about her waist, or in the middle of her favours?
> *Guildenstern* Faith, her privates we.
> *Hamlet* In the secret parts of fortune? O, most true, she is a strumpet. (Shakespeare, *Hamlet*)

secret (state) police an instrument of civil repression

The full phrase is a literal translation of *Geheime Staatspolizei*, which we all recognize in its shortened form, *Gestapo*. Every tyranny needs its *secret police* if it is to survive.

secret vice masturbation

Of either sex, but usually a male:

...the various lubricants I had used while practising the Secret Vice. (Styron, 1976)
Also as the *secret sin* or *secret indulgence*.

secretary a mistress
A usage when the parties are travelling together:
> Wives, daughters and mistresses too—documented as secretaries. (Deighton, 1978)

section *British* to detain involuntarily in a mental hospital
Social service jargon, from sections two and three of the Act which empowers such confinement:
> Should she be sectioned under the Mental Health Act and forced back into hospital? (*London Times*, 19 October 1991)
Under American service regulations during the Second World War, the equivalent section was numbered eight:
> You hold on... Or you get shipped home on a Section Eight. (Deighton, 1982, writing about American wartime fliers)

security an excuse for aggression, espionage, or repression
For Hitler, the invasion of neighbouring states:
> The old cry of 'Security', so shamelessly employed to cover the aggressions of the thirties. (A. Clark, 1995)
For Senator Joseph McCarthy, a *security risk* was anyone he disagreed with. For despots, a *security service* concerns itself with the survival of the rulers and not the safety of the ruled. The system was exported by Soviet Russia to client states through *security advisers*:
> Shehu made the way easy for the rapid growth at the end of 1945 of a Soviet military mission [to Albania] to which 'security advisers'—dull euphemism for torturers...—were already attached. (H. Thomas, 1986)
A *security service*, even in a democracy, is likely to act illegally:
> There was no sign of a smoking pistol pointing to ministerial knowledge of past illegal acts by the RCMP Security Service. (*Maclean's Toronto*, 9 April 1979)
During the Second World War, the Nazis made much use of *security battalions*, which were recruited from those they had conquered, to enforce their rule. These often acted with more ruthlessness and sadism than soldiers from the Wehrmacht:
> You can't tell by the uniform, you know. They recruited in Poland, the Ukraine, Latvia, Lithuania, Czechoslovakia, Croatia, Slovenia, Romania. You name it. You don't know it, but on the mainland [of Greece] they've got

Greeks they call 'Security Battalions'. (de Bernières, 1994)

seduce to persuade a woman to copulate with you extramaritally
Originally, to persuade a vassal to break his vows of loyalty:
> By long and vehement suit I was seduced
> To make room for him in my husband's bed. (Shakespeare, *King John*)
In modern use, there seems to be less long and vehement suit.

see[1] to have a sexual relationship with
Of either sex, from the sense to visit:
> What would you say if I told you I'd been seeing someone? (Theroux, 1989—a wife was admitting adultery)
A prostitute who *sees* a customer copulates with him, although you should not draw the same conclusion if a lawyer says he has seen a client, or a dentist, a patient. To *see company* is explicit.

see[2] to satisfy by bribery
As in the American *see the cops*:
> ...doing business without seeing the cops. (Lavine, 1930)
Lavine also uses *see* for sharing a bribe with a superior:
> Woe to the cop who collects anything...and doesn't 'see the sergeant'. (ibid.)

see a man about a dog to go to any place that is the subject of taboo or embarrassment
Dog fancying is a sport which might call you away unexpectedly. The dog's location depends on the company you keep—a lavatory, in mixed society; an inn, in the presence of your family at home; home, if you are with friends in an inn; and so on:
> 'See a man about a dog,' he replied tersely.
> 'It's a very late *dog*,' she said, hoping to tease him from his introspection. (le Carré, 1996)

see the rosebed (of a male) to urinate out of doors
Usually in mixed company, when the indoor lavatory is reserved for use by the females. He may elect to see many other outdoor locations, such as *the view* or the *compost heap*. To *see your aunt*, normally in female use, involves a visit to the lavatory, or AUNT 2, indoors.

seed the male semen
That which is sown:
> She that sets seeds and roots of shame and iniquity. (Shakespeare, *Pericles*—involving two of his vulgar puns)
and in modern use:

I felt my seed coming. (F. Harris, 1925)
The American *seed-ox* was a bull, when words
like *cock*, *bull*, *ram*, and *stallion* were taboo in
polite speech.

seek fresh challenges to be summarily
dismissed from employment
One of the excuses given when senior
managers are dismissed. Their main challenge
is often to find another job:
> However if, as he suspected, the shares
> rose, it would be goodnight George on
> some plausible pretext that the
> company's merchant bankers would
> supply—'seeking fresh challenges'
> ... anything would do so long as it wasn't
> 'to spend more time with his family', a
> euphemism that had always grated with
> the chairman. (*Sunday Telegraph*, 14 January
> 1996)

seen better days poor
It describes people who have fallen on hard
times or machinery which is worn out.

seepage the amount stolen from a retail
store
Literally, the liquid which has slowly escaped
from a container.

segregation the availability of inferior facilities for a minority ethnic group
Literally, no more than separating one thing
from another. A dysphemism in America and
South Africa for giving whites better conditions than blacks.
A *segregation unit*, in American prison jargon,
is a cell for the solitary confinement of a
prisoner.

select capable of being offered for sale
Shopkeepers' puff for perishable commodities which are unsaleable when rotten.
Things so described are unlikely to have been
subjected to any process of selection. For an
estate agent, *select* means no more than better
than average—you can reject any implication
that there has been any discrimination in
their choice of what they will try to sell.

selected out dismissed from employment
Sam Goldwyn, famous for such contradictory
catch-phrases as 'include me out', would have
been proud of it.

selective indiscriminate
It denotes various military activities, where
you wish to play down the horror. *Selective
ordnance* is usually napalm, less widely destructive than a nuclear blast but hardly
discriminating in its victims. A *selective strike*
or *response* is one where you don't intention-

ally wipe out civilians as well as soldiers.
Selective facts are lies.
Selective distribution, conversely, is a policy
whereby a manufacturer sells only to the
retail outlets which keep the prices high:
> The supermarkets say they are fighting a
> practice of 'selective distribution' whereby
> designer labels keep their prices high by
> selling only to shops that are not going to
> slash their recommended prices. (*Daily
> Telegraph*, 17 July 1998)

self-abuse masturbation
Usually by a male, from the supposition that
he may be damaging his body or soul—or go
blind. Also as *self-gratification*, *self-indulgence*, or
self-manipulation:
> ... two of them being pretty hopeless cases
> through self-abuse. (F. Richards, 1936)
> Nor would loutish self-gratification quail
> this imperious, feverish desire (Styron,
> 1976)
> Pandora says she is not going to risk being a
> single parent ... So I shall have to fall back
> on self-indulgence. (Townsend, 1982)
> I have started to become obsessed by sex.
> I have fallen to self-manipulation quite a
> lot lately. (Townsend, 1984)
Self-pollution and *self-pleasuring* are obsolete.
Self-love usually refers to female masturbation,
but without any implication of narcissism.

self-defence an unannounced military
attack
Specifically, the explanation given by Iraq for
its September 1980 unprovoked assault on
Iran.

self-deliverance suicide
Deliverance is the preferred usage of those who
advocate euthanasia:
> When there were enough [capsules], the
> father dictated, the mother typed a suicide
> farewell, proclamation of individual choice
> and self-deliverance. (Proulx, 1993)
You may also hear of *self-destruction*, *-execution*,
-immolation, or *-violence*.

sell out to betray
But not necessarily for cash:
> You'll sell me out fast. And you won't have
> any five thousand dollars. (Chandler, 1958)
A *sell-out* is such betrayal, or any agreement of
which you happen to disapprove, such as the
settlement of a trade dispute.

sell yourself to be a prostitute
Correctly viewed, the transaction is at best
one of hire, lease, or licence. Also as *sell your
back*, *body*, or *desires*:
> This woman went on the streets ... to keep
> them both alive ... so she sells herself.
> (Bradbury, 1959)

A housewife that, by selling her desires,
Buys herself bread and clothes.
(Shakespeare, *Othello*)

A politician or candidate who *sells himself* does
no more than to try to convince others of his
worth:

[Ross Perot] emphasises his business
experience—to sell himself as a manager
and penny-pincher. (*Esquire*, February 1994)

semi-detached (of a house) sharing a
party wall

The standard English usage avoids direct
mention of the fact that the house is not
separate from its neighbour:

And the novel's title was the first recorded
use (in 1859) of the word 'semi-detached'.
'Double cottages' built with a shared party
wall had been common in the eighteenth
century. (F. Muir, 1990)

send ashore to dismiss from the navy

A figurative use, covering misconduct on land
or at sea.

send away to commit involuntarily to an
institution

Not going on holiday:

You can stay with the firm...assuming the
IRS doesn't send you away. (Grisham,
1999—he had been evading tax)

send down¹ to dismiss from university

The opposite of *up*, in residence. Usually for
misconduct or failure to achieve academic
results:

When I was an undergraduate you got sent
down if you were caught riveting a dolly.
(Sharpe, 1974)

Send down the road, of summary dismissal from
employment, is obsolete.

send down² to sentence to imprisonment

Cells are often below courtrooms, whence the
injunction 'Send the prisoner down', when
sentence has been passed:

In all her nineteen years she had never
once been permitted to visit her father,
who had been sent down three months
before she was born. (Strong, 1994)

send in your papers *British* (of an officer)
to retire prematurely

From the figurative return to the sovereign of
the commission addressed individually to
each officer. The act describes voluntary as
well as unplanned retirement:

...I've put up a fearful black? I'm not sure
I shan't have to send in my papers.
(P. Scott, 1975)

send to heaven to kill

A Christian might also be sent *home, to heaven,
to his last or long account,* or *to the skies,* and an
American Indian, in a Western at least, to *his
happy hunting grounds:*

Now I seemed to see that warrior that my
hand had sent to his last account. (Haggard,
1885)
My faithful Jasper has gone to his
happy hunting grounds. (du Maurier,
1938—Jasper was a dog)

A Chinese might be sent to *the happy land* or
the land of the lotus blossom:

The only successful way to get rid of
a competitor...is to send him to
the happy land of his forefathers by
having him 'put on the spot'. (Lavine,
1930)
...send him to the land of the lotus
blossom. (ibid.)

To be *sent home in a body-bag* means that an
American military corpse is being repatriated
for a funeral. British casualties are normally
buried in 'some corner of a foreign field'.

send to the showers see TAKE AN EARLY BATH

send up to pass a prison sentence upon

The prisons of New York and New Orleans
were upstream of the cities, and convicts
were *sent up the river* or *line* of which this is a
shortened, and confusing, form, meaning the
same as SEND DOWN 2.

senior citizen an old person

As *senior* comes from the Latin *senex*, this is
arguably not a euphemism, merely a cloying
evasion. Also shortened to *seniors*:

I told them to send half a dozen senior
citizens who look a bit sad and just a little
threadbare. (L. Thomas, 1979)
Discover Tunisia in the Luxury of our
Air-conditioned Coach. Seniors a
Specialty. (le Carré, 1986)

senior moment (a) temporary forgetfulness

When *Memory Lane* runs into *Amnesia Avenue*.

sensible unfashionable but practical

It is used to describe women's shoes and
clothes, perhaps with supposed transference
from the wearer:

Her breasts, neatly harnessed under a dark
sweater, did not swing as she walked. She
wore the ultimate in 'sensible' shoes.
(Irvine, 1986)

sensitive payment a bribe

So described because of its impropriety and
probable illegality in the hands of the recipient, if others find out about it. If the person
paying the bribe is American, the payment is
illegal for him as well.

sent drunk or under the influence of illegal narcotics
The subject has passed to another stage of consciousness, if not unconsciousness.

separate¹ to dismiss from employment
Literally, to cause to part. Now rare.

separate² to cease living together as man and wife
As distinct from what happens when they go about their respective daily business. Those who are *separated* in this sense are living apart from their spouses without the intention of resuming cohabitation in future, but not, or not yet, divorced. Their condition, *separation*, has a precise legal meaning:
> Since her separation from a drunken husband some years ago, Sheila's friend Maureen Bowler had become a noted feminist. (Aldiss, 1988)

separate development see APARTHEID

separation death
Usually spoken of a spouse, although it might refer to the body and the soul going their different ways:
> The dreadful shock of separation took place in the night. (J. Boswell, 1791—Dr Johnson's wife had died)

seraglio a brothel
Originally, the palace of the Turkish sultan in the Golden Horn, of which a part only was the harem, or secret spot.

serpent a penis
The imagery is obvious. A girl STUNG BY A SERPENT has received an unwanted, though perhaps not unexpected, shock.

servant *obsolete American* a slave
An antebellum usage in the Southern states.

serve to copulate with
In standard usage, of male animals, and a fruitful ground for innuendo, as in the television comedy series set in a store and entitled *Are You Being Served*:
> It was a pity there wasn't time and leisure, or I'd have served her as I had once before. (Fraser, 1969)

Specifically as *serve your lust*:
> I would we had a thousand Roman dames
> At such a bay; by turn to serve our lust.
> (Shakespeare, *Titus Andronicus*)

service¹ to copulate with
In standard English, arranged copulation by a male mammal, usually a stallion or bull. Less often of humans:

> Aldo had walked in while he was servicing the cigarette girl over his desk. (J. Collins, 1981)

Whence the punning American *service station*, a brothel.

service² a charge additional to the cost of the goods supplied
As levied in some restaurants regardless of the quality of the attendance. The roadside *service station* is a misnomer, as the motorist is usually expected to attend to his own needs and get his hands stinking of fuel, except where he finds the tautological announcement *Attended Service*.

service lawyer *American* a clerk in a law office
Not unlike what the English used to call *managing clerks* (before status deprivation changed them into legal executives):
> He is what they call a 'service lawyer', like me, somebody who does the work that one of our hotshot partners has been hired for. (Turow, 1993)

services no longer required dismissed from employment
The blow is perhaps softened by the implication that the function no longer exists:
> I was given a discharge, ostensibly on the grounds that my services 'were no longer required', this being a curious euphemism. (R. V. Jones, 1978—Jones was the outstanding British scientist of the Second World War)

set back to cause (a person) to pay a cost that cannot easily be afforded
Literally, to cause a reverse or relapse:
> That luncheon set me back considerably. (N. Mitford, 1960)

set up¹ to provide accommodation for (a mistress)
From the meaning, to establish. The object of the setter-up is to keep her away from others, if he can:
> When Christine refused to leave Ward and be set up in a flat, [Profumo] refused to meet her. (S. Green, 1979)

set up² to incriminate falsely
As with skittles, for the purpose of knocking them down again:
> They 'set up' MacLennan in an attempt to discredit him. (*Private Eye*, July 1980)

set up shop on Goodwin Sands *obsolete* to be shipwrecked off the Kent coast
A low-lying island of some 4,000 acres in the English Channel was taken from (and named after) the Anglo-Saxon Earl Godwin by the

Norman conquerors and handed over to clerics who neglected the sea walls. A great storm overwhelmed it in 1100. Since then the land has remained a hazard to shipping, emerging above the waves to a varying extent at each low tide.

settle¹ to kill
Literally, to reach a conclusion:
> Jack Plenty had settled the Belagnini with a lovely back-hand cut. (Fraser, 1977)

settle² to conquer and appropriate
The language of aggression and imperialism. Whence the *settler*, who goes to live in conquered territory:
> Rubin resists calls to evict settlers. (*Daily Telegraph*, 7 March 1994, writing about Jews who had taken over part of the city of Hebron)

Such communities living among or replacing the indigenous population are called *settlements*:
> The settlements are usually built on hilltops outside Arab towns and villages. (ibid.)

settled *Irish* unlikely ever to marry
A use in a community where remoteness, differences in religion, and tribalism often combined to limit the catchment area, especially for a bride:
> Being generally regarded as 'settled' in the expressive Irish phrase, into single blessedness, he sprang it on all of us that was going to be married to a schoolteacher. (Fingall, 1977)

seven (chuck or throw a) *mainly Australian* to die or swoon
There is no seven on a dice cube.
> If she sees the thing she won't scream and throw a seven. She'll shoot. (Upfield, 1932)

Whence the catch-phrase: *Threw a seven, went to heaven.*

seven-year itch a wish for extramarital sexual variety
Seven years is the classic cycle of change:
> There's something called the seven-year itch ... middle-aged men quite suddenly cutting loose. (Moyes, 1980)

See also ITCH.

severance dismissal from employment
A kind of cutting:
> She would call her lawyer about the tedious details of her severance. (N. Evans, 1995—she had not lost a husband or a limb, but been dismissed)

Whence *severance pay*, the compensation for losing the job.

sewage see EFFLUENT

sewn up¹ pregnant
Perhaps from the meaning, stitched up, being placed in a compromising or difficult position; or from the meaning, finally arranged; or even from the distended appearance.

sewn up² *American* drunk
A variant of STITCHED.

sex¹ copulation
Literally, the classifications male and female, although the euphemistic use has long been standard English. Heterosexually or homosexually:
> I could have asked to wash after sex. (S. Green, 1979)

Sex love is obsolete:
> Katie told [Parnell] in 1891 ... that 'sex love' between herself and Willie was 'long-since dead'. (Kee, 1993—Katie was Mrs O'Shea and Willie was her husband)

The American *sex worker* is a prostitute, although I prefer, etymologically speaking, the alternative form *sex care provider*, whose therapy is strictly non-medical.

sex² the penis or vagina
Referring to the reproductive functions. The penis:
> I rubbed my hot sex against her little button. (F. Harris, 1925)

or the vagina:
> 'Oh how lovely your sex is!' I exclaimed ... my left hand drew down her head for a long kiss while my middle finger still continued its caress. (ibid.)

sexual act (the) see ACT (THE)

sexual ambiguity having bisexual tastes
Ambiguity here does not usually imply doubt or uncertainty—rather it indicates an excess of catholicism:
> ... over-stressing his sexual ambiguity, even his deviance with regard to drugs. (Davidson, 1978)

sexual assault *obsolete* an unsuccessful attempt at rape
Nowadays no longer a euphemism but:
> 'Sexual assault' is the euphemism for the rape that fails ... Sexual assault depended on the time and place. (Pearsall, 1969, writing about 19th-century usage)

sexual intercourse copulation
Not just dealings or conversation between individuals. Now standard English:
> If he gets pinched with a girl in a hotel room, stop sexual intercourse. (Chandler, 1953)

Sexual commerce is archaic, and there was no suggestion in the phrase that anybody was getting paid for their services.

Sexual congress does not refer to goings-on on or around Capitol Hill:

Eight days later in the little summer house, sexual congress took place. (Boyd, 1987)

Sexual conjunction sounds more like differentiating grammatically between the masculine and feminine cases:

...a woman who could not be held back from strangers' rooms, who would have sexual conjunction whether in stinking rest rooms or mop cupboards. (Proulx, 1993)

Sexual knowledge, which is usually had by an adult male with an under-age girl, does not mean simply that she has been told about the birds and the bees.

Sexual relations may also imply familiarities short of copulation, and *sexual relief* refers to what the male obtains, implying that his health might suffer from an excess of celibacy. *Sexual liaison* in this sense is rare:

[Mao] believed, as some Chinese emperors had believed, that sexual liaison with young virgins enhanced the chance of longevity in an old man. (Cheng, 1984—or it made a convenient excuse)

These concepts are further explored at COMMERCE, CONGRESS, INTERCOURSE, KNOW, etc.

sexual preference homosexuality

Not in the literal sense referring to gentlemen who prefer blondes or ladies who favour moustaches. Also as *sexual irregularity, orientation, proclivity*, or *tropism*:

...impossible to ask questions about (as they said on the current affairs programmes) Ron's 'sexual preference'. (Keneally, 1985)

She spoke of your sexual irregularities. (Burgess, 1980)

But my sexual orientation was the true instigator of apostasy. (ibid.)

She discovered her boyfriend's, uh, sexual proclivities. (Sanders, 1986)

...it is replacing your former militancy on behalf of the sexual tropism you and I both represent. (Burgess, 1980—*tropism* is normally a vegetable rather than an animal response to a stimulus, but the Greek source meant a turn)

To be *sexually non-conformist* is to be homosexual or bisexual:

His collaboration with the leading sexologist Wilhelm Reich...stood him in good stead when dealing with the sexually non-conformist Five from Cambridge. (*Daily Telegraph*, 5 April 1998, writing of their Russian controller, Arnold Deutsch and the homosexual British spies—Blunt, Philby, McLean, Burgess, and Cairncross)

Sexual variety usually means no more than promiscuity.

shack up (with) to cohabit in an extra-marital sexual relationship

A *shack* is a rudely built rural residence, but the arrangement so described usually has a degree of permanence:

Since she had shacked up with Joe, the youth had kicked over many traces. (R. Allen, 1971)

shade[1] to reduce in price

Commercial jargon, for making the price a *shade less than it was*. A genteel usage in a shop where overt haggling is frowned upon.

shade[2] *American* to influence illegally

It describes an act done out of the glare of full light:

My guess is they think your buddy Orleans there has been shading games. (Turow, 1993—Orleans was a basketball referee)

A *shade* is also a dealer in stolen goods, working in the shadows.

shaft[1] (of a male) to copulate with

The imagery is of the insertion of a spindle into a bore:

...he was out drinking or shafting someone older and uglier than she was. (Sanders, 1977)

Less often as a noun:

Well, it was clear enough that the old thing had no trouble, even across the dividing decades, in spotting him as a king of shaft. (Amis, 1988)

shaft[2] the penis

Like the handle of a tool or other rigid object:

As you thrust your shaft in and out of me, I felt a strange sort of pleasure. (F. Harris, 1925)

A rare meaning, the vagina, comes from a space into which an object may be inserted and moved smoothly up and down, such as an elevator shaft.

shag[1] to copulate with

The derivation is perhaps from the old meanings, to shake or to wrestle with—the cormorant is certainly not a renowned sexual performer. Men usually do the *shagging*:

Out shagging some quiff...(Sanders, 1982)

The main use of females is in the cliché She *shags like a rattlesnake*, using daunting imagery.

shag[2] to masturbate yourself

Usually of boys, again from the shaking.

shake[1] to rob

By violence or trickery:

How much you shake him for? (Chandler, 1953)

To *shake down* is to rob or cheat through trickery rather than violence:

Find out what they're all trying to shake us down for. (Bradbury, 1976)

and a *shakedown* is a fraudulent scheme:

It was a shakedown. For a two-hundred-dollar camera Sony made a hundred and the girl made a hundred. (Theroux, 1973)

shake² *American* an arrest

Police jargon, usually on trivial grounds to show activity, generate income, or fill a quota:

We ain't got no shakes yet today...Maybe we better write a couple of F.I.'s? (Wambaugh, 1981)

shake hands with the bishop (of a male) to urinate

An uncircumcized penis may resemble the chess piece:

Help me to the toilet...I have to go and shake the bishop's hand. (Theroux, 1979, quoting Borges)

Others may *shake hands with their best friend, their wife's best friend*, or, with melancholy humour, *the unemployed* or *the unemployable*. In modern use, a female may *shake the lettuce*.

shake the pagoda tree *obsolete* to make a rapid fortune in India

Punning on the *pagoda*, an Indian gold coin:

...won handsome fortunes by 'Shaking the Pagoda Tree', by the private trade that then was permitted to John Company's servants. (*Spectator*, 1912, quoted in *ODEP—John Company* was the East India Company which preceded the British Indian Empire)

shame extramarital copulation by a woman

What disgraced the female was thought less reprehensible in the male:

Is't not a kind of incest, to take life From thine own sister's shame? (Shakespeare, *Measure for Measure*)

The *shame* was also one of the devil's names:

The shame be on's. (W. Beattie, 1801)

shanghai forcibly to abduct (a person)

Originally, to render senseless and carry on board ship as a crew member from the crime-ridden Chinese city, because some of those with whom you arrived might be absent when you came to set sail, but now used of any involuntary removal:

...shanghai'd might be a more accurate description of all that happened to her during the last 24 hours. (Price, 1982)

share pusher see PUSH 4

share someone's affections to have an open adulterous relationship

Not just talking about the common love a parent will have for siblings:

The mistress even suggested that his wife should contemporaneously share his affections. (*Daily Telegraph*, 1979)

To *share someone's bed* is to copulate with someone, the phrase not being used of married couples. An assumption is made that such proximity outside marriage will always overcome chastity of disinclination:

I say you share his bed—*puta*. (Deighton, 1981—*puta* means prostitute in Spanish and Italian)

sharp elbows inconsiderate selfishness

Those so endowed thrust themselves forward in a throng:

Things were not helped by Brian Redhead who had, shall we say, sharp elbows for a cuddly-looking man. (*Daily Telegraph*, 20 March 2001)

sharp with the pencil inclined to over-charge

Punning on the necessity to resharpen lead pencils in the days before the ballpoint and word processor. Less often as *sharp with the pen*. Usually of rapacious lawyers (although for some the adjective may be considered tauto-logical).

sharpen your pencil to alter your stance in bargaining

An injunction to the seller who is asking too much or the buyer who is offering too little:

I am disappointed we didn't get another. But I did not want to sharpen my pencil as hard as some of the others have done and make such toppy forecasts. (*Sunday Telegraph*, 23 February 1997—a bidder was explaining why he had failed to secure a rail operating franchise when British Rail was privatized)

The phrase may also be used of other accounting inaccuracies short of fraud.

sharpener an intoxicating drink

Usually whisky or gin, which are supposed to liven you up:

I managed to escape from Colditz for a sharpener or twain with the Major at the RAC Club. (*Private Eye*, May 1981—*Colditz* was Number 10, Downing Street, where Denis Thatcher then lived)

sheath a contraceptive worn by a male

Literally, the covering in which a blade is kept:

It was typical of Murray to call it a sheath, he thought. (Boyd, 1981)

The rare *sheathe the sword* meant to copulate, using obvious imagery. In literal use, it meant to cease to fight.

sheep buck *obsolete American* a ram
Another example of 19th-century prudery about farm animals. Although a *buck* is a correct usage for the male of several quadrupeds, it is not of the genus *ovis aries*. See BIG ANIMAL for similar pruderies.

sheep's eyes (make) to indicate sexual attraction in a look
The derivation is from the ophthalmic dilation of those seeking to attract the attention of a potential mate, which makes them look ovine:
    Having had several glasses of beer, he now began to make sheep's eyes at me, and asked if I had a sweetheart. (Atwood, 1996)

sheet in the wind (a) mildly drunk
A *sheet* is a rope tying a sail to a spar, not the sail itself as landlubbers sometimes assume. If one or more breaks loose, the vessel is in some disarray:
    A thought tipsy—a sheet in the wind. (A. Trollope, 1885)
A drunkard may also be *three, four* or *several sheets in* or *to the wind*, but not, it seems, *two*:
    An American lady who was three sheets in the wind said I looked like a movie actor. (Theroux, 1973)
    He remembered coming in it with Jennifer a couple of times, both of them four sheets in the wind and giggling like kids. (Winton, 1994)
    There were French seamen at the next table—all several sheets to the wind. (R. Moss, 1987)

sheets an allusion to copulation
    Happiness to their sheets. (Shakespeare, *Othello*)
Pressing the sheets is not necessarily the action of a laundress going about her daily business.

shellacked *mainly American* very drunk
Literally, covered with shellac, a varnish which is stoved to give a glazed appearance. To be *shellacked* may also mean to be utterly defeated (WCND).

sheltered for those unable to look after themselves
It is used of accommodation where invalids or geriatrics can be watched over and helped, although it is no less likely to let in wind or water than the normal home:
    Her father went into sheltered accommodation and her daughter to a bedsit. (*Telegraph Magazine*, 1 July 1995)

shelved dismissed from employment
Normally describing those asked to retire early or overlooked for promotion because of their declining powers, from storing objects on a shelf:
    ... so that men who lack drive and imagination can, without undue cruelty, be shelved. (Colville, 1976)

sheriff's hotel *American* a prison
And in the old days to *dance at a sheriff's ball* used to mean you were killed by hanging.

shield *American* a policeman
From the badge.

shift¹ an act of defecation
When you *move your bowels* (see MOVEMENT 1), as in the male use *do a shift*.

shift² to copulate
Again I suppose from the movement involved:
    Let we shift...You give baby me. (Theroux, 1971)

ship *American* to dismiss from employment
Likening the departure to the dispatch of goods from a warehouse. Sometimes also referring to the dismissal of a student from a college.

shipped home in a box dead overseas
Not only of soldiers:
    Shelley had to get him out, or he'd be shipped home in a box. (C. Thomas, 1993)

ship's lawyer see BARRACK-ROOM LAWYER

shirtlifter a male homosexual
The usage ignores the occasions on which heterosexual men lift their shirts and shirt-tails in the normal course of dressing and undressing. Also shortened to *lifter*:
    ...when you sup with a shirtlifter you should use a very long spoon. (*Private Eye*, January 1987)
    Earlier this year Tasmanian 'lifters' handed themselves over to the police. (*Sunday Telegraph*, 4 September 1994)
Shirtlifting is sodomy:
    ...what the good old-fashioned 'bloke' sniggeringly refers to as shirt-lifting. (ibid.)

shit stabber a homosexual male
Originally British army usage:
    Arab men are very affectionate with each other, holding hands and so on. It's just their culture, of course. It doesn't mean they're shit stabbers. (McNab, 1993)

shoo-in a favoured successor

Originally, in America, it described a horse chosen to win a race fraudulently, which was *shooed into* the winning post. Now only figurative use, occasionally mis-spelt as *shoe-in*:

> The old guard preferred Chernenko,
> but they had run out of options even
> before Chernenko died of emphysema
> in 1985. By the time Gorbachev
> came to London he was a shoe-in.
> (Simpson, 1998)

shoot¹ to kill or wound by a firearm

Literally, to discharge a projectile. This standard use implies an accurate aim by the person who does the shooting:

> He was condemned to death and shot
> within two hours. (Goebbels, 1945, in
> translation)

shoot² **(the)** peremptory dismissal from employment

An unusual version of the FIRE theme.

shoot³ to inject an illegal narcotic intravenously

It has a direct passage into a vein:

> I'm going to shoot myself so full of junk
> I'll never come down. I'm gonna shoot it
> all up my arm in one blast. I'm gonna
> OD myself. (Gabriel, 1992)

shoot a line to boast

The imagery is probably not from whaling:

> He described his journey to Marseille, but
> left out the more adventurous episodes,
> deterred by some residual airman's code
> against what the men called shooting a
> line. (Faulks, 1998)

Nowadays you are as likely, if so inclined, to *shoot the bull*, of which more under BULL 3:

> No-one lingers, no-one sits down and
> shoots the bull. (Theroux, 1988, writing of
> the aftermath of a Chinese banquet, not of
> a Spanish *corrida*)

Shooting the breeze is usually of male flirtation:

> Inside, oblivious of all this, are the two
> highway policemen, sitting at the counter
> and shooting the breeze with the waitress.
> (Bryson, 1989)

The obsolete Scottish *shoot among the doves*, again meaning to boast, referred to the ease with which tame birds might be hit:

> A lady...had heard her husband
> mention...that such a gentleman...was
> thought to shoot among the doves.
> She immediately took the alarm
> and said to him with great
> eagerness...'My husband says ye
> shoot among the doves. Now as I am
> very fond of my pigeons, I beg you
> winna meddle wi' them.' (*EDD*)

shoot a lion (of a male) to urinate

Usually he goes out of doors to do it. In America you are more likely to say that you are going to *shoot a dog*.

shoot blanks to be sexually impotent

Unable effectively to SHOOT OFF and often said of themselves by those who have had a vasectomy:

> That's pretty big talk for a man shooting
> blanks. (Garner, 1994—and not of someone
> using a starting pistol)

shoot off to ejaculate semen

Usually prematurely, under intense sexual excitement:

> I had to change my underwear when I got
> back here. That's right. I shot off in my
> drawers. (Diehl, 1978)

The punning *shoot over the stubble* was to ejaculate in a woman's pubic hair. To *shoot your roe* or *shoot your load* refers to any ejaculation. The obsolete *shoot between wind and water* was to infect with venereal disease, punning on the crippling shot to a sailing ship.

shoot the agate *American* to seek out a woman for sexual purposes

Derived from the name of an affected form of strutting seen in some parades by black people.

shoot the cat to become drunk

Originally, to vomit, from a similar tendency in cats:

> He came to and shot the cat from
> the window, howling to wake
> the dead, and then we sent for
> more coffee and dosed him again.
> (Fraser, 1997)

shoot the moon see MOONLIGHT FLIT

shoot with a silver gun *obsolete* to be unable to provide meat by hunting

In those far-off days when a gentleman was supposed to keep the household supplied with fresh game birds in season by shooting them, and a lady was content to pluck, draw, hang, and cook them, it was thought demeaning if he had to go out and buy what he should have shot:

> Shooting with a *silver gun* is a saying among
> game eaters. That is to say, *purchasing* the
> game. (Cobbett, 1830)

See also CATCH FISH WITH A SILVER HOOK.

shop¹ *American* to dismiss summarily from employment

This usage may be obsolete and the etymology is uncertain:

> I would have shopped the fellow in an
> instant...He was most impertinent.
> (H. Wilson, 1915)

shop² to give information leading to arrest

You might suppose that, with the commercial imagery, the information would be sold, but most *shopping* occurs through malice or self-protection:

[He] volunteered for a fiver to 'shop' his pals. (*Tit-Bits*, 20 May, 1899)

This criminal slang usage has nothing to do with the *cop-shop*, or police station.

shop-door is open (the) your trousers are unfastened

An oblique warning, usually to another male, of an undone zip. If a portion of shirt-tail protrudes, you may be told you are *flying a flag*.

shoplift see LIFT 1

short¹ a measure of spirits

Shortened from *short drink* as different from a *long drink* like beer or cider.

short² a handgun

As different from a *long*, a rifle. Army jargon:

We had no shorts (pistols), they were all longs, and it was going to be almost impossible to bear them if we were compromised. (McNab, 1993)

short-arm inspection an examination for venereal disease among men

Punning on the regular small arms inspection of rifles etc. and on the *short-arm*, the penis. Army jargon.

short hairs the pubic hair

Even though they may be more luxuriant than those on other parts of the body. The use is almost always in the figurative cliché:

I think I've got them by the short hairs. (Sharpe, 1974)

The *short and curlies* is specific.

short illness (a) see LONG ILLNESS (A)

short-shipped lost in transit

Airlines do not like talking about the luggage which goes astray:

'It's not lost,' said a BA spokesman, 'it's short-shipped.' (*Daily Telegraph*, 25 September 1999)

short time a single act of copulation

Prostitutes' jargon for a contact with few preliminaries and no sequel. Also as *short session(s)*:

The price for a short time with massage stayed the same. (Theroux, 1973)
She's short sessions. Never lets a man stay for more than half an hour. (Archer, 1979)

If the hotel receptionist asks you whether you need the room for *short-time* occupation, he concludes you will be using the room for such activity and you will be charged accordingly. *Short-term* carries the same implication:

An overnight stay, sir? Or a short-term residency? (Keneally, 1985)

shorten the front (line)¹ to retreat under pressure

Soldiers and their apologists thus explain a defeat by implying that a salient is being voluntarily abandoned:

He was painfully familiar with the Fuehrer's attitude to 'shortening the front' under enemy pressure. (A. Clark, 1995)

shorten the front line² to lose weight

Punning on the military euphemism (above) and usually of men.

shortism¹ a supposed prejudice against small adults

Yet another category to whom we can be nasty:

Small step in battle to end shortism. (*Daily Telegraph*, 12 April 1994—the victims may well have been VERTICALLY CHALLENGED before battle commenced)

shortism² the greedy pursuit of short-term gain

Financial jargon for seeking profits quickly regardless of the consequences to third parties, rather than waiting for growth in the medium term.

shorts (the) indigence

Usually of a temporary nature, being short of cash until the next pay cheque:

... if you get the shorts, don't be bashful about asking me for help. (Sanders, 1986)

shot¹ a measure of spirits

Probably from the way it is discharged into the glass. In the British Isles it is usually measured with an excess of caution, a reprehensible habit that now seems to have spread to America.

shot² a narcotic taken illegally

Usually by injection:

The keepers could sell the balance ... to other prisoners in need of a shot. (Lavine, 1930)

shot³ drunk

Probably from the slang meaning, finished, although the variant, *shot away*, does not help that etymology. So long as you are still on your feet, you are unlikely to be more than *half-shot*:

...unlimited wine being dispensed in all the public buildings. The whole population seemed to be half-shot. (Fraser, 1970)

shot⁴ an ejaculation of semen
When you SHOOT OFF:
It's the only [brothel] where you get three shots for your money. The shot upstairs (fellatio). The shot downstairs (vaginal copulation). And the shot in the room (whisky). (Longstreet, 1956)

shot in the tail pregnant
A rather tasteless multiple pun.

shot while trying to escape murdered in custody
A favoured excuse of the Nazis and other tyrants. Also as *shot while fleeing*:
[They] had been shot from ranges of under a metre 'while trying to escape'. (Burleigh, 2000—the powder burns on the bodies indicated the proximity of the weapon)
...homosexuals were routinely 'shot while fleeing' in concentration camps. (ibid.)

shotgun marriage the marriage of a pregnant bride to the putative father
The man is supposed to have come to the altar or register office under duress. Also as *shotgun wedding*:
Princess Caroline of Monaco is finding it impossible to secure an annulment of her 1978 marriage...made even more difficult following a shotgun marriage last December to Italian Stefano Casiraghi. (*Private Eye*, August 1984)
Shotgun is used of other precipitate action taken under duress:
He understood only too well that my father was acting against all his personal inclination under the duress of a shot-gun Coalition caused by Lord Fisher's desertion. (V. B. Carter, 1965—her father was the British prime minister, H. H. Asquith)

shout¹ (the) peremptory dismissal from employment
Dismissed employees may say they have *had the shout*, even if dismissed *sotto voce* or in writing.

shout² an obligation to pay for a round of drinks in a bar
Only euphemistic when someone is said *not to pay his shout*, implying parsimony in one who is not prepared to take his turn:
My shout, now, Tug, I insist. (le Carré, 1996)
To *shout yourself hoarse* is to be drunk, from ordering too many rounds.

shove¹ (of a male) to copulate
The common pushing imagery.

shove² (the) peremptory dismissal from employment or courtship
No physical ejection or rejection can be assumed.

shove over *American* to kill
Not necessarily involving a cliff but into another state of existence, perhaps:
Did you—did anybody—have any idea that she was gonna get shoved over? (Diehl, 1978)

shovelled under dead
But not necessarily buried:
My last day in the Fourteenth Army will be the day they shovel me under. (Fraser, 1992—the British/Indian 14th Army under General Slim in the Far East, also known as the Forgotten Army because of scant publicity and no home leave for its British troops, was arguably the most consistently successful fighting formation of the Second World War)

show¹ to menstruate
Usually of animals and especially of mares when breeding is planned. In women, the noun a *show* indicates vaginal bleeding at the onset of menstruation or childbirth.

show² a battle
Mainly First World War usage, minimizing the danger by referring to a theatrical production or a pyrotechnic display:
'I am watching the show over on our right.' Some of our new divisions...had advanced through a gap. (F. Richards, 1933)

show your charms (of a prostitute) to seek a customer
She may in public reveal more than chaster women but less than the term might suggest, until terms have been agreed:
A woman was showing a man her private charms, and inviting him to enjoy them. (Masters, 1976)
See also CHARMS.

showers¹ deviant sexual activity
A code word in prostitutes' advertisements, from the penchant of some males for sexual antics involving the urine of another or, in the jargon, a *golden shower*:
The gangs control drugs. Hooking, that's mostly for oddball stuff now, golden showers, Greek, not straight sex. (Turow, 1993)
A *brown shower* is offered for customers who prefer faeces. A *showercap* in this company is either a contraceptive sheath or a diaphragm.

showers² see TAKE AN EARLY BATH

showers³ gas chambers
Part of the Nazi pretence that prisoners arriving at an extermination camp were merely being disinfected. Also as *shower baths*:
> His first job was to work in one of the ante-rooms where prisoners had to remove their clothes before going through a door to the 'showers'. (C. Booker in *Sunday Telegraph*, 29 January 1995, writing about Auschwitz)
> But it might be acceptable to evacuate the children and the old people (presumably to 'shower baths'). (A. Clark, 1995, describing German policy planned for Leningrad in 1942)

shown the door summarily dismissed from employment
The exit, not the entrance:
> About 500 other staff are also being shown the door. (*Daily Telegraph*, 15 June 2001)

shrink see HEADSHRINKER

shrinkage the amount stolen from retail stores
Literally, a reduction in weight or volume of packed goods due to settlement or dehydration. Retailers' jargon.

shroud waving a tactic for safeguarding or augmenting expenditure on medical projects or the salaries of those employed in the industry
The sponsor is threatened, usually with more publicity than veracity, that deaths will result if the funds are not forthcoming:
> She noted that shroud waving had 'quite a high success rate'. (*Sunday Telegraph*, 29 March 1992).
A *shroud waver* is a doctor or politician, or frequently a combination of the two, who so acts.

shuffle off this mortal coil to die
The Bard said it first, through the voice of Hamlet.
> ... left a hundred grand when he shuffled off his mortal coil. (Sanders, 1986)

sick menstruating
A rarer version of ILL 1.

sick-out a strike by public service employees
Those forbidden by law or contract from going on strike may absent themselves due to pretended illness. The usage is mainly found in the aircraft business, as with British Airways cabin attendants in 1998, and in America:
> The dispute over Reno ... led to a sick-out by pilots. (*New York Herald Tribune*, 10 August 1999)

side orders sexual practices of an unusual or depraved nature
Like the dishes available additional to the main course, although the phrase may also refer to plain adultery:
> Alvin C. had been having no side orders of sex; no arguments either, or drink or drugs. (Davidson, 1978)

sides pads worn to accentuate a woman's figure
From the days when men seemed to be attracted to big hips:
> She pulled off a pair of 'sides', artificial hips she wore to give herself a good figure. (L. Armstrong, 1955)

sight-deprived blind
It should literally mean blinded:
> The blind are now 'sight-deprived' as if to refute any suspicion that they got that way voluntarily. (Jennings, 1965)

sigma phi syphilis
Medical jargon from the Greek letters used as shorthand, which also conceals the diagnosis from the less-educated patient.

sign the pledge see PLEDGE (THE)

significant other a regular sexual companion without marriage
Normally heterosexual, but sometimes homosexual, as:
> I started the yacht upholstery, you know, after my friend died. In 1979. What these days they'd call a 'significant other'. (Proulx, 1993—they were both female)

silk (the) a parachute
Euphemistic only in the phrase *on the silk*, referring to a military air crew obliged to abandon an aircraft in flight:
> ... you've got to stick to your own air space or ride down on the silk. (Hackett, 1978—if you collide you will crash)
Whence the figurative *hit the silk*, to seek to escape from or avoid a calamity, as by using a parachute:
> In markets like this, if that happens, everyone'll hit the silk at once and no one'll get out the door. (M. Thomas, 1987)

simple of small intelligence
Not just lacking knowledge or experience, as in Simple Simon's commercial exchange with the Pieman. *Simple* is now widely used of those of limited mental powers considered fit to remain in society.

sin to copulate extramaritally
Literally, to commit a forbidden act but, since St Paul's obsession with that particular wrong-doing, used of any activity which is taboo sexually:
> Most dangerous
> In that temptation that doth goad us on
> To sin in loving virtue. (Shakespeare, *Measure for Measure*)

Sinful means relating to such copulation, as in *sinful commerce*, which is not trading in stolen goods To *live in sin* implies unmarried cohabitation.

sing (of a criminal) to give information to the police
The imagery is from the songbird in a cage, and may relate to your own misdeeds or those of other criminals:
> ...had him under the lights all fuckin' night...and about nine this morning he starts singin' like Frank Sinatra. (Diehl, 1978)

sing a different tune to change your story, attitude, or opinion
The same imagery recurs in various phrases. Thus the musical British politician Edward Heath, not especially renowned for the consistency of his policies, was said to *sing from a different song sheet*:
> Indeed, a former prime minister, Edward Heath (who was subsequently to sing from a different song sheet), admonished the government to press ahead with democratic reform. (Patten, 1998, writing about Hong Kong)

Those said to *sing off the same hymn sheet* or to *sing the same tune* are taking the same line or expressing publicly the same opinion.

sing soprano to be castrated
But not of young male choristers:
> 'If I discover you've been cheating, you know what will happen to you, don't you?' 'I'll be singing soprano?' (Sanders, 1992)

single parent a parent living with dependent offspring without an adult partner
A variant of LONE PARENT and no longer referring for the most part to someone who has lost a spouse. Also as *single mother*:
> The papers are always complaining about single mothers on social security. (P. D. James, 1994)

singles describing a place where individuals can meet strangers for companionship or sexual relations
From *single*, unmarried, although you will observe that females who frequent such places tend to hunt in pairs. Whence *singles bars, nights, joints* etc.:
> Used to be a singles joint but lately it's turned really rough. (Deighton, 1981)

sink[1] a lavatory
Originally, a drain or cesspit and now perhaps obsolete:
> Usuph pretended to wander off to the regimental sink. (Keneally, 1979, writing in 19th-century style)

sink[2] to be terminally ill
But not liable to drown:
> 'How is Grandad?' Her voice dropped as if she were reluctant to ask. 'He's being himself. But he's sinking'. (L. Thomas, 1994—Grandad died soon afterwards)

sip a drink of intoxicant
Literally, anything drunk in small quantities:
> By the time they had had a few sips there was damned little left for us. (F. Richards, 1933, describing a rum ration)

The Scottish and northern English *siper*, a drunkard, came from a dialect verb meaning to soak:
> The Hivverby lads at fair drinking are seypers. (R. Anderson, 1808)

siphon off to steal
Usually by embezzlement and not necessarily of liquids:
> No way he could have spent more than half of what was coming in...The best guess was that Birdsong...was siphoning it off. (Hailey, 1973)

Siphon is specific of stealing fuel from the tanks of motor vehicles.

siphon the python (of a male) to urinate
The common serpentine/penis imagery.

sissy *American* a male homosexual
An alternative spelling of CISSY, with the same derivation, and also used of effeminate heterosexuals:
> Little teeny sissy with gold hair. Looks enough like a girl to be a queen. (Wambaugh, 1983)

sister[1] a prostitute
Pimps in the Far East claim this kinship:
> ...pimps accosting you...with promises of their sister. (Fraser, 1977)

The dusky lad who invites strangers to copulate with his *sister, very white, very clean*, makes three assertions in which little confidence should be placed. Occasionally in the west as *sister of charity* or *sister of mercy*, both being of the same tendency as *nun* (see NUNNERY).

sister² *American* a black woman
Normally of African ancestry:
> The sister can tell you things about Jack
> Stanton. (Anonymous, 1996)

sit-down job an act of defecation
Usually of a male, who does not avail himself
of the modern pedestal seat for urination:
> Oh, a sit-down job is it? (Higgins, 1976)

sit-in a trespass to draw attention to a
grievance
By a body of people, often without violence,
sometimes in the course of a trade dispute. A
sleep-in continues overnight, and during a *love-
in* the participants may while the hours
promiscuously away.

sit-upon the buttocks
More common in Great Britain than in
America, where *sit-upons* were trousers, not
bottoms, the equivalent of the contemporary
British *sit-in-'ems*. Also as a *sit-down-upon* or as a
sitting:
> She had a tumour going from her sitting.
> (*EDD*, from 1887)

sitting by the window underemployed
A phenomenon of Japanese industrial society,
where paternalistic attitudes deterred the
dismissal of employees for whom there was
no longer a job:
> Either more and more underworked
> employees are left, as the Japanese say
> 'sitting by the window', or these jobs got
> vaporised in the white heat of the
> technological revolution. (*Daily Telegraph*,
> 4 April 1995)

six feet of earth death
The length of an average grave rather than its
depth:
> Six feet of earth make all men equal.
> (Proverb)
Six feet underground emphasizes the depth
rather than the length:
> I'm glad his father's six feet underground.
> (G. Greene, 1978)

six o'clock swill *Australian/New Zealand*
an excessive drinking of beer
An Antipodean phenomenon arising from
aridity, machismo, thirst, and unhelpful licensing laws:
> During those months we considered their
> sunlit way of life in every State, from
> koalas and the six o'clock swill to the
> farmer in Morse who hunted and
> killed snakes by grabbing their tails
> and cracking them like whips.
> (Whicker, 1982)
In New Zealand, for five decades until 1967,
all bars closed at 6 in the afternoon.

sixty-nine see SOIXANTE-NEUF

sizzle *American* to be killed by electrocution
One of several culinary images for the
process.

skewer (of a male) to copulate with
The imagery is from the action of transfixing
meat:
> The crooked shadow of Harvey skewering
> Hornette... (Theroux, 1978—they were
> copulating during a public performance)

skidmarks the stains of excrement on
underpants
Normally linear, like rubber on the road from
excessive braking:
> There was a lot of slagging of underpants
> and so on... 'Jaysis, look at those skid
> marks.' (R. Doyle, 1990)

skim to embezzle or extort
On a regular basis, like cream from milk:
> ...the two brokers set up the 'skimming'
> operation mainly dealing in overseas
> shares through overseas brokers and
> charging the Kuwait organization inflated
> prices. (*Daily Telegraph*, 16 April 1994—they
> were alleged to have stolen some £2
> million)
It is also American gambling jargon:
> Skimming is the term used to describe
> the removal of gambling revenues before
> they are counted for state or Federal
> taxes. (*Daily Telegraph*, September 1979)
A *skim* is a bribe or other sum regularly
received in one of these ways:
> A skim of a hundred and eighty was
> damned thin for a bull lieutenant.
> (Weverka, 1973)

skin¹ *American* a male contraceptive
sheath
Whence the punning *skin-diver* who uses that
form of contraception.

skin-² pornographic
From the implication of nudity. Thus a *skin-
flick* is a pornographic film, which used to be
shown in *skin-house*, a cinema specializing in
pornography, before becoming freely available to young and old alike in every video
shop. A *skin-magazine*, often shortened to *skin-
mag*, contains erotic pictures, mainly for male
edification or whatever. The *skin-business* is
operating such ventures:
> Rex had purchased... a string of topless
> bars and strip clubs... The skin business
> was lucrative. (Grisham, 1999)

skin off all dead horses to marry your
mistress

A *dead horse* is something of small value, which it is not worth flogging, although at one time it had had its uses. In obsolete Irish use, to *work on a dead horse* was to have to complete a job for which you had already been paid, and when the task was done, you were said to have *skinned a dead horse*.

skinful an excessive quantity of intoxicating drink
Usually of beer, which suggests derivation from a distended bladder rather than from a wine-skin:
    Take it easy, Larry. You've got a skinful. (Chandler, 1958)

skinny-dip to bathe in the nude
The subject of greater taboo in America than in Europe:
    I'm going skinny-dipping...Who's game? (Sanders, 1982)

skippy *American* a male homosexual taking the female role.
Using an affected walk. Black slang.

skirt a woman viewed sexually by a male
The garment is worn normally only by females. Men call them kilts:
    He's got a nice skirt all right...I wouldn't say pretty, but a good figure. (G. Greene, 1932)
A *bit* or *piece of skirt* may be a woman viewed sexually, a man's sexual partner, or the act of copulation in general:
    He enjoyed nothing better in the world than a nice bit of skirt. (F. Richards, 1933)

skivvy a prostitute
In standard use, a female domestic servant. The American *skivvie-house* is a brothel:
    Little chickie workin' the skivvie houses...(Herr, 1977)

sky-piece a wig
It used to mean a hat. Only of those worn by males, which an American may also call a *sky-rug*.

slack (of a male) to urinate
Sometimes as *slack off*, which indicates a relieving of pressure.

slack fill delivering less than the customer thinks has been sold
Commercial jargon for the design and manufacture of bottles and cartons which look as if they hold more than they do. Sometimes too of only partly filling them, with packing or air taking up the empty space.

slag a promiscuous woman

Usually young. Partridge (*DSUE*) suggested 'perhaps ex slagger', which was an old term used for a bawd but I just wonder if it is not simply back slang for *gals*, as *yob* is for *boy*.

slake your lust (of a male) to copulate
Usually extramaritally, from *slake*, to quench or satisfy. A man may also *slake his (base) passion*:
    ...let him slake his lust on one of his own serf-women. (Fraser, 1973)
    Having slaked what the lady novelists would call my base passion, I staggered up and collapsed on the bed. (Fraser, 1994)
In obsolete Westmorland dialect, a *sleck-trough* was a prostitute, the cooling place into which a smith plunged his red-hot iron.

slammer a prison
Either from the *slamming* of the door as you are admitted or the rough treatment you receive once inside. Also shortened to *slam*:
    'You'll turn her into an addict. And she's—what? Sixteen. Jesus.' 'She's already been in the slammer.' (Theroux, 1976)
    Now kin we just wrap this up and take me to the slam. (Wambaugh, 1983—a hobo wanted a night in jail)

slang *American* to sell illegal narcotics
A black usage of uncertain derivation:
    'And how, sir, did you make a living prior to your incarceration?' 'Slanging.' 'Slanging?' 'Slanging dope.' 'Hanging, banging and slanging' is the motto of gang life, in that street doggerel. Slang, which originally meant to talk the talk, now is the term for selling drugs. (Turow, 1996)

slap and tickle sexual play
Literally, no more than what might occur in any courtship, which is all this phrase normally implies:
    And what sells this year's new royal books but the same slap and tickle? (*Esquire*, December, 1993)

slash an act of urination
Originally, a splashing or bespattering. Common use by both sexes:
    All I was doing was quickly relieving myself or, in plain language, having a slash. (Sharpe, 1979)

slash and burn[1] gonorrhoea
You feel the pain during urination.

slash and burn[2] asset stripping and ruthless cost-cutting
Financial jargon copied from primitive agriculture:

One analyst said: 'We like slash-and-burn deals. The more people who get fired the better.' (*Daily Telegraph*, 9 May 2001)

slate-off a person with low intelligence or lacking common sense

Like an incomplete house roof:

He left aw 'at he hed to his slayatt hoff of a nevvy. (*EDD*—the beneficiary was his nephew)

Such a person is still said to *have a slate loose*.

sledge unsportingly to harass (an opponent)

Jargon of professional cricket where the rewards become more important than the game. *OED* suggests the origin may have been *sledgehammer*, but I prefer the imagery of what was once used to pull a man to his execution. The practice seems to have originated in Australia and is definitely not cricket, as they say.

sleep to be dead

While you await the resurrection of the body. Often in compounds according to the circumstance. Thus to *sleep in your leaden hammock* or in *Davy Jones's locker* was to have died and been buried at sea:

Though Drake their famous Captain now slept in his leaden hammock. (Monsarrat, 1978)

To *sleep in your shoes* was to be killed in battle:

The dreary eighteenth day of June
Made many a ane sleep in their shoon;
The British blood was spilt like dew
Upon the field of Waterloo. (G. Muir, 1816)

When F. D. Roosevelt died, the official White House statement said he had *slept away*, which did not refer to yet another overnight absence from Eleanor with his mistress at Mount David:

The four Roosevelt boys in the services have been sent a message by their mother which said, 'President slept away this afternoon'. (Ranfurly, 1994—1945 diary entry)

Sleep is death:

Anyone who went to sleep in a dug-out where there was not much air with one of those fires going...would soon drop into a sleep from which there would be no awakening. (F. Richards, 1933)

sleep around to copulate promiscuously

Of either sex, supposedly in various beds:

...sleeping around with a lot of West Indians. 'I never approved of Christine's lust for black men.' (S. Green, 1979)

sleep-in see SIT-IN

sleep over to stay overnight for extramarital sexual activity

Not involving the occupation of bunk beds:

He wanted to sleep over that night. (Sanders, 1982)

sleep together (of a couple) to copulate

Usually extramaritally on a regular basis, and also of homosexuals. *Not to sleep together*, of spouses, means that they have ceased to copulate with each other, even though they may continue to share the same bed or room.

sleep with to copulate with

Perhaps the commonest use, normally of extramarital copulation by either sex, or both, and now standard English:

One couldn't accept a fur coat without sleeping with a man. (G. Greene, 1932)

A *sleeping dictionary* is a native-speaking mistress from whom you hope to learn the language:

East African (European) officers as a whole maintained a very much stricter code in the matter of sleeping with African women...sometimes referred to as 'sleeping dictionaries', from their obvious advantages as language instructors. (C. Allen, 1975)

A *sleeping partner*, with whom you regularly copulate, puns on the part-owner who plays no active part in the running of the business:

...the services of a Somali girl-friend or sleeping partner. (ibid.)

Also rarely as *sleepy time girl*, who can be a mistress or a prostitute:

Seems like the bint was one of his sleepy time girls. (Chandler, 1953)

sleighride the condition of being under the influence of illegal drugs

Riding on SNOW 1, cocaine.

slewed drunk

Not going straight:

Mr Hornby was just a bit slewed by the liquor he'd taken. (Russell, *c*.1900)

Also as *half-slewed*, where as usual the half equals the whole.

slice to cheat (a customer)

Retailer's jargon for overcharging by removing a sliver of cheese etc. from what has been weighed and priced. I cherish the punning phrase *slice the gentry*, to cheat the better-off.

slice of the action see ACTION 1

slight chill a pretext for not keeping an engagement

An indisposition which the draughts of royal palaces seem to induce:

'What shall I tell them? A slight chill?'
'That sounds a deal too much like

Buckingham Palace. Just say I'm out.'
(Ustinov, 1971)

Royal personages are also martyrs to *slight colds* and *indispositions*. However, the phrases can also be used, as with geriatric Russian leaders, to try to conceal the gravity of an illness:

Every other paper reported that Attlee is now getting better from a slight indisposition. (Crossman, 1981—Attlee when Prime Minister had had an attack of cerebral thrombosis)

slip¹ to give premature birth to

Usually of domestic animals:

Cows slipped their calves, horses fell lame. (R. Hunt, 1865)

but not for the great diarist:

Fraizer is so great with my Lady Castlemain and Steward and all the ladies at Court, in helping them slip their calfes when there is occasion. (Pepys, 1664—Fraizer was a court physician and royal abortionist, without whom there might have been many more royal dukedoms)

To *slip a foot* or *slip a girth* was to give birth to an illegitimate child, both with imagery from a fall whilst riding:

Slipping a foot, casting a leglin-girth or the like. (W. Scott, 1822)

slip² to die

The concept of gliding easily away and usually in compounds. To *slip away* is to die painlessly, usually in old age or after long illness:

To 'slip away' within sight of ninety. (Maclaren, 1895)

Old people may also *slip off*. With nautical imagery you may *slip your breath, cable, grip* or *wind*:

He was going to slip his cable with all the good scandal untold. (Fraser, 1971)

I don't think people *slip to Nod* any more:

He the bizzy roun' hath trod,
An' quietly wants to slip to Nod. (W. Taylor, 1787—later in the verse his fate is to 'trudge on Pluto's gloomy shore')

slippage mental illness or decline

Not the ability to skate, nor used to denote physical deterioration:

I learned all this much later from my mother who, after my father's death, had begun to show signs of slippage. (Desai, 1988)

slippery palm see PALM 1

slops the police

Punning back slang indicating disrespect:

... sent out a girl for the slops. (Sims, 1902—she was asked to fetch a policeman, not the wasted food)

sloshed drunk

To *slosh* is to be a glutton but there is also the imagery of an over-full container:

... her career of piss artistry, when she could still pretend she got sloshed out of not knowing about alcohol. (Amis, 1986)

Usually as *half-sloshed*, which means no less drunk.

slot to kill

The imagery of piercing perhaps, or from the slang *slot away*, to place an object in an aperture, as scoring a goal at football:

If the ragheads had me tied down naked and were sharpening their knives, I'd do whatever I could to provoke them into slotting me. (McNab, 1993—the *ragheads* were Iraqis)

slow stupid

Mainly educational jargon of children, but also of adults of low mental capacity. *Slow upstairs* is used only of adults:

He's the Irish version of a street hood, very good with weapons but a little slow upstairs. (Clancy, 1987, repeating a common but fallacious myth about the intelligence of the Irish)

slowdown¹ American a deliberate failure to do work for which you are being paid

A variant of the British GO SLOW whereby employees exert pressure on their employer in a labour dispute, especially when, as in the case of Federal workers, striking might be illegal:

... air controllers or postal workers staged 'slowdowns'. (*Daily Telegraph*, August 1981—Reagan was soon to turn the air controllers' *slowdown* into a full stop by dismissing them all)

See also SICK-OUT.

slowdown² a recession

One of the soothing words used by politicians when referring to an economic collapse for which they may bear some blame.

slug¹ a bullet

In the olden days leaden bullets had much the same shape and colour as the gastropod:

... felt that a .38 slug could save a lot of time and the taxpayer's money. (Allbeury, 1976)

To *get a slug* means to be killed or wounded by a bullet, but *slugged* means being hit by any agency, including a fist, a baseball bat, or an excess of alcohol.

slug² a quantity of spirits

Probably punning on SHOT 1, although there is a rare meaning, to swallow:

Jackie sighed and took a slug from her
glass. (R. Doyle, 1990)

Usually in the cliché a *slug of whisky* and *slugged*
means drunk, from the hitting, the swallowing, and the measure.

sluice¹ to copulate with
Literally, to flush:
> ... she has been sluic'd in's absence,
> And his pond fish'd by his next neighbour.
> (Shakespeare, *The Winter's Tale*)

This may be a spurious entry based on a single
metaphorical use, but it is still more worthy
of notice than the American *sluice*, to shoot
eagles from a helicopter.

sluice² a lavatory
From the controlled flow of water:
> He's in the sluice. (Bradbury, 1959—he had
> not fallen into a millstream)

slumber *American* death
The common imagery of SLEEP but this usage
is mainly the jargon of the mortician. Thus a
slumber cot or *box* is a coffin, a *slumber robe* is a
shroud, and a *slumber room* is a morgue:
> Lavish slumber rooms where the deceased
> receives visitors for some days before the
> funeral. (J. Mitford, 1963)

slush bribery
Originally, a mixture of grease and oil and still
so used of waste cooking fat aboard ship,
which used to (or may still) be sold to create a
slush fund, to be shared among the favoured
few. For landlubbers the phrase means only
cash which may be used for corporate bribery:
> A non-existent British Leyland 'slush'
> fund... (*Private Eye*, May 1981)

smack illegal heroin
A corruption of the Yiddish *schmeck*, to sniff,
rather than what it does for you. Derivation
from the nickname of a bandleader who died
in 1952 is implausible:
> Hey, Johnny, you want smack? (Simon,
> 1979)

small folk (the) the fairies
Alluding to their stature in the days when
they were real to West Country folk and, with
their vicious natures, not to be trifled with or
talked about directly. Also as the *small men* or
the *small people*:
> The small men. I mean the pixies.
> (Mortimer, 1895)

> The small people are believed by some to
> be the spirits of the people who inhabited
> Cornwall many thousands of years ago.
> (R. Hunt, 1865)

smallest room (the) the lavatory
Even if, by geometric computation, it isn't:

smallest room, the The bathroom;
restroom. *A facetious euphem.* (*DAS*, which
contrives to define one euphemism by two
others)

smalls underpants and brassières
A shortened form of *small clothes*.

smashed drunk or under the influence of
illegal narcotics
Or, in these depraved times, both, your
consciousness having been destroyed by what
you have ingested:
> I was smashed last night. Some of the
> guys at this party were on methedrine with
> their acid. (Deighton, 1972)

To *smash the teapot* was to resume regular
drinking of alcohol after a period of abstinence.

smear¹ to bribe
Literally, to spread:
> A little smearing of the right
> palm... (Longstreet, 1956—not implying
> that the left palm would not have done
> equally well)

The American spelling *schmear* comes from
the German *schmieren* via Yiddish to mean the
same thing as a verb or a noun:
> I get the feeling that a schmear changed
> hands somewhere along the way. (Sanders,
> 1977)

smear² a test for cervical cancer
The usage avoids any reference to the dread
disease or the place from which the sample is
taken:
> Course I did ask once when I went to the
> family planning for a smear. Well, you
> wonder if all is well. (Lockhead, 1985)

smear³ to attempt to bring into disrepute
Spreading what the subject prefers to keep
hidden. The tabloid press often regales its
readership with *smear campaigns* against persons known to the public, and politicians who
adopt the same tactics also know that mud
sticks:
> The opposition has twice tried to smear
> me. (Crisp, 1982)

smear out to kill
A variant of WIPE OUT 1:
> The opposition had twice tried to smear
> me out. (Hall, 1969)

smeared *American* drunk
Using the same imagery as the slang *blotto*? Or
just unable to see things in focus.

smell of to be tainted with
What you are said to *smell of* is something
taboo. Thus to *smell of the counting-house* was,

among the landed gentry, to be contaminated by having actually earned your wealth:

> If she thought that any of her newcomers smelt of the counting-house, she would tell her friends 'Have nothing to do with them'. (Bence-Jones, 1987, writing about Anglo-Irish protestants in the 19th century)

smell the stuff *American* illegally to sniff cocaine

Usually of an addict and see STUFF 1.

smoke¹ (the) opium

From the method of ingestion:

> There isn't much record he went for tea-sticks or the smoke. (Longstreet, 1956)

smoke² to murder

Presumably from the discharge of burnt powder:

> So how is it, dude, you really be wantin me to smoke your daddy? (Turow, 1996)

To *smoke it* is to kill yourself, from putting the barrel of a handgun in your mouth:

> I hear some detective from West L.A. smoked it. (Wambaugh, 1983, referring to a suicide)

smoker (the) the devil

With his fire and brimstone:

> The old smoker takes the glittish gorbelly pig. (*EDD—gorbelly* means very fat)

smokey *American* a policeman

The *DAS* suggests this comes from *Smokey the Bear*, the US Forestry Service symbol, and see also BEAR 2:

> The only enemies are the weather and the occasional lawman, known as 'Smokey Bear'. (*Daily Telegraph*, 1995, writing about American truckers)

Whence many compounds: *smokey beaver*, a policewoman; *smokey on four legs*, a policeman on horseback; *smokey with camera*, police with radar; *smokey on rubber*, police in a car; *smokey with ears*, police listening or able to listen to CB; and so on.

smoking gun (a) conclusive evidence of guilt

From the emission from the barrel immediately after a shot has been fired:

> ...the tape is a 'smoking gun', that is, in police and prosecutional slang, direct evidence of criminal guilt. (Colodny and Gettlin, 1991, writing of a White House tape dated June, 1973)

smooth to distort (published accounts)

You conceal, or try to even out, fluctuations by carrying forward exceptional movements up or down, of cash and inventory, but especially of profit and loss. This keeps stock-holders and analysts quiet, for a time.

smother (of a male) to copulate

It alludes to his attitude on the female:

> I've smothered in too many hall bedrooms. (Chandler, 1939)

The meaning, to kill by suffocating, is standard English.

smut house *American* a place where pornographic programmes are screened.

Smut as in DIRTY 1, and nothing to do with an old-fashioned boiler-room:

> He had never watched queer movies before, and after this night he had no plans to watch another one. This was his third such smut house in the last ninety minutes. (Grisham, 1992)

snaffle to steal

Originally, to saunter, as many chance thieves do:

> He cud snaffle the raisins an' currins away. (Bagnall, 1852)

snag to pilfer

The allusion is to the involuntary catching, as a garment on a nail:

> He snagged my Texas toast when he thought no one was looking. (Anonymous, 1996)

snake pit a mental hospital

Probably from one of the common delusions of the mentally ill, but also a place where the sane hope not to find themselves:

> The old man was always threatening to stash her away in a snake pit. (Macdonald, 1971)

The less common *snake ranch* is a brothel, punning on the SERPENT imagery.

snapper an ampoule of amyl nitrite

The drug, used in the treatment of heart disease, is popularly supposed to be an aphrodisiac and is therefore sought after for illegal use. It is ingested by snapping the cap off an ampoule, and sniffing:

> ...a box of snappers in plain view on a dresser top. (Sanders, 1977)

snatch¹ a single act of copulation

Usually extramaritally. The derivation might be from any of several standard English meanings of *snatch*—a snare, an entanglement, a hasty meal, a sudden jerk—or merely from SNATCH 2, the vagina. Shakespeare could have been using the word in either sexual sense:

> ...it seems some certain snatch or so Would serve your turns. (*Titus Andronicus*)

but there is no equivocation in:

I could not abide marriage, but as a
rambler I took a snatch when I could get
it. (R. Burton, 1621)

snatch² the vagina

Perhaps from the meaning, a portion of hair,
or merely from its association with SNATCH 1:
... if the number of the vaginas... were
lined up orifice to orifice, there would be a
snatch long enough... (Styron, 1976)
A *snatch mouse* is a tampon in American slang.

snatch³ to kidnap or steal

The action of seizing:
Snatching Steven was going to be one
big piece of chocolate cake. (J. Collins,
1981)
A *snatch* is the commission of either type of
crime:
Harry the Horse and Spanish John and
Little Isadora... go on the snatch on a
pretty fair scale. (Runyon, 1990, written
in 1935)

snatch⁴ to arrest

Either singly, or taking a ringleader from a
mob. Whence the police *snatch squad*, which is
trained to make such arrests.

snatched from us dead

The figurative kidnapping is done by the
deity. Also as *snatched away*:
The depth and reality of his religious faith,
coupled with his practical wisdom, was
what supported us both when our only son
and then our only daughter were snatched
from us. (E. M. Wright, 1932—the children
of Joseph Wright, who gave us the *EDD*,
died respectively of septicaemia and
peritonitis)
... a routine operation went wrong and she
was snatched away. Her death was a
terrible shock. (J. Major, 1999)

sneak to steal

In standard English, to move furtively,
whence, in the children's use, to inform
against. In the 19th century it applied particularly to thefts from private houses:
He saw Seth Thimaltwig snake hawf
a pahnd o' fresh butter. (Treddlehoyle,
1893)
Today we only meet (but far too often) the
tautological *sneak thief*.

sneezer *American* a prison

Possibly a corruption of FREEZER. I thought it
might have come into the language because a
typist couldn't read Chandler's handwriting
until I found Runyon using the same word in
the 1930s:
... tossed in the sneezer by some patrol car
boys. (Chandler, 1953)

sniff to inhale narcotics or stimulants illegally

Either cocaine:
Department wives who drink, analysts who
are screwing their secretary, translators
who sniff. (Deighton, 1994—just the one
secretary, poor woman?)
or glue, especially by juveniles:
... an increasing number of
children... have adopted glue-sniffing. (*The
Practitioner*, 1977)
To be *on the sniff* is habitually to inhale in this
way:
'Is she on the sniff?' said Robyna... 'I
thought she was spaced out.' (Deighton,
1993/2)

sniff out to kill

Perhaps a corruption of SNUFF (OUT), because
it means literally no more than to detect:
... before some busybody at the top sniffs
out Sniffers. (Manning, 1977, writing about
a killing not a detection)
To *take a long (deep) sniff* indicates that you are
about to BREATHE YOUR LAST:
Half a dozen horsemen galloped past,
firing six-guns in the air. The young
cowboy said, 'Seems like you might be
taking yourself a long deep sniff.'
(Deighton, 1972)

snifter a drink of spirits

Literally, a sniff, whence a small portion of
brandy etc. offered so that the aroma can be
sampled, and then any spirits:
He turned, snifter in hand. (Wodehouse,
1934)

snip a vasectomy

Medical jargon which has passed into standard use. (The Kent trading standards officer,
dealing with a complaint that a surgeon's fee
for a vasectomy was too high, dismissed the
charge, remarking that it was a snip, for
which he found himself reported to the chief
executive.) *Snib* and *snick* were dialect words
for the castration of domestic and farm
animals.

snort¹ a drink of spirits

Also as a *snorter*, perhaps because it makes you
exhale noisily:
There's a pint in the glove compartment.
Want a snort? (Chandler, 1958)

snort² to ingest an illegal narcotic

By taking a big SNIFF. It also may mean the
substance ingested:
'I'm not worried about it,' she said with a
half-smile as she casually spooned two
snorts. (Robbins, 1981)

snout¹ a police informer

Underworld slang for the nose of the PIG:
> I know all about snouts. And I didn't have
> to pay for this. (P. D. James, 1986)

snout² tobacco
As this was a 19th-century usage, it may have
been derived from the sniffing of snuff. Now
British prison jargon, especially of tobacco
used as a currency inside a jail.

snow¹ cocaine
In its crystalline or powdered form, from the
colour and coldness:
> Not all jazz-players smoke marijuana or
> opium, or sniff snow. (Longstreet, 1956)

Whence many derivatives. A *snowball is a*
quantity or derivative of cocaine or heroin:
> Each was controlled by a mobile phone:
> one for heroin, two for crack and three for
> snowballs—a popular mix of crack and
> heroin. (Fiennes, 1996)

A *snowbird* is a person addicted to cocaine;
snowed in, *under*, or *up*, is under the influence
of narcotics; a *snow-storm* is a gathering where
cocaine is taken illegally. To be *snow-blind* is to
become addicted to cocaine:
> But Renzo got snow-blind real bad. He
> began to deal, and deal heavily enough to
> draw attention. (Anonymous, 1996—Renzo
> was not an arctic explorer or a card player)

An addict will turn into a *snowman*:
> Behind his back they call him G-nose or
> Snowman. (Turow, 1993)

snow² deliberately to obfuscate (an issue) or deceive (a person)
As a landscape may be obscured by a snowfall.
To *snow* a person is to produce masses of
documentation which will make it hard for
the recipient to pick out and understand the
relevant points:
> Little job? Don't let them snow you, old
> friend. (Price, 1970)

Such an operation is known as a *snow-job*:
> A lie, a cover-up, a snow-job was fatal.
> (Allbeury, 1980)

snowdrop *American* a military policeman
They wore white spats in the Second World
War:
> '...we've even put the 787th Military
> Police Company into the Junior
> Constitutional Club.'... 'Your snowdrops,
> you mean.' (Deighton, 1982)

snowing down south (it's) *American* the hem of your petticoat is showing
An oblique warning to the wearer. Petticoats
are normally white.

snuff (out) to kill
Like extinguishing a candle:

> You mean you make sure he doesn't go off
> like a mad dog, snuffing people left and
> right. (van Lustbaden, 1983)

> I'd have snuffed out every life in India.
> (Fraser, 1975)

To *snuff it* is to die:
> An' Ray Tuck's been running Lippy's
> errands—or was until Lippy snuffed it.
> (Price, 1982)

snug inconveniently small
The language of the estate agent seeking to
convey an impression of cosiness:
> Now he knew 'snug' meant tiny. (Theroux,
> 1974, giving a property description in an
> advertisement)

so in a condition the subject of a taboo
Pregnant:
> A euphemism for pregnant...Mrs Brown is
> so. (*EDD*)

or homosexual (*SOED*). Both uses may be
obsolete.

so-and-so a mild insult
Each *so* being a substitute for the abusive
epithet, as in the expression, *He's a right so-
and-so*.

so-so in a physical condition which differs from the normal
In common speech, it indicates mediocrity. It
is used of pregnancy and mild indisposition.

soak a drunkard
Formerly, it meant to drink alcohol to excess:
> A 'slug for the drink' is a man who soaks
> and never succumbs. (Douglas, 1901)

Soaked means drunk.

social disease a venereal disease
Mainly 19th-century usage, and as *social
infection*:
> 'He has contracted a social disease, which
> makes it impossible that he marry.' 'You
> mean he's got a dose of clap?' (Fraser, 1970,
> writing in 19th-century style)
> ...contracting certain indelicate social
> infections from—hem, hem—female
> camp-followers. (Fraser, 1975—again in
> 19th-century style)

social evil (the) *obsolete* prostitution
So considered in Victorian times, which may
be why Gladstone was so interested in meeting its practitioners.

social glass (a) see GLASS 1

social housing accommodation built for poor people
So named because the provision of such
premises for sale and rent, often with the

aid of subsidy, is looked upon as helping society:

> The associations took over from the councils as the main providers of social housing in 1988. (*Daily Telegraph*, 23 October 1995)

Social Science or *Social Studies* are the names given to the study of society and human behaviour, although, as Bullock and Stally-brass (1977) observe, 'Social Studies...frequently fail to exercise scientific stringency'. A *social worker* is primarily concerned with the poor, sick, or criminal members of society, which is not to suggest that other workers are anti-social.

social inclusion giving special advantages to selected groups of people

The jargon of social science. See also SOCIALLY EXCLUDED:

> The University [Lincolnshire at Humberside] performs well in the Government's social inclusion scale. More than 90 per cent of the 12,000 students come from state schools or colleges. (*Sunday Telegraph*, 3 February 2001 — unfortunately its academic performance was less noteworthy)

social justice an imprecise dogma based on a wish to improve the situation of the poor rather than on the rule of law

Some see it as being based on envy:

> The robbery of the rich is called social justice. (Michael Roberts, 1951)

For others, like those who set the courses at Haverford College in Pennsylvania, the phrase may refer to what is seen to be morally right:

> ...students must complete a 'Social Justice Requirement' in order to graduate. This means taking courses in Feminist Political Theory. (*Daily Telegraph*, 23 February 1991)

Goebbels saw *social justice* in January 1945 as one of the Nazi war aims. (A. Clark, 1995)
And so, as Alice discovered in Wonderland, the phrase tends to mean what you want it to mean.

social ownership control by politicians and bureaucrats

The control is achieved by expropriation, with or without compensation. In 1986 the British Labour Party needed another word than NATIONALIZE to describe a process in which much of the electorate had ceased to have confidence:

> ...the substitution of phrases like 'social ownership' for nasty brutal words like 'nationalization'. (*Daily Telegraph*, August 1986)

social security the payment of money by the state to the poor

A durable phrase among the many with which we have sought to mask the plight of, and charity to, fellow citizens. Sometimes shortened to *the social*:

> It was the morning most people went to collect their social security. (L. Thomas, 1979)
> You won't have to keep me. I'll get the social. (L. Thomas, 1994)

socialist justice arbitrary punishment

The Russian Communist euphemism for legalistic tyranny:

> [Gorbachev] read law; an unusual choice in a country where 'socialist justice'—the Gulag, the execution cellar—had for so long taken precedence over juridical nicety. (Moynahan, 1994)

socially excluded poor

Not denied the vote, refused free education, or forbidden to participate in public functions but unable to afford what others can buy or to have access to credit:

> According to this argument, those who are described as socially excluded—the jobless, urban poor—become permanently excluded. (Patten, 1998)

sodden habitually drunk

Permanently soaked, but with the wrong kind of liquid:

> She's lonely,—as well she might be, married to the sodden and straying Major. (Atwood, 1996)

soft¹ of low intelligence

A shortened form of *soft in the head*:

> She's saft at best, and something lazy. (Burns, 1785)

soft² inflicting less harm than an alternative

The opposite to HARD in pornography, illegal narcotics, etc. A *soft drink* is non-alcoholic, and will harm your teeth more than your liver. For the military, a *soft target* is one which you can attack with relative impunity. A *soft option* is a simple solution, with overtones of laziness or cowardice if you take it.

soft commission a bribe

Paid in addition to normal commercial commission for the introduction of business:

> It is the first time in Imro's history for a breach of rules on 'soft commissions'. (*Daily Telegraph*, 25 June 1994—the British Investment Management Regulatory Authority—IMRO—fined unit trust managers who had accepted £50,000 worth

of travel expenses from brokers in return for placing business with them)

soft-shoe a clandestine or indirect approach
From the silence of the tread and the association with shuffling:
Doing the same soft-shoe as you, talking to me about something else, then trying to slide this Litiplex name in so I wouldn't notice. (Turow, 1993)

soft skills application and discipline
If not taught in the home, hardest of all to acquire at school:
There are also problems with many basic skills such as literacy and numeracy and there are difficulties with 'soft skills' such as the ability to communicate with, or work in a team or show initiative. (*Daily Telegraph*, 14 March 2001, writing about unemployed young people)

soft soap flattery
Originally, what we now call *shampoo*, a word borrowed from the Hindi:
I protest I have done my share, but he merely condescends to ladle out soft soap about the colonel's good opinion. (Mark VII, 1927—an officer was being talked into extra and dangerous duties)
Also as a verb:
Don't you soft-soap me. Fancy trying to get round me like that. (Pérez-Réverté, in translation, 1994)
See also SADDLE SOAP.

softness in the economy a recession
When it would seem, conversely, that times are hard:
Instead he insists that the current campaign was planned five months ago and is running because of 'softness' in the economy. (*Daily Telegraph*, 29 October 1998, referring to advertising by a supermarket chain)

soil human excrement
In the days of the earth closet, solid (and liquid) matter had to be regularly removed, usually at night, whence NIGHT SOIL.
To *soil yourself* or *soil your pants*, *clothing* etc. is to defecate or urinate involuntarily without getting your clothing out of the way.

soil your reputation (of a woman) to copulate extramaritally
From the figurative dirtying:
A true geisha will never soil her reputation by making herself available to men on a nightly basis. (Golden, 1997)

soixante-neuf simultaneous fellatio and cunnilingus
The reversible numbers 6 and 9, indicating the position adopted by the participants. This French form is normal in the British Isles—I speak etymologically—with *six-à-neuf* being rare:
...six-à-neuf meaning a slightly contortive sexual diversion. (Jennings, 1965)
Another usage, more direct or less Francophone, is *sixty-nine*:
...every act from masturbation to 'sixty-nine' was indulged in. (ibid.)
The participants may also be described as *sixty-nining*.

solace extramarital copulation
Supposedly consolation during the absence or disinterestedness of a spouse:
[Lloyd George] was hardly the first or the last politician to find solace in a woman more clever and attractive than his own wife. (Graham Stewart, 1999)

soldier *American* a hoodlum
He executes the orders of his gangster boss, threatening, assaulting, or killing:
I lend you a couple of soldiers—you frighten the crap outta number one on the list. (J. Collins, 1981)

solicit to offer sexual services for money
Literally, to request or entreat in any context, as does the British *solicitor*, a lawyer who pleads for you in court, or the American *solicitor* who calls on customers seeking orders, often ignoring a notice ordering him to stay away:
She was soliciting to cover her air fare. (Gardner, 1983—she was a prostitute)
And homosexually:
The defendant was accused of having improperly solicited another man in a public lavatory. (Boyle, 1979, writing about Guy Burgess)

solid waste human excrement
Civil engineering jargon. The term does not include empty tins or potato peelings. Sometimes simply as *solids*, as in the cliché *when the solids hit the fan*.

solidarity participating in a strike on behalf of others
The word was used, as in modern Poland, for the coming together of workers in a single bargaining unit, whence support for other employees in dispute with their employer.

solitary sex masturbation
Not hermaphroditism. Also as *solitary sin* or *solitary vice*:

Carter had seen 'young unmarried women, of the middle-class of society reduced, by the constant use of the speculum, to the mental and moral condition of prostitutes; seeking to give themselves the same indulgence by the practice of solitary vice'. (Pearsall, 1969, quoting from a document of 1853)

something¹ an alcoholic drink
You may be asked if you would like a *little something*, although the amount may turn out to be substantial if you accept. Also as *something short, moist*, or *for the thirst*:
> 'May we offer you something?' Birkenhead said. Griffith did not reply but Collins shook his head. (Flanagan, 1995)
> She pulled out a bottle of gin, asking me if I would have a drop of something short. (Mayhew, 1862)
> I doubt if he were quite as fully sensible of the gentleman's merits under arid conditions, as when something moist was going. (C. Dickens, 1861)
> There's usually a little something for the thirst that's in it. (McCourt, 1997)

something² an expletive
Of the same tendency as BLANK 1 and, similarly, seldom used today:
> It's nothing but twists and turns, and there isn't a something fence you could go fast at without risking your something neck...and a nice hope I've got on that blank sketchy jumper. (Sassoon, 1928)
You may also hear *something-something* used in the same sense, in polite circles.

something for the weekend a contraceptive sheath
Or a packet of contraceptives, from the days when the main purveyors were barbers, and men had their hair cut more often:
> Condoms weren't called condoms, the euphemism was 'something for the weekend'. (Monkhouse, 1993)

something on you a damaging piece of knowledge about you
Not the clothes you are wearing. In this usage, *on* means against:
> He's got something on her and she's afraid of him. (Chandler, 1958)

somewhere in ... the location is secret
A usage in time of war, to conceal information about where specific regiments were located:
> As it was, most already had their soldier 'somewhere in France'—that delightful euphemism of the censors. (Horne, 1969)
You may still hear an embattled war correspondent be similarly evasive about a location.

somewhere where he (or she) can be looked after off our hands
Used of aged, ill, or burdensome dependants, implying that they, not you, will benefit from the impersonal care of paid attendants:
> Get him out of here as soon as possible, to somewhere where he can be looked after. (Bradbury, 1959)

son of a bitch an illegitimate child
Once a deadly insult to both mother and child, but now a mild insult or expletive, often abbreviated to *S.O.B.* For a dissertation on *son of a gun* see GUNNER'S DAUGHTER. The synonymous *son of a bachelor* is obsolete.

song and dance a male homosexual
Rhyming slang for *nance* (see NANCY) and punning on the supposed tastes of male professional dancers.

sop a drunkard
Literally, something dipped in liquid or the liquid in which it is dipped. It may just be confused with the common SOT.

sore a carcinoma
The symptom, in this case an ulcer, is used for the dread affliction:
> Her own mother had died of a 'sore'. (Mann, 1902)

sot a drunkard
The original meaning was a fool:
> If ony Whiggish whingin sot,
> To blame poor Matthew dare. (Burns, 1786)
whence to act foolishly in association with drunkenness:
> Drover blades, who drink and sot. (Nicholson, 1814)

sought after expensive
Estate agents' puff, when they want to imply that a buyer will have plenty of competition. Any property, however humble, is likely to be *sought after*, if the price is right.

sound bite a spoken phrase or sentence short and pithy enough to be broadcast in its entirety
An art form developed by politicians who know that any fuller statement is likely to be truncated or distorted prior to or on being broadcast:
> We are in the age of the satellite image, the spin-doctor, and the three-second sound bite. (McCrum, 1991)

souper *Irish* a Roman Catholic converted to Protestantism or someone attempting to bring about such conversion
In the recurrent periods of 19th-century famine, which gave rise to the phrase *the*

hungry forties in other places than Ireland, Protestant Church of Ireland clergy provided food for their congregations, including converts from the Church of Rome:

> Proselytizers, or soupers, from their offering soup to starving people...(Carleton, 1836)
> I'll turn souper this day for the male.
> (Barlow, 1892—*male* meant meal)

See also TAKE THE SOUP.

A *soup kitchen* affords the same relief to the hungry, but usually without strings attached.

souse a drunkard

The common culinary imagery, this time from soaking in vinegar or the like:

> That much would just get a real souse started. (Chandler, 1953)

Soused means drunk:

> I could see that mother was getting soused. (L. Armstrong, 1955)

south[1] (the) the poorer or less industrialized countries

The geographical location of many of them relative to western Europe and North America, although you are unlikely to use the term of or in the Antipodes. The usage seeks to avoid other patronizing or offensive language.

south[2] (the) a person's reproductive parts

Alluding to the fact that the trunk would be to the north of them, if you were a cartographer:

> I said it may be difficult to obtain elastic girdles and that bras are very dependant on elastic, but I dodged mentioning needs further south. (Ranfurly, 1994—diary entry of 26 May 1942, recording a conversation with the Duke of Gloucester about a shortage of rubber)

south[3] (going or moving) deteriorating

Alluding to business and share prices, from the direction taken on the wall charts. An improvement does not, however, lead to the comment that prices are *going north*.

South Chelsea Battersea

An example of what the snobs and estate agents do to upgrade an address in cities where a fashionable area is bounded by an unfashionable:

> Battersea...South Chelsea, the snobs call it. (Theroux, 1982)

Southern Comfort masturbation

Punning on the location of the area stimulated and the brand of spirits:

> I usually wind up giving myself another kind of Southern Comfort, you know what I mean? (Lodge, 1980)

souvenir an illegitimate child

Certainly a lasting memory for the mother:

> I expect in some cases [the troops] had left other souvenirs which would either be a blessing or a curse to the ladies concerned. (F. Richards, 1933)

For most wartime soldiers, *souvenirs* were things they stole.

sow your wild oats to behave wildly or irresponsibly

With extravagance or with promiscuous seminal distribution, like the persistent weed *Avena fatua*:

> We all sow our wild oats at some time or another. (Sharpe, 1974)

sozzle to drink to excess

Originally, to splash and in America, to soak or dowse:

> Life in India is horribly artificial and meaningless...It's just sozzling in the club and general scandal or petty romance. (Royle, 1989, quoting from a letter written by a Briton who had stayed after independence)

The past participle, meaning drunk, is more common:

> 'We were all rather sozzled that night.' 'I wonder if he was drunk when he killed himself.' (I. Murdoch, 1977)

space American a grave

Funeral jargon:

> As for other euphemisms...'space' for 'grave'. (J. Mitford, 1963)

A *space and bronze deal* was what you got if you bought your plot and casket in advance.

space-head a drug addict

From being SPACED OUT:

> Another fuckin' space-head [in Thailand]. Can't move for them, man. (Garland, 1996)

spaced out under the influence of illegal drugs

Referring to the floating sensation, especially after ingesting a hallucinogen:

> The doctor arrived, but to our dismay he was totally incompetent. I mean, he was spaced out on drugs or something. (Peck, 1987)

Less often of an abnormal physical or mental state not necessarily drug-induced:

> She looked sick, depressed, and spaced out. Someone had slipped her a mickey. (Greeley, 1986)

spam[1] a penis

The common MEAT 2 imagery, from the proprietary brand of processed sweet pork (which is said to taste like human flesh). In many vulgarisms such as *spam alley* or *chasm*, the vagina; *spam sceptre* or *javelin*, the penis viewed sexually.

spam² the malicious violation of computer security by overloading with messages

The derivation is uncertain. As noun and verb:

It has now tracked down a team of internal security specialists, to track down the source of the spam. (*Daily Telegraph*, 16 January 2001)

The mass 'spamming'... happened last Wednesday night when more than two million unsolicited messages arrived in UUNet's system at the same time, causing the crash. (ibid.)

Spanish gout syphilis

Honest British tarts thought that Spanish girls must have infected them, if not French, Italian, or other 'foreign' prostitutes.

Spanish practices regular cheating by employees

A feature of the old Fleet Street newspaper industry in London, where overmanning, falsification of time sheets, paid absenteeism, and other similar goings-on were endemic:

A year ago, as well, as overmanning, the exploitative 'Spanish practices' and the interrupted production...' (*Times*, January 1987)

(Eddie Shah, Robert Maxwell, 'Tiny' Rowland, Rupert Murdoch, and Conrad Black did not share the inhibitions of native managers when it came to cleaning out these stables.)

Spanish tummy diarrhoea

The British holidaymaker's equivalent of the American TOURISTAS.

spare tyre obesity at the waistline

Usually of a male, from the roll of fat overhanging his belt:

I longed to melt away that spare tyre before it was too late. (Matthew, 1983)

In America, sometimes as *rubber tire*.

spared still alive

The deity doesn't require your company just yet:

I thought: if I am spared, if I attain the age of eighty-five. (Theroux, 1995)

speak to *obsolete* to propose marriage to

This is a reminder of 19th-century reticence about marriage:

When Jamie 'spoke to' Janet Carson, who told her people at once, having no opposition to expect... (Strain, 1900)

Also as the Scottish *speak for* and *speak till*.

speak with forked tongue to dissimulate

Serpents want to have a word with animal rights enthusiasts about this usage, without which writers of screenplays for Westerns would have had to dream up another cliché:

Owners and players act as if there were no fans, as if the fans were a myth invented by sportswriters for days when there is no... multi-millionaire owner to scold for speaking with forked tongue. (*Guardian*, 11 August 1994)

spear a penis

A WEAPON of no greater length or threat than the coarse *mutton dagger* of army slang:

'No, Redmon,' said Leon with great seriousness, 'there is new diseases here. Your spear it rots.' (O'Hanlon, 1984—the new disease was syphilis)

special¹ requiring non-standard attention or facilities

Educational jargon which is not used for those of superior attainments. Whence *special* pupils who may go to *special* classes for REMEDIAL tuition or to *special schools* where those of restricted mobility may play *special* games, have *special* needs, and so on:

Mrs Evans was attacked by the boy, a special needs pupil who suffers from Attention Deficit Hyperactivity Disorder, after he was told he was not allowed to go swimming. (*Daily Telegraph*, 2 September 2000—the teacher, not the pupil, was then disciplined, suspended, and prosecuted)

Special care is what is given to the mentally ill:

To the outside world, it advertised itself as a 'Special Care unit', but that, like so much of the language employed by the authorities, was a euphemism. To a greater or lesser extent, its inmates were insane. (McCrum, 1991)

Poor areas are designated *special areas*:

The Commissioner for what were euphemistically called the Special Areas— later known as the Distressed Areas—had resigned his post. (Deedes, 1997, writing of Britain in the 1930s)

etc.

special² *British* an ancillary and voluntary police officer

Shortened form of *special constable* and without political overtones in England, Wales, and Scotland. In Northern Ireland the *Specials* were a paramilitary force which supported Protestant political dominance:

Originally there had been three classes of enlistment: Class A, which involved full-time duty; Class B, involving part-time duties; and Class C, comprising volunteers who could be called up in an emergency. In 1969, only Class B—the 'B-Specials'— remained... There was not a Catholic amongst them. (Deedes, 1997, describing the Ulster Special Constabulary)

special³ nuclear

In the jargon of the forces, *special stores* or *weapons*:

> ...a considerable number [of nuclear warheads] had been in Special Weapons Stores overrun by the offensive. (Hackett, 1978)

special⁴ exclusively provided for the use of senior party officials and their families

An abuse recognized, but not eliminated, by post-Communist Russian leaders:

> We must finally eliminate the special food 'perks' for the 'starving nomenklatura', and abolish both in substance and form the word 'Spets'—special stores, special clinics, special health resorts, and so forth—since we did not have any special communists. (Gorbachev, in translation 1995, quoting Yeltsin: 'spets' were special facilities for the *nomenklatura*, or privileged class)

special⁵ involving a personal sexual relationship

Some of us consider other friendships also as *special*:

> I was drinking...with Democritus—that's my friend, my special friend, you understand. (A. Massie, 1986—he was his catamite)

special⁶ ruthless and not complying with normal laws

In many phrases, of which a sample follows:

special action the rounding up and murdering of Jews by Nazis

> ...the incredible *numbers* involved in these Special Actions...These Jews, they come on and on. (Styron, 1976)

Special Branch *British* police specifically concerned with subversion or terrorism

> Here you call your political police the Special Branch, because you English are not so direct in these matters. (Deighton, 1978)
>
> I was working for the [Irish] Garda Special Branch and supplying extensive and important information. (O'Callaghan, 1998)

special court a tribunal with extra-legal powers and procedures

The Nazi *Sondergericht* set up in March 1933 to overrule and supersede the independent judiciary was a good example:

> Dr Bergshasser...—an aryan by the way— was sentenced to ten months by the special court. (Klemperer, 1998, in translation, diary entry of 13 January 1934—the doctor had been overheard repeating a joke about Hitler)

special detachment an army or police unit established to terrorize dissidents etc.

> Even the Jews of the Special Detachment were reluctant to pick the children up. (Styron, 1976, writing of Poland in the Second World War, where the Nazis so named a police force consisting of Jews working for the SS, mainly responsible for controlling other Jews)

special duty illegal or inhuman activity sanctioned by the state

> 'Special duty groups' is a close translation [of *Einsatzgruppen*]. But the amorphous word 'Einsatz' had another shade of meaning—knightliness. (Keneally, 1982, writing about Nazi gangs appointed to harass and round up Jews)

Other tyrannies employ the same language, methods, and concepts.

special education see SPECIAL REGIME

special investigations unit malefactors for political purposes

> ...the work of the Special Investigations Unit (Plumbers). (Colodny and Gettlin, 1991, writing about Watergate)

special operations state-sponsored bribery

> Sirven...knows more political secrets than any man in France as a result of his position in charge of Elf's 'special operations', a euphemism for wholesale bribery and political manipulation. (*Daily Telegraph*, 8 February 2001—Elf was the state-owned oil company which government used to finance and channel bribes)

special police police seconded from normal duties to control subversion and political disorder

A London variant, the *special patrol group*, was a riot squad which sometimes used excessive violence and unauthorized weaponry. In underworld slang, as *special fuzz*:

> A hairy hitchhiking student had only recently complained to him that the special fuzz were becoming hard to pinpoint. (Price, 1971)

special regime a treatment intended to kill, or destroy the health of, a prisoner

The most severe of the four categories of Russian treatment of prisoners; the others were *general* (the mildest), *intensified*, and *strict*. If you were classed as *special*, you would be required to do heavy manual work for long hours under harsh conditions on 800 calories of food a day, so long as you survived. The Chinese Communists call such treatment *special education*.

special services and investigations the covert monitoring of law-abiding citizens

> Caulfield had been a member of the NYPD and its undercover unit, the Bureau of Special Services and Investigations (BUSSI)... known for its ability to penetrate and keep track of left-wing and black groups. (Colodny and Gettlin, 1991)

special squad a unit set up by an autocracy to harass or eliminate its opponents

So named by many tyrants, especially in Latin America. The Nazis used their *Sonderkommandos* for this duty.

special task force an extra-legal police group

Another instrument of tyranny or religious bigotry:

> Their attempts at non-violent protests were brutally put down by the Special Task Force, a kind of Buddhist Gestapo. (Dalrymple, 1998, writing about Sri Lankan Tamils)

special treatment the torture and killing of your opponents

> ...what Sonderbehandlung means, that though it says *Special Treatment*, it means pyramids of cyanosed corpses. (Keneally, 1982)

A 1983 British Airways advertisement in Germany relied on a literal translation of 'You fly frequently. Don't you deserve a little special treatment?' Many travellers felt the use of *Sonderbehandlung* was a Freudian slip.

specimen a sample of urine

Medical jargon, sometimes confusing to patients:

> He should show his *specimen* privately to his family doctor. (T. Harris, 1988, referring to urine and not to some physical attribute)

speed an illegal stimulant

Usually amphetamine. To *speed*, punning on driving a car above the legal limit, is to take such a substance illegally:

> They were speeding and tripping at the same time. (Deighton, 1972—to TRIP is to ingest a hallucinogen)

A *speedball* may be a cocktail of illegal narcotics.

spend to ejaculate (semen)

Usually in copulation, despite the hint of premature ejaculation in:

> Spending his manly marrow in her arms. (Shakespeare, *All's Well That Ends Well*)

or, in modern use:

> I could after the first orgasm go on indefinitely without spending again. (F. Harris, 1925)

Spent is the male's post-coital condition:

> Spent as he was, his penis still made a lump under the bedclothes. (L. Thomas, 1997)

spend a penny to urinate

Normally referring to urination by either sex, although only women were required, for the purpose of urination, to produce that particular coin needed to operate the lock of a British public lavatory turnstile or cubicle.

spend more time with your family to be dismissed from employment

Usually of a senior employee who has been peremptorily dismissed:

> ...he has not resigned... He will be preparing for the trial and 'would like to spend some time with [his] family'. (*Daily Telegraph*, 2 March 1995—as he was accused of false accounting there was some risk of his seeing his family only on permitted visiting days)

spend the night with to copulate with

Of either sex, usually in a transient relationship:

> She wanted me to go and spend the night with her. (L. Armstrong, 1955)

There is a legal presumption that adult males and females cannot spend a night in each other's company without copulating, if they are not married to each other.

spicy pornographic

Literally, highly flavoured, whence salacious:

> ...she would be talking about a sexual episode—the man in the Norman Mailer story sodomizing his girlfriend, for example—and she would call it 'spicy'. (Theroux, 1989)

spifflicated drunk

Originally, beaten up, although the *EDD* gives dialect meanings which include to confound or kill, which are the more normal imageries of intoxication. The slang shortened form is *spiffed*.

spike[1] to adulterate or introduce an intoxicant to (a drink)

Perhaps from *spiking*, or destroying, a gun by driving a metal object through the touch-hole, or merely from the practice of inserting a hot piece of metal into a fluid. It is used of the addition of alcohol surreptitiously to a non-alcoholic drink:

> When I complained that it was my first day and I was afraid to drink, Mary reluctantly bought me an orange juice and then spiked it with vodka when my back was turned. (Bolger, 1990)

or, these days, of the adulteration of a drink by the addition of narcotics:

> A couple of hours later Beano spiked their tequilas with angel dust, which was his idea of a good New Year's joke. (O'Connor, 1991)

spike² to reject for publication
Editorial jargon, from the metal *spike* on which rejects were once impaled:

> The chances are that no sub-editor is going to spike the story. (Deighton, 1982)

spike³ a hypodermic needle
A specific sharp-pointed piece of metal:

> It was for the spike he held out toward her in his open hand... Her eyes never left the needle, or the loving smile her face. (Crews, 1990)

spill to give information of a criminal or damaging nature
A shortened form of the common *spill the beans*, to reveal a secret:

> If Hench shot somebody, she would have some idea... She would spill if he had. (Chandler, 1943)

spill yourself to ejaculate (semen)
Voluntarily or involuntarily:

> Ulf who is nothing and has no career had spilled himself on their precious sheets. (Seymour, 1980—they had copulated on the bed of the girl's parents)

spin the editing, suppression, or correction of a public statement
First noted in *New York Times* in 1984. Whether the derivation is from the twisting or from the entrapment techniques of the spider will never be known:

> It's gonna be different, guys. Things are really changing. That's the spin from Marks and Spencer's Baker Street labyrinth. (*Daily Telegraph*, 5 December 1998)

The activity is carried out by aides known as *spin doctors* or *spinners*:

> The Government and its 'spin doctors' like to pretend that a majority of the hereditary peers are the proud owners of 'broad acres'. (letter in *Daily Telegraph*, 2 December 1998)
> They would want a react to whatever the

opposing spinners had laid down. (Anonymous, 1996)

spirits¹ a man's semen
In obsolete use, the essence of maleness, whence the symbol of courage:

> Much use of Venus doth dim the light... The cause of dimness is the expense of spirits. (Bacon, 1627)

The modern SPUNK has the same duality of meaning.

spirits² spirituous intoxicant
Literally, no more than any liquid in the form of a distillation or essence:

> He gave me a piece of an honey-comb, and a little bottle of spirits. (Bunyan, 1684)

Now generically of whisky, gin, rum, vodka, brandy, schnapps, etc.:

> 'Spirits don't seem to agree with you.'
> 'They differed from me sharply this time.' (Amis, 1978)

splash to crash into the sea
Of aircraft, and also used transitively, meaning to force down into the sea:

> So, if Bronco... does have to splash the inbound druggie, nobody'll know about it. (Clancy, 1989—Bronco was a fighter pilot)

splash your boots to urinate
Usually of a male, but not necessarily out of doors or even wetting your footwear:

> I was up splashing my boots. (Theroux, 1971)

splice the mainbrace to drink intoxicants
The *mainbrace* was the rope which held the mainsail in position, and a vessel was in peril if it broke. In rough weather *splicing* it, or mending it by joining up the severed parts, was a hazardous operation and the seamen received as a reward a large tot of rum. The custom continues under the same style in the modern navy, to celebrate some national event. For the rest of us, *splicing the mainbrace* is more likely to involve whisky or gin and tonic than rum:

> Having, I hope, splic'd their Main-Brace well. (Pynchon, 1997—sailors had been drinking ashore)

split (of a male) to copulate with
With obvious imagery:

> If you want to split the black oak... then you'll find it great down Macpherson Road or among the taxi dancers at the Great World. (N. Barber, 1981, writing about hiring a black prostitute)

In obsolete use *split a woman's shape* was to impregnate her. Whence too *split-mutton*, the penis, and other vulgarities.

To *split on* is merely to inform against, mainly in the speech of children:

> It's the meanest thing out—that splitting on a pal. (A. Trollope, 1885)

spoken for retained as an exclusive mistress

Literally, engaged to be married:

> You can spot these spoken for girls in the public trucks, sitting and smiling a lovely white smile. (Theroux, 1992—of the French colonial South Pacific where white soldiers provided their gummy mistresses with dentures, which they repossess to retain title when they go back to their wives and families on leave)

sponge a habitual drunkard

Punning perhaps on the soaking up of liquid and his willingness to accept free refills, *sponging on* others. The British *sponging-house* was not an inn but a temporary prison for debtors, where they might be relieved, or *sponged*, of their cash and valuables before passing into a long-stay debtors' prison.

sponsor an advertiser

Originally, a godparent, whence one who supports a candidate or public performance. Now standard use of paying for publicity by financing another activity, especially in American television programming:

> Sponsors didn't write the programmes any more, but they did impose a firm control on the contents. (Bryson, 1994)

And the sickening introduction to an advertising break—'A word from our sponsor'.

spoon to caress heterosexually

A boon to songwriters from having, for once, a whole series of unforced rhymes like *moon*, *June*, *swoon*, and so on. There was once a phrase to *lie spoons*, to nestle closely with the convex side of one against the concave side of the other. The Welsh too used to give their sweethearts suitably carved wooden spoons, as a token of their amorous interest. In the 19th century it referred also to homosexual relationships between males:

> 'Spooning' between master and boy was a subject for cruel jest. (Pearsall, 1969, writing of Victorian boarding schools for boys)

sport (the) copulation

Sometimes viewed as such by the male:

> He had some feeling for the sport; he knew the service. (Shakespeare, *Measure for Measure*—his vulgar puns did not refer to battledore and shuttlecock)

In literary use you will run across *amorous sport*, *sport for Jove*, and so on.

To *sport* has long meant to copulate:

> Now let us sport us while we may. (Marvell, c.1670)

although in modern use it usually refers to prostitution, as in *sport-trap*, a brothel area of a town:

> Storyville became and stayed the biggest tourist and sport-trap in the nation. (Longstreet, 1956—and so remained until 1917, when it was shut down to protect American servicemen from temptation and disease)

or in *sporting section*, which puns on the part of the newspaper given over to reporting ball games etc.:

> You came to the sporting section, the cathouses around 22nd street. (ibid.)

and a *sporting-house* is a brothel:

> She was like a lot of sporting-house landladies I've known through life. (L. Armstrong, 1955)

There you may find *sporting girls* or *women*, whose athleticism is concentrated in the boudoir rather than on the playing field.

However in a *sports bar* you may not find anything more titillating than a TOPLESS waitress:

> If nothing else it means the topless waitress in your local sports bar can now double as a salad-dressing dispenser. (Mark Stein in *Daily Telegraph*, 5 December 1998—reporting on soya-oil breast implants)

sports medicine illegal drugs

Although prevalent among professional athletes on an individual basis, the practice and language reflected state policy in Communist East Germany:

> . . . in order to win, everything possible must be done, and . . . sports medicine had its part to play. (*Sunday Telegraph*, 27 February 1994)

Cheating, or acting with exceptions (*mit Abstrichen*), also had its official part to play, and the use of drugs was called *laufende Versuche*, or continuing experiments.

sportsman a gambler

The modern equivalent of GAMESTER 2. Usually it refers to regular or spectacular punters on the results of horse- or dog-racing.

spot¹ a drink of spirituous intoxicant

I suppose a shortened form of a *spot of* whisky etc.:

> I think I could do with a spot. (E. Waugh, 1955)

spot² to kill

From the entry mark of the bullet, from noting the victim, or merely a shortened form of PUT ON THE SPOT:

> That's enough to spot a guy for. (Chandler, 1939)

spot³ a tubercular infection
Usually referring to pulmonary tuberculosis, when there is a hole in the lining of the lung which appears as a spot on the X-ray plate. In the days when the disease was prevalent and difficult to cure, a *spot on the lung* sounded better than a clinical description.

sprain your ankle *obsolete* to copulate with a man before marriage
Usually in the past tense, especially if the woman was pregnant. British women might also suffer similar injuries to their knees, elbows, and thighs, of which more at BREAK YOUR ELBOW.

spread for (of a female) to copulate with
Usually willingly, once, and outside marriage. Explicitly as *spread your legs*:
   They must both be paid, cash on the barrel-head, before she would spread her legs. (Monsarrat, 1978)
or more vulgarly as *spread your twat*:
   Spreading that twat of yours for a cheap, chiselling quack doctor ... (Styron, 1976)

spring to secure the release of (someone)
Either referring to a legal pardon, to an escape, or occasionally to bail before conviction, from the unexpected and positive action of a released coil:
   The proprietor knew how to 'spring' them, that is, get them out of jail. (L. Armstrong, 1955)

sprung slightly drunk
Like a ship which leaks but hasn't sunk:
   How's a chap to get sprung, much less drunk? (Westall, 1885)
Half-sprung is no more drunk or less sober.

spunk a man's semen
Originally, courage, and still so used in some innocent or naive circles:
   ... a term Lady Maud found almost as offensive as Colonel Chapman's comment that she was full of spunk. (Sharpe, 1975).
but for the less innocent:
   ... right off there, with my fresh spunk in her. (Keneally, 1979)
Occasionally also of the vaginal sexual discharge.
As with the modern SPIRITS 1, there was an obsolete use of whisky:
   Spunkie ance to make us mellow. (Burns, in an undated letter)

spur of the moment passion unpremeditated extramarital copulation
Not momentary anger or other forms of suffering:

... spur of the moment passion with a married woman ... (*Daily Telegraph*, April 1980)

spurious illegitimate
From the days when birth other than to married parents was viewed differently. Literally, it meant not real, although the resultant human beings certainly existed:
   He would not have spurious children to get any share of the family inheritance. (J. Boswell, 1791—Johnson was saying that adultery by a wife should be reported to her father-in-law)
Specifically as *spurious issue*:
   She only argues that she may indulge herself in gallantries with equal freedom as her husband does, provided she takes care not to introduce a spurious issue into his family. (ibid.)

spurt to ejaculate semen
Usually of premature ejaculation:
   That had been excitement until the stupid bugger had spurted before he even got into her. (Seymour, 1997—*bugger* is here a term of abuse rather than a technical description)

squash to kill
Of humans, treating them as we do insects:
   'At best? Two busted kneecaps.' 'And at worst?' 'They'll squash me.' (Sanders, 1980)

squashed drunk.
But not from drinking fruit squash.

squat¹ to defecate
The posture adopted and perhaps referring to the dialect meaning, to SQUIRT:
   The authorities were trying to teach the people not to squat behind their huts. (M. McCarthy, 1967)
For females, a *squat* may mean urination only. Some figurative use, as:
   ... the 52 has told me squat about the enemy now facing me. (Coyle, 1987—the 52 is an American staff officer responsible for obtaining and disseminating information about the enemy)
A *squatter* is a lavatory without a pedestal seat:
   I vowed never again to travel on a heap of coal slag, never again to stay in a hotel that smelt like a morgue, never again to use a squatter which belched up its contents over the user. (Dalrymple, 1989)

squat² to occupy (a building or land) by trespass
Squatters' rights is an English legal concept dating from the social and economic need in the Middle Ages to see land and buildings, vacated and ownerless through plague,

brought back into productive use. The verb is used both transitively:

> Hobo punks hop trains, squat abandoned buildings, collect welfare, and dumpster food. (*Esquire*, January 1994)

and intransitively:

> She was working...to identify and locate people who are homeless or squatting in abandoned buildings. (*Philadelphia Enquirer*, 17 December 1989)

A *squat* is such a trespass, or the property in which it happens:

> ...they eventually discovered his body in some squat. (B. Forbes, 1989)

A *squatter* is someone who so trespasses:

> Squatters of empty, unused houses may be evicted after a summary hearing at which they cannot defend themselves and may be imprisoned if they refuse to move within 24 hours. (*Kindred Spirit*, Autumn 1994)

except in New Zealand, where it meant a sheep farmer (Sinclair, 1991).

squeal (of a criminal) to give information to the police

There is an implication of duress, with the *squeal* indicating pain. It is used of informing on others or confessing your own guilt:

> ...loath to 'squeal' or harm him. (Lavine, 1930)

squeeze¹ to extort money etc. from illegally

From the pressure applied:

> The Red Eleven would stick by him and fight anyone who tried to squeeze him. (Theroux, 1973)

The squeeze is such extortion, and especially the developed and endemic version in the Far East:

> Perhaps the Englishman, like the French, wanted his squeeze. (R. Moss, 1987)

It may, however, refer to no more than a tip:

> Brooke nodded to the little chauffeur, then handed him some money as he had seen Jeremy do. *Squeeze*, they called it. (Reeman, 1994)

squeeze² a female sexual friend

You cuddle her:

> 'I'm just Oliver's new squeeze.' 'I'm in love with her,' Oliver explained. (le Carré, 1999)

squib off to murder

Usually by shooting, presumably from the noise made by the firework:

> The night Joe got squibbed off. (Chandler, 1939)

squiffy drunk

Literally, uneven or lopsided:

> 'The man was squiffy,' said Aunt Agnes. 'It was written all over him.' (E. Waugh, 1933)

squirrel *American* the patient of a psychiatrist

The animal has a penchant for a NUT 1. A *squirrel tank* is an institution for the insane:

> ...the perpetrator went nuts after the accident and is now in the squirrel tank. (Wambaugh, 1975)

squirt to defecate

Normally of diarrhoea:

> Wharton...once grabbed Percy and scared him so bad that Percy squirted in his pants. (King, 1996)

The squirts is diarrhoea, and also used as a mild insult, more in the singular than the plural:

> ...a very coarse name, which we can change euphemistically into...squirts. (Vachell, 1934)

Diarrhoea is also *skeet*, *squit*, *skitters*:

> 'Skitters,' I said. 'That'll wait for no man. Run for it. I'll wait.' I dashed for the toilet. (Steinbeck, 1961)

or the very common *squitters*, which can also be used as a verb:

> ...the senile Labrador that drools and squitters all over the stairs. (Theroux, 1982)

stab (of a male) to copulate with

The common imagery of violence and pushing:

> He'd stabb'd me in mine own house...he will foin like any devil. (Shakespeare, *2 Henry IV*—foin means thrust)

Being *stabbed with a Bridport dagger* was not copulating with a native of the Dorset town but suffering death by hanging, Bridport being famous for rope-making because of a climate in which flax flourished.

stabilization price control by government

Another political attempt to replace the law of supply and demand by statute:

> It cost then $888 a month, rent-stabilized. If it hadn't been for the rent-stabilization law, it would probably have cost $1,500. (Wolfe, 1987)

stable horse *obsolete American* a stallion

Another example of prudery about male animals kept for breeding: see BIG ANIMAL. A *stable-boss* does not keep stallions but is a pimp running more than one prostitute.

stacked having large breasts

Like the heavy loading of shelves etc. A male usage by those who see this as a desirable feature in a female:

> Anne was a London blonde, improbably imposing and statuesque—stacked, if you must know—who would have turned heads in Oxford Street. (Whicker, 1982—

she happened to be working in a bank in Paraguay)

staff a penis
A rarer version of ROD 2:
> ...the registrar of births had to increase his staff owing to the way he had exercised his. (Pearsall, 1969, quoting 19th-century pornography)

stag pornographic
It is incorrectly assumed that all-male parties favour such titillation:
> But you can go to late-night stag movies piped into our place. (C. Forbes, 1983)
For *stag month* see STEG MONTH.

stain *obsolete* (of a male) to copulate with outside marriage
He pollutes the female morally rather than seminally:
> Give up your body to such sweet uncleanness,
> As she that he hath stain'd. (Shakespeare, *Measure for Measure*)

staining bleeding
Medical jargon, from the seepage of blood through a bandage.

stake (the) killing by burning
The victim was tied to a pole. The significance of this form of death for heretics was that nothing remained to reappear and cause trouble at the Resurrection.

stake-out a police trap where a crime is anticipated
There has been a previous survey of the location:
> ...he was running a stake-out...over in the meat-packing department. (van Lustbaden, 1983)

stale[1] *obsolete* a prostitute
Her freshness having been already destroyed by others:
> ...poor I am but his stale. (Shakespeare, *The Comedy of Errors*)
Stale meat was a more experienced prostitute:
> ...since to the accustomed rake the most prized flesh is the newest, some now counted her stale meat. (Fowles, 1985)

stale[2] *obsolete* urine
From its retention in former times for laundry and other use:
> The dung and stale of cattle. (Marshall, 1817)

stalk to harass obsessively
Hunting game, but not on a single occasion with a view of photographing it or killing it. Men usually stalk women but:

Is that how you saw it—she was 'stalking' him? (R. N. Patterson, 1996)

stand[1] the erect penis
Of obvious derivation, and as a verb:
> When it stands well with him, it stands well with her. (Shakespeare, *The Comedy of Errors*)
The penis may also be said to *stand to attention*, from the upright posture in military drill:
> She finished...posing as a nude Britannia with helmet and union jack. I wondered how many of the audience would be standing to attention. (Monkhouse, 1993)
or *be brought to attention*:
> Man you should have seen that redhead bitch in the green thong. On a scale of one to ten, she's a twelve. Bring you all the way to attention. (Koontz, 1997)

stand[2] to be available for breeding
Standard English of a male quadruped, although MOUNT is more appropriate:
> ...the stallion has stood for three seasons and therefore covered a hundred and twenty mares. (D. Francis, 1982)

stand before your Maker to die
It would be presumptuous to sit. In various forms:
> ...none should accept Gratitude until it is his time to stand before the Father of us all. (le Carré, 1986)

stand down to be dismissed or prematurely retired from employment
Literally, to end a tour of duty or to revert to a lower state of preparedness after an alert. The term is used to protect the self-esteem of a departing, and usually senior, employee.

stand up[1] without notice or apology to fail to keep a date with (someone)
Usually in the past tense:
> Cannot believe it. Am stood up. Entire waste of whole day's effort. (Helen Fielding, 1996)
To *stand up and be counted* is to express in cliché form your support in public for an unpopular or minority cause.

stand-up[2] *American* a person paid to make an instant comment on television
What others may call a TALKING HEAD. Perhaps from the *stand-up comedian*, who stands alone before an audience to perform his act.

standard small or poor quality
No longer the level of size, quality, etc. against which judgement of other similar products can be made. You will find that a *standard pack* is small and a *standard* model of anything is

the cheapest version without any refinements.

standstill an attempt by government to restrict pay increases

Another, but equally ineffective, version of FREEZE 1 and PAUSE 2 in the days when British politicians still revered King Canute:

Thus, in the House of Commons on 6 November, 1972, when Heath announced a standstill on wages and prices, thereby introducing the kind of incomes policy which he had always sworn to eschew ... (Cosgrave, 1989)

star in the east (a) an undone fly-button

An oblique warning from one male to another which seems not to have survived the zip age.

stark naked

Stark in this sense means completely, and this is probably merely a shortened form of the idiom *stark naked*:

Stark as the day you were born. (Buchan, 1898)

The obsolete meaning, dead, came from a dialect meaning, stiff, often found in the tautological *stiff and stark*.

start bleeding to menstruate for the first time

The female concerned will certainly have bled from her nose or a wound on previous occasions:

Yes, I matured early ... I started bleeding at eleven. (Sanders, 1970)

starter home a small house

Not *you remember, you remember, the house where you were born* (with apologies to Thomas Hood) but the first you may be induced to buy. Less often as *starter house* or *starter*:

They were often what realtors liked to term 'starter houses', which means that they could be afforded by couples just starting out and not being bankrolled by a parent. (Katzenbach, 1995)

Biff had a real estate business and sold darling little starters to newly-weds. (Grisham, 1999)

stash a supply of illegal narcotics

Or the place where the hoard is hidden, as in *stash-pad*, a room or apartment used for that purpose:

This was one of Core's stash pads. (Turow, 1996)

To *stash* is to put such drugs in a hidden place, whence the addict adage *Never carry when you can stash*.

state farm *American* an institution where people are detained involuntarily

Where you consign forlorn children and geriatrics as well as criminals and lunatics. Also as *state home, hospital, training school*, etc.

state of excitement having an erection of the penis

Not merely awaiting the benevolence of Father Christmas:

Someone like me who delivers telegrams and winds up in a state of excitement on a green sofa with a girl dying of the galloping consumption. (McCourt, 1997)

state of nature (a) nudity

Not that being clothed is unnatural, but using the imagery of NATURE'S GARB:

Charles Boon, who scorned pyjamas and was often to be encountered walking about the apartment ... in a state of nature ... (Lodge, 1975)

state protection the preservation of tyranny

As in the *Department of State Protection*, which controlled political prisons and all forms of publication as well as routinely spying on citizens in Communist Russia. In Amin's Uganda the body charged with similar functions was called the *State Research Bureau*.

statement *British* to assess for corrective treatment

A bureaucratic shortening of *prepare a statement for consideration*:

... the mother of a child who was dyslexic and slightly deaf, describing how her daughter had been 'statemented' by the local authority. (P. D. James, 2001)

status deprivation being thought badly of

Educational jargon for a child who is objectionable or does badly at school and is not therefore respected or liked by teachers and fellow pupils.

statutory appointed other than on merit

It is used of membership of committees, boards, etc. where those perceived as being oppressed or the subject of prejudice secure appointment regardless of merit:

I realised that the government would wish to include certain 'statutory members' such as representatives of the trade unions and the Co-operative movements—though not, to my regret, a Statutory Lady. (Cork, 1988)

See also OBLIGATORY and TOKEN.

statutory offense *American* the rape of a female

Legal jargon. A *statutory rape* is copulation with a female below an age chosen by law rather than by her physical development—see JAIL BAIT. Although over the centuries females, better fed and less worked, have tended to achieve sexual maturity at ever younger ages, the statutory age of consent has risen from 10 years in medieval times to 15 or 16 in most western countries today.

steady company a person with whom you have regular extramarital sexual relationship
Usually in the phrase *keep steady company (with)*:
> We've been keeping steady company for the past five years now. (McBain, 1981, writing about a man and his mistress)
See also COMPANY 1 and KEEP COMPANY WITH.

steal privately to *obsolete* to copulate with extramaritally
From the surreptitious approach within a household:
> If, for instance, from mere wantonness of appetite, [a husband] steals privately to her chambermaid, Sir, a wife ought not greatly to resent this. (J. Boswell, 1791—
> Dr Johnson's views would find less favour today, but then there are fewer chambermaids about)

steer dishonestly to influence the placing of business
By pretending to give disinterested counsel in the selection of an adviser, vendor, or service when you are receiving a bribe, commission, or reciprocal benefit:
> ... bribery of hospital personnel to 'steer' cases. (J. Mitford, 1963, describing how funeral firms secured business)

steg month *obsolete* the period around childbirth when a husband might copulate extramaritally with relative impunity
From being a gander in northern English dialect, wandering about while the goose was hatching the goslings, a *steg* became an aimless male. The wife who was unavailable for copulation was known as a *steg-widow*. See also GANDER-MOONER. *Stag month* and *stag widow*, which you may find in other works of reference, are mistaken corruptions.
In modern, probably ephemeral, slang, a *steg*, a shortened form of *stegosaurus*, is a sexually unattractive woman.

stem a penis
Not in this case the opposite of stern, but of the same tendency as ROOT 1:
> Gently she tugged, guiding my stem between her sleepy breasts. (L. Thomas, 1989)

step away *obsolete* *Scottish* to die
Also as *step off*:
> Garskadden's been wi' his Maker these two hours; I saw him step awa. (E. B. Ramsay, 1861)

step down to be dismissed from employment
Used of retiring of your own volition, but also of when you are pushed:
> Sanders must step down. (*London Standard* headline, January 1987—the story was about a company chairman who was later dismissed, prosecuted, convicted, incarcerated, and then released from prison on account of an incurable disease from which he was to make a miraculous recovery)

step-ins *American* women's underpants
Not a bath tub or a pair of slippers. This usage has survived most of the evasions used for nether garments—see UNMENTIONABLES 1.

step on[1] to grow old
A shortened form of *step on in years*:
> I'm stepping on in years, and not so easy in the joints as once on a day. (Keith, 1897)

step on[2] to kill
Presumably from the way we kill insects:
> Jack and Hyme talk so casually about killing and death. 'Should I step on him?' 'We should have killed the cock-sucker.' Like that. (Sanders, 1980)

step out on to deceive (a regular sexual partner) by having a sexual relationship with another
Of either sex:
> Do you think Haveabud and your mother had a sexual relationship? Do you think I ever stepped out on her? (A. Beattie, 1989)
To *step out with* someone, or to *step out together* is to be courting:
> Before long they were stepping out together and although Thea was strictly chaperoned, they had soon become very close. (M. Clark, 1991)

stepney *obsolete* a pimp's favourite prostitute
I include this for the pleasure of explaining the derivation. A *stepney* was the spare wheel, carried on the step, or running-board, of a car, and only brought into use when one of the other four wheels was unserviceable.

sterilize to destroy
Literally, to render barren, whence to purify or make clean. It may refer to obliterating tapes or removing documents from files if they might prove embarrassing. In Vietnam

military jargon, it meant dropping bombs and trying to kill or drive out the Vietcong:

> We sterilize the area prior to the introduction of the R.D. teams. (M. McCarthy, 1967—R.D. stood for *rural development*, or trying to persuade villagers to reject the Viet-cong)

stern the buttocks

Naval imagery in general use. The punning *stern-chaser* may have heterosexual or homosexual preferences.

stewed drunk

The common culinary imagery:

> ...most of the time in camp...poor old Abel was stewed. (Keneally, 1979—Abel was not in the hands of cannibals)

You are no less drunk if *half-stewed*.
Sometimes also of being under the influence of narcotics:

> They kept piling the old hashish into the shisheh...He's totally stewed. (Deighton, 1991—a *shisheh* is a bowl made of shisham wood, or *Dalbergia sissoo*)

stews (the) *obsolete* a brothel

Originally a bath-house, and we know what the other use of those places usually was:

> An I could get me but a wife in the stews. (Shakespeare, *2 Henry IV*)

stick[1] to kill

Supposedly with a pointed weapon, of cattle in an abattoir and of wild pigs in hunting. It used also to mean to wound:

> The black thief has sticket the woman. (Carrick, 1835)

stick[2] a spirit added to another drink

Perhaps you have simply placed, or *stuck*, one liquid inside another:

> Coffee, if you like, with a 'stick' in it. (Praed, 1890)

stick[3] (of a male) to copulate with

A pun on *stick*, a slang name for a penis:

> Said he with a snicker,
> As he watched the guy stick
> her... (*Playboy's Book of Limericks*)

Also as to *give stick*, punning on the meaning, to offer violence, *stick it into*, or *stick it on*:

> Brother was sticking it into sister every night. (Mailer, 1965—they were committing incest)
> Men liked to think they were sticking it on some kind of technical virgin. (McBain, 1981)

stick[4] a marijuana cigarette

Usually already rolled, and probably a shortened form of *stick of tea*, a thin form of self-

rolled cigarette. Also in compounds like dream-stick and the punning *joy-stick*.

stick[5] a handgun

The ROD 1 imagery:

> He hit some East Side apartment for a bundle. Ice, mostly. Never carried a stick. (Sanders, 1970, and not about someone with a limp on a slippery surface sliding into a building)

A *stick of bombs* dropped from an aircraft may merely refer to their hitting the ground and exploding in a straight line.

stick it into[1] see STICK 3

stick it into[2] to extort money etc. from with threats

Figuratively wounding with a weapon:

> They had pictures, who the hell knows what else? But they stuck it into him. (Diehl, 1978—he was being blackmailed. The *pictures* were incriminating photographs)

stick up to rob with a threat of, or actual, violence

From the command to *stick up your hands* rather than the use of a STICK 5. A *stick-up* is such a robbery:

> 'You'll hold me up, I suppose?'...'I'm a stick-up artist now, am I?' (Chandler, 1939)

sticky a spirituous intoxicant

Usually a liqueur, from its tacky properties:

> I spend the next two hours...with a litre bottle of some colourless but potent sticky at my elbow. (*Private Eye*, August 1983)

sticky-fingered thieving

Other people's property adheres to the fingers. Usually of embezzlement or chance pilfering.

sticky stranger a clandestine electronic listening device

Espionage jargon—the device incorporates some form of glue or magnet for rapid deployment:

> You'll want to look around for a sticky stranger. If they think you've got something to hide, they'll plant another ear. (D. Francis, 1978)

stiff[1] a corpse

Referring to the rigor mortis:

> When anyone was killed they piled the stiffs outside the door. (*Scribner's Monthly*, July 1880)

In the 19th century also as a *stiff one*:

> Would she stick it till she was a stiff 'un. (Mayhew, 1862)

stiff² drunk

It tends to make you feel and look like a corpse:

> I was quite stiff by the time we got to the burial ground. (Styron, 1976—he was drunk)

stiff³ having an erection of the penis

Of obvious derivation:

> ... she approached me where I lay, stiff as a dagger. (Styron, 1976—but not drunk on this occasion)

In slang use, an erection of the penis is a *stiffy*.

stiff⁴ (out) to fail to meet your financial obligations (to someone)

It is a form of death:

> 'Suppose,' she asked, 'he was in trouble over drugs. Stiffed his supplier, somehow.' (R. N. Patterson, 1996)

stiff-arm to compel through threats or violence

From a disabling hold in wrestling:

> One more attempt to stiff-arm him occurred at 8.30 p.m. (Colodny and Gettlin, 1991—the White House was seeking to make the Attorney-General suppress the Nixon tapes)

stiff one¹ see STIFF 1

stiff one² a drink of spirits

Not soup or strong coffee, although the alcohol so described may be diluted by water, soda-water, or tonic:

> Mallards was filling quickly with weary young professionals who needed a couple of stiff ones for the drive to the suburbs. (Grisham, 1994)

stiffener a drink of spirits

A variant of the common BRACER, owing perhaps something to being a STIFF ONE 2:

> ... careless riders would fall away, in search of a few stiffeners. (Flanagan, 1988—and then fall off, you might suppose)

stimulant (a) spirits or an illegal narcotic

Not a bribe, a kiss, a gift, an encouraging word, or any of the other things you might find stimulating:

> ... if ever there was a man who needed a snappy stimulant, it was he. (Wodehouse, 1934)
>
> Their main source of revenue is from trafficking in stimulants, especially crystal methamphetamine (known as ice). (*Economist*, 29 February 1992)

sting to deprive by trickery

It refers to robbery, overcharging, cheating, or any other form of knavery:

> He has completely dead eyes, and looks at you with the warmth of one deciding how much he can sting you for your bridgework. (L. Barber, 1991)

The sting is the ultimate coup in an elaborate confidence trick or a complex police operation set up to catch criminals:

> The sting resulted in the serving of 198 arrest warrants for fewer than 100 individuals. (*Law and Order*, May 1990)

stink on *American* to betray or deceive

Usually of sexual conduct, with imagery perhaps from defecation:

> I stopped stinking on Rainey when she got sick. (Turow, 1999)

stinking very drunk

Probably not from your *stinking* of drink but from the meaning exceedingly, as in *stinking rich*. At one time corrupted to *stinko*:

> Are you stinko? (Chandler, 1953)

stir a prison

Probably from the Romany and not what you do to your breakfast PORRIDGE:

> A friend of mine who's in stir. (Chandler, 1939)

To be *stir-wise* is to be experienced in prison life:

> He's too stir-wise for me. (ibid.)

To *stir the porridge* is not to be incarcerated but to copulate with a woman shortly after she has copulated with another.

stitch up to fabricate evidence against

The imagery is from the securing of a canvas bag:

> 'Someone else did it, I tell you.' 'Who? Why?' 'To stitch me up.' (C. Thomas, 1993)

stitched drunk

Probably derived from the slang *stitched up*, embarrassed or compromised, rather than being sent home in a body bag. A *stitch in your wig* meant being mildly drunk in the days when a wig might be worn askew by those not totally sober, and to *stitch* meant to rumple.

stoat a libertine

It is unclear why the European ermine should have acquired such a reputation:

> He fancied everyone really. By way of being a stoat. (le Carré, 1989)

Forster in 1971 used the same animal to represent homosexual lust.

stock beast *obsolete American* a bull

More 19th-century prudery. Also as *stock animal*, *brute*, or *cow*. See also BIG ANIMAL.

stockade *American* a military prison

Literally, a strong fence forming an enclosure:
> ... you fly or you go to the stockade.
> (Deighton, 1982—they were Second World War fliers)

See also CHOKEY, which uses the same imagery, (Conversely, the imagery is also used in the word *paradise*, which comes from ancient Persian meaning a wall around, via Greek and Latin, being originally the description of the magnificent gardens built by (or for) the Emperor Cyrus at Sardis.)

stoke Lucifer's fires to be dead
Usually of one who has led a sinful life for which he is presumed to be doing penance into eternity at the devil's behest:
> There was a rumour of his death, or he's probably been stoking Lucifer's fires these thirty years. (Fraser, 1970, writing in 19th-century style)

Stoke-on-Trent *British* homosexual
Not from the inhabitants of that worthy town but cockney rhyming slang for BENT 2.

stomach (a) obesity around the waist
Usually of a male and incorrectly specifying the internal chamber through which food passes in the process of digestion. A *bit of a stomach* also implies obesity rather than post-surgical deprivation.

stomach cramps menstruation
One of the symptoms is used to avoid reference to the condition:
> ... the stomach cramps ... happen quite regularly in the first week of every month when a certain software salesman is in town. (J. Trollope, 1992—she was a malingerer)

stoned drunk or under the influence of illegal narcotics
It is hard to see what the discomfort of St Stephen and others had to do with this common use.
> The day Butler's Military Cross was gazetted they both got stoned out of their minds. (Price, 1979—they were very drunk)
> He did his best work half-stoned. When you stare at motels for a living, you need to be stoned. (Grisham, 1992, referring to an investigator who habitually smoked cannabis. Here, as usual in this context, the half equals the whole)

stones the testicles
On man and other mammals:
> A philosopher, with two stones more than his artificial one. (Shakespeare, *Timon of Athens*)

The obsolete *stoned horse man* was not a heroin addict but the groom who took a stallion—*stony*—around farms to impregnate mares.

stool pigeon a police informer
Pigeons were tied to stools to lure other pigeons for capture:
> Perhaps the incident would have passed without further consequences, for the stool pigeon was no more popular among the guards, most of whom thought he had it coming. (Dodds, 1991)

To *stool* is to inform against:
> ... stooled on a bank job in Michigan and git me four years. (Chandler, 1939)

stoop your body to pollution *obsolete* (of a female) to copulate extramaritally
She is more likely to be recumbent than bending down:
> Before her sister should her body stoop
> To such abhorred pollution
> Then, Isabel, live chaste. (Shakespeare, *Measure for Measure*)

stop a mouth to kill
Not necessarily by suffocation:
> 'That's all right,'I said, 'but their mouths must be stopped ... They mustn't be allowed to talk.' (A. Massie, 1986)

stop one to be killed or wounded
A common First World War usage:
> We old ones aren't lucky enough to stop one that way. (F. Richards, 1933—he was referring to a BLIGHTY)

To *stop a slug* is more specific:
> I wasn't hired to kill people. Until Frisky stopped that slug I didn't have no such ideas. (Chandler, 1939—Frisky was a gunman, not a gardener)

To *stop the big one* is to be killed:
> The guy stopped the big one. Cold. (ibid.)

stoppage¹ an inability to defecate
Medical jargon and also used of nasal and other physical blockages.

stoppage² a strike by employees
Trade union jargon which is still used despite the fact that the organization affected continues to function. If the employer stops people working it is called a LOCK OUT.

story a lie
Nursery usage, although the punning *story-teller* may also be used of an adult. A *tall story* implies exaggeration, and a *cock-and-bull story* (ROOSTER and BIG ANIMAL story in 19th-century America?) is an improbable fabrication.

straddle (of a male) to copulate with
Using the common riding imagery:

I had a moment's pang at the thought
that I'd straddled her for the last time.
(Fraser, 1985)

straighten out to bribe
You induce another to follow the line which
you indicate. We also use the phrase of our
forceful, but usually unavailing, correction of
someone with a different opinion to our own.

straighten the line to retreat under pressure
A military evasion:
Forrest in the *News Chronicle* called the
Catalonian retreat 'a straightening of the
Government line'. (Kee, 1984—it was the
start of the final collapse)

strain your greens (of a female) to urinate
Referring to the colour of the urine and
perhaps its mode of egress.

stranger to the truth a habitual liar
Not more than circumlocution perhaps, but
people still don't like being called liars outright:
He was an absolute stranger to the truth.
But a storyteller such as might have
beguiled Odysseus. (Turow, 1993)

strangle to cause (a horse) to run badly in
a race
You figuratively throttle it by tugging on the
bridle:
Sandie had 'strangled' a couple at one
stage. (D. Francis, 1962—Sandie was a
crooked jockey)

strap a handgun
The etymology is obscure, except that *strapped*
means carrying a gun in a harness:
'I can't bring no strap with me to school.' A
gun, she meant. (Turow, 1996)
She ain't strapped—armed—she know
better than that. (ibid.)
To be *strapped for cash* is not to act as a
mercenary but to be short of money.

strategic induced under pressure
The soldiers and propagandists pretend they
meant it. Thus a *strategic withdrawal* is a flight:
We've admitted a strategic
withdrawal...the Jerries are coming hell
for leather down the coast road. (Manning,
1965)
A *strategic movement to the rear* means the flight
is headlong and a *strategic retreat* is a rout:
The Germans announced an Allied
retreat. Merely a strategic retreat,
said the British News Service.
(Manning, 1960)
In commerce, a *strategic premium* is an over-
payment:

Tim Clarke, chief executive, admits the
group paid a 'strategic premium' (too
much) for Inter-Continental. (*Daily
Telegraph*, 5 April 2001)
A *strategic capability* is the possession of
nuclear weapons, and *strategic targets* in the
Second World War were, for the Anglo/
Americans, any part of Germany.

stray to copulate extramaritally
The *lust* in wanderlust. On its own:
She's lonely—as well she might be,
married to the sodden and straying major.
(Atwood, 1996)
And in phrases like *stray your affection* or *stray
from the hearth*:
Stray'd his affection in unlawful love.
(Shakespeare, *The Comedy of Errors*)
I know Harry William strays from
the hearth. (Sanders, 1992—a
servant was revealing his master's
adultery)

stray off the reservation to diverge from
an agreed line
This is another contribution to the language
from the Watergate conspirators:
... if Jeb 'strayed off the reservation'—the
phrase had come to be used in the Nixon
inner elite to mean refusing to adhere to
the approved story of the burglary and
the cover-up—Dean would not have
remained at liberty himself. (Colodny
and Gettlin, 1991)

streak to run naked in a public place
In this practice, which started in the mid-
1970s, the speed was meant to restrict the
visibility as well as to postpone capture. A
streaker so behaves:
Clarke was a JP for almost 20 years; he tried
the first case recorded in Norfolk involving
a streaker. (*Daily Telegraph*, 21 December
1998)

streamlining the simultaneous dismissal
of a number of employees
In the expectation, perhaps, that those remaining will go faster.

street (the) prostitution
The place where customers are picked up:
'You're the only person who can save us.'
'How?' 'Why, the street, of course.'
(Londres, 1928, in translation)
A *street-walker*, *street-corner girl*, or *street girl* is a
prostitute:
The modern equivalents of the old-time
disorderly house and of the street walker.
(Lavine, 1930)
I guess you must have taken up with the
wrong street-corner girl the last time you
were in Baton Rouge. (King, 1996)

...her wretched career from housewife to street girl. (S. Green, 1979)

On the street(s) is to be engaged in prostitution:
She fell in love with Mary Jack's pimp, who put her on the street. (L. Armstrong, 1955)

The American *street tricking* is finding customers as a prostitute on the street:
This old campaigner we call Mabel the Monster, been street trickin' must be ten years now. (Diehl, 1978)

street bets bets placed illegally through bookmakers' runners
In the days before off-course gambling was legalized.

street drugs narcotics, hallucinogens, etc. sold illegally
As distinct from those supplied on prescription from a pharmacy.

street money *American* electoral bribes
From the wide dissemination:
He claimed Mrs Whitman's campaign paid what is known as 'street money' to black clergy and elected officials to dissuade them from getting out the black vote. (*Daily Telegraph*, 23 November 1993)

street tax *American* regular payment to an extortionist
You have to differentiate this, if you can, from what municipal, state, and federal authorities take from you:
You keep a book, fine and dandy, but you give them a share—they call it paying the street tax. (Turow, 1993)

stretch¹ a period of imprisonment
A shortened form of *stretch of years*:
The bosses get the longest stretch in the penitentiary. (L. Thomas, 1979)

stretch² (the) a shortage of liquidity or assets
The jargon of businessmen who are short of cash, are unwilling to admit it outright, and would like published figures to enjoy the property of elasticity:
A deal with Keebler, whether it is sold or we find a joint venture partner, will substantially resolve the stretch in our balance sheet and leave us in a much more favourable cash position. (*Daily Telegraph*, 18 July 1998)

stretch the hemp to kill by hanging
From the material of the noose. The victim may be said to have effected the expansion:
Molly Maguire stretching the hemp in the last act. (*Pearson's Magazine*, October 1900)
More practically as *stretch the neck*:

At home it ran full tilt into the autocracy; into...provincial governors with powers to stretch a neck at whim. (Moynahan, 1994, writing of Russia under the Czars)

stretch your legs to urinate
Why we say we have breaks in meetings or stops on long journeys:
Another five or ten minutes, and you'll be able to stretch your legs. And then after that I fancy you'll be able to travel more comfortably. (Price, 1978)

stretcher a lie or exaggeration
From *stretching* your credulity and the truth:
Is old Wheat still telling Gus back there them stretchers regarding his gran'daddy? (Keneally, 1979)
Whence the punning *stretcher case*, a habitual liar; to *stretch* is to lie or boast:
There was things which he stretched, but mainly he told the truth. (Twain, 1884)

strike out *American* to die
As in baseball.

string up to kill by hanging
Usually of lynching, on a conveniently placed branch which always seems to be to hand in cowboy films.

stripper *American* a thief
Especially of radios etc. from cars:
...our motherfucking car stripper is halfway to Watts. (Wambaugh, 1975)
In standard English, a stripper removes clothes for sexual titillation.

stroke to attempt to persuade by flattery
As you might comfort a pet:
He asked himself over a glass of vodka whether Pokryshkin had handled—he didn't know the Western expression 'stroked'—him enough to create a false impression. (Clancy, 1988)
and the Watergate team reported:
We are giving him a lot of stroking. (Colodny and Gettlin, 1991—they were trying to persuade a witness to keep quiet)
A *stroke job* is such flattery:
'I want to be as candid as I can...' The stroke job's starting, Barcella thought. (Maas, 1986)
(*Stroke* is a word which occupies several pages in the *OED*. Inevitably it has had a number of euphemistic uses, including copulation (Grose) and death, as well as being the standard English for a cerebral haemorrhage.)

stroke off to masturbate
Usually of the male. Sundry vulgar compounds also as *stroke the bishop, dummy, lizard,*

etc. A *stroke-mag* is a pornographic publication for males.

stroller *Irish* a habitual itinerant
But not ON THE STROLL:
> You'll not trick me, stroller. I saw you pull up and there's no-one with you. (O'Donoghue, 1988—addressing a lone gypsy)

strong-arm to steal
With the use or a threat of force:
> If he had not strong-armed that money out of me I would have given him lots more. (L. Armstrong, 1955—his own surname originated from the English/Scottish borders where for centuries such activities were endemic)

strong waters spirituous intoxicants
Not a fast-flowing stream:
> ...[opium] does not one-tenth of the harm that strong waters cause among the poorer class. (Fraser, 1985)

In Ireland the delightful *strong weakness* was dipsomania:
> Bob would be marked as a man with what our countryside calls 'a strong weakness'. (Flanagan, 1988)

strop your beak (of a male) to copulate or masturbate
The allusion is to the movements in sharpening an open razor and punning on the slang *beak*, the penis.

structured arranged as a cartel
The imagery is the same as in ORDERLY MARKET. The American *structured competition* describes attempts to disguise illegal agreements on price, market share, and so on.

struggle for national existence the extermination of Jews, gypsies, and Slavs
For some Nazis the fight against the Anglo-Americans and the Russians had a lower linguistic priority:
> ...a struggle for national existence meant racial warfare. (Keneally, 1982—for the SS)

In a political campaign, *struggle* is used to make look important what most of us would consider trivial. See also ARMED STRUGGLE.

strung out addicted to illegal narcotics
From the haggard appearance? Also of anyone under their influence:
> Now half these young men, more than half, they in here for narcotics and quite a number come in strung out. (Turow, 1996)

stubble see TAKE A TURN IN THE STUBBLE

stuck cheated

Probably a shortened form of *stuck with a poor bargain*:
> I experienced that peculiar sinking that accompanies the birth of the conviction that one has been stuck. (Somerville and Ross, 1897, telling of a horse deal)

stuck on infatuated with
No doubt from the desire to enjoy propinquity:
> Archer, are you stuck on the girl or something? (Macdonald, 1976)

stud a male viewed sexually
The imagery is from the place where stallions are kept for breeding, rather than a projecting lug. Of heterosexuals or homosexuals:
> Sex?... No stud in the world is worth two million dollars. (M. West, 1979)
> I don't go to no leather joints lookin' for some stud to fistfuck. (M. Thomas, 1980)

The punning *stud farm* is a place where homosexuals congregate:
> It was hard, my dear, not to feel like some old queen mincing around at a stud farm. (Pérez-Réverté, 1994, in translation)

stuff¹ any taboo or forbidden substance
Literally, any substance or material. Among other things, it may refer to semen, to contraband spirits, or to illegal drugs:
> ...put stuff
> To some she-beggar. (Shakespeare, *Timon of Athens*)
> A considerable amount of 'stuff' finds its way to the consumers without the formality of the Custom House. (Stoker, 1895)
> ...he smokes too much, and 'stuff'. (Bogarde, 1981)

stuff² to copulate with
From the physical entry rather than impregnation, despite:
> A maid, and stuff'd! there's goodly catching of cold. (Shakespeare, *Much Ado About Nothing*)

Now also of sodomy. There is much figurative use:
> As for the flute, he knew where he could stuff that. (Davidson, 1978)

and in abusive phrases like *get stuffed* and *stuff that*.

stump liquor *American* illegal spirits
Probably made by a *stump-jumper*, or hillbilly:
> People in these hills still made moonshine, or stump liquor as they call it. (Bryson, 1989, writing about Tennessee)

stung by a serpent pregnant
The common imagery of the penis as a snake, in this instance leaving an unwanted mark. *Stung* may also mean drunk.

stunned *American* drunk
Common slang, with obvious imagery.

stunt a limited battle
Much more than just a trick, but soldiers in
the First World War understood the horrors:
  If he don't get the Victoria Cross for this
  stunt I'm a bloody Dutchman. (F. Richards,
  1933)

stunted hare a rabbit
For seamen, the mention of rabbit is taboo
although it is a long time since chandlers
substituted salted rabbit meat, which decays
quickly, for the conventional salted pork. See
also FURRY THING.

stupid drunk
Derived from the drunkard's behaviour rather
than from the folly of getting like it. Common
still in Scotland as *stupid-fou*:
  He was na stupid-fou, as was his wont on
  market days. (Strain, 1900)

subdue to your will to copulate with
  extramaritally
Males do it, overcoming, so it suggests, female
fears or scruples. The woman has to be royal
or rich to reciprocate:
  ... the queen has only two uses for foreign
  men—first to subdue them to her will, if
  you follow me ... (Fraser, 1977)

submit to (of a female) to copulate with
Usually extramaritally and with a hint of
reluctance:
  They refuse to submit to his pleasure, and
  will not return him the money. (Mayhew,
  1862, referring to cheating prostitutes)

subsidy publishing the publication of a
  book at the author's expense
VANITY PUBLISHING, which means the same
thing, is nearer to the truth.

substance an illegal narcotic
Literally, any matter. Normally in compounds
like *illegal substance*, which could just as well
mean Semtex in the hands of a terrorist:
  To everyone's surprise, not least his own,
  he had not touched alcohol or illegal
  substances since. (Bryson, 1997)
Substance abuse is the ingestion of illegal
narcotics, or sniffing glue or solvents:
  ... she'd been a nurse too long, had too
  often seen the results of substance abuse.
  (Clancy, 1989)

succubus a prostitute
Originally, a female demon who copulates
with men in their sleep, thus for the fastidious providing an excuse for involuntary
nocturnal seminal ejaculation:

  'Yes, thou barbarian,' said she, turning to
  Wagtail, 'thou tiger, thou succubus!'
  (Smollett, 1748)
Succuba would seem the correct gender, but is
wrong:
  'She's a witch. She'll destroy everything!'
  'A succuba, is she? I'd like to meet her.'
  (B. Cornwell, 1993)

succumb[1] to die
Literally, to give way to anything, and usually
of natural death:
  Hibbert ... succumbed to a heart attack at
  his desk. (Condon, 1966)

succumb[2] to copulate outside marriage
Another form of giving way, or something, by
either sex:
  I'm willing to bet you five dollars she
  doesn't succumb even to the charms of
  William. (Archer, 1979)

suck off to practise fellatio or cunnilin-
  gus on
Of obvious derivation:
  One American GI is forcing a Vietnamese
  woman to suck him off. (*Guardian*, 27
  September 1971)
  Equilibrists suck each other off deftly.
  (Burroughs, 1959)
Sucker, a dupe, came from the supposed
gullibility of a 19th-century American piglet
rather than any sexual association.

suck the monkey *British* to steal rum
A naval practice, by inserting a straw surreptitiously in a cask. It also referred to the
practice of filling a coconut with rum to drink
on board ship. The obsolete *suck the daisy roots*
meant to be dead.

suffer to be killed
An obsolete use, as in the Apostles' Creed,
which tells us 'He suffered and was buried':
  In it is a pyramid erected to the memory of
  Thomas Lord Lovat, by his son Lord Simon,
  who suffered on Tower-hill. (J. Boswell,
  1773—Thomas, not Simon, had sided with
  the Stuart Prince Charles and had his head
  chopped off as a result)
To *suffer the supreme penalty* is explicit:
  As for ... the murder of her Indian
  subordinate ... eventually one or two men
  suffered the supreme penalty. (P. Scott,
  1973)

suffer fools gladly to tolerate incompetence
Euphemistic only in the negative, especially
of impatient people:
  I could not easily forgive the mistakes of
  others, what is euphemistically called not
  suffering fools gladly. (Lomax, 1995)

sugar¹ a bribe
The common imagery when you SWEETEN 1 a deal.

sugar² a mild oath
Common genteel use, for the taboo *shit*.

sugar³ an illegal narcotic
It describes any white narcotic in crystalline form, or LSD deposited on a lump of sugar to make it palatable.

sugar daddy a man with a mistress much younger than himself
Daddy from the generation gap and *sugar* from the sweet things of life which she may expect of him:
    Kathy's Sugar Daddy Evicted.
    (Headline in *Western Daily Press*, May 1981)
Sometimes shortened to *daddy*.

suggestion the unauthorized disclosure of privileged or confidential information
How an INSIDER tips off his friends:
    He'll get a commission of five percent of all profits generated by his 'suggestions'.
    (Erdman, 1987, writing about share dealing)
Although to make such a *suggestion* may be improper, an *improper suggestion* is specifically making a sexual proposal to someone who resents receiving it.

suits (the) men in professional or managerial jobs
A derogatory term used by those over whom they think they can exercise authority and who may be less formally attired:
    They put an end to working-class fantasies about the gentleness of professional life. It was the suits you had to fear. (Winton, 1994)

sun has been hot today (the) *obsolete* there are signs of drunkenness
At harvest time, cider or small beer was provided for the workers in the fields, who would become progressively more tipsy as they slaked their thirst. A drunkard might also be said to *have the sun in his eyes* or to *have been in the sunshine*:
    We guessed by his rackle as he's bin i' the sunshine. (Pinnock, 1895—rackle was riotous conduct)

sun has gone over the yardarm (the) let us drink some alcohol
By naval tradition, you might start drinking alcohol when the sun had fallen below the *yardarm*, a horizontal spar from the mast. Landlubbers may use the phrase at the end of a day's work:

Ah well, sun is over the yardarm, so down to work. (*Private Eye*, May 1981—the 'work' was drinking intoxicants)

Sunday incompetent or amateur
As different from those who perform functions during the week for a living. Thus a *Sunday driver* may try your patience by dawdling or threaten your life by incompetence. It can, however, mean no more than doing something as a hobby:
    [Ira Gershwin] was an enthusiastic, gently gifted, Sunday painter. (F. Muir, 1997)

Sunday traveller *obsolete Irish* an illegal drinker of intoxicants at an inn
At one time only a bona fide traveller could legally be served with intoxicants on Sundays in Ireland:
    ...a door consecrated to the unobtrusive visits of so-called 'Sunday Travellers'. (Somerville and Ross, 1897)

sundowner a drink of intoxicants
From the habit of drinking alcohol in the tropics after the risk of dehydration is lessened:
    As he sits there [in Zaire] on a hot evening swilling his sundowners...(G. Greene, 1978)

sunset years old age
Those who appreciate the beauty of sunset normally do not relish the darkness which must follow. Less sickly however than the GOLDEN YEARS.

supercharged drunk or under the influence of illegal narcotics
Having had a CHARGE 2 too many.

supporters' club investors who act in concert
Often following the lead or career of a successful investor or manager, forming a FAN CLUB which skirts the fringes of the law. Less often it may refer to the employees of a potential customer who favour a specific vendor, from whom they may receive bribes.

supportive obsessive
Literally, ready to support, but the use may imply a deep commitment to, and obsession with, a cause, and contempt for those who may not share the same opinions or emotions:
    ...if the caring and supportive wanted a political focus, it was necessary to drive...to meet others with similar ambitions for the use of the planet. (*Daily Telegraph*, May 1990—the ecological point might have been better made by leaving the car in the garage)

supreme measure of punishment death by execution
Not suffered voluntarily by those who MAKE THE SUPREME SACRIFICE. Also as *the supreme penalty*:
> With an affectionate pat, he assured the historian Yuri Staklov that he was safe; the NKVD came for Staklov that night. The scribbled letters SMP, Supreme Measure of Punishment, filled the margins of his lists. (Moynahan, 1994, writing of Stalin and his terror)
> In the Soviet Union [they] will face the supreme penalty. (Seymour, 1977)

sure thing a promiscuous woman
And considered likely by male acquaintances to be so. The derivation is from the racehorse so described by a tipster, although there are no certainties in either sport:
> ...hardly at all like someone who in her time had been one of the surest things between Bridgend and Carmarthen. (Amis, 1986)

surgical appliance see APPLIANCE

surgical strike a bombing raid
Supposedly as accurate as the first incision of the scalpel:
> ...precision bombing is 'surgical strikes'. (Commager, 1972, writing about Vietnam, where carpet bombing was liable to be classified as *precision*)

surplus *American* to dismiss from employment
Discharging the excess quantity:
> IBM has reportedly 'surplused' 25,000 jobs corporate-wide. (*Computer Shopper*, July 1993)
Perhaps less euphemistic as a noun:
> BT expects no significant job losses from the tie-up but AT&T president John Zeglis admitted his company might find some 'pockets of potential surplus'. (*Daily Telegraph*, 27 July 1998)

surrender to (of a female) to copulate with
The common imagery of male aggression and dominance:
> Girls seemed to prefer the story of her surrendering to Koolman in exchange for a leading role. (Deighton, 1972)

surrendered personnel Japanese prisoners of war
An evasion used by the British 14th Army, which had killed about 500,000 of the enemy and wanted to dissuade the remainder from obeying their martial code—fighting to the death or committing *hara kiri*:
> By October, thousands of Japanese Surrendered Personnel (as a salve to their dignity they were never referred to as prisoners)...(M. Clark, 1991)

surveillance spying
Literally, no more than keeping a watch over. Police and espionage jargon for clandestine observation. *Electronic* or *technical surveillance* is the use of hidden microphones, wire-taps, or other gadgetry of spying.

suspect cigarette an illegal narcotic
Normally marijuana, smoked as you would legal tobacco:
> An unsuccessful party to welcome Mrs Neville culminated in a black saxophonist, playing with the blatant inspiration of a suspect cigarette, strolling overboard into the Thames. (*Daily Telegraph*, 13 June 1997—the party was being held on a houseboat)

swallow the anchor to retire from a career at sea
Originally a British naval use but also adopted by yachtsmen and others:
> At sixty-three, their painful knees and hands were making it increasingly difficult to work the foredeck, but at the same time neither of them relished the prospect of swallowing the anchor. (M. Clark, 1991)

swallow the Bible *American* to perjure yourself
From swearing on the Bible when you take the oath in court:
> They will stick together, stretch conscience and at times 'swallow the Bible'. (Lavine, 1930)
See also EAT THE BIBLE and SWITCH THE PRIMER.

sweat it out of to obtain information from by coercion
Police jargon, sometimes shortened to *sweat*:
> I don't believe Frank Gloriana is a strong character. Sweat him. (Sanders, 1992—Frank was under arrest)
The coercion usually takes place in a cell named a *sweat-box*, which, significantly, used to be 19th-century criminal slang for any cell in a British police station.

Sweeney see FLYING SQUAD

sweet equity shares issued to favoured parties at below their value
As a reward for those on the inside arranging a deal or to satisfy the greed of their advisers and other associates:
> ...those ubiquitous buy-out teams with their dazzling 'sweet equity' incentive packages. (*Daily Telegraph*, 8 April 1999)

sweet man *American* a woman's regular extramarital sexual partner
Mainly black usage. A *sweet momma* was once any black woman of a kindly disposition but now is a mistress who is black.

sweet tooth an addiction to illegal narcotics
A fondness for CANDY.

sweetbreads animal glands used for food
Literally, the thymus or pancreas, but also the testicles. See also VARIETY MEATS and PRAIRIE OYSTER 1.

sweeten¹ to bribe
Using the common imagery of making something more toothsome:
  Now-a-days ane canna' phraise,
  An' sooth, an' lie, an' sweeten,
  An' palm, an' sconse. (Lauderdale, 1796—referring to flattery, bribery, and trickery)
And in modern use of an improper inducement:
  Construction had been held up by the Pollution Control Board. A $30,000 fee was negotiated, sweetened with the offer of a job. (Evans-Pritchard, 1997)
A *sweetener* is such a bribe, not necessarily in cash:
  Giving big commissions, sweeteners, call it bribery if you like ... (Lyall, 1980)

sweeten² (of a public auction) improperly to force up bidding
Auctioneers' jargon for the practice of purporting to accept spurious or nonexistent bids.

sweeten³ to attempt to improve by deception
Showbusiness jargon of the practice whereby a producer introduces pre-recorded laughter to give the impression that an audience found a show funnier than in fact they did:
  Producers ... devised what they believed was a totally justified method of sweetening a show. (F. Muir, 1997—they had a comedian tell a vulgar joke, and cut the resultant laughter into another recording)

sweetheart indicative of an arrangement which improperly benefits two parties at the expense of a third
It may describe deals between an employer and union officials, like channelling pension funds through the union with the officials taking a commission, at the expense of the wages paid to the workforce; or insiders cheating stockholders on a share deal:

And at a good sweetheart price, too. Less than $6 billion over four years. (M. Thomas, 1980)

swell to be pregnant
Of obvious imagery, and not used of male or female obesity:
  Unless it swell past hiding, and then it's past watching. (Shakespeare, *Troilus and Cressida*)

swill to be a habitual drunkard
Literally, to rinse out, but long standard English for drunkenness. The usual stream of derivatives—*swilled, swiller, swill-pot*, and the like—seem to have passed into disuse. See also SIX O'CLOCK SWILL.

swim for a wizard *obsolete Lancashire* to test for magical powers of evil
Witchcraft was a fruitful subject for taboo and euphemism. I include this sample entry to remind us of the social behaviour and beliefs of our recent ancestors, which were not confined to Salem:
  So late as 1863, an old man was flung into a mill-stream ... being what was called 'swimming for a wizard'. (Harland and Wilkinson, 1867—presumably, he drowned if he was human and you killed him if he proved himself a wizard by not drowning)
See also WAKE A WITCH.

swing¹ to be killed by hanging
The rotation of a suspended corpse:
  On high as ever on a tow
  Swing's in the widdie. (Sanderson, 1826—*tow* is hemp and *in the widdie* was twisting around)
Still used figuratively of receiving punishment, in the term *I'll swing for this*.

swing² to engage in any taboo act
From the meaning, to act in a modern or unrestrained fashion. It is used of ingesting illegal drugs, extramarital copulation, and any other conduct which may offend conventional mores, including homosexuality:
  Thomas Did you ever swing with her?
  Cynthia Twice. No more.
  Thomas Bent—isn't she? (Sanders, 1970)
Married couples jointly participating in a taboo activity may be said to *swing together*:
  One couple we know are Godparents of the other couple's children—but they swing together. It's just a friendly way of showing friendship. (Whicker, 1982, quoting a wife who, like her husband, regularly copulated with third parties)
To *swing both ways* is to have both heterosexual and homosexual tastes:
  You swing both ways, uh? (Sanders, 1982)

swing around the buoy *British* to have an easy job
Naval imagery, from a ship at anchor moving with the tides, and the consequent inactivity for the crew.

swing off to die
Not by hanging or even by violence. The imagery is possibly avian, as with HOP OFF:
> She placed flowers on his grave on the day he swung off. (Longstreet, 1956—its anniversary, I would suggest, unless there had been an unusually rapid interment)

swing the lamp *British* to boast
Naval usage and imagery, probably from the action of a signaller passing a message between ships at night rather than from the movement of a suspended lamp below decks:
> There were several groans and Andy Laird, the chief stoker, shouted, 'Swing the bloody lamp, somebody!' (Reeman, 1994—a crew member had been bragging)

swing the lead to pretend unfitness to avoid work or duty
The association with the function of the leadsman is unclear:
> The majority were swinging the lead and would do anything to protect themselves being marked A1. (F. Richards, 1933—soldiers in the First World War tried to avoid being returned to the trenches)

swipe to steal
The *SOED* gives the origin as American but an old English dialect use meant to take possession of:
> When awd man deed, Bob swipet all bit o' brass he had. (*EDD*, mid-19th century)

swish *American* (of a male) to flaunt your homosexuality
He conducts himself in a manner recognized by fellow homosexuals, possibly from the slang meaning, smart. A *swish* is a homosexual male.

switch-hitter a person with both homosexual and heterosexual tastes
From the American ambidextrous baseball player. In obsolete British use, to *switch* was to copulate, along with to *swinge* and to *swive* (Grose). To *switch on* means to excite sexually, being a variant of TURN ON.

switch-selling dishonest advertising of cheap goods designed to induce a customer to buy something dearer
Not offering for sale whips or false hair but a scam outlawed in 1962 by the British Code of Advertising Practices:
> ...there must be no 'switch selling', namely advertising one article at a cheap price in the hope of persuading the customer to switch to a more expensive one. (E. S. Turner, 1952)

switch the primer *Irish* to perjure yourself
The *primer* was a prayer book, and a Roman Catholic would have small regard for the mana of the Protestant Bible produced in court for him to swear upon:
> He switched the primer himself that he was innocent. (Carleton, 1836)

sword the penis
Viewed sexually as in the male vulgarism *pork sword*. A *sword-swallower* is the patient in fellatio. A *swordsman* is a male profligate:
> 'Bit of a swordsman, was he?' ... 'The post-mortem suggests there was sexual activity on the night of the murder.' (Blacker, 1992)

sympathetic ear a self-righteous person forcing his attention on those suffering a misfortune
Literally, someone prepared to listen with sympathy:
> No tragedy is too immense and no personal anxiety too insignificant to be absorbed by Britain's vast emotional sponge of psychotherapists, social workers, trauma experts, do-gooders, and assorted sympathetic ears. (*Daily Telegraph*, 31 March 1994—what about the omnipresent COUNSELLOR?)

syndicate *American* an association of powerful criminals
Literally, any group of business associates:
> 'When we talk about the rackets, are we talking about the same guys?' 'We're talking about the syndicate.' (Ustinov, 1971)

syndrome any taboo medical condition
Originally, a set of symptoms of which the cause was conjectural or unknown, but now denoting established afflictions like DOWN'S SYNDROME, *Acquired Immune Deficiency Syndrome* (AIDS), *Korsakoff's Syndrome* (delirium tremens) and the deadly *School Phobia Syndrome*, which makes the life of an EDUCATION WELFARE MANAGER so stressful.

syrup a wig
Rhyming slang on *syrup of figs*. Usually of one worn by a male, against which the taboo remains stronger in Britain than in America:
> ...a hairline down to his eyebrows... It can't be an iffy syrup, because he's too drunk to put it on. (P. McCarthy, 2000)

T

tackle the male genitalia
Literally, equipment:
> He's certainly got the tackle. I saw
> him in the showers the other day.
> (Lodge, 1995)

Also as *marriage* or *wedding tackle*, which does
not refer to the buttonhole or morning-coat,
the veil, the bouquet, or bridal gown:
> He lifted his T-shirt, pulled in his stomach
> and looked down at his marriage tackle.
> (R. Doyle, 1991)
> There were the usual comments about the
> size of one's wedding tackle; 'Cor, wot a
> beauty', or 'he's bloody well hung', or
> 'Christ, his poor wife,' etc. (Milligan, 1971,
> reporting talk in communal male showers)

tactical done involuntarily under pressure
Originally, relating to the deployment of
troops, but something announced as a *tactical
regrouping* is a forced retreat. A *tactical nuclear
weapon*, for use against troops, is correctly
described.

tagged[1] hit by a bullet
Literally, labelled, from the old superstition
among soldiers that the bullet which hits you
has your name on it:
> 'Tagged,' he realized. There was no
> mistaking it, he had been hit before.
> (W. Smith, 1979)

tagged[2] *American* detected in the commission of a crime
Being caught and named:
> Ralph got tagged for stealing stamps.
> (Steinbeck, 1961)

tail[1] a woman or women viewed sexually
by a male
> It's tail, Lew. Women. (Bradbury, 1976)
An individual female may be described as a *bit*
(see BIT 1) or *piece* (see PIECE 1) *of tail*:
> She was a piece of Scandinavian tail that
> he'd picked up. (Matthew, 1978)
See also *flash-tail* under FLASH-KEN.

tail[2] to follow surreptitiously
Staying close behind. Whence a *tail*, who does
the following, and a *tail-job*, such an operation:
> You can do a tail job on him.
> (Allbeury, 1976)

tail-pulling the publication of a book at
the author's expense

Publishers' punning usage, from the meaning, teasing.

take[1] to steal
OED gives a first use in this sense in 1200,
since when it had been standard English. In
modern use it may refer to being bribed:
> The judges who took were said to be
> carefully isolated. There were bagmen and
> code words. (Turow, 1999)

take[2] to copulate with
Usually of the male, in ancient or modern use:
> To take her in her heart's extremest hate.
> (Shakespeare, *Richard III*)
> It didn't stop the waves of lust as he took
> her. (Allbeury, 1976)
Rarely, although with rather more logic, the
female *takes* the male:
> Chandra...had been the cause of his love
> affair...for she had taken him just to
> forget Chandra. (Masters, 1976)

take[3] to kill
The victims are animals, by culling or hunting:
> And many of the creatures she allowed to
> escape. 'You take him,' she would say.
> (Mailer, 1965, writing about shooting
> squirrels)

take[4] to cause or allow to die
When your deity says your time is up:
> I felt wretchedly old...and began to
> wonder, for the first time in my life, when
> it would please God to take me. (W. Collins,
> 1868)

take[5] to conceive
Used of domestic animals, as of cuttings or
grafts of plants:
> Some mares won't take. (D. Francis,
> 1982)

take[6] to overcome or master
An omnibus usage which may describe any
action from aggressively passing another
vehicle on the highway to any kind of villainy:
> He had no doubts he could 'take' the
> apartment at Fontenoy House. He was,
> after all, one of the best cracksmen in
> London. (Forsyth, 1984)

take a bath to suffer a heavy financial loss
Your boat is capsized:
> His old man took a bath in real estate about
> ten years ago, got in the shower, and
> emptied his brains out with a .45.
> (Diehl, 1978)

take a bit from to copulate with promiscuously
Usually of a female, on a regular basis:

Margot Dunlop-Huynegen is taking a little
bit now and then from her husband's valet.
(Condon, 1966)
And see BIT 1.

take a break to allow the intrusion of advertisements
Television jargon, especially when the same
programme will be resumed.

take a drink to be an alcoholic
As in DRINK 1:
Do you take a drink, Missis Spencer?
(R. Doyle, 1996—a doctor was quizzing
his patient)

take a hike¹ to be dismissed from emp-
loyment
A variant of the more common WALK 2:
They told him to take a hike, because it was
so gross. (Theroux, 1993)
See also HIKE 1 (OFF).

take a hike² to become a fugitive
Usually after escaping from prison:
'No fences, no locks, no guns. But also no
swimming pool or tennis court.' 'So why
doesn't everybody just take a hike?'
'Because if you do, when they catch you,
you get a mandatory extra five years.'
(Erdman, 1993)
but also of evading your creditors:
When gold finally moved up, a lot of his
investors tried to exercise their options,
which prompted my former colleague...to
take a hike. (ibid.)

take a leak see LEAK 1

take a leap to kill yourself by jumping off
a high place
This is an example of many similar expressions for suicide. Thus he who *takes a long walk
off a short pier* is assumed to be a non-
swimmer, and the water deep.

take a liberty with to make an unwanted
sexual approach
Always by the male:
Nobody ever tried to take a liberty with
her. (M. McCarthy, 1963)
Take liberties, meaning the same thing, is
obsolete:
...[the licentious monk] proceeded to take
still further liberties. (M. Lewis, 1795—a
girl was saved from rape by her mother's
entry)

take a powder to leave hurriedly to avoid
an obligation or publicity
Alluding to the rapid departure necessitated
after taking a laxative. It may refer to
checking out of a hotel without paying,

deserting a spouse, running away in battle,
avoiding the press, etc.:
...she's the one who took the powder. I
didn't ask her to leave. (Turow, 1987)
...you guys took a powder and the Krauts
just came rolling over your support areas.
(Deighton, 1981)
Dean commented it would be a good
thing...for Hunt to take a powder.
(Colodny and Gettlin, 1991—Hunt was a
Watergate witness)

take a stick to to punish by beating
Not giving a lame person an aid in walking:
If it happens again, I'll take a stick to you.
(Sayers, 1937)

take a turn in the stubble *obsolete* (of a
male) to copulate
One of many vulgar puns of which our
forefathers were so fond, a *turn*, being a stroll
or outing, and the *stubble*, pubic hair. To *shoot
over the stubble* was to suffer premature ejaculation or the withdrawal method of contraception. Grose tells us that a man might take many
other similar *turns*, *in Cupid's Corner, Love Lane,
Mount Pleasant*, and other punning addresses in
London. A female might *take a turn on her back*
in any part of the Kingdom.

take a walk¹ *American* to leave employment
Either voluntarily or involuntarily:
I think he should take a walk. Who
needs this shit? (M. Thomas, 1985—he
referred to a troublesome affair and not
to the employee or to his digestive system)
See also WALK 2.

take a walk² to defect
You go and do not return:
Years ago—before Fiona took a
walk...(Deighton, 1988—Fiona had
defected to Russia)
It is also used of a spouse leaving home
permanently.

take a walk³ to be stolen
The implication that inanimate objects can
remove themselves may avoid a direct accusation of theft or fraud:
If half a million pounds took a
walk...(Deighton, 1988)

take a wheel off the cart to force another
into bankruptcy
Bankers' jargon. If the lender recovers one
wheel out of four, the vehicle collapses.

take advantage of (of a male) to copulate
with casually
Alluding to the female's weakness and his
ungentlemanly conduct:

My later behaviour in taking advantage of
her did no more than damage her
self-respect. (Amis, 1978)

An obsolete form was *take vantages*:
'I fear her not, unless she chance to
fall.'...'God forbid that for he'll take
vantages.' (Shakespeare, *3 Henry VI*)

take an early bath to be dismissed for
foul play or poor performance

Sporting jargon, but some figurative use also
of dismissal from employment:
The week started with the farce of Sunday
newspaper stories about...the chairman
taking an early bath. (*Daily Telegraph*, 7
October 2000)

See also EARLY BATH.

take care of¹ to kill or render impotent

Literally, to look after, whence to account for:
Clearly, the commissionaire of the
night-watch could easily be 'taken care
of'. (Forsyth, 1994)

take care of² to bribe

Another form of looking after:
Osborne had always known which officials
should be taken care of. (Archer 1979)

take electricity *American* to be judicially
killed

In the *electric chair*:
The world forgot them until they saw a
squib in the paper saying a certain fellow
had taken a little electricity along about
midnight. (King, 1996)

take for a ride to murder

You bundled your victim into a car and killed
him in a secluded place:
...taken for a ride. His death is
attributed...(Lavine, 1930)
Whence the current figurative meaning, to
cheat.

take home to die of natural causes

The devout, for whom heaven is *home*, are led
there by their deity or his representative:
If it would please the Lord to take it
home...(*EDD*)

take in your coals *American* to contract
venereal disease

Naval usage, punning on the burning sensation.

take leave of life to die

Circumlocution as much as euphemism,
although it suggests a voluntary decision
where dying is concerned:
He could eat nothing, not rally his
strength, and within ten days he took leave
of life. (Monsarrat, 1978)

take little interest in the opposite sex to
be a homosexual

The case of the British naval spy Vassall
highlighted the danger of using euphemism
instead of direct speech. One of Vassall's
referees, when he was being considered for
a job which involved access to secret material,
instead of warning of his homosexuality (and,
at that time, the possibility of his being
blackmailed), merely said that:
...he took very little interest in the
opposite sex. (N. West, 1982)
Also as *take no interest in the opposite sex*.

take needle to inject narcotics illegally

Not the action of a sempstress:
...[a drug addict] about to take the needle.
(Mailer, 1965)

take off *obsolete Scottish* to die

Before any visible manifestation of wings:
You were in the house at the time of his
taking off. (Beatty, 1897)
There are also various ephemeral uses of *take
off* in drug jargon, some of which appear
contradictory. Thus it may mean you can be
denied a narcotic, or experience its effect; rob
for money to buy illegal drugs, or buy them
from a dealer.

take out¹ (of a male) to court a female

The action may take place in the front room,
if secluded enough.

take out² to render ineffective

By killing or other violent action:
If a KGB agent named Talaniekov
appeared on the scene, he was to be
taken out as ruthlessly as Schofield.
(Ludlum, 1979)
Japanese counter-terrorist people had
decided to take out the headquarters of the
fanatical ultra-left Red Army Faction.
(Forsyth, 1984)

take pleasure with to copulate with

Not just sharing an enjoyable meal or trip:
Later, stirred by the curry, he took
pleasure with his second wife.
(Sanders, 1977)
See also PLEASURE.

take refuge in a better world to die

Or so it is to be hoped:
A shy, sensitive, painfully principled man,
a few years later he took refuge in a better
world by his own hand. (J. Major, 1999,
writing about a politician who
committed suicide)

take someone's (good or **dear) name
away** (of a male) to copulate with casually

It is her reputation, not her form of address, which is at stake:
> The captain of the football team spent a whole year trying to take my dear name away from me. (Mailer, 1965—he was not suggesting marriage)

take someone's pants off *American* to reduce to penury
In this usage at least, of financial rather than sexual activity:
> What about a game of poker...I'm going to take the pants off you. (C. Forbes, 1992—but not strip poker)

Also as *take someone's shirt off*.

take something to drink an intoxicant or use an illegal narcotic
In various phrases:
> 'Have you taken anything?' (This meant drugs.) (I. Murdoch, 1977)

take the air to urinate
As in the days when the lavatory was not indoors:
> Danny rose and said he needed to take the air, a gentlemanly statement of his wish to use the outhouse. (Keneally, 1979)

take the air abroad to leave the country to avoid arrest
Not for health reasons:
> We did endure what you might call a slight low directly after the US invasion when some of the General's higher officials felt obliged to take the air abroad for a time. (le Carré, 1996—the General was the infamous Noriega of Panama)

take the can back to be held responsible
See CARRY THE CAN for a dissertation on this usage:
> Nobody wanted to take the can back. (B. Forbes, 1986)

take the drop to be killed by hanging
From the scaffold:
> He's as good as taken the drop already. (G. Greene, 1934)

To *take a drop* means regularly to drink alcohol.

take the mick(e)y to taunt or mimic
Rhyming slang on *Michael*, *Mike*, or *Micky Bliss*, TAKE THE PISS. Seldom *tout court* as *micky*:
> Look at Bill wobbling his belly—mickying her, he is (Cookson, 1967)

take the piss to taunt or mimic
The etymology is unclear:
> It hadn't occurred to me that people take the piss out of Bugs. (Garland, 1996—Bugs did not have a catheter)

take the pledge see PLEDGE

take the soup *Irish* to convert under duress to Protestantism
See SOUPER for an explanation:
> I think our little friend here has taken the soup. That's the worst thing you can say to any Catholic in Limerick or Ireland. (McCourt, 1997)

take the walk *American* to be judicially killed
The *walk* to the electric chair:
> The little Frenchman would take the walk shortly before Halloween. (King, 1996)

To *take a walk* means no more than to depart:
> In Pittsburgh I'd have told him to take a walk. (McBain, 1994)

take the wall *obsolete* to be socially superior
Those who walked closer to the buildings were less likely to be splashed or jostled. It therefore became a status symbol to occupy that space:
> When I returned to Lichfield, after having been in London, my mother asked me whether I was one of those who gave the wall, or those who took it. *Now* it is fixed that every man keeps to the right; or, if one is taking the wall, another yields it; and it is never a dispute. (J. Boswell, 1791, quoting Dr Johnson)

take the wind *American* to be summarily dismissed from employment or courtship
Usually of the person dismissed but occasionally of the one who rejects:
> She takes the wind on me a couple of months ago for my friend Frankie Ferocious. (Runyon, 1990, written in the 1930s)

Also as *take the breeze*.

take to bed to copulate with
Of either sex, and see BED 2:
> What does it matter to me if she lets a man take her to bed? (G. Greene, 1932)

take to the cleaners to rob or cheat
The process thoroughly removes all surplus matter:
> Dantzler's sporting a new Ferrari, braggin' on the street how he took some cowboy to the cleaners. (Diehl, 1978)

take to the hills to escape
You are free from captivity, real or figurative:
> I really thought seriously of taking to the hills with our little Laura. (B. Forbes, 1983—he was thinking of deserting his wife)

take too much to be drunk
Either on a single occasion or habitually:
> I very much fear he has taken too much.
> (E. Waugh, 1933)

take up with to have an extramarital
sexual relationship with
Literally, no more than to consort with or
support:
> After a quarrel too, a lad goes and takes up
> with another girl. (Mayhew, 1851)

take with you to kill
When you also expect to be killed:
> ...a few desperate wretches taking as
> many Sioux with them as they could.
> (Fraser, 1982)

take your end *American* to accept bribes
regularly
Your *end* of the bargain:
> Chicago was a right town then. The fix was
> in. The dicks took their end without a beef.
> (Weverka, 1973)

take your leave of to bereave
The final parting:
> ...so absolutely unlike the way Frank
> would have wished to take his leave of us.
> (M. Thomas, 1982—Frank had died)

take (your) life to kill yourself
As distinct from *take life in your hands*, to risk
your life rashly, or just *take life as it comes*, to
live in a casual way:
> Beautiful Young Society Matron Takes
> Life in Plunge. (Mailer, 1965—headline
> relating to a suicide)

take your trousers off (of a male) to copulate
Not just retiring for the night:
> The belief...that they were 'the best
> people in the world' did not stop them
> taking their trousers off. (Paxman, 1998—
> writing of British colonial administrators)

taken dead
Not being killed, as in TAKE 3, but conducted
from this world to another, or as the case may
be:
> He was taken with leukemia. (Ustinov,
> 1971)
> Took he was—in the pride of his prime.
> (Ollivant, 1898)

taken short needing to urinate at an inconvenient time or place
From the days when coaches, and trains
without corridors, made no intermediate
stops between staging posts or stations:
> We used to empty bully-beef tines for
> urinating in. If a man was taken short

during the day, he had to use the trench.
(F. Richards, 1933)

taking (a) death
What happens when you are TAKEN hence:
> I was present at her taking, and though I be
> partial to death-beds...(Zack, 1901)
> The early days before the taking hence of
> her brother John. (Jane, 1897)

talent a woman viewed sexually by a man
Singly or collectively, hoping to find a *talent*
for sexual activity perhaps:
> He had no plans to get trapped by just
> any piece of gash. The talent in the
> place had to be seen to be believed.
> (J. Collins, 1983)
The punning *talent-spotting* is male searching
for such females.

talk to to bribe
More than verbal persuasion is involved:
> Pincus handled all arrangements with the
> lawyers who 'talked' to the judge. (Turow,
> 1999)

talking cardigan a broadcaster with staid
and conventional views
Dressed perhaps in old-style attire, unlike his
more aggressive, dismissive, and sometimes
arrogant colleagues who appear to be given
more airtime:
> The Oxbridge mafia of the BBC regards him
> as a talking cardigan, a left-over from the
> Richard Baker era. (*Daily Telegraph*, 10 June
> 1997—the cultured Baker was polite and
> fair to those whom he interviewed)

talking head a lay person appearing on
television on a current issue
The pundit is expected to pontificate and
make an instant judgement, often filling
airtime rather than adding to the stock of
human knowledge:
> An entire industry existed to analyze such
> things, a universe of scorps, talking heads,
> pollsters, consultants, free-range wisemen
> and gurus. (Anonymous, 1996—*scorps* is
> short for *scorpions*, or journalists)

Tampax time the period of menstruation
Of obvious derivation:
> When it's Tampax time, the lady is a
> tramp. (B. Forbes, 1989)

tank fight *American* a fraudulent boxing
match
One of the contestants *dives* into a figurative
water tank—collapses voluntarily on to the
canvas—whence the pun on a contest between armoured vehicles.

tanked up *American* drunk

Motoring imagery, which may owe something
to the German *tanken*, to fill with fuel:
> He got tanked up one night and stood on
> his chair and sang. (Theroux, 1973)

See also IN THE TANK.

tap¹ to drink intoxicants
From piercing a cask to draw off liquid
through a *tap*:
> I got the square bottle out and tapped it
> with discretion. (Chandler, 1939)

tap² to obtain an advantageous loan or
other finance from
Again the imagery of the faucet, with a
suggestion that repayment may be uncertain:
> He's invested in movies, I believe, though
> being a chum I've never tapped him.
> (C. Forbes, 1983)

tap³ the constant availability of stock
from willing sellers
Whence the market adage, *Where there's a tip,
there's a tap*.

tap⁴ see DO-LALLY-TAP

tap a kidney to urinate
Of either sex, from the renal function:
> I tapped a kidney in the ladies' room.
> (Theroux, 1978)

taps (the) *American* death
Military use, from the roll of a drum at a
funeral.

tarbrush (the) partial descent from a
non-white ancestor
If a brush is used for tarring, it will retain dark
streaks when you seek to use it later for a
lighter colour. The genes controlling dark
skin pigmentation are also dominant:
> ... her body was slightly darker than could
> be expected even by a rich girl's sunburn,
> her breasts were brown. ('Touch of the
> tarbrush there,' murmured Pinn.)
> (I. Murdoch, 1974)

The use, once prevalent, especially among the
British in India, is offensive.

target of opportunity (a) random bombing
The common instruction to bomber crews in
the Second World War, giving them an
excuse to jettison their bombs if they failed
to reach or identify their designated target:
> They bombed 'targets of
> opportunity' ... shutting your eyes,
> toggling the bombload, gaining
> height, and getting the hell out.
> (Deighton, 1982)

tart a prostitute or promiscuous person

The derivation is from *jam tart*, rhyming slang
for sweetheart:
> Young lady indeed. She's a tart. (G. Greene,
> 1932)

Now used of both sexes. One of my grand-
daughters used the word of a philanderer in
January 2001.

Tartans (the) *Macbeth*
It is taboo among actors to mention that
particular tragedy:
> What I'd like to do next year is the First
> Witch in 'The Tartans'. (Atwood, 1988)

taste *obsolete* (of a male) to copulate with
Another of the Bard's images:
> If you can make't apparent
> That you have tasted her in bed.
> (Shakespeare, *Cymbeline*)

taste for the bottle an addiction to alcohol
See BOTTLE 1:
> A letter from her daughter Norah to
> Henry Harrison delicately hinted at a
> taste for the bottle. (R. F. Foster, 1993,
> describing Mrs C. S. Parnell in later life)

tax *American* to steal with a threat of violence
Our contributions to central and municipal
funds, involuntary and onerous though they
may be, are not made under threat to our
persons:
> The principle of 'taxing'—mugging to steal
> shoes—is well established in the tough
> cauldrons of America's inner cities. (*Daily
> Telegraph*, June 1990)

tea *American* marijuana
From its likeness, when chopped, to tea
leaves. Also as *tea-sticks* or *sticks of tea*:
> ... marijuana; he called it tea. (Styron, 1976)
> There isn't much record he went for tea-
> sticks or the smoke. (Longstreet, 1956)
> Three highballs and three sticks of tea.
> (Chandler, 1940)

Thus *tea-heads* may smoke marijuana at a
punning *tea party*.

tea leaf *British* a thief
Rhyming slang:
> Or go and be a straightforward tea-leaf—
> thieve, rob. (Kersh, 1936)

tea money *British* a bribe
Paying for the essential need of the working
man and woman, in field, factory, or office:
> Day-to-day we survive with bribery and
> black market. It used to be that a
> bribe was called tea money. Now we
> pay so much it is called beer money.
> (Maclean, 1998)

team player *American* a non-critical supporter

Even if it involves condoning illegality:
> The case had been closed long before.
> Hickman Ewing was a team player. (Evans-Pritchard, 1997—Ewing had shown little enthusiasm for reopening an enquiry into the mysterious death of Vincent Foster)

See also PLAYER.

tearoom *American* a public lavatory frequented by homosexuals

Another sort of meeting place frequented for refreshment and gossip. Whence the *tearoom trade*, those who frequent such haunts:
> The Tea Room trade they call it in America; in England, Cottaging. (Fry, 1991)

A Japanese *teahouse* is something else again:
> A teahouse isn't for tea, you see; it's the place the men go to be entertained by geisha. (Golden, 1997)

technical adjustment a sudden fall in stock market prices

The phrase seeks to imply that market-makers are merely covering their positions without anything so worrying as an absence of buyers or bad news. Be equally wary of a *technical correction* or a *technical reaction*.

technicolor yawn (a) vomiting due to drunkenness

Of obvious imagery:
> No sooner was Lord Matey allowed back than he failed to stifle a technicolour yawn and swamped the entire bar. (*Private Eye*, February, 1988—note the Anglicization of the American film process)

tell me about it I am already aware of that unfortunate fact

You are likely to get a withering look if you accept the invitation:
> 'It's the worst idea I ever heard.' 'Tell me about it,' said Keaty. (Garland, 1996—Keaty already knew it was a bad idea)

temperance see INTEMPERANCE

temporary permanent and embarrassing

An evasion called in aid by politicians, soldiers, and others. Thus the British Prime Minister Macmillan described the unprecedented resignation of his three treasury ministers, Thornycroft, Powell, and Birch on 3 January 1958 as a *temporary local difficulty*. Setbacks in Vietnam for the US army tended also to be *temporary*:
> [The news service] caused heavy casualties, to be announced as light, routs and ambushes to be described as temporary tactical ploys. (Herr, 1997)

So too of personal or corporate insolvency:
> Your old man's got a temporary problem of liquidity. (le Carré, 1986—he was bankrupt)

ten commandments (the) scratches by a woman's fingernails

When she says to a man 'Thou shalt not':
> Could I come near your beauty with my nails,
> I'd set my ten commandments in your face. (Shakeapeare, *2 Henry VI*)

In occasional modern use it may refer to punches by either sex.

ten one hundred *American* stopping at the roadside to urinate

CB code which I have not unravelled. A *ten two thousand* is a seller of illegal narcotics.

tender a fool *obsolete* to give birth to an illegitimate child

To *tender* is to attend or wait upon, whence to offer or present. So spoke the punning Polonius to Ophelia:
> Tender yourself more dearly;
> Or—not to crack the wind of the poor phrase,
> Running it thus—you'll tender me a fool. (Shakespeare, *Hamlet*)

tender loving care allow to die

Hospital jargon of those mortally ill without hope of recovery. If you see the initials TLC on the charts at the foot of your bed, put your affairs in order.

tenderloin *American* associated with promiscuity and other illegality

Alluding to the choice cuts which the police might take in bribery:
> ...she was a dancer or an entertainer met on one of his tenderloin expeditions. (Winchester, 1998)

A *tenderloin district* is the precinct where prostitution, illegal gambling, and other rackets are rife:
> He had a long history of frequenting ...the 'tenderloin districts' of the cities in which he had been posted—most notably New York. (ibid.)

tenure *British* a job for life

University jargon for security of employment until retirement of a teacher confirmed in his post, to encourage and ensure academic freedom but sometimes providing for the idle, the ageing, the tired, and the incompetent at the expense of their fellows, their students, and research:
> He set up his tents in various different universities, from all of which he was

tactfully evicted. He never achieved
'tenure'. (I. Murdoch, 1983)

term¹ *obsolete* the period of menstruation

Literally, any specific period:
My wife, after absence of her terms for
seven weeks...(Pepys, 1660)

term² (a) imprisonment
The duration need not be stated:
He was a two-bit porch-climber with a few
small terms on him. (Chandler, 1939)

terminate¹ to kill
Literally, to end:
The people he terminated died for specific
reasons. (M. Thomas, 1980)
When killing illegally, the CIA *terminated with
extreme prejudice*:
I'm afraid the project's been terminated.
There was prejudice, extreme prejudice.
(Lyall, 1980, describing a CIA killing)

terminate² to dismiss from employment
Another form of ending:
...they had been sent home and demoted
or else fired—'terminated' was the word.
(Theroux, 1982)

termination an induced abortion
Either referring to an unwanted pregnancy or
on medical advice:
A nice girl from a nice home...the
thought of termination was unthinkable.
(Seymour, 1980)

terminological inexactitude a lie
The term was coined by Winston Churchill in
a speech quoted by Hansard on 22 February
1906, meaning inaccuracy rather than un-
truth:
[Chinese labour in South Africa] cannot in
the opinion of His Majesty's Government
be classified as slavery in the extreme
acceptance of the word without some
risk of terminological inexactitude.
(V. B. Carter, 1965)
But clearly too elegant a phrase to countenance desuetude:
...half lies, or as Erskine May finds more
acceptable, terminological inexactitudes.
(Howard, 1977)

testing unfavourable
Literally, no more than problematic:
Rexam shares fell 19.5 to 264p yesterday
after the packaging group reported 'testing
trading conditions'. (*Daily Telegraph*, 9
March 2001)

thank to bribe

In many places, verbal appreciation is not
sufficient:
'Have you thanked the captain?' 'I always
thank everybody,' I replied naively. (Simon,
1979—he was passing through a North
African frontier on a motorcycle)

that way¹ homosexual
Of either sex:
I never picked you for a sapphic...were
you always that way? (M. McCarthy,
1963)

that way² pregnant
Female use, normally of an unexpected or
unwanted pregnancy.

the worse drunk
A shortened form of *the worse for drink* or
liquor:
She had never known him the worse for
liquor. (Mayhew, 1862)

them a woman's breasts viewed sexually
by a male
A similar evasion to IT 3:
...clothing disarranged to reveal a, to him,
rare glimpse of 'them'. (F. Muir, 1990,
quoting K. Amis's *Jake's Thing*)

thick stupid
A shortened form of *thick in the head*:
—I don't know! said Linda.—It's thick.
She's useless. (R. Doyle, 1991)

thick of hearing *obsolete* deaf
Now replaced by HARD OF HEARING:
Doubtless I may be thick of
hearing...(Quiller-Couch, 1890)

thief (of the world) *mainly Irish* the devil
Often further particularized as *old* or *black*:
May the thief o' the world turn it all
into...whishky an' he be choked wid it.
(Bartram, 1898)

thing any taboo object to which you refer
allusively
Such as a ghost, for which:
'Summut' or 'Things' is preferred.
(*Spectator*, February 1902, quoted in *EDD*)
or the penis, in uses both ancient and
modern:
So that's a maid now...shall not be a maid
long, unless things be cut shorter.
(Shakespeare, *King Lear*)
Measured my 'thing'. It was eleven
centimeters. (Townsend, 1982)
The penis may also be called a *thingy* or
thingamajig:
You stand there with your thingamajig in
my toothmug...(Sharpe, 1979—he had
scratched it on a rosebush)

thing about a sexual feeling for
Either sex may have a *thing about* the other, or
homosexually:

> Iris, who I'd had a thing about...
> (R. Thompson, 1996)

thing going an extramarital sexual relationship between two people
Unlike a THING ABOUT, this is always reciprocal:

> We did have a thing going in London.
> (Reeman, 1994—the speaker was married
> to a third party)

third age (the) senescence
As in the *University of the Third Age*, a British
lecture and discussion group for elderly
people.

third degree police violence to extract
information
Probably from the scale of seriousness of
burns, of which the *third degree* is the worst.
Also as *third*:

> A veritable catalogue of police third-degree
> methods is contained in a recent (February
> 1930) issue of *Harvard Law Review*. (Lavine,
> 1930)
> He's giving me a third about a gun.
> (Chandler, 1934)

third leg the penis
Also vulgarly as the *middle leg*:

> He had to learn to live with the fact
> that his third leg had proved
> faulty. (Goldman, 1984—he was sexually
> impotent)

third party payment a bribe
The favourite commercial euphemism of the
1990s. A *third party* is someone with a casual
connection to the matter in hand.

third world poor
As different from the FIRST WORLD, rich
countries, and the former *second* (Communist)
world:

> ...a wealthy Bostonian, from a family of
> some distinction, adventuring in Third
> World philanthropy. (Theroux, 1980)

thirst (a) an addiction to alcohol
Whether or not dehydrated:

> There's a man that had a thirst, as the Irish
> would say. (Follett, 1991, and not just the
> Irish)

those days menstruation
A common female usage:

> Girls were separated off from the boys so
> they could be told about the curse. Not that
> the word was used. 'Those days' was the
> accepted, official phrase. (Atwood, 1988)

three-letter man¹ *obsolete* a swindler or
cheat
From the Latin *fur*, a thief.

three-letter man² *American* a male homo-
sexual
The letters are, or perhaps were, f-a-g; and see
FAG.

three-point play *American* the recruitment of a non-white woman
The imagery is from basketball. The employer
got a point for taking on another worker, a
second point if the worker was a female,
to show that he was not prejudiced about
employing women, and a third point when
he contributed to his quota of non-white
employees. He hit the jackpot only if the
recruit had American-Indian ancestry.

three sheets in the wind see SHEET IN THE
WIND

threepennies (the) *British* diarrhoea
Rhyming slang on the duodecimal *threepenny
bits* (for shits), useful as currency apart from
their insertion in Christmas puddings to be
prodded for eagerly on Christmas Day before
you swallowed them or broke a tooth.
Now obsolete apart from among those ancient enough to remember the ritual prod-
ding.

thrill a sexual orgasm
Literally, a sudden feeling of excitement or
pleasure. Whence to *thrill to your own touch* is
to masturbate yourself:

> I listened as her breath slowly rose,
> reaching its summit and briefly ceasing as
> she thrilled to her own touch. (Turow,
> 1996)

throat a wish to drink intoxicants
Possibly a shortened form of *dry throat*, which
makes you thirsty:

> I'd go to bed with yeh only I've a throat on
> me. (R. Doyle, 1987—he preferred to go to
> the pub)

throne a pedestal lavatory
From the shape, elevation, and solitary location. A person sitting on it is said to be
enthroned:

> ...she looked along the vista and saw,
> at the far end, Lord Doneraile enthroned
> playing the violin. (Bence-Jones, 1987,
> writing about an Irish mansion where the
> lavatory had been sited in the conservatory
> facing the hall)

throw¹ to give premature birth to
Usually of cattle, and still used in western
England:

Sight o' yoes've a-drow'd their lambs.
(*EDD*—a *sight o' yoes* is many ewes)

throw² to lose deliberately
Usually involving gambling fraud, and a
shortened form of *throw away*:

I heard you were supposed to throw it.
(Chandler, 1939—it was a boxing match,
not a discus)

throw down *obsolete* to copulate with
The common violent imagery, or the Bard's
wordplay:

And better would it fit Achilles much
To throw down Hector than Polyxena.
(Shakespeare, *Troilus and Cressida*)

Today a male may in vulgar speech *throw a leg
over* or *throw a bop into* his sexual partner.

throw in the towel to concede defeat
Boxing imagery, from what the second does
when his fighter is unable to continue:

I've got to go to Rummidge to see my
lawyer tomorrow. I could instruct him to
throw in the towel. (Lodge, 1995)

throw the book at to charge with every
feasible offence
Mainly police jargon, the *book* being the
manual setting out criminal offences:

You'll just have to throw the book at
me . . . I don't sell out—even to good police
officers. (Chandler, 1958)

throw the switches to become mentally
unbalanced
The imagery is probably from electric power,
although it might just refer to some sporting
manoeuvre:

When you get faith you throw the
switches, blow a gasket, you deliberately go
soft in the head. (O'Hanlon, 1996)

throw up to vomit
The oral expulsion, often due to drunkenness,
is usually directed downwards:

I got so mad I actually threw up. Puked!
(Theroux, 1982)

An Australian may claim to *throw a map*. To
throw up your toenails is to vomit excessively.

thump (of a male) to copulate with
Then and now, with the usual violent imagery:

Jump her and thump her. (Shakespeare,
The Winter's Tale)
Well, if I'd had my way, he'd still have been
thumping her every night. (Fraser, 1973)

thunderbox a portable lavatory
The sitter produces the sounds overhead:

When it rained the clients had to
row themselves to the thunder-box

at the bottom of the yard. (Simon,
1979)

The Second World War American military
thunder-mug, for urination, was not to be
found in less lavishly equipped armies:

. . . have a water pitcher, wash-basin, fancy
soap dish, and a thunder-mug. (Butcher,
1946)

tick a person clandestinely following another
Referring to the parasitic arachnid, which
sticks to your skin:

He saw his tick come in through the
revolving doors, look around, and, spotting
Kim, make for the elevator. (van Lustbaden,
1983)

ticker the heart
You only refer to it in this way if you have a
fear it will shortly wind down, and cease
ticking:

'In any case I have a bad heart.' 'My ticker
was none too good,' said Mr Flack.
(Theroux, 1974)

tickle to copulate with
Perhaps from the preliminary caresses, or
from the association with TICKLER 1:

When the swollen little girl told her
father the name of the man who'd been
tickling them—and I defy you to find a
more revolting terminology . . .
(Condon, 1966)

tickler¹ the clitoris
From its role in sexual arousal:

I went back to caressing her tickler.
(F. Harris, 1925)

tickler² see *French tickler* under FRENCH
LETTER

tiddly slightly drunk
Rhyming and punning slang on *tiddly-wink*, a
drink, which was an unlicensed inn or
pawnshop before it came to mean the game
played in pubs with counters:

I poured her wine carefully. 'Ma, you'll get
tiddly.' (Bogarde, 1983)

tie a can on *American* to dismiss from employment
Punning on CAN 2 and the cruel practice of
tying an old can to the tail of a stray cat to
drive it away.

tie one on *American* to go on a carouse
The etymology of this phrase is unex-
plained:

We could tie one good one on, two days,
three days, five empty bottles at the foot of
the bed. (Mailer, 1965)

tied up unwilling to see or speak to a caller
The phrase has no connection with the old meaning, constipated, or with a fetish for bondage:
> Wouldn't it be better to say 'I'm tied up' or 'in a meeting'? (P. D. James, 1994)

tiger-sweat *American* an impure intoxicant
It may be beer or spirits, with no aspersions being cast at very potable *Tiger* beer from Singapore:
> King Kong is not a movie. It's cheap alcohol, also known as Tigersweat. (Longstreet, 1956)

Also as *tiger juice*, *milk*, or *piss*. See also PANTHER SWEAT.

tight¹ drunk
Perhaps a pun on SCREWED, as the *OED* suggests, but I am not sure which usage came first:
> Well, he got in at last, and he lit a candle then. That took him five minutes. He was pretty tight. (Somerville and Ross, 1897)

tight² stingy
Tight with the purse-strings and *tight-fisted*:
> A wunt gie 'e nothun, a allus was a tight man. (*EDD*)

A *tightwad* is a miser:
> Cost him a hundred bucks to cancel which must have killed the old tightwad. (M. Thomas, 1987)

time the happening of something subject to a taboo
Childbirth, death, imprisonment, or menstruation:
> Elizabeth's full time came that she should be delivered; and she brought forth a son. (*Luke* 1: 57)
> My wife—she be near her time wi' the eleventh. (M. Francis, 1901)
> Mr Ralph wuz to die, his toime had coom. (Antrobus, 1901)
> 'Listen,' he said softly. 'I did my time.' (Chandler, 1939—he had served his sentence)
> I must cut up some more clouts. I have those pains in my stomach and my back, and it's about time. (de Bernières, 1994, writing about menstruation)

time of the month menstruation
Common female usage:
> Could it be that time of the day, that time of the month? (Bradbury, 1965)

tin ear (a) arrogant disregard
It hears only what you want it to hear:
> Since leaving the White House, Mrs Clinton has displayed a tin ear to public opinion. (*Daily Telegraph*, 20 March 2001)

tin handshake a derisory payment on dismissal from employment
He who leaves would prefer it to be GOLDEN:
> He's sacked, given a tin handshake and left to rot. (Allbeury, 1981)

tincture¹ a partial descent from other than white ancestry
Literally, a pigment, and used offensively of those whose dark skin pigmentation indicates a non-white ancestor:
> She had a tincture herself or she would not have mentioned their race. (Theroux, 1977)

tincture² an intoxicant
Literally, in pharmacy, a medical solution in alcohol:
> So while I was shunted off for tinctures with a lot of silly women in leotards... (*Private Eye*, February 1981)

tinhead a stupid person
Tin was wrongly associated with things of small worth, as is explained under TINPOT:
> ... Constantly one goes into a barbershop and reads all sorts of garbage that some tinhead has put out. (Whicker, 1982, quoting Sean Connery)

tinker *Irish* a gypsy or itinerant
At one time he made a living travelling from door to door mending pans:
> I've had more than one tink woman to *chavver*...I'll take a bet a big girl like you's been *chavvered* by half the gyppos in Ireland. (O'Donoghue, 1988—*chavver*, to copulate with, is a variant of *chauver*, from the Romany *charver*, to touch)

tinkle to urinate
Onomatopoeic nursery usage, from the noise of urinating into a mild steel (not tin) receptacle:
> Then that stopped...as a punishment for 'tinkling' behind the cupboard on the top floor. (A. Clark, 2000)

tinpot pretentiously assuming the trappings and manner of authority
The usage arose because a TINKER was loath to use expensive *tin* when repairing a *pot*. The substitute, prior to the availability of alumunium, was mild steel, which rusted and did not make a good repair:
> ...give away every scrap of Empire that remains to any tinpot potentate that asks for it. (*Private Eye*, July 1981)

tint to dye (hair)

Literally, to colour slightly:
> ...we drove sixty miles to Banbury to get her hair dyed—'tinted' they said in the shop. (Kyle, 1988)

tip¹ to copulate with

In former Scottish use, the rams *tipped* the ewes, whence the proverb:
> Tip where you will, you shall lamb with the leave.

In modern American use, to *tip* means to copulate with other than your regular sexual partner.

tip² (the bottle) to drink intoxicants to excess

From the motion of *tipping* the container:
> If she 'tips the bottle' he knocks her about a little more to teach her to keep sober. (Burmester, 1902)

Tipped and *tipsy* mean drunk:
> You're tipped darling. You're hurting. (Steinbeck, 1961)

> 'Was he tipsy?' I dare say...now you mention it. (E. Waugh, 1933)

A *tiper* or *tipper* was a drunkard; and see TIPPLE.

tip³(off) to warn or inform against

The usage implies betrayal or a breach of confidence:
> 'Who tipped you? He said, smiling...'If I find him...I'll have his balls.' (Sanders, 1983)

tip off *obsolete* to die

The common avian imagery:
> They all tipped off an' deed. (Binns, 1889)

tip off your trolley see OFF 2

tip over¹ to rob

Originally, from upsetting a stall and stealing some of the goods in the ensuing confusion, rather than from knocking over the victim. In modern American use it can apply to any theft.

tip over² *American* (of the police) to make a thorough search

After an unannounced raid, when the place is turned upside down looking for evidence.

tipple an intoxicating drink

Probably, despite its venerable ancestry, from *tip*, which meant beer:
> Helpers had brought in the drinks and bits. 'Do dig into the tipple,' said Serena. (Bradbury, 1976)

A *tippler*, who today drinks alcohol to excess, used to be an innkeeper, who kept a *tippling-house*:

> No vyattler nor tipler to sell any ale or beer brewed out of town. (*Lincoln Corporation Records*, 1575)

tired¹ unwilling to copulate with your regular partner

A female explanation or excuse which may or may not have to do with weariness:
> ...a kind of marital signal, looking to her for sexual encouragement, the unspoken suggestion that they would make love. 'I'm tired' or 'I'm not tired.' (Theroux, 1976)

tired² drunk

The symptoms of weariness and intoxication can be the same:
> Mr Brown had been tired and overwrought on many occasions. (*Private Eye*, 29 September 1967—George Brown was a drunken British Cabinet minister; the more common phrase to describe his condition was *tired and emotional*)

to one side of the truth untrue

A political evasion in a club where liars are not called liars:
> 'Nothing asked and nothing taken,' was how Gladstone put it which, if not strictly falsehood, was certainly to one side of the truth. (Kee, 1993)

to the knuckle devoid of resources

All the meat has gone:
> It's to the knuckle. It's not MGM or anything. There's no money. (Bogarde, 1983)

together having a permanent sexual relationship with each other

But not the *togetherness* of marriage:
> 'What about women?' Brett looked startled, then defensive. With an edge, she answered, 'We were together.' (R. N. Patterson, 1996)

toilet a lavatory

Originally, a towel, whence washing and the place where the washing was done. *Toilet paper* is used for wiping rather than washing.

token appointed other than on merit

The female or black member of the committee etc. whose presence is POLITICALLY CORRECT:
> The token black, Dr Clifton R. Wharton Jr. had gone in 1975. (Lacey, 1986, writing of the board of directors of the Ford Motor Company)

Whence *tokenism*, making such an appointment:
> There was evidence of 'tokenism', employing black staff purely for their colour. (*Daily Telegraph*, June 1984)

tolbooth *obsolete Scottish* a prison

Originally, the Town Hall, where tolls were paid. The jail was often in the same building:
> How many gypsies were sent to the tolbooth? (W. Scott, 1815)

Tom¹ (Tit) an act of defecation

Rhyming slang, always of defecation and never used as an insult:
> All that Tom Tit blown up in the air. (R. Forbes, 1986—a sewage plant had been bombed)

Tom² *American* a black man who defers unduly to whites

A shortened form of UNCLE TOM:
> He'd been at constant odds with the Black Power types at Easton, who called him a Tom for rooming with a white guy. (Turow, 1996)

tomboy *obsolete* a prostitute

From the reputation of male felines, perhaps, and also punning on TUMBLE 1:
> A lady
> So fair... to be partner'd
> With tomboys. (Shakespeare, *Cymbeline*)

Today it means no more than a girl who enjoys the athletic and other traditional pursuits of a boy.

tomcatting sexual excess

The reference is to the lustful feline:
> The tomcatting made history in the form of songs. (Longstreet, 1956, of New Orleans)

Tommy the penis

Rarer than DICK 1, commoner than *Harry*:
> She... had to use her hand to get my Tommy in again. (F. Harris, 1925)

tongue an enemy prisoner captured for interrogation

In the Stalingrad campaign neither side was content with limiting a captive's speech to what the Geneva Convention stipulated, namely name, rank, and number:
> NVD officers and interpreters worked late into the night interrogating German prisoners, including the first deserters, as well as 'tongues' captured by reconnaissance companies. (Beevor, 1998)

tool the penis

Literally, any instrument:
> 'Draw thy tool.'... 'My naked weapon is out.' (Shakespeare, *Romeo and Juliet*— another of the Bard's vulgar puns)
> No accountability could be apportioned anywhere for how his tool behaved, or failed to behave, while he slept. (Amis, 1978)

Grose has:
> *Tools*. the private parts of a man.

toot¹ a carouse

Perhaps from the noise, but *toot* is one of those words with many slang meanings for taboos down the centuries, including the devil, lunacy, defecation, and farting:
> Her husband was off on a toot. (Chandler, 1953—he was on a drunken spree)

toot² to ingest illegal narcotics

This follows the common linguistic progression from alcoholic to narcotic excess:
> Word was, down here, they were even tooting up on the White House. (Anonymous, 1996)

And as a noun:
> He'd just had his morning toot, and he was feeling cool, alert, happy. (Gabriel, 1992)

top¹ *obsolete* to copulate with

Either a corruption of the standard English TUP, or from the position adopted by the male, or from his supposed dominance:
> Behold her top'd? (Shakespeare, *Othello*)

top² to kill

Illegally or legally, but not necessarily by beheading:
> Just who did top Ambassador Mobuto? It came as a great relief to all concerned to find he had topped himself. (*Private Eye*, March 1980)
> Those fellows you are topping in batches... (Flanagan, 1979, writing of a public hanging)

The obsolete *topping fellow* was a public hangman and a gruesome pun.

top and tail to clean up a baby

Nursery usage, with imagery from preparing gooseberries or root crops for cooking. The baby may have vomited as well as defecated.

top floor (the) senior management

Not necessarily sinister, as are the *boys upstairs*, under BOYS 2, but occupying the best offices, wielding the power, and best spoken of obliquely:
> My shout, now, Tug. There's jeopardy here, which I like. So will the Top Floor. (le Carré, 1996)

top-heavy drunk

Unable to stand up without swaying:
> We kept on drinking until stop-tap. At that time we were getting a little top-heavy. (F. Richards, 1933)

top shelf pornographic

The publications so described are displayed there in newsagents, supposedly out of the reach of children:

He publishes a number of top-shelf titles. (BBC News 24, 7 February 2001, reporting on the purchaser of Express Newspapers)

top up to conceal inferior goods below those of higher quality
Usually of fruit sold by weight, where only part of the purchase is visible:
      ... a few tempting strawberries
      being displayed on top of the pottle.
      'Topping up,' said a fruit dealer.
      (Mayhew, 1851)

topless exposing your breasts in public
Beach, bar, and entertainment usage:
      As one of the show-girls who had to strut
      around the stage topless...(S. Green, 1979)
Thus a *topless bar* is not one which is open to the skies, and it is no longer prudent to use the adjective of a bare-headed man.

torch to set light to as an arsonist
Matches are more commonly used to start the fire:
      Then you see how neatly it will be solved
      by torching your office. (Deighton, 1993/
      2—to destroy some incriminating files)

torch of Hymen (the) copulation only within marriage
Hymen, the god of marriage, was depicted carrying a torch:
      The torch of Hymen burns less brightly
      than of yore. (Mayhew, 1862—and has by
      now probably gone out)

toss¹ to search (another's property)
Usually without consent and throwing things carelessly into the air as you rummage through drawers etc.:
      'How did you know the apartment had
      been searched?'...'She...knew where
      everything was kept. She swears the place
      was tossed.' (Sanders, 1986)

toss² summarily to dismiss
As might a bull:
      He was tossed from college when he was
      nineteen for selling drugs. (Grisham, 1999)

toss down to drink (an intoxicant)
Not hay off a stack but down the throat from the movement of the glass:
      'We need to talk,' he said, 'and toss down a
      few before you go.' (Shirer, 1984)

toss in the hay an act of copulation
The normal hay and BED 2 association which is noted in IN THE HAY:
      He had a toss in the hay with his tootsie
      tonight. (Sanders, 1981)
Whence the common vulgarism *I don't give a toss*.

toss off (of a male) to masturbate
The imagery is obvious:
      I could have another whisky and toss
      myself off in the loo. (Theroux, 1973)
The figurative *tosser* is a term of male abuse:
      What would they know? Bunch of tossers.
      (C. Thomas, 1993)

tot a drink of sprits
Literally, anything small, whence a small drinking vessel or measure, which used to be from quarter to half a pint. Formerly, to *tot* was to drink intoxicants
      An' th' women folk...can tot
      That Dunville's Irish whiskey. (Doherty,
      1884)

totty *British* a prostitute
DSUE suggests it is a corruption of the name *Dorothy*, but it had the old meaning, of bad character:
      I tyell yu bestways 'ave nort tu du wi' she;
      er's nort but a totty twoad. (Hewett, 1892)

touch¹ (of a male) to copulate with
And not of the female, despite the mutuality of the transaction. Still some dialect use:
      ...you have touch'd his queen
      Forbiddenly...(Shakespeare, *The Winter's
      Tale*)
Grose has *touch up* in the same sense.

touch² an act of cadging
Normally described by the recipient as a loan, but do not expect repayment:
      A quick ten or twenty dollar *touch*, which of
      course was never intended to be returned.
      (Lavine, 1930)
In former use, to *touch* was to steal, usually from a pocket, except in a a *touch-crib*, or low brothel, where the loot was taken from the victim's clothing.

touch signature a fingerprint
Bankers' jargon, when they want positively to identify their customers without using the language of criminal investigation:
      The practice [of fingerprinting] is known by
      the euphemism 'touch signature', an
      approach which one banker described as
      'part of our back-up security system'. (*Daily
      Telegraph*, September 1980)

touch up¹ digitally to excite the genitals (of another)
Usually the male does it to the female:
      ... it would be ridiculous to keep you from
      your work just because you touched up
      some Jewess. (Keneally, 1982, writing of
      territory occupied by the Germans in the
      Second World War)

touch up² to dye (hair)

Barbers' jargon, implying a partial application where in fact the whole is treated.

touch yourself to masturbate yourself
Usually of a female:
> You want to know whether I have touched myself. Sure; all girls have. (F. Harris, 1925)

touched[1] *obsolete* drunk
A shortened form of *touched with liquor* and usually of mild drunkenness:
> In respect of her liquor-traffic, she was seen 'touched' about once a week. (Tweeddale, 1896)

touched[2] **(in the head)** of unsound mind
Not necessary by the sun:
> The doctor gave me a woeful account of his absurdity and is of the opinion he is touched. (Bathurst, 1999)
> ...an uncle who had a passion for concrete dwarves...who his mother said was a bit touched in the head. (Sharpe, 1974)

touchy-feely demonstrating insincere expressions of sympathy, generosity, or bonhomie
A politician or businessman so described does not need to make physical contact with those he seeks to impress:
> Any more of this touchy-feely stuff and I'll have to make my excuses. (*Sunday Telegraph*, 3 February 2001—a journalist was interviewing a tycoon)

tourist inferior
The jargon of air transport. Richer-sounding names are thought up for those who pay more, such as *club*, *sovereign*, *executive*, or *clipper*.

touristas (the) *American* diarrhoea
Suffered by many a tourist, or *turista* (including myself), on a Mexican vacation.

tout *Irish* a police informer
The derivation is from the tipster who covertly observes racehorses in training. Terrorist jargon:
> ...if there's a tout on the mountain and he's dead you won't find tears on me. (Seymour, 1992)

town bike a prostitute or promiscuous woman
So called because she is available for men to RIDE 1. Less often as *town pump*, the source, in the days before piped water, to which men went for refreshment.

toy boy a man consorting sexually with a much older woman

Not necessarily a gigolo, but often lavished with gifts:
> At 48 she is a teenage girl again—raving it up with four different lovers including a toyboy of 27. (*News of the World*, 15 November 1987)

tracks the scars left by repeated injections of illegal narcotics
Like railroad lines:
> Russell inconclusively scanned her arm for tracks. (McInerney, 1992)
Track-marks seems tautological:
> 'Needle marks,' he whispered. 'Those are track-marks, aren't they?' (Gabriel, 1992)

trade (the) prostitution
Or PROFESSION:
> Oh, there's no doubt they live by trading. (*EDD*, referring to prostitutes)
The *trade* can also refer to the customer:
> She doesn't like the trade, she packs it in and goes home. (Diehl, 1978)

traffic with yourself *obsolete* masturbation
Another form of TRADE:
> For having traffic with thyself alone,
> Thou of thyself thy sweet self doth deceive. (Shakespeare, *Sonnets*)

trail to release information without attribution
The train that follows behind:
> Mr Campbell's rules now require 'trailing' (the euphemism for leaking) to 'position' issues. (*Sunday Telegraph*, 9 July 2000— Campbell was the Prime Minister's forceful press secretary; *position* meant to place in a favourable context)

trainspotter a boring person
Derogatory use of those who have non-intellectual hobbies, such as watching railway operations:
> For years people have been going around doing the wally voice for anoraks and trainspotters. (*Guardian*, 7 October 1994— not many people, fortunately)

tramp a prostitute or promiscuous woman
Originally, from her walking the streets:
> When it's Tampax time, the lady is a tramp. (B. Forbes, 1989)

transfer the forcible deportation of a population
Those made to move do not go voluntarily to another place:
> Ze'evi, 62, is an advocate of transfer, the euphemism employed by the supporters for the removal from Israel and the

Occupied Territories of the Arab population. (*Daily Telegraph*, October 1988) The same euphemism was used for the forced movement of Jews by the Nazis and the Vichy French.

transfer pricing the excessive adjustment of prices between subsidiaries

A *transfer price* is the price charged by one subsidiary of a corporation to another subsidiary for goods and services. Where the subsidiaries operate in different countries, with differing tax rules and excise duties, the price structure may be influenced by other considerations than cost:

This could be achieved by the delicately contrived device of transfer pricing, by which companies with branches in Ireland understated the cost incurred by their Irish enterprises, which exaggerated their earnings. (J. J. Lee, 1989—the growth of the Irish economy was largely fuelled by the low rates of tax on corporate earnings and the consequent encouragement of investment)

transfusion an alcoholic drink

Ingested, not injected:

I was badly in need of a transfusion. I was certain a frozen daiquiri would bring roses back to the McNally cheeks. (Sanders, 1992)

translated *obsolete* drunk

Literally, transferred from one state or place to another, as from life to death or, in the jargon of the church, from one clerical living to another:

Bless thee, Bottom, bless thee! thou art translated. (Shakespeare, *A Midsummer Night's Dream*)

transported *obsolete British* sentenced to exile for a criminal offence

Not merely carried from one place to another:

One old offender, who stole the Duke of Beaufort's dog, was transported, not for selling the dog, but his collar. (Mayhew, 1851—under English Common Law there was no property in dogs or corpses)

trash *American* unsportingly to harass (an opponent)

Literally, garbage or rubbish:

They are fast and noisy and they 'trash' their opponents while playing. (*Sunday Telegraph*, 20 March 1994, writing about regular chess players in Washington Square Park, New York)

travel agent a dealer in illegal narcotics

He allows his customers to go on a TRIP:

Big John necked the embalming fluid and connected Cecil with pasta from the travel agent. (Fiennes, 1996—*Big John* is the police, *Cecil* is cocaine, and *pasta* is coca paste)

travel expenses bribes or money claimed dishonestly

Paid for trips which were not made, or for first class when you rode second:

Owen, a former miner, had been recruited during a 1957 visit to Czechoslovakia and had been supplied with his 'travel expenses'. Thereafter he received regular cash payments from the Czechs. (N. West, 1982—Owen, a British Member of Parliament, was named by the defector Forlik as being in the pay of the Communists. Nobody was more surprised than the accused when he was later acquitted of charges of spying)

traveller *Irish* a habitual itinerant

Often gypsies, although it is also a way of life for many families without Romany blood. Also as *travelling community* or *people*:

...there must have been fifty or sixty travellers crammed in the back of the close, malodorous cave. (O'Donoghue, 1988)

Up to 100 members of the travelling community were involved in the fracas. (*Daily Telegraph*, 25 June, 2001—six people were stabbed at a wedding reception)

News was passed on with the speed of Morse among the travelling people. (O'Donoghue, 1988)

See also NEW AGE TRAVELLERS.

tread to copulate

It is used of birds, from their foot movements:

The cock that treads them shall not know. (Shakespeare, *Sonnets to Sundry Notes of Music*)

treasonable activity losing a battle or retreating

What Russian generals were guilty of in the Second World War, however gallant or outgunned:

General Rychagov...was under sentence of death for 'treasonable activity' (that is to say having been defeated). (A. Clark, 1995)

treasure (of a female) a willingness to copulate

Figurative use by a rejected suitor:

I fall crazy in love...and she keeps her sweet treasure all locked up. (Styron, 1976)

treat to bribe

Literally, to pay for another's enjoyment of an outing etc. In the 19th century, it was specific of bribing voters:

...the emollience with which the established Radical election agent offers treating at the polls. (R. F. Foster, 1993—a limited franchise allowed for individual bribery, a practice economically less harmful perhaps than today's pre-electoral governmental profligacy)

treatment the use of violence to extract information
Far removed from the medication which cures sickness:
> I guess if this was a KGB operation, we should get Leggat out and give him the treatment. (Allbeury, 1977—Leggat's real name was Pyatokov, which was why they were prepared to be beastly to him)

tree rat a prostitute
The small mammal infests the bashas used by troops as billets in India:
> ...any man who availed himself of the 'tree rats' or 'grass bidis' was properly dealt with. (C. Allen, 1975—a *grass bidi* was also a prostitute)

triangular where two people wish to enjoy an exclusive sexual relationship with a third
The *eternal triangle*, as different from a MÉNAGE À TROIS:
> ...not only was much left intentionally unsolved on the political scene, but also much in the triangular situation at Eltham. (Kee, 1993—reporting a conversation between Parnell and Mrs O'Shea)

triangular trade (the) trading in slaves
On the first leg, manufactured goods went from England to Africa; on the second leg, slaves went from Africa to America; on the third leg, commodities went from America to Europe. It was also known as the *African Trade*.

tribute a regular payment to an extortionist
This use calls to mind the Latin linguistic progression, from the payments by *tribes* to the Romans to leave them in peace, *tributum*, through to taxes, then to presents, and so to acknowledging virtues in another.
> I had problems in Spain when ETA demanded 'tribute' for operating in 'their territory'. (*Sunday Telegraph*, 31 January 1999—ETA is the Basque terrorist separatist movement)

trick *American* a prostitute's customer
From the limited turn of duty rather than any deception:
> Lots of women walking the streets for tricks to take to their 'pads'. (L. Armstrong, 1955)

Whence to *trick*, as a prostitute to copulate with a customer:
> And I never tricked him. He never asked for it. (Wambaugh, 1981)
See also the punning CALL THE TRICKS.

trim (your wick) (of a male) to copulate
Cutting into shape and what used to be done to candles:
> 'You're just getting old. Lucky to be able to—'Ah, shut up. I got my wick trimmed all right'. (Lyall, 1975)

trip a condition induced by the ingestion of illegal hallucinogens
What your TRAVEL AGENT may arrange for you:
> The kind of thing that hippies switch into when the trips turn sour. (Bradbury, 1975)
To *trip* is to hallucinate as a result of taking a drug:
> They were speeding and tripping at the same time. (Deighton, 1972)

triple a sexual act involving three people
Usually, of one man with two women:
> Oh, and they don't do triples. As a rule. These are respectable girls. (R. Harris, 1998—but not that respectable, it would seem)

triple entry fraudulent
It refers to book-keeping; and see DOUBLE ENTRY:
> ...carried with him, like bad breath, the reek of the back-streets—of furtive deals and triple-entry accountancy. (R. Harris, 1992)
In France, it means having separate sets of accounts for your wife, your mistress, and the taxman.

troll to seek a casual sexual partner
From a car or on foot, homosexual or heterosexual, paid or free. The imagery is from dangling a lure in the water while fishing:
> Cars were cruising the early morning street, trolling. (McBain, 1994)

trollop a prostitute
Originally, an untidy or slatternly woman and to *trollop* was to work in a slovenly manner. The euphemism dates from the 18th century:
> That impudent trollop, who is with child by you. (Henry Fielding, 1742)

trophy wife a younger spouse chosen because her appearance indicates her husband's enhanced status
Or what he conceives his enhanced status to be. Also as *trophy* or *trophy model*:
> By now Alex had metamorphosed into the country-dwelling driver of a studiedly-

mudded Range Rover, with trophy wife, son and gundog. (*Daily Telegraph*, 31 August 1998)

... the grieving, abandoned yet dutiful first wife who got traded in for a trophy. (Grisham, 1998):

More often than not the tycoon dumps the first wife for a trophy model. (*Sunday Telegraph*, 21 March 1999)

trot *obsolete* a prostitute

The common equine imagery, whence the punning:

Marry him to ... an old trot ... though she have as many diseases as two and fifty horses. (Shakespeare, *The Taming of the Shrew*)

trots (the) diarrhoea

The need is too immediate for walking:

I'd already got the trots. They're supposed to cement you up. (P. Scott, 1975, describing pills)

A sufferer is said to be *on the trot*.

trouble any unpleasant or unwanted experience

Euphemistic when the subject is taboo, such as unplanned pregnancy, childbirth, menstruation, piles, varicose veins, and the like:

She got into trouble. Through an old white fellow who used to have those coloured girls up to an old ramshackle house of his. I do not have to tell you what he was up to. (L. Armstrong, 1955—she was pregnant)

When I'm over my trouble I'll come to see you. (M. Francis, 1901, referring to childbirth)

I was confident that it was nae rheumatics, though what his trouble was I couldna just say. (Service, 1890)

trouble with his flies (of a male) sexually licentious

Not finding the salmon hard to catch:

Always had trouble with his flies, that man. (*Sunday Telegraph*, 7 May 1995—Denis Thatcher was talking about Cecil Parkinson)

troubles (the) *Irish* fighting or violence against the British or between rival communities

The differences between those participating are frequently more tribal than religious:

The 'troubles'—that quaint ... word for murder and mayhem. (Theroux, 1983)

troubles in this world are over (his) he is dead

But not anticipating what is to follow:

I have the certainty in my own mind that her troubles in this world are over. (W. Collins, 1860)

trouser to accept an improper payment

The garment which holds the pocket into which the bribe or other receipt is actually or figuratively deposited:

I am having a fairly fizzing time ... but have already trousered £20 in solid hard paper. (French, 1995)

Livingstone summed up the national mood yesterday when he asked why the Labour Party had trousered £1 million from the head of Formula One. (*Daily Telegraph*, 13 November 1997—the payer's desire to avoid a ban on tobacco advertising on racing cars was subsequently gratified, albeit fortuitously, if ministers were to be believed)

trouser test the forced inspection of a prepuce to determine religion

A feature of the horrendous events which followed the partition of India in 1947:

Muslims in Mumbai were given the 'trouser test' by mobs of Sena activists, a euphemism which refers to the ripping off of a man's trousers in search of a foreskin. If he lacks one, he is drenched in kerosene and lit. (French, 1997—*Mumbai* was then called, as it still is by many, Bombay)

truant with your bed *obsolete* to copulate extramaritally

A *truant* was a professional beggar, whence an absconder, and so a child absenting himself from school:

The double wrong to truant with your bed, And let her read it in thy looks at board. (Shakespeare, *The Comedy of Errors*)

true not copulating with other than your regular sexual partner

The opposite of FALSE and UNTRUE.

trull *obsolete* a prostitute

A corruption of TROLLOP:

Am sure I scared the Dauphin and his trull, When arm in arm they both came swiftly running. (Shakespeare, *I Henry VI*)

trunk *American* falsely to conceal

Referring to the hiding of evidence etc. and the place where it might be hidden:

And so you gave her that file to trunk. (Turow, 1987)

trustee *American* a placid prisoner

Not to be confused with those charged with looking after an estate for a third party. In Britain spelt *trusty*. He is *trusted* by the warders not to step out of line:

Two trustees in blue prison pants with white stripes down the legs swept the front steps. (Grisham, 1994)

truth-shader *American* a liar
To *shade* is to discolour or darken slightly:
> The second Republican choice,
> businessman John Laklan, has shown
> himself to be a truth-shader impressive
> even by the generous standards of
> Massachusetts. (*Sunday Telegraph*,
> 14 August 1994)

trying to escape see SHOT WHILE TRYING TO
ESCAPE

tub of grease *American* a place or situation where corruption is endemic
GREASE 1 and bribery have been long associated:
> In times past, the Park District was a
> notorious tub of grease, with patronage
> jobs and no-bid contracts, the haven for no-
> nose politicians. (Turow, 1996)

tube *American* sodomy
In prison jargon *had* or *laid*, with obvious imagery:
> ...about eight of them's going to lay more
> tube than the motherfucking Alaska
> pipeline...(Weverka, 1973, writing about
> the ordeal facing a prisoner)

tube of meat the penis
See also MEAT 2:
> All because of that lousy tube of meat. I
> want to hump every woman I see. (Sanders,
> 1982)

tuck the cosmetic removal of surplus fat or flesh by surgery
The imagery is from adjusting clothing, whence also to *tuck*, to perform such a procedure:
> And the people who live here have all got
> tucks in their faces, porcelain teeth, plastic
> hair, and ten-thousand dollar wristwatches.
> (Deighton, 1993/2)
> ...their women with chiselled faces they
> never had when they were young, and
> tucked stomachs and tucked bottoms, and
> artificial brightness in their unpouched
> eyes. (le Carré, 1993)

tuck away/under to kill or inter
Describing natural or unnatural death, with imagery from bedtime:
> He was going to be quietly tucked away in
> earth at the frontier station after dark.
> (G. Greene, 1932)
> After me poor old man was tucked under
> the daisies...(MacDonagh, 1898)

tuft-hunter a sycophant
From seeking the company of wealthier Oxford undergraduates sporting gold tassels on their mortar-boards rather than black:
> An unabashed tuft-hunter, he faithfully
> followed the Jesuit tradition established in
> England of concentrating on the upper
> echelons of society. (S. Hastings, 1994)

tumble¹ to copulate with
Of either sex, from the alacrity of the move into the prone position:
> Quoth she, before you tumbled me,
> You promised me to wed. (Shakespeare,
> *Hamlet*)

Modern use can be intransitive, or, as a noun, of a single act:
> I'm not a regular girl and you expect me to
> tumble. (Weverka, 1973)
> A discreet visit in a rickshaw for a tumble
> at Dunromin. (Theroux, 1973)

tumble² (down the sink) a drink of an intoxicant
From the rhyming slang, and occasionally used in full:
> Afterwards, Dickie Leeman...surmised
> that I'd had 'a tumble down the sink' at
> lunchtime. I never drink before 6 p.m.
> (Monkhouse, 1993)

tumescent having an erection of the penis
Literally, swelling, of anything:
> I don't in the least mind letting girls see
> my penis. I suppose it's because I
> fear...becoming lightly, or indeed
> heavily, tumescent and attracting the
> attention of other men. (A. Clark, 1993,
> explaining why he was reluctant that
> men also should be so favoured)

tumour (a) cancer
Originally, any swelling, as with Dryden's *tender tumour*, or erect penis.

tup to copulate with
Dr Johnson coyly says 'To but like a ram'. The use in connection with ovine behaviour remains standard English, being euphemistic only when applied to humans:
> ...but then he cruelly upped and tupped a
> PR girl leaving Patricia simply squelching
> in misery. (Fry, 1994)

turkey farmer *American* an unsuccessful businessman
A *turkey* is an enterprise which turns out badly, especially if it is a film or play:
> ...at least I'm not a turkey farmer. My last
> three films made money. (B. Forbes, 1983)

turkey shoot *American* a business easily concluded
Based on the size and relative immobility of the bird, which originated in the Americas, and not the Levant. Used of making money

easily, killing a victim without a problem, etc.:

> ...a chance for a real turkey shoot just turned up. (M. Thomas, 1982—a wealthy customer had appeared)
> Already there was mounting criticism in the Press that the battle had turned into a turkey shoot. (de la Billière, 1992, writing about the Gulf War)

Turkish ally an unreliable supporter
From their supposed cowardice and treachery, although etymologically the Greeks fare little better:

> ...the rock was a Turkish ally, ready to change sides if the going got rough. (Trevanian, 1972)

Turkish medal *obsolete British* an inadvertently exposed trouser fly-button
A warning in the pre-zip days from one male to another, from the casual way in which some Turks wear Western-style dress:

> Their flybuttons were undone, and now I could understand why these buttons were called 'Turkish medals' by British soldiers in the First World War. (Theroux, 1975)

turn¹ an act of copulation
The imagery is from the stage:

> To obtain lodgings she fell prey to a Jamaican pimp whose girls worked Wilberforce Road in Finsbury Park at £5 a turn. (Fiennes, 1996)

turn² (round/around) to subvert from allegiance
Espionage jargon:

> The case might be a textbook Soviet attempt to 'turn' an American military officer. (*Daily Telegraph*, February 1981)
> 'Why does a feller earning a handsome salary in the American State Department decide to chuck it all in and join a bomb factory?' 'I got turned around.' (Theroux, 1976)

turn³ a sudden illness
Anything from dizziness to a cerebral haemorrhage. Perhaps a shortened form of a *turn for the worse*.

turn⁴ *American* (of a residential district) to have inhabitants of different colours or religions
Where the residents were once predominantly white Christians.

turn away to dismiss summarily from employment
Not refusing a job to those who apply:

> She said that as soon as it was known what sort of trouble she was in, she would be

turned away. (Atwood, 1996—a housemaid was pregnant)

turn in to betray to authority
Literally, to hand over to another, as a piece of work to a tutor:

> ...fearing the other might reveal something or even connive to turn in the other. (Sanders, 1980)

turn off¹ to kill
Usually judicially by hanging, with imagery from a lamp rather than the *turning tree*, the gallows on which a corpse rotated:

> ...it gives a man a wonderful appetite for his breakfast to assist in turning off a dozen or more rebels. (F. Richards, 1936)

turn off² not to excite sexually
As we might expect, the converse of TURN ON.

turn off³ *obsolete* to dismiss from employment or courtship
The imagery of the faucet:

> He can turn a poor gal off, as soon as he tires of her. (Mayhew, 1851)

turn on to excite
Sexually, with illicit narcotics, or by whatever you fancy most:

> He left bruises! I suppose he thought he was—what's the expression—turning me on. (Theroux, 1977)
> 'Hey, want to turn on with me? Here, I'll make you one.' He fumbled with his cigarette papers and took one out of his stash. (Theroux, 1976)

turn to to have sexual relations with
Relying on, as much as moving towards, another. To *turn to yourself* is to masturbate:

> In the last hour of the day... Sonny turns to him, as formerly she turned to herself. (Turow, 1996)

turn up *American* to betray to authority
A variant of TURN IN:

> He would be set free if he 'turned up the gang'. (Lavine, 1930)

turn up your little finger to be a habitual drunkard
From the way of holding a glass, although many hold a teacup in the same fashion. Also in Scotland as *turn up pinkie*:

> Ye maun keep unco sober, an no be turnin' up your wee finger sae aften. (Ballantine, 1869)
> So very fond was Tam of 'turnin' up his pinkie' that he latterly lost both his credit and his character. (A. Murdoch, 1895)

turn up your tail *obsolete* to defecate or (of a woman) to urinate
Al fresco:
> ... it being very pleasant to see how everyone turns up his tail, here one and there another, in a bush, and the women in their Quarters the like. (Pepys, 1663—the lavatory facilities at Epsom for race-goers were clearly insufficient for those moved by the spectacle and the famous salts)

turn up your toes to die
Most people die in bed and are buried on their backs:
> I'll turn merrier toes to th' sky nor thee, lad, when it comes to deeing. (Sutcliffe, 1899)

turn your coat dishonourably to desert a cause
A survival from the days when livery facilitated recognition and personal allegiance, on and off the battlefield:
> Perhaps wisely they turned coat and told us where he was. (C. Allen, 1975—Ali Dinar's spies betrayed him)

turn your face to the wall to die
Not from the reversal of a picture of a disgraced person but from the privacy sought by the dying:
> Sahib turns his face to the wall and all is up with him. (P. Scott, 1977)

twelve annas to the rupee of mixed Indian and white ancestry
British Indian derogatory use of those of mixed race, especially if they pretended to be white. There were sixteen annas to the rupee:
> I took the conventional attitude ... of making jokes about 'blackie-whitie' and 'twelve annas to the rupee'. (C. Allen, 1975)
See also NOT SIXTEEN ANNAS TO THE RUPEE.

twenty-four-hour service we have a telephone recording device
A misleading advertisement, and not much help when you have a burst pipe in the early hours.

twilight home an institution for the geriatric
Not a summer house facing the west but from the cliché *twilight of your life*:
> ... arranged for her mother to be packed off to a comfortable and expensive 'twilight home'. (I. Murdoch, 1978)

twin-tracking *British* sinecures reciprocally given to each other by sympathetic politicians in neighbouring administrations
Thus the councillors of one district are paid, albeit absent, employees of another, to the councillors of which they provide similar situations, leaving both of them able to devote their energies to retaining office without the distraction of having to earn a living:
> ... the bill will seek to limit the politicisation of local authorities ... ending so-called 'twin-tracking', where councillors are offered well-paid posts in sympathetic neighbouring councils. This has been used by left-wingers to build up a power base. (*Daily Telegraph*, June 1989—an example was the notorious arrangement between the politicians in Leeds and Wakefield)

twisted *obsolete* killed by hanging
Referring to the rotation of the corpse on the gibbet:
> You'll be the first Christian twisted in this awful place. (Keneally, 1987, writing of Australia)

two-backed beast see BEAST WITH TWO BACKS

two-by-four *British* a prostitute
Rhyming slang for whore, punning on the rag used as a pull-through to clean the barrel of a .303 rifle, although soldiers in the Second World War called it *four-by-two*.

two-fingered involving a vulgar gesture
The Latins use a single digit:
> I must find something else first before I give the Captain the two-fingered farewell. (B. Forbes, 1989—he was seeking other employment)

two-on-one two people sexually using a third
Two prostitutes with a single man, or three male homosexuals:
> If you'd be interested in a two-on-one ... (McBain, 1981—two prostitutes were propositioning a man)
> Enjoyed more damn two-on-ones with Jimmy up there in Castleviews ... (ibid.—they were convicts)

two-time contemporaneously to have a sexual relationship with two people
Literally, in slang, to CHEAT:
> Lonsdale ... who is the latest escort of the gracious Princess Margaret, is reputed to be still two-timing with his old flame. (*Private Eye*, December 1981)

Tyburn *obsolete* appertaining to death by hanging
The London gallows were located in the parish named after two *burns*, or streams, but now called St Marylebone. The *Tyburn dance*, *hornpipe*, or *jig* was a hanging, by the

Tyburn tippet, the noose, on the *Tyburn tree* or *triple tree*, the gallows. The *King of Tyburn*, the hangman, used to conduct a *Tyburn scragging*, a ceremony, at which he would hang a *Tyburn blossom*, a young convict, who would be said to *preach at Tyburn Cross*. A *Tyburn ticket* was a certificate of exemption from payment of all taxes in the parish in which a felony had been committed (or other reward) given to an informer who secured a conviction and hanging. A *Tyburn top* was a wig worn 'in a knowing style...by the gentlemen pads, scamps, divers, and other knowing hands' (Grose), all of whom might expect to be sentenced to death in the fullness of time:

> He should have had a Tyburn tippet, a half-penny halter, and all such proud prelates. (Latimer in sermon, 1549, quoted in *ODEP*)
> That souldiers sterne, or prech at Tiborne crosse. (Gascoigne, 1576, quoted in *ODEP*)
> The old Nag and Brewer was crowded like a Tyburn scragging. (Fraser, 1997)

U-turn a fundamental change of policy
Political use, usually where a previous policy
has failed:
> Powell, in a speech to the Oxford Union,
> dismissed [Heath] as 'the old virtuoso of
> the U-turn'. (Heffer, 1998—as Prime
> Minister, Heath abandoned the
> monetarist policies on which he
> had been elected)

Uganda a promiscuous sexual relationship
A long-running *Private Eye* in-joke based on
an alleged incident in which an African
princess, found in compromising circumstances, said that she had been discussing
Ugandan affairs with the man involved. It is
used of heterosexual or homosexual behaviour:
> One second-year student called 'Elsie'
> offers to discuss Uganda with anyone
> as an act of Christian love.
> (*Private Eye*, May 1981—Elsie was
> a male candidate for ordination as a
> priest)

ultimate (the) copulation
The final act of courtship and specifically as
the *ultimate connection*:
> Much seems to have happened during the
> four weeks at sea—though not, perhaps,
> the ultimate. (Winchester, 1998)
> The ultimate connection took place ... I
> must have been something more than a
> man to have held out any longer. (William
> Dalrymple, in *Sunday Telegraph*, 20 February
> 2000)

ultimate intentions the killing of all Jews
The FINAL SOLUTION:
> How did you know this? About ultimate
> intentions? (Keneally, 1982—the question
> was asked of a Polish Jew in the Second
> World War)

un-American *American* differing from an
accepted or assumed standard
Originally, in 1844, used to deride the Know
Nothing movement. Subsequent political use
of any opponent with whose philosophy you
disagree, especially by Senator Joseph
McCarthy:
> They'd be branded for ever as
> un-American. (N. Mitford, 1960, writing
> about those who resisted McCarthy's
> attacks)

unassigned *American* dismissed from employment
Not awaiting another *assignment* in the same
organization:
> ... despite the fact that your company is
> doing rather well, you have just been
> sacked or ... 'unassigned'. (*Sunday Telegraph*,
> 27 October 1996)

unavailable[1] unwilling to accept a call
Social and business jargon, whether the call is
by telephone or in person.

unavailable[2] evading arrest
Police and underworld jargon:
> Ray Tuck is 'unavailable' at the moment.
> And we've got a three-line whip out on
> him. (Price, 1982)

unbalanced of unsound mind
Not just dizziness:
> We have to accept the position that Ed was
> unbalanced. (Condon, 1966)

unbiblical sex *American* incest
It is certainly frowned on in the Scriptures,
although the Tables of Consanguinity, which
allow first cousins to marry but bar in-laws,
might have benefited from the advice of a
geneticist:
> Loony hillbillies destabilized by gross
> quantities of impure corn liquor and
> generations of profoundly unbiblical sex.
> (Bryson. 1997)

unbundling asset stripping
The word chosen by those who successfully
attacked the British conglomerate British-
American Tobacco Company:
> This would be a highly-geared company.
> Our purpose is unbundling, and the
> proceeds would be used immediately to
> repay debt. (*Daily Telegraph*, July 1989,
> quoting James Goldsmith)

uncertain economically depressed
The future is always *uncertain*. This is the
jargon of economists who fear that to talk of
recession will bring it about:
> ... the economic situation in the
> UK remains uncertain. (M. Thomas,
> 1980)

uncertain sexual preferences homosexual tendencies
The phrase is only used when there is a high
degree of certainty. Also as *uncertain proclivities*:
> Boys with uncertain sexual preferences,
> only happy in male company ... (Deighton,
> 1990)
> His initial discomfort at finding himself in
> a strange place in the presence of a pretty

young woman, an antiquarian of uncertain
proclivities and a painting of equivocal
appearance...(Pérez-Réverté, 1994, in
translation)

uncle a pawnbroker
Punning on the Latin *uncus*, the hook on his
scale, and the supposed benevolence of your
relative. This does not explain why the French
called him an aunt.

Uncle Tom a black person who defers
unduly to whites
From the character in *Uncle Tom's Cabin, or, Life
among the Lowly*, published in 1851:
> ...kissed the right asses, moved on up
> there. Fuckin' Uncle Tom shit. (Diehl,
> 1978)

See also TOM 2.

uncontaminated free from sexual activity
Literally, not subjected to impurity or pollution:
> Every mother must be yearning that her
> own son should keep himself
> uncontaminated. (French, 1995)

uncover nakedness *obsolete* to copulate
An evasion favoured by the translators of the
Authorized Version of the Bible:
> Frequently the words used to cover the sex
> act are 'uncover nakedness' (another
> example of the literal translation of a
> Hebrew metaphor). (Peter Mullen in
> Enright, 1985—and see his essay 'The
> Religious Speak-Easy' for further
> enlightenment and linguistic delight)

under-invoicing a fraudulent device to
avoid import duties
The practice is found where the importing
country imposes high tariffs and the buyer
has access to external funds. The documentation shows a lower price than that agreed
between the parties, on which duty is levied,
the balance being paid free of duty offshore.
See also OVER-INVOICING.

under the counter illegal
The physical reality with many scarce goods
in war-torn countries:
> This gave him access to what extras were
> being kept under the counter. (Teisser du
> Croix, 1962, writing of Paris in the Second
> World War)

Now used figuratively of transactions involving stolen goods, wages paid without deduction of tax, etc.:
> ...called for an end of 'shamateurism', the
> nudge-nudge, wink-wink under-the-
> counter payments and perks to leading
> players. (*Daily Telegraph*, 5 February 1994)

under the daisies dead
And buried. Also as *under the sod, under the
grass, underground*, or *undersod*:
> If he dhraws thim mountainy men down
> on me, I may as well go under the sod.
> (Somerville and Ross, 1908)
> You can live there when I'm underground,
> which will be any day now. (I. Murdoch,
> 1983)
> Small wonder then that th' ghosties
> stir up an' dahn, time an' time, when
> them as lig undersod fall to thinkin' o'
> th' unquiet things that hev happened
> just aboon their heads. (Sutcliffe, 1900)

under the influence drunk
Shortened form of the legal jargon *under the
influence of drink or drugs. Half under* is no less
drunk.

under the table[1] very drunk
You are supposed to end up there after
dropping senseless from your chair. Now used
figuratively:
> I'll drink you under the table, Max. Be
> warned. (Deighton, 1981—he was
> suggesting that Max would become drunk
> first)

See also GET YOUR FEET UNDER THE TABLE.

under the table[2] illegal or surreptitious
From the actual or figurative concealed
passing of money. It is used of bribery,
wages paid in cash without deduction of tax,
etc.

under the weather unwell
Standard English, despite it being the condition of all other than mountaineers, aviators,
and astronauts. The phrase is also used of
those recovering from drunkenness or of
women menstruating.

under water showing a loss or worthless
And drowning:
> All of his 287,884 share options are under
> water after three profit warnings in the
> past two years. (*Daily Telegraph*, 24 July
> 1999)
> He said that many of the directors' existing
> options were 'underwater'. (*Daily Telegraph*,
> 12 May 2000)

underachiever an idle or stupid child
Literally, a child capable of doing better,
especially in examinations, but failing
through nervousness or ill-health. As educational jargon, it seeks to excuse wilfulness
under a cloak of misfortune:
> ...'we do have a special course for the
> Over-active Underachiever,' continued the
> Headmaster. (Sharpe, 1982)

underdeveloped poor
The inference is that a greater degree of *development* was or is attainable and desirable. It may describe sovereign states or regions:
> The use of underdeveloped is a clue to a state of mind, that of the international do-gooders. (Pei, 1969)
> All big cities have these little underdeveloped areas in them. (Theroux, 1982)

underground railroad *obsolete American* the protection of escaped slaves organized by philanthropists in the North
An antebellum phenomenon:
> The escape route for runaway slaves was known as the 'underground railway' because it was so reliable. (Faith, 1990—in using the word 'reliable' in this context, he showed unfamiliarity with the network run by London Transport, which is also obsolete)

underprivileged poor or illiterate
Literally, lacking honourable distinction, so that it embraces us all, unless we are royalty, Nobel prize-winners, or have been decorated for gallantry:
> One righted the balance by being more than fair to the underprivileged. (Bradbury, 1959)

undiscovered country (the) death
The
> Undiscover'd country, from whose bourn
> No traveller returns. (Shakespeare, *Hamlet*)
and in later use:
> I shall have entered the great 'Perhaps', as Danton I think called 'the undiscovered country'. (F. Harris, 1925)

undo *obsolete* to copulate with (a female) outside marriage
From the loss of reputation rather than the removal of clothing:
> Thou hast undone our mother.
> (Shakespeare, *Titus Andronicus*)

undocumented *American* illegal
Especially referring to Hispanic migrants into the United States working without Green Cards or other permits.

unearned income the proceeds of crime
Not, as formerly and misleadingly in Britain, the income from savings and investments, the cost of which had previously been *earned* by the recipient and taxed, nor the money paid by the state to those who do not work:
> Things were beginning to get out of hand with the May, 1986 decision to step up the battle with 'unearned income'. These measures were supposed to be aimed at thieves, grafters, and extortionists, but in fact they more often affected those individual workers...who were trying to make a little money. (Gorbachev, 1995, in translation)

uneven bad
A code message in financial statements, of which the cypher was broken long ago:
> Shares in Coates Viyella...yesterday slipped 4 to 163p as chairman Sir James Spooner told the annual meeting that trading conditions were uneven. (*Daily Telegraph*, June 1989)

unfaithful having had a sexual relationship with other than your regular sexual partner
Of either sex, within marriage or of other heterosexual and homosexual arrangements:
> 'She's been unfaithful to me.'...'He thinks it's a violation of our marriage because it was someone he didn't like.' (Bradbury, 1965)
> ...the [male] person he loved was being unfaithful to him in Paris. (N. Mitford, 1949)

unfortified not having drunk alcohol
Describing those whose courage is less when sober:
> One of them had already been unwise enough to drink too much before turning up to our beginning of term party, giving the impression that he could not face the usurper unfortified. (Rae, 1993)

unfortunate *obsolete* engaged in prostitution
A common 18th- and 19th-century use, especially by women who earned their living in other ways, or not at all:
> ...those unfortunate young women, who...were the juster objects of compassion. (Cleland, 1749)

unglued *American* mentally ill
Your mind had become unstuck:
> She was completely unglued. You know, I tried to reassure her. (Turow, 1990)

unhealthy homosexual
Not because of an increased risk of contracting AIDS:
> Hattie heard one of the mistresses, talking about her and Pearl, say, 'It's an unhealthy relationship'. (I. Murdoch, 1983)

unheard presence someone dismissed from employment
Television and radio jargon of a character WRITTEN OUT OF THE SCRIPT:
> The failure of his relationship to Lizzie Archer was the fate of Nigel Pargeter, who

will become an 'unheard presence'—radio terminology for sacked. (*Daily Telegraph*, February 1990)

unhinged mad

The common *gate* imagery:

> Gordon Masters is quite unhinged—has taken to coming into the Department wearing his old territorial Army uniform. (Lodge, 1975)

union[1] copulation

Venerable use, making two into one, or three:

> The union of your bed...(Shakespeare, *The Tempest*)

union[2] *obsolete British* an institution for the homeless poor

Shortened form of *union house*, set up by a Poor Law Union (of parishes) which had an obligation to provide food and shelter to the indigent:

> We used to...tramp from one union to another. (Mayhew, 1862)

uniquely *American* (in compound adjectives) suffering from a defect

As though nobody else had the same disability. Thus the *uniquely abled* are crippled, the *uniquely co-ordinated* are clumsy, the *uniquely proficient* are incompetent, etc.

united dead

You have joined, or rejoined, your Maker, or a spouse who has predeceased you. Monumental usage.

university a political prison

Where Napoleon III developed his economic theory, alongside a romantic attachment, and, on Robben Island, where Nelson Mandela studied:

> At the height of his career as Emperor, he was fond of saying...'I took my honours at the University of Ham.' (Corley, 1961)

unknown to men a virgin

And, less often, a man might be *unknown to woman*:

> I am yet
> Unknown to woman. (Shakespeare, *Macbeth*)

unlawful *obsolete* (of children) illegitimate

A matter of great concern to our ancestors, especially where primogeniture was concerned. In various phrases:

> ...in his unlawful bed, he got
> This Edward. (Shakespeare, *Richard III*)
> ...the unlawful issue that their lust
> Since then has made between them.

(Shakespeare, *Antony and Cleopatra*)

> I had rather my brother die by the law than that my son should be unlawfully born. (Shakespeare, *(Measure for Measure)*)
> May be the amorous count solicits her in the unlawful purpose. (Shakespeare, *All's Well That Ends Well*)

unlimber your joint (of a male) to urinate

See JOINT 2:

> ...graffiti...where males unlimbered their joints. (Styron, 1976)

unmarried homosexual

Most bachelors are not homosexual, and, as ever, the euphemistic use depends on the context:

> Neighbours of unmarried Mr Hamilton contacted police six months ago...a male model and a tenant at Mr Hamilton's house...is acting as Mr Hamilton's agent. (*Sunday Telegraph*, December 1986)

The phrase *He was unmarried* at the end of an obituary sometimes indicates that the subject was homosexual.

unmentionable crime (the) buggery or sodomy

Once one of the great taboos:

> The practice of bedding the men by threes and not in pairs was supposed, optimistically, to reduce unmentionable crime. (R. Hughes, 1987, describing the treatment of convicts)

unmentionable disease a venereal disease

Still the subject of taboo:

> ...adding an unmentionable disease to the old lady's dossier of Wilt's faults. (Sharpe, 1979)

unmentionables[1] *obsolete* trousers or undergarments

19th-century prudery forbade the mention of anything to do with legs:

> She had vowed never to change her unmentionables until her husband, Archduke Albert, took the city of Ostend by siege. (Jennings, 1965—as it held out for three years, she must have kept her vow at the expense of her friends and her marriage)

Also as *unexpressibles*, *unspeakables*, *unwhisperables*, *ineffables*, *indescribables*, and *inexpressibles*:

> They wear all manner of pantaloons and inexpressibles. (H. James, 1816)

unmentionables[2] haemorrhoids

A female evasion. Men seem to suffer from FARMER GILES.

unnatural (of sexual behaviour) not conventionally heterosexual
Legal jargon of bestiality and formerly of sodomy, as in *unnatural act, crime, practice, vice,* etc.:
> ...the severe penalties imposed on unnatural practices in our own country by an Act of 1886 have merely had the effect of advertising them. (F. Richards, 1936)
> ...seeing a Turk severely whipped and his beard singed for attempting unnatural vice. (Ollard, 1974—we may ask what a Turk was doing in St Helena in 1683, apart from his sexual exploit)
> ...trying to sort out which portion of anatomy fitted the next...in what... appeared to be a series of extremely unnatural acts. (Sharpe, 1975)

unofficial action a strike in breach of an agreement
The *action* is inaction, especially where the strike, if officially sanctioned by a trade union, might involve legal penalties:
> Was it another day of 'unofficial action?' Had an epidemic of sunstroke decimated the staff of London Transport? (Blacker, 1992—the trains were not running)

unofficial relations corrupt practices
Not your illegitimate offspring but the way business was conducted in Communist Russia:
> Economic ties were entangled in a dense network of 'unofficial relations' (extortions and gifts, bribery, exaggeration of results, embezzlement). (Gorbachev, 1995, in translation)

unplugged mentally ill
The supply of electricity for the light has been removed:
> All these unplugged folks and me, with a busted solar heater. (Anonymous, 1996—describing being a patient in a mental institution)

unprotected sex copulation without using a condom
The phrase could equally apply to batting against a hard ball without using a box. Also as *unsafe sex*:
> Except that he's into unsafe sex, according to another mistress...(*Sunday Telegraph*, 15 July 2001—he was the aptly titled *Congressman* Condit)

unscheduled caused by accident or necessity
Airline jargon, which seeks to avoid any implication of loss of reliability or safety:

> Engineers have a nice phrase for engine breakdowns. An 'unscheduled engine removal'. (Moynahan, 1983)

unscrewed mad
What happens after you have a SCREW LOOSE:
> ...this is pure banana oil! You've come unscrewed. (Wodehouse, 1934)

unsighted blind
Literally, prevented from seeing by an intervening obstruction.

unslated *obsolete* of unsound mind
The outcome if you have a SLATE-OFF:
> He's gone clean off his head, unslated. (Brierley, 1886)

unsociable (be) to perform a taboo act
Such as vomiting at the table through excess, or urinating elsewhere than is acceptable by convention:
> ...biting the property company chairman on the ear, or being unsociable on the carpet. (F. Muir, 1997—the biting was threatened by a dog, not a disaffected shareholder)

unsound not to be trusted
More from a faulty ship than from the legal jargon for mental illness, *of unsound mind.* Among bureaucrats, of judgement rather than honesty. Among autocrats, *unsoundness* indicates unwelcome independence of thought or action:
> '...Tyler was unsound.' 'And you can't say worse than that in Whitehall.' (Lyall, 1980)
> German troops were reassigned to Italy where...their former confederates...had long demonstrated their 'unsoundness' in dealing with the Jews. (Burleigh, 2000)

unstaunched *obsolete* (of a woman) virgin
A *staunch* is something which stops the flow of blood. I think the imagery is from the cessation of menstruation during pregnancy, although it might apply to the absence of a protective towel. No doubt his audience knew:
> As leaky as an unstaunch'd wench. (Shakespeare, *The Tempest*)

untrimmed *obsolete* (of a woman) virgin
The imagery is from a wick rather than from the meaning, to put in order:
> In likeness of a new untrimmed bride. (Shakespeare, *King John*)

untrue having copulated outside marriage
The reverse of TRUE, and also applicable to those who have eschewed the trip up the aisle:

The thought that you might have been
untrue...would have broken my heart.
(Fraser, 1975)

unwaged involuntarily unemployed
Not the war which was averted but the pay
which is not earned:
Claire is trying to get her father to give
cheap food to the unwaged. (Townsend,
1982)

unwell[1] menstruating
Being ILL 1:
...all's well that ends unwell. (F. Harris,
1925—he feared he had impregnated a
woman)

unwell[2] drunk
Covering up the taboo condition with one of
its symptoms:
'Our Mr Fellowes had been 'very unwell' at
the time of the move.' 'He wasn't unwell,'
said my sister. 'He was drunk.' (Bogarde,
1983)

unwired mentally unbalanced
Like an electrical device which is not connected to a power supply:
I've seen him completely unwired after a
night of boozing. (Sanders, 1994)

up[1] (of a male) copulating with
Tout court and in a variety of vulgar phrases:
'When you're up who, Barbara's down on
whom?' asks Flora. 'Flora, you're coarse,'
says Howard. (Bradbury, 1975)

up[2] under the influence of illegal narcotics
The result of getting HIGH. *Ups* or *uppers* are
the drugs, usually amphetamine:
I knew one 4th Division Lurp who took his
pills by the fistful, downs from the left
pocket of his tiger suit and ups from the
right. (Herr, 1977)

up along old
Shortened form of *up along in years* and still
common in English West Country dialect. The
Scottish *up in life* is obsolete:
Though up in life, I'll get a wife.
(A. Boswell, 1871)

up-and-coming dilapidated
Estate agents' jargon of run-down areas,
where property is cheaper:
Estate agents would call Brixton an up-and-
coming neighbourhood—it has more than
its fair share of drive-by shootings. (*Daily
Telegraph*, 26 July 1999—Brixton is a run-
down district in south London)

up for it agreeable to casual copulation

Literally, prepared for what is coming:
A thuggish, dim young man with a short
fuse and a lot of aggression is going to
expect that a pretty girl who visits his hotel
bedroom in the small hours is up for it.
(Mary Kenny, in *Sunday Telegraph*, 16
January 2000)

up the creek in severe difficulties
The British army waterway, in which you
might find yourself *without a paddle*, was *shit
creek*, a vulgarism for the anus. Today most
people who use the phrase figuratively are
unaware of its provenance, and the association with sodomy:
...telling them that if they'd followed this
far up shit creek it's a long way to walk
back. (*Private Eye*, July 1981, with some
choice mixing of metaphors)

up the loop mad
The imagery was from railway shunting
practices, where a wagon might be misdir-
ected on to the wrong *loop*, or siding:
A lot of us believed he was really up the
loop for having played at it so long.
(F. Richards, 1936—a soldier was feigning
madness to secure his discharge)

up the pole pregnant
Where the monkey ends up. The phrase puns
on the meaning, in trouble, and the vulgar
POLE, the penis. Also as *up the spout*, with
imagery from a shell rammed in a rifled barrel
from which, the copper band having been
engaged, it can be extracted only with danger
and difficulty; and *up the stick*, reverting to the
simian imagery:
'We've planned [marriage] for a long time.'
'When you discovered she was up the pole.'
(Binchy, 1985)
The chorus, four times repeated, was 'She
was up the bleeding spout'. (F. Richards,
1936)
I believe Garry Foster's young fella's after
puttin' some young one from Coolock up
the stick. (R. Doyle, 1987)
All these phrases can also be used of financial
difficulties.

up top relating to intelligence
Where the brain is located, but euphemisti-
cally always in the negative:
She didn't have much to offer up top.
Pretty face, though. (J. Patterson, 1999)
Also as *upstairs*.

upstairs[1] an allusion to a taboo act or
place
In former times, *she's gone upstairs* meant that
a birth was imminent. An invalid who *has been
upstairs for two months* indicates the duration of
his infirmity. Socially, *Would you like to go*

upstairs? invites urination. *Upstairs* is also
where the bedrooms are, for copulation:
> Was he going to haul her off upstairs,
> leaving first-years honours [students] to riot
> away among the cakes below while he
> satisfied his passion? (Bradbury, 1959)

upstairs² death
Where God lives and heaven is to be found.
However, to *go upstairs out of this world* was to be
hanged, punning on the climb up the scaffold.

upstairs³ in authority
The senior staff occupy the higher floors:
> And now the pressure put on from upstairs
> to put the clamp on the case...(van
> Lustbaden, 1983)

And see *boys upstairs* under BOYS 2.

Uranian *obsolete* a male homosexual
From *Urania*, another name for Aphrodite,
although there may be some who hanker
after a coarse planetary pun. Also as a *child of
Uranus*:
> Many of the Uranians or Urnings (favourite
> term among the literati) were disgusted by
> the physical manifestations of their
> tendencies. (Pearsall, 1969)
> O child of Uranus...
> Thy woman-soul within a man's form
> dwelling. (ibid., quoting Carpenter, *c*.1895)

urban renewal slum clearance
Not just a tidied up business district:
> The abandoned warehouse was in a
> depressed area long overdue for urban
> renewal. (Bagley, 1982)

use¹ (of a male) to copulate with
Normally outside marriage:
> Be a whore still: they love thee not that use
> thee. (Shakespeare, *Timon of Athens*)
> The fact that her father had used her killed
> my liking for Kätchen. (F. Harris, 1925)

use² to be addicted to illegal narcotics
A shortened form of *use drugs* or, in the jargon
use some help. A *user* is an addict:
> 'I think we can use some help,'...he said,
> passing the vial and the gold spoon to her.
> (Robbins, 1981)
> This deranged, a late-period Vasco, had
> become a heavy user. (Rushdie, 1995)

use³ (in) capable of conception
It is used of those mammals which indicate
their readiness by bleeding:
> ...none of the mares he covered three
> weeks or more ago has come back into use.
> (D. Francis, 1982)

use a wheelchair to be physically incapable of walking
The word *cripple* is taboo:
> You should not say that someone
> 'cannot walk'. Instead say 'uses a
> wheelchair'. (M. Holman, in *Financial Times*,
> October 1994)

use of Venus *obsolete* copulation
Much use of Venus doth dim the sight.
(Bacon, 1627—Shakespeare would never
have written that)

use paper to defecate
Hospital jargon, and not of writing a letter.

use your tin *American* to identify yourself
as a policeman
From the badge;
> I'd be in civilian clothes...Could I use my
> tin? (Sanders, 1973)

used second-hand
To remove the stigma of prior ownership,
especially of cars.

useful expenditure a bribe
True, we might suppose, if it lands you the
contract:
> A German who bribes a French official in
> an EU-wide open tender procedure
> cannot be prosecuted in Germany and the
> bribe can be written off against tax. Such
> costs on the tax form are called *nuetzliche
> Ausgaben*—'useful expenditures'. (*Sunday
> Telegraph*, 20 January 1997)

useful fool a dupe of the Communists
Lenin's phrase for the shallow thinkers in the
West whom the Communists manipulated.
Also as *useful idiot*:
> ...the Judas goats leading what they call
> 'the useful fools' up the garden path to the
> knacker's yard—the brave sons of Ireland
> in the IRA and the honest pacifists in CND.
> (Price, 1982)
> It had taken courage to write his kind of
> books, thirty years ago, on the Famine
> and the Terror, when every other useful
> idiot in academia was screeching for
> détente. (R. Harris, 1998)

useful girl *?obsolete American* a domestic
servant
The phrase avoids any implication of subser-
vience:
> I was urged to accept the position of
> 'useful girl', a silly name to designate a
> maid's maid. (*Daily Telegraph*, 10 March 2001)

usual trouble (the) menstruation
See TROUBLE:
> Here on the twelfth of May, she's got
> 'the usual trouble at this time'.
> (R. Harris, 1998)

V

vacation *American* a prison sentence
Literally, a holiday which involves any absence from home:
   ...won a twenty years' vacation in the Big House. (Lavine, 1930)

vacuum to destroy incriminating evidence
Sweeping it out of sight:
   [Associate White House Counsel William H. Kennedy III] was summoned before the Senate Banking Committee to explain why he had written 'Vacuum Rose law files...Documents never know, go out quietly' in his notes at a White House meeting on November 5, 1993. (Evans-Pritchard, 1997—perhaps on that particular day it would have been better to put them on the bonfire with the guy)

valentine *American* a warning or notice of dismissal
Punning on the CARDS received by some on 14 February:
   The captain...may distribute a few complaints or 'valentines' for dereliction of duty. (Lavine, 1930)

vanity publishing the publication of a book or article at the author's expense
Where the venture is not commercially attractive to a professional publisher:
   And persuading his friend, Sir Roland Smith, to interview him on his career must count as an exercise in vanity publishing. (*Daily Telegraph*, 16 April 1994—the article was on (Lord) Swarj Paul)

variety meats *American* offal
Lungs, liver, testicles, and all the bits you would rather not spell out with precision. See also SWEETBREADS.

Vatican roulette the use of the safe period method of contraception
Punning on the Roman Catholic dogma against contraception and Russian roulette. In either case you cannot be quite sure there isn't one *up the spout*, as it were:
   But it seems that Vatican roulette had failed them again and a fourth little faithful is on the way. (Penguin blurb for Lodge's *The British Museum is Falling Down*, 1965)

vault¹ *obsolete* (of a male) to copulate with
Pre-dating the modern JUMP 2:
   While he is vaulting variable ramps. (Shakespeare, *Cymbeline*)
The punning *vaulting-school* was a brothel.

vault² *American* a cupboard for the storage of a corpse
Literally, any structure with an arched roof, which is how many early tombs were built:
   The vault we are describing here is designed as an outer receptacle to protect the casket and its contents from the elements during their eternal sojourn in the grave. (J. Mitford, 1963)

velvet¹ an opportunity for copulation offered by a woman
Like the fabric with the smooth, rich, luxurious pile:
   ...pitiless calculation of a woman with velvet to sell. (Mailer, 1965)

velvet² associated with a payment for which there is no consideration
Either a bribe or an exceptional profit, again from the properties of the cloth:
   Money is dropped in the 'velvet-lined' drawer of my desk...(Lavine, 1930)
   ...to get back his original investment in order to be able to work in 'velvet'. (ibid.)

venerous act (the) *obsolete* copulation
From VENUS, and pursuing women rather than deer:
   ...it did afford him some pleasure to see the venerous act performed. (Fowles, 1985, using archaic language about a VOYEUR)

Venus appertaining to copulation
The Roman goddess of love appears in many compounds and variations:
   ...his heart
   Inflam'd with Venus...(Shakespeare, *Troilus and Cressida*)
The adjectival form, *venereal*, which once meant beautiful or lustful, is now used only of sexually transmitted diseases.

verbal *British* an oral admission of guilt
Police jargon, for something which may or may not have been given voluntarily. To *verbal* an accused is falsely to record such an alleged admission.

verbally deficient unable to read
Not merely having a restricted vocabulary. Jennings (1965) pointed out how odd it is that those who cannot read need a written euphemism to conceal their ignorance, but that was before we became POLITICALLY CORRECT.

vertically challenged of short stature
But not a mountaineer. See also CHAL-
LENGED:
> A better deal for the vertically challenged
> was urged yesterday by Dr David Weeks, a
> consultant psychiatrist, who said that
> 'shortism' was as pernicious as sexism and
> racism. (*Daily Telegraph*, 12 April 1994—the
> doctor should know, being himself 5ft 2in
> tall)

vicar of Bray a cowardly or opportunistic
trimmer
A cleric held this living in the 16th century
during the reign of four English monarchs,
two of whom were Roman Catholic and three
Protestant, Henry VIII being both. Other
incumbents were replaced as the state religion altered, as can be seen from the records
of incumbents displayed in many English
parish churches. When he was accused of
being of a changeable turn, he replied:
> No, I am steadfast, however other folk
> change I remain Vicar of Bray. (reported by
> Alleyn, Bishop of Exeter)

victualler *obsolete* the keeper of a brothel
He provided the MEAT 1:
> *Falstaff*... suffering flesh to be eaten in thy
> house contrary to the law; for the which I
> think thou wilt howl.
> *Hostess* All victuallers do so. (Shakespeare, *2
> Henry IV*—note the two sexual puns)
A *victualling-house* was a brothel.

vigilance (in a totalitarian state) informing to the authorities on fellow citizens
Literally, keeping a good look-out:
> ...everyone informs right from the
> nursery...They call it 'vigilance'. (M. C.
> Smith, 1981, writing of Communist Russia)

violate (of a male) to copulate with extramaritally
The common violent imagery, although the
word is also used where there have been
blandishments and no force:
> With unchaste purpose, and with oath to
> violate
> My lady's honour. (Shakespeare, *Cymbeline*)

virtue the property of not having copulated extramaritally
Literally, conformity with all moral standards,
but in this use of women since the 16th
century, and in the centuries subsequently
when wives were expected to be *virtuous*:
> Their triumphs over the virtue of
> girls...(Mayhew, 1851)
> Betimes in the morning I will beseech the
> virtuous Desdemona. (Shakespeare, *Othello*)

visible (of people) not white

Although white people have not somehow
become *invisible* in societies where they form a
majority:
> An Ad from Concordia University in
> Montreal, Canada, says it especially
> encourages applications from women,
> 'visible minorities', and the disabled. (*Daily
> Telegraph*, 17 February 1992):
> When referring to groups of Asian, African
> Caribbean or a mixture of people from
> both groups, the individual may feel it is
> more appropriate to adopt the term 'visibly
> minority ethnic groups'. (Statement issued
> by London Metropolitan Police, June 1999)
> Why 'visibly ethnic' is the new black.
> (*Sunday Telegraph* headline, 6 June 1999)
> The BBC does not attract as many people as
> it should from the 'visible community'.
> (*Daily Telegraph*, 10 January 2001—as
> employees rather than listeners or viewers)

visiting card traces of urine or faeces left
in a public place
Left by domestic pets:
> He's left his visiting card. (Ross, 1956, of a
> dog)
See also PAY A VISIT.

visiting fireman[1] *American* a boisterous
reveller
Especially at conventions etc. some distance
from home:
> ...a visiting fireman in search of a cheap
> thrill would get mugged and robbed.
> (McBain, 1981)

visiting fireman[2] a person sent from
headquarters to investigate the situation
or correct mistakes in a subsidiary organization
Looking for a fire or trying to extinguish it:
> He should not get into any arguments or
> debates with visiting firemen who take his
> time. (Butcher, 1946, writing of General
> Eisenhower in Algiers)
> When visiting 'firemen' move in, the bodel
> has to move out. (Forsyth, 1994—a *bodel* is a
> young Israeli living abroad and spying for
> the Israeli secret service, MOSSAD)

visitor (a) menstruation
Common female usage. In America she may
come from a place called *Redbank*.

visually challenged ugly
Not by a sentry but an extension of the
CHALLENGED theme. The phrase was used by
Auberon Waugh in the *Daily Telegraph* on 4
October 1993 when describing a politician.

visually impaired blind or with very poor
eyesight

Literally, *impaired* means damaged or weakened:

> Two more blind magistrates have been appointed to establish whether the visually impaired should become JPs. (*Daily Telegraph*, 7 August 1999)

vital statistics the measurement of a woman's chest, waist, and buttocks

As so often, here *vital* means no more than interesting or important, which the information seems to be in the world of entertainment.

vitals the testicles

Literally, the parts of the body essential to the continuation of life, whence usually the organs located in the trunk:

> ...him so bad with the mumps and all, so that his poor vitals were swelled to pumpkin size. (Graves, 1941)

void water *obsolete* to urinate

Not spitting or sweating. To *void your bowels* was to defecate:

> When, at the end, they went too far, she voided her water on the deck. (Monsarrat, 1978, writing in archaic style)
> If the battalion had not been going into battle he would have galloped away, found a private spot and voided his bowels. (B. Cornwell, 1997—again using archaic speech)

voluntary done under duress or compulsion

Such as attendance at a church parade in the army or an admission of guilt obtained under duress:

> ...denied that any coercive measures had been used in obtaining the 'voluntary confession'. (Lavine, 1930)

See also VOLUNTEER.

voluntary patient a patient in a psychiatric hospital supposedly free to leave on request

Those who are confined through legal process have no such choice. The expression is not used of those in-patients undergoing treatment for physical illness

voluntary pregnancy interruption see PREGNANCY INTERRUPTION

volunteer a person instructed to fight for a third party

Used originally of those who intervened in military formations for the Nazis, Fascists, and Communists during the Spanish Civil War. Now of any organized military interference where you wish to influence events without a declaration of war:

> ...intervention on the enemy's side of overwhelming reinforcements of Chinese 'volunteers'. (Boyle, 1979, writing about the Korean War)

voyeur a person who enjoys watching the sexual activity of others

Literally, a watcher of anything:

> Hamilton had been an enthusiastic voyeur...In one home, microphones had been installed throughout the bedrooms. (S. Green, 1979—an ÉCOUTEUR also, it would seem)

Vulcan's badge (wear) *literary* to be a cuckold

Venus, while married to Vulcan, committed adultery with Mars.

vulnerable poor or inadequate

None of us is incapable of being wounded but some appear to be more at risk than others.

W

W/WC See WATER CLOSET

wad-shifter *obsolete British* a person who never drinks intoxicants
The army in India used to take *wads*, doughy buns, with their *char*, tea. In that society, temperance was taboo:
> If a teetaller, he was known as a 'char-wallah', 'bun-puncher', or 'wad-shifter'. (F. Richards, 1933)

waddle to be unsuccessful in business or with an investment
See LAME DUCK 2 for the derivation:
> The speculation became most unfortunate as they *waddled*, and became *lame ducks*. (Foreman, 1998)

wages of sin (the) death
The venerable inducement to virtue was that only the good people survive in this life and the next. The modern usage may be more literal:
> For the wages of sin is death; but the gift of God is eternal life . . . (*Romans* 6: 23)
> I could have mentioned that the wages of sin are death—that the Union Captain's carnal desire for the powdered, rouged, weeping old woman we'd left that evening had brought him a well-deserved end. (Baldwin, 1993)

waiting for employment involuntarily unemployed
A Chinese Communist usage:
> He told me he had plenty of time since he was 'waiting for employment'—an expression used by the People's Government for 'unemployment' which was supposed not to exist in a socialist state. (Cheng, 1984)

wake a death
From the verbal form, which meant to stay awake to watch over a corpse, to prevent anyone trying to take it for sale:
> 'There's a wake in the family,' an euphemistic expression for death. (*EDD*)
> For nobody cared to wake Sir Robert Redgauntlet like another corpse. (W. Scott, 1824)
To *wake the churchyard* was not to sound the last trump but to keep an eye out for grave-robbers:
> Wauk the kirkyard . . . to prevent the inroads of resurrection-men. (*EDD*)

wake a witch *obsolete Scottish* to force a woman to confess to witchcraft
As with SWIM FOR A WIZARD, this entry illustrates the behaviour of our recent ancestors. In this procedure an iron hoop was placed over the victim's face, with four prongs in her mouth. Chained to a wall so that she could not lie down, she was kept awake by relays of men until she admitted she was a witch, after which she might be ducked or burnt to death.

walk[1] (the streets) to be a prostitute
Seldom *tout court*, but if so used, the confusion may be considerable. In 1891 Daisy Hopkins was sentenced to fourteen days in prison by the University Court of Cambridge after being accused of *walking with a member of the university*. A higher court on appeal, perhaps unversed in euphemism, held this to have been no offence:
> Women walking the streets for tricks to take to their 'pads'. (L. Armstrong, 1955)

walk[2] to be dismissed from employment
The usage wrongly implies a voluntary departure:
> Thing is, I give you maybe three, four years, you'll walk. (Diehl, 1978, suggesting such dismissal)
Also of dismissal from courtship or cohabitation.

walk[3] to be stolen
Normally of small tools or army kit, attributing powers of locomotion to inanimate objects rather than accusing one of your mates of theft. Such objects may also *go for a walk*:
> Hitherto, under state control, the biggest problem had been bits disappearing off the engines—even whole exhibits going for a walk. (*Sunday Telegraph*, 7 February 1999, reporting on the Nairobi Railway Museum)

walk[4] (in cricket) to acknowledge dismissal before the umpire's adjudication
Euphemistic only in the negative, where *not to walk* implies bad sportsmanship:
> Gooch's initial movement suggested that he was going to walk, which might have deceived the umpire. (*Daily Telegraph*, 27 January 1995—he was given out incorrectly)

walk[5] to escape deserved punishment or obtain early release from prison
A shortened form of *walk free from court* or *jail*:
> 'Havistock is going to walk, isn't he?' 'Sure he is,' Al said. 'What could we charge him with?' (Sanders, 1986)
> . . . the most they'll get is twenty years, walk in seven or eight. (Clancy, 1989)
Whence, to secure an acquittal:

I've never had a client I've walked on a murder charge go out and do it again. (R. N. Patterson, 1996/2—but how could an innocent man be a recidivist?)

walk⁶ *American* unsportingly to throw a ball at a striker which he cannot reach
From baseball:

They boo their own pitchers if they 'walk' him—that is, deliberately throw wides he cannot reach, allowing him a free saunter to first base rather than run the risk of letting him blast one into the stands. (*Daily Telegraph*, 5 September 1998)

walk⁷(out/with/out with) to court
The usage has survived the days when preliminary courtship was a pedestrian affair:

You'll dance at the hops with me, ride with me, but you won't walk with me. (Cookson, 1967)
Caleb was 'walkin' a maid out'. (Agnus, 1900)
Donald Campbell... who for many years has walked out with Julie Christie, the actress... (*Daily Telegraph*, 28 December 2000)

walk out to go on strike
Not just the departure of workers on foot at the end of a shift. Also, as a noun, to describe concerted strike action, usually taken at short notice.

walk penniless in Mark Lane see MARK 2

walk the plank to be killed by drowning
Favoured by pirates for the disposal of their captives. Some figurative use:

A 15-year-old daughter broke out upon sexual adventures [on a cruise] and a singer with the ship's band was only saved from walking the plank by some polaroid pictures of her performance in other cabins. (Whicker, 1982)

To *walk the golden gangplank* implies departure from employment with a generous payoff:

Grand Met's finance director has walked the golden gangplank without waiting for consummation of the deal. (*Daily Telegraph*, 28 June 1997)

walk the snake (of a male) to copulate
The common serpentine imagery:

'Y'all come back there, we gonna walk the snake.' 'The *snake*?' she snorted. 'More like a worm, I'll bet.'... 'It's a fucking *python*,' he shouted. 'You don't believe me'... He was unzipping his pants. (Anonymous, 1996)

walker a male paid by a female to accompany her on a social occasion

The imagery, and word, comes from being employed to exercise someone's dog, or take it *walkies*:

A dependable date for charity events... Woolley has fallen into the category of 'walker'. (*Vanity Fair*, January 1993)

walking papers a notice of dismissal from employment
Your instructions to WALK 2, but not to hike:

I should give you your walking papers. (Theroux, 1989)

wall-eyed drunk
Literally, strabismic, with difficulty in focusing, and drunkenness can cause that too.

wallflower a young woman who is failing to attract a male companion
From the far-off days when girls sat around the periphery of dance halls, waiting for a male partner to ask them to take the floor with him:

Suddenly came the sweet green age of chlorophyll, offering new hope for wallflowers and old maids. (E. S. Turner, 1952)

Wallflower week is the time of menstruation.

wander to philander within marriage
It is the male who tends to STRAY:

... her pain, particularly with her husband's wandering, was sometimes intense. (Turow, 1990)

wandered *Scottish* mentally confused
From the inability to concentrate:

... sick in mind as in body. He seemed, as my wife's relatives would have said, to be 'wandered'. (Fraser, 1969—the relatives were Scottish)

wandering eye a tendency to promiscuity
An affliction of husbands rather than wives:

No wonder Bill has a wandering eye. (Michael Sheldon in *Sunday Telegraph*, 3 March 1996, reviewing a book by Hillary Clinton)

wang-house *American* a brothel
Possibly a corruption of WANK 1, and not from a Chinese dialect:

I had expected the opium parlour to be something like a wang-house filled with sleepy hookers. (Theroux, 1973)

wank¹(off) to masturbate
Literally, to beat or thrash. As both verb and noun, while *wanker* is a common term of male insult:

He himself felt only guilt and depression like as a lad he used to feel when he wanked off. (Lodge, 1988)

He seems to be recording, in his own graceful way, a wank in the woods. (Fry, 1994)

Harrison's are a load of wankers. (Sharpe, 1982, illustrating schoolboy, rather than sexual, abuse)

wank² a penis

Presumably from its function in WANK 1:

Her father escaped from a lunatic asylum with bunions on his balls and warts on his wank. (McCourt, 1997)

wankery pornographic literature

An aid to male titillation:

... locking himself in with a load of new-bought wankery. (Amis, 1978)

want¹ (a) low mental ability

A shortened form of a *want of understanding* etc.:

I had a want and been daft likewise. (Galt, 1826)

And in several phrases, indicating a shortage from a full complement, such as *want some pence in a shilling*:

... of rather a wild frantic nature, and seem to want 'some pence in the shilling'. (Mactaggart, 1824)

Whence the common adjective, *wanting*, for a slow-witted person.

Junior had always been slightly wanting. (Fraser, 1994)

want² to lust after

This kind of *want* is not for social intercourse:

Yet he wanted my mother, his half-sister, and in trying to get his way with her caused her untold agony of mind. (Cookson, 1969)

Specifically, as *want sex, a body, intercourse, it, love, relations*, etc.:

Since she was fifteen, men had wanted her body. (Allbeury, 1976)

want out to wish to kill yourself

Literally, to wish to extract yourself from a deal or arrangement:

'Does the letter signify anything to you?'

'Only that he wanted out.' (B. Forbes, 1983—it was a suicide note)

ward off invasion to launch a pre-emptive strike

The language of Nazism, and one of the excuses given for the German invasion of Poland in August 1939, and of Holland and Belgium in May 1940:

Naturally a 'counter-attack' to 'ward off the hostile invasion'. (Klemperer, 1998, in translation—diary entry of 11 May 1940,

noting the reason given for the attack on the Low Countries).

warehouse to hold (securities) for a principal to conceal his interest

Stock exchange jargon when the arrangement is clandestine or illegal:

It is even suggested that the diminutive legal person could have 'warehoused' some of the Howard shares. (*Private Eye*, March 1981)

warm¹ sexually aroused

And not noticeably cooler than HOT 1:

The warm effects which she in him finds missing. (Shakespeare, *Venus and Adonis*)

In obsolete use, a *warm one* was a prostitute, whom you might find in a *warm shop*, or brothel.

warm² wealthy

Denoting a fortune thought to be undeserved, the possessor of which may be miserly:

He's a warm man, is Mr Noakes. (Sayers, 1937)

warm³ (with wine) tipsy

Rum or whisky warm better:

Col's bowl was finished; and by that time we were well warmed. (J. Boswell, 1773—he himself felt far from well the next morning)

Addison wrote some of his best papers in *The Spectator* when warm with wine. (J. Boswell, 1791)

warm a backside to thrash

Not by standing before the fire on a cold day:

Please don't think I don't know how to warm your backside. (Theroux, 1993—the threat was made to a child)

warm a bed to copulate with someone promiscuously

Not by using a hot-water bottle or electric blanket:

It was equally possible she was warming another man's bed. (R. Moss, 1987)

warm up old porridge to renew a discontinued sexual relationship

It never tastes the same, so they say.

warn off to expel from participation in horse-racing for dishonesty

A shortened form of *warn off the turf*:

[He] realized that he might be warned-off. Might suffer the ultimate disgrace. (D. Francis, 1998)

warning *obsolete* a notice of termination of employment

Usually, but not always, given by the employer to the employee:

> If respectable young girls are set picking grass out of your gravel, in place of their proper work, they will give warning. (Somerville and Ross, 1897)

warpaint facial cosmetics

Punning jocular female usage (although the process of application and its purpose are serious):

> Baby was down with a fresh dressing of warpaint. (Sharpe, 1977—*Baby* was an adult female)

wash¹ *obsolete* stale urine

As once commonly used in laundry:

> Dochter, here is a bottle o' my father's wash. (D. Graham, 1883—it was for medical examination)

A *wash-mug* was a piss-pot.

wash² *British* to deal unnecessarily in securities to obtain commission

Stock exchange jargon. It is one way in which the broker can TAKE TO THE CLEANERS a trusting client. See also CHURN.

wash³ to bring into open circulation

It indicates money or assets obtained illegally, and a less common version of LAUNDER:

> We must wash the money... if that money isn't broken down... (Freemantle, 1977)

wash and brush up *American* a lavatory

You are unlikely to find anyone to do the *brushing up* in one these days.

wash its face not to incur a loss

Coming clean, I suppose, or not needing help from another:

> He was forced to concede that, with some small adjustments, it managed to wash its face. (McCrum, 1991, describing a dubious venture)

wash out to destroy or bankrupt

Literally, an event which has to be abandoned because of rain:

> We do not beat a race in four days. In fact... we go overboard today. We are washed out. (Runyon, 1990, written in the 1930s)

wash the baby's head to drink intoxicants in celebration of a birth

A less common variant of *wet the baby's head*, given under WET 2:

> To wesh ther heeads e bumper toasts. (Treddlehoyle, 1846)

wash your hands¹ to urinate

The hand wash basin and the lavatory bowl are usually in close proximity. It is what arriving guests may be invited to do.

wash your hands² (of) to dissociate yourself from (anything embarrassing or unpleasant)

Like Pilate who 'took water and washed his hands before the multitude, saying, I am innocent of the blood of this just person, see ye to it'. (*Matthew* 27: 24)

washed up bankrupt

Like flotsam:

> Mr and Mrs Dan Prescott were washed up for the rest of their days. They'd end up in a trailer park in South Florida. (Erdman, 1993, describing the direst of destinies)

washroom *American* a lavatory

Not a laundry:

> In the washroom the two of them sit side by side in separate cubicles, talking over the noise of the gushing pee. (Atwood, 1988)

waste¹ *American* to kill

Literally, to destroy or use up:

> You wanted a photo of Roger Kope, the cop who got wasted. (Sanders, 1973—British cops are only *wasted* by excessive bureaucracy)

waste² *American* urine or faeces

Canine faeces on the sidewalk or *house waste*, from an earth closet. A spacecraft is said to have no lavatory but it will boast a *waste management compartment*. In Britain a *waste management centre*, in Oxford and elsewhere, is a rubbish dump.

waste time *American* to masturbate

It is suggested that the time would be better spent with a sexual partner.

wasted *American* drunk

Not from spilling the liquid or resultant bodily emaciation:

> To an American, the word *bar* suggests a place to get either happily squiffed or unhappily wasted. (*Travel and Leisure*, 1990)

watch *Irish* to sit with a corpse

The tradition of the WAKE persists in Ireland, where mourners visit the house to view the body, being suitably refreshed, before subsequently attending the funeral:

> He hits me in the back with the whiskey bottle, pleads, Will you not watch one hour with me. (McCourt, 1997)

water urine

Used in this sense since the 14th century even though urine differs significantly from the clear and potable compound of hydrogen and oxygen:

> Sirrah, you giant, what says the doctor to my water? (Shakespeare, *2 Henry IV*)

To *water* something, such as *the garden, the roses*, or whatever, is to urinate on it:

> When Brutal asked if he wouldn't like to step down and help us water the bushes, he just shook his head. (King, 1996)
> Then the officer excused himself to Jean-Marie, turned away, undid a fly, watered a rock...(Furst, 1995)

water closet a lavatory with a flush mechanism

Standard English, abbreviated to *WC*, and occasionally in Britain to *W*:

> The W is a frequent non-U expression for 'lavatory' (W.C. is also non-U). (Ross, 1956)

This is a euphemism we have passed on to the French, as *le water* or *le water-closet*.

water cure a form of torture

Much different from attending a spa to cure your rheumatism. The water is applied in persistent drips externally, or in excessive quantities orally.

water gardener someone who improperly releases confidential information to the media

Cultivating the press, preparing the ground for policy changes, and the source of many a LEAK 2:

> The markets sensed some change of mood, some well-placed drips from the Treasury's water-gardeners, and Friday of last week was their best day ever. (*Daily Telegraph*, 4 October 1997)

water of life (the) *Scottish/Irish* whisky

The Gaelic *usquebaugh* (and in various spellings) rather than the French *eau de vie*:

> 'Usquebeatha?' Murdoch said in Gaelic. 'The water of life.' (Higgins, 1976)
> A glass of brandy or usquabae. (W. Scott, 1824)

water sports sexual activity involving urination

Not swimming, diving, etc.:

> ...they're interested in leather and water sports. (Theroux, 1990, describing sexual deviants)

water stock *American* to render securities less valuable by constant dilution

As a drover, Daniel Drew, as was usual, fed salt to cattle as they were being driven to market, so that they drank a lot and put on weight, making up for the flesh they lost during the drive. He adopted the same principle when he started financing railroads, especially the Erie. (Faith, 1990)

watering hole a place licensed to sell intoxicants

Punning jocular usage, although there would be no smiles if only water was on offer:

> A blinking sign I took to be a watering hole...(Theroux, 1979)

watermelon *American* an indication of pregnancy

In phrases such as *have a watermelon on the vine* or *swallow a watermelon seed*. *Watermelons*, in vulgar male talk, may be female breasts.

waterworks[1] the human urinary system

The pun is only used in the case of malfunction, to avoid mentioning a taboo condition:

> ...busily at work cauterizing his waterworks...(Sharpe, 1979)

waterworks[2] tears

Especially those of a woman or child thought to be producing them to obtain sympathy:

> It's impossible to reason with Ma; she just turns on the waterworks. (Seth, 1993)

wax[1] to remove unwanted hair from (a part of the body)

Mainly female usage and practice:

> Mumsy and I are motoring up to London to have our legs waxed at Fortnums. (*Private Eye*, April 1981)

wax[2] *American* to kill

Perhaps only in the past participle, from the appearance of a corpse rather than the immobility of a dummy in a *waxworks*:

> After you saw Sophie Millstein get waxed ... (Katzenbach, 1995—Sophie had not had cosmetic treatment but was murdered)

way of all flesh (the) death

From the Douay Bible:

> I am going the way of all flesh. (*Joshua* 23:14)

Made a cliché by Samuel Butler's novel of the same title, published posthumously in 1903.

way out under the influence of illegal narcotics

In standard usage, showing any wide deviance from a norm, whence a drug-induced elation in which some instrumentalists consider they work best.

weaker half (the) females

Euphemism, dysphemism, chauvinist insult, assessment of physical strength, or merely how our male ancestors, and many female ones also, regarded the comparison between the sexes. A shortened form of *weaker half of the human family* or *race*:

At this latter proceeding, the weaker half
of the human family went distracted on
the spot. (W. Collins, 1868—he might have
written 'the women became excited')

weakness a tendency towards self-indulgence
Often *tout court* of drunkenness, and in
phrases such as a *weakness for the drink*, a
weakness for men or *women* (profligacy), a *weakness for boys* (homosexuality in men), a *weakness
for the horses* (addiction to gambling), etc.:
    ...their Mr Fellowes *did* have a weakness.
    (Bogarde, 1983—he was a drunkard)
    ...it was a weakness for one of the
    secretaries in the P.A.'s office that
    had ended his first marriage. (Turow,
    1999)
See also the delightful Irish *strong weakness*
under STRONG WATERS.

weapon the erect penis
Of obvious and venerable derivation:
    My naked weapon is out. (Shakespeare,
    Romeo and Juliet)
    ...my weapon sheathed itself in her
    naturally. (F. Harris, 1925)

wear a bullet *American* to be killed or
wounded by shooting
Although unlikely to be visible on the outer
garments:
    'Who's wearing a bullet?' I asked her.
    (Chandler, 1958)

wear a fork *obsolete* to be cuckolded
The *fork*, or antlers, was a traditional indica-
tion of cuckoldry. Also as *wear horns*:
    I wondered how many sets of horns
    Griswald III was wearing. (Sanders,
    1994—he had just added one more
    himself)
See also FORKED PLAGUE and HORN 2.

wear a pad to be menstruating
The phrase is not used of female hockey
players.

wear a smile to be naked
And nothing else.

wear away *obsolete* to die a lingering
death
Usually from the CONSUMPTION or pulmonary
tuberculosis:
    Sickened. Took the bed, an' wear awa'.
    (Grant, 1884)

wear Dick's hatband see DICK'S HATBAND

wear down *Scottish* to grow old
Physically accurate and an allusion to the
burdens of a long life:

I and my Jenny are baith wearin' down.
(Rodger, 1838)

wear green garters *obsolete* *Scottish* to
remain unmarried after a younger sister's wedding
By tradition, the unmarried elder sister wore
green or yellow garters at the wedding of a
younger. The taboos surrounding spinster-
hood arose from the plight of those women
who failed to obtain the support of a husband
and were forbidden by convention to seek
work to support themselves.

wear iron knickers (of a female) to refrain
from copulation
Men are not figuratively so attired:
    Her Italian father...wanted her to wear
    iron knickers until she was twenty-one.
    (Follett, 1979)

wear lead boots *American* to be ineli-
gible for promotion
As worn by the deep-sea diver, to keep him
down:
    All his buddies in the department'll do
    him favors today...but as for as
    going higher, he smelled bad, to the
    brass he was wearing lead boots.
    (Turow, 1993)

wear lead buttons *American* to be murdered
The common association between LEAD and
shooting:
    Talk to me like that...and you're liable to
    be wearing lead buttons on your vest.
    (Chandler, 1943)
See also WEAR A BULLET.

wear the breeches to be the dominant
partner in a relationship between a
man and a woman
Usually of the woman, from the days when
only men wore *the breech*, *breeches*, *trousers*, or
(in America) *pants*:
    That you might still have worn the
    petticoat,
    And ne'er have stol'n the breech from
    Lancaster. (Shakespeare, *3 Henry IV*)
    Helpmate, a thick, stubborn-looking lady of
    40, childless, and most likely wearing the
    breeches. (*Century Magazine*, July 1882)
    [She] is even more predatory than he
    is...This film's brassy flouting of
    money, power, and sex appeal would
    appear naïve no matter who wore the
    pants, as they used to say. (*New York
    Times*, 12 July 1992)

wear your heart upon your sleeve to fail
to conceal heterosexual longing

At one time men might advertise their intentions or desires by displaying some keepsake from the woman:

> But I will wear my heart upon my sleeve
> For daws to peck at. (Shakespeare, *Othello*—
> a *daw* was a jackdaw)

wedding tackle see TACKLE

wee(-wee) to urinate
The derivation is from *little* as in LITTLE JOBS, or is a corruption of *eau*, with the common WATER imagery. The repetition of *wee* does not indicate a double effusion:

> 'Just a minute,' said Viola, 'I want to wee-wee.' (Bradbury, 1959)

wee drop *mainly Irish/Scottish* a drink of whisky
As a with a LITTLE SOMETHING, the volume is seldom small. Also as *wee dram* or *wee half*:

> Manis was always fond of the wee dhrap. (MacManus, 1899)
> ...a 'wee hauf' held my heart in cheer. (A. Murdoch, 1873)

wee folk *obsolete mainly Irish* the fairies
Malevolent creatures of whom you had to speak nicely to appease them. Also as the *wee people*:

> The belief in the 'wee folk', or 'gentry', is very much more wisely spread. (*Cornhill Magazine*, February, 1877, quoted in *EDD*)
> ...they attribute it to the wee people. (W. Mason, 1815)

weed (the) a taboo substance which is smoked
Formerly tobacco, to smoke which in Victorian times was antisocial outside the Smoking Room, but now marijuana:

> ...a man whose private worth is only to be equalled by the purity of his milk-punch and the excellence of his weeds. (Bradley, 1853, meaning cigars)
> ...opened the door and sniffed the weed. (Chandler, 1958—he could smell cannabis smoke)

weekend dishonestly to use a customer's money after the close of business on Friday
Banking jargon and practice. By delaying the transfer of funds, the banker earns, on the customer's credit balance or transfer, interest which is accrued on a daily business. For some banks, this kind of *weekend* starts on a Thursday and ends on a Tuesday.

weenie *American* a penis
Possibly from the German *wienerworst*, Vienna sausage, whence *wienie*, and the Anglicized *weenie*, a frankfurter, and the common *sausage* imagery. To *step on* or *shoot your weenie* is a variant of the cliché, to shoot yourself in the foot:

> So long as I don't step upon my weenie. (Clancy, 1989)

weigh the thumb deliberately to overcharge
From the practice of surreptitiously depressing the scales to give a heavier reading, but now used figuratively of any overcharging.

weight problem see PROBLEM

weight watcher an obese person
But at least conscious of it and often trying to do something about it. See CALORIE COUNTER.

welfare state aid to the poor
It originally meant prosperity, which is not how all the recipients today see it:

> ...his girl friend threatened to call the cops when he took half of her welfare money. (Wambaugh, 1983)

The British *Welfare State*, a Utopian concept introduced after the Second World War, had the laudable intention of providing all citizens with free medical care, free schooling, and provision for adequate shelter, food, and clothing, regardless of whether they were in employment or paid taxes.

well away drunk
Also as *well bottled*, *in the way*, *corned*, *oiled*, *sprung*, etc.:

> The Colonel... overcomes his resistance to vodka to such an extent that he is soon well away and sings songs of Old Kentucky. (A. Carter, 1984)
> I'll nut say drunk, but gay weel cwonr'd. (A. Whitehead, 1896)

Some forms are obsolete.

well built fat
Used of men and women, and of children also, because manufacturers know better than to describe somebody's little darling as obese. Less often as *well-fleshed*:

> ...there is a well-built girl attendant who is chased about the stage. (*Daily Telegraph*, 31 October 1972)
> Well-fleshed men could niver stand up long agen an ale-pot. (Sutcliffe, 1901)

well endowed having large genitals or breasts
It is unlikely that a female so described will bring a dowry to the marriage settlement. The possession of such characteristics is known as *endowment*:

> ...she was probably as pretty, if considerably less well-endowed. (Price, 1972—she had smaller breasts)

Exceptionally good-looking, personable,
muscular athlete is available. Hot bottom
plus large endowment equals a good time.
(*Sunday Telegraph*, September 1989, quoting
the advertisement answered by
Representative Frank, who later appointed
the personable, if immodest, prostitute as a
personal aide)

well hung having large genitalia
Used critically of bulls, stallions, and rams,
and lewdly of men:
> He had a deep voice and looked from his
> tight pants to be fairly well hung. (Phillips,
> 1991)

well-informed sources the person involved
Political usage when the passer of the information wishes to remain anonymous, to
influence public opinion without making a
direct statement, or to reveal confidential
details. As the attribution no longer deceives
many people, the information now tends to
come from *friends* of the politician in question:
> Friends reported Michael Portillo's
> opinion as being in the same vein.
> (J. Major, 1999)

well rewarded overpaid
It is better not to be seen to accuse the
beneficiary of greed:
> ...Lord Young, C & W's well-rewarded
> chairman. (*Daily Telegraph*, 6 December
> 1994)

welly a contraceptive sheath
A shortened form of *Wellington boot*, which is
also made of rubber and has protective
properties:
> **wellies from the Queen** are condoms held
> by the QM at the brow during foreign port
> visits. (Jolly, 1988—the *brow* is the gang-
> way)

wench *archaic* a prostitute
Originally, a girl, whence a promiscuous
woman:
> Let my lord take wenches by the score.
> (Blackhall, 1849)
He who *wenches* is a womanizer.

West Briton *Irish* an Anglicized Irishman
Often Protestant, educated in England, and
affecting the speech and manners of the
British professional classes. Used derogatively
by some other Irish people:
> Those on the other side, he said, were mere
> 'West Britons'. (Kee, 1993—this was rather
> rich coming from C. S. Parnell, a Protestant
> cricket-lover educated at Cambridge who
> spoke with a British upper-class accent)

Whence the obsolete *West Britonism*, the
policy of advocating the continuation of the
union with Great Britain:
> The O'Conor Don is a sample of West
> Britonism in Ireland—he is a sample of the
> rights of England and Englishmen to rule
> Ireland. (ibid.)
And the adjectival *West British*:
> After a short time the paper's policy could
> no longer with any justice be called 'West
> British'. (Fleming, 1965, of the *Irish Times*,
> which maintained a Unionist stance for
> some time after the creation of the Irish
> Free State)

wet¹ (the bed) to urinate in an inappropriate place
And in various other phrases, such as *wet
yourself*, to urinate in your clothing; *wet your
pants*, to urinate in your trousers, etc.:
> Boys and girls who steal, vandalize, or wet
> the bed...(Bradbury, 1976)
> Grooters felt her legs almost doubling
> underneath her and she wet herself.
> (Davidson, 1978)
> Merriman thought he was going to wet his
> pants. (M. Thomas, 1980)

wet² a drink of an intoxicant
Seldom on its own:
> Bring me a wet. I feel parched. (Cookson,
> 1967)
A *wet canteen* or *bar* is a place where
intoxicants are served:
> We spent a very pleasant evening, the First
> Battalion having a wet canteen, and when
> we started back we were three sheets in
> the wind. (F. Richards, 1933)
> The sitting room of his cottage had a
> fully stocked wet bar. (Erdman, 1993)
Wet goods or *stuff* were intoxicants, especially
in American Prohibition use:
> The wet goods flowed. You couldn't move
> all of it. (Longstreet, 1956, describing the
> Prohibition years)
A *wet-hand* is a drunkard, who might be said
too often to *wet his mouth, beard, quill,* or
whistle:
> Simply must wet m'whistle. (Manning,
> 1960)
To *wet a bargain* was to drink together to seal
it:
> ...and be dam we'll wet our bargain.
> (Somerville and Ross, 1908)
To *wet the baby's head* is to drink intoxicants to
celebrate a birth.

wet-back *American* an illegal Mexican
immigrant into the United States
At one time many swam across the border:
> A lot of [Californian orange pickers] were
> wet-backs. (Macdonald, 1971)

wet deck *obsolete* copulation with a woman who had recently copulated with someone else

Nautical use and imagery:

> And who would have the first bout, in any case? I'll not take your wet-decks.
> (Monsarrat, 1978, writing in archaic style)

A *wet hen* was a prostitute.

wet dream an involuntary seminal ejaculation while asleep

The experience may be accompanied by an erotic dream:

> Any dreams, wet or non-wet . . . (Amis, 1978)

Figurative use only of female lust:

> Sharing a bed is nothing, in college we girls do it all the time. But curling up is your Philomena's wet dream. (Rushdie, 1995—it was suggested that Philomena was a homosexual)

wet for (of a woman) lusting after

From the enhanced. secretion. Also *wet your drawers, knickers, pants,* or *yourself*:

> I am rotten-ripe, soft and wet for you.
> (F. Harris, 1925)

> It's a stock joke that all the women in the club wet their knickers at the sight of him.
> (Lodge, 1980)

> —Women like your women go for money, Jimmy Sr told Bimbo.—They'll wet themselves abou' any ugly fucker or spastic just as long as they're rich. (R. Doyle, 1991)

wet job a murder

But not necessarily by drowning. Also as *wet operations* or *work*:

> If anyone fancied the idea of doing a 'wet job' on me then the bomb would go off in hours. (Allbeury, 1983)

> Max was an expert at what the checkists tactfully described as mokrie dela, 'wet operations'. (R. Moss, 1987)

> Heydrich [had] his more donnish subordinates carry out what is uncharmingly called 'wet-work'. (Burleigh, 2000)

wet nurse a woman paid to suckle another's baby

Standard English:

> Most women then got their kids wet-nursed by somebody else, if they could afford it. (Atwood, 1988)

wet weekend *Australian* a period of menstruation

Weather during which the opportunity for sport is curtailed.

wet your wick (of a male) to copulate

Not by taking a shower—see WICK:

> Carlo had tried to wet his wick, because in Oregon that was no big deal, and before the sun was up her father had opened his throat for the ants to have a drink.
> (Seymour, 1984)

wetness sweat

Female usage and advertising jargon:

> The confident, knowledgeable people with public lives which transcend choices about bathroom bowl cleaners and products to prevent underarm 'wetness' have been males. (Mackie, 1983)

wetting[1] *obsolete* an intoxicating drink

Not being caught in the rain:

> The young chaps bring their bottles out, And ilk ane gets a wettin'. (Lumsden, 1892)

wetting[2] *obsolete* stale urine

Used in domestic laundry and cloth manufacture before chemists formulated more expensive alternatives:

> I slat a pot of wettin in his face. (Wheeler, 1790)

whack to kill

The common hitting imagery:

> Joe, you know when Geoff got whacked, don't you? (Sanders, 1977—Joe was hit not by a cane but by the train under which he was pushed in Union Square station)

whack off to masturbate

To *whack* is to pull, among other meanings:

> . . . Zoona—who was eventually thrown out of school for whacking off in full sight of three mothers during parents day.
> (J. Collins, 1981)

whacked drunk

From the slang meaning, exhausted. The symptoms can be the same:

> . . . a very wet party. Everyone got whacked out of their skulls. (Sanders, 1982)

wham (of a male) to copulate with

The usual violent imagery, and also in the phrase *wham, bang, and thank you ma'am,* of a selfish philanderer:

> Monotonous, you know: the wham, bang and thank you ma'am type. (Pérez-Réverté, 1994, in translation—a woman was expressing dissatisfaction with her sexual partner)

what the traffic will bear an excessive but obtainable price

The imagery is from transport pricing policy. The cliché is most used by lawyers, merchant bankers, etc. when setting fee levels for corporate, careless, or care-worn customers.

what you may call it any taboo object
The lavatory for many females, or a part of
the body associated with sex or urination.
Often shortened to *whatsit*, less often to
whatzis:
> The whatsit is through there if you want it.
> (B. Forbes, 1983—a woman was indicating
> where the lavatory lay)
> ...you'll probably use it to shoot off your
> whatzis. (Sanders, 1982—*it* was a handgun)

whelp to give birth to a child
A *whelp* is literally the cub of a bitch, a lioness,
or a tigress:
> ...she was so close to what she called
> 'whelpin' that she couldn't be moved.
> (Keneally, 1979)

whiff *American* to kill
Perhaps obsolete, from the slang meaning, to
hit out at:
> He wasn't alone when you whiffed him.
> (Chandler, 1939)

whiff of associated with something il-
legal or taboo
From the smell:
> ...we got a definite whiff of march hare.
> (Monkhouse, 1993—somebody was acting
> strangely)
Carlyle's *whiff of grapeshot* was the firing on the
Paris mob by Napoleon which established
order and his personal authority.

whiffled drunk
To *whiffle* was to be unsteady, as drunkards
often are:
> 'I did thirty days without the option
> for punching a policeman in the
> stomach on Boat-Race night.' 'But you
> were whiffled at the time.' (Wodehouse,
> 1930)

whip to steal
Usually of small objects, perhaps from the
moving of a distant article with the use of a
whip. Common slang use.

whip the cat to be drunk
Cats are associated with vomiting and vomiting with drunkenness, although that does not
explain the *whipping*.

whistle the penis
Nursery usage, from the shape in a young boy.

whistleblower a person who reveals
damaging confidential information
The position of a referee, who stops the game
when he detects foul play:
> But the marginalizing of local government,
> and giving powers and public funds to
> unelected, unaccountable quangos (with

rules that punish 'whistleblowers')...(*Daily
Telegraph*, 5 February 1994)
See also BLOW THE WHISTLE ON.

whistled *?obsolete* drunk
A *whistle* in slang is a mouth, which we still
WET 2. A *whistle-shop* was an unlicensed inn,
operated by a *whistler*:
> The whistler, otherwise the spirit-
> merchant. (Moncrieff, 1821)

white elephant an unwanted or onerous
possession
The King of Siam, also titled 'the King of the
White Elephant', was said to present such a
beast to any courtier he wished to ruin.
Unable to sell or work the animal, the
recipient had to provide for it with no return:
> The £2000 million white elephant. (*Private
> Eye*, March 1981, referring to Concorde)

white feather cowardice
Such a feather in the plumage of a fighting
cock was said to indicate poor breeding
whence less aggressive behaviour:
> There's a white feather somewhere in the
> chield's wing, for all he's so big and
> buirdly. (Hamilton, 1898—*buirdly* means
> fine-looking)

white girl cocaine or heroin
In addict jargon. Also as *white lady*, *line*, *powder*,
or *stuff*:
> She could tell you each and every
> nickname for cocaine. Snow or Peruvian
> lady or blow or white girl. (McBain, 1994)
> Trade in the 'red, green and white lines'—
> rubies, jade and heroin—lay behind the
> dramatic growth of business in Mandalay.
> (Maclean, 1998)
> He was still getting $100,000 a
> year...and that bought a goodly amount
> of the sweet white powder.
> (M. Thomas, 1982)

white-knuckler *American* a small aircraft
on a scheduled service
Alluding to the anxious grip of the passengers
on the arms of the seats, especially in bad
weather:
> You take a white-knuckler...from Hyannis
> Airport through the fog to Logan. (Theroux,
> 1978)
Various local carriers are called the *White-
Knuckle Line* by their regular passengers.

white lightning[1] LSD
From its effect on those who ingest it:
> Ellen...unfolded some tinfoil which she
> said contained three tabs of Owsley's
> original 'white lightning', the Mouton-
> Rothschild of LSD. (*Village Voice*, 1 June
> 1972)

white lightning² a spirituous intoxicant
Either illegally distilled, and uncoloured,
whisky, or standard gin or vodka. Also as
white eye, *mule* (from the kick), *satin*, or *stuff*:
> ... 'white lightning', 'white mule', or
> just plain 'corn', as the local
> moonshine whiskey is called.
> (*Double Dealer*, July 1921)
> White satin, if I must know, was gin.
> (Mayhew, 1862)
> He was drunk ... He'd been on the white
> stuff all day long and was drinking it like
> water. (le Carré, 1989)

white marriage a marriage in which the
parties do not copulate
The traditional virginal colour, so often seen
inappropriately in the bridal gown, remains
appropriate here:
> I don't think there's much sex in poor
> Tom. What's known as a white marriage.
> (Burgess, 1980)

white meat¹ the breast of cooked poultry
As with DARK MEAT 1, now standard English,
with Victorian prudery forgotten.

white meat² a white woman viewed
sexually
The converse of DARK MEAT 2, but also used of
the aspirations of a white man living among
black people:
> If it's white meat you want, ji, you won't
> find-o much on her. (Rushdie, 1995—it was
> suggested that Jawaharlal Nehru would find
> Edwina, Countess Mountbatten, an
> unsatisfactory sexual partner)
> If there's one thing an English officer abroad
> wants once in a while, Sharpie, it's a spot of
> the white meat ... They get bored with the
> dark meat. (B. Cornwell, 1997, writing in
> archaic style)

white plague (the) *obsolete* pulmonary
tuberculosis
The illness attracted much euphemism because it killed many young adults:
> When scarlet fever, cholera, typhoid
> fever, and the 'white plague'
> (tuberculosis) took such a toll of
> young ladies in their
> prime ... (Pearsall, 1969, writing of
> the 19th century)

white rabbit scut (the) cowardice
The *scut* is the short white erect tail, the sign
of the fleeing rabbit:
> What, leave Marsh and show the white
> rabbit scut to Nicholas Radcliffe? (Sutcliffe,
> 1900)

white sale an occasion when concessions
are freely given

There is recurrent heavy discounting by
retailers of *white goods*, bedlinen, and domestic
appliances. Some figurative use:
> I got him everything. It was a white sale at
> the U.S. Attorney's office. (Turow, 1990)

white slave a white prostitute working
outside Europe
Usually under a pimp's strict control or in a
brothel. *White slavery* is the business in which
a *white slaver* is engaged as a pimp:
> London, or rather those who carry on the
> White Slave Traffic, provides the largest
> market in the world for the sale of human
> flesh. (Paxman, 1998, quoting Stead,
> *c.*1882)
> White slavery—the seduction and selling,
> and of course buying, of women for
> immoral purposes ... (Londres, 1928, in
> translation)
> I'm not a white slaver in case they exist.
> (P. D. James, 1972—a young woman was
> being invited to go on a journey with a
> stranger)

white tail a completed but unsold new
aircraft
The manufacturer leaves it in a white finish
until the buyer stipulates the livery. *White tails*
are a treble disaster for the maker: his finance
charges continue, his cash flow is interrupted,
and the presence of unsold aircraft spoils the
market.

white top a geriatric
A man so described may be bald, and a
woman may have BLUE HAIR:
> The problem with 'white tops', old folks
> with failing reflexes, impaired faculties or
> the effects of prescription drugs, let loose
> on the highways, is causing concern in
> Florida. (*Daily Telegraph*, December 1988)

whitewash an attempt to hush up an embarrassing or shameful event
The compound of lime and water, or similar
non-permanent materials, easily and liberally
applied to a surface, may provide temporary
cover for the blemishes underneath:
> Then, in Hughes's opinion, the committee
> had produced a whitewash. (Colodny and
> Gettlin, 1991, writing about a report on the
> secret bombing of Vietnam)
The author of a British report in February 2001
on the granting of citizenship to wealthy
Indians with what seemed to many to be
unseemly haste, despite their apparent inelig-
ibility and their financial prodigality to causes
dear to the heart of Government, was given, in
the press if not elsewhere, the nickname *Dulux*,
from a brand of paint, possibly because it was
thought the affair had been more effectively
covered up than by a simple *whitewash*.

whizz *American* an act of urination
Onomatopoeic use:
> 'I just came in for a whizz.' He recoiled at
> the vulgarity. (Theroux, 1978)

whole hog (the) copulation
Usually after courtship involving exploratory
sexual acts, and in the phrase *go the whole hog*,
meaning to do something completely, which
was derived either from eating a male pig at a
sitting or from drinking all of a hogshead of
ale:
> She was disappointed. That I didn't go the
> whole hog. (Amis, 1980)

wholesome *obsolete* not suffering from
venereal disease
Literally, no more than healthy:
> The woman, endeed, is a most lovely
> woman; but I had no courage to meddle
> with her, for fear of her not being
> wholesome. (Pepys, 1664—perhaps too he
> was feeling weary, having already 'had his
> pleasure of' Mrs Lane twice that day)

wick the penis
Rhyming slang on the London neighbourhood
Hampton Wick and PRICK. This is a unique
example of both parts of a rhyming slang
phrase being used individually, although they
are not synonyms, *wick* alone being used
figuratively as well as literally:
> It gets on my, you know, wick. (Bradbury,
> 1976)
See also HAMPTON.

wicked way (your) copulation
It is the male who seeks this path, which is
not to be confused with Jermyn Street or
the Reeperbahn. The phrase is mostly used
humorously, and as *wicked design*, *purposes*,
etc.:
> James MacDermott was hauling me all
> around the house at Mr Kinnear's,
> looking for a bed for his wicked purposes.
> (Atwood, 1996)

wide-on (a) *American* female heterosex-
ual lust
I suppose from the inappropriateness of
HARD-ON. Also figurative use:
> That's the one thing about lady
> analysts...once in a while they fall in love
> with a stock, usually because they get a
> wide-on for the management. (M. Thomas,
> 1985)

wiener a penis
The derivation is explained under WEENIE:
> And keep your hands off yer wiener. (King,
> 1996)

will *obsolete* a homosexual

Widespread dialect use of either sex. *EDD* says
'an effeminate man; a mannish woman',
which is as close to defining homosexuality
as Dr Wright would venture. It is a shortened
form of *will-o-the-wisp*, the *ignis fatuus*, of which
first appearances are deceptive.

will there be anything else? *obsolete* do
you wish to buy condoms?
The question was asked of adult males by
their barber, when condoms were not sold
openly in places to which women went and
were freely available through barbers' shops:
> ...the days when one's barber, hoping to
> sell a packet of Durex, used to murmur
> discreetly, 'Will there be anything else,
> sir?' (*Sunday Telegraph*, 27 March 1994—and
> they still called a customer 'sir')

willie-waught *obsolete Scottish* a drink of
intoxicant
Good willie meant hospitable and *waught*
meant to drink deeply:
> 'And we'll take a right guid willie-waught'
> was changed to, 'We'll give a right guid
> hearty shake', in deference to temperance
> principles. (E. Murray, 1977, writing of Sir
> James Murray, the creator of the *OED* and
> domestically the bowdlerizer of Robert
> Burns. He also omitted from the *OED* the
> common vulgarisms noted by Grose, and
> other taboo words)

willy a penis
Or *willie*, in nursery and adult use:
> Does your willy rise like a snake out of a
> basket? (Theroux, 1978)
> There are almost as many names for a
> man's most intimate possession as there
> are for himself...from Tom, Dick and
> Harry to Jean-Claude, Giorgio and Fritz. The
> villain of this book is called Willie. (Joliffe
> and Mayle, 1984)
A *willie-puller*, a masturbater, is a term of
vulgar abuse:
> Enter Willie-Puller Hays, the man in charge
> of President Harding's election
> campaign. (Vanderhaeghe, 1997—Hays
> also ran the 'Hays Office', which sought
> to monitor and control the morality of
> Hollwood stars)

win¹ to steal
Old general use and still current among
soldiers:
> The cull has won a couple of glimsticks.
> (Grose—a *glimstick* was a candlestick)
> In the army it is always considered more
> excusable to 'win' or 'borrow' things from
> men belonging to other companies.
> (F. Richards, 1936)

win² to copulate with

In a bygone age, to *win* a woman was to secure her consent to marriage. It now refers to extramarital sexual conquest:

> I resolved to win her altogether. (F. Harris, 1925—but not with a proposal of wedlock)

win home *obsolete Scottish* to die
Christian devout use of the death of another, although the speaker seldom seemed anxious to secure a similar victory for himself. Also as *win your way* or *win to rest*:

> Thro' a' life's troubles we'll win home at e'en. (J. Wright, 1897)
> Auld Jamie has gi'en up the ghost
> And won his way. (Hetrick, 1826)
> He's been troubled lang; but now
> He's won to rest. (ibid.)

wind[1] a belch or fart
In genteel use, only of belching, about which there are fewer taboos than farting:

> Baked beans, which always give me terrible wind... (Matthew, 1978)

See also WINDY 1.

wind[2] **(the)** *American* dismissal from employment, courtship, or occupancy
Something which you may be *given*:

> My rent is over due for the shovel and broom... She says she will give me the wind if I do not lay something on the line at once. (Runyon, 1990, written in the 1930s—the *shovel and broom* was the room)

Or *taken*, which implies voluntary departure:

> She takes the wind on me a couple of months ago for my friend Frankie Ferocious. (ibid.)

wind up (the) cowardice
The result of being WINDY 2:

> Been sick, has he? He's got the wind up, that's his trouble. (Faulks, 1993, writing of a soldier in the trenches in 1916)

winded (of a male) incapacitated by a blow to the genitalia
Supposedly, having received a blow in the stomach:

> 'Just winded,' groaned Harry, though in fact a flying brick had struck him a painful blow in the groin... he was holding his genitals in his hand for they were too painful to massage. (Farrell, 1973)

The evasion is much favoured by sports commentators.

windfall a bribe
Fruit which fell to the ground used to be given to whomsoever wished to gather it. Thus a *windfall* was something of value for which you did not have to pay, including a legacy or other unexpected benefit:

> The cop and those higher up share in the windfall. (Lavine, 1930—describing bribery, not apples)

window dressing falsely or fraudulently issuing figures or statements relating to a business
Commercial and banking jargon, using imagery from retail trading:

> The cheques were part of the 'window dressing' of the balance sheet at London and County Securities. (*Private Eye*, September 1981—beware always the words *security* or *trust* in any financial organization which asks you to invest)

windy[1] suffering from or likely to cause flatulence or flatus
See ALSO WIND 1:

> ... taters... es windy zort o grub. (Agrikler, 1872)

windy[2] frightened
With a suggestion of cowardice:

> ... he may be what the British soldier would call 'slightly windy'. (W. S. Moss, 1950)

See also WIND UP.

winged wounded
Second World War use of humans, from the shooting of birds which, if hit in the wing, fall to the ground alive.

winkle a penis
Nursery usage, perhaps from the *Willie* in *Wee Willie Winkie*. Occasionally also as *winkie*:

> ... unlikely to haul himself diagonally across the polished walnut and scratch at his winkle. (Amis, 1978)
> Very butch, and he's got a gun trained on your winkie. (B. Forbes, 1986)

wipe off to kill
The imagery is from erasing chalk from a blackboard. The phrase is used of death through the forces of nature or by virtue of man's inhumanity:

> What more useful bird can you find, as wipes off worms an' grubs as they did? (A. Patterson, 1895)
> He'll wipe you off. (Chandler, 1939, referring to a killing, not a spilt bowl of soup)

wipe out[1] to kill
From the erasure:

> I worked with three gangs who got wiped out, all except me. (L. Thomas, 1979)

wipe out[2] to cause to lose wealth or reputation

Either through bankruptcy or being discrediting:

> ...was it fair to take a nice, dumb little guy like Lehman for such a ride, one that would inevitably wipe him out? (Erdman, 1987—Lehman was about to be cheated, not killed)
>
> It would wipe me out, of course. No one would employ me. (Deighton, 1988—he was facing a criminal charge)

wire to render ineffective a tachograph (on a commercial vehicle)

The tachograph records the times when the vehicle is moving, thus providing evidence that statutory rest periods are taken by the driver:

> A driver who wishes to exceed his permitted hours may disconnect the tachograph, either by removing the fuse or by seeking to by-pass it electrically, which is known as 'wiring'. (Holder, 2000)

See also HOT-WIRE.

wire-pulling the covert use of influence or pressure

Like the actuation of a puppet:

> ...promises were held out of 'wire-pulling tactics in high political circles'. (R. F. Foster, 1993, referring to the advance publicity for Mrs Parnell's 1914 autobiography)

wired¹ drunk or under the influence of narcotics

Of the same tendency as LIT and more of drug-taking than alcohol:

> 'Do you have to go to bed?' he asked. 'I'm wired. I can't sleep.' (Robbins, 1981, after taking drugs)

wired² (up) subject to clandestine surveillance

This espionage and police jargon has survived the introduction of devices which are almost always *wire-less*:

> Even the damn cats are wired, no exaggeration. (le Carré, 1980)
>
> ...the defendant remained unaware...that their interrogators were...'wired up'. (*Private Eye*, March, 1981)

An investigator or person seeking evidence clandestinely may be said to *wear a wire*:

> Because of that [Linda Tripp] decided to wear a wire for Ken Starr? (*Sunday Telegraph*, 4 October 1998)

A *wireman* is an expert in the technology:

> What we need is a first-class wireman, somebody who can do it right. The apartment. The phone. (Diehl, 1978)

wired to the moon mentally abnormal

A variant of the common *lunar* theme:

> She was wired to the moon but she was harmless. (R. Doyle, 1996)

wise woman *obsolete* a witch

And a *wise man* was a wizard:

> Sure a wise woman came in from Finnigan...and she said it's what ailed him he had the Fallen Palate. (Somerville and Ross, 1908)

with child pregnant

Standard English, and not just somebody left holding the baby:

> Once he had got a girl with child. (G. Greene, 1932)

with learning difficulties unable to keep up with your peers in class

All of us suffer from *learning difficulties* from time to time, especially the elderly when it comes to computers and other electronic gadgets, and children who prefer watching television to doing their homework. A favoured educational jargon use.

with respect you are wrong

Used in polite discussion and jargon of the courts where an advocate wishes to contradict a judge without prejudicing his case:

> There is high authority for the view that (with respect) means 'You are wrong'...just as 'with great respect' means 'you are utterly wrong' and 'with the utmost respect' equals 'send for the men in white coats'. (Mr Justice Staughton, quoted in *Daily Telegraph*, February 1987)

with us no more dead

Or having left employment, voluntarily or otherwise. See also NO LONGER WITH US.

with your Maker dead

Christian usage in various forms, from the posthumous heavenly gathering of the righteous and others, who may also aspire to meet *God, Jesus, the Lord*, etc.:

> If you make a wrong move, you're with your maker. (Fraser, 1970)

withdraw from life to kill yourself

The destination is unspecified:

> Due to the hopelessness of the state of her health, she decided to withdraw from life. (*Daily Telegraph*, 6 July 2001—reporting a statement about the suicide of Hannelore, the wife of Helmut Kohl)

withdraw your labour to go on strike

Trade union jargon. It could simply mean to go home or to change your employment.

withdrawal to prepared positions a forced retreat

One way in which the defeated seek to play down or mitigate failure. A *withdrawal in good order* is probably a rout.

within-group norming *American* giving lower marks to white candidates than to blacks

An attempt to meet a QUOTA in employment ratios by penalizing those who are likely to have had better educational opportunities:
> ...referred to in government and employment circles as 'within-group norming' or 'score adjustment'. (*Chicago Times*, 14 May 1991)

See also RACE-NORMING.

without a head *obsolete Scottish* unmarried

This expression refers to the time when many unmarried women had little security outside their parents' house, few opportunities to maintain themselves, and almost no protection in law:
> It's no easy thing...for a woman to go through the world without a head. (Miller, 1879)

(Males who are vexed by the antics of modern feminists should remember that this pendulum once swung the other way.)

without baggage *obsolete* to execution

One of the coded phrases used by the Russians under Communism for prisoners taken out of jail to be killed. Also as *without the right to correspondence*, which at least acknowledged that dead people can't read:
> From time to time someone would depart from the camp 'without baggage'. Those were sinister words—we all knew what they meant. (Horrocks, 1960—he was imprisoned in Moscow in 1920 after serving with the White Russian forces)
> A doctor who complained that his sister had died of hunger was sentenced to ten years 'without the right of correspondence', the euphemism for a death sentence. (Moynahan, 1994)

without the highest IQ in the world slow-witted

A sample entry to cover many similar phrases, which logically might refer to all of us, bar one:
> He was a good man—without the highest IQ in the world. (Monty Roberts, 1996)

woman a female viewed lustfully by a man

He who says *I feel like a woman tonight* does not postulate an incipient sex-change. A *womanizer* is a male profligate.

woman friend a mistress

As distinct from a FRIEND who is a *woman*:
> Somoza, his woman friend...and four of his five children. (*Daily Telegraph*, August 1979)

woman in a gilded cage a mistress

In the 19th-century she might be provided with separate accommodation by her wealthy keeper:
> The companion of a girl's fall might himself be the utterer of a divine message...the woman...breaking away from her gilded cage. (H. Hunt, *c.*1854)

In modern America, she may be the young (second or subsequent) bride of a much older wealthy man.

woman named *British* a woman accused by the wife of an adulterous association with her husband

Legal jargon in a divorce suit. A man accused by the husband of a similar involvement with his wife might be joined in the proceedings as a CO-RESPONDENT, thereby making him liable for damages and costs. *Naming* the woman brought nothing worse than unwelcome publicity.

woman of intrigue *obsolete* a dissolute woman

As different from an *intriguing woman*:
> Praise me...for my good qualities—you know them; but tell also how odd, how constant, how impetuous, how much accustomed to women of intrigue. (Lynd, 1946—Boswell was instructing Temple about approaching Miss Blair on his behalf)

woman of the town a prostitute

Not just someone who does not live in the country:
> It is ordered that hereafter when any female shall...show contempt for any officer or soldier of the United States, she shall be regarded and held liable as a woman of the town, plying her avocation. (G. C. Ward, 1990, quoting an order by the Yankee military governor of New Orleans in 1862)

Also as a *woman of the world*, although to be a *man of the world* implies knowledge of, rather than participation in, shameful activities.

woman's thing (the) female homosexuality

Homosexual jargon:
> The virago and her soulmate into, as they would say, the woman's thing...(Theroux, 1978)

women a lavatory for exclusively female use

Not generally less salubrious than a lavatory marked LADIES. Also as *women's room* etc.

women's liberation aggressive feminism
For most men, and many women, a dysphemism, especially when shortened to *women's lib*:

> Women's lib meant more than burning your bra. It meant total commitment to the programme of women's superiority over men. (Sharpe, 1976)

An enthusiast may be called a *women's libber* or *libber*, which latter was once the job title of a castrator of pigs—further comment seems inappropriate:

> You make me sound like the worst sort of Women's Libber, an aggressive great Lesbian with a foul placard. (Pilcher, 1988)
> She's gone to join some women friends. Libbers, you know. (I. Murdoch, 1980)

women's movement (the) an association of committed feminists
Nothing to do with calisthenics; and see MOVEMENT 2.

women's rights the claim to or enjoyment of economic and social conditions historically exclusive to or awarded in priority to men
As different from the normal rights of females as citizens:

> ...extensive literature on Women's Rights and the Feminist movement. (Bradbury, 1976)

women's things any taboo matter or article exclusive to women
Usually the phrase refers to a medical condition exclusive to females, or to absorbent matter worn during menstruation:

> For the Curse—you know. Women's things. (W. Smith, 1979)

wooden box a coffin
A current usage. *Wooden breeches, breeks, coat, overcoat*, etc. are obsolete:

> A pair of wooden breeks
> Now him doth clede. (W. Sutherland, 1821—to *clead* was to clothe)

Whence figurative use of death:

> The Winston treatment when it finally comes to the wooden box. (*Private Eye*, June 1981—Churchill had an elaborate state funeral)

wooden hill the staircase
Nursery usage. Children may be told to climb it when reluctant to go to bed or, in the hallowed punning phrase, *to Bedfordshire*.

wooden log a human used involuntarily for dangerous medical research
A Second World War usage by both Russians and Japanese:

> White Russian Jews, nearly all living in Manchuria or Northern China, were already subject to appalling discrimination, not as Jews but as stateless White Russians, and potential 'wooden logs'. (Behr, 1989)

The Japanese General Ishii, commanding Unit 731, used prisoners of war for medical experimentation until the end of the Second World War. He also tried to land plague-bearing fleas by submarine on Saipan to infect US troops. Fortunately the submarine was sunk. Neither he nor his emperor, Hirohito, was charged as a war criminal.

word from our sponsor (a) *American* an advertisement on television
Would that it were only one.

word to the wise a warning or threat
There is a suggestion that it would be unwise to ignore the message:

> When questions of the legitimacy of the Zogoiby children began to be hinted at...the editors of all the major newspapers...had a word-to-the-wise in their ears; and after that the press campaign stopped instantly. (Rushdie, 1995)

words *American* an advertisement on television
Another way of covering up the intrusion:

> We'll have a filmed report after these words. (Bryson, 1989)

work at yourself to masturbate
As different from *working on yourself*, a process of self-improvement:

> To obliterate these thoughts, she slid her hand between her legs and felt herself, worked on herself...until at last her loins twisted and she was lost. (N. Evans, 1995)

Remember also Shakespeare's 'You rise to play, and go to bed to work' (*Othello*).

work both sides of the street to serve people with conflicting interests
To *work a street* was to attempt to sell goods from door to door, not always honestly, as different from to WORK THE STREETS:

> For years he'd been a Mr Fixit, working both sides of the street. (Deighton, 1988)

work on[1] to extract information from through violence
Literally, to have an effect on physically:

> 'Shellacking', 'massaging', 'breaking the news', 'working on the——'...'giving him the works'...express how [the NYC police] compel reluctant prisoners to refresh their memories. (Lavine, 1930)

work on² (of a male) to copulate with
The concept is of rough handling rather than referring to the posture assumed:
> We could...give you an examination too, and see if you've been working on her tonight. (Mailer, 1965)

work the streets to be a prostitute
From her public solicitation:
> She worked each side of the street with a skill shared...by the best of streetwalkers. (Mailer, 1965)

work to rule *British* (as an employee) to behave at work in a way calculated to obstruct and cause loss
Trade union jargon for a device which, if successful, allows an employee to be paid while damaging the employer's business by purporting to be following strictly an actual or fictional *rule book*. Less often as a noun:
> Within months, he was asking me whether we ought not to be writing more about a work-to-rule on the Circle Line of the Underground. (Cole, 1995)

See also GO SLOW and SLOWDOWN 1.

workers' control the oppressive rule by an oligarchy
Communist jargon which implied that the populace controlled the ruling and self-perpetuating oligarchs, rather than the contrary:
> Within the Leninist model... 'Worker's control' here means control of the workers. (*Sunday Telegraph*, August 1980, referring to Poland where before long the *workers* did take *control*)

workhouse an institution for the homeless indigent
The intention was that the unfortunate inmates should work to pay for their keep, although the name outlived the concept:
> I was put in the workhouse when I was young...I never knew my father or my mother. (Mayhew, 1862)

working girl a prostitute
But hoping not, as a consequence, to go into labour:
> The Marquess of Aberdeen, 80, describes his experiences as a bachelor in the Forties in a magazine article reminiscing about the working girls of London, Paris, Brussels and Beirut. (*Daily Telegraph*, 1 March 2001)

working people *British* industrial workers not self-employed or in management
Those who once claimed to belong to the *working class*, but the people who use the phrase tend to ignore others who also work for a living. Also as *working men*:
> I doubt whether working people will be willing to go on making sacrifices of this nature for much longer. (*Daily Telegraph*, January 1977—the *sacrifice* was not to receive a wage increase much exceeding the rate of inflation)
> ...most working men obeyed their trade union leaders. (Faulks, 1996, writing about the General Strike)

World Peace Council an instrument of Soviet foreign policy
A weapon of the Cold War; and see PEACE: World Peace Council, see under *front organization*. (Bullock and Stallybrass, 1977—a magisterially dismissive comment)

worry to make sexual advances to an unwilling partner
Originally, of dogs and animals, to kill by gripping the throat, whence, by transference, mental distress in, or harassment of, humans:
> It is perfectly dreadful that Wifie should be so worried at night. (Kee, 1993—Parnell was writing to his mistress Katie O'Shea, commiserating with her on the fact that her husband wished to copulate with her)

worse for wear (the) drunk
No longer in pristine condition:
> Arrived home at four, rather the worse for wear. (Matthew, 1978)

See also THE WORSE.

worship at the shrine of to be unhealthily addicted to
Usually of alcohol, illegal narcotics, or sexual excess:
> Among newspapermen, most of whom worshipped more frequently at the shrine of Bacchus than Ariadne...(Deighton, 1991—Bacchus was the god of wine. Ariadne was of an inquiring mind, helping Theseus to escape from the maze devised by Daedalus, from which subsequently Daedalus himself and his son Icarus made their aerial escape)

wrack *obsolete* to copulate with (a female virgin)
Literally, to destroy, being another form of *wreck*:
> I fear'd he did but trifle,
> And meant to wrack thee. (Shakespeare, *Hamlet*)

The *wrack of maidenhead* was the loss of virginity before marriage:
> ...the misery is, example, that so terrible shows in the wrack of maidenhead. (Shakespeare, *All's Well That Ends Well*)

wreak your passion on to copulate with
Passion, originally the suffering of pain, has
been used of lust, especially in males, since
the 16th century:
> ...overborne by desire, he had wreak'd his
> passion on a mere lifeless, spiritless body.
> (Cleland, 1749)

wrecked drunk or under the influence of
illegal narcotics
The way you may feel and look:
> They were half blitzed, but both Dolly and
> Dilford were totally wrecked. (Wambaugh,
> 1983)

wretched calendar (the) I am menstruating
Referring to the practice of noting the date of
the expected onset:
> You must be kind. The wretched calendar.
> (Fowles, 1977)

wrinkly an old person
Used by the young, mindless of 'time's
wingéd chariot':
> ...helping the wrinklies with their heating
> bills. (*Private Eye*, January 1987)

wrist job (a) masturbation
Referring to the act and, figuratively as an
insult, the actor:
> Keen? In my book he's a wrist-job.
> (C. Forbes, 1983)

write off to kill or destroy
The imagery is from the removal of an
unserviceable item from an inventory.

written out of the script dismissed from
employment
Literally, in theatrical use, in a serial play, soap
opera, etc. and metaphorically for others:
> ...he had played a psychiatrist in a soap

opera for seven years until he was written
out of the script. (Sanders, 1981)
> I wouldn't write the D-G out of the script
> too early. (Deighton, 1988)
Whence the figurative use of death:
> One jalopy like that in the flight could get
> us all written out of the script. (Deighton,
> 1982)

wrong[1] *obsolete* (of a male) to copulate
with extramaritally
Even if the female concerned said it was all
right:
> Ravish'd and wrong'd, as Philemena was.
> (Shakespeare, *Titus Andronicus*)

wrong[2] homosexual
Possibly obsolete, with the change in attitudes
to homosexuality:
> Mildred genuinely suspected something
> 'wrong' with the girl, and 'wrong' with
> Libbie. (P. Scott, 1971)
Specifically as *wrong sexual preference* etc.:
> Chris was a genuine Eastern aristocrat
> with the right name, right family, right
> connections, and the wrong sexual
> preference. (Sohmer, 1988)

wrong side of the blanket an allusion to
illegitimacy
The impregnation supposedly took place on
or out of the marital bed, not in it:
> Frank Kennedy, he said, was a gentleman
> though on the wrong side of the blanket.
> (W. Scott, 1815)

wrong time of the month the period of
menstruation
Female usage:
> It's always the wrong time of the month.
> (Weissman, quoted in Dickson, 1978)
See also TIME OF THE MONTH.

yak *American* a human carrier of illegal narcotics in bulk
See also MULE—different continent, same concept:
> Maybe some of your yaks are mouthy guys. (Sanders, 1990)

yard *obsolete* a penis
I hesitate to venture a derivation:
> 'Loves her by the foot.' 'He may not by the yard.' (Shakespeare, *Love's Labour's Lost*)

yardbird *American* a convict
He uses the exercise *yard* in a penitentiary:
> The yardbirds ignored their chief and slacked off. (Adams, 1985)

year of progress *American* a period of irreversible decline
Progress, in the statements of politicians or company chairman, usually indicates that things have gone badly:
> In the year leading up to the Tet Offensive ('1987—Year of progress' was the name of the official year-end report)...(Herr, 1977)

yellow[1] cowardly
Probably from the pallor of fright. In many phrases, with a *yellow belly* being a coward, who might display a *yellow streak* or *stripe*:
> What we have here is a demonstration of what can only be referred to as a yellow stripe down the back of the Irish Government. (*Daily Telegraph*, 7 September 1995—it had postponed a meeting with the British Prime Minister at the behest of terrorists)

However, Shakespeare's yellow stockings were a sign of jealousy:
> Remember who commended thy yellow stockings. (*Twelfth Night*)

yellow[2] *American* (especially of a prostitute) of mixed black and white ancestry
Originally, describing a light-skinned female slave, often used as a house servant. Also as *high-yellow*:
> The yellow girls stood around giggling. (Longstreet, 1956, describing New Orleans, not Hong Kong)
> ...end up being shot in the saloon by a high-yellow girl. (ibid.)

yellow page common or inferior
The implication is that those offering high-quality goods or services do not have to advertise in the popular directory, *Yellow Pages*:
> They followed Wally Bright, their yellow

page lawyer. (Grisham, 1999)

yield to copulate with a man outside marriage
Literally, to submit, and of venerable ancestry:
> There is no woman, Euphues, but she will yield in time. (Lyly, 1579, quoted in *ODEP*)
> My sisterly remorse confuted mine honour, And did I yield to him. (Shakespeare, *Measure for Measure*)

The female may *yield to desire, solicitation*, etc., *yielding her body, person, virginity*, etc.:
> Without much demur I yielded to his desire. (Mayhew, 1862)
> The pretty lady's maid will often yield to soft solicitation. (ibid.—the maid was pretty, not the lady)
> Yielding up thy body to my will. (Shakespeare, *Measure for Measure*)
> If I would yield him my virginity...(ibid.)
> ...the innocent young woman, with full knowledge, usually yields, without remorse, her person to any man. (Pearsall, 1969, quoting Patmore, c.1890)

you-know-what any taboo subject within the context
Copulation, usually as a *bit of you-know-what*, a lavatory, or parts of the body:
> 'The you-know-what's in there,' she said helpfully. Frensic staggered into the bathroom and shut the door. (Sharpe, 1977)
> ...scratching one another's you-know-whats. (le Carré, 1989)

young not over 45 years old
Mainly journalistic use, often to describe public figures who have achieved prominence at an earlier age than most of their contemporaries:
> Nick was very young, still in his early thirties. (M. Thomas, 1982)

See also MIDDLE-AGE.

young lady a man's premarital sexual partner
As with the more severe *young woman*, it may imply no more than courtship:
> The marriage has been annulled by the papal courts and it would be very painful to me & my young lady to have it referred to. (S. Hastings, 1994, quoting a letter written by E. Waugh in January, 1937)

youth (guidance) center *American* an institution for the punishment of young offenders
Unlike the British *youth centre*, which provides leisure facilities, it may require a young criminal to attend on a daily or permanent basis.

Z

zap to kill violently
Perhaps from the American cartoon language:
    Clever bastards like us, who care about
    getting zapped. (Seymour, 1984—the
    Afghans fighting the Russian invader
    were braver or more reckless than their
    opponents)

zero grazing intensive farming of cattle
The animals are confined to a barn or yard
instead of being put out to pasture:
    Heifer Project International is now
    pushing 'Zero Grazing', a
    euphemism for factory-style
    confinement farming. (*Animals Agenda*,
    March 1990)

zipper a male profligate
One who readily un*zips* his trousers other than
to urinate or retire for the night:
    The quickest zipper in the west, someone
    had once called him. (Turow, 1990, of a

philanderer)
He may also be said to have a *zipper problem*:
    I knew all about the President's alleged
    attractiveness. His 'zipper problem' had
    provided hours of dinner-party
    amusement for his friends and me.
    (Nina Burleigh, in *Daily Telegraph*,
    3 August 1998—it is to be hoped that the
    amusement was confined to the dinner
    parties)
See also TROUBLE WITH HIS FLIES.

zoned out *American* drunk or under the
influence of illegal narcotics
The imagery is from a defensive play in
football and basketball.

zonked *American* drunk or under the influence of illegal drugs
Literally in slang, hit:
    ...he should be banging women zonked
    out of their gourds on high-quality coke.
    (Sanders, 1990)

zoo *American* a brothel
A variety of creatures are available to the
visitor.

Thematic Index

Classification under specific headings is necessarily inexact and is intended only to give the reader a quick guide to the most common areas of euphemism. It is not possible to avoid an overlap between such categories as, for example, *Death*, *Funerals*, and *Killing and Suicide*. A word or phrase which does not have its own entry but which appears under another entry is listed in one of two ways. If its headword is listed in the index under the same subject heading and is alphabetically adjacent, it will appear indented beneath it:

blue hair
  blue rinse

If the headword is listed under a different subject heading or is at some remove alphabetically, it will be presented in this way:

male beast *at* big animal

The specific headings are as follows:

Abortion and Miscarriage
Age
Aircraft
Animals
Auctions and Real Estate

Bankruptcy and
  Indebtedness
Bawds and Pimps
Boasting and Flattery
Breasts
Bribery
Brothels

Charity
Cheating
Childbirth and Pregnancy
Clothing
Commerce, Banking, and
  Industry
Contraception
Copulation
Cosmetics
Courtship and Marriage
Cowardice
Crime (other than Stealing)
Cuckoldry

Death
Defecation

Dismissal
Drunkenness

Education
Employment
Entertainment
Erections and Orgasms
Espionage
Extortion and Violence

Farting
Female Genitalia
Funerals

Gambling

Illegitimacy and Parentage
Illness and Injury
Intoxicants

Killing and Suicide

Lavatories
Low Intelligence
Lying

Male Genitalia
Masturbation
Menstruation
Mental Illness
Mistresses and Lovers

Nakedness

Narcotics

Obesity

Parts of the Body (other
  than Genitalia and
  Breasts)
Police
Politics
Pornography
Poverty and Parsimony
Pregnancy
Prison
Prostitution

Race
Religion and Superstition

Sexual Pursuit
Sexual Variations
Stealing
Sweat

Urination

Venereal Disease
Vulgarisms

Warfare

Unclassified entries are listed at the end of the thematic index.

Abortion and Miscarriage

bring off [2]
criminal operation
D and C
drop a bundle *at* drop[4]

female pills
French renovating pills
hoovering
illegal operation
misgo *at* misfortune
mis(s) *at* miss[2]

part with Patrick
  part with child
pick[2]
planned parenthood
planned termination
pregnancy interruption

pro-choice
pro-life
reproductive freedom
slip[1]
termination
voluntary pregnancy
    interruption

Age

active
ageful
blue hair
    blue rinse
boy
certain age (a)
chair-days
convalescent home
crinkly
crumbly
Darby and Joan[1]
eventide home
fail
forward at the knees
get along
get on
girl[2]
God's waiting room
golden age
golden years (the)
home[1]
honourable age
kid
long in the tooth
longer-living
make old bones
mature
    matured
middle age
mutton dressed as lamb
no (spring) chicken
not as young as I was
not in the first flush of youth
nursing home
of mature years
older woman (the)
residential provision
    resident
rest home
Roman spring (a)
senior citizen
    seniors
senior moment (a)
sheltered
somewhere where he (or she)
    can be looked after
state farm
    state home
state hospital
step on[1]
sunset years
third age (the)
    University of the Third Age
twilight home

up along
wear down
white top
wrinkly
young

Aircraft

air hostess at hostess
blue room
Chinese (three-point) landing
clipper at tourist
club at tourist
Dutch roll
economy
executive at tourist
fall[7]
go-around
go down[3]
go in
gross height excursion
heavy landing
hijack
hit the silk
involuntary conversion
loss of separation
motion discomfort
    motion discomfort bag
no show
on the silk at silk (the)
operational difficulties
out of the envelope
overdue[2]
overflight
pancake[2]
paper aeroplane
    paper helicopter
red eye (special) at
    red-eye
roman candle
short-shipped
silk (the)
sovereign at tourist
splash
tourist
unscheduled
white-knuckler
    White Knuckle Line
white tail

Animals

big animal
brute
bunny hugger
cleanse[2]
crower
dark meat[1]
drumstick
French pigeon
fry[2]
furry thing
game[1]
he-cow

he-biddy
he-thing
in season
Irish horse
Johnny bum at arse
lady dog
male beast at big animal
man-cow
mountain chicken
prairie oyster[1]
roach[2]
    rooster-roach
roof rabbit
rooster
seed-ox at seed
sheep buck
sluice[1]
stable horse
stand[2]
stock beast
    stock animal
    stock brute
    stock cow
stoned-horse-man at stones
stony at stones
stunted hare
sweetbreads
take[5]
throw[1]
use[3] (in)
variety meats
white meat[1]

Auctions and Real Estate

agent
bijou
blockbuster[1]
boost[2]
character
colonial
convenient[2]
Dutch auction
East Village
eat-in kitchen
efficiency
estate agent at agent
gated community at gate[1]
Georgian
handyman special
historic
home[2]
ideal for modernization
immaculate
in the ring
inner city
knock-out
landscaped
lower ground floor
monkey[2]
negotiable
    neg
off the chandelier
    off the ceiling

off the wall
old-fashioned
period[2]
planning
prestigious
ring[2]
secluded
select
semi-detached
snug
sought after
South Chelsea
starter home
   starter
   starter house
sweeten[2]
up-and-coming
urban renewal

Bankruptcy and Indebtedness

arrangement *at* arrange
bank
   banker
belly up
bolt
bolt the moon
bounce[2]
bust
cash flow problem
catch a packet *at* packet[2]
Chapter Eleven
close its doors
come to a sticky end
corporate recovery
Deed of Arrangement
   at arrange
do a runner
done for
drown the miller
fall off the wire
fall out of bed
file Chapter Eleven
flit[2] (do a)
fly-by-night[1]
fold
get the shorts
go[2]
   go at staves
   go Chapter Eleven
   go crash
   go for a Burton
   go smash
   go under
   go west
go down the tube(s)
go south
go to the wall
haircut
hammer[1]
in Carey Street
in the cart

in the glue
in the nightsoil *at* in the glue
lame duck[2]
liquidator *at* liquidate
liquidity
   liquidity crisis
lose your shirt
   lose your pants
   lose your vest
moonlight flit
   moonlight flight
   moonlight march
   moonlight touch
   moonlight walk
need help
negative cash
negative equity
negatively impacted
non-performing asset
on the skids
over-geared
pear-shaped
phoenix
pull the rug
put the skids under
red ink
refer to drawer
   RD
roller-coaster
rubber cheque
run[3]
set back
shoot the moon
stiff[4] (out)
strapped for cash
stretch[2] (the)
take a bath
take a hike[2]
take a powder
take a wheel off the cart
take someone's pants off
   take someone's shirt off
temporary liquidity problem *at*
   temporary
up the creek
up the pole
   up the spout
   up the stick
waddle
walk penniless in Mark Lane
wash out
washed up
wipe out[2]

Bawds and Pimps

abbess
bawd
Charlie Ronce
Covent Garden abbess *at* Covent
   Garden
governess
husband[1]
joe[1]

Joe Ronce
madam
mother[1]
procure
   procurer
   procuress
victualler
white slaver *at* white slave

Boasting and Flattery

angle with a silver hook
apple-polish
   apple-polisher
BS *at* bull[3]
blow[5]
   blow smoke
   blow your own horn
   blow your own trumpet
blow the whistle on
brown nose
   brown-noser
brownie points
bull
   bull-rinky
   bullshit
   bullshitter
bunk flying
catch fish with a silver hook
Chinese whisper
come up with the rations
dog and pony show
   dog and pony act
draw the long bow
embroidery
fact sheet
fish story
give a line
gong
   gong-hunter
grandstand
   grandstand play
handout[2]
have your ticket punched
hose[2]
increase in head
   measurement
Japanese
joiner
log-rolling
massage[5]
Monday morning quarter-back
pay lip service
piggyback
poor-mouth
poodle
put down[2]
recognition
ride abroad with St George but
   at home with St Michael
saddle soap
shoot a line
   shoot the breeze
   shoot the bull

soft soap
stroke
  stroke job
swing the lamp
tall story *at* story
tuft hunter
whistle-blower

Breasts

amply endowed
boobies *at* booby-trap
boobs *at* booby-trap
bouncers
bristols
Charlies *at* Charlie
cleavage
couple[3]
dairies
décolletage
endowed
feed
glands
globes
headlights
hawk your meat *at* hawk your
  mutton
intimate part
jugs
knobs
knockers
lungs
melons
nurse
pair
stacked
them
topless
vital statistics
watermelons *at*
  watermelon
well endowed
wet nurse

Bribery

adjustment[2]
angle with a silver hook
anoint a palm
Asian levy
backdoor[3]
backhander
bag[4]
  bagman
boot money
brown envelope
business entertainment *at*
  corporate entertainment
clean hands
  at clean
collect
come across[1]
come through
commission

concessionary fare *at* corporate
  entertainment
conference *at* corporate
  entertainment
connections
cop the drop
corporate entertainment
cough syrup *at* cough medicine
cross your palm
cumshaw
cut[4]
distribution
double dipper
douceur
drink[2]
drop[5]
entertain[2]
  entertainment
facilitator
facility trip *at* corporate
  entertainment
fix[1]
fixer
freebie *at* corporate
  entertainment
glove money
golden hello *at* golden
governmental relations
graft[2]
gratify
grease[1]
  grease hands
  grease palms
  grease paws
  grease the skids
  grease the system
handout[1]
honours
hospitality
  hospitality room
hush money
  hush payment
incentive travel
introducer's fee
jaunt *at* corporate
  entertainment
jolly[2]
junket
kickback
kindness
lay pipes
lubricate
lunchtime engineering
massage[1]
oil
on the pad
on the side
on the take
open palm
over-invoicing
palm[1]
  palm grease
  palm oil

palm soap
palmistry
payoff
piece of
present
pourboire
questionable payment *at*
  questionable rake-off
recognition
sale preview *at* corporate
  entertainment
schmear *at* smear[1]
secondary distribution *at*
  distribution
see[2]
  see the cops
sensitive payment
shade[2]
skim
slippery palm
slush
  slush fund
smear[1]
soft commission
special operations
straighten out
street money
sugar[1]
supporters' club
sweeten[1]
  sweetener
take[1]
take care of[2]
take your end
talk to
tea money
tenderloin
thank
third party payment
travel expenses
treat
tub of grease
under the table[2]
unofficial relations
useful expenditure
velvet[2]
windfall

Brothels

abode of love
academy
accommodation house
barrel-house
bawdy house *at* bawd
bird-cage *at* bird[1]
bitch
call house
canhouse
case[1]
  casa
  casito
  caso
cat-house *at* cat[1]

cheap john *at* john[5]
chickie house *at* chick
chippie-joint *at* chippy[1]
common house[1]
coupling house *at* couple[1]
creep-joint
crib
disorderly house
dress-house *at* dress for sale
escort agency *at* escort
fish market *at* fishmonger's
    daughter
flash-ken
    flash-house
    flash-panney
fleshpot
fun house
garden house
girlie bar *at* girl[1]
girlie parlor *at* girl[1]
goat-house
grind-mill *at* grind
hook-shop *at* hooker
hot-house
hot-pillow
    hot-pillow hotel
    hot-pillow joint
    hot-pillow motel
hot sheet *at* hot pillow
hourly hotel
house[1]
    house in the suburbs
    house of accommodation
    house of assignation
    house of civil reception
    house of evil repute
    house of ill-fame
    house of ill-repute
    house of pleasure
    house of profession
    house of resort
    house of sale
    house of sin
    house of tolerance
ill-famed house *at* house[1]
immoral house *at* immoral
improper house *at* improper
jag house
joy house *at* joy[1]
knocking-shop
    knocker's shop
    knocking-house
    knocking-joint
ladies' college *at* lady
leaping house
    leaping academy
loose house
make-out joint *at* make
massage parlour
meat-house *at* meat rack
nanny-house
naughty house
nunnery

panel-house *at* panel[2]
panel-joint *at* panel[2]
parlor house
place of ill fame
play house *at* play
pleasure house *at* pleasure
pushing academy
    pushing shop
queen-house *at* queen[1]
rag (the)
ramps (the)
rap club
    rap parlor
    rap studio
red lamp
    red light
    red-light district
    red-light precinct
    red-lighted number
rib joint
sauna
scalding house *at* scald
seraglio
service station *at* service[1]
skivvie-house *at* skivvy
snake-ranch *at* snake pit
sport-trap *at* sport (the)
sporting-house *at* sport (the)
sporting section *at* sport (the)
stews (the)
touch-crib *at* touch[2]
vaulting-school *at* vault[1]
victualling house *at* victualler
wang-house
warm shop *at* warm[1]
zoo

Charity

aid
assistance
benefit
care
caring
concessional
    concessional fares
    concessional financing
    concessional loans
dole
    dole-bread
    dole-meats
    dole-money
entitlement
financial assistance
fly a kite[2]
giro day
handout[1]
house[3]
    house of industry
in care
income support
national assistance
negative (income-) tax
on assistance *at* assistance

on the dole
on the labour
on the parish
    on the parochial
out of benefit *at* benefit
panel[1] (the)
public assistance
relief[1]
remittance man
rock and roll
social housing
social security
    social (the)
soup kitchen *at* souper
tied aid *at* aid
welfare
    welfare state
workhouse

Cheating

catch a cold[3]
chant
    chanter
cheese-eater
chisel
clip[1]
    clip-artist
    clip-joint
coffee-housing
comic
con
    con artist
    con man
    confidence trick
concoct
cut[2]
do[3] (over)
fix[1]
horse-chanter *at* chant
hose[1]
leaner
nickel and dime
on the chisel
operator
palm[2]
plant the books
ramp
rip off
salt
scalp
screw[3]
shake down *at* shake
slice
stuck
take for a ride
take to the cleaners
tank fight
three-letter man
throw[2]

Childbirth and Pregnancy

accouchement

bear[1]
bed[1]
  brought to bed
cast[1]
child-bed (in)
click[2]
confinement
  confined
doorstep[1]
drop[4]
  drop a bundle
facts (of life)
  facts (the)
fall[6]
fiddle
gooseberry bush
groper *at* grope
happy event
hatch
kid
lady in the straw
  lady in waiting
lay in *at* lie in
lie in
little stranger
lying-in wife *at* lie in
miss[2]
mistake[1]
parsley bed
pup
slip[1]
steg month
time
trouble
upstairs[1]
whelp

Clothing

abandoned habits
  at abandoned
appliance
at half mast
athletic supporter
bags
body shaper
  body briefer
  body hugger
  body outline
booby trap
box[2]
brassière
  bra
bust bodice
canteen medal
catch a cold[2]
Charlie's dead *at* Charlie
cheaters
continuations
co-respondent's shoes *at* co-
  respondent
Cuban heels
decent
don't-name-'ems

enhanced contouring *at*
  enhance
falsies
flapper
fly a flag
flying low
foundation garment
gazelles are in the garden
indescribables
ineffables *at* unmentionables[1]
inexpressibles
jock-strap *at* jock
Johnnie's out of jail
leg-bags *at* bags
lift[4]
linen
medal showing
one o'clock at the waterworks
petite
riser
sartorially challenged
sensible
shop door is open (the)
sides
sit-in-'ems *at* sit-upon
sit-upons *at* sit-upon
smalls
snowing down south (it's)
star in the east (a)
surgical appliance *at* appliance
Turkish medal
unmentionables[1]
  unexpressibles
  unspeakables
  unwhisperables

Commerce, Banking, and Industry

accumulate
adjustment[4]
affordable
agent
ambulance-chaser
arrange
  arrangement
as planned *at* planned
assistant
association
attended service *at* service[2]
back-up in retail inventories
bad-mouth
bait and switch
bandwagon
  band-wagoner
bean counter
Best Brian
bite the bullet
black economy
blind copy
boiler room
  boiler house
  boiler shop

boost[3]
bottom line
bounce[2]
bounce[5]
bucket shop
budget
bump[6]
carpetbagger
catch a cold[3]
category killer
chair[2]
challenging
cherry-pick
Chinese bookkeeping
Chinese copy
Chinese paper
Chinese wall
churn
clicker *at* click[1]
clock
club[2]
club[3]
come-on[3]
complimentary
concert party
conference (in)
confident pricing
consultant[2]
controversial[2]
corner[1]
correction
country
courtesy
creative
  creative bookkeeping
  creative tension
critical power excursion
cross-firing
crumbling edge
cuff[2]
currency adjustment
daisy chain
dawn raid
dead-cat bounce
Deed of Arrangement *at* arrange
demonstrator
direct mail
directional selling
doctor
downward adjustment
drop the boom on
Dutch bargain
Dutch reckoning
easy terms
economy
effluent
energy release
equity equivalent
  contingent
  participation
ethical investment
excess[2]
exclusive

expenses
   expense account
experienced[2]
expert
exterminating engineer
facilitator
facility[2]
family *at* large[2]
fan club
fast buck (a)
fat cat
feather your nest
fee note
filler[2]
financial engineering
   financial engineer
financial products
financial services
financially excluded
fireman[2]
float paper
fly a kite[1]
for your convenience
free
freeze out
fringe
front-running
fudge
go south
grab[1]
gravy train (the)
greenmailer
grey[1]
   grey goods
   grey marketer
guest[2]
guidance to
   the market
haircut
hang a red light on
hike[2]
holiday ownership
home equity loan
hospital job
hot[2]
hot seating
   hot-desking
HR *at* human resources
human resources
identification
improvement[2]
in conference
in the red
income protection
informal
   informal market
inside track
insider
   insider dealing
inventory adjustment
jawbone
kick the tyres
kitchen-sinking

kite
   kite-man
knight of the Golden Fleece *at*
   knight
lack of visibility
lame duck[2]
large[2]
late booking
leveraged
link prices
loaded[2]
load-shedding
long-term buy
low-budget
   low-cost
lower the boom on[2]
massage[4]
medium
meeting (in/at a)
men in suits
merger accounting
me-too
mirror operation
mom-and-pop
near[2]
negative containment
negative contribution
   negative profit contribution
negative growth
negative stockholding
networking
neutral
never-never (the)
Newgate solicitor *at* Newgate
NIH *at* not invented here
non-performing asset
non-profit
not invented here
on jawbone *at* jawbone
on the black
on the cuff *at* cuff[2]
operator
orderly market
orderly progress
pad
paint the tape
paper-hanger[2]
parallel
   parallel importing
   parallel pricing
   parallel traders
park[2]
past its sell-by date
pencil[2]
personal assistant
ping-ponging
planned
poison pill
positive contribution *at*
   negative contribution
pre-driven
premium
pre-owned

pressure of work
previously owned
price-crowding
prime
product
product shrinkage
proposition selling
provision
pull out of a hat
   pull out of the air
qualify accounts
   qualification
R-word (the)
rainmaker
RD
rebased
redlining
refer to drawer
refresher[2]
regular[3]
remainder[2]
restructured
reverse engineering
ride the gravy train *at* gravy
   train (the)
ring[2]
Rio trade
rodent operator *at*
   exterminating engineer
save
scandal sheet
select
selective distribution *at*
   selective
service[2]
   service station
shade[1]
share pusher
sharp with the pencil
sharpen your pencil
shoe the colt *at* colt[2]
shortism[2]
silent copy *at* blind copy
slack fill
slowdown[2]
smooth
snow[2]
   snow-job
softness in the economy
soft-shoe
south[3] (going or moving)
spam[2]
strategic premium *at* strategic
structured
   structured competition
suggestion
supporters' club
sweet equity
sweetheart
switch-selling
tap[2]
tap[3]
technical adjustment

technical correction
technical reaction
testing
tied up
top floor (the)
top up
touch signature
transfer pricing
triple entry
turkey farmer
turkey shoot
twenty-four-hour service
unavailable[1]
unbundling
uncertain
under water
under-invoicing
uneven
upstairs[3]
used
velvet[2]
visiting fireman[2]
warehouse
wash[2]
wash[3]
wash its face
water stock
weekend
weigh the thumb
what the traffic will bear
white sale
window dressing
work both sides of the street
yellow page
zero-grazing

Contraception

armour
bareback
  bareback rider
birth control
cardigan
circular protector
collapsible container
device
dry run *at* dry bob
Dutch cap *at* Dutch
    family planning
    family planning requisites
fight in armour
FL *at* French letter
French letter
  French tickler
  Frenchie
froggie
get fitted
johnny
  Johnnie
leave before the gospel
on the pill
play Onan
pill[2] (the)
precautions

preventative
pro-pack *at* pro
prophylactic
protected sex
protector[2]
raincoat[1]
rubber
  rubber cookie
  rubber goods
  rubber johnny
safe
  safe sex
safety
sheath
skin[1]
  skin-diver
something for the weekend
tickler[2]
unprotected sex
Vatican roulette
welly
will there be anything else?

Copulation

abuse
act (the)
    act of generation
    act of intercourse
    act of love
    act of shame
act like a husband
all the way
amatory rites
amorous favours
  amorous sport
  amorous tie
amour[2]
appetites
arouse
  arousal
arse
ass
assignation
associate with
astride
at it
athwart your hawse
attentions
avail yourself of
ball
bang[1]
bareback
baser needs
basket-making *at* basket[1]
be nice to
be with
beast
beast with two backs (the)
beastliness
beat the gun
bed[2]
    bed-hopping
    bed with

bedtime business
bed and breakfast
beddable
been there *at* be with
beg a child of
belt
bestow your
    enthusiasm on
bestride
betray
between the sheets
between the thighs of
big prize (the)
bit[2] (a)
  bit of the other
block
blow[1]
  blow the groundsels
board
  board a train
boff[1]
bonk
boom-boom[2]
bother
bounce[1]
  bouncy-bouncy
bout
break a commandment
break the pale
break your knee *at* break your
    elbow
bring off[1]
buff[2]
bull[1]
bum-fighting *at* bum
bump[4]
  bump bones
bundle
bung up and bilge free
business
buttered bun
buttock
  buttock ball
  buttock-mail
calisthenics in bed
canoe
carnal
  carnal act
  carnal knowledge
  carnal necessities
  carnal relations
carry on with
carwash (a)
casting couch
cattle[2]
chambering
change your luck
cheat
clean up[2]
cleave *at* chopper[2]
clicket
climb
  climb aboard

climb in with
climb into bed (with)
climb the ladder on her back *at*
   climb the ladder
close the bedroom door
cock
   cock a leg across
   cock a leg athwart
   cock a leg over
cohabit
coition
come across[2]
come to
come together
comfort[1]
commerce
commit misconduct
compound with
congress
conjugal rights
connect[1]
   connection
connubial pleasures
conquer a bed
console
   consolation
consummate a relationship
   consummate your desires
   consummation
contact with
content[2] (your desire)
continence *at* incontinent[1]
continency *at* incontinent[1]
continent *at* incontinent[1]
conversation
copulate
   copulation
corn[2]
   cornification
corrupt
couple[1] (with)
cover[1]
crack a Jane
   crack a doll
   crack a Judy
   crack a pipkin
   crack a pitcher
crack your whip
creep around
criminal assault
criminal connection
criminal conversation
   crim con
cross
cut the mustard
   cut it
Cythera
dally
   dalliance
debauch
deceive (your regular sexual
   partner)
deed (the)

defend your virtue
defile
   defile a bed
   defile yourself
   defilement
   defiler
deflower
   defloration
degraded *at* degrade
deny yourself
   deny a bed
destruction
diddle[3]
dip Cecil in the hot grease *at*
   Cecil
dip your wick
dirty deed *at* dirty[1]
dirty weekend *at* dirty[1]
dishonoured
disport amorously
dissolution[2]
do[1]
   do it
do the business
do what comes naturally
do wrong (to someone)
dock
double in stud
double time
double-header
droit de seigneur
drop your drawers
   drop your pants
dry bob
   dry run
East African activities
easy woman
eat flesh
embraces
   embrace
employ
enjoy
   enjoy favours
   enjoy hospitality
   enjoyment of her person
enter
entertain[1]
err
   errant
exchange flesh
excitement (the)
exercise
   exercise your marital rights
experienced
extras
fall[1]
fall on your back
false
fate worse than death
favour
feed from home
fidelity
flat on your back

flesh your will
flop
foin
follow your passion
force yourself on
   force your ardour on
   force your attentions on
fork
foul desire
   foul designs
   foul way with
frailty
frank[1]
fraternization
free love
free of Fumbler's Hall
free relationship
freeze[2]
frig[1]
fulfilment
full treatment (the)
fumble
fun
   fun and games
gallant
gallop
get
   get a leg over
   get busy with
   get in/into her bloomers
   get in/into her girdle
   get in/into her knickers
   get in/into her pants
   get into bed with
   get it
   get it in
   get it together
   get laid
   get lucky
   get off
   get off with
   get on
   get round
   get there
   get through
   get up
   get your end in
   get your greens
   get your hook into
   get your muttons
   get your nuts off
   get your rocks off
   get your share
   get your way with
   get your will(s) of
get in the saddle *at* saddle up
   with
get stuffed *at* stuff[2]
get your corner *at* corner[3]
gift of your body (the)
give
   give a little
   give access to your body

give it
give in to
give it to
give out
give the ferret a run
give the time to
give (up) your treasure
give way
give your all
give your body
give yourself
go all the way
go (any) further
go beyond friendship
go into
go the whole hog *at* whole hog
  (the)
go the whole way
go through[1]
go to bed with
go to it
go with
go wrong
gratify your passion(s)
  gratification
  gratify your (amorous)
    desires/works
green gown
grind
half-and-half
hammer away *at* hammer[2]
haul your ashes
have
  have a bit
  have a man/woman
  have at
  have it
  have it off
  have sex
  have (sexual) relations (with)
  have something to do with
  have your end away
  have your nose in the butter
  have your (wicked) way with
  have your will of
headache[2]
heart's desire
hit-and-run
hit the sack with
hochle
hoist your skirt
hole[2]
honest
honour
hop into bed
horizontal
  horizontal aerobics
  horizontal collaboration
  horizontal conquest
  horizontal jogging
  horizontal position
how's your father
human relations

hump
  hump the mutton
illicit
  illicit commerce
  illicit connection
  illicit embraces
  illicit intercourse
impale
impotent
improper
  improper connection
  improper suggestion
in[2]
in circulation
in flagrante delicto
  en flagrant délit
in mid-job *at* on the job
in name only
in relation with
in rut
in season
in the box
in the hay
in the sack
  into the sack
in the saddle
inconstancy
incontinent[1]
infidelity
initiation
insatiable
intact
intercourse
intimacy
  intimate
introduce yourself to a bed
invade
irregular
it[2]
itch
Jack in the orchard *at* jack[1]
jail bait
jam
jig-a-jig
  jig
  jig-jig
  jiggle
  jiggy-jig
join[1]
jolly[3]
joy[1]
joy ride[1]
juggle
jump[2]
keep your legs crossed
  keep your legs together
keep your pants on
  keep your pants zipped
kind
kiss
knock
knock off[2]
knot

know
know the score *at* score[1]
lance
last favour (the)
  last intimacies
  last thing
lay[1]
  lay a leg across
  lay a leg on
  lay a leg over
lay some pipe *at* lay pipes
lead apes in hell
leap on
  leap at
  leap into
  leap into bed with
leave shoes under a bed
led astray
leg-over
leg-sliding
let in
lie with[1]
  lie on
  lie together
lift a leg[1]
line[1]
linked with
lose your (good) character
lose your cherry
  lose your snood
lose your reputation
  lose your virtue
love
lovemaking
lower part
lumber
main thing (the)
make[1]
  make it
make a (an improper)
    suggestion
make babies together
make little of
make love to
make nice-nice
make sweat with
make the (bed) springs creak
  make the (bed) springs
    squeak
make whoopee
management privileges
  managerial privileges
marital rights
marriage joys
mate
  mating (a)
mattress
  mattress drill
  mattress extortion
mess[1]
migraine
mingle bodies
misbehave

missionary position (the)
misuse
momentary trick (the)
monkey business
mount
  mounting drill
mutual joy(s) *at* joy[1]
nail[1]
national indoor game (the)
needs of manhood *at* manhood
nibble
night games
  night baseball
night physic
nightwork
nocturnal exercise
oats
occupy
offer yourself
  offer kindness
on the couch
on the job
on top of
on your back
one-night stand
  one-nighter
one thing
open your legs
other (the)
outrage
pasture
peel a banana
penetrate[1]
perform[2]
  performer
personal relations
pile into
play
play around
play away
play hookie
play in the hay
play mothers and fathers
  play mummies and daddies
  play mums and dads
play on your back
play the ace against the jack
play the beast with two backs
play the organ
play tricks
please yourself on
pleasure
  pleasures
  pleasuring
plough[1]
pluck
  pluck a rose
plug[2]
plumb
pocket the red *at* pocket job (a)
poke[2]
poontang
  poontan

pop[2]
pork[3]
possess
pound
press conjugal rights on
press your attentions on
probe
prong
pull a train
pump up
punch
push[1]
put
  put a man in a belly
  put and take
  put it about
  put it in
  put it up
put out
put to
quickie[2]
R and R *at* rest and recreation
racy
ram[1]
rattle[1]
ravish
relate
relations
release[4]
relief[3]
relieve of virginity
rest and recreation
ride[1]
  ride St George
rip off a piece of arse/ass *at* rip
  off
rivet
roger
roll[1]
  roll in the hay
roll over[1]
romp
root[2] (about)
  root rat
rub groins together
rub the bacon
  rub the pork
ruin
  ruined in character
saddle up with
sauce[2]
sausage sandwich *at*
  sausage
save it *at* save
score[1]
screw
  screw around
sensual intercourse *at*
  intercourse
serve
  serve your lust
service[1]
sex[1]

sex love
sexual act (the)
sexual intercourse
  sexual commerce
  sexual congress
  sexual conjunction
  sexual knowledge
  sexual liaison
  sexual relief
shaft[1]
shag[1]
shame
share someone's bed *at* share
  someone's affections
sheathe the sword *at* sheath
sheets
shift[2]
short time
  short session(s)
  short-term
shove[1]
sin
  sinful commerce
skewer
slake your lust
  slake your (base) passion
slap and tickle
sleep around
sleep over
sleep together
sleep with
sluice[1]
smother
snatch[1]
soil your reputation
solace
spend the night with
split
sport (the)
  sport for Jove
sprain your ankle
spread for
  spread your legs
  spread your twat
spur of the moment passion
stab
stain
statutory offense
  statutory rape
steal privately to
stick[3]
  stick it on
  stick it into[1]
stir the porridge *at* stir
stoop your body to pollution
straddle
stray
  stray from the hearth
  stray your affection
strop your beak
stuff[2]
subdue to your will
submit to

succumb[2]
surrender to
swing[2]
swinge *at* switch-hitter
swive *at* switch-hitter
take[2]
take a bit from
take a turn in the stubble
  take a turn in Cupid's Corner
  take a turn in Love Lane
  take a turn in Mount Pleasant
  take a turn on her back
take advantage of
  take vantages
take pleasure with
take someone's (good or dear)
    name away
take to bed
take up with
take your trousers off
throw down
  throw a bop into
  throw a leg over
thump
tickle
tip[1]
tired[1]
top[1]
torch of Hymen (the)
toss in the hay
touch[1]
touch up[1]
tread
treasure
truant with your bed
true
tumble[1]
tup
turn[1]
twixt the sheets *at* between the
    sheets
two-backed beast
two-backed game *at* beast with
    two backs (the)
ultimate (the)
uncover nakedness
undo
unfaithful
union[1]
unknown to men
  unknown to women
unstaunched
untrimmed
untrue
up[1]
up for it
upstairs[1]
use[1]
use of Venus
vault[1]
velvet[1]
venerous act
Venus

violate
virtue
  virtuous
walk the snake
warm a bed
wear iron knickers
wet deck
wet your wick
wham
whole hog (the)
wicked way (your)
  wicked design
  wicked purposes
work on[2]
worry
wrack
  wrack of maidenhead
wreak your passion on
wrong[1]
yield
  yield her body
  yield her person
  yield her virginity
  yield to desire
  yield to solicitation
you-know-what
zig-zig *at* jig-a-jig

Cosmetics

adapt
aesthetic procedure
after-shave
below medium height
bikini wax
blue rinse *at* blue hair
body image
bottle-blonde
carpet[2]
colour-tinted
  colour-correct
coloured[2]
conditioner
cover[2]
designer stubble
enhance
  enhanced contouring
enlist the aid of science
follicularly challenged *at*
    challenged
forehead challenged
hairpiece
high forehead (a)
homely
improving knife (the)
less attractive *at* less
lift[4]
mutate
no oil painting/beauty
nose job (a)
odorously challenged
partner with Revlon
receding
restricted growth

rinse
scalp dolly *at* scalp
shortism[1]
sky-piece
  sky-rug
syrup
tint
touch up[2]
Tyburn top *at* Tyburn
visually challenged
warpaint
wax[1]

Courtship and Marriage

air (the)
alternative
apron-string-hold
arranged by circumstances
axe[2]
baby-snatcher
  baby-farmer
bag[2]
ball money
beat the gun
bell money
blind date *at* date
bolt
boondock
bounce[3]
breach of promise *at* promised
break your elbow in the church
    at break your elbow
broken home
broomstick match
bundle
bunny
bush marriage
by-courting *at* by(e)
by-shot *at* by(e)
California widow
call down
catch
chap
  chapping
chuck (the)
come out
come to see
commit misconduct
community of wives
compromise
conjugal rights
co-respondent
correspondent *at* co-respondent
couple[2]
cradle-snatcher
  cradle robber
cuckold the parson *at* cuckoo[1]
damaged[2]
  damaged goods
dance at
dance barefoot
  dance in the half-peck
dark moon

date
dear John
do a runner
do the right thing
empty-nesters
extramarital excursion
fancy[2]
feather your nest
fishing fleet
flexible[2]
flower[1]
follower
    follow
forum shopping
free relationship
free samples
French kiss
friend
game fee *at* game[2] (the)
gander-mooner
get off[2]
give green stockings *at* green
    gown
go out with
go steady
gold-digger[2]
(good) catch *at* catch
grass widow
green gown
    green sickness
hand-fasting
handful[2]
hang in the bell-ropes
hang on the bough
hang out the besom
hang out the broomstick
hang up your hat
    hang up your ladle
heavy
    heavy date
    heavy involvement
    heavy necking
hen
    hen-brass
    hen-drinking
    hen-night
    hen-party
    hen silver
hop-pole marriage
house-proud
indiscretions
intentions
leap the broomstick
    leap the besom
leave[1]
    leave your pillow
        unpressed
make a hit with *at*
    hit on
make an honest woman of
neck
new cookie *at* cookie
not seeing anybody

not to live as man and wife *at*
    live as man and wife
old maid
on the shelf
    on the peg
open marriage
out[1]
party cited *at* co-respondent
petticoat
    petticoat government
petting-stone
play gooseberry *at* gooseberry
pop the question
promised
pursue
ram-riding (a)
    riding *at* ram-riding (a)
rob the cradle
run away
run off[1]
season (the)
separate[2]
    separation
settled
seven-year itch
shove[2] (the)
singles
    singles bar
    singles joint
    singles night
speak to
    speak for
    speak till
special[5]
stand up[1]
steg month
    steg-widow
step out together *at* step out on
step out with *at* step out on
take a walk[2]
take out[1]
take the wind
    take the breeze
trophy wife
    trophy model
turn off[3]
walk[7] (out/with/out with)
    walk out
    walk out with
    walk with
wander
wear the breeches
    wear the pants
    wear the trousers
white marriage
wind[2] (the)
without a head
woman named
young lady
    young woman

Cowardice

acute environmental reaction

allergic to lead
battle fatigue
bottle[4]
bug-out
    bug-out fever
chicken[2]
cold feet
combat fatigue
Dutch courage
far from staunch
force protection
go off[2]
head for the hills
lack of moral fibre
    LMF
run[2]
take a powder
Turkish ally
vicar of Bray
white feather
white rabbit scut (the)
wind up (the)
windy[2]
yellow[1]
    yellow belly
    yellow streak
    yellow stripe

Crime (other than Stealing)

abuse
action[1]
adjustment[2]
anti-social
    anti-social behaviour
apportion
armed struggle
artillery[2]
at it
bend the rules
bent[1]
    bent copper
bird dog[3]
black market
black money
    black cash
    black dollars
    black francs
    black marks
    black pounds
boning *at* bone[1]
bootleg
    bootlegger
    bootlegger turn
carry the can
cherry-pick
claim responsibility
    for
clean[1]
clean up[1]
clock
cobbler

come to the attention of the
    police
community alienation
con
    con artist
    con man
    confidence fraud
    confidence trick
cook^2
cop out
corner^1
cough^1
covert act
criminal assault
criminally used
damaged^3
dive^3
do^5
doctor
dodgy
    dodgy night
double entry
draw the king's picture
drop car
ethically challenged *at*
    challenged
fall money *at* fall^5
family^2
feed the bears
feed the meter
finger^1
finger^2
    finger guy
finger-man$^{1/2/3}$
fireman^1
firm (the)
fit up
fix^1
fixer
fleece
form
frame
    frame-up
fringe
front^2
fudge
funny money
go state
gold-brick swindle *at* gold-brick
gooseberry lay
grass^1
green goods
    green-goods man
gun
hang paper
hard case *at* case^2
Havana rider
hillside men
hook^3
in trouble^2
informal
    informal dealer
    informal market

irregularity *at* irregular
jacket
job
junior jumper *at* jump^2
kangaroo court
King's evidence *at* Queen's
    evidence
known to the police
lard the books
launder
    laundry
lay paper
line your pocket
    line your coat
    line your vest
lose your (good) character
low flying
Lydford law
men of respect
Mickey Mouse
mob
no show
off the rails^2
off-line
on the chisel *at* chisel
on the left
on the panel^2
on the square
organization (the)
out of line *at* off-line
outfit
past (your)
penman
piece of the action
pigeon
    pigeon-drop
plant^2
put the clock back
put the finger on *at* finger^1
Queen's evidence
queer^4 (the)
questionable
    questionable act
    questionable motive
ramp
rap
record (a)
    record sheet
refresh your memory^2
resolved without trial
revolving-door^1
ride-by
roll over^2
run^5
run (a)round the Horn
score^2
send to the cleaners *at* clean up^1
set up^2
sexual assault
shakedown *at* shake^1
shanghai
share pusher
shop^2

sing
slice of the action
smoking gun (a)
spill
    spill the beans
split on *at* split
squeal
sting
stink on
stitch up
syndicate
tagged^2
take^6
take the air abroad
take the can back
throw the book at
tip^3 (off)
torch
trunk
unavailable^2
under the counter
under the table^2
unearned income
vacuum
walk^5
waltz around the Horn *at* run
    (a)round the Horn
wash^3

Cuckoldry

abuse a bed
Actaeon
antlers
co-respondent
forked plague (the)
freeman of Bucks
horn^2
    horn-maker
    horned
knight of Hornsey *at* knight
member for Horncastle *at*
    member
prey to the bicorn *at* prey to (a)
Vulcan's badge (wear)
wear a fork
wear horns
wind the horn *at* horn^2

Death

above ground
adverse event
afterlife
all night man
all over with
anointed
another state (in)
answer the call
asleep
at rest
    at peace
at the last day
at your last

auction of kit
away[1]
back-gate parole
better country
　better state
　better world
beyond help
big D
　big jump
　big stand-easy
bite the dust
bonds of life being gradually
　dissolved
bone[2]
breathe your last
bring your heart to its final
　pause
buy it
　buy the farm
call (the)
　called
　called away
　called home
　called to higher service
call a soul
call off all bets
cardiac arrest *at* cardiac
　incident
cash in your checks
　cash in your chips
cast for death *at* cast[2]
catch a packet[1]
cease to be
check out
chop shot *at* chop[1]
chuck seven
church triumphant
close your eyes
clunk
cold[1]
combat ineffective
come again
　come back
come home feet first
come to a sticky end
come to your resting place
　come to the end of the
　　road
　come to yourself
conk (out)
cool[1]
　cool out
cop a packet
　cop it
cough[2]
count (the)
　count the daisies
croak[1]
cross the Styx
　cross the River Jordan
curtains
cut off
cut the painter

cut adrift
cut your cable
dance a two-step to another
　world *at* dance[1]
Davy Jones's locker
depart this life
　departed
　departure
diet of worms
disappear[1]
dissolution[1]
done for
drop in your tracks
　drop off
end
　end of the road
enter the next world
eternal life
eternity (in)
everlasting life
exchange this life for a better
expended
expire[1]
extremely ill
face your maker
fade away
fall[3]
fall asleep
fall off the perch
fall out
fallen (the)
feet first
finished *at* finish[1]
flit[1]
follow
food for worms
freed from earthly limitations
gathered to his fathers
　gathered to God
　gathered to his ancestors
　gathered to Jesus
　gathered to Mohammed
get away
get it
get the chop *at* chop[1]
give up the ghost
　give up your spoon
give up your life
go[1]
　go aloft
　go away
　go corbie
　go down the nick
　go for a Burton
　go forth in your cerements
　go home
　go into the ground
　go off
　go off the hooks
　go on
　go out
　go over
　go right

　go round land
　go the wrong way
　go to a better place
　go to heaven
　go to our rest
　go to the wall
　go to our reward
　go to yourself
　go under
　go west
goner
　gonner
grave (the)
　gravestone gentry
great certainty (the)
　great change
　great leveller
　great out
　great perhaps
　great secret
great majority
Grim Reaper (the)
ground
had it
hand in your dinner pail
hang up your hat[2]
　hang up your dinner-pail
　hang up your mug
　hang up your spoon
happen to
happy release
　happier seat
　happy dispatch
　happy hunting grounds
heels foremost
hereafter (the)
higher state (of existence) (a)
in Abraham's bosom
in heaven
　in the arms of Jesus
in the churchyard
in the soil
jack it in
join[2]
　join the (great) majority
jump the last hurdle
keel over
kick[1]
　kick in
　kick it
　kick off
　kick the bucket
　kick the wind
　kick up
　kick your heels
kingdom come
kiss off[1]
kiss the ground
konk off
laid to rest
　laid in the lockers
land of forgetfulness (the)
　last bow

last call (the)
  last debt
  last journey
  last resting place
  last round-up
  last trump
  last voyage
late[1]
latter end[2]
lay down your life
  lay down the clay
  lay down your burden
  lay down your knife and fork
leave[2]
leave the building
  leave the land of the living
lick the dust
life[2]
  life assurance
  life cover
  life office
  life policy
little gentleman in black velvet
long count *at* count (the)
long home (your)
  long day
  long journey
Lord sends for you (the)
lose[3]
lose the vital signs
loss
lost[2]
  lost at sea
make it
make the supreme sacrifice
meet your Maker
  meet the Prophet
move on
negative patient care outcome
night (the)
no longer with us
no more
no right to correspondence
  (have)
not dead but gone before
  not lost but gone before
NYR
off the voting list
off-line
on your shield
on your way out
other side (the)
over Jordan
pack it in
packet[1]
part
pass[1]
  pass away
  pass beyond the veil
  pass in your checks
  pass into the next world
  pass off the earth
  pass on

  pass over
passing
pay nature's debt
  pay nature's last debt
pay the supreme sacrifice
  pay the supreme price
peace at last
peg out
plucked from us
pop off
pop your clogs
popping up the daisies
promoted to Glory
push up the daisies
put in your ticket
put to rest
quietus
quit
  quit breathing
  quit cold
  quit the scene
reaper (the)
release[2]
relieve of your sufferings
remain above ground
removed
repose
resign your spirit
return to
ring eight bells
sale before the mast *at* auction
  of kit
say Kaddish for
screwed down
send home in a body bag *at* send
  to heaven
separation
seven (chuck or throw) a
shipped home in a box
shuffle off this mortal coil
six feet of earth
  six feet underground
sleep
  sleep in Davy Jones's locker
  sleep in your leaden
    hammock
  sleep in your shoes
sleep away
slip[2]
  slip away
  slip off
  slip to Nod
  slip your breath
  slip your cable
  slip your grip
  slip your wind
slumber
snatched from us
  snatched away
snuff it *at* snuff (out)
spared
stand before your Maker
stark

step away
  step off
stoke Lucifer's fires
stop one
  stop a slug
  stop the big one
strike out
succumb[1]
swing off
take[4]
take a long (deep) sniff *at* sniff
  out
take home
take leave of life
take off
take refuge in a better world
take your leave of
taken
taking (a)
taps (the)
throw a seven *at* seven (throw
  or chuck a)
time
tip off
took *at* taken
troubles in this world are over
  (the)
turn up your toes
turn your face to the wall
under the daisies
  under the grass
  under the sod
  underground
  undersod
undiscovered country (the)
united
upstairs[2]
wages of sin (the)
wake
way of all flesh (the)
wear away
win home
  win to rest
  win your way
with us no more
with your Maker
  with God
  with Jesus
  with the Lord
wooden box
worm-food *at* food for worms
written out of the script

Defecation

accident[1]
Aztec two-step
  Aztec hop
back-door trot *at* back door
be excused
been
big jobs
bind
bodily functions

bodily wastes
boom-boom[1]
bowel movement (a)
brown stuff (the)
bucket[1]
bun[2]
bury a Quaker
business
Cairo crud *at* crud
call of nature
cast your pellet
caught short
CC pills *at* C
cement
change[3]
cleanliness training
confined *at* confinement
continent
cowpat *at* horse apples
crap
crud
defecate
  defecation
Delhi belly
demands of nature
deposit
dirty your pants/trousers *at* dirty[2]
do a bunk
  do a dike
  do a rural
doo-doo
drop the crotte
  drop a log
  drop wax
drop your arse
droppings
dump
duty
ease nature
  ease your bowels
Edgar Brits *at* Jimmy Brits
empty yourself *at* empty out
essential purposes
evacuation[1]
excrete
fertilizer
flying handicap
flux[2]
foul
  foul yourself
go[3]
  go about your business
  go for a walk (with a spade)
  go places
  go to ground
  go to the toilet
  go upstairs
  going
grunt
gyppy tummy
honey
  honey-barge

honey bucket
  honey cart
  honey-dipper
hooky
horse apples
house-trained
human waste
incontinent[2]
  incontinency
irregularity *at* irregular
Jimmy Brits
job
loose[2]
  loose disease
loosen the bowels
mail a letter
make a deposit *at* deposit
make a mess
manure
mess[2]
Mexican fox-trot/toothache/
  two-step *at* Montezuma's
  revenge
mistake[2]
Montezuma's revenge
move your bowels
movement[1]
mud in your trousers
my word
Napoleon's revenge
nappy
natural functions (the)
  natural necessities
  natural purposes
nature's needs
night soil
  nightman
number nine
number two(s)
on the trot *at* trots (the)
open your bowels
opening medicine
ordure
pancake[1]
perform[1]
  perform a natural function
physic
pony
poop[1]
pooper-scooper
post a letter
prairie chips *at* horse apples
privacy
pure[2]
purge[3]
Rangoon runs *at* Rangoon itch
rear
regular[1]
relief[2]
relieve your bowels *at* relieve
  yourself
Richard
road apples

runny tummy (a)
  runs
sausage
scour
  scours
sewage
shift[1]
sit-down job
skidmarks
soil
  soil your clothing
  soil your pants
  soil yourself
solid waste
Spanish tummy
squat[1]
squirt
  skeet
  skitters
  squit
  squitters
stoppage[1]
threepennies (the)
Tom[1] (Tit)
top and tail
touristas (the)
trots (the)
turn up your tail
visiting card
void your bowels *at* void water
waste[2]
wedding *at* night soil

Dismisssal

administrative leave
air (the)
axe
bag
bench
  bench-warmer
bobtail
boot (the)
bounce[3]
bowler hat
bullet (the)
bump[1] (the)
bump[2]
California kiss-off *at*
  kiss-off
can[2]
cards (your)
career change
  career transition center
carpet[1]
chop[2] (the)
chuck (the)
clear your desk
consultant
cut numbers
DCM
de-accession
dehire
delayering

demanning
deselect
dispense with (someone's)
    assistance
dose of P45 medicine
down population
downsize
drop the boom on
drop-dead list
early release
    early retirement
excess[1]
fire
flush down the drain
for the chop at chop[2] (the)
for the high jump
furlough
gardening leave
gate[2] (the)
general discharge
get on your bike
get the shaft
give a P45
give (someone) the air
give time to other
    commitments
    give time to other interests
given new responsibilities
golden bowler at bowler hat
golden goodbye at golden
golden handshake at golden
golden parachute at golden
goodbye
graze on the common at graze
graze on the plain at graze
halve the footprint
handshake
have the shout at shout[1] (the)
headcount reduction
heave (the)
hike (off)[1]
human sacrifice
in the barrel
in the departure lounge
interim
Irish promotion
Irishman's rise
job turning
kick[2] (the)
kiss-off[2]
lay off
leave of absence
let go
let out
liberate[4]
look after (your) other interests
lose[2]
marching orders
measure for the drop
Mexican raise
negative employee situation at
    negative employment
New York kiss-off at kiss-off[2]

notice
off the payroll[1]
on health grounds
on the beach
on your way out
order of the boot
    order of the push
overhaul of profit margins
payroll adjustment
people cuts
pink slip
poke[1] (the)
pursue other interests
push[2] (the)
put in the mobility pool
put on file
put out to grass
railroad
rationalize
reduce the headcount
reduce your commitments
reduction in force
    riff
redundant
re-engineer
release[1]
relieve
    relieve of duties
relinquish
removal[2]
repositioning
reshuffle
resign
restructure
retire[3]
retrenched
revolving door[2]
right-sizing
run[4] (the)
    running shoes
sack (the)
seek fresh challenges
selected out
send ashore
send down the road
separate[1]
services no longer required
severance
    severance pay
shelved
ship
shoot[2] (the)
shop[1]
shout[1] (the)
shove[2] (the)
shown the door
slash and burn[2]
spend more time with your
    family
stand down
step down
streamling
surplus

swallow the anchor
take a hike[1]
take a walk[1]
take an early bath
take the wind
    take the breeze
terminate[2]
tie a can on
tin handshake
toss[2]
turn away
turn off[3]
unassigned
unheard presence
valentine
walk[2]
walk the golden gangplank at
    walk the plank
walking papers
warning
wind[2] (the)
with us no more
written out of the script

Drunkenness

abstinence
abuse
aerated
afternoon man
bacchanalian
    bacchanals
    Bag o' Nails
back teeth floating
bagged
bamboozled
bar-fly at bar
barley-fever
    barley-cap
basted
bat
battered
been in the sunshine at sun has
    been hot today (the)
belt
bend
bender
bevvied at beverage
binge
blasted
blind
    blind drunk
    blind-fou
blitzed
blotto at smeared
blow me one
blue ribbon
boiled
bombed out
bother the bottle at bottle[1] (the)
bottle (the)
    bottled
Brahms
break the pledge at pledge (the)

bug-eyed
bun on (have/tie a)
bung[1]
    Bungay fair
bun-puncher
burn with a (low) blue flame
bust[3]
buy a brewery
buzz on (a)
    buzzed
can on (a)
canned
carry[4]
    carry a (heavy) load
celebrate
charwallah
chemically affected *at* chemical
chemically inconvenienced *at*
    chemical
chucked
circulate the bottle *at* bottle[1]
    (the)
clobbered
cock the little finger
cock-eyed
cocked
cold turkey
cold-water man
comfortable[1]
concerned
confused
convivial
    conviviality
cop an elephant's
corked
corned
cousin Cis
    cousin sis
crack a bottle
crocked
    crock
crook the elbow
cup too many
cut[3]
damaged[1]
debauch
decks awash
dependency[2]
devotee of Bacchus *at*
    Bacchanalian
dine well
dip[2]
    dip your beak
    dip your bill
disciple of Bacchus *at* disciple
drink[1]
    drink taken
    drink too much
    drinking problem
drink problem *at* problem
drink tank *at* in the tank
drop[2]
    drop on

drop taken
drown your sorrows
drunk
dry[2]
dry out
Dutch courage
Dutch feast
Dutch headache
edged
elbow-bending
    elbow-bender
elephant's
elevation
    elevated
embalmed
emotional
enjoy a drink
    enjoy a cup
    enjoy a drop
    enjoy a glass
    enjoy a nip
    enjoy the bottle
enjoy a jar *at* jar
excited by wine
fall among friends
    fall among thieves
far gone
feel no pain
five or seven
flawed
floating
fly-by-night[2]
fly one wing low
foggy
    fogged
fond of a glass *at* fond of
footless
forward
fou *at* full
four sheets in the wind
foxed
fractured
fragile
frail
fresh[1]
fresh[2]
    fresh in drink
fricasseed
fried
fuddled
full
    full as a tick
full of liquor *at* liquor
fun-loving
funny tummy *at* funny[1]
gage
    gaged
gay
geared up *at* gear
given to the drink
glass too many *at* glass[1]
glow on
gone[2]

good lunch (a)
grape-shot *at* grape (the)
greased
groggy
    grog on board
    grog-hound
half[2]
    half and half
    half canned
    half cooked
    half corned
    half cut
    half foxed
    half gone
    half in the bag
    half on
half under *at* under the influence
half-pint *at* half[1]
half-seas over
    half-sea
half-screwed *at* screwed
half-shot *at* shot[3]
half-slewed *at* slewed
half-sloshed *at* sloshed
half-sprung *at* sprung
half-stewed *at* stewed
hang a few on
    hang one on
hangover
have a load on *at* load[1]
have the sun in your eyes *at* sun
    has been hot today (the)
hen-drinking *at* hen
high
hit[1]
    hit it
    hit the bottle
    hit the hooch
hoist[2]
hold your liquor
hollow legs
hung
    hungover
hunt the brass rail
hunt the fox down the red lane
ill[3]
illuminated
imbibe
in bits
in drink
in liquor
in the bag[2]
in the down-pins *at* down
    among the dead men
in the rats
in the sunshine *at* sun has been
    hot today (the)
in the tank
in your cups
incapable
indisposed[2]
indulge
intemperance

Irish thing (the)
jag on *at* jag house
jagged
jet-lag
jolly[1]
juice[1] (the)
  juice head
  juiced
keelhauled
keep the pledge *at* pledge (the)
knock it back
knock off[4]
Korsakoff's syndrome *at*
  syndrome
laid out
leave your can
led astray
legless
lift your little finger
  lift your arm
  lift your elbow
  lift your wrist
like a drink
liquored *at* liquor
lit
  lit up
load[1]
loaded[1]
locked
look on the wine when it was
  red
looped
lose your lunch
lubricate your tonsils
  lubricated
lush
  lushed
  lushy
market-fresh *at* fresh[2]
mellow
merry
migraine
morning after (the)
Mozart
muddy
muggy
muzzy
nasty[2]
non-drinker *at* drink[1]
off the wagon
oiled
  oil the wig
on[1]
on the bat *at* bat
on the bottle
on the piss
on the roof
on the sauce *at* sauce[1] (the)
on the tiles
on the town[1]
on the wagon
one over the eight
one too many

over the bat
overdo the Dionysian rites
over-indulge
over-refreshed
  over-excited
  over-sedated
overtired
  overtiredness
package on (a)
paint the town red
paralytic
paralysed
parboiled
partake
peg[2]
petrified
pickled
pie-eyed
pioneer[2]
piran
pissed
plastered
pledge (the)
plowed *at* plough[2]
polluted *at* pollute
pooped
pot[2]
  pot valour
  potted
pot-walloper
preserved
priest of Bacchus *at*
  Bacchanalian
primed
problem drinker *at* problem
pruned
punish the bottle
put (it) away
queer[1]
racked
ragged
ran-dan *at* randy
rattled
raunchy
reading Geneva print
refreshed
ripe
ripped
ripples on
rocky[2]
rollocked
rosy
scorched
Scotch mist
screwed
scuttered
sent
several sheets in the wind *at*
  sheet in the wind (a)
sewn up[2]
sheet in the wind (a)
shellacked
shoot the cat

shot[3]
shout[2]
  shout yourself hoarse
sign the pledge
siper *at* sip
six o'clock swill
skinful
slewed
sloshed
slugged *at* slug[2]
smashed
  smash the teapot
smeared
soak
  soaked
sodden
son of Bacchus *at* Bacchanalian
sop
sot
souse
  soused
sozzle
spifflicated
  spiffed
splice the mainbrace
sponge
sprung
squashed
squiffy
stewed
stiff[2]
stinking
  stinko
stitched
  stitch in your wig
stoned
strong weakness *at* strong
  waters
stung *at* stung by a serpent
stunned
stupid
  stupid-fou
sun has been hot today (the)
  sun in your eyes
Sunday traveller
supercharged
swill
  swill-pot
  swilled
  swiller
take a drink
take a drop *at* take the drop
take something
take the pledge
take to the bottle *at* bottle (the)
take too much
tanked up
tap[1]
taste for the bottle
technicolor yawn (a)
temperance
the worse
thirst (a)

three sheets in the wind
throat
tiddly
tie one on
tight[1]
tip[2] (the bottle)
  tiper
  tipped
  tipper
  tipsy
tippler *at* tipple
tired[2]
  tired and emotional
toot[1]
top-heavy
toss down
tot
touched[1]
translated
turn up your little finger
  turn up pinkie
under the influence
under the table[1]
unfortified
unwell
visiting fireman[1]
wad-shifter
wall-eyed
warm[3] (with wine)
wash the baby's head
wasted
waterlogged
weakness for the drink *at*
  weakness
well away
  well bottled
  well corned
  well in the way
  well oiled
  well sprung
wet a bargain *at* wet[2]
wet-hand *at* wet[2]
wet your beard *at* wet[2]
wet your mouth *at* wet[2]
wet your whistle *at* wet[2]
whacked
whiffled
whip the cat
whistled
wired[1]
worse for drink *at* the worse
worse for wear (the)
wrecked
zoned out
zonked

Education

academic dismissal
academically subnormal
attention deficit disorder
  ADD
backward[1]
Blue Peter

can[2]
care
chalkboard
comprehension
  comprehensive
concentration problem (a)
confederation
convoy concept
creative freedom *at* creative
developmental
  developmental class
  developmental course
disparate impact
disturbed[1]
dumb down
educational welfare manager
fair[1]
foundation language arts *at*
  foundation
gate[1]
home economics
in care
jerk[1]
late developer
less prepared *at* less
limited
maladjusted
mature student *at* mature
no Einstein/genius/scholar
not a great reader
numeracy *at* comprehension
open access
overactive
plough[2]
plucked
precocious
referred
remedial
rusticate
school phobia syndrome *at*
  syndrome
send down[1]
ship
slow
soft skills
special[1]
  special needs
  special schools
special education
status deprivation
tenure
underachiever
verbally deficient

Employment

above your ceiling
affirmative action
ask for your papers
at liberty
available[2]
below stairs[1]
between shows
  between jobs

bug[2]
day of action
dispute
domestic
duvet day
economically inactive
employment
English disease (the)[2]
fairness at work
feather bed
flying picket
gentleman
ghost[1]
glass ceiling
go slow
golden
  golden hallo
  golden handcuffs
  golden parachute
  golden retriever
hand
headhunter[2]
help[1]
hit the bricks[1]
industrial action
job action
kangaroo court
labour[2]
moonlight[3]
movement[2]
negative employment
off the payroll[2]
on the labour *at* labour[2]
organize
parity
phantom
player
prairie-dogging
private enterprise
production difficulties
pull rank
pull the pin
resting
rights at work
scandal sheet
sell out
send in your papers
service lawyer
sick-out
sitting by the window
slowdown[1]
solidarity
Spanish practices
stoppage[2]
suits (the)
swing around the buoy
swing the lead
team player
unofficial action
unwaged
upstairs[3]
useful girl
waiting for employment

walk out
wear lead boots
well rewarded
withdraw your labour
work to rule
working people
   working men

Entertainment

airport novel
best-seller
between shows
blockbuster
celebrity
clog *at* put the clog in
collaborator[2]
corpse
cult
cut-and-paste job
dark[1]
doorstep[2]
dry[3]
dumb down
Dutch concert
early bath
filler[1]
fold your hand
fringe theatre *at* fringe
get a result
ghost[2]
ghost does not walk (the)
hang up your boots
hatchet (man)
   hatchet job
haute cuisine
help[2]
I must have notice of this
   question
instant bestseller *at* bestseller
integrated casting
intermission
international bestseller *at*
   bestseller
keep the pot boiling
   at potboiler
kiss-and-tell
   kiss money
less enjoyable *at* less
low-budget
   low-cost
message
natural break
negative incident
nouvelle cuisine
objective
paper the house
paying guest
personality
PG
pill[3]
plant[3]
plastic chicken circuit (the)
poughman's (a)

ploughman's lunch
plug[3]
potboiler
professional
   professional foul
pull[1]
put the clog in
rabbit
reluctant to depart
resting
result[1]
say a few words
scissor-and-paste job
send to the showers
sharp elbow
showers[2]
sledge
sound bite
spike[2]
sponsor
stand-up[2]
subsidy publishing
sweeten[3]
tail-pulling
take a break
talking cardigan
talking head
Tartans (the)
trail
trash
unheard presence
vanity publishing
walk[4]
warn off
   warn off the turf
water gardener
word from our sponsor
words
written out of the script

Erections and Orgasms

arousal *at* arouse
beat on
blow off *at* blow[1]
boner
bring off[1]
bugle
bulge
charge[1]
climax
come
come aloft
come off
completion
crank
cream
   cream your jeans
die
discharge
dry bob
earth moved for you
effusion
erection

erect
essence
expire[2]
finish[2]
fire a shot
flute
get off[1]
get the upshoot
go off[1]
hair trigger trouble
hard-on
horn[1]
Irish toothache[2]
juice[3]
lead in your pencil
man-root
Maria Monk
Mr Priapus
night loss
   night emission
nocturnal emission
over the top[2]
piss your tallow *at* piss pins and
   needles
present arms
priapus
   priapism
pride
   pride of the morning
pull his trigger
raise a beat
   raise a gallop
rise
ripple
roe *at* shoot off
run out of steam
seed
shoot blanks
shoot off
   shoot over the stubble
   shoot your load
   shoot your roe
shot[4]
spend
spill yourself
spirits[1]
spunk
spurt
stand[1]
   stand to attention
state of excitement
stiff[3]
   stiffy
stuff[1]
thrill
tumescent
weapon
wet dream

Espionage

agent
asset
baby-sitting

back-door[2]
beard
black bag
blow[7]
  blow away
  blow the gaff
  blow up
blow the whistle on
brief
bromide job
bubble
canary trap
clean house
cobbler
come across[1]
company[2] (the)
covert act
decontaminate[2]
doctor
dry clean
ear
earpiece
electrical surveillance *at* surveillance
electronic underwear
  electronic counter-measures
  electronic penetration
executive action *at* executive measure
extremely sensitive source
firm (the)
fishing expedition[1]
  fishing trip
go over
hospital[2]
human intelligence
illegal resident *at* legal resident
intelligence
joe[2]
legal resident
military intelligence
mole
no longer in service *at* no longer with us
overhear
penetrate[2]
persona non grata
place-man
safe house
secret agent *at* agent
security
  security service
sticky stranger
surveillance
tail[2]
  tail job
take a walk[2]
technical surveillance *at* surveillance
terminate with extreme prejudice *at* terminate[1]
turn[2] (round/around)

wear a wire *at* wired[2] (up)
wired[2] (up)
  wireman

Extortion and Violence

action[2]
Arkansas toothpick
badger game *at* badger
ball money
barker
bederipe *at* droit de seigneur
bell money
benevolence
biographic leverage
blackmail
bleed
blood money
boonwork *at* droit de seigneur
bottle[5]
bounce[4]
break the news
bunch of fives
burn[3]
call out
card[1]
carry[3]
change someone's voice
charity money
Chicago typewriter
chopper[1]
claim responsibility for
clean[1]
cooperate
colt[2]
come across[1]
come through
convince
dance[2]
direct action
dirt
do[2]
  do over
electric methods
energetic
enforcer
fill in
frightener
gang-bang
get the shaft
give (someone) the works
Glasgow kiss
glass[2]
go abroad
greenmailer
gunner's daughter
handle[2]
hatchet (man)
have the dirt on *at* dirt
heat[1]
heat[2]
  heater

heeled
heightened interrogation
help the police (with their inquiries)
honey trap
hook[2]
hurt
in protection *at* protection
inquisition
interrogation with prejudice
Irish hoist
iron[1]
joint[3]
juice[2]
  juice dealer
  juice man
kiss the gunner's daughter *at* gunner's daughter
kneecap
knock around
knuckle sandwich
lay hands on
lead
  lead ballast
  lead buttons
  lead pill
  lead poisoning
lean on
leather[1]
life preserver
lift a hand to
long *at* short[2]
love-boonwork *at* droit de seigneur
mark[3]
marry the gunner's daughter *at* gunner's daughter
massage[2]
molest
moonlight[2]
muscle
  muscleman
nut[2]
out[3]
personal correction
persuade
persuader
piece[2]
plink
pressure
protection
purge[2]
put the arm on
  put the bite on
  put the black on
  put the muscle on
  put the scissors on
put the boot in
put the burn on *at* burn[3]
rake-off
razor
reasonable
refresh your memory

retainer
ride the wooden horse
rod
  rodded
shoot[1]
skim
slug
  slugged
soldier
something on you
squeeze[1]
stick it into[2]
stiff-arm
strap
street tax
sweat it out of
  sweat-box
take a stick to
third degree
treatment
voluntary
warm a backside
water cure
word to the wise
work on[1]

Farting

anti-social (noise) *at* anti-social
bad powder
Bronx cheer
cheeser *at* cut a cheese
cut a cheese
  cut a leg
  cut one
emunctory
let off
  let fly
lift a gam
pass air
  pass gas
  pass wind
poop[2]
raspberry[1]
rude noise
unsociable (be)
wind[1]
  windy

Female Genitalia

beaver
below stairs[2]
between the legs
bird[3]
  bird's nest
box[3]
cat[2]
cock
  cockpit
Cupid's arbour
  Cupid's cave
  Cupid's cloister
  Cupid's corner

  Cupid's cupboard
down below
  down there
Eve's custom-house *at* Adam's
  arsenal
face between her forks *at* fork
fanny
feminine gender
finish yourself off
front door (the)
  front parlour
hole[2]
holy of holies
intimate part
it[3]
kitty[1]
lower stomach
mickey
monosyllable
mousehole
muff
nest
nether parts
  nether regions
  Netherlands (the)
organ
oval office
parts
private parts
  privates
privities
privy parts
pussy[1]
  pussy lift
ring[1]
secret parts
sex[2]
shaft[2]
snatch[2]
south (the)[2]
spam alley/chasm *at* spam[1]
tickler[1]
treasure
what you may call it
  whatsit
  whatzis

Funerals

all-night man
black job
body
body bag
  body-bag syndrome
bone[2]
  bone-house
  bone-hugging
  bone-orchard
  bone-yard
box[1]
bury
  burial
case[2]
chapel of ease[1]

  chapel of rest
clay *at* lay down your life
clunk
cold[1]
  cold-box
  cold cart
  cold cook
  cold meat party
  cold storage
Davy Jones's locker
decontaminate[1]
diet of worms
dismal trade
  dismal trader
  dismals
dole-meats *at* dole
dustbin *at* dust[2]
dustman *at* dust[2]
earth
  earth-dole
floater[2]
floral tribute
garden of remembrance
  garden crypt
  garden of honor
ground-lair *at* ground
ground-mail *at* ground
ground-sweat *at* ground
hic jacet
hick
hygienic treatment
ice box[2]
invalid coach
lay out
lay to rest
lie with
long pig
loved one
lump
  lump of meat
mausoleum crypt
meat[3]
  meat wagon
memorial
  memorial counsellor
  memorial house
  memorial park
  memorial society
narrow bed
narrow passageway to the
  unknown
non-heart beating donor
personal representatives
pine overcoat
plant[1]
pre-arrangement
pre-need
preparation room
prepare
  prepared biography
professional car
put away[2]
remains

removal[3]
repose
  reposing room
restroom *at* rest room
restorative art
resurrection man
  resurrection cove
  resurrectionist
slumber box *at* slumber
slumber cot *at* slumber
slumber robe *at* slumber
slumber room *at* slumber
space
  space and bronze deal
stiff[1]
  stiff one[1]
vault[2]
wake the churchyard *at* wake
watch
wooden box
  wooden breeches
  wooden breeks
  wooden coat
  wooden overcoat

Gambling

amusement with prizes
betting book *at* bookmaker
bird dog[1]
bookmaker
broads
casino *at* case[1]
cold deck
commission agent
coffee-housing
debt of honour
dissolution[2]
  dissolute
dope
drop anchor
flutter
fruit machine
gamester[2]
  gaming
investor
one-armed bandit
plant the books
pull[1]
  pull up
railroad bible
ringer
runner[1]
sportsman
strangle
street bets
tank fight
weakness for horses *at*
  weakness

Illegitimacy and Parentage

absent parent

base born
bend sinister
beyond the blanket
born in the vestry *at* born in
  Borough English
break your elbow
  break your leg (above the
  knee)
by(e)
  by(e)-begot
  by(e)-blow
  by(e)-chap
  by(e)-come
  by(e)-scape
cast a (laggin or leglin) girth *at*
  cast[1]
chance
  chance-bairn
  chance-begot
  chance-born
  chance-child
  chance-come
  chanceling
cheat the starter
child of sin
  child of grief
come in at the window
  come in at the back door
  come in at the hatch
  come in at the side door
  come o'will
doorstep[1]
flyblow
force-put job
grass-widow
illegitimate
indiscretion
latchkey
left-handed[1]
lone parent
love child
  love begotten
  love bird
  love-bairn
  love child
midnight baby
misfortune
  misbegot
  mishap
natural
nurse-child *at* nurse
one-parent family
parentally challenged *at*
  challenged
single parent
  single mother
slip a foot *at* slip[1]
slip a girth *at* slip[1]
son of a bitch
  SOB
  son of a bachelor
son of a gun *at* gunner's
  daughter

souvenir
spurious
  spurious issue
tender a fool
unlawful
  unlawful bed
  unlawful issue
  unlawful purpose
  unlawfully born
wrong side of the blanket

Illness and Injury

ableism
active
afflicted
aurally challenged *at*
  challenged
aurally handicapped *at*
  handicapped
aurally inconvenienced *at*
  inconvenienced
big C
blighty
buy it
C
card[1]
cardiac incident
  cardiac arrest
case[2]
catch a packet[1]
Chalfonts
challenged
change someone's voice
charming *at* charm
chuck up
claret
clip[2]
combat ineffective
comfortable[2]
condition[1]
consumption
cop a packet
coronary inefficiency
crack[2]
crease
decline
delicate
devil disease (the)
dicky
differently abled *at* differently
disability
disabled
do[2]
  do down
  do for
  do in
  do over
doctor
done for
Down's syndrome
eating disorder (an)
eliminate manhood *at*
  manhood

Emmas
  Emma Freuds
face your maker
falling sickness (the)
  falling evil
Farmer Giles
feed the fishes
feel funny *at* funny[1]
feminine complaint
fix[2]
fly the yellow flag
funny[1]
  funny tummy
gas
get a slug *at* slug[1]
get it
go on the box
groggy
groper *at* grope
growth
handicap
  handicapped
hard of hearing
have a heart *at* heart condition
health
  health care products
  health clinics
  health farms
  health insurance
heart condition
  heart
heart problem *at* problem
home[1]
hopping-Giles
  Hopkins
hospice
human difference
impaired hearing
inconvenienced
intervention[2]
Irish fever (the)
joint[3]
knackered *at* knackers
knocked out cold
Kraepelin's syndrome *at*
  Down's syndrome
lay a child
long illness (a)
martyr to (a)
meat wagon *at* meat[3]
medical correctness
misadventure
mitotic disease
mobility impaired
muster your bag
National Health Service *at*
  health
neoplasm
nick[4]
nick[5]
nil by mouth
nip[3]
no active treatment

no i/v access
no mayday
not long for this world
not very well
  not at all well
nursing home *at* home[1]
off-colour[2]
old man's friend
on the club
on the panel[1]
one foot in the grave
operation (an)
optically challenged
  optically handicapped
  optically inconvenienced
  optically marginalized
packet[1]
partially sighted
people with differing abilities *at*
  people of/with
people with impaired hearing *at*
  people of/with
person with AIDS *at* person of/
  with
PWA
physically challenged *at*
  challenged
physically handicapped *at*
  handicap
poorly[1]
prey to (a)
private patient
PRN
problem
procedure
put out for the count *at* count
  (the)
raspberry[2]
rather poorly *at* rather
residential provision
  resident
restricted growth
routine (nursing) care only
scratch[2]
sight deprived
sing soprano
sink[2]
smear[2]
snib *at* snip
snick *at* snip
snip
so-so
sore
spot[3]
staining
statement
stone deaf *at* hard of hearing
stop one
  stop a slug
surgical misadventure *at*
  misadventure
syndrome
tagged[1]

tap the claret *at* claret
TB *at* consumption
temporarily abled *at* ableism
ten commandments (the)
tender loving care
therapeutic misadventure *at*
  misadventure
thick of hearing
throw up
  throw a map
  throw up your tonsils
trouble
tumour (a)
turn[3]
Uncle Dick *at* Dicky
under the weather
uniquely
  uniquely abled
  uniquely coordinated
unmentionables[2]
unsighted
upstairs[1]
use a wheelchair
vertically challenged *at*
  challenged
visually handicapped *at*
  handicapped
visually impaired
visually inconvenienced *at*
  inconvenienced
waterworks[2]
wear a bullet
white plague (the)
winded
winged
women's problem *at* problem

Intoxicants

alcohol
amber fluid/liquid/nectar
ambrosia
angel foam *at* angel dust
anti-freeze
ardent spirits
auld kirk (the)
awful experiment (the)
bar
belt
beverage
  beverage host
  beverage room
  bevvy
  bevy
black stuff (the)
blast[4]
blind pig
blow me one
blue ruin
  blue stone
bottle[1] (the)
  bottle club
  bottle shop
bracer

branch water
brew[2]
brother of the bung *at* brother[1]
brownie
burra peg
bush-house
chaser
chota peg
club[3]
cocktail[2]
    cocktail bar
    cocktail hour
    cocktail lounge
cooler[2]
cordial[1]
corn[1]
    corn-juice
    corn mule
    corn waters
cough medicine
    cough syrup
creature (the)
    crater
    crathur
    cratur
cut[3]
dash[1]
dead soldier
dive[2]
doctor
dram
drink[1]
drop[2]
    drop of blood
drown the miller
dry[1]
Dutch cheer
duty not paid
embalming fluid *at* embalmed
eye-opener
fellow commoner
firewater
foot
    footing
French article
    French cream
    French elixir
    French lace
    Frenchman
freshen a drink
G
gargle
gas-house
gear
glass[1]
grape (the)
gravy
groceries sundries
half[1]
    half a can
    half and half
hard
    hard drink

hard stuff
    harden a drink
hardware[1]
heel-tap
highball
horn of the ox
hospitality
jar
John Barleycorn
jolt (a)
jug[2]
juice[1] (the)
    juice joint
    juice of the bear
juniper juice *at* juice[1]
libation
lightning
liquid
    liquid dinner
    liquid lunch
    liquid refreshment
    liquid restaurant
    liquid supper
liquor
little something
livener
load[1]
loaded[3]
local
    local pub
lotion
lush
medicine
mercy
Mickey (Finn)
Moll Thompson's mark
    at moll
moonlight[1]
moonshine
mother's ruin
    mother's milk
mountain dew
nasty[1] (the)
    nasty stuff
native elixir (the)
needle
Nelson's blood
nightcap
nineteenth (hole)
nip[2]
    nipperkin
no heel-taps *at* heel-tap
noggin
oil of malt *at* oiled
one for the road
pack *at* package on (a)
package store
panther sweat
    panther piss
parliament[2]
peg[1]
pick-me-up
pint (the)

piss (the)
plasma
poison
potation
prairie oyster[2]
    prairie dew
prune-juice *at* pruned
public house
    pub
purge[1]
quick one
quickie[1]
rag water
red eye
refresher[1]
restorative
reviver
rush the growler
sauce[1] (the)
scoop
scour-the-gate *at* scour
sea food
sharpener
short[1]
    short drink
shot[1]
sip
slug[2]
snifter
snort[1]
    snorter
social glass (a)
something
    something for the thirst
    something moist
    something short
spike[1]
spirits[2]
spot[1]
spunkie *at* spunk
stick[2]
sticky
stiff one[2]
stiffener
stimulant (a)
strong waters
stuff[1]
stump liquor
sundowner
tiddly-wink *at* tiddly
tiger sweat
    tiger juice
    tiger milk
    tiger piss
tincture[2]
tipple
    tippling house
tot
transfusion
tumble[2] (down the sink)
water of life
watering hole
wee drop

wee dram
wee half
wet[2]
    wet bar
    wet canteen
    wet goods
    wet stuff
wetting[1]
whistler *at* whistled
whistle-shop *at* whistled
white lightning[2]
    white eye
    white mule
    white satin
    white stuff
willie-waught

Killing and Suicide

account for
ace
auto-da-fé
axe[1]
bag[3]
bake
barker
bath-house
bellyful of lead
blank[2]
blast[2]
blip off
block out
blot (out)
blow away
brace
Bridport dagger
bring down
bucket[3]
bump[5] (off)
    bump-man
Burke
burn[2]
business
button[1] (man)
call out
capital
    capital charge
    capital crime
    capital punishment
    capital sentences unit
carry off
cement shoes
chair[1] (the)
chew a gun
chill
chop[1]
climb the ladder
clip[2]
clip his wick
close an account
collect a bullet
comb out
commit suicide
compromise

concrete shoes (in)
    concrete boots
    concrete overcoat
contract
cook[1]
cool[1]
country sports
    country pursuits
crack[2]
cramper *at* crap
crap
    crap merchant
    crapping cull
crease
croak[1]
    croak yourself
cull
cut[6]
cut down on
dance[1]
    dance a twostep to another
        world
    dance at the end of a rope
    dance off
    dance on air
    dance the Tyburn jig
    dance upon nothing
    dance-hall
    dancing master
daylight
deep six
demote maximally
destroy
die queer
die with your knees bent
disappear[1]
disinfection
dispatch
disposal
do[2]
    do for
    do in
    do yourself in
do away with
done for
draw a bead on
drill[1]
drink milk
drive a ball through
drop[1]
    drop down the chute
dull
dust[2]
Dutch (do the)
    Dutch act
earn a passport
East
easy way out (the)
eat a gun
electric cure
eliminate
    elimination
emigrated

end
erase
evacuation[2]
    evacuee
executive measure
    executive action
exemplary punishment
expedient demise
expose
extremely ill
fade
feed a slug
    feed a pill
fill full of holes
    filled with daylight
    filled with lead
finger-man[3]
finish[1]
    finish off
fix[4]
fog away
    fog
for the high jump
foul play
frag
freeze off
fry[1]
gaggler *at* crap
game[1]
gas
get a slug *at* slug[1]
get the chop *at* chop[1]
get the gas pipe *at* gas
get the needle
give (someone) the works
give the good news
go down[1]
go for your tea
go through[2]
go to heaven in a string
go up[1]
Grace of Wapping (the)
grease[2]
green needle (the)
hang
    hang-fair
    hanging judge
harvest
have his neck stretched *at*
    necktie party
head[1]
    heading
    heading-hill
    heading-man
hemp[1]
    hempen fever
    hempen widow
    hemp-quinsy
    Hempshire gentleman
    hemp-string
hit[2]
    hitman
hole[1]

hole in the head
hot seat
ice[1]
in the cart
iron out
   iron off
justify
kayo
keep sheep by moonlight
King of Tyburn *at* Tyburn
kiss St Giles' cup
kissed by the maiden
knock down
knock off[1]
   knock on the head
knock over
last drop *at* drop[3]
last waltz
lay hands on
leap in the dark (a)
lethal
lift your hair
liquidate
long drop *at* drop[3]
long walk off a short pier (a)
loop
make a hole in the water
make away with[1]
make dead meat of *at* dead
   meat
make use of a weapon *at* make
   use of
make your bones
maximum demote *at* demote
   maximally
measured for a necktie *at*
   necktie party
mercy death
   mercy killing
midwives' mercy
necklace
necktie party
   necktie sociable
neutralize
nine ounces of lead
nobble[2]
nullification
number is up (your)
OD yourself
off[1]
one-way ride
overdose
   OD
Paddington
paper out on
pay your debt
   to society
pick off
plough under
plug[1]
pop[4]
pot[1]
   pot-shot

preach at Tyburn Cross *at*
   Tyburn
pull the plug on
push the button on
put against a wall
put away[1]
put daylight through
put down[1]
put off
put on ice *at* ice[1]
put on the spot
put out a contract on (someone)
put out of your troubles
put the juice to
put to sleep
put to the sword
put underground *at* put under
   the sod
put yourself away
release[3]
remainder[1]
removal[1]
resettlement
retire[1]
ride backwards
ride up Holborn Hill
roll[3]
rope[1] (the)
roper *at* crap
rub out
run into a bullet
sanction
scalp
scrag
scragger *at* crap
scuppered
self-deliverance
   self-destruction
   self-execution
   self-immolation
   self-violence
send to heaven
   send home
   send to the happy hunting
      ground
   send to the happy land
   send to the land of the lotus
      blossom
   send to your long account
settle[1]
sheriff's journeyman
   at crap
shoot[1]
short illness (a)
shot while trying to
   escape
   shot while fleeing
shove over
showers[3]
   shower baths
sizzle
sluice[2]
smear out

smoke[2]
   smoke it
sniff out
snuff (out)
spot[2]
squash
squib off
stabbed with a Bridport dagger
   at stab
stake (the)
step on[2]
stick[1]
stop a mouth
stretch the hemp
   stretch the neck
string up
suffer
   suffer the supreme
      penalty
supreme measure of
   punishment
swing[1]
switcher *at* crap
take[3]
take a leap
take care of[1]
take electricity
take for a ride
take out[2]
take the drop
take the walk
take with you
take (your) life
terminate[1]
   terminate with
      extreme prejudice
top[2]
   topping fellow
topping cove *at* crap
trouble
tuck away
   tuck under
turn off[1]
   turning tree
twisted
Tyburn
   Tyburn blossom
   Tyburn dance
   Tyburn hornpipe
   Tyburn jig
   Tyburn ticket
   Tyburn tippet
   Tyburn tree
   Tyburn triple tree
walk the plank
want out
waste[1]
wax[2]
wear lead buttons
wet job
   wet operations
   wet work
whack

whiff
wipe off
wipe out
withdraw from life
without baggage
write off
upstairs out of this world (go) *at* upstairs[2]
zap

Lavatories

ablutions
Ajax
ammunition
army form blank
arrangement *at* arrange
article
aunt[2]
   Aunt Jones
basement
bathroom
   bathroom paper
   bathroom tissue
bedpan
blue room
bog
   bog-house
boys[1] (room)
bucket[1]
bum-fodder
can[1]
carsey
   carsy
chamber
chamber-pot
chic sale
cloakroom
close stool
closet[1]
comfort station *at* comfort[2]
commode
common house[2]
convenience
corner[2]
cottage *at* cottaging
cousin John *at* john[1]
dung
   dunnie van
EC
earth closet
effluent
facility[1]
fourth
gentlemen
   gentlemen's convenience
   gents
geography
girls room
going *at* go[3]
head(s)[2]
holy of holies[2]
hopper
house[2]

house of commons
house of ease
house of lords
house of office
hygienic facilities
jacks *at* jakes
jakes
jane[2]
jerry
   Jericho
john[1]
Jordan
karsey *at* carsey
kersey *at* carsey
ladies
   ladies' convenience
   ladies' room
latrine
lavabo
lavatory
little boys' room
   little girls' room
little house
loo
looking glass
male
men('s room)
modern convenience
Mrs Chant
necessary (house)
   necessary woman
night bucket
   night jar
night stool
on the seat
outdoor plumbing
outhouse
pan
parliament[1]
personal hygiene station
petty house
pig's ear
   pig
place
plumbing[1]
potty[2]
powder room
private office
privy
   privy stool
public convenience
Quaker's burial ground *at* bury a Quaker
rears
relief-station *at* relief[2]
rest room
retiring-room
sanctum sanctorum *at* holy of holies
sanitary man
sanitized
sink[1]
sluice[2]

smallest room (the)
squatter *at* squat[1]
tearoom
throne
thunderbox
   thunder-mug
toilet
   toilet paper
upstairs[1]
W/WC
wash and brush up
washroom
waste management
   compartment *at* waste[2]
water closet
what you may call it
   whatsit
   whatzis
women
women's room
you-know-what

Low Intelligence

academically subnormal
airhead
backward[1]
brick short of a load (a)
card short of a full deck (a)
cerebrally challenged *at* challenged
Charlie uncle
cupcake
developmentally challenged *at* challenged
differently abled *at* differently
disparate impact
dope
double dutch *at* Dutch
dummy[1]
Dutchman
   Dutchy
educable
elevator does not go to the top floor (the)
fifty cards in the pack
fogbound
have a slate loose
   at slate-off
intellectually challenged *at* challenged
jerk[2]
   jerk-off
learning difficulties (with)
light in the head
meathead
mentally challenged *at* mental
minus
   minus buttons
   minus screws
muggy
natural[1]
not all there

not sixteen annas to
    the rupee
    not sixteen ounces to the
        pound
penny short of a pound
people with learning difficulties
    at people of/with
play with a full deck
pointy head
retard
right Charlie *at* Charlie
simple
slate-off
slow
    slow upstairs
soft[1]
thick
    thick in the head
tinhead
uniquely proficient
up top
want[1] (a)
    want some pence in a shilling
    wanting
without the highest IQ in the
    world

Lying

cock-and-bull story *at* story
creative
credibility gap
deal from the bottom of the
    deck
deniably
    deniable
    deniability
disinformation *at* information
eat the Bible
economical with the truth
    economical with the actualité
elastic
    elasticity
embroidery
evasion
fact of life *at* facts (of life)
find[2]
flutterer
gild
    gild the facts
    gild the lily
    gild the proposition
    gild the truth
imaginative journalism
information
inoperative
investigate
    investigative journalism
    investigative reporting
Irish evidence
martyr to selective amnesia *at*
    martyr to (a)
Ministry of Information *at*
    information

misspeak
news management
no comment
not available to comment
out of context
paint a picture
poetic truth
polygraph
pork pies
    porkie pies
    porkies
psychological warfare
put on
selective facts *at* selective
serious credibility gap *at*
    credibility gap
snow[2]
    snow-job
speak with forked tongue
story
    story-teller
stranger to the truth
stray off the reservation
stretcher
    stretch
    stretcher-case
swallow the Bible
switch the primer
tall story *at* story
terminological inexactitude
to one side of the truth
truth-shader

Male Genitalia

abdominal protector
acorns
Adam's arsenal
amply endowed
appendage
apples
baldy fellow
ballocks *at* bollocks
balls
banana
basket[2]
beak *at* strop your beak
beef
below stairs[2]
between the legs
bollocks
box[2]
bush
Cecil
chopper[2]
cluster
cobblers
cobs
cock
cojones
complications
corner[3]
crank
crown jewels

cut[1]
dick
ding-a-ling
dong
down below
    down there
downstairs[2]
dummy[2]
eel
endowed
engine
equipment
essentials
exhibit yourself
expose yourself
family jewels
feed the ducks
finish yourself off
Fritz *at* willy
fruit bowl
gear
Giorgio *at* willy
glands
goolies
    goolie chits
groin
hampton
Harry *at* willy
honk
horn of plenty
hot meat *at* meat[2]
hung like
    hung like a bull
    hung like a horse
    hung like a rabbit
    hung like a stallion
instrument
intimate part
intimate person
it[3]
jack[1]
Jean-Claude *at* willy
jewels
jock
John Thomas
    John Peter
    JP
    JT
Johnson
joint[2]
knackers
knob
knocker
load[2]
loins
long-arm inspection
love muscle
lower abdomen
lower stomach
lunch-box
male parts
manhood
man-root

marbles
marriage tackle *at* tackle
masculinity
meat[2] (and two veg)
member
membrum virile
mickey
middle leg *at* third leg
most precious part
Netherlands (the)
nether parts
  nether regions
nuts
old man[2]
orchestras
organ
  organ of sex
  organs
parts
pecker
peculiar members *at* peculiar
pencil[1]
Percy
person
  personal parts
peter
pickle *at* pump your shaft
pill[1]
pills
pin
pistol
pole
pork[2]
  pork sword
pride
  prides
private parts
  privates
privities
privy parts
process
python
rocks
rod[2]
roger
root[1]
sausage
secret parts
serpent
sex[2]
sexual organ *at* organ
shaft[2]
short hairs
  short and curlies
short-arm inspection
  short-arm
south[2] (the)
spam[1]
  spam javelin
  spam sceptre
spear
split-mutton at split
staff

stem
stick[3]
stones
sword
tackle
tassel *at* pencil[1]
tender tumour *at* tumour (a)
thing
  thingamajig
  thingy
third leg
Tom *at* willy
Tommy
tool
tube of meat
vitals
wank[2]
weapon
wedding tackle
weenie
well endowed
well hung
what you may call it
whatzis
  whatsit
whip *at* crack your whip
whistle
wick
wiener
willy
  willie
winded
winkle
  winkie
yard

Masturbation

abuse
at yourself
auto-erotic practices
  auto-erotic habits
Barclays
bash the bishop
beastliness
beat your meat
  beat off
  beat your dummy
body rub (a)
bring off[1]
caress yourself
choke your chicken
  chicken-choker
come your mutton
diddle[2]
do yourself
duff[1]
easement
extras
fifty up
filthy
finger[3]
  finger yourself
five-fingered widow

flog off
  flog your beef
  flog your donkey
  flog your dummy
  flog your mutton
fluff your duff
fondle
fool (about) with yourself
frig[2]
go at yourself
hand job
  hand relief
lone love
J. Arthur
jack off
jerk off[1]
jiggle
make love to yourself *at* make
    love to
Mary Fivefingers
  Mary Palm
massage[3]
mess with yourself
mother five fingers
mount a corporal and four
onanism
one off the wrist
play
play at hot cockles
play the organ
play with yourself *at* play
    with
pleasuring *at* pleasure
pocket job (a)
  pocket billiards
  pocket pool
pollute yourself *at* pollute
pull (yourself) off
pull the pud(ding)
pump your shaft
  pump your pickle
release[4]
relief[3]
rub off
  rub up
  rub yourself
secret vice
  secret indulgence
  secret sin
self-abuse
  self-gratification
  self-indulgence
  self-love
  self-manipulation
  self-pleasuring
  self-pollution
shag[2]
solitary sex
  solitary sin
  solitary vice
Southern Comfort
stroke off
strop your beak

thrill to your own touch
   at thrill
toss off
touch yourself
traffic with yourself
wank[1] (off)
waste time
whack off
willy-puller *at* willy
work at yourself
wrist job (a)

Menstruation

Aunt Flo
baker flying
bends (the)
blood
   bloody
   bloody flag is up
bunny[2]
   buns on
caller (a)
captain is at home (the)
cardinal is at home (the)
cease to be
change[1] (the)
Charlie's come *at* Charlie
clear
come around
come on[1]
country cousins *at* relations
   have come (my)
courses
curse (the)
   curse of Eve
danger signal is up (the)
domestic afflictions
facts (of life)
fall off the roof
female physiology
feminine hygiene
flag is up (the)
   flag of defiance
fly the red flag *at* flag is up (the)
friend has come (my)
have the painters in
holy week
hygiene *at* personal hygiene
ill[1]
   ill of those
in purdah
indisposed[1]
irregularity *at* irregular
jam rag
Kit has come
late[2]
leaky
little friend
little visitor
   little sister
mense(s)
miss[2]
monthly flowers *at* flowers

monthly period
   month's
   monthlies
   monthly blues
   monthly courses
off duty
   off games
old faithful
others
out of circulation
painters are in (the)
pause[1]
period[1]
personal hygiene
poorly[2]
prince (the)
problem days *at* problem
rag(s) on
   rag week
   ragtime
red flag is up (the)
Red Sea is in
redhaired visitor (a)
reds (the)
regular[2]
relations have come (my)
ride the red horse
road is up for repair (the)
roses (your)
run on (a)
sanitary towel
   sanitary napkin
show[1]
sick
snatch mouse *at* snatch[2]
start bleeding
stomach cramps
Tampax time
term[1]
those days
time
time of the month
trouble
under the weather
unwell[1]
usual trouble (the)
visitor (a)
   visitor from Redbank
wallflower week *at* wallflower
wear a pad
women's things
wretched calendar (the)
wrong time of the month

Mental illness

acorn academy
adjustment[3]
afflicted
ape
asylum
balance of mind disturbed
bananas
barking

bats in the belfry
   bats
   batty
bin
black dog (the)
blow a gasket
booby
   booby hatch
   booby hutch
both oars in the water
bughouse
bust a string
by yourself
certifiable
change[2]
   changeling
change your bulbs
coco
   cocoa
commit
content[1]
counsellor
   counselling
cracked
crack-brained
crackers
   crackpot
cuckoo[2]
dateless
Deolalic tap *at* do-lally-tap
derailed
devil's mark (the)
dicked in the nob
diminished responsibility
disability
   disabled
distressed
disturbed[2]
do-lally-tap
dotty
East Ham *at* barking
eccentric
fatigue
flake[1]
flip your lid
for the birds
fruit[2]
fruitcake
funny
   funny farm
   funny home
   funny place
gears have slipped
go bush
God's child
gone in the nut *at* nut[1]
half-deck
handicapped
harpic
head case
headshrinker
headbanger
hospital[1]

ill[4]
  ill-adjusted
in left field
institutionalize
knock off your rudder
laughing academy
learning disabled *at* disability
left field
loopy
loose in the attic
  loose in the head
lose hold
lose your grip
lose your marbles *at* marbles
maladjustment
march to a different drummer
mental
  mentally challenged
mental fatigue *at* fatigue
mentally handicapped *at*
    handicap
meshugga
moon people
nervous breakdown
next door to a padded cell
nut[1]
  nut college
  nut farm
  nut house
  nut hutch
  nuts
  nutter
  nutty
off[2]
  off at the side
  off the wall
  off your chump
  off your gourd
  off your head
  off your napper
  off your nut
  off your rocker
  off your tree
  off your trolley
  off your turnip
off the rails[1]
one bubble left of level
out of the envelope
out of your skull
  out of your gourd
  out of your head
  out of your senses
  out of your tree
out to lunch
postal
potty[1]
psycho
put away[3]
· queer[2]
residential provision
  resident
rest home
rocky[1]

round the bend
screw loose (a)
  screw factory
  screwy
seclusion *at* secluded
section
send away
shrink
slippage
snake pit
special care *at* special[1]
squirrel
  squirrel tank
state farm
  state home
  state hospital
  state (training) school
throw the switches
tip off your trolley
touched[2] (in the head)
unbalanced
unglued
unhinged
unplugged
unslated
unwired
up the loop
voluntary patient
wandered
whiff of march hare *at* whiff of
wired to the moon

Mistresses and Lovers

à trois
admirer
adult[2]
adventure[2]
affair(e)
affinity
amour[1]
arm candy
assignation
attentions
baby-snatcher
back door man
  at back door[1]
beard
beau
bedfellow
bit of meat *at* meat[1]
bit on the side *at* bit[1]
boyfriend
brother starling *at* brother[1]
camp down with
canary[2]
carry on with
chère amie
close[2]
  close companion
  close friend
  close relationship
cohabit
commit misconduct

companion
company[1]
consort with
constant companion *at*
    companion
cookie
daddy *at* sugar daddy
dalliance *at* dally
dear friend
dirty weekend *at* dirty
err
  errant
escort
extra-curricular
familiar with
fancy man
  fancy bit
  fancy piece
  fancy woman
favours
fling (a)
friend
gallant
  gallantry
gentleman friend
girlfriend
go with
good friend(s)
grass widow
hand-fasting
hearth rival
housekeeper
housemate
in full fling
inamorata
  inamorato
inseparable
intimate *at* intimacy
intrigue (an)
involved with
item (an)
jocker
john[2]
jolly
judy
jump the broomstick
  jump the besom
just good friends
keep
  kept mistress
  kept wench
  kept woman
keep company with
lad
lady friend
lady of intrigue
lady of pleasure *at* lady
ladybird *at* lady
lass
leap the broomstick
  leap the besom
learn on the pillow
left-handed wife

liaison
light-housekeeping
linked with
little woman
live as man and wife
live in (mortal) sin
live tally
live together
live with
live-in girlfriend
long-term friend
long-term relationship
love affair
love nest
lover
make out with
make way with
man[1]
man friend
ménage à trois
miss[1]
mistress
more than a (good) friend
move in with
new cookie *at* cookie
niece[2]
on the side
open relationship
other woman (the)
over the broomstick
parallel parking
paramour
partner
patron
peculiar
person of the opposite sex
    sharing living quarters *at*
       person of/with
pet[2]
petite amie
    petite femme
piece on the side *at* piece[1]
pillow partner
play-fellow
    playmate
protector[1]
pure[1]
relationship
retread
rich friend
riding master
romance
romantic entanglement
    romantic affair
    romantic relationship
    romantically linked
rum-johnny
run around with
St Colman's girdle has lost its
    virtue
secretary
see[1]
    see company

set up[1]
shack up (with)
share someone's
    affections
significant other
skin off all dead horses
sleeping dictionary *at* sleep
    with
sleeping partner *at* sleep with
sleepy time girl *at* sleep with
spoken for
steady company
step out on
    step out with
sugar daddy
sweet man
    sweet momma
swing together *at* swing[2]
take into keeping *at* keep
take up with
thing going
together
toy boy
triangular
turn
two-time
warm up old porridge
woman friend
woman in a gilded cage

Nakedness

as Allah made him
    as God made him
au naturel
birthday suit
    birthday attire
    birthday finery
    birthday gear
bollocky
buff[1]
decent
garb of Eden
in his naturals *at* nature's garb
in the altogether
in the raw
in the skin
    in the buff
in your nip
nature's garb
naturist
raw
skin-[2]
skinny-dip
sports bar *at* sport
stark
state of nature (a)
streak
    streaker
wear a smile

Narcotics

A1

abuse
acid
    acid-head
acid freak
additional means
angel dust
artillery[1]
B
    B-pill
bagman
bang[2]
base-head
beat the gong
    beat pad
belt
black smoke
blast[3]
blocked
bloke
blow[8]
    blow a horse
    blow a stick
    blow Charlie
    blow snow
blue ruin
    blue devils
    blue flags
    blue heaven
    blue joy
    blue velvet
bombed out
    bomb
    bomber
    bombita
brown sugar
business
bust a cap
buyer
buzz on (a)
C
camel
candy
    candy man
    candy store
carry[2]
charge[2]
Charlie
    Charlie girl
chase the dragon
chemical
    chemically affected
    chemically inconvenienced
China white
Chinese tobacco
chippy[2]
chuck horrors
clean[1]
clear up
cocktail[2]
coffin nail *at* nail[2]
coke
    coke-hound
    coked

cold turkey
Colombian gold
come down
connect[2]
  connection
cook[3]
cookie *at* cookie-pusher
cool[2]
cool a turkey *at* cold turkey
cop[3]
crack[3]
  crackhead
crash
cruise[2]
crystal
cut[2]
deal
deck
  deck up
dependency[2]
dissolution[2]
do a line
doctor
doll[2]
dope
downer
downs
dragon (the)
dream
  dream dust
  dream stick
drop acid
dust[1]
Eastern substances
ecstasy
eye-opener
feed your nose
fix[3]
flake[2]
floating
fly[2]
freak[3]
  freak out
fruit salad
gage
gear
get off[3]
girl[3]
G-nose *at* G
go up[2]
God's own medicine
  gom
gone[2]
goods (the)
goof
  goofball
  goofed
grass-weed
green grass
H
habit
happy dust
hard drugs *at* hard

hash
  hash-head
head[3]
headache[1]
  headache-wine
heaven
  heaven dust
  heavenly blue
hemp[2]
high
highball
hit[4]
  hit the pipe
hold
hooked
hop
  hophead
  hop-joint
  hopped
horse[2]
hot shot
hustle[1]
ice[2]
  ice cream
Indian hemp
jab a vein
  jab off
jerk off[2]
joint[1]
jolt (a)
joy[2]
  joy flakes
  joy popper
  joy powder
  joy rider
  joy smoke
  joy stick
joy ride[2]
junk
  junked up
  junker
  junkie
  junkman
kick the habit
leave alone
lid
life[1] (the)
lift[2]
line[2]
lit
loaded[1]
Lucy in the sky with diamonds
M
Mary
  Mary Jane
Mexican brown
  Mexican green
  Mexican mushroom
  Mexican red
Mickey (Finn)
Miss Emma
MJ *at* Mary
monkey (the)

mood freshener
mother's blessing
mule
nail[2]
needlepusher
nose
  nose habit
O
on[3]
on a cloud
on the needle
on the sniff *at* sniff
operator
pharmaceuticals
pharmacy
pipe
pit-stop
polluted *at* pollute
pop[1]
  popper
porch-climber[2]
pot[4]
powder
  powdered lunch
powder your nose[2]
psychologically disadvantaged
punk[3]
  punk pills
push[4]
  pusher
racked
recreational drug
red devil
  red cross
reefer
ripped
roach[1]
rock
rope[2]
runny nose
scorched
score[2]
sent
shoot[3]
shot[2]
slang
sleighride
smack
smashed
smell the stuff
smoke[1] (the)
snapper
sniff
snort[2]
snow[1]
  snowball
  snowbird
  snow-blind
  snowed in
  snowed under
  snowed up
  snowman
  snow-storm

snow-head *at* head[3]
spaced out
space-head
speed
   speedball
spike[1]
spike[3]
sports medicine
stash
stewed
stick[4]
   stick of tea
stimulant (a)
stoned
street drugs
strung out
stuff[1]
substance
   substance abuse
sugar[3]
supercharged
suspect cigarette
sweet tooth
swing[2]
take needle
take off
take something
tea
   tea-head
   tea-party
   tea-stick
ten two thousand *at* ten one
   hundred
toot[2]
tracks
   track-marks
travel agent
trip
turn on
up[2]
   uppers
   ups
use[2]
   user
way out
weed (the)
white girl
   white lady
   white line
   white powder
   white stuff
white lightning[1]
wired[1]
wrecked
yak
zoned out
zonked

Obesity

ample
battle of the bulge
bay window
big-boned

bit of a stomach *at* stomach (a)
brewer's goitre
calorie counter
chubby
classic proportions
contour
corn-fed
couch potato
devoted to the table
differently weighted *at*
   differently
dine well
fond of food *at* fond of
full figure (a)
   fuller figure
go to the fat farm
heavily built
larger
led astray
many pounds heavier
maturer
   maturer figure
middle-aged spread
people of size *at* people of/with
puppy fat
quantitatively challenged
reduce your contour
   at contour
rubber tire
shorten the front line[2]
spare tyre
stomach (a)
tuck
weight problem
weight watcher
well-built
well-fleshed

Parts of the Body (other than genitalia and breasts)

antrum (amoris)
back door[1]
back passage
backside
behind
benders
bottom
bronze eye
brown[1]
cornhole
derrière
double jug *at* jugs
duff[2]
elephant and castle
eye
fanny
fleshy part of the thigh
heinie
Khyber
latter end[1]
   latter part

limb
little Mary
lower limbs *at* dark meat
moon
plumbing[2]
porthole
posterior(s)
rear end
ring[1]
seat
second eye
sit-upon
   sit-down-upon
   sitting
stern
ticker

Police

around the Horn
assist the police *at* help the
   police (with their
   inquiries)
badge
   badge bandit
bear[2]
   bear bait
   bear bite
   bear in the air
   bear trap
bent copper *at* bent[1]
bill
bird dog[3]
black-and-white
blue[1]
   blue-and-white
   blue-belly
   blue jeans
   blue lamp
   blue police
   blue suit
   bluebird
   bluebottle
   bluecoat
bobby
bogy[1]
boy scouts
Bridewell
B-Specials *at* special[2]
bull[4]
bust[2]
busy
button[2]
canary[3]
Charlie
chat
chirp
collar[3]
cop[2]
   cop house
   cop shop
copper
cough[1]

crack[4]
cuff[1]
dick[2]
　　Dickless Tracy
dip squad *at* dip[1]
do[5]
do a number
do your paperwork *at* paper-
　　hanger[1]
drop the hook on
fall[5]
　　fall money
feel a collar
fetch[2]
field associate
finger[1]
finger-man[1]
fireman[2]
flash your tin
fly[1]
flying squad
fuzz
　　fuzz-buster
Gestapo *at* secret (state) police
get your collar felt
G-man *at* G
goon squad
grass[1]
gumshoe
headhunter[1]
heat[1]
helmet
help the police (with their
　　inquiries)
hold paper on
horny[1]
house man
informer
internal affairs
jack[2]
john[4]
　　John Law
lady bear
lift[3]
limb of the law
　　limb
local bear
　　local boy
　　local yokel
lower the boom on[1]
man[2]
man in blue *at* blue[1]
meat wagon *at* meat[3]
Mr Plod
nick[3]
nightingale[1]
noddy
old bill
paddy wagon
paper-hanger[1]
parallel police *at* parallel
peeler
　　peel

peeper
pig
　　pig-feet
pinch[2]
plod
pull in (for a chat)
pull off
put the finger on *at* finger[1]
question[1]
Radical Squad *at* radical
raincoat[2]
red squad (the)
roach[2]
rubber heel
runner[1]
Sam
secret (state) police
shake[2]
shield
slops
smokey
　　smokey on four legs
　　smokey on rubber
　　smokey with camera
　　smokey with ears
　　smokey-bear
　　smokey-beaver
snatch[4]
　　snatch squad
snout[1]
snowdrop
special[2]
Special Branch
special detachment
special police
　　special fuzz
　　special patrol group
special task force
stake-out
stool pigeon
　　stool
Sweeney
tip over[2]
toss[1]
tout
turn in
turn up
use your tin
verbal
voluntary

Politics

action[2]
activist
adviser
alternative
America first
animal rights
anti-
　　anti-fascist
antisocial
appropriate[2]
armed struggle

Aryan
awful experiment (the)
bag job *at* bag[1]
bamboo curtain
banana skin
bederipe *at* droit de seigneur
benevolence
blow-in
boat people
boonwork *at* droit de seigneur
boys in the backroom *at* boys[2]
Buggins' turn
camp *at* concentration camp
carry a card
chair[2]
change your jacket
chiseller *at* chisel
Civil Co-operation Bureau
colony
come into the public domain
come up with the rations
committed
Committee (the)
　　Committee for the Protection
　　　of the Revolution
concern
concession
confederation
controversial[1]
convalescing
Cook County
cordial[2]
correct[1]
correct[2]
counter-revolution
cross the floor
Cultural Revolution *at* cultural
currency adjustment
cut[5]
decontaminate[2]
democrat/democracy
demonstration
　　demo
dependency[1]
deselect
dietary difficulties
diplomatic cold
　　diplomatic illness
direct action
disinvestment
　　divestiture
do business with
dollar shop
doorstep[2]
draw water
　　draw too much water
emergency[2]
encourage
Endlösung *at* final solution (the)
enlightenment
exchange of views
executive measure
fact-finding mission

fair[2]
fair-haired boy
fairness at work
fat cat
fellow-traveller
fifth column
final solution (the)
find Cook County
fireman[2]
flexible
  flexibility
former person
frank[2]
free trade
free world
freeze[1]
friendly
front[1]
full and frank *at* frank[2]
gaffe
gender norming
German
  German chemistry
  German mathematics
  German science
  Germanization
German Democratic Republic
go native
go over
golden boy
gold-plating
granny farming
great and the good (the)
Great Game
grey[2]
  grey suits
greymail
guiding light
  guidelines
hang out to dry
  hang-out
harmful elements
healthy
house-cleaning
house-trained
human rights
ideological supervision
initiative
internal security
involved
  involvement
king over the water
lame duck[1]
leak[2]
  leakage
  leaky
Lebensborn *at* living space
lend-lease *at* lend
lingua tertii imperii
little gentleman in black velvet
little local difficulty
living space
log-rolling

loose cannon
lose[1]
love-in *at* sit-in
low profile
mercy death
militia
movement[2]
national savings
national security guard
nationalize
negative aspect(s)
negative propaganda
negotiate
new
  New Deal
  New Labour
  New Order
new economic zones
no comment
non-aligned
non-person
obligatory
off the reservation
other place (the)
outsourcing
over-civilized
overhaul
own goal
PC
parallel justice *at* parallel
party member
pause[2]
peace
people's
  people's army
  people's car
  people's court
  people's democracy
  people's justice
  people's lottery
  people's militia
  people's palace
  people's republic
  people's tribunal
place of safety
player
Plum Book (the)
plumber
political and social order
politically correct
  political correctness
population transfer
pork[1]
  pork-chopper
pork barrel
Post-War Credit *at* benevolence
Potomac fever
prime the pump
procedure
progressive
proletarian
  proletarian democracy
  proletarian internationalism

protectorate
  protect
public ownership
public–private partnership
public sector borrowing
  requirement
public tranquility
question[2]
radical
rainbow fascist
rational
realign
redistribution of wealth
re-educate
  re-education
relocation
rent stabilization
resistance
restraint[1]
restraint[2]
revenue enhancement
  revenue emolument
revisionist
revolutionary
rusticate
salami tactics
sanitized
second world *at* first world
security
  security adviser
  security risk
  security service
shoo-in
shroud waving
  shroud waver
sit-in
sleep-in
so-called Austrian problem *at*
  problem
special[1]
special[4]
special[6]
special action
special court
special duty
special investigation unit
special squad
special treatment
spin
  spin doctor
  spinner
squat[2]
  squatter
stabilization
standstill
state protection
  State Research Bureau
sterilize
struggle for national existence
temporary local difficulty *at*
  temporary
troubles (the)
twin tracking

U-turn
ultimate intentions
un-American
unsound
urban renewal
useful fool
  useful idiot
vigilance
wage initiative
  at initiative
welfare state *at* welfare
well-informed sources
whitewash
wire-pulling
women's liberation
  women's libber
women's movement (the)
women's rights
work both sides of the
  street
workers' control
World Peace Council

Pornography

adult[1]
amusing
art
blue[2]
bodice-ripper
club[3]
dirty[1]
  dirty book
  dirty joke
family[1]
filthy
  filth
girlie flick *at* girl[1]
girlie magazine *at* girl[1]
girlie video *at* girl[1]
hard core *at* hard
horn emporium *at* horn[1]
laddish
less edited *at* less
men's magazine
off-colour[1]
raunchy
skin
  skin-business
  skin-flick
  skin-house
  skin magazine
smut house
soft[2]
stag
stripper
topless
top shelf

Poverty and Parsimony

aid
advantaged
assistance

backward[2]
banana republic
basket case
benefit
boracic
bum
careful
carry the banner
  carry the balloon
  carry the stick
cash flow problem
claimant
  Claimants' Union
close[1]
country in transition
deadhead
demographic strain
depleted
deprived
  deprivation
developing
differently advantaged *at*
    differently
dole
Dutch treat
economically disadvantaged
  economically abused
  economically exploited
  economically marginalized
emergent
  emerging
entitlement
excluded (the)
financial assistance
financially constrained
first world
floater[1]
fly a kite[2]
fumble for a check
gentleman
  gentleman of the road
get the shorts
go Dutch
hard up
hearts (of oak)
house[3]
  house of industry
in the red
industrializing country
jump a check *at* jump[3]
less developed *at* less
lesser developed *at* less
loaded[4]
moonlight flit
  moonlight flight
  moonlight march
  moonlight touch
  moonlight walk
moth in your wallet (a)
narrow
  narrowness
near[1]
negatively privileged

non-industrial
on a budget
on assistance *at* assistance
on the club
on the labour
on the parish
  on the parochial
on the ribs
on your bones
other side of the tracks (the)
over-privileged
panhandler
pavement people
pay with the roll of a drum
pop[3]
preliterate
privileged
remittance man
seen better days
shoot the moon
shorts (the)
socially excluded
south[2] (the)
special areas *at* special[1]
stroller
third world
tied aid *at* aid
tight[2]
  tight-fisted
  tightwad
to the knuckle
touch[2]
uncle
underdeveloped
underprivileged
union[2]
urban renewal
vulnerable
warm[2]
workhouse

Pregnancy

accident[2]
afterthought
anticipating
arranged by circumstances
bear[1]
beg a child of
belly plea
big
  big belly
bump[3] (the)
bun in the oven (a)
carry[1]
  carry a child
caught[1]
certain condition (a)
cheat the starter
click[2]
colt[2]
come to a sticky end
condition[2]
costume wedding

delicate condition
  at condition[2]
disgrace
do the right thing
do your duty by
eat for two
enceinte
expectant
  expecting
facts (of life)
fall[2]
  fall for a child
  fall in the family way
  fall pregnant
  fall wrong
family way
force-put job
free of Fumbler's Hall
full in the belly
get with child
gone
grass widow
great
  great bellied
  great with child
have a watermelon on the vine
  at watermelon
heavy of foot
how's your father
in calf
  in foal
  in pig
  in pod
  in pup
in for it
in season
in the club
  in the plum(p) pudding
    club
in the family way
  in that way
  in the increasing way
in trouble[1]
interesting condition
Irish toothache[1]
join the club
kid
knock up
lady in waiting[2]
large[1]
lined
little stranger
make a child *at* make babies
  together
make a decent woman of
make an honest woman of
mistake[1]
off-white wedding
on[2]
on heat[1]
on her way
on the nest
overdue[1]

plum(p) pudding club
premature
pup
quick
raise a belly
rank
ready for
riding time
ring the bell
sewn up[1]
shot in the tail
shotgun marriage
  shotgun wedding
so
so-so
split a woman's shape *at* split
stung by a serpent
swallow a watermelon seed *at*
  watermelon
swell
that way[2]
trouble
up the pole
  up the spout
  up the stick
watermelon
with child

Prison

approved school
assembly area
at government expense
at Her Majesty's pleasure
attendance centre
away[2]
back-gate parole
bag[5]
bang up
behind the wire
big house
  big pasture
  big school
bird[2]
black hole
blue[1]
board school *at* residential
  provision
boat *at* boat people
book
boom-passenger
Bridewell
brig
bucket[2]
bull pen
cage
camp *at* concentration camp
can[3]
canary[1]
chokey
chuck horrors
clink
cockchafer[1]

community treatment center
concentration camp
control unit
cooler[1]
coop
cop[2]
correctional
  correctional facility
  correctional officer
  correctional training
corrective training camp *at*
  correctional
cross-bar hotel
custody suite
dance-hall *at* dance[1]
deep freeze
detain
do a runner
do bird *at* bird[2]
down
  down the line
down for the count
drink tank *at* in the tank
eat porridge
end up with Her Majesty
enjoy Her Majesty's
  hospitality
everlasting staircase
fall[4]
Fanny Hill *at* fanny
fistful
five fingers
flowery[1]
freezer
G
glass house
go down[2]
go over the hill
  go over the wall
go to the Bay
go up the river
grind the wind
guest
  guest of Her Majesty
  guest of Uncle Sam
handful[1]
Hanoi Hilton
hard room
hit the bricks[2]
  hit the hump
hit the wall
hole *at* black hole
holiday
hoosegow
horse[1]
hospital[2]
house of correction
  house of detention
hulk
ice-box[1]
  ice-house
in[1]
in the bag[1]

individual behavior adjustment
　　unit
inside
Irish vacation
jolt (a)
jump bail *at* jump[3]
jug[1]
kangaroo club *at* kangaroo
　　court
kitty
labour education
last shame (the)
length
limbo *at* limb of the law
little school *at* big house
make tracks
man[2]
municipal farm
nab the stoop *at* nab
Newgate
nick[3]
North
ODC
on ice
on the run
on the trot
on the wall
on vacation
pacification camp *at* pacify
pacification center *at* pacify
periodic rest
place of correction
place of safety
poke[3]
political re-education
porridge
preventive detention
protective custody
put away[3]
quod
re-educate
　　re-education
relocation camp
residential provision
　　resident
resisting arrest
rock crusher
room and board with uncle Sam
runner[2]
school
screw[2]
seclusion *at* secluded
segregation unit *at* segregation
send away
send down
send up
sheriff's hotel
slammer
　　slam
sneezer
snout[2]
socialist justice

special education
special regime
sponging-house *at* sponge
spring
state farm
　　state home
　　state (training) school
stir
　　stir-wise
stockade
stretch[1]
sweat-box *at* sweat it out of
take a hike[2]
take to the hills
term[2]
time
tolbooth
transported
trustee
　　trusty
trying to escape
university
vacation
walk[5]
yardbird
youth (guidance) center

Prostitution

abandoned
academician *at* academy
accost
actress
alley-cat
all-nighter
amateur
angel of the night
arse-peddler *at* arse
at the game *at* game[2] (the)
available indigenous female
　　companion
B girl *at* bar girl
bad
badger
　　badger game
baggage
bang-tail *at* bang[1]
bar girl
bash
be nice to
belter *at* belt
bibi
　　bidi
biddy
bint
bird[1]
bit
bitch
black velvet
blow[2]
　　blowen
board lodger
bobtail[1]
body rub (a)

bona roba
bottom woman *at* bottom
brasser
break luck
bum
bun[1]
business
　　business woman
buttered bun
buttock and twang *at* buttock
buy
buy love
call girl
　　call-boy
　　call-button girl
call the tricks
camp follower
can *at* canhouse
cat[1]
cavalry
chick
　　chickie
child of Venus
chippy[1]
cockatrice *at* cocktail[1]
cockchafer[2]
cocktail[1]
coffee grinder
collabos horizontales *at*
　　horizontal
comfort women
commercial sex worker
common customer
　　common jack
　　common maid
　　common sewer
　　common tart
　　commoner o' th' camp
compensated dating
convenient[1]
country-club girls
courtesan
Covent Garden
　　Covent Garden goddess
crawl a kerb *at* kerb-crawling
creature of sale
Cressida
crib girl *at* crib
cross girl
cruiser *at* cruise[1]
currency girl
Cyprian
dance a Haymarket hornpipe
dasher
daughter of joy
daughter of the game
degradation *at* degrade
demi-mondaine
　　demi-rep
doe
dolly
　　dolly-common
　　dolly-mop

double header
doxy
dress for sale
    dress-lodger
Drury Lane vestal *at* Drury Lane
    ague
Dutch widow
Edie
entertainment lady *at*
    entertain[1]
escort
faggot *at* fag
fallen woman
feather-bed soldier *at* feather-
    bed
filth
fish[2]
fishmonger's daughter
fix up
flapper
flash girl *at* flash-ken
flash tail *at* flash-ken
flash woman *at* flash-ken
flat-backer *at* flat on your back
flirty fishing
flutter a skirt
forty-four
frail sister
freak trick *at* trick[2]
fresh meat *at* meat[1]
game[2] (the)
gamester[1]
gay girl *at* gay
gay lady *at* gay
gay life *at* gay
girl[1]
    girl of the streets
    girlie
go case
go into the streets
go to Paul's for a wife
good time
    good-time girl
goose[1]
grande horizontale *at*
    horizontal
grass bibi/bibi *at* bibi
guinea-hen
hawk your mutton
    hawk your meat
    hawk your pearly
head chick *at* head job (a)
high-yellow *at* yellow[2]
hobby-horse
hold-door trade (the)
hooker
horizontal life *at* horizontal
hostess
hustle[2]
    hustler
immoral
    immoral earnings
    immoral girls

immoral purposes
Immorality Act
importune
in circulation
in the game *at* game[2] (the)
in the trade
infamy
infantry
jam tart *at* tart
jane[1]
    Jane Shore
Jezebel
john[5]
joy-boy *at* joy[1]
joy-girl *at* joy[1]
Judy
kerb-crawling
lady
    lady of a certain description
    lady of easy virtue
    lady of no virtue
    lady of pleasure
    lady of the night
    lady of the stage
    lady of the streets
    ladybird
lady in waiting[1]
life[1] (the)
life of infamy
    life of shame
light ladies *at* light[1]
light the lamp
light wenches *at* light[1]
little bit
live by trade
loose woman *at* loose[1]
lost[1]
low girls
Magdalene
make use of
masseuse
model
moll
moose
mud-kicker
Murphy game (the)
mutton
nanny *at* nanny-house
naughty lady
nautch girl
nice time[1]
nightclub hostess
night girl
night job
nightingale[3]
noble game (the)
nocturne
nun *at* nunnery
nymph
    nymph of darkness
    nymph of delight
    nymph of the pavement
oldest profession (the)

on the bash *at* bash
on the cross
on the game *at* game[2] (the)
on the grind
on the loose
on the street(s)
on the stroll
on the town[2]
one of those
pagan
painted woman
panel[2]
Paphian
park women
party girl
pavement girl
    pavement princess
peddle your arse
personal services
pick-up joint *at* pick up
piece of trade *at* piece[1]
prima donna
princess
pro
profession (the)
professional (woman)
punk[1]
quail
queen[1]
quick time
quickie[2]
receiver-general
rent boy
renter
sand-rat
sausage jockey *at* sausage
scarlet woman
scrubber
sell yourself
    sell your back
    sell your body
    sell your desires
show your charms
sex care provider *at* sex[1]
sex worker *at* sex[1]
sinful commerce *at* commerce
sister[1]
    sister of charity
    sister of mercy
skivvy
sleck-trough *at* slake your lust
sleepy-time girl *at* sleep with
social evil (the)
solicit
    solicitor
sporting girls at sport (the)
sporting women *at* sport (the)
stale[1]
    stale meat
stepney
street (the)
    street girl
    street tricking

street-corner girl
street-walker
succubus
tart
teahouse *at* tearoom
tenderloin
tenderloin district
tomboy
totty
town bike
town pump
trade (the)
tramp
tree-rat
trick
trollop
trot
trull
two-by-four
unfortunate
walk[1] (the streets)
walk with
warm one *at* warm[1]
wench
wet hen *at* wet deck
white slave
white slavery
whore-hopping *at* hop into bed
Winchester goose *at* goose[1]
woman of the town
woman of the world
work the streets
working girl
yellow[2]

Race

affirmative action
African trade *at* triangular trade
   (the)
African-American
African-descended
apartheid
Aryan
black up
blackbird
black cattle
black hides
black pigs
black sheep
blackbirder
blockbuster[2]
blue-eyed brother *at* brother[2]
boy
brother[2]
Cape coloured *at* coloured[1]
card[2]
cattle[1]
chalk-board
chi-chi
clean[2]
cleanse[1]
colour
colour problem

colour-blind
coloured[1]
community relations
community affairs
   correspondent
community affairs officer
cultural
cultural bias
cultural deprivation
dark[2]
dark-complected
dark-skinned
darky
demographically correct
dietary difficulties
discrimination
disinfection
diversity[1]
diversity[2]
diversity training
ethnic
ethnic minority
ethnic cleansing
ethnic loading
fancy[3]
feel a draft
female-American
fiddle
first people
glass ceiling
guest worker
homelands
house[4]
immigrant
improvement[1]
indigenous
Inquiry and Control Section
insult
integrated casting
itinerant
Jewish question (the)
Jim Crow
letterhead
lick of the tarbrush *at* tarbrush
   (the)
light[3]
long acre
mainstreaming
marginalized
master race *at* racial
melanin enriched
migration
multicultural
multiculturalism
N-word (the)
native
Native American
negro
new Australian
New Commonwealth
NINA
non-Aryan
non-traditional casting

non-white
obligatory
open housing
peculiar institution (the)
person of/with
person of colour *at* coloured[1]
person of the coloured
   persuasion *at* coloured[1]
pigmentation problem *at*
   problem
play a card
purification of the race
quota
race defilement
race relations
Race Relations Board
race relations industry
race relations officer
racial
racial purification
racial purity
racial science
racial war
racism
racialism
racist
racialist
redneck
re-emigration
reservation
reverse discrimination
salt and pepper
scheduled classes
score adjustment
segregation
separate development
servant
sister[2]
social inclusion
statutory
tarbrush (the)
three-point play
tincture[1]
tinker
token
tokenism
Tom[2]
transfer
traveller
travelling people
triangular trade (the)
trouser test
turn[4]
twelve annas in the rupee
Uncle Tom
underground railroad
undocumented
visible
visible community
visible minorities
visible minority ethnic
   groups
visibly ethnic

weaker half (the)
West Briton
   West Britonism
   West British
wet-back
white meat[2]
within-group norming
wooden log
yellow[2]
   high yellow

Religion and Superstition

alternative
anti-
     anti-Arian
auld *at* old
auto-da-fé
bad fire (the)
bad man
   bad lad
black lad
   black gentleman
   black man
   black prince
   black Sam
   black spy
black thief *at* thief
blazes
butch
cast[2]
charm
child of God
cloot
   clootie
   Clootie's croft
creative conflict
   at creative
cunning man
dark man
David Jones *at* Davy Jones's
   locker
dickens
don the turban
Eumenides
   Euxine
father of lies
fly-by-night[1]
fly-lord *at* Lord of the Flies
foul[2]
   foul ane
   foul thief
furry thing
game fee *at* game[2] (the)
gentle
   gentle bushes
   gentle people
   gentle place
   gentle thorns
gentry
give to God
given rig
go again

go over
good folk
   good neighbours
   good people
gooseberry
grunter
gypsy's warning
Harry
holy wars
horn of fidelity
horny[1]
hot place (the)
ill-wished
irregular situation
    at irregular
left-footer
lift the books
   lift your lines
little people
   little folk
living Harry *at* Harry
look in a cup
Lord Harry *at* Harry
Lord of the Flies
mark[1]
nephew
Nick[1]
   Nicker
   Nickie
niece[1]
old
   old bendy
   old blazes
   old bogey
   old boots
   old boy
   old chap
   old child
   old cloot
   old cloutie
   old dad
   old Davy
   old driver
   old gentleman
   old gooseberry
   old Harry
   old hornie
   old lad
   old mahoon
   old man
   old Nick
   old one
   old poger
   old poker
   old Roger
   old ruffin
   old Sandy
   old scratch
   old serpent
   old smoker
   old sooty
   old thief
   old toast

oversee
   overlook
   overshadow
playboy
plotcock
Prince of Darkness
scratch[1]
shame
small folk
   small men
   small people
smoker (the)
souper
stunted hare
swim for a wizard
take the soup
thief (of the world)
thing
wake a witch
wee folk
   wee people
wise woman
   wise man

Sexual Pursuit

action[3] (the)
adventuress
alley-cat
appetites
arouse
   arousal
arse
   arse man
ass
asbestos drawers
assault
association with
athlete
attentions
available[1]
beau
beddable
bedroom eyes (with)
beef
beefcake
bicycle
biddy
bimbo
bird[1]
bit[1]
   bit of all right
   bit of arse/ass
   bit of crumpet
   bit of fluff
   bit of goods
   bit of hot stuff
   bit of how's your father
   bit of jam
   bit of meat
   bit of muslin
   bit of skirt
   bit of stuff

bit of you-know-what
bit on the side
bother
break the pale
broad
bull²
bunny
bush patrol
canary²
canned goods
canoodle *at* canoe
carry a torch for
cast sheep's eyes at *at* make
    sheep's eyes at
charity girl
  charity dame
charms
chase
  chase hump
  chase skirt
  chase tail
cherry-picker *at* cherry
click with
cocksman *at* cock
cold²
come across²
come on²
consensual relationship
consort with
contact with
  contact sex
cookie
cop⁴
cop a feel *at* feel/cop⁴
crackling
cream for
  creamer
cruise¹
crumpet
crush
cuckoo¹
dangerous to women
dark meat²
dead to
  dead to honour
  dead to propriety
defend your honour
designs on (have)
dick around
dirty old man *at* dirty¹
dish
distracted by
doe
doll¹
Don Juan
down boy
easy woman
  easy affections
end of desire
entanglement
Eve
eye-candy
facile

fallen woman
familiar with
fancy¹
fast
feel
  feel up
  feel-up
fell design
femme fatale
filly
flapper
fond of the women *at* fond of
fondle
fool around with
forget yourself
foxy
frail
frank¹
freelance
fresh³
frippet
frottage
fumble
fun
fun and games
gash
get off with
get your feet under the table
girler
give the eye
goat *at* goat-house
goer
gone about
goose²
grope
  groper
hammer²
hand trouble
handle¹
hanky-panky
have a hard-on for *at* hard-on
hit on
horny²
hot¹
  hots (the)
hot back (a)
hot pants
hot stuff
  hot time
hot-tailing
ice queen
in heat *at* on heat
in the mood
inflame
it¹
itch
  itchy feet
jail bait
Judy
juiced up
  juicy
ladies' man
lady-killer

lay²
liberal
light¹
light-footed
like the ladies
little bit
loose¹
  loose in the hilts
lose your reputation
  lose your virtue
Lothario
make¹
make sheep's eyes at
make time with
make up to
make yourself available
man about town
man of pleasure
maul
meat¹
mouse
mutton
  mutton-monger
natural vigours
naughty
no better than she should be
  no better than she ought to be
nonsense
nose open
not all she should be
  not all she ought to be
not inconsolable
old Adam (the)
on⁴
on heat²
on the make
on the pull
open legged
over-familiar
overfriendly
over-gallant
pant after
party-goer *at* goer
pass²
past (your)
paw
permissive
pet¹
physical involvement
pick up
  pick-up
  pick-up joint
piece¹
  piece of arse/ass
  piece of buttered bun
  piece of crackling
  piece of crumpet
  piece of gash
  piece of goods
  piece of muslin
  piece of rump
  piece of skirt
  piece of spare

piece on a fork
piece of tail *at* tail[1]
play games *at* play
play the field
play the goat
play with
popsy
privileges
proposition
pull[2]
push (someone's) buttons
pussy[2]
pussy-whipped *at* pussy[1]
put a move on
put yourself about
ram[2]
randy
rattle[2]
raunchy
result[2]
roundheels
rover
roving eye
salute upon the lips
scarlet fever *at* scarlet woman
seat cover *at* seat
seduce
seven-year itch
sexual variety *at* sexual
    preference
sheep's eyes (make)
shoot the agate
shoot the breeze *at* shoot
    a line
slap and tickle
skirt
slag
sow your wild oats
spoon
squeeze[2]
stalk
stern-chaser *at* stern
stoat
strong-arm
stuck on
stud
sure thing
swordsman
tail[1]
take liberties
    take a liberty
talent
    talent-spotting
thing about
tomcatting
trouble with his flies
turn off[2]
turn on
two-time
Uganda
uncontaminated
walker
wallflower

wandering eye
want[2]
    want a body
    want intercourse
    want it
    want love
    want relations
    want sex
warm[1]
weakness for men/women *at*
    weakness
wear your heart upon your
    sleeve
wet for
    wet your drawers
    wet your knickers
    wet your pants
    wet yourself
wide-on (a)
woman
    womanizer
woman of intrigue
zipper
    zipper problem

Sexual Variations

aberration
abnormal
    abnormality
AC/DC
    acey-deecy
aesthete
    aestheticism
affair(e)
agent
all-rounder
alternative
    alternative proclivity
    alternative sexuality
ambidextrous
ambiguous
ambivalent
antrum (amoris)
arouse
    arousal
arse
    arse-bandit
    arse peddler
ass
Aussie kiss *at* French kiss
aunt
    auntie
back door[1]
backward[3]
bait *at* jail bait
batting and bowling
battyboy
behind
bent[2]
bestiality
bird circuit
bisexual

bi
bitch
blow[3]
blow job
bondage
boondagger *at* boondock
both-way
bottle[3]
Brighton pier
brown[2]
brown shower *at* showers
brown-hatter
bull[5]
    bull-dyke
bum-boy *at* bum
butch
butterfly
camp
    camp about
    camp it up
capon
Charlie
chew
chicken[1]
    chickenhawk
child molester *at* molest
child of Uranus *at* Uranian
cissy
closet[2]
    closet lez
    closet queen
    closet queer
come home by Clapham
come out
    come out of the closet
companion
confirmed bachelor
connection *at* connect[1]
consenting adults
cookie pusher
cornhole
cottaging
crime against nature (a)
cross-dress
cruise[1]
crush
cupcake
curious
Darby and Joan[2]
decadent
degenerate
dick[1]
Dick's hatband
disciple of Oscar Wilde *at*
    disciple of
discipline *at* dominance
dissolution[2]
    dissolute
diver
divergence
dodgy deacon *at* dodgy
dominance
double-gaited

doubtful sexuality
down on
drag
dress on/to the left
drop beads
earnest
eat
   eat out
écouteur
effeminate
English
   English arts
   English discipline
   English guidance
   English treatment
English disease (the)[1]
English vice (the)
even numbers or odd
expose yourself
fag
faggot
fairy
female domination
female oriented
   female identified
fish[1]
   fishwife
fishy
flamboyant
flash
flit[3]
   flit about
flower[2]
fluter *at* flute
frame[2]
freak[1]
freak trick *at* freak[2]
French[1]
French vice (the)
   French way
friend
fruit[1]
funny[2]
gang-bang
gear
gender-bending
get it off *at* get
ginger
   ginger beer
give head
give yourself *at* give
go down on
go the other way
go to bed with
gobble
golden shower
   at showers[1]
Greek way (the)
gross indecency
group sex
half-and-half
hand job (a)
have it off *at* have

head job (a)
hermaphrodite
homo
hunt
husband[2]
in the closet
indecency
   indecent assault
   indecent exposure
   indecent offence
interfere with
intermediate
invert
   inversion
   inverted
iron[2]
Jack of both sides
jag house
Jasper
jocker
john[3]
   John and Joan
jolly[3]
King Lear
kinky
lavender
   lavender boy
   lavender convention
leather[2]
   leather-queen
left-footer
left-handed[2]
lesbian
   lesbianism
   lesbic
   lez
   lezzer
lifestyle
lifter *at* shirtlifter
light[2] (a)
light on his toes
light-footed[2]
like that
lily
limp-wrist
live with
lizzie
love that durst not speak its
   name (the)
lover
male
   male identified
   male movies
   male oriented
   male videos
marital aid
meat[1]
meat-rack
misbehave
Miss Nancy *at* nancy
mother[1]
muff-diver *at* muff
musical

nameless crime (the)
nancy
   nancy boy
Nelly
not interested in the opposite
   sex
oblique
odd
one of those
one-way street
oral sex
   oral service
orientation
Oscar
other way (the)
out[2]
   outing
out of the closet *at* out[2]
pansy
pash
pass[2]
peculiar
peddle your arse/ass
Peeping Tom
perform[2]
permissive
personal relations
petit ami
pink pound
plater
   plate of ham
play
   play the pink oboe
   play the skin flute
plug[2]
pogey bait *at* poke[2]
porthole
posterior assault
pouff
   pooftah
predilection
preference (a)
proclivities
proposition
punk[2]
queen[2]
queer[2]
   queertalk
raisin
ream
rent boy
Roman
   Roman culture
   Roman way
rough trade
same gender oriented
Sapphic
sexual ambiguity
sexual preference
   sexual irregularity
   sexual orientation
   sexual proclivity
   sexual tropism

sexually non-conformist
shirtlifter
  shirt-lifting
shit stabber
showers[1]
side orders
sissy
six-à-neuf *at* soixante-neuf
sixty-nine
skippy
so
soixante-neuf
song and dance
stern-chaser *at* stern
Stoke-on-Trent
stud farm *at* stud
stuff[2]
súck off
swing[2]
swing both ways
swish
switch-hitter
sword-swallower *at* sword
take little interest in the
    opposite sex
  take no interest in the
    opposite sex
tearoom
  tearoom trade
that way[1]
three-letter man
triple
tube
two left hands *at* left-handed
two-on-one
unbiblical sex
uncertain sexual preferences
unfaithful
unhealthy
unmarried
unmentionable crime (the)
unnatural
  unnatural act
  unnatural crime
  unnatural practice
  unnatural vice
up the creek
Uranian
voyeur
water sports
weakness for boys *at* weakness
wear Dick's hatband
will
woman's thing (the)
wrong[2]
  wrong sexual preference

Stealing

acquire
  acquisition
alienate
appropriate[1]
aryanize

bag[1]
  bag job
bleed the monkey *at* bleed
blindside
bone[1]
  boning
boost[1]
  booster
  booster bag
  booster bloomers
bootleg
  bootlegger
  bootlegger turn
borrow
browse
butler's perks
cabbage
cadge
cannon
gentleman of the road *at*
    gentleman
gentleman of fortune *at*
    gentleman
ghost[1]
glean
glue
gone walkabout
goods (the)
gooseberry *at* gooseberry lay
grab[2]
graze
half-inch
heist
help yourself
highgrade
hijack
highwayman
  high law
  high lawyer
  high pad
hit[3]
hoist[1]
hold-up
hook[1]
  hooker
hot[2]
  hot market
  hot money
hot-wire
hustle[1]
in the ring
informal dealer *at* informal
inventory leakage
it's a big firm
job
joyride[3]
jump[1]
knight of the road *at* knight
knock off[3]
liberate[2]
life[1] (the)
lift[1]
  lifter

light-fingered
made at one heat
make[2]
make a purse for yourself
make away with[2]
make off with
milk
mooch
moonlight[1]
moonraker
mudlark
mug
  mugger
mush
nab
  nab the snow
nationalize
Newgate bird *at* Newgate
nibble[2]
nick[2]
nip[1]
no show
nobble[1]
obtain
on the chisel *at* chisel
on the cross
pick[1]
  pick a pocket
  pickle
  pickpocket
pigeon
pike *at* pick[1]
pinch[1]
pocket
porch climber[1]
pouch
punter
ramp
receiver
redistribution of property
requisition
rip off
roll[2]
rumble
  running rumbler
run[1]
safe man *at* dip[1]
salvage
seepage
shade[2]
shake[1]
  shake down
  shakedown
shoplift
shoplifter *at* lift[1]
shrinkage
siphon off
snag
snatch[3]
sneak
souvenir
stick up
sticky-fingered

stripper
strong-arm
suck the monkey
swipe
take[1]
take a walk[3]
take to the cleaners
tax
tea leaf
three-letter man
tip over[1]
touch[2]
Tyburn blossom *at* Tyburn
walk[3]
whip
win[1]

Sweat

bedewed
BO
body odour
glow
odorously challenged
wetness

Urination

accident[1]
accommodate yourself
adjust your dress
answer the call[2]
arrange yourself *at* arrange
article
back teeth floating
bale out
be excused
bedwetting
been
bodily functions
bodily wastes
break your neck
burst
business
call of nature
caught short
chamber
    chamber-lye
    chamber-pot
choke your chicken
cleanliness training
cock the leg
comfort[2]
    comfort break
    comfort station
commit a nuisance
continent
cover your boots
decant
demands of nature
Dicky Diddle *at* diddle[1]
diddle[1]
dirty[2]

dirty your pants
dirty your trousers
dirty yourself
disappear[2]
do a bunk
    do a dike
    do a shift
drain off
duck
ease nature
    ease your bladder
    ease yourself
ease springs
empty out
    empty your bladder
essential purposes
find a tree
freshen up
gather a daisy/rose/pea *at* pick a
    daisy
go[3]
    go about your business
    go for a walk (with a spade
        etc.)
    go on the coal
    go over the heap
    go places
    go round the corner
    go to ground
    go to the toilet
    go upstairs
house-trained
incontinent[2]
    incontinency
jerry
Jimmy
    Jimmy Riddle
kill a snake
leak[1]
leaky
leave the room
    leave the class
lift a leg[2]
little jobs
look at the garden
    look at the compost heap
    look at the lawn
    look at the roses
make a call
make a mess
make room for tea
make water
mess[2]
minor function (the)
mistake[2]
natural function (the)
    natural necessities
    natural purposes
nature stop
nature's needs
night water *at* night soil
number one(s)[1]
P

pass water
pay a visit
pee
    pee-pee
perform[1]
    perform a natural function
pick a daisy
    pick a pea
    pick a rose
pig's ear
pit-stop
pluck a daisy/pea/rose *at* pick a
    daisy
point Percy at the porcelain
polish the mahogany
powder your nose[1]
privacy
puddle
pull a daisy
pump bilges
    pump ship
rattle[3]
relief[2]
relieve yourself
retire[2]
run off[2]
sample
see a man about a dog
see the rosebed
    see the compost heap
    see the view
    see your aunt
shake hands with the bishop
    shake hands with the
        unemployable
    shake hands with the
        unemployed
    shake hands with your best
        friend
    shake hands with your wife's
        best friend
    shake the lettuce
shoot a lion
    shoot a dog
siphon the python
slack
    slack off
slash
specimen
spend a penny
splash your boots
squat[1]
stale[2]
strain your greens
stretch your legs
take a leak
take the air
taken short
tap a kidney
ten one hundred
tinkle
turn up your tail
unlimber your joint

unsociable (be)
upstairs[2]
visiting card
void water
wash[1]
   wash-mug
wash your hands
waste[2]
water
   water the garden
   water the roses
waterworks[1]
wee(-wee)
wet[1] (the bed)
   wet your pants
   wet yourself
wetting[2]
whizz

Venereal Disease

affliction of the loins *at* afflicted
bang and biff *at* bang[2]
bareback rider *at* bareback
blood disease
   blood poison
bone-ache
break your shins against Covent
   Garden rails
burn[1]
   burn your poker
   burner
catch a cold[1]
catch a packet[2]
catch the boat up
caught[2]
Clapham
clean[1]
cold[2]
come home by Clapham
communicable disease
contagious and disgraceful
   disease
cop a packet
Covent Garden gout *at* Covent
   Garden
Cupid's measles
   Cupid's itch
disease of love
docked smack smooth *at* dock
dose
Drury Lane ague
dry pox (the)
early treatment room
free from infection
   FFI
French ache
   French compliment
   French disease
   French fever
   French measles
   French pox
   Frenchified
garden gout

general paralysis of the insane
   at incurable bone-ache
get a marked tray
hot[3]
hygienic
ill[2]
incurable bone-ache
ladies' fever *at* lady
malady of France
mental disease
nasty complaint (a)
Neapolitan bone-ache
   Neapolitan favour
packet[2]
pick up a nail
piled with French velvet
piss pins and needles
   piss pure cream
preventable disease
Rangoon itch
Sandy McNabs
scald
secret disease *at* blood
   disease
shoot between wind and water
   at shoot off
short-arm inspection
sigma phi
slash and burn[1]
social disease
   social infection
Spanish gout
specific blood poison *at* blood
   disease
take in your coals
unmentionable disease
wholesome
Winchester goose *at* goose[1]

Vulgarisms

adjective deleted *at* expletive
   deleted
affair of honour
B
   B fool
   B off
bad-mouth
ball bearing
bar steward *at* bar
basket[1]
Billingsgate
blank[1]
   blanking
blast[1]
bleeding
bleep
bloody *at* B
blooming
blow[6]
blow a raspberry
bugger *at* B
by gum *at* golly

characterization deleted *at*
   expletive deleted
chicken-choker *at* choke your
   chicken
club[3]
D
   damn
   damnable
   damned
darn
dash[2]
ding-a-ling
effing
expletive deleted
F
F-word
Fanny Adams
flowery[2]
forget yourself
foul may care *at* foul[2]
foul skelp ye *at* foul[2]
four-letter man
four-letter word
French[2]
frigging *at* frig[1]
G
gee
give the finger to
gold-brick
golly
   goles
   golles
   gollin
   golls
   gom
   gommy
   goms
   gomz
   goom
   gull
   gum
Gordon Bennet(t)
H
Hail Columbia
hell *at* H
horse-collar
in your brown *at* brown[1]
jerk *at* jerk off
language
merchant banker
monkey's
mother[2]
Mrs Duckett
naff off
P off *at* P
pin-up
pillock *at* pill[1]
pissed off *at* pissed
P.O. *at* pissed
poor-mouth
pound salt
   pound sand
prick

questionable remark
  questionable joke
ruddy
silly B *at* B
so-and-so
something
  something-something
stuff that *at* stuff[2]
sugar[2]
sweet FA *at* Fanny Adams
sweet Fanny Adams *at* Fanny
  Adams
take the mick(e)y
  take the Michael
take the piss
tinpot
tosser *at* toss off
two-fingered
up your Khyber *at* Khyber
wanker *at* wank[1] (off)
what the H *at* H
willy-puller *at* willie

Warfare

absorption
adventure[1]
Agent Orange *at* agent
air support
alternative defence *at*
  alternative
annex
Anschluss
anti-personnel
barrack-room lawyer
  barracks lawyer
blocking detachment
blue-on-blue
bog(e)y[2]
border incident *at* incident
boys in the bush *at* boys[2]
brew[1]
  brew up
brushfire war
bug out
bushwhack
ceasefire
Charlie
chopper[1]
civilian impacting
clean[1]
cleanse[1]
co-belligerent
cooperate
collaborator[1]
  collaborate
  collaborationist
collateral damage
come up with the rations
coming of peace
conflict
confrontation
constructed
conventional

counter-attack
counter-insurgency
defence
  D notice
  defence notice
defensive victory
degrade
deliver
  delivery vehicle
device
dirty[1]
disengage
  disengagement
ditch
do[4]
done for
dove
draw the enemy into a trap
duration
emergency
enhanced radiation weapon *at*
  enhance
expendable *at* expended
fact-finding mission
fail to win
fifth column
first strike
  first strike capability
fish[3]
fizzer
fly the blue pigeon[2]
fragmentation device *at* frag
fraternal assistance
fratricide
freedom fighters
French leave
friendly fire
frontier guards
garden
Ginza cowboy
go over the hill
  go over the side
go over the top
    at over the top[1]
good voyage
guardhouse lawyer
guardian
hardware[2]
hawk
heat[2]
hit the bricks[2]
incident
incontinent ordnance
incursion
intervention[1]
intruder
jump ship *at* jump[3]
late disturbances
  late nastiness
  late unpleasantness
liberate[1]
limited action
  limited covert war

living space
lot
medium machine
milice *at* militia
milk run
Ministry of Defence *at* defence
modern
Molotov cocktail
mop up
national emergency
national service
nerve agent
nightingale[2]
non-fraternization *at*
  fraternization
normalization
nuclear device *at* device
NYR
  not yet returned
occupied
over the top[1]
over there
pacify
  pacification
party
patriotic front
peace
  peace council
  peace offensive
  peace-keeping action
  peace-keeping force
pioneer[1]
police action
political change
positive
pre-dawn vertical insertion
pre-emptive
  pre-emptive action
  pre-emptive offensive
  pre-emptive self-defence
  pre-emptive strike
press
  press gang *at* press
protect
protect your interests
protectorate
purge[2]
push[2]
Quaker gun
quarantine
rebuilding costs
recent unpleasantness
reconstructed *at* constructed
rectification of frontiers
regroup
regularize
relocation camp
resources control
restore order
return fire
returned to unit
  RTU
run[2]

sea-lawyer
second-strike
   second-strike capability
   second-strike destruction
security
   security battalion
self-defence
settle[2]
   settlement
   settler
ship's lawyer
shorten the front (line)[1]
show[2]
soft[2]
   soft target
somewhere in...
special[3]
   special stores
   special weapons
sterilize
straighten the line
strategic
   strategic capability
   strategic movement to the
     rear
   strategic retreat
   strategic targets
   strategic withdrawal
stunt
surgical strike
surrendered personnel
tactical
   tactical nuclear weapon
tactical regrouping
target of opportunity (a)
temporary
   temporary tactical ploy
tongue
treasonable activity
turn your coat
voluntary
volunteer

ward off invasion
withdrawal to prepared
   positions
   withdrawal in good order
year of progress

Unclassified Entries

behind the eight ball
below the salt
bleeding heart
born in
bouncer *at* bounce[3]
brass-rags
Chinese fire-drill (a)
Chinese parliament
circular file
country pay
difficult
do-gooder
   do-gooding
downstairs[1]
Dutch comfort
Dutch consolation
Dutch fuck
Dutch uncle
eat stale dog
file thirteen
   file seventeen
gang
Greek Calends (the)
Greek gift
hold the bag
I hear what you say
in Dutch
in the arms of Morpheus
inclusive language
invigorating
Irish hurricane
Irish pennant
keep up with the Jones's
kick over the traces

land of Nod (the)
lend
liberate[3]
   liberation
lived-in
magic word (the)
morally challenging
not at home
not in
not rocket science
oblige
one of us
Paris Mean Time
pick up a knife
receive
set up shop on Goodwin Sands
shake the pagoda tree
shoot with a silver gun
sing a different tune
   sing from a different song
     sheet
slight chill
   slight cold
   slight indisposition
smell of
suffer fools gladly
Sunday
supportive
sympathetic ear
take the wall
tell me about it
temporary
throw in the towel
tin ear (a)
touchy-feely
trainspotter
wash your hands of
whiff of
white elephant
with respect
wooden hill
worship at the shrine of